Place-of-Service Codes for Professional Claims

The following is a list of place-of-service codes. The list contains the code, name, and description. These codes should be used on professional claims to specify the entity where service(s) were rendered. Check with your individual payer (eg, Medicare, Medicaid, other private insurance) to determine whether a particular code will be recognized for payment purposes. The codes are maintained by the Centers for Medicare and Medicaid Services (CMS). More information regarding the review and modification process as well as updates to the code set can be found at the CMS Web site www.cms.hhs.gov/states/posdata.pdf. If you would like to comment on a code(s) or description(s), please send your request to posinfo@cms.hhs.gov.

Place of Service Code(s)	Place of Service Name	Place of Service Description
01	Pharmacy	A facility or location where drugs and other medically related items and services are sold, dispensed, or otherwise provided directly to patients. (effective 10/1/05)
02	Unassigned	N/A
03	School	A facility whose primary purpose is education.
04	Homeless Shelter	A facility or location whose primary purpose is to provide temporary housing to homeless individuals (eg, emergency shelters, individual, or family shelters).
05	Indian Health Service Free-standing Facility	A facility or location, owned and operated by the Indian Health Service, that provides diagnostic, therapeutic (surgical and non-surgical), and rehabilitation services to American Indians and Alaska Natives who do not require hospitalization.
06	Indian Health Service Provider-based Facility	A facility or location, owned and operated by the Indian Health Service, that provides diagnostic, therapeutic (surgical and nonsurgical), and rehabilitation services rendered by, or under the supervision of, physicians to American Indians and Alaska Natives admitted as inpatients or outpatients.
07	Tribal 638 Free-standing Facility	A facility or location owned and operated by a federally recognized American Indian or Alaska Native tribe or tribal organization under a 638 agreement that which provides diagnostic, therapeutic (surgical and non-surgical), and rehabilitation services to tribal members who do not require hospitalization.
08	Tribal 638 Provider-based Facility	A facility or location owned and operated by a federally recognized American Indian or Alaska Native tribe or tribal organization under a 638 agreement that provides diagnostic, therapeutic (surgical and nonsurgical), and rehabilitation services to tribal members admitted as inpatients or outpatients.
09-10	Unassigned	N/A
11	Office	Location, other than a hospital, skilled nursing facility (SNF), military treatment facility, community health center, state or local public health clinic, or intermediate care facility (ICF), where the health professional routinely provides health examinations, diagnosis, and treatment of illness or injury on an ambulatory basis.
12	Home	Location, other than a hospital or other facility, where the patient receives care in a private residence.
13	Assisted Living Facility	Congregate residential facility with self-contained living units providing assessment of each resident's needs and on-site support 24 hours a day, 7 days a week, with the capacity to deliver or arrange for services including some health care and other services. (effective 10/1/03)
14	Group Home	A residence, with shared living areas, where clients receive supervision and other services such as social and/or behavioral services, custodial service, and minimal services (eg, medication administration).
15	Mobile Unit	A facility or unit that moves from place-to-place equipped to provide preventive, screening, diagnostic, and/or treatment services.
16-19	Unassigned	N/A
20	Urgent Care Facility	Location, distinct from a hospital emergency department, an office, or a clinic, whose purpose is to diagnose and treat illness or injury for unscheduled, ambulatory patients seeking immediate medical attention.
21	Inpatient Hospital	A facility, other than psychiatric, that primarily provides diagnostic, therapeutic (both surgical and nonsurgical), and rehabilitation services by, or under, the supervision of physicians to patients admitted for a variety of medical conditions.
22	Outpatient Hospital	A portion of a hospital that provides diagnostic, therapeutic (both surgical and nonsurgical), and rehabilitation services to sick or injured persons who do not require hospitalization or institutionalization.
23	Emergency Room — Hospital	A portion of a hospital where emergency diagnosis and treatment of illness or injury is provided.
24	Ambulatory Surgical Center	A freestanding facility, other than a physician's office, where surgical and diagnostic services are provided on an ambulatory basis.
25	Birthing Center	A facility, other than a hospital's maternity facilities or a physician's office, that provides a setting for labor, delivery, and immediate postpartum care as well as immediate care of new born infants.
26	Military Treatment Facility	A medical facility operated by one or more of the Uniformed Services. Military treatment facility (MTF) also refers to certain former US Public Health Service (USPHS) facilities now designated as uniformed service treatment facilities (USTF).
27-30	Unassigned	N/A
31	Skilled Nursing Facility	A facility that primarily provides inpatient skilled nursing care and related services to patients who require medical, nursing, or rehabilitative services but does not provide the level of care or treatment available in a hospital.

32	Nursing Facility	A facility that primarily provides to residents skilled nursing care and related services for the rehabilitation of injured, disabled, or sick persons, or, on a regular basis, health-related care services above the level of custodial care to other than mentally retarded individuals.
33	Custodial Care Facility	A facility that provides room, board, and other personal assistance services, generally on a long-term basis, and does not include a medical component.
34	Hospice	A facility, other than a patient's home, in which palliative and supportive care for terminally ill patients and their families are provided.
35-40	Unassigned	N/A
41	Ambulance — Land	A land vehicle specifically designed, equipped, and staffed for lifesaving and transporting the sick or injured.
42	Ambulance — Air or Water	An air or water vehicle specifically designed, equipped, and staffed for lifesaving and transporting the sick or injured.
43-48	Unassigned	N/A
49	Independent Clinic	A location, not part of a hospital and not described by any other place-of-service code, that is organized and operated to provide preventive, diagnostic, therapeutic, rehabilitative, or palliative services to outpatients only. (effective 10/1/03)
50	Federally Qualified Health Center	A facility located in a medically underserved area that provides Medicare beneficiaries preventive primary medical care under the general direction of a physician.
51	Inpatient Psychiatric Facility	A facility that provides inpatient psychiatric services for the diagnosis and treatment of mental illness on a 24-hour basis, by or under the supervision of a physician.
52	Psychiatric Facility — Partial Hospitalization	A facility for the diagnosis and treatment of mental illness that provides a planned therapeutic program for patients who do not require full time hospitalization but who need broader programs than are possible from outpatient visits to a hospital-based or hospital-affiliated facility.
53	Community Mental Health Center	A facility that provides the following services: outpatient services, including specialized outpatient services for children, the elderly, individuals who are chronically ill, and residents of the CMHC's mental health services area who have been discharged from inpatient treatment at a mental health facility; 24-hour-a-day emergency care services; day treatment, other partial hospitalization services, or psychosocial rehabilitation services; screening for patients being considered for admission to state mental health facilities to determine the appropriateness of such admission; and consultation and education services.
54	Intermediate Care Facility/Mentally Retarded	A facility that primarily provides health-related care and services above the level of custodial care to mentally retarded individuals but does not provide the level of care or treatment available in a hospital or SNF.
55	Residential Substance Abuse Treatment Facility	A facility that provides treatment for substance (alcohol and drug) abuse to live-in residents who do not require acute medical care. Services include individual and group therapy and counseling, family counseling, laboratory tests, drugs and supplies, psychological testing, and room and board.
56	Psychiatric Residential Treatment Center	A facility or distinct part of a facility for psychiatric care that provides a total 24-hour therapeutically planned and professionally staffed group living and learning environment.
57	Nonresidential Substance Abuse Treatment Facility	A location that provides treatment for substance (alcohol and drug) abuse on an ambulatory basis. Services include individual and group therapy and counseling, family counseling, laboratory tests, drugs and supplies, and psychological testing. (effective 10/1/03)
58-59	Unassigned	N/A
60	Mass Immunization Center	A location where providers administer pneumococcal pneumonia and influenza virus vaccinations and submit these services as electronic media claims, paper claims, or using the roster billing method. This generally takes place in a mass immunization setting, such as a public health center, pharmacy, or mall but may include a physician office setting.
61	Comprehensive Inpatient Rehabilitation Facility	A facility that provides comprehensive rehabilitation services under the supervision of a physician to inpatients with physical disabilities. Services include physical therapy, occupational therapy, speech pathology, social or psychological services, and orthotics and prosthetics services.
62	Comprehensive Outpatient Rehabilitation Facility	A facility that provides comprehensive rehabilitation services under the supervision of a physician to outpatients with physical disabilities. Services include physical therapy, occupational therapy, and speech pathology services.
63-64	Unassigned	N/A
65	End-Stage Renal Disease Treatment Facility	A facility, other than a hospital, that provides dialysis treatment, maintenance, and/or training to patients or caregivers on an ambulatory or home-care basis.
66-70	Unassigned	N/A
71	Public Health Clinic	A facility maintained by either state or local health departments that provides ambulatory primary medical care under the general direction of a physician. (effective 10/1/03)
72	Rural Health Clinic	A certified facility located in a rural medically underserved area that provides ambulatory primary medical care under the general direction of a physician.
73-80	Unassigned	N/A
81	Independent Laboratory	A laboratory certified to perform diagnostic and/or clinical tests independent of an institution or a physician's office.
82-98	Unassigned	N/A
99	Other Place of Service	Other place of service not identified above.

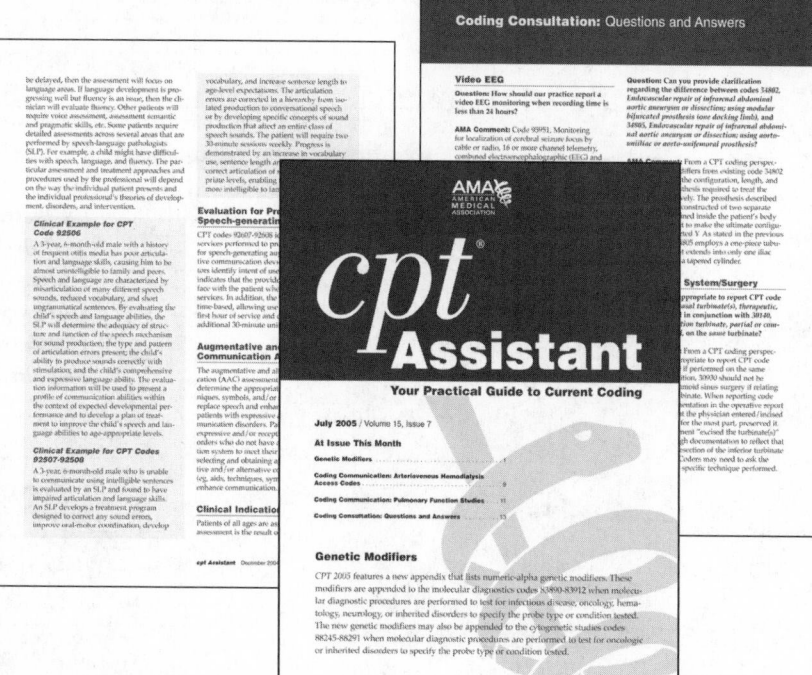

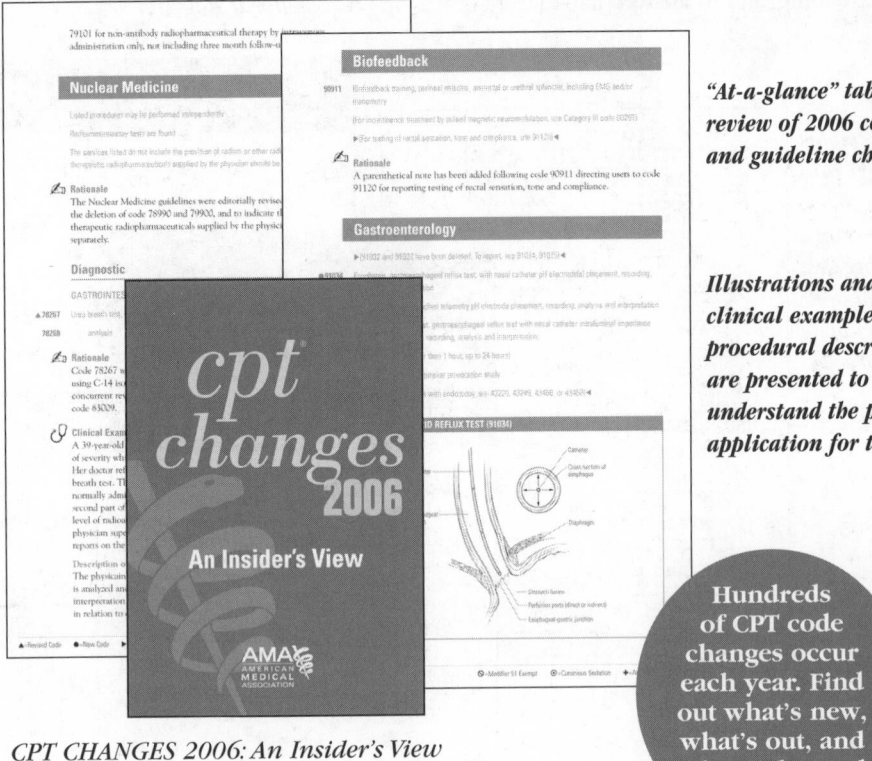

cpt®

2006

Current Procedural Terminology
Standard Edition

Michael Beebe
Joyce A. Dalton
Catherine Duffy, BS, RHIT
Martha Espronceda, AAS
Desiree D. Evans, AAS
Rejina L. Glenn
Gloria Green, BA

DeHandro Hayden, BS
Elizabeth Lumakovska, BS, RHIT
Anita Majerowicz, MS, RHIA
Marie L. Mindeman, BA, RHIT
Karen E. O'Hara, BS, CCS-P
Mary R. O'Heron, RHIA, CCS-P
Danielle Pavloski, BS, RHIT, CCS-P

Desiree Rozell, MPA
Lianne Stancik, RHIT
Peggy Thompson, MS, RHIA, CCS
Susan Tracy, BA, RHIT
Jennifer Trajkovski, BS, RHIT
Ada Walker, CCA

AMA
AMERICAN
MEDICAL
ASSOCIATION

Standard ISBN: 1-57947-697-X
ISSN: 0276-8283

1st Edition printed 1966
2nd Edition printed 1970
3rd Edition printed 1973
4th Edition printed 1977
Revised: 1978, 1979, 1980, 1981, 1982, 1984, 1985,
1986, 1987, 1988, 1989, 1990, 1991, 1992, 1993, 1994,
1995, 1996, 1997, 1998, 1999, 2000, 2001, 2002, 2003, 2004, 2005

To purchase additional CPT products, contact the American Medical Association Customer Service
at 800 621-8335.

To request a license for distribution of products containing or reprinting CPT codes and/or guidelines,
please see our Web site at *www.ama-assn.org/go/cpt* or contact the American Medical Association CPT
Intellectual Property Services, 515 N. State Street, Chicago, Illinois 60610, 312 464-5022.

AC35:OP054106:10/05

Foreword

Current Procedural Terminology (CPT®), Fourth Edition, is a listing of descriptive terms and identifying codes for reporting medical services and procedures performed by physicians. The purpose of the terminology is to provide a uniform language that will accurately describe medical, surgical, and diagnostic services, and will thereby provide an effective means for reliable nationwide communication among physicians, patients, and third parties. *CPT 2006* is the most recent revision of a work that first appeared in 1966.

CPT descriptive terms and identifying codes currently serve a wide variety of important functions in the field of medical nomenclature. The CPT codebook is useful for administrative management purposes such as claims processing and for the development of guidelines for medical care review. The uniform language is also applicable to medical education and outcomes, health services and quality research by providing a useful basis for local, regional, and national utilization comparisons. The CPT codebook is the most widely accepted nomenclature for the reporting of physician procedures and services under government and private health insurance programs. In 2000, the CPT code set was designated by the Department of Health and Human Services as the national coding standard for physician and other health care professional services and procedures under the Health Insurance Portability and Accountability Act (HIPAA). This means that for all financial and administrative health care transactions sent electronically, the CPT code set will need to be used.

The changes that appear in this revision have been prepared by the CPT Editorial Panel with the assistance of physicians representing all specialties of medicine, and with important contributions from many third-party payers and governmental agencies.

The American Medical Association trusts that this revision will continue the usefulness of its predecessors in identifying, describing, and coding medical, surgical, and diagnostic services.

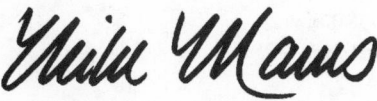

Michael D. Maves, MD, MBA
Executive Vice President, CEO

Acknowledgments

Publication of the annual CPT codebook represents many challenges and opportunities. From reconciling the many differences of opinion about the best way to describe a procedure, to the last details on placement of a semicolon, many individuals and organizations devote their energies and expertise to the preparation of this revision.

The editorial staff wishes to express sincere thanks to the many national medical specialty societies, health insurance organizations and agencies, and individual physicians and other health professionals who have made contributions.

Thanks are due to Robert A. Musacchio, PhD, Sr VP, American Medical Association; Claudia Bonnell, Blue Cross and Blue Shield Association; Nelly Leon-Chisen, American Hospital Association; Tom Wilder, America's Health Insurance Plans; and Sue Bowman, RHIA, American Health Information Management Association, for their invaluable assistance in enhancing the CPT code set.

And finally, our gratitude to the following staff of the American Medical Association for their assistance in producing the books, diskettes, and CD-ROMs that contain the CPT code set: Anthony J. Frankos, Vice President, Business Products; Mike Desposito, Publisher; Elise Schumacher, Senior Acquisition Editor; Dan Reyes, Director, CPT Product Development; J. D. Kinney, Director of Marketing; Jean Roberts, Director, Production and Manufacturing; Erin Kalitowski, Marketing Manager; Carol Brockman, Technical Developmental Editor; Rosalyn Carlton, Senior Production Coordinator; Boon Ai Tan, Senior Production Coordinator; Ronnie Summers, Senior Print Coordinator; Angela Boudreau, Electronic Products Support and Development Manager; and Todd Feinstein, Application Developer.

Coding Questions

For questions regarding the use of CPT codes, please contact the American Medical Association CPT Information Services (CPTIS) at 800 634-6922. Please note that AMA members receive a complimentary subscription to CPTIS, while for all others, this is a fee-for-service resource. Subscription information on CPTIS can be obtained at www.ama-assn.org/go/cpt.

AMA CPT Editorial Panel

American Roentgen Ray Society
Geraldine B. McGinty, MD, MBA
American Society for Aesthetic Plastic Surgery, Inc.
Paul R. Weiss, MD
American Society for Clinical Pathology
Mark S. Synovec, MD
American Society for Dermatologic Surgery
Pamela K. Phillips, MD
American Society for Gastrointestinal Endoscopy
Klaus Mergener, MD
American Society for Reproductive Medicine
John T. Queenan, Jr, MD
American Society for Surgery of the Hand
Daniel J. Nagle, MD
American Society for Therapeutic Radiology and Oncology
Michael L. Steinberg, MD
American Society of Abdominal Surgeons
Louis F. Alfano, Jr, MD
American Society of Anesthesiologists
H. J. Przybylo, Jr, MD
American Society of Bariatric Physicians
Mary C. Vernon, MD‡
American Society of Cataract and Refractive Surgery
Stephen S. Lane, MD
American Society of Clinical Oncology
William C. Penley, MD
American Society of Colon and Rectal Surgeons
David A. Margolin, MD
American Society of Cytopathology
David C. Hoak, MD
Patricia A. Gregg, MD‡
American Society of General Surgeons
Charles Drueck, III, MD, FACS
American Society of Hematology
Samuel M. Silver, MD, PhD
American Society of Neuroimaging
Mircea A. Morariu, Jr, MD
American Society of Neuroradiology
Robert A. Murray, MD
American Society of Ophthalmic Plastic and Reconstructive Surgery
L. Neal Freeman, MD, MBA, CCS-P, FACS
American Society of Plastic Surgeons
Raymond V. Janevicius, MD
American Thoracic Society
Stephen P. Hoffmann, MD‡
American Urological Association
Jeffrey A. Dann, MD
Association of University Radiologists
Bob W. Gayler, MD
College of American Pathologists
Stephen N. Bauer, MD
Congress of Neurological Surgeons
R. Patrick Jacob, MD
Contact Lens Association of Ophthalmologists
Charles B. Slonim, MD, FACS
Infectious Disease Society of America
Lawrence P. Martinelli, MD‡
International Spinal Injection Society
Claire Tibiletti, MD
National Association of Medical Examiners
Paul A. Raslavicus, MD
North American Spine Society
William Mitchell, MD
Radiological Society of North America
Richard E. Fulton, MD

Renal Physicians Association
Richard J. Hamburger, MD
Society for Investigative Dermatology
Stephen P. Stone, MD
Society for Vascular Surgery
Anton N. Sidawy, MD
Society of American Gastrointestinal Endoscopic Surgeons
Paresh C. Shah, MD
Society of Critical Care Medicine
George A. Sample, MD
Society of Interventional Radiology
Katharine L. Krol, MD‡
Society of Nuclear Medicine
Kenneth A. McKusick, MD
Society of Radiologists in Ultrasound
Robert L. Bree, MD
Society of Thoracic Surgeons
Keith S. Naunheim, MD
The Endocrine Society
Richard A. Dickey, MD
The Triological Society
James H. Kelly, MD
United States and Canadian Academy of Pathology
David S. Wilkinson, MD, PhD‡

AMA Health Care Professionals Advisory Committee (HCPAC)

Tracy R. Gordy, MD, Co-Chair
AMA CPT Editorial Panel
Helene Fearon, PT, Co-Chair
AMA CPT Editorial Panel
American Academy of Physician Assistants
Patrick J. Cafferty, MPAS, PA-C
American Association of Naturopathic Physicians
Wendell B. Milliman, ND
American Association for Respiratory Care
Susan Rinaldo-Gallo, Med, RRT
American Chiropractic Association
Craig S. Little, DC
American Dietetic Association
Jane V. White, PhD, RD, FADA
Keith Thomas-Ayoob, EdD, RD, FADA, CSP‡
American Massage Therapy Association
Whitney W. Lowe
American Nurses Association
David Keepnews, PhD, JD, RN‡
American Occupational Therapy Association
Leslie F. Davison, MS, Ed, OTR/L
American Optometric Association
Douglas C. Morrow, OD
Pharmacist Services Technical Advisory Coalition
Daniel E. Buffington, PharmD, MBA
American Physical Therapy Association
Paul A. Rockar, Jr, PT, MS
American Podiatric Medical Association
Michael J. King, DPM
American Psychological Association
Antonio E. Puente, PhD
American Speech-Language Hearing Association
R. Wayne Holland, EdD
National Association of Social Workers
Nelda Spyres, ACSW, LCSW
National Society of Genetic Counselors
Debra L. Doyle, MS, CGC

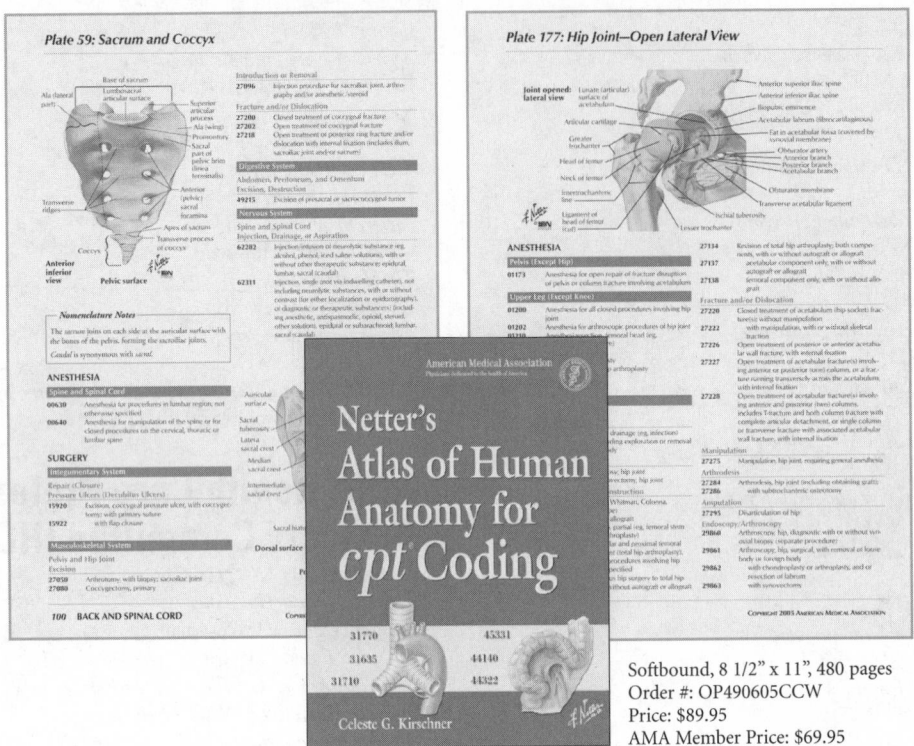

Contents

Introduction . . . .**.xiii**

  Section Numbers and Their Sequences xiii

  Instructions for Use of the CPT Codebook xiii

    Format of the Terminology .xiii

    Requests to Update the CPT Nomenclature xiv

    Guidelines xiv

    Add-on Codes xiv

    Modifiers xiv

    Unlisted Procedure or Service xv

    Special Report xv

    Code Symbols xv

    Alphabetical Reference Index xv

    CPT 2006 in Electronic Formats xv

**Evaluation and Management (E/M) Services
Guidelines** **1**

Evaluation and Management **9**

  Office or Other Outpatient Services 9

  Hospital Observation Services 10

  Hospital Inpatient Services 11

  Consultations 14

  Emergency Department Services 16

  Pediatric Critical Care Patient Transport 17

  Critical Care Services 17

  Inpatient Neonatal and Pediatric Critical
  Care Services 19

  Inpatient Pediatric Critical Care 20

  Inpatient Neonatal Critical Care 20

  ►Continuing Intensive Care Services . . . . .20◄

  Nursing Facility Services 21

  Domiciliary, Rest Home (eg, Boarding Home), or Custodial
  Care Services 23

  ►Domiciliary Rest Home (eg, Assisted Living Facility), or
  Home Care Plan Oversight Services . . . . .24◄

  Home Services 25

  Prolonged Services 26

  Case Management Services .27

  Care Plan Oversight Services 28

  Preventive Medicine Services 28

  Newborn Care 30

  Special Evaluation and Management Services 30

  Other Evaluation and Management Services 31

Anesthesia Guidelines **33**

Anesthesia **35**

  Head 35

  Neck 35

  Thorax (Chest Wall and Shoulder Girdle) 35

  Intrathoracic 36

  Spine and Spinal Cord 36

  Upper Abdomen 36

  Lower Abdomen 37

  Perineum 37

  Pelvis (Except Hip) 38

  Upper Leg (Except Knee) 38

  Knee and Popliteal Area 38

  Lower Leg (Below Knee, Includes Ankle and Foot) 38

  Shoulder and Axilla 39

  Upper Arm and Elbow 39

  Forearm, Wrist, and Hand 39

  Radiological Procedures 40

  Burn Excisions or Debridement 40

  Obstetric 40

  Other Procedures 40

Surgery Guidelines **41**

Surgery **47**

  General 47

  Integumentary System 47

  Musculoskeletal System 63

  Respiratory System 103

  Cardiovascular System 113

  Hemic and Lymphatic Systems 137

  Mediastinum and Diaphragm 139

  Digestive System 141

  Urinary System 167

  Male Genital System 179

  Intersex Surgery 183

  Female Genital System 185

  Maternity Care and Delivery .191

  Endocrine System 195

Contents

Nervous System 197

Eye and Ocular Adnexa 213

Auditory System 223

Operating Microscope 225

Radiology Guidelines (Including Nuclear Medicine and Diagnostic Ultrasound) 227

Radiology 229

Diagnostic Radiology (Diagnostic Imaging) 229

Diagnostic Ultrasound 242

Radiation Oncology 245

Nuclear Medicine 248

Pathology and Laboratory Guidelines 253

Pathology and Laboratory 255

Organ or Disease Oriented Panels 255

Drug Testing 256

Therapeutic Drug Assays 256

Evocative/Suppression Testing 257

Consultations (Clinical Pathology) 258

Urinalysis 258

Chemistry 259

Hematology and Coagulation 268

Immunology 270

Transfusion Medicine 274

Microbiology 275

Anatomic Pathology 279

Cytopathology 279

Cytogenetic Studies 280

Surgical Pathology 281

Transcutaneous Procedures 284

Other Procedures 285

Reproductive Medicine Procedures 285

Medicine Guidelines 287

Medicine 289

Immune Globulins 289

Immunization Administration for Vaccines/Toxoids 289

Vaccines, Toxoids 290

►Hydration, Therapeutic, Prophylactic, and Diagnostic Injections and Infusion (Excludes Chemotherapy) ..... 291◄

Psychiatry 293

Biofeedback 295

Dialysis 295

Gastroenterology 297

Ophthalmology 298

Special Otorhinolaryngologic Services 300

Cardiovascular 303

Non-Invasive Vascular Diagnostic Studies 310

Pulmonary 311

Allergy and Clinical Immunology 313

Endocrinology 314

Neurology and Neuromuscular Procedures 314

Central Nervous System Assessments/Tests 318

Health and Behavior Assessment/Intervention 319

Chemotherapy Administration 319

Photodynamic Therapy 321

Special Dermatological Procedures 321

Physical Medicine and Rehabilitation 322

Medical Nutrition Therapy 324

Acupuncture 324

Osteopathic Manipulative Treatment 324

Chiropractic Manipulative Treatment 324

►Education and Training for Patient Self-Management .... 325◄

Special Services, Procedures and Reports 325

Qualifying Circumstances for Anesthesia 326

►Moderate (Conscious) Sedation .... 327◄

Other Services and Procedures 327

Home Health Procedures/Services 328

Category II Codes 329

Category III Codes 333

Appendix A—Modifiers 339

Appendix B—Summary of Additions, Deletions, and Revisions 344

Appendix C—Clinical Examples 353

Appendix D—Summary of CPT Add-on Codes 371

Appendix E—Summary of CPT Codes Exempt from Modifier 51 372

Appendix F—Summary of CPT Codes Exempt from Modifier 63 373

Appendix G—Summary of CPT Codes That Include Moderate (Conscious) Sedation 374

Appendix H—Alphabetic Index of Performance Measures by Clinical Condition or Topic 376

Appendix I—Genetic Testing Code Modifiers 384

►Appendix J—Electrodiagnostic Medicine Listing of Sensory, Motor, and Mixed Nerves .... 387◄

►Appendix K—Product Pending FDA Approval ...... 391◄

►Appendix L—Vascular Families .... 392◄

Index 395

Introduction

Current Procedural Terminology (*CPT*®), Fourth Edition, is a set of codes, descriptions, and guidelines intended to describe procedures and services performed by physicians and other health care providers. Each procedure or service is identified with a five-digit code. The use of CPT codes simplifies the reporting of services.

Inclusion of a descriptor and its associated five-digit code number in the CPT codebook is based on whether the procedure is consistent with contemporary medical practice and is performed by many practitioners in clinical practice in multiple locations. Inclusion in the CPT codebook does not represent endorsement by the American Medical Association (AMA) of any particular diagnostic or therapeutic procedure. Inclusion or exclusion of a procedure does not imply any health insurance coverage or reimbursement policy.

The CPT code set is published annually in the late summer or early fall as both electronic data files and books. The release of CPT data files on the Internet typically precedes the book by several weeks. In any case, January 1 is the effective date for use of the update of the CPT code set. The interval between the release of the update and the effective date is considered the implementation period and is intended to allow physicians and other providers, payers, and vendors to incorporate CPT changes into their systems. The exception to this schedule of release and effective dates are CPT Category II, Category III, and vaccine product codes, which are released twice a year on January 1 or July 1 with effective dates for use six months later.

The main body of the material is listed in six sections. Each section is divided into subsections with anatomic, procedural, condition, or descriptor subheadings. The procedures and services with their identifying codes are presented in numeric order with one exception—the entire **Evaluation and Management** section (99201-99499) appears at the beginning of the listed procedures. These items are used by most physicians in reporting a significant portion of their services.

Section Numbers and Their Sequences

Evaluation and Management 99201-99499
Anesthesiology 00100-01999, 99100-99140
Surgery 10021-69990
Radiology (Including Nuclear Medicine and Diagnostic
    Ultrasound) 70010-79999
Pathology and Laboratory 80048-89356
Medicine
(except Anesthesiology) 90281-99199, 99500-99602

The first and last code numbers and the subsection name of the items appear at the top margin of most pages (eg, "11010-11306 Surgery/Integumentary System"). The continuous pagination of the *CPT* codebook is found on the lower margin of each page along with explanation of any code symbols that are found on that page.

Instructions for Use of the CPT Codebook

Select the name of the procedure or service that accurately identifies the service performed. Do not select a CPT code that merely approximates the service provided. If no such procedure or service exists, then report the service using the appropriate unlisted procedure or service code. In surgery, it may be an operation; in medicine, a diagnostic or therapeutic procedure; in radiology, a radiograph. Other additional procedures performed or pertinent special services are also listed. When necessary, any modifying or extenuating circumstances are added. Any service or procedure should be adequately documented in the medical record.

It is important to recognize that the listing of a service or procedure and its code number in a specific section of this book does not restrict its use to a specific specialty group. Any procedure or service in any section of this book may be used to designate the services rendered by any qualified physician or other qualified health care professional.

Instructions, typically included as parenthetical notes, with selected codes indicate that a code should not be reported with another code or codes. These instructions are intended to prevent errors of significant probability and are not all inclusive. For example, the code with such instructions may be a component of another code and therefore it would be incorrect to report both codes even when the component service is performed. These instructions are not intended as a listing of all possible code combinations that should not be reported, nor to indicate all possible code combinations that are appropriately reported.

Format of the Terminology

The CPT code set has been developed as stand-alone descriptions of medical procedures. However, some of the procedures in the CPT codebook are not printed in their entirety but refer back to a common portion of the procedure listed in a preceding entry. This is evident when an entry is followed by one or more indentations. This is done in an effort to conserve space.

Example

25100   Arthrotomy, wrist joint; with biopsy

25105   with synovectomy

Note that the common part of code 25100 (the part before the semicolon) should be considered part of code 25105. Therefore, the full procedure represented by code 25105 should read:

25105   Arthrotomy, wrist joint; with synovectomy

Requests to Update the CPT Nomenclature

The effectiveness of the CPT nomenclature depends on constant updating to reflect changes in medical practice. This can only be accomplished through the interest and timely suggestions of practicing physicians, medical specialty societies, state medical associations, and other organizations and agencies. Accordingly, the AMA welcomes correspondence, inquiries, and suggestions concerning old and new procedures, as well as other matters such as codes and indices.

To submit a suggestion to add, delete, or revise procedures contained in the CPT codebook, please contact:
CPT Editorial Research & Development
American Medical Association
515 North State Street
Chicago, Illinois 60610

Coding change request forms are also available at the AMA's CPT Web site: www.ama-assn.org/ama/pub/article/3866.html.

All proposed changes of the CPT codebook will be considered by the CPT Editorial Panel with consultation of appropriate medical specialty societies.

Guidelines

Specific guidelines are presented at the beginning of each of the six sections. These guidelines define items that are necessary to appropriately interpret and report the procedures and services contained in that section. For example, in the **Medicine** section, specific instructions are provided for handling unlisted services or procedures, special reports, and supplies and materials provided. Guidelines also provide explanations regarding terms that apply only to a particular section. For instance, **Radiology Guidelines** provide a definition of the unique term, "radiological supervision and interpretation." While in **Anesthesia**, a discussion of reporting time is included.

Add-on Codes

Some of the listed procedures are commonly carried out in addition to the primary procedure performed. These additional or supplemental procedures are designated as add-on codes with the "+" symbol and they are listed in Appendix D of the CPT codebook. Add-on codes in *CPT 2006* can be readily identified by specific descriptor nomenclature that includes phrases such as "each additional" or "(List separately in addition to primary procedure)."

The add-on code concept in *CPT 2006* applies only to add-on procedures or services performed by the same physician. Add-on codes describe additional intra-service work associated with the primary procedure, eg, additional digit(s), lesion(s), neurorrhaphy(s), vertebral segment(s), tendon(s), joint(s).

Add-on codes are always performed in addition to the primary service or procedure and must never be reported as a stand-alone code. All add-on codes found in the CPT codebook are exempt from the multiple procedure concept (see the modifier 51 definition in **Appendix A**).

Modifiers

A modifier provides the means by which the reporting physician can indicate that a service or procedure that has been performed has been altered by some specific circumstance but not changed in its definition or code. The judicious application of modifiers obviates the necessity for separate procedure listings that may describe the modifying circumstance. Modifiers may be used to indicate to the recipient of a report that:

- A service or procedure had both a professional and technical component.
- A service or procedure was performed by more than one physician and/or in more than one location.
- A service or procedure was increased or reduced.
- Only part of a service was performed.
- An adjunctive service was performed.
- A bilateral procedure was performed.
- A service or procedure was provided more than once.
- Unusual events occurred.

Example

A physician providing diagnostic or therapeutic radiology services, ultrasound, or nuclear medicine services in a hospital would add modifier 26 to report the professional component.

73090 with modifier 26 = Professional component only for an X ray of the forearm

Example

Two surgeons may be required to manage a specific surgical problem. When two surgeons work together as primary surgeons performing distinct part(s) of a procedure, each surgeon should report his/her distinct operative work by adding modifier 62 to the procedure code and any associated code(s) for that procedure as long as both surgeons continue to work together as primary surgeons. Each surgeon should report the co-surgery once using the same procedure code. Modifier 62 would be applicable. For instance, a neurological surgeon and an otolaryngologist are working as co-surgeons in performing transsphenoidal excision of a pituitary neoplasm.

The first surgeon would report:

61548 with modifier 62 = Hypophysectomy or excision of pituitary tumor, transnasal or transseptal approach, nonstereotactic + two surgeons modifier

AND the second surgeon would report:

61548 with modifier 62 = Hypophysectomy or excision of pituitary tumor, transnasal or transseptal approach, nonstereotactic + two surgeons modifier

If additional procedure(s) (including add-on procedure[s]) are performed during the same surgical session, separate code(s) may also be reported with modifier 62 added. **Note:** If a co-surgeon acts as an assistant in the performance of additional procedure(s) during the same surgical session, those services may be reported using separate procedure code(s) with modifier 80 or modifier 82 added, as appropriate. A complete listing of modifiers is found in **Appendix A**.

Unlisted Procedure or Service

It is recognized that there may be services or procedures performed by physicians that are not found in the CPT codebook. Therefore, a number of specific code numbers have been designated for reporting unlisted procedures. When an unlisted procedure number is used, the service or procedure should be described. Each of these unlisted procedural code numbers (with the appropriate accompanying topical entry) relates to a specific section of the book and is presented in the guidelines of that section.

Special Report

A service that is rarely provided, unusual, variable, or new may require a special report in determining medical appropriateness of the service. Pertinent information should include an adequate definition or description of the nature, extent, and need for the procedure and the time, effort, and equipment necessary to provide the service. Additional items may include complexity of symptoms, final diagnosis, pertinent physical findings, diagnostic and therapeutic procedures, concurrent problems, and follow-up care.

Code Symbols

A summary listing of additions, deletions, and revisions applicable to the CPT codebook is found in **Appendix B**. New procedure numbers added to the CPT codebook are identified throughout the text with the symbol ● placed before the code number. In instances where a code revision has resulted in a substantially altered procedure descriptor, the symbol ▲ is placed before the code number. The symbols ► ◄ are used to indicate new and revised text other than the procedure descriptors. CPT add-on codes are annotated by the symbol ✚ and are listed in **Appendix D**. The symbol ⊘ is used to identify codes that are exempt from the use of modifier 51 but have not been designated as CPT add-on procedures or services. A list of codes exempt from modifier 51 usage is included in **Appendix E**. The symbol ⊙ is used to identify codes that include conscious sedation (see **Appendix G**). The symbol ⁄ is used to identify codes for vaccines that are pending FDA approval (see **Appendix K**).

Alphabetical Reference Index

This codebook features an expanded alphabetical index that includes listings by procedure and anatomic site. Procedures and services commonly known by their eponyms or other designations are also included.

CPT 2006 in Electronic Formats

CPT 2006 procedure codes and descriptions are also available on CD-ROM as data files and electronic software. Data files are available in ASCII and EBCDIC formats and can be imported into any billing and claims reporting software that accepts a text (TXT) file format. *CPT 2006 Electronic Professional* software places the entire *CPT 2006 Professional Edition* on your desktop in an easy-to-use, fully searchable format. For more information call 800 621-8335 or visit www.amapress.com.

Evaluation and Management (E/M) Services Guidelines

In addition to the information presented in the Introduction, several other items unique to this section are defined or identified here.

Classification of Evaluation and Management (E/M) Services

The E/M section is divided into broad categories such as office visits, hospital visits, and consultations. Most of the categories are further divided into two or more subcategories of E/M services. For example, there are two subcategories of office visits (new patient and established patient) and there are two subcategories of hospital visits (initial and subsequent). The subcategories of E/M services are further classified into levels of E/M services that are identified by specific codes. This classification is important because the nature of physician work varies by type of service, place of service, and the patient's status.

The basic format of the levels of E/M services is the same for most categories. First, a unique code number is listed. Second, the place and/or type of service is specified, eg, office consultation. Third, the content of the service is defined, eg, comprehensive history and comprehensive examination. (See "Levels of E/M Services," page 2, for details on the content of E/M services.) Fourth, the nature of the presenting problem(s) usually associated with a given level is described. Fifth, the time typically required to provide the service is specified. (A detailed discussion of time is provided on page 3.)

Definitions of Commonly Used Terms

Certain key words and phrases are used throughout the E/M section. The following definitions are intended to reduce the potential for differing interpretations and to increase the consistency of reporting by physicians in differing specialties.

New and Established Patient

Solely for the purposes of distinguishing between new and established patients, **professional services** are those face-to-face services rendered by a physician and reported by a specific CPT code(s). A new patient is one who has not received any professional services from the physician or another physician of the same specialty who belongs to the same group practice, within the past three years.

An established patient is one who has received professional services from the physician or another physician of the same specialty who belongs to the same group practice, within the past three years.

In the instance where a physician is on call for or covering for another physician, the patient's encounter will be classified as it would have been by the physician who is not available.

No distinction is made between new and established patients in the emergency department. E/M services in the emergency department category may be reported for any new or established patient who presents for treatment in the emergency department.

Chief Complaint

A chief complaint is a concise statement describing the symptom, problem, condition, diagnosis, or other factor that is the reason for the encounter, usually stated in the patient's words.

Concurrent Care

Concurrent care is the provision of similar services, eg, hospital visits, to the same patient by more than one physician on the same day. When concurrent care is provided, no special reporting is required. Modifier 75 has been deleted.

Counseling

Counseling is a discussion with a patient and/or family concerning one or more of the following areas:

- Diagnostic results, impressions, and/or recommended diagnostic studies
- Prognosis
- Risks and benefits of management (treatment) options
- Instructions for management (treatment) and/or follow-up

- Importance of compliance with chosen management (treatment) options
- Risk factor reduction
- Patient and family education

(For psychotherapy, see 90804-90857)

Family History

A review of medical events in the patient's family that includes significant information about:

- The health status or cause of death of parents, siblings, and children
- Specific diseases related to problems identified in the Chief Complaint or History of the Present Illness, and/or System Review
- Diseases of family members that may be hereditary or place the patient at risk

History of Present Illness

A chronological description of the development of the patient's present illness from the first sign and/or symptom to the present. This includes a description of location, quality, severity, timing, context, modifying factors, and associated signs and symptoms significantly related to the presenting problem(s).

Levels of E/M Services

Within each category or subcategory of E/M service, there are three to five levels of E/M services available for reporting purposes. Levels of E/M services are **not** interchangeable among the different categories or subcategories of service. For example, the first level of E/M services in the subcategory of office visit, new patient, does not have the same definition as the first level of E/M services in the subcategory of office visit, established patient.

The levels of E/M services include examinations, evaluations, treatments, conferences with or concerning patients, preventive pediatric and adult health supervision, and similar medical services, such as the determination of the need and/or location for appropriate care. Medical screening includes the history, examination, and medical decision-making required to determine the need and/or location for appropriate care and treatment of the patient (eg, office and other outpatient setting, emergency department, nursing facility). The levels of E/M services encompass the wide variations in skill, effort, time, responsibility, and medical knowledge required for the prevention or diagnosis and treatment of illness or injury and the promotion of optimal health. Each level of E/M services may be used by all physicians.

The descriptors for the levels of E/M services recognize seven components, six of which are used in defining the levels of E/M services. These components are:

- History
- Examination
- Medical decision making
- Counseling
- Coordination of care
- Nature of presenting problem
- Time

The first three of these components (history, examination, and medical decision making) are considered the **key** components in selecting a level of E/M services. (See "Determine the Extent of History Obtained," page 5.)

The next three components (counseling, coordination of care, and the nature of the presenting problem) are considered **contributory** factors in the majority of encounters. Although the first two of these contributory factors are important E/M services, it is not required that these services be provided at every patient encounter.

Coordination of care with other providers or agencies without a patient encounter on that day is reported using the case management codes.

The final component, time, is discussed in detail (see page 3).

Any specifically identifiable procedure (ie, identified with a specific CPT code) performed on or subsequent to the date of initial or subsequent E/M services should be reported separately.

The actual performance and/or interpretation of diagnostic tests/studies ordered during a patient encounter are not included in the levels of E/M services. Physician performance of diagnostic tests/studies for which specific CPT codes are available may be reported separately, in addition to the appropriate E/M code. The physician's interpretation of the results of diagnostic tests/studies (ie, professional component) with preparation of a separate distinctly identifiable signed written report may also be reported separately, using the appropriate CPT code with modifier 26 appended.

The physician may need to indicate that on the day a procedure or service identified by a CPT code was performed, the patient's condition required a significant separately identifiable E/M service above and beyond other services provided or beyond the usual preservice and postservice care associated with the procedure that was performed. The E/M service may be caused or prompted by the symptoms or condition for which the procedure and/or service was provided. This circumstance may be reported by adding modifier 25 to the appropriate level of E/M service. As such, different diagnoses are not required for reporting of the procedure and the E/M services on the same date.

Nature of Presenting Problem

A presenting problem is a disease, condition, illness, injury, symptom, sign, finding, complaint, or other reason for encounter, with or without a diagnosis being established at the time of the encounter. The E/M codes recognize five types of presenting problems that are defined as follows:

Minimal: A problem that may not require the presence of the physician, but service is provided under the physician's supervision.

Self-limited or minor: A problem that runs a definite and prescribed course, is transient in nature, and is not likely to permanently alter health status OR has a good prognosis with management/compliance.

Low severity: A problem where the risk of morbidity without treatment is low; there is little to no risk of mortality without treatment; full recovery without functional impairment is expected.

Moderate severity: A problem where the risk of morbidity without treatment is moderate; there is moderate risk of mortality without treatment; uncertain prognosis OR increased probability of prolonged functional impairment.

High severity: A problem where the risk of morbidity without treatment is high to extreme; there is a moderate to high risk of mortality without treatment OR high probability of severe, prolonged functional impairment.

Past History

A review of the patient's past experiences with illnesses, injuries, and treatments that includes significant information about:

- Prior major illnesses and injuries
- Prior operations
- Prior hospitalizations
- Current medications
- Allergies (eg, drug, food)
- Age appropriate immunization status
- Age appropriate feeding/dietary status

Social History

An age appropriate review of past and current activities that includes significant information about:

- Marital status and/or living arrangements
- Current employment
- Occupational history
- Use of drugs, alcohol, and tobacco
- Level of education
- Sexual history
- Other relevant social factors

System Review (Review of Systems)

An inventory of body systems obtained through a series of questions seeking to identify signs and/or symptoms that the patient may be experiencing or has experienced. For the purposes of the CPT codebook the following elements of a system review have been identified:

- Constitutional symptoms (fever, weight loss, etc)
- Eyes
- Ears, nose, mouth, throat
- Cardiovascular
- Respiratory
- Gastrointestinal
- Genitourinary
- Musculoskeletal
- Integumentary (skin and/or breast)
- Neurological
- Psychiatric
- Endocrine
- Hematologic/lymphatic
- Allergic/immunologic

The review of systems helps define the problem, clarify the differential diagnosis, identify needed testing, or serves as baseline data on other systems that might be affected by any possible management options.

Time

The inclusion of time in the definitions of levels of E/M services has been implicit in prior editions of the CPT codebook. The inclusion of time as an explicit factor beginning in *CPT 1992* is done to assist physicians in selecting the most appropriate level of E/M services. It should be recognized that the specific times expressed in the visit code descriptors are averages and, therefore, represent a range of times that may be higher or lower depending on actual clinical circumstances.

Time is **not** a descriptive component for the emergency department levels of E/M services because emergency department services are typically provided on a variable intensity basis, often involving multiple encounters with several patients over an extended period of time. Therefore, it is often difficult for physicians to provide accurate estimates of the time spent face-to-face with the patient.

Studies to establish levels of E/M services employed surveys of practicing physicians to obtain data on the amount of time and work associated with typical E/M services. Since "work" is not easily quantifiable, the codes must rely on other objective, verifiable measures that correlate with physicians' estimates of their "work." It has been demonstrated that physicians' estimations of **intraservice** time (as explained on the next page), both within and across specialties, is a variable that is predictive of the "work" of E/M services. This same research has shown there is a strong relationship between intraservice time and total time for E/M services. Intraservice time, rather than total time, was chosen for inclusion with the codes because of its relative ease of measurement and because of its direct correlation with measurements of the total amount of time and work associated with typical E/M services.

Intraservice times are defined as **face-to-face** time for office and other outpatient visits and as **unit/floor** time for hospital and other inpatient visits. This distinction is necessary because most of the work of typical office visits takes place during the face-to-face time with the patient, while most of the work of typical hospital visits takes place during the time spent on the patient's floor or unit.

Face-to-face time (office and other outpatient visits and office consultations): For coding purposes, face-to-face time for these services is defined as only that time that the physician spends face-to-face with the patient and/or family. This includes the time in which the physician performs such tasks as obtaining a history, performing an examination, and counseling the patient.

Physicians also spend time doing work before or after the face-to-face time with the patient, performing such tasks as reviewing records and tests, arranging for further services, and communicating further with other professionals and the patient through written reports and telephone contact.

This **non-face-to-face** time for office services—also called pre- and postencounter time—is not included in the time component described in the E/M codes. However, the pre- and post-face-to-face work associated with an encounter was included in calculating the total work of typical services in physician surveys.

Thus, the face-to-face time associated with the services described by any E/M code is a valid proxy for the total work done before, during, and after the visit.

Unit/floor time (hospital observation services, inpatient hospital care, initial and follow-up hospital consultations, nursing facility): For reporting purposes, intraservice time for these services is defined as unit/floor time, which includes the time that the physician is present on the patient's hospital unit and at the bedside rendering services for that patient. This includes the time in which the physician establishes and/or reviews the patient's chart, examines the patient, writes notes, and communicates with other professionals and the patient's family.

In the hospital, pre- and post-time includes time spent off the patient's floor performing such tasks as reviewing pathology and radiology findings in another part of the hospital.

This pre- and postvisit time is not included in the time component described in these codes. However, the pre- and postwork performed during the time spent off the floor or unit was included in calculating the total work of typical services in physician surveys.

Thus, the unit/floor time associated with the services described by any code is a valid proxy for the total work done before, during, and after the visit.

Unlisted Service

An E/M service may be provided that is not listed in this section of the CPT codebook. When reporting such a service, the appropriate "Unlisted" code may be used to indicate the service, identifying it by "Special Report," as discussed in the following paragraph. The "Unlisted Services" and accompanying codes for the E/M section are as follows:

99429   **Unlisted preventive** medicine service

99499   **Unlisted evaluation and management** service

Special Report

An unlisted service or one that is unusual, variable, or new may require a special report demonstrating the medical appropriateness of the service. Pertinent information should include an adequate definition or description of the nature, extent, and need for the procedure and the time, effort, and equipment necessary to provide the service. Additional items that may be included are complexity of symptoms, final diagnosis, pertinent physical findings, diagnostic and therapeutic procedures, concurrent problems, and follow-up care.

Clinical Examples

Clinical examples of the codes for E/M services are provided to assist physicians in understanding the meaning of the descriptors and selecting the correct code. The clinical examples are listed in Appendix C. Each example was developed by physicians in the specialties shown.

The same problem, when seen by physicians in different specialties, may involve different amounts of work. Therefore, the appropriate level of encounter should be reported using the descriptors rather than the examples.

The examples have been tested for validity and approved by the CPT Editorial Panel. Physicians were given the examples and asked to assign a code or assess the amount of time and work involved. Only examples that were rated consistently have been included in Appendix C.

Table 1
Categories and Subcategories of Service

Category/Subcategory	Code Numbers	Category/Subcategory	Code Numbers
Office or Other Outpatient Services		Domiciliary, Rest Home or	
New Patient	99201-99205	Custodial Care Services	
Established Patient	99211-99215	New Patient	►99307-99310◄
►Hospital Observation Services◄		Established Patient	►99334-99337◄
Hospital Observation Discharge Services	99217	►Domiciliary, Rest Home (eg, Assisted	
►Initial◄ Hospital Observation Services	99218-99220	Living Facility), or Home Care Plan	
Hospital Observation or Inpatient Care		Oversight Services	99339-99340◄
Services (Including Admission and		Home Services	
Discharge Services)	99234-99236	New Patient	99341-99345
Hospital Inpatient Services		Established Patient	99347-99350
Initial Hospital Care	99221-99223	Prolonged Services	
Subsequent Hospital Care	99231-99233	With Direct Patient Contact	99354-99357
Hospital Discharge Services	99238-99239	Without Direct Patient Contact	99358-99359
Consultations		Standby Services	99360
Office Consultations	99241-99245	Case Management Services	
Initial Inpatient Consultations	99251-99255	Team Conferences	99361-99362
Emergency Department Services	99281-99288	Telephone Calls	99371-99373
Pediatric Patient Transport	99289-99290	Care Plan Oversight Services	99374-99380
Critical Care Services		Preventive Medicine Services	
Adult (over 24 months of age)	99291-99292	New Patient	99381-99387
Pediatric	99293-99294	Established Patient	99391-99397
Neonatal	99295-99296	Individual Counseling	99401-99404
►Continuing◄ Intensive Care ►Services◄	99298-99300	Group Counseling	99411-99412
Nursing Facility Services		Other	99420-99429
►Initial Nursing Facility Care	99304-99306◄	Newborn Care	99431-99440
Subsequent Nursing Facility Care	►99307-99310◄	Special E/M Services	99450-99456
Nursing Facility Discharge Services	99315-99316	Other E/M Services	99499
►Other Nursing Facility Services	99318◄		

Instructions for Selecting a Level of E/M Service

Identify the Category and Subcategory of Service

The categories and subcategories of codes available for reporting E/M services are shown in Table 1.

Review the Reporting Instructions for the Selected Category or Subcategory

Most of the categories and many of the subcategories of service have special guidelines or instructions unique to that category or subcategory. Where these are indicated, eg, "Inpatient Hospital Care," special instructions will be presented preceding the levels of E/M services.

Review the Level of E/M Service Descriptors and Examples in the Selected Category or Subcategory

The descriptors for the levels of E/M services recognize seven components, six of which are used in defining the levels of E/M services. These components are:

- History
- Examination
- Medical decision making
- Counseling
- Coordination of care
- Nature of presenting problem
- Time

The first three of these components (ie, history, examination, and medical decision making) should be considered the **key** components in selecting the level of E/M services. An exception to this rule is in the case of visits that consist predominantly of counseling or coordination of care (see numbered paragraph 3, page 7).

The nature of the presenting problem and time are provided in some levels to assist the physician in determining the appropriate level of E/M service.

Determine the Extent of History Obtained

The extent of the history is dependent upon clinical judgment and on the nature of the presenting problems(s). The levels of E/M services recognize four types of history that are defined as follows:

Problem focused: Chief complaint; brief history of present illness or problem.

Expanded problem focused: Chief complaint; brief history of present illness; problem pertinent system review.

Detailed: Chief complaint; extended history of present illness; problem pertinent system review extended to include a review of a limited number of additional systems; **pertinent** past, family, and/or social history **directly related to the patient's problems.**

Comprehensive: Chief complaint; extended history of present illness; review of systems that is directly related to the problem(s) identified in the history of the present illness plus a review of all additional body systems; **complete** past, family, and social history.

The comprehensive history obtained as part of the preventive medicine E/M service is not problem-oriented and does not involve a chief complaint or present illness. It does, however, include a comprehensive system review and comprehensive or interval past, family, and social history as well as a comprehensive assessment/history of pertinent risk factors.

Determine the Extent of Examination Performed

The extent of the examination performed is dependent on clinical judgment and on the nature of the presenting problem(s). The levels of E/M services recognize four types of examination that are defined as follows:

Problem focused: A limited examination of the affected body area or organ system.

Expanded problem focused: A limited examination of the affected body area or organ system and other symptomatic or related organ system(s).

Detailed: An extended examination of the affected body area(s) and other symptomatic or related organ system(s).

Comprehensive: A general multisystem examination or a complete examination of a single organ system. **Note:** The comprehensive examination performed as part of the preventive medicine E/M service is multisystem, but its extent is based on age and risk factors identified.

For the purposes of these CPT definitions, the following body areas are recognized:

- Head, including the face
- Neck
- Chest, including breasts and axilla
- Abdomen
- Genitalia, groin, buttocks
- Back
- Each extremity

For the purposes of these CPT definitions, the following organ systems are recognized:

- Eyes
- Ears, nose, mouth, and throat
- Cardiovascular
- Respiratory
- Gastrointestinal
- Genitourinary
- Musculoskeletal
- Skin
- Neurologic
- Psychiatric
- Hematologic/lymphatic/immunologic

Determine the Complexity of Medical Decision Making

Medical decision making refers to the complexity of establishing a diagnosis and/or selecting a management option as measured by:

- The number of possible diagnoses and/or the number of management options that must be considered
- The amount and/or complexity of medical records, diagnostic tests, and/or other information that must be obtained, reviewed, and analyzed
- The risk of significant complications, morbidity, and/or mortality, as well as comorbidities, associated with the patient's presenting problems(s), the diagnostic procedure(s), and/or the possible management options

Four types of medical decision making are recognized: straightforward, low complexity, moderate complexity, and high complexity. To qualify for a given type of decision making, two of the three elements in Table 2 must be met or exceeded.

Comorbidities/underlying diseases, in and of themselves, are not considered in selecting a level of E/M services *unless* their presence significantly increases the complexity of the medical decision making.

Select the Appropriate Level of E/M Services Based on the Following

▶1. For the following categories/subcategories, **all of the key components,** ie, history, examination, and medical decision making, must meet or exceed the stated requirements to qualify for a particular level of E/M service: office, new patient; hospital observation services; initial hospital care; office consultations; initial inpatient consultations; emergency department services; initial nursing facility care; domiciliary care, new patient; and home, new patient.◀

Table 2
Complexity of Medical Decision Making

Number of Diagnoses or Management Options	Amount and/or Complexity of Data to be Reviewed	Risk of Complications and/or Morbidity or Mortality	Type of Decision Making
minimal	minimal or none	minimal	**straightforward**
limited	limited	low	**low complexity**
multiple	moderate	moderate	**moderate complexity**
extensive	extensive	high	**high complexity**

►2. For the following categories/subcategories, **two of the three key components** (ie, history, examination, and medical decision making) must meet or exceed the stated requirements to qualify for a particular level of E/M services: office, established patient; subsequent hospital care; subsequent nursing facility care; domiciliary care, established patient; and home, established patient.◄

3. When counseling and/or coordination of care dominates (more than 50%) the physician/patient and/or family encounter (face-to-face time in the office or other outpatient setting or floor/unit time in the hospital or nursing facility), then **time** may be considered the key or controlling factor to qualify for a particular level of E/M services. This includes time spent with parties who have assumed responsibility for the care of the patient or decision making whether or not they are family members (eg, foster parents, person acting in locum parentis, legal guardian). The extent of counseling and/or coordination of care must be documented in the medical record.

Notes

⊘=Modifier 51 exempt   ⊙=Conscious sedation   +=Add-on code   ✗=FDA approval pending

Evaluation and Management

Office or Other Outpatient Services

The following codes are used to report evaluation and management services provided in the physician's office or in an outpatient or other ambulatory facility. A patient is considered an outpatient until inpatient admission to a health care facility occurs.

►To report services provided to a patient who is admitted to a hospital or nursing facility in the course of an encounter in the office or other ambulatory facility, see the notes for initial hospital inpatient care (page 11) or initial nursing facility care (page 21).◄

For services provided by physicians in the emergency department, see 99281-99285.

For observation care, see 99217-99220.

For observation or inpatient care services (including admission and discharge services), see 99234-99236.

New Patient

99201   **Office or other outpatient visit** for the evaluation and management of a new patient, which requires these three key components:

- **a problem focused history;**
- **a problem focused examination;**
- **straightforward medical decision making.**

Counseling and/or coordination of care with other providers or agencies are provided consistent with the nature of the problem(s) and the patient's and/or family's needs.

Usually, the presenting problem(s) are self limited or minor. Physicians typically spend 10 minutes face-to-face with the patient and/or family.

99202   **Office or other outpatient visit** for the evaluation and management of a new patient, which requires these three key components:

- **an expanded problem focused history;**
- **an expanded problem focused examination;**
- **straightforward medical decision making.**

Counseling and/or coordination of care with other providers or agencies are provided consistent with the nature of the problem(s) and the patient's and/or family's needs.

Usually, the presenting problem(s) are of low to moderate severity. Physicians typically spend 20 minutes face-to-face with the patient and/or family.

99203   **Office or other outpatient visit** for the evaluation and management of a new patient, which requires these three key components:

- **a detailed history;**
- **a detailed examination;**
- **medical decision making of low complexity.**

Counseling and/or coordination of care with other providers or agencies are provided consistent with the nature of the problem(s) and the patient's and/or family's needs.

Usually, the presenting problem(s) are of moderate severity. Physicians typically spend 30 minutes face-to-face with the patient and/or family.

99204   **Office or other outpatient visit** for the evaluation and management of a new patient, which requires these three key components:

- **a comprehensive history;**
- **a comprehensive examination;**
- **medical decision making of moderate complexity.**

Counseling and/or coordination of care with other providers or agencies are provided consistent with the nature of the problem(s) and the patient's and/or family's needs.

Usually, the presenting problem(s) are of moderate to high severity. Physicians typically spend 45 minutes face-to-face with the patient and/or family.

99205   **Office or other outpatient visit** for the evaluation and management of a new patient, which requires these three key components:

- **a comprehensive history;**
- **a comprehensive examination;**
- **medical decision making of high complexity.**

Counseling and/or coordination of care with other providers or agencies are provided consistent with the nature of the problem(s) and the patient's and/or family's needs.

Usually, the presenting problem(s) are of moderate to high severity. Physicians typically spend 60 minutes face-to-face with the patient and/or family.

Established Patient

99211   **Office or other outpatient visit** for the evaluation and management of an established patient, that may not require the presence of a physician. Usually, the presenting problem(s) are minimal. Typically, 5 minutes are spent performing or supervising these services.

99212 **Office or other outpatient visit** for the evaluation and management of an established patient, which requires at least two of these three key components:

- **a problem focused history;**

- **a problem focused examination;**

- **straightforward medical decision making.**

Counseling and/or coordination of care with other providers or agencies are provided consistent with the nature of the problem(s) and the patient's and/or family's needs.

Usually, the presenting problem(s) are self limited or minor. Physicians typically spend 10 minutes face-to-face with the patient and/or family.

99213 **Office or other outpatient visit** for the evaluation and management of an established patient, which requires at least two of these three key components:

- **an expanded problem focused history;**

- **an expanded problem focused examination;**

- **medical decision making of low complexity.**

Counseling and coordination of care with other providers or agencies are provided consistent with the nature of the problem(s) and the patient's and/or family's needs.

Usually, the presenting problem(s) are of low to moderate severity. Physicians typically spend 15 minutes face-to-face with the patient and/or family.

99214 **Office or other outpatient visit** for the evaluation and management of an established patient, which requires at least two of these three key components:

- **a detailed history;**

- **a detailed examination;**

- **medical decision making of moderate complexity.**

Counseling and/or coordination of care with other providers or agencies are provided consistent with the nature of the problem(s) and the patient's and/or family's needs.

Usually, the presenting problem(s) are of moderate to high severity. Physicians typically spend 25 minutes face-to-face with the patient and/or family.

99215 **Office or other outpatient visit** for the evaluation and management of an established patient, which requires at least two of these three key components:

- **a comprehensive history;**

- **a comprehensive examination;**

- **medical decision making of high complexity.**

Counseling and/or coordination of care with other providers or agencies are provided consistent with the nature of the problem(s) and the patient's and/or family's needs.

Usually, the presenting problem(s) are of moderate to high severity. Physicians typically spend 40 minutes face-to-face with the patient and/or family.

Hospital Observation Services

The following codes are used to report evaluation and management services provided to patients designated/admitted as "observation status" in a hospital. It is not necessary that the patient be located in an observation area designated by the hospital.

If such an area does exist in a hospital (as a separate unit in the hospital, in the emergency department, etc), these codes are to be utilized if the patient is placed in such an area.

For definitions of key components and commonly used terms, please see **Evaluation and Management Services Guidelines.**

Typical times have not yet been established for this category of services.

Observation Care Discharge Services

Observation care discharge of a patient from "observation status" includes final examination of the patient, discussion of the hospital stay, instructions for continuing care, and preparation of discharge records. For observation or inpatient hospital care including the admission and discharge of the patient on the same date, see codes 99234-99236 as appropriate.

99217 **Observation care discharge** day management (This code is to be utilized by the physician to report all services provided to a patient on discharge from "observation status" if the discharge is on other than the initial date of "observation status." To report services to a patient designated as "observation status" or "inpatient status" and discharged on the same date, use the codes for Observation or Inpatient Care Services [including Admission and Discharge Services, 99234-99236 as appropriate.])

Initial Observation Care

New or Established Patient

The following codes are used to report the encounter(s) by the supervising physician with the patient when designated as "observation status." This refers to the initiation of observation status, supervision of the care plan for observation and performance of periodic reassessments. For observation encounters by other physicians, see Office or Other Outpatient Consultation codes (99241-99245).

Evaluation and Management

To report services provided to a patient who is admitted to the hospital after receiving hospital observation care services on the same date, see the notes for initial hospital inpatient care (page 11). For a patient admitted to the hospital on a date subsequent to the date of observation status, the hospital admission would be reported with the appropriate Initial Hospital Care code (99221-99223). For a patient admitted and discharged from observation or inpatient status on the same date, the services should be reported with codes 99234-99236 as appropriate. Do not report observation discharge (99217) in conjunction with a hospital admission.

When "observation status" is initiated in the course of an encounter in another site of service (eg, hospital emergency department, physician's office, nursing facility) all evaluation and management services provided by the supervising physician in conjunction with initiating "observation status" are considered part of the initial observation care when performed on the same date. The observation care level of service reported by the supervising physician should include the services related to initiating "observation status" provided in the other sites of service as well as in the observation setting.

Evaluation and management services on the same date provided in sites that are related to initiating "observation status" should NOT be reported separately.

These codes may not be utilized for post-operative recovery if the procedure is considered part of the surgical "package." These codes apply to all evaluation and management services that are provided on the same date of initiating "observation status."

99218   **Initial observation care,** per day, for the evaluation and management of a patient which requires these three key components:

- **a detailed or comprehensive history;**

- **a detailed or comprehensive examination; and**

- **medical decision making that is straightforward or of low complexity.**

Counseling and/or coordination of care with other providers or agencies are provided consistent with the nature of the problem(s) and the patient's and/or family's needs.

Usually, the problem(s) requiring admission to "observation status" are of low severity.

99219   **Initial observation care,** per day, for the evaluation and management of a patient, which requires these three key components:

- **a comprehensive history;**

- **a comprehensive examination; and**

- **medical decision making of moderate complexity.**

Counseling and/or coordination of care with other providers or agencies are provided consistent with the nature of the problem(s) and the patient's and/or family's needs.

Usually, the problem(s) requiring admission to "observation status" are of moderate severity.

99220   **Initial observation care,** per day, for the evaluation and management of a patient, which requires these three key components:

- **a comprehensive history;**

- **a comprehensive examination; and**

- **medical decision making of high complexity.**

Counseling and/or coordination of care with other providers or agencies are provided consistent with the nature of the problem(s) and the patient's and/or family's needs.

Usually, the problem(s) requiring admission to "observation status" are of high severity.

Hospital Inpatient Services

The following codes are used to report evaluation and management services provided to hospital inpatients. Hospital inpatient services include those services provided to patients in a "partial hospital" setting. These codes are to be used to report these partial hospitalization services. See also psychiatry notes in the full text of CPT codebook.

For definitions of key components and commonly used terms, please see **Evaluation and Management Services Guidelines.** For Hospital Observation Services, see 99218-99220. For a patient admitted and discharged from observation or inpatient status on the same date, the services should be reported with codes 99234-99236 as appropriate.

Initial Hospital Care

New or Established Patient

The following codes are used to report the first hospital inpatient encounter with the patient by the admitting physician.

For initial inpatient encounters by physicians other than the admitting physician, see initial inpatient consultation codes (99251-99255) or subsequent hospital care codes (99231-99233) as appropriate.

When the patient is admitted to the hospital as an inpatient in the course of an encounter in another site of service (eg, hospital emergency department, observation status in a hospital, physician's office, nursing facility) all evaluation and management services provided by that physician in conjunction with that admission are considered part of the initial hospital care when

---

▲=Revised code   ●=New code   ▶ ◀=Contains new or revised text

performed on the same date as the admission. The inpatient care level of service reported by the admitting physician should include the services related to the admission he/she provided in the other sites of service as well as in the inpatient setting.

Evaluation and management services on the same date provided in sites that are related to the admission "observation status" should NOT be reported separately. For a patient admitted and discharged from observation or inpatient status on the same date, the services should be reported with codes 99234-99236 as appropriate.

99221   **Initial hospital care,** per day, for the evaluation and management of a patient, which requires these three key components:

- **a detailed or comprehensive history;**
- **a detailed or comprehensive examination; and**
- **medical decision making that is straightforward or of low complexity.**

Counseling and/or coordination of care with other providers or agencies are provided consistent with the nature of the problem(s) and the patient's and/or family's needs.

Usually, the problem(s) requiring admission are of low severity. Physicians typically spend 30 minutes at the bedside and on the patient's hospital floor or unit.

99222   **Initial hospital care,** per day, for the evaluation and management of a patient, which requires these three key components:

- **a comprehensive history;**
- **a comprehensive examination; and**
- **medical decision making of moderate complexity.**

Counseling and/or coordination of care with other providers or agencies are provided consistent with the nature of the problem(s) and the patient's and/or family's needs.

Usually, the problem(s) requiring admission are of moderate severity. Physicians typically spend 50 minutes at the bedside and on the patient's hospital floor or unit.

99223   **Initial hospital care,** per day, for the evaluation and management of a patient, which requires these three key components:

- **a comprehensive history;**
- **a comprehensive examination; and**
- **medical decision making of high complexity.**

Counseling and/or coordination of care with other providers or agencies are provided consistent with the nature of the problem(s) and the patient's and/or family's needs.

Usually, the problem(s) requiring admission are of high severity. Physicians typically spend 70 minutes at the bedside and on the patient's hospital floor or unit.

Subsequent Hospital Care

All levels of subsequent hospital care include reviewing the medical record and reviewing the results of diagnostic studies and changes in the patient's status (ie, changes in history, physical condition and response to management) since the last assessment by the physician.

99231   **Subsequent hospital care,** per day, for the evaluation and management of a patient, which requires at least two of these three key components:

- **a problem focused interval history;**
- **a problem focused examination;**
- **medical decision making that is straightforward or of low complexity.**

Counseling and/or coordination of care with other providers or agencies are provided consistent with the nature of the problem(s) and the patient's and/or family's needs.

Usually, the patient is stable, recovering or improving. Physicians typically spend 15 minutes at the bedside and on the patient's hospital floor or unit.

99232   **Subsequent hospital care,** per day, for the evaluation and management of a patient, which requires at least two of these three key components:

- **an expanded problem focused interval history;**
- **an expanded problem focused examination;**
- **medical decision making of moderate complexity.**

Counseling and/or coordination of care with other providers or agencies are provided consistent with the nature of the problem(s) and the patient's and/or family's needs.

Usually, the patient is responding inadequately to therapy or has developed a minor complication. Physicians typically spend 25 minutes at the bedside and on the patient's hospital floor or unit.

99233   **Subsequent hospital care,** per day, for the evaluation and management of a patient, which requires at least two of these three key components:

- **a detailed interval history;**
- **a detailed examination;**
- **medical decision making of high complexity.**

Counseling and/or coordination of care with other providers or agencies are provided consistent with the nature of the problem(s) and the patient's and/or family's needs.

Usually, the patient is unstable or has developed a significant complication or a significant new problem. Physicians typically spend 35 minutes at the bedside and on the patient's hospital floor or unit.

Observation or Inpatient Care Services (Including Admission and Discharge Services)

The following codes are used to report observation or inpatient hospital care services provided to patients admitted and discharged on the same date of service. When a patient is admitted to the hospital from observation status on the same date, the physician should report only the initial hospital care code. The initial hospital care code reported by the admitting physician should include the services related to the observation status services he/she provided on the same date of inpatient admission.

When "observation status" is initiated in the course of an encounter in another site of service (eg, hospital emergency department, physician's office, nursing facility) all evaluation and management services provided by the supervising physician in conjunction with initiating "observation status" are considered part of the initial observation care when performed on the same date. The observation care level of service should include the services related to initiating "observation status" provided in the other sites of service as well as in the observation setting when provided by the same physician.

For patients admitted to observation or inpatient care and discharged on a different date, see codes 99218-99220 and 99217, or 99221-99223 and 99238, 99239.

99234   **Observation or inpatient hospital care,** for the evaluation and management of a patient including admission and discharge on the same date which requires these three key components:

- **a detailed or comprehensive history;**

- **a detailed or comprehensive examination; and**

- **medical decision making that is straightforward or of low complexity.**

Counseling and/or coordination of care with other providers or agencies are provided consistent with the nature of the problem(s) and the patient's and/or family's needs.

Usually the presenting problem(s) requiring admission are of low severity.

99235   **Observation or inpatient hospital care,** for the evaluation and management of a patient including admission and discharge on the same date which requires these three key components:

- **a comprehensive history;**

- **a comprehensive examination; and**

- **medical decision making of moderate complexity.**

Counseling and/or coordination of care with other providers or agencies are provided consistent with the nature of the problem(s) and the patient's and/or family's needs.

Usually the presenting problem(s) requiring admission are of moderate severity.

99236   **Observation or inpatient hospital care,** for the evaluation and management of a patient including admission and discharge on the same date which requires these three key components:

- **a comprehensive history;**

- **a comprehensive examination; and**

- **medical decision making of high complexity.**

Counseling and/or coordination of care with other providers or agencies are provided consistent with the nature of the problem(s) and the patient's and/or family's needs.

Usually the presenting problem(s) requiring admission are of high severity.

Hospital Discharge Services

The hospital discharge day management codes are to be used to report the total duration of time spent by a physician for final hospital discharge of a patient. The codes include, as appropriate, final examination of the patient, discussion of the hospital stay, even if the time spent by the physician on that date is not continuous, instructions for continuing care to all relevant caregivers, and preparation of discharge records, prescriptions and referral forms. For a patient admitted and discharged from observation or inpatient status on the same date, the services should be reported with codes 99234-99236 as appropriate.

99238   **Hospital discharge day management;** 30 minutes or less

99239   more than 30 minutes

(These codes are to be utilized by the physician to report all services provided to a patient on the date of discharge, if other than the initial date of inpatient status. To report services to a patient who is admitted as an inpatient, and discharged on the same date, see codes 99234-99236 for observation or inpatient hospital care including the admission and discharge of the patient on the same date. To report concurrent care services provided by a physician(s) other than the attending physician, use subsequent hospital care codes (99231-99233) on the day of discharge.)

(For Observation Care Discharge, use 99217)

(For observation or inpatient hospital care including the admission and discharge of the patient on the same date, see 99234-99236)

(For Nursing Facility Care Discharge, see 99315, 99316)

(For discharge services provided to newborns admitted and discharged on the same date, use 99435)

Consultations

A consultation is a type of service provided by a physician whose opinion or advice regarding evaluation and/or management of a specific problem is requested by another physician or other appropriate source.

A physician consultant may initiate diagnostic and/or therapeutic services at the same or subsequent visit.

The written or verbal request for a consult may be made by a physician or other appropriate source and documented in the patient's medical record. The consultant's opinion and any services that were ordered or performed must also be documented in the patient's medical record and communicated by written report to the requesting physician or other appropriate source.

▶A "consultation" initiated by a patient and/or family, and not requested by a physician, is not reported using the consultation codes but may be reported using the office visit codes, as appropriate.◀

▶If a consultation is mandated, eg, by a third-party payer, modifier 32 should also be reported.◀

Any specifically identifiable procedure (ie, identified with a specific CPT code) performed on or subsequent to the date of the initial consultation should be reported separately.

▶If subsequent to the completion of a consultation, the consultant assumes responsibility for management of a portion or all of the patient's condition(s), the appropriate **Evaluation and Management** services code for the site of service should be reported. In the hospital setting, the consulting physician should use the appropriate inpatient hospital consultation code for the initial encounter and then subsequent hospital care codes. In the office setting, the appropriate established patient code should be used.◀

For definitions of key components and commonly used terms, please see **Evaluation and Management Services Guidelines.**

Office or Other Outpatient Consultations

New or Established Patient

The following codes are used to report consultations provided in the physician's office or in an outpatient or other ambulatory facility, including hospital observation services, home services, domiciliary, rest home, custodial care, or emergency department (see consultation definition, above). Follow-up visits in the consultant's office or other outpatient facility that are initiated by the physician consultant are reported using office visit codes for established patients (99211-99215). If an additional request for an opinion or advice regarding the same or a new problem is received from the attending physician and documented in the medical record, the office consultation codes may be used again.

99241 **Office consultation** for a new or established patient, which requires these three key components:

- **a problem focused history;**
- **problem focused examination; and**
- **straightforward medical decision making.**

Counseling and/or coordination of care with other providers or agencies are provided consistent with the nature of the problem(s) and the patient's and/or family's needs.

Usually, the presenting problem(s) are self limited or minor. Physicians typically spend 15 minutes face-to-face with the patient and/or family.

99242 **Office consultation** for a new or established patient, which requires these three key components:

- **an expanded problem focused history;**
- **an expanded problem focused examination; and**
- **straightforward medical decision making.**

Counseling and/or coordination of care with other providers or agencies are provided consistent with the nature of the problem(s) and the patient's and/or family's needs.

Usually, the presenting problem(s) are of low severity. Physicians typically spend 30 minutes face-to-face with the patient and/or family.

99243 **Office consultation** for a new or established patient, which requires these three key components:

- **a detailed history;**
- **a detailed examination; and**
- **medical decision making of low complexity.**

Counseling and/or coordination of care with other providers or agencies are provided consistent with the nature of the problem(s) and the patient's and/or family's needs.

Usually, the presenting problem(s) are of moderate severity. Physicians typically spend 40 minutes face-to-face with the patient and/or family.

99244 **Office consultation** for a new or established patient, which requires these three key components:

- **a comprehensive history;**
- **a comprehensive examination; and**
- **medical decision making of moderate complexity.**

Counseling and/or coordination of care with other providers or agencies are provided consistent with the nature of the problem(s) and the patient's and/or family's needs.

Usually, the presenting problem(s) are of moderate to high severity. Physicians typically spend 60 minutes face-to-face with the patient and/or family.

99245   **Office consultation** for a new or established patient, which requires these three key components:

- **a comprehensive history;**

- **a comprehensive examination; and**

- **medical decision making of high complexity.**

Counseling and/or coordination of care with other providers or agencies are provided consistent with the nature of the problem(s) and the patient's and/or family's needs.

Usually, the presenting problem(s) are of moderate to high severity. Physicians typically spend 80 minutes face-to-face with the patient and/or family.

Initial Inpatient Consultations

New or Established Patient

The following codes are used to report physician consultations provided to hospital inpatients, residents of nursing facilities, or patients in a partial hospital setting. Only one initial consultation should be reported by a consultant per admission.

99251   **Initial inpatient consultation** for a new or established patient, which requires these three key components:

- **a problem focused history;**

- **a problem focused examination; and**

- **straightforward medical decision making.**

Counseling and/or coordination of care with other providers or agencies are provided consistent with the nature of the problem(s) and the patient's and/or family's needs.

Usually, the presenting problem(s) are self limited or minor. Physicians typically spend 20 minutes at the bedside and on the patient's hospital floor or unit.

99252   **Initial inpatient consultation** for a new or established patient, which requires these three key components:

- **an expanded problem focused history;**

- **an expanded problem focused examination; and**

- **straightforward medical decision making.**

Counseling and/or coordination of care with other providers or agencies are provided consistent with the nature of the problem(s) and the patient's and/or family's needs.

Usually, the presenting problem(s) are of low severity. Physicians typically spend 40 minutes at the bedside and on the patient's hospital floor or unit.

99253   **Initial inpatient consultation** for a new or established patient, which requires these three key components:

- **a detailed history;**

- **a detailed examination; and**

- **medical decision making of low complexity.**

Counseling and/or coordination of care with other providers or agencies are provided consistent with the nature of the problem(s) and the patient's and/or family's needs.

Usually, the presenting problem(s) are of moderate severity. Physicians typically spend 55 minutes at the bedside and on the patient's hospital floor or unit.

99254   **Initial inpatient consultation** for a new or established patient, which requires these three key components:

- **a comprehensive history;**

- **a comprehensive examination; and**

- **medical decision making of moderate complexity.**

Counseling and/or coordination of care with other providers or agencies are provided consistent with the nature of the problem(s) and the patient's and/or family's needs.

Usually, the presenting problem(s) are of moderate to high severity. Physicians typically spend 80 minutes at the bedside and on the patient's hospital floor or unit.

99255   **Initial inpatient consultation** for a new or established patient, which requires these three key components:

- **a comprehensive history;**

- **a comprehensive examination; and**

- **medical decision making of high complexity.**

Counseling and/or coordination of care with other providers or agencies are provided consistent with the nature of the problem(s) and the patient's and/or family's needs.

Usually, the presenting problem(s) are of moderate to high severity. Physicians typically spend 110 minutes at the bedside and on the patient's hospital floor or unit.

▶(99261-99263 have been deleted)◀

▶(For follow-up inpatient consultation, see 99231-99233, 99307-99310)◀

▶(99271-99275 have been deleted. For confirmatory consultation, see the appropriate E/M service code for the setting and type of service (eg, consultation))◀

Evaluation and Management

Emergency Department Services

New or Established Patient

The following codes are used to report evaluation and management services provided in the emergency department. No distinction is made between new and established patients in the emergency department.

An emergency department is defined as an organized hospital-based facility for the provision of unscheduled episodic services to patients who present for immediate medical attention. The facility must be available 24 hours a day.

For critical care services provided in the emergency department, see Critical Care notes and 99291, 99292.

For evaluation and management services provided to a patient in an observation area of a hospital, see 99217-99220.

For observation or inpatient care services (including admission and discharge services), see 99234-99236.

99281 **Emergency department visit** for the evaluation and management of a patient, which requires these three key components:

- **a problem focused history;**
- **a problem focused examination; and**
- **straightforward medical decision making.**

Counseling and/or coordination of care with other providers or agencies are provided consistent with the nature of the problem(s) and the patient's and/or family's needs.

Usually, the presenting problem(s) are self limited or minor.

99282 **Emergency department visit** for the evaluation and management of a patient, which requires these three key components:

- **an expanded problem focused history;**
- **an expanded problem focused examination; and**
- **medical decision making of low complexity.**

Counseling and/or coordination of care with other providers or agencies are provided consistent with the nature of the problem(s) and the patient's and/or family's needs.

Usually, the presenting problem(s) are of low to moderate severity.

99283 **Emergency department visit** for the evaluation and management of a patient, which requires these three key components:

- **an expanded problem focused history;**
- **an expanded problem focused examination; and**
- **medical decision making of moderate complexity.**

Counseling and/or coordination of care with other providers or agencies are provided consistent with the nature of the problem(s) and the patient's and/or family's needs.

Usually, the presenting problem(s) are of moderate severity.

99284 **Emergency department visit** for the evaluation and management of a patient, which requires these three key components:

- **a detailed history;**
- **a detailed examination; and**
- **medical decision making of moderate complexity.**

Counseling and/or coordination of care with other providers or agencies are provided consistent with the nature of the problem(s) and the patient's and/or family's needs.

Usually, the presenting problem(s) are of high severity, and require urgent evaluation by the physician but do not pose an immediate significant threat to life or physiologic function.

99285 **Emergency department visit** for the evaluation and management of a patient, which requires these three key components within the constraints imposed by the urgency of the patient's clinical condition and/or mental status:

- **a comprehensive history;**
- **a comprehensive examination; and**
- **medical decision making of high complexity.**

Counseling and/or coordination of care with other providers or agencies are provided consistent with the nature of the problem(s) and the patient's and/or family's needs.

Usually, the presenting problem(s) are of high severity and pose an immediate significant threat to life or physiologic function.

Other Emergency Services

In physician directed emergency care, advanced life support, the physician is located in a hospital emergency or critical care department, and is in two-way voice communication with ambulance or rescue personnel outside the hospital. The physician directs the performance of necessary medical procedures, including but not limited to: telemetry of cardiac rhythm; cardiac and/or pulmonary resuscitation; endotracheal or esophageal obturator airway intubation; administration of intravenous fluids and/or administration of intramuscular, intratracheal or subcutaneous drugs; and/or electrical conversion of arrhythmia.

99288 **Physician direction of** emergency medical systems (EMS) emergency care, advanced life support

Pediatric Critical Care Patient Transport

The following codes 99289 and 99290 are used to report the physical attendance and direct face-to-face care by a physician during the interfacility transport of a critically ill or critically injured pediatric patient. For the purpose of reporting codes 99289 and 99290, face-to-face care begins when the physician assumes primary responsibility of the pediatric patient at the referring hospital/facility, and ends when the receiving hospital/facility accepts responsibility for the pediatric patient's care. Only the time the physician spends in direct face-to-face contact with the patient during the transport should be reported. Pediatric patient transport services involving less than 30 minutes of face-to-face physician care should not be reported using codes 99289, 99290. Procedure(s) or service(s) performed by other members of the transporting team may not be reported by the supervising physician.

The following services are included when performed during the pediatric patient transport by the physician providing critical care and may not be reported separately: routine monitoring evaluations (eg, heart rate, respiratory rate, blood pressure, and pulse oximetry), the interpretation of cardiac output measurements (93561, 93562), chest x-rays (71010, 71015, 71020), pulse oximetry (94760, 94761, 94762), blood gases and information data stored in computers (eg, ECGs, blood pressures, hematologic data) (99090), gastric intubation (43752, 91105), temporary transcutaneous pacing (92953), ventilatory management (94656, 94660, 94662) and vascular access procedures (36000, 36400, 36405, 36406, 36410, 36415, 36540, 36600). Any services performed which are not listed above should be reported separately.

Critical care is the direct delivery by a physician(s) of medical care for a critically ill or critically injured patient. A critical illness or injury acutely impairs one or more

vital organ systems such that there is a high probability of imminent or life threatening deterioration in the patient's condition. Critical care involves high complexity decision making to assess, manipulate, and support vital system function(s) to treat single or multiple vital organ system failure and/or to prevent further life threatening deterioration of the patient's condition. Examples of vital organ system failure include, but are not limited to: central nervous system failure, circulatory failure, shock, renal, hepatic, metabolic, and/or respiratory failure.

Providing medical care to a critically ill, injured, or post-operative patient qualifies as a critical care service only if both the illness or injury and the treatment being provided meet the above requirements.

The direction of emergency care to transporting staff by a physician located in a hospital or other facility by two-way communication is not considered direct face-to-face care and should not be reported with codes 99289, 99290. Physician directed emergency care through outside voice communication to transporting staff personnel is reported with code 99288.

The emergency department services codes (99281-99285), initial hospital care codes (99221-99223), hourly critical care codes (99291, 99292), or initial date neonatal intensive care code (99295) are only reported after the patient has been admitted to the emergency department, the inpatient floor or the critical care unit of the receiving facility.

Code 99289 is used to report the first 30-74 minutes of direct face-to-face time with the transport pediatric patient and should be reported only once on a given date. Code 99290 is used to report each additional 30 minutes provided on a given date. Face-to-face services less than 30 minutes should not be reported with these codes.

99289 Critical care services delivered by a physician, face-to-face, during an interfacility transport of critically ill or critically injured pediatric patient, 24 months of age or less; first 30-74 minutes of hands on care during transport

+ 99290 each additional 30 minutes (List separately in addition to code for primary service)

(Use 99290 in conjunction with 99289)

(Critical care of less than 30 minutes total duration should be reported with the appropriate E/M code)

Critical Care Services

Critical care is the direct delivery by a physician(s) of medical care for a critically ill or critically injured patient. A critical illness or injury acutely impairs one or more vital organ systems such that there is a high probability of imminent or life threatening deterioration in the patient's condition. Critical care involves high complexity decision making to assess, manipulate, and support vital system function(s) to treat single or multiple vital organ system failure and/or to prevent further life threatening deterioration of the patient's condition. Examples of vital organ system failure include, but are not limited to: central nervous system failure, circulatory failure, shock, renal, hepatic, metabolic, and/or respiratory failure. Although critical care typically requires interpretation of multiple physiologic parameters and/or application of advanced technology(s), critical care may be provided in life threatening situations when these elements are not present. Critical care may be provided on multiple days, even if no changes are made in the treatment rendered to the patient, provided that the patient's condition continues to require the level of physician attention described above.

Providing medical care to a critically ill, injured, or post-operative patient qualifies as a critical care service only if both the illness or injury and the treatment being provided meet the above requirements. Critical care is usually, but not always, given in a critical care area, such as the coronary care unit, intensive care unit, pediatric intensive care unit, respiratory care unit, or the emergency care facility.

Inpatient critical care services provided to infants 29 days through 24 months of age are reported with pediatric critical care codes 99293 and 99294. The pediatric critical care codes are reported as long as the infant/young child qualifies for critical care services during the hospital stay through 24 months of age. Inpatient critical care services provided to neonates (28 days of age or less) are reported with the neonatal critical care codes 99295 and 99296. The neonatal critical care codes are reported as long as the neonate qualifies for critical care services during the hospital stay through the 28th postnatal day. The reporting of the pediatric and neonatal critical care services is not based on time or the type of unit (eg, pediatric or neonatal critical care unit) and it is not dependent upon the type of provider delivering the care. To report critical care services provided in the outpatient setting (eg, emergency department or office), for neonates and pediatric patients up through 24 months of age, see the hourly Critical Care codes 99291, 99292. If the same physician provides critical care services for a neonatal or pediatric patient in both the outpatient and inpatient settings on the same day, report only the appropriate Neonatal or Pediatric Critical Care code (99293-99296) for all critical care services provided on that day. For additional instructions on reporting these services, see the Neonatal and Pediatric Critical Care section and codes 99293-99296.

Services for a patient who is not critically ill but happens to be in a critical care unit are reported using other appropriate E/M codes.

Critical care and other E/M services may be provided to the same patient on the same date by the same physician.

The following services are included in reporting critical care when performed during the critical period by the physician(s) providing critical care: the interpretation of cardiac output measurements (93561, 93562), chest x-rays (71010, 71015, 71020), pulse oximetry (94760, 94761, 94762), blood gases, and information data stored in computers (eg, ECGs, blood pressures, hematologic data (99090)); gastric intubation (43752, 91105); temporary transcutaneous pacing (92953); ventilatory management (94656, 94657, 94660, 94662); and vascular access procedures (36000, 36410, 36415, 36540, 36600). Any services performed which are not listed above should be reported separately.

Codes 99291, 99292 should be reported for the physician's attendance during the transport of critically ill or critically injured patients over 24 months of age to or from a facility or hospital. For physician transport services of critically ill or critically injured pediatric patients 24 months of age or less see 99289, 99290.

The critical care codes 99291 and 99292 are used to report the total duration of time spent by a physician providing critical care services to a critically ill or critically injured patient, even if the time spent by the physician on that date is not continuous. For any given period of time spent providing critical care services, the physician must devote his or her full attention to the patient and, therefore, cannot provide services to any other patient during the same period of time.

Time spent with the individual patient should be recorded in the patient's record. The time that can be reported as critical care is the time spent engaged in work directly related to the individual patient's care whether that time was spent at the immediate bedside or elsewhere on the floor or unit. For example, time spent on the unit or at the nursing station on the floor reviewing test results or imaging studies, discussing the critically ill patient's care with other medical staff or documenting critical care services in the medical record would be reported as critical care, even though it does not occur at the bedside. Also, when the patient is unable or clinically incompetent to participate in discussions, time spent on the floor or unit with family members or surrogate decision makers obtaining a medical history, reviewing the patient's condition or prognosis, or discussing treatment or limitation(s) of treatment may be reported as critical care, provided that the conversation bears directly on the management of the patient.

Time spent in activities that occur outside of the unit or off the floor (eg, telephone calls, whether taken at home, in the office, or elsewhere in the hospital) may not be reported as critical care since the physician is not immediately available to the patient. Time spent in activities that do not directly contribute to the treatment of the patient may not be reported as critical care, even if they are performed in the critical care unit (eg, participation in administrative meetings or telephone calls to discuss other patients). Time spent performing separately reportable procedures or services should not be included in the time reported as critical care time.

Code 99291 is used to report the first 30-74 minutes of critical care on a given date. It should be used only once per date even if the time spent by the physician is not continuous on that date. Critical care of less than 30 minutes total duration on a given date should be reported with the appropriate E/M code.

Code 99292 is used to report additional block(s) of time, of up to 30 minutes each beyond the first 74 minutes. (See table below.)

The following examples illustrate the correct reporting of critical care services:

Total Duration of Critical Care	Codes
less than 30 minutes (less than 1/2 hour)	appropriate E/M codes
30-74 minutes (1/2 hr. - 1 hr. 14 min.)	99291 X 1
75-104 minutes (1 hr. 15 min. - 1 hr. 44 min.)	99291 X 1 AND 99292 X 1
105-134 minutes (1 hr. 45 min. - 2 hr. 14 min.)	99291 X 1 AND 99292 X 2
135 - 164 minutes (2 hr. 15 min. - 2 hr. 44 min.)	99291 X 1 AND 99292 X 3
165 - 194 minutes (2 hr. 45 min. - 3 hr. 14 min.)	99291 X 1 AND 99292 X 4
194 minutes or longer (3 hr. 14 min. - etc.)	99291 and 99292 as appropriate (see illustrated reporting examples above)

99291 **Critical care, evaluation and management** of the critically ill or critically injured patient; first 30-74 minutes

+ **99292** each additional 30 minutes (List separately in addition to code for primary service)

(Use 99292 in conjunction with 99291)

Inpatient Neonatal and Pediatric Critical Care Services

The following codes (99293-99296) are used to report services provided by a physician directing the inpatient care of a critically ill neonate/infant. The same definitions for critical care services apply for the adult, child, and neonate.

The initial day neonatal critical care code (99295) can be used in addition to codes 99360, 99436 or 99440 as appropriate, when the physician is present for the delivery

(99360 or 99436) and newborn resuscitation (99440) is required. Other procedures performed as a necessary part of the resuscitation (eg, endotracheal intubation (31500)) are also reported separately when performed as part of the pre-admission delivery room care. In order to report these procedures separately, they must be performed as a necessary component of the resuscitation and not simply as a convenience before admission to the neonatal intensive care unit.

►Codes 99295, 99296 are used to report services provided by a physician directing the inpatient care of a critically ill neonate through the first 28 days of life. They represent care starting with the date of admission (99295) and subsequent day(s) (99296) and may be reported only once per day, per patient. ◄

►Codes 99293, 99294 are used to report services provided by a physician directing the inpatient care of a critically ill infant or young child from 29 days of postnatal age through 24 months of age. They represent care starting with the date of admission (99293) and subsequent day(s) (99294) and may be reported by a single physician only once per day, per patient in a given setting. The critically ill or critically injured child older than 24 months of age would be reported with hourly critical care service codes (99291, 99292). ◄

►When a neonate or infant is not critically ill, but requires intensive observation, frequent interventions and other intensive care services, the Continuing Intensive Care Services codes (99298, 99299, 99300) should be used to report services for those neonates/infants with present body weight of 5000 grams or less. When the present body weight of those neonates/infants exceeds 5000 grams, the Subsequent Hospital Care Services codes (99231-99233) should be used.◄

►To report critical care services provided in the outpatient setting (eg, emergency department or office) for neonates and pediatric patients up through 24 months of age, see the hourly Critical Care codes 99291, 99292. If the same physician provides critical care services for a neonatal or pediatric patient in both the outpatient and inpatient settings on the same day, report only the appropriate Neonatal or Pediatric Critical Care code (99295-99296) for all critical care services provided on that day.◄

Care rendered under 99293-99296 includes management, monitoring, and treatment of the patient including respiratory, pharmacologic control of the circulatory system, enteral and parenteral nutrition, metabolic and hematologic maintenance, parent/family counseling, case management services, and personal direct supervision of the health care team in the performance of cognitive and procedural activities.

►The pediatric and neonatal critical care codes include those procedures listed above for the hourly critical care codes (99291, 99292). In addition, the following procedures are also included in the bundled (global)

pediatric and neonatal critical care service codes (99293-99296): umbilical venous (36510) and umbilical arterial catheters (36660), other arterial catheters (36140, 36620), central (36555) or peripheral vessel catheterization (36000), vascular access procedures (36400, 36405, 36406), vascular punctures (36420, 36600), oral or nasogastric tube placement (43752), endotracheal intubation (31500), lumbar puncture (62270), suprapubic bladder aspiration (51000), bladder catheterization (51701, 51702), initiation and management of mechanical ventilation (94656, 94657) or continuous positive airway pressure (CPAP) (94660), surfactant administration, intravascular fluid administration (90760-90761), transfusion of blood components (36430, 36440), invasive or non-invasive electronic monitoring of vital signs, bedside pulmonary function testing (94375), and/or monitoring or interpretation of blood gases or oxygen saturation (94760-94762). Any services performed which are not listed above should be reported separately.◄

For additional instructions, see descriptions listed for 99293-99296

Inpatient Pediatric Critical Care

99293 **Initial inpatient pediatric critical care,** per day, for the evaluation and management of a critically ill infant or young child, 29 days through 24 months of age

99294 **Subsequent inpatient pediatric critical care,** per day, for the evaluation and management of a critically ill infant or young child, 29 days through 24 months of age

Inpatient Neonatal Critical Care

99295 **Initial inpatient neonatal critical care,** per day, for the evaluation and management of a critically ill neonate, 28 days of age or less

This code is reserved for the date of admission for neonates who are critically ill. Critically ill neonates require cardiac and/or respiratory support (including ventilator or nasal CPAP when indicated), continuous or frequent vital sign monitoring, laboratory and blood gas interpretations, follow-up physician reevaluations, and constant observation by the health care team under direct physician supervision. Immediate preoperative evaluation and stabilization of neonates with life threatening surgical or cardiac conditions are included under this code. Neonates with life threatening surgical or cardiac conditions are included under this code.

Care for neonates who require an intensive care setting but who are not critically ill is reported using the initial hospital care codes (99221-99223).

99296 **Subsequent inpatient neonatal critical care,** per day, for the evaluation and management of a critically ill neonate, 28 days of age or less

A critically ill neonate will require cardiac and/or respiratory support (including ventilator or nasal CPAP when indicated), continuous or frequent vital sign monitoring, laboratory and blood gas interpretations, follow-up physician re-evaluations throughout a 24-hour period, and constant observation by the health care team under direct physician supervision.

(Subsequent care for neonates who require an intensive setting but who are not critically ill is reported using either the intensive low birth weight services codes (99298, 99299) or the subsequent hospital care codes (99231-99233))

►Continuing Intensive Care Services◄

►Codes 99298, 99299, 99300 are used to report services subsequent to the day of admission provided by a physician directing the continuing intensive care of the low birth weight (LBW, 1500-2500 grams present body weight) infant, very low birth weight (VLBW, less than 1500 grams present body weight) infant, or normal weight (2501-5000 grams present body weight) newborn who do not meet the definition of critically ill but continue to require intensive observation, frequent interventions, and other intensive services. Codes 99298, 99299, 99300 represent subsequent day(s) of care and may be reported only once per calendar day, per patient and are global codes with the same services bundled as outlined under codes 99293-99296.◄

►For additional instructions, see descriptions listed for 99298, 99299, 99300.◄

▲ **99298** **Subsequent intensive care,** per day, for the evaluation and management of the recovering very low birth weight infant (present body weight less than 1500 grams)

►Infants with present body weight less than 1500 grams who are not critically ill but continue to require intensive cardiac and respiratory monitoring, continuous and/or frequent vital sign monitoring, heat maintenance, enteral and/or parenteral nutritional adjustments, laboratory and oxygen monitoring and constant observation by the health care team under direct physician supervision.◄

▲ **99299** **Subsequent intensive care,** per day, for the evaluation and management of the recovering low birth weight infant (present body weight of 1500-2500 grams)

►Infants with present body weight of 1500-2500 grams who are not critically ill but continue to require intensive cardiac and respiratory monitoring, continuous and/or frequent vital sign monitoring, heat maintenance, enteral and/or parenteral nutritional adjustments, laboratory and oxygen monitoring, and constant observation by the health care team under direct physician supervision.◄

● **99300**   Subsequent intensive care, per day, for the evaluation and management of the recovering infant (present body weight of 2501-5000 grams)

►Infants with present body weight of 2501-5000 grams who are not critically ill but continue to require intensive cardiac and respiratory monitoring, continuous and/or frequent vital sign monitoring, heat maintenance, enteral and/or parenteral nutritional adjustments, laboratory and oxygen monitoring, and constant observation by the health care team under direct physician supervision.◄

Nursing Facility Services

The following codes are used to report evaluation and management services to patients in Nursing Facilities (formerly called Skilled Nursing Facilities (SNFs), Intermediate Care Facilities (ICFs) or Long Term Care Facilities (LTCFs)).

These codes should also be used to report evaluation and management services provided to a patient in a psychiatric residential treatment center (a facility or a distinct part of a facility for psychiatric care, which provides a 24-hour therapeutically planned and professionally staffed group living and learning environment). If procedures such as medical psychotherapy are provided in addition to evaluation and management services, these should be reported in addition to the evaluation and management services provided.

Nursing facilities that provide convalescent, rehabilitative, or long term care are required to conduct comprehensive, accurate, standardized, and reproducible assessments of each resident's functional capacity using a Resident Assessment Instrument (RAI). All RAIs include the Minimum Data Set (MDS), Resident Assessment Protocols (RAPs) and utilization guidelines. The MDS is the primary screening and assessment tool; the RAPs trigger the identification of potential problems and provide guidelines for follow-up assessments.

►Physicians have a central role in assuring that all residents receive thorough assessments and that medical plans of care are instituted or revised to enhance or maintain the residents' physical and psychosocial functioning. This role includes providing input in the development of the MDS and a multi-disciplinary plan of care, as required by regulations pertaining to the care of nursing facility residents.◄

►Two major subcategories of nursing facility services are recognized: Initial Nursing Facility Care and Subsequent Nursing Facility Care. Both subcategories apply to new or established patients. ◄

For definitions of key components and commonly used terms, please see **Evaluation and Management Services Guidelines.**

(For care plan oversight services provided to nursing facility residents, see 99379-99380)

►Initial Nursing Facility Care◄

New or Established Patient

When the patient is admitted to the nursing facility in the course of an encounter in another site of service (eg, hospital emergency department, physician's office), all evaluation and management services provided by that physician in conjunction with that admission are considered part of the initial nursing facility care when performed on the same date as the admission or readmission. The nursing facility care level of service reported by the admitting physician should include the services related to the admission he/she provided in the other sites of service as well as in the nursing facility setting.

Hospital discharge or observation discharge services performed on the same date of nursing facility admission or readmission may be reported separately. For a patient discharged from inpatient status on the same date of nursing facility admission or readmission, the hospital discharge services should be reported with codes 99238, 99239 as appropriate. For a patient discharged from observation status on the same date of nursing facility admission or readmission, the observation care discharge services should be reported with code 99217. For a patient admitted and discharged from observation or inpatient status on the same date, see codes 99234-99236.

(For nursing facility care discharge, see 99315, 99316)

►Typical unit times have not been established for 99304-99306.◄

►(99301-99303 have been deleted)◄

● **99304**   Initial nursing facility care, per day, for the evaluation and management of a patient which requires these three key components:

- **a detailed or comprehensive history;**

- **a detailed or comprehensive examination; and**

- **medical decision making that is straightforward or of low complexity.**

Counseling and/or coordination of care with other providers or agencies are provided consistent with the nature of the problem(s) and the patient's and/or family's needs.

Usually, the problem(s) requiring admission are of low severity.

● **99305**   Initial nursing facility care, per day, for the evaluation and management of a patient which requires these three key components:

- **a comprehensive history;**

- **a comprehensive examination; and**

- **medical decision making of moderate complexity.**

Evaluation and Management

Counseling and/or coordination of care with other providers or agencies are provided consistent with the nature of the problem(s) and the patient's and/or family's needs.

Usually, the problem(s) requiring admission are of moderate severity.

● 99306 Initial nursing facility care, per day, for the evaluation and management of a patient, which requires these three key components:

- **a comprehensive history;**

- **a comprehensive examination; and**

- **medical decision making of high complexity.**

Counseling and/or coordination of care with other providers or agencies are provided consistent with the nature of the problem(s) and the patient's and/or family's needs.

Usually, the problem(s) requiring admission are of high severity.

Subsequent Nursing Facility Care

▶All levels of subsequent nursing facility care include reviewing the medical record and reviewing the results of diagnostic studies and changes in the patient's status (ie, changes in history, physical condition, and response to management) since the last assessment by the physician.◀

● 99307 Subsequent nursing facility care, per day, for the evaluation and management of a patient, which requires at least two of these three key components:

- **a problem focused interval history;**

- **a problem focused examination;**

- **straightforward medical decision making.**

Counseling and/or coordination of care with other providers or agencies are provided consistent with the nature of the problem(s) and the patient's and/or family's needs.

Usually, the patient is stable, recovering, or improving.

● 99308 Subsequent nursing facility care, per day, for the evaluation and management of a patient, which requires at least two of these three key components:

- **an expanded problem focused interval history;**

- **an expanded problem focused examination;**

- **medical decision making of low complexity.**

Counseling and/or coordination of care with other providers or agencies are provided consistent with the nature of the problem(s) and the patient's and/or family's needs.

Usually, the patient is responding inadequately to therapy or has developed a minor complication.

● 99309 Subsequent nursing facility care, per day, for the evaluation and management of a patient, which requires at least two of these three key components:

- **a detailed interval history;**

- **a detailed examination;**

- **medical decision making of moderate complexity.**

Counseling and/or coordination of care with other providers or agencies are provided consistent with the nature of the problem(s) and the patient's and/or family's needs.

Usually, the patient has developed a significant complication or a significant new problem.

● 99310 Subsequent nursing facility care, per day, for the evaluation and management of a patient, which requires at least two of these three key components:

- **a comprehensive interval history;**

- **a comprehensive examination;**

- **medical decision making of high complexity.**

Counseling and/or coordination of care with other providers or agencies are provided consistent with the nature of the problem(s) and the patient's and/or family's needs.

The patient may be unstable or may have developed a significant new problem requiring immediate physician attention.

▶(99311-99313 have been deleted)◀

Nursing Facility Discharge Services

The nursing facility discharge day management codes are to be used to report the total duration of time spent by a physician for the final nursing facility discharge of a patient. The codes include, as appropriate, final examination of the patient, discussion of the nursing facility stay, even if the time spent by the physician on that date is not continuous. Instructions are given for continuing care to all relevant caregivers, and preparation of discharge records, prescriptions and referral forms.

99315 Nursing facility discharge day management; 30 minutes or less

99316 more than 30 minutes

▶Other Nursing Facility Services◀

● 99318 Evaluation and management of a patient involving an annual nursing facility assessment, which requires these three key components:

- **a detailed interval history;**

- **a comprehensive examination; and**

- **medical decision making that is of low to moderate complexity.**

Counseling and/or coordination of care with other providers or agencies are provided consistent with the nature of the problem(s) and the patient's and/or family's needs.

Usually, the patient is stable, recovering, or improving.

►(Do not report 99318 on the same date of service as nursing facility services codes 99304-99316)◄

Domiciliary, Rest Home (eg, Boarding Home), or Custodial Care Services

►The following codes are used to report evaluation and management services in a facility which provides room, board and other personal assistance services, generally on a long-term basis. They also are used to report evaluation and management services in an assisted living facility. ◄

►The facility's services do not include a medical component.◄

For definitions of key components and commonly used terms, please see **Evaluation and Management Services Guidelines.**

(For care plan oversight services provided to a patient in a domiciliary facility under the care of a home health agency, see 99374-99375)

►(For care plan oversight services provided to a patient in a domiciliary facility under the individual supervision of a physician, see 99339, 99340)◄

New Patient

►(99321-99323 have been deleted)◄

● 99324   Domiciliary or rest home visit for the evaluation and management of a new patient, which requires these three key components:

- **a problem focused history;**
- **a problem focused examination; and**
- **straightforward medical decision making.**

Counseling and/or coordination of care with other providers or agencies are provided consistent with the nature of the problem(s) and the patient's and/or family's needs.

Usually, the presenting problem(s) are of low severity. Physicians typically spend 20 minutes with the patient and/or family or caregiver.

● 99325   Domiciliary or rest home visit for the evaluation and management of a new patient, which requires these three key components:

- **an expanded problem focused history;**
- **an expanded problem focused examination; and**
- **medical decision making of low complexity.**

Counseling and/or coordination of care with other providers or agencies are provided consistent with the nature of the problem(s) and the patient's and/or family's needs.

Usually, the presenting problem(s) are of moderate severity. Physicians typically spend 30 minutes with the patient and/or family or caregiver.

● 99326   Domiciliary or rest home visit for the evaluation and management of a new patient, which requires these three key components:

- **a detailed history;**
- **a detailed examination; and**
- **medical decision making of moderate complexity.**

Counseling and/or coordination of care with other providers or agencies are provided consistent with the nature of the problem(s) and the patient's and/or family's needs.

Usually, the presenting problem(s) are of moderate to high severity. Physicians typically spend 45 minutes with the patient and/or family or caregiver.

● 99327   Domiciliary or rest home visit for the evaluation and management of a new patient, which requires these three key components:

- **a comprehensive history;**
- **a comprehensive examination; and**
- **medical decision making of moderate complexity.**

Counseling and/or coordination of care with other providers or agencies are provided consistent with the nature of the problem(s) and the patient's and/or family's needs.

Usually, the presenting problem(s) are of high severity. Physicians typically spend 60 minutes with the patient and/or family or caregiver.

● 99328   Domiciliary or rest home visit for the evaluation and management of a new patient, which requires these three key components:

- **a comprehensive history;**
- **a comprehensive examination; and**
- **medical decision making of high complexity.**

Evaluation and Management

Counseling and/or coordination of care with other providers or agencies are provided consistent with the nature of the problem(s) and the patient's and/or family's needs.

Usually, the patient is unstable or has developed a significant new problem requiring immediate physician attention. Physicians typically spend 75 minutes with the patient and/or family or caregiver.

Established Patient

▶(99331-99333 have been deleted)◀

● 99334 Domiciliary or rest home visit for the evaluation and management of an established patient, which requires at least two of these three key components:

■ **a problem focused interval history;**

■ **a problem focused examination;**

■ **straightforward medical decision making.**

Counseling and/or coordination of care with other providers or agencies are provided consistent with the nature of the problem(s) and the patient's and/or family's needs.

Usually, the presenting problem(s) are self-limited or minor. Physicians typically spend 15 minutes with the patient and/or family or caregiver.

● 99335 Domiciliary or rest home visit for the evaluation and management of an established patient, which requires at least two of these three key components:

■ **an expanded problem focused interval history;**

■ **an expanded problem focused examination;**

■ **medical decision making of low complexity.**

Counseling and/or coordination of care with other providers or agencies are provided consistent with the nature of the problem(s) and the patient's and/or family's needs.

Usually, the presenting problem(s) are of low to moderate severity. Physicians typically spend 25 minutes with the patient and/or family or caregiver.

● 99336 Domiciliary or rest home visit for the evaluation and management of an established patient, which requires at least two of these three key components:

■ **a detailed interval history;**

■ **a detailed examination;**

■ **medical decision making of moderate complexity.**

Counseling and/or coordination of care with other providers or agencies are provided consistent with the nature of the problem(s) and the patient's and/or family's needs.

Usually, the presenting problem(s) are of moderate to high severity. Physicians typically spend 40 minutes with the patient and/or family or caregiver.

● 99337 Domiciliary or rest home visit for the evaluation and management of an established patient, which requires at least two of these three key components:

■ **a comprehensive interval history;**

■ **a comprehensive examination; and**

■ **medical decision making of moderate to high complexity.**

Counseling and/or coordination of care with other providers or agencies are provided consistent with the nature of the problem(s) and the patient's and/or family's needs.

Usually, the presenting problem(s) are of moderate to high severity. The patient may be unstable or may have developed a significant new problem requiring immediate physician attention. Physicians typically spend 60 minutes with the patient and/or family or caregiver.

▶Domiciliary, Rest Home (eg, Assisted Living Facility), or Home Care Plan Oversight Services◀

▶(For instructions on the use of 99339, 99340, see introductory notes for 99374-99380)◀

▶(For care plan oversight services for patients under the care of a home health agency, hospice, or nursing facility, see 99374-99380)◀

● 99339 Individual physician supervision of a patient (patient not present) in home, domiciliary or rest home (eg, assisted living facility) requiring complex and multidisciplinary care modalities involving regular physician development and/or revision of care plans, review of subsequent reports of patient status, review of related laboratory and other studies, communication (including telephone calls) for purposes of assessment or care decisions with health care professional(s), family member(s), surrogate decision maker(s) (eg, legal guardian) and/or key caregiver(s) involved in patient's care, integration of new information into the medical treatment plan and/or adjustment of medical therapy, within a calendar month; 15-29 minutes

● 99340 30 minutes or more

▶(Do not report 99339, 99340 for patients under the care of a home health agency, enrolled in a hospice program, or for nursing facility residents)◀

Home Services

The following codes are used to report evaluation and management services provided in a private residence.

For definitions of key components and commonly used terms, please see **Evaluation and Management Services Guidelines.**

> (For care plan oversight services provided to a patient in the home under the care of a home health agency, see 99374-99375)
>
> ►(For care plan oversight services provided to a patient in the home under the individual supervision of a physician, see 99339, 99340)◄

New Patient

99341 **Home visit** for the evaluation and management of a new patient, which requires these three key components:

- **a problem focused history;**
- **a problem focused examination; and**
- **straightforward medical decision making.**

Counseling and/or coordination of care with other providers or agencies are provided consistent with the nature of the problem(s) and the patient's and/or family's needs.

Usually, the presenting problem(s) are of low severity. Physicians typically spend 20 minutes face-to-face with the patient and/or family.

99342 **Home visit** for the evaluation and management of a new patient, which requires these three key components:

- **an expanded problem focused history;**
- **an expanded problem focused examination; and**
- **medical decision making of low complexity.**

Counseling and/or coordination of care with other providers or agencies are provided consistent with the nature of the problem(s) and the patient's and/or family's needs.

Usually, the presenting problem(s) are of moderate severity. Physicians typically spend 30 minutes face-to-face with the patient and/or family.

99343 **Home visit** for the evaluation and management of a new patient, which requires these three key components:

- **a detailed history;**
- **a detailed examination; and**
- **medical decision making of moderate complexity.**

Counseling and/or coordination of care with other providers or agencies are provided consistent with the nature of the problem(s) and the patient's and/or family's needs.

Usually, the presenting problem(s) are of moderate to high severity. Physicians typically spend 45 minutes face-to-face with the patient and/or family.

99344 **Home visit** for the evaluation and management of a new patient, which requires these three components:

- **a comprehensive history;**
- **a comprehensive examination; and**
- **medical decision making of moderate complexity.**

Counseling and/or coordination of care with other providers or agencies are provided consistent with the nature of the problem(s) and the patient's and/or family's needs.

Usually, the presenting problem(s) are of high severity. Physicians typically spend 60 minutes face-to-face with the patient and/or family.

99345 **Home visit** for the evaluation and management of a new patient, which requires these three key components:

- **a comprehensive history;**
- **a comprehensive examination; and**
- **medical decision making of high complexity.**

Counseling and/or coordination of care with other providers or agencies are provided consistent with the nature of the problem(s) and the patient's and/or family's needs.

Usually, the patient is unstable or has developed a significant new problem requiring immediate physician attention. Physicians typically spend 75 minutes face-to-face with the patient and/or family.

Established Patient

99347 **Home visit** for the evaluation and management of an established patient, which requires at least two of these three key components:

- **a problem focused interval history;**
- **a problem focused examination;**
- **straightforward medical decision making.**

Counseling and/or coordination of care with other providers or agencies are provided consistent with the nature of the problem(s) and the patient's and/or family's needs.

Usually, the presenting problem(s) are self limited or minor. Physicians typically spend 15 minutes face-to-face with the patient and/or family.

99348 **Home visit** for the evaluation and management of an established patient, which requires at least two of these three key components:

- **an expanded problem focused interval history;**
- **an expanded problem focused examination;**
- **medical decision making of low complexity.**

Counseling and/or coordination of care with other providers or agencies are provided consistent with the nature of the problem(s) and the patient's and/or family's needs.

Usually, the presenting problem(s) are of low to moderate severity. Physicians typically spend 25 minutes face-to-face with the patient and/or family.

99349 **Home visit** for the evaluation and management of an established patient, which requires at least two of these three key components:

- **a detailed interval history;**

- **a detailed examination;**

- **medical decision making of moderate complexity.**

Counseling and/or coordination of care with other providers or agencies are provided consistent with the nature of the problem(s) and the patient's and/or family's needs.

Usually, the presenting problem(s) are moderate to high severity. Physicians typically spend 40 minutes face-to-face with the patient and/or family.

99350 **Home visit** for the evaluation and management of an established patient, which requires at least two of these three key components:

- **a comprehensive interval history;**

- **a comprehensive examination;**

- **medical decision making of moderate to high complexity.**

Counseling and/or coordination of care with other providers or agencies are provided consistent with the nature of the problem(s) and the patient's and/or family's needs.

Usually, the presenting problem(s) are of moderate to high severity. The patient may be unstable or may have developed a significant new problem requiring immediate physician attention. Physicians typically spend 60 minutes face-to-face with the patient and/or family.

Prolonged Services

Prolonged Physician Service With Direct (Face-To-Face) Patient Contact

Codes 99354-99357 are used when a physician provides prolonged service involving direct (face-to-face) patient contact that is beyond the usual service in either the inpatient or outpatient setting. This service is reported in addition to other physician services, including evaluation and management services at any level. Appropriate codes should be selected for supplies provided or procedures performed in the care of the patient during this period.

Codes 99354-99357 are used to report the total duration of face-to-face time spent by a physician on a given date providing prolonged service, even if the time spent by the physician on that date is not continuous.

Code 99354 or 99356 is used to report the first hour of prolonged service on a given date, depending on the place of service.

Either code also may be used to report a total duration of prolonged service of 30-60 minutes on a given date. Either code should be used only once per date, even if the time spent by the physician is not continuous on that date. Prolonged service of less than 30 minutes total duration on a given date is not separately reported because the work involved is included in the total work of the evaluation and management codes.

Code 99355 or 99357 is used to report each additional 30 minutes beyond the first hour, depending on the place of service. Either code may also be used to report the final 15-30 minutes of prolonged service on a given date. Prolonged service of less than 15 minutes beyond the first hour or less than 15 minutes beyond the final 30 minutes is not reported separately.

The following examples illustrate the correct reporting of prolonged physician service with direct patient contact in the office setting:

Total Duration of Prolonged Services	Code(s)
less than 30 minutes (less than 1/2 hour)	Not reported separately
30-74 minutes (1/2 hr. - 1 hr. 14 min.)	99354 X 1
75-104 minutes (1 hr. 15 min. - 1 hr. 44 min.)	99354 X 1 AND 99355 X 1
105-134 minutes (1 hr. 45 min. - 2 hr. 14 min.)	99354 X 1 AND 99355 X 2
135-164 minutes (2 hr. 15 min. - 2 hr. 44 min.)	99354 X 1 AND 99355 X 3
165-194 minutes (2 hr. 45 min. - 3 hr. 14 min.)	99354 X 1 AND 99355 X 4

Evaluation and Management

+ 99354   Prolonged physician service in the office or other outpatient setting requiring direct (face-to-face) patient contact beyond the usual service (eg, prolonged care and treatment of an acute asthmatic patient in an outpatient setting); first hour (List separately in addition to code for office or other outpatient **Evaluation and Management** service)

(Use 99354 in conjunction with 99201-99215, 99241-99245, 99304-99350)

+ 99355   each additional 30 minutes (List separately in addition to code for prolonged physician service)

(Use 99355 in conjunction with 99354)

+ 99356   Prolonged physician service in the inpatient setting, requiring direct (face-to-face) patient contact beyond the usual service (eg, maternal fetal monitoring for high risk delivery or other physiological monitoring, prolonged care of an acutely ill inpatient); first hour (List separately in addition to code for inpatient Evaluation and Management service)

▶(Use 99356 in conjunction with 99221-99233, 99251-99255)◀

+ 99357   each additional 30 minutes (List separately in addition to code for prolonged physician service)

(Use 99357 in conjunction with 99356)

Prolonged Physician Service Without Direct (Face-To-Face) Patient Contact

Codes 99358 and 99359 are used when a physician provides prolonged service not involving direct (face-to-face) care that is beyond the usual service in either the inpatient or outpatient setting.

This service is to be reported in addition to other physician service, including evaluation and management services at any level.

Codes 99358 and 99359 are used to report the total duration of non-face-to-face time spent by a physician on a given date providing prolonged service, even if the time spent by the physician on that date is not continuous. Code 99358 is used to report the first hour of prolonged service on a given date regardless of the place of service.

It may also be used to report a total duration of prolonged service of 30-60 minutes on a given date. It should be used only once per date even if the time spent by the physician is not continuous on that date.

Prolonged service of less than 30 minutes total duration on a given date is not separately reported.

Code 99359 is used to report each additional 30 minutes beyond the first hour regardless of the place of service. It may also be used to report the final 15-30 minutes of prolonged service on a given date.

Prolonged service of less than 15 minutes beyond the first hour or less than 15 minutes beyond the final 30 minutes is not reported separately.

+ 99358   **Prolonged evaluation and management service** before and/or after direct (face-to-face) patient care (eg, review of extensive records and tests, communication with other professionals and/or the patient/family); first hour (List separately in addition to code(s) for other physician service(s) and/or inpatient or outpatient Evaluation and Management service)

+ 99359   each additional 30 minutes (List separately in addition to code for prolonged physician service)

(Use 99359 in conjunction with 99358)

(To report telephone calls, see 99371-99373)

Physician Standby Services

Code 99360 is used to report physician standby service that is requested by another physician and that involves prolonged physician attendance without direct (face-to-face) patient contact. The physician may not be providing care or services to other patients during this period. This code is not used to report time spent proctoring another physician. It is also not used if the period of standby ends with the performance of a procedure subject to a "surgical" package by the physician who was on standby.

Code 99360 is used to report the total duration of time spent by a physician on a given date on standby. Standby service of less than 30 minutes total duration on a given date is not reported separately.

Second and subsequent periods of standby beyond the first 30 minutes may be reported only if a full 30 minutes of standby was provided for each unit of service reported.

99360   **Physician standby service,** requiring prolonged physician attendance, each 30 minutes (eg, operative standby, standby for frozen section, for cesarean/high risk delivery, for monitoring EEG)

(For hospital mandated on call services, see 99026, 99027)

(99360 may be reported in addition to 99431, 99440 as appropriate)

(Do not report 99360 in conjunction with 99436)

Case Management Services

Physician case management is a process in which a physician is responsible for direct care of a patient, and for coordinating and controlling access to or initiating and/or supervising other health care services needed by the patient.

▲=Revised code   ●=New code   ▶◀=Contains new or revised text

Evaluation and Management

Team Conferences

99361 **Medical conference** by a physician with interdisciplinary team of health professionals or representatives of community agencies to coordinate activities of patient care (patient not present); approximately 30 minutes

99362 approximately 60 minutes

Telephone Calls

99371 **Telephone call** by a physician to patient or for consultation or medical management or for coordinating medical management with other health care professionals (eg, nurses, therapists, social workers, nutritionists, physicians, pharmacists); simple or brief (eg, to report on tests and/or laboratory results, to clarify or alter previous instructions, to integrate new information from other health professionals into the medical treatment plan, or to adjust therapy)

99372 intermediate (eg, to provide advice to an established patient on a new problem, to initiate therapy that can be handled by telephone, to discuss test results in detail, to coordinate medical management of a new problem in an established patient, to discuss and evaluate new information and details, or to initiate new plan of care)

99373 complex or lengthy (eg, lengthy counseling session with anxious or distraught patient, detailed or prolonged discussion with family members regarding seriously ill patient, lengthy communication necessary to coordinate complex services of several different health professionals working on different aspects of the total patient care plan)

Care Plan Oversight Services

Care Plan Oversight Services are reported separately from codes for office/outpatient, hospital, home, nursing facility or domiciliary services. The complexity and approximate physician time of the care plan oversight services provided within a 30-day period determine code selection. Only one physician may report services for a given period of time, to reflect that physician's sole or predominant supervisory role with a particular patient. These codes should not be reported for supervision of patients in nursing facilities or under the care of home health agencies unless they require recurrent supervision of therapy.

The work involved in providing very low intensity or infrequent supervision services is included in the pre- and post-encounter work for home, office/outpatient and nursing facility or domiciliary visit codes.

▶(For care plan oversight services of patients in the home, domiciliary, or rest home (eg, assisted living facility) under the individual supervision of a physician, see 99339, 99340)◀

99374 **Physician supervision** of a patient under care of home health agency (patient not present) in home, domiciliary or equivalent environment (eg, Alzheimer's facility) requiring complex and multidisciplinary care modalities involving regular physician development and/or revision of care plans, review of subsequent reports of patient status, review of related laboratory and other studies, communication (including telephone calls) for purposes of assessment or care decisions with health care professional(s), family member(s), surrogate decision maker(s) (eg, legal guardian) and/or key caregiver(s) involved in patient's care, integration of new information into the medical treatment plan and/or adjustment of medical therapy, within a calendar month; 15-29 minutes

99375 30 minutes or more

99377 **Physician supervision** of a hospice patient (patient not present) requiring complex and multidisciplinary care modalities involving regular physician development and/or revision of care plans, review of subsequent reports of patient status, review of related laboratory and other studies, communication (including telephone calls) for purposes of assessment or care decisions with health care professional(s), family member(s), surrogate decision maker(s) (eg, legal guardian) and/or key caregiver(s) involved in patient's care, integration of new information into the medical treatment plan and/or adjustment of medical therapy, within a calendar month; 15-29 minutes

99378 30 minutes or more

99379 **Physician supervision** of a nursing facility patient (patient not present) requiring complex and multidisciplinary care modalities involving regular physician development and/or revision of care plans, review of subsequent reports of patient status, review of related laboratory and other studies, communication (including telephone calls) for purposes of assessment or care decisions with health care professional(s), family member(s), surrogate decision maker(s) (eg, legal guardian) and/or key caregiver(s) involved in patient's care, integration of new information into the medical treatment plan and/or adjustment of medical therapy, within a calendar month; 15-29 minutes

99380 30 minutes or more

Preventive Medicine Services

The following codes are used to report the preventive medicine evaluation and management of infants, children, adolescents and adults.

The extent and focus of the services will largely depend on the age of the patient.

If an abnormality/ies is encountered or a preexisting problem is addressed in the process of performing this preventive medicine evaluation and management service, and if the problem/abnormality is significant enough to require additional work to perform the key components of a problem-oriented E/M service, then the appropriate Office/Outpatient code 99201-99215 should also be reported. Modifier 25 should be added to the Office/Outpatient code to indicate that a significant, separately identifiable Evaluation and Management service was provided by the same physician on the same day as the preventive medicine service. The appropriate preventive medicine service is additionally reported.

An insignificant or trivial problem/abnormality that is encountered in the process of performing the preventive medicine evaluation and management service and which does not require additional work and the performance of the key components of a problem-oriented E/M service should not be reported.

The "comprehensive" nature of the Preventive Medicine Services codes 99381-99397 reflects an age and gender appropriate history/exam and is NOT synonymous with the "comprehensive" examination required in Evaluation and Management codes 99201-99350.

Codes 99381-99397 include counseling/anticipatory guidance/risk factor reduction interventions which are provided at the time of the initial or periodic comprehensive preventive medicine examination. (Refer to codes 99401-99412 for reporting those counseling/anticipatory guidance/risk factor reduction interventions that are provided at an encounter separate from the preventive medicine examination.)

Immunizations and ancillary studies involving laboratory, radiology, other procedures, or screening tests identified with a specific CPT code are reported separately. For immunizations, see 90465-90474 and 90476-90749.

New Patient

99381   **Initial comprehensive preventive medicine** evaluation and management of an individual including an age and gender appropriate history, examination, counseling/anticipatory guidance/risk factor reduction interventions, and the ordering of appropriate immunization(s), laboratory/diagnostic procedures, new patient; infant (age under 1 year)

99382   early childhood (age 1 through 4 years)

99383   late childhood (age 5 through 11 years)

99384   adolescent (age 12 through 17 years)

99385   18-39 years

99386   40-64 years

99387   65 years and over

Established Patient

99391   **Periodic comprehensive preventive medicine** reevaluation and management of an individual including an age and gender appropriate history, examination, counseling/anticipatory guidance/risk factor reduction interventions, and the ordering of appropriate immunization(s), laboratory/diagnostic procedures, established patient; infant (age under 1 year)

99392   early childhood (age 1 through 4 years)

99393   late childhood (age 5 through 11 years)

99394   adolescent (age 12 through 17 years)

99395   18-39 years

99396   40-64 years

99397   65 years and over

Counseling and/or Risk Factor Reduction Intervention

New or Established Patient

These codes are used to report services provided to individuals at a separate encounter for the purpose of promoting health and preventing illness or injury.

Preventive medicine counseling and risk factor reduction interventions provided as a separate encounter will vary with age and should address such issues as family problems, diet and exercise, substance abuse, sexual practices, injury prevention, dental health, and diagnostic and laboratory test results available at the time of the encounter.

These codes are not to be used to report counseling and risk factor reduction interventions provided to patients with symptoms or established illness. For counseling individual patients with symptoms or established illness, use the appropriate office, hospital or consultation or other evaluation and management codes. For counseling groups of patients with symptoms or established illness, use 99078.

Preventive Medicine, Individual Counseling

99401   **Preventive medicine counseling** and/or risk factor reduction intervention(s) provided to an individual (separate procedure); approximately 15 minutes

99402   approximately 30 minutes

99403   approximately 45 minutes

99404   approximately 60 minutes

▲=Revised code   ●=New code   ▶◀=Contains new or revised text

Evaluation and Management

Preventive Medicine, Group Counseling

99411   **Preventive medicine counseling** and/or risk factor reduction intervention(s) provided to individuals in a group setting (separate procedure); approximately 30 minutes

99412   approximately 60 minutes

Other Preventive Medicine Services

99420   **Administration and interpretation** of health risk assessment instrument (eg, health hazard appraisal)

99429   **Unlisted preventive** medicine service

Newborn Care

The following codes are used to report the services provided to newborns in several different settings.

For newborn hospital discharge services provided on a date subsequent to the admission date of the newborn, use 99238.

For discharge services provided to newborns admitted and discharged on the same date, use 99435.

99431   **History and examination** of the normal newborn infant, initiation of diagnostic and treatment programs and preparation of hospital records. (This code should also be used for birthing room deliveries.)

99432   **Normal newborn care** in other than hospital or birthing room setting, including physical examination of baby and conference(s) with parent(s)

99433   **Subsequent hospital care,** for the evaluation and management of a normal newborn, per day

99435   **History and examination** of the normal newborn infant, including the preparation of medical records. (This code should only be used for newborns assessed and discharged from the hospital or birthing room on the same date.)

99436   **Attendance** at delivery (when requested by delivering physician) and initial stabilization of newborn

(99436 may be reported in addition to 99431)

(Do not report 99436 in conjunction with 99440)

99440   **Newborn resuscitation**: provision of positive pressure ventilation and/or chest compressions in the presence of acute inadequate ventilation and/or cardiac output

Special Evaluation and Management Services

The following codes are used to report evaluations performed to establish baseline information prior to life or disability insurance certificates being issued. This service is performed in the office or other setting, and applies to both new and established patients. When using these codes, no active management of the problem(s) is undertaken during the encounter.

If other evaluation and management services and/or procedures are performed on the same date, the appropriate E/M or procedure code(s) should be reported in addition to these codes.

Basic Life and/or Disability Evaluation Services

99450   **Basic life** and/or disability examination that includes:

- **measurement of height, weight and blood pressure;**

- **completion of a medical history following a life insurance pro forma;**

- **collection of blood sample and/or urinalysis complying with "chain of custody" protocols; and**

- **completion of necessary documentation/certificates.**

Work Related or Medical Disability Evaluation Services

99455   **Work related** or medical disability examination by the treating physician that includes:

- **completion of a medical history commensurate with the patient's condition;**

- **performance of an examination commensurate with the patient's condition;**

- **formulation of a diagnosis, assessment of capabilities and stability, and calculation of impairment;**

- **development of future medical treatment plan; and**

- **completion of necessary documentation/certificates and report.**

99456 **Work related** or medical disability examination by other than the treating physician that includes:

- **completion of a medical history commensurate with the patient's condition;**

- **performance of an examination commensurate with the patient's condition;**

- **formulation of a diagnosis, assessment of capabilities and stability, and calculation of impairment;**

- **development of future medical treatment plan; and**

- **completion of necessary documentation/certificates and report.**

(Do not report 99455, 99456 in conjunction with 99080 for the completion of Workman's Compensation forms)

Other Evaluation and Management Services

99499 **Unlisted evaluation and management** service

Notes

⊘ =Modifier 51 exempt   ⊙ =Conscious sedation   **+** =Add-on code   ✗ =FDA approval pending

Anesthesia Guidelines

Services involving administration of anesthesia are reported by the use of the anesthesia five-digit procedure code (00100-01999) plus modifier codes (defined under "Anesthesia Modifiers" later in these Guidelines).

The reporting of anesthesia services is appropriate by or under the responsible supervision of a physician. These services may include but are not limited to general, regional, supplementation of local anesthesia, or other supportive services in order to afford the patient the anesthesia care deemed optimal by the anesthesiologist during any procedure. These services include the usual preoperative and postoperative visits, the anesthesia care during the procedure, the administration of fluids and/or blood and the usual monitoring services (eg, ECG, temperature, blood pressure, oximetry, capnography, and mass spectrometry). Unusual forms of monitoring (eg, intra-arterial, central venous, and Swan-Ganz) are not included.

Items used by all physicians in reporting their services are presented in the **Introduction.** Some of the commonalities are repeated in this section for the convenience of those physicians referring to this section on **Anesthesia.** Other definitions and items unique to anesthesia are also listed.

►To report moderate (conscious) sedation provided by a physician also performing the service for which conscious sedation is being provided, see codes 99143-99145.◄

►For the procedures listed in Appendix G, when a second physician other than the health care professional performing the diagnostic or therapeutic services provides moderate (conscious) sedation in the facility setting (eg, hospital, outpatient hospital/ambulatory surgery center, skilled nursing facility), the second physician reports the associated moderate sedation procedure/service 99148-99150; when these services are performed by the second physician in the nonfacility setting (eg, physician office, freestanding imaging center), codes 99148-99150 would not be reported. Moderate sedation does not include minimal sedation (anxiolysis), deep sedation, or monitored anesthesia care (00100-01999).◄

To report regional or general anesthesia provided by a physician also performing the services for which the anesthesia is being provided, see modifier 47 in Appendix A.

Time Reporting

Time for anesthesia procedures may be reported as is customary in the local area. Anesthesia time begins when the anesthesiologist begins to prepare the patient for the induction of anesthesia in the operating room or in an equivalent area and ends when the anesthesiologist is no longer in personal attendance, that is, when the patient may be safely placed under postoperative supervision.

Physician's Services

Physician's services rendered in the office, home, or hospital; consultation; and other medical services are listed in the section titled **Evaluation and Management Services** (99200 series) found on page 1. "Special Services and Reporting" (99000 series) are listed in the **Medicine** section.

Materials Supplied by Physician

Supplies and materials provided by the physician (eg, sterile trays, drugs) over and above those usually included with the office visit or other services rendered may be listed separately. Drugs, tray supplies, and materials provided should be listed and identified with 99070 or the appropriate supply code.

Separate or Multiple Procedures

When multiple surgical procedures are performed during a single anesthetic administration, the anesthesia code representing the most complex procedure is reported. The time reported is the combined total for all procedures.

Special Report

A service that is rarely provided, unusual, variable, or new may require a special report in determining medical appropriateness of the service. Pertinent information should include an adequate definition or description of the nature, extent, and need for the procedure and the time, effort, and equipment necessary to provide the service. Additional items may include:

- Complexity of symptoms
- Final diagnosis
- Pertinent physical findings
- Diagnostic and therapeutic procedures
- Concurrent problems
- Follow-up care

Anesthesia Modifiers

All anesthesia services are reported by use of the anesthesia five-digit procedure code (00100-01999) plus the addition of a physical status modifier. The use of other optional modifiers may be appropriate.

Physical Status Modifiers

Physical Status modifiers are represented by the initial letter 'P' followed by a single digit from 1 to 6 as defined in the following list.

P1: A normal healthy patient

P2: A patient with mild systemic disease

P3: A patient with severe systemic disease

P4: A patient with severe systemic disease that is a constant threat to life

P5: A moribund patient who is not expected to survive without the operation

P6: A declared brain-dead patient whose organs are being removed for donor purposes

These six levels are consistent with the American Society of Anesthesiologists (ASA) ranking of patient physical status. Physical status is included in the CPT codebook to distinguish among various levels of complexity of the anesthesia service provided.

Example: 00100-P1

Qualifying Circumstances

More than one qualifying circumstance may be selected.

Many anesthesia services are provided under particularly difficult circumstances, depending on factors such as extraordinary condition of patient, notable operative conditions, and/or unusual risk factors. This section includes a list of important qualifying circumstances that significantly affect the character of the anesthesia service provided. These procedures would not be reported alone but would be reported as additional procedure numbers qualifying an anesthesia procedure or service.

+ 99100   Anesthesia for patient of extreme age, under 1 year and over 70 (List separately in addition to code for primary anesthesia procedure)

(For procedure performed on infants less than 1 year of age at time of surgery, see 00326, 00561, 00834, 00836)

+ 99116   Anesthesia complicated by utilization of total body hypothermia (List separately in addition to code for primary anesthesia procedure)

+ 99135   Anesthesia complicated by utilization of controlled hypotension (List separately in addition to code for primary anesthesia procedure)

+ 99140   Anesthesia complicated by emergency conditions (specify) (List separately in addition to code for primary anesthesia procedure)

(An emergency is defined as existing when delay in treatment of the patient would lead to a significant increase in the threat to life or body part.)

Anesthesia

Head

00100	Anesthesia for procedures on salivary glands, including biopsy
00102	Anesthesia for procedures involving plastic repair of cleft lip
00103	Anesthesia for reconstructive procedures of eyelid (eg, blepharoplasty, ptosis surgery)
00104	Anesthesia for electroconvulsive therapy
00120	Anesthesia for procedures on external, middle, and inner ear including biopsy; not otherwise specified
00124	otoscopy
00126	tympanotomy
00140	Anesthesia for procedures on eye; not otherwise specified
00142	lens surgery
00144	corneal transplant
00145	vitreoretinal surgery
00147	iridectomy
00148	ophthalmoscopy
00160	Anesthesia for procedures on nose and accessory sinuses; not otherwise specified
00162	radical surgery
00164	biopsy, soft tissue
00170	Anesthesia for intraoral procedures, including biopsy; not otherwise specified
00172	repair of cleft palate
00174	excision of retropharyngeal tumor
00176	radical surgery
00190	Anesthesia for procedures on facial bones or skull; not otherwise specified
00192	radical surgery (including prognathism)
00210	Anesthesia for intracranial procedures; not otherwise specified
00212	subdural taps
00214	burr holes, including ventriculography
00215	cranioplasty or elevation of depressed skull fracture, extradural (simple or compound)
00216	vascular procedures
00218	procedures in sitting position
00220	cerebrospinal fluid shunting procedures
00222	electrocoagulation of intracranial nerve

Neck

00300	Anesthesia for all procedures on the integumentary system, muscles and nerves of head, neck, and posterior trunk, not otherwise specified
00320	Anesthesia for all procedures on esophagus, thyroid, larynx, trachea and lymphatic system of neck; not otherwise specified, age 1 year or older
00322	needle biopsy of thyroid

(For procedures on cervical spine and cord, see 00600, 00604, 00670)

00326	Anesthesia for all procedures on the larynx and trachea in children less than 1 year of age

(Do not report 00326 in conjunction with 99100)

00350	Anesthesia for procedures on major vessels of neck; not otherwise specified
00352	simple ligation

(For arteriography, use 01916)

Thorax (Chest Wall and Shoulder Girdle)

00400	Anesthesia for procedures on the integumentary system on the extremities, anterior trunk and perineum; not otherwise specified
00402	reconstructive procedures on breast (eg, reduction or augmentation mammoplasty, muscle flaps)
00404	radical or modified radical procedures on breast
00406	radical or modified radical procedures on breast with internal mammary node dissection
00410	electrical conversion of arrhythmias
00450	Anesthesia for procedures on clavicle and scapula; not otherwise specified
00452	radical surgery
00454	biopsy of clavicle
00470	Anesthesia for partial rib resection; not otherwise specified
00472	thoracoplasty (any type)
00474	radical procedures (eg, pectus excavatum)

Anesthesia

Intrathoracic

00500   Anesthesia for all procedures on esophagus

00520   Anesthesia for closed chest procedures; (including bronchoscopy) not otherwise specified

00522   needle biopsy of pleura

00524   pneumocentesis

00528   mediastinoscopy and diagnostic thoracoscopy not utilizing one lung ventilation

(For tracheobronchial reconstruction, use 00539)

00529   mediastinoscopy and diagnostic thoracoscopy utilizing one lung ventilation

00530   Anesthesia for permanent transvenous pacemaker insertion

00532   Anesthesia for access to central venous circulation

00534   Anesthesia for transvenous insertion or replacement of pacing cardioverter-defibrillator

(For transthoracic approach, use 00560)

00537   Anesthesia for cardiac electrophysiologic procedures including radiofrequency ablation

00539   Anesthesia for tracheobronchial reconstruction

00540   Anesthesia for thoracotomy procedures involving lungs, pleura, diaphragm, and mediastinum (including surgical thoracoscopy); not otherwise specified

00541   utilizing one lung ventilation

00542   decortication

(00544 has been deleted. To report, use 00542)

00546   pulmonary resection with thoracoplasty

00548   intrathoracic procedures on the trachea and bronchi

00550   Anesthesia for sternal debridement

00560   Anesthesia for procedures on heart, pericardial sac, and great vessels of chest; without pump oxygenator

00561   with pump oxygenator, under one year of age

(Do not report 00561 in conjunction with 99100, 99116, and 99135)

00562   with pump oxygenator

00563   with pump oxygenator with hypothermic circulatory arrest

00566   Anesthesia for direct coronary artery bypass grafting without pump oxygenator

00580   Anesthesia for heart transplant or heart/lung transplant

Spine and Spinal Cord

00600   Anesthesia for procedures on cervical spine and cord; not otherwise specified

(For myelography and diskography, see radiological procedures 01905)

00604   procedures with patient in the sitting position

00620   Anesthesia for procedures on thoracic spine and cord; not otherwise specified

00622   thoracolumbar sympathectomy

00630   Anesthesia for procedures in lumbar region; not otherwise specified

00632   lumbar sympathectomy

00634   chemonucleolysis

00635   diagnostic or therapeutic lumbar puncture

00640   Anesthesia for manipulation of the spine or for closed procedures on the cervical, thoracic or lumbar spine

00670   Anesthesia for extensive spine and spinal cord procedures (eg, spinal instrumentation or vascular procedures)

Upper Abdomen

00700   Anesthesia for procedures on upper anterior abdominal wall; not otherwise specified

00702   percutaneous liver biopsy

00730   Anesthesia for procedures on upper posterior abdominal wall

00740   Anesthesia for upper gastrointestinal endoscopic procedures, endoscope introduced proximal to duodenum

00750   Anesthesia for hernia repairs in upper abdomen; not otherwise specified

00752   lumbar and ventral (incisional) hernias and/or wound dehiscence

00754   omphalocele

00756   transabdominal repair of diaphragmatic hernia

00770   Anesthesia for all procedures on major abdominal blood vessels

00790   Anesthesia for intraperitoneal procedures in upper abdomen including laparoscopy; not otherwise specified

00792   partial hepatectomy or management of liver hemorrhage (excluding liver biopsy)

00794   pancreatectomy, partial or total (eg, Whipple procedure)

00796   liver transplant (recipient)

(For harvesting of liver, use 01990)

00797   gastric restrictive procedure for morbid obesity

Lower Abdomen

00800   Anesthesia for procedures on lower anterior abdominal wall; not otherwise specified

00802   panniculectomy

00810   Anesthesia for lower intestinal endoscopic procedures, endoscope introduced distal to duodenum

00820   Anesthesia for procedures on lower posterior abdominal wall

00830   Anesthesia for hernia repairs in lower abdomen; not otherwise specified

00832   ventral and incisional hernias

(For hernia repairs in the infant 1 year of age or younger, see 00834, 00836)

00834   Anesthesia for hernia repairs in the lower abdomen not otherwise specified, under 1 year of age

(Do not report 00834 in conjunction with 99100)

00836   Anesthesia for hernia repairs in the lower abdomen not otherwise specified, infants less than 37 weeks gestational age at birth and less than 50 weeks gestational age at time of surgery

(Do not report 00836 in conjunction with 99100)

00840   Anesthesia for intraperitoneal procedures in lower abdomen including laparoscopy; not otherwise specified

00842   amniocentesis

00844   abdominoperineal resection

00846   radical hysterectomy

00848   pelvic exenteration

00851   tubal ligation/transection

00860   Anesthesia for extraperitoneal procedures in lower abdomen, including urinary tract; not otherwise specified

00862   renal procedures, including upper 1/3 of ureter, or donor nephrectomy

00864   total cystectomy

00865   radical prostatectomy (suprapubic, retropubic)

00866   adrenalectomy

00868   renal transplant (recipient)

(For donor nephrectomy, use 00862)

(For harvesting kidney from brain-dead patient, use 01990)

00870   cystolithotomy

00872   Anesthesia for lithotripsy, extracorporeal shock wave; with water bath

00873   without water bath

00880   Anesthesia for procedures on major lower abdominal vessels; not otherwise specified

00882   inferior vena cava ligation

Perineum

(For perineal procedures on integumentary system, muscles and nerves, see 00300, 00400)

00902   Anesthesia for; anorectal procedure

00904   radical perineal procedure

00906   vulvectomy

00908   perineal prostatectomy

00910   Anesthesia for transurethral procedures (including urethrocystoscopy); not otherwise specified

00912   transurethral resection of bladder tumor(s)

00914   transurethral resection of prostate

00916   post-transurethral resection bleeding

00918   with fragmentation, manipulation and/or removal of ureteral calculus

00920   Anesthesia for procedures on male genitalia (including open urethral procedures); not otherwise specified

00921   vasectomy, unilateral or bilateral

00922   seminal vesicles

00924   undescended testis, unilateral or bilateral

00926   radical orchiectomy, inguinal

00928   radical orchiectomy, abdominal

00930   orchiopexy, unilateral or bilateral

00932   complete amputation of penis

00934   radical amputation of penis with bilateral inguinal lymphadenectomy

00936   radical amputation of penis with bilateral inguinal and iliac lymphadenectomy

00938   insertion of penile prosthesis (perineal approach)

00940   Anesthesia for vaginal procedures (including biopsy of labia, vagina, cervix or endometrium); not otherwise specified

00942   colpotomy, vaginectomy, colporrhaphy, and open urethral procedures

00944   vaginal hysterectomy

00948   cervical cerclage

00950   culdoscopy

00952   hysteroscopy and/or hysterosalpingography

Anesthesia

Pelvis (Except Hip)

01112   Anesthesia for bone marrow aspiration and/or biopsy, anterior or posterior iliac crest

01120   Anesthesia for procedures on bony pelvis

01130   Anesthesia for body cast application or revision

01140   Anesthesia for interpelviabdominal (hindquarter) amputation

01150   Anesthesia for radical procedures for tumor of pelvis, except hindquarter amputation

01160   Anesthesia for closed procedures involving symphysis pubis or sacroiliac joint

01170   Anesthesia for open procedures involving symphysis pubis or sacroiliac joint

01173   Anesthesia for open repair of fracture disruption of pelvis or column fracture involving acetabulum

01180   Anesthesia for obturator neurectomy; extrapelvic

01190   intrapelvic

Upper Leg (Except Knee)

01200   Anesthesia for all closed procedures involving hip joint

01202   Anesthesia for arthroscopic procedures of hip joint

01210   Anesthesia for open procedures involving hip joint; not otherwise specified

01212   hip disarticulation

01214   total hip arthroplasty

01215   revision of total hip arthroplasty

01220   Anesthesia for all closed procedures involving upper 2/3 of femur

01230   Anesthesia for open procedures involving upper 2/3 of femur; not otherwise specified

01232   amputation

01234   radical resection

01250   Anesthesia for all procedures on nerves, muscles, tendons, fascia, and bursae of upper leg

01260   Anesthesia for all procedures involving veins of upper leg, including exploration

01270   Anesthesia for procedures involving arteries of upper leg, including bypass graft; not otherwise specified

01272   femoral artery ligation

01274   femoral artery embolectomy

Knee and Popliteal Area

Surgical endoscopy/arthroscopy always includes a diagnostic endoscopy/arthroscopy.

01320   Anesthesia for all procedures on nerves, muscles, tendons, fascia, and bursae of knee and/or popliteal area

01340   Anesthesia for all closed procedures on lower 1/3 of femur

01360   Anesthesia for all open procedures on lower 1/3 of femur

01380   Anesthesia for all closed procedures on knee joint

01382   Anesthesia for diagnostic arthroscopic procedures of knee joint

01390   Anesthesia for all closed procedures on upper ends of tibia, fibula, and/or patella

01392   Anesthesia for all open procedures on upper ends of tibia, fibula, and/or patella

01400   Anesthesia for open or surgical arthroscopic procedures on knee joint; not otherwise specified

01402   total knee arthroplasty

01404   disarticulation at knee

01420   Anesthesia for all cast applications, removal, or repair involving knee joint

01430   Anesthesia for procedures on veins of knee and popliteal area; not otherwise specified

01432   arteriovenous fistula

01440   Anesthesia for procedures on arteries of knee and popliteal area; not otherwise specified

01442   popliteal thromboendarterectomy, with or without patch graft

01444   popliteal excision and graft or repair for occlusion or aneurysm

Lower Leg (Below Knee, Includes Ankle and Foot)

Surgical endoscopy/arthroscopy always includes a diagnostic endoscopy/arthroscopy.

01462   Anesthesia for all closed procedures on lower leg, ankle, and foot

01464   Anesthesia for arthroscopic procedures of ankle and/or foot

01470   Anesthesia for procedures on nerves, muscles, tendons, and fascia of lower leg, ankle, and foot; not otherwise specified

01472   repair of ruptured Achilles tendon, with or without graft

01474   gastrocnemius recession (eg, Strayer procedure)

01480	Anesthesia for open procedures on bones of lower leg, ankle, and foot; not otherwise specified
01482	radical resection (including below knee amputation)
01484	osteotomy or osteoplasty of tibia and/or fibula
01486	total ankle replacement
01490	Anesthesia for lower leg cast application, removal, or repair
01500	Anesthesia for procedures on arteries of lower leg, including bypass graft; not otherwise specified
01502	embolectomy, direct or with catheter
01520	Anesthesia for procedures on veins of lower leg; not otherwise specified
01522	venous thrombectomy, direct or with catheter

Shoulder and Axilla

Surgical endoscopy/arthroscopy always includes a diagnostic endoscopy/arthroscopy.

Includes humeral head and neck, sternoclavicular joint, acromioclavicular joint, and shoulder joint.

01610	Anesthesia for all procedures on nerves, muscles, tendons, fascia, and bursae of shoulder and axilla
01620	Anesthesia for all closed procedures on humeral head and neck, sternoclavicular joint, acromioclavicular joint, and shoulder joint
01622	Anesthesia for diagnostic arthroscopic procedures of shoulder joint
01630	Anesthesia for open or surgical arthroscopic procedures on humeral head and neck, sternoclavicular joint, acromioclavicular joint, and shoulder joint; not otherwise specified
01632	radical resection
01634	shoulder disarticulation
01636	interthoracoscapular (forequarter) amputation
01638	total shoulder replacement
01650	Anesthesia for procedures on arteries of shoulder and axilla; not otherwise specified
01652	axillary-brachial aneurysm
01654	bypass graft
01656	axillary-femoral bypass graft
01670	Anesthesia for all procedures on veins of shoulder and axilla
01680	Anesthesia for shoulder cast application, removal or repair; not otherwise specified
01682	shoulder spica

Upper Arm and Elbow

Surgical endoscopy/arthroscopy always includes a diagnostic endoscopy/arthroscopy.

01710	Anesthesia for procedures on nerves, muscles, tendons, fascia, and bursae of upper arm and elbow; not otherwise specified
01712	tenotomy, elbow to shoulder, open
01714	tenoplasty, elbow to shoulder
01716	tenodesis, rupture of long tendon of biceps
01730	Anesthesia for all closed procedures on humerus and elbow
01732	Anesthesia for diagnostic arthroscopic procedures of elbow joint
01740	Anesthesia for open or surgical arthroscopic procedures of the elbow; not otherwise specified
01742	osteotomy of humerus
01744	repair of nonunion or malunion of humerus
01756	radical procedures
01758	excision of cyst or tumor of humerus
01760	total elbow replacement
01770	Anesthesia for procedures on arteries of upper arm and elbow; not otherwise specified
01772	embolectomy
01780	Anesthesia for procedures on veins of upper arm and elbow; not otherwise specified
01782	phleborrhaphy

Forearm, Wrist, and Hand

01810	Anesthesia for all procedures on nerves, muscles, tendons, fascia, and bursae of forearm, wrist, and hand
01820	Anesthesia for all closed procedures on radius, ulna, wrist, or hand bones
01829	Anesthesia for diagnostic arthroscopic procedures on the wrist
01830	Anesthesia for open or surgical arthroscopic/endoscopic procedures on distal radius, distal ulna, wrist, or hand joints; not otherwise specified
01832	total wrist replacement
01840	Anesthesia for procedures on arteries of forearm, wrist, and hand; not otherwise specified
01842	embolectomy
01844	Anesthesia for vascular shunt, or shunt revision, any type (eg, dialysis)

▲=Revised code   ●=New code   ▶ ◀=Contains new or revised text

Anesthesia

01850 Anesthesia for procedures on veins of forearm, wrist, and hand; not otherwise specified

01852   phleborrhaphy

01860 Anesthesia for forearm, wrist, or hand cast application, removal, or repair

Radiological Procedures

01905 Anesthesia for myelography, diskography, vertebroplasty

01916 Anesthesia for diagnostic arteriography/venography

(Do not report 01916 in conjunction with therapeutic codes 01924-01926, 01930-01933)

01920 Anesthesia for cardiac catheterization including coronary angiography and ventriculography (not to include Swan-Ganz catheter)

01922 Anesthesia for non-invasive imaging or radiation therapy

01924 Anesthesia for therapeutic interventional radiologic procedures involving the arterial system; not otherwise specified

01925   carotid or coronary

01926   intracranial, intracardiac, or aortic

01930 Anesthesia for therapeutic interventional radiologic procedures involving the venous/lymphatic system (not to include access to the central circulation); not otherwise specified

01931   intrahepatic or portal circulation (eg, transcutaneous porto-caval shunt (TIPS))

01932   intrathoracic or jugular

01933   intracranial

Burn Excisions or Debridement

01951 Anesthesia for second and third degree burn excision or debridement with or without skin grafting, any site, for total body surface area (TBSA) treated during anesthesia and surgery; less than four percent total body surface area

01952   between four and nine percent of total body surface area

+ 01953   each additional nine percent total body surface area or part thereof (List separately in addition to code for primary procedure)

(Use 01953 in conjunction with 01952)

Obstetric

01958 Anesthesia for external cephalic version procedure

01960 Anesthesia for vaginal delivery only

01961 Anesthesia for cesarean delivery only

01962 Anesthesia for urgent hysterectomy following delivery

01963 Anesthesia for cesarean hysterectomy without any labor analgesia/anesthesia care

▶(01964 has been deleted. To report, see 01965, 01966)◀

● **01965** Anesthesia for incomplete or missed abortion procedures

● **01966** Anesthesia for induced abortion procedures

01967 Neuraxial labor analgesia/anesthesia for planned vaginal delivery (this includes any repeat subarachnoid needle placement and drug injection and/or any necessary replacement of an epidural catheter during labor)

+ 01968 Anesthesia for cesarean delivery following neuraxial labor analgesia/anesthesia (List separately in addition to code for primary procedure performed)

(Use 01968 in conjunction with 01967)

+ 01969 Anesthesia for cesarean hysterectomy following neuraxial labor analgesia/anesthesia (List separately in addition to code for primary procedure performed)

(Use 01969 in conjunction with 01967)

Other Procedures

01990 Physiological support for harvesting of organ(s) from brain-dead patient

01991 Anesthesia for diagnostic or therapeutic nerve blocks and injections (when block or injection is performed by a different provider); other than the prone position

01992   prone position

(Do not report 01991 or 01992 in conjunction with 99141)

01995 Regional intravenous administration of local anesthetic agent or other medication (upper or lower extremity)

▶(For intra-arterial or intravenous therapy for pain management, see 90774, 90775)◀

01996 Daily hospital management of epidural or subarachnoid continuous drug administration

(Report code 01996 for daily hospital management of continuous epidural or subarachnoid drug administration performed after insertion of an epidural or subarachnoid catheter)

01999 Unlisted anesthesia procedure(s)

Surgery Guidelines

Items used by all physicians in reporting their services are presented in the **Introduction.** Some of the commonalities are repeated here for the convenience of those physicians referring to this section on **Surgery.** Other definitions and items unique to Surgery are also listed.

Physicians' Services

Physicians' services rendered in the office, home, or hospital, consultations, and other medical services are listed in the section entitled **Evaluation and Management Services** (99201-99499) found in the front of the book, beginning on page 9. "Special Services and Reports" (99000 series) is presented in the **Medicine** section.

CPT Surgical Package Definition

The services provided by the physician to any patient by their very nature are variable. The CPT codes that represent a readily identifiable surgical procedure thereby include, on a procedure-by-procedure basis, a variety of services. In defining the specific services "included" in a given CPT surgical code, the following services are always included in addition to the operation per se:

- Local infiltration, metacarpal/metatarsal/digital block or topical anesthesia
- Subsequent to the decision for surgery, one related E/M encounter on the date immediately prior to or on the date of procedure (including history and physical)
- Immediate postoperative care, including dictating operative notes, talking with the family and other physicians
- Writing orders
- Evaluating the patient in the postanesthesia recovery area
- Typical postoperative follow-up care

Follow-Up Care for Diagnostic Procedures

Follow-up care for diagnostic procedures (eg, endoscopy, arthroscopy, injection procedures for radiography) includes only that care related to recovery from the diagnostic procedure itself. Care of the condition for which the diagnostic procedure was performed or of other concomitant conditions is not included and may be listed separately.

Follow-Up Care for Therapeutic Surgical Procedures

Follow-up care for therapeutic surgical procedures includes only that care which is usually a part of the surgical service. Complications, exacerbations, recurrence, or the presence of other diseases or injuries requiring additional services should be separately reported.

Materials Supplied by Physician

Supplies and materials provided by the physician (eg, sterile trays/drugs), over and above those usually included with the procedure(s) rendered are reported separately. List drugs, trays, supplies, and materials provided. Identify as 99070 or specific supply code.

Reporting More Than One Procedure/Service

When a physician performs more than one procedure/service on the same date, same session or during a post-operative period (subject to the "surgical package" concept), several CPT modifiers may apply (see Appendix A for definition).

27 Multiple Outpatient Hospital E/M Encounters on the Same Date

For hospital outpatient reporting purposes, utilization of hospital resources related to separate and distinct E/M encounters performed in multiple outpatient hospital settings on the same date may be reported by adding modifier 27 to each appropriate level outpatient and/or emergency department E/M code(s). This modifier provides a means of reporting circumstances involving evaluation and management services provided by physician(s) in more than one (multiple) outpatient hospital setting(s) (eg, hospital emergency department, clinic). **Note:** This modifier is not to be used for physician reporting of multiple E/M services performed by the same physician on the same date. For physician reporting of all outpatient evaluation and management services provided by the same physician on the same date and performed in multiple outpatient setting(s) (eg, hospital emergency department, clinic), see **Evaluation and Management, Emergency Department,** or **Preventive Medicine Services** codes.

51 Multiple Procedures

When multiple procedures/services (other than evaluation and management) are performed at the same session, report the most significant procedure first, with all other procedures listed with modifier 51 appended. For a list of procedures exempt from the use of modifier 51, see Appendices D and E.

58 Staged or Related Procedure or Service by the Same Physician During the Postoperative Period

When a procedure(s) is prospectively planned as a staged procedure, or when the secondary and subsequent procedure(s) is more extensive, or to indicate therapy following a diagnostic surgical procedure, use modifier 58 with the staged procedure(s).

59 Distinct Procedural Service

For procedure(s)/service(s) not ordinarily performed or encountered on the same day by the same physician, but appropriate under certain circumstances (eg, different site or organ system, separate excision or lesion), use modifier 59.

76 Repeat Procedure by Same Physician

When a procedure or service is repeated by the same physician subsequent to the original service, use modifier 76.

77 Repeat Procedure by Another Physician

When a procedure is repeated by another physician subsequent to the original service, use modifier 77.

78 Return to the Operating Room for a Related Procedure During the Postoperative Period

When a procedure, related to the initial procedure, requires a return to the operating room during the postoperative period of that initial procedure, use modifier 78.

79 Unrelated Procedure or Service by the Same Physician During the Postoperative Period

When a procedure, unrelated to the initial procedure, is performed by the same physician during the post-operative period of the initial procedure, use modifier 79.

91 Repeat Clinical Diagnostic Laboratory Test

In the course of treatment of the patient, it may be necessary to repeat the same laboratory test on the same day to obtain subsequent (multiple) test results. Under these circumstances, the laboratory test performed can be identified by its usual procedure number and the addition of modifier 91. **Note:** This modifier may not be used when tests are rerun to confirm initial results; due to testing problems with specimens or equipment; or for any other reason when a normal, one-time, reportable result is all that is required. This modifier may not be used when other code(s) describe a series of test results (eg, glucose tolerance tests, evocative/suppression testing). This modifier may only be used for laboratory test(s) performed more than once on the same day on the same patient.

Separate Procedure

Some of the procedures or services listed in the CPT codebook that are commonly carried out as an integral component of a total service or procedure have been identified by the inclusion of the term "separate procedure." The codes designated as "separate procedure" should not be reported in addition to the code for the total procedure or service of which it is considered an integral component.

However, when a procedure or service that is designated as a "separate procedure" is carried out independently or considered to be unrelated or distinct from other procedures/services provided at that time, it may be reported by itself, or in addition to other procedures/services by appending modifier 59 to the specific "separate procedure" code to indicate that the procedure is not considered to be a component of another procedure, but is a distinct, independent procedure. This may represent a different session or patient encounter, different procedure or surgery, different site or organ system, separate incision/excision, separate lesion, or separate injury (or area of injury in extensive injuries).

Subsection Information

Several of the subheadings or subsections have special needs or instructions unique to that section. Where these are indicated (eg, "Maternity Care and Delivery"), special **"Notes"** will be presented preceding those procedural terminology listings, referring to that subsection specifically. If there is an "Unlisted Procedure" code number (see below) for the individual subsection, it will also be shown. Those subsections within the **Surgery** section that have **"Notes"** are as follows:

Biopsy	11100-11101
Removal of Skin Tags	11200-11201
Shaving of Lesions	11300-11313
Excision—Benign Lesions	11400-11471
Excision—Malignant Lesions	11600-11646
Repair (Closure)	12001-13160
Adjacent Tissue Transfer or Rearrangement	14000-14350
▶Skin Replacement Surgery and Skin Substitutes	15000-15431
Allograft and Tissue Cultured Allogeneic Skin Substitutes	15300-15366
Xenograft	15400-15431◀
Flaps (Skin and/or Deep Tissue)	15570-15999
Burns, Local Treatment	16000-16036
Destruction	17000-17286
Mohs Micrographic Surgery	17304-17310
Breast—Excision	19100-19272
Musculoskeletal	20000-29999
Wound Exploration—Trauma	20100-20103
Grafts (or Implants)	20900-20999
Introduction or Removal	21076-21116
Spine: (Vertebral Column)	22100-22855
Spine: Excision	22100-22116
Spine: Osteotomy	22210-22226
Spine: Fracture/Dislocation	22305-22328
Spine: Arthrodesis	22548-22812
Spine: Exploration	22830
Spinal Instrumentation	22840-22855
Casting and Strapping	29000-29750
Musculoskeletal: Endoscopy/Arthroscopy	29800-29999
Respiratory: Endoscopy	31231-31294, 31505-31579, 31615-31656, 32601-32665
Cardiovascular System	33010-37799

Pacing Cardioverter-Pacemaker or Defibrillator	33200-33249
Venous—CABG	33510-33516
Arteries and Veins	34001-35907
Endovascular Repair of Abdominal Aortic Aneurysm	34800-34826
Endovascular Repair of Illiac Aneurysm	34900
Transluminal Angioplasty	35450-35476
Transluminal Atherectomy	35480-35495
Bypass Graft	35500-35572
Composite Grafts	35681-35683
Adjuvant Techniques	35685-35686
Vascular Injection Procedures: Intravenous	36000-36015
Central Venous Access Procedures	36555-36597
Transcatheter Procedures: Intravenous	37195-37216
Intravascular Ultrasound	37250-37251
Bone Marrow or Stem Cell Services/Procedures	38204-38242
Hemic and Lymphatic Systems: Laparoscopy	38570-38589
▶Digestive: Endoscopy/Laparoscopy	43200-43272, 43280-43289, 43651-43659, 43770-43774, 44180-44238, 44360-44397, 44970-44979, 45300-45387, 45395-45397, 45400-45402, 46600-46615, 47370-47379, 47550-47556, 47560-47562, 49320-49329, 49650-49659◀
Pancreas Transplantation	48550-48556
Herniotomy	49491-49611
Renal Transplantation	50300-50380
Urodynamics	51725-51798
Endoscopy/Laparoscopy	
Urinary	50541-50545, 50945-50980, 51990-52648
Male Genital	54690-54699, 55550-55559, 55866
Female Genital	58545-58579, 58660-58679
Endocrine	60650-60659
Maternity Care and Delivery	59000-59899
Nervous System: Surgery of Skull Base	61580-61619
Neurostimulators (Intracranial)	61850-61888, 62160-62319
Neurostimulators (Spinal)	63650-63688

Surgery Guidelines

Neurostimulators (Peripheral Nerve) . 64553-64595

Secondary Implants(s) 65125-65175

Removal Cataract. 66830-66999

Prophylaxis 67141-67145

Excision 67800-67820

Reconstruction 67930-67999

Operating Microscope 69990

Unlisted Service or Procedure

A service or procedure may be provided that is not listed in this edition of the CPT codebook. When reporting such a service, the appropriate "Unlisted Procedure" code may be used to indicate the service, identifying it by "Special Report" as discussed in the section below. The "Unlisted Procedures" and accompanying codes for **Surgery** are as follows:

15999 Unlisted procedure, excision pressure ulcer

17999 Unlisted procedure, skin, mucous membrane and subcutaneous tissue

19499 Unlisted procedure, breast

20999 Unlisted procedure, musculoskeletal system, general

21089 Unlisted maxillofacial prosthetic procedure

21299 Unlisted craniofacial and maxillofacial procedure

21499 Unlisted musculoskeletal procedure, head

21899 Unlisted procedure, neck or thorax

22899 Unlisted procedure, spine

22999 Unlisted procedure, abdomen, musculoskeletal system

23929 Unlisted procedure, shoulder

24999 Unlisted procedure, humerus or elbow

25999 Unlisted procedure, forearm or wrist

26989 Unlisted procedure, hands or fingers

27299 Unlisted procedure, pelvis or hip joint

27599 Unlisted procedure, femur or knee

27899 Unlisted procedure, leg or ankle

28899 Unlisted procedure, foot or toes

29799 Unlisted procedure, casting or strapping

29999 Unlisted procedure, arthroscopy

30999 Unlisted procedure, nose

31299 Unlisted procedure, accessory sinuses

31599 Unlisted procedure, larynx

31899 Unlisted procedure, trachea, bronchi

32999 Unlisted procedure, lungs and pleura

33999 Unlisted procedure, cardiac surgery

36299 Unlisted procedure, vascular injection

37501 Unlisted vascular endoscopy procedure

37799 Unlisted procedure, vascular surgery

38129 Unlisted laparoscopy procedure, spleen

38589 Unlisted laparoscopy procedure, lymphatic system

38999 Unlisted procedure, hemic or lymphatic system

39499 Unlisted procedure, mediastinum

39599 Unlisted procedure, diaphragm

40799 Unlisted procedure, lips

40899 Unlisted procedure, vestibule of mouth

41599 Unlisted procedure, tongue, floor of mouth

41899 Unlisted procedure, dentoalveolar structures

42299 Unlisted procedure, palate, uvula

42699 Unlisted procedure, salivary glands or ducts

42999 Unlisted procedure, pharynx, adenoids, or tonsils

43289 Unlisted laparoscopy procedure, esophagus

43499 Unlisted procedure, esophagus

43659 Unlisted laparoscopy procedure, stomach

43999 Unlisted procedure, stomach

44238 Unlisted laparoscopy procedure, intestine (except rectum)

44799 Unlisted procedure, intestine

44899 Unlisted procedure, Meckel's diverticulum and the mesentery

44979 Unlisted laparoscopy procedure, appendix

● **45499** Unlisted laparoscopy procedure, rectum

45999 Unlisted procedure, rectum

46999 Unlisted procedure, anus

47379 Unlisted laparoscopic procedure, liver

47399 Unlisted procedure, liver

47579 Unlisted laparoscopy procedure, biliary tract

47999 Unlisted procedure, biliary tract

48999 Unlisted procedure, pancreas

49329 Unlisted laparoscopy procedure, abdomen, peritoneum and omentum

49659 Unlisted laparoscopy procedure, hernioplasty, herniorrhaphy, herniotomy

49999 Unlisted procedure, abdomen, peritoneum and omentum

50549 Unlisted laparoscopy procedure, renal

50949 Unlisted laparoscopy procedure, ureter

● **51999** Unlisted laparoscopy procedure, bladder

53899 Unlisted procedure, urinary system

54699 Unlisted laparoscopy procedure, testis

55559	Unlisted laparoscopy procedure, spermatic cord
55899	Unlisted procedure, male genital system
58578	Unlisted laparoscopy procedure, uterus
58579	Unlisted hysteroscopy procedure, uterus
58679	Unlisted laparoscopy procedure, oviduct, ovary
58999	Unlisted procedure, female genital system (nonobstetrical)
59897	Unlisted fetal invasive procedure, including ultrasound guidance
59898	Unlisted laparoscopy procedure, maternity care and delivery
59899	Unlisted procedure, maternity care and delivery
60659	Unlisted laparoscopy procedure, endocrine system
60699	Unlisted procedure, endocrine system
64999	Unlisted procedure, nervous system
66999	Unlisted procedure, anterior segment of eye
67299	Unlisted procedure, posterior segment
67399	Unlisted procedure, ocular muscle
67599	Unlisted procedure, orbit
67999	Unlisted procedure, eyelids
68399	Unlisted procedure, conjunctiva
68899	Unlisted procedure, lacrimal system
69399	Unlisted procedure, external ear
69799	Unlisted procedure, middle ear
69949	Unlisted procedure, inner ear
69979	Unlisted procedure, temporal bone, middle fossa approach

Special Report

A service that is rarely provided, unusual, variable, or new may require a special report in determining medical appropriateness of the service. Pertinent information should include an adequate definition or description of the nature, extent, and need for the procedure, and the time, effort, and equipment necessary to provide the service. Additional items which may be included are:

- Complexity of symptoms
- Final diagnosis
- Pertinent physical findings (such as size, locations, and number of lesion(s), if appropriate)
- Diagnostic and therapeutic procedures (including major and supplementary surgical procedures, if appropriate)
- Concurrent problems
- Follow-up care

Surgical Destruction

Surgical destruction is a part of a surgical procedure and different methods of destruction are not ordinarily listed separately unless the technique substantially alters the standard management of a problem or condition. Exceptions under special circumstances are provided for by separate code numbers.

Surgery Guidelines

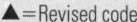 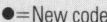

Notes

Surgery

General

10021 Fine needle aspiration; without imaging guidance

10022 with imaging guidance

(For radiological supervision and interpretation, see 76003, 76360, 76393, 76942)

(For percutaneous needle biopsy other than fine needle aspiration, see 20206 for muscle, 32400 for pleura, 32405 for lung or mediastinum, 42400 for salivary gland, 47000, 47001 for liver, 48102 for pancreas, 49180 for abdominal or retroperitoneal mass, 60100 for thyroid, 62269 for spinal cord)

(For evaluation of fine needle aspirate, see 88172, 88173)

Integumentary System

Skin, Subcutaneous and Accessory Structures

Incision and Drainage

(For excision, see 11400, et seq)

10040 Acne surgery (eg, marsupialization, opening or removal of multiple milia, comedones, cysts, pustules)

10060 Incision and drainage of abscess (eg, carbuncle, suppurative hidradenitis, cutaneous or subcutaneous abscess, cyst, furuncle, or paronychia); simple or single

10061 complicated or multiple

10080 Incision and drainage of pilonidal cyst; simple

10081 complicated

(For excision of pilonidal cyst, see 11770-11772)

10120 Incision and removal of foreign body, subcutaneous tissues; simple

10121 complicated

(To report wound exploration due to penetrating trauma without laparotomy or thoracotomy, see 20100-20103, as appropriate)

(To report debridement associated with open fracture(s) and/or dislocation(s), use 11010-11012, as appropriate)

10140 Incision and drainage of hematoma, seroma or fluid collection

(If imaging guidance is performed, see 76360, 76393, 76942)

10160 Puncture aspiration of abscess, hematoma, bulla, or cyst

(If imaging guidance is performed, see 76360, 76393, 76942)

10180 Incision and drainage, complex, postoperative wound infection

(For secondary closure of surgical wound, see 12020, 12021, 13160)

Excision—Debridement

(For dermabrasions, see 15780-15783)

(For nail debridement, see 11720-11721)

(For burn(s), see 16000-16035)

11000 Debridement of extensive eczematous or infected skin; up to 10% of body surface

(For abdominal wall or genitalia debridement for necrotizing soft tissue infection, see 11004-11006)

+ 11001 each additional 10% of the body surface (List separately in addition to code for primary procedure)

(Use 11001 in conjunction with 11000)

11004 Debridement of skin, subcutaneous tissue, muscle and fascia for necrotizing soft tissue infection; external genitalia and perineum

11005 abdominal wall, with or without fascial closure

11006 external genitalia, perineum and abdominal wall, with or without fascial closure

+ 11008 Removal of prosthetic material or mesh, abdominal wall for necrotizing soft tissue infection (List separately in addition to code for primary procedure)

(Use 11008 in conjunction with 11004-11006)

(Do not report 11008 in conjunction with 11000-11001, 11010-11044)

(Report skin grafts or flaps separately when performed for closure at the same session as 11004-11008)

►(When insertion of mesh is used for closure, use 49568)◄

(If orchiectomy is performed, use 54520)

(If testicular transplantation is performed, use 54680)

11010 Debridement including removal of foreign material associated with open fracture(s) and/or dislocation(s); skin and subcutaneous tissues

11011 skin, subcutaneous tissue, muscle fascia, and muscle

11012 skin, subcutaneous tissue, muscle fascia, muscle, and bone

11040 Debridement; skin, partial thickness

11041 skin, full thickness

Surgery: Integumentary System

11042   skin, and subcutaneous tissue

11043   skin, subcutaneous tissue, and muscle

11044   skin, subcutaneous tissue, muscle, and bone

(Do not report 11040-11044 in conjunction with 97597-97602)

Paring or Cutting

(To report destruction, see 17000-17004)

11055   Paring or cutting of benign hyperkeratotic lesion (eg, corn or callus); single lesion

11056   two to four lesions

11057   more than four lesions

Biopsy

During certain surgical procedures in the integumentary system, such as excision, destruction, or shave removals, the removed tissue is often submitted for pathologic examination. The obtaining of tissue for pathology during the course of these procedures is a routine component of such procedures. This obtaining of tissue is not considered a separate biopsy procedure and is not separately reported. The use of a biopsy procedure code (eg, 11100, 11101) indicates that the procedure to obtain tissue for pathologic examination was performed independently, or was unrelated or distinct from other procedures/services provided at that time. Such biopsies are not considered components of other procedures when performed on different lesions or different sites on the same date, and are to be reported separately.

(For biopsy of conjunctiva, use 68100; eyelid, use 67810)

11100   Biopsy of skin, subcutaneous tissue and/or mucous membrane (including simple closure), unless otherwise listed; single lesion

+ 11101   each separate/additional lesion (List separately in addition to code for primary procedure)

(Use 11101 in conjunction with 11100)

Removal of Skin Tags

Removal by scissoring or any sharp method, ligature strangulation, electrosurgical destruction or combination of treatment modalities including chemical or electrocauterization of wound, with or without local anesthesia.

11200   Removal of skin tags, multiple fibrocutaneous tags, any area; up to and including 15 lesions

+ 11201   each additional ten lesions (List separately in addition to code for primary procedure)

(Use 11201 in conjunction with 11200)

Shaving of Epidermal or Dermal Lesions

Shaving is the sharp removal by transverse incision or horizontal slicing to remove epidermal and dermal lesions without a full-thickness dermal excision. This includes local anesthesia, chemical or electrocauterization of the wound. The wound does not require suture closure.

11300   Shaving of epidermal or dermal lesion, single lesion, trunk, arms or legs; lesion diameter 0.5 cm or less

11301   lesion diameter 0.6 to 1.0 cm

11302   lesion diameter 1.1 to 2.0 cm

11303   lesion diameter over 2.0 cm

11305   Shaving of epidermal or dermal lesion, single lesion, scalp, neck, hands, feet, genitalia; lesion diameter 0.5 cm or less

11306   lesion diameter 0.6 to 1.0 cm

11307   lesion diameter 1.1 to 2.0 cm

11308   lesion diameter over 2.0 cm

11310   Shaving of epidermal or dermal lesion, single lesion, face, ears, eyelids, nose, lips, mucous membrane; lesion diameter 0.5 cm or less

11311   lesion diameter 0.6 to 1.0 cm

11312   lesion diameter 1.1 to 2.0 cm

11313   lesion diameter over 2.0 cm

Excision—Benign Lesions

Excision (including simple closure) of benign lesions of skin (eg, neoplasm, cicatricial, fibrous, inflammatory, congenital, cystic lesions), includes local anesthesia. See appropriate size and area below. For shave removal, see 11300 et seq., and for electrosurgical and other methods see 17000 et seq.

Excision is defined as full-thickness (through the dermis) removal of a lesion, including margins, and includes simple (non-layered) closure when performed. Report separately each benign lesion excised. Code selection is determined by measuring the greatest clinical diameter of the apparent lesion plus that margin required for complete excision (lesion diameter plus the most narrow margins required equals the excised diameter). The margins refer to the most narrow margin required to adequately excise the lesion, based on the physician's judgment. The measurement of lesion plus margin is made prior to excision. The excised diameter is the same whether the surgical defect is repaired in a linear fashion, or reconstructed (eg, with a skin graft).

The closure of defects created by incision, excision, or trauma may require intermediate or complex closure. Repair by intermediate or complex closure should be reported separately. For excision of benign lesions requiring more than simple closure, ie, requiring intermediate or complex closure, report 11400-11446 in addition to appropriate intermediate (12031-12057) or complex closure (13100-13153) codes. For reconstructive closure, see 14000-14300, 15000-15261, 15570-15770. See page 51 for definition of intermediate or complex closure.

11400   Excision, benign lesion including margins, except skin tag (unless listed elsewhere), trunk, arms or legs; excised diameter 0.5 cm or less

11401   excised diameter 0.6 to 1.0 cm

11402   excised diameter 1.1 to 2.0 cm

11403   excised diameter 2.1 to 3.0 cm

11404   excised diameter 3.1 to 4.0 cm

11406   excised diameter over 4.0 cm

        (For unusual or complicated excision, add modifier 22)

11420   Excision, benign lesion including margins, except skin tag (unless listed elsewhere), scalp, neck, hands, feet, genitalia; excised diameter 0.5 cm or less

11421   excised diameter 0.6 to 1.0 cm

11422   excised diameter 1.1 to 2.0 cm

11423   excised diameter 2.1 to 3.0 cm

11424   excised diameter 3.1 to 4.0 cm

11426   excised diameter over 4.0 cm

        (For unusual or complicated excision, add modifier 22)

11440   Excision, other benign lesion including margins, except skin tag (unless listed elsewhere), face, ears, eyelids, nose, lips, mucous membrane; excised diameter 0.5 cm or less

11441   excised diameter 0.6 to 1.0 cm

11442   excised diameter 1.1 to 2.0 cm

11443   excised diameter 2.1 to 3.0 cm

11444   excised diameter 3.1 to 4.0 cm

11446   excised diameter over 4.0 cm

        (For unusual or complicated excision, add modifier 22)

        (For eyelids involving more than skin, see also 67800 et seq)

11450   Excision of skin and subcutaneous tissue for hidradenitis, axillary; with simple or intermediate repair

11451   with complex repair

11462   Excision of skin and subcutaneous tissue for hidradenitis, inguinal; with simple or intermediate repair

11463   with complex repair

11470   Excision of skin and subcutaneous tissue for hidradenitis, perianal, perineal, or umbilical; with simple or intermediate repair

11471   with complex repair

        (When skin graft or flap is used for closure, use appropriate procedure code in addition)

        (For bilateral procedure, add modifier 50)

Excision—Malignant Lesions

Excision (including simple closure) of malignant lesions of skin (eg, basal cell carcinoma, squamous cell carcinoma, melanoma) includes local anesthesia. (See appropriate size and body area below.) For destruction of malignant lesions of skin, see destruction codes 17260-17286.

Excision is defined as full-thickness (through the dermis) removal of a lesion including margins, and includes simple (non-layered) closure when performed. Report separately each malignant lesion excised. Code selection is determined by measuring the greatest clinical diameter of the apparent lesion plus that margin required for complete excision (lesion diameter plus the most narrow margins required equals the excised diameter). The margins refer to the most narrow margin required to adequately excise the lesion, based on the physician's judgment. The measurement of lesion plus margin is made prior to excision. The excised diameter is the same whether the surgical defect is repaired in a linear fashion, or reconstructed (eg, with a skin graft).

The closure of defects created by incision, excision, or trauma may require intermediate or complex closure. Repair by intermediate or complex closure should be reported separately. For excision of malignant lesions requiring more than simple closure, ie, requiring intermediate or complex closure, report 11600-11646 in addition to appropriate intermediate (12031-12057) or complex closure (13100-13153) codes. For reconstructive closure, see 14000-14300, 15000-15261, 15570-15770. See page 51 for definition of intermediate or complex closure.

When frozen section pathology shows the margins of excision were not adequate, an additional excision may be necessary for complete tumor removal. Use only one code to report the additional excision and re-excision(s) based on the final widest excised diameter required for complete tumor removal at the same operative session. To report a re-excision procedure performed to widen margins at a subsequent operative session, see codes 11600-11646, as appropriate. Append modifier 58 if the re-excision procedure is performed during the postoperative period of the primary excision procedure.

11600   Excision, malignant lesion including margins, trunk, arms, or legs; excised diameter 0.5 cm or less

11601   excised diameter 0.6 to 1.0 cm

11602   excised diameter 1.1 to 2.0 cm

11603   excised diameter 2.1 to 3.0 cm

11604   excised diameter 3.1 to 4.0 cm

11606   excised diameter over 4.0 cm

Surgery: Integumentary System

11620   Excision, malignant lesion including margins, scalp, neck, hands, feet, genitalia; excised diameter 0.5 cm or less

11621   excised diameter 0.6 to 1.0 cm

11622   excised diameter 1.1 to 2.0 cm

11623   excised diameter 2.1 to 3.0 cm

11624   excised diameter 3.1 to 4.0 cm

11626   excised diameter over 4.0 cm

11640   Excision, malignant lesion including margins, face, ears, eyelids, nose, lips; excised diameter 0.5 cm or less

11641   excised diameter 0.6 to 1.0 cm

11642   excised diameter 1.1 to 2.0 cm

11643   excised diameter 2.1 to 3.0 cm

11644   excised diameter 3.1 to 4.0 cm

11646   excised diameter over 4.0 cm

(For eyelids involving more than skin, see also 67800 et seq)

Nails

(For drainage of paronychia or onychia, see 10060, 10061)

11719   Trimming of nondystrophic nails, any number

11720   Debridement of nail(s) by any method(s); one to five

11721   six or more

11730   Avulsion of nail plate, partial or complete, simple; single

+ 11732   each additional nail plate (List separately in addition to code for primary procedure)

(Use 11732 in conjunction with 11730)

11740   Evacuation of subungual hematoma

11750   Excision of nail and nail matrix, partial or complete, (eg, ingrown or deformed nail) for permanent removal;

11752   with amputation of tuft of distal phalanx

(For skin graft, if used, use 15050)

11755   Biopsy of nail unit (eg, plate, bed, matrix, hyponychium, proximal and lateral nail folds) (separate procedure)

11760   Repair of nail bed

11762   Reconstruction of nail bed with graft

11765   Wedge excision of skin of nail fold (eg, for ingrown toenail)

Pilonidal Cyst

11770   Excision of pilonidal cyst or sinus; simple

11771   extensive

11772   complicated

(For incision of pilonidal cyst, see 10080, 10081)

Introduction

11900   Injection, intralesional; up to and including seven lesions

11901   more than seven lesions

(11900, 11901 are not to be used for preoperative local anesthetic injection)

(For veins, see 36470, 36471)

(For intralesional chemotherapy administration, see 96405, 96406)

11920   Tattooing, intradermal introduction of insoluble opaque pigments to correct color defects of skin, including micropigmentation; 6.0 sq cm or less

11921   6.1 to 20.0 sq cm

+ 11922   each additional 20.0 sq cm (List separately in addition to code for primary procedure)

(Use 11922 in conjunction with 11921)

11950   Subcutaneous injection of filling material (eg, collagen); 1 cc or less

11951   1.1 to 5.0 cc

11952   5.1 to 10.0 cc

11954   over 10.0 cc

11960   Insertion of tissue expander(s) for other than breast, including subsequent expansion

(For breast reconstruction with tissue expander(s), use 19357)

11970   Replacement of tissue expander with permanent prosthesis

11971   Removal of tissue expander(s) without insertion of prosthesis

11975   Insertion, implantable contraceptive capsules

11976   Removal, implantable contraceptive capsules

11977   Removal with reinsertion, implantable contraceptive capsules

11980   Subcutaneous hormone pellet implantation (implantation of estradiol and/or testosterone pellets beneath the skin)

11981   Insertion, non-biodegradable drug delivery implant

11982   Removal, non-biodegradable drug delivery implant

11983   Removal with reinsertion, non-biodegradable drug delivery implant

Repair (Closure)

Use the codes in this section to designate wound closure utilizing sutures, staples, or tissue adhesives (eg, 2-cyanoacrylate), either singly or in combination with each other, or in combination with adhesive strips. Wound closure utilizing adhesive strips as the sole repair material should be coded using the appropriate E/M code.

Definitions

The repair of wounds may be classified as Simple, Intermediate, or Complex.

Simple repair is used when the wound is superficial; eg, involving primarily epidermis or dermis, or subcutaneous tissues without significant involvement of deeper structures, and requires simple one layer closure. This includes local anesthesia and chemical or electrocauterization of wounds not closed.

Intermediate repair includes the repair of wounds that, in addition to the above, require layered closure of one or more of the deeper layers of subcutaneous tissue and superficial (non-muscle) fascia, in addition to the skin (epidermal and dermal) closure. Single-layer closure of heavily contaminated wounds that have required extensive cleaning or removal of particulate matter also constitutes intermediate repair.

Complex repair includes the repair of wounds requiring more than layered closure, viz., scar revision, debridement (eg, traumatic lacerations or avulsions), extensive undermining, stents or retention sutures. Necessary preparation includes creation of a defect for repairs (eg, excision of a scar requiring a complex repair) or the debridement of complicated lacerations or avulsions. Complex repair does not include excision of benign (11400-11446) or malignant (11600-11646) lesions.

Instructions for listing services at time of wound repair:

1. The repaired wound(s) should be measured and recorded in centimeters, whether curved, angular, or stellate.

2. When multiple wounds are repaired, add together the lengths of those in the same classification (see above) and from all anatomic sites that are grouped together into the same code descriptor. For example, add together the lengths of intermediate repairs to the trunk and extremities. Do not add lengths of repairs from different groupings of anatomic sites (eg, face and extremities). Also, do not add together lengths of different classifications (eg, intermediate and complex repairs).

When more than one classification of wounds is repaired, list the more complicated as the primary procedure and the less complicated as the secondary procedure, using modifier 51.

3. Decontamination and/or debridement: Debridement is considered a separate procedure only when gross contamination requires prolonged cleansing, when appreciable amounts of devitalized or contaminated tissue are removed, or when debridement is carried out separately without immediate primary closure. (For extensive debridement of soft tissue and/or bone, see 11040-11044.)

(For extensive debridement of soft tissue and/or bone, not associated with open fracture(s) and/or dislocation(s) resulting from penetrating and/or blunt trauma, see 11040-11044.)

(For extensive debridement of subcutaneous tissue, muscle fascia, muscle, and/or bone associated with open fracture(s) and/or dislocation(s), see 11010-11012.)

4. Involvement of nerves, blood vessels and tendons: Report under appropriate system (Nervous, Cardiovascular, Musculoskeletal) for repair of these structures. The repair of these associated wounds is included in the primary procedure unless it qualifies as a complex wound, in which case modifier 51 applies.

Simple ligation of vessels in an open wound is considered as part of any wound closure.

Simple "exploration" of nerves, blood vessels or tendons exposed in an open wound is also considered part of the essential treatment of the wound and is not a separate procedure unless appreciable dissection is required. If the wound requires enlargement, extension of dissection (to determine penetration), debridement, removal of foreign body(s), ligation or coagulation of minor subcutaneous and/or muscular blood vessel(s) of the subcutaneous tissue, muscle fascia, and/or muscle, not requiring thoracotomy or laparotomy, use codes 20100-20103, as appropriate.

Repair—Simple

Sum of lengths of repairs for each group of anatomic sites.

12001	Simple repair of superficial wounds of scalp, neck, axillae, external genitalia, trunk and/or extremities (including hands and feet); 2.5 cm or less
12002	2.6 cm to 7.5 cm
12004	7.6 cm to 12.5 cm
12005	12.6 cm to 20.0 cm
12006	20.1 cm to 30.0 cm
12007	over 30.0 cm
12011	Simple repair of superficial wounds of face, ears, eyelids, nose, lips and/or mucous membranes; 2.5 cm or less
12013	2.6 cm to 5.0 cm
12014	5.1 cm to 7.5 cm
12015	7.6 cm to 12.5 cm
12016	12.6 cm to 20.0 cm
12017	20.1 cm to 30.0 cm
12018	over 30.0 cm

Surgery: Integumentary System

12020 Treatment of superficial wound dehiscence; simple closure

12021 with packing

(For extensive or complicated secondary wound closure, use 13160)

Repair—Intermediate

Sum of lengths of repairs for each group of anatomic sites.

12031 Layer closure of wounds of scalp, axillae, trunk and/or extremities (excluding hands and feet); 2.5 cm or less

12032 2.6 cm to 7.5 cm

12034 7.6 cm to 12.5 cm

12035 12.6 cm to 20.0 cm

12036 20.1 cm to 30.0 cm

12037 over 30.0 cm

12041 Layer closure of wounds of neck, hands, feet and/or external genitalia; 2.5 cm or less

12042 2.6 cm to 7.5 cm

12044 7.6 cm to 12.5 cm

12045 12.6 cm to 20.0 cm

12046 20.1 cm to 30.0 cm

12047 over 30.0 cm

12051 Layer closure of wounds of face, ears, eyelids, nose, lips and/or mucous membranes; 2.5 cm or less

12052 2.6 cm to 5.0 cm

12053 5.1 cm to 7.5 cm

12054 7.6 cm to 12.5 cm

12055 12.6 cm to 20.0 cm

12056 20.1 cm to 30.0 cm

12057 over 30.0 cm

Repair—Complex

Reconstructive procedures, complicated wound closure.

Sum of lengths of repairs for each group of anatomic sites.

(For full thickness repair of lip or eyelid, see respective anatomical subsections)

13100 Repair, complex, trunk; 1.1 cm to 2.5 cm

(For 1.0 cm or less, see simple or intermediate repairs)

13101 2.6 cm to 7.5 cm

+ 13102 each additional 5 cm or less (List separately in addition to code for primary procedure)

(Use 13102 in conjunction with 13101)

13120 Repair, complex, scalp, arms, and/or legs; 1.1 cm to 2.5 cm

(For 1.0 cm or less, see simple or intermediate repairs)

13121 2.6 cm to 7.5 cm

+ 13122 each additional 5 cm or less (List separately in addition to code for primary procedure)

(Use 13122 in conjunction with 13121)

13131 Repair, complex, forehead, cheeks, chin, mouth, neck, axillae, genitalia, hands and/or feet; 1.1 cm to 2.5 cm

(For 1.0 cm or less, see simple or intermediate repairs)

13132 2.6 cm to 7.5 cm

+ 13133 each additional 5 cm or less (List separately in addition to code for primary procedure)

(Use 13133 in conjunction with 13132)

13150 Repair, complex, eyelids, nose, ears and/or lips; 1.0 cm or less

(See also 40650-40654, 67961-67975)

13151 1.1 cm to 2.5 cm

13152 2.6 cm to 7.5 cm

+ 13153 each additional 5 cm or less (List separately in addition to code for primary procedure)

(Use 13153 in conjunction with 13152)

13160 Secondary closure of surgical wound or dehiscence, extensive or complicated

(For packing or simple secondary wound closure, see 12020, 12021)

Adjacent Tissue Transfer or Rearrangement

For full thickness repair of lip or eyelid, see respective anatomical subsections.

Excision (including lesion) and/or repair by adjacent tissue transfer or rearrangement (eg, Z-plasty, W-plasty, V-Y plasty, rotation flap, advancement flap, double pedicle flap). When applied in repairing lacerations, the procedures listed must be developed by the surgeon to accomplish the repair. They do not apply when direct closure or rearrangement of traumatic wounds incidentally result in these configurations.

Skin graft necessary to close secondary defect is considered an additional procedure. For purposes of code selection, the term "defect" includes the primary and secondary defects. The primary defect resulting from the excision and the secondary defect resulting from flap design to perform the reconstruction are measured together to determine the code.

14000 Adjacent tissue transfer or rearrangement, trunk; defect 10 sq cm or less

14001 defect 10.1 sq cm to 30.0 sq cm

14020   Adjacent tissue transfer or rearrangement, scalp, arms and/or legs; defect 10 sq cm or less

14021   defect 10.1 sq cm to 30.0 sq cm

14040   Adjacent tissue transfer or rearrangement, forehead, cheeks, chin, mouth, neck, axillae, genitalia, hands and/or feet; defect 10 sq cm or less

14041   defect 10.1 sq cm to 30.0 sq cm

14060   Adjacent tissue transfer or rearrangement, eyelids, nose, ears and/or lips; defect 10 sq cm or less

14061   defect 10.1 sq cm to 30.0 sq cm

      (For eyelid, full thickness, see 67961 et seq)

14300   Adjacent tissue transfer or rearrangement, more than 30 sq cm, unusual or complicated, any area

14350   Filleted finger or toe flap, including preparation of recipient site

▶Skin Replacement Surgery and Skin Substitutes◀

▶Identify by size and location of the defect (recipient area) and the type of graft or skin substitute; includes simple debridement of granulation tissue or recent avulsion.◀

▶When a primary procedure such as orbitectomy, radical mastectomy, or deep tumor removal requires skin graft for definitive closure, see appropriate anatomical subsection for primary procedure and this section for skin graft or skin substitute.◀

▶Use 15000, 15001 for initial wound recipient site preparation.◀

▶Use 15100-15261 for autologous skin grafts. For autologous tissue-cultured epidermal grafts, use 15150-15157. For harvesting of autologous keratinocytes and dermal tissue for tissue-cultured skin grafts, use 15040. Procedures are coded by recipient site. Use 15170-15176 for acellular dermal replacement. Use modifier 58 for staged application procedure(s).◀

Repair of donor site requiring skin graft or local flaps is to be added as an additional procedure.

▶Codes 15000 and 15001 describe burn and wound preparation or incisional or excisional release of scar contracture resulting in an open wound requiring a skin graft. Codes 15100-15431 describe the application of skin replacements and skin substitutes. The following definition should be applied to those codes that reference "100 sq cm or one percent of body area of infants and children" when determining the involvement of body size: The measurement of 100 sq cm is applicable to adults and children age 10 and older, percentages of body surface area apply to infants and children under the age of 10.◀

▶These codes are not intended to be reported for simple graft application alone or application stabilized with dressings (eg, by simple gauze wrap) without surgical fixation of the skin substitute/graft. The skin substitute/graft is anchored using the surgeon's choice of fixation. When services are performed in the office, the supply of the skin substitute/graft should be reported separately. Routine dressing supplies are not reported separately.◀

(For microvascular flaps, see 15756-15758)

▶Surgical Preparation◀

▲ **15000**   Surgical preparation or creation of recipient site by excision of open wounds, burn eschar, or scar (including subcutaneous tissues), or incisional release of scar contracture; first 100 sq cm or one percent of body area of infants and children

      ▶(For appropriate skin grafts or replacements, see 15050-15261, 15330-15336. List the graft or replacement separately by its procedure number when the graft, immediate or delayed, is applied)◀

+ **15001**   each additional 100 sq cm or each additional one percent of body area of infants and children (List separately in addition to code for primary procedure)

      (Use 15001 in conjunction with 15000)

      (For excision of benign lesions, see 11400-11471)

      (For excision of malignant lesions, see 11600-11646)

      ▶(For excision to prepare or create recipient site with dressings or materials not listed in 15040-15431, use 15000-15001 only)◀

      (For excision with immediate skin grafting use 15000, 15001 in conjunction with 15050-15261)

      ▶(For excision with immediate allograft skin placement, use 15000, 15001 in conjunction with 15300-15366)◀

      ▶(For excision with immediate xenogeneic dermis placement use 15000, 15001 in conjunction with 15400-15431)◀

▶Grafts◀

▶*Autograft/Tissue Cultured Autograft*◀

● **15040**   Harvest of skin for tissue cultured skin autograft, 100 sq cm or less

15050   Pinch graft, single or multiple, to cover small ulcer, tip of digit, or other minimal open area (except on face), up to defect size 2 cm diameter

Surgery: Integumentary System

Surgery: Integumentary System

▲ **15100** Split-thickness autograft, trunk, arms, legs; first 100 sq cm or less, or one percent of body area of infants and children (except 15050)

+ **15101** each additional 100 sq cm, or each additional one percent of body area of infants and children, or part thereof (List separately in addition to code for primary procedure)

(Use 15101 in conjunction with 15100)

● **15110** Epidermal autograft, trunk, arms, legs; first 100 sq cm or less, or one percent of body area of infants and children

+● **15111** each additional 100 sq cm, or each additional one percent of body area of infants and children, or part thereof (List separately in addition to code for primary procedure)

►(Use 15111 in conjunction with 15110)◄

● **15115** Epidermal autograft, face, scalp, eyelids, mouth, neck, ears, orbits, genitalia, hands, feet, and/or multiple digits; first 100 sq cm or less, or one percent of body area of infants and children

+● **15116** each additional 100 sq cm, or each additional one percent of body area of infants and children, or part thereof (List separately in addition to code for primary procedure)

►(Use 15116 in conjunction with 15115)◄

▲ **15120** Split-thickness autograft, face, scalp, eyelids, mouth, neck, ears, orbits, genitalia, hands, feet, and/or multiple digits; first 100 sq cm or less, or one percent of body area of infants and children (except 15050)

+ **15121** each additional 100 sq cm, or each additional one percent of body area of infants and children, or part thereof (List separately in addition to code for primary procedure)

(Use 15121 in conjunction with 15120)

(For eyelids, see also 67961 et seq)

● **15130** Dermal autograft, trunk, arms, legs; first 100 sq cm or less, or one percent of body area of infants and children

+● **15131** each additional 100 sq cm, or each additional one percent of body area of infants and children, or part thereof (List separately in addition to code for primary procedure)

►(Use 15131 in conjunction with 15130)◄

● **15135** Dermal autograft, face, scalp, eyelids, mouth, neck, ears, orbits, genitalia, hands, feet, and/or multiple digits; first 100 sq cm or less, or one percent of body area of infants and children

+● **15136** each additional 100 sq cm, or each additional one percent of body area of infants and children, or part thereof (List separately in addition to code for primary procedure)

►(Use 15136 in conjunction with 15135)◄

● **15150** Tissue cultured epidermal autograft, trunk, arms, legs; first 25 sq cm or less

+● **15151** additional 1 sq cm to 75 sq cm (List separately in addition to code for primary procedure)

►(Do not report 15151 more than once per session)◄

►(Use 15151 in conjunction with 15150)◄

+● **15152** each additional 100 sq cm, or each additional one percent of body area of infants and children, or part thereof (List separately in addition to code for primary procedure)

►(Use 15152 in conjunction with 15151)◄

● **15155** Tissue cultured epidermal autograft, face, scalp, eyelids, mouth, neck, ears, orbits, genitalia, hands, feet, and/or multiple digits; first 25 sq cm or less

+● **15156** additional 1 sq cm to 75 sq cm (List separately in addition to code for primary procedure)

►(Do not report 15156 more than once per session)◄

►(Use 15156 in conjunction with 15155)◄

+● **15157** each additional 100 sq cm, or each additional one percent of body area of infants and children, or part thereof (List separately in addition to code for primary procedure)

►(Use 15157 in conjunction with 15156)◄

►*Acellular Dermal Replacement*◄

● **15170** Acellular dermal replacement, trunk, arms, legs; first 100 sq cm or less, or one percent of body area of infants and children

+● **15171** each additional 100 sq cm, or each additional one percent of body area of infants and children, or part thereof (List separately in addition to code for primary procedure)

►(Use 15171 in conjunction with 15170)◄

● **15175** Acellular dermal replacement, face, scalp, eyelids, mouth, neck, ears, orbits, genitalia, hands, feet, and/or multiple digits; first 100 sq cm or less, or one percent of body area of infants and children

+● **15176** each additional 100 sq cm, or each additional one percent of body area of infants and children, or part thereof (List separately in addition to code for primary procedure)

►(Use 15176 in conjunction with 15175)◄

15200 Full thickness graft, free, including direct closure of donor site, trunk; 20 sq cm or less

+ **15201** each additional 20 sq cm (List separately in addition to code for primary procedure)

(Use 15201 in conjunction with 15200)

15220   Full thickness graft, free, including direct closure of donor site, scalp, arms, and/or legs; 20 sq cm or less

+ 15221   each additional 20 sq cm (List separately in addition to code for primary procedure)

        (Use 15221 in conjunction with 15220)

15240   Full thickness graft, free, including direct closure of donor site, forehead, cheeks, chin, mouth, neck, axillae, genitalia, hands, and/or feet; 20 sq cm or less

        (For finger tip graft, use 15050)

        (For repair of syndactyly, fingers, see 26560-26562)

+ 15241   each additional 20 sq cm (List separately in addition to code for primary procedure)

        (Use 15241 in conjunction with 15240)

15260   Full thickness graft, free, including direct closure of donor site, nose, ears, eyelids, and/or lips; 20 sq cm or less

+ 15261   each additional 20 sq cm (List separately in addition to code for primary procedure)

        (Use 15261 in conjunction with 15260)

        (For eyelids, see also 67961 et seq)

        (Repair of donor site requiring skin graft or local flaps, to be added as additional separate procedure)

►Allograft/Tissue Cultured Allogeneic Skin Substitute◄

►Application of a non-autologous human skin graft (ie, homograft) from a donor to a part of the recipient's body to resurface an area damaged by burns, traumatic injury, soft tissue infection and/or tissue necrosis or surgery.◄

● **15300**   Allograft skin for temporary wound closure, trunk, arms, legs; first 100 sq cm or less, or one percent of body area of infants and children

+● **15301**   each additional 100 sq cm, or each additional one percent of body area of infants and children, or part thereof (List separately in addition to code for primary procedure)

        ►(Use 15301 in conjunction with 15300)◄

● **15320**   Allograft skin for temporary wound closure, face, scalp, eyelids, mouth, neck, ears, orbits, genitalia, hands, feet, and/or multiple digits; first 100 sq cm or less, or one percent of body area of infants and children

+● **15321**   each additional 100 sq cm, or each additional one percent of body area of infants and children, or part thereof (List separately in addition to code for primary procedure)

        ►(Use 15321 in conjunction with 15320)◄

● **15330**   Acellular dermal allograft, trunk, arms, legs; first 100 sq cm or less, or one percent of body area of infants and children

+● **15331**   each additional 100 sq cm, or each additional one percent of body area of infants and children, or part thereof (List separately in addition to code for primary procedure)

        ►(Use 15331 in conjunction with 15330)◄

● **15335**   Acellular dermal allograft, face, scalp, eyelids, mouth, neck, ears, orbits, genitalia, hands, feet, and/or multiple digits; first 100 sq cm or less, or one percent of body area of infants and children

+● **15336**   each additional 100 sq cm, or each additional one percent of body area of infants and children, or part thereof (List separately in addition to code for primary procedure)

        ►(Use 15336 in conjunction with 15335)◄

● **15340**   Tissue cultured allogeneic skin substitute; first 25 sq cm or less

+● **15341**   each additional 25 sq cm

        ►(Use 15341 in conjunction with 15340)◄

        ►(Do not report 15340, 15341 in conjunction with 11040-11042, 15000)◄

        ►(15342 has been deleted. To report, see 15170, 15175, 15340, 15360, 15365)◄

        ►(15343 has been deleted. To report, see 15171, 15176, 15341, 15361, 15366)◄

        ►(15350 has been deleted. To report, see 15300, 15320, 15330, 15335)◄

        ►(15351 has been deleted. To report, see 15301, 15321, 15331, 15336)◄

● **15360**   Tissue cultured allogeneic dermal substitute; trunk, arms, legs; first 100 sq cm or less, or one percent of body area of infants and children

+● **15361**   each additional 100 sq cm, or each additional one percent of body area of infants and children, or part thereof (List separately in addition to code for primary procedure)

        ►(Use 15361 in conjunction with 15360)◄

● **15365**   Tissue cultured allogeneic dermal substitute, face, scalp, eyelids, mouth, neck, ears, orbits, genitalia, hands, feet, and/or multiple digits; first 100 sq cm or less, or one percent of body area of infants and children

+● **15366**   each additional 100 sq cm, or each additional one percent of body area of infants and children, or part thereof (List separately in addition to code for primary procedure)

        ►(Use 15366 in conjunction with 15365)◄

Surgery: Integumentary System

► *Xenograft* ◄

►Application of a non-human skin graft or biologic wound dressing (eg, porcine tissue or pigskin) to a part of the recipient's body following debridement of the burn wound or area of traumatic injury, soft tissue infection and/or tissue necrosis, or surgery.◄

▲ **15400** Xenograft, skin (dermal), for temporary wound closure; trunk, arms, legs; first 100 sq cm or less, or one percent of body area of infants and children

+▲ **15401** each additional 100 sq cm, or each additional one percent of body area of infants and children, or part thereof (List separately in addition to code for primary procedure)

(Use 15401 in conjunction with 15400)

● **15420** Xenograft skin (dermal), for temporary wound closure, face, scalp, eyelids, mouth, neck, ears, orbits, genitalia, hands, feet, and/or multiple digits; first 100 sq cm or less, or one percent of body area of infants and children

+● **15421** each additional 100 sq cm, or each additional one percent of body area of infants and children, or part thereof (List separately in addition to code for primary procedure)

►(Use 15421 in conjunction with 15420)◄

● **15430** Acellular xenograft implant; first 100 sq cm or less, or one percent of body area of infants and children

+● **15431** each additional 100 sq cm, or each additional one percent of body area of infants and children, or part thereof (List separately in addition to code for primary procedure)

►(Use 15431 in conjunction with 15430)◄

►(Do not report 15430, 15431 in conjunction with 11040-11042, 15000)◄

Flaps (Skin and/or Deep Tissues)

Regions listed refer to recipient area (not donor site) when flap is being attached in transfer or to final site.

Regions listed refer to donor site when tube is formed for later or when "delay" of flap is prior to transfer.

Procedures 15570-15738 do not include extensive immobilization (eg, large plaster casts and other immobilizing devices are considered additional separate procedures).

Repair of donor site requiring skin graft or local flaps is considered an additional separate procedure.

(For microvascular flaps, see 15756-15758)

15570 Formation of direct or tubed pedicle, with or without transfer; trunk

15572 scalp, arms, or legs

15574 forehead, cheeks, chin, mouth, neck, axillae, genitalia, hands or feet

15576 eyelids, nose, ears, lips, or intraoral

15600 Delay of flap or sectioning of flap (division and inset); at trunk

15610 at scalp, arms, or legs

15620 at forehead, cheeks, chin, neck, axillae, genitalia, hands, or feet

15630 at eyelids, nose, ears, or lips

15650 Transfer, intermediate, of any pedicle flap (eg, abdomen to wrist, Walking tube), any location

(For eyelids, nose, ears, or lips, see also anatomical area)

(For revision, defatting or rearranging of transferred pedicle flap or skin graft, see 13100-14300)

(Procedures 15732-15738 are described by donor site of the muscle, myocutaneous, or fasciocutaneous flap)

15732 Muscle, myocutaneous, or fasciocutaneous flap; head and neck (eg, temporalis, masseter muscle, sternocleidomastoid, levator scapulae)

15734 trunk

15736 upper extremity

15738 lower extremity

Other Flaps and Grafts

Repair of donor site requiring skin graft or local flaps should be reported as an additional procedure.

15740 Flap; island pedicle

15750 neurovascular pedicle

15756 Free muscle or myocutaneous flap with microvascular anastomosis

(Do not report code 69990 in addition to code 15756)

15757 Free skin flap with microvascular anastomosis

(Do not report code 69990 in addition to code 15757)

15758 Free fascial flap with microvascular anastomosis

(Do not report code 69990 in addition to code 15758)

15760 Graft; composite (eg, full thickness of external ear or nasal ala), including primary closure, donor area

15770 derma-fat-fascia

15775 Punch graft for hair transplant; 1 to 15 punch grafts

15776 more than 15 punch grafts

(For strip transplant, use 15220)

Other Procedures

15780   Dermabrasion; total face (eg, for acne scarring, fine wrinkling, rhytids, general keratosis)

15781   segmental, face

15782   regional, other than face

15783   superficial, any site, (eg, tattoo removal)

15786   Abrasion; single lesion (eg, keratosis, scar)

+ 15787   each additional four lesions or less (List separately in addition to code for primary procedure)

(Use 15787 in conjunction with 15786)

15788   Chemical peel, facial; epidermal

15789   dermal

15792   Chemical peel, nonfacial; epidermal

15793   dermal

▶(15810, 15811 have been deleted)◀

15819   Cervicoplasty

15820   Blepharoplasty, lower eyelid;

15821   with extensive herniated fat pad

15822   Blepharoplasty, upper eyelid;

15823   with excessive skin weighting down lid

(For bilateral blepharoplasty, add modifier 50)

15824   Rhytidectomy; forehead

(For repair of brow ptosis, use 67900)

15825   neck with platysmal tightening (platysmal flap, P-flap)

15826   glabellar frown lines

15828   cheek, chin, and neck

15829   superficial musculoaponeurotic system (SMAS) flap

(For bilateral rhytidectomy, add modifier 50)

15831   Excision, excessive skin and subcutaneous tissue (including lipectomy); abdomen (abdominoplasty)

15832   thigh

15833   leg

15834   hip

15835   buttock

15836   arm

15837   forearm or hand

15838   submental fat pad

15839   other area

(For bilateral procedure, add modifier 50)

15840   Graft for facial nerve paralysis; free fascia graft (including obtaining fascia)

(For bilateral procedure, add modifier 50)

15841   free muscle graft (including obtaining graft)

15842   free muscle flap by microsurgical technique

(Do not report code 69990 in addition to code 15842)

15845   .   regional muscle transfer

(For intravenous fluorescein examination of blood flow in graft or flap, use 15860)

(For nerve transfers, decompression, or repair, see 64831-64876, 64905, 64907, 69720, 69725, 69740, 69745, 69955)

15850   Removal of sutures under anesthesia (other than local), same surgeon

15851   Removal of sutures under anesthesia (other than local), other surgeon

15852   Dressing change (for other than burns) under anesthesia (other than local)

15860   Intravenous injection of agent (eg, fluorescein) to test vascular flow in flap or graft

15876   Suction assisted lipectomy; head and neck

15877   trunk

15878   upper extremity

15879   lower extremity

Pressure Ulcers (Decubitus Ulcers)

15920   Excision, coccygeal pressure ulcer, with coccygectomy; with primary suture

15922   with flap closure

15931   Excision, sacral pressure ulcer, with primary suture;

15933   with ostectomy

15934   Excision, sacral pressure ulcer, with skin flap closure;

15935   with ostectomy

15936   Excision, sacral pressure ulcer, in preparation for muscle or myocutaneous flap or skin graft closure;

15937   with ostectomy

(For repair of defect using muscle or myocutaneous flap, use code(s) 15734 and/or 15738 in addition to 15936, 15937. For repair of defect using split skin graft, use codes 15100 and/or 15101 in addition to 15936, 15937)

15940   Excision, ischial pressure ulcer, with primary suture;

15941   with ostectomy (ischiectomy)

15944   Excision, ischial pressure ulcer, with skin flap closure;

15945   with ostectomy

Surgery: Integumentary System

15946 Excision, ischial pressure ulcer, with ostectomy, in preparation for muscle or myocutaneous flap or skin graft closure

(For repair of defect using muscle or myocutaneous flap, use code(s) 15734 and/or 15738 in addition to 15946. For repair of defect using split skin graft, use codes 15100 and/or 15101 in addition to 15946)

15950 Excision, trochanteric pressure ulcer, with primary suture;

15951 with ostectomy

15952 Excision, trochanteric pressure ulcer, with skin flap closure;

15953 with ostectomy

15956 Excision, trochanteric pressure ulcer, in preparation for muscle or myocutaneous flap or skin graft closure;

15958 with ostectomy

(For repair of defect using muscle or myocutaneous flap, use code(s) 15734 and/or 15738 in addition to 15956, 15958. For repair of defect using split skin graft, use codes 15100 and/or 15101 in addition to 15956, 15958)

15999 Unlisted procedure, excision pressure ulcer

(For free skin graft to close ulcer or donor site, see 15000 et seq)

Burns, Local Treatment

▶Procedures 16000-16036 refer to local treatment of burned surface only. Codes 16020-16030 include the application of materials (eg, Biobrane®, other dressings) not described in 15100-15431.◀

List percentage of body surface involved and depth of burn.

For necessary related medical services (eg, hospital visits, detention) in management of burned patients, see appropriate services in **Evaluation and Management** and **Medicine** sections.

▶For the application of skin grafts or skin substitutes, see 15100-15650.◀

16000 Initial treatment, first degree burn, when no more than local treatment is required

▶(16010, 16015 have been deleted. To report, see 16020-16030)◀

▲ **16020** Dressings and/or debridement of partial-thickness burns, initial or subsequent; small (less than 5% total body surface area)

▲ **16025** medium (eg, whole face or whole extremity, or 5% to 10% total body surface area)

▲ **16030** large (eg, more than one extremity, or greater than 10% total body surface area)

16035 Escharotomy; initial incision

+ **16036** each additional incision (List separately in addition to code for primary procedure)

(Use 16036 in conjunction with 16035)

▶(For debridement, curettement of burn wound, see 16020-16030)◀

Destruction

Destruction means the ablation of benign, premalignant or malignant tissues by any method, with or without curettement, including local anesthesia, and not usually requiring closure.

Any method includes electrosurgery, cryosurgery, laser and chemical treatment. Lesions include condylomata, papillomata, molluscum contagiosum, herpetic lesions, warts (ie, common, plantar, flat), milia, or other benign, premalignant (eg, actinic keratoses), or malignant lesions.

(For destruction of lesion(s) in specific anatomic sites, see 40820, 46900-46917, 46924, 54050-54057, 54065, 56501, 56515, 57061, 57065, 67850, 68135)

(For paring or cutting of benign hyperkeratotic lesions (eg, corns or calluses), see 11055-11057)

(For sharp removal or electrosurgical destruction of skin tags and fibrocutaneous tags, see 11200, 11201)

(For cryotherapy of acne, use 17340)

(For initiation or follow-up care of topical chemotherapy (eg, 5-FU or similar agents), see appropriate office visits)

(For shaving of epidermal or dermal lesions, see 11300-11313)

Destruction, Benign or Premalignant Lesions

17000 Destruction (eg, laser surgery, electrosurgery, cryosurgery, chemosurgery, surgical curettement), all benign or premalignant lesions (eg, actinic keratoses) other than skin tags or cutaneous vascular proliferative lesions; first lesion

+ **17003** second through 14 lesions, each (List separately in addition to code for first lesion)

(Use 17003 in conjunction with 17000)

⊘ **17004** Destruction (eg, laser surgery, electrosurgery, cryosurgery, chemosurgery, surgical curettement), all benign or premalignant lesions (eg, actinic keratoses) other than skin tags or cutaneous vascular proliferative lesions, 15 or more lesions

(Do not report 17004 in conjunction with 17000-17003)

17106 Destruction of cutaneous vascular proliferative lesions (eg, laser technique); less than 10 sq cm

17107 10.0 to 50.0 sq cm

17108 over 50.0 sq cm

17110   Destruction (eg, laser surgery, electrosurgery, cryosurgery, chemosurgery, surgical curettement), of flat warts, molluscum contagiosum, or milia; up to 14 lesions

17111   15 or more lesions

(For destruction of common or plantar warts, see 17000, 17003, 17004)

17250   Chemical cauterization of granulation tissue (proud flesh, sinus or fistula)

(17250 is not to be used with removal or excision codes for the same lesion)

Destruction, Malignant Lesions, Any Method

17260   Destruction, malignant lesion (eg, laser surgery, electrosurgery, cryosurgery, chemosurgery, surgical curettement), trunk, arms or legs; lesion diameter 0.5 cm or less

17261   lesion diameter 0.6 to 1.0 cm

17262   lesion diameter 1.1 to 2.0 cm

17263   lesion diameter 2.1 to 3.0 cm

17264   lesion diameter 3.1 to 4.0 cm

17266   lesion diameter over 4.0 cm

17270   Destruction, malignant lesion (eg, laser surgery, electrosurgery, cryosurgery, chemosurgery, surgical curettement), scalp, neck, hands, feet, genitalia; lesion diameter 0.5 cm or less

17271   lesion diameter 0.6 to 1.0 cm

17272   lesion diameter 1.1 to 2.0 cm

17273   lesion diameter 2.1 to 3.0 cm

17274   lesion diameter 3.1 to 4.0 cm

17276   lesion diameter over 4.0 cm

17280   Destruction, malignant lesion (eg, laser surgery, electrosurgery, cryosurgery, chemosurgery, surgical curettement), face, ears, eyelids, nose, lips, mucous membrane; lesion diameter 0.5 cm or less

17281   lesion diameter 0.6 to 1.0 cm

17282   lesion diameter 1.1 to 2.0 cm

17283   lesion diameter 2.1 to 3.0 cm

17284   lesion diameter 3.1 to 4.0 cm

17286   lesion diameter over 4.0 cm

Mohs Micrographic Surgery

Mohs micrographic surgery, for the removal of complex or ill-defined skin cancer, requires a single physician to act in two integrated, but separate and distinct capacities: surgeon and pathologist. If either of these responsibilities are delegated to another physician who reports his services separately, these codes are not appropriate. If

repair is performed, use separate repair, flap, or graft codes. If a biopsy of a suspected skin cancer is performed on the same day as Mohs surgery because there was no prior pathology confirmation of a diagnosis, then report diagnostic skin biopsy (11100, 11101) and frozen section pathology (88331) with modifier 59 to distinguish from the subsequent definitive surgical procedure of Mohs surgery.

⊘ **17304**   Chemosurgery (Mohs micrographic technique), including removal of all gross tumor, surgical excision of tissue specimens, mapping, color coding of specimens, microscopic examination of specimens by the surgeon, and complete histopathologic preparation including the first routine stain (eg, hematoxylin and eosin, toluidine blue); first stage, fresh tissue technique, up to 5 specimens

(If additional special pathology procedures, stains or immunostains are required, use 88311-88314, 88342)

⊘ **17305**   second stage, fixed or fresh tissue, up to 5 specimens

⊘ **17306**   third stage, fixed or fresh tissue, up to 5 specimens

⊘ **17307**   additional stage(s), up to 5 specimens, each stage

+ **17310**   each additional specimen, after the first 5 specimens, fixed or fresh tissue, any stage (List separately in addition to code for primary procedure)

(Use 17310 in conjunction with 17304-17307)

Other Procedures

17340   Cryotherapy (CO_2 slush, liquid N_2) for acne

17360   Chemical exfoliation for acne (eg, acne paste, acid)

17380   Electrolysis epilation, each 1/2 hour

(For actinotherapy, use 96900)

17999   Unlisted procedure, skin, mucous membrane and subcutaneous tissue

Breast

Incision

19000   Puncture aspiration of cyst of breast;

+ **19001**   each additional cyst (List separately in addition to code for primary procedure)

(Use 19001 in conjunction with 19000)

(If imaging guidance is performed, see 76095, 76096, 76393, 76942)

19020   Mastotomy with exploration or drainage of abscess, deep

19030   Injection procedure only for mammary ductogram or galactogram

(For radiological supervision and interpretation, see 76086, 76088)

(For catheter lavage of mammary ducts for collection of cytology specimens, use Category III codes 0046T, 0047T)

Surgery: Integumentary System

Excision

(To report bilateral procedures, report modifier 50 with the procedure code)

Excisional breast surgery includes certain biopsy procedures, the removal of cysts or other benign or malignant tumors or lesions, and the surgical treatment of breast and chest wall malignancies. Biopsy procedures may be percutaneous or open, and they involve the removal of differing amounts of tissue for diagnosis.

Breast biopsies are reported using codes 19100-19103. The open excision of breast lesions (eg, lesions of the breast ducts, cysts, benign or malignant tumors), without specific attention to adequate surgical margins, with or without the preoperative placement of radiological markers, is reported using codes 19110-19126. Partial mastectomy procedures (eg, lumpectomy, tylectomy, quadrantectomy, or segmentectomy) describe open excisions of breast tissue with specific attention to adequate surgical margins.

Partial mastectomy procedures are reported using codes 19160 or 19162 as appropriate. Documentation for partial mastectomy procedures includes attention to the removal of adequate surgical margins surrounding the breast mass or lesion.

Total mastectomy procedures include simple mastectomy, complete mastectomy, subcutaneous mastectomy, modified radical mastectomy, radical mastectomy, and more extended procedures (eg, Urban type operation). Total mastectomy procedures are reported using codes 19180, 19182, 19200, 19220, or 19240 as appropriate.

Excisions or resections of chest wall tumors including ribs, with or without reconstruction, with or without mediastinal lymphadenectomy, are reported using codes 19260, 19271, or 19272. Codes 19260-19272 are not restricted to breast tumors and are used to report resections of chest wall tumors originating from any chest wall component. (For excision of lung or pleura, see 32310 et seq.)

19100 Biopsy of breast; percutaneous, needle core, not using imaging guidance (separate procedure)

(For fine needle aspiration, use 10021)

(For image guided breast biopsy, see 19102, 19103, 10022)

19101 open, incisional

19102 percutaneous, needle core, using imaging guidance

(For placement of percutaneous localization clip, use 19295)

19103 percutaneous, automated vacuum assisted or rotating biopsy device, using imaging guidance

(For imaging guidance performed in conjunction with 19102, 19103, see 76095, 76096, 76360, 76393, 76942)

(For placement of percutaneous localization clip, use 19295)

19110 Nipple exploration, with or without excision of a solitary lactiferous duct or a papilloma lactiferous duct

19112 Excision of lactiferous duct fistula

19120 Excision of cyst, fibroadenoma, or other benign or malignant tumor, aberrant breast tissue, duct lesion, nipple or areolar lesion (except 19140), open, male or female, one or more lesions

19125 Excision of breast lesion identified by preoperative placement of radiological marker, open; single lesion

+ 19126 each additional lesion separately identified by a preoperative radiological marker (List separately in addition to code for primary procedure)

(Use 19126 in conjunction with 19125)

19140 Mastectomy for gynecomastia

19160 Mastectomy, partial (eg, lumpectomy, tylectomy, quadrantectomy, segmentectomy);

19162 with axillary lymphadenectomy

(For placement of radiotherapy afterloading balloon/brachytherapy catheters, see 19296-19298)

19180 Mastectomy, simple, complete

(For immediate or delayed insertion of implant, use 19340 or 19342)

(For gynecomastia, use 19140)

19182 Mastectomy, subcutaneous

(For immediate or delayed insertion of implant, use 19340 or 19342)

19200 Mastectomy, radical, including pectoral muscles, axillary lymph nodes

(For immediate or delayed insertion of implant, use 19340 or 19342)

19220 Mastectomy, radical, including pectoral muscles, axillary and internal mammary lymph nodes (Urban type operation)

(For immediate or delayed insertion of implant, use 19340 or 19342)

19240 Mastectomy, modified radical, including axillary lymph nodes, with or without pectoralis minor muscle, but excluding pectoralis major muscle

(For immediate or delayed insertion of implant, use 19340 or 19342)

19260 Excision of chest wall tumor including ribs

19271 Excision of chest wall tumor involving ribs, with plastic reconstruction; without mediastinal lymphadenectomy

19272 with mediastinal lymphadenectomy

▶(Do not report 19260, 19271, 19272 in conjunction with 32002, 32020, 32100, 32503, 32504)◀

Introduction

19290 Preoperative placement of needle localization wire, breast;

+ 19291 each additional lesion (List separately in addition to code for primary procedure)

(Use 19291 in conjunction with 19290)

(For radiological supervision and interpretation, see 76095, 76096, 76942)

+ 19295 Image guided placement, metallic localization clip, percutaneous, during breast biopsy (List separately in addition to code for primary procedure)

(Use 19295 in conjunction with 19102, 19103)

19296 Placement of radiotherapy afterloading balloon catheter into the breast for interstitial radioelement application following partial mastectomy, includes imaging guidance; on date separate from partial mastectomy

+ 19297 concurrent with partial mastectomy (List separately in addition to code for primary procedure)

(Use 19297 in conjunction with 19160 or 19162)

⊙ **19298** Placement of radiotherapy afterloading brachytherapy catheters (multiple tube and button type) into the breast for interstitial radioelement application following (at the time of or subsequent to) partial mastectomy, includes imaging guidance

Repair and/or Reconstruction

(To report bilateral procedures, report modifier 50 with the procedure code)

19316 Mastopexy

19318 Reduction mammaplasty

19324 Mammaplasty, augmentation; without prosthetic implant

19325 with prosthetic implant

(For flap or graft, use also appropriate number)

19328 Removal of intact mammary implant

19330 Removal of mammary implant material

19340 Immediate insertion of breast prosthesis following mastopexy, mastectomy or in reconstruction

19342 Delayed insertion of breast prosthesis following mastopexy, mastectomy or in reconstruction

(For supply of implant, use 99070)

(For preparation of custom breast implant, use 19396)

19350 Nipple/areola reconstruction

19355 Correction of inverted nipples

19357 Breast reconstruction, immediate or delayed, with tissue expander, including subsequent expansion

19361 Breast reconstruction with latissimus dorsi flap, with or without prosthetic implant

19364 Breast reconstruction with free flap

(Do not report code 69990 in addition to code 19364)

(19364 includes harvesting of the flap, microvascular transfer, closure of the donor site, and inset shaping the flap into a breast)

19366 Breast reconstruction with other technique

(For operating microscope, use 69990)

(For insertion of prosthesis, use also 19340 or 19342)

19367 Breast reconstruction with transverse rectus abdominis myocutaneous flap (TRAM), single pedicle, including closure of donor site;

19368 with microvascular anastomosis (supercharging)

(Do not report code 69990 in addition to code 19368)

19369 Breast reconstruction with transverse rectus abdominis myocutaneous flap (TRAM), double pedicle, including closure of donor site

19370 Open periprosthetic capsulotomy, breast

19371 Periprosthetic capsulectomy, breast

19380 Revision of reconstructed breast

19396 Preparation of moulage for custom breast implant

Other Procedures

(For microwave thermotherapy of the breast, use Category III code 0061T)

19499 Unlisted procedure, breast

Surgery: Integumentary System

Notes

⊘=Modifier 51 exempt ⊙=Conscious sedation ✚=Add-on code ✂=FDA approval pending

Musculoskeletal System

Cast and strapping procedures appear at the end of this section.

The services listed below include the application and removal of the first cast or traction device only. Subsequent replacement of cast and/or traction device may require an additional listing.

Definitions

The terms "closed treatment," "open treatment," and "percutaneous skeletal fixation" have been carefully chosen to accurately reflect current orthopaedic procedural treatments.

Closed treatment specifically means that the fracture site is not surgically opened (exposed to the external environment and directly visualized). This terminology is used to describe procedures that treat fractures by three methods: 1) without manipulation; 2) with manipulation; or 3) with or without traction.

Open treatment is used when the fractured bone is either: 1) surgically opened (exposed to the external environment) and the fracture (bone ends) visualized and internal fixation may be used; or 2) the fractured bone is opened remote from the fracture site in order to insert an intramedullary nail across the fracture site (the fracture site is not opened and visualized).

Percutaneous skeletal fixation describes fracture treatment which is neither open nor closed. In this procedure, the fracture fragments are not visualized, but fixation (eg, pins) is placed across the fracture site, usually under X-ray imaging.

The type of fracture (eg, open, compound, closed) does not have any coding correlation with the type of treatment (eg, closed, open, or percutaneous) provided.

The codes for treatment of fractures and joint injuries (dislocations) are categorized by the type of manipulation (reduction) and stabilization (fixation or immobilization). These codes can apply to either open (compound) or closed fractures or joint injuries.

Skeletal traction is the application of a force (distracting or traction force) to a limb segment through a wire, pin, screw, or clamp that is attached (eg, penetrates) to bone.

Skin traction is the application of a force (longitudinal) to a limb using felt or strapping applied directly to skin only.

External fixation is the usage of skeletal pins plus an attaching mechanism/device used for temporary or definitive treatment of acute or chronic bony deformity.

Codes for obtaining autogenous bone grafts, cartilage, tendon, fascia lata grafts or other tissues through separate incisions are to be used only when the graft is not already listed as part of the basic procedure.

Re-reduction of a fracture and/or dislocation performed by the primary physician may be identified by the addition of the modifier 76 to the usual procedure number to indicate "Repeat Procedure by Same Physician." (See guidelines.)

Codes for external fixation are to be used only when external fixation is not already listed as part of the basic procedure.

All codes for suction irrigation have been deleted. To report, list only the primary surgical procedure performed (eg, sequestrectomy, deep incision).

Manipulation is used throughout the musculoskeletal fracture and dislocation subsections to specifically mean the attempted reduction or restoration of a fracture or joint dislocation to its normal anatomic alignment by the application of manually applied forces.

(For computer assisted musculoskeletal surgical navigational orthopedic procedures, report 0054T-0056T)

General

Incision

20000   Incision of soft tissue abscess (eg, secondary to osteomyelitis); superficial

20005   deep or complicated

Wound Exploration—Trauma (eg, Penetrating Gunshot, Stab Wound)

20100-20103 relate to wound(s) resulting from penetrating trauma. These codes describe surgical exploration and enlargement of the wound, extension of dissection (to determine penetration), debridement, removal of foreign body(s), ligation or coagulation of minor subcutaneous and/or muscular blood vessel(s), of the subcutaneous tissue, muscle fascia, and/or muscle, not requiring thoracotomy or laparotomy. If a repair is done to major structure(s) or major blood vessel(s) requiring thoracotomy or laparotomy, then those specific code(s) would supersede the use of codes 20100-20103. To report Simple, Intermediate, or Complex repair of wound(s) that do not require enlargement of the wound, extension of dissection, etc., as stated above, use specific Repair code(s) in the **Integumentary System** section.

20100   Exploration of penetrating wound (separate procedure); neck

20101   chest

20102   abdomen/flank/back

20103   extremity

▲=Revised code   ●=New code   ►◄=Contains new or revised text

Excision

20150   Excision of epiphyseal bar, with or without autogenous soft tissue graft obtained through same fascial incision

(For aspiration of bone marrow, use 38220)

20200   Biopsy, muscle; superficial

20205   deep

20206   Biopsy, muscle, percutaneous needle

(If imaging guidance is performed, see 76360, 76393, 76942)

(For fine needle aspiration, use 10021 or 10022)

(For evaulation of fine needle aspirate, see 88172-88173)

(For excision of muscle tumor, deep, see specific anatomic section)

20220   Biopsy, bone, trocar, or needle; superficial (eg, ilium, sternum, spinous process, ribs)

20225   deep (eg, vertebral body, femur)

(For bone marrow biopsy, use 38221)

(For radiologic supervision and interpretation, see 76003, 76360, 76393)

20240   Biopsy, bone, open; superficial (eg, ilium, sternum, spinous process, ribs, trochanter of femur)

20245   deep (eg, humerus, ischium, femur)

20250   Biopsy, vertebral body, open; thoracic

20251   lumbar or cervical

(For sequestrectomy, osteomyelitis or drainage of bone abscess, see anatomical area)

Introduction or Removal

(For injection procedure for arthrography, see anatomical area)

20500   Injection of sinus tract; therapeutic (separate procedure)

20501   diagnostic (sinogram)

(For radiological supervision and interpretation, use 76080)

20520   Removal of foreign body in muscle or tendon sheath; simple

20525   deep or complicated

20526   Injection, therapeutic (eg, local anesthetic, corticosteroid), carpal tunnel

20550   Injection(s); single tendon sheath, or ligament, aponeurosis (eg, plantar "fascia")

20551   single tendon origin/insertion

20552   Injection(s); single or multiple trigger point(s), one or two muscle(s)

20553   single or multiple trigger point(s), three or more muscle(s)

(If imaging guidance is performed, see 76003, 76393, 76942)

20600   Arthrocentesis, aspiration and/or injection; small joint or bursa (eg, fingers, toes)

20605   intermediate joint or bursa (eg, temporomandibular, acromioclavicular, wrist, elbow or ankle, olecranon bursa)

20610   major joint or bursa (eg, shoulder, hip, knee joint, subacromial bursa)

(If imaging guidance is performed, see 76003, 76360, 76393, 76942)

20612   Aspiration and/or injection of ganglion cyst(s) any location

(To report multiple ganglion cyst aspirations/injections, use 20612 and append modifier 59)

20615   Aspiration and injection for treatment of bone cyst

20650   Insertion of wire or pin with application of skeletal traction, including removal (separate procedure)

⊘ **20660**   Application of cranial tongs, caliper, or stereotactic frame, including removal (separate procedure)

20661   Application of halo, including removal; cranial

20662   pelvic

20663   femoral

20664   Application of halo, including removal, cranial, 6 or more pins placed, for thin skull osteology (eg, pediatric patients, hydrocephalus, osteogenesis imperfecta), requiring general anesthesia

20665   Removal of tongs or halo applied by another physician

20670   Removal of implant; superficial, (eg, buried wire, pin or rod) (separate procedure)

20680   deep (eg, buried wire, pin, screw, metal band, nail, rod or plate)

⊘ **20690**   Application of a uniplane (pins or wires in one plane), unilateral, external fixation system

⊘ **20692**   Application of a multiplane (pins or wires in more than one plane), unilateral, external fixation system (eg, Ilizarov, Monticelli type)

20693   Adjustment or revision of external fixation system requiring anesthesia (eg, new pin(s) or wire(s) and/or new ring(s) or bar(s))

20694   Removal, under anesthesia, of external fixation system

Replantation

20802   Replantation, arm (includes surgical neck of humerus through elbow joint), complete amputation

(To report replantation of incomplete arm amputation, see specific code(s) for repair of bone(s), ligament(s), tendon(s), nerve(s), or blood vessel(s) with modifier 52)

20805   Replantation, forearm (includes radius and ulna to radial carpal joint), complete amputation

(To report replantation of incomplete forearm amputation, see specific code(s) for repair of bone(s), ligament(s), tendon(s), nerve(s), or blood vessel(s) with modifier 52)

20808   Replantation, hand (includes hand through metacarpophalangeal joints), complete amputation

(To report replantation of incomplete hand amputation, see specific code(s) for repair of bone(s), ligament(s), tendon(s), nerve(s), or blood vessel(s) with modifier 52)

20816   Replantation, digit, excluding thumb (includes metacarpophalangeal joint to insertion of flexor sublimis tendon), complete amputation

(To report replantation of incomplete digit amputation, excluding thumb, see specific code(s) for repair of bone(s), ligament(s), tendon(s), nerve(s), or blood vessel(s) with modifier 52)

20822   Replantation, digit, excluding thumb (includes distal tip to sublimis tendon insertion), complete amputation

(To report replantation of incomplete digit amputation, excluding thumb, see specific code(s) for repair of bone(s), ligament(s), tendon(s), nerve(s), or blood vessel(s) with modifier 52)

20824   Replantation, thumb (includes carpometacarpal joint to MP joint), complete amputation

(To report replantation of incomplete thumb amputation, see specific code(s) for repair of bone(s), ligament(s), tendon(s), nerve(s), or blood vessel(s) with modifier 52)

20827   Replantation, thumb (includes distal tip to MP joint), complete amputation

(To report replantation of incomplete thumb amputation, see specific code(s) for repair of bone(s), ligament(s), tendon(s), nerve(s), or blood vessel(s) with modifier 52)

(To report replantation of complete leg amputation, see specific code(s) for repair of bone(s), ligament(s), tendon(s), nerve(s), or blood vessel(s) with modifier 52)

(To report replantation of incomplete leg amputation, see specific code(s) for repair of bone(s), ligament(s), tendon(s), nerve(s), or blood vessel(s) with modifier 52)

20838   Replantation, foot, complete amputation

(To report replantation of incomplete foot amputation, see specific code(s) for repair of bone(s), ligament(s), tendon(s), nerve(s), or blood vessel(s) with modifier 52)

Grafts (or Implants)

Codes for obtaining autogenous bone, cartilage, tendon, fascia lata grafts, or other tissues through separate skin/fascial incisions should be reported separately unless the code descriptor references the harvesting of the graft or implant (eg, includes obtaining graft).

Do not append modifier 62 to bone graft codes 20900-20938.

(For spinal surgery bone graft(s) see codes 20930-20938)

⊘ **20900**   Bone graft, any donor area; minor or small (eg, dowel or button)

⊘ **20902**   major or large

⊘ **20910**   Cartilage graft; costochondral

⊘ **20912**   nasal septum

(For ear cartilage, use 21235)

⊘ **20920**   Fascia lata graft; by stripper

⊘ **20922**   by incision and area exposure, complex or sheet

⊘ **20924**   Tendon graft, from a distance (eg, palmaris, toe extensor, plantaris)

⊘ **20926**   Tissue grafts, other (eg, paratenon, fat, dermis)

(Codes 20930-20938 are reported in addition to codes for the definitive procedure(s) without modifier 51)

⊘ **20930**   Allograft for spine surgery only; morselized

⊘ **20931**   structural

⊘ **20936**   Autograft for spine surgery only (includes harvesting the graft); local (eg, ribs, spinous process, or laminar fragments) obtained from same incision

⊘ **20937**   morselized (through separate skin or fascial incision)

⊘ **20938**   structural, bicortical or tricortical (through separate skin or fascial incision)

(For needle aspiration of bone marrow for the purpose of bone grafting, use 38220)

Other Procedures

20950   Monitoring of interstitial fluid pressure (includes insertion of device, eg, wick catheter technique, needle manometer technique) in detection of muscle compartment syndrome

20955   Bone graft with microvascular anastomosis; fibula

20956   iliac crest

20957   metatarsal

20962   other than fibula, iliac crest, or metatarsal

(Do not report code 69990 in addition to codes 20955-20962)

20969   Free osteocutaneous flap with microvascular anastomosis; other than iliac crest, metatarsal, or great toe

20970   iliac crest

20972   metatarsal

20973   great toe with web space

(Do not report code 69990 in addition to codes 20969-20973)

(For great toe, wrap-around procedure, use 26551)

⊘ 20974   Electrical stimulation to aid bone healing; noninvasive (nonoperative)

⊘ 20975   invasive (operative)

20979   Low intensity ultrasound stimulation to aid bone healing, noninvasive (nonoperative)

⊙ 20982   Ablation, bone tumor(s) (eg, osteoid osteoma, metastasis) radiofrequency, percutaneous, including computed tomographic guidance

20999   Unlisted procedure, musculoskeletal system, general

Head

Skull, facial bones, and temporomandibular joint.

Incision

(For drainage of superficial abscess and hematoma, use 20000)

(For removal of embedded foreign body from dentoalveolar structure, see 41805, 41806)

21010   Arthrotomy, temporomandibular joint

(To report bilateral procedures, report 21010 with modifier 50)

Excision

21015   Radical resection of tumor (eg, malignant neoplasm), soft tissue of face or scalp

(To report excision of skull tumor for osteomyelitis, use 61501)

21025   Excision of bone (eg, for osteomyelitis or bone abscess); mandible

21026   facial bone(s)

21029   Removal by contouring of benign tumor of facial bone (eg, fibrous dysplasia)

21030   Excision of benign tumor or cyst of maxilla or zygoma by enucleation and curettage

21031   Excision of torus mandibularis

21032   Excision of maxillary torus palatinus

21034   Excision of malignant tumor of maxilla or zygoma

21040   Excision of benign tumor or cyst of mandible, by enucleation and/or curettage

(For enucleation and/or curettage of benign cysts or tumors of mandible not requiring osteotomy, use 21040)

(For excision of benign tumor or cyst of mandible requiring osteotomy, see 21046-21047)

21044   Excision of malignant tumor of mandible;

21045   radical resection

(For bone graft, use 21215)

21046   Excision of benign tumor or cyst of mandible; requiring intra-oral osteotomy (eg, locally aggressive or destructive lesion(s))

21047   requiring extra-oral osteotomy and partial mandibulectomy (eg, locally aggressive or destructive lesion(s))

21048   Excision of benign tumor or cyst of maxilla; requiring intra-oral osteotomy (eg, locally aggressive or destructive lesion(s))

21049   requiring extra-oral osteotomy and partial maxillectomy (eg, locally aggressive or destructive lesion(s))

21050   Condylectomy, temporomandibular joint (separate procedure)

(For bilateral procedures, report 21050 with modifier 50)

21060   Meniscectomy, partial or complete, temporomandibular joint (separate procedure)

(For bilateral procedures, report 21060 with modifier 50)

21070   Coronoidectomy (separate procedure)

(For bilateral procedures, report 21070 with modifier 50)

Introduction or Removal

(For application or removal of caliper or tongs, see 20660, 20665.) Codes 21076-21089 describe professional services for the rehabilitation of patients with oral, facial or other anatomical deficiencies by means of prostheses such as an artificial eye, ear, or nose or intraoral obturator to close a cleft. Codes 21076-21089 should only be used when the physician actually designs and prepares the prosthesis (ie, not prepared by an outside laboratory).

21076   Impression and custom preparation; surgical obturator prosthesis

21077   orbital prosthesis

21079   interim obturator prosthesis

21080   definitive obturator prosthesis

21081   mandibular resection prosthesis

21082   palatal augmentation prosthesis

21083   palatal lift prosthesis

Surgery: Musculoskeletal System

21084   speech aid prosthesis

21085   oral surgical splint

21086   auricular prosthesis

21087   nasal prosthesis

21088   facial prosthesis

21089   Unlisted maxillofacial prosthetic procedure

21100   Application of halo type appliance for maxillofacial fixation, includes removal (separate procedure)

21110   Application of interdental fixation device for conditions other than fracture or dislocation, includes removal

(For removal of interdental fixation by another physician, see 20670-20680)

21116   Injection procedure for temporomandibular joint arthrography

(For radiological supervision and interpretation, use 70332. Do not report 76003 in addition to 70332)

Repair, Revision, and/or Reconstruction

(For cranioplasty, see 21179, 21180 and 62116, 62120, 62140-62147)

21120   Genioplasty; augmentation (autograft, allograft, prosthetic material)

21121   sliding osteotomy, single piece

21122   sliding osteotomies, two or more osteotomies (eg, wedge excision or bone wedge reversal for asymmetrical chin)

21123   sliding, augmentation with interpositional bone grafts (includes obtaining autografts)

21125   Augmentation, mandibular body or angle; prosthetic material

21127   with bone graft, onlay or interpositional (includes obtaining autograft)

21137   Reduction forehead; contouring only

21138   contouring and application of prosthetic material or bone graft (includes obtaining autograft)

21139   contouring and setback of anterior frontal sinus wall

21141   Reconstruction midface, LeFort I; single piece, segment movement in any direction (eg, for Long Face Syndrome), without bone graft

21142   two pieces, segment movement in any direction, without bone graft

21143   three or more pieces, segment movement in any direction, without bone graft

21145   single piece, segment movement in any direction, requiring bone grafts (includes obtaining autografts)

21146   two pieces, segment movement in any direction, requiring bone grafts (includes obtaining autografts) (eg, ungrafted unilateral alveolar cleft)

21147   three or more pieces, segment movement in any direction, requiring bone grafts (includes obtaining autografts) (eg, ungrafted bilateral alveolar cleft or multiple osteotomies)

21150   Reconstruction midface, LeFort II; anterior intrusion (eg, Treacher-Collins Syndrome)

21151   any direction, requiring bone grafts (includes obtaining autografts)

21154   Reconstruction midface, LeFort III (extracranial), any type, requiring bone grafts (includes obtaining autografts); without LeFort I

21155   with LeFort I

21159   Reconstruction midface, LeFort III (extra and intracranial) with forehead advancement (eg, mono bloc), requiring bone grafts (includes obtaining autografts); without LeFort I

21160   with LeFort I

21172   Reconstruction superior-lateral orbital rim and lower forehead, advancement or alteration, with or without grafts (includes obtaining autografts)

(For frontal or parietal craniotomy performed for craniosynostosis, use 61556)

21175   Reconstruction, bifrontal, superior-lateral orbital rims and lower forehead, advancement or alteration (eg, plagiocephaly, trigonocephaly, brachycephaly), with or without grafts (includes obtaining autografts)

(For bifrontal craniotomy performed for craniosynostosis, use 61557)

21179   Reconstruction, entire or majority of forehead and/or supraorbital rims; with grafts (allograft or prosthetic material)

21180   with autograft (includes obtaining grafts)

(For extensive craniectomy for multiple suture craniosynostosis, use only 61558 or 61559)

21181   Reconstruction by contouring of benign tumor of cranial bones (eg, fibrous dysplasia), extracranial

21182   Reconstruction of orbital walls, rims, forehead, nasoethmoid complex following intra- and extracranial excision of benign tumor of cranial bone (eg, fibrous dysplasia), with multiple autografts (includes obtaining grafts); total area of bone grafting less than 40 sq cm

21183   total area of bone grafting greater than 40 sq cm but less than 80 sq cm

21184   total area of bone grafting greater than 80 sq cm

(For excision of benign tumor of cranial bones, see 61563, 61564)

Surgery: Musculoskeletal System

21188 Reconstruction midface, osteotomies (other than LeFort type) and bone grafts (includes obtaining autografts)

21193 Reconstruction of mandibular rami, horizontal, vertical, C, or L osteotomy; without bone graft

21194 with bone graft (includes obtaining graft)

21195 Reconstruction of mandibular rami and/or body, sagittal split; without internal rigid fixation

21196 with internal rigid fixation

21198 Osteotomy, mandible, segmental;

21199 with genioglossus advancement

(To report total osteotomy of the maxilla, see 21141-21160)

21206 Osteotomy, maxilla, segmental (eg, Wassmund or Schuchard)

21208 Osteoplasty, facial bones; augmentation (autograft, allograft, or prosthetic implant)

21209 reduction

21210 Graft, bone; nasal, maxillary or malar areas (includes obtaining graft)

(For cleft palate repair, see 42200-42225)

21215 mandible (includes obtaining graft)

21230 Graft; rib cartilage, autogenous, to face, chin, nose or ear (includes obtaining graft)

21235 ear cartilage, autogenous, to nose or ear (includes obtaining graft)

(To report graft augmentation of facial bones, use 21208)

21240 Arthroplasty, temporomandibular joint, with or without autograft (includes obtaining graft)

21242 Arthroplasty, temporomandibular joint, with allograft

21243 Arthroplasty, temporomandibular joint, with prosthetic joint replacement

21244 Reconstruction of mandible, extraoral, with transosteal bone plate (eg, mandibular staple bone plate)

21245 Reconstruction of mandible or maxilla, subperiosteal implant; partial

21246 complete

21247 Reconstruction of mandibular condyle with bone and cartilage autografts (includes obtaining grafts) (eg, for hemifacial microsomia)

21248 Reconstruction of mandible or maxilla, endosteal implant (eg, blade, cylinder); partial

21249 complete

(To report midface reconstruction, see 21141-21160)

21255 Reconstruction of zygomatic arch and glenoid fossa with bone and cartilage (includes obtaining autografts)

21256 Reconstruction of orbit with osteotomies (extracranial) and with bone grafts (includes obtaining autografts) (eg, micro-ophthalmia)

21260 Periorbital osteotomies for orbital hypertelorism, with bone grafts; extracranial approach

21261 combined intra- and extracranial approach

21263 with forehead advancement

21267 Orbital repositioning, periorbital osteotomies, unilateral, with bone grafts; extracranial approach

21268 combined intra- and extracranial approach

21270 Malar augmentation, prosthetic material

(For malar augmentation with bone graft, use 21210)

21275 Secondary revision of orbitocraniofacial reconstruction

21280 Medial canthopexy (separate procedure)

(For medial canthoplasty, use 67950)

21282 Lateral canthopexy

21295 Reduction of masseter muscle and bone (eg, for treatment of benign masseteric hypertrophy); extraoral approach

21296 intraoral approach

Other Procedures

21299 Unlisted craniofacial and maxillofacial procedure

Fracture and/or Dislocation

21300 Closed treatment of skull fracture without operation

(For operative repair, see 62000-62010)

21310 Closed treatment of nasal bone fracture without manipulation

21315 Closed treatment of nasal bone fracture; without stabilization

21320 with stabilization

21325 Open treatment of nasal fracture; uncomplicated

21330 complicated, with internal and/or external skeletal fixation

21335 with concomitant open treatment of fractured septum

21336 Open treatment of nasal septal fracture, with or without stabilization

21337 Closed treatment of nasal septal fracture, with or without stabilization

21338 Open treatment of nasoethmoid fracture; without external fixation

21339 with external fixation

21340 Percutaneous treatment of nasoethmoid complex fracture, with splint, wire or headcap fixation, including repair of canthal ligaments and/or the nasolacrimal apparatus

21343 Open treatment of depressed frontal sinus fracture

21344   Open treatment of complicated (eg, comminuted or involving posterior wall) frontal sinus fracture, via coronal or multiple approaches

21345   Closed treatment of nasomaxillary complex fracture (LeFort II type), with interdental wire fixation or fixation of denture or splint

21346   Open treatment of nasomaxillary complex fracture (LeFort II type); with wiring and/or local fixation

21347   requiring multiple open approaches

21348   with bone grafting (includes obtaining graft)

21355   Percutaneous treatment of fracture of malar area, including zygomatic arch and malar tripod, with manipulation

21356   Open treatment of depressed zygomatic arch fracture (eg, Gillies approach)

21360   Open treatment of depressed malar fracture, including zygomatic arch and malar tripod

21365   Open treatment of complicated (eg, comminuted or involving cranial nerve foramina) fracture(s) of malar area, including zygomatic arch and malar tripod; with internal fixation and multiple surgical approaches

21366   with bone grafting (includes obtaining graft)

21385   Open treatment of orbital floor blowout fracture; transantral approach (Caldwell-Luc type operation)

21386   periorbital approach

21387   combined approach

21390   periorbital approach, with alloplastic or other implant

21395   periorbital approach with bone graft (includes obtaining graft)

21400   Closed treatment of fracture of orbit, except blowout; without manipulation

21401   with manipulation

21406   Open treatment of fracture of orbit, except blowout; without implant

21407   with implant

21408   with bone grafting (includes obtaining graft)

21421   Closed treatment of palatal or maxillary fracture (LeFort I type), with interdental wire fixation or fixation of denture or splint

21422   Open treatment of palatal or maxillary fracture (LeFort I type);

21423   complicated (comminuted or involving cranial nerve foramina), multiple approaches

21431   Closed treatment of craniofacial separation (LeFort III type) using interdental wire fixation of denture or splint

21432   Open treatment of craniofacial separation (LeFort III type); with wiring and/or internal fixation

21433   complicated (eg, comminuted or involving cranial nerve foramina), multiple surgical approaches

21435   complicated, utilizing internal and/or external fixation techniques (eg, head cap, halo device, and/or intermaxillary fixation)

(For removal of internal or external fixation device, use 20670)

21436   complicated, multiple surgical approaches, internal fixation, with bone grafting (includes obtaining graft)

21440   Closed treatment of mandibular or maxillary alveolar ridge fracture (separate procedure)

21445   Open treatment of mandibular or maxillary alveolar ridge fracture (separate procedure)

21450   Closed treatment of mandibular fracture; without manipulation

21451   with manipulation

21452   Percutaneous treatment of mandibular fracture, with external fixation

21453   Closed treatment of mandibular fracture with interdental fixation

21454   Open treatment of mandibular fracture with external fixation

21461   Open treatment of mandibular fracture; without interdental fixation

21462   with interdental fixation

21465   Open treatment of mandibular condylar fracture

21470   Open treatment of complicated mandibular fracture by multiple surgical approaches including internal fixation, interdental fixation, and/or wiring of dentures or splints

21480   Closed treatment of temporomandibular dislocation; initial or subsequent

21485   complicated (eg, recurrent requiring intermaxillary fixation or splinting), initial or subsequent

21490   Open treatment of temporomandibular dislocation

(For interdental wire fixation, use 21497)

▶(21493 and 21494 have been deleted. To report, use the applicable Evaluation and Management codes)◀

21495   Open treatment of hyoid fracture

▶(For laryngoplasty with open reduction of fracture, use 31584)◀

▶(To report treatment of closed fracture of larynx, use the applicable Evaluation and Management codes)◀

21497   Interdental wiring, for condition other than fracture

Other Procedures

21499   Unlisted musculoskeletal procedure, head

(For unlisted craniofacial or maxillofacial procedure, use 21299)

Surgery: Musculoskeletal System

Neck (Soft Tissues) and Thorax

(For cervical spine and back, see 21920 et seq)

(For injection of fracture site or trigger point, use 20550)

Incision

(For incision and drainage of abscess or hematoma, superficial, see 10060, 10140)

21501   Incision and drainage, deep abscess or hematoma, soft tissues of neck or thorax;

▶(For posterior spine subfascial incision and drainage, see 22010-22015)◀

21502   with partial rib ostectomy

21510   Incision, deep, with opening of bone cortex (eg, for osteomyelitis or bone abscess), thorax

Excision

(For bone biopsy, see 20220-20251)

21550   Biopsy, soft tissue of neck or thorax

(For needle biopsy of soft tissue, use 20206)

21555   Excision tumor, soft tissue of neck or thorax; subcutaneous

21556   deep, subfascial, intramuscular

21557   Radical resection of tumor (eg, malignant neoplasm), soft tissue of neck or thorax

21600   Excision of rib, partial

(For radical resection of chest wall and rib cage for tumor, use 19260)

(For radical debridement of chest wall and rib cage for injury, see 11040-11044)

21610   Costotransversectomy (separate procedure)

21615   Excision first and/or cervical rib;

21616   with sympathectomy

21620   Ostectomy of sternum, partial

21627   Sternal debridement

(For debridement and closure, use 21750)

21630   Radical resection of sternum;

21632   with mediastinal lymphadenectomy

Repair, Revision, and/or Reconstruction

(For superficial wound, see **Integumentary System** section under Repair—Simple)

21685   Hyoid myotomy and suspension

21700   Division of scalenus anticus; without resection of cervical rib

21705   with resection of cervical rib

21720   Division of sternocleidomastoid for torticollis, open operation; without cast application

(For transection of spinal accessory and cervical nerves, see 63191, 64722)

21725   with cast application

21740   Reconstructive repair of pectus excavatum or carinatum; open

21742   minimally invasive approach (Nuss procedure), without thoracoscopy

21743   minimally invasive approach (Nuss procedure), with thoracoscopy

21750   Closure of median sternotomy separation with or without debridement (separate procedure)

Fracture and/or Dislocation

21800   Closed treatment of rib fracture, uncomplicated, each

21805   Open treatment of rib fracture without fixation, each

21810   Treatment of rib fracture requiring external fixation (flail chest)

21820   Closed treatment of sternum fracture

21825   Open treatment of sternum fracture with or without skeletal fixation

(For sternoclavicular dislocation, see 23520-23532)

Other Procedures

21899   Unlisted procedure, neck or thorax

Back and Flank

Excision

21920   Biopsy, soft tissue of back or flank; superficial

21925   deep

(For needle biopsy of soft tissue, use 20206)

21930   Excision, tumor, soft tissue of back or flank

21935   Radical resection of tumor (eg, malignant neoplasm), soft tissue of back or flank

Spine (Vertebral Column)

Cervical, thoracic, and lumbar spine.

Within the SPINE section, bone grafting procedures are reported separately and in addition to arthrodesis. For bone grafts in other Musculoskeletal sections, see specific code(s) descriptor(s) and/or accompanying guidelines.

To report bone grafts performed after arthrodesis, see codes 20930-20938. Bone graft codes are reported without modifier 51 (multiple procedure). Do not append modifier 62 to bone graft codes 20900-20938.

Example:

Posterior arthrodesis of L5-S1 for degenerative disc disease utilizing morselized autogenous iliac bone graft harvested through a separate fascial incision.

Report as 22612 and 20937.

Within the SPINE section, instrumentation is reported separately and in addition to arthrodesis. To report instrumentation procedures performed with definitive vertebral procedure(s), see codes 22840-22855. Instrumentation procedure codes 22840-22848 and 22851 are reported in addition to the definitive procedure(s) without modifier 51. Modifier 62 may not be appended to the definitive or add-on spinal instrumentation procedure code(s) 22840-22848 and 22850-22852.

Example:

Posterior arthrodesis of L4-S1, utilizing morselized autogenous iliac bone graft harvested through separate fascial incision, and pedicle screw fixation.

Report as 22612, 22614, 22842, and 20937.

Vertebral procedures are sometimes followed by arthrodesis and in addition may include bone grafts and instrumentation.

When arthrodesis is performed in addition to another procedure, the arthrodesis should be reported in addition to the original procedure with modifier 51 (multiple procedures). Examples are after osteotomy, fracture care, vertebral corpectomy and laminectomy. Since bone grafts and instrumentation are never performed without arthrodesis, modifier 51 (multiple procedures) is not used.

Arthrodesis, however, may be performed in the absence of other procedures and therefore when it is combined with another definitive procedure, modifier 51 (multiple procedure) is appropriate.

Example:

Treatment of a burst fracture of L2 by corpectomy followed by arthrodesis of L1-L3, utilizing anterior instrumentation L1-L3 and structural allograft.

Report as 63090, 22558-51, 22585, 22845, and 20931.

When two surgeons work together as primary surgeons performing distinct part(s) of a single reportable procedure, each surgeon should report his/her distinct operative work by appending modifier 62 to the single definitive procedure code. If additional procedure(s) (including add-on procedure(s)) are performed during the same surgical session, separate code(s) may be reported by each co-surgeon, with modifier 62 appended (see Appendix A).

Example:

A 42-year-old male with a history of posttraumatic degenerative disc disease at L3-4 and L4-5 (internal disc disruption) underwent surgical repair. Surgeon A

performed an anterior exposure of the spine with mobilization of the great vessels. Surgeon B performed anterior (minimal) diskectomy and fusion at L3-4 and L4-5 using anterior interbody technique.

Report surgeon A: 22558 append modifier 62, 22585 append modifier 62
Report surgeon B: 22558 append modifier 62, 22585 append modifier 62, 20931

> (Do not append modifier 62 to bone graft code 20931)
>
> (For injection procedure for myelography, use 62284)
>
> (For injection procedure for diskography, see 62290, 62291)
>
> (For injection procedure, chemonucleolysis, single or multiple levels, use 62292)
>
> (For injection procedure for facet joints, see 64470-64476, 64622-64627)
>
> (For needle or trocar biopsy, see 20220-20225)

►Incision◄

● **22010**   Incision and drainage, open, of deep abscess (subfascial), posterior spine; cervical, thoracic, or cervicothoracic

● **22015**   lumbar, sacral, or lumbosacral

> ►(Do not report 22015 in conjunction with 22010)◄
>
> ►(Do not report 22015 in conjunction with instrumentation removal, 10180, 22850, 22852)◄
>
> ►(For incision and drainage of abscess or hematoma, superficial, see 10060, 10140)◄

Excision

For the following codes, when two surgeons work together as primary surgeons performing distinct part(s) of partial vertebral body excision, each surgeon should report his/her distinct operative work by appending modifier 62 to the procedure code. In this situation, modifier 62 may be appended to the procedure code(s) 22100-22102, 22110-22114 and, as appropriate, to the associated additional vertebral segment add-on code(s) 22103, 22116 as long as both surgeons continue to work together as primary surgeons.

> (For bone biopsy, see 20220-20251)
>
> (To report soft tissue biopsy of back or flank, see 21920-21925)
>
> (For needle biopsy of soft tissue, use 20206)
>
> (To report excision of soft tissue tumor of back or flank, use 21930)

22100   Partial excision of posterior vertebral component (eg, spinous process, lamina or facet) for intrinsic bony lesion, single vertebral segment; cervical

22101   thoracic

Surgery: Musculoskeletal System

22102 lumbar

+ 22103 each additional segment (List separately in addition to code for primary procedure)

(Use 22103 in conjunction with 22100, 22101, 22102)

22110 Partial excision of vertebral body, for intrinsic bony lesion, without decompression of spinal cord or nerve root(s), single vertebral segment; cervical

22112 thoracic

22114 lumbar

+ 22116 each additional vertebral segment (List separately in addition to code for primary procedure)

(Use 22116 in conjunction with 22110, 22112, 22114)

(For complete or near complete resection of vertebral body, see vertebral corpectomy, 63081-63091)

(For spinal reconstruction with bone graft (autograft, allograft) and/or methylmethacrylate of cervical vertebral body, use 63081 and 22554 and 20931 or 20938)

(For spinal reconstruction with bone graft (autograft, allograft) and/or methylmethacrylate of thoracic vertebral body, use 63085 or 63087 and 22556 and 20931 or 20938)

(For spinal reconstruction with bone graft (autograft, allograft) and/or methylmethacrylate of lumbar vertebral body, use 63087 or 63090 and 22558 and 20931 or 20938)

(For spinal reconstruction following vertebral body resection, use 63082 or 63086 or 63088 or 63091, and 22585)

(For harvest of bone autograft for vertebral reconstruction, see 20931 or 20938)

(For cervical spinal reconstruction with prosthetic replacement of resected vertebral bodies, see codes 63081 and 22554 and 20931 or 20938 and 22851)

(For thoracic spinal reconstruction with prosthetic replacement of resected vertebral bodies, see codes 63085 or 63087 and 22556 and 20931 or 20938 and 22851)

(For lumbar spinal reconstruction with prosthetic replacement of resected vertebral bodies, see codes 63087 or 63090 and 22558, and 20931 or 20938 and 22851)

(For osteotomy of spine, see 22210-22226)

Osteotomy

To report arthrodesis, see codes 22590-22632. (Report in addition to code(s) for the definitive procedure with modifier 51.)

To report instrumentation procedures, see codes 22840-22855. (Report in addition to code(s) for the definitive procedure(s) without modifier 51.) Do not append modifier 62 to spinal instrumentation codes 22840-22848 and 22850-22852.

To report bone graft procedures, see codes 20930-20938. (Report in addition to code(s) for the definitive procedure(s) without modifier 51.) Do not append modifier 62 to bone graft codes 20900-20938.

For the following codes, when two surgeons work together as primary surgeons performing distinct part(s) of an anterior spine osteotomy, each surgeon should report his/her distinct operative work by appending modifier 62 to the procedure code. In this situation, modifier 62 may be appended to the procedure code(s) 22210-22214, 22220-22224 and, as appropriate, to associated additional segment add-on code(s) 22216, 22226 as long as both surgeons continue to work together as primary surgeons.

22210 Osteotomy of spine, posterior or posterolateral approach, one vertebral segment; cervical

22212 thoracic

22214 lumbar

+ 22216 each additional vertebral segment (List separately in addition to primary procedure)

(Use 22216 in conjunction with 22210, 22212, 22214)

22220 Osteotomy of spine, including diskectomy, anterior approach, single vertebral segment; cervical

22222 thoracic

22224 lumbar

+ 22226 each additional vertebral segment (List separately in addition to code for primary procedure)

(Use 22226 in conjunction with 22220, 22222, 22224)

(For vertebral corpectomy, see 63081-63091)

Fracture and/or Dislocation

To report arthrodesis, see codes 22590-22632. (Report in addition to code(s) for the definitive procedure with modifier 51.)

To report instrumentation procedures, see codes 22840-22855. (Report in addition to code(s) for the definitive procedure(s) without modifier 51.) Do not append modifier 62 to spinal instrumentation codes 22840-22848 and 22850-22852.

To report bone graft procedures, see codes 20930-20938. (Report in addition to code(s) for the definitive procedure(s) without modifier 51.) Do not append modifier 62 to bone graft codes 20900-20938.

For the following codes, when two surgeons work together as primary surgeons performing distinct part(s) of open fracture and/or dislocation procedure(s), each surgeon should report his/her distinct operative work by appending modifier 62 to the procedure code. In this situation, modifier 62 may be appended to the procedure code(s) 22318-22327 and, as appropriate, the associated additional fracture vertebrae or dislocated segment add-on code 22328 as long as both surgeons continue to work together as primary surgeons.

22305   Closed treatment of vertebral process fracture(s)

22310   Closed treatment of vertebral body fracture(s), without manipulation, requiring and including casting or bracing

22315   Closed treatment of vertebral fracture(s) and/or dislocation(s) requiring casting or bracing, with and including casting and/or bracing, with or without anesthesia, by manipulation or traction

(For spinal subluxation, use 97140)

22318   Open treatment and/or reduction of odontoid fracture(s) and or dislocation(s) (including os odontoideum), anterior approach, including placement of internal fixation; without grafting

22319   with grafting

22325   Open treatment and/or reduction of vertebral fracture(s) and/or dislocation(s), posterior approach, one fractured vertebrae or dislocated segment; lumbar

22326   cervical

22327   thoracic

+ 22328   each additional fractured vertebrae or dislocated segment (List separately in addition to code for primary procedure)

(Use 22328 in conjunction with 22325, 22326, 22327)

(For treatment of vertebral fracture by the anterior approach, see corpectomy 63081-63091, and appropriate arthrodesis, bone graft and instrument codes)

(For decompression of spine following fracture, see 63001-63091; for arthrodesis of spine following fracture, see 22548-22632)

Manipulation

(For spinal manipulation without anesthesia, use 97140)

22505   Manipulation of spine requiring anesthesia, any region

Vertebral Body, Embolization or Injection

22520   Percutaneous vertebroplasty, one vertebral body, unilateral or bilateral injection; thoracic

22521   lumbar

+ 22522   each additional thoracic or lumbar vertebral body (List separately in addition to code for primary procedure)

(Use 22522 in conjunction with 22520, 22521 as appropriate)

(For radiological supervision and interpretation, see 76012, 76013)

● 22523   Percutaneous vertebral augmentation, including cavity creation (fracture reduction and bone biopsy included when performed) using mechanical device, one vertebral body, unilateral or bilateral cannulation (eg, kyphoplasty); thoracic

● 22524   lumbar

+● 22525   each additional thoracic or lumbar vertebral body (List separately in addition to code for primary procedure)

►(Do not report 22525 in conjunction with 20225 when performed at the same level as 22523-22525)◄

►(Use 22525 in conjunction with 22523, 22524)◄

►(For radiological supervision and interpretation, see 76012, 76013)◄

Arthrodesis

Arthrodesis may be performed in the absence of other procedures and therefore when it is combined with another definitive procedure (eg, osteotomy, fracture care, vertebral corpectomy or laminectomy), modifier 51 is appropriate. However, arthrodesis codes 22585, 22614, and 22632 are considered add-on procedure codes and should not be used with modifier 51.

To report instrumentation procedures, see 22840-22855. (Codes 22840-22848, 22851 are reported in conjunction with code(s) for the definitive procedure(s) without modifier 51. When instrumentation reinsertion or removal is reported in conjunction with other definitive procedures including arthrodesis, decompression, and exploration of fusion, append modifier 51 to 22849, 22850, 22852, and 22855.) To report exploration of fusion, use 22830. (When exploration is reported in conjunction with other definitive procedures, including arthrodesis and decompression, append modifier 51 to 22830.) Do not append modifier 62 to spinal instrumentation codes 22840-22848 and 22850-22852.

To report bone graft procedures, see codes 20930-20938. (Report in addition to code(s) for the definitive procedure(s) without modifier 51.) Do not append modifier 62 to bone graft codes 20900-20938.

Lateral Extracavitary Approach Technique

22532   Arthrodesis, lateral extracavitary technique, including minimal diskectomy to prepare interspace (other than for decompression); thoracic

22533   lumbar

+ 22534   thoracic or lumbar, each additional vertebral segment (List separately in addition to code for primary procedure)

(Use 22534 in conjunction with 22532 and 22533)

Surgery: Musculoskeletal System

Surgery: Musculoskeletal System

Anterior or Anterolateral Approach Technique

Procedure codes 22554-22558 are for SINGLE interspace; for additional interspaces, use 22585. A vertebral interspace is the non-bony compartment between two adjacent vertebral bodies, which contains the intervertebral disk, and includes the nucleus pulposus, annulus fibrosus, and two cartilagenous endplates.

For the following codes, when two surgeons work together as primary surgeons performing distinct part(s) of an anterior interbody arthrodesis, each surgeon should report his/her distinct operative work by appending modifier 62 to the procedure code. In this situation, modifier 62 may be appended to the procedure code(s) 22548-22558 and, as appropriate, to the associated additional interspace add-on code 22585 as long as both surgeons continue to work together as primary surgeons.

22548 Arthrodesis, anterior transoral or extraoral technique, clivus-C1-C2 (atlas-axis), with or without excision of odontoid process

(For intervertebral disk excision by laminotomy or laminectomy, see 63020-63042)

22554 Arthrodesis, anterior interbody technique, including minimal diskectomy to prepare interspace (other than for decompression); cervical below C2

22556 thoracic

22558 lumbar

+ 22585 each additional interspace (List separately in addition to code for primary procedure)

(Use 22585 in conjunction with 22554, 22556, 22558)

Posterior, Posterolateral or Lateral Transverse Process Technique

To report instrumentation procedures, see codes 22840-22855. (Report in addition to code(s) for the definitive procedure(s) without modifier 51.) Do not append modifier 62 to spinal instrumentation codes 22840-22848 and 22850-22852.

To report bone graft procedures, see codes 20930-20938. (Report in addition to code(s) for the definitive procedure(s) without modifier 51.) Do not append modifier 62 to bone graft codes 20900-20938.

A vertebral segment describes the basic constituent part into which the spine may be divided. It represents a single complete vertebral bone with its associated articular processes and laminae. A vertebral interspace is the non-bony compartment between two adjacent vertebral bodies which contains the intervertebral disk, and includes the nucleus pulposus, annulus fibrosus, and two cartilagenous endplates.

22590 Arthrodesis, posterior technique, craniocervical (occiput-C2)

22595 Arthrodesis, posterior technique, atlas-axis (C1-C2)

22600 Arthrodesis, posterior or posterolateral technique, single level; cervical below C2 segment

22610 thoracic (with or without lateral transverse technique)

22612 lumbar (with or without lateral transverse technique)

+ 22614 each additional vertebral segment (List separately in addition to code for primary procedure)

(Use 22614 in conjunction with 22600, 22610, 22612)

22630 Arthrodesis, posterior interbody technique, including laminectomy and/or diskectomy to prepare interspace (other than for decompression), single interspace; lumbar

+ 22632 each additional interspace (List separately in addition to code for primary procedure)

(Use 22632 in conjunction with 22630)

Spine Deformity (eg, Scoliosis, Kyphosis)

To report instrumentation procedures, see codes 22840-22855. (Report in addition to code(s) for the definitive procedure(s) without modifier 51.) Do not append modifier 62 to spinal instrumentation codes 22840-22848 and 22850-22852.

To report bone graft procedures, see codes 20930-20938. (Report in addition to code(s) for the definitive procedure(s) without modifier 51.) Do not append modifier 62 to bone graft codes 20900-20938.

A vertebral segment describes the basic constituent part into which the spine may be divided. It represents a single complete vertebral bone with its associated articular processes and laminae.

For the following codes, when two surgeons work together as primary surgeons performing distinct part(s) of an arthrodesis for spinal deformity, each surgeon should report his/her distinct operative work by appending modifier 62 to the procedure code. In this situation, modifier 62 may be appended to procedure code(s) 22800-22819 as long as both surgeons continue to work together as primary surgeons.

22800 Arthrodesis, posterior, for spinal deformity, with or without cast; up to 6 vertebral segments

22802 7 to 12 vertebral segments

22804 13 or more vertebral segments

22808 Arthrodesis, anterior, for spinal deformity, with or without cast; 2 to 3 vertebral segments

22810 4 to 7 vertebral segments

22812 8 or more vertebral segments

| 22818 | Kyphectomy, circumferential exposure of spine and resection of vertebral segment(s) (including body and posterior elements); single or 2 segments |
| 22819 | 3 or more segments |

(To report arthrodesis, see 22800-22804 and add modifier 51)

Exploration

To report instrumentation procedures, see 22840-22855. (Codes 22840-22848, 22851 are reported in conjunction with code(s) for the definitive procedure(s) without modifier 51. When instrumentation reinsertion or removal is reported in conjunction with other definitive procedures including arthrodesis, decompression, and exploration of fusion, append modifier 51 to 22849, 22850, 22852 and 22855.) To report exploration of fusion, see 22830. (When exploration is reported in conjunction with other definitive procedures, including arthrodesis and decompression, append modifier 51 to 22830.)

(To report bone graft procedures, see 20930-20938)

| 22830 | Exploration of spinal fusion |

Spinal Instrumentation

Segmental instrumentation is defined as fixation at each end of the construct and at least one additional interposed bony attachment.

Non-segmental instrumentation is defined as fixation at each end of the construct and may span several vertebral segments without attachment to the intervening segments.

Insertion of spinal instrumentation is reported separately and in addition to arthrodesis. Instrumentation procedure codes 22840-22848, 22851 are reported in addition to the definitive procedure(s) without modifier 51. Do not append modifier 62 to spinal instrumentation codes 22840-22848 and 22850-22852.

To report bone graft procedures, see codes 20930-20938. (Report in addition to code(s) for definitive procedure(s) without modifier 51.) Do not append modifier 62 to bone graft codes 20900-20938.

A vertebral segment describes the basic constituent part into which the spine may be divided. It represents a single complete vertebral bone with its associated articular processes and laminae. A vertebral interspace is the non-bony compartment between two adjacent vertebral bodies, which contains the intervertebral disk, and includes the nucleus pulposus, annulus fibrosus, and two cartilagenous endplates.

List 22840-22855 separately, in conjunction with code(s) for fracture, dislocation, arthrodesis or exploration of fusion of the spine 22325-22328, 22548-22812, and 22830. Codes 22840-22848, 22851 are reported in conjunction with code(s) for the definitive procedure(s) without modifier 51. Codes 22849, 22850, 22852, and 22855 are subject to modifier 51 if reported with other definitive procedure(s), including arthrodesis, decompression, and exploration of fusion. Code 22849 should not be reported with 22850, 22852, and 22855 at the same spinal levels.

⊘ 22840	Posterior non-segmental instrumentation (eg, Harrington rod technique, pedicle fixation across one interspace, atlantoaxial transarticular screw fixation, sublaminar wiring at C1, facet screw fixation)
⊘ 22841	Internal spinal fixation by wiring of spinous processes
⊘ 22842	Posterior segmental instrumentation (eg, pedicle fixation, dual rods with multiple hooks and sublaminar wires); 3 to 6 vertebral segments
⊘ 22843	7 to 12 vertebral segments
⊘ 22844	13 or more vertebral segments
⊘ 22845	Anterior instrumentation; 2 to 3 vertebral segments
⊘ 22846	4 to 7 vertebral segments
⊘ 22847	8 or more vertebral segments
⊘ 22848	Pelvic fixation (attachment of caudal end of instrumentation to pelvic bony structures) other than sacrum
22849	Reinsertion of spinal fixation device
22850	Removal of posterior nonsegmental instrumentation (eg, Harrington rod)
⊘ 22851	Application of intervertebral biomechanical device(s) (eg, synthetic cage(s), threaded bone dowel(s), methylmethacrylate) to vertebral defect or interspace
22852	Removal of posterior segmental instrumentation
22855	Removal of anterior instrumentation

Other Procedures

| 22899 | Unlisted procedure, spine |

Abdomen

Excision

| 22900 | Excision, abdominal wall tumor, subfascial (eg, desmoid) |

Other Procedures

| 22999 | Unlisted procedure, abdomen, musculoskeletal system |

Surgery: Musculoskeletal System

Shoulder

Clavicle, scapula, humerus head and neck, sterno-clavicular joint, acromioclavicular joint and shoulder joint.

Incision

23000 Removal of subdeltoid calcareous deposits, open

(For arthroscopic removal of bursal deposits, use 29999)

23020 Capsular contracture release (eg, Sever type procedure)

(For incision and drainage procedures, superficial, see 10040-10160)

23030 Incision and drainage, shoulder area; deep abscess or hematoma

23031 infected bursa

23035 Incision, bone cortex (eg, osteomyelitis or bone abscess), shoulder area

23040 Arthrotomy, glenohumeral joint, including exploration, drainage, or removal of foreign body

23044 Arthrotomy, acromioclavicular, sternoclavicular joint, including exploration, drainage, or removal of foreign body

Excision

23065 Biopsy, soft tissue of shoulder area; superficial

23066 deep

(For needle biopsy of soft tissue, use 20206)

23075 Excision, soft tissue tumor, shoulder area; subcutaneous

23076 deep, subfascial, or intramuscular

23077 Radical resection of tumor (eg, malignant neoplasm), soft tissue of shoulder area

23100 Arthrotomy, glenohumeral joint, including biopsy

23101 Arthrotomy, acromioclavicular joint or sternoclavicular joint, including biopsy and/or excision of torn cartilage

23105 Arthrotomy; glenohumeral joint, with synovectomy, with or without biopsy

23106 sternoclavicular joint, with synovectomy, with or without biopsy

23107 Arthrotomy, glenohumeral joint, with joint exploration, with or without removal of loose or foreign body

23120 Claviculectomy; partial

(For arthroscopic procedure, use 29824)

23125 total

23130 Acromioplasty or acromionectomy, partial, with or without coracoacromial ligament release

23140 Excision or curettage of bone cyst or benign tumor of clavicle or scapula;

23145 with autograft (includes obtaining graft)

23146 with allograft

23150 Excision or curettage of bone cyst or benign tumor of proximal humerus;

23155 with autograft (includes obtaining graft)

23156 with allograft

23170 Sequestrectomy (eg, for osteomyelitis or bone abscess), clavicle

23172 Sequestrectomy (eg, for osteomyelitis or bone abscess), scapula

23174 Sequestrectomy (eg, for osteomyelitis or bone abscess), humeral head to surgical neck

23180 Partial excision (craterization, saucerization, or diaphysectomy) bone (eg, osteomyelitis), clavicle

23182 Partial excision (craterization, saucerization, or diaphysectomy) bone (eg, osteomyelitis), scapula

23184 Partial excision (craterization, saucerization, or diaphysectomy) bone (eg, osteomyelitis), proximal humerus

23190 Ostectomy of scapula, partial (eg, superior medial angle)

23195 Resection, humeral head

(For replacement with implant, use 23470)

23200 Radical resection for tumor; clavicle

23210 scapula

23220 Radical resection of bone tumor, proximal humerus;

23221 with autograft (includes obtaining graft)

23222 with prosthetic replacement

Introduction or Removal

(For arthrocentesis or needling of bursa, use 20610)

(For K-wire or pin insertion or removal, see 20650, 20670, 20680)

23330 Removal of foreign body, shoulder; subcutaneous

23331 deep (eg, Neer hemiarthroplasty removal)

23332 complicated (eg, total shoulder)

23350 Injection procedure for shoulder arthrography or enhanced CT/MRI shoulder arthrography

(For radiographic arthrography, radiological supervision and interpretation, use 73040. Fluoroscopy (76003) is inclusive of radiographic arthrography)

(When fluoroscopic guided injection is performed for enhanced CT arthrography, use 23350, 76003, and 73201 or 73202)

(When fluoroscopic guided injection is performed for enhanced MR arthrography, use 23350, 76003, and 73222 or 73223)

(For enhanced CT or enhanced MRI arthrography, use 76003 and either 73201, 73202, 73222 or 73223)

(To report biopsy of the shoulder and joint, see 29805-29826)

Repair, Revision, and/or Reconstruction

23395　Muscle transfer, any type, shoulder or upper arm; single

23397　　　multiple

23400　Scapulopexy (eg, Sprengels deformity or for paralysis)

23405　Tenotomy, shoulder area; single tendon

23406　　　multiple tendons through same incision

23410　Repair of ruptured musculotendinous cuff (eg, rotator cuff) open; acute

23412　　　chronic

(For arthroscopic procedure, use 29827)

23415　Coracoacromial ligament release, with or without acromioplasty

(For arthroscopic procedure, use 29826)

23420　Reconstruction of complete shoulder (rotator) cuff avulsion, chronic (includes acromioplasty)

23430　Tenodesis of long tendon of biceps

23440　Resection or transplantation of long tendon of biceps

23450　Capsulorrhaphy, anterior; Putti-Platt procedure or Magnuson type operation

(To report arthroscopic thermal capsulorrhaphy, use 29999)

23455　　　with labral repair (eg, Bankart procedure)

(For arthroscopic procedure, use 29806)

23460　Capsulorrhaphy, anterior, any type; with bone block

23462　　　with coracoid process transfer

(To report open thermal capsulorrhaphy, use 23929)

23465　Capsulorrhaphy, glenohumeral joint, posterior, with or without bone block

(For sternoclavicular and acromioclavicular reconstruction, see 23530, 23550)

23466　Capsulorrhaphy, glenohumeral joint, any type multi-directional instability

23470　Arthroplasty, glenohumeral joint; hemiarthroplasty

23472　　　total shoulder (glenoid and proximal humeral replacement (eg, total shoulder))

(For removal of total shoulder implants, see 23331, 23332)

(For osteotomy, proximal humerus, use 24400)

23480　Osteotomy, clavicle, with or without internal fixation;

23485　　　with bone graft for nonunion or malunion (includes obtaining graft and/or necessary fixation)

23490　Prophylactic treatment (nailing, pinning, plating or wiring) with or without methylmethacrylate; clavicle

23491　　　proximal humerus

Fracture and/or Dislocation

23500　Closed treatment of clavicular fracture; without manipulation

23505　　　with manipulation

23515　Open treatment of clavicular fracture, with or without internal or external fixation

23520　Closed treatment of sternoclavicular dislocation; without manipulation

23525　　　with manipulation

23530　Open treatment of sternoclavicular dislocation, acute or chronic;

23532　　　with fascial graft (includes obtaining graft)

23540　Closed treatment of acromioclavicular dislocation; without manipulation

23545　　　with manipulation

23550　Open treatment of acromioclavicular dislocation, acute or chronic;

23552　　　with fascial graft (includes obtaining graft)

23570　Closed treatment of scapular fracture; without manipulation

23575　　　with manipulation, with or without skeletal traction (with or without shoulder joint involvement)

23585　Open treatment of scapular fracture (body, glenoid or acromion) with or without internal fixation

23600　Closed treatment of proximal humeral (surgical or anatomical neck) fracture; without manipulation

23605　　　with manipulation, with or without skeletal traction

23615　Open treatment of proximal humeral (surgical or anatomical neck) fracture, with or without internal or external fixation, with or without repair of tuberosity(s);

23616　　　with proximal humeral prosthetic replacement

23620　Closed treatment of greater humeral tuberosity fracture; without manipulation

23625　　　with manipulation

23630　Open treatment of greater humeral tuberosity fracture, with or without internal or external fixation

23650　Closed treatment of shoulder dislocation, with manipulation; without anesthesia

23655　　　requiring anesthesia

Surgery: Musculoskeletal System

23660   Open treatment of acute shoulder dislocation

(Repairs for recurrent dislocations, see 23450-23466)

23665   Closed treatment of shoulder dislocation, with fracture of greater humeral tuberosity, with manipulation

23670   Open treatment of shoulder dislocation, with fracture of greater humeral tuberosity, with or without internal or external fixation

23675   Closed treatment of shoulder dislocation, with surgical or anatomical neck fracture, with manipulation

23680   Open treatment of shoulder dislocation, with surgical or anatomical neck fracture, with or without internal or external fixation

Manipulation

23700   Manipulation under anesthesia, shoulder joint, including application of fixation apparatus (dislocation excluded)

Arthrodesis

23800   Arthrodesis, glenohumeral joint;

23802   with autogenous graft (includes obtaining graft)

Amputation

23900   Interthoracoscapular amputation (forequarter)

23920   Disarticulation of shoulder;

23921   secondary closure or scar revision

Other Procedures

23929   Unlisted procedure, shoulder

Humerus (Upper Arm) and Elbow

Elbow area includes head and neck of radius and olecranon process.

Incision

(For incision and drainage procedures, superficial, see 10040-10160)

23930   Incision and drainage, upper arm or elbow area; deep abscess or hematoma

23931   bursa

23935   Incision, deep, with opening of bone cortex (eg, for osteomyelitis or bone abscess), humerus or elbow

24000   Arthrotomy, elbow, including exploration, drainage, or removal of foreign body

24006   Arthrotomy of the elbow, with capsular excision for capsular release (separate procedure)

Excision

24065   Biopsy, soft tissue of upper arm or elbow area; superficial

24066   deep (subfascial or intramuscular)

(For needle biopsy of soft tissue, use 20206)

24075   Excision, tumor, soft tissue of upper arm or elbow area; subcutaneous

24076   deep (subfascial or intramuscular)

24077   Radical resection of tumor (eg, malignant neoplasm), soft tissue of upper arm or elbow area

24100   Arthrotomy, elbow; with synovial biopsy only

24101   with joint exploration, with or without biopsy, with or without removal of loose or foreign body

24102   with synovectomy

24105   Excision, olecranon bursa

24110   Excision or curettage of bone cyst or benign tumor, humerus;

24115   with autograft (includes obtaining graft)

24116   with allograft

24120   Excision or curettage of bone cyst or benign tumor of head or neck of radius or olecranon process;

24125   with autograft (includes obtaining graft)

24126   with allograft

24130   Excision, radial head

(For replacement with implant, use 24366)

24134   Sequestrectomy (eg, for osteomyelitis or bone abscess), shaft or distal humerus

24136   Sequestrectomy (eg, for osteomyelitis or bone abscess), radial head or neck

24138   Sequestrectomy (eg, for osteomyelitis or bone abscess), olecranon process

24140   Partial excision (craterization, saucerization, or diaphysectomy) bone (eg, osteomyelitis), humerus

24145   Partial excision (craterization, saucerization, or diaphysectomy) bone (eg, osteomyelitis), radial head or neck

24147   Partial excision (craterization, saucerization, or diaphysectomy) bone (eg, osteomyelitis), olecranon process

24149   Radical resection of capsule, soft tissue, and heterotopic bone, elbow, with contracture release (separate procedure)

(For capsular and soft tissue release only, use 24006)

24150   Radical resection for tumor, shaft or distal humerus;

24151   with autograft (includes obtaining graft)

24152	Radical resection for tumor, radial head or neck;
24153	with autograft (includes obtaining graft)
24155	Resection of elbow joint (arthrectomy)

Introduction or Removal

(For K-wire or pin insertion or removal, see 20650, 20670, 20680)

(For arthrocentesis or needling of bursa or joint, use 20605)

24160	Implant removal; elbow joint
24164	radial head
24200	Removal of foreign body, upper arm or elbow area; subcutaneous
24201	deep (subfascial or intramuscular)
24220	Injection procedure for elbow arthrography

(For radiological supervision and interpretation, use 73085. Do not report 76003 in addition to 73085)

(For injection for tennis elbow, use 20550)

Repair, Revision, and/or Reconstruction

24300	Manipulation, elbow, under anesthesia

(For application of external fixation, see 20690 or 20692)

24301	Muscle or tendon transfer, any type, upper arm or elbow, single (excluding 24320-24331)
24305	Tendon lengthening, upper arm or elbow, each tendon
24310	Tenotomy, open, elbow to shoulder, each tendon
24320	Tenoplasty, with muscle transfer, with or without free graft, elbow to shoulder, single (Seddon-Brookes type procedure)
24330	Flexor-plasty, elbow (eg, Steindler type advancement);
24331	with extensor advancement
24332	Tenolysis, triceps
24340	Tenodesis of biceps tendon at elbow (separate procedure)
24341	Repair, tendon or muscle, upper arm or elbow, each tendon or muscle, primary or secondary (excludes rotator cuff)
24342	Reinsertion of ruptured biceps or triceps tendon, distal, with or without tendon graft
24343	Repair lateral collateral ligament, elbow, with local tissue
24344	Reconstruction lateral collateral ligament, elbow, with tendon graft (includes harvesting of graft)
24345	Repair medial collateral ligament, elbow, with local tissue

24346	Reconstruction medial collateral ligament, elbow, with tendon graft (includes harvesting of graft)
24350	Fasciotomy, lateral or medial (eg, tennis elbow or epicondylitis);
24351	with extensor origin detachment
24352	with annular ligament resection
24354	with stripping
24356	with partial ostectomy
24360	Arthroplasty, elbow; with membrane (eg, fascial)
24361	with distal humeral prosthetic replacement
24362	with implant and fascia lata ligament reconstruction
24363	with distal humerus and proximal ulnar prosthetic replacement (eg, total elbow)
24365	Arthroplasty, radial head;
24366	with implant
24400	Osteotomy, humerus, with or without internal fixation
24410	Multiple osteotomies with realignment on intramedullary rod, humeral shaft (Sofield type procedure)
24420	Osteoplasty, humerus (eg, shortening or lengthening) (excluding 64876)
24430	Repair of nonunion or malunion, humerus; without graft (eg, compression technique)
24435	with iliac or other autograft (includes obtaining graft)

(For proximal radius and/or ulna, see 25400-25420)

24470	Hemiepiphyseal arrest (eg, cubitus varus or valgus, distal humerus)
24495	Decompression fasciotomy, forearm, with brachial artery exploration
24498	Prophylactic treatment (nailing, pinning, plating or wiring), with or without methylmethacrylate, humeral shaft

Fracture and/or Dislocation

24500	Closed treatment of humeral shaft fracture; without manipulation
24505	with manipulation, with or without skeletal traction
24515	Open treatment of humeral shaft fracture with plate/screws, with or without cerclage
24516	Treatment of humeral shaft fracture, with insertion of intramedullary implant, with or without cerclage and/or locking screws
24530	Closed treatment of supracondylar or transcondylar humeral fracture, with or without intercondylar extension; without manipulation
24535	with manipulation, with or without skin or skeletal traction

Surgery: Musculoskeletal System

24538   Percutaneous skeletal fixation of supracondylar or transcondylar humeral fracture, with or without intercondylar extension

24545   Open treatment of humeral supracondylar or transcondylar fracture, with or without internal or external fixation; without intercondylar extension

24546   with intercondylar extension

24560   Closed treatment of humeral epicondylar fracture, medial or lateral; without manipulation

24565   with manipulation

24566   Percutaneous skeletal fixation of humeral epicondylar fracture, medial or lateral, with manipulation

24575   Open treatment of humeral epicondylar fracture, medial or lateral, with or without internal or external fixation

24576   Closed treatment of humeral condylar fracture, medial or lateral; without manipulation

24577   with manipulation

24579   Open treatment of humeral condylar fracture, medial or lateral, with or without internal or external fixation

(To report closed treatment of fractures without manipulation, see 24530, 24560, 24576, 24650, 24670)

(To report closed treatment of fractures with manipulation, see 24535, 24565, 24577, 24675)

24582   Percutaneous skeletal fixation of humeral condylar fracture, medial or lateral, with manipulation

24586   Open treatment of periarticular fracture and/or dislocation of the elbow (fracture distal humerus and proximal ulna and/or proximal radius);

24587   with implant arthroplasty

(See also 24361)

24600   Treatment of closed elbow dislocation; without anesthesia

24605   requiring anesthesia

24615   Open treatment of acute or chronic elbow dislocation

24620   Closed treatment of Monteggia type of fracture dislocation at elbow (fracture proximal end of ulna with dislocation of radial head), with manipulation

24635   Open treatment of Monteggia type of fracture dislocation at elbow (fracture proximal end of ulna with dislocation of radial head), with or without internal or external fixation

24640   Closed treatment of radial head subluxation in child, nursemaid elbow, with manipulation

24650   Closed treatment of radial head or neck fracture; without manipulation

24655   with manipulation

24665   Open treatment of radial head or neck fracture, with or without internal fixation or radial head excision;

24666   with radial head prosthetic replacement

24670   Closed treatment of ulnar fracture, proximal end (olecranon process); without manipulation

24675   with manipulation

24685   Open treatment of ulnar fracture proximal end (olecranon process), with or without internal or external fixation

Arthrodesis

24800   Arthrodesis, elbow joint; local

24802   with autogenous graft (includes obtaining graft)

Amputation

24900   Amputation, arm through humerus; with primary closure

24920   open, circular (guillotine)

24925   secondary closure or scar revision

24930   re-amputation

24931   with implant

24935   Stump elongation, upper extremity

24940   Cineplasty, upper extremity, complete procedure

Other Procedures

24999   Unlisted procedure, humerus or elbow

Forearm and Wrist

Radius, ulna, carpal bones, and joints.

Incision

25000   Incision, extensor tendon sheath, wrist (eg, deQuervains disease)

(For decompression median nerve or for carpal tunnel syndrome, use 64721)

25001   Incision, flexor tendon sheath, wrist (eg, flexor carpi radialis)

25020   Decompression fasciotomy, forearm and/or wrist, flexor OR extensor compartment; without debridement of nonviable muscle and/or nerve

25023   with debridement of nonviable muscle and/or nerve

(For decompression fasciotomy with brachial artery exploration, use 24495)

(For incision and drainage procedures, superficial, see 10060-10160)

(For debridement, see also 11000-11044)

25024   Decompression fasciotomy, forearm and/or wrist, flexor AND extensor compartment; without debridement of nonviable muscle and/or nerve

25025   with debridement of nonviable muscle and/or nerve

25028   Incision and drainage, forearm and/or wrist; deep
         abscess or hematoma

25031   bursa

25035   Incision, deep, bone cortex, forearm and/or wrist (eg,
         osteomyelitis or bone abscess)

25040   Arthrotomy, radiocarpal or midcarpal joint, with
         exploration, drainage, or removal of foreign body

Excision

25065   Biopsy, soft tissue of forearm and/or wrist; superficial

25066   deep (subfascial or intramuscular)

         (For needle biopsy of soft tissue, use 20206)

25075   Excision, tumor, soft tissue of forearm and/or wrist area;
         subcutaneous

25076   deep (subfascial or intramuscular)

25077   Radical resection of tumor (eg, malignant neoplasm), soft
         tissue of forearm and/or wrist area

25085   Capsulotomy, wrist (eg, contracture)

25100   Arthrotomy, wrist joint; with biopsy

25101   with joint exploration, with or without biopsy, with or
              without removal of loose or foreign body

25105   with synovectomy

25107   Arthrotomy, distal radioulnar joint including repair of
         triangular cartilage, complex

25110   Excision, lesion of tendon sheath, forearm and/or wrist

25111   Excision of ganglion, wrist (dorsal or volar); primary

25112   recurrent

         (For hand or finger, use 26160)

25115   Radical excision of bursa, synovia of wrist, or forearm
         tendon sheaths (eg, tenosynovitis, fungus, Tbc, or other
         granulomas, rheumatoid arthritis); flexors

25116   extensors, with or without transposition of dorsal
              retinaculum

         (For finger synovectomies, use 26145)

25118   Synovectomy, extensor tendon sheath, wrist, single
         compartment;

25119   with resection of distal ulna

25120   Excision or curettage of bone cyst or benign tumor of
         radius or ulna (excluding head or neck of radius and
         olecranon process);

         (For head or neck of radius or olecranon process, see
         24120-24126)

25125   with autograft (includes obtaining graft)

25126   with allograft

25130   Excision or curettage of bone cyst or benign tumor of
         carpal bones;

25135   with autograft (includes obtaining graft)

25136   with allograft

25145   Sequestrectomy (eg, for osteomyelitis or bone abscess),
         forearm and/or wrist

25150   Partial excision (craterization, saucerization, or
         diaphysectomy) of bone (eg, for osteomyelitis); ulna

25151   radius

         (For head or neck of radius or olecranon process, see
         24145, 24147)

25170   Radical resection for tumor, radius or ulna

25210   Carpectomy; one bone

         (For carpectomy with implant, see 25441-25445)

25215   all bones of proximal row

25230   Radial styloidectomy (separate procedure)

25240   Excision distal ulna partial or complete (eg, Darrach type
         or matched resection)

         (For implant replacement, distal ulna, use 25442)

         (For obtaining fascia for interposition, see 20920, 20922)

Introduction or Removal

         (For K-wire, pin or rod insertion or removal, see 20650,
         20670, 20680)

25246   Injection procedure for wrist arthrography

         (For radiological supervision and interpretation, use
         73115. Do not report 76003 in addition to 73115)

         (For foreign body removal, superficial use 20520)

25248   Exploration with removal of deep foreign body, forearm or
         wrist

25250   Removal of wrist prosthesis; (separate procedure)

25251   complicated, including total wrist

25259   Manipulation, wrist, under anesthesia

         (For application of external fixation, see 20690 or 20692)

Repair, Revision, and/or Reconstruction

25260   Repair, tendon or muscle, flexor, forearm and/or wrist;
         primary, single, each tendon or muscle

25263   secondary, single, each tendon or muscle

25265   secondary, with free graft (includes obtaining graft),
              each tendon or muscle

25270   Repair, tendon or muscle, extensor, forearm and/or wrist;
         primary, single, each tendon or muscle

25272   secondary, single, each tendon or muscle

25274   secondary, with free graft (includes obtaining graft),
              each tendon or muscle

Surgery: Musculoskeletal System

25275   Repair, tendon sheath, extensor, forearm and/or wrist, with free graft (includes obtaining graft) (eg, for extensor carpi ulnaris subluxation)

25280   Lengthening or shortening of flexor or extensor tendon, forearm and/or wrist, single, each tendon

25290   Tenotomy, open, flexor or extensor tendon, forearm and/or wrist, single, each tendon

25295   Tenolysis, flexor or extensor tendon, forearm and/or wrist, single, each tendon

25300   Tenodesis at wrist; flexors of fingers

25301   extensors of fingers

25310   Tendon transplantation or transfer, flexor or extensor, forearm and/or wrist, single; each tendon

25312   with tendon graft(s) (includes obtaining graft), each tendon

25315   Flexor origin slide (eg, for cerebral palsy, Volkmann contracture), forearm and/or wrist;

25316   with tendon(s) transfer

25320   Capsulorrhaphy or reconstruction, wrist, open (eg, capsulodesis, ligament repair, tendon transfer or graft) (includes synovectomy, capsulotomy and open reduction) for carpal instability

25332   Arthroplasty, wrist, with or without interposition, with or without external or internal fixation

(For obtaining fascia for interposition, see 20920, 20922)

(For prosthetic replacement arthroplasty, see 25441-25446)

25335   Centralization of wrist on ulna (eg, radial club hand)

25337   Reconstruction for stabilization of unstable distal ulna or distal radioulnar joint, secondary by soft tissue stabilization (eg, tendon transfer, tendon graft or weave, or tenodesis) with or without open reduction of distal radioulnar joint

(For harvesting of fascia lata graft, see 20920, 20922)

25350   Osteotomy, radius; distal third

25355   middle or proximal third

25360   Osteotomy; ulna

25365   radius AND ulna

25370   Multiple osteotomies, with realignment on intramedullary rod (Sofield type procedure); radius OR ulna

25375   radius AND ulna

25390   Osteoplasty, radius OR ulna; shortening

25391   lengthening with autograft

25392   Osteoplasty, radius AND ulna; shortening (excluding 64876)

25393   lengthening with autograft

25394   Osteoplasty, carpal bone, shortening

25400   Repair of nonunion or malunion, radius OR ulna; without graft (eg, compression technique)

25405   with autograft (includes obtaining graft)

25415   Repair of nonunion or malunion, radius AND ulna; without graft (eg, compression technique)

25420   with autograft (includes obtaining graft)

25425   Repair of defect with autograft; radius OR ulna

25426   radius AND ulna

25430   Insertion of vascular pedicle into carpal bone (eg, Hori procedure)

25431   Repair of nonunion of carpal bone (excluding carpal scaphoid (navicular)) (includes obtaining graft and necessary fixation), each bone

25440   Repair of nonunion, scaphoid carpal (navicular) bone, with or without radial styloidectomy (includes obtaining graft and necessary fixation)

25441   Arthroplasty with prosthetic replacement; distal radius

25442   distal ulna

25443   scaphoid carpal (navicular)

25444   lunate

25445   trapezium

25446   distal radius and partial or entire carpus (total wrist)

25447   Arthroplasty, interposition, intercarpal or carpometacarpal joints

(For wrist arthroplasty, use 25332)

25449   Revision of arthroplasty, including removal of implant, wrist joint

25450   Epiphyseal arrest by epiphysiodesis or stapling; distal radius OR ulna

25455   distal radius AND ulna

25490   Prophylactic treatment (nailing, pinning, plating or wiring) with or without methylmethacrylate; radius

25491   ulna

25492   radius AND ulna

Fracture and/or Dislocation

25500   Closed treatment of radial shaft fracture; without manipulation

25505   with manipulation

25515   Open treatment of radial shaft fracture, with or without internal or external fixation

25520   Closed treatment of radial shaft fracture and closed treatment of dislocation of distal radioulnar joint (Galeazzi fracture/dislocation)

25525   Open treatment of radial shaft fracture, with internal and/ or external fixation and closed treatment of dislocation of distal radioulnar joint (Galeazzi fracture/dislocation), with or without percutaneous skeletal fixation

25526   Open treatment of radial shaft fracture, with internal and/or external fixation and open treatment, with or without internal or external fixation of distal radioulnar joint (Galeazzi fracture/dislocation), includes repair of triangular fibrocartilage complex

25530   Closed treatment of ulnar shaft fracture; without manipulation

25535   with manipulation

25545   Open treatment of ulnar shaft fracture, with or without internal or external fixation

25560   Closed treatment of radial and ulnar shaft fractures; without manipulation

25565   with manipulation

25574   Open treatment of radial AND ulnar shaft fractures, with internal or external fixation; of radius OR ulna

25575   of radius AND ulna

25600   Closed treatment of distal radial fracture (eg, Colles or Smith type) or epiphyseal separation, with or without fracture of ulnar styloid; without manipulation

25605   with manipulation

25611   Percutaneous skeletal fixation of distal radial fracture (eg, Colles or Smith type) or epiphyseal separation, with or without fracture of ulnar styloid, requiring manipulation, with or without external fixation

25620   Open treatment of distal radial fracture (eg, Colles or Smith type) or epiphyseal separation, with or without fracture of ulnar styloid, with or without internal or external fixation

25622   Closed treatment of carpal scaphoid (navicular) fracture; without manipulation

25624   with manipulation

25628   Open treatment of carpal scaphoid (navicular) fracture, with or without internal or external fixation

25630   Closed treatment of carpal bone fracture (excluding carpal scaphoid (navicular)); without manipulation, each bone

25635   with manipulation, each bone

25645   Open treatment of carpal bone fracture (other than carpal scaphoid (navicular)), each bone

25650   Closed treatment of ulnar styloid fracture

25651   Percutaneous skeletal fixation of ulnar styloid fracture

25652   Open treatment of ulnar styloid fracture

25660   Closed treatment of radiocarpal or intercarpal dislocation, one or more bones, with manipulation

25670   Open treatment of radiocarpal or intercarpal dislocation, one or more bones

25671   Percutaneous skeletal fixation of distal radioulnar dislocation

25675   Closed treatment of distal radioulnar dislocation with manipulation

25676   Open treatment of distal radioulnar dislocation, acute or chronic

25680   Closed treatment of trans-scaphoperilunar type of fracture dislocation, with manipulation

25685   Open treatment of trans-scaphoperilunar type of fracture dislocation

25690   Closed treatment of lunate dislocation, with manipulation

25695   Open treatment of lunate dislocation

Arthrodesis

25800   Arthrodesis, wrist; complete, without bone graft (includes radiocarpal and/or intercarpal and/or carpometacarpal joints)

25805   with sliding graft

25810   with iliac or other autograft (includes obtaining graft)

25820   Arthrodesis, wrist; limited, without bone graft (eg, intercarpal or radiocarpal)

25825   with autograft (includes obtaining graft)

25830   Arthrodesis, distal radioulnar joint with segmental resection of ulna, with or without bone graft (eg, Sauve-Kapandji procedure)

Amputation

25900   Amputation, forearm, through radius and ulna;

25905   open, circular (guillotine)

25907   secondary closure or scar revision

25909   re-amputation

25915   Krukenberg procedure

25920   Disarticulation through wrist;

25922   secondary closure or scar revision

25924   re-amputation

25927   Transmetacarpal amputation;

25929   secondary closure or scar revision

25931   re-amputation

Other Procedures

25999   Unlisted procedure, forearm or wrist

Hand and Fingers

Incision

26010   Drainage of finger abscess; simple

26011   complicated (eg, felon)

26020   Drainage of tendon sheath, digit and/or palm, each

26025   Drainage of palmar bursa; single, bursa

26030   multiple bursa

26034   Incision, bone cortex, hand or finger (eg, osteomyelitis or bone abscess)

26035   Decompression fingers and/or hand, injection injury (eg, grease gun)

26037   Decompressive fasciotomy, hand (excludes 26035)

(For injection injury, use 26035)

26040   Fasciotomy, palmar (eg, Dupuytren's contracture); percutaneous

26045   open, partial

(For fasciectomy, see 26121-26125)

26055   Tendon sheath incision (eg, for trigger finger)

26060   Tenotomy, percutaneous, single, each digit

26070   Arthrotomy, with exploration, drainage, or removal of loose or foreign body; carpometacarpal joint

26075   metacarpophalangeal joint, each

26080   interphalangeal joint, each

Excision

26100   Arthrotomy with biopsy; carpometacarpal joint, each

26105   metacarpophalangeal joint, each

26110   interphalangeal joint, each

26115   Excision, tumor or vascular malformation, soft tissue of hand or finger; subcutaneous

26116   deep (subfascial or intramuscular)

26117   Radical resection of tumor (eg, malignant neoplasm), soft tissue of hand or finger

26121   Fasciectomy, palm only, with or without Z-plasty, other local tissue rearrangement, or skin grafting (includes obtaining graft)

26123   Fasciectomy, partial palmar with release of single digit including proximal interphalangeal joint, with or without Z-plasty, other local tissue rearrangement, or skin grafting (includes obtaining graft);

+ 26125   each additional digit (List separately in addition to code for primary procedure)

(Use 26125 in conjunction with 26123)

(For fasciotomy, see 26040, 26045)

26130   Synovectomy, carpometacarpal joint

26135   Synovectomy, metacarpophalangeal joint including intrinsic release and extensor hood reconstruction, each digit

26140   Synovectomy, proximal interphalangeal joint, including extensor reconstruction, each interphalangeal joint

26145   Synovectomy, tendon sheath, radical (tenosynovectomy), flexor tendon, palm and/or finger, each tendon

(For tendon sheath synovectomies at wrist, see 25115, 25116)

26160   Excision of lesion of tendon sheath or joint capsule (eg, cyst, mucous cyst, or ganglion), hand or finger

(For wrist ganglion, see 25111, 25112)

(For trigger digit, use 26055)

26170   Excision of tendon, palm, flexor, single (separate procedure), each

26180   Excision of tendon, finger, flexor (separate procedure), each tendon

26185   Sesamoidectomy, thumb or finger (separate procedure)

26200   Excision or curettage of bone cyst or benign tumor of metacarpal;

26205   with autograft (includes obtaining graft)

26210   Excision or curettage of bone cyst or benign tumor of proximal, middle, or distal phalanx of finger;

26215   with autograft (includes obtaining graft)

26230   Partial excision (craterization, saucerization, or diaphysectomy) bone (eg, osteomyelitis); metacarpal

26235   proximal or middle phalanx of finger

26236   distal phalanx of finger

26250   Radical resection, metacarpal (eg, tumor);

26255   with autograft (includes obtaining graft)

26260   Radical resection, proximal or middle phalanx of finger (eg, tumor);

26261   with autograft (includes obtaining graft)

26262   Radical resection, distal phalanx of finger (eg, tumor)

Introduction or Removal

26320   Removal of implant from finger or hand

(For removal of foreign body in hand or finger, see 20520, 20525)

Repair, Revision, and/or Reconstruction

26340   Manipulation, finger joint, under anesthesia, each joint

(For application of external fixation, see 20690 or 20692)

26350   Repair or advancement, flexor tendon, not in zone 2 digital flexor tendon sheath (eg, no man's land); primary or secondary without free graft, each tendon

26352   secondary with free graft (includes obtaining graft), each tendon

26356   Repair or advancement, flexor tendon, in zone 2 digital flexor tendon sheath (eg, no man's land); primary, without free graft, each tendon

26357   secondary, without free graft, each tendon

26358   secondary, with free graft (includes obtaining graft), each tendon

26370   Repair or advancement of profundus tendon, with intact superficialis tendon; primary, each tendon

26372   secondary with free graft (includes obtaining graft), each tendon

26373   secondary without free graft, each tendon

26390   Excision flexor tendon, with implantation of synthetic rod for delayed tendon graft, hand or finger, each rod

26392   Removal of synthetic rod and insertion of flexor tendon graft, hand or finger (includes obtaining graft), each rod

26410   Repair, extensor tendon, hand, primary or secondary; without free graft, each tendon

26412   with free graft (includes obtaining graft), each tendon

26415   Excision of extensor tendon, with implantation of synthetic rod for delayed tendon graft, hand or finger, each rod

26416   Removal of synthetic rod and insertion of extensor tendon graft (includes obtaining graft), hand or finger, each rod

26418   Repair, extensor tendon, finger, primary or secondary; without free graft, each tendon

26420   with free graft (includes obtaining graft) each tendon

26426   Repair of extensor tendon, central slip, secondary (eg, boutonniere deformity); using local tissue(s), including lateral band(s), each finger

26428   with free graft (includes obtaining graft), each finger

26432   Closed treatment of distal extensor tendon insertion, with or without percutaneous pinning (eg, mallet finger)

26433   Repair of extensor tendon, distal insertion, primary or secondary; without graft (eg, mallet finger)

26434   with free graft (includes obtaining graft)

(For tenovaginotomy for trigger finger, use 26055)

26437   Realignment of extensor tendon, hand, each tendon

26440   Tenolysis, flexor tendon; palm OR finger, each tendon

26442   palm AND finger, each tendon

26445   Tenolysis, extensor tendon, hand OR finger, each tendon

26449   Tenolysis, complex, extensor tendon, finger, including forearm, each tendon

26450   Tenotomy, flexor, palm, open, each tendon

26455   Tenotomy, flexor, finger, open, each tendon

26460   Tenotomy, extensor, hand or finger, open, each tendon

26471   Tenodesis; of proximal interphalangeal joint, each joint

26474   of distal joint, each joint

26476   Lengthening of tendon, extensor, hand or finger, each tendon

26477   Shortening of tendon, extensor, hand or finger, each tendon

26478   Lengthening of tendon, flexor, hand or finger, each tendon

26479   Shortening of tendon, flexor, hand or finger, each tendon

26480   Transfer or transplant of tendon, carpometacarpal area or dorsum of hand; without free graft, each tendon

26483   with free tendon graft (includes obtaining graft), each tendon

26485   Transfer or transplant of tendon, palmar; without free tendon graft, each tendon

26489   with free tendon graft (includes obtaining graft), each tendon

26490   Opponensplasty; superficialis tendon transfer type, each tendon

26492   tendon transfer with graft (includes obtaining graft), each tendon

26494   hypothenar muscle transfer

26496   other methods

(For thumb fusion in opposition, use 26820)

26497   Transfer of tendon to restore intrinsic function; ring and small finger

26498   all four fingers

26499   Correction claw finger, other methods

26500   Reconstruction of tendon pulley, each tendon; with local tissues (separate procedure)

26502   with tendon or fascial graft (includes obtaining graft) (separate procedure)

26504   with tendon prosthesis (separate procedure)

26508   Release of thenar muscle(s) (eg, thumb contracture)

26510   Cross intrinsic transfer, each tendon

26516   Capsulodesis, metacarpophalangeal joint; single digit

26517   two digits

26518   three or four digits

▲=Revised code   ●=New code   ▶ ◀=Contains new or revised text

26520 Capsulectomy or capsulotomy; metacarpophalangeal joint, each joint

26525 interphalangeal joint, each joint

(To report carpometacarpal joint arthroplasty, use 25447)

26530 Arthroplasty, metacarpophalangeal joint; each joint

26531 with prosthetic implant, each joint

26535 Arthroplasty, interphalangeal joint; each joint

26536 with prosthetic implant, each joint

26540 Repair of collateral ligament, metacarpophalangeal or interphalangeal joint

26541 Reconstruction, collateral ligament, metacarpophalangeal joint, single; with tendon or fascial graft (includes obtaining graft)

26542 with local tissue (eg, adductor advancement)

26545 Reconstruction, collateral ligament, interphalangeal joint, single, including graft, each joint

26546 Repair non-union, metacarpal or phalanx, (includes obtaining bone graft with or without external or internal fixation)

26548 Repair and reconstruction, finger, volar plate, interphalangeal joint

26550 Pollicization of a digit

26551 Transfer, toe-to-hand with microvascular anastomosis; great toe wrap-around with bone graft

(For great toe with web space, use 20973)

26553 other than great toe, single

26554 other than great toe, double

(Do not report code 69990 in addition to codes 26551-26554)

26555 Transfer, finger to another position without microvascular anastomosis

26556 Transfer, free toe joint, with microvascular anastomosis

(Do not report code 69990 in addition to code 26556)

(To report great toe-to-hand transfer, use 20973)

26560 Repair of syndactyly (web finger) each web space; with skin flaps

26561 with skin flaps and grafts

26562 complex (eg, involving bone, nails)

26565 Osteotomy; metacarpal, each

26567 phalanx of finger, each

26568 Osteoplasty, lengthening, metacarpal or phalanx

26580 Repair cleft hand

26587 Reconstruction of polydactylous digit, soft tissue and bone

(For excision of polydactylous digit, soft tissue only, use 11200)

26590 Repair macrodactylia, each digit

26591 Repair, intrinsic muscles of hand, each muscle

26593 Release, intrinsic muscles of hand, each muscle

26596 Excision of constricting ring of finger, with multiple Z-plasties

(To report release of scar contracture or graft repairs see 11041-11042, 14040-14041, or 15120, 15240)

Fracture and/or Dislocation

26600 Closed treatment of metacarpal fracture, single; without manipulation, each bone

26605 with manipulation, each bone

26607 Closed treatment of metacarpal fracture, with manipulation, with external fixation, each bone

26608 Percutaneous skeletal fixation of metacarpal fracture, each bone

26615 Open treatment of metacarpal fracture, single, with or without internal or external fixation, each bone

26641 Closed treatment of carpometacarpal dislocation, thumb, with manipulation

26645 Closed treatment of carpometacarpal fracture dislocation, thumb (Bennett fracture), with manipulation

26650 Percutaneous skeletal fixation of carpometacarpal fracture dislocation, thumb (Bennett fracture), with manipulation, with or without external fixation

26665 Open treatment of carpometacarpal fracture dislocation, thumb (Bennett fracture), with or without internal or external fixation

26670 Closed treatment of carpometacarpal dislocation, other than thumb, with manipulation, each joint; without anesthesia

26675 requiring anesthesia

26676 Percutaneous skeletal fixation of carpometacarpal dislocation, other than thumb, with manipulation, each joint

26685 Open treatment of carpometacarpal dislocation, other than thumb; with or without internal or external fixation, each joint

26686 complex, multiple or delayed reduction

26700 Closed treatment of metacarpophalangeal dislocation, single, with manipulation; without anesthesia

26705 requiring anesthesia

26706 Percutaneous skeletal fixation of metacarpophalangeal dislocation, single, with manipulation

26715 Open treatment of metacarpophalangeal dislocation, single, with or without internal or external fixation

26720   Closed treatment of phalangeal shaft fracture, proximal or middle phalanx, finger or thumb; without manipulation, each

26725   with manipulation, with or without skin or skeletal traction, each

26727   Percutaneous skeletal fixation of unstable phalangeal shaft fracture, proximal or middle phalanx, finger or thumb, with manipulation, each

26735   Open treatment of phalangeal shaft fracture, proximal or middle phalanx, finger or thumb, with or without internal or external fixation, each

26740   Closed treatment of articular fracture, involving metacarpophalangeal or interphalangeal joint; without manipulation, each

26742   with manipulation, each

26746   Open treatment of articular fracture, involving metacarpophalangeal or interphalangeal joint, with or without internal or external fixation, each

26750   Closed treatment of distal phalangeal fracture, finger or thumb; without manipulation, each

26755   with manipulation, each

26756   Percutaneous skeletal fixation of distal phalangeal fracture, finger or thumb, each

26765   Open treatment of distal phalangeal fracture, finger or thumb, with or without internal or external fixation, each

26770   Closed treatment of interphalangeal joint dislocation, single, with manipulation; without anesthesia

26775   requiring anesthesia

26776   Percutaneous skeletal fixation of interphalangeal joint dislocation, single, with manipulation

26785   Open treatment of interphalangeal joint dislocation, with or without internal or external fixation, single

Arthrodesis

26820   Fusion in opposition, thumb, with autogenous graft (includes obtaining graft)

26841   Arthrodesis, carpometacarpal joint, thumb, with or without internal fixation;

26842   with autograft (includes obtaining graft)

26843   Arthrodesis, carpometacarpal joint, digit, other than thumb, each;

26844   with autograft (includes obtaining graft)

26850   Arthrodesis, metacarpophalangeal joint, with or without internal fixation;

26852   with autograft (includes obtaining graft)

26860   Arthrodesis, interphalangeal joint, with or without internal fixation;

+ 26861   each additional interphalangeal joint (List separately in addition to code for primary procedure)

(Use 26861 in conjunction with 26860)

26862   with autograft (includes obtaining graft)

+ 26863   with autograft (includes obtaining graft), each additional joint (List separately in addition to code for primary procedure)

(Use 26863 in conjunction with 26862)

Amputation

(For hand through metacarpal bones, use 25927)

26910   Amputation, metacarpal, with finger or thumb (ray amputation), single, with or without interosseous transfer

(For repositioning, see 26550, 26555)

26951   Amputation, finger or thumb, primary or secondary, any joint or phalanx, single, including neurectomies; with direct closure

26952   with local advancement flaps (V-Y, hood)

(For repair of soft tissue defect requiring split or full thickness graft or other pedicle flaps, see 15050-15758)

Other Procedures

26989   Unlisted procedure, hands or fingers

Pelvis and Hip Joint

Including head and neck of femur.

Incision

(For incision and drainage procedures, superficial, see 10040-10160)

26990   Incision and drainage, pelvis or hip joint area; deep abscess or hematoma

26991   infected bursa

26992   Incision, bone cortex, pelvis and/or hip joint (eg, osteomyelitis or bone abscess)

27000   Tenotomy, adductor of hip, percutaneous (separate procedure)

27001   Tenotomy, adductor of hip, open

(To report bilateral procedures, report 27001 with modifier 50)

27003   Tenotomy, adductor, subcutaneous, open, with obturator neurectomy

(To report bilateral procedures, report 27003 with modifier 50)

27005 Tenotomy, hip flexor(s), open (separate procedure)

27006 Tenotomy, abductors and/or extensor(s) of hip, open (separate procedure)

27025 Fasciotomy, hip or thigh, any type

(To report bilateral procedures, report 27025 with modifier 50)

27030 Arthrotomy, hip, with drainage (eg, infection)

27033 Arthrotomy, hip, including exploration or removal of loose or foreign body

27035 Denervation, hip joint, intrapelvic or extrapelvic intra-articular branches of sciatic, femoral, or obturator nerves

(For obturator neurectomy, see 64763, 64766)

27036 Capsulectomy or capsulotomy, hip, with or without excision of heterotopic bone, with release of hip flexor muscles (ie, gluteus medius, gluteus minimus, tensor fascia latae, rectus femoris, sartorius, iliopsoas)

Excision

27040 Biopsy, soft tissue of pelvis and hip area; superficial

27041 deep, subfascial or intramuscular

(For needle biopsy of soft tissue, use 20206)

27047 Excision, tumor, pelvis and hip area; subcutaneous tissue

27048 deep, subfascial, intramuscular

27049 Radical resection of tumor, soft tissue of pelvis and hip area (eg, malignant neoplasm)

27050 Arthrotomy, with biopsy; sacroiliac joint

27052 hip joint

27054 Arthrotomy with synovectomy, hip joint

27060 Excision; ischial bursa

27062 trochanteric bursa or calcification

(For arthrocentesis or needling of bursa, use 20610)

27065 Excision of bone cyst or benign tumor; superficial (wing of ilium, symphysis pubis, or greater trochanter of femur) with or without autograft

27066 deep, with or without autograft

27067 with autograft requiring separate incision

27070 Partial excision (craterization, saucerization) (eg, osteomyelitis or bone abscess); superficial (eg, wing of ilium, symphysis pubis, or greater trochanter of femur)

27071 deep (subfascial or intramuscular)

27075 Radical resection of tumor or infection; wing of ilium, one pubic or ischial ramus or symphysis pubis

27076 ilium, including acetabulum, both pubic rami, or ischium and acetabulum

27077 innominate bone, total

27078 ischial tuberosity and greater trochanter of femur

27079 ischial tuberosity and greater trochanter of femur, with skin flaps

27080 Coccygectomy, primary

(For pressure (decubitus) ulcer, see 15920, 15922 and 15931-15958)

Introduction or Removal

27086 Removal of foreign body, pelvis or hip; subcutaneous tissue

27087 deep (subfascial or intramuscular)

27090 Removal of hip prosthesis; (separate procedure)

27091 complicated, including total hip prosthesis, methylmethacrylate with or without insertion of spacer

27093 Injection procedure for hip arthrography; without anesthesia

(For radiological supervision and interpretation, use 73525. Do not report 76003 in addition to 73525)

27095 with anesthesia

(For radiological supervision and interpretation, use 73525. Do not report 76003 in addition to 73525)

27096 Injection procedure for sacroiliac joint, arthrography and/or anesthetic/steroid

(27096 is to be used only with imaging confirmation of intra-articular needle positioning)

(For radiological supervision and interpretation of sacroiliac joint arthrography, use 73542)

(For fluoroscopic guidance without formal arthrography, use 76005)

(Code 27096 is a unilateral procedure. For bilateral procedure, use modifier 50)

Repair, Revision, and/or Reconstruction

27097 Release or recession, hamstring, proximal

27098 Transfer, adductor to ischium

27100 Transfer external oblique muscle to greater trochanter including fascial or tendon extension (graft)

27105 Transfer paraspinal muscle to hip (includes fascial or tendon extension graft)

27110 Transfer iliopsoas; to greater trochanter of femur

27111 to femoral neck

27120 Acetabuloplasty; (eg, Whitman, Colonna, Haygroves, or cup type)

27122 resection, femoral head (eg, Girdlestone procedure)

27125   Hemiarthroplasty, hip, partial (eg, femoral stem prosthesis, bipolar arthroplasty)

(For prosthetic replacement following fracture of the hip, use 27236)

27130   Arthroplasty, acetabular and proximal femoral prosthetic replacement (total hip arthroplasty), with or without autograft or allograft

27132   Conversion of previous hip surgery to total hip arthroplasty, with or without autograft or allograft

27134   Revision of total hip arthroplasty; both components, with or without autograft or allograft

27137   acetabular component only, with or without autograft or allograft

27138   femoral component only, with or without allograft

27140   Osteotomy and transfer of greater trochanter of femur (separate procedure)

27146   Osteotomy, iliac, acetabular or innominate bone;

27147   with open reduction of hip

27151   with femoral osteotomy

27156   with femoral osteotomy and with open reduction of hip

27158   Osteotomy, pelvis, bilateral (eg, congenital malformation)

27161   Osteotomy, femoral neck (separate procedure)

27165   Osteotomy, intertrochanteric or subtrochanteric including internal or external fixation and/or cast

27170   Bone graft, femoral head, neck, intertrochanteric or subtrochanteric area (includes obtaining bone graft)

27175   Treatment of slipped femoral epiphysis; by traction, without reduction

27176   by single or multiple pinning, in situ

27177   Open treatment of slipped femoral epiphysis; single or multiple pinning or bone graft (includes obtaining graft)

27178   closed manipulation with single or multiple pinning

27179   osteoplasty of femoral neck (Heyman type procedure)

27181   osteotomy and internal fixation

27185   Epiphyseal arrest by epiphysiodesis or stapling, greater trochanter of femur

27187   Prophylactic treatment (nailing, pinning, plating or wiring) with or without methylmethacrylate, femoral neck and proximal femur

Fracture and/or Dislocation

27193   Closed treatment of pelvic ring fracture, dislocation, diastasis or subluxation; without manipulation

27194   with manipulation, requiring more than local anesthesia

27200   Closed treatment of coccygeal fracture

27202   Open treatment of coccygeal fracture

27215   Open treatment of iliac spine(s), tuberosity avulsion, or iliac wing fracture(s) (eg, pelvic fracture(s) which do not disrupt the pelvic ring), with internal fixation

27216   Percutaneous skeletal fixation of posterior pelvic ring fracture and/or dislocation (includes ilium, sacroiliac joint and/or sacrum)

27217   Open treatment of anterior ring fracture and/or dislocation with internal fixation (includes pubic symphysis and/or rami)

27218   Open treatment of posterior ring fracture and/or dislocation with internal fixation (includes ilium, sacroiliac joint and/or sacrum)

27220   Closed treatment of acetabulum (hip socket) fracture(s); without manipulation

27222   with manipulation, with or without skeletal traction

27226   Open treatment of posterior or anterior acetabular wall fracture, with internal fixation

27227   Open treatment of acetabular fracture(s) involving anterior or posterior (one) column, or a fracture running transversely across the acetabulum, with internal fixation

27228   Open treatment of acetabular fracture(s) involving anterior and posterior (two) columns, includes T-fracture and both column fracture with complete articular detachment, or single column or transverse fracture with associated acetabular wall fracture, with internal fixation

27230   Closed treatment of femoral fracture, proximal end, neck; without manipulation

27232   with manipulation, with or without skeletal traction

27235   Percutaneous skeletal fixation of femoral fracture, proximal end, neck

27236   Open treatment of femoral fracture, proximal end, neck, internal fixation or prosthetic replacement

27238   Closed treatment of intertrochanteric, pertrochanteric, or subtrochanteric femoral fracture; without manipulation

27240   with manipulation, with or without skin or skeletal traction

27244   Treatment of intertrochanteric, pertrochanteric, or subtrochanteric femoral fracture; with plate/screw type implant, with or without cerclage

27245   with intramedullary implant, with or without interlocking screws and/or cerclage

27246   Closed treatment of greater trochanteric fracture, without manipulation

27248   Open treatment of greater trochanteric fracture, with or without internal or external fixation

27250   Closed treatment of hip dislocation, traumatic; without anesthesia

27252   requiring anesthesia

Surgery: Musculoskeletal System

27253 Open treatment of hip dislocation, traumatic, without internal fixation

27254 Open treatment of hip dislocation, traumatic, with acetabular wall and femoral head fracture, with or without internal or external fixation

(For treatment of acetabular fracture with fixation, see 27226, 27227)

27256 Treatment of spontaneous hip dislocation (developmental, including congenital or pathological), by abduction, splint or traction; without anesthesia, without manipulation

27257 with manipulation, requiring anesthesia

27258 Open treatment of spontaneous hip dislocation (developmental, including congenital or pathological), replacement of femoral head in acetabulum (including tenotomy, etc);

27259 with femoral shaft shortening

27265 Closed treatment of post hip arthroplasty dislocation; without anesthesia

27266 requiring regional or general anesthesia

Manipulation

27275 Manipulation, hip joint, requiring general anesthesia

Arthrodesis

27280 Arthrodesis, sacroiliac joint (including obtaining graft)

(To report bilateral procedures, report 27280 with modifier 50)

27282 Arthrodesis, symphysis pubis (including obtaining graft)

27284 Arthrodesis, hip joint (including obtaining graft);

27286 with subtrochanteric osteotomy

Amputation

27290 Interpelviabdominal amputation (hindquarter amputation)

27295 Disarticulation of hip

Other Procedures

27299 Unlisted procedure, pelvis or hip joint

Femur (Thigh Region) and Knee Joint

Including tibial plateaus.

Incision

(For incision and drainage of abscess or hematoma, superficial, see 10040-10160)

27301 Incision and drainage, deep abscess, bursa, or hematoma, thigh or knee region

27303 Incision, deep, with opening of bone cortex, femur or knee (eg, osteomyelitis or bone abscess)

27305 Fasciotomy, iliotibial (tenotomy), open

(For combined Ober-Yount fasciotomy, use 27025)

27306 Tenotomy, percutaneous, adductor or hamstring; single tendon (separate procedure)

27307 multiple tendons

27310 Arthrotomy, knee, with exploration, drainage, or removal of foreign body (eg, infection)

27315 Neurectomy, hamstring muscle

27320 Neurectomy, popliteal (gastrocnemius)

Excision

27323 Biopsy, soft tissue of thigh or knee area; superficial

27324 deep (subfascial or intramuscular)

(For needle biopsy of soft tissue, use 20206)

27327 Excision, tumor, thigh or knee area; subcutaneous

27328 deep, subfascial, or intramuscular

27329 Radical resection of tumor (eg, malignant neoplasm), soft tissue of thigh or knee area

27330 Arthrotomy, knee; with synovial biopsy only

27331 including joint exploration, biopsy, or removal of loose or foreign bodies

27332 Arthrotomy, with excision of semilunar cartilage (meniscectomy) knee; medial OR lateral

27333 medial AND lateral

27334 Arthrotomy, with synovectomy, knee; anterior OR posterior

27335 anterior AND posterior including popliteal area

27340 Excision, prepatellar bursa

27345 Excision of synovial cyst of popliteal space (eg, Baker's cyst)

27347 Excision of lesion of meniscus or capsule (eg, cyst, ganglion), knee

27350 Patellectomy or hemipatellectomy

27355 Excision or curettage of bone cyst or benign tumor of femur;

27356 with allograft

27357 with autograft (includes obtaining graft)

+ 27358 with internal fixation (List in addition to code for primary procedure)

(Use 27358 in conjunction with 27355, 27356, or 27357)

27360   Partial excision (craterization, saucerization, or diaphysectomy) bone, femur, proximal tibia and/or fibula (eg, osteomyelitis or bone abscess)

27365   Radical resection of tumor, bone, femur or knee

(For radical resection of tumor, soft tissue, use 27329)

Introduction or Removal

27370   Injection procedure for knee arthrography

(For radiological supervision and interpretation, use 73580. Do not report 76003 in addition to 73580)

27372   Removal of foreign body, deep, thigh region or knee area

(For removal of knee prosthesis including "total knee," use 27488)

(For surgical arthroscopic knee procedures, see 29870-29887)

Repair, Revision, and/or Reconstruction

27380   Suture of infrapatellar tendon; primary

27381   secondary reconstruction, including fascial or tendon graft

27385   Suture of quadriceps or hamstring muscle rupture; primary

27386   secondary reconstruction, including fascial or tendon graft

27390   Tenotomy, open, hamstring, knee to hip; single tendon

27391   multiple tendons, one leg

27392   multiple tendons, bilateral

27393   Lengthening of hamstring tendon; single tendon

27394   multiple tendons, one leg

27395   multiple tendons, bilateral

27396   Transplant, hamstring tendon to patella; single tendon

27397   multiple tendons

27400   Transfer, tendon or muscle, hamstrings to femur (eg, Egger's type procedure)

27403   Arthrotomy with meniscus repair, knee

(For arthroscopic repair, use 29882)

27405   Repair, primary, torn ligament and/or capsule, knee; collateral

27407   cruciate

(For cruciate ligament reconstruction, use 27427)

27409   collateral and cruciate ligaments

(For ligament reconstruction, see 27427-27429)

27412   Autologous chondrocyte implantation, knee

(Do not report 27412 in conjunction with 20926, 27331, 27570)

(For harvesting of chondrocytes, use 29870)

27415   Osteochondral allograft, knee, open

(For arthroscopic implant of osteochondral allograft, use 29867)

27418   Anterior tibial tubercleplasty (eg, Maquet type procedure)

27420   Reconstruction of dislocating patella; (eg, Hauser type procedure)

27422   with extensor realignment and/or muscle advancement or release (eg, Campbell, Goldwaite type procedure)

27424   with patellectomy

27425   Lateral retinacular release, open

(For arthroscopic lateral release, use 29873)

27427   Ligamentous reconstruction (augmentation), knee; extra-articular

27428   intra-articular (open)

27429   intra-articular (open) and extra-articular

(For primary repair of ligament(s) performed in conjunction with reconstruction, report 27405, 27407 or 27409 in conjunction with 27427, 27428 or 27429)

27430   Quadricepsplasty (eg, Bennett or Thompson type)

27435   Capsulotomy, posterior capsular release, knee

27437   Arthroplasty, patella; without prosthesis

27438   with prosthesis

27440   Arthroplasty, knee, tibial plateau;

27441   with debridement and partial synovectomy

27442   Arthroplasty, femoral condyles or tibial plateau(s), knee;

27443   with debridement and partial synovectomy

27445   Arthroplasty, knee, hinge prosthesis (eg, Walldius type)

27446   Arthroplasty, knee, condyle and plateau; medial OR lateral compartment

27447   medial AND lateral compartments with or without patella resurfacing (total knee arthroplasty)

(For revision of total knee arthroplasty, use 27487)

(For removal of total knee prosthesis, use 27488)

27448   Osteotomy, femur, shaft or supracondylar; without fixation

(To report bilateral procedures, report 27448 with modifier 50)

27450   with fixation

(To report bilateral procedures, report 27450 with modifier 50)

Surgery: Musculoskeletal System

Surgery: Musculoskeletal System

27454 Osteotomy, multiple, with realignment on intramedullary rod, femoral shaft (eg, Sofield type procedure)

27455 Osteotomy, proximal tibia, including fibular excision or osteotomy (includes correction of genu varus (bowleg) or genu valgus (knock-knee)); before epiphyseal closure

(To report bilateral procedures, report 27455 with modifier 50)

27457 after epiphyseal closure

(To report bilateral procedures, report 27457 with modifier 50)

27465 Osteoplasty, femur; shortening (excluding 64876)

27466 lengthening

27468 combined, lengthening and shortening with femoral segment transfer

27470 Repair, nonunion or malunion, femur, distal to head and neck; without graft (eg, compression technique)

27472 with iliac or other autogenous bone graft (includes obtaining graft)

27475 Arrest, epiphyseal, any method (eg, epiphysiodesis); distal femur

27477 tibia and fibula, proximal

27479 combined distal femur, proximal tibia and fibula

27485 Arrest, hemiepiphyseal, distal femur or proximal tibia or fibula (eg, genu varus or valgus)

27486 Revision of total knee arthroplasty, with or without allograft; one component

27487 femoral and entire tibial component

27488 Removal of prosthesis, including total knee prosthesis, methylmethacrylate with or without insertion of spacer, knee

27495 Prophylactic treatment (nailing, pinning, plating or wiring) with or without methylmethacrylate, femur

27496 Decompression fasciotomy, thigh and/or knee, one compartment (flexor or extensor or adductor);

27497 with debridement of nonviable muscle and/or nerve

27498 Decompression fasciotomy, thigh and/or knee, multiple compartments;

27499 with debridement of nonviable muscle and/or nerve

Fracture and/or Dislocation

(For arthroscopic treatment of intercondylar spine(s) and tuberosity fracture(s) of the knee, see 29850, 29851)

(For arthroscopic treatment of tibial fracture, see 29855, 29856)

27500 Closed treatment of femoral shaft fracture, without manipulation

27501 Closed treatment of supracondylar or transcondylar femoral fracture with or without intercondylar extension, without manipulation

27502 Closed treatment of femoral shaft fracture, with manipulation, with or without skin or skeletal traction

27503 Closed treatment of supracondylar or transcondylar femoral fracture with or without intercondylar extension, with manipulation, with or without skin or skeletal traction

27506 Open treatment of femoral shaft fracture, with or without external fixation, with insertion of intramedullary implant, with or without cerclage and/or locking screws

27507 Open treatment of femoral shaft fracture with plate/screws, with or without cerclage

27508 Closed treatment of femoral fracture, distal end, medial or lateral condyle, without manipulation

27509 Percutaneous skeletal fixation of femoral fracture, distal end, medial or lateral condyle, or supracondylar or transcondylar, with or without intercondylar extension, or distal femoral epiphyseal separation

27510 Closed treatment of femoral fracture, distal end, medial or lateral condyle, with manipulation

27511 Open treatment of femoral supracondylar or transcondylar fracture without intercondylar extension, with or without internal or external fixation

27513 Open treatment of femoral supracondylar or transcondylar fracture with intercondylar extension, with or without internal or external fixation

27514 Open treatment of femoral fracture, distal end, medial or lateral condyle, with or without internal or external fixation

27516 Closed treatment of distal femoral epiphyseal separation; without manipulation

27517 with manipulation, with or without skin or skeletal traction

27519 Open treatment of distal femoral epiphyseal separation, with or without internal or external fixation

27520 Closed treatment of patellar fracture, without manipulation

27524 Open treatment of patellar fracture, with internal fixation and/or partial or complete patellectomy and soft tissue repair

27530 Closed treatment of tibial fracture, proximal (plateau); without manipulation

27532 with or without manipulation, with skeletal traction

(For arthroscopic treatment, see 29855, 29856)

27535 Open treatment of tibial fracture, proximal (plateau); unicondylar, with or without internal or external fixation

27536 bicondylar, with or without internal fixation

(For arthroscopic treatment, see 29855, 29856)

27538   Closed treatment of intercondylar spine(s) and/or tuberosity fracture(s) of knee, with or without manipulation

(For arthroscopic treatment, see 29850, 29851)

27540   Open treatment of intercondylar spine(s) and/or tuberosity fracture(s) of the knee, with or without internal or external fixation

27550   Closed treatment of knee dislocation; without anesthesia

27552   requiring anesthesia

27556   Open treatment of knee dislocation, with or without internal or external fixation; without primary ligamentous repair or augmentation/reconstruction

27557   with primary ligamentous repair

27558   with primary ligamentous repair, with augmentation/reconstruction

27560   Closed treatment of patellar dislocation; without anesthesia

(For recurrent dislocation, see 27420-27424)

27562   requiring anesthesia

27566   Open treatment of patellar dislocation, with or without partial or total patellectomy

Manipulation

27570   Manipulation of knee joint under general anesthesia (includes application of traction or other fixation devices)

Arthrodesis

27580   Arthrodesis, knee, any technique

Amputation

27590   Amputation, thigh, through femur, any level;

27591   immediate fitting technique including first cast

27592   open, circular (guillotine)

27594   secondary closure or scar revision

27596   re-amputation

27598   Disarticulation at knee

Other Procedures

27599   Unlisted procedure, femur or knee

Leg (Tibia and Fibula) and Ankle Joint

Incision

27600   Decompression fasciotomy, leg; anterior and/or lateral compartments only

27601   posterior compartment(s) only

27602   anterior and/or lateral, and posterior compartment(s)

(For incision and drainage procedures, superficial, see 10040-10160)

(For decompression fasciotomy with debridement, see 27892-27894)

27603   Incision and drainage, leg or ankle; deep abscess or hematoma

27604   infected bursa

27605   Tenotomy, percutaneous, Achilles tendon (separate procedure); local anesthesia

27606   general anesthesia

27607   Incision (eg, osteomyelitis or bone abscess), leg or ankle

27610   Arthrotomy, ankle, including exploration, drainage, or removal of foreign body

27612   Arthrotomy, posterior capsular release, ankle, with or without Achilles tendon lengthening

(See also 27685)

Excision

27613   Biopsy, soft tissue of leg or ankle area; superficial

27614   deep (subfascial or intramuscular)

(For needle biopsy of soft tissue, use 20206)

27615   Radical resection of tumor (eg, malignant neoplasm), soft tissue of leg or ankle area

27618   Excision, tumor, leg or ankle area; subcutaneous tissue

27619   deep (subfascial or intramuscular)

27620   Arthrotomy, ankle, with joint exploration, with or without biopsy, with or without removal of loose or foreign body

27625   Arthrotomy, with synovectomy, ankle;

27626   including tenosynovectomy

27630   Excision of lesion of tendon sheath or capsule (eg, cyst or ganglion), leg and/or ankle

27635   Excision or curettage of bone cyst or benign tumor, tibia or fibula;

27637   with autograft (includes obtaining graft)

27638   with allograft

27640   Partial excision (craterization, saucerization, or diaphysectomy) bone (eg, osteomyelitis or exostosis); tibia

27641   fibula

27645   Radical resection of tumor, bone; tibia

27646   fibula

27647   talus or calcaneus

Introduction or Removal

27648   Injection procedure for ankle arthrography

(For radiological supervision and interpretation, use 73615. Do not report 76003 in addition to 73615)

(For ankle arthroscopy, see 29894-29898)

Repair, Revision, and/or Reconstruction

27650   Repair, primary, open or percutaneous, ruptured Achilles tendon;

27652   with graft (includes obtaining graft)

27654   Repair, secondary, Achilles tendon, with or without graft

27656   Repair, fascial defect of leg

27658   Repair, flexor tendon, leg; primary, without graft, each tendon

27659   secondary, with or without graft, each tendon

27664   Repair, extensor tendon, leg; primary, without graft, each tendon

27665   secondary, with or without graft, each tendon

27675   Repair, dislocating peroneal tendons; without fibular osteotomy

27676   with fibular osteotomy

27680   Tenolysis, flexor or extensor tendon, leg and/or ankle; single, each tendon

27681   multiple tendons (through separate incision(s))

27685   Lengthening or shortening of tendon, leg or ankle; single tendon (separate procedure)

27686   multiple tendons (through same incision), each

27687   Gastrocnemius recession (eg, Strayer procedure)

(Toe extensors are considered as a group to be a single tendon when transplanted into midfoot)

27690   Transfer or transplant of single tendon (with muscle redirection or rerouting); superficial (eg, anterior tibial extensors into midfoot)

27691   deep (eg, anterior tibial or posterior tibial through interosseous space, flexor digitorum longus, flexor hallucis longus, or peroneal tendon to midfoot or hindfoot)

+ 27692   each additional tendon (List separately in addition to code for primary procedure)

(Use 27692 in conjunction with 27690, 27691)

27695   Repair, primary, disrupted ligament, ankle; collateral

27696   both collateral ligaments

27698   Repair, secondary, disrupted ligament, ankle, collateral (eg, Watson-Jones procedure)

27700   Arthroplasty, ankle;

27702   with implant (total ankle)

27703   revision, total ankle

27704   Removal of ankle implant

27705   Osteotomy; tibia

27707   fibula

27709   tibia and fibula

27712   multiple, with realignment on intramedullary rod (eg, Sofield type procedure)

(For osteotomy to correct genu varus (bowleg) or genu valgus (knock-knee), see 27455-27457)

27715   Osteoplasty, tibia and fibula, lengthening or shortening

27720   Repair of nonunion or malunion, tibia; without graft, (eg, compression technique)

27722   with sliding graft

27724   with iliac or other autograft (includes obtaining graft)

27725   by synostosis, with fibula, any method

27727   Repair of congenital pseudarthrosis, tibia

27730   Arrest, epiphyseal (epiphysiodesis), open; distal tibia

27732   distal fibula

27734   distal tibia and fibula

27740   Arrest, epiphyseal (epiphysiodesis), any method, combined, proximal and distal tibia and fibula;

27742   and distal femur

(For epiphyseal arrest of proximal tibia and fibula, use 27477)

27745   Prophylactic treatment (nailing, pinning, plating or wiring) with or without methylmethacrylate, tibia

Fracture and/or Dislocation

27750   Closed treatment of tibial shaft fracture (with or without fibular fracture); without manipulation

27752   with manipulation, with or without skeletal traction

27756   Percutaneous skeletal fixation of tibial shaft fracture (with or without fibular fracture) (eg, pins or screws)

27758   Open treatment of tibial shaft fracture, (with or without fibular fracture) with plate/screws, with or without cerclage

27759   Treatment of tibial shaft fracture (with or without fibular fracture) by intramedullary implant, with or without interlocking screws and/or cerclage

27760   Closed treatment of medial malleolus fracture; without manipulation

27762   with manipulation, with or without skin or skeletal traction

27766   Open treatment of medial malleolus fracture, with or without internal or external fixation

27780   Closed treatment of proximal fibula or shaft fracture; without manipulation

27781   with manipulation

27784   Open treatment of proximal fibula or shaft fracture, with or without internal or external fixation

27786   Closed treatment of distal fibular fracture (lateral malleolus); without manipulation

27788   with manipulation

27792   Open treatment of distal fibular fracture (lateral malleolus), with or without internal or external fixation

(For treatment of tibia and fibula shaft fractures, see 27750-27759)

27808   Closed treatment of bimalleolar ankle fracture, (including Potts); without manipulation

27810   with manipulation

27814   Open treatment of bimalleolar ankle fracture, with or without internal or external fixation

27816   Closed treatment of trimalleolar ankle fracture; without manipulation

27818   with manipulation

27822   Open treatment of trimalleolar ankle fracture, with or without internal or external fixation, medial and/or lateral malleolus; without fixation of posterior lip

27823   with fixation of posterior lip

27824   Closed treatment of fracture of weight bearing articular portion of distal tibia (eg, pilon or tibial plafond), with or without anesthesia; without manipulation

27825   with skeletal traction and/or requiring manipulation

27826   Open treatment of fracture of weight bearing articular surface/portion of distal tibia (eg, pilon or tibial plafond), with internal or external fixation; of fibula only

27827   of tibia only

27828   of both tibia and fibula

27829   Open treatment of distal tibiofibular joint (syndesmosis) disruption, with or without internal or external fixation

27830   Closed treatment of proximal tibiofibular joint dislocation; without anesthesia

27831   requiring anesthesia

27832   Open treatment of proximal tibiofibular joint dislocation, with or without internal or external fixation, or with excision of proximal fibula

27840   Closed treatment of ankle dislocation; without anesthesia

27842   requiring anesthesia, with or without percutaneous skeletal fixation

27846   Open treatment of ankle dislocation, with or without percutaneous skeletal fixation; without repair or internal fixation

27848   with repair or internal or external fixation

(For surgical or diagnostic arthroscopic procedures, see 29894-29898)

Manipulation

27860   Manipulation of ankle under general anesthesia (includes application of traction or other fixation apparatus)

Arthrodesis

27870   Arthrodesis, ankle, open

(For arthroscopic ankle arthrodesis, use 29899)

27871   Arthrodesis, tibiofibular joint, proximal or distal

Amputation

27880   Amputation, leg, through tibia and fibula;

27881   with immediate fitting technique including application of first cast

27882   open, circular (guillotine)

27884   secondary closure or scar revision

27886   re-amputation

27888   Amputation, ankle, through malleoli of tibia and fibula (eg, Syme, Pirogoff type procedures), with plastic closure and resection of nerves

27889   Ankle disarticulation

Other Procedures

27892   Decompression fasciotomy, leg; anterior and/or lateral compartments only, with debridement of nonviable muscle and/or nerve

(For decompression fasciotomy of the leg without debridement, use 27600)

27893   posterior compartment(s) only, with debridement of nonviable muscle and/or nerve

(For decompression fasciotomy of the leg without debridement, use 27601)

Surgery: Musculoskeletal System

27894   anterior and/or lateral, and posterior compartment(s), with debridement of nonviable muscle and/or nerve

(For decompression fasciotomy of the leg without debridement, use 27602)

27899   Unlisted procedure, leg or ankle

Foot and Toes

Incision

(For incision and drainage procedures, superficial, see 10040-10160)

28001   Incision and drainage, bursa, foot

28002   Incision and drainage below fascia, with or without tendon sheath involvement, foot; single bursal space

28003   multiple areas

28005   Incision, bone cortex (eg, osteomyelitis or bone abscess), foot

28008   Fasciotomy, foot and/or toe

(See also 28060, 28062, 28250)

28010   Tenotomy, percutaneous, toe; single tendon

28011   multiple tendons

(For open tenotomy, see 28230-28234)

28020   Arthrotomy, including exploration, drainage, or removal of loose or foreign body; intertarsal or tarsometatarsal joint

28022   metatarsophalangeal joint

28024   interphalangeal joint

28030   Neurectomy, intrinsic musculature of foot

28035   Release, tarsal tunnel (posterior tibial nerve decompression)

(For other nerve entrapments, see 64704, 64722)

Excision

28043   Excision, tumor, foot; subcutaneous tissue

28045   deep, subfascial, intramuscular

28046   Radical resection of tumor (eg, malignant neoplasm), soft tissue of foot

28050   Arthrotomy with biopsy; intertarsal or tarsometatarsal joint

28052   metatarsophalangeal joint

28054   interphalangeal joint

28060   Fasciectomy, plantar fascia; partial (separate procedure)

28062   radical (separate procedure)

(For plantar fasciotomy, see 28008, 28250)

28070   Synovectomy; intertarsal or tarsometatarsal joint, each

28072   metatarsophalangeal joint, each

28080   Excision, interdigital (Morton) neuroma, single, each

28086   Synovectomy, tendon sheath, foot; flexor

28088   extensor

28090   Excision of lesion, tendon, tendon sheath, or capsule (including synovectomy) (eg, cyst or ganglion); foot

28092   toe(s), each

28100   Excision or curettage of bone cyst or benign tumor, talus or calcaneus;

28102   with iliac or other autograft (includes obtaining graft)

28103   with allograft

28104   Excision or curettage of bone cyst or benign tumor, tarsal or metatarsal, except talus or calcaneus;

28106   with iliac or other autograft (includes obtaining graft)

28107   with allograft

28108   Excision or curettage of bone cyst or benign tumor, phalanges of foot

(For ostectomy, partial (eg, hallux valgus, Silver type procedure), use 28290)

28110   Ostectomy, partial excision, fifth metatarsal head (bunionette) (separate procedure)

28111   Ostectomy, complete excision; first metatarsal head

28112   other metatarsal head (second, third or fourth)

28113   fifth metatarsal head

28114   all metatarsal heads, with partial proximal phalangectomy, excluding first metatarsal (eg, Clayton type procedure)

28116   Ostectomy, excision of tarsal coalition

28118   Ostectomy, calcaneus;

28119   for spur, with or without plantar fascial release

28120   Partial excision (craterization, saucerization, sequestrectomy, or diaphysectomy) bone (eg, osteomyelitis or bossing); talus or calcaneus

28122   tarsal or metatarsal bone, except talus or calcaneus

(For partial excision of talus or calcaneus, use 28120)

(For cheilectomy for hallux rigidus, use 28289)

28124   phalanx of toe

28126   Resection, partial or complete, phalangeal base, each toe

28130   Talectomy (astragalectomy)

(For calcanectomy, use 28118)

28140   Metatarsectomy

28150   Phalangectomy, toe, each toe

28153   Resection, condyle(s), distal end of phalanx, each toe

28160   Hemiphalangectomy or interphalangeal joint excision, toe, proximal end of phalanx, each

28171   Radical resection of tumor, bone; tarsal (except talus or calcaneus)

28173   metatarsal

28175   phalanx of toe

         (For talus or calcaneus, use 27647)

Introduction or Removal

28190   Removal of foreign body, foot; subcutaneous

28192   deep

28193   complicated

Repair, Revision, and/or Reconstruction

28200   Repair, tendon, flexor, foot; primary or secondary, without free graft, each tendon

28202   secondary with free graft, each tendon (includes obtaining graft)

28208   Repair, tendon, extensor, foot; primary or secondary, each tendon

28210   secondary with free graft, each tendon (includes obtaining graft)

28220   Tenolysis, flexor, foot; single tendon

28222   multiple tendons

28225   Tenolysis, extensor, foot; single tendon

28226   multiple tendons

28230   Tenotomy, open, tendon flexor; foot, single or multiple tendon(s) (separate procedure)

28232   toe, single tendon (separate procedure)

28234   Tenotomy, open, extensor, foot or toe, each tendon

         (For tendon transfer to midfoot or hindfoot, see 27690, 27691)

28238   Reconstruction (advancement), posterior tibial tendon with excision of accessory tarsal navicular bone (eg, Kidner type procedure)

         (For subcutaneous tenotomy, see 28010, 28011)

         (For transfer or transplant of tendon with muscle redirection or rerouting, see 27690-27692)

         (For extensor hallucis longus transfer with great toe IP fusion (Jones procedure), use 28760)

28240   Tenotomy, lengthening, or release, abductor hallucis muscle

28250   Division of plantar fascia and muscle (eg, Steindler stripping) (separate procedure)

28260   Capsulotomy, midfoot; medial release only (separate procedure)

28261   with tendon lengthening

28262   extensive, including posterior talotibial capsulotomy and tendon(s) lengthening (eg, resistant clubfoot deformity)

28264   Capsulotomy, midtarsal (eg, Heyman type procedure)

28270   Capsulotomy; metatarsophalangeal joint, with or without tenorrhaphy, each joint (separate procedure)

28272   interphalangeal joint, each joint (separate procedure)

28280   Syndactylization, toes (eg, webbing or Kelikian type procedure)

28285   Correction, hammertoe (eg, interphalangeal fusion, partial or total phalangectomy)

28286   Correction, cock-up fifth toe, with plastic skin closure (eg, Ruiz-Mora type procedure)

28288   Ostectomy, partial, exostectomy or condylectomy, metatarsal head, each metatarsal head

28289   Hallux rigidus correction with cheilectomy, debridement and capsular release of the first metatarsophalangeal joint

28290   Correction, hallux valgus (bunion), with or without sesamoidectomy; simple exostectomy (eg, Silver type procedure)

28292   Keller, McBride, or Mayo type procedure

28293   resection of joint with implant

28294   with tendon transplants (eg, Joplin type procedure)

28296   with metatarsal osteotomy (eg, Mitchell, Chevron, or concentric type procedures)

28297   Lapidus-type procedure

28298   by phalanx osteotomy

28299   by double osteotomy

28300   Osteotomy; calcaneus (eg, Dwyer or Chambers type procedure), with or without internal fixation

28302   talus

28304   Osteotomy, tarsal bones, other than calcaneus or talus;

28305   with autograft (includes obtaining graft) (eg, Fowler type)

28306   Osteotomy, with or without lengthening, shortening or angular correction, metatarsal; first metatarsal

28307   first metatarsal with autograft (other than first toe)

28308   other than first metatarsal, each

28309   multiple (eg, Swanson type cavus foot procedure)

28310   Osteotomy, shortening, angular or rotational correction; proximal phalanx, first toe (separate procedure)

28312   other phalanges, any toe

Surgery: Musculoskeletal System

28313 Reconstruction, angular deformity of toe, soft tissue procedures only (eg, overlapping second toe, fifth toe, curly toes)

28315 Sesamoidectomy, first toe (separate procedure)

28320 Repair, nonunion or malunion; tarsal bones

28322 metatarsal, with or without bone graft (includes obtaining graft)

28340 Reconstruction, toe, macrodactyly; soft tissue resection

28341 requiring bone resection

28344 Reconstruction, toe(s); polydactyly

28345 syndactyly, with or without skin graft(s), each web

28360 Reconstruction, cleft foot

Fracture and/or Dislocation

28400 Closed treatment of calcaneal fracture; without manipulation

28405 with manipulation

28406 Percutaneous skeletal fixation of calcaneal fracture, with manipulation

28415 Open treatment of calcaneal fracture, with or without internal or external fixation;

28420 with primary iliac or other autogenous bone graft (includes obtaining graft)

28430 Closed treatment of talus fracture; without manipulation

28435 with manipulation

28436 Percutaneous skeletal fixation of talus fracture, with manipulation

28445 Open treatment of talus fracture, with or without internal or external fixation

28450 Treatment of tarsal bone fracture (except talus and calcaneus); without manipulation, each

28455 with manipulation, each

28456 Percutaneous skeletal fixation of tarsal bone fracture (except talus and calcaneus), with manipulation, each

28465 Open treatment of tarsal bone fracture (except talus and calcaneus), with or without internal or external fixation, each

28470 Closed treatment of metatarsal fracture; without manipulation, each

28475 with manipulation, each

28476 Percutaneous skeletal fixation of metatarsal fracture, with manipulation, each

28485 Open treatment of metatarsal fracture, with or without internal or external fixation, each

28490 Closed treatment of fracture great toe, phalanx or phalanges; without manipulation

28495 with manipulation

28496 Percutaneous skeletal fixation of fracture great toe, phalanx or phalanges, with manipulation

28505 Open treatment of fracture great toe, phalanx or phalanges, with or without internal or external fixation

28510 Closed treatment of fracture, phalanx or phalanges, other than great toe; without manipulation, each

28515 with manipulation, each

28525 Open treatment of fracture, phalanx or phalanges, other than great toe, with or without internal or external fixation, each

28530 Closed treatment of sesamoid fracture

28531 Open treatment of sesamoid fracture, with or without internal fixation

28540 Closed treatment of tarsal bone dislocation, other than talotarsal; without anesthesia

28545 requiring anesthesia

28546 Percutaneous skeletal fixation of tarsal bone dislocation, other than talotarsal, with manipulation

28555 Open treatment of tarsal bone dislocation, with or without internal or external fixation

28570 Closed treatment of talotarsal joint dislocation; without anesthesia

28575 requiring anesthesia

28576 Percutaneous skeletal fixation of talotarsal joint dislocation, with manipulation

28585 Open treatment of talotarsal joint dislocation, with or without internal or external fixation

28600 Closed treatment of tarsometatarsal joint dislocation; without anesthesia

28605 requiring anesthesia

28606 Percutaneous skeletal fixation of tarsometatarsal joint dislocation, with manipulation

28615 Open treatment of tarsometatarsal joint dislocation, with or without internal or external fixation

28630 Closed treatment of metatarsophalangeal joint dislocation; without anesthesia

28635 requiring anesthesia

28636 Percutaneous skeletal fixation of metatarsophalangeal joint dislocation, with manipulation

28645 Open treatment of metatarsophalangeal joint dislocation, with or without internal or external fixation

28660 Closed treatment of interphalangeal joint dislocation; without anesthesia

28665 requiring anesthesia

28666 Percutaneous skeletal fixation of interphalangeal joint dislocation, with manipulation

28675 Open treatment of interphalangeal joint dislocation, with or without internal or external fixation

Arthrodesis

28705 Arthrodesis; pantalar

28715 triple

28725 subtalar

28730 Arthrodesis, midtarsal or tarsometatarsal, multiple or transverse;

28735 with osteotomy (eg, flatfoot correction)

28737 Arthrodesis, with tendon lengthening and advancement, midtarsal, tarsal navicular-cuneiform (eg, Miller type procedure)

28740 Arthrodesis, midtarsal or tarsometatarsal, single joint

28750 Arthrodesis, great toe; metatarsophalangeal joint

28755 interphalangeal joint

28760 Arthrodesis, with extensor hallucis longus transfer to first metatarsal neck, great toe, interphalangeal joint (eg, Jones type procedure)

(For hammertoe operation or interphalangeal fusion, use 28285)

Amputation

28800 Amputation, foot; midtarsal (eg, Chopart type procedure)

28805 transmetatarsal

28810 Amputation, metatarsal, with toe, single

28820 Amputation, toe; metatarsophalangeal joint

28825 interphalangeal joint

(For amputation of tuft of distal phalanx, use 11752)

Other Procedures

● **28890** Extracorporeal shock wave, high energy, performed by a physician, requiring anesthesia other than local, including ultrasound guidance, involving the plantar fascia

▶(For extracorporeal shock wave therapy involving musculoskeletal system not otherwise specified, see Category III codes 0019T, 0101T, 0102T)◀

28899 Unlisted procedure, foot or toes

Application of Casts and Strapping

The listed procedures apply when the cast application or strapping is a replacement procedure used during or after the period of follow-up care, or when the cast application or strapping is an initial service performed without a restorative treatment or procedure(s) to stabilize or protect a fracture, injury, or dislocation and/or to afford comfort to a patient. Restorative treatment or procedure(s) rendered by another physician following the application of the initial cast/splint/strap may be reported with a treatment of fracture and/or dislocation code.

A physician who applies the initial cast, strap or splint and also assumes all of the subsequent fracture, dislocation, or injury care cannot use the application of casts and strapping codes as an initial service, since the first cast/splint or strap application is included in the treatment of fracture and/or dislocation codes. (See notes under Musculoskeletal System, page 63.) A temporary cast/splint/strap is not considered to be part of the preoperative care, and the use of the modifier 56 is not applicable. Additional evaluation and management services are reportable only if significant identifiable further services are provided at the time of the cast application or strapping.

If cast application or strapping is provided as an initial service (eg, casting of a sprained ankle or knee) in which no other procedure or treatment (eg, surgical repair, reduction of a fracture or joint dislocation) is performed or is expected to be performed by a physician rendering the initial care only, use the casting, strapping and/or supply code (99070) in addition to an evaluation and management code as appropriate.

Listed procedures include removal of cast or strapping.

▶(For orthotics management and training, see 97760-97762)◀

Body and Upper Extremity

Casts

29000 Application of halo type body cast (see 20661-20663 for insertion)

29010 Application of Risser jacket, localizer, body; only

29015 including head

29020 Application of turnbuckle jacket, body; only

29025 including head

29035 Application of body cast, shoulder to hips;

29040 including head, Minerva type

29044 including one thigh

29046 including both thighs

29049 Application, cast; figure-of-eight

29055 shoulder spica

29058 plaster Velpeau

29065 shoulder to hand (long arm)

29075 elbow to finger (short arm)

29085 hand and lower forearm (gauntlet)

29086 finger (eg, contracture)

Surgery: Musculoskeletal System

Splints

29105   Application of long arm splint (shoulder to hand)

29125   Application of short arm splint (forearm to hand); static

29126   dynamic

29130   Application of finger splint; static

29131   dynamic

Strapping—Any Age

29200   Strapping; thorax

29220   low back

29240   shoulder (eg, Velpeau)

29260   elbow or wrist

29280   hand or finger

Lower Extremity

Casts

29305   Application of hip spica cast; one leg

29325   one and one-half spica or both legs

(For hip spica (body) cast, including thighs only, use 29046)

29345   Application of long leg cast (thigh to toes);

29355   walker or ambulatory type

29358   Application of long leg cast brace

29365   Application of cylinder cast (thigh to ankle)

29405   Application of short leg cast (below knee to toes);

29425   walking or ambulatory type

29435   Application of patellar tendon bearing (PTB) cast

29440   Adding walker to previously applied cast

29445   Application of rigid total contact leg cast

29450   Application of clubfoot cast with molding or manipulation, long or short leg

(To report bilateral procedure, use 29450 with modifier 50)

Splints

29505   Application of long leg splint (thigh to ankle or toes)

29515   Application of short leg splint (calf to foot)

Strapping—Any Age

29520   Strapping; hip

29530   knee

29540   ankle and/or foot

29550   toes

29580   Unna boot

29590   Denis-Browne splint strapping

Removal or Repair

Codes for cast removals should be employed only for casts applied by another physician.

29700   Removal or bivalving; gauntlet, boot or body cast

29705   full arm or full leg cast

29710   shoulder or hip spica, Minerva, or Risser jacket, etc.

29715   turnbuckle jacket

29720   Repair of spica, body cast or jacket

29730   Windowing of cast

29740   Wedging of cast (except clubfoot casts)

29750   Wedging of clubfoot cast

(To report bilateral procedure, use 29750 with modifier 50)

Other Procedures

29799   Unlisted procedure, casting or strapping

Endoscopy/Arthroscopy

Surgical endoscopy/arthroscopy always includes a diagnostic endoscopy/arthroscopy.

When arthroscopy is performed in conjunction with arthrotomy, add modifier 51.

29800   Arthroscopy, temporomandibular joint, diagnostic, with or without synovial biopsy (separate procedure)

29804   Arthroscopy, temporomandibular joint, surgical

(For open procedure, use 21010)

29805   Arthroscopy, shoulder, diagnostic, with or without synovial biopsy (separate procedure)

(For open procedure, see 23065-23066, 23100-23101)

29806   Arthroscopy, shoulder, surgical; capsulorrhaphy

(For open procedure, see 23450-23466)

(To report thermal capsulorrhaphy, use 29999)

29807   repair of SLAP lesion

29819   with removal of loose body or foreign body

(For open procedure, see 23040-23044, 23107)

⊘=Modifier 51 exempt   ⊙=Conscious sedation   ✛=Add-on code   ✔=FDA approval pending

29820   synovectomy, partial

(For open procedure, see 23105)

29821   synovectomy, complete

(For open procedure, see 23105)

29822   debridement, limited

(For open procedure, see specific open shoulder procedure performed)

29823   debridement, extensive

(For open procedure, see specific open shoulder procedure performed)

29824   distal claviculectomy including distal articular surface (Mumford procedure)

(For open procedure, use 23120)

29825   with lysis and resection of adhesions, with or without manipulation

(For open procedure, see specific open shoulder procedure performed)

29826   decompression of subacromial space with partial acromioplasty, with or without coracoacromial release

(For open procedure, use 23130 or 23415)

29827   with rotator cuff repair

(For open or mini-open rotator cuff repair, use 23412)

(When arthroscopic subacromial decompression is performed at the same setting, use 29826 and append modifier 51)

(When arthroscopic distal clavicle resection is performed at the same setting, use 29824 and append modifier 51)

29830   Arthroscopy, elbow, diagnostic, with or without synovial biopsy (separate procedure)

29834   Arthroscopy, elbow, surgical; with removal of loose body or foreign body

29835   synovectomy, partial

29836   synovectomy, complete

29837   debridement, limited

29838   debridement, extensive

29840   Arthroscopy, wrist, diagnostic, with or without synovial biopsy (separate procedure)

29843   Arthroscopy, wrist, surgical; for infection, lavage and drainage

29844   synovectomy, partial

29845   synovectomy, complete

29846   excision and/or repair of triangular fibrocartilage and/or joint debridement

29847   internal fixation for fracture or instability

29848   Endoscopy, wrist, surgical, with release of transverse carpal ligament

(For open procedure, use 64721)

29850   Arthroscopically aided treatment of intercondylar spine(s) and/or tuberosity fracture(s) of the knee, with or without manipulation; without internal or external fixation (includes arthroscopy)

29851   with internal or external fixation (includes arthroscopy)

(For bone graft, use 20900, 20902)

29855   Arthroscopically aided treatment of tibial fracture, proximal (plateau); unicondylar, with or without internal or external fixation (includes arthroscopy)

29856   bicondylar, with or without internal or external fixation (includes arthroscopy)

(For bone graft, use 20900, 20902)

29860   Arthroscopy, hip, diagnostic with or without synovial biopsy (separate procedure)

29861   Arthroscopy, hip, surgical; with removal of loose body or foreign body

29862   with debridement/shaving of articular cartilage (chondroplasty), abrasion arthroplasty, and/or resection of labrum

29863   with synovectomy

29866   Arthroscopy, knee, surgical; osteochondral autograft(s) (eg, mosaicplasty) (includes harvesting of the autograft)

▶(Do not report 29866 in conjunction with 29870, 29871, 29875, 29884 when performed at the same session and/or 29874, 29877, 29879, 29885-29887 when performed in the same compartment)◀

29867   osteochondral allograft (eg, mosaicplasty)

▶(Do not report 29867 in conjunction with 27570, 29870, 29871, 29875, 29884 when performed at the same session and/or 29874, 29877, 29879, 29885-29887 when performed in the same compartment)◀

(Do not report 29867 in conjunction with 27415)

29868   meniscal transplantation (includes arthrotomy for meniscal insertion), medial or lateral

▶(Do not report 29868 in conjunction with 29870, 29871, 29875, 29880, 29883, 29884 when performed at the same session or 29874, 29877, 29881, 29882 when performed in the same compartment)◀

29870   Arthroscopy, knee, diagnostic, with or without synovial biopsy (separate procedure)

(For open autologous chondrocyte implantation of the knee, use 27412)

29871 Arthroscopy, knee, surgical; for infection, lavage and drainage

(For implantation of osteochondral graft for treatment of articular surface defect, see 27412, 27415, 29866, 29867)

29873 with lateral release

(For open lateral release, use 27425)

29874 for removal of loose body or foreign body (eg, osteochondritis dissecans fragmentation, chondral fragmentation)

29875 synovectomy, limited (eg, plica or shelf resection) (separate procedure)

29876 synovectomy, major, two or more compartments (eg, medial or lateral)

29877 debridement/shaving of articular cartilage (chondroplasty)

29879 abrasion arthroplasty (includes chondroplasty where necessary) or multiple drilling or microfracture

29880 with meniscectomy (medial AND lateral, including any meniscal shaving)

29881 with meniscectomy (medial OR lateral, including any meniscal shaving)

29882 with meniscus repair (medial OR lateral)

29883 with meniscus repair (medial AND lateral)

(For meniscal transplantation, medial or lateral, knee, use 29868)

29884 with lysis of adhesions, with or without manipulation (separate procedure)

29885 drilling for osteochondritis dissecans with bone grafting, with or without internal fixation (including debridement of base of lesion)

29886 drilling for intact osteochondritis dissecans lesion

29887 drilling for intact osteochondritis dissecans lesion with internal fixation

29888 Arthroscopically aided anterior cruciate ligament repair/augmentation or reconstruction

29889 Arthroscopically aided posterior cruciate ligament repair/augmentation or reconstruction

(Procedures 29888 and 29889 should not be used with reconstruction procedures 27427-27429)

29891 Arthroscopy, ankle, surgical, excision of osteochondral defect of talus and/or tibia, including drilling of the defect

29892 Arthroscopically aided repair of large osteochondritis dissecans lesion, talar dome fracture, or tibial plafond fracture, with or without internal fixation (includes arthroscopy)

29893 Endoscopic plantar fasciotomy

29894 Arthroscopy, ankle (tibiotalar and fibulotalar joints), surgical; with removal of loose body or foreign body

29895 synovectomy, partial

29897 debridement, limited

29898 debridement, extensive

29899 with ankle arthrodesis

(For open ankle arthrodesis, use 27870)

29900 Arthroscopy, metacarpophalangeal joint, diagnostic, includes synovial biopsy

(Do not report 29900 with 29901, 29902)

29901 Arthroscopy, metacarpophalangeal joint, surgical; with debridement

29902 with reduction of displaced ulnar collateral ligament (eg, Stenar lesion)

29999 Unlisted procedure, arthroscopy

Respiratory System

Nose

Incision

30000   Drainage abscess or hematoma, nasal, internal approach

(For external approach, see 10060, 10140)

30020   Drainage abscess or hematoma, nasal septum

(For lateral rhinotomy, see specific application (eg, 30118, 30320))

Excision

30100   Biopsy, intranasal

(For biopsy skin of nose, see 11100, 11101)

30110   Excision, nasal polyp(s), simple

(30110 would normally be completed in an office setting)

(To report bilateral procedure, use 30110 with modifier 50)

30115   Excision, nasal polyp(s), extensive

(30115 would normally require the facilities available in a hospital setting)

(To report bilateral procedure, use 30115 with modifier 50)

30117   Excision or destruction (eg, laser), intranasal lesion; internal approach

30118   external approach (lateral rhinotomy)

30120   Excision or surgical planing of skin of nose for rhinophyma

30124   Excision dermoid cyst, nose; simple, skin, subcutaneous

30125   complex, under bone or cartilage

▲ **30130**   Excision inferior turbinate, partial or complete, any method

▶(For excision of superior or middle turbinate, use 30999)◀

▲ **30140**   Submucous resection inferior turbinate, partial or complete, any method

▶(Do not report 30130 or 30140 in conjunction with 30801, 30802, 30930)◀

▶(For submucous resection of superior or middle turbinate, use 30999)◀

▶(For endoscopic resection of concha bullosa of middle turbinate, use 31240)◀

(For submucous resection of nasal septum, use 30520)

(For reduction of turbinates, use 30140 with modifier 52)

30150   Rhinectomy; partial

30160   total

(For closure and/or reconstruction, primary or delayed, see **Integumentary System,** 13150-13160, 14060-14300, 15120, 15121, 15260, 15261, 15760, 20900-20912)

Introduction

30200   Injection into turbinate(s), therapeutic

30210   Displacement therapy (Proetz type)

30220   Insertion, nasal septal prosthesis (button)

Removal of Foreign Body

30300   Removal foreign body, intranasal; office type procedure

30310   requiring general anesthesia

30320   by lateral rhinotomy

Repair

(For obtaining tissues for graft, see 20900-20926, 21210)

30400   Rhinoplasty, primary; lateral and alar cartilages and/or elevation of nasal tip

(For columellar reconstruction, see 13150 et seq)

30410   complete, external parts including bony pyramid, lateral and alar cartilages, and/or elevation of nasal tip

30420   including major septal repair

30430   Rhinoplasty, secondary; minor revision (small amount of nasal tip work)

30435   intermediate revision (bony work with osteotomies)

30450   major revision (nasal tip work and osteotomies)

30460   Rhinoplasty for nasal deformity secondary to congenital cleft lip and/or palate, including columellar lengthening; tip only

30462   tip, septum, osteotomies

30465   Repair of nasal vestibular stenosis (eg, spreader grafting, lateral nasal wall reconstruction)

(30465 excludes obtaining graft. For graft procedure, see 20900-20926, 21210)

(30465 is used to report a bilateral procedure. For unilateral procedure, use modifier 52)

30520   Septoplasty or submucous resection, with or without cartilage scoring, contouring or replacement with graft

(For submucous resection of turbinates, use 30140)

Surgery: Respiratory System

Surgery: Respiratory System

30540   Repair choanal atresia; intranasal

30545   transpalatine

(Do not report modifier 63 in conjunction with 30540, 30545)

30560   Lysis intranasal synechia

30580   Repair fistula; oromaxillary (combine with 31030 if antrotomy is included)

30600   oronasal

30620   Septal or other intranasal dermatoplasty (does not include obtaining graft)

30630   Repair nasal septal perforations

Destruction

▲ 30801   Cautery and/or ablation, mucosa of inferior turbinates, unilateral or bilateral, any method; superficial

►(For cautery and ablation of superior or middle turbinates, use 30999)◄

30802   intramural

►(Do not report 30801, 30802, 30930 in conjunction with 30130 or 30140)◄

►(For cautery performed for control of nasal hemorrhage, see 30901-30906)◄

Other Procedures

30901   Control nasal hemorrhage, anterior, simple (limited cautery and/or packing) any method

(To report bilateral procedure, use 30901 with modifier 50)

30903   Control nasal hemorrhage, anterior, complex (extensive cautery and/or packing) any method

(To report bilateral procedure, use 30903 with modifier 50)

30905   Control nasal hemorrhage, posterior, with posterior nasal packs and/or cautery, any method; initial

30906   subsequent

30915   Ligation arteries; ethmoidal

30920   internal maxillary artery, transantral

(For ligation external carotid artery, use 37600)

▲ 30930   Fracture nasal inferior turbinate(s), therapeutic

►(Do not report 30801, 30802, 30930 in conjunction with 30130 or 30140)◄

►(For fracture of superior or middle turbinate(s), use 30999)◄

30999   Unlisted procedure, nose

Accessory Sinuses

Incision

31000   Lavage by cannulation; maxillary sinus (antrum puncture or natural ostium)

(To report bilateral procedure, use 31000 with modifier 50)

31002   sphenoid sinus

31020   Sinusotomy, maxillary (antrotomy); intranasal

(To report bilateral procedure, use 31020 with modifier 50)

31030   radical (Caldwell-Luc) without removal of antrochoanal polyps

(To report bilateral procedure, use 31030 with modifier 50)

31032   radical (Caldwell-Luc) with removal of antrochoanal polyps

(To report bilateral procedure, use 31032 with modifier 50)

31040   Pterygomaxillary fossa surgery, any approach

(For transantral ligation of internal maxillary artery, use 30920)

31050   Sinusotomy, sphenoid, with or without biopsy;

31051   with mucosal stripping or removal of polyp(s)

31070   Sinusotomy frontal; external, simple (trephine operation)

(For frontal intranasal sinusotomy, use 31276)

31075   transorbital, unilateral (for mucocele or osteoma, Lynch type)

31080   obliterative without osteoplastic flap, brow incision (includes ablation)

31081   obliterative, without osteoplastic flap, coronal incision (includes ablation)

31084   obliterative, with osteoplastic flap, brow incision

31085   obliterative, with osteoplastic flap, coronal incision

31086   nonobliterative, with osteoplastic flap, brow incision

31087   nonobliterative, with osteoplastic flap, coronal incision

31090   Sinusotomy, unilateral, three or more paranasal sinuses (frontal, maxillary, ethmoid, sphenoid)

Excision

31200   Ethmoidectomy; intranasal, anterior

31201   intranasal, total

31205   extranasal, total

31225 Maxillectomy; without orbital exenteration

31230   with orbital exenteration (en bloc)

(For orbital exenteration only, see 65110 et seq)

(For skin grafts, see 15120 et seq)

Endoscopy

A surgical sinus endoscopy includes a sinusotomy (when appropriate) and diagnostic endoscopy.

Codes 31231-31294 are used to report unilateral procedures unless otherwise specified.

The codes 31231-31235 for diagnostic evaluation refer to employing a nasal/sinus endoscope to inspect the interior of the nasal cavity and the middle and superior meatus, the turbinates, and the spheno-ethmoid recess. Any time a diagnostic evaluation is performed all these areas would be inspected and a separate code is not reported for each area.

31231 Nasal endoscopy, diagnostic, unilateral or bilateral (separate procedure)

31233 Nasal/sinus endoscopy, diagnostic with maxillary sinusoscopy (via inferior meatus or canine fossa puncture)

31235 Nasal/sinus endoscopy, diagnostic with sphenoid sinusoscopy (via puncture of sphenoidal face or cannulation of ostium)

31237 Nasal/sinus endoscopy, surgical; with biopsy, polypectomy or debridement (separate procedure)

31238   with control of nasal hemorrhage

31239   with dacryocystorhinostomy

31240   with concha bullosa resection

(For endoscopic osteomeatal complex (OMC) resection with antrostomy and/or anterior ethmoidectomy, with or without removal of polyp(s), use 31254 and 31256)

(For endoscopic osteomeatal complex (OMC) resection with antrostomy, removal of antral mucosal disease, and/or anterior ethmoidectomy, with or without removal of polyp(s), use 31254 and 31267)

(For endoscopic frontal sinus exploration, osteomeatal complex (OMC) resection and/or anterior ethmoidectomy, with or without removal of polyp(s), use 31254 and 31276)

(For endoscopic frontal sinus exploration, osteomeatal complex (OMC) resection, antrostomy, and/or anterior ethmoidectomy, with or without removal of polyp(s), use 31254, 31256, and 31276)

(For endoscopic nasal diagnostic endoscopy, see 31231-31235)

(For endoscopic osteomeatal complex (OMC) resection, frontal sinus exploration, antrostomy, removal of antral mucosal disease, and/or anterior ethmoidectomy, with or without removal of polyp(s), use 31254, 31267, and 31276)

31254 Nasal/sinus endoscopy, surgical; with ethmoidectomy, partial (anterior)

31255   with ethmoidectomy, total (anterior and posterior)

31256 Nasal/sinus endoscopy, surgical, with maxillary antrostomy;

(For endoscopic anterior and posterior ethmoidectomy (APE) and antrostomy, with or without removal of polyp(s), use 31255 and 31256)

(For endoscopic anterior and posterior ethmoidectomy (APE), antrostomy and removal of antral mucosal disease, with or without removal of polyp(s), use 31255 and 31267)

(For endoscopic anterior and posterior ethmoidectomy (APE), and frontal sinus exploration, with or without removal of polyp(s), use 31255 and 31276)

31267   with removal of tissue from maxillary sinus

(For endoscopic anterior and posterior ethmoidectomy (APE), and frontal sinus exploration and antrostomy, with or without removal of polyp(s), use 31255, 31256, and 31276)

(For endoscopic anterior and posterior ethmoidectomy (APE), frontal sinus exploration, antrostomy, and removal of antral mucosal disease, with or without removal of polyp(s), use 31255, 31267, and 31276)

31276 Nasal/sinus endoscopy, surgical with frontal sinus exploration, with or without removal of tissue from frontal sinus

(For endoscopic anterior and posterior ethmoidectomy and sphenoidotomy (APS), with or without removal of polyp(s), use 31255, 31287 or 31288)

(For endoscopic anterior and posterior ethmoidectomy and sphenoidotomy (APS), and antrostomy, with or without removal of polyp(s), use 31255, 31256, and 31287 or 31288)

(For endoscopic anterior and posterior ethmoidectomy and sphenoidotomy (APS), antrostomy and removal of antral mucosal disease, with or without removal of polyp(s), use 31255, 31267, and 31287 or 31288)

(For endoscopic anterior and posterior ethmoidectomy and sphenoidotomy (APS), and frontal sinus exploration with or without removal of polyp(s), use 31255, 31287 or 31288, and 31276)

(For endoscopic anterior and posterior ethmoidectomy and sphenoidotomy (APS), with or without removal of polyp(s), with frontal sinus exploration and antrostomy, use 31255, 31256, 31287 or 31288, and 31276)

(For unilateral endoscopy of two or more sinuses, see 31231-31235)

(For endoscopic anterior and posterior ethmoidectomy and sphenoidotomy (APS), frontal sinus exploration, antrostomy and removal of antral mucosal disease, with or without removal of polyp(s), see 31255, 31267, 31287 or 31288 and 31276)

Surgery: Respiratory System

31287	Nasal/sinus endoscopy, surgical, with sphenoidotomy;
31288	with removal of tissue from the sphenoid sinus
31290	Nasal/sinus endoscopy, surgical, with repair of cerebrospinal fluid leak; ethmoid region
31291	sphenoid region
31292	Nasal/sinus endoscopy, surgical; with medial or inferior orbital wall decompression
31293	with medial orbital wall and inferior orbital wall decompression
31294	with optic nerve decompression

Other Procedures

(For hypophysectomy, transantral or transeptal approach, use 61548)

(For transcranial hypophysectomy, use 61546)

31299	Unlisted procedure, accessory sinuses

Larynx

Excision

31300	Laryngotomy (thyrotomy, laryngofissure); with removal of tumor or laryngocele, cordectomy
31320	diagnostic
31360	Laryngectomy; total, without radical neck dissection
31365	total, with radical neck dissection
31367	subtotal supraglottic, without radical neck dissection
31368	subtotal supraglottic, with radical neck dissection
31370	Partial laryngectomy (hemilaryngectomy); horizontal
31375	laterovertical
31380	anterovertical
31382	antero-latero-vertical
31390	Pharyngolaryngectomy, with radical neck dissection; without reconstruction
31395	with reconstruction
31400	Arytenoidectomy or arytenoidopexy, external approach

(For endoscopic arytenoidectomy, use 31560)

31420	Epiglottidectomy

Introduction

⊘ 31500	Intubation, endotracheal, emergency procedure

(For injection procedure for bronchography, see 31656, 31708, 31710)

31502	Tracheotomy tube change prior to establishment of fistula tract

Endoscopy

▶For endoscopic procedures, code appropriate endoscopy of each anatomic site examined. If using operating microscope, telescope, or both, use the applicable code only once per operative session.◀

31505	Laryngoscopy, indirect; diagnostic (separate procedure)
31510	with biopsy
31511	with removal of foreign body
31512	with removal of lesion
31513	with vocal cord injection
31515	Laryngoscopy direct, with or without tracheoscopy; for aspiration
31520	diagnostic, newborn

(Do not report modifier 63 in conjunction with 31520)

31525	diagnostic, except newborn
▲ 31526	diagnostic, with operating microscope or telescope

(Do not report code 69990 in addition to code 31526)

31527	with insertion of obturator
31528	with dilation, initial
31529	with dilation, subsequent
31530	Laryngoscopy, direct, operative, with foreign body removal;
▲ 31531	with operating microscope or telescope

(Do not report code 69990 in addition to code 31531)

31535	Laryngoscopy, direct, operative, with biopsy;
▲ 31536	with operating microscope or telescope

(Do not report code 69990 in addition to code 31536)

31540	Laryngoscopy, direct, operative, with excision of tumor and/or stripping of vocal cords or epiglottis;
▲ 31541	with operating microscope or telescope

(Do not report code 69990 in addition to code 31541)

31545	Laryngoscopy, direct, operative, with operating microscope or telescope, with submucosal removal of non-neoplastic lesion(s) of vocal cord; reconstruction with local tissue flap(s)
31546	reconstruction with graft(s) (includes obtaining autograft)

(Do not report 31546 in addition to 20926 for graft harvest)

(For reconstruction of vocal cord with allograft, use 31599)

(Do not report 31545 or 31546 in conjunction with 31540, 31541, 69990)

31560   Laryngoscopy, direct, operative, with arytenoidectomy;

▲ 31561   with operating microscope or telescope

        (Do not report code 69990 in addition to code 31561)

31570   Laryngoscopy, direct, with injection into vocal cord(s), therapeutic;

▲ 31571   with operating microscope or telescope

        (Do not report code 69990 in addition to code 31571)

31575   Laryngoscopy, flexible fiberoptic; diagnostic

31576   with biopsy

31577   with removal of foreign body

31578   with removal of lesion

        (To report flexible fiberoptic endoscopic evaluation of swallowing, see 92612-92613)

        (To report flexible fiberoptic endoscopic evaluation with sensory testing, see 92614-92615)

        (To report flexible fiberoptic endoscopic evaluation of swallowing with sensory testing, see 92616-92617)

        (For flexible fiberoptic laryngoscopy as part of flexible fiberoptic endoscopic evaluation of swallowing and/or laryngeal sensory testing by cine or video recording, see 92612-92617)

31579   Laryngoscopy, flexible or rigid fiberoptic, with stroboscopy

Repair

31580   Laryngoplasty; for laryngeal web, two stage, with keel insertion and removal

31582   for laryngeal stenosis, with graft or core mold, including tracheotomy

31584   with open reduction of fracture

        ▶(31585 and 31586 have been deleted. To report, use the appropriate Evaluation and Management codes)◀

31587   Laryngoplasty, cricoid split

31588   Laryngoplasty, not otherwise specified (eg, for burns, reconstruction after partial laryngectomy)

31590   Laryngeal reinnervation by neuromuscular pedicle

Destruction

31595   Section recurrent laryngeal nerve, therapeutic (separate procedure), unilateral

Other Procedures

31599   Unlisted procedure, larynx

Trachea and Bronchi

Incision

31600   Tracheostomy, planned (separate procedure);

31601   under two years

31603   Tracheostomy, emergency procedure; transtracheal

31605   cricothyroid membrane

31610   Tracheostomy, fenestration procedure with skin flaps

        (For endotracheal intubation, use 31500)

        (For tracheal aspiration under direct vision, use 31515)

31611   Construction of tracheoesophageal fistula and subsequent insertion of an alaryngeal speech prosthesis (eg, voice button, Blom-Singer prosthesis)

31612   Tracheal puncture, percutaneous with transtracheal aspiration and/or injection

31613   Tracheostoma revision; simple, without flap rotation

31614   complex, with flap rotation

Endoscopy

For endoscopy procedures, code appropriate endoscopy of each anatomic site examined. Surgical bronchoscopy always includes diagnostic bronchoscopy when performed by the same physician. Codes 31622-31646 include fluoroscopic guidance, when performed.

        (For tracheoscopy, see laryngoscopy codes 31515-31578)

⊙ 31615   Tracheobronchoscopy through established tracheostomy incision

⊙✚ 31620   Endobronchial ultrasound (EBUS) during bronchoscopic diagnostic or therapeutic intervention(s) (List separately in addition to code for primary procedure(s))

        ▶(Use 31620 in conjunction with 31622-31646)◀

⊙ 31622   Bronchoscopy, rigid or flexible, with or without fluoroscopic guidance; diagnostic, with or without cell washing (separate procedure)

⊙ 31623   with brushing or protected brushings

⊙ 31624   with bronchial alveolar lavage

⊙ 31625   with bronchial or endobronchial biopsy(s), single or multiple sites

⊙ 31628   with transbronchial lung biopsy(s), single lobe

        (31628 should be reported only once regardless of how many transbronchial lung biopsies are performed in a lobe)

        (To report transbronchial lung biopsies performed on additional lobe, use 31632)

Surgery: Respiratory System

⊙ **31629**   with transbronchial needle aspiration biopsy(s), trachea, main stem and/or lobar bronchus(i)

(31629 should be reported only once for upper airway biopsies regardless of how many transbronchial needle aspiration biopsies are performed in the upper airway or in a lobe)

(To report transbronchial needle aspiration biopsies performed on additional lobe(s), use 31633)

31630   with tracheal/bronchial dilation or closed reduction of fracture

31631   with placement of tracheal stent(s) (includes tracheal/bronchial dilation as required)

(For placement of bronchial stent, see 31636, 31637)

(For revision of tracheal/bronchial stent, use 31638)

+ **31632**   with transbronchial lung biopsy(s), each additional lobe (List separately in addition to code for primary procedure)

(Use 31632 in conjunction with 31628)

(31632 should be reported only once regardless of how many transbronchial lung biopsies are performed in a lobe)

+ **31633**   with transbronchial needle aspiration biopsy(s), each additional lobe (List separately in addition to code for primary procedure)

(Use 31633 in conjunction with 31629)

(31633 should be reported only once regardless of how many transbronchial needle aspiration biopsies are performed in the trachea or the additional lobe)

⊙ **31635**   with removal of foreign body

31636   with placement of bronchial stent(s) (includes tracheal/bronchial dilation as required), initial bronchus

+ **31637**   each additional major bronchus stented (List separately in addition to code for primary procedure)

(Use 31637 in conjunction with 31636)

31638   with revision of tracheal or bronchial stent inserted at previous session (includes tracheal/bronchial dilation as required)

31640   with excision of tumor

31641   Bronchoscopy, (rigid or flexible); with destruction of tumor or relief of stenosis by any method other than excision (eg, laser therapy, cryotherapy)

(For bronchoscopic photodynamic therapy, report 31641 in addition to 96570, 96571 as appropriate)

31643   with placement of catheter(s) for intracavitary radioelement application

(For intracavitary radioelement application, see 77761-77763, 77781-77784)

⊙ **31645**   with therapeutic aspiration of tracheobronchial tree, initial (eg, drainage of lung abscess)

⊙ **31646**   with therapeutic aspiration of tracheobronchial tree, subsequent

(For catheter aspiration of tracheobronchial tree at bedside, use 31725)

⊙ **31656**   with injection of contrast material for segmental bronchography (fiberscope only)

(For radiological supervision and interpretation, see 71040, 71060)

Introduction

(For endotracheal intubation, use 31500)

(For tracheal aspiration under direct vision, see 31515)

31700   Catheterization, transglottic (separate procedure)

31708   Instillation of contrast material for laryngography or bronchography, without catheterization

(For radiological supervision and interpretation, see 70373, 71040, 71060)

31710   Catheterization for bronchography, with or without instillation of contrast material

(For bronchoscopic catheterization for bronchography, fiberscope only, use 31656)

(For radiological supervision and interpretation, see 71040, 71060)

31715   Transtracheal injection for bronchography

(For radiological supervision and interpretation, see 71040, 71060)

(For prolonged services, see 99354-99360)

31717   Catheterization with bronchial brush biopsy

31720   Catheter aspiration (separate procedure); nasotracheal

⊙ **31725**   tracheobronchial with fiberscope, bedside

31730   Transtracheal (percutaneous) introduction of needle wire dilator/stent or indwelling tube for oxygen therapy

Repair

31750   Tracheoplasty; cervical

31755   tracheopharyngeal fistulization, each stage

31760   intrathoracic

31766   Carinal reconstruction

31770   Bronchoplasty; graft repair

31775   excision stenosis and anastomosis

(For lobectomy and bronchoplasty, use 32501)

31780   Excision tracheal stenosis and anastomosis; cervical

31781   cervicothoracic

Surgery: Respiratory System (side tab)

31785   Excision of tracheal tumor or carcinoma; cervical

31786   thoracic

31800   Suture of tracheal wound or injury; cervical

31805   intrathoracic

31820   Surgical closure tracheostomy or fistula; without plastic repair

31825   with plastic repair

         (For repair tracheoesophageal fistula, see 43305, 43312)

31830   Revision of tracheostomy scar

Other Procedures

31899   Unlisted procedure, trachea, bronchi

Lungs and Pleura

Incision

⊘ 32000   Thoracentesis, puncture of pleural cavity for aspiration, initial or subsequent

         (If imaging guidance is performed, see 76003, 76360, 76942)

         (For total lung lavage, use 32997)

⊘ 32002   Thoracentesis with insertion of tube with or without water seal (eg, for pneumothorax) (separate procedure)

         ▶(Do not report 32002 in conjunction with 19260, 19271, 19272, 32503, 32504)◀

         (If imaging guidance is performed, see 76003, 76360, 76942)

32005   Chemical pleurodesis (eg, for recurrent or persistent pneumothorax)

⊙ 32019   Insertion of indwelling tunneled pleural catheter with cuff

         (Do not report 32019 in conjunction with 32000-32005, 32020, 36000, 36410, 62318, 62319, 64450, 64470, 64475)

         (If imaging guidance is performed, use 75989)

⊙⊘ 32020   Tube thoracostomy with or without water seal (eg, for abscess, hemothorax, empyema) (separate procedure)

         ▶(Do not report 32020 in conjunction with 19260, 19271, 19272, 32503, 32504)◀

         (If imaging guidance is performed, use 75989)

32035   Thoracostomy; with rib resection for empyema

32036   with open flap drainage for empyema

32095   Thoracotomy, limited, for biopsy of lung or pleura

         (To report wound exploration due to penetrating trauma without thoractomy, use 20102)

32100   Thoracotomy, major; with exploration and biopsy

         ▶(Do not report 32100 in conjunction with 19260, 19271, 19272, 32503, 32504)◀

32110   with control of traumatic hemorrhage and/or repair of lung tear

32120   for postoperative complications

32124   with open intrapleural pneumonolysis

32140   with cyst(s) removal, with or without a pleural procedure

32141   with excision-plication of bullae, with or without any pleural procedure

         (For lung volume reduction, use 32491)

32150   with removal of intrapleural foreign body or fibrin deposit

32151   with removal of intrapulmonary foreign body

32160   with cardiac massage

         ▶(For segmental or other resections of lung, see 32480-32504)◀

32200   Pneumonostomy; with open drainage of abscess or cyst

⊙ 32201   with percutaneous drainage of abscess or cyst

         (For radiological supervision and interpretation, use 75989)

32215   Pleural scarification for repeat pneumothorax

32220   Decortication, pulmonary (separate procedure); total

32225   partial

Excision

32310   Pleurectomy, parietal (separate procedure)

32320   Decortication and parietal pleurectomy

32400   Biopsy, pleura; percutaneous needle

         (If imaging guidance is performed, see 76003, 76360, 76393, 76942)

         (For fine needle aspiration, use 10021 or 10022)

         (For evaluation of fine needle aspirate, see 88172, 88173)

32402   open

32405   Biopsy, lung or mediastinum, percutaneous needle

         (For radiological supervision and interpretation, see 76003, 76360, 76393, 76942)

         (For fine needle aspiration, use 10022)

         (For evaluation of fine needle aspirate, see 88172, 88173)

32420   Pneumocentesis, puncture of lung for aspiration

Surgery: Respiratory System

Surgery: Respiratory System

32440 Removal of lung, total pneumonectomy;

32442 with resection of segment of trachea followed by broncho-tracheal anastomosis (sleeve pneumonectomy)

32445 extrapleural

(For extrapleural pneumonectomy, with empyemectomy, use 32445 and 32540)

▶(If lung resection is performed with chest wall tumor resection, report the appropriate chest wall tumor resection code, 19260-19272, in addition to lung resection code 32440-32445)◀

32480 Removal of lung, other than total pneumonectomy; single lobe (lobectomy)

32482 two lobes (bilobectomy)

32484 single segment (segmentectomy)

(For removal of lung with bronchoplasty, use 32501)

32486 with circumferential resection of segment of bronchus followed by broncho-bronchial anastomosis (sleeve lobectomy)

32488 all remaining lung following previous removal of a portion of lung (completion pneumonectomy)

(For total or segmental lobectomy, with concomitant decortication, use 32320 and the appropriate removal of lung code)

32491 excision-plication of emphysematous lung(s) (bullous or non-bullous) for lung volume reduction, sternal split or transthoracic approach, with or without any pleural procedure

32500 wedge resection, single or multiple

▶(If lung resection is performed with chest wall tumor resection, report the appropriate chest wall tumor resection code, 19260-19272, in addition to lung resection code 32480-32500)◀

+ 32501 Resection and repair of portion of bronchus (bronchoplasty) when performed at time of lobectomy or segmentectomy (List separately in addition to code for primary procedure)

(Use 32501 in conjunction with 32480, 32482, 32484)

(32501 is to be used when a portion of the bronchus to preserved lung is removed and requires plastic closure to preserve function of that preserved lung. It is not to be used for closure for the proximal end of a resected bronchus)

● **32503** Resection of apical lung tumor (eg, Pancoast tumor), including chest wall resection, rib(s) resection(s), neurovascular dissection, when performed; without chest wall reconstruction(s)

● **32504** with chest wall reconstruction

▶(Do not report 32503, 32504 in conjunction with 19260, 19271, 19272, 32002, 32020, 32100)◀

▶(32520, 32522, and 32525 have been deleted)◀

▶(For performance of lung resection in conjunction with chest wall resection, see 19260, 19271, 19272 and 32480-32500, 32503, 32504)◀

32540 Extrapleural enucleation of empyema (empyemectomy)

(For extrapleural enucleation of empyema (empyemectomy) with lobectomy, use 32540 and the appropriate removal of lung code)

Endoscopy

Surgical thoracoscopy always includes diagnostic thoracoscopy.

For endoscopic procedures, code appropriate endoscopy of each anatomic site examined.

32601 Thoracoscopy, diagnostic (separate procedure); lungs and pleural space, without biopsy

32602 lungs and pleural space, with biopsy

32603 pericardial sac, without biopsy

32604 pericardial sac, with biopsy

32605 mediastinal space, without biopsy

32606 mediastinal space, with biopsy

(Surgical thoracoscopy always includes diagnostic thoracoscopy)

32650 Thoracoscopy, surgical; with pleurodesis (eg, mechanical or chemical)

32651 with partial pulmonary decortication

32652 with total pulmonary decortication, including intrapleural pneumonolysis

32653 with removal of intrapleural foreign body or fibrin deposit

32654 with control of traumatic hemorrhage

32655 with excision-plication of bullae, including any pleural procedure

32656 with parietal pleurectomy

32657 with wedge resection of lung, single or multiple

32658 with removal of clot or foreign body from pericardial sac

32659 with creation of pericardial window or partial resection of pericardial sac for drainage

32660 with total pericardiectomy

32661 with excision of pericardial cyst, tumor, or mass

32662 with excision of mediastinal cyst, tumor, or mass

32663 with lobectomy, total or segmental

32664   with thoracic sympathectomy

32665   with esophagomyotomy (Heller type)

(For exploratory thoracoscopy, and exploratory thoracoscopy with biopsy, see 32601-32606)

Repair

32800   Repair lung hernia through chest wall

32810   Closure of chest wall following open flap drainage for empyema (Clagett type procedure)

32815   Open closure of major bronchial fistula

32820   Major reconstruction, chest wall (posttraumatic)

Lung Transplantation

Lung allotransplantation involves three distinct components of physician work:

1) ***Cadaver donor pneumonectomy(s)***, which include(s) harvesting the allograft and cold preservation of the allograft (perfusing with cold preservation solution and cold maintenance) (use 32850).

2) ***Backbench work***:

Preparation of a cadaver donor single lung allograft prior to transplantation, including dissection of the allograft from surrounding soft tissues to prepare the pulmonary venous/atrial cuff, pulmonary artery, and bronchus unilaterally (use 32855).

Preparation of a cadaver donor double lung allograft prior to transplantation, including dissection of the allograft from surrounding soft tissues to prepare the pulmonary venous/atrial cuff, pulmonary artery, and bronchus bilaterally (use 32856).

3) ***Recipient lung allotransplantation***, which includes transplantation of a single or double lung allograft and care of the recipient (see 32851-32854).

32850   Donor pneumonectomy(s) (including cold preservation), from cadaver donor

32851   Lung transplant, single; without cardiopulmonary bypass

32852   with cardiopulmonary bypass

32853   Lung transplant, double (bilateral sequential or en bloc); without cardiopulmonary bypass

32854   with cardiopulmonary bypass

32855   Backbench standard preparation of cadaver donor lung allograft prior to transplantation, including dissection of allograft from surrounding soft tissues to prepare pulmonary venous/atrial cuff, pulmonary artery, and bronchus; unilateral

32856   bilateral

(For repair or resection procedures on the donor lung, see 32491, 32500, 35216, or 35276)

Surgical Collapse Therapy; Thoracoplasty

▶(See also 32503, 32504)◀

32900   Resection of ribs, extrapleural, all stages

32905   Thoracoplasty, Schede type or extrapleural (all stages);

32906   with closure of bronchopleural fistula

(For open closure of major bronchial fistula, use 32815)

(For resection of first rib for thoracic outlet compression, see 21615, 21616)

32940   Pneumonolysis, extraperiosteal, including filling or packing procedures

32960   Pneumothorax, therapeutic, intrapleural injection of air

Other Procedures

32997   Total lung lavage (unilateral)

(For bronchoscopic bronchial alveolar lavage, use 31624)

32999   Unlisted procedure, lungs and pleura

Surgery: Respiratory System

Notes

Cardiovascular System

Selective vascular catheterizations should be coded to include introduction and all lesser order selective catheterizations used in the approach (eg, the description for a selective right middle cerebral artery catheterization includes the introduction and placement catheterization of the right common and internal carotid arteries).

Additional second and/or third order arterial catheterizations within the same family of arteries supplied by a single first order artery should be expressed by 36218 or 36248. Additional first order or higher catheterizations in vascular families supplied by a first order vessel different from a previously selected and coded family should be separately coded using the conventions described above.

(For monitoring, operation of pump and other nonsurgical services, see 99190-99192, 99291, 99292, 99354-99360)

(For other medical or laboratory related services, see appropriate section)

(For radiological supervision and interpretation, see 75600-75978)

Heart and Pericardium

Pericardium

⊙ **33010**   Pericardiocentesis; initial

(For radiological supervision and interpretation, use 76930)

⊙ **33011**   subsequent

(For radiological supervision and interpretation, use 76930)

33015   Tube pericardiostomy

33020   Pericardiotomy for removal of clot or foreign body (primary procedure)

33025   Creation of pericardial window or partial resection for drainage

33030   Pericardiectomy, subtotal or complete; without cardiopulmonary bypass

33031   with cardiopulmonary bypass

33050   Excision of pericardial cyst or tumor

Cardiac Tumor

33120   Excision of intracardiac tumor, resection with cardiopulmonary bypass

33130   Resection of external cardiac tumor

Transmyocardial Revascularization

33140   Transmyocardial laser revascularization, by thoracotomy; (separate procedure)

+ 33141   performed at the time of other open cardiac procedure(s) (List separately in addition to code for primary procedure)

(Use 33141 in conjunction with 33400-33496, 33510-33536, 33542)

Pacemaker or Pacing Cardioverter-Defibrillator

A pacemaker system includes a pulse generator containing electronics and a battery, and one or more electrodes (leads). Pulse generators are placed in a subcutaneous "pocket" created in either a subclavicular site or underneath the abdominal muscles just below the ribcage. Electrodes may be inserted through a vein (transvenous) or they may be placed on the surface of the heart (epicardial). The epicardial location of electrodes requires a thoracotomy for electrode insertion.

A single chamber pacemaker system includes a pulse generator and one electrode inserted in either the atrium or ventricle. A dual chamber pacemaker system includes a pulse generator and one electrode inserted in the right atrium and one electrode inserted in the right ventricle. In certain circumstances, an additional electrode may be required to achieve pacing of the left ventricle (bi-ventricular pacing). In this event, transvenous (cardiac vein) placement of the electrode should be separately reported using code 33224 or 33225.

Like a pacemaker system, a pacing cardioverter-defibrillator system includes a pulse generator and electrodes, although pacing cardioverter-defibrillators may require multiple leads, even when only a single chamber is being paced. A pacing cardioverter-defibrillator system may be inserted in a single chamber (pacing in the ventricle) or in dual chambers (pacing in atrium and ventricle). These devices use a combination of antitachycardia pacing, low energy cardioversion or defibrillating shocks to treat ventricular tachycardia or ventricular fibrillation.

Pacing cardioverter-defibrillator pulse generators may be implanted in a subcutaneous infraclavicular pocket or in an abdominal pocket. Removal of a pacing cardioverter-defibrillator pulse generator requires opening of the existing subcutaneous pocket and disconnection of the pulse generator from its electrode(s). A thoracotomy (or laparotomy in the case of abdominally placed pulse generators) is not required to remove the pulse generator.

The electrodes (leads) of a pacing cardioverter-defibrillator system are positioned in the heart via the venous system (transvenously), in most circumstances. In certain circumstances, an additional electrode may be required to achieve pacing of the left ventricle (bi-ventricular pacing). In this event, transvenous (cardiac vein) placement of the electrode should be separately reported using code 33224 or 33225.

Electrode positioning on the epicardial surface of the heart requires a thoracotomy (codes 33245-33246). Removal of electrode(s) may first be attempted by transvenous extraction (code 33244). However, if transvenous extraction is unsuccessful, a thoracotomy may be required to remove the electrodes (code 33243).

When the "battery" of a pacemaker or pacing cardioverter-defibrillator is changed, it is actually the pulse generator that is changed. Replacement of a pulse generator should be reported with a code for removal of the pulse generator and another code for insertion of a pulse generator.

Repositioning of a pacemaker electrode, pacing cardioverter-defibrillator electrode(s), or a left ventricular pacing electrode is reported using 33215 or 33226, as appropriate. Replacement of a pacemaker electrode, pacing cardioverter-defibrillator electrode(s), or a left ventricular pacing electrode is reported using 33206-33208, 33210-33213, or 33224, as appropriate.

(For electronic, telephonic analysis of internal pacemaker system, see 93731-93736)

(For radiological supervision and interpretation with insertion of pacemaker, use 71090)

33200   Insertion of permanent pacemaker with epicardial electrode(s); by thoracotomy

33201   by xiphoid approach

⊙ **33206**   Insertion or replacement of permanent pacemaker with transvenous electrode(s); atrial

⊙ **33207**   ventricular

⊙ **33208**   atrial and ventricular

(Codes 33206-33208 include subcutaneous insertion of the pulse generator and transvenous placement of electrode(s))

⊙ **33210**   Insertion or replacement of temporary transvenous single chamber cardiac electrode or pacemaker catheter (separate procedure)

⊙ **33211**   Insertion or replacement of temporary transvenous dual chamber pacing electrodes (separate procedure)

⊙ **33212**   Insertion or replacement of pacemaker pulse generator only; single chamber, atrial or ventricular

⊙ **33213**   dual chamber

⊙ **33214**   Upgrade of implanted pacemaker system, conversion of single chamber system to dual chamber system (includes removal of previously placed pulse generator, testing of existing lead, insertion of new lead, insertion of new pulse generator)

33215   Repositioning of previously implanted transvenous pacemaker or pacing cardioverter-defibrillator (right atrial or right ventricular) electrode

⊙ **33216**   Insertion of a transvenous electrode; single chamber (one electrode) permanent pacemaker or single chamber pacing cardioverter-defibrillator

⊙ **33217**   dual chamber (two electrodes) permanent pacemaker or dual chamber pacing cardioverter-defibrillator

(Do not report 33216-33217 in conjunction with 33214)

⊙ **33218**   Repair of single transvenous electrode for a single chamber, permanent pacemaker or single chamber pacing cardioverter-defibrillator

(For atrial or ventricular single chamber repair of pacemaker electrode(s) with replacement of pulse generator, see 33212 or 33213 and 33218 or 33220)

⊙ **33220**   Repair of two transvenous electrodes for a dual chamber permanent pacemaker or dual chamber pacing cardioverter-defibrillator

⊙ **33222**   Revision or relocation of skin pocket for pacemaker

⊙ **33223**   Revision of skin pocket for single or dual chamber pacing cardioverter-defibrillator

33224   Insertion of pacing electrode, cardiac venous system, for left ventricular pacing, with attachment to previously placed pacemaker or pacing cardioverter-defibrillator pulse generator (including revision of pocket, removal, insertion and/or replacement of generator)

+ **33225**   Insertion of pacing electrode, cardiac venous system, for left ventricular pacing, at time of insertion of pacing cardioverter-defibrillator or pacemaker pulse generator (including upgrade to dual chamber system) (List separately in addition to code for primary procedure)

(Use 33225 in conjunction with 33206, 33207, 33208, 33212, 33213, 33214, 33216, 33217, 33222, 33233, 33234, 33235, 33240, 33249)

33226   Repositioning of previously implanted cardiac venous system (left ventricular) electrode (including removal, insertion and/or replacement of generator)

⊙ **33233**   Removal of permanent pacemaker pulse generator

⊙ **33234**   Removal of transvenous pacemaker electrode(s); single lead system, atrial or ventricular

⊙ **33235**   dual lead system

33236   Removal of permanent epicardial pacemaker and electrodes by thoracotomy; single lead system, atrial or ventricular

33237   dual lead system

33238   Removal of permanent transvenous electrode(s) by thoracotomy

⊙ **33240**   Insertion of single or dual chamber pacing cardioverter-defibrillator pulse generator

⊙ **33241**   Subcutaneous removal of single or dual chamber pacing cardioverter-defibrillator pulse generator

(For removal of electrode(s) by thoracotomy, use 33243 in conjunction with 33241)

(For removal of electrode(s) by transvenous extraction, use 33244 in conjunction with 33241)

(For removal and reinsertion of a pacing cardioverter-defibrillator system (pulse generator and electrodes), report 33241 and 33243 or 33244 and 33249)

(For repair of implantable cardioverter-defibrillator pulse generator and/or leads, see 33218, 33220)

33243   Removal of single or dual chamber pacing cardioverter-defibrillator electrode(s); by thoracotomy

⊙ **33244**   by transvenous extraction

(For subcutaneous removal of the pulse generator, use 33241 in conjunction with 33243 or 33244)

33245   Insertion of epicardial single or dual chamber pacing cardioverter-defibrillator electrodes by thoracotomy;

33246   with insertion of pulse generator

(For insertion of implantable cardioverter-defibrillator lead(s), without thoracotomy, use 33216)

⊙ **33249**   Insertion or repositioning of electrode lead(s) for single or dual chamber pacing cardioverter-defibrillator and insertion of pulse generator

(For removal and reinsertion of a pacing cardioverter-defibrillator system (pulse generator and electrodes), report 33241 and 33243 or 33244 and 33249)

Electrophysiologic Operative Procedures

33250   Operative ablation of supraventricular arrhythmogenic focus or pathway (eg, Wolff-Parkinson-White, atrioventricular node re-entry), tract(s) and/or focus (foci); without cardiopulmonary bypass

33251   with cardiopulmonary bypass

33253   Operative incisions and reconstruction of atria for treatment of atrial fibrillation or atrial flutter (eg, maze procedure)

33261   Operative ablation of ventricular arrhythmogenic focus with cardiopulmonary bypass

Patient-Activated Event Recorder

33282   Implantation of patient-activated cardiac event recorder

(Initial implantation includes programming. For subsequent electronic analysis and/or reprogramming, use 93727)

33284   Removal of an implantable, patient-activated cardiac event recorder

Wounds of the Heart and Great Vessels

33300   Repair of cardiac wound; without bypass

33305   with cardiopulmonary bypass

33310   Cardiotomy, exploratory (includes removal of foreign body, atrial or ventricular thrombus); without bypass

33315   with cardiopulmonary bypass

(Do not report removal of thrombus (33310-33315) in conjunction with other cardiac procedures unless a separate incision in the heart is required to remove the atrial or ventricular thrombus)

(If removal of thrombus with cardiopulmonary bypass (33315) is reported in conjunction with 33120, 33130, 33420-33430, 33460-33468, 33496, 33542, 33545, 33641-33647, 33670, 33681, 33975-33980 which requires a separate heart incision, report 33315 with modifier 59)

33320   Suture repair of aorta or great vessels; without shunt or cardiopulmonary bypass

33321   with shunt bypass

33322   with cardiopulmonary bypass

33330   Insertion of graft, aorta or great vessels; without shunt, or cardiopulmonary bypass

33332   with shunt bypass

33335   with cardiopulmonary bypass

Cardiac Valves

(For multiple valve procedures, see 33400-33478 and add modifier 51 to the secondary valve procedure code)

Aortic Valve

33400   Valvuloplasty, aortic valve; open, with cardiopulmonary bypass

33401   open, with inflow occlusion

33403   using transventricular dilation, with cardiopulmonary bypass

(Do not report modifier 63 in conjunction with 33401, 33403)

33404   Construction of apical-aortic conduit

33405   Replacement, aortic valve, with cardiopulmonary bypass; with prosthetic valve other than homograft or stentless valve

33406   with allograft valve (freehand)

(For aortic valve valvotomy, (commissurotomy) with inflow occlusion, use 33401)

(For aortic valve valvotomy, (commissurotomy) with cardiopulmonary bypass, use 33403)

33410   with stentless tissue valve

Surgery: Cardiovascular System

33411 Replacement, aortic valve; with aortic annulus enlargement, noncoronary cusp

33412 with transventricular aortic annulus enlargement (Konno procedure)

33413 by translocation of autologous pulmonary valve with allograft replacement of pulmonary valve (Ross procedure)

33414 Repair of left ventricular outflow tract obstruction by patch enlargement of the outflow tract

33415 Resection or incision of subvalvular tissue for discrete subvalvular aortic stenosis

33416 Ventriculomyotomy (-myectomy) for idiopathic hypertrophic subaortic stenosis (eg, asymmetric septal hypertrophy)

33417 Aortoplasty (gusset) for supravalvular stenosis

Mitral Valve

33420 Valvotomy, mitral valve; closed heart

33422 open heart, with cardiopulmonary bypass

33425 Valvuloplasty, mitral valve, with cardiopulmonary bypass;

33426 with prosthetic ring

33427 radical reconstruction, with or without ring

33430 Replacement, mitral valve, with cardiopulmonary bypass

Tricuspid Valve

33460 Valvectomy, tricuspid valve, with cardiopulmonary bypass

33463 Valvuloplasty, tricuspid valve; without ring insertion

33464 with ring insertion

33465 Replacement, tricuspid valve, with cardiopulmonary bypass

33468 Tricuspid valve repositioning and plication for Ebstein anomaly

Pulmonary Valve

33470 Valvotomy, pulmonary valve, closed heart; transventricular

(Do not report modifier 63 in conjunction with 33470)

33471 via pulmonary artery

(To report percutaneous valvuloplasty of pulmonary valve, use 92990)

33472 Valvotomy, pulmonary valve, open heart; with inflow occlusion

(Do not report modifier 63 in conjunction with 33472)

33474 with cardiopulmonary bypass

33475 Replacement, pulmonary valve

33476 Right ventricular resection for infundibular stenosis, with or without commissurotomy

33478 Outflow tract augmentation (gusset), with or without commissurotomy or infundibular resection

▶(Use 33478 in conjunction with 33768 when a cavopulmonary anastomosis to a second superior vena cava is performed)◀

Other Valvular Procedures

33496 Repair of non-structural prosthetic valve dysfunction with cardiopulmonary bypass (separate procedure)

(For reoperation, use 33530 in addition to 33496)

Coronary Artery Anomalies

Basic procedures include endarterectomy or angioplasty.

33500 Repair of coronary arteriovenous or arteriocardiac chamber fistula; with cardiopulmonary bypass

33501 without cardiopulmonary bypass

▲ **33502** Repair of anomalous coronary artery from pulmonary artery origin; by ligation

33503 by graft, without cardiopulmonary bypass

(Do not report modifier 63 in conjunction with 33502, 33503)

33504 by graft, with cardiopulmonary bypass

33505 with construction of intrapulmonary artery tunnel (Takeuchi procedure)

33506 by translocation from pulmonary artery to aorta

(Do not report modifier 63 in conjunction with 33505, 33506)

● **33507** Repair of anomalous (eg, intramural) aortic origin of coronary artery by unroofing or translocation

Endoscopy

Surgical vascular endoscopy always includes diagnostic endoscopy.

✚ **33508** Endoscopy, surgical, including video-assisted harvest of vein(s) for coronary artery bypass procedure (List separately in addition to code for primary procedure)

(Use 33508 in conjunction with 33510-33523)

(For open harvest of upper extremity vein procedure, use 35500)

Venous Grafting Only for Coronary Artery Bypass

The following codes are used to report coronary artery bypass procedures using venous grafts only. These codes should NOT be used to report the performance of coronary artery bypass procedures using arterial grafts and venous grafts during the same procedure. See 33517-33523 and 33533-33536 for reporting combined arterial-venous grafts.

Procurement of the saphenous vein graft is included in the description of the work for 33510-33516 and should not be reported as a separate service or co-surgery. To report harvesting of an upper extremity vein, use 35500 in addition to the bypass procedure. To report harvesting of a femoropopliteal vein segment, report 35572 in addition to the bypass procedure. When surgical assistant performs graft procurement, add modifier 80 to 33510-33516.

33510   Coronary artery bypass, vein only; single coronary venous graft

33511   two coronary venous grafts

33512   three coronary venous grafts

33513   four coronary venous grafts

33514   five coronary venous grafts

33516   six or more coronary venous grafts

Combined Arterial-Venous Grafting for Coronary Bypass

The following codes are used to report coronary artery bypass procedures using venous grafts and arterial grafts during the same procedure. These codes may NOT be used alone.

To report combined arterial-venous grafts it is necessary to report two codes: 1) the appropriate combined arterial-venous graft code (33517-33523); and 2) the appropriate arterial graft code (33533-33536).

Procurement of the saphenous vein graft is included in the description of the work for 33517-33523 and should not be reported as a separate service or co-surgery. Procurement of the artery for grafting is included in the description of the work for 33533-33536 and should not be reported as a separate service or co-surgery, except when an upper extremity artery (eg, radial artery) is procured. To report harvesting of an upper extremity artery, use 35600 in addition to the bypass procedure. To report harvesting of an upper extremity vein, use 35500 in addition to the bypass procedure. To report harvesting of a femoropopliteal vein segment, report 35572 in addition to the bypass procedure. When surgical assistant performs arterial and/or venous graft procurement, add modifier 80 to 33517-33523, 33533-33536, as appropriate.

⊘ **33517**   Coronary artery bypass, using venous graft(s) and arterial graft(s); single vein graft (List separately in addition to code for arterial graft)

⊘ **33518**   two venous grafts (List separately in addition to code for arterial graft)

⊘ **33519**   three venous grafts (List separately in addition to code for arterial graft)

⊘ **33521**   four venous grafts (List separately in addition to code for arterial graft)

⊘ **33522**   five venous grafts (List separately in addition to code for arterial graft)

⊘ **33523**   six or more venous grafts (List separately in addition to code for arterial graft)

+ **33530**   Reoperation, coronary artery bypass procedure or valve procedure, more than one month after original operation (List separately in addition to code for primary procedure)

(Use 33530 in conjunction with 33400-33496; 33510-33536, 33863)

Arterial Grafting for Coronary Artery Bypass

The following codes are used to report coronary artery bypass procedures using either arterial grafts only or a combination of arterial-venous grafts. The codes include the use of the internal mammary artery, gastroepiploic artery, epigastric artery, radial artery, and arterial conduits procured from other sites.

To report combined arterial-venous grafts it is necessary to report two codes: 1) the appropriate arterial graft code (33533-33536); and 2) the appropriate combined arterial-venous graft code (33517-33523).

Procurement of the artery for grafting is included in the description of the work for 33533-33536 and should not be reported as a separate service or co-surgery, except when an upper extremity artery (eg, radial artery) is procured. To report harvesting of an upper extremity artery, use 35600 in addition to the bypass procedure. To report harvesting of an upper extremity vein, use 35500 in addition to the bypass procedure. To report harvesting of a femoropopliteal vein segment, report 35572 in addition to the bypass procedure. When surgical assistant performs arterial and/or venous graft procurement, add modifier 80 to 33517-33523, 33533-33536, as appropriate.

33533   Coronary artery bypass, using arterial graft(s); single arterial graft

33534   two coronary arterial grafts

33535   three coronary arterial grafts

33536   four or more coronary arterial grafts

33542   Myocardial resection (eg, ventricular aneurysmectomy)

33545   Repair of postinfarction ventricular septal defect, with or without myocardial resection

● **33548**   Surgical ventricular restoration procedure, includes prosthetic patch, when performed (eg, ventricular remodeling, SVR, SAVER, DOR procedures)

▶(Do not report 33548 in conjunction with 32020, 33210, 33211, 33310, 33315)◀

▶(For Batista procedure or pachopexy, use 33999)◀

Surgery: Cardiovascular System

Coronary Endarterectomy

+ 33572 Coronary endarterectomy, open, any method, of left anterior descending, circumflex, or right coronary artery performed in conjunction with coronary artery bypass graft procedure, each vessel (List separately in addition to primary procedure)

(Use 33572 in conjunction with 33510-33516, 33533-33536)

Single Ventricle and Other Complex Cardiac Anomalies

33600 Closure of atrioventricular valve (mitral or tricuspid) by suture or patch

33602 Closure of semilunar valve (aortic or pulmonary) by suture or patch

33606 Anastomosis of pulmonary artery to aorta (Damus-Kaye-Stansel procedure)

33608 Repair of complex cardiac anomaly other than pulmonary atresia with ventricular septal defect by construction or replacement of conduit from right or left ventricle to pulmonary artery

▶(For repair of pulmonary artery arborization anomalies by unifocalization, see 33925-33926)◀

33610 Repair of complex cardiac anomalies (eg, single ventricle with subaortic obstruction) by surgical enlargement of ventricular septal defect

(Do not report modifier 63 in conjunction with 33610)

33611 Repair of double outlet right ventricle with intraventricular tunnel repair;

(Do not report modifier 63 in conjunction with 33611)

33612   with repair of right ventricular outflow tract obstruction

33615 Repair of complex cardiac anomalies (eg, tricuspid atresia) by closure of atrial septal defect and anastomosis of atria or vena cava to pulmonary artery (simple Fontan procedure)

33617 Repair of complex cardiac anomalies (eg, single ventricle) by modified Fontan procedure

▶(Use 33617 in conjunction with 33768 when a cavopulmonary anastomosis to a second superior vena cava is performed)◀

33619 Repair of single ventricle with aortic outflow obstruction and aortic arch hypoplasia (hypoplastic left heart syndrome) (eg, Norwood procedure)

(Do not report modifier 63 in conjunction with 33619)

Septal Defect

33641 Repair atrial septal defect, secundum, with cardiopulmonary bypass, with or without patch

33645 Direct or patch closure, sinus venosus, with or without anomalous pulmonary venous drainage

33647 Repair of atrial septal defect and ventricular septal defect, with direct or patch closure

(Do not report modifier 63 in conjunction with 33647)

(For repair of tricuspid atresia (eg, Fontan, Gago procedures), use 33615)

33660 Repair of incomplete or partial atrioventricular canal (ostium primum atrial septal defect), with or without atrioventricular valve repair

33665 Repair of intermediate or transitional atrioventricular canal, with or without atrioventricular valve repair

33670 Repair of complete atrioventricular canal, with or without prosthetic valve

(Do not report modifier 63 in conjunction with 33670)

33681 Closure of ventricular septal defect, with or without patch;

33684   with pulmonary valvotomy or infundibular resection (acyanotic)

33688   with removal of pulmonary artery band, with or without gusset

33690 Banding of pulmonary artery

(Do not report modifier 63 in conjunction with 33690)

33692 Complete repair tetralogy of Fallot without pulmonary atresia;

33694   with transannular patch

(Do not report modifier 63 in conjunction with 33694)

(For ligation and takedown of a systemic-to-pulmonary artery shunt, performed in conjunction with a congenital heart procedure; see 33924)

33697 Complete repair tetralogy of Fallot with pulmonary atresia including construction of conduit from right ventricle to pulmonary artery and closure of ventricular septal defect

(For ligation and takedown of a systemic-to-pulmonary artery shunt, performed in conjunction with a congenital heart procedure; see 33924)

Sinus of Valsalva

33702 Repair sinus of Valsalva fistula, with cardiopulmonary bypass;

33710   with repair of ventricular septal defect

33720 Repair sinus of Valsalva aneurysm, with cardiopulmonary bypass

33722 Closure of aortico-left ventricular tunnel

Total Anomalous Pulmonary Venous Drainage

33730 Complete repair of anomalous venous return (supracardiac, intracardiac, or infracardiac types)

(Do not report modifier 63 in conjunction with 33730)

(For partial anomalous return, see atrial septal defect)

33732 Repair of cor triatriatum or supravalvular mitral ring by resection of left atrial membrane

(Do not report modifier 63 in conjunction with 33732)

Shunting Procedures

33735 Atrial septectomy or septostomy; closed heart (Blalock-Hanlon type operation)

33736   open heart with cardiopulmonary bypass

(Do not report modifier 63 in conjunction with 33735, 33736)

33737   open heart, with inflow occlusion

(For transvenous method cardiac catheterization balloon atrial septectomy or septostomy (Rashkind type), use 92992)

(For blade method cardiac catheterization atrial septectomy or septostomy (Sang-Park septostomy), use 92993)

33750 Shunt; subclavian to pulmonary artery (Blalock-Taussig type operation)

33755   ascending aorta to pulmonary artery (Waterston type operation)

33762   descending aorta to pulmonary artery (Potts-Smith type operation)

(Do not report modifier 63 in conjunction with 33750, 33755, 33762)

33764   central, with prosthetic graft

33766   superior vena cava to pulmonary artery for flow to one lung (classical Glenn procedure)

33767   superior vena cava to pulmonary artery for flow to both lungs (bidirectional Glenn procedure)

+● **33768** Anastomosis, cavopulmonary, second superior vena cava (List separately in addition to primary procedure)

▶(Use 33768 in conjunction with 33478, 33617, 33767)◀

▶(Do not report 33768 in conjunction with 32020, 33210, 33211)◀

Transposition of the Great Vessels

33770 Repair of transposition of the great arteries with ventricular septal defect and subpulmonary stenosis; without surgical enlargement of ventricular septal defect

33771   with surgical enlargement of ventricular septal defect

33774 Repair of transposition of the great arteries, atrial baffle procedure (eg, Mustard or Senning type) with cardiopulmonary bypass;

33775   with removal of pulmonary band

33776   with closure of ventricular septal defect

33777   with repair of subpulmonic obstruction

33778 Repair of transposition of the great arteries, aortic pulmonary artery reconstruction (eg, Jatene type);

(Do not report modifier 63 in conjunction with 33778)

33779   with removal of pulmonary band

33780   with closure of ventricular septal defect

33781   with repair of subpulmonic obstruction

Truncus Arteriosus

33786 Total repair, truncus arteriosus (Rastelli type operation)

(Do not report modifier 63 in conjunction with 33786)

33788 Reimplantation of an anomalous pulmonary artery

(For pulmonary artery band, use 33690)

Aortic Anomalies

33800 Aortic suspension (aortopexy) for tracheal decompression (eg, for tracheomalacia) (separate procedure)

33802 Division of aberrant vessel (vascular ring);

33803   with reanastomosis

33813 Obliteration of aortopulmonary septal defect; without cardiopulmonary bypass

33814   with cardiopulmonary bypass

33820 Repair of patent ductus arteriosus; by ligation

33822   by division, under 18 years

33824   by division, 18 years and older

33840 Excision of coarctation of aorta, with or without associated patent ductus arteriosus; with direct anastomosis

33845   with graft

33851   repair using either left subclavian artery or prosthetic material as gusset for enlargement

33852 Repair of hypoplastic or interrupted aortic arch using autogenous or prosthetic material; without cardiopulmonary bypass

33853   with cardiopulmonary bypass

(For repair of hypoplastic left heart syndrome (eg, Norwood type), via excision of coarctation of aorta, use 33619)

Surgery: Cardiovascular System

Thoracic Aortic Aneurysm

33860 Ascending aorta graft, with cardiopulmonary bypass, with or without valve suspension;

33861   with coronary reconstruction

33863   with aortic root replacement using composite prosthesis and coronary reconstruction

(For graft of ascending aorta, with cardiopulmonary bypass and valve replacement, with or without coronary implant or valve suspension; use 33860 or 33861 and 33405 or 33406)

33870 Transverse arch graft, with cardiopulmonary bypass

33875 Descending thoracic aorta graft, with or without bypass

33877 Repair of thoracoabdominal aortic aneurysm with graft, with or without cardiopulmonary bypass

►Endovascular Repair of Descending Thoracic Aorta◄

►Codes 33880-33891 represent a family of procedures to report placement of an endovascular graft for repair of the descending thoracic aorta. These codes include all device introduction, manipulation, positioning, and deployment. All balloon angioplasty and/or stent deployment within the target treatment zone for the endoprosthesis, either before or after endograft deployment, are not separately reportable. Open arterial exposure and associated closure of the arteriotomy sites (eg, 34812, 34820, 34833, 34834), introduction of guidewires and catheters (eg, 36140, 36200-36218), and extensive repair or replacement of an artery (eg, 35226, 35286) should be additionally reported. Transposition of subclavian artery to carotid, and carotid-carotid bypass performed in conjunction with endovascular repair of the descending thoracic aorta (eg, 33889, 33891) should be separately reported. The primary codes, 33880 and 33881, include placement of all distal extensions, if required, in the distal thoracic aorta, while proximal extensions, if needed, are reported separately.◄

►For fluoroscopic guidance in conjunction with endovascular repair of the thoracic aorta, see codes 75956-75959 as appropriate. Codes 75956 and 75957 include all angiography of the thoracic aorta and its branches for diagnostic imaging prior to deployment of the primary endovascular devices (including all routine components of modular devices), fluoroscopic guidance in the delivery of the endovascular components, and intraprocedural arterial angiography (eg, confirm position, detect endoleak, evaluate runoff). Code 75958 includes the analogous services for placement of each proximal thoracic endovascular extension. Code 75959 includes the analogous services for placement of a distal thoracic endovascular extension(s) placed during a procedure after the primary repair.◄

►Other interventional procedures performed at the time of endovascular repair of the descending thoracic aorta should be additionally reported (eg, innominate, carotid, subclavian, visceral, or iliac artery transluminal angioplasty or stenting, arterial embolization, intravascular ultrasound) when performed before or after deployment of the aortic prostheses.◄

● **33880** Endovascular repair of descending thoracic aorta (eg, aneurysm, pseudoaneurysm, dissection, penetrating ulcer, intramural hematoma, or traumatic disruption); involving coverage of left subclavian artery origin, initial endoprosthesis plus descending thoracic aortic extension(s), if required, to level of celiac artery origin

►(For radiological supervision and interpretation, use 75956 in conjunction with 33880)◄

● **33881**   not involving coverage of left subclavian artery origin, initial endoprosthesis plus descending thoracic aortic extension(s), if required, to level of celiac artery origin

►(For radiological supervision and interpretation, use 75957 in conjunction with 33881)◄

● **33883** Placement of proximal extension prosthesis for endovascular repair of descending thoracic aorta (eg, aneurysm, pseudoaneurysm, dissection, penetrating ulcer, intramural hematoma, or traumatic disruption); initial extension

►(For radiological supervision and interpretation, use 75958 in conjunction with 33883)◄

►(Do not report 33881, 33883 when extension placement converts repair to cover left subclavian origin. Use only 33880)◄

+● **33884**   each additional proximal extension (List separately in addition to code for primary procedure)

►(Use 33884 in conjunction with 33883)◄

►(For radiological supervision and interpretation, use 75958 in conjunction with 33884)◄

● **33886** Placement of distal extension prosthesis(s) delayed after endovascular repair of descending thoracic aorta

►(Do not report 33886 in conjunction with 33880, 33881)◄

►(Report 33886 once, regardless of number of modules deployed)◄

►(For radiological supervision and interpretation, use 75959 in conjunction with 33886)◄

● **33889** Open subclavian to carotid artery transposition performed in conjunction with endovascular repair of descending thoracic aorta, by neck incision, unilateral

►(Do not report 33889 in conjunction with 35694)◄

● **33891** Bypass graft, with other than vein, transcervical retropharyngeal carotid-carotid, performed in conjunction with endovascular repair of descending thoracic aorta, by neck incision

►(Do not report 33891 in conjunction with 35509, 35601)◄

Pulmonary Artery

33910   Pulmonary artery embolectomy; with cardiopulmonary bypass

33915   without cardiopulmonary bypass

33916   Pulmonary endarterectomy, with or without embolectomy, with cardiopulmonary bypass

33917   Repair of pulmonary artery stenosis by reconstruction with patch or graft

     ▶(33918, 33919 have been deleted. To report, see 33925, 33926)◀

33920   Repair of pulmonary atresia with ventricular septal defect, by construction or replacement of conduit from right or left ventricle to pulmonary artery

     (For repair of other complex cardiac anomalies by construction or replacement of right or left ventricle to pulmonary artery conduit, use 33608)

33922   Transection of pulmonary artery with cardiopulmonary bypass

     (Do not report modifier 63 in conjunction with 33922)

+ 33924   Ligation and takedown of a systemic-to-pulmonary artery shunt, performed in conjunction with a congenital heart procedure (List separately in addition to code for primary procedure)

     ▶(Use 33924 in conjunction with 33470-33475, 33600-33619, 33684-33688, 33692-33697, 33735-33767, 33770-33781, 33786, 33920-33922)◀

● 33925   Repair of pulmonary artery arborization anomalies by unifocalization; without cardiopulmonary bypass

● 33926   with cardiopulmonary bypass

     ▶(Do not report 33925, 33926 in conjunction with 33697)◀

Heart/Lung Transplantation

Heart with or without lung allotransplantation involves three distinct components of physician work:

1) *Cadaver donor cardiectomy with or without pneumonectomy*, which includes harvesting the allograft and cold preservation of the allograft (perfusing with cold preservation solution and cold maintenance) (see 33930, 33940).

2) *Backbench work*:

Preparation of a cadaver donor heart and lung allograft prior to transplantation, including dissection of the allograft from surrounding soft tissues to prepare the aorta, superior vena cava, inferior vena cava, and trachea for implantation (use 33933).

Preparation of a cadaver donor heart allograft prior to transplantation, including dissection of the allograft

from surrounding soft tissues to prepare aorta, superior vena cava, inferior vena cava, pulmonary artery, and left atrium for implantation (use 33944).

3) *Recipient heart with or without lung allotransplantation*, which includes transplantation of allograft and care of the recipient (see 33935, 33945).

     (For implantation of a total replacement heart system (artificial heart) with recipient cardiectomy or heart replacement system components, see Category III codes 0051T-0053T)

33930   Donor cardiectomy-pneumonectomy (including cold preservation)

33933   Backbench standard preparation of cadaver donor heart/lung allograft prior to transplantation, including dissection of allograft from surrounding soft tissues to prepare aorta, superior vena cava, inferior vena cava, and trachea for implantation

33935   Heart-lung transplant with recipient cardiectomy-pneumonectomy

33940   Donor cardiectomy (including cold preservation)

33944   Backbench standard preparation of cadaver donor heart allograft prior to transplantation, including dissection of allograft from surrounding soft tissues to prepare aorta, superior vena cava, inferior vena cava, pulmonary artery, and left atrium for implantation

     (For repair or resection procedures on the donor heart, see 33300, 33310, 33320, 33400, 33463, 33464, 33510, 33641, 35216, 35276 or 35685)

33945   Heart transplant, with or without recipient cardiectomy

Cardiac Assist

     (For percutaneous implantation of extracorporeal ventricular assist device or for removal of percutaneously implanted extracorporeal ventricular assist device, see Category III codes 0048T-0050T)

33960   Prolonged extracorporeal circulation for cardiopulmonary insufficiency; initial 24 hours

+ 33961   each additional 24 hours (List separately in addition to code for primary procedure)

     (Do not report modifier 63 in conjunction with 33960, 33961)

     (Use 33961 in conjunction with 33960)

     (For insertion of cannula for prolonged extracorporeal circulation, use 36822)

33967   Insertion of intra-aortic balloon assist device, percutaneous

33968   Removal of intra-aortic balloon assist device, percutaneous

33970   Insertion of intra-aortic balloon assist device through the femoral artery, open approach

Surgery: Cardiovascular System

Surgery: Cardiovascular System

33971 Removal of intra-aortic balloon assist device including repair of femoral artery, with or without graft

33973 Insertion of intra-aortic balloon assist device through the ascending aorta

33974 Removal of intra-aortic balloon assist device from the ascending aorta, including repair of the ascending aorta, with or without graft

33975 Insertion of ventricular assist device; extracorporeal, single ventricle

33976   extracorporeal, biventricular

33977 Removal of ventricular assist device; extracorporeal, single ventricle

33978   extracorporeal, biventricular

33979 Insertion of ventricular assist device, implantable intracorporeal, single ventricle

33980 Removal of ventricular assist device, implantable intracorporeal, single ventricle

Other Procedures

33999 Unlisted procedure, cardiac surgery

Arteries and Veins

Primary vascular procedure listings include establishing both inflow and outflow by whatever procedures necessary. Also included is that portion of the operative arteriogram performed by the surgeon, as indicated. Sympathectomy, when done, is included in the listed aortic procedures. For unlisted vascular procedure, use 37799.

Embolectomy/Thrombectomy

Arterial, With or Without Catheter

34001 Embolectomy or thrombectomy, with or without catheter; carotid, subclavian or innominate artery, by neck incision

34051 innominate, subclavian artery, by thoracic incision

34101 axillary, brachial, innominate, subclavian artery, by arm incision

34111 radial or ulnar artery, by arm incision

34151 renal, celiac, mesentery, aortoiliac artery, by abdominal incision

34201 femoropopliteal, aortoiliac artery, by leg incision

34203 popliteal-tibio-peroneal artery, by leg incision

Venous, Direct or With Catheter

34401 Thrombectomy, direct or with catheter; vena cava, iliac vein, by abdominal incision

34421 vena cava, iliac, femoropopliteal vein, by leg incision

34451 vena cava, iliac, femoropopliteal vein, by abdominal and leg incision

34471 subclavian vein, by neck incision

34490 axillary and subclavian vein, by arm incision

Venous Reconstruction

34501 Valvuloplasty, femoral vein

34502 Reconstruction of vena cava, any method

34510 Venous valve transposition, any vein donor

34520 Cross-over vein graft to venous system

34530 Saphenopopliteal vein anastomosis

Endovascular Repair of Abdominal Aortic Aneurysm

Codes 34800-34826 represent a family of component procedures to report placement of an endovascular graft for abdominal aortic aneurysm repair. These codes describe open femoral or iliac artery exposure, device manipulation and deployment, and closure of the arteriotomy sites. Balloon angioplasty and/or stent deployment within the target treatment zone for the endoprosthesis, either before or after endograft deployment, are not separately reportable. Introduction of guidewires and catheters should be reported separately (eg, 36200, 36245-36248, 36140). Extensive repair or replacement of an artery should be additionally reported (eg, 35226 or 35286).

For fluoroscopic guidance in conjunction with endovascular aneurysm repair, see code 75952 or 75953, as appropriate. Code 75952 includes angiography of the aorta and its branches for diagnostic imaging prior to deployment of the endovascular device (including all routine components of modular devices), fluoroscopic guidance in the delivery of the endovascular components, and intraprocedural arterial angiography (eg, confirm position, detect endoleak, evaluate runoff). Code 75953 includes the analogous services for placement of additional extension prostheses (not for routine components of modular devices).

Other interventional procedures performed at the time of endovascular abdominal aortic aneurysm repair should be additionally reported (eg, renal transluminal angioplasty, arterial embolization, intravascular ultrasound, balloon angioplasty or stenting of native artery(s) outside the endoprosthesis target zone, when done before or after deployment of graft).

34800 Endovascular repair of infrarenal abdominal aortic aneurysm or dissection; using aorto-aortic tube prosthesis

34802 using modular bifurcated prosthesis (one docking limb)

34803   using modular bifurcated prosthesis (two docking limbs)

(For endovascular repair of abdominal aortic aneurysm or dissection involving visceral vessels using a fenestrated modular bifurcated prosthesis (two docking limbs), use Category III codes 0078T, 0079T)

34804   using unibody bifurcated prosthesis

34805   using aorto-uniiliac or aorto-unifemoral prosthesis

+ 34808   Endovascular placement of iliac artery occlusion device (List separately in addition to code for primary procedure)

(Use 34808 in conjunction with 34800, 34805, 34813, 34825, 34826)

(For radiological supervision and interpretation, use 75952 in conjunction with 34800-34808)

(For open arterial exposure, report 34812, 34820, 34833, 34834 as appropriate, in addition to 34800-34808)

34812   Open femoral artery exposure for delivery of endovascular prosthesis, by groin incision, unilateral

(For bilateral procedure, use modifier 50)

+ 34813   Placement of femoral-femoral prosthetic graft during endovascular aortic aneurysm repair (List separately in addition to code for primary procedure)

(Use 34813 in conjunction with 34812)

(For femoral artery grafting, see 35521, 35533, 35546, 35551-35558, 35566, 35621, 35646, 35651-35661, 35666, 35700)

34820   Open iliac artery exposure for delivery of endovascular prosthesis or iliac occlusion during endovascular therapy, by abdominal or retroperitoneal incision, unilateral

(For bilateral procedure, use modifier 50)

34825   Placement of proximal or distal extension prosthesis for endovascular repair of infrarenal abdominal aortic or iliac aneurysm, false aneurysm, or dissection; initial vessel

+ 34826   each additional vessel (List separately in addition to code for primary procedure)

(Use 34826 in conjunction with 34825)

(Use 34825, 34826 in addition to 34800-34808, 34900 as appropriate)

(For staged procedure, use modifier 58)

(For radiological supervision and interpretation, use 75953)

34830   Open repair of infrarenal aortic aneurysm or dissection, plus repair of associated arterial trauma, following unsuccessful endovascular repair; tube prosthesis

34831   aorto-bi-iliac prosthesis

34832   aorto-bifemoral prosthesis

▲ 34833   Open iliac artery exposure with creation of conduit for delivery of aortic or iliac endovascular prosthesis, by abdominal or retroperitoneal incision, unilateral

(For bilateral procedure, use modifier 50)

(Do not report 34833 in addition to 34820)

▲ 34834   Open brachial artery exposure to assist in the deployment of aortic or iliac endovascular prosthesis by arm incision, unilateral

(For bilateral procedure, use modifier 50)

Endovascular Repair of Iliac Aneurysm

Code 34900 represents a procedure to report introduction, positioning, and deployment of an endovascular graft for treatment of aneurysm, pseudoaneurysm, or arteriovenous malformation or trauma of the iliac artery (common, hypogastric, external). All balloon angioplasty and/or stent deployments within the target treatment zone for the endoprosthesis, either before or after endograft deployment, are included in the work of 34900 and are not separately reportable. Open femoral or iliac artery exposure (eg, 34812, 34820), introduction of guidewires and catheters (eg, 36200, 36215-36218), and extensive repair or replacement of an artery (eg, 35206-35286) should be additionally reported.

For fluoroscopic guidance in conjunction with endovascular iliac aneurysm repair, see code 75954. Code 75954 includes angiography of the aorta and iliac arteries for diagnostic imaging prior to deployment of the endovascular device (including all routine components), fluoroscopic guidance in the delivery of the endovascular components, and intraprocedural arterial angiography to confirm appropriate position of the graft, detect endoleaks, and evaluate the status of the runoff vessels (eg, evaluation for dissection, stenosis, thrombosis, distal embolization, or iatrogenic injury).

Other interventional procedures performed at the time of endovascular aortic aneurysm repair should be additionally reported (eg, transluminal angioplasty outside the aneurysm target zone, arterial embolization, intravascular ultrasound).

34900   Endovascular graft placement for repair of iliac artery (eg, aneurysm, pseudoaneurysm, arteriovenous malformation, trauma)

(For radiological supervision and interpretation, use 75954)

(For placement of extension prosthesis during endovascular iliac artery repair, use 34825)

(For bilateral procedure, use modifier 50)

Surgery: Cardiovascular System

Direct Repair of Aneurysm or Excision (Partial or Total) and Graft Insertion for Aneurysm, Pseudoaneurysm, Ruptured Aneurysm, and Associated Occlusive Disease

Procedures 35001-35152 include preparation of artery for anastomosis including endarterectomy.

(For direct repairs associated with occlusive disease only, see 35201-35286)

(For intracranial aneurysm, see 61700 et seq)

(For endovascular repair of abdominal aortic aneurysm, see 34800-34826)

(For endovascular repair of iliac artery aneurysm, see 34900)

(For thoracic aortic aneurysm, see 33860-33875)

►(For endovascular repair of descending thoracic aorta, involving coverage of left subclavian artery origin, use 33880)◄

35001 Direct repair of aneurysm, pseudoaneurysm, or excision (partial or total) and graft insertion, with or without patch graft; for aneurysm and associated occlusive disease, carotid, subclavian artery, by neck incision

35002 for ruptured aneurysm, carotid, subclavian artery, by neck incision

35005 for aneurysm, pseudoaneurysm, and associated occlusive disease, vertebral artery

35011 for aneurysm and associated occlusive disease, axillary-brachial artery, by arm incision

35013 for ruptured aneurysm, axillary-brachial artery, by arm incision

35021 for aneurysm, pseudoaneurysm, and associated occlusive disease, innominate, subclavian artery, by thoracic incision

35022 for ruptured aneurysm, innominate, subclavian artery, by thoracic incision

35045 for aneurysm, pseudoaneurysm, and associated occlusive disease, radial or ulnar artery

35081 for aneurysm, pseudoaneurysm, and associated occlusive disease, abdominal aorta

35082 for ruptured aneurysm, abdominal aorta

35091 for aneurysm, pseudoaneurysm, and associated occlusive disease, abdominal aorta involving visceral vessels (mesenteric, celiac, renal)

35092 for ruptured aneurysm, abdominal aorta involving visceral vessels (mesenteric, celiac, renal)

35102 for aneurysm, pseudoaneurysm, and associated occlusive disease, abdominal aorta involving iliac vessels (common, hypogastric, external)

35103 for ruptured aneurysm, abdominal aorta involving iliac vessels (common, hypogastric, external)

35111 for aneurysm, pseudoaneurysm, and associated occlusive disease, splenic artery

35112 for ruptured aneurysm, splenic artery

35121 for aneurysm, pseudoaneurysm, and associated occlusive disease, hepatic, celiac, renal, or mesenteric artery

35122 for ruptured aneurysm, hepatic, celiac, renal, or mesenteric artery

35131 for aneurysm, pseudoaneurysm, and associated occlusive disease, iliac artery (common, hypogastric, external)

35132 for ruptured aneurysm, iliac artery (common, hypogastric, external)

35141 for aneurysm, pseudoaneurysm, and associated occlusive disease, common femoral artery (profunda femoris, superficial femoral)

35142 for ruptured aneurysm, common femoral artery (profunda femoris, superficial femoral)

35151 for aneurysm, pseudoaneurysm, and associated occlusive disease, popliteal artery

35152 for ruptured aneurysm, popliteal artery

(35161, 35162 have been deleted. To report, use 37799)

Repair Arteriovenous Fistula

35180 Repair, congenital arteriovenous fistula; head and neck

35182 thorax and abdomen

35184 extremities

35188 Repair, acquired or traumatic arteriovenous fistula; head and neck

35189 thorax and abdomen

35190 extremities

Repair Blood Vessel Other Than for Fistula, With or Without Patch Angioplasty

(For AV fistula repair, see 35180-35190)

35201 Repair blood vessel, direct; neck

35206 upper extremity

35207 hand, finger

35211 intrathoracic, with bypass

35216 intrathoracic, without bypass

35221 intra-abdominal

35226 lower extremity

35231	Repair blood vessel with vein graft; neck
35236	upper extremity
35241	intrathoracic, with bypass
35246	intrathoracic, without bypass
35251	intra-abdominal
35256	lower extremity
35261	Repair blood vessel with graft other than vein; neck
35266	upper extremity
35271	intrathoracic, with bypass
35276	intrathoracic, without bypass
35281	intra-abdominal
35286	lower extremity

Thromboendarterectomy

(For coronary artery, see 33510-33536 and 33572)

35301	Thromboendarterectomy, with or without patch graft; carotid, vertebral, subclavian, by neck incision
35311	subclavian, innominate, by thoracic incision
35321	axillary-brachial
35331	abdominal aorta
35341	mesenteric, celiac, or renal
35351	iliac
35355	iliofemoral
35361	combined aortoiliac
35363	combined aortoiliofemoral
35371	common femoral
35372	deep (profunda) femoral
35381	femoral and/or popliteal, and/or tibioperoneal
+ 35390	Reoperation, carotid, thromboendarterectomy, more than one month after original operation (List separately in addition to code for primary procedure)

(Use 35390 in conjunction with 35301)

Angioscopy

+ 35400	Angioscopy (non-coronary vessels or grafts) during therapeutic intervention (List separately in addition to code for primary procedure)

Transluminal Angioplasty

If done as part of another operation, use modifier 51 or use modifier 52.

(For radiological supervision and interpretation, see 75962-75968 and 75978)

Open

35450	Transluminal balloon angioplasty, open; renal or other visceral artery
35452	aortic
35454	iliac
35456	femoral-popliteal
35458	brachiocephalic trunk or branches, each vessel
35459	tibioperoneal trunk and branches
35460	venous

Percutaneous

Codes for catheter placement and the radiologic supervision and interpretation should also be reported, in addition to the code(s) for the therapeutic aspect of the procedure.

⊙ 35470	Transluminal balloon angioplasty, percutaneous; tibioperoneal trunk or branches, each vessel
⊙ 35471	renal or visceral artery
⊙ 35472	aortic
⊙ 35473	iliac
⊙ 35474	femoral-popliteal
⊙ 35475	brachiocephalic trunk or branches, each vessel
⊙ 35476	venous

(For radiological supervision and interpretation, use 75978)

Transluminal Atherectomy

If done as part of another operation, use modifier 51 or use modifier 52.

(For radiological supervision and interpretation, see 75992-75996)

Open

35480	Transluminal peripheral atherectomy, open; renal or other visceral artery
35481	aortic
35482	iliac
35483	femoral-popliteal
35484	brachiocephalic trunk or branches, each vessel
35485	tibioperoneal trunk and branches

Surgery: Cardiovascular System

Surgery: Cardiovascular System

Percutaneous

Codes for catheter placement and the radiologic supervision and interpretation should also be reported, in addition to the code(s) for the therapeutic aspect of the procedure.

35490   Transluminal peripheral atherectomy, percutaneous; renal or other visceral artery

35491   aortic

35492   iliac

35493   femoral-popliteal

35494   brachiocephalic trunk or branches, each vessel

35495   tibioperoneal trunk and branches

Bypass Graft

Vein

Procurement of the saphenous vein graft is included in the description of the work for 35501-35587 and should not be reported as a separate service or co-surgery. To report harvesting of an upper extremity vein, use 35500 in addition to the bypass procedure. To report harvesting of a femoropopliteal vein segment, use 35572 in addition to the bypass procedure. To report harvesting and construction of an autogenous composite graft of two segments from two distant locations, report 35682 in addition to the bypass procedure, for autogenous composite of three or more segments from distant sites, report 35683.

+ 35500   Harvest of upper extremity vein, one segment, for lower extremity or coronary artery bypass procedure (List separately in addition to code for primary procedure)

          (Use 35500 in conjunction with 33510-33536, 35556, 35566, 35571, 35583-35587)

          (For harvest of more than one vein segment, see 35682, 35683)

          (For endoscopic procedure, use 33508)

35501   Bypass graft, with vein; carotid

35506   carotid-subclavian

35507   subclavian-carotid

35508   carotid-vertebral

35509   carotid-carotid

35510   carotid-brachial

35511   subclavian-subclavian

35512   subclavian-brachial

35515   subclavian-vertebral

35516   subclavian-axillary

35518   axillary-axillary

35521   axillary-femoral

          (For bypass graft performed with synthetic graft, use 35621)

35522   axillary-brachial

35525   brachial-brachial

35526   aortosubclavian or carotid

          (For bypass graft performed with synthetic graft, use 35626)

35531   aortoceliac or aortomesenteric

35533   axillary-femoral-femoral

          (For bypass graft performed with synthetic graft, use 35654)

35536   splenorenal

35541   aortoiliac or bi-iliac

          (For bypass graft performed with synthetic graft, use 35641)

35546   aortofemoral or bifemoral

          (For bypass graft performed with synthetic graft, use 35646)

35548   aortoiliofemoral, unilateral

          (For bypass graft performed with synthetic graft, use 37799)

35549   aortoiliofemoral, bilateral

          (For bypass graft performed with synthetic graft, use 37799)

35551   aortofemoral-popliteal

35556   femoral-popliteal

35558   femoral-femoral

35560   aortorenal

35563   ilioiliac

35565   iliofemoral

35566   femoral-anterior tibial, posterior tibial, peroneal artery or other distal vessels

35571   popliteal-tibial, -peroneal artery or other distal vessels

+ 35572   Harvest of femoropopliteal vein, one segment, for vascular reconstruction procedure (eg, aortic, vena caval, coronary, peripheral artery) (List separately in addition to code for primary procedure)

          (Use 35572 in conjunction with 33510-33516, 33517-33523, 33533-33536, 34502, 34520, 35001, 35002, 35011-35022, 35102, 35103, 35121-35152, 35231-35256, 35501-35587, 35879-35907)

          (For bilateral procedure, use modifier 50)

In-Situ Vein

(35582 has been deleted)

35583   In-situ vein bypass; femoral-popliteal

(To report aortobifemoral bypass using synthetic conduit, and femoral-popliteal bypass with vein conduit in-situ, use 35646 and 35583. To report aorto(uni)femoral bypass with synthetic conduit, and femoral-popliteal bypass with vein conduit in-situ, use 35647 and 35583. To report aortofemoral bypass using vein conduit, and femoral-popliteal bypass with vein conduit in-situ, use 35546 and 35583)

35585   femoral-anterior tibial, posterior tibial, or peroneal artery

35587   popliteal-tibial, peroneal

Other Than Vein

(For arterial transposition and/or reimplantation, see 35691-35695)

⊘ 35600   Harvest of upper extremity artery, one segment, for coronary artery bypass procedure

35601   Bypass graft, with other than vein; carotid

35606   carotid-subclavian

►(For open transcervical common carotid-common carotid bypass performed in conjunction with endovascular repair of descending thoracic aorta, use 33891)◄

►(For open subclavian to carotid artery transposition performed in conjunction with endovascular thoracic aneurysm repair by neck incision, use 33889)◄

35612   subclavian-subclavian

35616   subclavian-axillary

35621   axillary-femoral

35623   axillary-popliteal or -tibial

35626   aortosubclavian or carotid

35631   aortoceliac, aortomesenteric, aortorenal

35636   splenorenal (splenic to renal arterial anastomosis)

35641   aortoiliac or bi-iliac

(For open placement of aorto-bi-iliac prosthesis following unsuccessful endovascular repair, use 34831)

35642   carotid-vertebral

35645   subclavian-vertebral

35646   aortobifemoral

(For open placement of aortobifemoral prosthesis following unsuccessful endovascular repair, use 34832)

35647   aortofemoral

35650   axillary-axillary

35651   aortofemoral-popliteal

35654   axillary-femoral-femoral

35656   femoral-popliteal

35661   femoral-femoral

35663   ilioiliac

35665   iliofemoral

35666   femoral-anterior tibial, posterior tibial, or peroneal artery

35671   popliteal-tibial or -peroneal artery

Composite Grafts

Codes 35682-35683 are used to report harvest and anastomosis of multiple vein segments from distant sites for use as arterial bypass graft conduits. These codes are intended for use when the two or more vein segments are harvested from a limb other than that undergoing bypass. Add-on codes 35682 and 35683 may be reported in addition to codes 35556, 35566, 35571, 35583-35587, as appropriate.

+ 35681   Bypass graft; composite, prosthetic and vein (List separately in addition to code for primary procedure)

(Do not report 35681 in addition to 35682, 35683)

+ 35682   autogenous composite, two segments of veins from two locations (List separately in addition to code for primary procedure)

(Do not report 35682 in addition to 35681, 35683)

+ 35683   autogenous composite, three or more segments of vein from two or more locations (List separately in addition to code for primary procedure)

(Do not report 35683 in addition to 35681, 35682)

Adjuvant Techniques

Adjuvant (additional) technique(s) may be required at the time a bypass graft is created to improve patency of the lower extremity autogenous or synthetic bypass graft (eg, femoral-popliteal, femoral-tibial, or popliteal-tibial arteries). Code 35685 should be reported in addition to the primary synthetic bypass graft procedure, when an interposition of venous tissue (vein patch or cuff) is placed at the anastomosis between the synthetic bypass conduit and the involved artery (includes harvest).

Code 35686 should be reported in addition to the primary bypass graft procedure, when autogenous vein is used to create a fistula between the tibial or peroneal artery and vein at or beyond the distal bypass anastomosis site of the involved artery.

(For composite graft(s), see 35681-35683)

Surgery: Cardiovascular System

+ 35685   Placement of vein patch or cuff at distal anastomosis of bypass graft, synthetic conduit (List separately in addition to code for primary procedure)

(Use 35685 in conjunction with 35656, 35666, or 35671)

+ 35686   Creation of distal arteriovenous fistula during lower extremity bypass surgery (non-hemodialysis) (List separately in addition to code for primary procedure)

(Use 35686 in conjunction with 35556, 35566, 35571, 35583-35587, 35623, 35656, 35666, 35671)

Arterial Transposition

35691   Transposition and/or reimplantation; vertebral to carotid artery

35693   vertebral to subclavian artery

35694   subclavian to carotid artery

▶(For open subclavian to carotid artery transposition performed in conjunction with endovascular repair of descending thoracic aorta, use 33889)◀

35695   carotid to subclavian artery

+ 35697   Reimplantation, visceral artery to infrarenal aortic prosthesis, each artery (List separately in addition to code for primary procedure)

(Do not report 35697 in conjunction with 33877)

Exploration/Revision

+ 35700   Reoperation, femoral-popliteal or femoral (popliteal)-anterior tibial, posterior tibial, peroneal artery or other distal vessels, more than one month after original operation (List separately in addition to code for primary procedure)

(Use 35700 in conjunction with 35556, 35566, 35571, 35583, 35585, 35587, 35656, 35666, 35671)

35701   Exploration (not followed by surgical repair), with or without lysis of artery; carotid artery

35721   femoral artery

35741   popliteal artery

35761   other vessels

35800   Exploration for postoperative hemorrhage, thrombosis or infection; neck

35820   chest

35840   abdomen

35860   extremity

35870   Repair of graft-enteric fistula

35875   Thrombectomy of arterial or venous graft (other than hemodialysis graft or fistula);

35876   with revision of arterial or venous graft

(For thrombectomy of hemodialysis graft or fistula, see 36831, 36833)

Codes 35879 and 35881 describe open revision of graft-threatening stenoses of lower extremity arterial bypass graft(s) (previously constructed with autogenous vein conduit) using vein patch angioplasty or segmental vein interposition techniques. For thrombectomy with revision of any non-coronary arterial or venous graft, including those of the lower extremity, (other than hemodialysis graft or fistula), use 35876. For direct repair (other than for fistula) of a lower extremity blood vessel (with or without patch angioplasty), use 35226. For repair (other than for fistula) of a lower extremity blood vessel using a vein graft, use 35256.

35879   Revision, lower extremity arterial bypass, without thrombectomy, open; with vein patch angioplasty

35881   with segmental vein interposition

(For excision of infected graft, see 35901-35907 and appropriate revascularization code)

35901   Excision of infected graft; neck

35903   extremity

35905   thorax

35907   abdomen

Vascular Injection Procedures

Listed services for injection procedures include necessary local anesthesia, introduction of needles or catheter, injection of contrast media with or without automatic power injection, and/or necessary pre- and postinjection care specifically related to the injection procedure.

Catheters, drugs, and contrast media are not included in the listed service for the injection procedures.

Selective vascular catheterization should be coded to include introduction and all lesser order selective catheterization used in the approach (eg, the description for a selective right middle cerebral artery catheterization includes the introduction and placement catheterization of the right common and internal carotid arteries).

Additional second and/or third order arterial catheterization within the same family of arteries or veins supplied by a single first order vessel should be expressed by 36012, 36218 or 36248.

Additional first order or higher catheterization in vascular families supplied by a first order vessel different from a previously selected and coded family should be separately coded using the conventions described above.

(For radiological supervision and interpretation, see **Radiology**)

(For injection procedures in conjunction with cardiac catheterization, see 93541-93545)

(For chemotherapy of malignant disease, see 96400-96549)

⊘ =Modifier 51 exempt   ⊙ =Conscious sedation   ✛ =Add-on code   ✗ =FDA approval pending

Intravenous

An intracatheter is a sheathed combination of needle and short catheter.

36000 Introduction of needle or intracatheter, vein

36002 Injection procedures (eg, thrombin) for percutaneous treatment of extremity pseudoaneurysm

(For imaging guidance, see 76003, 76360, 76393, or 76942)

(For ultrasound guided compression repair of pseudoaneurysms, use 76936)

(Do not report 36002 for vascular sealant of an arteriotomy site)

36005 Injection procedure for extremity venography (including introduction of needle or intracatheter)

(For radiological supervision and interpretation, see 75820, 75822)

36010 Introduction of catheter, superior or inferior vena cava

36011 Selective catheter placement, venous system; first order branch (eg, renal vein, jugular vein)

36012   second order, or more selective, branch (eg, left adrenal vein, petrosal sinus)

36013 Introduction of catheter, right heart or main pulmonary artery

36014 Selective catheter placement, left or right pulmonary artery

36015 Selective catheter placement, segmental or subsegmental pulmonary artery

(For insertion of flow directed catheter (eg, Swan-Ganz), use 93503)

(For venous catheterization for selective organ blood sampling, use 36500)

Intra-Arterial—Intra-Aortic

(For radiological supervision and interpretation, see **Radiology**)

36100 Introduction of needle or intracatheter, carotid or vertebral artery

(For bilateral procedure, report 36100 with modifier 50)

36120 Introduction of needle or intracatheter; retrograde brachial artery

36140   extremity artery

36145   arteriovenous shunt created for dialysis (cannula, fistula, or graft)

(For insertion of arteriovenous cannula, see 36810-36821)

36160 Introduction of needle or intracatheter, aortic, translumbar

36200 Introduction of catheter, aorta

36215 Selective catheter placement, arterial system; each first order thoracic or brachiocephalic branch, within a vascular family

(For catheter placement for coronary angiography, use 93508)

36216   initial second order thoracic or brachiocephalic branch, within a vascular family

36217   initial third order or more selective thoracic or brachiocephalic branch, within a vascular family

+ 36218   additional second order, third order, and beyond, thoracic or brachiocephalic branch, within a vascular family (List in addition to code for initial second or third order vessel as appropriate)

(Use 36218 in conjunction with 36216, 36217)

(For angiography, see 75600-75790)

(For angioplasty, see 35470-35475)

(For transcatheter therapies, see 37200-37208, 61624, 61626)

(When coronary artery, arterial conduit (eg, internal mammary, inferior epigastric or free radical artery) or venous bypass graft angiography is performed in conjunction with cardiac catheterization, see the appropriate cardiac catheterization, injection procedure, and imaging supervision code(s) (93501-93556) in the **Medicine** section of the CPT codebook. When coronary artery, arterial coronary conduit or venous bypass graft angiography is performed without concomitant left heart cardiac catheterization, use 93508. When internal mammary artery angiography only is performed without a concomitant left heart cardiac catheterization, use 36216 or 36217 as appropriate.)

36245 Selective catheter placement, arterial system; each first order abdominal, pelvic, or lower extremity artery branch, within a vascular family

36246   initial second order abdominal, pelvic, or lower extremity artery branch, within a vascular family

36247   initial third order or more selective abdominal, pelvic, or lower extremity artery branch, within a vascular family

+ 36248   additional second order, third order, and beyond, abdominal, pelvic, or lower extremity artery branch, within a vascular family (List in addition to code for initial second or third order vessel as appropriate)

(Use 36248 in conjunction with 36246, 36247)

36260 Insertion of implantable intra-arterial infusion pump (eg, for chemotherapy of liver)

36261 Revision of implanted intra-arterial infusion pump

36262 Removal of implanted intra-arterial infusion pump

36299 Unlisted procedure, vascular injection

Surgery: Cardiovascular System

Venous

Venipuncture, needle or catheter for diagnostic study or intravenous therapy, percutaneous.

36400 Venipuncture, under age 3 years, necessitating physician's skill, not to be used for routine venipuncture; femoral or jugular vein

36405 scalp vein

36406 other vein

36410 Venipuncture, age 3 years or older, necessitating physician's skill (separate procedure), for diagnostic or therapeutic purposes (not to be used for routine venipuncture)

36415 Collection of venous blood by venipuncture

(Do not report modifier 63 in conjunction with 36415)

36416 Collection of capillary blood specimen (eg, finger, heel, ear stick)

36420 Venipuncture, cutdown; under age 1 year

(Do not report modifier 63 in conjunction with 36420)

36425 age 1 or over

36430 Transfusion, blood or blood components

36440 Push transfusion, blood, 2 years or under

36450 Exchange transfusion, blood; newborn

(Do not report modifier 63 in conjunction with 36450)

36455 other than newborn

36460 Transfusion, intrauterine, fetal

(Do not report modifier 63 in conjunction with 36460)

(For radiological supervision and interpretation, use 76941)

36468 Single or multiple injections of sclerosing solutions, spider veins (telangiectasia); limb or trunk

36469 face

36470 Injection of sclerosing solution; single vein

36471 multiple veins, same leg

36475 Endovenous ablation therapy of incompetent vein, extremity, inclusive of all imaging guidance and monitoring, percutaneous, radiofrequency; first vein treated

+ 36476 second and subsequent veins treated in a single extremity, each through separate access sites (List separately in addition to code for primary procedure)

(Use 36476 in conjunction with 36475)

(Do not report 36475, 36476 in conjunction with 36000-36005, 36410, 36425, 36478, 36479, 37204, 75894, 76000-76003, 76937, 76942, 93970, 93971)

36478 Endovenous ablation therapy of incompetent vein, extremity, inclusive of all imaging guidance and monitoring, percutaneous, laser; first vein treated

+ 36479 second and subsequent veins treated in a single extremity, each through separate access sites (List separately in addition to code for primary procedure)

(Use 36479 in conjunction with 36478)

(Do not report 36478, 36479 in conjunction with 36000-36005, 36410, 36425, 36475, 36476, 37204, 75894, 76000-76003, 76937, 76942, 93970, 93971)

36481 Percutaneous portal vein catheterization by any method

(For radiological supervision and interpretation, see 75885, 75887)

(36488-36491 have been deleted. To report, see 36555-36556, 36568-36569, 36580, 36584)

(36493 has been deleted. To report, use 36597)

36500 Venous catheterization for selective organ blood sampling

(For catheterization in superior or inferior vena cava, use 36010)

(For radiological supervision and interpretation, use 75893)

36510 Catheterization of umbilical vein for diagnosis or therapy, newborn

(Do not report modifier 63 in conjunction with 36510)

36511 Therapeutic apheresis; for white blood cells

36512 for red blood cells

36513 for platelets

36514 for plasma pheresis

36515 with extracorporeal immunoadsorption and plasma reinfusion

36516 with extracorporeal selective adsorption or selective filtration and plasma reinfusion

(For physician evaluation, use modifier 26)

36522 Photopheresis, extracorporeal

(36530 has been deleted. To report, use 36563)

(36531 has been deleted. To report, see 36575-36576, 36578, 36581-36582, 36584-36585)

(36532 has been deleted. To report, use 36590)

(36533 has been deleted. To report, see 36557-36561, 36565-36566, 36570-36571)

(36534 has been deleted. To report, see 36575-36578, 36581-36583, 36585)

(36535 has been deleted. To report, use 36589)

(36536 has been deleted. To report, use 36595)

(36537 have been deleted. To report, use 36596)

○=Modifier 51 exempt ⊙=Conscious sedation ✚=Add-on code ✗=FDA approval pending

36540   Collection of blood specimen from a completely implantable venous access device

(Do not report 36540 in conjunction with 36415, 36416)

(For collection of venous blood specimen by venipuncture, use 36415)

(For collection of capillary blood specimen, use 36416)

36550   Declotting by thrombolytic agent of implanted vascular access device or catheter

Central Venous Access Procedures

To qualify as a central venous access catheter or device, the tip of the catheter/device must terminate in the subclavian, brachiocephalic (innominate) or iliac veins, the superior or inferior vena cava, or the right atrium. The venous access device may be either centrally inserted (jugular, subclavian, femoral vein or inferior vena cava catheter entry site) or peripherally inserted (eg, basilic or cephalic vein). The device may be accessed for use either via exposed catheter (external to the skin), via a subcutaneous port or via a subcutaneous pump.

The procedures involving these types of devices fall into five categories:

1) *Insertion* (placement of catheter through a newly established venous access)

2) *Repair* (fixing device without replacement of either catheter or port/pump, other than pharmacologic or mechanical correction of intracatheter or pericatheter occlusion (see 36595 or 36596))

3) *Partial replacement* of only the catheter component associated with a port/pump device, but not entire device

4) *Complete replacement* of entire device via same venous access site (complete exchange)

5) *Removal* of entire device.

There is no coding distinction between venous access achieved percutaneously versus by cutdown or based on catheter size.

For the repair, partial (catheter only) replacement, complete replacement, or removal of both catheters (placed from separate venous access sites) of a multi-catheter device, with or without subcutaneous ports/pumps, use the appropriate code describing the service with a frequency of two.

If an existing central venous access device is removed and a new one placed via a separate venous access site, appropriate codes for both procedures (removal of old, if code exists, and insertion of new device) should be reported.

When imaging is used for these procedures, either for gaining access to the venous entry site or for manipulating the catheter into final central position, use 76937, 75998.

(For refilling and maintenance of an implantable pump or reservoir for intravenous or intra-arterial drug delivery, use 96530)

Insertion of Central Venous Access Device

⊙ **36555**   Insertion of non-tunneled centrally inserted central venous catheter; under 5 years of age

(For peripherally inserted non-tunneled central venous catheter, under 5 years of age, use 36568)

36556   age 5 years or older

(For peripherally inserted non-tunneled central venous catheter, age 5 years or older, use 36569)

⊙ **36557**   Insertion of tunneled centrally inserted central venous catheter, without subcutaneous port or pump; under 5 years of age

⊙ **36558**   age 5 years or older

(For peripherally inserted central venous catheter with port, 5 years or older, use 36571)

⊙ **36560**   Insertion of tunneled centrally inserted central venous access device, with subcutaneous port; under 5 years of age

(For peripherally inserted central venous access device with subcutaneous port, under 5 years of age, use 36570)

⊙ **36561**   age 5 years or older

(For peripherally inserted central venous catheter with subcutaneous port, 5 years or older, use 36571)

⊙ **36563**   Insertion of tunneled centrally inserted central venous access device with subcutaneous pump

⊙ **36565**   Insertion of tunneled centrally inserted central venous access device, requiring two catheters via two separate venous access sites; without subcutaneous port or pump (eg, Tesio type catheter)

⊙ **36566**   with subcutaneous port(s)

⊙ **36568**   Insertion of peripherally inserted central venous catheter (PICC), without subcutaneous port or pump; under 5 years of age

(For placement of centrally inserted non-tunneled central venous catheter, without subcutaneous port or pump, under 5 years of age, use 36555)

36569   age 5 years or older

(For placement of centrally inserted non-tunneled central venous catheter, without subcutaneous port or pump, age 5 years or older, use 36556)

⊙ **36570** Insertion of peripherally inserted central venous access device, with subcutaneous port; under 5 years of age

(For insertion of tunneled centrally inserted central venous access device with subcutaneous port, under 5 years of age, use 36560)

⊙ **36571**   age 5 years or older

(For insertion of tunneled centrally inserted central venous access device with subcutaneous port, age 5 years or older, use 36561)

Repair of Central Venous Access Device

(For mechanical removal of pericatheter obstructive material, use 36595)

(For mechanical removal of intracatheter obstructive material, use 36596)

36575 Repair of tunneled or non-tunneled central venous access catheter, without subcutaneous port or pump, central or peripheral insertion site

⊙ **36576** Repair of central venous access device, with subcutaneous port or pump, central or peripheral insertion site

Partial Replacement of Central Venous Access Device (Catheter Only)

⊙ **36578** Replacement, catheter only, of central venous access device, with subcutaneous port or pump, central or peripheral insertion site

(For complete replacement of entire device through same venous access, use 36582 or 36583)

Complete Replacement of Central Venous Access Device Through Same Venous Access Site

36580 Replacement, complete, of a non-tunneled centrally inserted central venous catheter, without subcutaneous port or pump, through same venous access

⊙ **36581** Replacement, complete, of a tunneled centrally inserted central venous catheter, without subcutaneous port or pump, through same venous access

⊙ **36582** Replacement, complete, of a tunneled centrally inserted central venous access device, with subcutaneous port, through same venous access

⊙ **36583** Replacement, complete, of a tunneled centrally inserted central venous access device, with subcutaneous pump, through same venous access

36584 Replacement, complete, of a peripherally inserted central venous catheter (PICC), without subcutaneous port or pump, through same venous access

⊙ **36585** Replacement, complete, of a peripherally inserted central venous access device, with subcutaneous port, through same venous access

Removal of Central Venous Access Device

36589 Removal of tunneled central venous catheter, without subcutaneous port or pump

⊙ **36590** Removal of tunneled central venous access device, with subcutaneous port or pump, central or peripheral insertion

(Do not report 36589 or 36590 for removal of non-tunneled central venous catheters)

Mechanical Removal of Obstructive Material

36595 Mechanical removal of pericatheter obstructive material (eg, fibrin sheath) from central venous device via separate venous access

(Do not report 36550 in addition to 36595)

(For venous catheterization, see 36010-36012)

(For radiological supervision and interpretation, use 75901)

36596 Mechanical removal of intraluminal (intracatheter) obstructive material from central venous device through device lumen

(Do not report 36550 in addition to 36596)

(For venous catheterization, see 36010-36012)

(For radiological supervision and interpretation, use 75902)

Other Central Venous Access Procedures

36597 Repositioning of previously placed central venous catheter under fluoroscopic guidance

(For fluoroscopic guidance, use 76000)

● **36598** Contrast injection(s) for radiologic evaluation of existing central venous access device, including fluoroscopy, image documentation and report

▶(Do not report 36598 in conjunction with 76000)◀

▶(Do not report 36598 in conjunction with 36595, 36596)◀

▶(For complete diagnostic studies, see 75820, 75825, 75827)◀

Arterial

36600 Arterial puncture, withdrawal of blood for diagnosis

⊘ **36620** Arterial catheterization or cannulation for sampling, monitoring or transfusion (separate procedure); percutaneous

36625   cutdown

36640   Arterial catheterization for prolonged infusion therapy (chemotherapy), cutdown

(See also 96420-96425)

(For arterial catheterization for occlusion therapy, see 75894)

⊘ **36660**   Catheterization, umbilical artery, newborn, for diagnosis or therapy

(Do not report modifier 63 in conjunction with 36660)

Intraosseous

36680   Placement of needle for intraosseous infusion

Hemodialysis Access, Intervascular Cannulation for Extracorporeal Circulation, or Shunt Insertion

36800   Insertion of cannula for hemodialysis, other purpose (separate procedure); vein to vein

36810   arteriovenous, external (Scribner type)

36815   arteriovenous, external revision, or closure

36818   Arteriovenous anastomosis, open; by upper arm cephalic vein transposition

(Do not report 36818 in conjunction with 36819, 36820, 36821, 36830 during a unilateral upper extremity procedure. For bilateral upper extremity open arteriovenous anastomoses performed at the same operative session, use modifier 50 or 59 as appropriate)

36819   by upper arm basilic vein transposition

(Do not report 36819 in conjunction with 36818, 36820, 36821, 36830 during a unilateral upper extremity procedure. For bilateral upper extremity open arteriovenous anastomoses performed at the same operative session, use modifier 50 or 59 as appropriate)

36820   by forearm vein transposition

36821   direct, any site (eg, Cimino type) (separate procedure)

36822   Insertion of cannula(s) for prolonged extracorporeal circulation for cardiopulmonary insufficiency (ECMO) (separate procedure)

(For maintenance of prolonged extracorporeal circulation, see 33960, 33961)

36823   Insertion of arterial and venous cannula(s) for isolated extracorporeal circulation including regional chemotherapy perfusion to an extremity, with or without hyperthermia, with removal of cannula(s) and repair of arteriotomy and venotomy sites

(36823 includes chemotherapy perfusion supported by a membrane oxygenator/perfusion pump. Do not report 96408-96425 in conjunction with 36823)

36825   Creation of arteriovenous fistula by other than direct arteriovenous anastomosis (separate procedure); autogenous graft

(For direct arteriovenous anastomosis, use 36821)

36830   nonautogenous graft (eg, biological collagen, thermoplastic graft)

(For direct arteriovenous anastomosis, use 36821)

36831   Thrombectomy, open, arteriovenous fistula without revision, autogenous or nonautogenous dialysis graft (separate procedure)

36832   Revision, open, arteriovenous fistula; without thrombectomy, autogenous or nonautogenous dialysis graft (separate procedure)

36833   with thrombectomy, autogenous or nonautogenous dialysis graft (separate procedure)

36834   Plastic repair of arteriovenous aneurysm (separate procedure)

36835   Insertion of Thomas shunt (separate procedure)

36838   Distal revascularization and interval ligation (DRIL), upper extremity hemodialysis access (steal syndrome)

(Do not report 36838 in conjunction with 35512, 35522, 36832, 37607, 37618)

36860   External cannula declotting (separate procedure); without balloon catheter

36861   with balloon catheter

(If imaging guidance is performed, use 76000)

⊙ **36870**   Thrombectomy, percutaneous, arteriovenous fistula, autogenous or nonautogenous graft (includes mechanical thrombus extraction and intra-graft thrombolysis)

(Do not report 36550 in conjunction with 36870)

(For catheterization, use 36145)

(For radiological supervision and interpretation, use 75790)

Portal Decompression Procedures

37140   Venous anastomosis, open; portocaval

(For peritoneal-venous shunt, use 49425)

37145   renoportal

37160   caval-mesenteric

37180   splenorenal, proximal

37181   splenorenal, distal (selective decompression of esophagogastric varices, any technique)

(For percutaneous procedure, use 37182)

Surgery: Cardiovascular System

37182 Insertion of transvenous intrahepatic portosystemic shunt(s) (TIPS) (includes venous access, hepatic and portal vein catheterization, portography with hemodynamic evaluation, intrahepatic tract formation/dilatation, stent placement and all associated imaging guidance and documentation)

(Do not report 75885 or 75887 in conjunction with 37182)

(For open procedure, use 37140)

37183 Revision of transvenous intrahepatic portosystemic shunt(s) (TIPS) (includes venous access, hepatic and portal vein catheterization, portography with hemodynamic evaluation, intrahepatic tract recanulization/dilatation, stent placement and all associated imaging guidance and documentation)

(Do not report 75885 or 75887 in conjunction with 37183)

(For repair of arteriovenous aneurysm, use 36834)

Transcatheter Procedures

Codes for catheter placement and the radiologic supervision and interpretation should also be reported, in addition to the code(s) for the therapeutic aspect of the procedure.

▶*Mechanical Thrombectomy*◀

▶Code(s) for catheter placement(s), diagnostic studies, and other percutaneous interventions (eg, transluminal balloon angioplasty, stent placement) provided are separately reportable.◀

▶Codes 37184-37188 specifically include intraprocedural fluoroscopic radiological supervision and interpretation services for guidance of the procedure.◀

▶Intraprocedural injection(s) of a thrombolytic agent is an included service and not separately reportable in conjunction with mechanical thrombectomy. However, subsequent or prior continuous infusion of a thrombolytic is not an included service and is separately reportable (see 37201, 75896, 75898).◀

▶For coronary mechanical thrombectomy, use 92973.◀

▶For mechanical thrombectomy for dialysis fistula, use 36870.◀

▶*Arterial Mechanical Thrombectomy*◀

▶Arterial mechanical thrombectomy may be performed as a "primary" transcatheter procedure with pretreatment planning, performance of the procedure, and postprocedure evaluation focused on providing this service. Primary mechanical thrombectomy is reported per vascular family using 37184 for the initial vessel treated and 37185 for second or all subsequent vessel(s) within the same vascular family. To report mechanical thrombectomy of an additional vascular family treated through a separate access site, use modifier 51 in conjunction with 37184-37185.◀

▶Do NOT report 37184-37185 for mechanical thrombectomy performed for treatment of thrombus or embolus complicating other percutaneous interventional procedures. See 37186 for these procedures.◀

▶Arterial mechanical thrombectomy is considered a "secondary" transcatheter procedure for removal or retrieval of short segments of thrombus or embolus when performed either before or after another percutaneous intervention (eg, percutaneous transluminal balloon angioplasty, stent placement). Secondary mechanical thrombectomy is reported using 37186. Do NOT report 37186 in conjunction with 37184-37185.◀

▶*Venous Mechanical Thrombectomy*◀

▶Use code 37188 to report the initial application of venous mechanical thrombectomy. To report bilateral venous mechanical thrombectomy performed through a separate access site(s), use modifier 50 in conjunction with 37188. For repeat treatment on a subsequent day during a course of thrombolytic therapy, use 37188.◀

▶Arterial Mechanical Thrombectomy◀

⊙● **37184** Primary percutaneous transluminal mechanical thrombectomy, noncoronary, arterial or arterial bypass graft, including fluoroscopic guidance and intraprocedural pharmacological thrombolytic injection(s); initial vessel

▶(Do not report 37184 in conjunction with 76000, 76001, 90774, 99143-99150)◀

⊙+● **37185** second and all subsequent vessel(s) within the same vascular family (List separately in addition to code for primary mechanical thrombectomy procedure)

▶(Do not report 37185 in conjunction with 76000, 76001, 90775)◀

⊙+● **37186** Secondary percutaneous transluminal thrombectomy (eg, nonprimary mechanical, snare basket, suction technique), noncoronary, arterial or arterial bypass graft, including fluoroscopic guidance and intraprocedural pharmacological thrombolytic injections, provided in conjunction with another percutaneous intervention other than primary mechanical thrombectomy (List separately in addition to code for primary procedure)

▶(Do not report 37186 in conjunction with 76000, 76001, 90775)◀

▶Venous Mechanical Thrombectomy◀

⊙● **37187** Percutaneous transluminal mechanical thrombectomy, vein(s), including intraprocedural pharmacological thrombolytic injections and fluoroscopic guidance

▶(Do not report 37187 in conjunction with 76000, 76001, 90775)◀

⊙● **37188**   Percutaneous transluminal mechanical thrombectomy, vein(s), including intraprocedural pharmacological thrombolytic injections and fluoroscopic guidance, repeat treatment on subsequent day during course of thrombolytic therapy

►(Do not report 37188 in conjunction with 76000, 76001, 90775)◄

►Other Procedures◄

37195   Thrombolysis, cerebral, by intravenous infusion

37200   Transcatheter biopsy

(For radiological supervision and interpretation, use 75970)

37201   Transcatheter therapy, infusion for thrombolysis other than coronary

(For radiological supervision and interpretation, use 75896)

37202   Transcatheter therapy, infusion other than for thrombolysis, any type (eg, spasmolytic, vasoconstrictive)

(For thrombolysis of coronary vessels, see 92975, 92977)

(For radiological supervision and interpretation, use 75896)

⊙ **37203**   Transcatheter retrieval, percutaneous, of intravascular foreign body (eg, fractured venous or arterial catheter)

(For radiological supervision and interpretation, use 75961)

37204   Transcatheter occlusion or embolization (eg, for tumor destruction, to achieve hemostasis, to occlude a vascular malformation), percutaneous, any method, non-central nervous system, non-head or neck

(See also 61624, 61626)

(For radiological supervision and interpretation, use 75894)

37205   Transcatheter placement of an intravascular stent(s), (except coronary, carotid, and vertebral vessel), percutaneous; initial vessel

(For radiological supervision and interpretation, use 75960)

►(For coronary stent placement, see 92980, 92981; intracranial, use 61635)◄

+ **37206**   each additional vessel (List separately in addition to code for primary procedure)

(Use 37206 in conjunction with 37205)

(For transcatheter placement of intravascular cervical carotid artery stent(s), see 37215, 37216)

(For transcatheter placement of extracranial vertebral or intrathoracic carotid artery stent(s), see Category III codes 0075T, 0076T)

(For radiological supervision and interpretation, use 75960)

37207   Transcatheter placement of an intravascular stent(s), (non-coronary vessel), open; initial vessel

+ **37208**   each additional vessel (List separately in addition to code for primary procedure)

(Use 37208 in conjunction with 37207)

(For radiological supervision and interpretation, use 75960)

(For catheterizations, see 36215-36248)

(For transcatheter placement of intracoronary stent(s), see 92980, 92981)

▲ **37209**   Exchange of a previously placed intravascular catheter during thrombolytic therapy

(For radiological supervision and interpretation, use 75900)

⊙ **37215**   Transcatheter placement of intravascular stent(s), cervical carotid artery, percutaneous; with distal embolic protection

⊙ **37216**   without distal embolic protection

(37215 and 37216 include all ipsilateral selective carotid catheterization, all diagnostic imaging for ipsilateral, cervical and cerebral carotid arteriography, and all related radiological supervision and interpretation. When ipsilateral carotid arteriogram (including imaging and selective catheterization) confirms the need for carotid stenting, 37215 and 37216 are inclusive of these services. If carotid stenting is not indicated, then the appropriate codes for carotid catheterization and imaging should be reported in lieu of 37215 and 37216)

(Do not report 37215, 37216 in conjunction with 75671, 75680)

(For transcatheter placement of extracranial vertebral or intrathoracic carotid artery stent(s), see Category III codes 0075T, 0076T)

(For percutaneous transcatheter placement of intravascular stents other than coronary, carotid, or vertebral, see 37205, 37206)

Intravascular Ultrasound Services

Intravascular ultrasound services include all transducer manipulations and repositioning within the specific vessel being examined, both before and after therapeutic intervention (eg, stent placement).

Vascular access for intravascular ultrasound performed during a therapeutic intervention is not reported separately.

Surgery: Cardiovascular System

+ **37250** Intravascular ultrasound (non-coronary vessel) during diagnostic evaluation and/or therapeutic intervention; initial vessel (List separately in addition to code for primary procedure)

+ **37251** each additional vessel (List separately in addition to code for primary procedure)

(Use 37251 in conjunction with 37250)

(For catheterizations, see 36215-36248)

(For transcatheter therapies, see 37200-37208, 61624, 61626)

(For radiological supervision and interpretation see 75945, 75946)

Endoscopy

Surgical vascular endoscopy always includes diagnostic endoscopy.

37500 Vascular endoscopy, surgical, with ligation of perforator veins, subfascial (SEPS)

(For open procedure, use 37760)

37501 Unlisted vascular endoscopy procedure

Ligation

(For phleborraphy and arteriorraphy, see 35201-35286)

37565 Ligation, internal jugular vein

37600 Ligation; external carotid artery

37605 internal or common carotid artery

37606 internal or common carotid artery, with gradual occlusion, as with Selverstone or Crutchfield clamp

(For transcatheter permanent arterial occlusion or embolization, see 61624-61626)

(For endovascular temporary arterial balloon occlusion, use 61623)

(For ligation treatment of intracranial aneurysm, use 61703)

37607 Ligation or banding of angioaccess arteriovenous fistula

37609 Ligation or biopsy, temporal artery

37615 Ligation, major artery (eg, post-traumatic, rupture); neck

37616 chest

37617 abdomen

37618 extremity

37620 Interruption, partial or complete, of inferior vena cava by suture, ligation, plication, clip, extravascular, intravascular (umbrella device)

(For radiological supervision and interpretation, use 75940)

37650 Ligation of femoral vein

(For bilateral procedure, report 37650 with modifier 50)

37660 Ligation of common iliac vein

37700 Ligation and division of long saphenous vein at saphenofemoral junction, or distal interruptions

▶(Do not report 37700 in conjunction with 37718, 37722)◀

(For bilateral procedure, report 37700 with modifier 50)

● **37718** Ligation, division, and stripping, short saphenous vein

▶(For bilateral procedure, use modifier 50)◀

▶(Do not report 37718 in conjunction with 37735, 37780)◀

▶(37720 has been deleted)◀

● **37722** Ligation, division, and stripping, long (greater) saphenous veins from saphenofemoral junction to knee or below

▶(For ligation and stripping of the short saphenous vein, use 37718)◀

▶(For bilateral procedure, report 37722 with modifier 50)◀

▶(Do not report 37722 in conjunction with 37700, 37735)◀

▶(37730 has been deleted. For ligation, division, and stripping of the greater saphenous vein, use 37722. For ligation, division, and stripping of the short saphenous vein, use 37718)◀

37735 Ligation and division and complete stripping of long or short saphenous veins with radical excision of ulcer and skin graft and/or interruption of communicating veins of lower leg, with excision of deep fascia

▶(Do not report 37735 in conjunction with 37700, 37718, 37722, 37780)◀

(For bilateral procedure, report 37735 with modifier 50)

37760 Ligation of perforator veins, subfascial, radical (Linton type), with or without skin graft, open

(For endoscopic procedure, use 37500)

37765 Stab phlebectomy of varicose veins, one extremity; 10-20 stab incisions

(For less than 10 incisions, use 37799)

(For more than 20 incisions, use 37766)

37766 more than 20 incisions

37780 Ligation and division of short saphenous vein at saphenopopliteal junction (separate procedure)

(For bilateral procedure, report 37780 with modifier 50)

37785 Ligation, division, and/or excision of varicose vein cluster(s), one leg

(For bilateral procedure, report 37785 with modifier 50)

Other Procedures

37788   Penile revascularization, artery, with or without vein graft

37790   Penile venous occlusive procedure

37799   Unlisted procedure, vascular surgery

Hemic and Lymphatic Systems

Spleen

Excision

38100   Splenectomy; total (separate procedure)

38101   partial (separate procedure)

+ 38102   total, en bloc for extensive disease, in conjunction with other procedure (List in addition to code for primary procedure)

Repair

38115   Repair of ruptured spleen (splenorrhaphy) with or without partial splenectomy

Laparoscopy

Surgical laparoscopy always includes diagnostic laparoscopy. To report a diagnostic laparoscopy (peritoneoscopy) (separate procedure), use 49320.

38120   Laparoscopy, surgical, splenectomy

38129   Unlisted laparoscopy procedure, spleen

Introduction

38200   Injection procedure for splenoportography

(For radiological supervision and interpretation, use 75810)

General

Bone Marrow or Stem Cell Services/Procedures

Codes 38207-38215 describe various steps used to preserve, prepare and purify bone marrow/stem cells prior to transplantation or reinfusion. Each code may be reported only once per day regardless of the quantity of bone marrow/stem cells manipulated.

38204   Management of recipient hematopoietic progenitor cell donor search and cell acquisition

38205   Blood-derived hematopoietic progenitor cell harvesting for transplantation, per collection; allogenic

38206   autologous

38207   Transplant preparation of hematopoietic progenitor cells; cryopreservation and storage

(For diagnostic cryopreservation and storage, see 88240)

38208   thawing of previously frozen harvest, without washing

(For diagnostic thawing and expansion of frozen cells, see 88241)

38209   thawing of previously frozen harvest, with washing

38210   specific cell depletion within harvest, T-cell depletion

38211   tumor cell depletion

38212   red blood cell removal

38213   platelet depletion

38214   plasma (volume) depletion

38215   cell concentration in plasma, mononuclear, or buffy coat layer

(Do not report 38207-38215 in conjunction with 88182, 88184-88189)

38220   Bone marrow; aspiration only

38221   biopsy, needle or trocar

(For bone marrow biopsy interpretation, use 88305)

38230   Bone marrow harvesting for transplantation

(For autologous and allogenic blood-derived peripheral stem cell harvesting for transplantation, see 38205-38206)

38240   Bone marrow or blood-derived peripheral stem cell transplantation; allogenic

38241   autologous

38242   allogeneic donor lymphocyte infusions

(For bone marrow aspiration, use 38220)

(For modification, treatment, and processing of bone marrow or blood-derived stem cell specimens for transplantation, use 38210-38213)

(For cryopreservation, freezing and storage of blood-derived stem cells for transplantation, use 88240)

(For thawing and expansion of blood-derived stem cells for transplantation, use 88241)

(For compatibility studies, see 86812-86822)

Lymph Nodes and Lymphatic Channels

Incision

38300   Drainage of lymph node abscess or lymphadenitis; simple

38305   extensive

38308   Lymphangiotomy or other operations on lymphatic channels

Surgery: Cardiovascular System

Surgery: Cardiovascular System

38380	Suture and/or ligation of thoracic duct; cervical approach
38381	thoracic approach
38382	abdominal approach

Excision

(For injection for sentinel node identification, use 38792)

38500	Biopsy or excision of lymph node(s); open, superficial

(Do not report 38500 with 38700-38780)

38505	by needle, superficial (eg, cervical, inguinal, axillary)

(If imaging guidance is performed, see 76360, 76393, 76942)

(For fine needle aspiration, use 10021 or 10022)

(For evaluation of fine needle aspirate, see 88172, 88173)

38510	open, deep cervical node(s)
38520	open, deep cervical node(s) with excision scalene fat pad
38525	open, deep axillary node(s)
38530	open, internal mammary node(s)

(Do not report 38530 with 38720-38746)

(For percutaneous needle biopsy, retroperitoneal lymph node or mass, use 49180. For fine needle aspiration, use 10022)

38542	Dissection, deep jugular node(s)

(For radical cervical neck dissection, use 38720)

38550	Excision of cystic hygroma, axillary or cervical; without deep neurovascular dissection
38555	with deep neurovascular dissection

Limited Lymphadenectomy for Staging

38562	Limited lymphadenectomy for staging (separate procedure); pelvic and para-aortic

(When combined with prostatectomy, use 55812 or 55842)

(When combined with insertion of radioactive substance into prostate, use 55862)

38564	retroperitoneal (aortic and/or splenic)

Laparoscopy

Surgical laparoscopy always includes diagnostic laparoscopy. To report a diagnostic laparoscopy (peritoneoscopy) (separate procedure), use 49320.

38570	Laparoscopy, surgical; with retroperitoneal lymph node sampling (biopsy), single or multiple
38571	with bilateral total pelvic lymphadenectomy
38572	with bilateral total pelvic lymphadenectomy and peri-aortic lymph node sampling (biopsy), single or multiple

(For drainage of lymphocele to peritoneal cavity, use 49323)

38589	Unlisted laparoscopy procedure, lymphatic system

Radical Lymphadenectomy (Radical Resection of Lymph Nodes)

(For limited pelvic and retroperitoneal lymphadenectomies, see 38562, 38564)

38700	Suprahyoid lymphadenectomy

(For bilateral procedure, report 38700 with modifier 50)

38720	Cervical lymphadenectomy (complete)

(For bilateral procedure, report 38720 with modifier 50)

38724	Cervical lymphadenectomy (modified radical neck dissection)
38740	Axillary lymphadenectomy; superficial
38745	complete
+ 38746	Thoracic lymphadenectomy, regional, including mediastinal and peritracheal nodes (List separately in addition to code for primary procedure)
+ 38747	Abdominal lymphadenectomy, regional, including celiac, gastric, portal, peripancreatic, with or without para-aortic and vena caval nodes (List separately in addition to code for primary procedure)
38760	Inguinofemoral lymphadenectomy, superficial, including Cloquets node (separate procedure)

(For bilateral procedure, report 38760 with modifier 50

38765	Inguinofemoral lymphadenectomy, superficial, in continuity with pelvic lymphadenectomy, including external iliac, hypogastric, and obturator nodes (separate procedure)

(For bilateral procedure, report 38765 with modifier 50)

38770	Pelvic lymphadenectomy, including external iliac, hypogastric, and obturator nodes (separate procedure)

(For bilateral procedure, report 38770 with modifier 50)

38780	Retroperitoneal transabdominal lymphadenectomy, extensive, including pelvic, aortic, and renal nodes (separate procedure)

(For excision and repair of lymphedematous skin and subcutaneous tissue, see 15000, 15570-15650)

Introduction

38790   Injection procedure; lymphangiography

(For bilateral procedure, report 38790 with modifier 50)

(For radiological supervision and interpretation, see 75801-75807)

⊘ **38792**   for identification of sentinel node

(For excision of sentinel node, see 38500-38542)

(For nuclear medicine lymphatics and lymph gland imaging, use 78195)

38794   Cannulation, thoracic duct

Other Procedures

38999   Unlisted procedure, hemic or lymphatic system

Mediastinum and Diaphragm

Mediastinum

Incision

39000   Mediastinotomy with exploration, drainage, removal of foreign body, or biopsy; cervical approach

39010   transthoracic approach, including either transthoracic or median sternotomy

Excision

39200   Excision of mediastinal cyst

39220   Excision of mediastinal tumor

(For substernal thyroidectomy, use 60270)

(For thymectomy, use 60520)

Endoscopy

39400   Mediastinoscopy, with or without biopsy

Other Procedures

39499   Unlisted procedure, mediastinum

Diaphragm

Repair

(For transabdominal repair of diaphragmatic (esophageal hiatal) hernia, see 43324, 43325)

39501   Repair, laceration of diaphragm, any approach

39502   Repair, paraesophageal hiatus hernia, transabdominal, with or without fundoplasty, vagotomy, and/or pyloroplasty, except neonatal

39503   Repair, neonatal diaphragmatic hernia, with or without chest tube insertion and with or without creation of ventral hernia

(Do not report modifier 63 in conjunction with 39503)

39520   Repair, diaphragmatic hernia (esophageal hiatal); transthoracic

39530   combined, thoracoabdominal

39531   combined, thoracoabdominal, with dilation of stricture (with or without gastroplasty)

39540   Repair, diaphragmatic hernia (other than neonatal), traumatic; acute

39541   chronic

39545   Imbrication of diaphragm for eventration, transthoracic or transabdominal, paralytic or nonparalytic

39560   Resection, diaphragm; with simple repair (eg, primary suture)

39561   with complex repair (eg, prosthetic material, local muscle flap)

Other Procedures

39599   Unlisted procedure, diaphragm

Surgery: Cardiovascular System

Notes

⊘=Modifier 51 exempt   ⊙=Conscious sedation   **+**=Add-on code   ⊁=FDA approval pending

Digestive System

Lips

(For procedures on skin of lips, see 10040 et seq)

Excision

40490   Biopsy of lip

40500   Vermilionectomy (lip shave), with mucosal advancement

40510   Excision of lip; transverse wedge excision with primary closure

40520   V-excision with primary direct linear closure

(For excision of mucous lesions, see 40810-40816)

40525   full thickness, reconstruction with local flap (eg, Estlander or fan)

40527   full thickness, reconstruction with cross lip flap (Abbe-Estlander)

40530   Resection of lip, more than one-fourth, without reconstruction

(For reconstruction, see 13131 et seq)

Repair (Cheiloplasty)

40650   Repair lip, full thickness; vermilion only

40652   up to half vertical height

40654   over one-half vertical height, or complex

40700   Plastic repair of cleft lip/nasal deformity; primary, partial or complete, unilateral

40701   primary bilateral, one stage procedure

40702   primary bilateral, one of two stages

40720   secondary, by recreation of defect and reclosure

(For bilateral procedure, report 40720 with modifier 50)

(To report rhinoplasty only for nasal deformity secondary to congenital cleft lip, see 30460, 30462)

(For repair of cleft lip, with cross lip pedicle flap (Abbe-Estlander type), use 40527)

40761   with cross lip pedicle flap (Abbe-Estlander type), including sectioning and inserting of pedicle

(For repair cleft palate, see 42200 et seq)

(For other reconstructive procedures, see 14060, 14061, 15120-15261, 15574, 15576, 15630)

Other Procedures

40799   Unlisted procedure, lips

Vestibule of Mouth

The vestibule is the part of the oral cavity outside the dentoalveolar structures; it includes the mucosal and submucosal tissue of lips and cheeks.

Incision

40800   Drainage of abscess, cyst, hematoma, vestibule of mouth; simple

40801   complicated

40804   Removal of embedded foreign body, vestibule of mouth; simple

40805   complicated

40806   Incision of labial frenum (frenotomy)

Excision, Destruction

40808   Biopsy, vestibule of mouth

40810   Excision of lesion of mucosa and submucosa, vestibule of mouth; without repair

40812   with simple repair

40814   with complex repair

40816   complex, with excision of underlying muscle

40818   Excision of mucosa of vestibule of mouth as donor graft

40819   Excision of frenum, labial or buccal (frenumectomy, frenulectomy, frenectomy)

40820   Destruction of lesion or scar of vestibule of mouth by physical methods (eg, laser, thermal, cryo, chemical)

Repair

40830   Closure of laceration, vestibule of mouth; 2.5 cm or less

40831   over 2.5 cm or complex

40840   Vestibuloplasty; anterior

40842   posterior, unilateral

40843   posterior, bilateral

40844   entire arch

40845   complex (including ridge extension, muscle repositioning)

(For skin grafts, see 15000 et seq)

Other Procedures

40899   Unlisted procedure, vestibule of mouth

Tongue and Floor of Mouth

Incision

41000   Intraoral incision and drainage of abscess, cyst, or hematoma of tongue or floor of mouth; lingual

41005   sublingual, superficial

41006   sublingual, deep, supramylohyoid

41007   submental space

41008   submandibular space

41009   masticator space

41010   Incision of lingual frenum (frenotomy)

41015   Extraoral incision and drainage of abscess, cyst, or hematoma of floor of mouth; sublingual

41016   submental

41017   submandibular

41018   masticator space

(For frenoplasty, use 41520)

Excision

41100   Biopsy of tongue; anterior two-thirds

41105   posterior one-third

41108   Biopsy of floor of mouth

41110   Excision of lesion of tongue without closure

41112   Excision of lesion of tongue with closure; anterior two-thirds

41113   posterior one-third

41114   with local tongue flap

(List 41114 in addition to code 41112 or 41113)

41115   Excision of lingual frenum (frenectomy)

41116   Excision, lesion of floor of mouth

41120   Glossectomy; less than one-half tongue

41130   hemiglossectomy

41135   partial, with unilateral radical neck dissection

41140   complete or total, with or without tracheostomy, without radical neck dissection

41145   complete or total, with or without tracheostomy, with unilateral radical neck dissection

41150   composite procedure with resection floor of mouth and mandibular resection, without radical neck dissection

41153   composite procedure with resection floor of mouth, with suprahyoid neck dissection

41155   composite procedure with resection floor of mouth, mandibular resection, and radical neck dissection (Commando type)

Repair

41250   Repair of laceration 2.5 cm or less; floor of mouth and/or anterior two-thirds of tongue

41251   posterior one-third of tongue

41252   Repair of laceration of tongue, floor of mouth, over 2.6 cm or complex

Other Procedures

41500   Fixation of tongue, mechanical, other than suture (eg, K-wire)

41510   Suture of tongue to lip for micrognathia (Douglas type procedure)

41520   Frenoplasty (surgical revision of frenum, eg, with Z-plasty)

(For frenotomy, see 40806, 41010)

41599   Unlisted procedure, tongue, floor of mouth

Dentoalveolar Structures

Incision

41800   Drainage of abscess, cyst, hematoma from dentoalveolar structures

41805   Removal of embedded foreign body from dentoalveolar structures; soft tissues

41806   bone

Excision, Destruction

41820   Gingivectomy, excision gingiva, each quadrant

41821   Operculectomy, excision pericoronal tissues

41822   Excision of fibrous tuberosities, dentoalveolar structures

41823   Excision of osseous tuberosities, dentoalveolar structures

41825   Excision of lesion or tumor (except listed above), dentoalveolar structures; without repair

41826   with simple repair

41827   with complex repair

(For nonexcisional destruction, use 41850)

41828   Excision of hyperplastic alveolar mucosa, each quadrant (specify)

41830   Alveolectomy, including curettage of osteitis or sequestrectomy

41850   Destruction of lesion (except excision), dentoalveolar structures

Other Procedures

41870   Periodontal mucosal grafting

41872   Gingivoplasty, each quadrant (specify)

41874   Alveoloplasty, each quadrant (specify)

(For closure of lacerations, see 40830, 40831)

(For segmental osteotomy, use 21206)

(For reduction of fractures, see 21421-21490)

41899   Unlisted procedure, dentoalveolar structures

Palate and Uvula

Incision

42000   Drainage of abscess of palate, uvula

Excision, Destruction

42100   Biopsy of palate, uvula

42104   Excision, lesion of palate, uvula; without closure

42106   with simple primary closure

42107   with local flap closure

(For skin graft, see 14040-14300)

(For mucosal graft, use 40818)

42120   Resection of palate or extensive resection of lesion

(For reconstruction of palate with extraoral tissue, see 14040-14300, 15050, 15120, 15240, 15576)

42140   Uvulectomy, excision of uvula

42145   Palatopharyngoplasty (eg, uvulopalatopharyngoplasty, uvulopharyngoplasty)

(For removal of exostosis of the bony palate, see 21031, 21032)

42160   Destruction of lesion, palate or uvula (thermal, cryo or chemical)

Repair

42180   Repair, laceration of palate; up to 2 cm

42182   over 2 cm or complex

42200   Palatoplasty for cleft palate, soft and/or hard palate only

42205   Palatoplasty for cleft palate, with closure of alveolar ridge; soft tissue only

42210   with bone graft to alveolar ridge (includes obtaining graft)

42215   Palatoplasty for cleft palate; major revision

42220   secondary lengthening procedure

42225   attachment pharyngeal flap

42226   Lengthening of palate, and pharyngeal flap

42227   Lengthening of palate, with island flap

42235   Repair of anterior palate, including vomer flap

(For repair of oronasal fistula, use 30600)

42260   Repair of nasolabial fistula

(For repair of cleft lip, see 40700 et seq)

42280   Maxillary impression for palatal prosthesis

42281   Insertion of pin-retained palatal prosthesis

Other Procedures

42299   Unlisted procedure, palate, uvula

Salivary Gland and Ducts

Incision

42300   Drainage of abscess; parotid, simple

42305   parotid, complicated

42310   Drainage of abscess; submaxillary or sublingual, intraoral

42320   submaxillary, external

▶(42325, 42326 have been deleted)◀

42330   Sialolithotomy; submandibular (submaxillary), sublingual or parotid, uncomplicated, intraoral

42335   submandibular (submaxillary), complicated, intraoral

42340   parotid, extraoral or complicated intraoral

Excision

42400   Biopsy of salivary gland; needle

(For fine needle aspiration, see 10021, 10022)

(For evaluation of fine needle aspirate, see 88172, 88173)

(If imaging guidance is performed, see 76003, 76360, 76393, 76942)

42405   incisional

(If imaging guidance is performed, see 76003, 76360, 76393, 76942)

42408   Excision of sublingual salivary cyst (ranula)

42409   Marsupialization of sublingual salivary cyst (ranula)

42410   Excision of parotid tumor or parotid gland; lateral lobe, without nerve dissection

42415   lateral lobe, with dissection and preservation of facial nerve

42420   total, with dissection and preservation of facial nerve

42425   total, en bloc removal with sacrifice of facial nerve

42426   total, with unilateral radical neck dissection

(For suture or grafting of facial nerve, see 64864, 64865, 69740, 69745)

Surgery: Digestive System

42440 Excision of submandibular (submaxillary) gland

42450 Excision of sublingual gland

Repair

42500 Plastic repair of salivary duct, sialodochoplasty; primary or simple

42505   secondary or complicated

42507 Parotid duct diversion, bilateral (Wilke type procedure);

42508   with excision of one submandibular gland

42509   with excision of both submandibular glands

42510   with ligation of both submandibular (Wharton's) ducts

Other Procedures

42550 Injection procedure for sialography

(For radiological supervision and interpretation, use 70390)

42600 Closure salivary fistula

42650 Dilation salivary duct

42660 Dilation and catheterization of salivary duct, with or without injection

42665 Ligation salivary duct, intraoral

42699 Unlisted procedure, salivary glands or ducts

Pharynx, Adenoids, and Tonsils

Incision

42700 Incision and drainage abscess; peritonsillar

42720   retropharyngeal or parapharyngeal, intraoral approach

42725   retropharyngeal or parapharyngeal, external approach

Excision, Destruction

42800 Biopsy; oropharynx

42802   hypopharynx

42804   nasopharynx, visible lesion, simple

42806   nasopharynx, survey for unknown primary lesion

(For laryngoscopic biopsy, see 31510, 31535, 31536)

42808 Excision or destruction of lesion of pharynx, any method

42809 Removal of foreign body from pharynx

42810 Excision branchial cleft cyst or vestige, confined to skin and subcutaneous tissues

42815 Excision branchial cleft cyst, vestige, or fistula, extending beneath subcutaneous tissues and/or into pharynx

42820 Tonsillectomy and adenoidectomy; under age 12

42821   age 12 or over

42825 Tonsillectomy, primary or secondary; under age 12

42826   age 12 or over

42830 Adenoidectomy, primary; under age 12

42831   age 12 or over

42835 Adenoidectomy, secondary; under age 12

42836   age 12 or over

42842 Radical resection of tonsil, tonsillar pillars, and/or retromolar trigone; without closure

42844   closure with local flap (eg, tongue, buccal)

42845   closure with other flap

(For closure with other flap(s), use appropriate number for flap(s))

(When combined with radical neck dissection, use also 38720)

42860 Excision of tonsil tags

42870 Excision or destruction lingual tonsil, any method (separate procedure)

(For resection of the nasopharynx (eg, juvenile angiofibroma) by bicoronal and/or transzygomatic approach, see 61586 and 61600)

42890 Limited pharyngectomy

42892 Resection of lateral pharyngeal wall or pyriform sinus, direct closure by advancement of lateral and posterior pharyngeal walls

(When combined with radical neck dissection, use also 38720)

42894 Resection of pharyngeal wall requiring closure with myocutaneous flap

(When combined with radical neck dissection, use also 38720)

(For limited pharyngectomy with radical neck dissection, use 38720 with 42890)

Repair

42900 Suture pharynx for wound or injury

42950 Pharyngoplasty (plastic or reconstructive operation on pharynx)

(For pharyngeal flap, use 42225)

42953 Pharyngoesophageal repair

(For closure with myocutaneous or other flap, use appropriate number in addition)

Other Procedures

42955   Pharyngostomy (fistulization of pharynx, external for feeding)

42960   Control oropharyngeal hemorrhage, primary or secondary (eg, post-tonsillectomy); simple

42961   complicated, requiring hospitalization

42962   with secondary surgical intervention

42970   Control of nasopharyngeal hemorrhage, primary or secondary (eg, postadenoidectomy); simple, with posterior nasal packs, with or without anterior packs and/or cautery

42971   complicated, requiring hospitalization

42972   with secondary surgical intervention

42999   Unlisted procedure, pharynx, adenoids, or tonsils

Esophagus

Incision

(For esophageal intubation with laparotomy, use 43510)

43020   Esophagotomy, cervical approach, with removal of foreign body

43030   Cricopharyngeal myotomy

43045   Esophagotomy, thoracic approach, with removal of foreign body

Excision

(For gastrointestinal reconstruction for previous esophagectomy, see 43360, 43361)

43100   Excision of lesion, esophagus, with primary repair; cervical approach

43101   thoracic or abdominal approach

(For wide excision of malignant lesion of cervical esophagus, with total laryngectomy without radical neck dissection, see 43107, 43116, 43124, and 31360)

(For wide excision of malignant lesion of cervical esophagus, with total laryngectomy with radical neck dissection, see 43107, 43116, 43124, and 31365)

43107   Total or near total esophagectomy, without thoracotomy; with pharyngogastrostomy or cervical esophagogastrostomy, with or without pyloroplasty (transhiatal)

43108   with colon interposition or small intestine reconstruction, including intestine mobilization, preparation and anastomosis(es)

43112   Total or near total esophagectomy, with thoracotomy; with pharyngogastrostomy or cervical esophagogastrostomy, with or without pyloroplasty

43113   with colon interposition or small intestine reconstruction, including intestine mobilization, preparation, and anastomosis(es)

43116   Partial esophagectomy, cervical, with free intestinal graft, including microvascular anastomosis, obtaining the graft and intestinal reconstruction

(Do not report code 69990 in addition to code 43116)

(Report 43116 with the modifier 52 appended if intestinal or free jejunal graft with microvascular anastomosis is performed by another physician)

(For free jejunal graft with microvascular anastomosis performed by another physician, use 43496)

43117   Partial esophagectomy, distal two-thirds, with thoracotomy and separate abdominal incision, with or without proximal gastrectomy; with thoracic esophagogastrostomy, with or without pyloroplasty (Ivor Lewis)

43118   with colon interposition or small intestine reconstruction, including intestine mobilization, preparation, and anastomosis(es)

(For total esophagectomy with gastropharyngostomy, see 43107, 43124)

(For esophagogastrectomy (lower third) and vagotomy, use 43122)

43121   Partial esophagectomy, distal two-thirds, with thoracotomy only, with or without proximal gastrectomy, with thoracic esophagogastrostomy, with or without pyloroplasty

43122   Partial esophagectomy, thoracoabdominal or abdominal approach, with or without proximal gastrectomy; with esophagogastrostomy, with or without pyloroplasty

43123   with colon interposition or small intestine reconstruction, including intestine mobilization, preparation, and anastomosis(es)

43124   Total or partial esophagectomy, without reconstruction (any approach), with cervical esophagostomy

43130   Diverticulectomy of hypopharynx or esophagus, with or without myotomy; cervical approach

43135   thoracic approach

Endoscopy

For endoscopic procedures, code appropriate endoscopy of each anatomic site examined.

Surgical endoscopy always includes diagnostic endoscopy.

⊙ **43200**   Esophagoscopy, rigid or flexible; diagnostic, with or without collection of specimen(s) by brushing or washing (separate procedure)

⊙ **43201**   with directed submucosal injection(s), any substance

(For injection sclerosis of esophageal varices, use 43204)

⊙ **43202**   with biopsy, single or multiple

Surgery: Digestive System

⊙ **43204**   with injection sclerosis of esophageal varices

⊙ **43205**   with band ligation of esophageal varices

⊙ **43215**   with removal of foreign body

(For radiological supervision and interpretation, use 74235)

⊙ **43216**   with removal of tumor(s), polyp(s), or other lesion(s) by hot biopsy forceps or bipolar cautery

⊙ **43217**   with removal of tumor(s), polyp(s), or other lesion(s) by snare technique

⊙ **43219**   with insertion of plastic tube or stent

⊙ **43220**   with balloon dilation (less than 30 mm diameter)

(If imaging guidance is performed, use 74360)

(For endoscopic dilation with balloon 30 mm diameter or larger, use 43458)

(For dilation without visualization, use 43450-43453)

(For diagnostic fiberoptic esophagogastroscopy, use 43200, 43235)

(For fiberoptic esophagogastroscopy with biopsy or collection of specimen, use 43200, 43202, 43235, 43239)

(For fiberoptic esophagogastroscopy with removal of foreign body, use 43215, 43247)

(For fiberoptic esophagogastroscopy with removal of polyp(s), use 43217, 43251)

⊙ **43226**   with insertion of guide wire followed by dilation over guide wire

(For radiological supervision and interpretation, use 74360)

⊙ **43227**   with control of bleeding (eg, injection, bipolar cautery, unipolar cautery, laser, heater probe, stapler, plasma coagulator)

⊙ **43228**   with ablation of tumor(s), polyp(s), or other lesion(s), not amenable to removal by hot biopsy forceps, bipolar cautery or snare technique

(For esophagoscopic photodynamic therapy, report 43228 in addition to 96570, 96571 as appropriate)

⊙ **43231**   with endoscopic ultrasound examination

(Do not report 43231 in conjunction with 76975)

⊙ **43232**   with transendoscopic ultrasound-guided intramural or transmural fine needle aspiration/biopsy(s)

(Do not report 43232 in conjunction with 76942, 76975)

(For interpretation of specimen, see 88172-88173)

⊙ **43234** Upper gastrointestinal endoscopy, simple primary examination (eg, with small diameter flexible endoscope) (separate procedure)

⊙ **43235** Upper gastrointestinal endoscopy including esophagus, stomach, and either the duodenum and/or jejunum as appropriate; diagnostic, with or without collection of specimen(s) by brushing or washing (separate procedure)

⊙ **43236**   with directed submucosal injection(s), any substance

(For injection sclerosis of esophageal and/or gastric varices, use 43243)

⊙ **43237**   with endoscopic ultrasound examination limited to the esophagus

(Do not report 43237 in conjunction with 76942, 76975)

⊙ **43238**   with transendoscopic ultrasound-guided intramural or transmural fine needle aspiration/biopsy(s), esophagus (includes endoscopic ultrasound examination limited to the esophagus)

(Do not report 43238 in conjunction with 76942 or 76975)

⊙ **43239**   with biopsy, single or multiple

(For upper gastrointestinal endoscopy with suturing of the esophagogastric junction, use Category III code 0008T)

▶(For upper gastrointestinal endoscopy with injection of implant material into and along the muscle of the lower esophageal sphincter, use Category III code 0133T)◄

⊙ **43240**   with transmural drainage of pseudocyst

⊙ **43241**   with transendoscopic intraluminal tube or catheter placement

⊙ **43242**   with transendoscopic ultrasound-guided intramural or transmural fine needle aspiration/biopsy(s) (includes endoscopic ultrasound examination of the esophagus, stomach, and either the duodenum and/or jejunum as appropriate)

(Do not report 43242 in conjunction with 76942, 76975)

(For transendoscopic fine needle aspiration/biopsy limited to esophagus, use 43238)

(For interpretation of specimen, see 88172-88173)

⊙ **43243**   with injection sclerosis of esophageal and/or gastric varices

⊙ **43244**   with band ligation of esophageal and/or gastric varices

⊙ **43245**   with dilation of gastric outlet for obstruction (eg, balloon, guide wire, bougie)

(Do not report 43245 in conjunction with 43256)

⊙ **43246**   with directed placement of percutaneous gastrostomy tube

(For radiological supervision and interpretation, use 74350)

⊙ **43247**   with removal of foreign body

(For radiological supervision and interpretation, use 74235)

Surgery: Digestive System

⊙ **43248** with insertion of guide wire followed by dilation of esophagus over guide wire

⊙ **43249** with balloon dilation of esophagus (less than 30 mm diameter)

⊙ **43250** with removal of tumor(s), polyp(s), or other lesion(s) by hot biopsy forceps or bipolar cautery

⊙ **43251** with removal of tumor(s), polyp(s), or other lesion(s) by snare technique

⊙ **43255** with control of bleeding, any method

⊙ **43256** with transendoscopic stent placement (includes predilation)

⊙ **43257** with delivery of thermal energy to the muscle of lower esophageal sphincter and/or gastric cardia, for treatment of gastroesophageal reflux disease

⊙ **43258** with ablation of tumor(s), polyp(s), or other lesion(s) not amenable to removal by hot biopsy forceps, bipolar cautery or snare technique

(For injection sclerosis of esophageal varices, use 43204, 43243)

⊙ **43259** with endoscopic ultrasound examination, including the esophagus, stomach, and either the duodenum and/or jejunum as appropriate

(Do not report 43259 in conjunction with 76975)

⊙ **43260** Endoscopic retrograde cholangiopancreatography (ERCP); diagnostic, with or without collection of specimen(s) by brushing or washing (separate procedure)

(For radiological supervision and interpretation, see 74328, 74329, 74330)

⊙ **43261** with biopsy, single or multiple

(For radiological supervision and interpretation, see 74328, 74329, 74330)

⊙ **43262** with sphincterotomy/papillotomy

(For radiological supervision and interpretation, see 74328, 74329, 74330)

⊙ **43263** with pressure measurement of sphincter of Oddi (pancreatic duct or common bile duct)

(For radiological supervision and interpretation, see 74328, 74329, 74330)

⊙ **43264** with endoscopic retrograde removal of calculus/calculi from biliary and/or pancreatic ducts

(When done with sphincterotomy, also use 43262)

(For radiological supervision and interpretation, see 74328, 74329, 74330)

⊙ **43265** with endoscopic retrograde destruction, lithotripsy of calculus/calculi, any method

(When done with sphincterotomy, also use 43262)

(For radiological supervision and interpretation, see 74328, 74329, 74330)

⊙ **43267** with endoscopic retrograde insertion of nasobiliary or nasopancreatic drainage tube

(When done with sphincterotomy, also use 43262)

(For radiological supervision and interpretation, see 74328, 74329, 74330)

⊙ **43268** with endoscopic retrograde insertion of tube or stent into bile or pancreatic duct

(When done with sphincterotomy, also use 43262)

(For radiological supervision and interpretation, see 74328, 74329, 74330)

⊙ **43269** with endoscopic retrograde removal of foreign body and/or change of tube or stent

(When done with sphincterotomy, also use 43262)

(For radiological supervision and interpretation, see 74328, 74329, 74330)

⊙ **43271** with endoscopic retrograde balloon dilation of ampulla, biliary and/or pancreatic duct(s)

(When done with sphincterotomy, also use 43262)

(For radiological supervision and interpretation, see 74328, 74329, 74330)

⊙ **43272** with ablation of tumor(s), polyp(s), or other lesion(s) not amenable to removal by hot biopsy forceps, bipolar cautery or snare technique

(For radiological supervision and interpretation, see 74328, 74329, 74330)

Laparoscopy

Surgical laparoscopy always includes diagnostic laparoscopy. To report a diagnostic laparoscopy (peritoneoscopy) (separate procedure), use 49320.

43280 Laparoscopy, surgical, esophagogastric fundoplasty (eg, Nissen, Toupet procedures)

(For open approach, use 43324)

43289 Unlisted laparoscopy procedure, esophagus

Repair

43300 Esophagoplasty (plastic repair or reconstruction), cervical approach; without repair of tracheoesophageal fistula

43305 with repair of tracheoesophageal fistula

43310 Esophagoplasty (plastic repair or reconstruction), thoracic approach; without repair of tracheoesophageal fistula

43312 with repair of tracheoesophageal fistula

43313 Esophagoplasty for congenital defect (plastic repair or reconstruction), thoracic approach; without repair of congenital tracheoesophageal fistula

43314 with repair of congenital tracheoesophageal fistula

(Do not report modifier 63 in conjunction with 43313, 43314)

43320   Esophagogastrostomy (cardioplasty), with or without vagotomy and pyloroplasty, transabdominal or transthoracic approach

43324   Esophagogastric fundoplasty (eg, Nissen, Belsey IV, Hill procedures)

(For laparoscopic procedure, use 43280)

43325   Esophagogastric fundoplasty; with fundic patch (Thal-Nissen procedure)

(For cricopharyngeal myotomy, use 43030)

43326   with gastroplasty (eg, Collis)

43330   Esophagomyotomy (Heller type); abdominal approach

43331   thoracic approach

(For thoracoscopic esophagomyotomy, use 32665)

43340   Esophagojejunostomy (without total gastrectomy); abdominal approach

43341   thoracic approach

43350   Esophagostomy, fistulization of esophagus, external; abdominal approach

43351   thoracic approach

43352   cervical approach

43360   Gastrointestinal reconstruction for previous esophagectomy, for obstructing esophageal lesion or fistula, or for previous esophageal exclusion; with stomach, with or without pyloroplasty

43361   with colon interposition or small intestine reconstruction, including intestine mobilization, preparation, and anastomosis(es)

43400   Ligation, direct, esophageal varices

43401   Transection of esophagus with repair, for esophageal varices

43405   Ligation or stapling at gastroesophageal junction for pre-existing esophageal perforation

43410   Suture of esophageal wound or injury; cervical approach

43415   transthoracic or transabdominal approach

43420   Closure of esophagostomy or fistula; cervical approach

43425   transthoracic or transabdominal approach

(For repair of esophageal hiatal hernia, see 39520 et seq)

Manipulation

(For associated esophagogram, use 74220)

43450   Dilation of esophagus, by unguided sound or bougie, single or multiple passes

(For radiological supervision and interpretation, use 74360)

⊙ **43453**   Dilation of esophagus, over guide wire

(For dilation with direct visualization, use 43220)

(For dilation of esophagus, by balloon or dilator, see 43220, 43458, and 74360)

(For radiological supervision and interpretation, use 74360)

⊙ **43456**   Dilation of esophagus, by balloon or dilator, retrograde

(For radiological supervision and interpretation, use 74360)

⊙ **43458**   Dilation of esophagus with balloon (30 mm diameter or larger) for achalasia

(For dilation with balloon less than 30 mm diameter, use 43220)

(For radiological supervision and interpretation, use 74360)

43460   Esophagogastric tamponade, with balloon (Sengstaaken type)

(For removal of esophageal foreign body by balloon catheter, see 43215, 43247, 74235)

Other Procedures

43496   Free jejunum transfer with microvascular anastomosis

(Do not report code 69990 in addition to code 43496)

43499   Unlisted procedure, esophagus

Stomach

Incision

43500   Gastrotomy; with exploration or foreign body removal

43501   with suture repair of bleeding ulcer

43502   with suture repair of pre-existing esophagogastric laceration (eg, Mallory-Weiss)

43510   with esophageal dilation and insertion of permanent intraluminal tube (eg, Celestin or Mousseaux-Barbin)

43520   Pyloromyotomy, cutting of pyloric muscle (Fredet-Ramstedt type operation)

(Do not report modifier 63 in conjunction with 43520)

Excision

43600   Biopsy of stomach; by capsule, tube, peroral (one or more specimens)

43605   by laparotomy

43610   Excision, local; ulcer or benign tumor of stomach

43611   malignant tumor of stomach

43620   Gastrectomy, total; with esophagoenterostomy

43621   with Roux-en-Y reconstruction

43622   with formation of intestinal pouch, any type

43631   Gastrectomy, partial, distal; with gastroduodenostomy

43632   with gastrojejunostomy

43633   with Roux-en-Y reconstruction

43634   with formation of intestinal pouch

+ 43635   Vagotomy when performed with partial distal gastrectomy (List separately in addition to code(s) for primary procedure)

> (Use 43635 in conjunction with 43631, 43632, 43633, 43634)

> ►(43638, 43639 have been deleted)◄

43640   Vagotomy including pyloroplasty, with or without gastrostomy; truncal or selective

> (For pyloroplasty, use 43800)

> (For vagotomy, see 64752-64760)

43641   parietal cell (highly selective)

> (For upper gastrointestinal endoscopy, see 43234-43259)

Laparoscopy

Surgical laparoscopy always includes diagnostic laparoscopy. To report a diagnostic laparoscopy (peritoneoscopy) (separate procedure), use 49320.

> (For upper gastrointestinal endoscopy including esophagus, stomach, and either the duodenum and/or jejunum, see 43235-43259)

43644   Laparoscopy, surgical, gastric restrictive procedure; with gastric bypass and Roux-en-Y gastroenterostomy (roux limb 150 cm or less)

> (Do not report 43644 in conjunction with 43846, 49320)

> (Esophagogastroduodenoscopy (EGD) performed for a separate condition should be reported with modifier 59)

> (For greater than 150 cm, use 43645)

> (For open procedure, use 43846)

43645   with gastric bypass and small intestine reconstruction to limit absorption

> (Do not report 43645 in conjunction with 49320, 43847)

43651   Laparoscopy, surgical; transection of vagus nerves, truncal

43652   transection of vagus nerves, selective or highly selective

43653   gastrostomy, without construction of gastric tube (eg, Stamm procedure) (separate procedure)

43659   Unlisted laparoscopy procedure, stomach

Introduction

43750   Percutaneous placement of gastrostomy tube

> (For radiological supervision and interpretation, use 74350)

43752   Naso- or oro-gastric tube placement, requiring physician's skill and fluoroscopic guidance (includes fluoroscopy, image documentation and report)

> (For enteric tube placement, see 44500, 74340)

> (Do not report 43752 in conjunction with critical care codes 99291-99292, neonatal critical care codes 99295-99296, pediatric critical care codes 99293-99294 or low birth weight intensive care service codes 99298-99299)

43760   Change of gastrostomy tube

> (For endoscopic placement of gastrostomy tube, use 43246)

> (For radiological supervision and interpretation, use 75984)

43761   Repositioning of the gastric feeding tube, any method, through the duodenum for enteric nutrition

> (If imaging guidance is performed, use 75984)

►Bariatric Surgery◄

►Bariatric surgical procedures may involve the stomach, duodenum, jejunum, and/or the ileum.◄

►Laparoscopy◄

►Surgical laparoscopy always includes diagnostic laparoscopy. To report a diagnostic laparoscopy (separate procedure), use 49320.◄

►Typical postoperative follow-up care (see Surgery Guidelines, CPT Surgical Package Definition) after gastric restriction using the adjustable gastric band technique includes subsequent band adjustment(s) through the postoperative period for the typical patient. Band adjustment refers to changing the gastric band component diameter by injection or aspiration of fluid through the subcutaneous port component.◄

● **43770**   Laparoscopy, surgical, gastric restrictive procedure; placement of adjustable gastric band (gastric band and subcutaneous port components)

> ►(For individual component placement, report 43770 with modifier 52)◄

● **43771**   revision of adjustable gastric band component only

● **43772**   removal of adjustable gastric band component only

Surgery: Digestive System

● **43773** removal and replacement of adjustable gastric band component only

▶(Do not report 43773 in conjunction with 43772)◀

● **43774** removal of adjustable gastric band and subcutaneous port components

▶(For removal and replacement of both gastric band and subcutaneous port components, use 43659)◀

Other Procedures

43800 Pyloroplasty

(For pyloroplasty and vagotomy, use 43640)

43810 Gastroduodenostomy

43820 Gastrojejunostomy; without vagotomy

43825 with vagotomy, any type

43830 Gastrostomy, open; without construction of gastric tube (eg, Stamm procedure) (separate procedure)

43831 neonatal, for feeding

(For change of gastrostomy tube, use 43760)

(Do not report modifier 63 in conjunction with 43831)

43832 with construction of gastric tube (eg, Janeway procedure)

(For percutaneous endoscopic gastrostomy, use 43246)

43840 Gastrorrhaphy, suture of perforated duodenal or gastric ulcer, wound, or injury

43842 Gastric restrictive procedure, without gastric bypass, for morbid obesity; vertical-banded gastroplasty

43843 other than vertical-banded gastroplasty

43845 Gastric restrictive procedure with partial gastrectomy, pylorus-preserving duodenoileostomy and ileoileostomy (50 to 100 cm common channel) to limit absorption (biliopancreatic diversion with duodenal switch)

(Do not report 43845 in conjunction with 43633, 43847, 44130, 49000)

43846 Gastric restrictive procedure, with gastric bypass for morbid obesity; with short limb (150 cm or less) Roux-en-Y gastroenterostomy

(For greater than 150 cm, use 43847)

(For laparoscopic procedure, use 43644)

43847 with small intestine reconstruction to limit absorption

▲ **43848** Revision, open, of gastric restrictive procedure for morbid obesity, other than adjustable gastric band (separate procedure)

▶(For adjustable gastric band procedures, see 43770-43774, 43886-43888)◀

43850 Revision of gastroduodenal anastomosis (gastroduodenostomy) with reconstruction; without vagotomy

43855 with vagotomy

43860 Revision of gastrojejunal anastomosis (gastrojejunostomy) with reconstruction, with or without partial gastrectomy or intestine resection; without vagotomy

43865 with vagotomy

43870 Closure of gastrostomy, surgical

43880 Closure of gastrocolic fistula

● **43886** Gastric restrictive procedure, open; revision of subcutaneous port component only

● **43887** removal of subcutaneous port component only

● **43888** removal and replacement of subcutaneous port component only

▶(Do not report 43888 in conjunction with 43774, 43887)◀

▶(For laparoscopic removal of both gastric band and subcutaneous port components, use 43774)◀

▶(For removal and replacement of both gastric band and subcutaneous port components, use 43659)◀

43999 Unlisted procedure, stomach

Intestines (Except Rectum)

Incision

44005 Enterolysis (freeing of intestinal adhesion) (separate procedure)

(Do not report 44005 in addition to 45136)

▶(For laparoscopic approach, use 44180)◀

44010 Duodenotomy, for exploration, biopsy(s), or foreign body removal

+ **44015** Tube or needle catheter jejunostomy for enteral alimentation, intraoperative, any method (List separately in addition to primary procedure)

44020 Enterotomy, small intestine, other than duodenum; for exploration, biopsy(s), or foreign body removal

44021 for decompression (eg, Baker tube)

44025 Colotomy, for exploration, biopsy(s), or foreign body removal

(For exteriorization of intestine (Mikulicz resection with crushing of spur), see 44602-44605)

44050 Reduction of volvulus, intussusception, internal hernia, by laparotomy

44055 Correction of malrotation by lysis of duodenal bands and/or reduction of midgut volvulus (eg, Ladd procedure)

(Do not report modifier 63 in conjunction with 44055)

Excision

Intestinal allotransplantation involves three distinct components of physician work:

1) ***Cadaver donor enterectomy***, which includes harvesting the intestine graft and cold preservation of the graft (perfusing with cold preservation solution and cold maintenance) (use 44132). ***Living donor enterectomy***, which includes harvesting the intestine graft, cold preservation of the graft (perfusing with cold preservation solution and cold maintenance), and care of the donor (use 44133).

2) ***Backbench work***:

Standard preparation of an intestine allograft prior to transplantation includes mobilization and fashioning of the superior mesenteric artery and vein (see 44715).

Additional reconstruction of an intestine allograft prior to transplantation may include venous and/or arterial anastomosis(es) (see 44720-44721).

3) ***Recipient intestinal allotransplantation with or without recipient enterectomy***, which includes transplantation of allograft and care of the recipient (see 44135, 44136).

44100 Biopsy of intestine by capsule, tube, peroral (one or more specimens)

44110 Excision of one or more lesions of small or large intestine not requiring anastomosis, exteriorization, or fistulization; single enterotomy

44111   multiple enterotomies

44120 Enterectomy, resection of small intestine; single resection and anastomosis

         (Do not report 44120 in addition to 45136)

+ 44121   each additional resection and anastomosis (List separately in addition to code for primary procedure)

         (Use 44121 in conjunction with 44120)

44125   with enterostomy

44126 Enterectomy, resection of small intestine for congenital atresia, single resection and anastomosis of proximal segment of intestine; without tapering

44127   with tapering

+ 44128   each additional resection and anastomosis (List separately in addition to code for primary procedure)

         (Use 44128 in conjunction with 44126, 44127)

         (Do not report modifier 63 in conjunction with 44126, 44127, 44128)

44130 Enteroenterostomy, anastomosis of intestine, with or without cutaneous enterostomy (separate procedure)

44132 Donor enterectomy (including cold preservation), open; from cadaver donor

44133   partial, from living donor

         (For backbench intestinal graft preparation or reconstruction, see 44715, 44720, 44721)

44135 Intestinal allotransplantation; from cadaver donor

44136   from living donor

44137 Removal of transplanted intestinal allograft, complete

         (For partial removal of transplant allograft, see 44120, 44121, 44140)

+ 44139 Mobilization (take-down) of splenic flexure performed in conjunction with partial colectomy (List separately in addition to primary procedure)

         (Use 44139 in conjunction with 44140-44147)

44140 Colectomy, partial; with anastomosis

         (For laparoscopic procedure, use 44204)

44141   with skin level cecostomy or colostomy

44143   with end colostomy and closure of distal segment (Hartmann type procedure)

         (For laparoscopic procedure, use 44206)

44144   with resection, with colostomy or ileostomy and creation of mucofistula

44145   with coloproctostomy (low pelvic anastomosis)

         (For laparoscopic procedure, use 44207)

44146   with coloproctostomy (low pelvic anastomosis), with colostomy

         (For laparoscopic procedure, use 44208)

44147   abdominal and transanal approach

44150 Colectomy, total, abdominal, without proctectomy; with ileostomy or ileoproctostomy

         (For laparoscopic procedure, use 44210)

44151   with continent ileostomy

44152   with rectal mucosectomy, ileoanal anastomosis, with or without loop ileostomy

         (For laparoscopic procedure, use 44211)

44153   with rectal mucosectomy, ileoanal anastomosis, creation of ileal reservoir (S or J), with or without loop ileostomy

         (For laparoscopic procedure, use 44211)

44155 Colectomy, total, abdominal, with proctectomy; with ileostomy

         (For laparoscopic procedure, use 44212)

44156   with continent ileostomy

44160 Colectomy, partial, with removal of terminal ileum with ileocolostomy

         (For laparoscopic procedure, use 44205)

Surgery: Digestive System

Laparoscopy

Surgical laparoscopy always includes diagnostic laparoscopy. To report a diagnostic laparoscopy (peritoneoscopy) (separate procedure), use 49320.

►Incision◄

● **44180** Laparoscopy, surgical, enterolysis (freeing of intestinal adhesion) (separate procedure)

(For laparoscopy with salpingolysis, ovariolysis, use 58660)

►Enterostomy—External Fistulization of Intestines◄

● **44186** Laparoscopy, surgical; jejunostomy (eg, for decompression or feeding)

● **44187** ileostomy or jejunostomy, non-tube

►(For open procedure, use 44310)◄

● **44188** Laparoscopy, surgical, colostomy or skin level cecostomy

►(For open procedure, use 44320)◄

►(Do not report 44188 in conjunction with 44970)◄

►(44200 has been deleted. To report, use 44180)◄

►(44201 has been deleted. To report, use 44186)◄

►Excision◄

▲ **44202** Laparoscopy, surgical; enterectomy, resection of small intestine, single resection and anastomosis

+ **44203** each additional small intestine resection and anastomosis (List separately in addition to code for primary procedure)

(Use 44203 in conjunction with 44202)

(For open procedure, see 44120, 44121)

44204 colectomy, partial, with anastomosis

(For open procedure, use 44140)

44205 colectomy, partial, with removal of terminal ileum with ileocolostomy

(For open procedure, use 44160)

44206 colectomy, partial, with end colostomy and closure of distal segment (Hartmann type procedure)

(For open procedure, use 44143)

44207 colectomy, partial, with anastomosis, with coloproctostomy (low pelvic anastomosis)

(For open procedure, use 44145)

44208 colectomy, partial, with anastomosis, with coloproctostomy (low pelvic anastomosis) with colostomy

(For open procedure, use 44146)

44210 colectomy, total, abdominal, without proctectomy, with ileostomy or ileoproctostomy

(For open procedure, use 44150)

44211 colectomy, total, abdominal, with proctectomy, with ileoanal anastomosis, creation of ileal reservoir (S or J), with loop ileostomy, with or without rectal mucosectomy

(For open procedure, see 44152, 44153)

44212 colectomy, total, abdominal, with proctectomy, with ileostomy

(For open procedure, use 44155)

+● **44213** Laparoscopy, surgical, mobilization (take-down) of splenic flexure performed in conjunction with partial colectomy (List separately in addition to primary procedure)

►(Use 44213 in conjunction with 44204-44208)◄

►(For open procedure, use 44139)◄

►Repair◄

● **44227** Laparoscopy, surgical, closure of enterostomy, large or small intestine, with resection and anastomosis

►(For open procedure, see 44625, 44626)◄

►Other Procedures◄

44238 Unlisted laparoscopy procedure, intestine (except rectum)

►(44239 has been deleted. To report, use 45499)◄

Enterostomy—External Fistulization of Intestines

44300 Enterostomy or cecostomy, tube (eg, for decompression or feeding) (separate procedure)

▲ **44310** Ileostomy or jejunostomy, non-tube

►(For laparoscopic procedure, use 44187)◄

►(Do not report 44310 in conjunction with 44144, 44150-44153, 44155, 44156, 45113, 45119, 45136)◄

44312 Revision of ileostomy; simple (release of superficial scar) (separate procedure)

44314 complicated (reconstruction in-depth) (separate procedure)

44316 Continent ileostomy (Kock procedure) (separate procedure)

(For fiberoptic evaluation, use 44385)

▲ 44320   Colostomy or skin level cecostomy;

►(For laparoscopic procedure, use 44188)◄

►(Do not report 44320 in conjunction with 44141, 44144, 44146, 44605, 45110, 45119, 45126, 45563, 45805, 45825, 50810, 51597, 57307, or 58240)◄

44322   with multiple biopsies (eg, for congenital megacolon) (separate procedure)

44340   Revision of colostomy; simple (release of superficial scar) (separate procedure)

44345   complicated (reconstruction in-depth) (separate procedure)

44346   with repair of paracolostomy hernia (separate procedure)

Endoscopy, Small Intestine and Stomal

Surgical endoscopy always includes diagnostic endoscopy.

(For upper gastrointestinal endoscopy, see 43234-43258)

⊙ 44360   Small intestinal endoscopy, enteroscopy beyond second portion of duodenum, not including ileum; diagnostic, with or without collection of specimen(s) by brushing or washing (separate procedure)

⊙ 44361   with biopsy, single or multiple

⊙ 44363   with removal of foreign body

⊙ 44364   with removal of tumor(s), polyp(s), or other lesion(s) by snare technique

⊙ 44365   with removal of tumor(s), polyp(s), or other lesion(s) by hot biopsy forceps or bipolar cautery

⊙ 44366   with control of bleeding (eg, injection, bipolar cautery, unipolar cautery, laser, heater probe, stapler, plasma coagulator)

⊙ 44369   with ablation of tumor(s), polyp(s), or other lesion(s) not amenable to removal by hot biopsy forceps, bipolar cautery or snare technique

⊙ 44370   with transendoscopic stent placement (includes predilation)

⊙ 44372   with placement of percutaneous jejunostomy tube

⊙ 44373   with conversion of percutaneous gastrostomy tube to percutaneous jejunostomy tube

(For fiberoptic jejunostomy through stoma, use 43235)

⊙ 44376   Small intestinal endoscopy, enteroscopy beyond second portion of duodenum, including ileum; diagnostic, with or without collection of specimen(s) by brushing or washing (separate procedure)

⊙ 44377   with biopsy, single or multiple

⊙ 44378   with control of bleeding (eg, injection, bipolar cautery, unipolar cautery, laser, heater probe, stapler, plasma coagulator)

⊙ 44379   with transendoscopic stent placement (includes predilation)

⊙ 44380   Ileoscopy, through stoma; diagnostic, with or without collection of specimen(s) by brushing or washing (separate procedure)

⊙ 44382   with biopsy, single or multiple

⊙ 44383   with transendoscopic stent placement (includes predilation)

⊙ 44385   Endoscopic evaluation of small intestinal (abdominal or pelvic) pouch; diagnostic, with or without collection of specimen(s) by brushing or washing (separate procedure)

⊙ 44386   with biopsy, single or multiple

⊙ 44388   Colonoscopy through stoma; diagnostic, with or without collection of specimen(s) by brushing or washing (separate procedure)

⊙ 44389   with biopsy, single or multiple

⊙ 44390   with removal of foreign body

⊙ 44391   with control of bleeding (eg, injection, bipolar cautery, unipolar cautery, laser, heater probe, stapler, plasma coagulator)

⊙ 44392   with removal of tumor(s), polyp(s), or other lesion(s) by hot biopsy forceps or bipolar cautery

⊙ 44393   with ablation of tumor(s), polyp(s), or other lesion(s) not amenable to removal by hot biopsy forceps, bipolar cautery or snare technique

⊙ 44394   with removal of tumor(s), polyp(s), or other lesion(s) by snare technique

(For colonoscopy per rectum, see 45330-45385)

⊙ 44397   with transendoscopic stent placement (includes predilation)

Introduction

⊙⊘ 44500   Introduction of long gastrointestinal tube (eg, Miller-Abbott) (separate procedure)

(For radiological supervision and interpretation, use 74340)

(For naso- or oro-gastric tube placement, use 43752)

Repair

44602   Suture of small intestine (enterorrhaphy) for perforated ulcer, diverticulum, wound, injury or rupture; single perforation

44603   multiple perforations

44604   Suture of large intestine (colorrhaphy) for perforated ulcer, diverticulum, wound, injury or rupture (single or multiple perforations); without colostomy

44605   with colostomy

44615   Intestinal stricturoplasty (enterotomy and enterorrhaphy) with or without dilation, for intestinal obstruction

44620 Closure of enterostomy, large or small intestine;

44625 with resection and anastomosis other than colorectal

44626 with resection and colorectal anastomosis (eg, closure of Hartmann type procedure)

▶(For laparoscopic procedure, use 44188)◀

44640 Closure of intestinal cutaneous fistula

44650 Closure of enteroenteric or enterocolic fistula

44660 Closure of enterovesical fistula; without intestinal or bladder resection

44661 with intestine and/or bladder resection

(For closure of renocolic fistula, see 50525, 50526)

(For closure of gastrocolic fistula, use 43880)

(For closure of rectovesical fistula, see 45800, 45805)

44680 Intestinal plication (separate procedure)

Other Procedures

44700 Exclusion of small intestine from pelvis by mesh or other prosthesis, or native tissue (eg, bladder or omentum)

(For therapeutic radiation clinical treatment, see **Radiation Oncology** section)

+ 44701 Intraoperative colonic lavage (List separately in addition to code for primary procedure)

(Use 44701 in conjunction with 44140, 44145, 44150, or 44604 as appropriate)

(Do not report 44701 in conjunction with 44300, 44950-44960)

44715 Backbench standard preparation of cadaver or living donor intestine allograft prior to transplantation, including mobilization and fashioning of the superior mesenteric artery and vein

44720 Backbench reconstruction of cadaver or living donor intestine allograft prior to transplantation; venous anastomosis, each

44721 arterial anastomosis, each

44799 Unlisted procedure, intestine

(For unlisted laparoscopic procedure, intestine except rectum, use 44238)

Meckel's Diverticulum and the Mesentery

Excision

44800 Excision of Meckel's diverticulum (diverticulectomy) or omphalomesenteric duct

44820 Excision of lesion of mesentery (separate procedure)

(With intestine resection, see 44120 or 44140 et seq)

Suture

44850 Suture of mesentery (separate procedure)

(For reduction and repair of internal hernia, use 44050)

Other Procedures

44899 Unlisted procedure, Meckel's diverticulum and the mesentery

Appendix

Incision

44900 Incision and drainage of appendiceal abscess; open

⊙ **44901** percutaneous

(For radiological supervision and interpretation, use 75989)

Excision

44950 Appendectomy;

(Incidental appendectomy during intra-abdominal surgery does not usually warrant a separate identification. If necessary to report, add modifier 52)

+ 44955 when done for indicated purpose at time of other major procedure (not as separate procedure) (List separately in addition to code for primary procedure)

44960 for ruptured appendix with abscess or generalized peritonitis

Laparoscopy

Surgical laparoscopy always includes diagnostic laparoscopy. To report a diagnostic laparoscopy (peritoneoscopy) (separate procedure), use 49320.

44970 Laparoscopy, surgical, appendectomy

44979 Unlisted laparoscopy procedure, appendix

Rectum

Incision

45000 Transrectal drainage of pelvic abscess

45005 Incision and drainage of submucosal abscess, rectum

45020 Incision and drainage of deep supralevator, pelvirectal, or retrorectal abscess

(See also 46050, 46060)

Excision

45100 Biopsy of anorectal wall, anal approach (eg, congenital megacolon)

(For endoscopic biopsy, use 45305)

45108 Anorectal myomectomy

45110 Proctectomy; complete, combined abdominoperineal, with colostomy

►(For laparoscopic procedure, use 45395)◄

45111   partial resection of rectum, transabdominal approach

45112 Proctectomy, combined abdominoperineal, pull-through procedure (eg, colo-anal anastomosis)

(For colo-anal anastomosis with colonic reservoir or pouch, use 45119)

45113 Proctectomy, partial, with rectal mucosectomy, ileoanal anastomosis, creation of ileal reservoir (S or J), with or without loop ileostomy

45114 Proctectomy, partial, with anastomosis; abdominal and transsacral approach

45116   transsacral approach only (Kraske type)

▲ **45119** Proctectomy, combined abdominoperineal pull-through procedure (eg, colo-anal anastomosis), with creation of colonic reservoir (eg, J-pouch), with diverting enterostomy when performed

►(For laparoscopic procedure, use 45397)◄

45120 Proctectomy, complete (for congenital megacolon), abdominal and perineal approach; with pull-through procedure and anastomosis (eg, Swenson, Duhamel, or Soave type operation)

45121   with subtotal or total colectomy, with multiple biopsies

45123 Proctectomy, partial, without anastomosis, perineal approach

45126 Pelvic exenteration for colorectal malignancy, with proctectomy (with or without colostomy), with removal of bladder and ureteral transplantations, and/or hysterectomy, or cervicectomy, with or without removal of tube(s), with or without removal of ovary(s), or any combination thereof

45130 Excision of rectal procidentia, with anastomosis; perineal approach

45135   abdominal and perineal approach

45136 Excision of ileoanal reservoir with ileostomy

(Do not report 45136 in addition to 44005, 44120, 44310)

45150 Division of stricture of rectum

45160 Excision of rectal tumor by proctotomy, transsacral or transcoccygeal approach

45170 Excision of rectal tumor, transanal approach

Destruction

45190 Destruction of rectal tumor (eg, electrodessication, electrosurgery, laser ablation, laser resection, cryosurgery) transanal approach

Endoscopy

Definitions

Proctosigmoidoscopy is the examination of the rectum and sigmoid colon.

Sigmoidoscopy is the examination of the entire rectum, sigmoid colon and may include examination of a portion of the descending colon.

Colonoscopy is the examination of the entire colon, from the rectum to the cecum, and may include the examination of the terminal ileum.

For an incomplete colonoscopy, with full preparation for a colonoscopy, use a colonoscopy code with the modifier 52 and provide documentation.

Surgical endoscopy always includes diagnostic endoscopy.

45300 Proctosigmoidoscopy, rigid; diagnostic, with or without collection of specimen(s) by brushing or washing (separate procedure)

⊙ **45303**   with dilation (eg, balloon, guide wire, bougie)

(For radiological supervision and interpretation, use 74360)

⊙ **45305**   with biopsy, single or multiple

⊙ **45307**   with removal of foreign body

⊙ **45308**   with removal of single tumor, polyp, or other lesion by hot biopsy forceps or bipolar cautery

⊙ **45309**   with removal of single tumor, polyp, or other lesion by snare technique

⊙ **45315**   with removal of multiple tumors, polyps, or other lesions by hot biopsy forceps, bipolar cautery or snare technique

⊙ **45317**   with control of bleeding (eg, injection, bipolar cautery, unipolar cautery, laser, heater probe, stapler, plasma coagulator)

⊙ **45320**   with ablation of tumor(s), polyp(s), or other lesion(s) not amenable to removal by hot biopsy forceps, bipolar cautery or snare technique (eg, laser)

⊙ **45321**   with decompression of volvulus

⊙ **45327**   with transendoscopic stent placement (includes predilation)

45330 Sigmoidoscopy, flexible; diagnostic, with or without collection of specimen(s) by brushing or washing (separate procedure)

45331   with biopsy, single or multiple

⊙ **45332**   with removal of foreign body

Surgery: Digestive System

⊙ **45333** with removal of tumor(s), polyp(s), or other lesion(s) by hot biopsy forceps or bipolar cautery

⊙ **45334** with control of bleeding (eg, injection, bipolar cautery, unipolar cautery, laser, heater probe, stapler, plasma coagulator)

⊙ **45335** with directed submucosal injection(s), any substance

⊙ **45337** with decompression of volvulus, any method

⊙ **45338** with removal of tumor(s), polyp(s), or other lesion(s) by snare technique

⊙ **45339** with ablation of tumor(s), polyp(s), or other lesion(s) not amenable to removal by hot biopsy forceps, bipolar cautery or snare technique

⊙ **45340** with dilation by balloon, 1 or more strictures

(Do not report 45340 in conjunction with 45345)

⊙ **45341** with endoscopic ultrasound examination

⊙ **45342** with transendoscopic ultrasound guided intramural or transmural fine needle aspiration/biopsy(s)

(Do not report 45341, 45342 in conjunction with 76942)

(Do not report 45341, 45342 in conjunction with 76975)

(For interpretation of specimen, see 88172-88173)

(For transrectal ultrasound utilizing rigid probe device, use 76872)

⊙ **45345** with transendoscopic stent placement (includes predilation)

⊙ **45355** Colonoscopy, rigid or flexible, transabdominal via colotomy, single or multiple

(For fiberoptic colonoscopy beyond 25cm to splenic flexure, see 45330-45345)

⊙ **45378** Colonoscopy, flexible, proximal to splenic flexure; diagnostic, with or without collection of specimen(s) by brushing or washing, with or without colon decompression (separate procedure)

⊙ **45379** with removal of foreign body

⊙ **45380** with biopsy, single or multiple

⊙ **45381** with directed submucosal injection(s), any substance

⊙ **45382** with control of bleeding (eg, injection, bipolar cautery, unipolar cautery, laser, heater probe, stapler, plasma coagulator)

⊙ **45383** with ablation of tumor(s), polyp(s), or other lesion(s) not amenable to removal by hot biopsy forceps, bipolar cautery or snare technique

⊙ **45384** with removal of tumor(s), polyp(s), or other lesion(s) by hot biopsy forceps or bipolar cautery

⊙ **45385** with removal of tumor(s), polyp(s), or other lesion(s) by snare technique

(For small intestine and stomal endoscopy, see 44360-44393)

⊙ **45386** with dilation by balloon, 1 or more strictures

(Do not report 45386 in conjunction with 45387)

⊙ **45387** with transendoscopic stent placement (includes predilation)

⊙ **45391** with endoscopic ultrasound examination

(Do not report 45391 in conjunction with 45330, 45341, 45342, 45378, 76872)

⊙ **45392** with transendoscopic ultrasound guided intramural or transmural fine needle aspiration/biopsy(s)

(Do not report 45392 in conjunction with 45330, 45341, 45342, 45378, 76872)

▶Laparoscopy◀

▶Surgical laparoscopy always includes diagnostic laparoscopy. To report a diagnostic laparoscopy (peritoneoscopy) (separate procedure), use 49320.◀

▶Excision◀

● **45395** Laparoscopy, surgical; proctectomy, complete, combined abdominoperineal, with colostomy

▶(For open procedure, use 45110)◀

● **45397** proctectomy, combined abdominoperineal pull-through procedure (eg, colo-anal anastomosis), with creation of colonic reservoir (eg, J-pouch), with diverting enterostomy, when performed

▶(For open procedure, use 45119)◀

▶Repair◀

● **45400** Laparoscopy, surgical; proctopexy (for prolapse)

▶(For open procedure, use 45540, 45541)◀

● **45402** proctopexy (for prolapse), with sigmoid resection

▶(For open procedure, use 45550)◀

● **45499** Unlisted laparoscopy procedure, rectum

Repair

45500 Proctoplasty; for stenosis

45505 for prolapse of mucous membrane

45520 Perirectal injection of sclerosing solution for prolapse

▲ **45540** Proctopexy (eg, for prolapse); abdominal approach

▶(For laparoscopic procedure, use 45400)◀

45541 perineal approach

▲ **45550** with sigmoid resection, abdominal approach

▶(For laparoscopic procedure, use 45402)◀

45560 Repair of rectocele (separate procedure)

(For repair of rectocele with posterior colporrhaphy, use 57250)

45562 Exploration, repair, and presacral drainage for rectal injury;

45563   with colostomy

45800 Closure of rectovesical fistula;

45805   with colostomy

45820 Closure of rectourethral fistula;

45825   with colostomy

(For rectovaginal fistula closure, see 57300-57308)

Manipulation

45900 Reduction of procidentia (separate procedure) under anesthesia

45905 Dilation of anal sphincter (separate procedure) under anesthesia other than local

45910 Dilation of rectal stricture (separate procedure) under anesthesia other than local

45915 Removal of fecal impaction or foreign body (separate procedure) under anesthesia

Other Procedures

►Surgical diagnostic anorectal exam (45990) includes the following elements: external perineal exam, digital rectal exam, pelvic exam (when performed), diagnostic anoscopy, and diagnostic rigid proctoscopy.◄

● **45990** Anorectal exam, surgical, requiring anesthesia (general, spinal, or epidural), diagnostic

►(Do not report 45990 in conjunction with 45300- 45327, 46600, 57410, 99170)◄

45999 Unlisted procedure, rectum

►(For unlisted laparoscopic procedure, rectum, use 45499)◄

Anus

Incision

(For subcutaneous fistulotomy, use 46270)

46020 Placement of seton

(Do not report 46020 in addition to 46060, 46280, 46600)

46030 Removal of anal seton, other marker

46040 Incision and drainage of ischiorectal and/or perirectal abscess (separate procedure)

46045 Incision and drainage of intramural, intramuscular, or submucosal abscess, transanal, under anesthesia

46050 Incision and drainage, perianal abscess, superficial

(See also 45020, 46060)

46060 Incision and drainage of ischiorectal or intramural abscess, with fistulectomy or fistulotomy, submuscular, with or without placement of seton

(Do not report 46060 in addition to 46020)

(See also 45020)

46070 Incision, anal septum (infant)

(For anoplasty, see 46700-46705)

(Do not report modifier 63 in conjunction with 46070)

46080 Sphincterotomy, anal, division of sphincter (separate procedure)

46083 Incision of thrombosed hemorrhoid, external

Excision

46200 Fissurectomy, with or without sphincterotomy

46210 Cryptectomy; single

46211   multiple (separate procedure)

46220 Papillectomy or excision of single tag, anus (separate procedure)

46221 Hemorrhoidectomy, by simple ligature (eg, rubber band)

46230 Excision of external hemorrhoid tags and/or multiple papillae

46250 Hemorrhoidectomy, external, complete

46255 Hemorrhoidectomy, internal and external, simple;

46257   with fissurectomy

46258   with fistulectomy, with or without fissurectomy

46260 Hemorrhoidectomy, internal and external, complex or extensive;

46261   with fissurectomy

46262   with fistulectomy, with or without fissurectomy

(For injection of hemorrhoids, use 46500; for destruction, see 46934-46936; for ligation, see 46945, 46946; for hemorrhoidopexy, use 46947)

46270 Surgical treatment of anal fistula (fistulectomy/fistulotomy); subcutaneous

46275   submuscular

46280   complex or multiple, with or without placement of seton

(Do not report 46280 in addition to 46020)

46285   second stage

46288 Closure of anal fistula with rectal advancement flap

46320 Enucleation or excision of external thrombotic hemorrhoid

Surgery: Digestive System

Introduction

46500 Injection of sclerosing solution, hemorrhoids

(For excision of hemorrhoids, see 46250-46262; for destruction, see 46934-46936; for ligation, see 46945, 46946; for hemorrhoidopexy, use 46947)

● **46505** Chemodenervation of internal anal sphincter

▶(For chemodenervation of other muscles, see 64612-64614, 64640)◀

▶(Report the specific service in conjunction with the specific substance(s) or drug(s) provided)◀

Endoscopy

Surgical endoscopy always includes diagnostic endoscopy.

46600 Anoscopy; diagnostic, with or without collection of specimen(s) by brushing or washing (separate procedure)

(Do not report 46600 in addition to 46020)

46604   with dilation (eg, balloon, guide wire, bougie)

46606   with biopsy, single or multiple

46608   with removal of foreign body

46610   with removal of single tumor, polyp, or other lesion by hot biopsy forceps or bipolar cautery

46611   with removal of single tumor, polyp, or other lesion by snare technique

46612   with removal of multiple tumors, polyps, or other lesions by hot biopsy forceps, bipolar cautery or snare technique

46614   with control of bleeding (eg, injection, bipolar cautery, unipolar cautery, laser, heater probe, stapler, plasma coagulator)

46615   with ablation of tumor(s), polyp(s), or other lesion(s) not amenable to removal by hot biopsy forceps, bipolar cautery or snare technique

Repair

46700 Anoplasty, plastic operation for stricture; adult

46705   infant

(For simple incision of anal septum, use 46070)

(Do not report modifier 63 in conjunction with 46705)

46706 Repair of anal fistula with fibrin glue

● **46710** Repair of ileoanal pouch fistula/sinus (eg, perineal or vaginal), pouch advancement; transperineal approach

● **46712**   combined transperineal and transabdominal approach

46715 Repair of low imperforate anus; with anoperineal fistula (cut-back procedure)

46716   with transposition of anoperineal or anovestibular fistula

(Do not report modifier 63 in conjunction with 46715, 46716)

46730 Repair of high imperforate anus without fistula; perineal or sacroperineal approach

46735   combined transabdominal and sacroperineal approaches

(Do not report modifier 63 in conjunction with 46730, 46735)

46740 Repair of high imperforate anus with rectourethral or rectovaginal fistula; perineal or sacroperineal approach

46742   combined transabdominal and sacroperineal approaches

(Do not report modifier 63 in conjunction with 46740, 46742)

46744 Repair of cloacal anomaly by anorectovaginoplasty and urethroplasty, sacroperineal approach

(Do not report modifier 63 in conjunction with 46744)

46746 Repair of cloacal anomaly by anorectovaginoplasty and urethroplasty, combined abdominal and sacroperineal approach;

46748   with vaginal lengthening by intestinal graft or pedicle flaps

46750 Sphincteroplasty, anal, for incontinence or prolapse; adult

46751   child

46753 Graft (Thiersch operation) for rectal incontinence and/or prolapse

46754 Removal of Thiersch wire or suture, anal canal

46760 Sphincteroplasty, anal, for incontinence, adult; muscle transplant

46761   levator muscle imbrication (Park posterior anal repair)

46762   implantation artificial sphincter

Destruction

46900 Destruction of lesion(s), anus (eg, condyloma, papilloma, molluscum contagiosum, herpetic vesicle), simple; chemical

46910   electrodesiccation

46916   cryosurgery

46917   laser surgery

46922   surgical excision

46924 Destruction of lesion(s), anus (eg, condyloma, papilloma, molluscum contagiosum, herpetic vesicle), extensive (eg, laser surgery, electrosurgery, cryosurgery, chemosurgery)

Surgery: Digestive System

46934	Destruction of hemorrhoids, any method; internal
46935	external
46936	internal and external

(For excision of hemorrhoids, see 46250-46262; for injection, use 46500; for ligation, see 46945, 46946; for hemorrhoidopexy, use 46947)

46937	Cryosurgery of rectal tumor; benign
46938	malignant
46940	Curettage or cautery of anal fissure, including dilation of anal sphincter (separate procedure); initial
46942	subsequent

Suture

46945	Ligation of internal hemorrhoids; single procedure
46946	multiple procedures
46947	Hemorrhoidopexy (eg, for prolapsing internal hemorrhoids) by stapling

(For excision of hemorrhoids, see 46250-46262; for injection, use 46500; for destruction, see 46934-46936)

Other Procedures

46999	Unlisted procedure, anus

Liver

Incision

47000	Biopsy of liver, needle; percutaneous

(If imaging guidance is performed, see 76003, 76360, 76393, 76942)

+ 47001	when done for indicated purpose at time of other major procedure (List separately in addition to code for primary procedure)

(If imaging guidance is performed, see 76003, 76942)

(For fine needle aspiration in conjunction with 47000, 47001, see 10021, 10022)

(For evaluation of fine needle aspirate in conjunction with 47000, 47001, see 88172, 88173)

47010	Hepatotomy; for open drainage of abscess or cyst, one or two stages
⊙ 47011	for percutaneous drainage of abscess or cyst, one or two stages

(For radiological supervision and interpretation, use 75989)

47015	Laparotomy, with aspiration and/or injection of hepatic parasitic (eg, amoebic or echinococcal) cyst(s) or abscess(es)

Excision

47100	Biopsy of liver, wedge
47120	Hepatectomy, resection of liver; partial lobectomy
47122	trisegmentectomy
47125	total left lobectomy
47130	total right lobectomy

Liver Transplantation

Liver allotransplantation involves three distinct components of physician work:

1) *Cadaver donor hepatectomy*, which includes harvesting the graft and cold preservation of the graft (perfusing with cold preservation solution and cold maintenance) (use 47133). *Living donor hepatectomy*, which includes harvesting the graft, cold preservation of the graft (perfusing with cold preservation solution and cold maintenance), and care of the donor (see 47140-47142).

2) *Backbench work*:

Standard preparation of the whole liver graft will include one of the following:

Preparation of whole liver graft (including cholecystectomy, if necessary, and dissection and removal of surrounding soft tissues to prepare vena cava, portal vein, hepatic artery, and common bile duct for implantation) (use 47143).

Preparation as described for whole liver graft, plus trisegment split into two partial grafts (use 47144).

Preparation as described for whole liver graft, plus lobe split into two partial grafts (use 47145).

Additional reconstruction of the liver graft may include venous and/or arterial anastomosis(es) (see 47146, 47147).

3) *Recipient liver allotransplantation*, which includes recipient hepatectomy (partial or whole), transplantation of the allograft (partial or whole), and care of the recipient (see 47135, 47136).

47133	Donor hepatectomy (including cold preservation), from cadaver donor

(47134 has been deleted. To report, use 47140)

47135	Liver allotransplantation; orthotopic, partial or whole, from cadaver or living donor, any age
47136	heterotopic, partial or whole, from cadaver or living donor, any age
47140	Donor hepatectomy (including cold preservation), from living donor; left lateral segment only (segments II and III)
47141	total left lobectomy (segments II, III and IV)
47142	total right lobectomy (segments V, VI, VII and VIII)

Surgery: Digestive System

47143 Backbench standard preparation of cadaver donor whole liver graft prior to allotransplantation, including cholecystectomy, if necessary, and dissection and removal of surrounding soft tissues to prepare the vena cava, portal vein, hepatic artery, and common bile duct for implantation; without trisegment or lobe split

47144 with trisegment split of whole liver graft into two partial liver grafts (ie, left lateral segment (segments II and III) and right trisegment (segments I and IV through VIII))

47145 with lobe split of whole liver graft into two partial liver grafts (ie, left lobe (segments II, III, and IV) and right lobe (segments I and V through VIII))

47146 Backbench reconstruction of cadaver or living donor liver graft prior to allotransplantation; venous anastomosis, each

47147 arterial anastomosis, each

(Do not report 47143-47147 in conjunction with 47120-47125, 47600, 47610)

Repair

47300 Marsupialization of cyst or abscess of liver

47350 Management of liver hemorrhage; simple suture of liver wound or injury

47360 complex suture of liver wound or injury, with or without hepatic artery ligation

47361 exploration of hepatic wound, extensive debridement, coagulation and/or suture, with or without packing of liver

47362 re-exploration of hepatic wound for removal of packing

Laparoscopy

Surgical laparoscopy always includes diagnostic laparoscopy. To report a diagnostic laparoscopy (peritoneoscopy) (separate procedure), use 49320.

47370 Laparoscopy, surgical, ablation of one or more liver tumor(s); radiofrequency

(For imaging guidance, use 76940)

47371 cryosurgical

(For imaging guidance, use 76940)

47379 Unlisted laparoscopic procedure, liver

Other Procedures

47380 Ablation, open, of one or more liver tumor(s); radiofrequency

(For imaging guidance, use 76940)

47381 cryosurgical

(For imaging guidance, use 76940)

47382 Ablation, one or more liver tumor(s), percutaneous, radiofrequency

(For imaging guidance and monitoring, see code 76362, 76394, or 76940)

47399 Unlisted procedure, liver

Biliary Tract

Incision

47400 Hepaticotomy or hepaticostomy with exploration, drainage, or removal of calculus

47420 Choledochotomy or choledochostomy with exploration, drainage, or removal of calculus, with or without cholecystotomy; without transduodenal sphincterotomy or sphincteroplasty

47425 with transduodenal sphincterotomy or sphincteroplasty

47460 Transduodenal sphincterotomy or sphincteroplasty, with or without transduodenal extraction of calculus (separate procedure)

47480 Cholecystotomy or cholecystostomy with exploration, drainage, or removal of calculus (separate procedure)

47490 Percutaneous cholecystostomy

(For radiological supervision and interpretation, use 75989)

Introduction

47500 Injection procedure for percutaneous transhepatic cholangiography

(For radiological supervision and interpretation, use 74320)

47505 Injection procedure for cholangiography through an existing catheter (eg, percutaneous transhepatic or T-tube)

(For radiological supervision and interpretation, use 74305)

47510 Introduction of percutaneous transhepatic catheter for biliary drainage

(For radiological supervision and interpretation, use 75980)

47511 Introduction of percutaneous transhepatic stent for internal and external biliary drainage

(For radiological supervision and interpretation, use 75982)

47525 Change of percutaneous biliary drainage catheter

(For radiological supervision and interpretation, use 75984)

47530 Revision and/or reinsertion of transhepatic tube

(For radiological supervision and interpretation, use 75984)

Endoscopy

Surgical endoscopy always includes diagnostic endoscopy.

+ **47550** Biliary endoscopy, intraoperative (choledochoscopy) (List separately in addition to code for primary procedure)

47552 Biliary endoscopy, percutaneous via T-tube or other tract; diagnostic, with or without collection of specimen(s) by brushing and/or washing (separate procedure)

47553 with biopsy, single or multiple

47554 with removal of calculus/calculi

47555 with dilation of biliary duct stricture(s) without stent

(For ERCP, see 43260-43272, 74363)

(If imaging guidance is performed, see 74363, 75982)

47556 with dilation of biliary duct stricture(s) with stent

(If imaging guidance is performed, see 74363, 75982)

Laparoscopy

Surgical laparoscopy always includes diagnostic laparoscopy. To report a diagnostic laparoscopy (peritoneoscopy) (separate procedure), use 49320.

47560 Laparoscopy, surgical; with guided transhepatic cholangiography, without biopsy

47561 with guided transhepatic cholangiography with biopsy

47562 cholecystectomy

47563 cholecystectomy with cholangiography

47564 cholecystectomy with exploration of common duct

47570 cholecystoenterostomy

47579 Unlisted laparoscopy procedure, biliary tract

Excision

47600 Cholecystectomy;

47605 with cholangiography

(For laparoscopic approach, see 47562-47564)

47610 Cholecystectomy with exploration of common duct;

(For cholecystectomy with exploration of common duct with biliary endoscopy, use 47610 with 47550)

47612 with choledochoenterostomy

47620 with transduodenal sphincterotomy or sphincteroplasty, with or without cholangiography

47630 Biliary duct stone extraction, percutaneous via T-tube tract, basket, or snare (eg, Burhenne technique)

(For radiological supervision and interpretation, use 74327)

47700 Exploration for congenital atresia of bile ducts, without repair, with or without liver biopsy, with or without cholangiography

(Do not report modifier 63 in conjunction with 47700)

47701 Portoenterostomy (eg, Kasai procedure)

(Do not report modifier 63 in conjunction with 47701)

47711 Excision of bile duct tumor, with or without primary repair of bile duct; extrahepatic

47712 intrahepatic

(For anastomosis, see 47760-47800)

47715 Excision of choledochal cyst

47716 Anastomosis, choledochal cyst, without excision

Repair

47720 Cholecystoenterostomy; direct

(For laparoscopic approach, use 47570)

47721 with gastroenterostomy

47740 Roux-en-Y

47741 Roux-en-Y with gastroenterostomy

47760 Anastomosis, of extrahepatic biliary ducts and gastrointestinal tract

47765 Anastomosis, of intrahepatic ducts and gastrointestinal tract

47780 Anastomosis, Roux-en-Y, of extrahepatic biliary ducts and gastrointestinal tract

47785 Anastomosis, Roux-en-Y, of intrahepatic biliary ducts and gastrointestinal tract

47800 Reconstruction, plastic, of extrahepatic biliary ducts with end-to-end anastomosis

47801 Placement of choledochal stent

47802 U-tube hepaticoenterostomy

47900 Suture of extrahepatic biliary duct for pre-existing injury (separate procedure)

Other Procedures

47999 Unlisted procedure, biliary tract

Pancreas

(For peroral pancreatic endoscopic procedures, see 43260-43272)

Incision

48000 Placement of drains, peripancreatic, for acute pancreatitis;

48001 with cholecystostomy, gastrostomy, and jejunostomy

Surgery: Digestive System

48005   Resection or debridement of pancreas and peripancreatic tissue for acute necrotizing pancreatitis

48020   Removal of pancreatic calculus

Excision

48100   Biopsy of pancreas, open (eg, fine needle aspiration, needle core biopsy, wedge biopsy)

48102   Biopsy of pancreas, percutaneous needle

(For radiological supervision and interpretation, see 76003, 76360, 76393, 76942)

(For fine needle aspiration, use 10022)

(For evaluation of fine needle aspirate, see 88172, 88173)

48120   Excision of lesion of pancreas (eg, cyst, adenoma)

48140   Pancreatectomy, distal subtotal, with or without splenectomy; without pancreaticojejunostomy

48145   with pancreaticojejunostomy

48146   Pancreatectomy, distal, near-total with preservation of duodenum (Child-type procedure)

48148   Excision of ampulla of Vater

48150   Pancreatectomy, proximal subtotal with total duodenectomy, partial gastrectomy, choledochoenterostomy and gastrojejunostomy (Whipple-type procedure); with pancreatojejunostomy

48152   without pancreatojejunostomy

48153   Pancreatectomy, proximal subtotal with near-total duodenectomy, choledochoenterostomy and duodenojejunostomy (pylorus-sparing, Whipple-type procedure); with pancreatojejunostomy

48154   without pancreatojejunostomy

48155   Pancreatectomy, total

48160   Pancreatectomy, total or subtotal, with autologous transplantation of pancreas or pancreatic islet cells

48180   Pancreaticojejunostomy, side-to-side anastomosis (Puestow-type operation)

Introduction

+ 48400   Injection procedure for intraoperative pancreatography (List separately in addition to code for primary procedure)

(For radiological supervision and interpretation, see 74300-74305)

Repair

48500   Marsupialization of pancreatic cyst

48510   External drainage, pseudocyst of pancreas; open

⊙ 48511   percutaneous

(For radiological supervision and interpretation, use 75989)

48520   Internal anastomosis of pancreatic cyst to gastrointestinal tract; direct

48540   Roux-en-Y

48545   Pancreatorrhaphy for injury

48547   Duodenal exclusion with gastrojejunostomy for pancreatic injury

Pancreas Transplantation

Pancreas allotransplantation involves three distinct components of physician work:

1) *Cadaver donor pancreatectomy*, which includes harvesting the pancreas graft, with or without duodenal segment, and cold preservation of the graft (perfusing with cold preservation solution and cold maintenance) (use 48550).

2) *Backbench work*:

Standard preparation of a cadaver donor pancreas allograft prior to transplantation includes dissection of the allograft from surrounding soft tissues, splenectomy, duodenotomy, ligation of bile duct, ligation of mesenteric vessels, and Y-graft arterial anastomoses from the iliac artery to the superior mesenteric artery and to the splenic artery (use 48551).

Additional reconstruction of a cadaver donor pancreas allograft prior to transplantation may include venous anastomosis(es) (use 48552).

3) *Recipient pancreas allotransplantation*, which includes transplantation of allograft, and care of the recipient (use 48554).

48550   Donor pancreatectomy (including cold preservation), with or without duodenal segment for transplantation

48551   Backbench standard preparation of cadaver donor pancreas allograft prior to transplantation, including dissection of allograft from surrounding soft tissues, splenectomy, duodenotomy, ligation of bile duct, ligation of mesenteric vessels, and Y-graft arterial anastomoses from iliac artery to superior mesenteric artery and to splenic artery

48552   Backbench reconstruction of cadaver donor pancreas allograft prior to transplantation, venous anastomosis, each

(Do not report 48551 and 48552 in conjunction with 35531, 35563, 35685, 38100-38102, 44010, 44820, 44850, 47460, 47505-47525, 47550-47556, 48100-48120, 48545)

48554   Transplantation of pancreatic allograft

48556   Removal of transplanted pancreatic allograft

Other Procedures

48999   Unlisted procedure, pancreas

Abdomen, Peritoneum, and Omentum

Incision

49000   Exploratory laparotomy, exploratory celiotomy with or without biopsy(s) (separate procedure)

(To report wound exploration due to penetrating trauma without laparotomy, use 20102)

49002   Reopening of recent laparotomy

(To report re-exploration of hepatic wound for removal of packing, use 47362)

49010   Exploration, retroperitoneal area with or without biopsy(s) (separate procedure)

(To report wound exploration due to penetrating trauma without laparotomy, use 20102)

49020   Drainage of peritoneal abscess or localized peritonitis, exclusive of appendiceal abscess; open

(For appendiceal abscess, use 44900)

⊙ **49021**   percutaneous

(For radiological supervision and interpretation, use 75989)

49040   Drainage of subdiaphragmatic or subphrenic abscess; open

⊙ **49041**   percutaneous

(For radiological supervision and interpretation, use 75989)

49060   Drainage of retroperitoneal abscess; open

⊙ **49061**   percutaneous

(For laparoscopic drainage, use 49323)

(For radiological supervision and interpretation, use 75989)

49062   Drainage of extraperitoneal lymphocele to peritoneal cavity, open

49080   Peritoneocentesis, abdominal paracentesis, or peritoneal lavage (diagnostic or therapeutic); initial

49081   subsequent

(If imaging guidance is performed, see 76360, 76942)

49085   Removal of peritoneal foreign body from peritoneal cavity

(For lysis of intestinal adhesions, use 44005)

Excision, Destruction

49180   Biopsy, abdominal or retroperitoneal mass, percutaneous needle

(If imaging guidance is performed, see 76003, 76360, 76393, 76942)

(For fine needle aspiration, use 10021 or 10022)

(For evaluation of fine needle aspirate, see 88172, 88173)

49200   Excision or destruction, open, intra-abdominal or retroperitoneal tumors or cysts or endometriomas;

49201   extensive

▶(For open cryoablation of renal tumor, use 50250)◀

▶(For percutaneous cryotherapy ablation of renal tumors, use Category III code 0135T)◀

49215   Excision of presacral or sacrococcygeal tumor

(Do not report modifier 63 in conjunction with 49215)

49220   Staging laparotomy for Hodgkins disease or lymphoma (includes splenectomy, needle or open biopsies of both liver lobes, possibly also removal of abdominal nodes, abdominal node and/or bone marrow biopsies, ovarian repositioning)

49250   Umbilectomy, omphalectomy, excision of umbilicus (separate procedure)

49255   Omentectomy, epiploectomy, resection of omentum (separate procedure)

Laparoscopy

Surgical laparoscopy always includes diagnostic laparoscopy. To report a diagnostic laparoscopy (peritoneoscopy), (separate procedure), use 49320.

For laparoscopic fulguration or excision of lesions of the ovary, pelvic viscera, or peritoneal surface use 58662.

49320   Laparoscopy, abdomen, peritoneum, and omentum, diagnostic, with or without collection of specimen(s) by brushing or washing (separate procedure)

49321   Laparoscopy, surgical; with biopsy (single or multiple)

49322   with aspiration of cavity or cyst (eg, ovarian cyst) (single or multiple)

49323   with drainage of lymphocele to peritoneal cavity

(For percutaneous or open drainage, see 49060, 49061)

49329   Unlisted laparoscopy procedure, abdomen, peritoneum and omentum

Surgery: Digestive System

Introduction, Revision, and/or Removal

49400 Injection of air or contrast into peritoneal cavity (separate procedure)

(For radiological supervision and interpretation, use 74190)

49419 Insertion of intraperitoneal cannula or catheter, with subcutaneous reservoir, permanent (ie, totally implantable)

(For removal, use 49422)

49420 Insertion of intraperitoneal cannula or catheter for drainage or dialysis; temporary

49421   permanent

49422 Removal of permanent intraperitoneal cannula or catheter

(For removal of a temporary catheter/cannula, use appropriate E/M code)

49423 Exchange of previously placed abscess or cyst drainage catheter under radiological guidance (separate procedure)

(For radiological supervision and interpretation, use 75984)

49424 Contrast injection for assessment of abscess or cyst via previously placed drainage catheter or tube (separate procedure)

(For radiological supervision and interpretation, use 76080)

49425 Insertion of peritoneal-venous shunt

49426 Revision of peritoneal-venous shunt

(For shunt patency test, use 78291)

49427 Injection procedure (eg, contrast media) for evaluation of previously placed peritoneal-venous shunt

(For radiological supervision and interpretation, see 75809, 78291)

49428 Ligation of peritoneal-venous shunt

49429 Removal of peritoneal-venous shunt

Repair

Hernioplasty, Herniorrhaphy, Herniotomy

The hernia repair codes in this section are categorized primarily by the type of hernia (inguinal, femoral, incisional, etc).

Some types of hernias are further categorized as "initial" or "recurrent" based on whether or not the hernia has required previous repair(s).

Additional variables accounted for by some of the codes include patient age and clinical presentation (reducible vs incarcerated or strangulated).

With the exception of the incisional hernia repairs (see 49560-49566) the use of mesh or other prostheses is not separately reported.

The excision/repair of strangulated organs or structures such as testicle(s), intestine, ovaries are reported by using the appropriate code for the excision/repair (eg, 44120, 54520, and 58940) in addition to the appropriate code for the repair of the strangulated hernia.

(For reduction and repair of intra-abdominal hernia, use 44050)

(For debridement of abdominal wall, see 11042, 11043)

(Codes 49491-49651 are unilateral procedures. To report bilateral procedures, report modifier 50 with the appropriate procedure code)

49491 Repair, initial inguinal hernia, preterm infant (less than 37 weeks gestation at birth), performed from birth up to 50 weeks postconception age, with or without hydrocelectomy; reducible

49492   incarcerated or strangulated

(Do not report modifier 63 in conjunction with 49491, 49492)

(Postconception age equals gestational age at birth plus age of infant in weeks at the time of the hernia repair. Initial inguinal hernia repairs that are performed on preterm infants who are over 50 weeks postconception age and under age 6 months at the time of surgery, should be reported using codes 49495, 49496)

49495 Repair, initial inguinal hernia, full term infant under age 6 months, or preterm infant over 50 weeks postconception age and under age 6 months at the time of surgery, with or without hydrocelectomy; reducible

49496   incarcerated or strangulated

(Do not report modifier 63 in conjunction with 49495, 49496)

(Postconception age equals gestational age at birth plus age in weeks at the time of the hernia repair. Initial inguinal hernia repairs that are performed on preterm infants who are under or up to 50 weeks postconception age but under 6 months of age since birth, should be reported using codes 49491, 49492. Inguinal hernia repairs on infants age 6 months to under 5 years should be reported using codes 49500-49501)

49500 Repair initial inguinal hernia, age 6 months to under 5 years, with or without hydrocelectomy; reducible

49501   incarcerated or strangulated

49505 Repair initial inguinal hernia, age 5 years or over; reducible

49507   incarcerated or strangulated

(For inguinal hernia repair, with simple orchiectomy, see 49505 or 49507 and 54520)

(For inguinal hernia repair, with excision of hydrocele or spermatocele, see 49505 or 49507 and 54840 or 55040)

49520   Repair recurrent inguinal hernia, any age; reducible

49521   incarcerated or strangulated

49525   Repair inguinal hernia, sliding, any age

         (For incarcerated or strangulated inguinal hernia repair, see 49496, 49501, 49507, 49521)

49540   Repair lumbar hernia

49550   Repair initial femoral hernia, any age; reducible

49553   incarcerated or strangulated

49555   Repair recurrent femoral hernia; reducible

49557   incarcerated or strangulated

49560   Repair initial incisional or ventral hernia; reducible

49561   incarcerated or strangulated

49565   Repair recurrent incisional or ventral hernia; reducible

49566   incarcerated or strangulated

+ 49568   Implantation of mesh or other prosthesis for incisional or ventral hernia repair (List separately in addition to code for the incisional or ventral hernia repair)

49570   Repair epigastric hernia (eg, preperitoneal fat); reducible (separate procedure)

49572   incarcerated or strangulated

49580   Repair umbilical hernia, under age 5 years; reducible

49582   incarcerated or strangulated

49585   Repair umbilical hernia, age 5 years or over; reducible

49587   incarcerated or strangulated

49590   Repair spigelian hernia

49600   Repair of small omphalocele, with primary closure

         (Do not report modifier 63 in conjunction with 49600)

49605   Repair of large omphalocele or gastroschisis; with or without prosthesis

49606   with removal of prosthesis, final reduction and closure, in operating room

         (Do not report modifier 63 in conjunction with 49605, 49606)

49610   Repair of omphalocele (Gross type operation); first stage

49611   second stage

         (Do not report modifier 63 in conjunction with 49610, 49611)

         (For diaphragmatic or hiatal hernia repair, see 39502-39541)

         (For surgical repair of omentum, use 49999)

Laparoscopy

Surgical laparoscopy always includes diagnostic laparoscopy. To report a diagnostic laparoscopy (peritoneoscopy) (separate procedure), use 49320.

49650   Laparoscopy, surgical; repair initial inguinal hernia

49651   repair recurrent inguinal hernia

49659   Unlisted laparoscopy procedure, hernioplasty, herniorrhaphy, herniotomy

Suture

49900   Suture, secondary, of abdominal wall for evisceration or dehiscence

         (For suture of ruptured diaphragm, see 39540, 39541)

         (For debridement of abdominal wall, see 11042, 11043)

Other Procedures

49904   Omental flap, extra-abdominal (eg, for reconstruction of sternal and chest wall defects)

         (Code 49904 includes harvest and transfer. If a second surgeon harvests the omental flap, then the two surgeons should code 49904 as co-surgeons, using modifier 62)

+ 49905   Omental flap, intra-abdominal (List separately in addition to code for primary procedure)

         (Do not report 49905 in conjunction with 44700)

49906   Free omental flap with microvascular anastomosis

         (Do not report code 69990 in addition to 49906)

49999   Unlisted procedure, abdomen, peritoneum and omentum

Surgery: Digestive System

Notes

⊘=Modifier 51 exempt   ⊙=Conscious sedation   +=Add-on code   ⋊=FDA approval pending

Urinary System

(For provision of chemotherapeutic agents, use 96545 in addition to code for primary procedure)

Kidney

Incision

(For retroperitoneal exploration, abscess, tumor, or cyst, see 49010, 49060, 49200, 49201)

50010   Renal exploration, not necessitating other specific procedures

(For laparoscopic ablation of renal mass lesion(s), use 50542)

50020   Drainage of perirenal or renal abscess; open

⊙ **50021**   percutaneous

(For radiological supervision and interpretation, use 75989)

50040   Nephrostomy, nephrotomy with drainage

50045   Nephrotomy, with exploration

(For renal endoscopy performed in conjunction with this procedure, see 50570-50580)

50060   Nephrolithotomy; removal of calculus

50065   secondary surgical operation for calculus

50070   complicated by congenital kidney abnormality

50075   removal of large staghorn calculus filling renal pelvis and calyces (including anatrophic pyelolithotomy)

50080   Percutaneous nephrostolithotomy or pyelostolithotomy, with or without dilation, endoscopy, lithotripsy, stenting, or basket extraction; up to 2 cm

50081   over 2 cm

(For establishment of nephrostomy without nephrostolithotomy, see 50040, 50395, 52334)

(For fluoroscopic guidance, see 76000, 76001)

50100   Transection or repositioning of aberrant renal vessels (separate procedure)

50120   Pyelotomy; with exploration

(For renal endoscopy performed in conjunction with this procedure, see 50570-50580)

50125   with drainage, pyelostomy

50130   with removal of calculus (pyelolithotomy, pelviolithotomy, including coagulum pyelolithotomy)

50135   complicated (eg, secondary operation, congenital kidney abnormality)

(For supply of anticarcinogenic agents, use 99070 in addition to code for primary procedure)

Excision

(For excision of retroperitoneal tumor or cyst, see 49200, 49201)

(For laparoscopic ablation of renal mass lesion(s), use 50542)

50200   Renal biopsy; percutaneous, by trocar or needle

(For radiological supervision and interpretation, see 76003, 76360, 76393, 76942)

(For fine needle aspiration, use 10022)

(For evaluation of fine needle aspirate, see 88172, 88173)

50205   by surgical exposure of kidney

50220   Nephrectomy, including partial ureterectomy, any open approach including rib resection;

50225   complicated because of previous surgery on same kidney

50230   radical, with regional lymphadenectomy and/or vena caval thrombectomy

(When vena caval resection with reconstruction is necessary, use 37799)

50234   Nephrectomy with total ureterectomy and bladder cuff; through same incision

50236   through separate incision

50240   Nephrectomy, partial

(For laparoscopic partial nephrectomy, use 50543)

● **50250**   Ablation, open, one or more renal mass lesion(s), cryosurgical, including intraoperative ultrasound, if performed

▶(For laparoscopic ablation of renal mass lesions, use 50542)◀

▶(For percutaneous cryotherapy ablation of renal tumors, use 0135T)◀

50280   Excision or unroofing of cyst(s) of kidney

(For laparoscopic ablation of renal cysts, use 50541)

50290   Excision of perinephric cyst

Renal Transplantation

Renal *auto*transplantation includes reimplantation of the autograft as the primary procedure, along with secondary extra-corporeal procedure(s) (eg, partial nephrectomy, nephrolithotomy) reported with modifier 51 (see 50380 and applicable secondary procedure(s)).

Renal *allo*transplantation involves three distinct components of physician work:

Surgery: Urinary System

1) ***Cadaver donor nephrectomy, unilateral or bilateral***, which includes harvesting the graft(s) and cold preservation of the graft(s) (perfusing with cold preservation solution and cold maintenance) (use 50300). ***Living donor nephrectomy***, which includes harvesting the graft, cold preservation of the graft (perfusing with cold preservation solution and cold maintenance), and care of the donor (see 50320, 50547).

2) ***Backbench work***:

Standard preparation of a cadaver donor renal allograft prior to transplantation including dissection and removal of perinephric fat, diaphragmatic and retroperitoneal attachments; excision of adrenal gland; and preparation of ureter(s), renal vein(s), and renal artery(s), ligating branches, as necessary (use 50323).

Standard preparation of a living donor renal allograft (open or laparoscopic) prior to transplantation including dissection and removal of perinephric fat and preparation of ureter(s), renal vein(s), and renal artery(s), ligating branches, as necessary (use 50325).

Additional reconstruction of a cadaver or living donor renal allograft prior to transplantation may include venous, arterial, and/or ureteral anastomosis(es) necessary for implantation (see 50327-50329).

3) ***Recipient renal allotransplantation***, which includes transplantation of the allograft (with or without recipient nephrectomy) and care of the recipient (see 50360, 50365).

(For dialysis, see 90935-90999)

(For laparoscopic donor nephrectomy, use 50547)

(For laparoscopic drainage of lymphocele to peritoneal cavity, use 49323)

50300   Donor nephrectomy (including cold preservation); from cadaver donor, unilateral or bilateral

50320   open, from living donor

50323   Backbench standard preparation of cadaver donor renal allograft prior to transplantation, including dissection and removal of perinephric fat, diaphragmatic and retroperitoneal attachments, excision of adrenal gland, and preparation of ureter(s), renal vein(s), and renal artery(s), ligating branches, as necessary

(Do not report 50323 in conjunction with 60540, 60545)

50325   Backbench standard preparation of living donor renal allograft (open or laparoscopic) prior to transplantation, including dissection and removal of perinephric fat and preparation of ureter(s), renal vein(s), and renal artery(s), ligating branches, as necessary

50327   Backbench reconstruction of cadaver or living donor renal allograft prior to transplantation; venous anastomosis, each

50328   arterial anastomosis, each

50329   ureteral anastomosis, each

50340   Recipient nephrectomy (separate procedure)

(For bilateral procedure, report 50340 with modifier 50)

50360   Renal allotransplantation, implantation of graft; without recipient nephrectomy

50365   with recipient nephrectomy

(For bilateral procedure, report 50365 with modifier 50)

50370   Removal of transplanted renal allograft

50380   Renal autotransplantation, reimplantation of kidney

(For renal autotransplantation extra-corporeal (bench) surgery, use autotransplantation as the primary procedure and report secondary procedure(s) (eg, partial nephrectomy, nephrolithotomy) with modifier 51)

Introduction

▶Renal Pelvis Catheter Procedures◀

▶*Internally Dwelling*◀

⊙● **50382**   Removal (via snare/capture) and replacement of internally dwelling ureteral stent via percutaneous approach, including radiological supervision and interpretation

▶(For bilateral procedure, use modifier 50)◀

⊙● **50384**   Removal (via snare/capture) of internally dwelling ureteral stent via percutaneous approach, including radiological supervision and interpretation

▶(For bilateral procedure, use modifier 50)◀

▶(Do not report 50382, 50384 in conjunction with 50395)◀

▶*Externally Accessible*◀

⊙● **50387**   Removal and replacement of externally accessible transnephric ureteral stent (eg, external/internal stent) requiring fluoroscopic guidance, including radiological supervision and interpretation

▶(For bilateral procedure, use modifier 50)◀

▶(For removal and replacement of externally accessible ureteral stent via ureterostomy or ilieal conduit, use 50688)◀

▶(For removal without replacement of an externally accessible ureteral stent not requiring fluoroscopic guidance, see **Evaluation and Management** services codes)◀

● **50389**   Removal of nephrostomy tube, requiring fluoroscopic guidance (eg, with concurrent indwelling ureteral stent)

▶(Removal of nephrostomy tube not requiring fluoroscopic guidance is considered inherent to E/M services. Report the appropriate level of E/M service provided)◀

Surgery: Urinary System

▶Other Introduction Procedures◄

50390   Aspiration and/or injection of renal cyst or pelvis by needle, percutaneous

(For radiological supervision and interpretation, see 74425, 74470, 76003, 76360, 76393, 76942)

(For evaluation of fine needle aspirate, see 88172, 88173)

50391   Instillation(s) of therapeutic agent into renal pelvis and/or ureter through established nephrostomy, pyelostomy or ureterostomy tube (eg, anticarcinogenic or antifungal agent)

50392   Introduction of intracatheter or catheter into renal pelvis for drainage and/or injection, percutaneous

(For radiological supervision and interpretation, see 74475, 76360, 76942)

50393   Introduction of ureteral catheter or stent into ureter through renal pelvis for drainage and/or injection, percutaneous

(For radiological supervision and interpretation, see 74480, 76003, 76360, 76942)

50394   Injection procedure for pyelography (as nephrostogram, pyelostogram, antegrade pyeloureterograms) through nephrostomy or pyelostomy tube, or indwelling ureteral catheter

(For radiological supervision and interpretation, use 74425)

50395   Introduction of guide into renal pelvis and/or ureter with dilation to establish nephrostomy tract, percutaneous

(For radiological supervision and interpretation, see 74475, 74480, 74485)

(For nephrostolithotomy, see 50080, 50081)

(For retrograde percutaneous nephrostomy, use 52334)

(For endoscopic surgery, see 50551-50561)

50396   Manometric studies through nephrostomy or pyelostomy tube, or indwelling ureteral catheter

(For radiological supervision and interpretation, see 74425, 74475, 74480)

50398   Change of nephrostomy or pyelostomy tube

(For radiological supervision and interpretation, use 75984)

Repair

50400   Pyeloplasty (Foley Y-pyeloplasty), plastic operation on renal pelvis, with or without plastic operation on ureter, nephropexy, nephrostomy, pyelostomy, or ureteral splinting; simple

50405   complicated (congenital kidney abnormality, secondary pyeloplasty, solitary kidney, calycoplasty)

(For laparoscopic approach, use 50544)

50500   Nephrorrhaphy, suture of kidney wound or injury

50520   Closure of nephrocutaneous or pyelocutaneous fistula

50525   Closure of nephrovisceral fistula (eg, renocolic), including visceral repair; abdominal approach

50526   thoracic approach

50540   Symphysiotomy for horseshoe kidney with or without pyeloplasty and/or other plastic procedure, unilateral or bilateral (one operation)

Laparoscopy

Surgical laparoscopy always includes diagnostic laparoscopy. To report a diagnostic laparoscopy (peritoneoscopy) (separate procedure), use 49320.

50541   Laparoscopy, surgical; ablation of renal cysts

50542   ablation of renal mass lesion(s)

(For open procedure, see 50220-50240)

▶(For open cryosurgical ablation, use 50250)◄

▶(For percutaneous cryotherapy ablation of renal tumors, use 0135T)◄

50543   partial nephrectomy

(For open procedure, use 50240)

50544   pyeloplasty

50545   radical nephrectomy (includes removal of Gerota's fascia and surrounding fatty tissue, removal of regional lymph nodes, and adrenalectomy)

(For open procedure, use 50230)

50546   nephrectomy, including partial ureterectomy

50547   donor nephrectomy (including cold preservation), from living donor

(For open procedure, use 50320)

(For backbench renal allograft standard preparation prior to transplantation, use 50325)

(For backbench renal allograft reconstruction prior to transplantation, see 50327-50329)

50548   nephrectomy with total ureterectomy

(For open procedure, see 50234, 50236)

50549   Unlisted laparoscopy procedure, renal

(For laparoscopic drainage of lymphocele to peritoneal cavity, use 49323)

Surgery: Urinary System

Endoscopy

(For supplies and materials, use 99070)

50551 Renal endoscopy through established nephrostomy or pyelostomy, with or without irrigation, instillation, or ureteropyelography, exclusive of radiologic service;

50553 with ureteral catheterization, with or without dilation of ureter

50555 with biopsy

50557 with fulguration and/or incision, with or without biopsy

(50559 has been deleted)

50561 with removal of foreign body or calculus

50562 with resection of tumor

(When procedures 50570-50580 provide a significant identifiable service, they may be added to 50045 and 50120)

50570 Renal endoscopy through nephrotomy or pyelotomy, with or without irrigation, instillation, or ureteropyelography, exclusive of radiologic service;

(For nephrotomy, use 50045)

(For pyelotomy, use 50120)

50572 with ureteral catheterization, with or without dilation of ureter

50574 with biopsy

50575 with endopyelotomy (includes cystoscopy, ureteroscopy, dilation of ureter and ureteral pelvic junction, incision of ureteral pelvic junction and insertion of endopyelotomy stent)

50576 with fulguration and/or incision, with or without biopsy

(50578 has been deleted)

50580 with removal of foreign body or calculus

Other Procedures

50590 Lithotripsy, extracorporeal shock wave

⊙● **50592** Ablation, one or more renal tumor(s), percutaneous, unilateral, radiofrequency

▶(50592 is a unilateral procedure. For bilateral procedure, report 50592 with modifier 50)◀

▶(For imaging guidance and monitoring, see 76362, 76394, 76940)◀

▶(For percutaneous cryotherapy ablation of renal tumors, use 0135T)◀

Ureter

Incision

50600 Ureterotomy with exploration or drainage (separate procedure)

(For ureteral endoscopy performed in conjunction with this procedure, see 50970-50980)

50605 Ureterotomy for insertion of indwelling stent, all types

50610 Ureterolithotomy; upper one-third of ureter

50620 middle one-third of ureter

50630 lower one-third of ureter

(For laparoscopic approach, use 50945)

(For transvesical ureterolithotomy, use 51060)

(For cystotomy with stone basket extraction of ureteral calculus, use 51065)

(For endoscopic extraction or manipulation of ureteral calculus, see 50080, 50081, 50561, 50961, 50980, 52320-52330, 52352, 52353)

Excision

(For ureterocele, see 51535, 52300)

50650 Ureterectomy, with bladder cuff (separate procedure)

50660 Ureterectomy, total, ectopic ureter, combination abdominal, vaginal and/or perineal approach

Introduction

50684 Injection procedure for ureterography or ureteropyelography through ureterostomy or indwelling ureteral catheter

(For radiological supervision and interpretation, use 74425)

50686 Manometric studies through ureterostomy or indwelling ureteral catheter

▲ **50688** Change of ureterostomy tube or externally accessible ureteral stent via ileal conduit

(If imaging guidance is performed, use 75984)

50690 Injection procedure for visualization of ileal conduit and/or ureteropyelography, exclusive of radiologic service

(For radiological supervision and interpretation, use 74425)

Repair

50700 Ureteroplasty, plastic operation on ureter (eg, stricture)

50715 Ureterolysis, with or without repositioning of ureter for retroperitoneal fibrosis

(For bilateral procedure, report 50715 with modifier 50)

50722   Ureterolysis for ovarian vein syndrome

50725   Ureterolysis for retrocaval ureter, with reanastomosis of upper urinary tract or vena cava

50727   Revision of urinary-cutaneous anastomosis (any type urostomy);

50728   with repair of fascial defect and hernia

50740   Ureteropyelostomy, anastomosis of ureter and renal pelvis

50750   Ureterocalycostomy, anastomosis of ureter to renal calyx

50760   Ureteroureterostomy

50770   Transureteroureterostomy, anastomosis of ureter to contralateral ureter

(Codes 50780-50785 include minor procedures to prevent vesicoureteral reflux)

50780   Ureteroneocystostomy; anastomosis of single ureter to bladder

(For bilateral procedure, report 50780 with modifier 50)

(When combined with cystourethroplasty or vesical neck revision, use 51820)

50782   anastomosis of duplicated ureter to bladder

50783   with extensive ureteral tailoring

50785   with vesico-psoas hitch or bladder flap

(For bilateral procedure, report 50785 with modifier 50)

50800   Ureteroenterostomy, direct anastomosis of ureter to intestine

(For bilateral procedure, report 50800 with modifier 50)

50810   Ureterosigmoidostomy, with creation of sigmoid bladder and establishment of abdominal or perineal colostomy, including intestine anastomosis

50815   Ureterocolon conduit, including intestine anastomosis

(For bilateral procedure, report 50815 with modifier 50)

50820   Ureteroileal conduit (ileal bladder), including intestine anastomosis (Bricker operation)

(For bilateral procedure, report 50820 with modifier 50)

(For combination of 50800-50820 with cystectomy, see 51580-51595)

50825   Continent diversion, including intestine anastomosis using any segment of small and/or large intestine (Kock pouch or Camey enterocystoplasty)

50830   Urinary undiversion (eg, taking down of ureteroileal conduit, ureterosigmoidostomy or ureteroenterostomy with ureteroureterostomy or ureteroneocystostomy)

50840   Replacement of all or part of ureter by intestine segment, including intestine anastomosis

(For bilateral procedure, report 50840 with modifier 50)

50845   Cutaneous appendico-vesicostomy

50860   Ureterostomy, transplantation of ureter to skin

(For bilateral procedure, report 50860 with modifier 50)

50900   Ureterorrhaphy, suture of ureter (separate procedure)

50920   Closure of ureterocutaneous fistula

50930   Closure of ureterovisceral fistula (including visceral repair)

50940   Deligation of ureter

(For ureteroplasty, ureterolysis, see 50700-50860)

Laparoscopy

Surgical laparoscopy always includes diagnostic laparoscopy. To report a diagnostic laparoscopy (peritoneoscopy) (separate procedure), use 49320.

50945   Laparoscopy, surgical; ureterolithotomy

50947   ureteroneocystostomy with cystoscopy and ureteral stent placement

50948   ureteroneocystostomy without cystoscopy and ureteral stent placement

(For open ureteroneocystostomy, see 50780-50785)

50949   Unlisted laparoscopy procedure, ureter

Endoscopy

50951   Ureteral endoscopy through established ureterostomy, with or without irrigation, instillation, or ureteropyelography, exclusive of radiologic service;

50953   with ureteral catheterization, with or without dilation of ureter

50955   with biopsy

50957   with fulguration and/or incision, with or without biopsy

(50959 has been deleted)

50961   with removal of foreign body or calculus

(When procedures 50970-50980 provide a significant identifiable service, they may be added to 50600)

50970   Ureteral endoscopy through ureterotomy, with or without irrigation, instillation, or ureteropyelography, exclusive of radiologic service;

(For ureterotomy, use 50600)

50972   with ureteral catheterization, with or without dilation of ureter

50974   with biopsy

50976   with fulguration and/or incision, with or without biopsy

(50978 has been deleted)

50980   with removal of foreign body or calculus

Surgery: Urinary System

Bladder

Incision

51000 Aspiration of bladder by needle

51005 Aspiration of bladder; by trocar or intracatheter

51010 with insertion of suprapubic catheter

(If imaging guidance is performed, see 76003, 76360, 76942)

51020 Cystotomy or cystostomy; with fulguration and/or insertion of radioactive material

51030 with cryosurgical destruction of intravesical lesion

51040 Cystostomy, cystotomy with drainage

51045 Cystotomy, with insertion of ureteral catheter or stent (separate procedure)

51050 Cystolithotomy, cystotomy with removal of calculus, without vesical neck resection

51060 Transvesical ureterolithotomy

51065 Cystotomy, with calculus basket extraction and/or ultrasonic or electrohydraulic fragmentation of ureteral calculus

51080 Drainage of perivesical or prevesical space abscess

Excision

51500 Excision of urachal cyst or sinus, with or without umbilical hernia repair

51520 Cystotomy; for simple excision of vesical neck (separate procedure)

51525 for excision of bladder diverticulum, single or multiple (separate procedure)

51530 for excision of bladder tumor

(For transurethral resection, see 52234-52240, 52305)

51535 Cystotomy for excision, incision, or repair of ureterocele

(For bilateral procedure, report 51535 with modifier 50)

(For transurethral excision, use 52300)

51550 Cystectomy, partial; simple

51555 complicated (eg, postradiation, previous surgery, difficult location)

51565 Cystectomy, partial, with reimplantation of ureter(s) into bladder (ureteroneocystostomy)

51570 Cystectomy, complete; (separate procedure)

51575 with bilateral pelvic lymphadenectomy, including external iliac, hypogastric, and obturator nodes

51580 Cystectomy, complete, with ureterosigmoidostomy or ureterocutaneous transplantations;

51585 with bilateral pelvic lymphadenectomy, including external iliac, hypogastric, and obturator nodes

51590 Cystectomy, complete, with ureteroileal conduit or sigmoid bladder, including intestine anastomosis;

51595 with bilateral pelvic lymphadenectomy, including external iliac, hypogastric, and obturator nodes

51596 Cystectomy, complete, with continent diversion, any open technique, using any segment of small and/or large intestine to construct neobladder

51597 Pelvic exenteration, complete, for vesical, prostatic or urethral malignancy, with removal of bladder and ureteral transplantations, with or without hysterectomy and/or abdominoperineal resection of rectum and colon and colostomy, or any combination thereof

(For pelvic exenteration for gynecologic malignancy, use 58240)

Introduction

51600 Injection procedure for cystography or voiding urethrocystography

(For radiological supervision and interpretation, see 74430, 74455)

51605 Injection procedure and placement of chain for contrast and/or chain urethrocystography

(For radiological supervision and interpretation, use 74430)

51610 Injection procedure for retrograde urethrocystography

(For radiological supervision and interpretation, use 74450)

51700 Bladder irrigation, simple, lavage and/or instillation

(Codes 51701-51702 are reported only when performed independently. Do not report 51701-51702 when catheter insertion is an inclusive component of another procedure.)

51701 Insertion of non-indwelling bladder catheter (eg, straight catheterization for residual urine)

51702 Insertion of temporary indwelling bladder catheter; simple (eg, Foley)

51703 complicated (eg, altered anatomy, fractured catheter/balloon)

51705 Change of cystostomy tube; simple

51710 complicated

(If imaging guidance is performed, use 75984)

51715 Endoscopic injection of implant material into the submucosal tissues of the urethra and/or bladder neck

51720 Bladder instillation of anticarcinogenic agent (including detention time)

Urodynamics

The following section (51725-51797) lists procedures that may be used separately or in many and varied combinations.

When multiple procedures are performed in the same investigative session, modifier 51 should be employed.

All procedures in this section imply that these services are performed by, or are under the direct supervision of, a physician and that all instruments, equipment, fluids, gases, probes, catheters, technician's fees, medications, gloves, trays, tubing and other sterile supplies be provided by the physician. When the physician only interprets the results and/or operates the equipment, a professional component, modifier 26, should be used to identify physicians' services.

51725   Simple cystometrogram (CMG) (eg, spinal manometer)

51726   Complex cystometrogram (eg, calibrated electronic equipment)

51736   Simple uroflowmetry (UFR) (eg, stop-watch flow rate, mechanical uroflowmeter)

51741   Complex uroflowmetry (eg, calibrated electronic equipment)

51772   Urethral pressure profile studies (UPP) (urethral closure pressure profile), any technique

51784   Electromyography studies (EMG) of anal or urethral sphincter, other than needle, any technique

51785   Needle electromyography studies (EMG) of anal or urethral sphincter, any technique

51792   Stimulus evoked response (eg, measurement of bulbocavernosus reflex latency time)

51795   Voiding pressure studies (VP); bladder voiding pressure, any technique

51797   intra-abdominal voiding pressure (AP) (rectal, gastric, intraperitoneal)

51798   Measurement of post-voiding residual urine and/or bladder capacity by ultrasound, non-imaging

Repair

51800   Cystoplasty or cystourethroplasty, plastic operation on bladder and/or vesical neck (anterior Y-plasty, vesical fundus resection), any procedure, with or without wedge resection of posterior vesical neck

51820   Cystourethroplasty with unilateral or bilateral ureteroneocystostomy

51840   Anterior vesicourethropexy, or urethropexy (eg, Marshall-Marchetti-Krantz, Burch); simple

51841   complicated (eg, secondary repair)

     (For urethropexy (Pereyra type), use 57289)

51845   Abdomino-vaginal vesical neck suspension, with or without endoscopic control (eg, Stamey, Raz, modified Pereyra)

51860   Cystorrhaphy, suture of bladder wound, injury or rupture; simple

51865   complicated

51880   Closure of cystostomy (separate procedure)

51900   Closure of vesicovaginal fistula, abdominal approach

     (For vaginal approach, see 57320-57330)

51920   Closure of vesicouterine fistula;

51925   with hysterectomy

     (For closure of vesicoenteric fistula, see 44660, 44661)

     (For closure of rectovesical fistula, see 45800-45805)

51940   Closure, exstrophy of bladder

     (See also 54390)

51960   Enterocystoplasty, including intestinal anastomosis

51980   Cutaneous vesicostomy

Laparoscopy

Surgical laparoscopy always includes diagnostic laparoscopy. To report a diagnostic laparoscopy (peritoneoscopy) (separate procedure), use 49320.

51990   Laparoscopy, surgical; urethral suspension for stress incontinence

51992   sling operation for stress incontinence (eg, fascia or synthetic)

     (For open sling operation for stress incontinence, use 57288)

     (For reversal or removal of sling operation for stress incontinence, use 57287)

● **51999**   Unlisted laparoscopy procedure, bladder

Endoscopy—Cystoscopy, Urethroscopy, Cystourethroscopy

Endoscopic descriptions are listed so that the main procedure can be identified without having to list all the minor related functions performed at the same time. For example: meatotomy, urethral calibration and/or dilation, urethro-scopy, and cystoscopy prior to a transurethral resection of prostate; ureteral catheterization following extraction of ureteral calculus; internal urethrotomy and bladder neck fulguration when performing a cystourethroscopy for the female urethral syndrome. When the secondary procedure requires significant additional time and effort, it may be identified by the addition of modifier 22.

For example: urethrotomy performed for a documented pre-existing stricture or bladder neck contracture.

Surgery: Urinary System

52000 Cystourethroscopy (separate procedure)

52001 Cystourethroscopy with irrigation and evacuation of multiple obstructing clots

(Do not report 52001 in addition to 52000)

52005 Cystourethroscopy, with ureteral catheterization, with or without irrigation, instillation, or ureteropyelography, exclusive of radiologic service;

52007 with brush biopsy of ureter and/or renal pelvis

52010 Cystourethroscopy, with ejaculatory duct catheterization, with or without irrigation, instillation, or duct radiography, exclusive of radiologic service

(For radiological supervision and interpretation, use 74440)

Transurethral Surgery

Urethra and Bladder

52204 Cystourethroscopy, with biopsy

52214 Cystourethroscopy, with fulguration (including cryosurgery or laser surgery) of trigone, bladder neck, prostatic fossa, urethra, or periurethral glands

52224 Cystourethroscopy, with fulguration (including cryosurgery or laser surgery) or treatment of MINOR (less than 0.5 cm) lesion(s) with or without biopsy

52234 Cystourethroscopy, with fulguration (including cryosurgery or laser surgery) and/or resection of; SMALL bladder tumor(s) (0.5 up to 2.0 cm)

52235 MEDIUM bladder tumor(s) (2.0 to 5.0 cm)

52240 LARGE bladder tumor(s)

52250 Cystourethroscopy with insertion of radioactive substance, with or without biopsy or fulguration

52260 Cystourethroscopy, with dilation of bladder for interstitial cystitis; general or conduction (spinal) anesthesia

52265 local anesthesia

52270 Cystourethroscopy, with internal urethrotomy; female

52275 male

52276 Cystourethroscopy with direct vision internal urethrotomy

52277 Cystourethroscopy, with resection of external sphincter (sphincterotomy)

52281 Cystourethroscopy, with calibration and/or dilation of urethral stricture or stenosis, with or without meatotomy, with or without injection procedure for cystography, male or female

52282 Cystourethroscopy, with insertion of urethral stent

52283 Cystourethroscopy, with steroid injection into stricture

52285 Cystourethroscopy for treatment of the female urethral syndrome with any or all of the following: urethral meatotomy, urethral dilation, internal urethrotomy, lysis of urethrovaginal septal fibrosis, lateral incisions of the bladder neck, and fulguration of polyp(s) of urethra, bladder neck, and/or trigone

52290 Cystourethroscopy; with ureteral meatotomy, unilateral or bilateral

52300 with resection or fulguration of orthotopic ureterocele(s), unilateral or bilateral

52301 with resection or fulguration of ectopic ureterocele(s), unilateral or bilateral

52305 with incision or resection of orifice of bladder diverticulum, single or multiple

52310 Cystourethroscopy, with removal of foreign body, calculus, or ureteral stent from urethra or bladder (separate procedure); simple

52315 complicated

52317 Litholapaxy: crushing or fragmentation of calculus by any means in bladder and removal of fragments; simple or small (less than 2.5 cm)

52318 complicated or large (over 2.5 cm)

Ureter and Pelvis

Surgical cystourethroscopy always includes diagnostic cystourethroscopy. To report a diagnostic cystourethroscopy, use 52351.

Do not report 52351 in conjunction with 52341-52346, 52352-52355.

The insertion and removal of a temporary stent during diagnostic or therapeutic cystourethroscopic intervention(s) is included in 52320-52355 and should not be reported separately.

To report insertion of a self-retaining, indwelling stent performed during cystourethroscopic diagnostic or therapeutic intervention(s), report 52332, in addition to primary procedure(s) performed, and append modifier 51. 52332 is used to report a unilateral procedure unless otherwise specified.

For bilateral insertion of self-retaining, indwelling ureteral stents, use code 52332, and append modifier 50.

To report cystourethroscopic removal of a self-retaining, indwelling ureteral stent, see 52310, 52315, and append modifier 58.

52320 Cystourethroscopy (including ureteral catheterization); with removal of ureteral calculus

52325 with fragmentation of ureteral calculus (eg, ultrasonic or electro-hydraulic technique)

52327 with subureteric injection of implant material

52330 with manipulation, without removal of ureteral calculus

52332 Cystourethroscopy, with insertion of indwelling ureteral stent (eg, Gibbons or double-J type)

52334 Cystourethroscopy with insertion of ureteral guide wire through kidney to establish a percutaneous nephrostomy, retrograde

(For percutaneous nephrostolithotomy, see 50080, 50081; for establishment of nephrostomy tract only, use 50395)

(For cystourethroscopy, with ureteroscopy and/or pyeloscopy, see 52351-52355)

(For cystourethroscopy with incision, fulguration, or resection of congenital posterior urethral valves or obstructive hypertrophic mucosal folds, use 52400)

52341 Cystourethroscopy; with treatment of ureteral stricture (eg, balloon dilation, laser, electrocautery, and incision)

52342 with treatment of ureteropelvic junction stricture (eg, balloon dilation, laser, electrocautery, and incision)

52343 with treatment of intra-renal stricture (eg, balloon dilation, laser, electrocautery, and incision)

52344 Cystourethroscopy with ureteroscopy; with treatment of ureteral stricture (eg, balloon dilation, laser, electrocautery, and incision)

52345 with treatment of ureteropelvic junction stricture (eg, balloon dilation, laser, electrocautery, and incision)

52346 with treatment of intra-renal stricture (eg, balloon dilation, laser, electrocautery, and incision)

(52347 has been deleted)

(For transurethral resection or incision of ejaculatory ducts, use 52402)

52351 Cystourethroscopy, with ureteroscopy and/or pyeloscopy; diagnostic

(For radiological supervision and interpretation, use 74485)

(Do not report 52351 in conjunction with 52341-52346, 52352-52355)

52352 with removal or manipulation of calculus (ureteral catheterization is included)

52353 with lithotripsy (ureteral catheterization is included)

52354 with biopsy and/or fulguration of ureteral or renal pelvic lesion

52355 with resection of ureteral or renal pelvic tumor

Vesical Neck and Prostate

52400 Cystourethroscopy with incision, fulguration, or resection of congenital posterior urethral valves, or congenital obstructive hypertrophic mucosal folds

52402 Cystourethroscopy with transurethral resection or incision of ejaculatory ducts

52450 Transurethral incision of prostate

52500 Transurethral resection of bladder neck (separate procedure)

52510 Transurethral balloon dilation of the prostatic urethra

52601 Transurethral electrosurgical resection of prostate, including control of postoperative bleeding, complete (vasectomy, meatotomy, cystourethroscopy, urethral calibration and/or dilation, and internal urethrotomy are included)

(For other approaches, see 55801-55845)

52606 Transurethral fulguration for postoperative bleeding occurring after the usual follow-up time

52612 Transurethral resection of prostate; first stage of two-stage resection (partial resection)

52614 second stage of two-stage resection (resection completed)

52620 Transurethral resection; of residual obstructive tissue after 90 days postoperative

52630 of regrowth of obstructive tissue longer than one year postoperative

52640 of postoperative bladder neck contracture

▲ **52647** Laser coagulation of prostate, including control of postoperative bleeding, complete (vasectomy, meatotomy, cystourethroscopy, urethral calibration and/or dilation, and internal urethrotomy are included if performed)

▲ **52648** Laser vaporization of prostate, including control of postoperative bleeding, complete (vasectomy, meatotomy, cystourethroscopy, urethral calibration and/or dilation, internal urethrotomy and transurethral resection of prostate are included if performed)

52700 Transurethral drainage of prostatic abscess

(For litholapaxy, use 52317, 52318)

Urethra

(For endoscopy, see cystoscopy, urethroscopy, cystourethroscopy, 52000-52700)

(For injection procedure for urethrocystography, see 51600-51610)

Incision

53000 Urethrotomy or urethrostomy, external (separate procedure); pendulous urethra

53010 perineal urethra, external

53020 Meatotomy, cutting of meatus (separate procedure); except infant

53025 infant

(Do not report modifier 63 in conjunction with 53025)

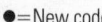

53040 Drainage of deep periurethral abscess

(For subcutaneous abscess, see 10060, 10061)

53060 Drainage of Skene's gland abscess or cyst

53080 Drainage of perineal urinary extravasation; uncomplicated (separate procedure)

53085 complicated

Excision

53200 Biopsy of urethra

53210 Urethrectomy, total, including cystostomy; female

53215 male

53220 Excision or fulguration of carcinoma of urethra

53230 Excision of urethral diverticulum (separate procedure); female

53235 male

53240 Marsupialization of urethral diverticulum, male or female

53250 Excision of bulbourethral gland (Cowper's gland)

53260 Excision or fulguration; urethral polyp(s), distal urethra

(For endoscopic approach, see 52214, 52224)

53265 urethral caruncle

53270 Skene's glands

53275 urethral prolapse

Repair

(For hypospadias, see 54300-54352)

53400 Urethroplasty; first stage, for fistula, diverticulum, or stricture (eg, Johannsen type)

53405 second stage (formation of urethra), including urinary diversion

53410 Urethroplasty, one-stage reconstruction of male anterior urethra

53415 Urethroplasty, transpubic or perineal, one stage, for reconstruction or repair of prostatic or membranous urethra

53420 Urethroplasty, two-stage reconstruction or repair of prostatic or membranous urethra; first stage

53425 second stage

53430 Urethroplasty, reconstruction of female urethra

53431 Urethroplasty with tubularization of posterior urethra and/or lower bladder for incontinence (eg, Tenago, Leadbetter procedure)

53440 Sling operation for correction of male urinary incontinence (eg, fascia or synthetic)

53442 Removal or revision of sling for male urinary incontinence (eg, fascia or synthetic)

53444 Insertion of tandem cuff (dual cuff)

53445 Insertion of inflatable urethral/bladder neck sphincter, including placement of pump, reservoir, and cuff

53446 Removal of inflatable urethral/bladder neck sphincter, including pump, reservoir, and cuff

53447 Removal and replacement of inflatable urethral/bladder neck sphincter including pump, reservoir, and cuff at the same operative session

53448 Removal and replacement of inflatable urethral/bladder neck sphincter including pump, reservoir, and cuff through an infected field at the same operative session including irrigation and debridement of infected tissue

(Do not report 11040-11043 in addition to 53448)

53449 Repair of inflatable urethral/bladder neck sphincter, including pump, reservoir, and cuff

53450 Urethromeatoplasty, with mucosal advancement

(For meatotomy, see 53020, 53025)

53460 Urethromeatoplasty, with partial excision of distal urethral segment (Richardson type procedure)

53500 Urethrolysis, transvaginal, secondary, open, including cystourethroscopy (eg, postsurgical obstruction, scarring)

(For urethrolysis by retropubic approach, use 53899)

(Do not report 53500 in conjunction with 52000)

53502 Urethrorrhaphy, suture of urethral wound or injury, female

53505 Urethrorrhaphy, suture of urethral wound or injury; penile

53510 perineal

53515 prostatomembranous

53520 Closure of urethrostomy or urethrocutaneous fistula, male (separate procedure)

(For closure of urethrovaginal fistula, use 57310)

(For closure of urethrorectal fistula, see 45820, 45825)

Manipulation

(For radiological supervision and interpretation, use 74485)

53600 Dilation of urethral stricture by passage of sound or urethral dilator, male; initial

53601 subsequent

53605 Dilation of urethral stricture or vesical neck by passage of sound or urethral dilator, male, general or conduction (spinal) anesthesia

53620 Dilation of urethral stricture by passage of filiform and follower, male; initial

53621 subsequent

53660   Dilation of female urethra including suppository and/or instillation; initial

53661   subsequent

53665   Dilation of female urethra, general or conduction (spinal) anesthesia

(For urethral catheterization, see 51701-51703)

Other Procedures

(For two or three glass urinalysis, use 81020)

53850   Transurethral destruction of prostate tissue; by microwave thermotherapy

53852   by radiofrequency thermotherapy

53853   by water-induced thermotherapy

53899   Unlisted procedure, urinary system

Surgery: Urinary System

Notes

⊘=Modifier 51 exempt   ⊙=Conscious sedation   ✚=Add-on code   ⊮=FDA approval pending

Male Genital System

Penis

Incision

(For abdominal perineal gangrene debridement, see 11004-11006)

54000 Slitting of prepuce, dorsal or lateral (separate procedure); newborn

(Do not report modifier 63 in conjunction with 54000)

54001   except newborn

54015 Incision and drainage of penis, deep

(For skin and subcutaneous abscess, see 10060-10160)

Destruction

54050 Destruction of lesion(s), penis (eg, condyloma, papilloma, molluscum contagiosum, herpetic vesicle), simple; chemical

54055   electrodesiccation

54056   cryosurgery

54057   laser surgery

54060   surgical excision

54065 Destruction of lesion(s), penis (eg, condyloma, papilloma, molluscum contagiosum, herpetic vesicle), extensive (eg, laser surgery, electrosurgery, cryosurgery, chemosurgery)

(For destruction or excision of other lesions, see **Integumentary System**)

Excision

54100 Biopsy of penis; (separate procedure)

54105   deep structures

54110 Excision of penile plaque (Peyronie disease);

54111   with graft to 5 cm in length

54112   with graft greater than 5 cm in length

54115 Removal foreign body from deep penile tissue (eg, plastic implant)

54120 Amputation of penis; partial

54125   complete

54130 Amputation of penis, radical; with bilateral inguinofemoral lymphadenectomy

54135   in continuity with bilateral pelvic lymphadenectomy, including external iliac, hypogastric and obturator nodes

(For lymphadenectomy (separate procedure), see 38760-38770)

54150 Circumcision, using clamp or other device; newborn

(Do not report modifier 63 in conjunction with 54150)

54152   except newborn

54160 Circumcision, surgical excision other than clamp, device or dorsal slit; newborn

(Do not report modifier 63 in conjunction with 54160)

54161   except newborn

54162 Lysis or excision of penile post-circumcision adhesions

54163 Repair incomplete circumcision

54164 Frenulotomy of penis

(Do not report 54164 with circumcision codes 54150-54161, 54162, 54163)

Introduction

54200 Injection procedure for Peyronie disease;

54205   with surgical exposure of plaque

54220 Irrigation of corpora cavernosa for priapism

54230 Injection procedure for corpora cavernosography

(For radiological supervision and interpretation, use 74445)

54231 Dynamic cavernosometry, including intracavernosal injection of vasoactive drugs (eg, papaverine, phentolamine)

54235 Injection of corpora cavernosa with pharmacologic agent(s) (eg, papaverine, phentolamine)

54240 Penile plethysmography

54250 Nocturnal penile tumescence and/or rigidity test

Repair

(For other urethroplasties, see 53400-53430)

(For penile revascularization, use 37788)

54300 Plastic operation of penis for straightening of chordee (eg, hypospadias), with or without mobilization of urethra

54304 Plastic operation on penis for correction of chordee or for first stage hypospadias repair with or without transplantation of prepuce and/or skin flaps

54308 Urethroplasty for second stage hypospadias repair (including urinary diversion); less than 3 cm

54312   greater than 3 cm

54316 Urethroplasty for second stage hypospadias repair (including urinary diversion) with free skin graft obtained from site other than genitalia

54318 Urethroplasty for third stage hypospadias repair to release penis from scrotum (eg, third stage Cecil repair)

Surgery: Male/Female Genital System

Surgery: Male/Female Genital System

54322   One stage distal hypospadias repair (with or without chordee or circumcision); with simple meatal advancement (eg, Magpi, V-flap)

54324   with urethroplasty by local skin flaps (eg, flip-flap, prepucial flap)

54326   with urethroplasty by local skin flaps and mobilization of urethra

54328   with extensive dissection to correct chordee and urethroplasty with local skin flaps, skin graft patch, and/or island flap

(For urethroplasty and straightening of chordee, use 54308)

54332   One stage proximal penile or penoscrotal hypospadias repair requiring extensive dissection to correct chordee and urethroplasty by use of skin graft tube and/or island flap

54336   One stage perineal hypospadias repair requiring extensive dissection to correct chordee and urethroplasty by use of skin graft tube and/or island flap

54340   Repair of hypospadias complications (ie, fistula, stricture, diverticula); by closure, incision, or excision, simple

54344   requiring mobilization of skin flaps and urethroplasty with flap or patch graft

54348   requiring extensive dissection and urethroplasty with flap, patch or tubed graft (includes urinary diversion)

54352   Repair of hypospadias cripple requiring extensive dissection and excision of previously constructed structures including re-release of chordee and reconstruction of urethra and penis by use of local skin as grafts and island flaps and skin brought in as flaps or grafts

54360   Plastic operation on penis to correct angulation

54380   Plastic operation on penis for epispadias distal to external sphincter;

54385   with incontinence

54390   with exstrophy of bladder

54400   Insertion of penile prosthesis; non-inflatable (semi-rigid)

54401   inflatable (self-contained)

(For removal or replacement of penile prosthesis, see 54415, 54416)

54405   Insertion of multi-component, inflatable penile prosthesis, including placement of pump, cylinders, and reservoir

(For reduced services, report 54405 with modifier 52)

54406   Removal of all components of a multi-component, inflatable penile prosthesis without replacement of prosthesis

(For reduced services, report 54406 with modifier 52)

54408   Repair of component(s) of a multi-component, inflatable penile prosthesis

54410   Removal and replacement of all component(s) of a multi-component, inflatable penile prosthesis at the same operative session

54411   Removal and replacement of all components of a multi-component inflatable penile prosthesis through an infected field at the same operative session, including irrigation and debridement of infected tissue

(For reduced services, report 54411 with modifier 52)

(Do not report 11040-11043 in addition to 54411)

54415   Removal of non-inflatable (semi-rigid) or inflatable (self-contained) penile prosthesis, without replacement of prosthesis

54416   Removal and replacement of non-inflatable (semi-rigid) or inflatable (self-contained) penile prosthesis at the same operative session

54417   Removal and replacement of non-inflatable (semi-rigid) or inflatable (self-contained) penile prosthesis through an infected field at the same operative session, including irrigation and debridement of infected tissue

(Do not report 11040-11043 in addition to 54417)

54420   Corpora cavernosa-saphenous vein shunt (priapism operation), unilateral or bilateral

54430   Corpora cavernosa-corpus spongiosum shunt (priapism operation), unilateral or bilateral

54435   Corpora cavernosa-glans penis fistulization (eg, biopsy needle, Winter procedure, rongeur, or punch) for priapism

54440   Plastic operation of penis for injury

Manipulation

54450   Foreskin manipulation including lysis of preputial adhesions and stretching

Testis

Excision

(For abdominal perineal gangrene debridement, see 11004-11006)

54500   Biopsy of testis, needle (separate procedure)

(For fine needle aspiration, see 10021, 10022)

(For evaluation of fine needle aspirate, see 88172, 88173)

54505   Biopsy of testis, incisional (separate procedure)

(For bilateral procedure, report 54505 with modifier 50)

(When combined with vasogram, seminal vesiculogram, or epididymogram, use 55300)

54512   Excision of extraparenchymal lesion of testis

54520   Orchiectomy, simple (including subcapsular), with or without testicular prosthesis, scrotal or inguinal approach

(For bilateral procedure, report 54520 with modifier 50)

54522	Orchiectomy, partial
54530	Orchiectomy, radical, for tumor; inguinal approach
54535	with abdominal exploration

(For orchiectomy with repair of hernia, see 49505 or 49507 and 54520)

(For radical retroperitoneal lymphadenectomy, use 38780)

54550	Exploration for undescended testis (inguinal or scrotal area)

(For bilateral procedure, report 54550 with modifier 50)

54560	Exploration for undescended testis with abdominal exploration

(For bilateral procedure, report 54560 with modifier 50)

Repair

54600	Reduction of torsion of testis, surgical, with or without fixation of contralateral testis
54620	Fixation of contralateral testis (separate procedure)
54640	Orchiopexy, inguinal approach, with or without hernia repair

(For bilateral procedure, report 54640 with modifier 50

(For inguinal hernia repair performed in conjunction with inguinal orchiopexy, see 49495-49525)

54650	Orchiopexy, abdominal approach, for intra-abdominal testis (eg, Fowler-Stephens)

(For laparoscopic approach, use 54692)

54660	Insertion of testicular prosthesis (separate procedure)

(For bilateral procedure, report 54660 with modifier 50)

54670	Suture or repair of testicular injury
54680	Transplantation of testis(es) to thigh (because of scrotal destruction)

Laparoscopy

Surgical laparoscopy always includes diagnostic laparoscopy. To report a diagnostic laparoscopy (peritoneoscopy) (separate procedure), use 49320.

54690	Laparoscopy, surgical; orchiectomy
54692	orchiopexy for intra-abdominal testis
54699	Unlisted laparoscopy procedure, testis

Epididymis

Incision

54700	Incision and drainage of epididymis, testis and/or scrotal space (eg, abscess or hematoma)

Excision

54800	Biopsy of epididymis, needle

(For fine needle aspiration, see 10021, 10022)

(For evaluation of fine needle aspirate, see 88172, 88173)

54820	Exploration of epididymis, with or without biopsy
54830	Excision of local lesion of epididymis
54840	Excision of spermatocele, with or without epididymectomy
54860	Epididymectomy; unilateral
54861	bilateral

Repair

54900	Epididymovasostomy, anastomosis of epididymis to vas deferens; unilateral
54901	bilateral

(For operating microscope, use 69990)

Tunica Vaginalis

Incision

55000	Puncture aspiration of hydrocele, tunica vaginalis, with or without injection of medication

Excision

55040	Excision of hydrocele; unilateral
55041	bilateral

(With hernia repair, see 49495-49501)

Repair

55060	Repair of tunica vaginalis hydrocele (Bottle type)

Scrotum

Incision

55100	Drainage of scrotal wall abscess

(See also 54700)

55110	Scrotal exploration
55120	Removal of foreign body in scrotum

Excision

(For excision of local lesion of skin of scrotum, see **Integumentary System**)

55150	Resection of scrotum

Surgery: Male/Female Genital System

Repair

55175 Scrotoplasty; simple

55180 complicated

Vas Deferens

Incision

55200 Vasotomy, cannulization with or without incision of vas, unilateral or bilateral (separate procedure)

Excision

55250 Vasectomy, unilateral or bilateral (separate procedure), including postoperative semen examination(s)

Introduction

55300 Vasotomy for vasograms, seminal vesiculograms, or epididymograms, unilateral or bilateral

(For radiological supervision and interpretation, use 74440)

(When combined with biopsy of testis, see 54505 and use modifier 51)

Repair

55400 Vasovasostomy, vasovasorrhaphy

(For bilateral procedure, report 55400 with modifier 50)

(For operating microscope, use 69990)

Suture

55450 Ligation (percutaneous) of vas deferens, unilateral or bilateral (separate procedure)

Spermatic Cord

Excision

55500 Excision of hydrocele of spermatic cord, unilateral (separate procedure)

55520 Excision of lesion of spermatic cord (separate procedure)

55530 Excision of varicocele or ligation of spermatic veins for varicocele; (separate procedure)

55535 abdominal approach

55540 with hernia repair

Laparoscopy

Surgical laparoscopy always includes diagnostic laparoscopy. To report a diagnostic laparoscopy (peritoneoscopy) (separate procedure), use 49320.

55550 Laparoscopy, surgical, with ligation of spermatic veins for varicocele

55559 Unlisted laparoscopy procedure, spermatic cord

Seminal Vesicles

Incision

55600 Vesiculotomy;

(For bilateral procedure, report 55600 with modifier 50)

55605 complicated

Excision

55650 Vesiculectomy, any approach

(For bilateral procedure, report 55650 with modifier 50)

55680 Excision of Mullerian duct cyst

(For injection procedure, see 52010, 55300)

Prostate

Incision

55700 Biopsy, prostate; needle or punch, single or multiple, any approach

▶(For prostate needle biopsy saturation sampling for prostate mapping, use Category III code 0137T)◀

(If imaging guidance is performed, use 76942)

(For fine needle aspiration, see 10021, 10022)

(For evaluation of fine needle aspirate, see 88172, 88173)

55705 incisional, any approach

55720 Prostatotomy, external drainage of prostatic abscess, any approach; simple

55725 complicated

(For transurethral drainage, use 52700)

Excision

(For transurethral removal of prostate, see 52601-52640)

(For transurethral destruction of prostate, see 53850-53852)

(For limited pelvic lymphadenectomy for staging (separate procedure), use 38562)

(For independent node dissection, see 38770-38780)

55801   Prostatectomy, perineal, subtotal (including control of postoperative bleeding, vasectomy, meatotomy, urethral calibration and/or dilation, and internal urethrotomy)

55810   Prostatectomy, perineal radical;

55812   with lymph node biopsy(s) (limited pelvic lymphadenectomy)

55815   with bilateral pelvic lymphadenectomy, including external iliac, hypogastric and obturator nodes

(If 55815 is carried out on separate days, use 38770 with modifier 50 and 55810)

55821   Prostatectomy (including control of postoperative bleeding, vasectomy, meatotomy, urethral calibration and/or dilation, and internal urethrotomy); suprapubic, subtotal, one or two stages

55831   retropubic, subtotal

55840   Prostatectomy, retropubic radical, with or without nerve sparing;

55842   with lymph node biopsy(s) (limited pelvic lymphadenectomy)

55845   with bilateral pelvic lymphadenectomy, including external iliac, hypogastric, and obturator nodes

(If 55845 is carried out on separate days, use 38770 with modifier 50 and 55840)

(For laparoscopic retropubic radical prostatectomy, use 55866)

55859   Transperineal placement of needles or catheters into prostate for interstitial radioelement application, with or without cystoscopy

(For interstitial radioelement application, see 77776-77784)

(For ultrasonic guidance for interstitial radioelement application, use 76965)

55860   Exposure of prostate, any approach, for insertion of radioactive substance;

(For application of interstitial radioelement, see 77776-77778)

55862   with lymph node biopsy(s) (limited pelvic lymphadenectomy)

55865   with bilateral pelvic lymphadenectomy, including external iliac, hypogastric and obturator nodes

Laparoscopy

Surgical laparoscopy always includes diagnostic laparoscopy. To report a diagnostic laparoscopy (peritoneoscopy) (separate procedure), use 49320.

55866   Laparoscopy, surgical prostatectomy, retropubic radical, including nerve sparing

(For open procedure, use 55840)

Other Procedures

(For artificial insemination, see 58321, 58322)

55870   Electroejaculation

55873   Cryosurgical ablation of the prostate (includes ultrasonic guidance for interstitial cryosurgical probe placement)

55899   Unlisted procedure, male genital system

Intersex Surgery

55970   Intersex surgery; male to female

55980   female to male

Surgery: Male/Female Genital System

Notes

Female Genital System

(For pelvic laparotomy, use 49000)

(For excision or destruction of endometriomas, open method, see 49200, 49201)

(For paracentesis, see 49080, 49081)

(For secondary closure of abdominal wall evisceration or disruption, use 49900)

(For fulguration or excision of lesions, laparoscopic approach, use 58662)

(For chemotherapy, see 96400-96549)

Vulva, Perineum and Introitus

Definitions

The following definitions apply to the vulvectomy codes (56620-56640).

A *simple* procedure is the removal of skin and superficial subcutaneous tissues.

A *radical* procedure is the removal of skin and deep subcutaneous tissue.

A *partial* procedure is the removal of less than 80% of the vulvar area.

A *complete* procedure is the removal of greater than 80% of the vulvar area.

Incision

(For incision and drainage of sebaceous cyst, furuncle, or abscess, see 10040, 10060, 10061)

56405   Incision and drainage of vulva or perineal abscess

56420   Incision and drainage of Bartholin's gland abscess

(For incision and drainage of Skene's gland abscess or cyst, use 53060)

56440   Marsupialization of Bartholin's gland cyst

56441   Lysis of labial adhesions

Destruction

56501   Destruction of lesion(s), vulva; simple (eg, laser surgery, electrosurgery, cryosurgery, chemosurgery)

56515   extensive (eg, laser surgery, electrosurgery, cryosurgery, chemosurgery)

(For destruction of Skene's gland cyst or abscess, use 53270)

(For cautery destruction of urethral caruncle, use 53265)

Excision

56605   Biopsy of vulva or perineum (separate procedure); one lesion

+ 56606   each separate additional lesion (List separately in addition to code for primary procedure)

(Use 56606 in conjunction with 56605)

(For excision of local lesion, see 11420-11426, 11620-11626)

56620   Vulvectomy simple; partial

56625   complete

(For skin graft, see 15000 et seq)

56630   Vulvectomy, radical, partial;

(For skin graft, if used, see 15000, 15120, 15121, 15240, 15241)

56631   with unilateral inguinofemoral lymphadenectomy

56632   with bilateral inguinofemoral lymphadenectomy

56633   Vulvectomy, radical, complete;

56634   with unilateral inguinofemoral lymphadenectomy

56637   with bilateral inguinofemoral lymphadenectomy

56640   Vulvectomy, radical, complete, with inguinofemoral, iliac, and pelvic lymphadenectomy

(For bilateral procedure, report 56640 with modifier 50)

(For lymphadenectomy, see 38760-38780)

56700   Partial hymenectomy or revision of hymenal ring

56720   Hymenotomy, simple incision

56740   Excision of Bartholin's gland or cyst

(For excision of Skene's gland, use 53270)

(For excision of urethral caruncle, use 53265)

(For excision or fulguration of urethral carcinoma, use 53220)

(For excision or marsupialization of urethral diverticulum, see 53230, 53240)

Repair

(For repair of urethra for mucosal prolapse, use 53275)

56800   Plastic repair of introitus

56805   Clitoroplasty for intersex state

56810   Perineoplasty, repair of perineum, nonobstetrical (separate procedure)

(See also 56800)

(For repair of wounds to genitalia, see 12001-12007, 12041-12047, 13131-13133)

(For repair of recent injury of vagina and perineum, nonobstetrical, use 57210)

Surgery: Male/Female Genital System

(For anal sphincteroplasty, see 46750, 46751)

(For episiorrhaphy, episioperineorrhaphy for recent injury of vulva and/or perineum, nonobstetrical, use 57210)

Endoscopy

56820   Colposcopy of the vulva;

56821   with biopsy(s)

(For colposcopic examinations/procedures involving the vagina, see 57420, 57421; cervix, see 57452-57461)

Vagina

Incision

57000   Colpotomy; with exploration

57010   with drainage of pelvic abscess

57020   Colpocentesis (separate procedure)

57022   Incision and drainage of vaginal hematoma; obstetrical/postpartum

57023   non-obstetrical (eg, post-trauma, spontaneous bleeding)

Destruction

57061   Destruction of vaginal lesion(s); simple (eg, laser surgery, electrosurgery, cryosurgery, chemosurgery)

57065   extensive (eg, laser surgery, electrosurgery, cryosurgery, chemosurgery)

Excision

57100   Biopsy of vaginal mucosa; simple (separate procedure)

57105   extensive, requiring suture (including cysts)

57106   Vaginectomy, partial removal of vaginal wall;

57107   with removal of paravaginal tissue (radical vaginectomy)

57109   with removal of paravaginal tissue (radical vaginectomy) with bilateral total pelvic lymphadenectomy and para-aortic lymph node sampling (biopsy)

57110   Vaginectomy, complete removal of vaginal wall;

57111   with removal of paravaginal tissue (radical vaginectomy)

57112   with removal of paravaginal tissue (radical vaginectomy) with bilateral total pelvic lymphadenectomy and para-aortic lymph node sampling (biopsy)

57120   Colpocleisis (Le Fort type)

57130   Excision of vaginal septum

57135   Excision of vaginal cyst or tumor

Introduction

57150   Irrigation of vagina and/or application of medicament for treatment of bacterial, parasitic, or fungoid disease

57155   Insertion of uterine tandems and/or vaginal ovoids for clinical brachytherapy

(For insertion of radioelement sources or ribbons, see 77761-77763, 77781-77784)

57160   Fitting and insertion of pessary or other intravaginal support device

57170   Diaphragm or cervical cap fitting with instructions

57180   Introduction of any hemostatic agent or pack for spontaneous or traumatic nonobstetrical vaginal hemorrhage (separate procedure)

Repair

(For urethral suspension, Marshall-Marchetti-Krantz type, abdominal approach, see 51840, 51841)

(For laparoscopic suspension, use 51990)

57200   Colporrhaphy, suture of injury of vagina (nonobstetrical)

57210   Colpoperineorrhaphy, suture of injury of vagina and/or perineum (nonobstetrical)

57220   Plastic operation on urethral sphincter, vaginal approach (eg, Kelly urethral plication)

57230   Plastic repair of urethrocele

57240   Anterior colporrhaphy, repair of cystocele with or without repair of urethrocele

57250   Posterior colporrhaphy, repair of rectocele with or without perineorrhaphy

(For repair of rectocele (separate procedure) without posterior colporrhaphy, use 45560)

57260   Combined anteroposterior colporrhaphy;

57265   with enterocele repair

+ 57267   Insertion of mesh or other prosthesis for repair of pelvic floor defect, each site (anterior, posterior compartment), vaginal approach (List separately in addition to code for primary procedure)

(Use 57267 in addition to 45560, 57240-57265)

57268   Repair of enterocele, vaginal approach (separate procedure)

57270   Repair of enterocele, abdominal approach (separate procedure)

57280   Colpopexy, abdominal approach

57282   Colpopexy, vaginal; extra-peritoneal approach (sacrospinous, iliococcygeus)

57283   intra-peritoneal approach (uterosacral, levator myorrhaphy)

Surgery: Male/Female Genital System

57284   Paravaginal defect repair (including repair of cystocele, stress urinary incontinence, and/or incomplete vaginal prolapse)

57287   Removal or revision of sling for stress incontinence (eg, fascia or synthetic)

57288   Sling operation for stress incontinence (eg, fascia or synthetic)

(For laparoscopic approach, use 51992)

57289   Pereyra procedure, including anterior colporrhaphy

57291   Construction of artificial vagina; without graft

57292   with graft

● **57295**   Revision (including removal) of prosthetic vaginal graft, vaginal approach

57300   Closure of rectovaginal fistula; vaginal or transanal approach

57305   abdominal approach

57307   abdominal approach, with concomitant colostomy

57308   transperineal approach, with perineal body reconstruction, with or without levator plication

57310   Closure of urethrovaginal fistula;

57311   with bulbocavernosus transplant

57320   Closure of vesicovaginal fistula; vaginal approach

(For concomitant cystostomy, see 51005-51040)

57330   transvesical and vaginal approach

(For abdominal approach, use 51900)

57335   Vaginoplasty for intersex state

Manipulation

57400   Dilation of vagina under anesthesia

57410   Pelvic examination under anesthesia

57415   Removal of impacted vaginal foreign body (separate procedure) under anesthesia

(For removal without anesthesia of an impacted vaginal foreign body, use the appropriate E/M code)

Endoscopy

(For speculoscopy, see Category III codes 0031T, 0032T)

57420   Colposcopy of the entire vagina, with cervix if present;

▲ **57421**   with biopsy(s) of vagina/cervix

(For colposcopic visualization of cervix and adjacent upper vagina, use 57452)

(When reporting colposcopies of multiple sites, use modifier 51 as appropriate. For colposcopic examinations/procedures involving the vulva, see 56820, 56821; cervix, see 57452-57461)

▶(For endometrial sampling (biopsy) performed in conjunction with colposcopy, use 58110)◀

57425   Laparoscopy, surgical, colpopexy (suspension of vaginal apex)

Cervix Uteri

(For cervicography, see Category III code 0003T)

Endoscopy

(For colposcopic examinations/procedures involving the vulva, see 56820, 56821; vagina, see 57420, 57421)

57452   Colposcopy of the cervix including upper/adjacent vagina;

(Do not report 57452 in addition to 57454-57461)

57454   with biopsy(s) of the cervix and endocervical curettage

57455   with biopsy(s) of the cervix

57456   with endocervical curettage

57460   with loop electrode biopsy(s) of the cervix

57461   with loop electrode conization of the cervix

(Do not report 57456 in addition to 57461)

▶(For endometrial sampling (biopsy) performed in conjunction with colposcopy, use 58110)◀

Excision

(For radical surgical procedures, see 58200-58240)

57500   Biopsy, single or multiple, or local excision of lesion, with or without fulguration (separate procedure)

57505   Endocervical curettage (not done as part of a dilation and curettage)

57510   Cautery of cervix; electro or thermal

57511   cryocautery, initial or repeat

57513   laser ablation

57520   Conization of cervix, with or without fulguration, with or without dilation and curettage, with or without repair; cold knife or laser

(See also 58120)

57522   loop electrode excision

57530   Trachelectomy (cervicectomy), amputation of cervix (separate procedure)

57531   Radical trachelectomy, with bilateral total pelvic lymphadenectomy and para-aortic lymph node sampling biopsy, with or without removal of tube(s), with or without removal of ovary(s)

(For radical abdominal hysterectomy, use 58210)

57540   Excision of cervical stump, abdominal approach;

57545   with pelvic floor repair

Surgery: Male/Female Genital System

57550 Excision of cervical stump, vaginal approach;

57555   with anterior and/or posterior repair

57556   with repair of enterocele

(For insertion of intrauterine device, use 58300)

(For insertion of any hemostatic agent or pack for control of spontaneous non-obstetrical hemorrhage, see 57180)

Repair

57700 Cerclage of uterine cervix, nonobstetrical

57720 Trachelorrhaphy, plastic repair of uterine cervix, vaginal approach

Manipulation

57800 Dilation of cervical canal, instrumental (separate procedure)

57820 Dilation and curettage of cervical stump

Corpus Uteri

Excision

58100 Endometrial sampling (biopsy) with or without endocervical sampling (biopsy), without cervical dilation, any method (separate procedure)

(For endocervical curettage only, use 57505)

▶(For endometrial sampling (biopsy) performed in conjunction with colposcopy (57420, 57421, 57452-57461), use 58110)◀

+● 58110 Endometrial sampling (biopsy) performed in conjunction with colposcopy (List separately in addition to code for primary procedure)

▶(Use 58110 in conjunction with 57420, 57421, 57452-57461)◀

58120 Dilation and curettage, diagnostic and/or therapeutic (nonobstetrical)

(For postpartum hemorrhage, use 59160)

58140 Myomectomy, excision of fibroid tumor(s) of uterus, 1 to 4 intramural myoma(s) with total weight of 250 grams or less and/or removal of surface myomas; abdominal approach

58145   vaginal approach

58146 Myomectomy, excision of fibroid tumor(s) of uterus, 5 or more intramural myomas and/or intramural myomas with total weight greater than 250 grams, abdominal approach

(Do not report 58146 in addition to 58140-58145, 58150-58240)

58150 Total abdominal hysterectomy (corpus and cervix), with or without removal of tube(s), with or without removal of ovary(s);

58152   with colpo-urethrocystopexy (eg, Marshall-Marchetti-Krantz, Burch)

(For urethrocystopexy without hysterectomy, see 51840, 51841)

58180 Supracervical abdominal hysterectomy (subtotal hysterectomy), with or without removal of tube(s), with or without removal of ovary(s)

58200 Total abdominal hysterectomy, including partial vaginectomy, with para-aortic and pelvic lymph node sampling, with or without removal of tube(s), with or without removal of ovary(s)

58210 Radical abdominal hysterectomy, with bilateral total pelvic lymphadenectomy and para-aortic lymph node sampling (biopsy), with or without removal of tube(s), with or without removal of ovary(s)

(For radical hysterectomy with ovarian transposition, use also 58825)

58240 Pelvic exenteration for gynecologic malignancy, with total abdominal hysterectomy or cervicectomy, with or without removal of tube(s), with or without removal of ovary(s), with removal of bladder and ureteral transplantations, and/or abdominoperineal resection of rectum and colon and colostomy, or any combination thereof

(For pelvic exenteration for lower urinary tract or male genital malignancy, use 51597)

58260 Vaginal hysterectomy, for uterus 250 grams or less;

58262   with removal of tube(s), and/or ovary(s)

58263   with removal of tube(s), and/or ovary(s), with repair of enterocele

(Do not report 58263 in addition to 57283)

58267   with colpo-urethrocystopexy (Marshall-Marchetti-Krantz type, Pereyra type) with or without endoscopic control

58270   with repair of enterocele

(For repair of enterocele with removal of tubes and/or ovaries, use 58263)

58275 Vaginal hysterectomy, with total or partial vaginectomy;

58280   with repair of enterocele

58285 Vaginal hysterectomy, radical (Schauta type operation)

58290 Vaginal hysterectomy, for uterus greater than 250 grams;

58291   with removal of tube(s) and/or ovary(s)

58292   with removal of tube(s) and/or ovary(s), with repair of enterocele

58293   with colpo-urethrocystopexy (Marshall-Marchetti-Krantz type, Pereyra type) with or without endoscopic control

58294   with repair of enterocele

Surgery: Male/Female Genital System

Introduction

(For insertion/removal of implantable contraceptive capsules, see 11975, 11976, 11977)

58300   Insertion of intrauterine device (IUD)

58301   Removal of intrauterine device (IUD)

58321   Artificial insemination; intra-cervical

58322   intra-uterine

58323   Sperm washing for artificial insemination

58340   Catheterization and introduction of saline or contrast material for saline infusion sonohysterography (SIS) or hysterosalpingography

(For radiological supervision and interpretation of saline infusion sonohysterography, use 76831)

(For radiological supervision and interpretation of hysterosalpingography, use 74740)

58345   Transcervical introduction of fallopian tube catheter for diagnosis and/or re-establishing patency (any method), with or without hysterosalpingography

(For radiological supervision and interpretation, use 74742)

58346   Insertion of Heyman capsules for clinical brachytherapy

(For insertion of radioelement sources or ribbons, see 77761-77763, 77781-77784)

58350   Chromotubation of oviduct, including materials

(For materials supplied by physician, use 99070)

58353   Endometrial ablation, thermal, without hysteroscopic guidance

(For hysteroscopic procedure, use 58563)

58356   Endometrial cryoablation with ultrasonic guidance, including endometrial curettage, when performed

(Do not report 58356 in conjunction with 58100, 58120, 58340, 76700, 76856)

Repair

58400   Uterine suspension, with or without shortening of round ligaments, with or without shortening of sacrouterine ligaments; (separate procedure)

58410   with presacral sympathectomy

(For anastomosis of tubes to uterus, use 58752)

58520   Hysterorrhaphy, repair of ruptured uterus (nonobstetrical)

58540   Hysteroplasty, repair of uterine anomaly (Strassman type)

(For closure of vesicouterine fistula, use 51920)

Laparoscopy/Hysteroscopy

Surgical laparoscopy always includes diagnostic laparoscopy. To report a diagnostic laparoscopy (peritoneoscopy) (separate procedure), use 49320. To report a diagnostic hysteroscopy (separate procedure), use 58555.

58545   Laparoscopy, surgical, myomectomy, excision; 1 to 4 intramural myomas with total weight of 250 grams or less and/or removal of surface myomas

58546   5 or more intramural myomas and/or intramural myomas with total weight greater than 250 grams

58550   Laparoscopy surgical, with vaginal hysterectomy, for uterus 250 grams or less;

58552   with removal of tube(s) and/or ovary(s)

58553   Laparoscopy, surgical, with vaginal hysterectomy, for uterus greater than 250 grams;

58554   with removal of tube(s) and/or ovary(s)

58555   Hysteroscopy, diagnostic (separate procedure)

58558   Hysteroscopy, surgical; with sampling (biopsy) of endometrium and/or polypectomy, with or without D & C

58559   with lysis of intrauterine adhesions (any method)

58560   with division or resection of intrauterine septum (any method)

58561   with removal of leiomyomata

58562   with removal of impacted foreign body

58563   with endometrial ablation (eg, endometrial resection, electrosurgical ablation, thermoablation)

58565   with bilateral fallopian tube cannulation to induce occlusion by placement of permanent implants

(Do not report 58565 in conjunction with 58555 or 57800)

(For unilateral procedure, use modifier 52)

58578   Unlisted laparoscopy procedure, uterus

58579   Unlisted hysteroscopy procedure, uterus

Oviduct/Ovary

Incision

58600   Ligation or transection of fallopian tube(s), abdominal or vaginal approach, unilateral or bilateral

58605   Ligation or transection of fallopian tube(s), abdominal or vaginal approach, postpartum, unilateral or bilateral, during same hospitalization (separate procedure)

(For laparoscopic procedures, use 58670, 58671)

+ 58611   Ligation or transection of fallopian tube(s) when done at the time of cesarean delivery or intra-abdominal surgery (not a separate procedure) (List separately in addition to code for primary procedure)

Surgery: Male/Female Genital System

58615 Occlusion of fallopian tube(s) by device (eg, band, clip, Falope ring) vaginal or suprapubic approach

(For laparoscopic approach, use 58671)

(For lysis of adnexal adhesions, use 58740)

Laparoscopy

Surgical laparoscopy always includes diagnostic laparoscopy. To report a diagnostic laparoscopy (peritoneoscopy) (separate procedure), use 49320.

(For laparoscopic biopsy of the ovary or fallopian tube, use 49321)

58660 Laparoscopy, surgical; with lysis of adhesions (salpingolysis, ovariolysis) (separate procedure)

58661   with removal of adnexal structures (partial or total oophorectomy and/or salpingectomy)

58662   with fulguration or excision of lesions of the ovary, pelvic viscera, or peritoneal surface by any method

58670   with fulguration of oviducts (with or without transection)

58671   with occlusion of oviducts by device (eg, band, clip, or Falope ring)

58672   with fimbrioplasty

58673   with salpingostomy (salpingoneostomy)

(Codes 58672 and 58673 are used to report unilateral procedures. For bilateral procedure, use modifier 50)

58679 Unlisted laparoscopy procedure, oviduct, ovary

Excision

58700 Salpingectomy, complete or partial, unilateral or bilateral (separate procedure)

58720 Salpingo-oophorectomy, complete or partial, unilateral or bilateral (separate procedure)

Repair

58740 Lysis of adhesions (salpingolysis, ovariolysis)

(For laparoscopic approach, use 58660)

(For excision or destruction of endometriomas, open method, see 49200, 49201)

(For fulguration or excision of lesions, laparoscopic approach, use 58662)

58750 Tubotubal anastomosis

58752 Tubouterine implantation

58760 Fimbrioplasty

(For laparoscopic approach, use 58672)

58770 Salpingostomy (salpingoneostomy)

(For laparoscopic approach, use 58673)

Ovary

Incision

58800 Drainage of ovarian cyst(s), unilateral or bilateral, (separate procedure); vaginal approach

58805   abdominal approach

58820 Drainage of ovarian abscess; vaginal approach, open

58822   abdominal approach

⊙ 58823 Drainage of pelvic abscess, transvaginal or transrectal approach, percutaneous (eg, ovarian, pericolic)

(For radiological supervision and interpretation, use 75989)

58825 Transposition, ovary(s)

Excision

58900 Biopsy of ovary, unilateral or bilateral (separate procedure)

(For laparoscopic biopsy of the ovary or fallopian tube, use 49321)

58920 Wedge resection or bisection of ovary, unilateral or bilateral

58925 Ovarian cystectomy, unilateral or bilateral

58940 Oophorectomy, partial or total, unilateral or bilateral;

(For oophorectomy with concomitant debulking for ovarian malignancy, use 58952)

58943   for ovarian, tubal or primary peritoneal malignancy, with para-aortic and pelvic lymph node biopsies, peritoneal washings, peritoneal biopsies, diaphragmatic assessments, with or without salpingectomy(s), with or without omentectomy

58950 Resection of ovarian, tubal or primary peritoneal malignancy with bilateral salpingo-oophorectomy and omentectomy;

58951   with total abdominal hysterectomy, pelvic and limited para-aortic lymphadenectomy

58952   with radical dissection for debulking (ie, radical excision or destruction, intra-abdominal or retroperitoneal tumors)

58953 Bilateral salpingo-oophorectomy with omentectomy, total abdominal hysterectomy and radical dissection for debulking;

58954   with pelvic lymphadenectomy and limited para-aortic lymphadenectomy

58956 Bilateral salpingo-oophorectomy with total omentectomy, total abdominal hysterectomy for malignancy

(Do not report 58956 in conjunction with 49255, 58150, 58180, 58262, 58263, 58550, 58661, 58700, 58720, 58900, 58925, 58940)

58960   Laparotomy, for staging or restaging of ovarian, tubal or primary peritoneal malignancy (second look), with or without omentectomy, peritoneal washing, biopsy of abdominal and pelvic peritoneum, diaphragmatic assessment with pelvic and limited para-aortic lymphadenectomy

In Vitro Fertilization

58970   Follicle puncture for oocyte retrieval, any method

(For radiological supervision and interpretation, use 76948)

58974   Embryo transfer, intrauterine

58976   Gamete, zygote, or embryo intrafallopian transfer, any method

(For laparoscopic adnexal procedures, see 58660-58673)

Other Procedures

58999   Unlisted procedure, female genital system (nonobstetrical)

Maternity Care and Delivery

The services normally provided in uncomplicated maternity cases include antepartum care, delivery, and postpartum care.

Antepartum care includes the initial and subsequent history, physical examinations, recording of weight, blood pressures, fetal heart tones, routine chemical urinalysis, and monthly visits up to 28 weeks gestation, biweekly visits to 36 weeks gestation, and weekly visits until delivery. Any other visits or services within this time period should be coded separately.

Delivery services include admission to the hospital, the admission history and physical examination, management of uncomplicated labor, vaginal delivery (with or without episiotomy, with or without forceps), or cesarean delivery. Medical problems complicating labor and delivery management may require additional resources and should be identified by utilizing the codes in the **Medicine** and **Evaluation and Management Services** section in addition to codes for maternity care.

Postpartum care includes hospital and office visits following vaginal or cesarean section delivery.

For medical complications of pregnancy (eg, cardiac problems, neurological problems, diabetes, hypertension, toxemia, hyperemesis, pre-term labor, premature rupture of membranes), see services in the **Medicine** and **Evaluation and Management Services** section.

For surgical complications of pregnancy (eg, appendectomy, hernia, ovarian cyst, Bartholin cyst), see services in the **Surgery** section.

If a physician provides all or part of the antepartum and/or postpartum patient care but does not perform delivery due to termination of pregnancy by abortion or referral to another physician for delivery, see the antepartum and postpartum care codes 59425-59426 and 59430.

(For circumcision of newborn, see 54150, 54160)

Antepartum Services

(For insertion of transcervical or transvaginal fetal oximetry sensor, use Category III code 0021T)

59000   Amniocentesis; diagnostic

(For radiological supervision and interpretation, use 76946)

59001   therapeutic amniotic fluid reduction (includes ultrasound guidance)

59012   Cordocentesis (intrauterine), any method

(For radiological supervision and interpretation, use 76941)

59015   Chorionic villus sampling, any method

(For radiological supervision and interpretation, use 76945)

59020   Fetal contraction stress test

59025   Fetal non-stress test

59030   Fetal scalp blood sampling

(For repeat fetal scalp blood sampling, use 59030 and see modifiers 76 and 77)

59050   Fetal monitoring during labor by consulting physician (ie, non-attending physician) with written report; supervision and interpretation

59051   interpretation only

59070   Transabdominal amnioinfusion, including ultrasound guidance

59072   Fetal umbilical cord occlusion, including ultrasound guidance

59074   Fetal fluid drainage (eg, vesicocentesis, thoracocentesis, paracentesis), including ultrasound guidance

59076   Fetal shunt placement, including ultrasound guidance

(For unlisted fetal invasive procedure, use 59897)

Excision

59100   Hysterotomy, abdominal (eg, for hydatidiform mole, abortion)

(When tubal ligation is performed at the same time as hysterotomy, use 58611 in addition to 59100)

Surgery: Male/Female Genital System

59120 Surgical treatment of ectopic pregnancy; tubal or ovarian, requiring salpingectomy and/or oophorectomy, abdominal or vaginal approach

59121   tubal or ovarian, without salpingectomy and/or oophorectomy

59130 abdominal pregnancy

59135 interstitial, uterine pregnancy requiring total hysterectomy

59136 interstitial, uterine pregnancy with partial resection of uterus

59140 cervical, with evacuation

59150 Laparoscopic treatment of ectopic pregnancy; without salpingectomy and/or oophorectomy

59151   with salpingectomy and/or oophorectomy

59160 Curettage, postpartum

Introduction

(For intrauterine fetal transfusion, use 36460)

(For introduction of hypertonic solution and/or prostaglandins to initiate labor, see 59850-59857)

59200 Insertion of cervical dilator (eg, laminaria, prostaglandin) (separate procedure)

Repair

(For tracheloplasty, use 57700)

59300 Episiotomy or vaginal repair, by other than attending physician

59320 Cerclage of cervix, during pregnancy; vaginal

59325   abdominal

59350 Hysterorrhaphy of ruptured uterus

Vaginal Delivery, Antepartum and Postpartum Care

(For insertion of transcervical or transvaginal fetal oximetry sensor, use Category III code 0021T)

59400 Routine obstetric care including antepartum care, vaginal delivery (with or without episiotomy, and/or forceps) and postpartum care

59409 Vaginal delivery only (with or without episiotomy and/or forceps);

59410   including postpartum care

59412 External cephalic version, with or without tocolysis

(Use 59412 in addition to code(s) for delivery)

59414 Delivery of placenta (separate procedure)

(For antepartum care only, see 59425, 59426 or appropriate E/M code(s))

(For 1-3 antepartum care visits, see appropriate E/M code(s))

59425 Antepartum care only; 4-6 visits

59426   7 or more visits

59430 Postpartum care only (separate procedure)

Cesarean Delivery

(For insertion of transcervical or transvaginal fetal oximetry sensor, use Category III code 0021T)

(For standby attendance for infant, use 99360)

(For low cervical cesarean section, see 59510, 59515, 59525)

59510 Routine obstetric care including antepartum care, cesarean delivery, and postpartum care

59514 Cesarean delivery only;

59515   including postpartum care

(For classic cesarean section, see 59510, 59515, 59525)

+ 59525 Subtotal or total hysterectomy after cesarean delivery (List separately in addition to code for primary procedure)

(Use 59525 in conjunction with 59510, 59514, 59515, 59618, 59620, 59622)

(For extraperitoneal cesarean section, or cesarean section with subtotal or total hysterectomy, see 59510, 59515, 59525)

Delivery After Previous Cesarean Delivery

Patients who have had a previous cesarean delivery and now present with the expectation of a vaginal delivery are coded using codes 59610-59622. If the patient has a successful vaginal delivery after a previous cesarean delivery (VBAC), use codes 59610-59614. If the attempt is unsuccessful and another cesarean delivery is carried out, use codes 59618-59622. To report elective cesarean deliveries use code 59510, 59514 or 59515.

(For insertion of transcervical or transvaginal fetal oximetry sensor, use Category III code 0021T)

59610 Routine obstetric care including antepartum care, vaginal delivery (with or without episiotomy, and/or forceps) and postpartum care, after previous cesarean delivery

59612 Vaginal delivery only, after previous cesarean delivery (with or without episiotomy and/or forceps);

59614   including postpartum care

59618 Routine obstetric care including antepartum care, cesarean delivery, and postpartum care, following attempted vaginal delivery after previous cesarean delivery

Surgery: Male/Female Genital System

59620   Cesarean delivery only, following attempted vaginal delivery after previous cesarean delivery;

59622   including postpartum care

Abortion

(For medical treatment of spontaneous complete abortion, any trimester, use E/M codes 99201-99233)

(For surgical treatment of spontaneous abortion, use 59812)

59812   Treatment of incomplete abortion, any trimester, completed surgically

59820   Treatment of missed abortion, completed surgically; first trimester

59821   second trimester

59830   Treatment of septic abortion, completed surgically

59840   Induced abortion, by dilation and curettage

59841   Induced abortion, by dilation and evacuation

59850   Induced abortion, by one or more intra-amniotic injections (amniocentesis-injections), including hospital admission and visits, delivery of fetus and secundines;

59851   with dilation and curettage and/or evacuation

59852   with hysterotomy (failed intra-amniotic injection)

(For insertion of cervical dilator, use 59200)

59855   Induced abortion, by one or more vaginal suppositories (eg, prostaglandin) with or without cervical dilation (eg, laminaria), including hospital admission and visits, delivery of fetus and secundines;

59856   with dilation and curettage and/or evacuation

59857   with hysterotomy (failed medical evacuation)

Other Procedures

59866   Multifetal pregnancy reduction(s) (MPR)

59870   Uterine evacuation and curettage for hydatidiform mole

59871   Removal of cerclage suture under anesthesia (other than local)

59897   Unlisted fetal invasive procedure, including ultrasound guidance

59898   Unlisted laparoscopy procedure, maternity care and delivery

59899   Unlisted procedure, maternity care and delivery

Surgery: Male/Female Genital System

Notes

⊘=Modifier 51 exempt   ⊙=Conscious sedation   +=Add-on code   ✗=FDA approval pending

Endocrine System

(For pituitary and pineal surgery, see **Nervous System**)

Thyroid Gland

Incision

60000 Incision and drainage of thyroglossal duct cyst, infected

Excision

60001 Aspiration and/or injection, thyroid cyst

(For fine needle aspiration, see 10021, 10022)

(If imaging guidance is performed, see 76360, 76942)

60100 Biopsy thyroid, percutaneous core needle

(If imaging guidance is performed, see 76003, 76360, 76393, 76942)

(For fine needle aspiration, use 10021 or 10022)

(For evaluation of fine needle aspirate, see 88172, 88173)

60200 Excision of cyst or adenoma of thyroid, or transection of isthmus

60210 Partial thyroid lobectomy, unilateral; with or without isthmusectomy

60212   with contralateral subtotal lobectomy, including isthmusectomy

60220 Total thyroid lobectomy, unilateral; with or without isthmusectomy

60225   with contralateral subtotal lobectomy, including isthmusectomy

60240 Thyroidectomy, total or complete

(For thyroidectomy, subtotal or partial, use 60271)

60252 Thyroidectomy, total or subtotal for malignancy; with limited neck dissection

60254   with radical neck dissection

60260 Thyroidectomy, removal of all remaining thyroid tissue following previous removal of a portion of thyroid

(For bilateral procedure, report 60260 with modifier 50)

60270 Thyroidectomy, including substernal thyroid; sternal split or transthoracic approach

60271   cervical approach

60280 Excision of thyroglossal duct cyst or sinus;

60281   recurrent

(For thyroid ultrasonography, use 76536)

Parathyroid, Thymus, Adrenal Glands, Pancreas, and Carotid Body

Excision

(For pituitary and pineal surgery, see **Nervous System**)

60500 Parathyroidectomy or exploration of parathyroid(s);

60502   re-exploration

60505   with mediastinal exploration, sternal split or transthoracic approach

+ 60512 Parathyroid autotransplantation (List separately in addition to code for primary procedure)

(Use 60512 in conjunction with 60500, 60502, 60505, 60212, 60225, 60240, 60252, 60254, 60260, 60270, 60271)

60520 Thymectomy, partial or total; transcervical approach (separate procedure)

60521   sternal split or transthoracic approach, without radical mediastinal dissection (separate procedure)

60522   sternal split or transthoracic approach, with radical mediastinal dissection (separate procedure)

60540 Adrenalectomy, partial or complete, or exploration of adrenal gland with or without biopsy, transabdominal, lumbar or dorsal (separate procedure);

60545   with excision of adjacent retroperitoneal tumor

(Do not report 60540, 60545 in conjunction with 50323)

(For bilateral procedure, report 60540 with modifier 50)

(For excision of remote or disseminated pheochromocytoma, see 49200, 49201)

(For laparoscopic approach, use 60650)

60600 Excision of carotid body tumor; without excision of carotid artery

60605   with excision of carotid artery

Laparoscopy

Surgical laparoscopy always includes diagnostic laparoscopy. To report a diagnostic laparoscopy (peritoneoscopy) (separate procedure), use 49320.

60650 Laparoscopy, surgical, with adrenalectomy, partial or complete, or exploration of adrenal gland with or without biopsy, transabdominal, lumbar or dorsal

60659 Unlisted laparoscopy procedure, endocrine system

Other Procedures

60699 Unlisted procedure, endocrine system

Surgery: Nervous System

Notes

⊘=Modifier 51 exempt   ⊙=Conscious sedation   ✚=Add-on code   ✗=FDA approval pending

Nervous System

Skull, Meninges, and Brain

(For injection procedure for cerebral angiography, see 36100-36218)

(For injection procedure for ventriculography, see 61026, 61120)

(For injection procedure for pneumoencephalography, use 61055)

Injection, Drainage, or Aspiration

61000 Subdural tap through fontanelle, or suture, infant, unilateral or bilateral; initial

61001 subsequent taps

61020 Ventricular puncture through previous burr hole, fontanelle, suture, or implanted ventricular catheter/reservoir; without injection

61026 with injection of medication or other substance for diagnosis or treatment

61050 Cisternal or lateral cervical (C1-C2) puncture; without injection (separate procedure)

61055 with injection of medication or other substance for diagnosis or treatment (eg, C1-C2)

(For radiological supervision and interpretation, see **Radiology**)

61070 Puncture of shunt tubing or reservoir for aspiration or injection procedure

(For radiological supervision and interpretation, use 75809)

Twist Drill, Burr Hole(s), or Trephine

61105 Twist drill hole for subdural or ventricular puncture;

⊘ **61107** for implanting ventricular catheter or pressure recording device

(For intracranial neuroendoscopic ventricular catheter placement, use 62160)

(For twist drill or burr hole performed to place thermal perfusion probe, use Category III code 0077T)

61108 for evacuation and/or drainage of subdural hematoma

61120 Burr hole(s) for ventricular puncture (including injection of gas, contrast media, dye, or radioactive material)

61140 Burr hole(s) or trephine; with biopsy of brain or intracranial lesion

61150 with drainage of brain abscess or cyst

61151 with subsequent tapping (aspiration) of intracranial abscess or cyst

61154 Burr hole(s) with evacuation and/or drainage of hematoma, extradural or subdural

(For bilateral procedure, report 61154 with modifier 50)

61156 Burr hole(s); with aspiration of hematoma or cyst, intracerebral

⊘ **61210** for implanting ventricular catheter, reservoir, EEG electrode(s) or pressure recording device (separate procedure)

(For intracranial neuroendoscopic ventricular catheter placement, use 62160)

61215 Insertion of subcutaneous reservoir, pump or continuous infusion system for connection to ventricular catheter

(For refilling and maintenance of an implantable infusion pump for spinal or brain drug therapy, use 95990)

(For chemotherapy, use 96450)

61250 Burr hole(s) or trephine, supratentorial, exploratory, not followed by other surgery

(For bilateral procedure, report 61250 with modifier 50)

61253 Burr hole(s) or trephine, infratentorial, unilateral or bilateral

(If burr hole(s) or trephine are followed by craniotomy at same operative session, use 61304-61321; do not use 61250 or 61253)

Craniectomy or Craniotomy

61304 Craniectomy or craniotomy, exploratory; supratentorial

61305 infratentorial (posterior fossa)

61312 Craniectomy or craniotomy for evacuation of hematoma, supratentorial; extradural or subdural

61313 intracerebral

61314 Craniectomy or craniotomy for evacuation of hematoma, infratentorial; extradural or subdural

61315 intracerebellar

+ **61316** Incision and subcutaneous placement of cranial bone graft (List separately in addition to code for primary procedure)

(Use 61316 in conjunction with 61304, 61312, 61313, 61322, 61323, 61340, 61570, 61571, 61680-61705)

61320 Craniectomy or craniotomy, drainage of intracranial abscess; supratentorial

61321 infratentorial

61322 Craniectomy or craniotomy, decompressive, with or without duraplasty, for treatment of intracranial hypertension, without evacuation of associated intraparenchymal hematoma; without lobectomy

(Do not report 61313 in addition to 61322)

(For subtemporal decompression, use 61340)

Surgery: Nervous System

Surgery: Nervous System

61323   with lobectomy

(Do not report 61313 in addition to 61323)

(For subtemporal decompression, use 61340)

61330   Decompression of orbit only, transcranial approach

(For bilateral procedure, report 61330 with modifier 50)

61332   Exploration of orbit (transcranial approach); with biopsy

61333   with removal of lesion

61334   with removal of foreign body

61340   Subtemporal cranial decompression (pseudotumor cerebri, slit ventricle syndrome)

(For bilateral procedure, report 61340 with modifier 50)

(For decompressive craniotomy or craniectomy for intracranial hypertension, without hematoma evacuation, see 61322, 61323)

61343   Craniectomy, suboccipital with cervical laminectomy for decompression of medulla and spinal cord, with or without dural graft (eg, Arnold-Chiari malformation)

61345   Other cranial decompression, posterior fossa

(For orbital decompression by lateral wall approach, Kroenlein type, use 67445)

61440   Craniotomy for section of tentorium cerebelli (separate procedure)

61450   Craniectomy, subtemporal, for section, compression, or decompression of sensory root of gasserian ganglion

61458   Craniectomy, suboccipital; for exploration or decompression of cranial nerves

61460   for section of one or more cranial nerves

61470   for medullary tractotomy

61480   for mesencephalic tractotomy or pedunculotomy

61490   Craniotomy for lobotomy, including cingulotomy

(For bilateral procedure, report 61490 with modifier 50)

61500   Craniectomy; with excision of tumor or other bone lesion of skull

61501   for osteomyelitis

61510   Craniectomy, trephination, bone flap craniotomy; for excision of brain tumor, supratentorial, except meningioma

61512   for excision of meningioma, supratentorial

61514   for excision of brain abscess, supratentorial

61516   for excision or fenestration of cyst, supratentorial

(For excision of pituitary tumor or craniopharyngioma, see 61545, 61546, 61548)

+ 61517   Implantation of brain intracavitary chemotherapy agent (List separately in addition to code for primary procedure)

(Use 61517 only in conjunction with 61510 or 61518)

(Do not report 61517 for brachytherapy insertion. For intracavitary insertion of radioelement sources or ribbons, see 77781-77784)

61518   Craniectomy for excision of brain tumor, infratentorial or posterior fossa; except meningioma, cerebellopontine angle tumor, or midline tumor at base of skull

61519   meningioma

61520   cerebellopontine angle tumor

61521   midline tumor at base of skull

61522   Craniectomy, infratentorial or posterior fossa; for excision of brain abscess

61524   for excision or fenestration of cyst

61526   Craniectomy, bone flap craniotomy, transtemporal (mastoid) for excision of cerebellopontine angle tumor;

61530   combined with middle/posterior fossa craniotomy/craniectomy

61531   Subdural implantation of strip electrodes through one or more burr or trephine hole(s) for long term seizure monitoring

(For stereotactic implantation of electrodes, use 61760)

(For craniotomy for excision of intracranial arteriovenous malformation, see 61680-61692)

61533   Craniotomy with elevation of bone flap; for subdural implantation of an electrode array, for long term seizure monitoring

(For continuous EEG monitoring, see 95950-95954)

61534   for excision of epileptogenic focus without electrocorticography during surgery

61535   for removal of epidural or subdural electrode array, without excision of cerebral tissue (separate procedure)

61536   for excision of cerebral epileptogenic focus, with electrocorticography during surgery (includes removal of electrode array)

61537   for lobectomy, temporal lobe, without electrocorticography during surgery

61538   for lobectomy, temporal lobe, with electrocorticography during surgery

61539   for lobectomy, other than temporal lobe, partial or total, with electrocorticography during surgery

61540   for lobectomy, other than temporal lobe, partial or total, without electrocorticography during surgery

61541   for transection of corpus callosum

61542   for total hemispherectomy

61543   for partial or subtotal (functional) hemispherectomy

61544   for excision or coagulation of choroid plexus

61545   for excision of craniopharyngioma

(For craniotomy for selective amygdalohippocampectomy, use 61566)

(For craniotomy for multiple subpial transections during surgery, use 61567)

61546   Craniotomy for hypophysectomy or excision of pituitary tumor, intracranial approach

61548   Hypophysectomy or excision of pituitary tumor, transnasal or transseptal approach, nonstereotactic

(Do not report code 69990 in addition to code 61548)

61550   Craniectomy for craniosynostosis; single cranial suture

61552   multiple cranial sutures

(For cranial reconstruction for orbital hypertelorism, see 21260-21263)

(For reconstruction, see 21172-21180)

61556   Craniotomy for craniosynostosis; frontal or parietal bone flap

61557   bifrontal bone flap

61558   Extensive craniectomy for multiple cranial suture craniosynostosis (eg, cloverleaf skull); not requiring bone grafts

61559   recontouring with multiple osteotomies and bone autografts (eg, barrel-stave procedure) (includes obtaining grafts)

(For reconstruction, see 21172-21180)

61563   Excision, intra and extracranial, benign tumor of cranial bone (eg, fibrous dysplasia); without optic nerve decompression

61564   with optic nerve decompression

(For reconstruction, see 21181-21183)

61566   Craniotomy with elevation of bone flap; for selective amygdalohippocampectomy

61567   for multiple subpial transections, with electrocorticography during surgery

61570   Craniectomy or craniotomy; with excision of foreign body from brain

61571   with treatment of penetrating wound of brain

(For sequestrectomy for osteomyelitis, use 61501)

61575   Transoral approach to skull base, brain stem or upper spinal cord for biopsy, decompression or excision of lesion;

61576   requiring splitting of tongue and/or mandible (including tracheostomy)

(For arthrodesis, use 22548)

Surgery of Skull Base

The surgical management of lesions involving the skull base (base of anterior, middle, and posterior cranial fossae) often requires the skills of several surgeons of different surgical specialties working together or in tandem during the operative session. These operations are usually not staged because of the need for definitive closure of dura, subcutaneous tissues, and skin to avoid serious infections such as osteomyelitis and/or meningitis.

The procedures are categorized according to: 1) *approach procedure* necessary to obtain adequate exposure to the lesion (pathologic entity), 2) *definitive procedure(s)* necessary to biopsy, excise or otherwise treat the lesion, and 3) *repair/reconstruction* of the defect present following the definitive procedure(s).

The *approach procedure* is described according to anatomical area involved, ie, anterior cranial fossa, middle cranial fossa, posterior cranial fossa, and brain stem or upper spinal cord.

The *definitive procedure(s)* describes the repair, biopsy, resection, or excision of various lesions of the skull base and, when appropriate, primary closure of the dura, mucous membranes, and skin.

The *repair/reconstruction procedure(s)* is reported separately if extensive dural grafting, cranioplasty, local or regional myocutaneous pedicle flaps, or extensive skin grafts are required.

For primary closure, see the appropriate codes, ie, 15732, 15756-15758.

When one surgeon performs the approach procedure, another surgeon performs the definitive procedure, and another surgeon performs the repair/reconstruction procedure, each surgeon reports only the code for the specific procedure performed.

If one surgeon performs more than one procedure (ie, approach procedure and definitive procedure), then both codes are reported, adding modifier 51 to the secondary, additional procedure(s).

Approach Procedures

Anterior Cranial Fossa

61580   Craniofacial approach to anterior cranial fossa; extradural, including lateral rhinotomy, ethmoidectomy, sphenoidectomy, without maxillectomy or orbital exenteration

61581   extradural, including lateral rhinotomy, orbital exenteration, ethmoidectomy, sphenoidectomy and/or maxillectomy

Surgery: Nervous System

61582   extradural, including unilateral or bifrontal craniotomy, elevation of frontal lobe(s), osteotomy of base of anterior cranial fossa

61583   intradural, including unilateral or bifrontal craniotomy, elevation or resection of frontal lobe, osteotomy of base of anterior cranial fossa

61584   Orbitocranial approach to anterior cranial fossa, extradural, including supraorbital ridge osteotomy and elevation of frontal and/or temporal lobe(s); without orbital exenteration

61585   with orbital exenteration

61586   Bicoronal, transzygomatic and/or LeFort I osteotomy approach to anterior cranial fossa with or without internal fixation, without bone graft

Middle Cranial Fossa

61590   Infratemporal pre-auricular approach to middle cranial fossa (parapharyngeal space, infratemporal and midline skull base, nasopharynx), with or without disarticulation of the mandible, including parotidectomy, craniotomy, decompression and/or mobilization of the facial nerve and/or petrous carotid artery

61591   Infratemporal post-auricular approach to middle cranial fossa (internal auditory meatus, petrous apex, tentorium, cavernous sinus, parasellar area, infratemporal fossa) including mastoidectomy, resection of sigmoid sinus, with or without decompression and/or mobilization of contents of auditory canal or petrous carotid artery

61592   Orbitocranial zygomatic approach to middle cranial fossa (cavernous sinus and carotid artery, clivus, basilar artery or petrous apex) including osteotomy of zygoma, craniotomy, extra- or intradural elevation of temporal lobe

Posterior Cranial Fossa

61595   Transtemporal approach to posterior cranial fossa, jugular foramen or midline skull base, including mastoidectomy, decompression of sigmoid sinus and/or facial nerve, with or without mobilization

61596   Transcochlear approach to posterior cranial fossa, jugular foramen or midline skull base, including labyrinthectomy, decompression, with or without mobilization of facial nerve and/or petrous carotid artery

61597   Transcondylar (far lateral) approach to posterior cranial fossa, jugular foramen or midline skull base, including occipital condylectomy, mastoidectomy, resection of C1-C3 vertebral body(s), decompression of vertebral artery, with or without mobilization

61598   Transpetrosal approach to posterior cranial fossa, clivus or foramen magnum, including ligation of superior petrosal sinus and/or sigmoid sinus

Definitive Procedures

Base of Anterior Cranial Fossa

61600   Resection or excision of neoplastic, vascular or infectious lesion of base of anterior cranial fossa; extradural

61601   intradural, including dural repair, with or without graft

Base of Middle Cranial Fossa

61605   Resection or excision of neoplastic, vascular or infectious lesion of infratemporal fossa, parapharyngeal space, petrous apex; extradural

61606   intradural, including dural repair, with or without graft

61607   Resection or excision of neoplastic, vascular or infectious lesion of parasellar area, cavernous sinus, clivus or midline skull base; extradural

61608   intradural, including dural repair, with or without graft

Codes 61609-61612 are reported in addition to code(s) for primary procedure(s) 61605-61608. Report only one transection or ligation of carotid artery code per operative session.

+ 61609   Transection or ligation, carotid artery in cavernous sinus; without repair (List separately in addition to code for primary procedure)

+ 61610   with repair by anastomosis or graft (List separately in addition to code for primary procedure)

+ 61611   Transection or ligation, carotid artery in petrous canal; without repair (List separately in addition to code for primary procedure)

+ 61612   with repair by anastomosis or graft (List separately in addition to code for primary procedure)

61613   Obliteration of carotid aneurysm, arteriovenous malformation, or carotid-cavernous fistula by dissection within cavernous sinus

Base of Posterior Cranial Fossa

61615   Resection or excision of neoplastic, vascular or infectious lesion of base of posterior cranial fossa, jugular foramen, foramen magnum, or C1-C3 vertebral bodies; extradural

61616   intradural, including dural repair, with or without graft

Repair and/or Reconstruction of Surgical Defects of Skull Base

61618   Secondary repair of dura for cerebrospinal fluid leak, anterior, middle or posterior cranial fossa following surgery of the skull base; by free tissue graft (eg, pericranium, fascia, tensor fascia lata, adipose tissue, homologous or synthetic grafts)

61619   by local or regionalized vascularized pedicle flap or myocutaneous flap (including galea, temporalis, frontalis or occipitalis muscle)

Surgery: Nervous System

Endovascular Therapy

61623 Endovascular temporary balloon arterial occlusion, head or neck (extracranial/intracranial) including selective catheterization of vessel to be occluded, positioning and inflation of occlusion balloon, concomitant neurological monitoring, and radiologic supervision and interpretation of all angiography required for balloon occlusion and to exclude vascular injury post occlusion

(If selective catheterization and angiography of arteries other than artery to be occluded is performed, use appropriate catheterization and radiologic supervision and interpretation codes)

(If complete diagnostic angiography of the artery to be occluded is performed immediately prior to temporary occlusion, use appropriate radiologic supervision and interpretation codes only)

61624 Transcatheter permanent occlusion or embolization (eg, for tumor destruction, to achieve hemostasis, to occlude a vascular malformation), percutaneous, any method; central nervous system (intracranial, spinal cord)

(See also 37204)

(For radiological supervision and interpretation, use 75894)

61626   non-central nervous system, head or neck (extracranial, brachiocephalic branch)

(See also 37204)

(For radiological supervision and interpretation, use 75894)

● **61630** Balloon angioplasty, intracranial (eg, atherosclerotic stenosis), percutaneous

● **61635** Transcatheter placement of intravascular stent(s), intracranial (eg, atherosclerotic stenosis), including balloon angioplasty, if performed

▶(61630 and 61635 include all selective vascular catheterization of the target vascular family, all diagnostic imaging for arteriography of the target vascular family, and all related radiological supervision and interpretation. When diagnostic arteriogram (including imaging and selective catheterization) confirms the need for angioplasty or stent placement, 61630 and 61635 are inclusive of these services. If angioplasty or stenting are not indicated, then the appropriate codes for selective catheterization and imaging should be reported in lieu of 61630 and 61635)◀

● **61640** Balloon dilatation of intracranial vasospasm, percutaneous; initial vessel

+● **61641**   each additional vessel in same vascular family (List separately in addition to code for primary procedure)

+● **61642**   each additional vessel in different vascular family (List separately in addition to code for primary procedure)

▶(Use 61641 and 61642 in conjunction with 61640)◀

▶(61640, 61641, 61642 include all selective vascular catheterization of the target vessel, contrast injection(s), vessel measurement, roadmapping, postdilatation angiography, and fluoroscopic guidance for the balloon dilatation)◀

Surgery for Aneurysm, Arteriovenous Malformation or Vascular Disease

Includes craniotomy when appropriate for procedure.

61680 Surgery of intracranial arteriovenous malformation; supratentorial, simple

61682   supratentorial, complex

61684   infratentorial, simple

61686   infratentorial, complex

61690   dural, simple

61692   dural, complex

61697 Surgery of complex intracranial aneurysm, intracranial approach; carotid circulation

61698   vertebrobasilar circulation

(61697, 61698 involve aneurysms that are larger than 15 mm or with calcification of the aneurysm neck, or with incorporation of normal vessels into the aneurysm neck, or a procedure requiring temporary vessel occlusion, trapping or cardiopulmonary bypass to successfully treat the aneurysm)

61700 Surgery of simple intracranial aneurysm, intracranial approach; carotid circulation

61702   vertebrobasilar circulation

61703 Surgery of intracranial aneurysm, cervical approach by application of occluding clamp to cervical carotid artery (Selverstone-Crutchfield type)

(For cervical approach for direct ligation of carotid artery, see 37600-37606)

61705 Surgery of aneurysm, vascular malformation or carotid-cavernous fistula; by intracranial and cervical occlusion of carotid artery

61708   by intracranial electrothrombosis

(For ligation or gradual occlusion of internal/common carotid artery, see 37605, 37606)

61710   by intra-arterial embolization, injection procedure, or balloon catheter

61711 Anastomosis, arterial, extracranial-intracranial (eg, middle cerebral/cortical) arteries

(For carotid or vertebral thromboendarterectomy, use 35301)

(Use 69990 when the surgical microscope is employed for the microsurgical procedure. Do not use 69990 for visualization with magnifying loupes or corrected vision)

Surgery: Nervous System

Stereotaxis

61720 Creation of lesion by stereotactic method, including burr hole(s) and localizing and recording techniques, single or multiple stages; globus pallidus or thalamus

61735 subcortical structure(s) other than globus pallidus or thalamus

61750 Stereotactic biopsy, aspiration, or excision, including burr hole(s), for intracranial lesion;

61751 with computed tomography and/or magnetic resonance guidance

(For radiological supervision and interpretation of computerized tomography, see 70450, 70460, or 70470 as appropriate)

(For radiological supervision and interpretation of magnetic resonance imaging, see 70551, 70552, or 70553 as appropriate)

61760 Stereotactic implantation of depth electrodes into the cerebrum for long term seizure monitoring

61770 Stereotactic localization, including burr hole(s), with insertion of catheter(s) or probe(s) for placement of radiation source

61790 Creation of lesion by stereotactic method, percutaneous, by neurolytic agent (eg, alcohol, thermal, electrical, radiofrequency); gasserian ganglion

61791 trigeminal medullary tract

61793 Stereotactic radiosurgery (particle beam, gamma ray or linear accelerator), one or more sessions

(For intensity modulated beam delivery plan and treatment, see 77301, 77418)

✛ 61795 Stereotactic computer assisted volumetric (navigational) procedure, intracranial, extracranial, or spinal (List separately in addition to code for primary procedure)

Neurostimulators (Intracranial)

Codes 61850-61888 apply to both simple and complex neurostimulators. For initial or subsequent electronic analysis and programming of neurostimulator pulse generators, see codes 95970-95975.

Microelectrode recording, when performed by the operating surgeon in association with implantation of neurostimulator electrode arrays, is an inclusive service and should not be reported separately. If another physician participates in neurophysiological mapping during a deep brain stimulator implantation procedure, this service may be reported by the other physician with codes 95961-95962.

61850 Twist drill or burr hole(s) for implantation of neurostimulator electrodes, cortical

61860 Craniectomy or craniotomy for implantation of neurostimulator electrodes, cerebral, cortical

(61862 has been deleted. To report, see 61867, 61868)

61863 Twist drill, burr hole, craniotomy, or craniectomy with stereotactic implantation of neurostimulator electrode array in subcortical site (eg, thalamus, globus pallidus, subthalamic nucleus, periventricular, periaqueductal gray), without use of intraoperative microelectrode recording; first array

✛ 61864 each additional array (List separately in addition to primary procedure)

(Use 61864 in conjunction with 61863)

61867 Twist drill, burr hole, craniotomy, or craniectomy with stereotactic implantation of neurostimulator electrode array in subcortical site (eg, thalamus, globus pallidus, subthalamic nucleus, periventricular, periaqueductal gray), with use of intraoperative microelectrode recording; first array

✛ 61868 each additional array (List separately in addition to primary procedure)

(Use 61868 in conjunction with 61867)

61870 Craniectomy for implantation of neurostimulator electrodes, cerebellar; cortical

61875 subcortical

61880 Revision or removal of intracranial neurostimulator electrodes

61885 Insertion or replacement of cranial neurostimulator pulse generator or receiver, direct or inductive coupling; with connection to a single electrode array

61886 with connection to two or more electrode arrays

(For open placement of cranial nerve (eg, vagal, trigeminal) neurostimulator electrode(s), use 64573)

(For percutaneous placement of cranial nerve (eg, vagal, trigeminal) neurostimulator electrode(s), use 64553)

(For revision or removal of cranial nerve (eg, vagal, trigeminal) neurostimulator electrode(s), use 64585)

61888 Revision or removal of cranial neurostimulator pulse generator or receiver

(Do not report 61888 in conjunction with 61885 or 61886 for the same pulse generator)

Repair

62000 Elevation of depressed skull fracture; simple, extradural

62005 compound or comminuted, extradural

62010 with repair of dura and/or debridement of brain

62100 Craniotomy for repair of dural/cerebrospinal fluid leak, including surgery for rhinorrhea/otorrhea

(For repair of spinal dural/CSF leak, see 63707, 63709)

62115 Reduction of craniomegalic skull (eg, treated hydrocephalus); not requiring bone grafts or cranioplasty

62116 with simple cranioplasty

62117 requiring craniotomy and reconstruction with or without bone graft (includes obtaining grafts)

Surgery: Nervous System

62120   Repair of encephalocele, skull vault, including cranioplasty

62121   Craniotomy for repair of encephalocele, skull base

62140   Cranioplasty for skull defect; up to 5 cm diameter

62141   larger than 5 cm diameter

62142   Removal of bone flap or prosthetic plate of skull

62143   Replacement of bone flap or prosthetic plate of skull

62145   Cranioplasty for skull defect with reparative brain surgery

62146   Cranioplasty with autograft (includes obtaining bone grafts); up to 5 cm diameter

62147   larger than 5 cm diameter

+ 62148   Incision and retrieval of subcutaneous cranial bone graft for cranioplasty (List separately in addition to code for primary procedure)

    (Use 62148 in conjunction with 62140-62147)

Neuroendoscopy

Surgical endoscopy always includes diagnostic endoscopy.

+ 62160   Neuroendoscopy, intracranial, for placement or replacement of ventricular catheter and attachment to shunt system or external drainage (List separately in addition to code for primary procedure)

    (Use 62160 only in conjunction with 61107, 61210, 62220, 62223, 62225, or 62230)

62161   Neuroendoscopy, intracranial; with dissection of adhesions, fenestration of septum pellucidum or intraventricular cysts (including placement, replacement, or removal of ventricular catheter)

62162   with fenestration or excision of colloid cyst, including placement of external ventricular catheter for drainage

62163   with retrieval of foreign body

62164   with excision of brain tumor, including placement of external ventricular catheter for drainage

62165   with excision of pituitary tumor, transnasal or trans-sphenoidal approach

Cerebrospinal Fluid (CSF) Shunt

62180   Ventriculocisternostomy (Torkildsen type operation)

62190   Creation of shunt; subarachnoid/subdural-atrial, -jugular, -auricular

62192   subarachnoid/subdural-peritoneal, -pleural, other terminus

62194   Replacement or irrigation, subarachnoid/subdural catheter

62200   Ventriculocisternostomy, third ventricle;

62201   stereotactic, neuroendoscopic method

    (For intracranial neuroendoscopic procedures, see 62161-62165)

62220   Creation of shunt; ventriculo-atrial, -jugular, -auricular

    (For intracranial neuroendoscopic ventricular catheter placement, use 62160)

62223   ventriculo-peritoneal, -pleural, other terminus

    (For intracranial neuroendoscopic ventricular catheter placement, use 62160)

62225   Replacement or irrigation, ventricular catheter

    (For intracranial neuroendoscopic ventricular catheter placement, use 62160)

62230   Replacement or revision of cerebrospinal fluid shunt, obstructed valve, or distal catheter in shunt system

    (For intracranial neuroendoscopic ventricular catheter placement, use 62160)

62252   Reprogramming of programmable cerebrospinal shunt

62256   Removal of complete cerebrospinal fluid shunt system; without replacement

62258   with replacement by similar or other shunt at same operation

    (For percutaneous irrigation or aspiration of shunt reservoir, use 61070)

    (For reprogramming of programmable CSF shunt, use 62252)

Spine and Spinal Cord

    (For application of caliper or tongs, use 20660)

    (For treatment of fracture or dislocation of spine, see 22305-22327)

Injection, Drainage, or Aspiration

Injection of contrast during fluoroscopic guidance and localization is an inclusive component of codes 62263-62264, 62270-62273, 62280-62282, 62310-62319, 0027T. Fluoroscopic guidance and localization is reported by code 76005, unless a formal contrast study (myelography, epidurography, or arthrography) is performed, in which case the use of fluoroscopy is included in the supervision and interpretation codes.

For radiologic supervision and interpretation of epidurography, use 72275. Code 72275 is only to be used when an epidurogram is performed, images documented, and a formal radiologic report is issued.

Code 62263 describes a catheter-based treatment involving targeted injection of various substances (eg, hypertonic saline, steroid, anesthetic) via an indwelling epidural catheter. Code 62263 includes percutaneous insertion and removal of an epidural catheter (remaining

Surgery: Nervous System

in place over a several-day period), for the administration of multiple injections of a neurolytic agent(s) performed during serial treatment sessions (ie, spanning two or more treatment days). If required, adhesions or scarring may also be lysed by mechanical means. Code 62263 is NOT reported for each adhesiolysis treatment, but should be reported ONCE to describe the entire series of injections/infusions spanning two or more treatment days. For endoscopic lysis of adhesions, use 0027T.

Code 62264 describes multiple adhesiolysis treatment sessions performed on the same day. Adhesions or scarring may be lysed by injections of neurolytic agent(s). If required, adhesions or scarring may also be lysed mechanically using a percutaneously-deployed catheter.

Codes 62263 and 62264 include the procedure of injections of contrast for epidurography (72275) and fluoroscopic guidance and localization (76005) during initial or subsequent sessions.

> (Report 01996 for daily hospital management of continuous epidural or subarachnoid drug administration performed in conjunction with 62318-62319)

> (For endoscopic lysis of epidural adhesions, use Category III code 0027T)

62263 Percutaneous lysis of epidural adhesions using solution injection (eg, hypertonic saline, enzyme) or mechanical means (eg, catheter) including radiologic localization (includes contrast when administered), multiple adhesiolysis sessions; 2 or more days

> (62263 includes codes 76005 and 72275)

62264   1 day

> (Do not report 62264 with 62263)

> (62264 includes codes 76005 and 72275)

62268 Percutaneous aspiration, spinal cord cyst or syrinx

> (For radiological supervision and interpretation, see 76003, 76360, 76942)

62269 Biopsy of spinal cord, percutaneous needle

> (For radiological supervision and interpretation, see 76003, 76360, 76942)

> (For fine needle aspiration, see 10021, 10022)

> (For evaluation of fine needle aspirate, see 88172, 88173)

62270 Spinal puncture, lumbar, diagnostic

62272 Spinal puncture, therapeutic, for drainage of cerebrospinal fluid (by needle or catheter)

62273 Injection, epidural, of blood or clot patch

> (For injection of diagnostic or therapeutic substance(s), see 62310, 62311, 62318, 62319)

62280 Injection/infusion of neurolytic substance (eg, alcohol, phenol, iced saline solutions), with or without other therapeutic substance; subarachnoid

62281   epidural, cervical or thoracic

62282   epidural, lumbar, sacral (caudal)

⊘ **62284** Injection procedure for myelography and/or computed tomography, spinal (other than C1-C2 and posterior fossa)

> (For injection procedure at C1-C2, use 61055)

> (For radiological supervision and interpretation, see **Radiology**)

62287 Aspiration or decompression procedure, percutaneous, of nucleus pulposus of intervertebral disk, any method, single or multiple levels, lumbar (eg, manual or automated percutaneous diskectomy, percutaneous laser diskectomy)

> (For fluoroscopic guidance, use 76003)

> (For injection of non-neurolytic diagnostic or therapeutic substance(s), see 62310, 62311)

62290 Injection procedure for diskography, each level; lumbar

62291   cervical or thoracic

> (For radiological supervision and interpretation, see 72285, 72295)

62292 Injection procedure for chemonucleolysis, including diskography, intervertebral disk, single or multiple levels, lumbar

62294 Injection procedure, arterial, for occlusion of arteriovenous malformation, spinal

62310 Injection, single (not via indwelling catheter), not including neurolytic substances, with or without contrast (for either localization or epidurography), of diagnostic or therapeutic substance(s) (including anesthetic, antispasmodic, opioid, steroid, other solution), epidural or subarachnoid; cervical or thoracic

62311   lumbar, sacral (caudal)

62318 Injection, including catheter placement, continuous infusion or intermittent bolus, not including neurolytic substances, with or without contrast (for either localization or epidurography), of diagnostic or therapeutic substance(s) (including anesthetic, antispasmodic, opioid, steroid, other solution), epidural or subarachnoid; cervical or thoracic

62319   lumbar, sacral (caudal)

> (For transforaminal epidural injection, see 64479-64484)

> (Report 01996 for daily hospital management of continuous epidural or subarachnoid drug administration performed in conjunction with 62318-62319)

Surgery: Nervous System

Catheter Implantation

(For percutaneous placement of intrathecal or epidural catheter, see codes 62270-62273, 62280-62284, 62310-62319)

62350 Implantation, revision or repositioning of tunneled intrathecal or epidural catheter, for long-term medication administration via an external pump or implantable reservoir/infusion pump; without laminectomy

62351 with laminectomy

(For refilling and maintenance of an implantable infusion pump for spinal or brain drug therapy, see 95990, 95991)

62355 Removal of previously implanted intrathecal or epidural catheter

Reservoir/Pump Implantation

62360 Implantation or replacement of device for intrathecal or epidural drug infusion; subcutaneous reservoir

62361 non-programmable pump

62362 programmable pump, including preparation of pump, with or without programming

62365 Removal of subcutaneous reservoir or pump, previously implanted for intrathecal or epidural infusion

62367 Electronic analysis of programmable, implanted pump for intrathecal or epidural drug infusion (includes evaluation of reservoir status, alarm status, drug prescription status); without reprogramming

62368 with reprogramming

(For refilling and maintenance of an implantable infusion pump for spinal or brain drug therapy, use 95990-95991)

Posterior Extradural Laminotomy or Laminectomy for Exploration/ Decompression of Neural Elements or Excision of Herniated Intervertebral Disks

(When 63001-63048 are followed by arthrodesis, see 22590-22614)

63001 Laminectomy with exploration and/or decompression of spinal cord and/or cauda equina, without facetectomy, foraminotomy or diskectomy, (eg, spinal stenosis), one or two vertebral segments; cervical

63003 thoracic

63005 lumbar, except for spondylolisthesis

63011 sacral

63012 Laminectomy with removal of abnormal facets and/or pars inter-articularis with decompression of cauda equina and nerve roots for spondylolisthesis, lumbar (Gill type procedure)

63015 Laminectomy with exploration and/or decompression of spinal cord and/or cauda equina, without facetectomy, foraminotomy or diskectomy, (eg, spinal stenosis), more than 2 vertebral segments; cervical

63016 thoracic

63017 lumbar

63020 Laminotomy (hemilaminectomy), with decompression of nerve root(s), including partial facetectomy, foraminotomy and/or excision of herniated intervertebral disk; one interspace, cervical

(For bilateral procedure, report 63020 with modifier 50)

63030 one interspace, lumbar (including open or endoscopically-assisted approach)

(For bilateral procedure, report 63030 with modifier 50)

+ 63035 each additional interspace, cervical or lumbar (List separately in addition to code for primary procedure)

(Use 63035 in conjunction with 63020-63030)

(For bilateral procedure, report 63035 with modifier 50)

63040 Laminotomy (hemilaminectomy), with decompression of nerve root(s), including partial facetectomy, foraminotomy and/or excision of herniated intervertebral disk, reexploration, single interspace; cervical

(For bilateral procedure, report 63040 with modifier 50)

63042 lumbar

(For bilateral procedure, report 63042 with modifier 50)

+ 63043 each additional cervical interspace (List separately in addition to code for primary procedure)

(Use 63043 in conjunction with 63040)

(For bilateral procedure, report 63043 with modifier 50)

+ 63044 each additional lumbar interspace (List separately in addition to code for primary procedure)

(Use 63044 in conjunction with 63042)

(For bilateral procedure, report 63044 with modifier 50)

63045 Laminectomy, facetectomy and foraminotomy (unilateral or bilateral with decompression of spinal cord, cauda equina and/or nerve root(s), (eg, spinal or lateral recess stenosis)), single vertebral segment; cervical

63046 thoracic

63047 lumbar

+ 63048 each additional segment, cervical, thoracic, or lumbar (List separately in addition to code for primary procedure)

(Use 63048 in conjunction with 63045-63047)

63050   Laminoplasty, cervical, with decompression of the spinal cord, two or more vertebral segments;

63051   with reconstruction of the posterior bony elements (including the application of bridging bone graft and non-segmental fixation devices (eg, wire, suture, mini-plates), when performed)

(Do not report 63050 or 63051 in conjunction with 22600, 22614, 22840-22842, 63001, 63015, 63045, 63048, 63295 for the same vertebral segment(s))

Transpedicular or Costovertebral Approach for Posterolateral Extradural Exploration/Decompression

63055   Transpedicular approach with decompression of spinal cord, equina and/or nerve root(s) (eg, herniated intervertebral disk), single segment; thoracic

63056   lumbar (including transfacet, or lateral extraforaminal approach) (eg, far lateral herniated intervertebral disk)

+ 63057   each additional segment, thoracic or lumbar (List separately in addition to code for primary procedure)

(Use 63057 in conjunction with 63055, 63056)

63064   Costovertebral approach with decompression of spinal cord or nerve root(s), (eg, herniated intervertebral disk), thoracic; single segment

+ 63066   each additional segment (List separately in addition to code for primary procedure)

(Use 63066 in conjunction with 63064)

(For excision of thoracic intraspinal lesions by laminectomy, see 63266, 63271, 63276, 63281, 63286)

Anterior or Anterolateral Approach for Extradural Exploration/Decompression

For the following codes, when two surgeons work together as primary surgeons performing distinct part(s) of spinal cord exploration/decompression operation, each surgeon should report his/her distinct operative work by appending modifier 62 to the procedure code (and any associated add-on codes for that procedure code as long as both surgeons continue to work together as primary surgeons). In this situation, modifier 62 may be appended to the definitive procedure code(s) 63075, 63077, 63081, 63085, 63087, 63090 and, as appropriate, to associated additional interspace add-on code(s) 63076, 63078 or additional segment add-on code(s) 63082, 63086, 63088, 63091 as long as both surgeons continue to work together as primary surgeons.

63075   Diskectomy, anterior, with decompression of spinal cord and/or nerve root(s), including osteophytectomy; cervical, single interspace

+ 63076   cervical, each additional interspace (List separately in addition to code for primary procedure)

(Use 63076 in conjunction with 63075)

63077   thoracic, single interspace

+ 63078   thoracic, each additional interspace (List separately in addition to code for primary procedure)

(Use 63078 in conjunction with 63077)

(Do not report code 69990 in addition to codes 63075-63078)

63081   Vertebral corpectomy (vertebral body resection), partial or complete, anterior approach with decompression of spinal cord and/or nerve root(s); cervical, single segment

+ 63082   cervical, each additional segment (List separately in addition to code for primary procedure)

(Use 63082 in conjunction with 63081)

(For transoral approach, see 61575, 61576)

63085   Vertebral corpectomy (vertebral body resection), partial or complete, transthoracic approach with decompression of spinal cord and/or nerve root(s); thoracic, single segment

+ 63086   thoracic, each additional segment (List separately in addition to code for primary procedure)

(Use 63086 in conjunction with 63085)

63087   Vertebral corpectomy (vertebral body resection), partial or complete, combined thoracolumbar approach with decompression of spinal cord, cauda equina or nerve root(s), lower thoracic or lumbar; single segment

+ 63088   each additional segment (List separately in addition to code for primary procedure)

(Use 63088 in conjunction with 63087)

63090   Vertebral corpectomy (vertebral body resection), partial or complete, transperitoneal or retroperitoneal approach with decompression of spinal cord, cauda equina or nerve root(s), lower thoracic, lumbar, or sacral; single segment

+ 63091   each additional segment (List separately in addition to code for primary procedure)

(Use 63091 in conjunction with 63090)

(Procedures 63081-63091 include diskectomy above and/or below vertebral segment)

(If followed by arthrodesis, see 22548-22812)

(For reconstruction of spine, use appropriate vertebral corpectomy codes 63081-63091, bone graft codes 20930-20938, arthrodesis codes 22548-22812, and spinal instrumentation codes 22840-22855)

Surgery: Nervous System

Lateral Extracavitary Approach for Extradural Exploration/Decompression

63101   Vertebral corpectomy (vertebral body resection), partial or complete, lateral extracavitary approach with decompression of spinal cord and/or nerve root(s) (eg, for tumor or retropulsed bone fragments); thoracic, single segment

63102   lumbar, single segment

+ **63103**   thoracic or lumbar, each additional segment (List separately in addition to code for primary procedure)

               (Use 63103 in conjunction with 63101 and 63102)

Incision

63170   Laminectomy with myelotomy (eg, Bischof or DREZ type), cervical, thoracic, or thoracolumbar

63172   Laminectomy with drainage of intramedullary cyst/syrinx; to subarachnoid space

63173   to peritoneal or pleural space

63180   Laminectomy and section of dentate ligaments, with or without dural graft, cervical; one or two segments

63182   more than two segments

63185   Laminectomy with rhizotomy; one or two segments

63190   more than two segments

63191   Laminectomy with section of spinal accessory nerve

               (For bilateral procedure, report 63191 with modifier 50)

               (For resection of sternocleidomastoid muscle, use 21720)

63194   Laminectomy with cordotomy, with section of one spinothalamic tract, one stage; cervical

63195   thoracic

63196   Laminectomy with cordotomy, with section of both spinothalamic tracts, one stage; cervical

63197   thoracic

63198   Laminectomy with cordotomy with section of both spinothalamic tracts, two stages within 14 days; cervical

63199   thoracic

63200   Laminectomy, with release of tethered spinal cord, lumbar

Excision by Laminectomy of Lesion Other Than Herniated Disk

63250   Laminectomy for excision or occlusion of arteriovenous malformation of spinal cord; cervical

63251   thoracic

63252   thoracolumbar

63265   Laminectomy for excision or evacuation of intraspinal lesion other than neoplasm, extradural; cervical

63266   thoracic

63267   lumbar

63268   sacral

63270   Laminectomy for excision of intraspinal lesion other than neoplasm, intradural; cervical

63271   thoracic

63272   lumbar

63273   sacral

63275   Laminectomy for biopsy/excision of intraspinal neoplasm; extradural, cervical

63276   extradural, thoracic

63277   extradural, lumbar

63278   extradural, sacral

63280   intradural, extramedullary, cervical

63281   intradural, extramedullary, thoracic

63282   intradural, extramedullary, lumbar

63283   intradural, sacral

63285   intradural, intramedullary, cervical

63286   intradural, intramedullary, thoracic

63287   intradural, intramedullary, thoracolumbar

63290   combined extradural-intradural lesion, any level

               (For drainage of intramedullary cyst/syrinx, use 63172, 63173)

+ **63295**   Osteoplastic reconstruction of dorsal spinal elements, following primary intraspinal procedure (List separately in addition to code for primary procedure)

               (Use 63295 in conjunction with 63172, 63173, 63185, 63190, 63200-63290)

               (Do not report 63295 in conjunction with 22590-22614, 22840-22844, 63050, 63051 for the same vertebral segment(s))

Excision, Anterior or Anterolateral Approach, Intraspinal Lesion

For the following codes, when two surgeons work together as primary surgeons performing distinct part(s) of an anterior approach for an intraspinal excision, each surgeon should report his/her distinct operative work by appending modifier 62 to the single definitive procedure code. In this situation, modifier 62 may be appended to the definitive procedure code(s) 63300-63307 and, as appropriate, to the associated additional segment add-on code 63308 as long as both surgeons continue to work together as primary surgeons.

               (For arthrodesis, see 22548-22585)

               (For reconstruction of spine, see 20930-20938)

Surgery: Nervous System

63300 Vertebral corpectomy (vertebral body resection), partial or complete, for excision of intraspinal lesion, single segment; extradural, cervical

63301 extradural, thoracic by transthoracic approach

63302 extradural, thoracic by thoracolumbar approach

63303 extradural, lumbar or sacral by transperitoneal or retroperitoneal approach

63304 intradural, cervical

63305 intradural, thoracic by transthoracic approach

63306 intradural, thoracic by thoracolumbar approach

63307 intradural, lumbar or sacral by transperitoneal or retroperitoneal approach

＋ 63308 each additional segment (List separately in addition to codes for single segment)

(Use 63308 in conjunction with 63300-63307)

Stereotaxis

63600 Creation of lesion of spinal cord by stereotactic method, percutaneous, any modality (including stimulation and/or recording)

63610 Stereotactic stimulation of spinal cord, percutaneous, separate procedure not followed by other surgery

63615 Stereotactic biopsy, aspiration, or excision of lesion, spinal cord

Neurostimulators (Spinal)

Codes 63650-63688 apply to both simple and complex neurostimulators. For initial or subsequent electronic analysis and programming of neurostimulator pulse generators, see codes 95970-95975.

Codes 63650, 63655, and 63660 describe the operative placement, revision, or removal of the spinal neuro-stimulator system components to provide spinal electrical stimulation. A neurostimulator system includes an implanted neurostimulator, external controller, extension, and collection of contacts. Multiple contacts or electrodes (4 or more) provide the actual electrical stimulation in the epidural space.

For percutaneously placed neurostimulator systems (63650, 63660), the contacts are on a catheter-like lead. An array defines the collection of contacts that are on one catheter.

For systems placed via an open surgical exposure (63655, 63660), the contacts are on a plate or paddle-shaped surface.

63650 Percutaneous implantation of neurostimulator electrode array, epidural

63655 Laminectomy for implantation of neurostimulator electrodes, plate/paddle, epidural

63660 Revision or removal of spinal neurostimulator electrode percutaneous array(s) or plate/paddle(s)

63685 Insertion or replacement of spinal neurostimulator pulse generator or receiver, direct or inductive coupling

(Do not report 63685 in conjunction with 63688 for the same pulse generator or receiver)

63688 Revision or removal of implanted spinal neurostimulator pulse generator or receiver

(For electronic analysis of implanted neurostimulator pulse generator system, see 95970-95975)

Repair

63700 Repair of meningocele; less than 5 cm diameter

63702 larger than 5 cm diameter

(Do not use modifier 63 in conjunction with 63700, 63702)

63704 Repair of myelomeningocele; less than 5 cm diameter

63706 larger than 5 cm diameter

(Do not use modifier 63 in conjunction with 63704, 63706)

(For complex skin closure, see **Integumentary System**)

63707 Repair of dural/cerebrospinal fluid leak, not requiring laminectomy

63709 Repair of dural/cerebrospinal fluid leak or pseudomeningocele, with laminectomy

63710 Dural graft, spinal

(For laminectomy and section of dentate ligaments, with or without dural graft, cervical, see 63180, 63182)

Shunt, Spinal CSF

63740 Creation of shunt, lumbar, subarachnoid-peritoneal, -pleural, or other; including laminectomy

63741 percutaneous, not requiring laminectomy

63744 Replacement, irrigation or revision of lumbosubarachnoid shunt

63746 Removal of entire lumbosubarachnoid shunt system without replacement

(For insertion of subarachnoid catheter with reservoir and/or pump for intermittent or continuous infusion of drug including laminectomy, see 62351 and 62360, 62361 or 62362)

(For insertion or replacement of subarachnoid or epidural catheter, with reservoir and/or pump for drug infusion without laminectomy, see 62350 and 62360, 62361 or 62362)

Surgery: Nervous System

Extracranial Nerves, Peripheral Nerves, and Autonomic Nervous System

(For intracranial surgery on cranial nerves, see 61450, 61460, 61790)

Introduction/Injection of Anesthetic Agent (Nerve Block), Diagnostic or Therapeutic

Somatic Nerves

64400 Injection, anesthetic agent; trigeminal nerve, any division or branch

64402 facial nerve

64405 greater occipital nerve

64408 vagus nerve

64410 phrenic nerve

64412 spinal accessory nerve

64413 cervical plexus

64415 brachial plexus, single

64416 brachial plexus, continuous infusion by catheter (including catheter placement) including daily management for anesthetic agent administration

(Do not report 01996 in addition to 64416)

64417 axillary nerve

64418 suprascapular nerve

64420 intercostal nerve, single

64421 intercostal nerves, multiple, regional block

64425 ilioinguinal, iliohypogastric nerves

64430 pudendal nerve

64435 paracervical (uterine) nerve

64445 sciatic nerve, single

64446 sciatic nerve, continuous infusion by catheter, (including catheter placement) including daily management for anesthetic agent administration

(Do not report 01996 in addition to 64446)

64447 femoral nerve, single

(Do not report 01996 in addition to 64447)

64448 femoral nerve, continuous infusion by catheter (including catheter placement) including daily management for anesthetic agent administration

(Do not report 01996 in addition to 64448)

64449 lumbar plexus, posterior approach, continuous infusion by catheter (including catheter placement) including daily management for anesthetic agent administration

(Do not report 01996 in conjunction with 64449)

64450 other peripheral nerve or branch

(For phenol destruction, see 64622-64627)

(For subarachnoid or subdural injection, see 62280, 62310-62319)

(For epidural or caudal injection, see 62273, 62281-62282, 62310-62319)

(Codes 64470-64484 are unilateral procedures. For bilateral procedures, use modifier 50)

(For fluoroscopic guidance and localization for needle placement and injection in conjunction with 64470-64484, use code 76005)

64470 Injection, anesthetic agent and/or steroid, paravertebral facet joint or facet joint nerve; cervical or thoracic, single level

+ 64472 cervical or thoracic, each additional level (List separately in addition to code for primary procedure)

(Use 64472 in conjunction with 64470)

64475 lumbar or sacral, single level

+ 64476 lumbar or sacral, each additional level (List separately in addition to code for primary procedure)

(Use 64476 in conjunction with 64475)

64479 Injection, anesthetic agent and/or steroid, transforaminal epidural; cervical or thoracic, single level

+ 64480 cervical or thoracic, each additional level (List separately in addition to code for primary procedure)

(Use 64480 in conjunction with 64479)

64483 lumbar or sacral, single level

+ 64484 lumbar or sacral, each additional level (List separately in addition to code for primary procedure)

(Use 64484 in conjunction with 64483)

Sympathetic Nerves

64505 Injection, anesthetic agent; sphenopalatine ganglion

64508 carotid sinus (separate procedure)

64510 stellate ganglion (cervical sympathetic)

64517 superior hypogastric plexus

64520 lumbar or thoracic (paravertebral sympathetic)

64530 celiac plexus, with or without radiologic monitoring

Surgery: Nervous System

Neurostimulators (Peripheral Nerve)

Codes 64553-64595 apply to both simple and complex neurostimulators. For initial or subsequent electronic analysis and programming of neurostimulator pulse generators, see codes 95970-95975.

64550   Application of surface (transcutaneous) neurostimulator

64553   Percutaneous implantation of neurostimulator electrodes; cranial nerve

(For open placement of cranial nerve (eg, vagal, trigeminal) neurostimulator pulse generator or receiver, see 61885, 61886, as appropriate)

64555   peripheral nerve (excludes sacral nerve)

64560   autonomic nerve

64561   sacral nerve (transforaminal placement)

64565   neuromuscular

64573   Incision for implantation of neurostimulator electrodes; cranial nerve

(For open placement of cranial nerve (eg, vagal, trigeminal) neurostimulator pulse generator or receiver, see 61885, 61886, as appropriate)

(For revision or removal of cranial nerve (eg, vagal, trigeminal) neurostimulator pulse generator or receiver, use 61888)

64575   peripheral nerve (excludes sacral nerve)

64577   autonomic nerve

64580   neuromuscular

64581   sacral nerve (transforaminal placement)

64585   Revision or removal of peripheral neurostimulator electrodes

64590   Insertion or replacement of peripheral neurostimulator pulse generator or receiver, direct or inductive coupling

(Do not report 64590 in conjunction with 64595)

64595   Revision or removal of peripheral neurostimulator pulse generator or receiver

Destruction by Neurolytic Agent (eg, Chemical, Thermal, Electrical or Radiofrequency)

(Codes 64600-64681 include the injection of other therapeutic agents (eg, corticosteroids).

Somatic Nerves

64600   Destruction by neurolytic agent, trigeminal nerve; supraorbital, infraorbital, mental, or inferior alveolar branch

64605   second and third division branches at foramen ovale

64610   second and third division branches at foramen ovale under radiologic monitoring

64612   Chemodenervation of muscle(s); muscle(s) innervated by facial nerve (eg, for blepharospasm, hemifacial spasm)

▲ 64613   neck muscle(s) (eg, for spasmodic torticollis, spasmodic dysphonia)

64614   extremity(s) and/or trunk muscle(s) (eg, for dystonia, cerebral palsy, multiple sclerosis)

►(For chemodenervation guided by needle electromyography or muscle electrical stimulation, see 95873, 95874)◄

(For chemodenervation for strabismus involving the extraocular muscles, use 67345)

►(For chemodenervation of internal anal sphincter, use 46505)◄

64620   Destruction by neurolytic agent, intercostal nerve

(For fluoroscopic guidance and localization for needle placement and neurolysis in conjunction with 64622-64627, use 76005)

64622   Destruction by neurolytic agent, paravertebral facet joint nerve; lumbar or sacral, single level

(For bilateral procedure, report 64622 with modifier 50)

+ 64623   lumbar or sacral, each additional level (List separately in addition to code for primary procedure)

(Use 64623 in conjunction with 64622)

(For bilateral procedure, report 64623 with modifier 50)

64626   cervical or thoracic, single level

(For bilateral procedure, report 64626 with modifier 50)

+ 64627   cervical or thoracic, each additional level (List separately in addition to code for primary procedure)

(Use 64627 in conjunction with 64626)

(For bilateral procedure, report 64627 with modifier 50)

64630   Destruction by neurolytic agent; pudendal nerve

64640   other peripheral nerve or branch

Sympathetic Nerves

● 64650   Chemodenervation of eccrine glands; both axillae

● 64653   other area(s) (eg, scalp, face, neck), per day

►(Report the specific service in conjunction with code(s) for the specific substance(s) or drug(s) provided)◄

►(For chemodenervation of extremities (eg, hands or feet), use 64999)◄

64680   Destruction by neurolytic agent, with or without radiologic monitoring; celiac plexus

64681   superior hypogastric plexus

Neuroplasty (Exploration, Neurolysis or Nerve Decompression)

Neuroplasty is the decompression or freeing of intact nerve from scar tissue, including external neurolysis and/or transposition.

(For internal neurolysis requiring use of operating microscope, use 64727)

(For facial nerve decompression, use 69720)

64702   Neuroplasty; digital, one or both, same digit

64704   nerve of hand or foot

64708   Neuroplasty, major peripheral nerve, arm or leg; other than specified

64712   sciatic nerve

64713   brachial plexus

64714   lumbar plexus

64716   Neuroplasty and/or transposition; cranial nerve (specify)

64718   ulnar nerve at elbow

64719   ulnar nerve at wrist

64721   median nerve at carpal tunnel

(For arthroscopic procedure, use 29848)

64722   Decompression; unspecified nerve(s) (specify)

64726   plantar digital nerve

+ **64727**   Internal neurolysis, requiring use of operating microscope (List separately in addition to code for neuroplasty) (Neuroplasty includes external neurolysis)

(Do not report code 69990 in addition to code 64727)

Transection or Avulsion

(For stereotactic lesion of gasserian ganglion, use 61790)

64732   Transection or avulsion of; supraorbital nerve

64734   infraorbital nerve

64736   mental nerve

64738   inferior alveolar nerve by osteotomy

64740   lingual nerve

64742   facial nerve, differential or complete

64744   greater occipital nerve

64746   phrenic nerve

(For section of recurrent laryngeal nerve, use 31595)

64752   vagus nerve (vagotomy), transthoracic

64755   vagus nerves limited to proximal stomach (selective proximal vagotomy, proximal gastric vagotomy, parietal cell vagotomy, supra- or highly selective vagotomy)

(For laparoscopic approach, use 43652)

64760   vagus nerve (vagotomy), abdominal

(For laparoscopic approach, use 43651)

64761   pudendal nerve

(For bilateral procedure, report 64761 with modifier 50)

64763   Transection or avulsion of obturator nerve, extrapelvic, with or without adductor tenotomy

(For bilateral procedure, report 64763 with modifier 50)

64766   Transection or avulsion of obturator nerve, intrapelvic, with or without adductor tenotomy

(For bilateral procedure, report 64766 with modifier 50)

64771   Transection or avulsion of other cranial nerve, extradural

64772   Transection or avulsion of other spinal nerve, extradural

(For excision of tender scar, skin and subcutaneous tissue, with or without tiny neuroma, see 11400-11446, 13100-13153)

Excision

Somatic Nerves

(For Morton neurectomy, use 28080)

64774   Excision of neuroma; cutaneous nerve, surgically identifiable

64776   digital nerve, one or both, same digit

+ **64778**   digital nerve, each additional digit (List separately in addition to code for primary procedure)

(Use 64778 in conjunction with 64776)

64782   hand or foot, except digital nerve

+ **64783**   hand or foot, each additional nerve, except same digit (List separately in addition to code for primary procedure)

(Use 64783 in conjunction with 64782)

64784   major peripheral nerve, except sciatic

64786   sciatic nerve

+ **64787**   Implantation of nerve end into bone or muscle (List separately in addition to neuroma excision)

(Use 64787 in conjunction with 64774-64786)

64788   Excision of neurofibroma or neurolemmoma; cutaneous nerve

64790   major peripheral nerve

64792   extensive (including malignant type)

64795   Biopsy of nerve

Surgery: Nervous System

Sympathetic Nerves

64802 Sympathectomy, cervical

(For bilateral procedure, report 64802 with modifier 50)

64804 Sympathectomy, cervicothoracic

(For bilateral procedure, report 64804 with modifier 50)

64809 Sympathectomy, thoracolumbar

(For bilateral procedure, report 64809 with modifier 50)

64818 Sympathectomy, lumbar

(For bilateral procedure, report 64818 with modifier 50)

64820 Sympathectomy; digital arteries, each digit

(Do not report 69990 in addition to code 64820)

64821 radial artery

(Do not report 69990 in addition to code 64821)

64822 ulnar artery

(Do not report 69990 in addition to code 64822)

64823 superficial palmar arch

(Do not report 69990 in addition to code 64823)

Neurorrhaphy

64831 Suture of digital nerve, hand or foot; one nerve

+ 64832 each additional digital nerve (List separately in addition to code for primary procedure)

(Use 64832 in conjunction with 64831)

64834 Suture of one nerve, hand or foot; common sensory nerve

64835 median motor thenar

64836 ulnar motor

+ 64837 Suture of each additional nerve, hand or foot (List separately in addition to code for primary procedure)

(Use 64837 in conjunction with 64834-64836)

64840 Suture of posterior tibial nerve

64856 Suture of major peripheral nerve, arm or leg, except sciatic; including transposition

64857 without transposition

64858 Suture of sciatic nerve

+ 64859 Suture of each additional major peripheral nerve (List separately in addition to code for primary procedure)

(Use 64859 in conjunction with 64856, 64857)

64861 Suture of; brachial plexus

64862 lumbar plexus

64864 Suture of facial nerve; extracranial

64865 infratemporal, with or without grafting

64866 Anastomosis; facial-spinal accessory

64868 facial-hypoglossal

64870 facial-phrenic

+ 64872 Suture of nerve; requiring secondary or delayed suture (List separately in addition to code for primary neurorrhaphy)

(Use 64872 in conjunction with 64831-64865)

+ 64874 requiring extensive mobilization, or transposition of nerve (List separately in addition to code for nerve suture)

(Use 64874 in conjunction with 64831-64865)

+ 64876 requiring shortening of bone of extremity (List separately in addition to code for nerve suture)

(Use 64876 in conjunction with 64831-64865)

Neurorrhaphy With Nerve Graft

64885 Nerve graft (includes obtaining graft), head or neck; up to 4 cm in length

64886 more than 4 cm length

64890 Nerve graft (includes obtaining graft), single strand, hand or foot; up to 4 cm length

64891 more than 4 cm length

64892 Nerve graft (includes obtaining graft), single strand, arm or leg; up to 4 cm length

64893 more than 4 cm length

64895 Nerve graft (includes obtaining graft), multiple strands (cable), hand or foot; up to 4 cm length

64896 more than 4 cm length

64897 Nerve graft (includes obtaining graft), multiple strands (cable), arm or leg; up to 4 cm length

64898 more than 4 cm length

+ 64901 Nerve graft, each additional nerve; single strand (List separately in addition to code for primary procedure)

(Use 64901 in conjunction with 64885-64893)

+ 64902 multiple strands (cable) (List separately in addition to code for primary procedure)

(Use 64902 in conjunction with 64885, 64886, 64895-64898)

64905 Nerve pedicle transfer; first stage

64907 second stage

Other Procedures

64999 Unlisted procedure, nervous system

Eye and Ocular Adnexa

(For diagnostic and treatment ophthalmological services, see **Medicine, Ophthalmology,** and 92002 et seq)

(Do not report code 69990 in addition to codes 65091-68850)

Eyeball

Removal of Eye

65091   Evisceration of ocular contents; without implant

65093   with implant

65101   Enucleation of eye; without implant

65103   with implant, muscles not attached to implant

65105   with implant, muscles attached to implant

(For conjunctivoplasty after enucleation, see 68320 et seq)

65110   Exenteration of orbit (does not include skin graft), removal of orbital contents; only

65112   with therapeutic removal of bone

65114   with muscle or myocutaneous flap

(For skin graft to orbit (split skin), see 15120, 15121; free, full thickness, see 15260, 15261)

(For eyelid repair involving more than skin, see 67930 et seq)

Secondary Implant(s) Procedures

An ocular implant is an implant inside muscular cone; an orbital implant is an implant outside muscular cone.

65125   Modification of ocular implant with placement or replacement of pegs (eg, drilling receptacle for prosthesis appendage) (separate procedure)

65130   Insertion of ocular implant secondary; after evisceration, in scleral shell

65135   after enucleation, muscles not attached to implant

65140   after enucleation, muscles attached to implant

65150   Reinsertion of ocular implant; with or without conjunctival graft

65155   with use of foreign material for reinforcement and/or attachment of muscles to implant

65175   Removal of ocular implant

(For orbital implant (implant outside muscle cone) insertion, use 67550; removal, use 67560)

Removal of Foreign Body

(For removal of implanted material: ocular implant, use 65175; anterior segment implant, use 65920; posterior segment implant, use 67120; orbital implant, use 67560)

(For diagnostic x-ray for foreign body, use 70030)

(For diagnostic echography for foreign body, use 76529)

(For removal of foreign body from orbit: frontal approach, use 67413; lateral approach, use 67430; transcranial approach, use 61334)

(For removal of foreign body from eyelid, embedded, use 67938)

(For removal of foreign body from lacrimal system, use 68530)

65205   Removal of foreign body, external eye; conjunctival superficial

65210   conjunctival embedded (includes concretions), subconjunctival, or scleral nonperforating

65220   corneal, without slit lamp

65222   corneal, with slit lamp

(For repair of corneal laceration with foreign body, use 65275)

65235   Removal of foreign body, intraocular; from anterior chamber of eye or lens

(For removal of implanted material from anterior segment, use 65920)

65260   from posterior segment, magnetic extraction, anterior or posterior route

65265   from posterior segment, nonmagnetic extraction

(For removal of implanted material from posterior segment, use 67120)

Repair of Laceration

(For fracture of orbit, see 21385 et seq)

(For repair of wound of eyelid, skin, linear, simple, see 12011-12018; intermediate, layered closure, see 12051-12057; linear, complex, see 13150-13160; other, see 67930, 67935)

(For repair of wound of lacrimal system, use 68700)

(For repair of operative wound, use 66250)

65270   Repair of laceration; conjunctiva, with or without nonperforating laceration sclera, direct closure

65272   conjunctiva, by mobilization and rearrangement, without hospitalization

65273   conjunctiva, by mobilization and rearrangement, with hospitalization

65275   cornea, nonperforating, with or without removal foreign body

Surgery: Ocular/Auditory System

65280   cornea and/or sclera, perforating, not involving uveal tissue

65285   cornea and/or sclera, perforating, with reposition or resection of uveal tissue

65286   application of tissue glue, wounds of cornea and/or sclera

(Repair of laceration includes use of conjunctival flap and restoration of anterior chamber, by air or saline injection when indicated)

(For repair of iris or ciliary body, use 66680)

65290   Repair of wound, extraocular muscle, tendon and/or Tenon's capsule

Anterior Segment

Cornea

Excision

65400   Excision of lesion, cornea (keratectomy, lamellar, partial), except pterygium

65410   Biopsy of cornea

65420   Excision or transposition of pterygium; without graft

65426   with graft

Removal or Destruction

65430   Scraping of cornea, diagnostic, for smear and/or culture

65435   Removal of corneal epithelium; with or without chemocauterization (abrasion, curettage)

65436   with application of chelating agent (eg, EDTA)

65450   Destruction of lesion of cornea by cryotherapy, photocoagulation or thermocauterization

65600   Multiple punctures of anterior cornea (eg, for corneal erosion, tattoo)

Keratoplasty

Corneal transplant includes use of fresh or preserved grafts, and preparation of donor material.

(Keratoplasty excludes refractive keratoplasty procedures, 65760, 65765, and 65767)

65710   Keratoplasty (corneal transplant); lamellar

65730   penetrating (except in aphakia)

65750   penetrating (in aphakia)

65755   penetrating (in pseudophakia)

Other Procedures

65760   Keratomileusis

65765   Keratophakia

65767   Epikeratoplasty

65770   Keratoprosthesis

65771   Radial keratotomy

65772   Corneal relaxing incision for correction of surgically induced astigmatism

65775   Corneal wedge resection for correction of surgically induced astigmatism

(For fitting of contact lens for treatment of disease, use 92070)

(For unlisted procedures on cornea, use 66999)

65780   Ocular surface reconstruction; amniotic membrane transplantation

65781   limbal stem cell allograft (eg, cadaveric or living donor)

65782   limbal conjunctival autograft (includes obtaining graft)

(For harvesting conjunctival allograft, living donor, use 68371)

Anterior Chamber

Incision

65800   Paracentesis of anterior chamber of eye (separate procedure); with diagnostic aspiration of aqueous

65805   with therapeutic release of aqueous

65810   with removal of vitreous and/or discission of anterior hyaloid membrane, with or without air injection

65815   with removal of blood, with or without irrigation and/or air injection

(For injection, see 66020-66030)

(For removal of blood clot, use 65930)

65820   Goniotomy

(Do not report modifier 63 in conjunction with 65820)

65850   Trabeculotomy ab externo

65855   Trabeculoplasty by laser surgery, one or more sessions (defined treatment series)

(If re-treatment is necessary after several months because of disease progression, a new treatment or treatment series should be reported with a modifier, if necessary, to indicate lesser or greater complexity)

(For trabeculectomy, use 66170)

65860   Severing adhesions of anterior segment, laser technique (separate procedure)

Other Procedures

65865   Severing adhesions of anterior segment of eye, incisional technique (with or without injection of air or liquid) (separate procedure); goniosynechiae

(For trabeculoplasty by laser surgery, use 65855)

65870   anterior synechiae, except goniosynechiae

65875   posterior synechiae

65880   corneovitreal adhesions

(For laser surgery, use 66821)

65900   Removal of epithelial downgrowth, anterior chamber of eye

65920   Removal of implanted material, anterior segment of eye

65930   Removal of blood clot, anterior segment of eye

66020   Injection, anterior chamber of eye (separate procedure); air or liquid

66030   medication

(For unlisted procedures on anterior segment, use 66999)

Anterior Sclera

Excision

(For removal of intraocular foreign body, use 65235)

(For operations on posterior sclera, use 67250, 67255)

66130   Excision of lesion, sclera

66150   Fistulization of sclera for glaucoma; trephination with iridectomy

66155   thermocauterization with iridectomy

66160   sclerectomy with punch or scissors, with iridectomy

66165   iridencleisis or iridotasis

66170   trabeculectomy ab externo in absence of previous surgery

(For trabeculotomy ab externo, use 65850)

(For repair of operative wound, use 66250)

66172   trabeculectomy ab externo with scarring from previous ocular surgery or trauma (includes injection of antifibrotic agents)

▶(For transciliary body sclera fistulization, use Category III code 0123T)◀

66180   Aqueous shunt to extraocular reservoir (eg, Molteno, Schocket, Denver-Krupin)

66185   Revision of aqueous shunt to extraocular reservoir

(For removal of implanted shunt, use 67120)

Repair or Revision

(For scleral procedures in retinal surgery, see 67101 et seq)

66220   Repair of scleral staphyloma; without graft

66225   with graft

(For scleral reinforcement, see 67250, 67255)

66250   Revision or repair of operative wound of anterior segment, any type, early or late, major or minor procedure

(For unlisted procedures on anterior sclera, use 66999)

Iris, Ciliary Body

Incision

66500   Iridotomy by stab incision (separate procedure); except transfixion

66505   with transfixion as for iris bombe

(For iridotomy by photocoagulation, use 66761)

Excision

66600   Iridectomy, with corneoscleral or corneal section; for removal of lesion

66605   with cyclectomy

66625   peripheral for glaucoma (separate procedure)

66630   sector for glaucoma (separate procedure)

66635   optical (separate procedure)

(For coreoplasty by photocoagulation, use 66762)

Repair

66680   Repair of iris, ciliary body (as for iridodialysis)

(For reposition or resection of uveal tissue with perforating wound of cornea or sclera, use 65285)

66682   Suture of iris, ciliary body (separate procedure) with retrieval of suture through small incision (eg, McCannel suture)

Destruction

66700   Ciliary body destruction; diathermy

66710   cyclophotocoagulation, transscleral

66711   cyclophotocoagulation, endoscopic

(Do not report 66711 in conjunction with 66990)

⊙ **66720**   cryotherapy

66740   cyclodialysis

Surgery: Ocular/Auditory System

66761 Iridotomy/iridectomy by laser surgery (eg, for glaucoma) (one or more sessions)

66762 Iridoplasty by photocoagulation (one or more sessions) (eg, for improvement of vision, for widening of anterior chamber angle)

66770 Destruction of cyst or lesion iris or ciliary body (nonexcisional procedure)

(For excision lesion iris, ciliary body, see 66600, 66605; for removal of epithelial downgrowth, use 65900)

(For unlisted procedures on iris, ciliary body, use 66999)

Lens

Incision

66820 Discission of secondary membranous cataract (opacified posterior lens capsule and/or anterior hyaloid); stab incision technique (Ziegler or Wheeler knife)

66821 laser surgery (eg, YAG laser) (one or more stages)

66825 Repositioning of intraocular lens prosthesis, requiring an incision (separate procedure)

Removal Cataract

Lateral canthotomy, iridectomy, iridotomy, anterior capsulotomy, posterior capsulotomy, the use of viscoelastic agents, enzymatic zonulysis, use of other pharmacologic agents, and subconjunctival or sub-tenon injections are included as part of the code for the extraction of lens.

66830 Removal of secondary membranous cataract (opacified posterior lens capsule and/or anterior hyaloid) with corneo-scleral section, with or without iridectomy (iridocapsulotomy, iridocapsulectomy)

66840 Removal of lens material; aspiration technique, one or more stages

66850 phacofragmentation technique (mechanical or ultrasonic) (eg, phacoemulsification), with aspiration

66852 pars plana approach, with or without vitrectomy

66920 intracapsular

66930 intracapsular, for dislocated lens

66940 extracapsular (other than 66840, 66850, 66852)

(For removal of intralenticular foreign body without lens extraction, use 65235)

(For repair of operative wound, use 66250)

66982 Extracapsular cataract removal with insertion of intraocular lens prosthesis (one stage procedure), manual or mechanical technique (eg, irrigation and aspiration or phacoemulsification), complex, requiring devices or techniques not generally used in routine cataract surgery (eg, iris expansion device, suture support for intraocular lens, or primary posterior capsulorrhexis) or performed on patients in the amblyogenic developmental stage

66983 Intracapsular cataract extraction with insertion of intraocular lens prosthesis (one stage procedure)

66984 Extracapsular cataract removal with insertion of intraocular lens prosthesis (one stage procedure), manual or mechanical technique (eg, irrigation and aspiration or phacoemulsification)

(For complex extracapsular cataract removal, use 66982)

66985 Insertion of intraocular lens prosthesis (secondary implant), not associated with concurrent cataract removal

(To code implant at time of concurrent cataract surgery, see 66982, 66983, 66984)

(For intraocular lens prosthesis supplied by physician, use 99070)

(For ultrasonic determination of intraocular lens power, use 76519)

(For removal of implanted material from anterior segment, use 65920)

(For secondary fixation (separate procedure), use 66682)

66986 Exchange of intraocular lens

+ 66990 Use of ophthalmic endoscope (List separately in addition to code for primary procedure)

(66990 may be used only with codes 65820, 65875, 65920, 66985, 66986, 67038, 67039, 67040)

Other Procedures

66999 Unlisted procedure, anterior segment of eye

Posterior Segment

Vitreous

67005 Removal of vitreous, anterior approach (open sky technique or limbal incision); partial removal

67010 subtotal removal with mechanical vitrectomy

(For removal of vitreous by paracentesis of anterior chamber, use 65810)

(For removal of corneovitreal adhesions, use 65880)

67015 Aspiration or release of vitreous, subretinal or choroidal fluid, pars plana approach (posterior sclerotomy)

67025 Injection of vitreous substitute, pars plana or limbal approach, (fluid-gas exchange), with or without aspiration (separate procedure)

Surgery: Ocular/Auditory System

67027   Implantation of intravitreal drug delivery system (eg, ganciclovir implant), includes concomitant removal of vitreous

(For removal, use 67121)

67028   Intravitreal injection of a pharmacologic agent (separate procedure)

67030   Discission of vitreous strands (without removal), pars plana approach

67031   Severing of vitreous strands, vitreous face adhesions, sheets, membranes or opacities, laser surgery (one or more stages)

67036   Vitrectomy, mechanical, pars plana approach;

67038   with epiretinal membrane stripping

67039   with focal endolaser photocoagulation

67040   with endolaser panretinal photocoagulation

(For use of ophthalmic endoscope with 67038, 67039, 67040, use 66990)

(For associated lensectomy, use 66850)

(For use of vitrectomy in retinal detachment surgery, use 67108)

(For associated removal of foreign body, see 65260, 65265)

(For unlisted procedures on vitreous, use 67299)

Retina or Choroid

Repair

(If diathermy, cryotherapy and/or photocoagulation are combined, report under principal modality used)

67101   Repair of retinal detachment, one or more sessions; cryotherapy or diathermy, with or without drainage of subretinal fluid

67105   photocoagulation, with or without drainage of subretinal fluid

67107   Repair of retinal detachment; scleral buckling (such as lamellar scleral dissection, imbrication or encircling procedure), with or without implant, with or without cryotherapy, photocoagulation, and drainage of subretinal fluid

67108   with vitrectomy, any method, with or without air or gas tamponade, focal endolaser photocoagulation, cryotherapy, drainage of subretinal fluid, scleral buckling, and/or removal of lens by same technique

67110   by injection of air or other gas (eg, pneumatic retinopexy)

67112   by scleral buckling or vitrectomy, on patient having previous ipsilateral retinal detachment repair(s) using scleral buckling or vitrectomy techniques

(For aspiration or drainage of subretinal or subchoroidal fluid, use 67015)

67115   Release of encircling material (posterior segment)

67120   Removal of implanted material, posterior segment; extraocular

67121   intraocular

(For removal from anterior segment, use 65920)

(For removal of foreign body, see 65260, 65265)

Prophylaxis

Repetitive services. The services listed below are often performed in multiple sessions or groups of sessions. The methods of reporting vary.

The following descriptors are intended to include all sessions in a defined treatment period.

67141   Prophylaxis of retinal detachment (eg, retinal break, lattice degeneration) without drainage, one or more sessions; cryotherapy, diathermy

67145   photocoagulation (laser or xenon arc)

Destruction

67208   Destruction of localized lesion of retina (eg, macular edema, tumors), one or more sessions; cryotherapy, diathermy

67210   photocoagulation

67218   radiation by implantation of source (includes removal of source)

67220   Destruction of localized lesion of choroid (eg, choroidal neovascularization); photocoagulation (eg, laser), one or more sessions

(For destruction of macular drusen, photocoagulation, use Category III code 0017T)

(For destruction of localized lesion of choroid by transpupillary thermotherapy, use Category III code 0016T)

67221   photodynamic therapy (includes intravenous infusion)

+ 67225   photodynamic therapy, second eye, at single session (List separately in addition to code for primary eye treatment)

(Use 67225 in conjunction with 67221)

67227   Destruction of extensive or progressive retinopathy (eg, diabetic retinopathy), one or more sessions; cryotherapy, diathermy

67228   photocoagulation (laser or xenon arc)

(For unlisted procedures on retina, use 67299)

Surgery: Ocular/Auditory System

Sclera

Repair

(For excision lesion sclera, use 66130)

67250   Scleral reinforcement (separate procedure); without graft

67255   with graft

(For repair scleral staphyloma, see 66220, 66225)

Other Procedures

67299   Unlisted procedure, posterior segment

Ocular Adnexa

Extraocular Muscles

67311   Strabismus surgery, recession or resection procedure; one horizontal muscle

67312   two horizontal muscles

67314   one vertical muscle (excluding superior oblique)

67316   two or more vertical muscles (excluding superior oblique)

(For adjustable sutures, use 67335 in addition to codes 67311-67334 for primary procedure reflecting number of muscles operated on)

67318   Strabismus surgery, any procedure, superior oblique muscle

+ 67320   Transposition procedure (eg, for paretic extraocular muscle), any extraocular muscle (specify) (List separately in addition to code for primary procedure)

(Use 67320 in conjunction with 67311-67318)

+ 67331   Strabismus surgery on patient with previous eye surgery or injury that did not involve the extraocular muscles (List separately in addition to code for primary procedure)

(Use 67331 in conjunction with 67311-67318)

+ 67332   Strabismus surgery on patient with scarring of extraocular muscles (eg, prior ocular injury, strabismus or retinal detachment surgery) or restrictive myopathy (eg, dysthyroid ophthalmopathy) (List separately in addition to code for primary procedure)

(Use 67332 in conjunction with 67311-67318)

+ 67334   Strabismus surgery by posterior fixation suture technique, with or without muscle recession (List separately in addition to code for primary procedure)

(Use 67334 in conjunction with 67311-67318)

+ 67335   Placement of adjustable suture(s) during strabismus surgery, including postoperative adjustment(s) of suture(s) (List separately in addition to code for specific strabismus surgery)

(Use 67335 in conjunction with 67311-67334)

+ 67340   Strabismus surgery involving exploration and/or repair of detached extraocular muscle(s) (List separately in addition to code for primary procedure)

(Use 67340 in conjunction with 67311-67334)

67343   Release of extensive scar tissue without detaching extraocular muscle (separate procedure)

(Use 67343 in conjunction with 67311-67340, when such procedures are performed other than on the affected muscle)

67345   Chemodenervation of extraocular muscle

(For chemodenervation for blepharospasm and other neurological disorders, see 64612 and 64613)

Other Procedures

67350   Biopsy of extraocular muscle

(For repair of wound, extraocular muscle, tendon or Tenon's capsule, use 65290)

67399   Unlisted procedure, ocular muscle

Orbit

Exploration, Excision, Decompression

67400   Orbitotomy without bone flap (frontal or transconjunctival approach); for exploration, with or without biopsy

67405   with drainage only

67412   with removal of lesion

67413   with removal of foreign body

67414   with removal of bone for decompression

67415   Fine needle aspiration of orbital contents

(For exenteration, enucleation, and repair, see 65101 et seq; for optic nerve decompression, use 67570)

67420   Orbitotomy with bone flap or window, lateral approach (eg, Kroenlein); with removal of lesion

67430   with removal of foreign body

67440   with drainage

67445   with removal of bone for decompression

(For optic nerve sheath decompression, use 67570)

67450   for exploration, with or without biopsy

(For orbitotomy, transcranial approach, see 61330-61334)

(For orbital implant, see 67550, 67560)

(For removal of eyeball or for repair after removal, see 65091-65175)

Surgery: Ocular/Auditory System

Other Procedures

67500   Retrobulbar injection; medication (separate procedure, does not include supply of medication)

67505   alcohol

67515   Injection of medication or other substance into Tenon's capsule

(For subconjunctival injection, use 68200)

67550   Orbital implant (implant outside muscle cone); insertion

67560   removal or revision

(For ocular implant (implant inside muscle cone), see 65093-65105, 65130-65175)

(For treatment of fractures of malar area, orbit, see 21355 et seq)

67570   Optic nerve decompression (eg, incision or fenestration of optic nerve sheath)

67599   Unlisted procedure, orbit

Eyelids

Incision

67700   Blepharotomy, drainage of abscess, eyelid

67710   Severing of tarsorrhaphy

67715   Canthotomy (separate procedure)

(For canthoplasty, use 67950)

(For division of symblepharon, use 68340)

Excision

Codes for removal of lesion include more than skin (ie, involving lid margin, tarsus, and/or palpebral conjunctiva).

(For removal of lesion, involving mainly skin of eyelid, see 11310-11313; 11440-11446; 11640-11646; 17000-17004)

(For repair of wounds, blepharoplasty, grafts, reconstructive surgery, see 67930-67975)

67800   Excision of chalazion; single

67801   multiple, same lid

67805   multiple, different lids

67808   under general anesthesia and/or requiring hospitalization, single or multiple

67810   Biopsy of eyelid

67820   Correction of trichiasis; epilation, by forceps only

67825   epilation by other than forceps (eg, by electrosurgery, cryotherapy, laser surgery)

67830   incision of lid margin

67835   incision of lid margin, with free mucous membrane graft

67840   Excision of lesion of eyelid (except chalazion) without closure or with simple direct closure

(For excision and repair of eyelid by reconstructive surgery, see 67961, 67966)

67850   Destruction of lesion of lid margin (up to 1 cm)

(For Mohs micrographic surgery, see 17304-17310)

(For initiation or follow-up care of topical chemotherapy (eg, 5-FU or similar agents), see appropriate office visits)

Tarsorrhaphy

67875   Temporary closure of eyelids by suture (eg, Frost suture)

67880   Construction of intermarginal adhesions, median tarsorrhaphy, or canthorrhaphy;

67882   with transposition of tarsal plate

(For severing of tarsorrhaphy, use 67710)

(For canthoplasty, reconstruction canthus, use 67950)

(For canthotomy, use 67715)

Repair (Brow Ptosis, Blepharoptosis, Lid Retraction, Ectropion, Entropion)

67900   Repair of brow ptosis (supraciliary, mid-forehead or coronal approach)

(For forehead rhytidectomy, use 15824)

▲ **67901**   Repair of blepharoptosis; frontalis muscle technique with suture or other material (eg, banked fascia)

▲ **67902**   frontalis muscle technique with autologous fascial sling (includes obtaining fascia)

67903   (tarso) levator resection or advancement, internal approach

67904   (tarso) levator resection or advancement, external approach

67906   superior rectus technique with fascial sling (includes obtaining fascia)

67908   conjunctivo-tarso-Muller's muscle-levator resection (eg, Fasanella-Servat type)

67909   Reduction of overcorrection of ptosis

67911   Correction of lid retraction

(For obtaining autogenous graft materials, see 20920, 20922 or 20926)

(For correction of trichiasis by mucous membrane graft, use 67835)

Surgery: Ocular/Auditory System

67912   Correction of lagophthalmos, with implantation of upper eyelid lid load (eg, gold weight)

67914   Repair of ectropion; suture

67915   thermocauterization

67916   excision tarsal wedge

67917   extensive (eg, tarsal strip operations)

(For correction of everted punctum, use 68705)

67921   Repair of entropion; suture

67922   thermocauterization

67923   excision tarsal wedge

67924   extensive (eg, tarsal strip or capsulopalpebral fascia repairs operation)

(For repair of cicatricial ectropion or entropion requiring scar excision or skin graft, see also 67961 et seq)

Reconstruction

Codes for blepharoplasty involve more than skin (ie, involving lid margin, tarsus, and/or palpebral conjunctiva).

67930   Suture of recent wound, eyelid, involving lid margin, tarsus, and/or palpebral conjunctiva direct closure; partial thickness

67935   full thickness

67938   Removal of embedded foreign body, eyelid

(For repair of skin of eyelid, see 12011-12018; 12051-12057; 13150-13153)

(For tarsorrhaphy, canthorrhaphy, see 67880, 67882)

(For repair of blepharoptosis and lid retraction, see 67901-67911)

(For blepharoplasty for entropion, ectropion, see 67916, 67917, 67923, 67924)

(For correction of blepharochalasis (blepharorhytidectomy), see 15820-15823)

(For repair of skin of eyelid, adjacent tissue transfer, see 14060, 14061; preparation for graft, use 15000; free graft, see 15120, 15121, 15260, 15261)

(For excision of lesion of eyelid, use 67800 et seq)

(For repair of lacrimal canaliculi, use 68700)

67950   Canthoplasty (reconstruction of canthus)

67961   Excision and repair of eyelid, involving lid margin, tarsus, conjunctiva, canthus, or full thickness, may include preparation for skin graft or pedicle flap with adjacent tissue transfer or rearrangement; up to one-fourth of lid margin

67966   over one-fourth of lid margin

(For canthoplasty, use 67950)

(For free skin grafts, see 15120, 15121, 15260, 15261)

(For tubed pedicle flap preparation, use 15576; for delay, use 15630; for attachment, use 15650)

67971   Reconstruction of eyelid, full thickness by transfer of tarsoconjunctival flap from opposing eyelid; up to two-thirds of eyelid, one stage or first stage

67973   total eyelid, lower, one stage or first stage

67974   total eyelid, upper, one stage or first stage

67975   second stage

Other Procedures

67999   Unlisted procedure, eyelids

Conjunctiva

(For removal of foreign body, see 65205 et seq)

Incision and Drainage

68020   Incision of conjunctiva, drainage of cyst

68040   Expression of conjunctival follicles (eg, for trachoma)

Excision and/or Destruction

68100   Biopsy of conjunctiva

68110   Excision of lesion, conjunctiva; up to 1 cm

68115   over 1 cm

68130   with adjacent sclera

68135   Destruction of lesion, conjunctiva

Injection

(For injection into Tenon's capsule or retrobulbar injection, see 67500-67515)

68200   Subconjunctival injection

Conjunctivoplasty

(For wound repair, see 65270-65273)

68320   Conjunctivoplasty; with conjunctival graft or extensive rearrangement

68325   with buccal mucous membrane graft (includes obtaining graft)

68326 Conjunctivoplasty, reconstruction cul-de-sac; with conjunctival graft or extensive rearrangement

68328   with buccal mucous membrane graft (includes obtaining graft)

68330 Repair of symblepharon; conjunctivoplasty, without graft

68335   with free graft conjunctiva or buccal mucous membrane (includes obtaining graft)

68340   division of symblepharon, with or without insertion of conformer or contact lens

Other Procedures

68360 Conjunctival flap; bridge or partial (separate procedure)

68362   total (such as Gunderson thin flap or purse string flap)

(For conjunctival flap for perforating injury, see 65280, 65285)

(For repair of operative wound, use 66250)

(For removal of conjunctival foreign body, see 65205, 65210)

68371 Harvesting conjunctival allograft, living donor

68399 Unlisted procedure, conjunctiva

Lacrimal System

Incision

68400 Incision, drainage of lacrimal gland

68420 Incision, drainage of lacrimal sac (dacryocystotomy or dacryocystostomy)

68440 Snip incision of lacrimal punctum

Excision

68500 Excision of lacrimal gland (dacryoadenectomy), except for tumor; total

68505   partial

68510 Biopsy of lacrimal gland

68520 Excision of lacrimal sac (dacryocystectomy)

68525 Biopsy of lacrimal sac

68530 Removal of foreign body or dacryolith, lacrimal passages

68540 Excision of lacrimal gland tumor; frontal approach

68550   involving osteotomy

Repair

68700 Plastic repair of canaliculi

68705 Correction of everted punctum, cautery

68720 Dacryocystorhinostomy (fistulization of lacrimal sac to nasal cavity)

68745 Conjunctivorhinostomy (fistulization of conjunctiva to nasal cavity); without tube

68750   with insertion of tube or stent

68760 Closure of the lacrimal punctum; by thermocauterization, ligation, or laser surgery

68761   by plug, each

68770 Closure of lacrimal fistula (separate procedure)

Probing and/or Related Procedures

68801 Dilation of lacrimal punctum, with or without irrigation

(To report a bilateral procedure, use 68801 with modifier 50)

68810 Probing of nasolacrimal duct, with or without irrigation;

(For bilateral procedure, report 68810 with modifier 50)

68811   requiring general anesthesia

(For bilateral procedure, report 68811 with modifier 50)

68815   with insertion of tube or stent

(See also 92018)

(For bilateral procedure, report 68815 with modifier 50)

68840 Probing of lacrimal canaliculi, with or without irrigation

68850 Injection of contrast medium for dacryocystography

(For radiological supervision and interpretation, see 70170, 78660)

Other Procedures

68899 Unlisted procedure, lacrimal system

Surgery: Ocular/Auditory System

Notes

⊘=Modifier 51 exempt   ⊙=Conscious sedation   ✚=Add-on code   ✔=FDA approval pending

Auditory System

(For diagnostic services (eg, audiometry, vestibular tests), see 92502 et seq)

External Ear

Incision

69000   Drainage external ear, abscess or hematoma; simple

69005   complicated

69020   Drainage external auditory canal, abscess

69090   Ear piercing

Excision

69100   Biopsy external ear

69105   Biopsy external auditory canal

69110   Excision external ear; partial, simple repair

69120   complete amputation

(For reconstruction of ear, see 15120 et seq)

69140   Excision exostosis(es), external auditory canal

69145   Excision soft tissue lesion, external auditory canal

69150   Radical excision external auditory canal lesion; without neck dissection

69155   with neck dissection

(For resection of temporal bone, use 69535)

(For skin grafting, see 15000-15261)

Removal of Foreign Body

69200   Removal foreign body from external auditory canal; without general anesthesia

69205   with general anesthesia

69210   Removal impacted cerumen (separate procedure), one or both ears

69220   Debridement, mastoidectomy cavity, simple (eg, routine cleaning)

(For bilateral procedure, report 69220 with modifier 50)

69222   Debridement, mastoidectomy cavity, complex (eg, with anesthesia or more than routine cleaning)

(For bilateral procedure, report 69222 with modifier 50)

Repair

(For suture of wound or injury of external ear, see 12011-14300)

⊙ **69300**   Otoplasty, protruding ear, with or without size reduction

(For bilateral procedure, report 69300 with modifier 50)

69310   Reconstruction of external auditory canal (meatoplasty) (eg, for stenosis due to injury, infection) (separate procedure)

69320   Reconstruction external auditory canal for congenital atresia, single stage

(For combination with middle ear reconstruction, see 69631, 69641)

(For other reconstructive procedures with grafts (eg, skin, cartilage, bone), see 13150-15760, 21230-21235)

Other Procedures

(For otoscopy under general anesthesia, use 92502)

69399   Unlisted procedure, external ear

Middle Ear

Introduction

69400   Eustachian tube inflation, transnasal; with catheterization

69401   without catheterization

69405   Eustachian tube catheterization, transtympanic

▶(69410 has been deleted)◀

Incision

69420   Myringotomy including aspiration and/or eustachian tube inflation

69421   Myringotomy including aspiration and/or eustachian tube inflation requiring general anesthesia

69424   Ventilating tube removal requiring general anesthesia

(For bilateral procedure, report 69424 with modifier 50)

(Do not report code 69424 in conjunction with 69205, 69210, 69420, 69421, 69433-69676, 69710-69745, 69801-69930)

69433   Tympanostomy (requiring insertion of ventilating tube), local or topical anesthesia

(For bilateral procedure, report 69433 with modifier 50)

69436   Tympanostomy (requiring insertion of ventilating tube), general anesthesia

(For bilateral procedure, report 69436 with modifier 50)

69440   Middle ear exploration through postauricular or ear canal incision

(For atticotomy, see 69601 et seq)

69450   Tympanolysis, transcanal

Excision

69501 Transmastoid antrotomy (simple mastoidectomy)

69502 Mastoidectomy; complete

69505   modified radical

69511   radical

(For skin graft, see 15000 et seq)

(For mastoidectomy cavity debridement, see 69220, 69222)

69530 Petrous apicectomy including radical mastoidectomy

69535 Resection temporal bone, external approach

(For middle fossa approach, see 69950-69970)

69540 Excision aural polyp

69550 Excision aural glomus tumor; transcanal

69552   transmastoid

69554   extended (extratemporal)

Repair

69601 Revision mastoidectomy; resulting in complete mastoidectomy

69602   resulting in modified radical mastoidectomy

69603   resulting in radical mastoidectomy

69604   resulting in tympanoplasty

(For planned secondary tympanoplasty after mastoidectomy, see 69631, 69632)

69605   with apicectomy

(For skin graft, see 15120, 15121, 15260, 15261)

69610 Tympanic membrane repair, with or without site preparation of perforation for closure, with or without patch

69620 Myringoplasty (surgery confined to drumhead and donor area)

69631 Tympanoplasty without mastoidectomy (including canalplasty, atticotomy and/or middle ear surgery), initial or revision; without ossicular chain reconstruction

69632   with ossicular chain reconstruction (eg, postfenestration)

69633   with ossicular chain reconstruction and synthetic prosthesis (eg, partial ossicular replacement prosthesis (PORP), total ossicular replacement prosthesis (TORP))

69635 Tympanoplasty with antrotomy or mastoidotomy (including canalplasty, atticotomy, middle ear surgery, and/or tympanic membrane repair); without ossicular chain reconstruction

69636   with ossicular chain reconstruction

69637   with ossicular chain reconstruction and synthetic prosthesis (eg, partial ossicular replacement prosthesis (PORP), total ossicular replacement prosthesis (TORP))

69641 Tympanoplasty with mastoidectomy (including canalplasty, middle ear surgery, tympanic membrane repair); without ossicular chain reconstruction

69642   with ossicular chain reconstruction

69643   with intact or reconstructed wall, without ossicular chain reconstruction

69644   with intact or reconstructed canal wall, with ossicular chain reconstruction

69645   radical or complete, without ossicular chain reconstruction

69646   radical or complete, with ossicular chain reconstruction

69650 Stapes mobilization

69660 Stapedectomy or stapedotomy with reestablishment of ossicular continuity, with or without use of foreign material;

69661   with footplate drill out

69662 Revision of stapedectomy or stapedotomy

69666 Repair oval window fistula

69667 Repair round window fistula

69670 Mastoid obliteration (separate procedure)

69676 Tympanic neurectomy

(For bilateral procedure, report 69676 with modifier 50)

Other Procedures

69700 Closure postauricular fistula, mastoid (separate procedure)

69710 Implantation or replacement of electromagnetic bone conduction hearing device in temporal bone

(Replacement procedure includes removal of old device)

69711 Removal or repair of electromagnetic bone conduction hearing device in temporal bone

69714 Implantation, osseointegrated implant, temporal bone, with percutaneous attachment to external speech processor/cochlear stimulator; without mastoidectomy

69715   with mastoidectomy

69717 Replacement (including removal of existing device), osseointegrated implant, temporal bone, with percutaneous attachment to external speech processor/cochlear stimulator; without mastoidectomy

69718   with mastoidectomy

Surgery: Ocular/Auditory System

69720   Decompression facial nerve, intratemporal; lateral to geniculate ganglion

69725   including medial to geniculate ganglion

69740   Suture facial nerve, intratemporal, with or without graft or decompression; lateral to geniculate ganglion

69745   including medial to geniculate ganglion

(For extracranial suture of facial nerve, use 64864)

69799   Unlisted procedure, middle ear

Inner Ear

Incision and/or Destruction

69801   Labyrinthotomy, with or without cryosurgery including other nonexcisional destructive procedures or perfusion of vestibuloactive drugs (single or multiple perfusions); transcanal

(69801 includes all required infusions performed on initial and subsequent days of treatment)

69802   with mastoidectomy

69805   Endolymphatic sac operation; without shunt

69806   with shunt

69820   Fenestration semicircular canal

69840   Revision fenestration operation

Excision

69905   Labyrinthectomy; transcanal

69910   with mastoidectomy

69915   Vestibular nerve section, translabyrinthine approach

(For transcranial approach, use 69950)

Introduction

69930   Cochlear device implantation, with or without mastoidectomy

Other Procedures

69949   Unlisted procedure, inner ear

Temporal Bone, Middle Fossa Approach

(For external approach, use 69535)

69950   Vestibular nerve section, transcranial approach

69955   Total facial nerve decompression and/or repair (may include graft)

69960   Decompression internal auditory canal

69970   Removal of tumor, temporal bone

Other Procedures

69979   Unlisted procedure, temporal bone, middle fossa approach

Operating Microscope

▶The surgical microscope is employed when the surgical services are performed using the techniques of microsurgery. Code 69990 should be reported (without modifier 51 appended) in addition to the code for the primary procedure performed. Do not use 69990 for visualization with magnifying loupes or corrected vision. Do not report code 69990 in addition to procedures where use of the operating microscope is an inclusive component (15756-15758, 15842, 19364, 19368, 20955-20962, 20969-20973, 26551-26554, 26556, 31526, 31531, 31536, 31541, 31545, 31546, 31561, 31571, 43116, 43496, 49906, 61548, 63075-63078, 64727, 64820-64823, 65091-68850).◀

+ 69990   Microsurgical techniques, requiring use of operating microscope (List separately in addition to code for primary procedure)

Surgery: Ocular/Auditory System

Notes

⊘=Modifier 51 exempt   ⊙=Conscious sedation   +=Add-on code   ✔=FDA approval pending

Radiology Guidelines (Including Nuclear Medicine and Diagnostic Ultrasound)

Items used by all physicians in reporting their services are presented in the **Introduction.** Some of the commonalities are repeated here for the convenience of those physicians referring to this section on **Radiology (Including Nuclear Medicine and Diagnostic Ultrasound).** Other definitions and items unique to Radiology are also listed.

Subject Listings

Subject listings apply when radiological services are performed by or under the responsible supervision of a physician.

Separate Procedures

Some of the procedures or services listed in the CPT codebook that are commonly carried out as an integral component of a total service or procedure have been identified by the inclusion of the term "separate procedure." The codes designated as "separate procedure" should not be reported in addition to the code for the total procedure or service of which it is considered an integral component.

However, when a procedure or service that is designated as a "separate procedure" is carried out independently or considered to be unrelated or distinct from other procedures/services provided at that time, it may be reported by itself, or in addition to other procedures/services by appending modifier 59 to the specific "separate procedure" code to indicate that the procedure is not considered to be a component of another procedure, but is a distinct, independent procedure. This may represent a different session or patient encounter, different procedure or surgery, different site or organ system, separate incision/excision, separate lesion, or separate injury (or area of injury in extensive injuries).

Subsection Information

Several of the subheadings or subsections have special needs or instructions unique to that section. Where these are indicated (eg, "Radiation Oncology") special **"Notes"** will be presented preceding those procedural terminology listings, referring to that subsection specifically. If there is an "Unlisted Procedure" code number (see section below) for the individual subsection, it will be shown. Those subsections with **"Notes"** are as follows:

Aorta and Arteries 75600-75790
Veins and Lymphatics 75801-75893
Transcatheter Procedures 75894-75989
Diagnostic Ultrasound 76506-76999
Abdomen and Retroperitoneum 76700-76778
Obstetrical 76801-76828
Non-Obstetrical 76830-76857
Radiation Oncology 77261-77799
Clinical Treatment Planning 77261-77299
Radiation Treatment
Management 77427-77499
Proton Beam Treatment
Delivery 77520-77525
Hyperthermia 77600-77620
Clinical Brachytherapy 77750-77799
Nuclear Medicine 78000-78299
Musculoskeletal System 78300-78399
Cardiovascular System 78414-78499
Therapeutic 79005-79999

Unlisted Service or Procedure

A service or procedure may be provided that is not listed in this edition of the CPT codebook. When reporting such a service, the appropriate "Unlisted Procedure" code may be used to indicate the service, identifying it by "Special Report" as discussed below. The "Unlisted Procedures" and accompanying codes for **Radiology (Including Nuclear Medicine and Diagnostic Ultrasound)** are as follows:

76496 Unlisted fluoroscopic procedure (eg, diagnostic, interventional)

76497 Unlisted computed tomography procedure (eg, diagnostic, interventional)

76498 Unlisted magnetic resonance procedure (eg, diagnostic, interventional)

76499	Unlisted diagnostic radiographic procedure
76999	Unlisted ultrasound procedure (eg, diagnostic, interventional)
77299	Unlisted procedure, therapeutic radiology clinical treatment planning
77399	Unlisted procedure, medical radiation physics, dosimetry and treatment devices, and special services
77499	Unlisted procedure, therapeutic radiology treatment management
77799	Unlisted procedure, clinical brachytherapy
78099	Unlisted endocrine procedure, diagnostic nuclear medicine
78199	Unlisted hematopoietic, reticuloendothelial and lymphatic procedure, diagnostic nuclear medicine
78299	Unlisted gastrointestinal procedure, diagnostic nuclear medicine
78399	Unlisted musculoskeletal procedure, diagnostic nuclear medicine
78499	Unlisted cardiovascular procedure, diagnostic nuclear medicine
78599	Unlisted respiratory procedure, diagnostic nuclear medicine
78699	Unlisted nervous system procedure, diagnostic nuclear medicine
78799	Unlisted genitourinary procedure, diagnostic nuclear medicine
78999	Unlisted miscellaneous procedure, diagnostic nuclear medicine
79999	Radiopharmaceutical therapy, unlisted procedure

Special Report

A service that is rarely provided, unusual, variable, or new may require a special report in determining medical appropriateness of the service. Pertinent information should include an adequate definition or description of the nature, extent, and need for the procedure; and the time, effort, and equipment necessary to provide the service. Additional items that may be included are:

- Complexity of symptoms
- Final diagnosis
- Pertinent physical findings
- Diagnostic and therapeutic procedures
- Concurrent problems
- Follow-up care

Supervision and Interpretation

When a procedure is performed by two physicians, the radiologic portion of the procedure is designated as "radiological supervision and interpretation." When a physician performs both the procedure and provides imaging supervision and interpretation, a combination of procedure codes outside the 70000 series and imaging supervision and interpretation codes are to be used.

(The Radiological Supervision and Interpretation codes are not applicable to the Radiation Oncology subsection.)

Administration of Contrast Material(s)

The phrase "with contrast" used in the codes for procedures performed using contrast for imaging enhancement represents contrast material administered intravascularly, intra-articularly or intrathecally.

For intra-articular injection, use the appropriate joint injection code. If radiographic arthrography is performed, also use the arthrography supervision and interpretation code for the appropriate joint (which includes fluoroscopy). If computed tomography (CT) or magnetic resonance (MR) arthrography are performed without radiographic arthrography, use the appropriate joint injection code, the appropriate CT or MR code ("with contrast" or "without followed by contrast"), and the appropriate imaging guidance code for needle placement for contrast injection.

For spine examinations using computed tomography, magnetic resonance imaging, magnetic resonance angiography, "with contrast" includes intrathecal or intravascular injection. For intrathecal injection, use also 61055 or 62284.

Injection of intravascular contrast material is part of the "with contrast" CT, computed tomographic angiography (CTA), magnetic resonance imaging (MRI), and magnetic resonance angiography (MRA) procedures.

Oral and/or rectal contrast administration alone does not qualify as a study "with contrast."

Written Report(s)

A written report, signed by the interpreting physician, should be considered an integral part of a radiologic procedure or interpretation.

Radiology

Diagnostic Radiology (Diagnostic Imaging)

Head and Neck

70010 Myelography, posterior fossa, radiological supervision and interpretation

70015 Cisternography, positive contrast, radiological supervision and interpretation

70030 Radiologic examination, eye, for detection of foreign body

70100 Radiologic examination, mandible; partial, less than four views

70110   complete, minimum of four views

70120 Radiologic examination, mastoids; less than three views per side

70130   complete, minimum of three views per side

70134 Radiologic examination, internal auditory meati, complete

70140 Radiologic examination, facial bones; less than three views

70150   complete, minimum of three views

70160 Radiologic examination, nasal bones, complete, minimum of three views

70170 Dacryocystography, nasolacrimal duct, radiological supervision and interpretation

70190 Radiologic examination; optic foramina

70200   orbits, complete, minimum of four views

70210 Radiologic examination, sinuses, paranasal, less than three views

70220 Radiologic examination, sinuses, paranasal, complete, minimum of three views

70240 Radiologic examination, sella turcica

70250 Radiologic examination, skull; less than four views

70260   complete, minimum of four views

70300 Radiologic examination, teeth; single view

70310   partial examination, less than full mouth

70320   complete, full mouth

70328 Radiologic examination, temporomandibular joint, open and closed mouth; unilateral

70330   bilateral

70332 Temporomandibular joint arthrography, radiological supervision and interpretation

(Do not report 76003 in addition to 70332)

70336 Magnetic resonance (eg, proton) imaging, temporomandibular joint(s)

70350 Cephalogram, orthodontic

70355 Orthopantogram

70360 Radiologic examination; neck, soft tissue

70370   pharynx or larynx, including fluoroscopy and/or magnification technique

70371 Complex dynamic pharyngeal and speech evaluation by cine or video recording

70373 Laryngography, contrast, radiological supervision and interpretation

70380 Radiologic examination, salivary gland for calculus

70390 Sialography, radiological supervision and interpretation

70450 Computed tomography, head or brain; without contrast material

70460   with contrast material(s)

70470   without contrast material, followed by contrast material(s) and further sections

►(To report 3D rendering, see 76376, 76377)◄

70480 Computed tomography, orbit, sella, or posterior fossa or outer, middle, or inner ear; without contrast material

70481   with contrast material(s)

70482   without contrast material, followed by contrast material(s) and further sections

►(To report 3D rendering, see 76376, 76377)◄

70486 Computed tomography, maxillofacial area; without contrast material

70487   with contrast material(s)

70488   without contrast material, followed by contrast material(s) and further sections

►(To report 3D rendering, see 76376, 76377)◄

70490 Computed tomography, soft tissue neck; without contrast material

70491   with contrast material(s)

70492   without contrast material followed by contrast material(s) and further sections

►(To report 3D rendering, see 76376, 76377)◄

(For cervical spine, see 72125, 72126)

Radiology

70496 Computed tomographic angiography, head, without contrast material(s), followed by contrast material(s) and further sections, including image post-processing

70498 Computed tomographic angiography, neck, without contrast material(s), followed by contrast material(s) and further sections, including image post-processing

70540 Magnetic resonance (eg, proton) imaging, orbit, face, and neck; without contrast material(s)

(For head or neck magnetic resonance angiography studies, see 70544-70546, 70547-70549)

70542 with contrast material(s)

70543 without contrast material(s), followed by contrast material(s) and further sequences

70544 Magnetic resonance angiography, head; without contrast material(s)

70545 with contrast material(s)

70546 without contrast material(s), followed by contrast material(s) and further sequences

70547 Magnetic resonance angiography, neck; without contrast material(s)

70548 with contrast material(s)

70549 without contrast material(s), followed by contrast material(s) and further sequences

70551 Magnetic resonance (eg, proton) imaging, brain (including brain stem); without contrast material

70552 with contrast material(s)

70553 without contrast material, followed by contrast material(s) and further sequences

(For magnetic spectroscopy, use 76390)

70557 Magnetic resonance (eg, proton) imaging, brain (including brain stem and skull base), during open intracranial procedure (eg, to assess for residual tumor or residual vascular malformation); without contrast material

70558 with contrast material(s)

70559 without contrast material(s), followed by contrast material(s) and further sequences

(For stereotactic biopsy of intracranial lesion with magnetic resonance guidance, use 61751. 70557, 70558 or 70559 may be reported only if a separate report is generated. Report only one of the above codes once per operative session. Do not use these codes in conjunction with 61751, 76393, 76394)

Chest

(For fluoroscopic or ultrasonic guidance for needle placement procedures (eg, biopsy, aspiration, injection, localization device) of the thorax, see 76003, 76942)

71010 Radiologic examination, chest; single view, frontal

71015 stereo, frontal

71020 Radiologic examination, chest, two views, frontal and lateral;

71021 with apical lordotic procedure

71022 with oblique projections

71023 with fluoroscopy

71030 Radiologic examination, chest, complete, minimum of four views;

71034 with fluoroscopy

(For separate chest fluoroscopy, use 76000)

71035 Radiologic examination, chest, special views (eg, lateral decubitus, Bucky studies)

71040 Bronchography, unilateral, radiological supervision and interpretation

71060 Bronchography, bilateral, radiological supervision and interpretation

71090 Insertion pacemaker, fluoroscopy and radiography, radiological supervision and interpretation

(For procedure, see appropriate organ or site)

71100 Radiologic examination, ribs, unilateral; two views

71101 including posteroanterior chest, minimum of three views

71110 Radiologic examination, ribs, bilateral; three views

71111 including posteroanterior chest, minimum of four views

71120 Radiologic examination; sternum, minimum of two views

71130 sternoclavicular joint or joints, minimum of three views

71250 Computed tomography, thorax; without contrast material

71260 with contrast material(s)

71270 without contrast material, followed by contrast material(s) and further sections

▶(To report 3D rendering, see 76376, 76377)◀

71275 Computed tomographic angiography, chest, without contrast material(s), followed by contrast material(s) and further sections, including image post-processing

71550 Magnetic resonance (eg, proton) imaging, chest (eg, for evaluation of hilar and mediastinal lymphadenopathy); without contrast material(s)

71551 with contrast material(s)

71552 without contrast material(s), followed by contrast material(s) and further sequences

(For breast MRI, see 76093 and 76094)

71555 Magnetic resonance angiography, chest (excluding myocardium), with or without contrast material(s)

Radiology

⊘=Modifier 51 exempt   ⊙=Conscious sedation   ✚=Add-on code   ⊿=FDA approval pending

Spine and Pelvis

72010 Radiologic examination, spine, entire, survey study, anteroposterior and lateral

72020 Radiologic examination, spine, single view, specify level

72040 Radiologic examination, spine, cervical; two or three views

72050   minimum of four views

72052   complete, including oblique and flexion and/or extension studies

72069 Radiologic examination, spine, thoracolumbar, standing (scoliosis)

72070 Radiologic examination, spine; thoracic, two views

72072   thoracic, three views

72074   thoracic, minimum of four views

72080   thoracolumbar, two views

72090   scoliosis study, including supine and erect studies

72100 Radiologic examination, spine, lumbosacral; two or three views

72110   minimum of four views

72114   complete, including bending views

72120 Radiologic examination, spine, lumbosacral, bending views only, minimum of four views

(Contrast material in CT of spine is either by intrathecal or intravenous injection. For intrathecal injection, use also 61055 or 62284. IV injection of contrast material is part of the CT procedure)

72125 Computed tomography, cervical spine; without contrast material

72126   with contrast material

72127   without contrast material, followed by contrast material(s) and further sections

(For intrathecal injection procedure, see 61055, 62284)

72128 Computed tomography, thoracic spine; without contrast material

72129   with contrast material

(For intrathecal injection procedure, see 61055, 62284)

72130   without contrast material, followed by contrast material(s) and further sections

(For intrathecal injection procedure, see 61055, 62284)

72131 Computed tomography, lumbar spine; without contrast material

72132   with contrast material

72133   without contrast material, followed by contrast material(s) and further sections

(For intrathecal injection procedure, see 61055, 62284)

►(To report 3D rendering, see 76376, 76377)◄

72141 Magnetic resonance (eg, proton) imaging, spinal canal and contents, cervical; without contrast material

72142   with contrast material(s)

(For cervical spinal canal imaging without contrast material followed by contrast material, use 72156)

72146 Magnetic resonance (eg, proton) imaging, spinal canal and contents, thoracic; without contrast material

72147   with contrast material(s)

(For thoracic spinal canal imaging without contrast material followed by contrast material, use 72157)

72148 Magnetic resonance (eg, proton) imaging, spinal canal and contents, lumbar; without contrast material

72149   with contrast material(s)

(For lumbar spinal canal imaging without contrast material followed by contrast material, use 72158)

72156 Magnetic resonance (eg, proton) imaging, spinal canal and contents, without contrast material, followed by contrast material(s) and further sequences; cervical

72157   thoracic

72158   lumbar

72159 Magnetic resonance angiography, spinal canal and contents, with or without contrast material(s)

72170 Radiologic examination, pelvis; one or two views

72190   complete, minimum of three views

(For pelvimetry, use 74710)

72191 Computed tomographic angiography, pelvis, without contrast material(s), followed by contrast material(s) and further sections, including image post-processing

(For CTA aorto-iliofemoral runoff, use 75635)

72192 Computed tomography, pelvis; without contrast material

72193   with contrast material(s)

72194   without contrast material, followed by contrast material(s) and further sections

►(To report 3D rendering, see 76376, 76377)◄

(For computed tomographic colonography, see Category III codes 0066T, 0067T. Do not report 72192-72194 in conjunction with 0066T, 0067T)

72195 Magnetic resonance (eg, proton) imaging, pelvis; without contrast material(s)

72196   with contrast material(s)

72197   without contrast material(s), followed by contrast material(s) and further sequences

72198 Magnetic resonance angiography, pelvis, with or without contrast material(s)

72200 Radiologic examination, sacroiliac joints; less than three views

72202   three or more views

Radiology

▲=Revised code   ●=New code   ►◄=Contains new or revised text

72220 Radiologic examination, sacrum and coccyx, minimum of two views

72240 Myelography, cervical, radiological supervision and interpretation

(For complete cervical myelography, see 61055, 62284, 72240)

72255 Myelography, thoracic, radiological supervision and interpretation

(For complete thoracic myelography, see 61055, 62284, 72255)

72265 Myelography, lumbosacral, radiological supervision and interpretation

(For complete lumbosacral myelography, see 61055, 62284, 72265)

72270 Myelography, two or more regions (eg, lumbar/thoracic, cervical/thoracic, lumbar/cervical, lumbar/thoracic/cervical), radiological supervision and interpretation

(For complete myelography of entire spinal canal, see 61055, 62284, 72270)

72275 Epidurography, radiological supervision and interpretation

(72275 includes 76005)

(For injection procedure, see 62280-62282, 62310-62319, 64479-64484, 0027T)

(Use 72275 only when an epidurogram is performed, images documented, and a formal radiologic report is issued)

72285 Diskography, cervical or thoracic, radiological supervision and interpretation

72295 Diskography, lumbar, radiological supervision and interpretation

Upper Extremities

(For stress views, any joint, use 76006)

73000 Radiologic examination; clavicle, complete

73010   scapula, complete

73020 Radiologic examination, shoulder; one view

73030   complete, minimum of two views

73040 Radiologic examination, shoulder, arthrography, radiological supervision and interpretation

(Do not report 76003 in addition to 73040)

73050 Radiologic examination; acromioclavicular joints, bilateral, with or without weighted distraction

73060   humerus, minimum of two views

73070 Radiologic examination, elbow; two views

73080   complete, minimum of three views

73085 Radiologic examination, elbow, arthrography, radiological supervision and interpretation

(Do not report 76003 in addition to 73085)

73090 Radiologic examination; forearm, two views

73092   upper extremity, infant, minimum of two views

73100 Radiologic examination, wrist; two views

73110   complete, minimum of three views

73115 Radiologic examination, wrist, arthrography, radiological supervision and interpretation

(Do not report 76003 in addition to 73115)

73120 Radiologic examination, hand; two views

73130   minimum of three views

73140 Radiologic examination, finger(s), minimum of two views

73200 Computed tomography, upper extremity; without contrast material

73201   with contrast material(s)

73202   without contrast material, followed by contrast material(s) and further sections

►(To report 3D rendering, see 76376, 76377)◄

73206 Computed tomographic angiography, upper extremity, without contrast material(s), followed by contrast material(s) and further sections, including image post-processing

73218 Magnetic resonance (eg, proton) imaging, upper extremity, other than joint; without contrast material(s)

73219   with contrast material(s)

73220   without contrast material(s), followed by contrast material(s) and further sequences

73221 Magnetic resonance (eg, proton) imaging, any joint of upper extremity; without contrast material(s)

73222   with contrast material(s)

73223   without contrast material(s), followed by contrast material(s) and further sequences

73225 Magnetic resonance angiography, upper extremity, with or without contrast material(s)

Lower Extremities

(For stress views, any joint, use 76006)

73500 Radiologic examination, hip, unilateral; one view

73510   complete, minimum of two views

73520 Radiologic examination, hips, bilateral, minimum of two views of each hip, including anteroposterior view of pelvis

73525 Radiologic examination, hip, arthrography, radiological supervision and interpretation

(Do not report 76003 in addition to 73525)

  ⊘=Modifier 51 exempt   ⊙=Conscious sedation   ✚=Add-on code   ✗=FDA approval pending

Radiology

73530 Radiologic examination, hip, during operative procedure

73540 Radiologic examination, pelvis and hips, infant or child, minimum of two views

73542 Radiological examination, sacroiliac joint arthrography, radiological supervision and interpretation

(Do not report 76003 in addition to 73542)

(For procedure, use 27096. If formal arthrography is not performed, recorded, and a formal radiologic report is not issued, use 76005 for fluoroscopic guidance for sacroiliac joint injections)

73550 Radiologic examination, femur, two views

73560 Radiologic examination, knee; one or two views

73562 three views

73564 complete, four or more views

73565 both knees, standing, anteroposterior

73580 Radiologic examination, knee, arthrography, radiological supervision and interpretation

(Do not report 76003 in addition to 73580)

73590 Radiologic examination; tibia and fibula, two views

73592 lower extremity, infant, minimum of two views

73600 Radiologic examination, ankle; two views

73610 complete, minimum of three views

73615 Radiologic examination, ankle, arthrography, radiological supervision and interpretation

(Do not report 76003 in addition to 73615)

73620 Radiologic examination, foot; two views

73630 complete, minimum of three views

73650 Radiologic examination; calcaneus, minimum of two views

73660 toe(s), minimum of two views

73700 Computed tomography, lower extremity; without contrast material

73701 with contrast material(s)

73702 without contrast material, followed by contrast material(s) and further sections

▶(To report 3D rendering, see 76376, 76377)◀

73706 Computed tomographic angiography, lower extremity, without contrast material(s), followed by contrast material(s) and further sections, including image post-processing

(For CTA aorto-iliofemoral runoff, use 75635)

73718 Magnetic resonance (eg, proton) imaging, lower extremity other than joint; without contrast material(s)

73719 with contrast material(s)

73720 without contrast material(s), followed by contrast material(s) and further sequences

73721 Magnetic resonance (eg, proton) imaging, any joint of lower extremity; without contrast material

73722 with contrast material(s)

73723 without contrast material(s), followed by contrast material(s) and further sequences

73725 Magnetic resonance angiography, lower extremity, with or without contrast material(s)

Abdomen

74000 Radiologic examination, abdomen; single anteroposterior view

74010 anteroposterior and additional oblique and cone views

74020 complete, including decubitus and/or erect views

74022 complete acute abdomen series, including supine, erect, and/or decubitus views, single view chest

74150 Computed tomography, abdomen; without contrast material

74160 with contrast material(s)

74170 without contrast material, followed by contrast material(s) and further sections

▶(To report 3D rendering, see 76376, 76377)◀

(For computed tomographic colonography, see Category III codes 0066T, 0067T. Do not report 74150-74170 in conjunction with 0066T, 0067T)

74175 Computed tomographic angiography, abdomen, without contrast material(s), followed by contrast material(s) and further sections, including image post-processing

(For CTA aorto-iliofemoral runoff, use 75635)

74181 Magnetic resonance (eg, proton) imaging, abdomen; without contrast material(s)

74182 with contrast material(s)

74183 without contrast material(s), followed by with contrast material(s) and further sequences

74185 Magnetic resonance angiography, abdomen, with or without contrast material(s)

74190 Peritoneogram (eg, after injection of air or contrast), radiological supervision and interpretation

(For procedure, use 49400)

(For computed tomography, see 72192 or 74150)

Gastrointestinal Tract

(For percutaneous placement of gastrostomy tube, use 43750)

74210 Radiologic examination; pharynx and/or cervical esophagus

74220 esophagus

74230 Swallowing function, with cineradiography/videoradiography

Radiology

74235 Removal of foreign body(s), esophageal, with use of balloon catheter, radiological supervision and interpretation

(For procedure, see 43215, 43247)

74240 Radiologic examination, gastrointestinal tract, upper; with or without delayed films, without KUB

74241 with or without delayed films, with KUB

74245 with small intestine, includes multiple serial films

74246 Radiological examination, gastrointestinal tract, upper, air contrast, with specific high density barium, effervescent agent, with or without glucagon; with or without delayed films, without KUB

74247 with or without delayed films, with KUB

74249 with small intestine follow-through

74250 Radiologic examination, small intestine, includes multiple serial films;

74251 via enteroclysis tube

74260 Duodenography, hypotonic

74270 Radiologic examination, colon; barium enema, with or without KUB

74280 air contrast with specific high density barium, with or without glucagon

74283 Therapeutic enema, contrast or air, for reduction of intussusception or other intraluminal obstruction (eg, meconium ileus)

74290 Cholecystography, oral contrast;

74291 additional or repeat examination or multiple day examination

74300 Cholangiography and/or pancreatography; intraoperative, radiological supervision and interpretation

+ 74301 additional set intraoperative, radiological supervision and interpretation (List separately in addition to code for primary procedure)

(Use 74301 in conjunction with 74300)

74305 through existing catheter, radiological supervision and interpretation

(For procedure, see 47505, 48400, 47560-47561, 47563)

(For biliary duct stone extraction, percutaneous, see 47630, 74327)

74320 Cholangiography, percutaneous, transhepatic, radiological supervision and interpretation

74327 Postoperative biliary duct calculus removal, percutaneous via T-tube tract, basket, or snare (eg, Burhenne technique), radiological supervision and interpretation

(For procedure, use 47630)

74328 Endoscopic catheterization of the biliary ductal system, radiological supervision and interpretation

(For procedure, see 43260-43272 as appropriate)

74329 Endoscopic catheterization of the pancreatic ductal system, radiological supervision and interpretation

(For procedure, see 43260-43272 as appropriate)

74330 Combined endoscopic catheterization of the biliary and pancreatic ductal systems, radiological supervision and interpretation

(For procedure, see 43260-43272 as appropriate)

74340 Introduction of long gastrointestinal tube (eg, Miller-Abbott), including multiple fluoroscopies and films, radiological supervision and interpretation

(For tube placement, use 44500)

74350 Percutaneous placement of gastrostomy tube, radiological supervision and interpretation

74355 Percutaneous placement of enteroclysis tube, radiological supervision and interpretation

74360 Intraluminal dilation of strictures and/or obstructions (eg, esophagus), radiological supervision and interpretation

74363 Percutaneous transhepatic dilation of biliary duct stricture with or without placement of stent, radiological supervision and interpretation

(For procedure, see 47510, 47511, 47555, 47556)

Urinary Tract

74400 Urography (pyelography), intravenous, with or without KUB, with or without tomography

74410 Urography, infusion, drip technique and/or bolus technique;

74415 with nephrotomography

74420 Urography, retrograde, with or without KUB

74425 Urography, antegrade, (pyelostogram, nephrostogram, loopogram), radiological supervision and interpretation

74430 Cystography, minimum of three views, radiological supervision and interpretation

74440 Vasography, vesiculography, or epididymography, radiological supervision and interpretation

74445 Corpora cavernosography, radiological supervision and interpretation

74450 Urethrocystography, retrograde, radiological supervision and interpretation

74455 Urethrocystography, voiding, radiological supervision and interpretation

74470 Radiologic examination, renal cyst study, translumbar, contrast visualization, radiological supervision and interpretation

74475 Introduction of intracatheter or catheter into renal pelvis for drainage and/or injection, percutaneous, radiological supervision and interpretation

Radiology

74480   Introduction of ureteral catheter or stent into ureter through renal pelvis for drainage and/or injection, percutaneous, radiological supervision and interpretation

(For transurethral surgery (ureter and pelvis), see 52320-52355)

74485   Dilation of nephrostomy, ureters, or urethra, radiological supervision and interpretation

(For dilation of ureter without radiologic guidance, use 52341, 52344)

(For change of nephrostomy or pyelostomy tube, use 50398)

Gynecological and Obstetrical

(For abdomen and pelvis, see 72170-72190, 74000-74170)

74710   Pelvimetry, with or without placental localization

74740   Hysterosalpingography, radiological supervision and interpretation

(For introduction of saline or contrast for hysterosalpingography, see 58340)

74742   Transcervical catheterization of fallopian tube, radiological supervision and interpretation

(For procedure, use 58345)

74775   Perineogram (eg, vaginogram, for sex determination or extent of anomalies)

Heart

(For separate injection procedures for vascular radiology, see **Surgery** section, 36000-36299)

(For cardiac catheterization procedures, see 93501-93556)

75552   Cardiac magnetic resonance imaging for morphology; without contrast material

75553   with contrast material

75554   Cardiac magnetic resonance imaging for function, with or without morphology; complete study

75555   limited study

75556   Cardiac magnetic resonance imaging for velocity flow mapping

Vascular Procedures

Aorta and Arteries

Selective vascular catheterizations should be coded to include introduction and all lesser order selective catheterizations used in the approach (eg, the description for a selective right middle cerebral artery catheterization includes the introduction and placement catheterization of the right common and internal carotid arteries).

Additional second and/or third order arterial catheterizations within the same family of arteries supplied by a single first order artery should be expressed by 36218 or 36248. Additional first order or higher catheterizations in vascular families supplied by a first order vessel different from a previously selected and coded family should be separately coded using the conventions described above.

For angiography performed in conjunction with therapeutic transcatheter radiological supervision and interpretation services, see the Radiology Transcatheter Procedures guidelines.

Diagnostic angiography (radiological supervision and interpretation) codes should NOT be used with interventional procedures for:

1. Contrast injections, angiography, roadmapping, and/or fluoroscopic guidance for the intervention,

2. Vessel measurement, and

3. Post-angioplasty/stent angiography,

as this work is captured in the radiological supervision and interpretation code(s).

Diagnostic angiography performed at the time of an interventional procedure is separately reportable if:

1. No prior catheter-based angiographic study is available and a full diagnostic study is performed, and the decision to intervene is based on the diagnostic study, OR

2. A prior study is available, but as documented in the medical record:

    a. The patient's condition with respect to the clinical indication has changed since the prior study, OR

    b. There is inadequate visualization of the anatomy and/or pathology, OR

    c. There is a clinical change during the procedure that requires new evaluation outside the target area of intervention.

Diagnostic angiography performed at a separate setting from an interventional procedure is separately reported.

Diagnostic angiography performed at the time of an interventional procedure is NOT separately reportable if it is specifically included in the interventional code descriptor.

(For intravenous procedure, see 36000-36013, 36400-36425 and 36100-36248 for intra-arterial procedure)

(For radiological supervision and interpretation, see 75600-75978)

75600   Aortography, thoracic, without serialography, radiological supervision and interpretation

(For injection procedure, use 93544)

Radiology

75605   Aortography, thoracic, by serialography, radiological supervision and interpretation

(For injection procedure, use 93544)

75625   Aortography, abdominal, by serialography, radiological supervision and interpretation

(For injection procedure, use 93544)

75630   Aortography, abdominal plus bilateral iliofemoral lower extremity, catheter, by serialography, radiological supervision and interpretation

75635   Computed tomographic angiography, abdominal aorta and bilateral iliofemoral lower extremity runoff, radiological supervision and interpretation, without contrast material(s), followed by contrast material(s) and further sections, including image post-processing

75650   Angiography, cervicocerebral, catheter, including vessel origin, radiological supervision and interpretation

75658   Angiography, brachial, retrograde, radiological supervision and interpretation

75660   Angiography, external carotid, unilateral, selective, radiological supervision and interpretation

75662   Angiography, external carotid, bilateral, selective, radiological supervision and interpretation

75665   Angiography, carotid, cerebral, unilateral, radiological supervision and interpretation

75671   Angiography, carotid, cerebral, bilateral, radiological supervision and interpretation

75676   Angiography, carotid, cervical, unilateral, radiological supervision and interpretation

75680   Angiography, carotid, cervical, bilateral, radiological supervision and interpretation

75685   Angiography, vertebral, cervical, and/or intracranial, radiological supervision and interpretation

75705   Angiography, spinal, selective, radiological supervision and interpretation

75710   Angiography, extremity, unilateral, radiological supervision and interpretation

75716   Angiography, extremity, bilateral, radiological supervision and interpretation

75722   Angiography, renal, unilateral, selective (including flush aortogram), radiological supervision and interpretation

75724   Angiography, renal, bilateral, selective (including flush aortogram), radiological supervision and interpretation

75726   Angiography, visceral, selective or supraselective, (with or without flush aortogram), radiological supervision and interpretation

(For selective angiography, each additional visceral vessel studied after basic examination, use 75774)

75731   Angiography, adrenal, unilateral, selective, radiological supervision and interpretation

75733   Angiography, adrenal, bilateral, selective, radiological supervision and interpretation

75736   Angiography, pelvic, selective or supraselective, radiological supervision and interpretation

75741   Angiography, pulmonary, unilateral, selective, radiological supervision and interpretation

(For injection procedure, use 93541)

75743   Angiography, pulmonary, bilateral, selective, radiological supervision and interpretation

(For injection procedure, use 93541)

75746   Angiography, pulmonary, by nonselective catheter or venous injection, radiological supervision and interpretation

(For injection procedure, use 93541)

(For introduction of catheter, injection procedure, see 93501-93533, 93539, 93540, 93545, 93556)

(For introduction of catheter, injection procedure, see 93501-93533, 93545, 93556)

(For introduction of catheter, injection procedure, see 93501-93533, 93539, 93540, 93545, 93556)

75756   Angiography, internal mammary, radiological supervision and interpretation

(For introduction of catheter, injection procedure, see 93501-93533, 93545, 93556)

+ **75774**   Angiography, selective, each additional vessel studied after basic examination, radiological supervision and interpretation (List separately in addition to code for primary procedure)

(Use 75774 in addition to code for specific initial vessel studied)

(For angiography, see codes 75600-75790)

(For catheterizations, see codes 36215-36248)

(For introduction of catheter, injection procedure, see 93501-93533, 93545, 93555, 93556)

75790   Angiography, arteriovenous shunt (eg, dialysis patient), radiological supervision and interpretation

(For introduction of catheter, use 36140, 36145, 36215-36217, 36245-36247)

Veins and Lymphatics

For venography performed in conjunction with therapeutic transcatheter radiological supervision and interpretation services, see the Radiology Transcatheter Procedures guidelines.

Diagnostic venography (radiological supervision and interpretation) codes should NOT be used with interventional procedures for:

1. Contrast injections, venography, roadmapping, and/or fluoroscopic guidance for the intervention,

2. Vessel measurement, and

3. Post-angioplasty/stent venography,

as this work is captured in the radiological supervision and interpretation code(s).

Diagnostic venography performed at the time of an interventional procedure is separately reportable if:

1. No prior catheter-based venographic study is available and a full diagnostic study is performed, and decision to intervene is based on the diagnostic study, OR

2. A prior study is available, but as documented in the medical record:

    a. The patient's condition with respect to the clinical indication has changed since the prior study, OR

    b. There is inadequate visualization of the anatomy and/or pathology, OR

    c. There is a clinical change during the procedure that requires new evaluation outside the target area of intervention.

Diagnostic venography performed at a separate setting from an interventional procedure is separately reported.

Diagnostic venography performed at the time of an interventional procedure is NOT separately reportable if it is specifically included in the interventional code descriptor.

(For injection procedure for venous system, see 36000-36015, 36400-36510)

(For injection procedure for lymphatic system, use 38790)

75801 Lymphangiography, extremity only, unilateral, radiological supervision and interpretation

75803 Lymphangiography, extremity only, bilateral, radiological supervision and interpretation

75805 Lymphangiography, pelvic/abdominal, unilateral, radiological supervision and interpretation

75807 Lymphangiography, pelvic/abdominal, bilateral, radiological supervision and interpretation

75809 Shuntogram for investigation of previously placed indwelling nonvascular shunt (eg, LeVeen shunt, ventriculoperitoneal shunt, indwelling infusion pump), radiological supervision and interpretation

(For procedure, see 49427 or 61070)

75810 Splenoportography, radiological supervision and interpretation

75820 Venography, extremity, unilateral, radiological supervision and interpretation

75822 Venography, extremity, bilateral, radiological supervision and interpretation

75825 Venography, caval, inferior, with serialography, radiological supervision and interpretation

75827 Venography, caval, superior, with serialography, radiological supervision and interpretation

75831 Venography, renal, unilateral, selective, radiological supervision and interpretation

75833 Venography, renal, bilateral, selective, radiological supervision and interpretation

75840 Venography, adrenal, unilateral, selective, radiological supervision and interpretation

75842 Venography, adrenal, bilateral, selective, radiological supervision and interpretation

75860 Venography, venous sinus (eg, petrosal and inferior sagittal) or jugular, catheter, radiological supervision and interpretation

75870 Venography, superior sagittal sinus, radiological supervision and interpretation

75872 Venography, epidural, radiological supervision and interpretation

75880 Venography, orbital, radiological supervision and interpretation

75885 Percutaneous transhepatic portography with hemodynamic evaluation, radiological supervision and interpretation

75887 Percutaneous transhepatic portography without hemodynamic evaluation, radiological supervision and interpretation

75889 Hepatic venography, wedged or free, with hemodynamic evaluation, radiological supervision and interpretation

75891 Hepatic venography, wedged or free, without hemodynamic evaluation, radiological supervision and interpretation

75893 Venous sampling through catheter, with or without angiography (eg, for parathyroid hormone, renin), radiological supervision and interpretation

(For procedure, use 36500)

Transcatheter Procedures

Therapeutic transcatheter radiological supervision and interpretation code(s) include the following services associated with that intervention:

1. Contrast injections, angiography/venography, roadmapping, and fluoroscopic guidance for the intervention,

2. Vessel measurement, and

3. Completion angiography/venography (except for those uses permitted by 75898).

Unless specifically included in the code descriptor, diagnostic angiography/venography performed at the time of transcatheter therapeutic radiological and interpretation service(s) is separately reportable (eg, no prior catheter-based diagnostic angiography/venography study of the target vessel is available, prior diagnostic

Radiology

study is inadequate, patient's condition with respect to the clinical indication has changed since the prior study or during the intervention). See 75600-75893.

▶Codes 75956 and 75957 include all angiography of the thoracic aorta and its branches for diagnostic imaging prior to deployment of the primary endovascular devices (including all routine components of modular devices), fluoroscopic guidance in the delivery of the endovascular components, and intraprocedural arterial angiography (eg, confirm position, detect endoleak, evaluate runoff).◀

▶Code 75958 includes the analogous services for placement of each proximal thoracic endovascular extension. Code 75959 includes the analogous services for placement of a distal thoracic endovascular extension(s) placed during a procedure after the primary repair.◀

75894 Transcatheter therapy, embolization, any method, radiological supervision and interpretation

75896 Transcatheter therapy, infusion, any method (eg, thrombolysis other than coronary), radiological supervision and interpretation

(For infusion for coronary disease, see 92975, 92977)

75898 Angiography through existing catheter for follow-up study for transcatheter therapy, embolization or infusion

▲ **75900** Exchange of a previously placed intravascular catheter during thrombolytic therapy with contrast monitoring, radiological supervision and interpretation

(For procedure, use 37209)

75901 Mechanical removal of pericatheter obstructive material (eg, fibrin sheath) from central venous device via separate venous access, radiologic supervision and interpretation

(For procedure, use 36595)

(For venous catheterization, see 36010-36012)

75902 Mechanical removal of intraluminal (intracatheter) obstructive material from central venous device through device lumen, radiologic supervision and interpretation

(For procedure, use 36596)

(For venous catheterization, see 36010-36012)

75940 Percutaneous placement of IVC filter, radiological supervision and interpretation

75945 Intravascular ultrasound (non-coronary vessel), radiological supervision and interpretation; initial vessel

+ **75946** each additional non-coronary vessel (List separately in addition to code for primary procedure)

(Use 75946 in conjunction with 75945)

(For catheterizations, see codes 36215-36248)

(For transcatheter therapies, see codes 37200-37208, 61624, 61626)

(For procedure, see 37250, 37251)

75952 Endovascular repair of infrarenal abdominal aortic aneurysm or dissection, radiological supervision and interpretation

(For implantation of endovascular grafts, see 34800-34808)

(For radiologic supervision and interpretation of endovascular repair of abdominal aortic aneurysm involving visceral vessels, see Category III codes 0078T-0081T)

75953 Placement of proximal or distal extension prosthesis for endovascular repair of infrarenal aortic or iliac artery aneurysm, pseudoaneurysm, or dissection, radiological supervision and interpretation

(For implantation of endovascular extension prostheses, see 34825, 34826)

75954 Endovascular repair of iliac artery aneurysm, pseudoaneurysm, arteriovenous malformation, or trauma, radiological supervision and interpretation

(For implantation of endovascular graft, see 34900)

● **75956** Endovascular repair of descending thoracic aorta (eg, aneurysm, pseudoaneurysm, dissection, penetrating ulcer, intramural hematoma, or traumatic disruption); involving coverage of left subclavian artery origin, initial endoprosthesis plus descending thoracic aortic extension(s), if required, to level of celiac artery origin, radiological supervision and interpretation

▶(For implantation of endovascular graft, use 33880)◀

● **75957** not involving coverage of left subclavian artery origin, initial endoprosthesis plus descending thoracic aortic extension(s), if required, to level of celiac artery origin, radiological supervision and interpretation

▶(For implantation of endovascular graft, use 33881)◀

● **75958** Placement of proximal extension prosthesis for endovascular repair of descending thoracic aorta (eg, aneurysm, pseudoaneurysm, dissection, penetrating ulcer, intramural hematoma, or traumatic disruption), radiological supervision and interpretation

▶(Report 75958 for each proximal extension)◀

▶(For implantation of proximal endovascular extension, see 33883, 33884)◀

● **75959** Placement of distal extension prosthesis(s) (delayed) after endovascular repair of descending thoracic aorta, as needed, to level of celiac origin, radiological supervision and interpretation

▶(Do not report 75959 in conjunction with 75956, 75957)◀

▶(Report 75959 once, regardless of number of modules deployed)◀

▶(For implantation of distal endovascular extension, use 33886)◀

75960 Transcatheter introduction of intravascular stent(s), (except coronary, carotid, and vertebral vessel), percutaneous and/or open, radiological supervision and interpretation, each vessel

(For procedure, see 37205-37208)

(For radiologic supervision and interpretation for transcatheter placement of extracranial vertebral or intrathoracic carotid artery stent(s), see Category III codes 0075T, 0076T)

75961 Transcatheter retrieval, percutaneous, of intravascular foreign body (eg, fractured venous or arterial catheter), radiological supervision and interpretation

(For procedure, use 37203)

75962 Transluminal balloon angioplasty, peripheral artery, radiological supervision and interpretation

+ 75964 Transluminal balloon angioplasty, each additional peripheral artery, radiological supervision and interpretation (List separately in addition to code for primary procedure)

(Use 75964 in conjunction with 75962)

75966 Transluminal balloon angioplasty, renal or other visceral artery, radiological supervision and interpretation

+ 75968 Transluminal balloon angioplasty, each additional visceral artery, radiological supervision and interpretation (List separately in addition to code for primary procedure)

(Use 75968 in conjunction with 75966)

(For percutaneous transluminal coronary angioplasty, see 92982-92984)

75970 Transcatheter biopsy, radiological supervision and interpretation

(For injection procedure only for transcatheter therapy or biopsy, see 36100-36299)

(For transcatheter renal and ureteral biopsy, use 52007)

(For percutaneous needle biopsy of pancreas, use 48102; of retroperitoneal lymph node or mass, use 49180)

75978 Transluminal balloon angioplasty, venous (eg, subclavian stenosis), radiological supervision and interpretation

75980 Percutaneous transhepatic biliary drainage with contrast monitoring, radiological supervision and interpretation

75982 Percutaneous placement of drainage catheter for combined internal and external biliary drainage or of a drainage stent for internal biliary drainage in patients with an inoperable mechanical biliary obstruction, radiological supervision and interpretation

75984 Change of percutaneous tube or drainage catheter with contrast monitoring (eg, gastrointestinal system, genitourinary system, abscess), radiological supervision and interpretation

(For change of nephrostomy or pyelostomy tube only, use 50398)

(For introduction procedure only for percutaneous biliary drainage, see 47510, 47511)

(For percutaneous cholecystostomy, use 47490)

(For change of percutaneous biliary drainage catheter only, use 47525)

(For percutaneous nephrostolithotomy or pyelostolithotomy, see 50080, 50081)

75989 Radiological guidance (ie, fluoroscopy, ultrasound, or computed tomography), for percutaneous drainage (eg, abscess, specimen collection), with placement of catheter, radiological supervision and interpretation

Transluminal Atherectomy

75992 Transluminal atherectomy, peripheral artery, radiological supervision and interpretation

(For procedure, see 35481-35485, 35491-35495)

+ 75993 Transluminal atherectomy, each additional peripheral artery, radiological supervision and interpretation (List separately in addition to code for primary procedure)

(Use 75993 in conjunction with 75992)

(For procedure, see 35481-35485, 35491-35495)

75994 Transluminal atherectomy, renal, radiological supervision and interpretation

(For procedure, see 35480, 35490)

75995 Transluminal atherectomy, visceral, radiological supervision and interpretation

(For procedure, see 35480, 35490)

+ 75996 Transluminal atherectomy, each additional visceral artery, radiological supervision and interpretation (List separately in addition to code for primary procedure)

(Use 75996 in conjunction with 75995)

(For procedure, see 35480, 35490)

Other Procedures

(For computed tomography cerebral perfusion analysis, see Category III code 0042T)

(For arthrography of shoulder, use 73040; elbow, use 73085; wrist, use 73115; hip, use 73525; knee, use 73580; ankle, use 73615)

+ 75998 Fluoroscopic guidance for central venous access device placement, replacement (catheter only or complete), or removal (includes fluoroscopic guidance for vascular access and catheter manipulation, any necessary contrast injections through access site or catheter with related venography radiologic supervision and interpretation, and radiographic documentation of final catheter position) (List separately in addition to code for primary procedure)

(Do not use 76003 in conjunction with 75998)

Radiology

(If formal extremity venography is performed from separate venous access and separately interpreted, use 36005 and 75820, 75822, 75825 or 75827)

76000   Fluoroscopy (separate procedure), up to one hour physician time, other than 71023 or 71034 (eg, cardiac fluoroscopy)

76001   Fluoroscopy, physician time more than one hour, assisting a non-radiologic physician (eg, nephrostilithotomy, ERCP, bronchoscopy, transbronchial biopsy)

76003   Fluoroscopic guidance for needle placement (eg, biopsy, aspiration, injection, localization device)

(See appropriate surgical code for procedure and anatomic location)

(Fluoroscopy 76003 is considered inclusive of all radiographic arthrography with the exception of supervision and interpretation for CT and MR arthrography)

(Do not report 76003 in addition to 70332, 73040, 73085, 73115, 73525, 73580, 73615)

(Fluoroscopy 76003 is considered inclusive of organ/anatomic specific radiological supervision and interpretation procedures 74320, 74350, 74355, 74445, 74470, 74475, 75809, 75810, 75885, 75887, 75980, 75982, 75989)

76005   Fluoroscopic guidance and localization of needle or catheter tip for spine or paraspinous diagnostic or therapeutic injection procedures (epidural, transforaminal epidural, subarachnoid, paravertebral facet joint, paravertebral facet joint nerve or sacroiliac joint), including neurolytic agent destruction

(Injection of contrast during fluoroscopic guidance and localization is an inclusive component of codes 62263, 62264, 62270-62273, 62280-62282, 62310-62319, 0027T)

(Fluoroscopic guidance for subarachnoid puncture for diagnostic radiographic myelography is included in supervision and interpretation codes 72240, 72255, 72265, 72270)

(For epidural or subarachnoid needle or catheter placement and injection, see codes 62270-62273, 62280-62282, 62310-62319)

(For sacroiliac joint arthrography, see 27096, 73542. If formal arthrography is not performed, recorded, and a formal radiographic report is not issued, use 76005 for fluoroscopic guidance for sacroiliac joint injections)

(For paravertebral facet joint injection, see 64470-64476. For transforaminal epidural needle placement and injection, see 64479-64484)

(For destruction by neurolytic agent, see 64600-64680)

(For percutaneous or endoscopic lysis of epidural adhesions, codes 62263, 62264, 0027T include fluoroscopic guidance and localization)

76006   Manual application of stress performed by physician for joint radiography, including contralateral joint if indicated

(For radiographic interpretation of stressed images, see appropriate anatomic site and number of views)

76010   Radiologic examination from nose to rectum for foreign body, single view, child

▲ **76012**   Radiological supervision and interpretation, percutaneous vertebroplasty or vertebral augmentation including cavity creation, per vertebral body; under fluoroscopic guidance

76013   under CT guidance

►(For procedure, see 22520-22522, 22523-22525)◄

76020   Bone age studies

76040   Bone length studies (orthoroentgenogram, scanogram)

76061   Radiologic examination, osseous survey; limited (eg, for metastases)

76062   complete (axial and appendicular skeleton)

76065   Radiologic examination, osseous survey, infant

76066   Joint survey, single view, two or more joints (specify)

76070   Computed tomography, bone mineral density study, one or more sites; axial skeleton (eg, hips, pelvis, spine)

76071   appendicular skeleton (peripheral) (eg, radius, wrist, heel)

76075   Dual energy X-ray absorptiometry (DXA), bone density study, one or more sites; axial skeleton (eg, hips, pelvis, spine)

76076   appendicular skeleton (peripheral) (eg, radius, wrist, heel)

76077   vertebral fracture assessment

(To report dual energy X-ray absorptiometry (DXA) body composition study, one or more sites, use Category III code 0028T)

76078   Radiographic absorptiometry (eg, photodensitometry, radiogrammetry), one or more sites

76080   Radiologic examination, abscess, fistula or sinus tract study, radiological supervision and interpretation

+ **76082**   Computer aided detection (computer algorithm analysis of digital image data for lesion detection) with further physician review for interpretation, with or without digitization of film radiographic images; diagnostic mammography (List separately in addition to code for primary procedure)

(Use 76082 in conjunction with 76090 or 76091)

+ **76083**   screening mammography (List separately in addition to code for primary procedure)

(Use 76083 in conjunction with 76092)

(76085 has been deleted. To report, see 76082, 76083)

76086 Mammary ductogram or galactogram, single duct, radiological supervision and interpretation

(For mammary ductogram or galactogram injection, use 19030)

76088 Mammary ductogram or galactogram, multiple ducts, radiological supervision and interpretation

76090 Mammography; unilateral

76091   bilateral

(Use 76082 in conjunction with 76090 or 76091 for computer aided detection applied to a diagnostic mammogram)

76092 Screening mammography, bilateral (two view film study of each breast)

(Use 76083 in conjunction with 76092 for computer aided detection applied to a screening mammogram)

(To report electrical impedance scan of the breast, bilateral, use Category III code 0060T)

76093 Magnetic resonance imaging, breast, without and/or with contrast material(s); unilateral

76094   bilateral

76095 Stereotactic localization guidance for breast biopsy or needle placement (eg, for wire localization or for injection), each lesion, radiological supervision and interpretation

(For procedure, see 10022, 19000, 19001, 19102, 19103, 19290, 19291)

(For injection for sentinel node localization without lymphoscintigraphy, use 38792)

76096 Mammographic guidance for needle placement, breast (eg, for wire localization or for injection), each lesion, radiological supervision and interpretation

(For procedure, see 10022, 19000, 19102, 19103, 19290, 19291)

(For injection for sentinel node localization without lymphoscintigraphy, use 38792)

76098 Radiological examination, surgical specimen

76100 Radiologic examination, single plane body section (eg, tomography), other than with urography

76101 Radiologic examination, complex motion (ie, hypercycloidal) body section (eg, mastoid polytomography), other than with urography; unilateral

76102   bilateral

(For nephrotomography, use 74415)

76120 Cineradiography/videoradiography, except where specifically included

+ 76125 Cineradiography/videoradiography to complement routine examination (List separately in addition to code for primary procedure)

76140 Consultation on X-ray examination made elsewhere, written report

76150 Xeroradiography

(76150 is to be used for non-mammographic studies only)

76350 Subtraction in conjunction with contrast studies

76355 Computed tomography guidance for stereotactic localization

76360 Computed tomography guidance for needle placement (eg, biopsy, aspiration, injection, localization device), radiological supervision and interpretation

76362 Computed tomography guidance for, and monitoring of, visceral tissue ablation

►(For percutaneous cryotherapy ablation of renal tumors, use 0135T)◄

►(For percutaneous radiofrequency ablation, see 47382, 50592)◄

76370 Computed tomography guidance for placement of radiation therapy fields

►(76375 has been deleted)◄

►(2D reformatting is no longer separately reported. To report 3D rendering, see 76376, 76377)◄

►(Codes 76376, 76377 require concurrent physician supervision of image postprocessing 3D manipulation of volumetric data set and image rendering)◄

● **76376** 3D rendering with interpretation and reporting of computed tomography, magnetic resonance imaging, ultrasound, or other tomographic modality; not requiring image postprocessing on an independent workstation

►(Use 76376 in conjunction with code(s) for base imaging procedure(s))◄

►(Do not report 76376 in conjunction with 70496, 70498, 70544-70549, 71275, 71555, 72159, 72191, 72198, 73206, 73225, 73706, 73725, 74175, 74185, 75635, 78814-78816, 0066T, 0067T)◄

● **76377**   requiring image postprocessing on an independent workstation

►(Use 76377 in conjunction with code(s) for base imaging procedure(s))◄

►(Do not report 76377 in conjunction with 70496, 70498, 70544-70549, 71275, 71555, 72159, 72191, 72198, 73206, 73225, 73706, 73725, 74175, 74185, 75635, 78814, 78815, 78816, 0066T, 0067T)◄

76380 Computed tomography, limited or localized follow-up study

76390 Magnetic resonance spectroscopy

(For magnetic resonance imaging, use appropriate MRI body site code)

Radiology

▲=Revised code   ●=New code   ► ◄=Contains new or revised text

76393   Magnetic resonance guidance for needle placement (eg, for biopsy, needle aspiration, injection, or placement of localization device) radiological supervision and interpretation

(For procedure see appropriate organ or site)

76394   Magnetic resonance guidance for, and monitoring of, visceral tissue ablation

▶(For percutaneous radiofrequency ablation, see 47382, 50592)◀

(For focused ultrasound ablation treatment of uterine leiomyomata, see Category III codes 0071T, 0072T)

▶(For percutaneous cryotherapy ablation of renal tumors, use 0135T)◀

76400   Magnetic resonance (eg, proton) imaging, bone marrow blood supply

(76490 has been deleted. To report, use 76940)

76496   Unlisted fluoroscopic procedure (eg, diagnostic, interventional)

76497   Unlisted computed tomography procedure (eg, diagnostic, interventional)

76498   Unlisted magnetic resonance procedure (eg, diagnostic, interventional)

76499   Unlisted diagnostic radiographic procedure

Diagnostic Ultrasound

All diagnostic ultrasound examinations require permanently recorded images with measurements, when such measurements are clinically indicated. For those codes whose sole diagnostic goal is a biometric measure (ie, 76514, 76516, and 76519), permanently recorded images are not required. A final, written report should be issued for inclusion in the patient's medical record. The prescription form for the intraocular lens satisfies the written report requirement for 76519. For those anatomic regions that have "complete" and "limited" ultrasound codes, note the elements that comprise a "complete" exam. The report should contain a description of these elements or the reason that an element could not be visualized (eg, obscured by bowel gas, surgically absent).

If less than the required elements for a "complete" exam are reported (eg, limited number of organs or limited portion of region evaluated), the "limited" code for that anatomic region should be used once per patient exam session. A "limited" exam of an anatomic region should not be reported for the same exam session as a "complete" exam of that same region.

Doppler evaluation of vascular structures (other than color flow used only for anatomic structure identification) is separately reportable. To report, see Non-Invasive Vascular Diagnostic Studies (93875-93990).

Ultrasound guidance procedures also require permanently recorded images of the site to be localized, as well as a documented description of the localization process, either separately or within the report of the procedure for which the guidance is utilized.

Use of ultrasound, without thorough evaluation of organ(s) or anatomic region, image documentation, and final, written report, is not separately reportable.

Definitions

A-mode implies a one-dimensional ultrasonic measurement procedure.

M-mode implies a one-dimensional ultrasonic measurement procedure with movement of the trace to record amplitude and velocity of moving echo-producing structures.

B-scan implies a two-dimensional ultrasonic scanning procedure with a two-dimensional display.

Real-time scan implies a two-dimensional ultrasonic scanning procedure with display of both two-dimensional structure and motion with time.

(To report diagnostic vascular ultrasound studies, see 93875-93990)

(For focused ultrasound ablation treatment of uterine leiomyomata, see Category III codes 0071T, 0072T)

Head and Neck

76506   Echoencephalography, B-scan and/or real time with image documentation (gray scale) (for determination of ventricular size, delineation of cerebral contents and detection of fluid masses or other intracranial abnormalities), including A-mode encephalography as secondary component where indicated

76510   Ophthalmic ultrasound, diagnostic; B-scan and quantitative A-scan performed during the same patient encounter

76511   quantitative A-scan only

76512   B-scan (with or without superimposed non-quantitative A-scan)

76513   anterior segment ultrasound, immersion (water bath) B-scan or high resolution biomicroscopy

76514   corneal pachymetry, unilateral or bilateral (determination of corneal thickness)

76516   Ophthalmic biometry by ultrasound echography, A-scan;

76519   with intraocular lens power calculation

(For partial coherence interferometry, use 92136)

76529   Ophthalmic ultrasonic foreign body localization

76536   Ultrasound, soft tissues of head and neck (eg, thyroid, parathyroid, parotid), B-scan and/or real time with image documentation

Radiology

Chest

76604   Ultrasound, chest, B-scan (includes mediastinum) and/or real time with image documentation

76645   Ultrasound, breast(s) (unilateral or bilateral), B-scan and/or real time with image documentation

Abdomen and Retroperitoneum

A complete ultrasound examination of the abdomen (76700) consists of B mode scans of the liver, gall bladder, common bile duct, pancreas, spleen, kidneys, and the upper abdominal aorta and inferior vena cava including any demonstrated abdominal abnormality.

A complete ultrasound examination of the retroperitoneum (76770) consists of B mode scans of the kidneys, abdominal aorta, common iliac artery origins, and inferior vena cava, including any demonstrated retroperitoneal abnormality. Alternatively, if clinical history suggests urinary tract pathology, complete evaluation of the kidneys and urinary bladder also comprises a complete retroperitoneal ultrasound.

Use of ultrasound, without thorough evaluation of organ(s) or anatomic region, image documentation and final, written report, is not separately reportable.

76700   Ultrasound, abdominal, B-scan and/or real time with image documentation; complete

76705   limited (eg, single organ, quadrant, follow-up)

76770   Ultrasound, retroperitoneal (eg, renal, aorta, nodes), B-scan and/or real time with image documentation; complete

76775   limited

76778   Ultrasound, transplanted kidney, B-scan and/or real time with image documentation, with or without duplex Doppler study

Spinal Canal

76800   Ultrasound, spinal canal and contents

Pelvis

Obstetrical

Codes 76801 and 76802 include determination of the number of gestational sacs and fetuses, gestational sac/fetal measurements appropriate for gestation (less than 14 weeks 0 days), survey of visible fetal and placental anatomic structure, qualitative assessment of amniotic fluid volume/gestational sac shape and examination of the maternal uterus and adnexa.

Codes 76805 and 76810 include determination of number of fetuses and amniotic/chorionic sacs, measurements appropriate for gestational age (greater than or equal to 14 weeks 0 days), survey of intracranial/spinal/abdominal anatomy, 4 chambered heart, umbilical cord insertion site, placenta location and amniotic fluid assessment and, when visible, examination of maternal adnexa.

Codes 76811 and 76812 include all elements of codes 76805 and 76810 plus detailed anatomic evaluation of the fetal brain/ventricles, face, heart/outflow tracts and chest anatomy, abdominal organ specific anatomy, number/length/architecture of limbs and detailed evaluation of the umbilical cord and placenta and other fetal anatomy as clinically indicated.

Report should document the results of the evaluation of each element described above or the reason for non-visualization.

Code 76815 represents a focused "quick look" exam limited to the assessment of one or more of the elements listed in code 76815.

Code 76816 describes an examination designed to reassess fetal size and interval growth or reevaluate one or more anatomic abnormalities of a fetus previously demonstrated on ultrasound, and should be coded once for each fetus requiring reevaluation using modifier 59 for each fetus after the first.

Code 76817 describes a transvaginal obstetric ultrasound performed separately or in addition to one of the transabdominal examinations described above. For transvaginal examinations performed for non-obstetrical purposes, use code 76830.

76801   Ultrasound, pregnant uterus, real time with image documentation, fetal and maternal evaluation, first trimester (< 14 weeks 0 days), transabdominal approach; single or first gestation

+ 76802   each additional gestation (List separately in addition to code for primary procedure)

        (Use 76802 in conjunction with 76801)

76805   Ultrasound, pregnant uterus, real time with image documentation, fetal and maternal evaluation, after first trimester (> or = 14 weeks 0 days), transabdominal approach; single or first gestation

+ 76810   each additional gestation (List separately in addition to code for primary procedure)

        (Use 76810 in conjunction with 76805)

76811   Ultrasound, pregnant uterus, real time with image documentation, fetal and maternal evaluation plus detailed fetal anatomic examination, transabdominal approach; single or first gestation

+ 76812   each additional gestation (List separately in addition to code for primary procedure)

        (Use 76812 in conjunction with 76811)

76815   Ultrasound, pregnant uterus, real time with image documentation, limited (eg, fetal heart beat, placental location, fetal position and/or qualitative amniotic fluid volume), one or more fetuses

        (Use 76815 only once per exam and not per element)

▲=Revised code   ●=New code   ▶ ◀=Contains new or revised text

Radiology

76816 Ultrasound, pregnant uterus, real time with image documentation, follow-up (eg, re-evaluation of fetal size by measuring standard growth parameters and amniotic fluid volume, re-evaluation of organ system(s) suspected or confirmed to be abnormal on a previous scan), transabdominal approach, per fetus

(Report 76816 with modifier 59 for each additional fetus examined in a multiple pregnancy)

76817 Ultrasound, pregnant uterus, real time with image documentation, transvaginal

(For non-obstetrical transvaginal ultrasound, use 76830)

(If transvaginal examination is done in addition to transabdominal obstetrical ultrasound exam, use 76817 in addition to appropriate transabdominal exam code)

76818 Fetal biophysical profile; with non-stress testing

76819   without non-stress testing

(Fetal biophysical profile assessments for the second and any additional fetuses, should be reported separately by code 76818 or 76819 with the modifier 59 appended)

(For amniotic fluid index without non-stress test, use 76815)

76820 Doppler velocimetry, fetal; umbilical artery

76821   middle cerebral artery

76825 Echocardiography, fetal, cardiovascular system, real time with image documentation (2D), with or without M-mode recording;

76826   follow-up or repeat study

76827 Doppler echocardiography, fetal, pulsed wave and/or continuous wave with spectral display; complete

76828   follow-up or repeat study

(To report the use of color mapping, use 93325)

Non-Obstetrical

Code 76856 includes the complete evaluation of the female pelvic anatomy. Elements of this examination include a description and measurements of the uterus and adnexal structures, measurement of the endometrium, measurement of the bladder (when applicable), and a description of any pelvic pathology (eg, ovarian cysts, uterine leiomyomata, free pelvic fluid).

Code 76856 is also applicable to a complete evaluation of the male pelvis. Elements of the examination include evaluation and measurement (when applicable) of the urinary bladder, evaluation of the prostate and seminal vesicles to the extent that they are visualized transabdominally, and any pelvic pathology (eg, bladder tumor, enlarged prostate, free pelvic fluid, pelvic abscess).

Code 76857 represents a focused examination limited to the assessment of one or more elements listed in code 76856 and/or the reevaluation of one or more pelvic abnormalities previously demonstrated on ultrasound. Code 76857, rather than 76770, should be utilized if the urinary bladder alone (ie, not including the kidneys) is imaged, whereas code 51798 should be utilized if a bladder volume or post-void residual measurement is obtained without imaging the bladder.

Use of ultrasound, without thorough evaluation of organ(s) or anatomic region, image documentation, and final, written report, is not separately reportable.

76830 Ultrasound, transvaginal

(For obstetrical transvaginal ultrasound, use 76817)

(If transvaginal examination is done in addition to transabdominal non-obstetrical ultrasound exam, use 76830 in addition to appropriate transabdominal exam code)

76831 Saline infusion sonohysterography (SIS), including color flow Doppler, when performed

(For introduction of saline for saline infusion sonohysterography, use 58340)

76856 Ultrasound, pelvic (nonobstetric), B-scan and/or real time with image documentation; complete

76857   limited or follow-up (eg, for follicles)

Genitalia

76870 Ultrasound, scrotum and contents

76872 Ultrasound, transrectal;

76873   prostate volume study for brachytherapy treatment planning (separate procedure)

Extremities

76880 Ultrasound, extremity, non-vascular, B-scan and/or real time with image documentation

76885 Ultrasound, infant hips, real time with imaging documentation; dynamic (requiring physician manipulation)

76886   limited, static (not requiring physician manipulation)

Ultrasonic Guidance Procedures

76930 Ultrasonic guidance for pericardiocentesis, imaging supervision and interpretation

76932 Ultrasonic guidance for endomyocardial biopsy, imaging supervision and interpretation

76936 Ultrasound guided compression repair of arterial pseudoaneurysm or arteriovenous fistulae (includes diagnostic ultrasound evaluation, compression of lesion and imaging)

Radiology

+ 76937 Ultrasound guidance for vascular access requiring ultrasound evaluation of potential access sites, documentation of selected vessel patency, concurrent realtime ultrasound visualization of vascular needle entry, with permanent recording and reporting (List separately in addition to code for primary procedure)

(Do not use 76937 in conjunction with 76942)

(If extremity venous non-invasive vascular diagnostic study is performed separate from venous access guidance, use 93965, 93970 or 93971)

76940 Ultrasound guidance for, and monitoring of, visceral tissue ablation

(Do not report 76940 in conjunction with 76986)

►(For ablation, see 47370-47382, 50592)◄

►(For percutaneous cryotherapy ablation of renal tumors, use 0135T)◄

76941 Ultrasonic guidance for intrauterine fetal transfusion or cordocentesis, imaging supervision and interpretation

(For procedure, see 36460, 59012)

76942 Ultrasonic guidance for needle placement (eg, biopsy, aspiration, injection, localization device), imaging supervision and interpretation

(Do not report 76942 in conjunction with 43232, 43237, 43242, 45341, 45342, or 76975)

(For microwave thermotherapy of the breast, use Category III code 0061T)

76945 Ultrasonic guidance for chorionic villus sampling, imaging supervision and interpretation

(For procedure, use 59015)

76946 Ultrasonic guidance for amniocentesis, imaging supervision and interpretation

76948 Ultrasonic guidance for aspiration of ova, imaging supervision and interpretation

76950 Ultrasonic guidance for placement of radiation therapy fields

76965 Ultrasonic guidance for interstitial radioelement application

Other Procedures

76970 Ultrasound study follow-up (specify)

76975 Gastrointestinal endoscopic ultrasound, supervision and interpretation

(Do not report 76975 in conjunction with 43231, 43232, 43237, 43238, 43242, 43259, 45341, 45342, or 76942)

76977 Ultrasound bone density measurement and interpretation, peripheral site(s), any method

76986 Ultrasonic guidance, intraoperative

(Do not report 76986 in addition to 47370-47382)

(For ultrasound guidance for open and laparoscopic radiofrequency tissue ablation, use 76940)

76999 Unlisted ultrasound procedure (eg, diagnostic, interventional)

Radiation Oncology

Listings for Radiation Oncology provide for teletherapy and brachytherapy to include initial consultation, clinical treatment planning, simulation, medical radiation physics, dosimetry, treatment devices, special services, and clinical treatment management procedures. They include normal follow-up care during course of treatment and for three months following its completion.

When a service or procedure is provided that is not listed in this edition of the CPT codebook it should be identified by a Special Report (see page 228) and one of the following unlisted procedure codes:

77299 Unlisted procedure, therapeutic radiology clinical treatment planning

77399 Unlisted procedure, medical radiation physics, dosimetry and treatment devices, and special services

77499 Unlisted procedure, therapeutic radiology treatment management

77799 Unlisted procedure, clinical brachytherapy

For treatment by injectable or ingestible isotopes, see subsection **Nuclear Medicine.**

Consultation: Clinical Management

Preliminary consultation, evaluation of patient prior to decision to treat, or full medical care (in addition to treatment management) when provided by the therapeutic radiologist may be identified by the appropriate procedure codes from **Evaluation and Management, Medicine,** or **Surgery** sections.

Clinical Treatment Planning (External and Internal Sources)

The clinical treatment planning process is a complex service including interpretation of special testing, tumor localization, treatment volume determination, treatment time/dosage determination, choice of treatment modality, determination of number and size of treatment ports, selection of appropriate treatment devices, and other procedures.

Definitions

Simple planning requires a single treatment area of interest encompassed in a single port or simple parallel opposed ports with simple or no blocking.

Intermediate planning requires three or more converging ports, two separate treatment areas, multiple blocks, or special time dose constraints.

Complex planning requires highly complex blocking, custom shielding blocks, tangential ports, special wedges or compensators, three or more separate treatment areas, rotational or special beam considerations, combination of therapeutic modalities.

77261	Therapeutic radiology treatment planning; simple
77262	intermediate
77263	complex

Definitions

Simple simulation of a single treatment area with either a single port or parallel opposed ports. Simple or no blocking.

Intermediate simulation of three or more converging ports, two separate treatment areas, multiple blocks.

Complex simulation of tangential portals, three or more treatment areas, rotation or arc therapy, complex blocking, custom shielding blocks, brachytherapy source verification, hyperthermia probe verification, any use of contrast materials.

Three-dimensional (3D) computer-generated 3D reconstruction of tumor volume and surrounding critical normal tissue structures from direct CT scans and/or MRI data in preparation for non-coplanar or coplanar therapy. The simulation uses documented 3D beam's eye view volume-dose displays of multiple or moving beams. Documentation with 3D volume reconstruction and dose distribution is required.

Simulation may be carried out on a dedicated simulator, a radiation therapy treatment unit, or diagnostic X-ray machine.

77280	Therapeutic radiology simulation-aided field setting; simple
77285	intermediate
77290	complex
77295	3-dimensional
77299	Unlisted procedure, therapeutic radiology clinical treatment planning

Medical Radiation Physics, Dosimetry, Treatment Devices, and Special Services

77300	Basic radiation dosimetry calculation, central axis depth dose calculation, TDF, NSD, gap calculation, off axis factor, tissue inhomogeneity factors, calculation of non-ionizing radiation surface and depth dose, as required during course of treatment, only when prescribed by the treating physician

77301	Intensity modulated radiotherapy plan, including dose-volume histograms for target and critical structure partial tolerance specifications

(Dose plan is optimized using inverse or forward planning technique for modulated beam delivery (eg, binary, dynamic MLC) to create highly conformal dose distribution. Computer plan distribution must be verified for positional accuracy based on dosimetric verification of the intensity map with verification of treatment set-up and interpretation of verification methodology)

77305	Teletherapy, isodose plan (whether hand or computer calculated); simple (one or two parallel opposed unmodified ports directed to a single area of interest)
77310	intermediate (three or more treatment ports directed to a single area of interest)
77315	complex (mantle or inverted Y, tangential ports, the use of wedges, compensators, complex blocking, rotational beam, or special beam considerations)

(Only one teletherapy isodose plan may be reported for a given course of therapy to a specific treatment area)

77321	Special teletherapy port plan, particles, hemibody, total body
77326	Brachytherapy isodose plan; simple (calculation made from single plane, one to four sources/ribbon application, remote afterloading brachytherapy, 1 to 8 sources)

(For definition of source/ribbon, see page 248)

77327	intermediate (multiplane dosage calculations, application involving 5 to 10 sources/ribbons, remote afterloading brachytherapy, 9 to 12 sources)
77328	complex (multiplane isodose plan, volume implant calculations, over 10 sources/ribbons used, special spatial reconstruction, remote afterloading brachytherapy, over 12 sources)
77331	Special dosimetry (eg, TLD, microdosimetry) (specify), only when prescribed by the treating physician
77332	Treatment devices, design and construction; simple (simple block, simple bolus)
77333	intermediate (multiple blocks, stents, bite blocks, special bolus)
77334	complex (irregular blocks, special shields, compensators, wedges, molds or casts)
77336	Continuing medical physics consultation, including assessment of treatment parameters, quality assurance of dose delivery, and review of patient treatment documentation in support of the radiation oncologist, reported per week of therapy
77370	Special medical radiation physics consultation
77399	Unlisted procedure, medical radiation physics, dosimetry and treatment devices, and special services

Radiology

Radiation Treatment Delivery

(Radiation treatment delivery (77401-77416) recognizes the technical component and the various energy levels.)

(For stereotactic body radiation therapy treatment delivery, use Category III code 0082T)

77401 Radiation treatment delivery, superficial and/or ortho voltage

77402 Radiation treatment delivery, single treatment area, single port or parallel opposed ports, simple blocks or no blocks; up to 5 MeV

77403 6-10 MeV

77404 11-19 MeV

77406 20 MeV or greater

77407 Radiation treatment delivery, two separate treatment areas, three or more ports on a single treatment area, use of multiple blocks; up to 5 MeV

77408 6-10 MeV

77409 11-19 MeV

77411 20 MeV or greater

▲ **77412** Radiation treatment delivery, three or more separate treatment areas, custom blocking, tangential ports, wedges, rotational beam, compensators, electron beam; up to 5 MeV

77413 6-10 MeV

77414 11-19 MeV

77416 20 MeV or greater

77417 Therapeutic radiology port film(s)

77418 Intensity modulated treatment delivery, single or multiple fields/arcs, via narrow spatially and temporally modulated beams, binary, dynamic MLC, per treatment session

(For intensity modulated treatment planning, use 77301)

(For compensator-based beam modulation treatment delivery, use Category III code 0073T)

● **77421** Stereoscopic X-ray guidance for localization of target volume for the delivery of radiation therapy

►(Do not report 77421 in conjunction with 77432, 0083T)◄

►Neutron Beam Treatment Delivery◄

● **77422** High energy neutron radiation treatment delivery; single treatment area using a single port or parallel-opposed ports with no blocks or simple blocking

● **77423** 1 or more isocenter(s) with coplanar or non-coplanar geometry with blocking and/or wedge, and/or compensator(s)

Radiation Treatment Management

Radiation treatment management is reported in units of five fractions or treatment sessions, regardless of the actual time period in which the services are furnished. The services need not be furnished on consecutive days. Multiple fractions representing two or more treatment sessions furnished on the same day may be counted separately as long as there has been a distinct break in therapy sessions, and the fractions are of the character usually furnished on different days. Code 77427 is also reported if there are three or four fractions beyond a multiple of five at the end of a course of treatment; one or two fractions beyond a multiple of five at the end of a course of treatment are not reported separately. The professional services furnished during treatment management typically consist of:

■ Review of port films;

■ Review of dosimetry, dose delivery, and treatment parameters;

■ Review of patient treatment set-up;

■ Examination of patient for medical evaluation and management (eg, assessment of the patient's response to treatment, coordination of care and treatment, review of imaging and/or lab test results).

77427 Radiation treatment management, five treatments

77431 Radiation therapy management with complete course of therapy consisting of one or two fractions only

(77431 is not to be used to fill in the last week of a long course of therapy)

77432 Stereotactic radiation treatment management of cerebral lesion(s) (complete course of treatment consisting of one session)

(For stereotactic body radiation therapy treatment management, use Category III code 0083T)

77470 Special treatment procedure (eg, total body irradiation, hemibody radiation, per oral, endocavitary or intraoperative cone irradiation)

(77470 assumes that the procedure is performed one or more times during the course of therapy, in addition to daily or weekly patient management)

77499 Unlisted procedure, therapeutic radiology treatment management

Proton Beam Treatment Delivery

Definitions

Simple proton treatment delivery to a single treatment area utilizing a single non-tangential/oblique port, custom block with compensation (77522) and without compensation (77520).

Radiology

Intermediate proton treatment delivery to one or more treatment areas utilizing two or more ports or one or more tangential/oblique ports, with custom blocks and compensators.

Complex proton treatment delivery to one or more treatment areas utilizing two or more ports per treatment area with matching or patching fields and/or multiple isocenters, with custom blocks and compensators.

77520	Proton treatment delivery; simple, without compensation
77522	simple, with compensation
77523	intermediate
77525	complex

Hyperthermia

Hyperthermia treatments as listed in this section include external (superficial and deep), interstitial, and intracavitary.

Radiation therapy when given concurrently is listed separately.

Hyperthermia is used only as an adjunct to radiation therapy or chemotherapy. It may be induced by a variety of sources (eg, microwave, ultrasound, low energy radio-frequency conduction, or by probes).

The listed treatments include management during the course of therapy and follow-up care for three months after completion.

Preliminary consultation is not included (see **Evaluation and Management** 99241-99255).

Physics planning and interstitial insertion of temperature sensors, and use of external or interstitial heat generating sources are included.

The following descriptors are included in the treatment schedule:

⊙	**77600**	Hyperthermia, externally generated; superficial (ie, heating to a depth of 4 cm or less)
⊙	**77605**	deep (ie, heating to depths greater than 4 cm)
⊙	**77610**	Hyperthermia generated by interstitial probe(s); 5 or fewer interstitial applicators
⊙	**77615**	more than 5 interstitial applicators

Clinical Intracavitary Hyperthermia

77620	Hyperthermia generated by intracavitary probe(s)

Clinical Brachytherapy

Clinical brachytherapy requires the use of either natural or man-made radioelements applied into or around a treatment field of interest. The supervision of radioelements and dose interpretation are performed solely by the therapeutic radiologist.

Services 77750-77799 include admission to the hospital and daily visits.

For insertion of ovoids and tandems, use 57155.

For insertion of Heyman capsules, use 58346.

Definitions

(Sources refer to intracavitary placement or permanent interstitial placement; ribbons refer to temporary interstitial placement)

A simple application has one to four sources/ribbons.

An intermediate application has five to 10 sources/ribbons.

A complex application has greater than 10 sources/ribbons.

77750	Infusion or instillation of radioelement solution (includes 3 months follow-up care)
	(For administration of radiolabeled monoclonal antibodies, use 79403)
	(For non-antibody radiopharmaceutical therapy by intravenous administration only, not including 3-month follow-up care, use 79101)
77761	Intracavitary radiation source application; simple
77762	intermediate
77763	complex
77776	Interstitial radiation source application; simple
77777	intermediate
77778	complex
77781	Remote afterloading high intensity brachytherapy; 1-4 source positions or catheters
77782	5-8 source positions or catheters
77783	9-12 source positions or catheters
77784	over 12 source positions or catheters
77789	Surface application of radiation source
77790	Supervision, handling, loading of radiation source
77799	Unlisted procedure, clinical brachytherapy

Nuclear Medicine

Listed procedures may be performed independently or in the course of overall medical care. If the physician providing these services is also responsible for diagnostic work-up and/or follow-up care of patient, see appropriate sections also.

Radioimmunoassay tests are found in the **Clinical Pathology** section (codes 82000-84999). These codes can be appropriately used by any specialist performing such tests in a laboratory licensed and/or certified for radioimmunoassays. The reporting of these tests is not confined to clinical pathology laboratories alone.

►The services listed do not include the radiopharmaceutical or drug. Diagnostic and therapeutic radiopharmaceuticals and drugs supplied by the physician should be reported separately using the appropriate supply code(s), in addition to the procedure code.◄

Diagnostic

Endocrine System

78000	Thyroid uptake; single determination
78001	multiple determinations
78003	stimulation, suppression or discharge (not including initial uptake studies)
78006	Thyroid imaging, with uptake; single determination
78007	multiple determinations
78010	Thyroid imaging; only
78011	with vascular flow
78015	Thyroid carcinoma metastases imaging; limited area (eg, neck and chest only)
78016	with additional studies (eg, urinary recovery)
78018	whole body
+ **78020**	Thyroid carcinoma metastases uptake (List separately in addition to code for primary procedure)
	(Use 78020 in conjunction with 78018 only)
78070	Parathyroid imaging
78075	Adrenal imaging, cortex and/or medulla
78099	Unlisted endocrine procedure, diagnostic nuclear medicine
	(For chemical analysis, see **Chemistry** section)

Hematopoietic, Reticuloendothelial and Lymphatic System

78102	Bone marrow imaging; limited area
78103	multiple areas
78104	whole body
78110	Plasma volume, radiopharmaceutical volume-dilution technique (separate procedure); single sampling
78111	multiple samplings
78120	Red cell volume determination (separate procedure); single sampling
78121	multiple samplings
78122	Whole blood volume determination, including separate measurement of plasma volume and red cell volume (radiopharmaceutical volume-dilution technique)

78130	Red cell survival study;
78135	differential organ/tissue kinetics, (eg, splenic and/or hepatic sequestration)
78140	Labeled red cell sequestration, differential organ/tissue, (eg, splenic and/or hepatic)
	►(78160, 78162, 78170, 78172 have been deleted)◄
78185	Spleen imaging only, with or without vascular flow
	(If combined with liver study, use procedures 78215 and 78216)
78190	Kinetics, study of platelet survival, with or without differential organ/tissue localization
78191	Platelet survival study
78195	Lymphatics and lymph nodes imaging
	(For sentinel node identification without scintigraphy imaging, use 38792)
	(For sentinal node excision, see 38500-38542)
78199	Unlisted hematopoietic, reticuloendothelial and lymphatic procedure, diagnostic nuclear medicine
	(For chemical analysis, see **Chemistry** section)

Gastrointestinal System

78201	Liver imaging; static only
78202	with vascular flow
	(For spleen imaging only, use 78185)
78205	Liver imaging (SPECT);
78206	with vascular flow
78215	Liver and spleen imaging; static only
78216	with vascular flow
78220	Liver function study with hepatobiliary agents, with serial images
78223	Hepatobiliary ductal system imaging, including gallbladder, with or without pharmacologic intervention, with or without quantitative measurement of gallbladder function
78230	Salivary gland imaging;
78231	with serial images
78232	Salivary gland function study
78258	Esophageal motility
78261	Gastric mucosa imaging
78262	Gastroesophageal reflux study
78264	Gastric emptying study
78267	Urea breath test, C-14 (isotopic); acquisition for analysis
78268	analysis

Radiology

78270   Vitamin B-12 absorption study (eg, Schilling test); without intrinsic factor

78271   with intrinsic factor

78272   Vitamin B-12 absorption studies combined, with and without intrinsic factor

78278   Acute gastrointestinal blood loss imaging

78282   Gastrointestinal protein loss

78290   Intestine imaging (eg, ectopic gastric mucosa, Meckel's localization, volvulus)

78291   Peritoneal-venous shunt patency test (eg, for LeVeen, Denver shunt)

         (For injection procedure, use 49427)

78299   Unlisted gastrointestinal procedure, diagnostic nuclear medicine

Musculoskeletal System

Bone and joint imaging can be used in the diagnosis of a variety of inflammatory processes (eg, osteomyelitis), as well as for localization of primary and/or metastatic neoplasms.

78300   Bone and/or joint imaging; limited area

78305   multiple areas

78306   whole body

78315   three phase study

78320   tomographic (SPECT)

78350   Bone density (bone mineral content) study, one or more sites; single photon absorptiometry

78351   dual photon absorptiometry, one or more sites

         (For radiographic bone density (photodensitometry), use 76078)

78399   Unlisted musculoskeletal procedure, diagnostic nuclear medicine

Cardiovascular System

Myocardial perfusion and cardiac blood pool imaging studies may be performed at rest and/or during stress. When performed during exercise and/or pharmacologic stress, the appropriate stress testing code from the 93015-93018 series should be reported in addition to 78460-78465, 78472-78492.

78414   Determination of central c-v hemodynamics (non-imaging) (eg, ejection fraction with probe technique) with or without pharmacologic intervention or exercise, single or multiple determinations

78428   Cardiac shunt detection

78445   Non-cardiac vascular flow imaging (ie, angiography, venography)

         ▶(78455 has been deleted)◀

78456   Acute venous thrombosis imaging, peptide

78457   Venous thrombosis imaging, venogram; unilateral

78458   bilateral

78459   Myocardial imaging, positron emission tomography (PET), metabolic evaluation

         (For myocardial perfusion study, see 78491-78492)

78460   Myocardial perfusion imaging; (planar) single study, at rest or stress (exercise and/or pharmacologic), with or without quantification

78461   multiple studies, (planar) at rest and/or stress (exercise and/or pharmacologic), and redistribution and/or rest injection, with or without quantification

78464   tomographic (SPECT), single study (including attenuation correction when performed), at rest or stress (exercise and/or pharmacologic), with or without quantification

78465   tomographic (SPECT), multiple studies (including attenuation correction when performed), at rest and/or stress (exercise and/or pharmacologic) and redistribution and/or rest injection, with or without quantification

78466   Myocardial imaging, infarct avid, planar; qualitative or quantitative

78468   with ejection fraction by first pass technique

78469   tomographic SPECT with or without quantification

78472   Cardiac blood pool imaging, gated equilibrium; planar, single study at rest or stress (exercise and/or pharmacologic), wall motion study plus ejection fraction, with or without additional quantitative processing

         ▶(For assessment of right ventricular ejection fraction by first pass technique, use 78496)◀

78473   multiple studies, wall motion study plus ejection fraction, at rest and stress (exercise and/or pharmacologic), with or without additional quantification

+ 78478   Myocardial perfusion study with wall motion, qualitative or quantitative study (List separately in addition to code for primary procedure)

         (Use 78478 in conjunction with 78460, 78461, 78464, 78465)

+ 78480   Myocardial perfusion study with ejection fraction (List separately in addition to code for primary procedure)

         (Use 78480 in conjunction with 78460, 78461, 78464, 78465)

78481   Cardiac blood pool imaging, (planar), first pass technique; single study, at rest or with stress (exercise and/or pharmacologic), wall motion study plus ejection fraction, with or without quantification

78483   multiple studies, at rest and with stress (exercise and/or pharmacologic), wall motion study plus ejection fraction, with or without quantification

         (For cerebral blood flow study, use 78615)

Radiology

78491 Myocardial imaging, positron emission tomography (PET), perfusion; single study at rest or stress

78492 multiple studies at rest and/or stress

78494 Cardiac blood pool imaging, gated equilibrium, SPECT, at rest, wall motion study plus ejection fraction, with or without quantitative processing

+ **78496** Cardiac blood pool imaging, gated equilibrium, single study, at rest, with right ventricular ejection fraction by first pass technique (List separately in addition to code for primary procedure)

(Use 78496 in conjunction with 78472)

78499 Unlisted cardiovascular procedure, diagnostic nuclear medicine

Respiratory System

78580 Pulmonary perfusion imaging, particulate

78584 Pulmonary perfusion imaging, particulate, with ventilation; single breath

78585 rebreathing and washout, with or without single breath

78586 Pulmonary ventilation imaging, aerosol; single projection

78587 multiple projections (eg, anterior, posterior, lateral views)

78588 Pulmonary perfusion imaging, particulate, with ventilation imaging, aerosol, one or multiple projections

78591 Pulmonary ventilation imaging, gaseous, single breath, single projection

78593 Pulmonary ventilation imaging, gaseous, with rebreathing and washout with or without single breath; single projection

78594 multiple projections (eg, anterior, posterior, lateral views)

78596 Pulmonary quantitative differential function (ventilation/perfusion) study

78599 Unlisted respiratory procedure, diagnostic nuclear medicine

Nervous System

78600 Brain imaging, limited procedure; static

78601 with vascular flow

78605 Brain imaging, complete study; static

78606 with vascular flow

78607 tomographic (SPECT)

78608 Brain imaging, positron emission tomography (PET); metabolic evaluation

78609 perfusion evaluation

78610 Brain imaging, vascular flow only

78615 Cerebral vascular flow

78630 Cerebrospinal fluid flow, imaging (not including introduction of material); cisternography

(For injection procedure, see 61000-61070, 62270-62319)

78635 ventriculography

(For injection procedure, see 61000-61070, 62270-62294)

78645 shunt evaluation

(For injection procedure, see 61000-61070, 62270-62294)

78647 tomographic (SPECT)

78650 Cerebrospinal fluid leakage detection and localization

(For injection procedure, see 61000-61070, 62270-62294)

78660 Radiopharmaceutical dacryocystography

78699 Unlisted nervous system procedure, diagnostic nuclear medicine

Genitourinary System

78700 Kidney imaging; static only

78701 with vascular flow

78704 with function study (ie, imaging renogram)

78707 Kidney imaging with vascular flow and function; single study without pharmacological intervention

78708 single study, with pharmacological intervention (eg, angiotensin converting enzyme inhibitor and/or diuretic)

78709 multiple studies, with and without pharmacological intervention (eg, angiotensin converting enzyme inhibitor and/or diuretic)

78710 Kidney imaging, tomographic (SPECT)

78715 Kidney vascular flow only

78725 Kidney function study, non-imaging radioisotopic study

78730 Urinary bladder residual study

(For introduction of radioactive substance in association with cystotomy or cystostomy, use 51020; in association with cystourethroscopy, use 52250)

78740 Ureteral reflux study (radiopharmaceutical voiding cystogram)

(For catheterization, see 51701, 51702, 51703)

78760 Testicular imaging;

78761 with vascular flow

78799 Unlisted genitourinary procedure, diagnostic nuclear medicine

(For chemical analysis, see **Chemistry** section)

Other Procedures

(For specific organ, see appropriate heading)

(For radiophosphorus tumor identification, ocular, see 78800)

Radiology

78800 Radiopharmaceutical localization of tumor or distribution of radiopharmaceutical agent(s); limited area

(For specific organ, see appropriate heading)

78801 multiple areas

78802 whole body, single day imaging

78803 tomographic (SPECT)

78804 whole body, requiring two or more days imaging

78805 Radiopharmaceutical localization of inflammatory process; limited area

78806 whole body

78807 tomographic (SPECT)

(For imaging bone infectious or inflammatory disease with a bone imaging radiopharmaceutical, see 78300, 78305, 78306)

(78810 has been deleted. To report, see 78811-78813)

(For PET of brain, see 78608, 78609)

►(For PET myocardial imaging, see 78459, 78491, 78492)◄

78811 Tumor imaging, positron emission tomography (PET); limited area (eg, chest, head/neck)

78812 skull base to mid-thigh

78813 whole body

78814 Tumor imaging, positron emission tomography (PET) with concurrently acquired computed tomography (CT) for attenuation correction and anatomical localization; limited area (eg, chest, head/neck)

78815 skull base to mid-thigh

78816 whole body

(Report 78811-78816 only once per imaging session)

(Computed tomography (CT) performed for other than attenuation correction and anatomical localization is reported using the appropriate site specific CT code with modifier 59)

78890 Generation of automated data: interactive process involving nuclear physician and/or allied health professional personnel; simple manipulations and interpretation, not to exceed 30 minutes

78891 complex manipulations and interpretation, exceeding 30 minutes

(Use 78890 or 78891 in addition to primary procedure)

(78990 has been deleted)

78999 Unlisted miscellaneous procedure, diagnostic nuclear medicine

Therapeutic

The oral and intravenous administration codes in this section are inclusive of the mode of administration. For intra-arterial, intra-cavitary, and intra-articular administration, also use the appropriate injection and/or procedure codes, as well as imaging guidance and radiological supervision and interpretation codes, when appropriate.

(79000, 79001 have been deleted. To report, use 79005)

79005 Radiopharmaceutical therapy, by oral administration

(79020, 79030, 79035 have been deleted. To report, use 79005)

(79100 has been deleted. To report, use 79101)

(For monoclonal antibody therapy, use 79403)

79101 Radiopharmaceutical therapy, by intravenous administration

(Do not report 79101 in conjunction with 36400, 36410, 79403, 90760, 90774 or 90775, 96409)

(For radiolabeled monoclonal antibody by intravenous infusion, use 79403)

(For infusion or instillation of non-antibody radioelement solution that includes 3 months follow-up care, use 77750)

79200 Radiopharmaceutical therapy, by intracavitary administration

79300 Radiopharmaceutical therapy, by interstitial radioactive colloid administration

(79400 has been deleted. To report, use 79101)

79403 Radiopharmaceutical therapy, radiolabeled monoclonal antibody by intravenous infusion

(For pre-treatment imaging, see 78802, 78804)

(Do not report 79403 in conjunction with 79101)

(79420 has been deleted. To report use 79445)

79440 Radiopharmaceutical therapy, by intra-articular administration

79445 Radiopharmaceutical therapy, by intra-arterial particulate administration

(Do not report 79445 in conjunction with 90783, 96420)

(Use appropriate procedural and radiological supervision and interpretation codes for the angiographic and interventional procedures provided prerequisite to intra-arterial radiopharmaceutical therapy)

(79900 has been deleted)

79999 Radiopharmaceutical therapy, unlisted procedure

Radiology

Pathology and Laboratory Guidelines

Items used by all physicians in reporting their services are presented in the **Introduction.** Some of the commonalities are repeated here for the convenience of those physicians referring to this section on **Pathology and Laboratory.** Other definitions and items unique to Pathology and Laboratory are also listed.

Services in Pathology and Laboratory

Services in Pathology and Laboratory are provided by a physician or by technologists under responsible supervision of a physician.

Separate or Multiple Procedures

It is appropriate to designate multiple procedures that are rendered on the same date by separate entries.

Subsection Information

Several of the subheadings or subsections have special needs or instructions unique to that section. Where these are indicated (eg, "Panel Tests"), special **"Notes"** will be presented preceding those procedural terminology listings referring to that subsection specifically. If there is an "Unlisted Procedure" code number (see the following section) for the individual subsection, it will be shown. Those subsections with **"Notes"** are as follows:

Organ or Disease Panels 80048-80076
Drug Testing 80100-80103
Therapeutic Drug Assays 80150-80299
Evocative/Suppression Testing 80400-80440
Consultations
   (Clinical Pathology) 80500-80502
Urinalysis 81000-81099
Chemistry 82000-84999
Molecular Diagnostics 83890-83912
Infectious Agent: Detection
   of Antibodies 86602-86804
Microbiology 87001-87255
   Infectious Agent Detection 87260-87999
Anatomic Pathology 88000-88099
Cytopathology 88104-88199
Cytogenetic Studies 88230-88299
Surgical Pathology 88300-88399

Unlisted Service or Procedure

A service or procedure may be provided that is not listed in this edition of the CPT codebook. When reporting such a service, the appropriate "Unlisted Procedure" code may be used to indicate the service, identifying it by "Special Report" as discussed below. The "Unlisted Procedures" and accompanying codes for **Pathology and Laboratory** are as follows:

81099	Unlisted urinalysis procedure
84999	Unlisted chemistry procedure
85999	Unlisted hematology and coagulation procedure
86586	Unlisted antigen, each
86849	Unlisted immunology procedure
86999	Unlisted transfusion medicine procedure
87999	Unlisted microbiology procedure
88099	Unlisted necropsy (autopsy) procedure
88199	Unlisted cytopathology procedure
88299	Unlisted cytogenetic study
88399	Unlisted surgical pathology procedure
89240	Unlisted miscellaneous pathology test

Special Report

A service that is rarely provided, unusual, variable, or new may require a special report in determining medical appropriateness of the service. Pertinent information should include an adequate definition or description of the nature, extent, and need for the procedure; and the time, effort, and equipment necessary to provide the service. Additional items that may be included are:

- Complexity of symptoms
- Final diagnosis
- Pertinent physical findings
- Diagnostic and therapeutic procedures
- Concurrent problems
- Follow-up care

Notes

Pathology and Laboratory

Organ or Disease Oriented Panels

These panels were developed for coding purposes only and should not be interpreted as clinical parameters. The tests listed with each panel identify the defined components of that panel.

These panel components are not intended to limit the performance of other tests. If one performs tests in addition to those specifically indicated for a particular panel, those tests should be reported separately in addition to the panel code.

80048   Basic metabolic panel

This panel must include the following:

Calcium (82310)

Carbon dioxide (82374)

Chloride (82435)

Creatinine (82565)

Glucose (82947)

Potassium (84132)

Sodium (84295)

Urea nitrogen (BUN) (84520)

(Do not use 80048 in addition to 80053)

80050   General health panel

This panel must include the following:

Comprehensive metabolic panel (80053)

Blood count, complete (CBC), automated and automated differential WBC count (85025 or 85027 and 85004)

OR

Blood count, complete (CBC), automated (85027) and appropriate manual differential WBC count (85007 or 85009)

Thyroid stimulating hormone (TSH) (84443)

80051   Electrolyte panel

This panel must include the following:

Carbon dioxide (82374)

Chloride (82435)

Potassium (84132)

Sodium (84295)

80053   Comprehensive metabolic panel

This panel must include the following:

Albumin (82040)

Bilirubin, total (82247)

Calcium (82310)

Carbon dioxide (bicarbonate) (82374)

Chloride (82435)

Creatinine (82565)

Glucose (82947)

Phosphatase, alkaline (84075)

Potassium (84132)

Protein, total (84155)

Sodium (84295)

Transferase, alanine amino (ALT) (SGPT) (84460)

Transferase, aspartate amino (AST) (SGOT) (84450)

Urea nitrogen (BUN) (84520)

(Do not use 80053 in addition to 80048, 80076)

80055   Obstetric panel

This panel must include the following:

Blood count, complete (CBC), automated and automated differential WBC count (85025 or 85027 and 85004)

OR

Blood count, complete (CBC), automated (85027) and appropriate manual differential WBC count (85007 or 85009)

Hepatitis B surface antigen (HBsAg) (87340)

Antibody, rubella (86762)

Syphilis test, qualitative (eg, VDRL, RPR, ART) (86592)

Antibody screen, RBC, each serum technique (86850)

Blood typing, ABO (86900) AND

Blood typing, Rh (D) (86901)

80061   Lipid panel

This panel must include the following:

Cholesterol, serum, total (82465)

Lipoprotein, direct measurement, high density cholesterol (HDL cholesterol) (83718)

Triglycerides (84478)

80069   Renal function panel

This panel must include the following:

Albumin (82040)

Calcium (82310)

Carbon dioxide (bicarbonate) (82374)

Chloride (82435)

Creatinine (82565)

Glucose (82947)

Phosphorus inorganic (phosphate) (84100)

Potassium (84132)

Sodium (84295)

Urea nitrogen (BUN) (84520)

80074 Acute hepatitis panel

This panel must include the following:

Hepatitis A antibody (HAAb), IgM antibody (86709)

Hepatitis B core antibody (HBcAb), IgM antibody (86705)

Hepatitis B surface antigen (HBsAg) (87340)

Hepatitis C antibody (86803)

80076 Hepatic function panel

This panel must include the following:

Albumin (82040)

Bilirubin, total (82247)

Bilirubin, direct (82248)

Phosphatase, alkaline (84075)

Protein, total (84155)

Transferase, alanine amino (ALT) (SGPT) (84460)

Transferase, aspartate amino (AST) (SGOT) (84450)

(Do not use 80076 in addition to 80053)

Drug Testing

The following list contains examples of drugs or classes of drugs that are commonly assayed by qualitative screen, followed by confirmation with a second method:

- Alcohols
- Amphetamines
- Barbiturates
- Benzodiazepines
- Cocaine and metabolites
- Methadones
- Methaqualones
- Opiates
- Phencyclidines
- Phenothiazines
- Propoxyphenes
- Tetrahydrocannabinoids
- Tricyclic antidepressants

Confirmed drugs may also be quantitated.

Use 80100 for each multiple drug class chromatographic procedure. Use 80102 for each procedure necessary for confirmation. For chromatography, each combination of stationary and mobile phase is to be counted as one procedure. For example, if detection of three drugs by chromatography requires one stationary phase with three mobile phases, use 80100 three (3) times. However, if multiple drugs can be detected using a single analysis (eg, one stationary phase with one mobile phase), use 80100 only once.

For quantitation of drugs screened, use appropriate code in **Chemistry** section (82000-84999) or **Therapeutic Drug Assay** section (80150-80299).

80100 Drug screen, qualitative; multiple drug classes chromatographic method, each procedure

80101 single drug class method (eg, immunoassay, enzyme assay), each drug class

80102 Drug confirmation, each procedure

80103 Tissue preparation for drug analysis

Therapeutic Drug Assays

The material for examination may be from any source. Examination is quantitative. For nonquantitative testing, see Drug Testing (80100-80103).

80150 Amikacin

80152 Amitriptyline

80154 Benzodiazepines

80156 Carbamazepine; total

80157 free

80158 Cyclosporine

80160 Desipramine

80162 Digoxin

80164 Dipropylacetic acid (valproic acid)

80166 Doxepin

80168 Ethosuximide

80170 Gentamicin

80172 Gold

80173 Haloperidol

80174 Imipramine

80176 Lidocaine

80178 Lithium

80182 Nortriptyline

80184 Phenobarbital

80185 Phenytoin; total

80186 free

80188	Primidone
80190	Procainamide;
80192	with metabolites (eg, n-acetyl procainamide)
80194	Quinidine
● **80195**	Sirolimus
80196	Salicylate
80197	Tacrolimus
80198	Theophylline
80200	Tobramycin
80201	Topiramate
80202	Vancomycin
80299	Quantitation of drug, not elsewhere specified

Evocative/Suppression Testing

The following test panels involve the administration of evocative or suppressive agents, and the baseline and subsequent measurement of their effects on chemical constituents. These codes are to be used for the reporting of the laboratory component of the overall testing protocol. For the physician's administration of the evocative or suppressive agents, see 90760, 90761, 90772-90774, 90775; for the supplies and drugs, see 99070. To report physician attendance and monitoring during the testing, use the appropriate evaluation and management code, including the prolonged physician care codes if required. Prolonged physician care codes are not separately reported when evocative/suppression testing involves prolonged infusions reported with 90760-90761. In the code descriptors where reference is made to a particular analyte (eg, Cortisol (82533 x 2)) the "x 2" refers to the number of times the test for that particular analyte is performed.

80400   ACTH stimulation panel; for adrenal insufficiency

This panel must include the following:

Cortisol (82533 x 2)

80402   for 21 hydroxylase deficiency

This panel must include the following:

Cortisol (82533 x 2)

17 hydroxyprogesterone (83498 x 2)

80406   for 3 beta-hydroxydehydrogenase deficiency

This panel must include the following:

Cortisol (82533 x 2)

17 hydroxypregnenolone (84143 x 2)

80408   Aldosterone suppression evaluation panel (eg, saline infusion)

This panel must include the following:

Aldosterone (82088 x 2)

Renin (84244 x 2)

80410   Calcitonin stimulation panel (eg, calcium, pentagastrin)

This panel must include the following:

Calcitonin (82308 x 3)

80412   Corticotropic releasing hormone (CRH) stimulation panel

This panel must include the following:

Cortisol (82533 x 6)

Adrenocorticotropic hormone (ACTH) (82024 x 6)

80414   Chorionic gonadotropin stimulation panel; testosterone response

This panel must include the following:

Testosterone (84403 x 2 on three pooled blood samples)

80415   estradiol response

This panel must include the following:

Estradiol (82670 x 2 on three pooled blood samples)

80416   Renal vein renin stimulation panel (eg, captopril)

This panel must include the following:

Renin (84244 x 6)

80417   Peripheral vein renin stimulation panel (eg, captopril)

This panel must include the following:

Renin (84244 x 2)

80418   Combined rapid anterior pituitary evaluation panel

This panel must include the following:

Adrenocorticotropic hormone (ACTH) (82024 x 4)

Luteinizing hormone (LH) (83002 x 4)

Follicle stimulating hormone (FSH) (83001 x 4)

Prolactin (84146 x 4)

Human growth hormone (HGH) (83003 x 4)

Cortisol (82533 x 4)

Thyroid stimulating hormone (TSH) (84443 x 4)

80420   Dexamethasone suppression panel, 48 hour

This panel must include the following:

Free cortisol, urine (82530 x 2)

Cortisol (82533 x 2)

Volume measurement for timed collection (81050 x 2)

(For single dose dexamethasone, use 82533)

Pathology and Laboratory

80422 Glucagon tolerance panel; for insulinoma

This panel must include the following:

Glucose (82947 x 3)

Insulin (83525 x 3)

80424 for pheochromocytoma

This panel must include the following:

Catecholamines, fractionated (82384 x 2)

80426 Gonadotropin releasing hormone stimulation panel

This panel must include the following:

Follicle stimulating hormone (FSH) (83001 x 4)

Luteinizing hormone (LH) (83002 x 4)

80428 Growth hormone stimulation panel (eg, arginine infusion, l-dopa administration)

This panel must include the following:

Human growth hormone (HGH) (83003 x 4)

80430 Growth hormone suppression panel (glucose administration)

This panel must include the following:

Glucose (82947 x 3)

Human growth hormone (HGH) (83003 x 4)

80432 Insulin-induced C-peptide suppression panel

This panel must include the following:

Insulin (83525)

C-peptide (84681 x 5)

Glucose (82947 x 5)

80434 Insulin tolerance panel; for ACTH insufficiency

This panel must include the following:

Cortisol (82533 x 5)

Glucose (82947 x 5)

80435 for growth hormone deficiency

This panel must include the following:

Glucose (82947 x 5)

Human growth hormone (HGH) (83003 x 5)

80436 Metyrapone panel

This panel must include the following:

Cortisol (82533 x 2)

11 deoxycortisol (82634 x 2)

80438 Thyrotropin releasing hormone (TRH) stimulation panel; one hour

This panel must include the following:

Thyroid stimulating hormone (TSH) (84443 x 3)

80439 two hour

This panel must include the following:

Thyroid stimulating hormone (TSH) (84443 x 4)

80440 for hyperprolactinemia

This panel must include the following:

Prolactin (84146 x 3)

Consultations (Clinical Pathology)

A clinical pathology consultation is a service, including a written report, rendered by the pathologist in response to a request from an attending physician in relation to a test result(s) requiring additional medical interpretive judgment.

Reporting of a test result(s) without medical interpretive judgment is not considered a clinical pathology consultation.

80500 Clinical pathology consultation; limited, without review of patient's history and medical records

80502 comprehensive, for a complex diagnostic problem, with review of patient's history and medical records

(These codes may also be used for pharmacokinetic consultations)

(For consultations involving the examination and evaluation of the patient, see 99241-99255)

Urinalysis

For specific analyses, see appropriate section.

(For urinalysis, infectious agent detection, semi-quantitative analysis of volatile compounds, use Category III code 0041T)

81000 Urinalysis, by dip stick or tablet reagent for bilirubin, glucose, hemoglobin, ketones, leukocytes, nitrite, pH, protein, specific gravity, urobilinogen, any number of these constituents; non-automated, with microscopy

81001 automated, with microscopy

81002 non-automated, without microscopy

81003 automated, without microscopy

81005 Urinalysis; qualitative or semiquantitative, except immunoassays

(For non-immunoassay reagent strip urinalysis, see 81000, 81002)

(For immunoassay, qualitative or semiquantitative, use 83518)

(For microalbumin, see 82043, 82044)

81007	bacteriuria screen, except by culture or dipstick

(For culture, see 87086-87088)

(For dipstick, use 81000 or 81002)

81015	microscopic only
81020	two or three glass test
81025	Urine pregnancy test, by visual color comparison methods
81050	Volume measurement for timed collection, each
81099	Unlisted urinalysis procedure

Chemistry

The material for examination may be from any source unless otherwise specified in the code descriptor. When an analyte is measured in multiple specimens from different sources, or in specimens that are obtained at different times, the analyte is reported separately for each source and for each specimen. The examination is quantitative unless specified. To report an organ or disease oriented panel, see codes 80048-80076.

When a code describes a method where measurement of multiple analytes may require one or several procedures, each procedure is coded separately (eg, 82491-82492, 82541-82544). For example, if two (2) analytes are measured using column chromatography using a single stationary or mobile phase, use 82492. If the same two analytes are measured using different stationary or mobile phase conditions, 82491 would be used twice. If a total of four (4) analytes are measured where two (2) analytes are measured with a single stationary and mobile phase, and the other two (2) analytes are measured using a different stationary and mobile phase, use 82492 twice. If a total of three (3) analytes are measured where two (2) analytes are measured using a single stationary or mobile phase condition, and the third analyte is measured separately using a different stationary or mobile phase procedure, use 82492 once for the two (2) analytes measured under the same condition, and use 82491 once for the third analyte measured separately.

Clinical information derived from the results of laboratory data that is mathematically calculated (eg, free thyroxine index (T7)) is considered part of the test procedure and therefore is not a separately reportable service.

82000	Acetaldehyde, blood
82003	Acetaminophen
82009	Acetone or other ketone bodies, serum; qualitative
82010	quantitative
82013	Acetylcholinesterase

(Acid, gastric, see gastric acid, 82926, 82928)

(Acid phosphatase, see 84060-84066)

82016	Acylcarnitines; qualitative, each specimen
82017	quantitative, each specimen

(For carnitine, use 82379)

82024	Adrenocorticotropic hormone (ACTH)
82030	Adenosine, 5-monophosphate, cyclic (cyclic AMP)
82040	Albumin; serum
82042	urine or other source, quantitative, each specimen
82043	urine, microalbumin, quantitative
82044	urine, microalbumin, semiquantitative (eg, reagent strip assay)

(For prealbumin, use 84134)

82045	ischemia modified
82055	Alcohol (ethanol); any specimen except breath

(For other volatiles, alcohol, use 84600)

82075	breath
82085	Aldolase
82088	Aldosterone

(Alkaline phosphatase, see 84075, 84080)

82101	Alkaloids, urine, quantitative

(Alphaketoglutarate, see 82009, 82010)

(Alpha tocopherol (Vitamin E), use 84446)

82103	Alpha-1-antitrypsin; total
82104	phenotype
82105	Alpha-fetoprotein; serum
82106	amniotic fluid
82108	Aluminum
82120	Amines, vaginal fluid, qualitative

(For combined pH and amines test for vaginitis, use 82120 and 83986)

82127	Amino acids; single, qualitative, each specimen
82128	multiple, qualitative, each specimen
82131	single, quantitative, each specimen
82135	Aminolevulinic acid, delta (ALA)
82136	Amino acids, 2 to 5 amino acids, quantitative, each specimen
82139	Amino acids, 6 or more amino acids, quantitative, each specimen
82140	Ammonia
82143	Amniotic fluid scan (spectrophotometric)

(For L/S ratio, use 83661)

(Amobarbital, see 80100-80103 for qualitative analysis, 82205 for quantitative analysis)

82145   Amphetamine or methamphetamine

(For qualitative analysis, see 80100-80103)

82150   Amylase

82154   Androstanediol glucuronide

82157   Androstenedione

82160   Androsterone

82163   Angiotensin II

82164   Angiotensin I - converting enzyme (ACE)

(Antidiuretic hormone (ADH), use 84588)

(Antimony, use 83015)

(Antitrypsin, alpha-1-, see 82103, 82104)

82172   Apolipoprotein, each

82175   Arsenic

(For heavy metal screening, use 83015)

82180   Ascorbic acid (Vitamin C), blood

(Aspirin, see acetylsalicylic acid, 80196)

(Atherogenic index, blood, ultracentrifugation, quantitative, use 83701)

82190   Atomic absorption spectroscopy, each analyte

82205   Barbiturates, not elsewhere specified

(For qualitative analysis, see 80100-80103)

(For B-Natriuretic peptide, use 83880)

82232   Beta-2 microglobulin

(Bicarbonate, use 82374)

82239   Bile acids; total

82240   cholylglycine

(For bile pigments, urine, see 81000-81005)

82247   Bilirubin; total

82248   direct

82252   feces, qualitative

82261   Biotinidase, each specimen

▲ 82270   Blood, occult, by peroxidase activity (eg, guaiac), qualitative; feces, consecutive collected specimens with single determination, for colorectal neoplasm screening (ie, patient was provided three cards or single triple card for consecutive collection)

● 82271   other sources

● 82272   Blood, occult, by peroxidase activity (eg, guaiac), qualitative, feces, single specimen (eg, from digital rectal exam)

►(82273 has been deleted. To report, use 82271)◄

(Blood urea nitrogen (BUN), see 84520, 84525)

82274   Blood, occult, by fecal hemoglobin determination by immunoassay, qualitative, feces, 1-3 simultaneous determinations

82286   Bradykinin

82300   Cadmium

82306   Calcifediol (25-OH Vitamin D-3)

82307   Calciferol (Vitamin D)

(For 1,25-Dihydroxyvitamin D, use 82652)

82308   Calcitonin

82310   Calcium; total

82330   ionized

82331   after calcium infusion test

82340   urine quantitative, timed specimen

82355   Calculus; qualitative analysis

82360   quantitative analysis, chemical

82365   infrared spectroscopy

82370   x-ray diffraction

(Carbamates, see individual listings)

82373   Carbohydrate deficient transferrin

82374   Carbon dioxide (bicarbonate)

(See also 82803)

82375   Carbon monoxide, (carboxyhemoglobin); quantitative

82376   qualitative

(To report end-tidal carbon monoxide, use Category III code 0043T)

82378   Carcinoembryonic antigen (CEA)

82379   Carnitine (total and free), quantitative, each specimen

(For acylcarnitine, see 82016, 82017)

82380   Carotene

82382   Catecholamines; total urine

82383   blood

82384   fractionated

(For urine metabolites, see 83835, 84585)

82387   Cathepsin-D

82390   Ceruloplasmin

82397   Chemiluminescent assay

82415   Chloramphenicol

82435   Chloride; blood

82436   urine

82438   other source

(For sweat collection by iontophoresis, use 89230)

82441	Chlorinated hydrocarbons, screen
	(Chlorpromazine, use 84022)
	(Cholecalciferol (Vitamin D), use 82307)
82465	Cholesterol, serum or whole blood, total
	(For high density lipoprotein (HDL), use 83718)
82480	Cholinesterase; serum
82482	RBC
82485	Chondroitin B sulfate, quantitative
	(Chorionic gonadotropin, see gonadotropin, 84702, 84703)
82486	Chromatography, qualitative; column (eg, gas liquid or HPLC), analyte not elsewhere specified
82487	paper, 1-dimensional, analyte not elsewhere specified
82488	paper, 2-dimensional, analyte not elsewhere specified
82489	thin layer, analyte not elsewhere specified
82491	Chromatography, quantitative, column (eg, gas liquid or HPLC); single analyte not elsewhere specified, single stationary and mobile phase
82492	multiple analytes, single stationary and mobile phase
82495	Chromium
82507	Citrate
82520	Cocaine or metabolite
	(Cocaine, qualitative analysis, see 80100-80103)
	(Codeine, qualitative analysis, see 80100-80103)
	(Codeine, quantitative analysis, see 82101)
	(Complement, see 86160-86162)
82523	Collagen cross links, any method
82525	Copper
	(Coproporphyrin, see 84119, 84120)
	(Corticosteroids, use 83491)
82528	Corticosterone
82530	Cortisol; free
82533	total
	(C-peptide, use 84681)
82540	Creatine
82541	Column chromatography/mass spectrometry (eg, GC/MS, or HPLC/MS), analyte not elsewhere specified; qualitative, single stationary and mobile phase
82542	quantitative, single stationary and mobile phase
82543	stable isotope dilution, single analyte, quantitative, single stationary and mobile phase
82544	stable isotope dilution, multiple analytes, quantitative, single stationary and mobile phase

82550	Creatine kinase (CK), (CPK); total
82552	isoenzymes
82553	MB fraction only
82554	isoforms
82565	Creatinine; blood
82570	other source
82575	clearance
82585	Cryofibrinogen
82595	Cryoglobulin, qualitative or semi-quantitative (eg, cryocrit)
	(For quantitative, cryoglobulin, see 82784, 82785)
	(Crystals, pyrophosphate vs. urate, use 89060)
82600	Cyanide
82607	Cyanocobalamin (Vitamin B-12);
82608	unsaturated binding capacity
	(Cyclic AMP, use 82030)
	(Cyclic GMP, use 83008)
	(Cyclosporine, use 80158)
82615	Cystine and homocystine, urine, qualitative
82626	Dehydroepiandrosterone (DHEA)
82627	Dehydroepiandrosterone-sulfate (DHEA-S)
	(Delta-aminolevulinic acid (ALA), use 82135)
82633	Desoxycorticosterone, 11-
82634	Deoxycortisol, 11-
	(Dexamethasone suppression test, use 80420)
	(Diastase, urine, use 82150)
82638	Dibucaine number
	(Dichloroethane, use 84600)
	(Dichloromethane, use 84600)
	(Diethylether, use 84600)
82646	Dihydrocodeinone
	(For qualitative analysis, see 80100-80103)
82649	Dihydromorphinone
	(For qualitative analysis, see 80100-80103)
82651	Dihydrotestosterone (DHT)
82652	Dihydroxyvitamin D, 1,25-
82654	Dimethadione
	(For qualitative analysis, see 80100-80103)
	(Diphenylhydantoin, use 80185)
	(Dipropylacetic acid, use 80164)

Pathology and Laboratory

(Dopamine, see 82382-82384)

(Duodenal contents, see individual enzymes; for intubation and collection, use 89100)

82656 Elastase, pancreatic (EL-1), fecal, qualitative or semi-quantitative

82657 Enzyme activity in blood cells, cultured cells, or tissue, not elsewhere specified; nonradioactive substrate, each specimen

82658 radioactive substrate, each specimen

82664 Electrophoretic technique, not elsewhere specified

(Endocrine receptor assays, see 84233-84235)

82666 Epiandrosterone

(Epinephrine, see 82382-82384)

82668 Erythropoietin

82670 Estradiol

82671 Estrogens; fractionated

82672 total

(Estrogen receptor assay, use 84233)

82677 Estriol

82679 Estrone

(Ethanol, see 82055 and 82075)

82690 Ethchlorvynol

(Ethyl alcohol, see 82055 and 82075)

82693 Ethylene glycol

82696 Etiocholanolone

(For fractionation of ketosteroids, use 83593)

82705 Fat or lipids, feces; qualitative

82710 quantitative

82715 Fat differential, feces, quantitative

82725 Fatty acids, nonesterified

82726 Very long chain fatty acids

▶(For long-chain (C20-22) omega-3 fatty acids in red blood cell (RBC) membranes, use Category III code 0111T)◀

82728 Ferritin

(Fetal hemoglobin, see hemoglobin 83030, 83033, and 85460)

(Fetoprotein, alpha-1, see 82105, 82106)

82731 Fetal fibronectin, cervicovaginal secretions, semi-quantitative

82735 Fluoride

82742 Flurazepam

(For qualitative analysis, see 80100-80103)

(Foam stability test, use 83662)

82746 Folic acid; serum

82747 RBC

(Follicle stimulating hormone (FSH), use 83001)

82757 Fructose, semen

(Fructosamine, use 82985)

(Fructose, TLC screen, use 84375)

82759 Galactokinase, RBC

82760 Galactose

82775 Galactose-1-phosphate uridyl transferase; quantitative

82776 screen

82784 Gammaglobulin; IgA, IgD, IgG, IgM, each

82785 IgE

(For allergen specific IgE, see 86003, 86005)

82787 immunoglobulin subclasses, (IgG1, 2, 3, or 4), each

(Gamma-glutamyltransferase (GGT), use 82977)

82800 Gases, blood, pH only

82803 Gases, blood, any combination of pH, pCO_2, pO_2, CO_2, HCO_3 (including calculated O_2 saturation);

(Use 82803 for two or more of the above listed analytes)

82805 with O_2 saturation, by direct measurement, except pulse oximetry

82810 Gases, blood, O_2 saturation only, by direct measurement, except pulse oximetry

(For pulse oximetry, use 94760)

82820 Hemoglobin-oxygen affinity (pO_2 for 50% hemoglobin saturation with oxygen)

82926 Gastric acid, free and total, each specimen

82928 Gastric acid, free or total, each specimen

82938 Gastrin after secretin stimulation

82941 Gastrin

(Gentamicin, use 80170)

(GGT, use 82977)

(GLC, gas liquid chromatography, use 82486)

82943 Glucagon

82945 Glucose, body fluid, other than blood

82946 Glucagon tolerance test

82947 Glucose; quantitative, blood (except reagent strip)

82948 blood, reagent strip

82950 post glucose dose (includes glucose)

82951 tolerance test (GTT), three specimens (includes glucose)

82952 tolerance test, each additional beyond three specimens

82953 tolbutamide tolerance test

(For insulin tolerance test, see 80434, 80435)

(For leucine tolerance test, use 80428)

(For semiquantitative urine glucose, see 81000, 81002, 81005, 81099)

82955 Glucose-6-phosphate dehydrogenase (G6PD); quantitative

82960 screen

(For glucose tolerance test with medication, use 90784 in addition)

82962 Glucose, blood by glucose monitoring device(s) cleared by the FDA specifically for home use

82963 Glucosidase, beta

82965 Glutamate dehydrogenase

82975 Glutamine (glutamic acid amide)

82977 Glutamyltransferase, gamma (GGT)

82978 Glutathione

82979 Glutathione reductase, RBC

82980 Glutethimide

(Glycohemoglobin, use 83036)

82985 Glycated protein

(Gonadotropin, chorionic, see 84702, 84703)

83001 Gonadotropin; follicle stimulating hormone (FSH)

83002 luteinizing hormone (LH)

(For luteinizing releasing factor (LRH), use 83727)

83003 Growth hormone, human (HGH) (somatotropin)

(For antibody to human growth hormone, use 86277)

83008 Guanosine monophosphate (GMP), cyclic

83009 Helicobacter pylori, blood test analysis for urease activity, non-radioactive isotope (eg, C-13)

(For H. pylori, breath test analysis for urease activity, see 83013, 83014)

83010 Haptoglobin; quantitative

83012 phenotypes

83013 Helicobacter pylori; breath test analysis for urease activity, non-radioactive isotope (eg, C-13)

83014 drug administration

(For H. pylori, stool, use 87338. For H. pylori, liquid scintillation counter, see 78267, 78268. For H. pylori, enzyme immunoassay, use 87339)

(For H. pylori, blood test analysis for urease activity, use 83009)

83015 Heavy metal (eg, arsenic, barium, beryllium, bismuth, antimony, mercury); screen

83018 quantitative, each

83020 Hemoglobin fractionation and quantitation; electrophoresis (eg, A2, S, C, and/or F)

83021 chromatography (eg, A2, S, C, and/or F)

83026 Hemoglobin; by copper sulfate method, non-automated

83030 F (fetal), chemical

83033 F (fetal), qualitative

▲ **83036** glycosylated (A1C)

(For fecal hemoglobin detection by immunoassay, use 82274)

● **83037** glycosylated (A1C) by device cleared by FDA for home use

83045 methemoglobin, qualitative

83050 methemoglobin, quantitative

83051 plasma

83055 sulfhemoglobin, qualitative

83060 sulfhemoglobin, quantitative

83065 thermolabile

83068 unstable, screen

83069 urine

83070 Hemosiderin; qualitative

83071 quantitative

(Heroin, see 80100-80103)

(HIAA, use 83497)

(High performance liquid chromatography (HPLC), use 82486)

83080 b-Hexosaminidase, each assay

83088 Histamine

(Hollander test, use 91052)

83090 Homocysteine

83150 Homovanillic acid (HVA)

(Hormones, see individual alphabetic listings in **Chemistry** section)

(Hydrogen breath test, use 91065)

83491 Hydroxycorticosteroids, 17- (17-OHCS)

(For cortisol, see 82530, 82533. For deoxycortisol, use 82634)

83497 Hydroxyindolacetic acid, 5-(HIAA)

(For urine qualitative test, use 81005)

(5-Hydroxytryptamine, use 84260)

83498 Hydroxyprogesterone, 17-d

Pathology and Laboratory

83499	Hydroxyprogesterone, 20-
83500	Hydroxyproline; free
83505	total
83516	Immunoassay for analyte other than infectious agent antibody or infectious agent antigen, qualitative or semiquantitative; multiple step method
83518	single step method (eg, reagent strip)
83519	Immunoassay, analyte, quantitative; by radiopharmaceutical technique (eg, RIA)
83520	not otherwise specified

(For immunoassays for antibodies to infectious agent antigens, see analyte and method specific codes in the **Immunology** section)

(For immunoassay of tumor antigen not elsewhere specified, use 86316)

(Immunoglobulins, see 82784, 82785)

83525	Insulin; total

(For proinsulin, use 84206)

83527	free
83528	Intrinsic factor

(For intrinsic factor antibodies, use 86340)

83540	Iron
83550	Iron binding capacity
83570	Isocitric dehydrogenase (IDH)

(Isonicotinic acid hydrazide, INH, see code for specific method)

(Isopropyl alcohol, use 84600)

83582	Ketogenic steroids, fractionation

(Ketone bodies, for serum, see 82009, 82010; for urine, see 81000-81003)

83586	Ketosteroids, 17- (17-KS); total
83593	fractionation
83605	Lactate (lactic acid)
83615	Lactate dehydrogenase (LD), (LDH);
83625	isoenzymes, separation and quantitation
▲ 83630	Lactoferrin, fecal; qualitative
● 83631	quantitative
83632	Lactogen, human placental (HPL) human chorionic somatomammotropin
83633	Lactose, urine; qualitative
83634	quantitative

(For tolerance, see 82951, 82952)

(For breath hydrogen test for lactase deficiency, use 91065)

83655	Lead
83661	Fetal lung maturity assessment; lecithin sphingomyelin (L/S) ratio
83662	foam stability test
83663	fluorescence polarization
83664	lamellar body density

(For phosphatidylglycerol, use 84081)

83670	Leucine aminopeptidase (LAP)
83690	Lipase
● 83695	Lipoprotein (a)
● 83700	Lipoprotein, blood; electrophoretic separation and quantitation
● 83701	high resolution fractionation and quantitation of lipoproteins including lipoprotein subclasses when performed (eg, electrophoresis, ultracentrifugation)
● 83704	quantitation of lipoprotein particle numbers and lipoprotein particle subclasses (eg, by nuclear magnetic resonance spectroscopy)

►(83715, 83716 have been deleted. To report, use 83700, 83701)◄

83718	Lipoprotein, direct measurement; high density cholesterol (HDL cholesterol)
83719	VLDL cholesterol
83721	LDL cholesterol

►(For fractionation by high resolution electrophoresis or ultracentrifugation, use 83701)◄

►(For lipoprotein particle numbers and subclasses analysis by nuclear magnetic resonance spectroscopy, use 83695)◄

(To report direct measurement, intermediate density lipoproteins (remnant lipoproteins), use Category III code 0026T)

83727	Luteinizing releasing factor (LRH)

(Luteinizing hormone (LH), use 83002)

(For qualitative analysis, see 80100-80103)

(Macroglobulins, alpha-2, use 86329)

83735	Magnesium
83775	Malate dehydrogenase

(Maltose tolerance, see 82951, 82952)

(Mammotropin, use 84146)

83785	Manganese

(Marijuana, see 80100-80103)

83788	Mass spectrometry and tandem mass spectrometry (MS, MS/MS), analyte not elsewhere specified; qualitative, each specimen
83789	quantitative, each specimen

83805 Meprobamate

(For qualitative analysis, see 80100-80103)

83825 Mercury, quantitative

(Mercury screen, use 83015)

83835 Metanephrines

(For catecholamines, see 82382-82384)

83840 Methadone

(For methadone qualitative analysis, see 80100-80103)

(Methamphetamine, see 80100-80103, 82145)

(Methanol, use 84600)

83857 Methemalbumin

(Methemoglobin, see hemoglobin 83045, 83050)

83858 Methsuximide

(Methyl alcohol, use 84600)

(Microalbumin, see 82043 for quantitative, see 82044 for semiquantitative)

(Microglobulin, beta-2, use 82232)

83864 Mucopolysaccharides, acid; quantitative

83866   screen

83872 Mucin, synovial fluid (Ropes test)

83873 Myelin basic protein, cerebrospinal fluid

(For oligoclonal bands, use 83916)

83874 Myoglobin

(Nalorphine, use 83925)

83880 Natriuretic peptide

83883 Nephelometry, each analyte not elsewhere specified

83885 Nickel

83887 Nicotine

►Codes 83890-83914 are intended for use with molecular diagnostic techniques for analysis of nucleic acids.◄

►Codes 83890-83914 are coded by procedure rather than analyte.◄

Code separately for each procedure used in an analysis. For example, a procedure requiring isolation of DNA, restriction endonuclease digestion, electrophoresis, and nucleic acid probe amplification would be coded 83890, 83892, 83894, and 83898.

►When molecular diagnostic procedures are performed to test for oncology, hematology, neurology or inherited disorder, use the appropriate modifier to specify probe type or condition tested. (See **Appendix I** for a listing of appropriate modifiers to report with molecular diagnostic and cytogenetic procedures.)◄

(For microbial identification, see 87797, 87798)

►(For array technology using more than 10 probes, see 88384-88386)◄

83890 Molecular diagnostics; molecular isolation or extraction

83891   isolation or extraction of highly purified nucleic acid

83892   enzymatic digestion

83893   dot/slot blot production

83894   separation by gel electrophoresis (eg, agarose, polyacrylamide)

83896   nucleic acid probe, each

83897   nucleic acid transfer (eg, Southern, Northern)

▲ **83898**   amplification of patient nucleic acid, each nucleic acid sequence

● **83900**   amplification of patient nucleic acid, multiplex, first two nucleic acid sequences

+▲ **83901**   amplification of patient nucleic acid, multiplex, each additional nucleic acid sequence (List separately in addition to code for primary procedure)

►(Use 83901 in conjunction with 83900)◄

83902   reverse transcription

83903   mutation scanning, by physical properties (eg, single strand conformational polymorphisms (SSCP), heteroduplex, denaturing gradient gel electrophoresis (DGGE), RNA'ase A), single segment, each

83904   mutation identification by sequencing, single segment, each segment

83905   mutation identification by allele specific transcription, single segment, each segment

83906   mutation identification by allele specific translation, single segment, each segment

● **83907**   lysis of cells prior to nucleic acid extraction (eg, stool specimens, paraffin embedded tissue)

● **83908**   signal amplification of patient nucleic acid, each nucleic acid sequence

►(For multiplex amplification, see 83900, 83901)◄

● **83909**   separation and identification by high resolution technique (eg, capillary electrophoresis)

83912   interpretation and report

● **83914** Mutation identification by enzymatic ligation or primer extension, single segment, each segment (eg, oligonucleotide ligation assay (OLA), single base chain extension (SBCE), or allele-specific primer extension (ASPE))

83915 Nucleotidase 5'-

83916 Oligoclonal immune (oligoclonal bands)

83918 Organic acids; total, quantitative, each specimen

83919   qualitative, each specimen

83921 Organic acid, single, quantitative

▲=Revised code   ●=New code   ► ◄=Contains new or revised text

83925	Opiates, (eg, morphine, meperidine)
83930	Osmolality; blood
83935	urine
83937	Osteocalcin (bone g1a protein)
83945	Oxalate
83950	Oncoprotein, HER-2/neu
	(For tissue, see 88342, 88365)
83970	Parathormone (parathyroid hormone)
	(Pesticide, quantitative, see code for specific method. For screen for chlorinated hydrocarbons, use 82441)
83986	pH, body fluid, except blood
	(For blood pH, see 82800, 82803)
83992	Phencyclidine (PCP)
	(For qualitative analysis, see 80100-80103)
	(Phenobarbital, use 80184)
84022	Phenothiazine
	(For qualitative analysis, see 80100, 80101)
84030	Phenylalanine (PKU), blood
	(Phenylalanine-tyrosine ratio, see 84030, 84510)
84035	Phenylketones, qualitative
84060	Phosphatase, acid; total
84061	forensic examination
84066	prostatic
84075	Phosphatase, alkaline;
84078	heat stable (total not included)
84080	isoenzymes
84081	Phosphatidylglycerol
	(Phosphates inorganic, use 84100)
	(Phosphates, organic, see code for specific method. For cholinesterase, see 82480, 82482)
84085	Phosphogluconate, 6-, dehydrogenase, RBC
84087	Phosphohexose isomerase
84100	Phosphorus inorganic (phosphate);
84105	urine
	(Pituitary gonadotropins, see 83001-83002)
	(PKU, see 84030, 84035)
84106	Porphobilinogen, urine; qualitative
84110	quantitative
84119	Porphyrins, urine; qualitative
84120	quantitation and fractionation

84126	Porphyrins, feces; quantitative
84127	qualitative
	(Porphyrin precursors, see 82135, 84106, 84110)
	(For protoporphyrin, RBC, see 84202, 84203)
84132	Potassium; serum
84133	urine
84134	Prealbumin
	(For microalbumin, see 82043, 82044)
84135	Pregnanediol
84138	Pregnanetriol
84140	Pregnenolone
84143	17-hydroxypregnenolone
84144	Progesterone
	(Progesterone receptor assay, use 84234)
	(For proinsulin, use 84206)
84146	Prolactin
84150	Prostaglandin, each
84152	Prostate specific antigen (PSA); complexed (direct measurement)
84153	total
84154	free
84155	Protein, total, except by refractometry; serum
84156	urine
84157	other source (eg, synovial fluid, cerebrospinal fluid)
84160	Protein, total, by refractometry, any source
	(For urine total protein by dipstick method, use 81000-81003)
84163	Pregnancy-associated plasma protein-A (PAPP-A)
84165	Protein; electrophoretic fractionation and quantitation, serum
84166	electrophoretic fractionation and quantitation, other fluids with concentration (eg, urine, CSF)
84181	Western Blot, with interpretation and report, blood or other body fluid
84182	Western Blot, with interpretation and report, blood or other body fluid, immunological probe for band identification, each
	(For Western Blot tissue analysis, use 88371)
84202	Protoporphyrin, RBC; quantitative
84203	screen
84206	Proinsulin
	(Pseudocholinesterase, use 82480)
84207	Pyridoxal phosphate (Vitamin B-6)

Pathology and Laboratory

84210	Pyruvate
84220	Pyruvate kinase
84228	Quinine
84233	Receptor assay; estrogen
84234	progesterone
84235	endocrine, other than estrogen or progesterone (specify hormone)
▲ 84238	non-endocrine (specify receptor)
84244	Renin
84252	Riboflavin (Vitamin B-2)

(Salicylates, use 80196)

(Secretin test, see 99070, 89100 and appropriate analyses)

84255	Selenium
84260	Serotonin

(For urine metabolites (HIAA), use 83497)

84270	Sex hormone binding globulin (SHBG)
84275	Sialic acid

(Sickle hemoglobin, use 85660)

84285	Silica
84295	Sodium; serum
84300	urine
84302	other source

(Somatomammotropin, use 83632)

(Somatotropin, use 83003)

84305	Somatomedin
84307	Somatostatin
84311	Spectrophotometry, analyte not elsewhere specified
84315	Specific gravity (except urine)

(For specific gravity, urine, see 81000-81003)

(Stone analysis, see 82355-82370)

84375	Sugars, chromatographic, TLC or paper chromatography
84376	Sugars (mono-, di-, and oligosaccharides); single qualitative, each specimen
84377	multiple qualitative, each specimen
84378	single quantitative, each specimen
84379	multiple quantitative, each specimen
84392	Sulfate, urine

(Sulfhemoglobin, see hemoglobin, 83055, 83060)

(T-3, see 84479-84481)

(T-4, see 84436-84439)

84402	Testosterone; free
84403	total
84425	Thiamine (Vitamin B-1)
84430	Thiocyanate
84432	Thyroglobulin

(Thyroglobulin, antibody, use 86800)

(Thyrotropin releasing hormone (TRH) test, see 80438, 80439)

84436	Thyroxine; total
84437	requiring elution (eg, neonatal)
84439	free
84442	Thyroxine binding globulin (TBG)
84443	Thyroid stimulating hormone (TSH)
84445	Thyroid stimulating immune globulins (TSI)

(Tobramycin, use 80200)

84446	Tocopherol alpha (Vitamin E)

(Tolbutamide tolerance, use 82953)

84449	Transcortin (cortisol binding globulin)
84450	Transferase; aspartate amino (AST) (SGOT)
84460	alanine amino (ALT) (SGPT)
84466	Transferrin

(Iron binding capacity, use 83550)

84478	Triglycerides
84479	Thyroid hormone (T3 or T4) uptake or thyroid hormone binding ratio (THBR)
84480	Triiodothyronine T3; total (TT-3)
84481	free
84482	reverse
84484	Troponin, quantitative

(For troponin, qualitative assay, use 84512)

84485	Trypsin; duodenal fluid
84488	feces, qualitative
84490	feces, quantitative, 24-hour collection
84510	Tyrosine

(Urate crystal identification, use 89060)

84512	Troponin, qualitative

(For troponin, quantitative assay, use 84484)

84520	Urea nitrogen; quantitative
84525	semiquantitative (eg, reagent strip test)
84540	Urea nitrogen, urine
84545	Urea nitrogen, clearance

Pathology and Laboratory

84550 Uric acid; blood

84560   other source

84577 Urobilinogen, feces, quantitative

84578 Urobilinogen, urine; qualitative

84580   quantitative, timed specimen

84583   semiquantitative

(Uroporphyrins, use 84120)

(Valproic acid (dipropylacetic acid), use 80164)

84585 Vanillylmandelic acid (VMA), urine

84586 Vasoactive intestinal peptide (VIP)

84588 Vasopressin (antidiuretic hormone, ADH)

84590 Vitamin A

(Vitamin B-1, use 84425)

(Vitamin B-2, use 84252)

(Vitamin B-6, use 84207)

(Vitamin B-12, use 82607)

(Vitamin B-12, absorption (Schilling), see 78270, 78271)

(Vitamin C, use 82180)

(Vitamin D, see 82306, 82307, 82652)

(Vitamin E, use 84446)

84591 Vitamin, not otherwise specified

84597 Vitamin K

(VMA, use 84585)

84600 Volatiles (eg, acetic anhydride, carbon tetrachloride, dichloroethane, dichloromethane, diethylether, isopropyl alcohol, methanol)

(For acetaldehyde, use 82000)

(Volume, blood, RISA or Cr-51, see 78110, 78111)

84620 Xylose absorption test, blood and/or urine

(For administration, use 99070)

84630 Zinc

84681 C-peptide

84702 Gonadotropin, chorionic (hCG); quantitative

84703   qualitative

(For urine pregnancy test by visual color comparison, use 81025)

84830 Ovulation tests, by visual color comparison methods for human luteinizing hormone

84999 Unlisted chemistry procedure

Hematology and Coagulation

(For blood banking procedures, see **Transfusion Medicine**)

(Agglutinins, see **Immunology**)

(Antiplasmin, use 85410)

(Antithrombin III, see 85300, 85301)

85002 Bleeding time

85004 Blood count; automated differential WBC count

85007   blood smear, microscopic examination with manual differential WBC count

85008   blood smear, microscopic examination without manual differential WBC count

(For other fluids (eg, CSF), see 89050, 89051)

85009   manual differential WBC count, buffy coat

(Eosinophils, nasal smear, use 89190)

85013   spun microhematocrit

85014   hematocrit (Hct)

85018   hemoglobin (Hgb)

(For other hemoglobin determination, see 83020-83069)

(For immunoassay, hemoglobin, fecal, use 82274)

85025   complete (CBC), automated (Hgb, Hct, RBC, WBC and platelet count) and automated differential WBC count

85027   complete (CBC), automated (Hgb, Hct, RBC, WBC and platelet count)

85032   manual cell count (erythrocyte, leukocyte, or platelet) each

85041   red blood cell (RBC), automated

(Do not report code 85041 in conjunction with 85025 or 85027)

85044   reticulocyte, manual

85045   reticulocyte, automated

85046   reticulocytes, automated, including one or more cellular parameters (eg, reticulocyte hemoglobin content (CHr), immature reticulocyte fraction (IRF), reticulocyte volume (MRV), RNA content), direct measurement

85048   leukocyte (WBC), automated

85049   platelet, automated

85055 Reticulated platelet assay

85060 Blood smear, peripheral, interpretation by physician with written report

85097 Bone marrow, smear interpretation

(For special stains, see 88312, 88313)

(For bone biopsy, see 20220, 20225, 20240, 20245, 20250, 20251)

Pathology and Laboratory

85130   Chromogenic substrate assay

         (Circulating anti-coagulant screen (mixing studies), see 85611, 85732)

85170   Clot retraction

85175   Clot lysis time, whole blood dilution

         (Clotting factor I (fibrinogen), see 85384, 85385)

85210   Clotting; factor II, prothrombin, specific

         (See also 85610-85613)

85220   factor V (AcG or proaccelerin), labile factor

85230   factor VII (proconvertin, stable factor)

85240   factor VIII (AHG), one stage

85244   factor VIII related antigen

85245   factor VIII, VW factor, ristocetin cofactor

85246   factor VIII, VW factor antigen

85247   factor VIII, von Willebrand factor, multimetric analysis

85250   factor IX (PTC or Christmas)

85260   factor X (Stuart-Prower)

85270   factor XI (PTA)

85280   factor XII (Hageman)

85290   factor XIII (fibrin stabilizing)

85291   factor XIII (fibrin stabilizing), screen solubility

85292   prekallikrein assay (Fletcher factor assay)

85293   high molecular weight kininogen assay (Fitzgerald factor assay)

85300   Clotting inhibitors or anticoagulants; antithrombin III, activity

85301   antithrombin III, antigen assay

85302   protein C, antigen

85303   protein C, activity

85305   protein S, total

85306   protein S, free

85307   Activated Protein C (APC) resistance assay

85335   Factor inhibitor test

85337   Thrombomodulin

         (For mixing studies for inhibitors, use 85732)

85345   Coagulation time; Lee and White

85347   activated

85348   other methods

         (Differential count, see 85007 et seq)

         (Duke bleeding time, use 85002)

         (Eosinophils, nasal smear, use 89190)

85360   Euglobulin lysis

         (Fetal hemoglobin, see 83030, 83033, 85460)

85362   Fibrin(ogen) degradation (split) products (FDP)(FSP); agglutination slide, semiquantitative

         (Immunoelectrophoresis, use 86320)

85366   paracoagulation

85370   quantitative

85378   Fibrin degradation products, D-dimer; qualitative or semiquantitative

85379   quantitative

         (For ultrasensitive and standard sensitivity quantitative D-dimer, use 85379)

85380   ultrasensitive (eg, for evaluation for venous thromboembolism), qualitative or semiquantitative

85384   Fibrinogen; activity

85385   antigen

85390   Fibrinolysins or coagulopathy screen, interpretation and report

85396   Coagulation/fibrinolysis assay, whole blood (eg, viscoelastic clot assessment), including use of any pharmacologic additive(s), as indicated, including interpretation and written report, per day

85400   Fibrinolytic factors and inhibitors; plasmin

85410   alpha-2 antiplasmin

85415   plasminogen activator

85420   plasminogen, except antigenic assay

85421   plasminogen, antigenic assay

         (Fragility, red blood cell, see 85547, 85555-85557)

85441   Heinz bodies; direct

85445   induced, acetyl phenylhydrazine

         (Hematocrit (PCV), see 85014, 85025, 85027)

         (Hemoglobin, see 83020-83068, 85018, 85025, 85027)

85460   Hemoglobin or RBCs, fetal, for fetomaternal hemorrhage; differential lysis (Kleihauer-Betke)

         (See also 83030, 83033)

         (Hemolysins, see 86940, 86941)

85461   rosette

85475   Hemolysin, acid

         (See also 86940, 86941)

85520   Heparin assay

85525   Heparin neutralization

85530   Heparin-protamine tolerance test

85536   Iron stain, peripheral blood

         (For iron stains on bone marrow or other tissues with physician evaluation, use 88313)

Pathology and Laboratory

Pathology and Laboratory

85540	Leukocyte alkaline phosphatase with count
85547	Mechanical fragility, RBC
85549	Muramidase
	(Nitroblue tetrazolium dye test, use 86384)
85555	Osmotic fragility, RBC; unincubated
85557	incubated
	(Packed cell volume, use 85013)
	(Partial thromboplastin time, see 85730, 85732)
	(Parasites, blood (eg, malaria smears), use 87207)
	(Plasmin, use 85400)
	(Plasminogen, use 85420)
	(Plasminogen activator, use 85415)
85576	Platelet, aggregation (in vitro), each agent
85597	Platelet neutralization
85610	Prothrombin time;
85611	substitution, plasma fractions, each
85612	Russell viper venom time (includes venom); undiluted
85613	diluted
	(Red blood cell count, see 85025, 85027, 85041)
85635	Reptilase test
	(Reticulocyte count, see 85044, 85045)
85651	Sedimentation rate, erythrocyte; non-automated
85652	automated
85660	Sickling of RBC, reduction
	(Hemoglobin electrophoresis, use 83020)
	(Smears (eg, for parasites, malaria), use 87207)
85670	Thrombin time; plasma
85675	titer
85705	Thromboplastin inhibition, tissue
	(For individual clotting factors, see 85245-85247)
85730	Thromboplastin time, partial (PTT); plasma or whole blood
85732	substitution, plasma fractions, each
85810	Viscosity
	(von Willebrand factor assay, see 85245-85247)
	(WBC count, see 85025, 85027, 85048, 89050)
85999	Unlisted hematology and coagulation procedure

Immunology

► (Acetylcholine receptor antibody, see 83519, 86255, 86256) ◄

(Actinomyces, antibodies to, use 86602)

(Adrenal cortex antibodies, see 86255, 86256)

86000	Agglutinins, febrile (eg, Brucella, Francisella, Murine typhus, Q fever, Rocky Mountain spotted fever, scrub typhus), each antigen
	(For antibodies to infectious agents, see 86602-86804)
86001	Allergen specific IgG quantitative or semiquantitative, each allergen
	(Agglutinins and autohemolysins, see 86940, 86941)
86003	Allergen specific IgE; quantitative or semiquantitative, each allergen
	(For total quantitative IgE, use 82785)
86005	qualitative, multiallergen screen (dipstick, paddle or disk)
	(For total qualitative IgE, use 83518)
	(Alpha-1 antitrypsin, see 82103, 82104)
	(Alpha-1 feto-protein, see 82105, 82106)
	(Anti-AChR (acetylcholine receptor) antibody titer, see 86255, 86256)
	(Anticardiolipin antibody, use 86147)
	(Anti-DNA, use 86225)
	(Anti-deoxyribonuclease titer, use 86215)
86021	Antibody identification; leukocyte antibodies
86022	platelet antibodies
86023	platelet associated immunoglobulin assay
86038	Antinuclear antibodies (ANA);
86039	titer
	(Antistreptococcal antibody, ie, anti-DNAse, use 86215)
	(Antistreptokinase titer, use 86590)
86060	Antistreptolysin O; titer
	(For antibodies to infectious agents, see 86602-86804)
86063	screen
	(For antibodies to infectious agents, see 86602-86804)
	(Blastomyces, antibodies to, use 86612)
	► (86064 has been deleted. For B cells, total count, use 86355) ◄

86077   Blood bank physician services; difficult cross match and/or evaluation of irregular antibody(s), interpretation and written report

86078   investigation of transfusion reaction including suspicion of transmissible disease, interpretation and written report

86079   authorization for deviation from standard blood banking procedures (eg, use of outdated blood, transfusion of Rh incompatible units), with written report

(Brucella, antibodies to, use 86622)

(Candida, antibodies to, use 86628. For skin testing, use 86485)

86140   C-reactive protein;

(Candidiasis, use 86628)

86141   high sensitivity (hsCRP)

86146   Beta 2 Glycoprotein I antibody, each

86147   Cardiolipin (phospholipid) antibody, each Ig class

86148   Anti-phosphatidylserine (phospholipid) antibody

(To report antiprothrombin (phospholipid cofactor) antibody, use Category III code 0030T)

86155   Chemotaxis assay, specify method

(Clostridium difficile toxin, use 87230)

(Coccidioides, antibodies to, see 86635. For skin testing, use 86490)

86156   Cold agglutinin; screen

86157   titer

86160   Complement; antigen, each component

86161   functional activity, each component

86162   total hemolytic (CH50)

86171   Complement fixation tests, each antigen

(Coombs test, see 86880-86886)

86185   Counterimmunoelectrophoresis, each antigen

(Cryptococcus, antibodies to, use 86641)

● **86200**   Cyclic citrullinated peptide (CCP), antibody

86215   Deoxyribonuclease, antibody

86225   Deoxyribonucleic acid (DNA) antibody; native or double stranded

(Echinococcus, antibodies to, see code for specific method)

(For HIV antibody tests, see 86701-86703)

86226   single stranded

(Anti D.S., DNA, IFA, eg, using C.Lucilae, see 86255 and 86256)

86235   Extractable nuclear antigen, antibody to, any method (eg, nRNP, SS-A, SS-B, Sm, RNP, Sc170, J01), each antibody

86243   Fc receptor

(Filaria, antibodies to, see code for specific method)

86255   Fluorescent noninfectious agent antibody; screen, each antibody

86256   titer, each antibody

(Fluorescent technique for antigen identification in tissue, use 88346; for indirect fluorescence, use 88347)

(FTA, see 86781)

(Gel (agar) diffusion tests, use 86331)

86277   Growth hormone, human (HGH), antibody

86280   Hemagglutination inhibition test (HAI)

(For rubella, use 86762)

(For antibodies to infectious agents, see 86602-86804)

86294   Immunoassay for tumor antigen, qualitative or semiquantitative (eg, bladder tumor antigen)

86300   Immunoassay for tumor antigen, quantitative; CA 15-3 (27.29)

86301   CA 19-9

86304   CA 125

(For measurement of serum HER-2/neu oncoprotein, see 83950)

(For hepatitis delta agent, antibody, use 86692)

86308   Heterophile antibodies; screening

(For antibodies to infectious agents, see 86602-86804)

86309   titer

(For antibodies to infectious agents, see 86602-86804)

86310   titers after absorption with beef cells and guinea pig kidney

(Histoplasma, antibodies to, use 86698. For skin testing, use 86510)

(For antibodies to infectious agents, see 86602-86804)

(Human growth hormone antibody, use 86277)

86316   Immunoassay for tumor antigen, other antigen, quantitative (eg, CA 50, 72-4, 549), each

86317   Immunoassay for infectious agent antibody, quantitative, not otherwise specified

(For immunoassay techniques for antigens, see 83516, 83518, 83519, 83520, 87301-87450, 87810-87899)

(For particle agglutination procedures, use 86403)

86318   Immunoassay for infectious agent antibody, qualitative or semiquantitative, single step method (eg, reagent strip)

86320	Immunoelectrophoresis; serum
86325	other fluids (eg, urine, cerebrospinal fluid) with concentration
86327	crossed (2-dimensional assay)
86329	Immunodiffusion; not elsewhere specified
86331	gel diffusion, qualitative (Ouchterlony), each antigen or antibody
86332	Immune complex assay
86334	Immunofixation electrophoresis; serum
86335	other fluids with concentration (eg, urine, CSF)
86336	Inhibin A
86337	Insulin antibodies
86340	Intrinsic factor antibodies

(Leptospira, antibodies to, use 86720)

(Leukoagglutinins, use 86021)

86341	Islet cell antibody
86343	Leukocyte histamine release test (LHR)
86344	Leukocyte phagocytosis
86353	Lymphocyte transformation, mitogen (phytomitogen) or antigen induced blastogenesis

(Malaria antibodies, use 86750)

● 86355	B cells, total count
● 86357	Natural killer (NK) cells, total count
86359	T cells; total count
86360	absolute CD4 and CD8 count, including ratio
86361	absolute CD4 count
● 86367	Stem cells (ie, CD34), total count

►(For flow cytometric immunophenotyping for the assessment of potential hematolymphoid neoplasia, see 88184-88189)◄

86376	Microsomal antibodies (eg, thyroid or liver-kidney), each
86378	Migration inhibitory factor test (MIF)

(Mitochondrial antibody, liver, see 86255, 86256)

(Mononucleosis, see 86308-86310)

►(86379 has been deleted. For natural killer cells, total count, use 86357)◄

86382	Neutralization test, viral
86384	Nitroblue tetrazolium dye test (NTD)

(Ouchterlony diffusion, use 86331)

(Platelet antibodies, see 86022, 86023)

86403	Particle agglutination; screen, each antibody
86406	titer, each antibody

(Pregnancy test, see 84702, 84703)

(Rapid plasma reagin test (RPR), see 86592, 86593)

86430	Rheumatoid factor; qualitative
86431	quantitative

(Serologic test for syphilis, see 86592, 86593)

● 86480	Tuberculosis test, cell mediated immunity measurement of gamma interferon antigen response
86485	Skin test; candida

(For antibody, candida, use 86628)

86490	coccidioidomycosis
86510	histoplasmosis

(For histoplasma, antibody, use 86698)

86580	tuberculosis, intradermal

►(For tuberculosis test, cell mediated immunity measurement of gamma interferon antigen response, use 86480)◄

►(86585 has been deleted. To report tuberculosis testing by intradermal (Mantoux) test, use 86580)◄

(For skin tests for allergy, see 95010-95199)

(Smooth muscle antibody, see 86255, 86256)

(Sporothrix, antibodies to, see code for specific method)

86586	Unlisted antigen, each

►(86587 has been deleted. For stem cells, total count, use 86367)◄

86590	Streptokinase, antibody

(For antibodies to infectious agents, see 86602-86804)

(Streptolysin O antibody, see antistreptolysin O, 86060, 86063)

86592	Syphilis test; qualitative (eg, VDRL, RPR, ART)

(For antibodies to infectious agents, see 86602-86804)

86593	quantitative

(For antibodies to infectious agents, see 86602-86804)

(Tetanus antibody, use 86774)

(Thyroglobulin antibody, use 86800)

(Thyroglobulin, use 84432)

(Thyroid microsomal antibody, use 86376)

(For toxoplasma antibody, see 86777-86778)

The following codes (86602-86804) are qualitative or semiquantitative immunoassays performed by multiple step methods for the detection of antibodies to infectious agents. For immunoassays by single step method (eg, reagent strips), use code 86318. Procedures for the identification of antibodies should be coded as precisely

Pathology and Laboratory

as possible. For example, an antibody to a virus could be coded with increasing specificity for virus, family, genus, species, or type. In some cases, further precision may be added to codes by specifying the class of immunoglobulin being detected. When multiple tests are done to detect antibodies to organisms classified more precisely than the specificity allowed by available codes, it is appropriate to code each as a separate service. For example, a test for antibody to an enterovirus is coded as 86658. Coxsackie viruses are enteroviruses, but there are no codes for the individual species of enterovirus. If assays are performed for antibodies to coxsackie A and B species, each assay should be separately coded. Similarly, if multiple assays are performed for antibodies of different immunoglobulin classes, each assay should be coded separately.

(For the detection of antibodies other than those to infectious agents, see specific antibody (eg, 86021, 86022, 86023, 86376, 86800, 86850-86870) or specific method (eg, 83516, 86255, 86256)).

(For infectious agent/antigen detection, see 87260-87899)

86602	Antibody; actinomyces
86603	adenovirus
86606	Aspergillus
86609	bacterium, not elsewhere specified
86611	Bartonella
86612	Blastomyces
86615	Bordetella
86617	Borrelia burgdorferi (Lyme disease) confirmatory test (eg, Western Blot or immunoblot)
86618	Borrelia burgdorferi (Lyme disease)
86619	Borrelia (relapsing fever)
86622	Brucella
86625	Campylobacter
86628	Candida

(For skin test, candida, use 86485)

86631	Chlamydia
86632	Chlamydia, IgM

(For chlamydia antigen, see 87270, 87320. For fluorescent antibody technique, see 86255, 86256)

86635	Coccidioides
86638	Coxiella burnetii (Q fever)
86641	Cryptococcus
86644	cytomegalovirus (CMV)
86645	cytomegalovirus (CMV), IgM
86648	Diphtheria
86651	encephalitis, California (La Crosse)

86652	encephalitis, Eastern equine
86653	encephalitis, St. Louis
86654	encephalitis, Western equine
86658	enterovirus (eg, coxsackie, echo, polio)

(Trichinella, antibodies to, use 86784)

(Trypanosoma, antibodies to, see code for specific method)

(Tuberculosis, use 86580 for skin testing)

(Viral antibodies, see code for specific method)

86663	Epstein-Barr (EB) virus, early antigen (EA)
86664	Epstein-Barr (EB) virus, nuclear antigen (EBNA)
86665	Epstein-Barr (EB) virus, viral capsid (VCA)
86666	Ehrlichia
86668	Francisella tularensis
86671	fungus, not elsewhere specified
86674	Giardia lamblia
86677	Helicobacter pylori
86682	helminth, not elsewhere specified
86684	Haemophilus influenza
86687	HTLV-I
86688	HTLV-II
86689	HTLV or HIV antibody, confirmatory test (eg, Western Blot)
86692	hepatitis, delta agent

(For hepatitis delta agent, antigen, use 87380)

86694	herpes simplex, non-specific type test
86695	herpes simplex, type 1
86696	herpes simplex, type 2
86698	histoplasma
86701	HIV-1
86702	HIV-2
86703	HIV-1 and HIV-2, single assay

(For HIV-1 antigen, use 87390)

(For HIV-2 antigen, use 87391)

(For confirmatory test for HIV antibody (eg, Western Blot), use 86689)

86704	Hepatitis B core antibody (HBcAb); total
86705	IgM antibody
86706	Hepatitis B surface antibody (HBsAb)
86707	Hepatitis Be antibody (HBeAb)
86708	Hepatitis A antibody (HAAb); total
86709	IgM antibody

▲=Revised code   ●=New code   ▶ ◀=Contains new or revised text

86710	Antibody; influenza virus
86713	Legionella
86717	Leishmania
86720	Leptospira
86723	Listeria monocytogenes
86727	lymphocytic choriomeningitis
86729	lymphogranuloma venereum
86732	mucormycosis
86735	mumps
86738	mycoplasma
86741	Neisseria meningitidis
86744	Nocardia
86747	parvovirus
86750	Plasmodium (malaria)
86753	protozoa, not elsewhere specified
86756	respiratory syncytial virus
86757	Rickettsia
86759	rotavirus
86762	rubella
86765	rubeola
86768	Salmonella
86771	Shigella
86774	tetanus
86777	Toxoplasma
86778	Toxoplasma, IgM
86781	Treponema pallidum, confirmatory test (eg, FTA-abs)
86784	Trichinella
86787	varicella-zoster
86790	virus, not elsewhere specified
86793	Yersinia
86800	Thyroglobulin antibody

(For thyroglobulin, use 84432)

86803	Hepatitis C antibody;
86804	confirmatory test (eg, immunoblot)

Tissue Typing

(For pretransplant cross-match, see appropriate code or codes)

86805	Lymphocytotoxicity assay, visual crossmatch; with titration
86806	without titration

86807	Serum screening for cytotoxic percent reactive antibody (PRA); standard method
86808	quick method
86812	HLA typing; A, B, or C (eg, A10, B7, B27), single antigen
86813	A, B, or C, multiple antigens
86816	DR/DQ, single antigen
86817	DR/DQ, multiple antigens
86821	lymphocyte culture, mixed (MLC)
86822	lymphocyte culture, primed (PLC)
86849	Unlisted immunology procedure

Transfusion Medicine

(For apheresis, use 36511, 36512)

(For therapeutic phlebotomy, use 99195)

86850	Antibody screen, RBC, each serum technique
86860	Antibody elution (RBC), each elution
86870	Antibody identification, RBC antibodies, each panel for each serum technique
86880	Antihuman globulin test (Coombs test); direct, each antiserum
86885	indirect, qualitative, each antiserum
86886	indirect, titer, each antiserum
86890	Autologous blood or component, collection processing and storage; predeposited
86891	intra- or postoperative salvage

(For physician services to autologous donors, see 99201-99204)

86900	Blood typing; ABO
86901	Rh (D)
86903	antigen screening for compatible blood unit using reagent serum, per unit screened
86904	antigen screening for compatible unit using patient serum, per unit screened
86905	RBC antigens, other than ABO or Rh (D), each
86906	Rh phenotyping, complete
86910	Blood typing, for paternity testing, per individual; ABO, Rh and MN
86911	each additional antigen system
86920	Compatibility test each unit; immediate spin technique
86921	incubation technique
86922	antiglobulin technique
● 86923	electronic

▶(Do not use 86923 in conjunction with 86920-86922 for same unit crossmatch)◀

86927	Fresh frozen plasma, thawing, each unit
86930	Frozen blood, each unit; freezing (includes preparation)
86931	thawing
86932	freezing (includes preparation) and thawing
86940	Hemolysins and agglutinins; auto, screen, each
86941	incubated
86945	Irradiation of blood product, each unit
86950	Leukocyte transfusion

(For leukapheresis, use 36511)

● **86960**   Volume reduction of blood or blood product (eg, red blood cells or platelets), each unit

86965   Pooling of platelets or other blood products

86970   Pretreatment of RBCs for use in RBC antibody detection, identification, and/or compatibility testing; incubation with chemical agents or drugs, each

86971   incubation with enzymes, each

86972   by density gradient separation

86975   Pretreatment of serum for use in RBC antibody identification; incubation with drugs, each

86976   by dilution

86977   incubation with inhibitors, each

86978   by differential red cell absorption using patient RBCs or RBCs of known phenotype, each absorption

86985   Splitting of blood or blood products, each unit

86999   Unlisted transfusion medicine procedure

Microbiology

Includes bacteriology, mycology, parasitology, and virology.

Presumptive identification of microorganisms is defined as identification by colony morphology, growth on selective media, Gram stains, or up to three tests (eg, catalase, oxidase, indole, urease). Definitive identification of microorganisms is defined as an identification to the genus or species level that requires additional tests (eg, biochemical panels, slide cultures). If additional studies involve molecular probes, chromatography, or immunologic techniques, these should be separately coded in addition to definitive identification codes (87140-87158). For multiple specimens/sites use modifier 59. For repeat laboratory tests performed on the same day, use modifier 91.

87001   Animal inoculation, small animal; with observation

87003   with observation and dissection

87015   Concentration (any type), for infectious agents

(Do not report 87015 in conjunction with 87177)

87040   Culture, bacterial; blood, aerobic, with isolation and presumptive identification of isolates (includes anaerobic culture, if appropriate)

87045   stool, aerobic, with isolation and preliminary examination (eg, KIA, LIA), Salmonella and Shigella species

87046   stool, aerobic, additional pathogens, isolation and presumptive identification of isolates, each plate

87070   any other source except urine, blood or stool, aerobic, with isolation and presumptive identification of isolates

(For urine, use 87088)

87071   quantitative, aerobic with isolation and presumptive identification of isolates, any source except urine, blood or stool

(For urine, use 87088)

87073   quantitative, anaerobic with isolation and presumptive identification of isolates, any source except urine, blood or stool

(For definitive identification of isolates, use 87076 or 87077. For typing of isolates see 87140-87158)

87075   any source, except blood, anaerobic with isolation and presumptive identification of isolates

87076   anaerobic isolate, additional methods required for definitive identification, each isolate

(For gas liquid chromatography (GLC) or high pressure liquid chromatography (HPLC), use 87143)

87077   aerobic isolate, additional methods required for definitive identification, each isolate

(For gas liquid chromatography (GLC) or high pressure liquid chromatography (HPLC), use 87143)

87081   Culture, presumptive, pathogenic organisms, screening only;

87084   with colony estimation from density chart

87086   Culture, bacterial; quantitative colony count, urine

87088   with isolation and presumptive identification of isolates, urine

87101   Culture, fungi (mold or yeast) isolation, with presumptive identification of isolates; skin, hair, or nail

87102   other source (except blood)

87103   blood

87106   Culture, fungi, definitive identification, each organism; yeast

(Use 87106 in addition to codes 87101, 87102, or 87103 when appropriate)

87107   mold

87109   Culture, mycoplasma, any source

Pathology and Laboratory

▲=Revised code   ●=New code   ▶ ◀=Contains new or revised text

87110 Culture, chlamydia, any source

(For immunofluorescence staining of shell vials, use 87140)

87116 Culture, tubercle or other acid-fast bacilli (eg, TB, AFB, mycobacteria) any source, with isolation and presumptive identification of isolates

(For concentration, use 87015)

87118 Culture, mycobacterial, definitive identification, each isolate

(For nucleic acid probe identification, use 87149)

(For GLC or HPLC identification, use 87143)

87140 Culture, typing; immunofluorescent method, each antiserum

87143 gas liquid chromatography (GLC) or high pressure liquid chromatography (HPLC) method

87147 immunologic method, other than immunofluoresence (eg, agglutination grouping), per antiserum

87149 identification by nucleic acid probe

87152 identification by pulse field gel typing

87158 other methods

87164 Dark field examination, any source (eg, penile, vaginal, oral, skin); includes specimen collection

87166 without collection

87168 Macroscopic examination; arthropod

87169 parasite

87172 Pinworm exam (eg, cellophane tape prep)

87176 Homogenization, tissue, for culture

87177 Ova and parasites, direct smears, concentration and identification

(Do not report 87177 in conjunction with 87015)

(For direct smears from a primary source, use 87207)

(For coccidia or microsporidia exam, use 87207)

►(For complex special stain (trichrome, iron hematoxylin), use 87209)◄

(For nucleic acid probes in cytologic material, use 88365)

(For molecular diagnostics, see 83890-83898, 87470-87799)

87181 Susceptibility studies, antimicrobial agent; agar dilution method, per agent (eg, antibiotic gradient strip)

87184 disk method, per plate (12 or fewer agents)

87185 enzyme detection (eg, beta lactamase), per enzyme

87186 microdilution or agar dilution (minimum inhibitory concentration (MIC) or breakpoint), each multi-antimicrobial, per plate

+ 87187 microdilution or agar dilution, minimum lethal concentration (MLC), each plate (List separately in addition to code for primary procedure)

(Use 87187 in conjunction with 87186 or 87188)

87188 macrobroth dilution method, each agent

87190 mycobacteria, proportion method, each agent

(For other mycobacterial susceptibility studies, see 87181, 87184, 87186, or 87188)

87197 Serum bactericidal titer (Schlicter test)

87205 Smear, primary source with interpretation; Gram or Giemsa stain for bacteria, fungi, or cell types

87206 fluorescent and/or acid fast stain for bacteria, fungi, parasites, viruses or cell types

87207 special stain for inclusion bodies or parasites (eg, malaria, coccidia, microsporidia, trypanosomes, herpes viruses)

(For direct smears with concentration and identification, use 87177)

(For thick smear preparation, use 87015)

(For fat, meat, fibers, nasal eosinophils, and starch, see miscellaneous section)

● **87209** complex special stain (eg, trichrome, iron hemotoxylin) for ova and parasites

87210 wet mount for infectious agents (eg, saline, India ink, KOH preps)

(For KOH examination of skin, hair or nails, see 87220)

87220 Tissue examination by KOH slide of samples from skin, hair, or nails for fungi or ectoparasite ova or mites (eg, scabies)

87230 Toxin or antitoxin assay, tissue culture (eg, Clostridium difficile toxin)

87250 Virus isolation; inoculation of embryonated eggs, or small animal, includes observation and dissection

87252 tissue culture inoculation, observation, and presumptive identification by cytopathic effect

87253 tissue culture, additional studies or definitive identification (eg, hemabsorption, neutralization, immunofluoresence stain), each isolate

(Electron microscopy, use 88348)

(Inclusion bodies in tissue sections, see 88304-88309; in smears, see 87207-87210; in fluids, use 88106)

87254 centrifuge enhanced (shell vial) technique, includes identification with immunofluorescence stain, each virus

(Report 87254 in addition to 87252 as appropriate)

87255 including identification by non-immunologic method, other than by cytopathic effect (eg, virus specific enzymatic activity)

These codes are intended for primary source only. For similar studies on culture material, refer to codes 87140-87158. Infectious agents by antigen detection, immunofluorescence microscopy, or nucleic acid probe techniques should be reported as precisely as possible. The most specific code possible should be reported. If there is no specific agent code, the general methodology code (eg, 87299, 87449, 87450, 87797, 87798, 87799, 87899) should be used. For identification of antibodies to many of the listed infectious agents, see 86602-86804. When separate assays are performed for different species or strain(s) of organisms, each assay should be reported separately.

87260 Infectious agent antigen detection by immunofluorescent technique; adenovirus

87265 Bordetella pertussis/parapertussis

87267 Enterovirus, direct fluorescent antibody (DFA)

87269 giardia

87270 Chlamydia trachomatis

87271 Cytomegalovirus, direct fluorescent antibody (DFA)

87272 cryptosporidium

87273 Herpes simplex virus type 2

87274 Herpes simplex virus type 1

87275 influenza B virus

87276 influenza A virus

87277 Legionella micdadei

87278 Legionella pneumophila

87279 Parainfluenza virus, each type

87280 respiratory syncytial virus

87281 Pneumocystis carinii

87283 Rubeola

87285 Treponema pallidum

87290 Varicella zoster virus

87299 not otherwise specified, each organism

87300 Infectious agent antigen detection by immunofluorescent technique, polyvalent for multiple organisms, each polyvalent antiserum

(For physician evaluation of infectious disease agents by immunofluorescence, use 88346)

87301 Infectious agent antigen detection by enzyme immunoassay technique, qualitative or semiquantitative, multiple step method; adenovirus enteric types 40/41

87320 Chlamydia trachomatis

87324 Clostridium difficile toxin(s)

87327 Cryptococcus neoformans

(For Cryptococcus latex agglutination, use 86403)

87328 cryptosporidium

87329 giardia

87332 cytomegalovirus

87335 Escherichia coli 0157

(For giardia antigen, use 87329)

87336 Entamoeba histolytica dispar group

87337 Entamoeba histolytica group

87338 Helicobacter pylori, stool

87339 Helicobacter pylori

(For H. pylori, stool, use 87338. For H. pylori, breath and blood by mass spectrometry, see 83013, 83014. For H. pylori, liquid scintillation counter, see 78267, 78268)

87340 hepatitis B surface antigen (HBsAg)

87341 hepatitis B surface antigen (HBsAg) neutralization

87350 hepatitis Be antigen (HBeAg)

87380 hepatitis, delta agent

87385 Histoplasma capsulatum

87390 HIV-1

87391 HIV-2

87400 Influenza, A or B, each

87420 respiratory syncytial virus

87425 rotavirus

87427 Shiga-like toxin

87430 Streptococcus, group A

87449 Infectious agent antigen detection by enzyme immunoassay technique qualitative or semiquantitative; multiple step method, not otherwise specified, each organism

87450 single step method, not otherwise specified, each organism

87451 multiple step method, polyvalent for multiple organisms, each polyvalent antiserum

87470 Infectious agent detection by nucleic acid (DNA or RNA); Bartonella henselae and Bartonella quintana, direct probe technique

87471 Bartonella henselae and Bartonella quintana, amplified probe technique

87472 Bartonella henselae and Bartonella quintana, quantification

87475 Borrelia burgdorferi, direct probe technique

87476 Borrelia burgdorferi, amplified probe technique

87477 Borrelia burgdorferi, quantification

87480 Candida species, direct probe technique

87481 Candida species, amplified probe technique

87482 Candida species, quantification

87485 Chlamydia pneumoniae, direct probe technique

Pathology and Laboratory

87486	Chlamydia pneumoniae, amplified probe technique
87487	Chlamydia pneumoniae, quantification
87490	Chlamydia trachomatis, direct probe technique
87491	Chlamydia trachomatis, amplified probe technique
87492	Chlamydia trachomatis, quantification
87495	cytomegalovirus, direct probe technique
87496	cytomegalovirus, amplified probe technique
87497	cytomegalovirus, quantification
87510	Gardnerella vaginalis, direct probe technique
87511	Gardnerella vaginalis, amplified probe technique
87512	Gardnerella vaginalis, quantification
87515	hepatitis B virus, direct probe technique
87516	hepatitis B virus, amplified probe technique
87517	hepatitis B virus, quantification
87520	hepatitis C, direct probe technique
87521	hepatitis C, amplified probe technique
87522	hepatitis C, quantification
87525	hepatitis G, direct probe technique
87526	hepatitis G, amplified probe technique
87527	hepatitis G, quantification
87528	Herpes simplex virus, direct probe technique
87529	Herpes simplex virus, amplified probe technique
87530	Herpes simplex virus, quantification
87531	Herpes virus-6, direct probe technique
87532	Herpes virus-6, amplified probe technique
87533	Herpes virus-6, quantification
87534	HIV-1, direct probe technique
87535	HIV-1, amplified probe technique
87536	HIV-1, quantification
87537	HIV-2, direct probe technique
87538	HIV-2, amplified probe technique
87539	HIV-2, quantification
87540	Legionella pneumophila, direct probe technique
87541	Legionella pneumophila, amplified probe technique
87542	Legionella pneumophila, quantification
87550	Mycobacteria species, direct probe technique
87551	Mycobacteria species, amplified probe technique
87552	Mycobacteria species, quantification
87555	Mycobacteria tuberculosis, direct probe technique
87556	Mycobacteria tuberculosis, amplified probe technique
87557	Mycobacteria tuberculosis, quantification

87560	Mycobacteria avium-intracellulare, direct probe technique
87561	Mycobacteria avium-intracellulare, amplified probe technique
87562	Mycobacteria avium-intracellulare, quantification
87580	Mycoplasma pneumoniae, direct probe technique
87581	Mycoplasma pneumoniae, amplified probe technique
87582	Mycoplasma pneumoniae, quantification
87590	Neisseria gonorrhoeae, direct probe technique
87591	Neisseria gonorrhoeae, amplified probe technique
87592	Neisseria gonorrhoeae, quantification
87620	papillomavirus, human, direct probe technique
87621	papillomavirus, human, amplified probe technique
87622	papillomavirus, human, quantification
87650	Streptococcus, group A, direct probe technique
87651	Streptococcus, group A, amplified probe technique
87652	Streptococcus, group A, quantification
87660	Trichomonas vaginalis, direct probe technique
87797	Infectious agent detection by nucleic acid (DNA or RNA), not otherwise specified; direct probe technique, each organism
87798	amplified probe technique, each organism
87799	quantification, each organism
87800	Infectious agent detection by nucleic acid (DNA or RNA), multiple organisms; direct probe(s) technique
87801	amplified probe(s) technique
87802	Infectious agent antigen detection by immunoassay with direct optical observation; Streptococcus, group B
87803	Clostridium difficile toxin A
87804	Influenza
87807	respiratory syncytial virus
87810	Infectious agent detection by immunoassay with direct optical observation; Chlamydia trachomatis
87850	Neisseria gonorrhoeae
87880	Streptococcus, group A
87899	not otherwise specified
● 87900	Infectious agent drug susceptibility phenotype prediction using regularly updated genotypic bioinformatics
87901	Infectious agent genotype analysis by nucleic acid (DNA or RNA); HIV 1, reverse transcriptase and protease
	►(For infectious agent drug susceptibility phenotype prediction for HIV-1, use 87900)◄
87902	Hepatitis C virus

⊘ =Modifier 51 exempt   ⊙ =Conscious sedation   ✦ =Add-on code   ✚ =FDA approval pending

87903 Infectious agent phenotype analysis by nucleic acid (DNA or RNA) with drug resistance tissue culture analysis, HIV 1; first through 10 drugs tested

+▲ **87904**   each additional drug tested (List separately in addition to code for primary procedure)

          (Use 87904 in conjunction with 87903)

87999 Unlisted microbiology procedure

Anatomic Pathology

Postmortem Examination

Procedures 88000 through 88099 represent physician services only. Use modifier 90 for outside laboratory services.

88000 Necropsy (autopsy), gross examination only; without CNS

88005   with brain

88007   with brain and spinal cord

88012   infant with brain

88014   stillborn or newborn with brain

88016   macerated stillborn

88020 Necropsy (autopsy), gross and microscopic; without CNS

88025   with brain

88027   with brain and spinal cord

88028   infant with brain

88029   stillborn or newborn with brain

88036 Necropsy (autopsy), limited, gross and/or microscopic; regional

88037   single organ

88040 Necropsy (autopsy); forensic examination

88045   coroner's call

88099 Unlisted necropsy (autopsy) procedure

Cytopathology

          (For cervicography, see Category III code 0003T)

          (For collection of cytology specimens via mammary duct catheter lavage, report 0045T-0046T)

88104 Cytopathology, fluids, washings or brushings, except cervical or vaginal; smears with interpretation

88106   filter method only with interpretation

88107   smears and filter preparation with interpretation

88108 Cytopathology, concentration technique, smears and interpretation (eg, Saccomanno technique)

          (For cervical or vaginal smears, see 88150-88155)

          (For gastric intubation with lavage, see 89130-89141, 91055)

          (For x-ray localization, use 74340)

88112 Cytopathology, selective cellular enhancement technique with interpretation (eg, liquid based slide preparation method), except cervical or vaginal

          (Do not report 88112 with 88108)

88125 Cytopathology, forensic (eg, sperm)

88130 Sex chromatin identification; Barr bodies

88140   peripheral blood smear, polymorphonuclear drumsticks

          (For Guard stain, use 88313)

▶Codes 88141-88155, 88164-88167, 88174-88175 are used to report cervical or vaginal screening by various methods and to report physician interpretation services. Use codes 88150-88154 to report conventional Pap smears that are examined using non-Bethesda reporting. Use codes 88164-88167 to report conventional Pap smears that are examined using the Bethesda System of reporting. Use codes 88142-88143 to report liquid-based specimens processed as thin-layer preparations that are examined using any system of reporting (Bethesda or non-Bethesda). Use codes 88174-88175 to report automated screening of liquid-based specimens that are examined using any system of reporting (Bethesda or non-Bethesda). Within each of these three code families choose the one code that describes the screening method(s) used. Codes 88141 and 88155 should be reported in addition to the screening code chosen when the additional services are provided. Manual rescreening requires a complete visual reassessment of the entire slide initially screened by either an automated or manual process. Manual review represents an assessment of selected cells or regions of a slide identified by initial automated review.◀

88141 Cytopathology, cervical or vaginal (any reporting system), requiring interpretation by physician

          (Use 88141 in conjunction with 88142-88154, 88164-88167, 88174-88175)

88142 Cytopathology, cervical or vaginal (any reporting system), collected in preservative fluid, automated thin layer preparation; manual screening under physician supervision

88143   with manual screening and rescreening under physician supervision

          (For automated screening of automated thin layer preparation, see 88174, 88175)

Pathology and Laboratory

88147   Cytopathology smears, cervical or vaginal; screening by automated system under physician supervision

88148   screening by automated system with manual rescreening under physician supervision

88150   Cytopathology, slides, cervical or vaginal; manual screening under physician supervision

88152   with manual screening and computer-assisted rescreening under physician supervision

88153   with manual screening and rescreening under physician supervision

88154   with manual screening and computer-assisted rescreening using cell selection and review under physician supervision

+ 88155   Cytopathology, slides, cervical or vaginal, definitive hormonal evaluation (eg, maturation index, karyopyknotic index, estrogenic index) (List separately in addition to code(s) for other technical and interpretation services)

(Use 88155 in conjunction with 88142-88154, 88164-88167, 88174-88175)

88160   Cytopathology, smears, any other source; screening and interpretation

88161   preparation, screening and interpretation

88162   extended study involving over 5 slides and/or multiple stains

(For aerosol collection of sputum, use 89220)

(For special stains, see 88312-88314)

88164   Cytopathology, slides, cervical or vaginal (the Bethesda System); manual screening under physician supervision

88165   with manual screening and rescreening under physician supervision

88166   with manual screening and computer-assisted rescreening under physician supervision

88167   with manual screening and computer-assisted rescreening using cell selection and review under physician supervision

(88170, 88171 have been deleted)

(To report collection of specimen via fine needle aspiration, see 10021, 10022)

88172   Cytopathology, evaluation of fine needle aspirate; immediate cytohistologic study to determine adequacy of specimen(s)

88173   interpretation and report

▶(For fine needle aspirate, see 10021, 10022)◀

▶(Do not report 88172, 88173 in conjunction with 88333 and 88334 for the same specimen)◀

88174   Cytopathology, cervical or vaginal (any reporting system), collected in preservative fluid, automated thin layer preparation; screening by automated system, under physician supervision

▲ 88175   with screening by automated system and manual rescreening or review, under physician supervision

(For manual screening, see 88142, 88143)

(88180 has been deleted. To report, see 88184-88189)

88182   Flow cytometry, cell cycle or DNA analysis

(For DNA ploidy analysis by morphometric technique, use 88358)

88184   Flow cytometry, cell surface, cytoplasmic, or nuclear marker, technical component only; first marker

+ 88185   each additional marker (List separately in addition to code for first marker)

(Report 88185 in conjunction with 88184)

88187   Flow cytometry, interpretation; 2 to 8 markers

88188   9 to 15 markers

88189   16 or more markers

88199   Unlisted cytopathology procedure

(For electron microscopy, see 88348, 88349)

Cytogenetic Studies

When molecular diagnostic procedures are performed to test for oncologic or inherited disorder, use the appropriate modifier to specify probe type or condition tested. (See **Appendix I** for a listing of appropriate modifiers to report with molecular diagnostic and cytogenetic procedures.)

(For acetylcholinesterase, use 82013)

(For alpha-fetoprotein, serum or amniotic fluid, see 82105, 82106)

(For laser microdissection of cells from tissue sample, see 88380)

88230   Tissue culture for non-neoplastic disorders; lymphocyte

88233   skin or other solid tissue biopsy

88235   amniotic fluid or chorionic villus cells

88237   Tissue culture for neoplastic disorders; bone marrow, blood cells

88239   solid tumor

88240   Cryopreservation, freezing and storage of cells, each cell line

(For therapeutic cryopreservation and storage, use 38207)

88241   Thawing and expansion of frozen cells, each aliquot

(For therapeutic thawing of previous harvest, use 38208)

⊘ =Modifier 51 exempt   ⊙ =Conscious sedation   ✚ =Add-on code   ⋌ =FDA approval pending

88245	Chromosome analysis for breakage syndromes; baseline Sister Chromatid Exchange (SCE), 20-25 cells
88248	baseline breakage, score 50-100 cells, count 20 cells, 2 karyotypes (eg, for ataxia telangiectasia, Fanconi anemia, fragile X)
88249	score 100 cells, clastogen stress (eg, diepoxybutane, mitomycin C, ionizing radiation, UV radiation)
88261	Chromosome analysis; count 5 cells, 1 karyotype, with banding
88262	count 15-20 cells, 2 karyotypes, with banding
88263	count 45 cells for mosaicism, 2 karyotypes, with banding
88264	analyze 20-25 cells
88267	Chromosome analysis, amniotic fluid or chorionic villus, count 15 cells, 1 karyotype, with banding
88269	Chromosome analysis, in situ for amniotic fluid cells, count cells from 6-12 colonies, 1 karyotype, with banding
88271	Molecular cytogenetics; DNA probe, each (eg, FISH)
88272	chromosomal in situ hybridization, analyze 3-5 cells (eg, for derivatives and markers)
88273	chromosomal in situ hybridization, analyze 10-30 cells (eg, for microdeletions)
88274	interphase in situ hybridization, analyze 25-99 cells
88275	interphase in situ hybridization, analyze 100-300 cells
88280	Chromosome analysis; additional karyotypes, each study
88283	additional specialized banding technique (eg, NOR, C-banding)
88285	additional cells counted, each study
88289	additional high resolution study
88291	Cytogenetics and molecular cytogenetics, interpretation and report
88299	Unlisted cytogenetic study

Surgical Pathology

Services 88300 through 88309 include accession, examination, and reporting. They do not include the services designated in codes 88311 through 88365 and 88399, which are coded in addition when provided.

The unit of service for codes 88300 through 88309 is the specimen.

A specimen is defined as tissue or tissues that is (are) submitted for individual and separate attention, requiring individual examination and pathologic diagnosis. Two or more such specimens from the same patient (eg, separately identified endoscopic biopsies, skin lesions) are each appropriately assigned an individual code reflective of its proper level of service.

Service code 88300 is used for any specimen that in the opinion of the examining pathologist can be accurately diagnosed without microscopic examination. Service code 88302 is used when gross and microscopic examination is performed on a specimen to confirm identification and the absence of disease. Service codes 88304 through 88309 describe all other specimens requiring gross and microscopic examination, and represent additional ascending levels of physician work. Levels 88302 through 88309 are specifically defined by the assigned specimens.

Any unlisted specimen should be assigned to the code which most closely reflects the physician work involved when compared to other specimens assigned to that code.

88300	**Level I** - Surgical pathology, gross examination only
88302	**Level II** - Surgical pathology, gross and microscopic examination

Appendix, Incidental

Fallopian Tube, Sterilization

Fingers/Toes, Amputation, Traumatic

Foreskin, Newborn

Hernia Sac, Any Location

Hydrocele Sac

Nerve

Skin, Plastic Repair

Sympathetic Ganglion

Testis, Castration

Vaginal Mucosa, Incidental

Vas Deferens, Sterilization

88304	**Level III** - Surgical pathology, gross and microscopic examination

Abortion, Induced

Abscess

Aneurysm - Arterial/Ventricular

Anus, Tag

Appendix, Other than Incidental

Artery, Atheromatous Plaque

Bartholin's Gland Cyst

Bone Fragment(s), Other than Pathologic Fracture

Bursa/Synovial Cyst

Carpal Tunnel Tissue

Cartilage, Shavings

Cholesteatoma

Colon, Colostomy Stoma

Conjunctiva - Biopsy/Pterygium

Cornea

Pathology and Laboratory

Pathology and Laboratory

Diverticulum - Esophagus/Small Intestine

Dupuytren's Contracture Tissue

Femoral Head, Other than Fracture

Fissure/Fistula

Foreskin, Other than Newborn

Gallbladder

Ganglion Cyst

Hematoma

Hemorrhoids

Hydatid of Morgagni

Intervertebral Disc

Joint, Loose Body

Meniscus

Mucocele, Salivary

Neuroma - Morton's/Traumatic

Pilonidal Cyst/Sinus

Polyps, Inflammatory - Nasal/Sinusoidal

Skin - Cyst/Tag/Debridement

Soft Tissue, Debridement

Soft Tissue, Lipoma

Spermatocele

Tendon/Tendon Sheath

Testicular Appendage

Thrombus or Embolus

Tonsil and/or Adenoids

Varicocele

Vas Deferens, Other than Sterilization

Vein, Varicosity

88305   Level IV - Surgical pathology, gross and microscopic examination

Abortion - Spontaneous/Missed

Artery, Biopsy

Bone Marrow, Biopsy

Bone Exostosis

Brain/Meninges, Other than for Tumor Resection

Breast, Biopsy, Not Requiring Microscopic Evaluation of Surgical Margins

Breast, Reduction Mammoplasty

Bronchus, Biopsy

Cell Block, Any Source

Cervix, Biopsy

Colon, Biopsy

Duodenum, Biopsy

Endocervix, Curettings/Biopsy

Endometrium, Curettings/Biopsy

Esophagus, Biopsy

Extremity, Amputation, Traumatic

Fallopian Tube, Biopsy

Fallopian Tube, Ectopic Pregnancy

Femoral Head, Fracture

Fingers/Toes, Amputation, Non-traumatic

Gingiva/Oral Mucosa, Biopsy

Heart Valve

Joint, Resection

Kidney, Biopsy

Larynx, Biopsy

Leiomyoma(s), Uterine Myomectomy - without Uterus

Lip, Biopsy/Wedge Resection

Lung, Transbronchial Biopsy

Lymph Node, Biopsy

Muscle, Biopsy

Nasal Mucosa, Biopsy

Nasopharynx/Oropharynx, Biopsy

Nerve, Biopsy

Odontogenic/Dental Cyst

Omentum, Biopsy

Ovary with or without Tube, Non-neoplastic

Ovary, Biopsy/Wedge Resection

Parathyroid Gland

Peritoneum, Biopsy

Pituitary Tumor

Placenta, Other than Third Trimester

Pleura/Pericardium - Biopsy/Tissue

Polyp, Cervical/Endometrial

Polyp, Colorectal

Polyp, Stomach/Small Intestine

Prostate, Needle Biopsy

Prostate, TUR

Salivary Gland, Biopsy

Sinus, Paranasal Biopsy

Skin, Other than Cyst/Tag/Debridement/Plastic Repair

Small Intestine, Biopsy

Soft Tissue, Other than Tumor/Mass/Lipoma/Debridement

Spleen

Stomach, Biopsy

Synovium

Testis, Other than Tumor/Biopsy/Castration

Thyroglossal Duct/Brachial Cleft Cyst

Tongue, Biopsy

Tonsil, Biopsy

Trachea, Biopsy

Ureter, Biopsy

Urethra, Biopsy

Urinary Bladder, Biopsy

Uterus, with or without Tubes and Ovaries, for Prolapse

Vagina, Biopsy

Vulva/Labia, Biopsy

88307   **Level V** - Surgical pathology, gross and microscopic examination

Adrenal, Resection

Bone - Biopsy/Curettings

Bone Fragment(s), Pathologic Fracture

Brain, Biopsy

Brain/Meninges, Tumor Resection

Breast, Excision of Lesion, Requiring Microscopic Evaluation of Surgical Margins

Breast, Mastectomy - Partial/Simple

Cervix, Conization

Colon, Segmental Resection, Other than for Tumor

Extremity, Amputation, Non-traumatic

Eye, Enucleation

Kidney, Partial/Total Nephrectomy

Larynx, Partial/Total Resection

Liver, Biopsy - Needle/Wedge

Liver, Partial Resection

Lung, Wedge Biopsy

Lymph Nodes, Regional Resection

Mediastinum, Mass

Myocardium, Biopsy

Odontogenic Tumor

Ovary with or without Tube, Neoplastic

Pancreas, Biopsy

Placenta, Third Trimester

Prostate, Except Radical Resection

Salivary Gland

Sentinel Lymph Node

Small Intestine, Resection, Other than for Tumor

Soft Tissue Mass (except Lipoma) - Biopsy/Simple Excision

Stomach - Subtotal/Total Resection, Other than for Tumor

Testis, Biopsy

Thymus, Tumor

Thyroid, Total/Lobe

Ureter, Resection

Urinary Bladder, TUR

Uterus, with or without Tubes and Ovaries, Other than Neoplastic/Prolapse

88309   **Level VI** - Surgical pathology, gross and microscopic examination

Bone Resection

Breast, Mastectomy - with Regional Lymph Nodes

Colon, Segmental Resection for Tumor

Colon, Total Resection

Esophagus, Partial/Total Resection

Extremity, Disarticulation

Fetus, with Dissection

Larynx, Partial/Total Resection - with Regional Lymph Nodes

Lung - Total/Lobe/Segment Resection

Pancreas, Total/Subtotal Resection

Prostate, Radical Resection

Small Intestine, Resection for Tumor

Soft Tissue Tumor, Extensive Resection

Stomach - Subtotal/Total Resection for Tumor

Testis, Tumor

Tongue/Tonsil - Resection for Tumor

Urinary Bladder, Partial/Total Resection

Uterus, with or without Tubes and Ovaries, Neoplastic

Vulva, Total/Subtotal Resection

(For fine needle aspiration, see 10021, 10022)

(For evaluation of fine needle aspirate, see 88172-88173)

+ 88311   Decalcification procedure (List separately in addition to code for surgical pathology examination)

Pathology and Laboratory

+ 88312 Special stains (List separately in addition to code for primary service); Group I for microorganisms (eg, Gridley, acid fast, methenamine silver), each

+ 88313 Group II, all other, (eg, iron, trichrome), except immunocytochemistry and immunoperoxidase stains, each

(For immunocytochemistry and immunoperoxidase tissue studies, use 88342)

+ 88314 histochemical staining with frozen section(s)

88318 Determinative histochemistry to identify chemical components (eg, copper, zinc)

88319 Determinative histochemistry or cytochemistry to identify enzyme constituents, each

88321 Consultation and report on referred slides prepared elsewhere

88323 Consultation and report on referred material requiring preparation of slides

88325 Consultation, comprehensive, with review of records and specimens, with report on referred material

88329 Pathology consultation during surgery;

88331 first tissue block, with frozen section(s), single specimen

88332 each additional tissue block with frozen section(s)

● 88333 cytologic examination (eg, touch prep, squash prep), initial site

● 88334 cytologic examination (eg, touch prep, squash prep), each additional site

►(For intraoperative consultation on a specimen requiring both frozen section and cytologic evaluation, use 88331 and 88334)◄

►(For percutaneous needle biopsy requiring intraprocedural cytologic examination, use 88333)◄

►(Do not report 88333 and 88334 for non-intraoperative cytologic examination, see 88160-88162)◄

►(Do not report 88333 and 88334 for intraprocedural cytologic evaluation of fine needle aspirate, see 88172)◄

88342 Immunohistochemistry (including tissue immunoperoxidase), each antibody

(Do not report 88342 in conjunction with 88360 or 88361 for the same antibody)

(For quantitative or semiquantitative immunohistochemistry, see 88360, 88361)

88346 Immunofluorescent study, each antibody; direct method

88347 indirect method

88348 Electron microscopy; diagnostic

88349 scanning

88355 Morphometric analysis; skeletal muscle

88356 nerve

88358 tumor (eg, DNA ploidy)

(Do not report 88358 with 88313 unless each procedure is for a different special stain)

88360 Morphometric analysis, tumor immunohistochemistry (eg, Her-2/neu, estrogen receptor/progesterone receptor), quantitative or semiquantitative, each antibody; manual

88361 using computer-assisted technology

(Do not report 88360, 88361 with 88342 unless each procedure is for a different antibody)

(For morphometric analysis using in situ hybridization techniques, see 88367, 88368)

(When semi-thin plastic-embedded sections are performed in conjunction with morphometric analysis, only the morphometric analysis should be reported; if performed as an independent procedure, see codes 88300-88309 for surgical pathology.)

88362 Nerve teasing preparations

88365 In situ hybridization (eg, FISH), each probe

(Do not report 88365 in conjunction with 88367, 88368 for the same probe)

88367 Morphometric analysis, in situ hybridization, (quantitative or semi-quantitative) each probe; using computer-assisted technology

88368 manual

88371 Protein analysis of tissue by Western Blot, with interpretation and report;

88372 immunological probe for band identification, each

88380 Microdissection (eg, mechanical, laser capture)

● 88384 Array-based evaluation of multiple molecular probes; 11 through 50 probes

● 88385 51 through 250 probes

● 88386 251 through 500 probes

►(For preparation of array-based evaluation, see 83890-83892, 83898-83901)◄

►(For preparation and analyses of less than 11 probes, see 83890-83914)◄

88399 Unlisted surgical pathology procedure

Transcutaneous Procedures

88400 Bilirubin, total, transcutaneous

Other Procedures

● **89049**   Caffeine halothane contracture test (CHCT) for malignant hyperthermia susceptibility, including interpretation and report

89050   Cell count, miscellaneous body fluids (eg, cerebrospinal fluid, joint fluid), except blood;

89051   with differential count

89055   Leukocyte assessment, fecal, qualitative or semiquantitative

89060   Crystal identification by light microscopy with or without polarizing lens analysis, any body fluid (except urine)

89100   Duodenal intubation and aspiration; single specimen (eg, simple bile study or afferent loop culture) plus appropriate test procedure

89105   collection of multiple fractional specimens with pancreatic or gallbladder stimulation, single or double lumen tube

(For radiological localization, use 74340)

(For chemical analyses, see **Chemistry,** this section)

(Electrocardiogram, see 93000-93268)

(Esophagus acid perfusion test (Bernstein), see 91030)

89125   Fat stain, feces, urine, or respiratory secretions

89130   Gastric intubation and aspiration, diagnostic, each specimen, for chemical analyses or cytopathology;

89132   after stimulation

89135   Gastric intubation, aspiration, and fractional collections (eg, gastric secretory study); one hour

89136   two hours

89140   two hours including gastric stimulation (eg, histalog, pentagastrin)

89141   three hours, including gastric stimulation

(For gastric lavage, therapeutic, use 91105)

(For radiologic localization of gastric tube, use 74340)

(For chemical analyses, see 82926, 82928)

(Joint fluid chemistry, see **Chemistry,** this section)

89160   Meat fibers, feces

89190   Nasal smear for eosinophils

(Occult blood, feces, use 82270)

(Paternity tests, use 86910)

89220   Sputum, obtaining specimen, aerosol induced technique (separate procedure)

89225   Starch granules, feces

89230   Sweat collection by iontophoresis

89235   Water load test

89240   Unlisted miscellaneous pathology test

Reproductive Medicine Procedures

89250   Culture of oocyte(s)/embryo(s), less than 4 days;

89251   with co-culture of oocyte(s)/embryos

(For extended culture of oocyte(s)/embryo(s), see 89272)

(89252 has been deleted. To report, use 89280-89281)

89253   Assisted embryo hatching, microtechniques (any method)

89254   Oocyte identification from follicular fluid

89255   Preparation of embryo for transfer (any method)

(89256 has been deleted. To report, use 89352)

89257   Sperm identification from aspiration (other than seminal fluid)

(For semen analysis, see 89300-89320)

(For sperm identification from testis tissue, use 89264)

89258   Cryopreservation; embryo(s)

89259   sperm

(For cryopreservation of reproductive tissue, testicular, use 89335)

(For cryopreservation of reproductive tissue, ovarian, use Category III code 0058T)

(For cryopreservation of oocyte(s), use Category III code 0059T)

89260   Sperm isolation; simple prep (eg, sperm wash and swim-up) for insemination or diagnosis with semen analysis

89261   complex prep (eg, Percoll gradient, albumin gradient) for insemination or diagnosis with semen analysis

(For semen analysis without sperm wash or swim-up, use 89320)

89264   Sperm identification from testis tissue, fresh or cryopreserved

(For biopsy of testis, see 54500, 54505)

(For sperm identification from aspiration, use 89257)

(For semen analysis, see 89300-89320)

89268   Insemination of oocytes

89272   Extended culture of oocyte(s)/embryo(s), 4-7 days

89280   Assisted oocyte fertilization, microtechnique; less than or equal to 10 oocytes

89281   greater than 10 oocytes

89290   Biopsy, oocyte polar body or embryo blastomere, microtechnique (for pre-implantation genetic diagnosis); less than or equal to 5 embryos

89291   greater than 5 embryos

Pathology and Laboratory

▲=Revised code   ●=New code   ▶◀=Contains new or revised text

89300   Semen analysis; presence and/or motility of sperm including Huhner test (post coital)

89310   motility and count (not including Huhner test)

89320   complete (volume, count, motility, and differential)

(Skin tests, see 86485-86580 and 95010-95199)

89321   Semen analysis, presence and/or motility of sperm

(To report Hyaluronan binding assay (HBA), use Category III code 0087T)

89325   Sperm antibodies

(For medicolegal identification of sperm, use 88125)

89329   Sperm evaluation; hamster penetration test

89330   cervical mucus penetration test, with or without spinnbarkeit test

89335   Cryopreservation, reproductive tissue, testicular

(For cryopreservation of embryo(s), use 89258. For cryopreservation of sperm, use 89259)

(For cryopreservation of reproductive tissue, ovarian, use Category III code 0058T)

(For cryopreservation of oocyte, use Category III code 0059T)

89342   Storage, (per year); embryo(s)

89343   sperm/semen

89344   reproductive tissue, testicular/ovarian

89346   oocyte(s)

(89350 has been deleted. To report, use 89220)

89352   Thawing of cryopreserved; embryo(s)

89353   sperm/semen, each aliquot

89354   reproductive tissue, testicular/ovarian

(89355 has been deleted. To report, use 89225)

89356   oocytes, each aliquot

(89360 has been deleted. To report, use 89230)

(89365 has been deleted. To report, use 89235)

(89399 has been deleted. To report, use 89240)

⊘ =Modifier 51 exempt   ⊙=Conscious sedation   ✚=Add-on code   ✗ =FDA approval pending

Medicine Guidelines

In addition to the definitions and commonly used terms presented in the **Introduction**, several other items unique to this section on **Medicine** are defined or identified here.

Multiple Procedures

It is appropriate to designate multiple procedures that are rendered on the same date by separate entries. For example: If individual medical psychotherapy (90829) is rendered in addition to subsequent hospital care (eg, 99231), the psychotherapy would be reported separately from the hospital visit. In this instance, both 99231 and 90829 would be reported.

Add-on Codes

Some of the listed procedures are commonly carried out in addition to the primary procedure performed. All add-on codes found in the CPT codebook are exempt from the multiple procedure concept. They are exempt from the use of modifier 51, as these procedures are not reported as stand-alone codes. These additional or supplemental procedures are designated as "add-on" codes. Add-on codes in the CPT codebook can be readily identified by specific descriptor nomenclature which includes phrases such as "each additional" or "(List separately in addition to primary procedure)."

Separate Procedures

Some of the procedures or services listed in the CPT codebook that are commonly carried out as an integral component of a total service or procedure have been identified by the inclusion of the term "separate procedure." The codes designated as "separate procedure" should not be reported in addition to the code for the total procedure or service of which it is considered an integral component.

However, when a procedure or service that is designated as a "separate procedure" is carried out independently or considered to be unrelated or distinct from other procedures/services provided at that time, it may be reported by itself, or in addition to other procedures/services by appending modifier 59 to the specific "separate procedure" code to indicate that the procedure is not considered to be a component of another procedure, but is a distinct, independent procedure. This may represent a different session or patient encounter, different procedure or surgery, different site or organ system, separate incision/excision, separate lesion, or separate injury (or area of injury in extensive injuries).

Subsection Information

Several of the subheadings or subsections have special instructions unique to that section. These special instructions will be presented preceding those procedural terminology listings, referring to that subsection specifically. If there is an "Unlisted Procedure" code number (see section below) for the individual subsection, it will also be shown. Those subsections within the **Medicine** section that have special instructions are as follows:

Immune Globulins 90281-90399
Immunization Administration for
    Vaccines/Toxoids 90465-90474
Vaccines, Toxoids 90476-90749
▶Hydration, Therapeutic, Prophylactic,
    and Diagnostic Injections and
    Infusions . . . . 90760-90779◀
Psychiatry 90801-90899
Dialysis 90918-90999
Ophthalmology 92002-92499
Contact Lens Services 92310-92326
▶Spectacle Services . . . . 92340-92371◀
Otorhinolaryngology 92502-92700
Audiologic Function Tests 92551-92597
Evaluative and Therapeutic Services . 92601-92625
Echocardiography 93303-93350
Cardiac Catheterization 93501-93581
Intracardiac Electrophysiological
    Procedures/Studies 93600-93662
Peripheral Arterial Disease
    Rehabilitation 93668
Non-Invasive Vascular
    Diagnostic Studies 93875-93990
Pulmonary 94010-94799
Allergy and Clinical Immunology . . . 95004-95199
Neurology and Neuromuscular 95805-95999
▶Electromyography and Nerve Conduction
    Tests . . . . 95860-95904◀
Neurostimulators,
    Analysis-Programming 95970-95979
Motion Analysis 96000-96004
▶Central Nervous System
    Assessments/Tests . . . . 96100-96120◀
Health and Behavior
    Assessment/Intervention 96150-96155
▶Chemotherapy Administration . . . . 96401-96549◀
Dermatological Procedures 96900-96999

Physical Medicine and Rehabilitation 97001-97755
　Modalities 97010-97039
　Constant Attendance 97032-97039
　Therapeutic Procedures 97110-97546
　Active Wound
　　Care Management 97597-97606
▶Tests and Measurements . . . . 97750-97755◀
Acupuncture 97810-97814
Osteopathic Manipulative
　Treatment 98925-98929
Chiropractic Manipulative
　Treatment 98940-98943
▶Education and Training for
　Patient Self-Management . . . . 98960-98962◀
Special Services, Procedures and
　Reports 99000-99091
▶Moderate (Conscious) Sedation . . . 99143-99150◀
Home Health
　Procedures/Services 99500-99600

Unlisted Service or Procedure

A service or procedure may be provided that is not listed in this edition of the CPT codebook. When reporting such a service, the appropriate "Unlisted Procedure" code may be used to indicate the service, identifying it by "Special Report" as discussed on this page. The "Unlisted Procedures" and accompanying codes for **Medicine** are as follows:

⊘ **90399**　Unlisted immune globulin

⊘ **90749**　Unlisted vaccine/toxoid

● **90779**　Unlisted therapeutic, prophylactic or diagnostic intravenous or intra-arterial injection or infusion

90899　Unlisted psychiatric service or procedure

90999　Unlisted dialysis procedure, inpatient or outpatient

91299　Unlisted diagnostic gastroenterology procedure

92499　Unlisted ophthalmological service or procedure

92700　Unlisted otorhinolaryngological service or procedure

93799　Unlisted cardiovascular service or procedure

94799　Unlisted pulmonary service or procedure

95199　Unlisted allergy/clinical immunologic service or procedure

95999　Unlisted neurological or neuromuscular diagnostic procedure

96549　Unlisted chemotherapy procedure

96999　Unlisted special dermatological service or procedure

97039　Unlisted modality (specify type and time if constant attendance)

97139　Unlisted therapeutic procedure (specify)

97799　Unlisted physical medicine/rehabilitation service or procedure

99199　Unlisted special service, procedure or report

99600　Unlisted home visit service or procedure

Special Report

A service that is rarely provided, unusual, variable, or new may require a special report in determining medical appropriateness of the service. Pertinent information should include an adequate definition or description of the nature, extent, and need for the procedure; and the time, effort, and equipment necessary to provide the service. Additional items that may be included are:

- Complexity of symptoms
- Final diagnosis
- Pertinent physical findings
- Diagnostic and therapeutic procedures
- Concurrent problems
- Follow-up care

Materials Supplied by Physician

Supplies and materials provided by the physician (eg, sterile trays/drugs), over and above those usually included with the procedure(s) rendered are reported separately. List drugs, trays, supplies, and materials provided. Identify as 99070 or specific supply code.

Medicine

Immune Globulins

►Codes 90281-90399 identify the immune globulin product only and must be reported in addition to the administration codes 90765-90768, 90772, 90774, 90775 as appropriate. Immune globulin products listed here include broad-spectrum and anti-infective immune globulins, antitoxins, and various isoantibodies.◄

⊘ **90281** Immune globulin (Ig), human, for intramuscular use

⊘ **90283** Immune globulin (IgIV), human, for intravenous use

⊘ **90287** Botulinum antitoxin, equine, any route

⊘ **90288** Botulism immune globulin, human, for intravenous use

⊘ **90291** Cytomegalovirus immune globulin (CMV-IgIV), human, for intravenous use

⊘ **90296** Diphtheria antitoxin, equine, any route

⊘ **90371** Hepatitis B immune globulin (HBIg), human, for intramuscular use

⊘ **90375** Rabies immune globulin (RIg), human, for intramuscular and/or subcutaneous use

⊘ **90376** Rabies immune globulin, heat-treated (RIg-HT), human, for intramuscular and/or subcutaneous use

⊘ **90378** Respiratory syncytial virus immune globulin (RSV-IgIM), for intramuscular use, 50 mg, each

⊘ **90379** Respiratory syncytial virus immune globulin (RSV-IgIV), human, for intravenous use

⊘ **90384** Rho(D) immune globulin (RhIg), human, full-dose, for intramuscular use

⊘ **90385** Rho(D) immune globulin (RhIg), human, mini-dose, for intramuscular use

⊘ **90386** Rho(D) immune globulin (RhIgIV), human, for intravenous use

⊘ **90389** Tetanus immune globulin (TIg), human, for intramuscular use

⊘ **90393** Vaccinia immune globulin, human, for intramuscular use

⊘ **90396** Varicella-zoster immune globulin, human, for intramuscular use

⊘ **90399** Unlisted immune globulin

Immunization Administration for Vaccines/Toxoids

Codes 90465-90474 must be reported in addition to the vaccine and toxoid code(s) 90476-90749.

Report codes 90465-90468 only when the physician provides face-to-face counseling of the patient and family during the administration of a vaccine. For immunization administration of any vaccine that is not accompanied by face-to-face physician counseling to the patient/family, report codes 90471-90474.

If a significant separately identifiable Evaluation and Management service (eg, office or other outpatient services, preventive medicine services) is performed, the appropriate E/M service code should be reported in addition to the vaccine and toxoid administration codes.

(For allergy testing, see 95004 et seq)

(For skin testing of bacterial, viral, fungal extracts, see 86485-86586)

►(For therapeutic or diagnostic injections, see 90772-90779)◄

90465 Immunization administration under 8 years of age (includes percutaneous, intradermal, subcutaneous, or intramuscular injections) when the physician counsels the patient/family; first injection (single or combination vaccine/toxoid), per day

(Do not report 90465 in conjunction with 90467)

+ 90466 each additional injection (single or combination vaccine/toxoid), per day (List separately in addition to code for primary procedure)

(Use 90466 in conjunction with 90465 or 90467)

90467 Immunization administration under age 8 years (includes intranasal or oral routes of administration) when the physician counsels the patient/family; first administration (single or combination vaccine/toxoid), per day

(Do not report 90467 in conjunction with 90465)

+ 90468 each additional administration (single or combination vaccine/toxoid), per day (List separately in addition to code for primary procedure)

(Use 90468 in conjunction with 90465 or 90467)

90471 Immunization administration (includes percutaneous, intradermal, subcutaneous, or intramuscular injections); one vaccine (single or combination vaccine/toxoid)

(Do not report 90471 in conjunction with 90473)

+ 90472 each additional vaccine (single or combination vaccine/toxoid) (List separately in addition to code for primary procedure)

(Use 90472 in conjunction with 90471 or 90473)

(For administration of immune globulins, use 90780-90784, and see 90281-90399)

(For intravesical administration of BCG vaccine, use 51720, and see 90586)

90473   Immunization administration by intranasal or oral route; one vaccine (single or combination vaccine/toxoid)

(Do not report 90473 in conjunction with 90471)

+ 90474   each additional vaccine (single or combination vaccine/toxoid) (List separately in addition to code for primary procedure)

(Use 90474 in conjunction with 90471 or 90473)

Vaccines, Toxoids

►To assist users to report the most recent new or revised vaccine product codes, the American Medical Association currently uses the CPT Web-site, which features updates of CPT Editorial Panel actions regarding these products. Once approved by the CPT Editorial Panel, these codes will be made available for release on a semi-annual (twice a year—July 1 and January 1) basis. As part of the electronic distribution, there is a 6-month implementation period from the initial release date (ie, codes released on January 1 are eligible for use on July 1 and codes released on July 1 are eligible for use January 1).◄

►The CPT Editorial Panel, in recognition of the public health interest in vaccine products, has chosen to publish new vaccine product codes prior to FDA approval. These codes are indicated with the ∕ symbol and will be tracked by the AMA to monitor FDA approval status. Once the FDA status changes to approval, the ∕ symbol will be removed. CPT users should refer to the AMA Internet site (www.ama-assn.org/ama/pub/category/10902.html) for the most up-to-date information on codes with the ∕ symbol.◄

Codes 90476-90748 identify the vaccine product **only.** To report the administration of a vaccine/toxoid, the vaccine/toxoid product codes 90476-90749 must be used in addition to an immunization administration code(s) 90465-90474. Do not append modifier 51 to the vaccine/toxoid product codes 90476-90749.

If a significantly separately identifiable Evaluation and Management (E/M) service (eg, office or other outpatient services, preventive medicine services) is performed, the appropriate E/M service code should be reported in addition to the vaccine and toxoid administration codes.

To meet the reporting requirements of immunization registries, vaccine distribution programs, and reporting systems (eg, Vaccine Adverse Event Reporting System) the exact vaccine product administered needs to be reported. Multiple codes for a particular vaccine are provided in the CPT codebook when the schedule (number of doses or timing) differs for two or more products of the same vaccine type (eg, hepatitis A, Hib) or the vaccine product is available in more than one chemical formulation, dosage, or route of administration.

Separate codes are available for combination vaccines (eg, DTP-Hib, DtaP-Hib, HepB-Hib). It is inappropriate to code each component of a combination vaccine separately. If a specific vaccine code is not available, the unlisted procedure code should be reported, until a new code becomes available.

(For immune globulins, see codes 90281-90399, 90765-90768, 90772-90775 for administration of immune globulins)

⊘ **90476**   Adenovirus vaccine, type 4, live, for oral use

⊘ **90477**   Adenovirus vaccine, type 7, live, for oral use

⊘ **90581**   Anthrax vaccine, for subcutaneous use

⊘ **90585**   Bacillus Calmette-Guerin vaccine (BCG) for tuberculosis, live, for percutaneous use

⊘ **90586**   Bacillus Calmette-Guerin vaccine (BCG) for bladder cancer, live, for intravesical use

⊘ **90632**   Hepatitis A vaccine, adult dosage, for intramuscular use

⊘ **90633**   Hepatitis A vaccine, pediatric/adolescent dosage-2 dose schedule, for intramuscular use

⊘ **90634**   Hepatitis A vaccine, pediatric/adolescent dosage-3 dose schedule, for intramuscular use

⊘ **90636**   Hepatitis A and hepatitis B vaccine (HepA-HepB), adult dosage, for intramuscular use

⊘ **90645**   Hemophilus influenza b vaccine (Hib), HbOC conjugate (4 dose schedule), for intramuscular use

⊘ **90646**   Hemophilus influenza b vaccine (Hib), PRP-D conjugate, for booster use only, intramuscular use

⊘ **90647**   Hemophilus influenza b vaccine (Hib), PRP-OMP conjugate (3 dose schedule), for intramuscular use

⊘ **90648**   Hemophilus influenza b vaccine (Hib), PRP-T conjugate (4 dose schedule), for intramuscular use

∕⊘● **90649**   Human Papilloma virus (HPV) vaccine, types 6, 11, 16, 18 (quadrivalent), 3 dose schedule, for intramuscular use

⊘ **90655**   Influenza virus vaccine, split virus, preservative free, for children 6-35 months of age, for intramuscular use

⊘ **90656**   Influenza virus vaccine, split virus, preservative free, for use in individuals 3 years and above, for intramuscular use

⊘ **90657**   Influenza virus vaccine, split virus, for children 6-35 months of age, for intramuscular use

⊘ **90658**   Influenza virus vaccine, split virus, for use in individuals 3 years of age and above, for intramuscular use

(90659 has been deleted. To report influenza virus vaccine, split virus, see 90657 or 90658)

⊘ **90660**   Influenza virus vaccine, live, for intranasal use

⊘ **90665**   Lyme disease vaccine, adult dosage, for intramuscular use

⊘ **90669**   Pneumococcal conjugate vaccine, polyvalent, for children under 5 years, for intramuscular use

⊘ **90675** Rabies vaccine, for intramuscular use

⊘ **90676** Rabies vaccine, for intradermal use

✎⊘▲ **90680** Rotavirus vaccine, pentavalent, 3 dose schedule, live, for oral use

⊘ **90690** Typhoid vaccine, live, oral

⊘ **90691** Typhoid vaccine, Vi capsular polysaccharide (ViCPs), for intramuscular use

⊘ **90692** Typhoid vaccine, heat- and phenol-inactivated (H-P), for subcutaneous or intradermal use

⊘ **90693** Typhoid vaccine, acetone-killed, dried (AKD), for subcutaneous use (U.S. military)

✎⊘ **90698** Diphtheria, tetanus toxoids, acellular pertussis vaccine, haemophilus influenza Type B, and poliovirus vaccine, inactivated (DTaP - Hib - IPV), for intramuscular use

⊘ **90700** Diphtheria, tetanus toxoids, and acellular pertussis vaccine (DTaP), for use in individuals younger than 7 years, for intramuscular use

⊘ **90701** Diphtheria, tetanus toxoids, and whole cell pertussis vaccine (DTP), for intramuscular use

⊘ **90702** Diphtheria and tetanus toxoids (DT) adsorbed for use in individuals younger than 7 years, for intramuscular use

⊘ **90703** Tetanus toxoid adsorbed, for intramuscular use

⊘ **90704** Mumps virus vaccine, live, for subcutaneous use

⊘ **90705** Measles virus vaccine, live, for subcutaneous use

⊘ **90706** Rubella virus vaccine, live, for subcutaneous use

⊘ **90707** Measles, mumps and rubella virus vaccine (MMR), live, for subcutaneous use

⊘ **90708** Measles and rubella virus vaccine, live, for subcutaneous use

✎⊘ **90710** Measles, mumps, rubella, and varicella vaccine (MMRV), live, for subcutaneous use

⊘ **90712** Poliovirus vaccine, (any type(s)) (OPV), live, for oral use

⊘▲ **90713** Poliovirus vaccine, inactivated, (IPV), for subcutaneous or intramuscular use

⊘● **90714** Tetanus and diphtheria toxoids (Td) adsorbed, preservative free, for use in individuals 7 years or older, for intramuscular use

✎⊘▲ **90715** Tetanus, diphtheria toxoids and acellular pertussis vaccine (Tdap), for use in individuals 7 years or older, for intramuscular use

⊘ **90716** Varicella virus vaccine, live, for subcutaneous use

⊘ **90717** Yellow fever vaccine, live, for subcutaneous use

⊘ **90718** Tetanus and diphtheria toxoids (Td) adsorbed for use in individuals 7 years or older, for intramuscular use

⊘ **90719** Diphtheria toxoid, for intramuscular use

⊘ **90720** Diphtheria, tetanus toxoids, and whole cell pertussis vaccine and Hemophilus influenza B vaccine (DTP-Hib), for intramuscular use

⊘ **90721** Diphtheria, tetanus toxoids, and acellular pertussis vaccine and Hemophilus influenza B vaccine (DtaP-Hib), for intramuscular use

⊘ **90723** Diphtheria, tetanus toxoids, acellular pertussis vaccine, Hepatitis B, and poliovirus vaccine, inactivated (DtaP-HepB-IPV), for intramuscular use

⊘ **90725** Cholera vaccine for injectable use

⊘ **90727** Plague vaccine, for intramuscular use

⊘ **90732** Pneumococcal polysaccharide vaccine, 23-valent, adult or immunosuppressed patient dosage, for use in individuals 2 years or older, for subcutaneous or intramuscular use

⊘ **90733** Meningococcal polysaccharide vaccine (any group(s)), for subcutaneous use

⊘ **90734** Meningococcal conjugate vaccine, serogroups A, C, Y and W-135 (tetravalent), for intramuscular use

⊘ **90735** Japanese encephalitis virus vaccine, for subcutaneous use

✎⊘● **90736** Zoster (shingles) vaccine, live, for subcutaneous injection

⊘ **90740** Hepatitis B vaccine, dialysis or immunosuppressed patient dosage (3 dose schedule), for intramuscular use

⊘ **90743** Hepatitis B vaccine, adolescent (2 dose schedule), for intramuscular use

⊘ **90744** Hepatitis B vaccine, pediatric/adolescent dosage (3 dose schedule), for intramuscular use

⊘ **90746** Hepatitis B vaccine, adult dosage, for intramuscular use

⊘ **90747** Hepatitis B vaccine, dialysis or immunosuppressed patient dosage (4 dose schedule), for intramuscular use

⊘ **90748** Hepatitis B and Hemophilus influenza b vaccine (HepB-Hib), for intramuscular use

⊘ **90749** Unlisted vaccine/toxoid

▶Hydration, Therapeutic, Prophylactic, and Diagnostic Injections and Infusions (Excludes Chemotherapy)◀

▶Physician work related to hydration, injection, and infusion services predominantly involves affirmation of treatment plan and direct supervision of staff.◀

▶If a significant separately identifiable Evaluation and Management service is performed, the appropriate E/M service code should be reported using modifier 25 in addition to 90760-90779. For same day E/M service a different diagnosis is not required.◀

▶If performed to facilitate the infusion or injection, the following services are included and are not reported separately:

Medicine

a. Use of local anesthesia

b. IV start

c. Access to indwelling IV, subcutaneous catheter or port

d. Flush at conclusion of infusion

e. Standard tubing, syringes, and supplies◄

►(For declotting a catheter or port, see 36550)◄

►When multiple drugs are administered, report the service(s) and the specific materials or drugs for each.◄

►When administering multiple infusions, injections or combinations, only one "initial" service code should be reported, unless protocol requires that two separate IV sites must be used. The "initial" code that best describes the key or primary reason for the encounter should always be reported irrespective of the order in which the infusions or injections occur. If an injection or infusion is of a subsequent or concurrent nature, even if it is the first such service within that group of services, then a subsequent or concurrent code from the appropriate section should be reported (eg, the first IV push given subsequent to an initial one-hour infusion is reported using a subsequent IV push code).◄

►When reporting codes for which infusion time is a factor, use the actual time over which the infusion is administered.◄

►Hydration◄

►Codes 90760-90761 are intended to report a hydration IV infusion to consist of a pre-packaged fluid and electrolytes (eg, normal saline, D5-$\frac{1}{2}$ normal saline+30mEq KCl/liter), but are not used to report infusion of drugs or other substances. Hydration IV infusions typically require direct physician supervision for purposes of consent, safety oversight, or intraservice supervision of staff. Typically such infusions require little special handling to prepare or dispose of, and staff that administer these do not typically require advanced practice training. After initial set-up, infusion typically entails little patient risk and thus little monitoring.◄

● **90760** Intravenous infusion, hydration; initial, up to 1 hour

►(Do not report 90760 if performed as a concurrent infusion service)◄

+● **90761** each additional hour, up to 8 hours (List separately in addition to code for primary procedure)

►(Use 90761 in conjunction with 90760)◄

►(Report 90761 for hydration infusion intervals of greater than 30 minutes beyond 1 hour increments)◄

►(Report 90761 to identify hydration if provided as a secondary or subsequent service after a different initial service [90760, 90765, 90774, 96409, 96413] is provided)◄

►Therapeutic, Prophylactic, and Diagnostic Injections and Infusions◄

►A therapeutic, prophylactic, or diagnostic IV infusion or injection (90765-90799) (other than hydration) is for the administration of substances/drugs. The fluid used to administer the drug(s) is incidental hydration and is not separately reportable. These services typically require direct physician supervision for any or all purposes of patient assessment, provision of consent, safety oversight, and intra-service supervision of staff. Typically, such infusions require special consideration to prepare, dose or dispose of, require practice training and competency for staff who administer the infusions, and require periodic patient assessment with vital sign monitoring during the infusion.◄

►Intravenous or intra-arterial push is defined as: a) an injection in which the health care professional who administers the substance/drug is continuously present to administer the injection and observe the patient, or b) an infusion of 15 minutes or less.◄

►(Do not report 90765-90779 with codes for which IV push or infusion is an inherent part of the procedure (eg, administration of contrast material for a diagnostic imaging study))◄

● **90765** Intravenous infusion, for therapy, prophylaxis, or diagnosis (specify substance or drug); initial, up to 1 hour

+● **90766** each additional hour, up to 8 hours (List separately in addition to code for primary procedure)

►(Report 90766 in conjunction with 90765, 90767)◄

►(Report 90766 for additional hour(s) of sequential infusion)◄

►(Report 90766 for infusion intervals of greater than 30 minutes beyond 1 hour increments)◄

+● **90767** additional sequential infusion, up to 1 hour (List separately in addition to code for primary procedure)

►(Report 90767 in conjunction with 90765, 90774, 96409, 96413 if provided as a secondary or subsequent service after a different initial service. Report 90767 only once per sequential infusion of same infusate mix)◄

+● **90768** concurrent infusion (List separately in addition to code for primary procedure)

►(Report 90768 only once per encounter)◄

►(Report 90768 in conjunction with 90765, 96413)◄

● **90772** Therapeutic, prophylactic or diagnostic injection (specify substance or drug); subcutaneous or intramuscular

►(For administration of vaccines/toxoids, see 90465-90466, 90471-90472)◄

►(Report 90772 for non-antineoplastic hormonal therapy injections)◄

►(Report 96401 for anti-neoplastic nonhormonal injection therapy)◄

►(Report 96402 for anti-neoplastic hormonal injection therapy)◄

►(Do not report 90772 for injections given without direct physician supervision. To report, use 99211)◄

● **90773**   intra-arterial

● **90774**   intravenous push, single or initial substance/drug

►(90772-90774 do not include injections for allergen immunotherapy. For allergen immunotherapy injections, see 95115-95117)◄

+● **90775**   each additional sequential intravenous push of a new substance/drug (List separately in addition to code for primary procedure)

►(Use 90775 in conjunction with 90765, 90774, 96409, 96413)◄

►(Report 90775 to identify intravenous push of a new substance/drug if provided as a secondary or subsequent service after a different initial service is provided)◄

● **90779**   Unlisted therapeutic, prophylactic or diagnostic intravenous or intra-arterial injection or infusion

►(For allergy immunizations, see 95004 et seq)◄

►(90780 and 90781 have been deleted. To report, see 90760, 90761, 90765-90768)◄

►(90782 has been deleted. To report, use 90772)◄

►(90783 has been deleted. To report, use 90773)◄

►(90784 has been deleted. To report, use 90774)◄

►(90788 has been deleted. To report, use 90772)◄

►(90799 has been deleted. To report, use 90779)◄

Psychiatry

Hospital care by the attending physician in treating a psychiatric inpatient or partial hospitalization may be initial or subsequent in nature (see 99221-99233) and may include exchanges with nursing and ancillary personnel. Hospital care services involve a variety of responsibilities unique to the medical management of inpatients, such as physician hospital orders, interpretation of laboratory or other medical diagnostic studies and observations.

Some patients receive hospital evaluation and management services only and others receive evaluation and management services and other procedures. If other procedures such as electroconvulsive therapy or psychotherapy are rendered in addition to hospital evaluation and management services, these should be listed separately (ie, hospital care service plus electroconvulsive therapy or when psychotherapy is done, an appropriate code defining psychotherapy with medical evaluation and management services). Modifier 22 may

be used to indicate a more extensive service. Modifier 52 may be used to signify a service that is reduced or less extensive than the usual procedure.

Other evaluation and management services, such as office medical service or other patient encounters, may be described as listed in the section on **Evaluation and Management,** if appropriate.

The evaluation and management services should not be reported separately, when reporting codes 90805, 90807, 90809, 90811, 90813, 90815, 90817, 90819, 90822, 90824, 90827, 90829.

Consultation for psychiatric evaluation of a patient includes examination of a patient and exchange of information with the primary physician and other informants such as nurses or family members, and preparation of a report. These consultation services (99241-99255) are limited to initial or follow-up evaluation and do not involve psychiatric treatment.

Psychiatric Diagnostic or Evaluative Interview Procedures

Psychiatric diagnostic interview examination includes a history, mental status, and a disposition, and may include communication with family or other sources, ordering and medical interpretation of laboratory or other medical diagnostic studies. In certain circumstances other informants will be seen in lieu of the patient.

Interactive psychiatric diagnostic interview examination is typically furnished to children. It involves the use of physical aids and non-verbal communication to overcome barriers to therapeutic interaction between the clinician and a patient who has not yet developed, or has lost, either the expressive language communication skills to explain his/her symptoms and response to treatment, or the receptive communication skills to understand the clinician if he/she were to use ordinary adult language for communication.

90801   Psychiatric diagnostic interview examination

90802   Interactive psychiatric diagnostic interview examination using play equipment, physical devices, language interpreter, or other mechanisms of communication

Psychiatric Therapeutic Procedures

Psychotherapy is the treatment for mental illness and behavioral disturbances in which the clinician establishes a professional contract with the patient and, through definitive therapeutic communication, attempts to alleviate the emotional disturbances, reverse or change maladaptive patterns of behavior, and encourage personality growth and development. The codes for reporting psychotherapy are divided into two broad categories: Interactive Psychotherapy; and Insight Oriented, Behavior Modifying and/or Supportive Psychotherapy.

▲=Revised code   ●=New code   ► ◄=Contains new or revised text

Interactive psychotherapy is typically furnished to children. It involves the use of physical aids and non-verbal communication to overcome barriers to therapeutic interaction between the clinician and a patient who has not yet developed, or has lost, either the expressive language communication skills to explain his/her symptoms and response to treatment, or the receptive communication skills to understand the clinician if he/she were to use ordinary adult language for communication.

Insight oriented, behavior modifying and/or supportive psychotherapy refers to the development of insight or affective understanding, the use of behavior modification techniques, the use of supportive interactions, the use of cognitive discussion of reality, or any combination of the above to provide therapeutic change.

Some patients receive psychotherapy only and others receive psychotherapy and medical evaluation and management services. These evaluation and management services involve a variety of responsibilities unique to the medical management of psychiatric patients, such as medical diagnostic evaluation (eg, evaluation of comorbid medical conditions, drug interactions, and physical examinations), drug management when indicated, physician orders, interpretation of laboratory or other medical diagnostic studies and observations.

In reporting psychotherapy, the appropriate code is chosen on the basis of the type of psychotherapy (interactive using non-verbal techniques versus insight oriented, behavior modifying and/or supportive using verbal techniques), the place of service (office versus inpatient), the face-to-face time spent with the patient during psychotherapy, and whether evaluation and management services are furnished on the same date of service as psychotherapy.

To report medical evaluation and management services furnished on a day when psychotherapy is not provided, select the appropriate code from the **Evaluation and Management Services Guidelines.**

Office or Other Outpatient Facility

Insight Oriented, Behavior Modifying and/or Supportive Psychotherapy

90804 Individual psychotherapy, insight oriented, behavior modifying and/or supportive, in an office or outpatient facility, approximately 20 to 30 minutes face-to-face with the patient;

90805 with medical evaluation and management services

90806 Individual psychotherapy, insight oriented, behavior modifying and/or supportive, in an office or outpatient facility, approximately 45 to 50 minutes face-to-face with the patient;

90807 with medical evaluation and management services

90808 Individual psychotherapy, insight oriented, behavior modifying and/or supportive, in an office or outpatient facility, approximately 75 to 80 minutes face-to-face with the patient;

90809 with medical evaluation and management services

Interactive Psychotherapy

90810 Individual psychotherapy, interactive, using play equipment, physical devices, language interpreter, or other mechanisms of non-verbal communication, in an office or outpatient facility, approximately 20 to 30 minutes face-to-face with the patient;

90811 with medical evaluation and management services

90812 Individual psychotherapy, interactive, using play equipment, physical devices, language interpreter, or other mechanisms of non-verbal communication, in an office or outpatient facility, approximately 45 to 50 minutes face-to-face with the patient;

90813 with medical evaluation and management services

90814 Individual psychotherapy, interactive, using play equipment, physical devices, language interpreter, or other mechanisms of non-verbal communication, in an office or outpatient facility, approximately 75 to 80 minutes face-to-face with the patient;

90815 with medical evaluation and management services

Inpatient Hospital, Partial Hospital or Residential Care Facility

Insight Oriented, Behavior Modifying and/or Supportive Psychotherapy

90816 Individual psychotherapy, insight oriented, behavior modifying and/or supportive, in an inpatient hospital, partial hospital or residential care setting, approximately 20 to 30 minutes face-to-face with the patient;

90817 with medical evaluation and management services

90818 Individual psychotherapy, insight oriented, behavior modifying and/or supportive, in an inpatient hospital, partial hospital or residential care setting, approximately 45 to 50 minutes face-to-face with the patient;

90819 with medical evaluation and management services

90821 Individual psychotherapy, insight oriented, behavior modifying and/or supportive, in an inpatient hospital, partial hospital or residential care setting, approximately 75 to 80 minutes face-to-face with the patient;

90822 with medical evaluation and management services

Interactive Psychotherapy

90823   Individual psychotherapy, interactive, using play equipment, physical devices, language interpreter, or other mechanisms of non-verbal communication, in an inpatient hospital, partial hospital or residential care setting, approximately 20 to 30 minutes face-to-face with the patient;

90824   with medical evaluation and management services

90826   Individual psychotherapy, interactive, using play equipment, physical devices, language interpreter, or other mechanisms of non-verbal communication, in an inpatient hospital, partial hospital or residential care setting, approximately 45 to 50 minutes face-to-face with the patient;

90827   with medical evaluation and management services

90828   Individual psychotherapy, interactive, using play equipment, physical devices, language interpreter, or other mechanisms of non-verbal communication, in an inpatient hospital, partial hospital or residential care setting, approximately 75 to 80 minutes face-to-face with the patient;

90829   with medical evaluation and management services

Other Psychotherapy

90845   Psychoanalysis

90846   Family psychotherapy (without the patient present)

90847   Family psychotherapy (conjoint psychotherapy) (with patient present)

90849   Multiple-family group psychotherapy

90853   Group psychotherapy (other than of a multiple-family group)

90857   Interactive group psychotherapy

Other Psychiatric Services or Procedures

▶(For repetitive transcranial magnetic stimulation for treatment of clinical depression, use Category III code 0018T)◀

90862   Pharmacologic management, including prescription, use, and review of medication with no more than minimal medical psychotherapy

90865   Narcosynthesis for psychiatric diagnostic and therapeutic purposes (eg, sodium amobarbital (Amytal) interview)

▲ **90870**   Electroconvulsive therapy (includes necessary monitoring)

▶(90871 has been deleted)◀

90875   Individual psychophysiological therapy incorporating biofeedback training by any modality (face-to-face with the patient), with psychotherapy (eg, insight oriented, behavior modifying or supportive psychotherapy); approximately 20-30 minutes

90876   approximately 45-50 minutes

90880   Hypnotherapy

90882   Environmental intervention for medical management purposes on a psychiatric patient's behalf with agencies, employers, or institutions

90885   Psychiatric evaluation of hospital records, other psychiatric reports, psychometric and/or projective tests, and other accumulated data for medical diagnostic purposes

90887   Interpretation or explanation of results of psychiatric, other medical examinations and procedures, or other accumulated data to family or other responsible persons, or advising them how to assist patient

90889   Preparation of report of patient's psychiatric status, history, treatment, or progress (other than for legal or consultative purposes) for other physicians, agencies, or insurance carriers

90899   Unlisted psychiatric service or procedure

Biofeedback

(For psychophysiological therapy incorporating biofeedback training, see 90875, 90876)

90901   Biofeedback training by any modality

90911   Biofeedback training, perineal muscles, anorectal or urethral sphincter, including EMG and/or manometry

(For incontinence treatment by pulsed magnetic neuromodulation, use Category III code 0029T)

(For testing of rectal sensation, tone and compliance, use 91120)

Dialysis

Codes 90918-90921 are reported ONCE per month to distinguish age-specific services related to the patient's end-stage renal disease (ESRD) performed in an outpatient setting. ESRD-related physician services include establishment of a dialyzing cycle, outpatient evaluation and management of the dialysis visits, telephone calls, and patient management during the dialysis, provided during a full month. These codes are not used if the physician also submits hospitalization codes during the month.

Codes 90918-90921 describe a full month of ESRD-related services provided in an outpatient setting. For ESRD and non-ESRD dialysis services performed in an inpatient setting, and for non-ESRD dialysis services performed in an outpatient setting, see 90935-90937 and 90945-90947.

Evaluation and management services unrelated to ESRD services that cannot be performed during the dialysis session may be reported separately.

Medicine

Codes 90922-90925 are reported when outpatient ESRD-related services are not performed consecutively during an entire full month (eg, when the patient spends part of the month as a hospital inpatient, or when the outpatient ESRD-related services are initiated after the first of the month). The appropriate age-related code from this series (90922-90925) is reported daily less the days of hospitalization. For reporting purposes, each month is considered 30 days.

Example:

Outpatient ESRD-related services are initiated on July 1 for a 57-year-old male. On July 11, he is admitted to the hospital as an inpatient and is discharged on July 27.

In this example, code 90925 should be reported for each day outside of the inpatient hospitalization (30 days/month less 17 days/hospitalization = 13 days). Report inpatient E/M services as appropriate. Dialysis procedures rendered during the hospitalization (July 11-27) should be reported as appropriate (90935-90937, 90945-90947).

End-Stage Renal Disease Services

90918   End-stage renal disease (ESRD) related services per full month; for patients under two years of age to include monitoring for the adequacy of nutrition, assessment of growth and development, and counseling of parents

90919   for patients between two and eleven years of age to include monitoring for the adequacy of nutrition, assessment of growth and development, and counseling of parents

90920   for patients between twelve and nineteen years of age to include monitoring for the adequacy of nutrition, assessment of growth and development, and counseling of parents

90921   for patients twenty years of age and over

90922   End-stage renal disease (ESRD) related services (less than full month), per day; for patients under two years of age

90923   for patients between two and eleven years of age

90924   for patients between twelve and nineteen years of age

90925   for patients twenty years of age and over

Hemodialysis

Codes 90935, 90937 are reported to describe the hemodialysis procedure with all evaluation and management services related to the patient's renal disease on the day of the hemodialysis procedure. These codes are used for inpatient ESRD and non-ESRD procedures or for outpatient non-ESRD dialysis services. Code 90935 is reported if only one evaluation of the patient is required related to that hemodialysis procedure. Code 90937 is reported when patient re-evaluation(s) is required during a hemodialysis procedure. Use modifier 25 with

Evaluation and Management codes for separately identifiable services unrelated to the dialysis procedure or renal failure which cannot be rendered during the dialysis session.

(For home visit hemodialysis services performed by a non-physician health care professional, use 99512)

(For cannula declotting, see 36831, 36833, 36860, 36861)

(For declotting of implanted vascular access device or catheter by thrombolytic agent, use 36550)

(For collection of blood specimen from a partially or completely implantable venous access device, use 36540)

(For prolonged physician attendance, see 99354-99360)

90935   Hemodialysis procedure with single physician evaluation

90937   Hemodialysis procedure requiring repeated evaluation(s) with or without substantial revision of dialysis prescription

▶(90939 has been deleted. To report, use 90940)◀

▲ **90940**   Hemodialysis access flow study to determine blood flow in grafts and arteriovenous fistulae by an indicator method

(For duplex scan of hemodialysis access, use 93990)

Miscellaneous Dialysis Procedures

Codes 90945, 90947 describe dialysis procedures other than hemodialysis (eg, peritoneal dialysis, hemofiltration or continuous renal replacement therapies), and all evaluation and management services related to the patient's renal disease on the day of the procedure. Code 90945 is reported if only one evaluation of the patient is required related to that procedure. Code 90947 is reported when patient re-evaluation(s) is required during a procedure. Utilize modifier 25 with Evaluation and Management codes for separately identifiable services unrelated to the procedure or the renal failure which cannot be rendered during the dialysis session.

(For insertion of intraperitoneal cannula or catheter, see 49420, 49421)

(For prolonged physician attendance, see 99354-99360)

90945   Dialysis procedure other than hemodialysis (eg, peritoneal dialysis, hemofiltration, or other continuous renal replacement therapies), with single physician evaluation

(For home infusion of peritoneal dialysis, use 99601, 99602)

90947   Dialysis procedure other than hemodialysis (eg, peritoneal dialysis, hemofiltration, or other continuous renal replacement therapies) requiring repeated physician evaluations, with or without substantial revision of dialysis prescription

90989   Dialysis training, patient, including helper where applicable, any mode, completed course

90993 Dialysis training, patient, including helper where applicable, any mode, course not completed, per training session

90997 Hemoperfusion (eg, with activated charcoal or resin)

90999 Unlisted dialysis procedure, inpatient or outpatient

Gastroenterology

(For duodenal intubation and aspiration, see 89100-89105)

(For gastrointestinal radiologic procedures, see 74210-74363)

(For esophagoscopy procedures, see 43200-43228; upper GI endoscopy 43234-43259; endoscopy, small intestine and stomal 44360-44393; proctosigmoidoscopy 45300-45321; sigmoidoscopy 45330-45339; colonoscopy 45355-45385; anoscopy 46600-46615)

91000 Esophageal intubation and collection of washings for cytology, including preparation of specimens (separate procedure)

91010 Esophageal motility (manometric study of the esophagus and/or gastroesophageal junction) study;

91011 with mecholyl or similar stimulant

91012 with acid perfusion studies

91020 Gastric motility (manometric) studies

● **91022** Duodenal motility (manometric) study

►(If gastrointestinal endoscopy is performed, use 43235)◄

►(If fluoroscopy is performed, use 76000)◄

►(If gastric motility study is performed, use 91020)◄

91030 Esophagus, acid perfusion (Bernstein) test for esophagitis

(91032 and 91033 have been deleted. To report, see 91034, 91035)

91034 Esophagus, gastroesophageal reflux test; with nasal catheter pH electrode(s) placement, recording, analysis and interpretation

91035 with mucosal attached telemetry pH electrode placement, recording, analysis and interpretation

91037 Esophageal function test, gastroesophageal reflux test with nasal catheter intraluminal impedance electrode(s) placement, recording, analysis and interpretation;

91038 prolonged (greater than 1 hour, up to 24 hours)

91040 Esophageal balloon distension provocation study

(For balloon dilatation with endoscopy, see 43220, 43249, 43456, or 43458)

91052 Gastric analysis test with injection of stimulant of gastric secretion (eg, histamine, insulin, pentagastrin, calcium and secretin)

(For gastric biopsy by capsule, peroral, via tube, one or more specimens, use 43600)

(For gastric laboratory procedures, see also 89130-89141)

91055 Gastric intubation, washings, and preparing slides for cytology (separate procedure)

(For gastric lavage, therapeutic, use 91105)

91060 Gastric saline load test

(For biopsy by capsule, small intestine, per oral, via tube (one or more specimens), use 44100)

91065 Breath hydrogen test (eg, for detection of lactase deficiency, fructose intolerance, bacterial overgrowth, or oro-cecal gastrointestinal transit)

(For H. pylori breath test analysis, use 83013 for non-radioactive (C-13) isotope or 78268 for radioactive (C-14) isotope)

91100 Intestinal bleeding tube, passage, positioning and monitoring

91105 Gastric intubation, and aspiration or lavage for treatment (eg, for ingested poisons)

(For cholangiography, see 47500, 74320)

(For abdominal paracentesis, see 49080, 49081; with instillation of medication, see 96440, 96445)

(For peritoneoscopy, use 49320; with biopsy, use 49321)

(For peritoneoscopy and guided transhepatic cholangiography, use 47560; with biopsy, use 47561)

(For splenoportography, see 38200, 75810)

91110 Gastrointestinal tract imaging, intraluminal (eg, capsule endoscopy), esophagus through ileum, with physician interpretation and report

(Visualization of the colon is not reported separately)

(Append modifier 52 if the ileum is not visualized)

91120 Rectal sensation, tone, and compliance test (ie, response to graded balloon distention)

(For biofeedback training, use 90911)

(For anorectal manometry, use 91122)

91122 Anorectal manometry

91123 Pulsed irrigation of fecal impaction

Gastric Physiology

91132 Electrogastrography, diagnostic, transcutaneous;

91133 with provocative testing

Other Procedures

91299 Unlisted diagnostic gastroenterology procedure

Medicine

Ophthalmology

(For surgical procedures, see **Surgery,** Eye and Ocular Adnexa, 65091 et seq)

Definitions

Intermediate ophthalmological services describes an evaluation of a new or existing condition complicated with a new diagnostic or management problem not necessarily relating to the primary diagnosis, including history, general medical observation, external ocular and adnexal examination and other diagnostic procedures as indicated; may include the use of mydriasis for ophthalmoscopy.

For example:

a. Review of history, external examination, ophthalmoscopy, biomicroscopy for an acute complicated condition (eg, iritis) not requiring comprehensive ophthalmological services.

b. Review of interval history, external examination, ophthalmoscopy, biomicroscopy and tonometry in established patient with known cataract not requiring comprehensive ophthalmological services.

Comprehensive ophthalmological services describes a general evaluation of the complete visual system. The comprehensive services constitute a single service entity but need not be performed at one session. The service includes history, general medical observation, external and ophthalmoscopic examinations, gross visual fields and basic sensorimotor examination. It often includes, as indicated: biomicroscopy, examination with cycloplegia or mydriasis and tonometry. It always includes initiation of diagnostic and treatment programs.

Intermediate and comprehensive ophthalmological services constitute integrated services in which medical decision making cannot be separated from the examining techniques used. Itemization of service components, such as slit lamp examination, keratometry, routine ophthalmoscopy, retinoscopy, tonometry, or motor evaluation is not applicable.

For example:

The comprehensive services required for diagnosis and treatment of a patient with symptoms indicating possible disease of the visual system, such as glaucoma, cataract or retinal disease, or to rule out disease of the visual system, new or established patient.

Initiation of diagnostic and treatment program includes the prescription of medication, and arranging for special ophthalmological diagnostic or treatment services, consultations, laboratory procedures and radiological services.

Special ophthalmological services describes services in which a special evaluation of part of the visual system is made, which goes beyond the services included under general ophthalmological services, or in which special treatment is given. Special ophthalmological services may be reported in addition to the general ophthalmological services or evaluation and management services.

For example:

Fluorescein angioscopy, quantitative visual field examination, refraction or extended color vision examination (such as Nagel's anomaloscope) should be separately reported.

Prescription of lenses, when required, is included in 92015. It includes specification of lens type (monofocal, bifocal, other), lens power, axis, prism, absorptive factor, impact resistance, and other factors.

Interpretation and report by the physician is an integral part of special ophthalmological services where indicated. Technical procedures (which may or may not be performed by the physician personally) are often part of the service, but should not be mistaken to constitute the service itself.

General Ophthalmological Services

New Patient

Solely for the purposes of distinguishing between new and established patients, **professional services** are those face-to-face services rendered by a physician and reported by a specific code(s). A new patient is one who has not received any professional services from the physician or another physician of the same specialty who belongs to the same group practice within the past three years.

92002   Ophthalmological services: medical examination and evaluation with initiation of diagnostic and treatment program; intermediate, new patient

92004   comprehensive, new patient, one or more visits

Established Patient

Solely for the purposes of distinguishing between new and established patients, **professional services** are those face-to-face services rendered by a physician and reported by a specific code(s). An established patient is one who has received professional services from the physician or another physician of the same specialty who belongs to the same group practice within the past three years.

92012   Ophthalmological services: medical examination and evaluation, with initiation or continuation of diagnostic and treatment program; intermediate, established patient

92014   comprehensive, established patient, one or more visits

(For surgical procedures, see **Surgery,** Eye and Ocular Adnexa, 65091 et seq)

Special Ophthalmological Services

92015   Determination of refractive state

92018   Ophthalmological examination and evaluation, under general anesthesia, with or without manipulation of globe for passive range of motion or other manipulation to facilitate diagnostic examination; complete

92019   limited

92020   Gonioscopy (separate procedure)

(For gonioscopy under general anesthesia, use 92018)

92060   Sensorimotor examination with multiple measurements of ocular deviation (eg, restrictive or paretic muscle with diplopia) with interpretation and report (separate procedure)

92065   Orthoptic and/or pleoptic training, with continuing medical direction and evaluation

92070   Fitting of contact lens for treatment of disease, including supply of lens

92081   Visual field examination, unilateral or bilateral, with interpretation and report; limited examination (eg, tangent screen, Autoplot, arc perimeter, or single stimulus level automated test, such as Octopus 3 or 7 equivalent)

92082   intermediate examination (eg, at least 2 isopters on Goldmann perimeter, or semiquantitative, automated suprathreshold screening program, Humphrey suprathreshold automatic diagnostic test, Octopus program 33)

92083   extended examination (eg, Goldmann visual fields with at least 3 isopters plotted and static determination within the central 30°, or quantitative, automated threshold perimetry, Octopus program G-1, 32 or 42, Humphrey visual field analyzer full threshold programs 30-2, 24-2, or 30/60-2)

(Gross visual field testing (eg, confrontation testing) is a part of general ophthalmological services and is not reported separately)

92100   Serial tonometry (separate procedure) with multiple measurements of intraocular pressure over an extended time period with interpretation and report, same day (eg, diurnal curve or medical treatment of acute elevation of intraocular pressure)

92120   Tonography with interpretation and report, recording indentation tonometer method or perilimbal suction method

92130   Tonography with water provocation

92135   Scanning computerized ophthalmic diagnostic imaging (eg, scanning laser) with interpretation and report, unilateral

92136   Ophthalmic biometry by partial coherence interferometry with intraocular lens power calculation

92140   Provocative tests for glaucoma, with interpretation and report, without tonography

Ophthalmoscopy

Routine ophthalmoscopy is part of general and special ophthalmologic services whenever indicated. It is a non-itemized service and is not reported separately.

92225   Ophthalmoscopy, extended, with retinal drawing (eg, for retinal detachment, melanoma), with interpretation and report; initial

92226   subsequent

92230   Fluorescein angioscopy with interpretation and report

92235   Fluorescein angiography (includes multiframe imaging) with interpretation and report

92240   Indocyanine-green angiography (includes multiframe imaging) with interpretation and report

92250   Fundus photography with interpretation and report

92260   Ophthalmodynamometry

(For ophthalmoscopy under general anesthesia, use 92018)

Other Specialized Services

92265   Needle oculoelectromyography, one or more extraocular muscles, one or both eyes, with interpretation and report

92270   Electro-oculography with interpretation and report

92275   Electroretinography with interpretation and report

(For electronystagmography for vestibular function studies, see 92541 et seq)

(For ophthalmic echography (diagnostic ultrasound), see 76511-76529)

92283   Color vision examination, extended, eg, anomaloscope or equivalent

(Color vision testing with pseudoisochromatic plates (such as HRR or Ishihara) is not reported separately. It is included in the appropriate general or ophthalmological service, or 99172)

92284   Dark adaptation examination with interpretation and report

92285   External ocular photography with interpretation and report for documentation of medical progress (eg, close-up photography, slit lamp photography, goniophotography, stereo-photography)

92286   Special anterior segment photography with interpretation and report; with specular endothelial microscopy and cell count

92287   with fluorescein angiography

Contact Lens Services

The prescription of contact lens includes specification of optical and physical characteristics (such as power, size, curvature, flexibility, gas-permeability). It is NOT a part of the general ophthalmological services.

Medicine

The fitting of contact lens includes instruction and training of the wearer and incidental revision of the lens during the training period.

Follow-up of successfully fitted extended wear lenses is reported as part of a general ophthalmological service (92012 et seq).

►The supply of contact lenses may be reported as part of the service of fitting. It may also be reported separately by using the appropriate supply codes.◄

(For therapeutic or surgical use of contact lens, see 68340, 92070)

92310   Prescription of optical and physical characteristics of and fitting of contact lens, with medical supervision of adaptation; corneal lens, both eyes, except for aphakia

(For prescription and fitting of one eye, add modifier 52)

92311   corneal lens for aphakia, one eye

92312   corneal lens for aphakia, both eyes

92313   corneoscleral lens

92314   Prescription of optical and physical characteristics of contact lens, with medical supervision of adaptation and direction of fitting by independent technician; corneal lens, both eyes except for aphakia

(For prescription and fitting of one eye, add modifier 52)

92315   corneal lens for aphakia, one eye

92316   corneal lens for aphakia, both eyes

92317   corneoscleral lens

92325   Modification of contact lens (separate procedure), with medical supervision of adaptation

92326   Replacement of contact lens

►(92330, 92335 have been deleted)◄

►(For prescription, fitting, and/or medical supervision of ocular prosthetic adaptation by a physician, see Evaluation and Management services or General Ophthalmological service codes 92002-92014)◄

Spectacle Services (Including Prosthesis for Aphakia)

Prescription of lenses, when required, is included in 92015 Determination of refractive state. It includes specification of lens type (monofocal, bifocal, other), lens power, axis, prism, absorptive factor, impact resistance, and other factors.

Fitting of spectacles is a separate service; when provided by the physician, it is reported as indicated by 92340-92371.

Fitting includes measurement of anatomical facial characteristics, the writing of laboratory specifications, and the final adjustment of the spectacles to the visual axes and anatomical topography. Presence of physician is not required.

Supply of materials is a separate service component; it is not part of the service of fitting spectacles.

92340   Fitting of spectacles, except for aphakia; monofocal

92341   bifocal

92342   multifocal, other than bifocal

92352   Fitting of spectacle prosthesis for aphakia; monofocal

92353   multifocal

92354   Fitting of spectacle mounted low vision aid; single element system

92355   telescopic or other compound lens system

92358   Prosthesis service for aphakia, temporary (disposable or loan, including materials)

92370   Repair and refitting spectacles; except for aphakia

92371   spectacle prosthesis for aphakia

►(Codes 92390-92396 have been deleted. For supply of spectacles or contact lenses, use the appropriate supply codes)◄

Other Procedures

92499   Unlisted ophthalmological service or procedure

Special Otorhinolaryngologic Services

Diagnostic or treatment procedures usually included in a comprehensive otorhinolaryngologic evaluation or office visit, are reported as an integrated medical service, using appropriate descriptors from the 99201 series. Itemization of component procedures (eg, otoscopy, rhinoscopy, tuning fork test) does not apply.

Special otorhinolaryngologic services are those diagnostic and treatment services not usually included in a comprehensive otorhinolaryngologic evaluation or office visit. These services are reported separately, using codes 92502-92700.

All services include medical diagnostic evaluation. Technical procedures (which may or may not be performed by the physician personally) are often part of the service, but should not be mistaken to constitute the service itself.

►Code 92506 is used to report evaluation of speech production, receptive language, and expressive language abilities. Tests may examine speech sound production, articulatory movements of oral musculature, the patient's ability to understand the meaning and intent of written and verbal expressions, and the appropriate formulation and utterance of expressive thought. In contrast, 92626 and 92627 are reported for an evaluation of auditory rehabilitation status determining the patient's ability to use residual hearing in order to identify the acoustic characteristics of sounds associated with speech communication.◄

(For laryngoscopy with stroboscopy, use 31579)

92502   Otolaryngologic examination under general anesthesia

92504   Binocular microscopy (separate diagnostic procedure)

▲ **92506**   Evaluation of speech, language, voice, communication, and/or auditory processing

▲ **92507**   Treatment of speech, language, voice, communication, and/or auditory processing disorder; individual

92508   group, 2 or more individuals

►(92510 has been deleted)◄

►(For auditory rehabilitation, prelingual hearing loss, use 92630)◄

►(For auditory rehabilitation, postlingual hearing loss, use 92633)◄

►(For cochlear implant programming, see 92601-92604)◄

92511   Nasopharyngoscopy with endoscope (separate procedure)

92512   Nasal function studies (eg, rhinomanometry)

92516   Facial nerve function studies (eg, electroneuronography)

▲ **92520**   Laryngeal function studies (ie, aerodynamic testing and acoustic testing)

►(For performance of a single test, use modifier 52)◄

►(To report flexible fiberoptic laryngeal evaluation of swallowing and laryngeal sensory testing, see 92611-92617)◄

►(To report other testing of laryngeal function (eg, electroglottography), use 92700)◄

92526   Treatment of swallowing dysfunction and/or oral function for feeding

Vestibular Function Tests, With Observation and Evaluation by Physician, Without Electrical Recording

92531   Spontaneous nystagmus, including gaze

92532   Positional nystagmus test

92533   Caloric vestibular test, each irrigation (binaural, bithermal stimulation constitutes four tests)

92534   Optokinetic nystagmus test

Vestibular Function Tests, With Recording (eg, ENG, PENG), and Medical Diagnostic Evaluation

92541   Spontaneous nystagmus test, including gaze and fixation nystagmus, with recording

92542   Positional nystagmus test, minimum of 4 positions, with recording

92543   Caloric vestibular test, each irrigation (binaural, bithermal stimulation constitutes four tests), with recording

92544   Optokinetic nystagmus test, bidirectional, foveal or peripheral stimulation, with recording

92545   Oscillating tracking test, with recording

92546   Sinusoidal vertical axis rotational testing

+ **92547**   Use of vertical electrodes (List separately in addition to code for primary procedure)

(Use 92547 in conjunction with 92541-92546)

(For unlisted vestibular tests, use 92700)

92548   Computerized dynamic posturography

Audiologic Function Tests With Medical Diagnostic Evaluation

The audiometric tests listed below imply the use of calibrated electronic equipment. Other hearing tests (such as whispered voice, tuning fork) are considered part of the general otorhinolaryngologic services and are not reported separately. All services include testing of both ears. Use modifier 52 if a test is applied to one ear instead of to two ears. All codes (except 92559) apply to testing of individuals; for testing of groups, use 92559 and specify test(s) used.

(For evaluation of speech, language and/or hearing problems through observation and assessment of performance, use 92506)

92551   Screening test, pure tone, air only

92552   Pure tone audiometry (threshold); air only

92553   air and bone

92555   Speech audiometry threshold;

92556   with speech recognition

92557   Comprehensive audiometry threshold evaluation and speech recognition (92553 and 92556 combined)

(For hearing aid evaluation and selection, see 92590-92595)

92559   Audiometric testing of groups

92560   Bekesy audiometry; screening

92561   diagnostic

92562   Loudness balance test, alternate binaural or monaural

92563   Tone decay test

Medicine

92564 Short increment sensitivity index (SISI)

92565 Stenger test, pure tone

92567 Tympanometry (impedance testing)

▲ **92568** Acoustic reflex testing; threshold

▲ **92569** decay

92571 Filtered speech test

92572 Staggered spondaic word test

92573 Lombard test

92575 Sensorineural acuity level test

92576 Synthetic sentence identification test

92577 Stenger test, speech

92579 Visual reinforcement audiometry (VRA)

92582 Conditioning play audiometry

92583 Select picture audiometry

92584 Electrocochleography

92585 Auditory evoked potentials for evoked response audiometry and/or testing of the central nervous system; comprehensive

92586 limited

92587 Evoked otoacoustic emissions; limited (single stimulus level, either transient or distortion products)

92588 comprehensive or diagnostic evaluation (comparison of transient and/or distortion product otoacoustic emissions at multiple levels and frequencies)

(92589 has been deleted)

(For central auditory function evaluation, see 92620, 92621)

92590 Hearing aid examination and selection; monaural

92591 binaural

92592 Hearing aid check; monaural

92593 binaural

92594 Electroacoustic evaluation for hearing aid; monaural

92595 binaural

92596 Ear protector attenuation measurements

92597 Evaluation for use and/or fitting of voice prosthetic device to supplement oral speech

(To report augmentative and alternative communication device services, see 92605, 92607, 92608)

Evaluative and Therapeutic Services

Codes 92601 and 92603 describe post-operative analysis and fitting of previously placed external devices, connection to the cochlear implant, and programming of the stimulator. Codes 92602 and 92604 describe

subsequent sessions for measurements and adjustment of the external transmitter and re-programming of the internal stimulator.

(For placement of cochlear implant, use 69930)

92601 Diagnostic analysis of cochlear implant, patient under 7 years of age; with programming

92602 subsequent reprogramming

(Do not report 92602 in addition to 92601)

▶(For aural rehabilitation services following cochlear implant, including evaluation of rehabilitation status, see 92626-92627, 92630-92633)◀

92603 Diagnostic analysis of cochlear implant, age 7 years or older; with programming

92604 subsequent reprogramming

(Do not report 92604 in addition to 92603)

92605 Evaluation for prescription of non-speech-generating augmentative and alternative communication device

92606 Therapeutic service(s) for the use of non-speech-generating device, including programming and modification

92607 Evaluation for prescription for speech-generating augmentative and alternative communication device, face-to-face with the patient; first hour

(For evaluation for prescription of a non-speech-generating device, use 92605)

+ **92608** each additional 30 minutes (List separately in addition to code for primary procedure)

(Use 92608 in conjunction with 92607)

92609 Therapeutic services for the use of speech-generating device, including programming and modification

(For therapeutic service(s) for the use of a non-speech-generating device, use 92606)

92610 Evaluation of oral and pharyngeal swallowing function

(For motion fluoroscopic evaluation of swallowing function, use 92611)

(For flexible endoscopic examination, use 92612-92617)

92611 Motion fluoroscopic evaluation of swallowing function by cine or video recording

(For radiological supervision and interpretation, use 74230)

(For evaluation of oral and pharyngeal swallowing function, use 92610)

(For flexible fiberoptic diagnostic laryngoscopy, use 31575. Do not report 31575 in conjunction with 92612-92617)

⊘=Modifier 51 exempt   ⊙=Conscious sedation   ✚=Add-on code   ✗=FDA approval pending

92612   Flexible fiberoptic endoscopic evaluation of swallowing by cine or video recording;

(If flexible fiberoptic or endoscopic evaluation of swallowing is performed without cine or video recording, use 92700)

92613   physician interpretation and report only

(To report an evaluation of oral and pharyngeal swallowing function, use 92610)

(To report motion fluoroscopic evaluation of swallowing function, use 92611)

92614   Flexible fiberoptic endoscopic evaluation, laryngeal sensory testing by cine or video recording;

(If flexible fiberoptic or endoscopic evaluation of swallowing is performed without cine or video recording, use 92700)

92615   physician interpretation and report only

92616   Flexible fiberoptic endoscopic evaluation of swallowing and laryngeal sensory testing by cine or video recording;

(If flexible fiberoptic or endoscopic evaluation of swallowing is performed without cine or video recording, use 92700)

92617   physician interpretation and report only

92620   Evaluation of central auditory function, with report; initial 60 minutes

92621   each additional 15 minutes

(Do not report 92620, 92621 in conjunction with 92506)

92625   Assessment of tinnitus (includes pitch, loudness matching, and masking)

(Do not report 92625 in conjunction with 92562)

(For unilateral assessment, use modifier 52)

● **92626**   Evaluation of auditory rehabilitation status; first hour

+● **92627**   each additional 15 minutes (List separately in addition to code for primary procedure)

▶(Use 92627 in conjunction with 92626)◀

▶(When reporting 92626, 92627, use the face-to-face time with the patient or family)◀

● **92630**   Auditory rehabilitation; pre-lingual hearing loss

● **92633**   post-lingual hearing loss

Other Procedures

92700   Unlisted otorhinolaryngological service or procedure

Cardiovascular

Therapeutic Services

(For non-surgical septal reduction therapy (eg, alcohol ablation), use Category III code 0024T)

92950   Cardiopulmonary resuscitation (eg, in cardiac arrest)

(See also critical care services, 99291, 99292)

⊙ **92953**   Temporary transcutaneous pacing

(For physician direction of ambulance or rescue personnel outside the hospital, use 99288)

⊙ **92960**   Cardioversion, elective, electrical conversion of arrhythmia; external

⊙ **92961**   internal (separate procedure)

(Do not report 92961 in addition to codes 93662, 93618-93624, 93631, 93640-93642, 93650-93652, 93741-93744)

92970   Cardioassist-method of circulatory assist; internal

92971   external

(For balloon atrial-septostomy, use 92992)

(For placement of catheters for use in circulatory assist devices such as intra-aortic balloon pump, use 33970)

⊙+ **92973**   Percutaneous transluminal coronary thrombectomy (List separately in addition to code for primary procedure)

(Use 92973 in conjunction with 92980, 92982)

⊙+ **92974**   Transcatheter placement of radiation delivery device for subsequent coronary intravascular brachytherapy (List separately in addition to code for primary procedure)

(Use 92974 in conjunction with 92980, 92982, 92995, 93508)

(For intravascular radioelement application, see 77781-77784)

⊙ **92975**   Thrombolysis, coronary; by intracoronary infusion, including selective coronary angiography

92977   by intravenous infusion

(For thrombolysis of vessels other than coronary, see 37201, 75896)

(For cerebral thrombolysis, use 37195)

⊙+ **92978**   Intravascular ultrasound (coronary vessel or graft) during diagnostic evaluation and/or therapeutic intervention including imaging supervision, interpretation and report; initial vessel (List separately in addition to code for primary procedure)

⊙+ **92979**   each additional vessel (List separately in addition to code for primary procedure)

(Use 92979 in conjunction with 92978)

(Intravascular ultrasound services include all transducer manipulations and repositioning within the specific vessel being examined, both before and after therapeutic intervention (eg, stent placement))

Medicine

⊙ **92980**   Transcatheter placement of an intracoronary stent(s), percutaneous, with or without other therapeutic intervention, any method; single vessel

⊙✛ **92981**   each additional vessel (List separately in addition to code for primary procedure)

(Use 92981 in conjunction with 92980)

(Codes 92980, 92981 are used to report coronary artery stenting. Coronary angioplasty (92982, 92984) or atherectomy (92995, 92996), in the same artery, is considered part of the stenting procedure and is not reported separately. Codes 92973 (percutaneous transluminal coronary thombectomy), 92974 (coronary brachytherapy) and 92978, 92979 (intravascular ultrasound) are add-on codes for reporting procedures performed in addition to coronary stenting, atherectomy, and angioplasty and are not included in the "therapeutic interventions" in 92980)

(To report additional vessels treated by angioplasty or atherectomy only during the same session, see 92984, 92996)

(To report transcatheter placement of radiation delivery device for coronary intravascular brachytherapy, use 92974)

(For intravascular radioelement application, see 77781-77784)

⊙ **92982**   Percutaneous transluminal coronary balloon angioplasty; single vessel

⊙✛ **92984**   each additional vessel (List separately in addition to code for primary procedure)

(Use 92984 in conjunction with 92980, 92982, 92995)

(For stent placement following completion of angioplasty or atherectomy, see 92980, 92981)

(To report transcatheter placement of radiation delivery device for coronary intravascular brachytherapy, use 92974)

(For intravascular radioelement application, see 77781-77784)

⊙ **92986**   Percutaneous balloon valvuloplasty; aortic valve

⊙ **92987**   mitral valve

92990   pulmonary valve

92992   Atrial septectomy or septostomy; transvenous method, balloon (eg, Rashkind type) (includes cardiac catheterization)

92993   blade method (Park septostomy) (includes cardiac catheterization)

⊙ **92995**   Percutaneous transluminal coronary atherectomy, by mechanical or other method, with or without balloon angioplasty; single vessel

⊙✛ **92996**   each additional vessel (List separately in addition to code for primary procedure)

(Use 92996 in conjunction with 92980, 92982, 92995)

(For stent placement following completion of angioplasty or atherectomy, see 92980, 92981)

(To report additional vessels treated by angioplasty only during the same session, use 92984)

92997   Percutaneous transluminal pulmonary artery balloon angioplasty; single vessel

✛ **92998**   each additional vessel (List separately in addition to code for primary procedure)

(Use 92998 in conjunction with 92997)

Cardiography

(For echocardiography, see 93303-93350)

93000   Electrocardiogram, routine ECG with at least 12 leads; with interpretation and report

93005   tracing only, without interpretation and report

93010   interpretation and report only

(For ECG monitoring, see 99354-99360)

93012   Telephonic transmission of post-symptom electrocardiogram rhythm strip(s), 24-hour attended monitoring, per 30 day period of time; tracing only

93014   physician review with interpretation and report only

93015   Cardiovascular stress test using maximal or submaximal treadmill or bicycle exercise, continuous electrocardiographic monitoring, and/or pharmacological stress; with physician supervision, with interpretation and report

93016   physician supervision only, without interpretation and report

93017   tracing only, without interpretation and report

93018   interpretation and report only

▶(For inert gas rebreathing measurement, see Category III codes 0104T, 0105T)◀

93024   Ergonovine provocation test

93025   Microvolt T-wave alternans for assessment of ventricular arrhythmias

93040   Rhythm ECG, one to three leads; with interpretation and report

93041   tracing only without interpretation and report

93042   interpretation and report only

93224   Electrocardiographic monitoring for 24 hours by continuous original ECG waveform recording and storage, with visual superimposition scanning; includes recording, scanning analysis with report, physician review and interpretation

93225   recording (includes hook-up, recording, and disconnection)

93226   scanning analysis with report

93227   physician review and interpretation

93230   Electrocardiographic monitoring for 24 hours by continuous original ECG waveform recording and storage without superimposition scanning utilizing a device capable of producing a full miniaturized printout; includes recording, microprocessor-based analysis with report, physician review and interpretation

93231   recording (includes hook-up, recording, and disconnection)

93232   microprocessor-based analysis with report

93233   physician review and interpretation

93235   Electrocardiographic monitoring for 24 hours by continuous computerized monitoring and non-continuous recording, and real-time data analysis utilizing a device capable of producing intermittent full-sized waveform tracings, possibly patient activated; includes monitoring and real-time data analysis with report, physician review and interpretation

93236   monitoring and real-time data analysis with report

93237   physician review and interpretation

93268   Patient demand single or multiple event recording with presymptom memory loop, 24-hour attended monitoring, per 30 day period of time; includes transmission, physician review and interpretation

93270   recording (includes hook-up, recording, and disconnection)

93271   monitoring, receipt of transmissions, and analysis

93272   physician review and interpretation only

        (For postsymptom recording, see 93012, 93014)

        (For implanted patient activated cardiac event recording, see 33282, 93727)

93278   Signal-averaged electrocardiography (SAECG), with or without ECG

        (For interpretation and report only, use 93278 with modifier 26)

        (For unlisted cardiographic procedure, use 93799)

Echocardiography

Echocardiography includes obtaining ultrasonic signals from the heart and great arteries, with two-dimensional image and/or Doppler ultrasonic signal documentation, and interpretation and report. When interpretation is performed separately use modifier 26.

Echocardiography is an ultrasound examination of the cardiac chambers and valves, the adjacent great vessels, and the pericardium. A complete transthoracic echocardiogram (93307) is a comprehensive procedure that includes 2-dimensional and selected M-mode examination of the left and right atria, left and right ventricles, the aortic, mitral, and tricuspid valves, the pericardium, and adjacent portions of the aorta. These structures are assessed using multiple views as required to obtain a complete functional and anatomic evaluation, and appropriate measurements are obtained and recorded. Despite significant effort, identification and measurement of some structures may not always be possible. In such instances, the reason that an element could not be visualized must be documented. Additional structures that may be visualized (eg, pulmonary veins, pulmonary artery, pulmonic valve, inferior vena cava) would be included as part of the service.

A follow-up or limited echocardiographic study (93308) is an examination that does not evaluate or document the attempt to evaluate all the structures that comprise the complete echocardiographic exam. This is typically performed in follow-up of a complete echocardiographic examination when a repeat complete exam is unnecessary due to the more focused clinical concern. In some emergent clinical situations, a limited echocardiographic study may be performed primarily.

Report of an echocardiographic study, whether complete or limited, includes an interpretation of all obtained information, documentation of all clinically relevant findings including quantitative measurements obtained, plus a description of any recognized abnormalities. Pertinent images, videotape, and/or digital data are archived for permanent storage and are available for subsequent review. Use of echocardiography not meeting these criteria is not separately reportable.

Use of ultrasound, without thorough evaluation of organ(s) or anatomic region, image documentation and final, written report, is not separately reportable.

        (For fetal echocardiography, see 76825-76828)

93303   Transthoracic echocardiography for congenital cardiac anomalies; complete

93304   follow-up or limited study

93307   Echocardiography, transthoracic, real-time with image documentation (2D) with or without M-mode recording; complete

93308   follow-up or limited study

⊙ **93312**   Echocardiography, transesophageal, real time with image documentation (2D) (with or without M-mode recording); including probe placement, image acquisition, interpretation and report

⊙ **93313**   placement of transesophageal probe only

⊙ **93314**   image acquisition, interpretation and report only

▲=Revised code   ●=New code   ► ◄=Contains new or revised text

⊙ **93315**   Transesophageal echocardiography for congenital cardiac anomalies; including probe placement, image acquisition, interpretation and report

⊙ **93316**   placement of transesophageal probe only

⊙ **93317**   image acquisition, interpretation and report only

⊙ **93318**   Echocardiography, transesophageal (TEE) for monitoring purposes, including probe placement, real time 2-dimensional image acquisition and interpretation leading to ongoing (continuous) assessment of (dynamically changing) cardiac pumping function and to therapeutic measures on an immediate time basis

+ **93320**   Doppler echocardiography, pulsed wave and/or continuous wave with spectral display (List separately in addition to codes for echocardiographic imaging); complete

(Use 93320 in conjunction with 93303, 93304, 93307, 93308, 93312, 93314, 93315, 93317, 93350)

+ **93321**   follow-up or limited study (List separately in addition to codes for echocardiographic imaging)

(Use 93321 in conjunction with 93303, 93304, 93307, 93308, 93312, 93314, 93315, 93317, 93350)

+ **93325**   Doppler echocardiography color flow velocity mapping (List separately in addition to codes for echocardiography)

(Use 93325 in conjunction with 76825, 76826, 76827, 76828, 93303, 93304, 93307, 93308, 93312, 93314, 93315, 93317, 93320, 93321, 93350)

93350   Echocardiography, transthoracic, real-time with image documentation (2D), with or without M-mode recording, during rest and cardiovascular stress test using treadmill, bicycle exercise and/or pharmacologically induced stress, with interpretation and report

(The appropriate stress testing code from the 93015-93018 series should be reported in addition to 93350 to capture the exercise stress portion of the study)

Cardiac Catheterization

Cardiac catheterization is a diagnostic medical procedure which includes introduction, positioning and repositioning of catheter(s), when necessary, recording of intracardiac and intravascular pressure, obtaining blood samples for measurement of blood gases or dilution curves and cardiac output measurements (Fick or other method, with or without rest and exercise and/or studies) with or without electrode catheter placement, final evaluation and report of procedure. When selective injection procedures are performed without a preceding cardiac catheterization, these services should be reported using codes in the Vascular Injection Procedures section, 36011-36015 and 36215-36218.

When coronary artery, arterial coronary conduit or venous bypass graft angiography is performed without concomitant left heart cardiac catheterization, use 93508. Injection procedures 93539, 93540, 93544, and 93545

represent separate identifiable services and may be reported in conjunction with one another in addition to 93508, as appropriate. To report imaging supervision, interpretation and report in conjunction with 93508, use 93556.

Modifier 51 should not be appended to 93501-93533, 93539-93556.

⊙⊘ **93501**   Right heart catheterization

(For bundle of His recording, use 93600)

⊘ **93503**   Insertion and placement of flow directed catheter (eg, Swan-Ganz) for monitoring purposes

(For subsequent monitoring, see 99356-99357)

⊙⊘ **93505**   Endomyocardial biopsy

⊙⊘ **93508**   Catheter placement in coronary artery(s), arterial coronary conduit(s), and/or venous coronary bypass graft(s) for coronary angiography without concomitant left heart catheterization

(93508 is to be used only when left heart catheterization 93510, 93511, 93524, 93526 is not performed)

(93508 is to be used only once per procedure)

(To report transcatheter placement of radiation delivery device for coronary intravascular brachytherapy, use 92974)

(For intravascular radioelement application, see 77781-77784)

⊙⊘ **93510**   Left heart catheterization, retrograde, from the brachial artery, axillary artery or femoral artery; percutaneous

⊙⊘ **93511**   by cutdown

⊙⊘ **93514**   Left heart catheterization by left ventricular puncture

⊙⊘ **93524**   Combined transseptal and retrograde left heart catheterization

⊙⊘ **93526**   Combined right heart catheterization and retrograde left heart catheterization

⊙⊘ **93527**   Combined right heart catheterization and transseptal left heart catheterization through intact septum (with or without retrograde left heart catheterization)

⊙⊘ **93528**   Combined right heart catheterization with left ventricular puncture (with or without retrograde left heart catheterization)

⊙⊘ **93529**   Combined right heart catheterization and left heart catheterization through existing septal opening (with or without retrograde left heart catheterization)

⊙⊘ **93530**   Right heart catheterization, for congenital cardiac anomalies

⊘ **93531**   Combined right heart catheterization and retrograde left heart catheterization, for congenital cardiac anomalies

⊘ **93532**   Combined right heart catheterization and transseptal left heart catheterization through intact septum with or without retrograde left heart catheterization, for congenital cardiac anomalies

⊘ **93533**   Combined right heart catheterization and transseptal left heart catheterization through existing septal opening, with or without retrograde left heart catheterization, for congenital cardiac anomalies

(When injection procedures are performed in conjunction with cardiac catheterization, these services do not include introduction of catheters but do include repositioning of catheters when necessary and use of automatic power injectors. Injection procedures 93539-93545 represent separate identifiable services and may be coded in conjunction with one another when appropriate. The technical details of angiography, supervision of filming and processing, interpretation and report are not included. To report imaging supervision, interpretation and report, use 93555 and/or 93556. Modifier 51 should not be appended to 93539-93556.)

⊙⊘ **93539**   Injection procedure during cardiac catheterization; for selective opacification of arterial conduits (eg, internal mammary), whether native or used for bypass

⊙⊘ **93540**   for selective opacification of aortocoronary venous bypass grafts, one or more coronary arteries

⊙⊘ **93541**   for pulmonary angiography

⊙⊘ **93542**   for selective right ventricular or right atrial angiography

⊙⊘ **93543**   for selective left ventricular or left atrial angiography

⊙⊘ **93544**   for aortography

⊙⊘ **93545**   for selective coronary angiography (injection of radiopaque material may be by hand)

(To report imaging supervision and interpretation, use 93555)

⊙⊘ **93555**   Imaging supervision, interpretation and report for injection procedure(s) during cardiac catheterization; ventricular and/or atrial angiography

⊙⊘ **93556**   pulmonary angiography, aortography, and/or selective coronary angiography including venous bypass grafts and arterial conduits (whether native or used in bypass)

(Codes 93561 and 93562 are not to be used with cardiac catheterization codes)

⊙ **93561**   Indicator dilution studies such as dye or thermal dilution, including arterial and/or venous catheterization; with cardiac output measurement (separate procedure)

⊙ **93562**   subsequent measurement of cardiac output

(For radioisotope method of cardiac output, see 78472, 78473, or 78481)

⊙+ **93571**   Intravascular Doppler velocity and/or pressure derived coronary flow reserve measurement (coronary vessel or graft) during coronary angiography including pharmacologically induced stress; initial vessel (List separately in addition to code for primary procedure)

⊙+ **93572**   each additional vessel (List separately in addition to code for primary procedure)

(Intravascular distal coronary blood flow velocity measurements include all Doppler transducer manipulations and repositioning within the specific vessel being examined, during coronary angiography or therapeutic intervention (eg, angioplasty))

(For unlisted cardiac catheterization procedure, use 93799)

Repair of Septal Defect

93580   Percutaneous transcatheter closure of congenital interatrial communication (ie, Fontan fenestration, atrial septal defect) with implant

(Percutaneous transcatheter closure of atrial septal defect includes a right heart catheterization procedure. Code 93580 includes injection of contrast for atrial and ventricular angiograms. Codes 93501, 93529-93533, 93539, 93543, 93555 should not be reported separately in addition to code 93580)

93581   Percutaneous transcatheter closure of a congenital ventricular septal defect with implant

(Percutaneous transcatheter closure of ventricular septal defect includes a right heart catheterization procedure. Code 93581 includes injection of contrast for atrial and ventricular angiograms. Codes 93501, 93529-93533, 93539, 93543, 93555 should not be reported separately in addition to code 93581)

(For echocardiographic services performed in addition to 93580, 93581, see 93303-93317, 93662 as appropriate)

Intracardiac Electrophysiological Procedures/Studies

Intracardiac electrophysiologic studies (EPS) are an invasive diagnostic medical procedure which include the insertion and repositioning of electrode catheters, recording of electrograms before and during pacing or programmed stimulation of multiple locations in the heart, analysis of recorded information, and report of the procedure. Electrophysiologic studies are most often performed with two or more electrode catheters. In many circumstances, patients with arrhythmias are evaluated and treated at the same encounter. In this situation, a diagnostic *electrophysiologic study* is performed, induced tachycardia(s) are *mapped*, and on the basis of the diagnostic and mapping information, the tissue is *ablated*. Electrophysiologic study(ies), mapping, and ablation represent distinctly different procedures, requiring individual reporting whether performed on the same or subsequent dates.

Medicine

Definitions

Arrhythmia Induction: In most electrophysiologic studies, an attempt is made to induce arrhythmia(s) from single or multiple sites within the heart. Arrhythmia induction is achieved by performing pacing at different rates, programmed stimulation (introduction of critically timed electrical impulses), and other techniques. Because arrhythmia induction occurs via the same catheter(s) inserted for the electrophysiologic study(ies), catheter insertion and temporary pacemaker codes are not additionally reported. Codes 93600-93603, 93610-93612 and 93618 are used to describe unusual situations where there may be recording, pacing or an attempt at arrhythmia induction from only one site in the heart. Code 93619 describes only evaluation of the sinus node, atrioventricular node and His-Purkinje conduction system, without arrhythmia induction. Codes 93620-93624 and 93640-93642 all include recording, pacing and attempted arrhythmia induction from one or more site(s) in the heart.

Mapping: Mapping is a distinct procedure performed in addition to a diagnostic electrophysiologic procedure and should be separately reported using 93609 or 93613. Do not report standard mapping (93609) in addition to 3-D mapping (93613). When a tachycardia is induced, the site of tachycardia origination or its electrical path through the heart is often defined by mapping. Mapping creates a multidimensional depiction of a tachycardia by recording multiple electrograms obtained sequentially or simultaneously from multiple catheter sites in the heart. Depending upon the technique, certain types of mapping catheters may be repositioned from point-to-point within the heart, allowing sequential recording from the various sites to construct maps. Other types of mapping catheters allow mapping without a point-to-point technique by allowing simultaneous recording from many electrodes on the same catheter and computer-assisted three dimensional reconstruction of the tachycardia activation sequence.

Ablation: Once the part of the heart involved in the tachycardia is localized, the tachycardia may be treated by ablation (the delivery of a radiofrequency energy to the area to selectively destroy cardiac tissue). Ablation procedures (93651-93652) may be performed: independently on a date subsequent to a diagnostic electrophysiologic study and mapping; or, at the time a diagnostic electrophysiologic study, tachycardia(s) induction and mapping is performed. When an electrophysiologic study, mapping, and ablation are performed on the same date, each procedure should be separately reported. In reporting catheter ablation, 93651 and/or 93652 should be reported once to describe ablation of cardiac arrhythmias, regardless of the number of arrhythmias ablated.

Modifier 51 should not be appended to 93600-93660.

⊘ **93600** Bundle of His recording

⊘ **93602** Intra-atrial recording

⊘ **93603** Right ventricular recording

⊙➕ **93609** Intraventricular and/or intra-atrial mapping of tachycardia site(s) with catheter manipulation to record from multiple sites to identify origin of tachycardia (List separately in addition to code for primary procedure)

(Use 93609 in conjunction with 93620, 93651, 93652)

(Do not report 93609 in addition to 93613)

⊘ **93610** Intra-atrial pacing

⊘ **93612** Intraventricular pacing

(Do not report 93612 in conjunction with 93620-93622)

⊙➕ **93613** Intracardiac electrophysiologic 3-dimensional mapping (List separately in addition to code for primary procedure)

(Use 93613 in conjunction with 93620, 93651, 93652)

(Do not report 93613 in addition to 93609)

⊙⊘ **93615** Esophageal recording of atrial electrogram with or without ventricular electrogram(s);

⊙⊘ **93616** with pacing

⊙⊘ **93618** Induction of arrhythmia by electrical pacing

(For intracardiac phonocardiogram, use 93799)

⊙⊘ **93619** Comprehensive electrophysiologic evaluation with right atrial pacing and recording, right ventricular pacing and recording, His bundle recording, including insertion and repositioning of multiple electrode catheters, without induction or attempted induction of arrhythmia

(Do not report 93619 in conjunction with 93600, 93602, 93610, 93612, 93618, or 93620-93622)

⊙⊘ **93620** Comprehensive electrophysiologic evaluation including insertion and repositioning of multiple electrode catheters with induction or attempted induction of arrhythmia; with right atrial pacing and recording, right ventricular pacing and recording, His bundle recording

(Do not report 93620 in conjunction with 93600, 93602, 93610, 93612, 93618 or 93619)

⊙➕ **93621** with left atrial pacing and recording from coronary sinus or left atrium (List separately in addition to code for primary procedure)

(Use 93621 in conjunction with 93620)

⊙➕ **93622** with left ventricular pacing and recording (List separately in addition to code for primary procedure)

(Use 93622 in conjunction with 93620)

➕ **93623** Programmed stimulation and pacing after intravenous drug infusion (List separately in addition to code for primary procedure)

(Use 93623 in conjunction with 93619, 93620)

⊙⊘ **93624** Electrophysiologic follow-up study with pacing and recording to test effectiveness of therapy, including induction or attempted induction of arrhythmia

⊘ **93631** Intra-operative epicardial and endocardial pacing and mapping to localize the site of tachycardia or zone of slow conduction for surgical correction

⊙⊘ **93640** Electrophysiologic evaluation of single or dual chamber pacing cardioverter-defibrillator leads including defibrillation threshold evaluation (induction of arrhythmia, evaluation of sensing and pacing for arrhythmia termination) at time of initial implantation or replacement;

⊙⊘ **93641** with testing of single or dual chamber pacing cardioverter-defibrillator pulse generator

(For subsequent or periodic electronic analysis and/or reprogramming of single or dual chamber pacing cardioverter-defibrillators, see 93642, 93741-93744)

⊙⊘ **93642** Electrophysiologic evaluation of single or dual chamber pacing cardioverter-defibrillator (includes defibrillation threshold evaluation, induction of arrhythmia, evaluation of sensing and pacing for arrhythmia termination, and programming or reprogramming of sensing or therapeutic parameters)

⊙⊘ **93650** Intracardiac catheter ablation of atrioventricular node function, atrioventricular conduction for creation of complete heart block, with or without temporary pacemaker placement

⊙⊘ **93651** Intracardiac catheter ablation of arrhythmogenic focus; for treatment of supraventricular tachycardia by ablation of fast or slow atrioventricular pathways, accessory atrioventricular connections or other atrial foci, singly or in combination

⊙⊘ **93652** for treatment of ventricular tachycardia

⊘ **93660** Evaluation of cardiovascular function with tilt table evaluation, with continuous ECG monitoring and intermittent blood pressure monitoring, with or without pharmacological intervention

(For testing of autonomic nervous system function, see 95921-95923)

+ **93662** Intracardiac echocardiography during therapeutic/diagnostic intervention, including imaging supervision and interpretation (List separately in addition to code for primary procedure)

▶(Use 93662 in conjunction with 92987, 93527, 93532, 93580, 93581, 93621, 93622, 93651, or 93652, as appropriate)◀

(Do not report 92961 in addition to 93662)

Peripheral Arterial Disease Rehabilitation

Peripheral arterial disease (PAD) rehabilitative physical exercise consists of a series of sessions, lasting 45-60 minutes per session, involving use of either a motorized treadmill or a track to permit each patient to achieve symptom-limited claudication. Each session is supervised by an exercise physiologist or nurse. The supervising provider monitors the individual patient's claudication threshold and other cardiovascular limitations for adjustment of workload. During this supervised rehabilitation program, the development of new arrhythmias, symptoms that might suggest angina or the continued inability of the patient to progress to an adequate level of exercise may require physician review and examination of the patient. These physician services would be separately reported with an appropriate level E/M service code.

93668 Peripheral arterial disease (PAD) rehabilitation, per session

Other Vascular Studies

(For arterial cannulization and recording of direct arterial pressure, use 36620)

(For radiographic injection procedures, see 36000-36299)

(For vascular cannulization for hemodialysis, see 36800-36821)

(For chemotherapy for malignant disease, see 96408-96549)

(For penile plethysmography, use 54240)

93701 Bioimpedance, thoracic, electrical

93720 Plethysmography, total body; with interpretation and report

93721 tracing only, without interpretation and report

93722 interpretation and report only

(For regional plethysmography, see 93875-93931)

93724 Electronic analysis of antitachycardia pacemaker system (includes electrocardiographic recording, programming of device, induction and termination of tachycardia via implanted pacemaker, and interpretation of recordings)

93727 Electronic analysis of implantable loop recorder (ILR) system (includes retrieval of recorded and stored ECG data, physician review and interpretation of retrieved ECG data and reprogramming)

93731 Electronic analysis of dual-chamber pacemaker system (includes evaluation of programmable parameters at rest and during activity where applicable, using electrocardiographic recording and interpretation of recordings at rest and during exercise, analysis of event markers and device response); without reprogramming

93732 with reprogramming

Medicine

93733 Electronic analysis of dual chamber internal pacemaker system (may include rate, pulse amplitude and duration, configuration of wave form, and/or testing of sensory function of pacemaker), telephonic analysis

93734 Electronic analysis of single chamber pacemaker system (includes evaluation of programmable parameters at rest and during activity where applicable, using electrocardiographic recording and interpretation of recordings at rest and during exercise, analysis of event markers and device response); without reprogramming

93735   with reprogramming

93736 Electronic analysis of single chamber internal pacemaker system (may include rate, pulse amplitude and duration, configuration of wave form, and/or testing of sensory function of pacemaker), telephonic analysis

93740 Temperature gradient studies

93741 Electronic analysis of pacing cardioverter-defibrillator (includes interrogation, evaluation of pulse generator status, evaluation of programmable parameters at rest and during activity where applicable, using electrocardiographic recording and interpretation of recordings at rest and during exercise, analysis of event markers and device response); single chamber or wearable cardioverter-defibrillator system, without reprogramming

(Do not report 93741 in conjunction with 93745)

93742   single chamber or wearable cardioverter-defibrillator system, with reprogramming

(Do not report 93742 in conjunction with 93745)

93743   dual chamber, without reprogramming

93744   dual chamber, with reprogramming

93745 Initial set-up and programming by a physician of wearable cardioverter-defibrillator includes initial programming of system, establishing baseline electronic ECG, transmission of data to data repository, patient instruction in wearing system and patient reporting of problems or events

(Do not report 93745 in conjunction with 93741, 93742)

93760 Thermogram; cephalic

93762   peripheral

93770 Determination of venous pressure

(For central venous cannulization see 36555-36556, 36500)

93784 Ambulatory blood pressure monitoring, utilizing a system such as magnetic tape and/or computer disk, for 24 hours or longer; including recording, scanning analysis, interpretation and report

93786   recording only

93788   scanning analysis with report

93790   physician review with interpretation and report

Other Procedures

93797 Physician services for outpatient cardiac rehabilitation; without continuous ECG monitoring (per session)

93798   with continuous ECG monitoring (per session)

93799 Unlisted cardiovascular service or procedure

Non-Invasive Vascular Diagnostic Studies

Vascular studies include patient care required to perform the studies, supervision of the studies and interpretation of study results with copies for patient records of hard copy output with analysis of all data, including bidirectional vascular flow or imaging when provided.

The use of a simple hand-held or other Doppler device that does not produce hard copy output, or that produces a record that does not permit analysis of bidirectional vascular flow, is considered to be part of the physical examination of the vascular system and is not separately reported.

Duplex scan (eg, 93880, 93882) describes an ultrasonic scanning procedure for characterizing the pattern and direction of blood flow in arteries or veins with the production of real time images integrating B-mode two-dimensional vascular structure with spectral and/or color flow Doppler mapping or imaging.

Non-invasive physiologic studies are performed using equipment separate and distinct from the duplex scanner. Codes 93875, 93965, 93922, 93923, and 93924 describe the evaluation of non-imaging physiologic recordings of pressures, Doppler analysis of bi-directional blood flow, plethysmography, and/or oxygen tension measurements appropriate for the anatomic area studied.

Cerebrovascular Arterial Studies

A complete transcranial Doppler (TCD) study (93886) includes ultrasound evaluation of the right and left anterior circulation territories and the posterior circulation territory (to include vertebral arteries and basilar artery). In a limited TCD study (93888) there is ultrasound evaluation of two or fewer of these territories. For TCD, ultrasound evaluation is a reasonable and concerted attempt to identify arterial signals through an acoustic window.

93875 Non-invasive physiologic studies of extracranial arteries, complete bilateral study (eg, periorbital flow direction with arterial compression, ocular pneumoplethys-mography, Doppler ultrasound spectral analysis)

93880   Duplex scan of extracranial arteries; complete bilateral study

93882   unilateral or limited study

      ►(To report common carotid intima-media thickness (IMT) study for evaluation of atherosclerotic burden or coronary heart disease risk factor assessment, use Category III code 0126T)◄

93886   Transcranial Doppler study of the intracranial arteries; complete study

93888   limited study

93890   vasoreactivity study

93892   emboli detection without intravenous microbubble injection

93893   emboli detection with intravenous microbubble injection

      (Do not report 93890-93893 in conjunction with 93888)

Extremity Arterial Studies (Including Digits)

93922   Non-invasive physiologic studies of upper or lower extremity arteries, single level, bilateral (eg, ankle/brachial indices, Doppler waveform analysis, volume plethysmography, transcutaneous oxygen tension measurement)

93923   Non-invasive physiologic studies of upper or lower extremity arteries, multiple levels or with provocative functional maneuvers, complete bilateral study (eg, segmental blood pressure measurements, segmental Doppler waveform analysis, segmental volume plethysmography, segmental transcutaneous oxygen tension measurements, measurements with postural provocative tests, measurements with reactive hyperemia)

93924   Non-invasive physiologic studies of lower extremity arteries, at rest and following treadmill stress testing, complete bilateral study

93925   Duplex scan of lower extremity arteries or arterial bypass grafts; complete bilateral study

93926   unilateral or limited study

93930   Duplex scan of upper extremity arteries or arterial bypass grafts; complete bilateral study

93931   unilateral or limited study

Extremity Venous Studies (Including Digits)

93965   Non-invasive physiologic studies of extremity veins, complete bilateral study (eg, Doppler waveform analysis with responses to compression and other maneuvers, phleborheography, impedance plethysmography)

93970   Duplex scan of extremity veins including responses to compression and other maneuvers; complete bilateral study

93971   unilateral or limited study

Visceral and Penile Vascular Studies

93975   Duplex scan of arterial inflow and venous outflow of abdominal, pelvic, scrotal contents and/or retroperitoneal organs; complete study

93976   limited study

93978   Duplex scan of aorta, inferior vena cava, iliac vasculature, or bypass grafts; complete study

93979   unilateral or limited study

93980   Duplex scan of arterial inflow and venous outflow of penile vessels; complete study

93981   follow-up or limited study

Extremity Arterial-Venous Studies

93990   Duplex scan of hemodialysis access (including arterial inflow, body of access and venous outflow)

      (For measurement of hemodialysis access flow using indicator dilution methods, use 90940)

Pulmonary

Codes 94010-94799 include laboratory procedure(s) and interpretation of test results. If a separate identifiable Evaluation and Management service is performed, the appropriate E/M service code should be reported in addition to 94010-94799.

94010   Spirometry, including graphic record, total and timed vital capacity, expiratory flow rate measurement(s), with or without maximal voluntary ventilation

94014   Patient-initiated spirometric recording per 30-day period of time; includes reinforced education, transmission of spirometric tracing, data capture, analysis of transmitted data, periodic recalibration and physician review and interpretation

94015   recording (includes hook-up, reinforced education, data transmission, data capture, trend analysis, and periodic recalibration)

94016   physician review and interpretation only

94060   Bronchodilation responsiveness, spirometry as in 94010, pre- and post-bronchodilator administration

      (Report bronchodilator supply separately with 99070 or appropriate supply code)

      (For prolonged exercise test for bronchospasm with pre- and post-spirometry, use 94620)

Medicine

94070   Bronchospasm provocation evaluation, multiple spirometric determinations as in 94010, with administered agents (eg, antigen(s), cold air, methacholine)

(Report antigen(s) administration separately with 99070 or appropriate supply code)

94150   Vital capacity, total (separate procedure)

94200   Maximum breathing capacity, maximal voluntary ventilation

94240   Functional residual capacity or residual volume: helium method, nitrogen open circuit method, or other method

94250   Expired gas collection, quantitative, single procedure (separate procedure)

94260   Thoracic gas volume

(For plethysmography, see 93720-93722)

94350   Determination of maldistribution of inspired gas: multiple breath nitrogen washout curve including alveolar nitrogen or helium equilibration time

94360   Determination of resistance to airflow, oscillatory or plethysmographic methods

94370   Determination of airway closing volume, single breath tests

94375   Respiratory flow volume loop

94400   Breathing response to CO_2 (CO_2 response curve)

94450   Breathing response to hypoxia (hypoxia response curve)

(For high altitude simulation test (HAST), see 94452, 94453)

94452   High altitude simulation test (HAST), with physician interpretation and report;

(For obtaining arterial blood gases, use 36600)

(Do not report 94452 in conjunction with 94453, 94760, 94761)

94453   with supplemental oxygen titration

(For obtaining arterial blood gases, use 36600)

(Do not report 94453 in conjunction with 94452, 94760, 94761)

94620   Pulmonary stress testing; simple (eg, prolonged exercise test for bronchospasm with pre- and post-spirometry)

94621   complex (including measurements of CO_2 production, O_2 uptake, and electrocardiographic recordings)

94640   Pressurized or nonpressurized inhalation treatment for acute airway obstruction or for sputum induction for diagnostic purposes (eg, with an aerosol generator, nebulizer, metered dose inhaler or intermittent positive pressure breathing (IPPB) device)

(For more than one inhalation treatment performed on the same date, append modifier 76)

94642   Aerosol inhalation of pentamidine for pneumocystis carinii pneumonia treatment or prophylaxis

94656   Ventilation assist and management, initiation of pressure or volume preset ventilators for assisted or controlled breathing; first day

94657   subsequent days

94660   Continuous positive airway pressure ventilation (CPAP), initiation and management

94662   Continuous negative pressure ventilation (CNP), initiation and management

94664   Demonstration and/or evaluation of patient utilization of an aerosol generator, nebulizer, metered dose inhaler or IPPB device

(94664 can be reported one time only per day of service)

94667   Manipulation chest wall, such as cupping, percussing, and vibration to facilitate lung function; initial demonstration and/or evaluation

94668   subsequent

94680   Oxygen uptake, expired gas analysis; rest and exercise, direct, simple

94681   including CO_2 output, percentage oxygen extracted

94690   rest, indirect (separate procedure)

(For single arterial puncture, use 36600)

94720   Carbon monoxide diffusing capacity (eg, single breath, steady state)

94725   Membrane diffusion capacity

94750   Pulmonary compliance study (eg, plethysmography, volume and pressure measurements)

94760   Noninvasive ear or pulse oximetry for oxygen saturation; single determination

(For blood gases, see 82803-82810)

94761   multiple determinations (eg, during exercise)

94762   by continuous overnight monitoring (separate procedure)

94770   Carbon dioxide, expired gas determination by infrared analyzer

(For bronchoscopy, see 31622-31656)

(For placement of flow directed catheter, use 93503)

(For venipuncture, use 36410)

(For central venous catheter placement, see 36555-36556)

(For arterial puncture, use 36600)

(For arterial catheterization, use 36620)

(For thoracentesis, use 32000)

(For phlebotomy, therapeutic, use 99195)

(For lung biopsy, needle, use 32405)

(For intubation, orotracheal or nasotracheal, use 31500)

94772   Circadian respiratory pattern recording (pediatric pneumogram), 12 to 24 hour continuous recording, infant

(Separate procedure codes for electromyograms, EEG, ECG, and recordings of respiration are excluded when 94772 is reported)

94799   Unlisted pulmonary service or procedure

Allergy and Clinical Immunology

Definitions

Allergy sensitivity tests describe the performance and evaluation of selective cutaneous and mucous membrane tests in correlation with the history, physical examination, and other observations of the patient. The number of tests performed should be judicious and dependent upon the history, physical findings, and clinical judgment. All patients should not necessarily receive the same tests nor the same number of sensitivity tests.

Immunotherapy (desensitization, hyposensitization) is the parenteral administration of allergenic extracts as antigens at periodic intervals, usually on an increasing dosage scale to a dosage which is maintained as maintenance therapy. Indications for immunotherapy are determined by appropriate diagnostic procedures coordinated with clinical judgment and knowledge of the natural history of allergic diseases.

Other therapy: for medical conferences on the use of mechanical and electronic devices (precipitators, air conditioners, air filters, humidifiers, dehumidifiers), climatotherapy, physical therapy, occupational and recreational therapy, see **Evaluation and Management** section.

Allergy Testing

95004   Percutaneous tests (scratch, puncture, prick) with allergenic extracts, immediate type reaction, specify number of tests

95010   Percutaneous tests (scratch, puncture, prick) sequential and incremental, with drugs, biologicals or venoms, immediate type reaction, specify number of tests

95015   Intracutaneous (intradermal) tests, sequential and incremental, with drugs, biologicals, or venoms, immediate type reaction, specify number of tests

95024   Intracutaneous (intradermal) tests with allergenic extracts, immediate type reaction, specify number of tests

95027   Intracutaneous (intradermal) tests, sequential and incremental, with allergenic extracts for airborne allergens, immediate type reaction, specify number of tests

95028   Intracutaneous (intradermal) tests with allergenic extracts, delayed type reaction, including reading, specify number of tests

95044   Patch or application test(s) (specify number of tests)

95052   Photo patch test(s) (specify number of tests)

95056   Photo tests

95060   Ophthalmic mucous membrane tests

95065   Direct nasal mucous membrane test

95070   Inhalation bronchial challenge testing (not including necessary pulmonary function tests); with histamine, methacholine, or similar compounds

95071   with antigens or gases, specify

(For pulmonary function tests, see 94060, 94070)

95075   Ingestion challenge test (sequential and incremental ingestion of test items, eg, food, drug or other substance such as metabisulfite)

95078   Provocative testing (eg, Rinkel test)

(For allergy laboratory tests, see 86000-86999)

▶(For intravenous therapy for severe or intractable allergic disease, see 90765-90768, 90772, 90774, 90775)◀

Allergen Immunotherapy

Codes 95115-95199 include the professional services necessary for allergen immunotherapy. Office visit codes may be used in addition to allergen immunotherapy if other identifiable services are provided at that time.

95115   Professional services for allergen immunotherapy not including provision of allergenic extracts; single injection

95117   two or more injections

95120   Professional services for allergen immunotherapy in prescribing physicians office or institution, including provision of allergenic extract; single injection

95125   two or more injections

95130   single stinging insect venom

95131   two stinging insect venoms

95132   three stinging insect venoms

95133   four stinging insect venoms

95134   five stinging insect venoms

95144   Professional services for the supervision of preparation and provision of antigens for allergen immunotherapy, single dose vial(s) (specify number of vials)

(A single dose vial contains a single dose of antigen administered in one injection)

Medicine

95145 Professional services for the supervision of preparation and provision of antigens for allergen immunotherapy (specify number of doses); single stinging insect venom

95146 two single stinging insect venoms

95147 three single stinging insect venoms

95148 four single stinging insect venoms

95149 five single stinging insect venoms

95165 Professional services for the supervision of preparation and provision of antigens for allergen immunotherapy; single or multiple antigens (specify number of doses)

95170 whole body extract of biting insect or other arthropod (specify number of doses)

(For allergy immunotherapy reporting, a dose is the amount of antigen(s) administered in a single injection from a multiple dose vial)

95180 Rapid desensitization procedure, each hour (eg, insulin, penicillin, equine serum)

95199 Unlisted allergy/clinical immunologic service or procedure

(For skin testing of bacterial, viral, fungal extracts, see 95028, 86485-86586)

(For special reports on allergy patients, use 99080)

(For testing procedures such as radioallergosorbent testing (RAST), rat mast cell technique (RMCT), mast cell degranulation test (MCDT), lymphocytic transformation test (LTT), leukocyte histamine release (LHR), migration inhibitory factor test (MIF), transfer factor test (TFT), nitroblue tetrazolium dye test (NTD), see Immunology section in **Pathology** or use 95199)

Endocrinology

▲ **95250** Ambulatory continuous glucose monitoring of interstitial tissue fluid via a subcutaneous sensor for up to 72 hours; sensor placement, hook-up, calibration of monitor, patient training, removal of sensor, and printout of recording

(Do not report 95250 in conjunction with 99091)

● **95251** physician interpretation and report

▶(Do not report 95250, 95251 in conjunction with 99091)◀

Neurology and Neuromuscular Procedures

▶Neurologic services are typically consultative, and any of the levels of consultation (99241-99255) may be appropriate.◀

In addition, services and skills outlined under **Evaluation and Management** levels of service appropriate to neurologic illnesses should be reported similarly.

▶The EEG, autonomic function, evoked potential, reflex tests, EMG, NCV, and MEG services (95812-95829 and 95860-95967) include recording, interpretation by a physician, and report. For interpretation only, use modifier 26. For EMG guidance, see 95873, 95874.◀

(For repetitive transcranial magnetic stimulation for treatment of clinical depression, use Category III code 0018T)

(Do not report codes 95860-95875 in addition to 96000-96004)

Sleep Testing

Sleep studies and polysomnography refer to the continuous and simultaneous monitoring and recording of various physiological and pathophysiological parameters of sleep for 6 or more hours with physician review, interpretation and report. The studies are performed to diagnose a variety of sleep disorders and to evaluate a patient's response to therapies such as nasal continuous positive airway pressure (NCPAP). Polysomnography is distinguished from sleep studies by the inclusion of sleep staging which is defined to include a 1-4 lead electroencephalogram (EEG), an electro-oculogram (EOG), and a submental electromyogram (EMG). Additional parameters of sleep include: 1) ECG; 2) airflow; 3) ventilation and respiratory effort; 4) gas exchange by oximetry, transcutaneous monitoring, or end tidal gas analysis; 5) extremity muscle activity, motor activity-movement; 6) extended EEG monitoring; 7) penile tumescence; 8) gastroesophageal reflux; 9) continuous blood pressure monitoring; 10) snoring; 11) body positions; etc.

The sleep services (95805-95811) include recording, interpretation and report. For interpretation only, use modifier 26.

For a study to be reported as polysomnography, sleep must be recorded and staged.

(Report with modifier 52 if less than 6 hours of recording or in other cases of reduced services as appropriate)

(For unattended sleep study, use 95806)

95805 Multiple sleep latency or maintenance of wakefulness testing, recording, analysis and interpretation of physiological measurements of sleep during multiple trials to assess sleepiness

95806 Sleep study, simultaneous recording of ventilation, respiratory effort, ECG or heart rate, and oxygen saturation, unattended by a technologist

95807 Sleep study, simultaneous recording of ventilation, respiratory effort, ECG or heart rate, and oxygen saturation, attended by a technologist

95808   Polysomnography; sleep staging with 1-3 additional parameters of sleep, attended by a technologist

95810   sleep staging with 4 or more additional parameters of sleep, attended by a technologist

95811   sleep staging with 4 or more additional parameters of sleep, with initiation of continuous positive airway pressure therapy or bilevel ventilation, attended by a technologist

Routine Electroencephalography (EEG)

EEG codes 95812-95822 include hyperventilation and/or photic stimulation when appropriate. Routine EEG codes 95816-95822 include 20 to 40 minutes of recording. Extended EEG codes 95812-95813 include reporting times longer than 40 minutes.

95812   Electroencephalogram (EEG) extended monitoring; 41-60 minutes

95813   greater than one hour

95816   Electroencephalogram (EEG); including recording awake and drowsy

95819   including recording awake and asleep

95822   recording in coma or sleep only

95824   cerebral death evaluation only

95827   all night recording

(For 24-hour EEG monitoring, see 95950-95953 or 95956)

(For EEG during nonintracranial surgery, use 95955)

(For Wada test, use 95958)

(For digital analysis of EEG, use 95957)

95829   Electrocorticogram at surgery (separate procedure)

95830   Insertion by physician of sphenoidal electrodes for electroencephalographic (EEG) recording

Muscle and Range of Motion Testing

95831   Muscle testing, manual (separate procedure) with report; extremity (excluding hand) or trunk

95832   hand, with or without comparison with normal side

95833   total evaluation of body, excluding hands

95834   total evaluation of body, including hands

95851   Range of motion measurements and report (separate procedure); each extremity (excluding hand) or each trunk section (spine)

95852   hand, with or without comparison with normal side

95857   Tensilon test for myasthenia gravis

►(95858 has been deleted)◄

Electromyography and Nerve Conduction Tests

►Needle electromyographic procedures include the interpretation of electrical waveforms measured by equipment that produces both visible and audible components of electrical signals recorded from the muscle(s) studied by the needle electrode.◄

95860   Needle electromyography; one extremity with or without related paraspinal areas

95861   two extremities with or without related paraspinal areas

(For dynamic electromyography performed during motion analysis studies, see 96002-96003)

95863   three extremities with or without related paraspinal areas

95864   four extremities with or without related paraspinal areas

● 95865   larynx

►(Do not report modifier 50 in conjunction with 95865)◄

►(For unilateral procedure, report modifier 52 in conjunction with 95865)◄

● 95866   hemidiaphragm

95867   cranial nerve supplied muscle(s), unilateral

95868   cranial nerve supplied muscles, bilateral

95869   thoracic paraspinal muscles (excluding T1 or T12)

95870   limited study of muscles in one extremity or non-limb (axial) muscles (unilateral or bilateral), other than thoracic paraspinal, cranial nerve supplied muscles, or sphincters

(To report a complete study of the extremities, see 95860-95864)

(For anal or urethral sphincter, detrusor, urethra, perineum musculature, see 51785-51792)

(For eye muscles, use 92265)

95872   Needle electromyography using single fiber electrode, with quantitative measurement of jitter, blocking and/or fiber density, any/all sites of each muscle studied

+● 95873   Electrical stimulation for guidance in conjunction with chemodenervation (List separately in addition to code for primary procedure)

+● 95874   Needle electromyography for guidance in conjunction with chemodenervation (List separately in addition to code for primary procedure)

►(Use 95873, 95874 in conjunction with 64612-64614)◄

►(Do not report 95874 in conjunction with 95873)◄

►(Do not report 95873, 95874 in conjunction with 95860-95870)◄

Medicine

▲=Revised code   ●=New code   ► ◄=Contains new or revised text

95875 Ischemic limb exercise test with serial specimen(s) acquisition for muscle(s) metabolite(s)

▶(For listing of nerves considered for separate study, see Appendix J)◀

⊘ **95900** Nerve conduction, amplitude and latency/velocity study, each nerve; motor, without F-wave study

⊘ **95903** motor, with F-wave study

⊘ **95904** sensory

(Report 95900, 95903, and/or 95904 only once when multiple sites on the same nerve are stimulated or recorded)

Intraoperative Neurophysiology

+ **95920** Intraoperative neurophysiology testing, per hour (List separately in addition to code for primary procedure)

(Use 95920 in conjunction with the study performed, 92585, 95822, 95860, 95861, 95867, 95868, 95870, 95900, 95904, 95925-95937)

(Code 95920 describes ongoing electrophysiologic testing and monitoring performed during surgical procedures. Code 95920 is reported per hour of service, and includes only the ongoing electrophysiologic monitoring time distinct from performance of specific type(s) of baseline electrophysiologic study(s) (95860, 95861, 95867, 95868, 95870, 95900, 95904, 95928, 95929, 95933-95937) or interpretation of specific type(s) of baseline electrophysiologic study(s) (92585, 95822, 95870, 95925-95928, 95929, 95930). The time spent performing or interpreting the baseline electrophysiologic study(s) should not be counted as intraoperative monitoring, but represents separately reportable procedures. Code 95920 should be used once per hour even if multiple electrophysiologic studies are performed. The baseline electrophysiologic study(s) should be used once per operative session.)

(For electrocorticography, use 95829)

(For intraoperative EEG during nonintracranial surgery, use 95955)

(For intraoperative functional cortical or subcortical mapping, see 95961-95962)

(For intraoperative neurostimulator programming and analysis, see 95970-95975)

Autonomic Function Tests

95921 Testing of autonomic nervous system function; cardiovagal innervation (parasympathetic function), including two or more of the following: heart rate response to deep breathing with recorded R-R interval, Valsalva ratio, and 30:15 ratio

95922 vasomotor adrenergic innervation (sympathetic adrenergic function), including beat-to-beat blood pressure and R-R interval changes during Valsalva maneuver and at least five minutes of passive tilt

95923 sudomotor, including one or more of the following: quantitative sudomotor axon reflex test (QSART), silastic sweat imprint, thermoregulatory sweat test, and changes in sympathetic skin potential

Evoked Potentials and Reflex Tests

95925 Short-latency somatosensory evoked potential study, stimulation of any/all peripheral nerves or skin sites, recording from the central nervous system; in upper limbs

95926 in lower limbs

95927 in the trunk or head

(To report a unilateral study, use modifier 52)

(For auditory evoked potentials, use 92585)

95928 Central motor evoked potential study (transcranial motor stimulation); upper limbs

95929 lower limbs

95930 Visual evoked potential (VEP) testing central nervous system, checkerboard or flash

95933 Orbicularis oculi (blink) reflex, by electrodiagnostic testing

95934 H-reflex, amplitude and latency study; record gastrocnemius/soleus muscle

95936 record muscle other than gastrocnemius/soleus muscle

(To report a bilateral study, use modifier 50)

95937 Neuromuscular junction testing (repetitive stimulation, paired stimuli), each nerve, any one method

Special EEG Tests

95950 Monitoring for identification and lateralization of cerebral seizure focus, electroencephalographic (eg, 8 channel EEG) recording and interpretation, each 24 hours

95951 Monitoring for localization of cerebral seizure focus by cable or radio, 16 or more channel telemetry, combined electroencephalographic (EEG) and video recording and interpretation (eg, for presurgical localization), each 24 hours

95953 Monitoring for localization of cerebral seizure focus by computerized portable 16 or more channel EEG, electroencephalographic (EEG) recording and interpretation, each 24 hours

95954 Pharmacological or physical activation requiring physician attendance during EEG recording of activation phase (eg, thiopental activation test)

95955 Electroencephalogram (EEG) during nonintracranial surgery (eg, carotid surgery)

95956 Monitoring for localization of cerebral seizure focus by cable or radio, 16 or more channel telemetry, electroencephalographic (EEG) recording and interpretation, each 24 hours

95957   Digital analysis of electroencephalogram (EEG) (eg, for epileptic spike analysis)

95958   Wada activation test for hemispheric function, including electroencephalographic (EEG) monitoring

95961   Functional cortical and subcortical mapping by stimulation and/or recording of electrodes on brain surface, or of depth electrodes, to provoke seizures or identify vital brain structures; initial hour of physician attendance

+ 95962   each additional hour of physician attendance (List separately in addition to code for primary procedure)

(Use 95962 in conjunction with 95961)

95965   Magnetoencephalography (MEG), recording and analysis; for spontaneous brain magnetic activity (eg, epileptic cerebral cortex localization)

95966   for evoked magnetic fields, single modality (eg, sensory, motor, language, or visual cortex localization)

+ 95967   for evoked magnetic fields, each additional modality (eg, sensory, motor, language, or visual cortex localization) (List separately in addition to code for primary procedure)

(Use 95967 in conjunction with 95966)

(For electroencephalography performed in addition to magnetoencephalography, see 95812-95827)

(For somatosensory evoked potentials, auditory evoked potentials, and visual evoked potentials performed in addition to magnetic evoked field responses, see 92585, 95925, 95926, and/or 95930)

(For computerized tomography performed in addition to magnetoencephalography, see 70450-70470, 70496)

(For magnetic resonance imaging performed in addition to magnetoencephalography, see 70551-70553)

Neurostimulators, Analysis-Programming

A simple neurostimulator pulse generator/transmitter (95970, 95971) is one capable of affecting 3 or fewer of the following: pulse amplitude, pulse duration, pulse frequency, 8 or more electrode contacts, cycling, stimulation train duration, train spacing, number of programs, number of channels, alternating electrode polarities, dose time (stimulation parameters changing in time periods of minutes including dose lockout times), more than 1 clinical feature (eg, rigidity, dyskinesia, tremor). A complex neurostimulator pulse generator/transmitter (95970-95975) is one capable of affecting more than 3 of the above.

Code 95970 describes subsequent electronic analysis of a previously-implanted simple or complex brain, spinal cord, or peripheral neurostimulator pulse generator system, without reprogramming. Code 95971 describes intraoperative or subsequent electronic analysis of an implanted simple spinal cord or peripheral (ie, peripheral

nerve, autonomic nerve, neuromuscular) neurostimulator pulse generator system, with programming. Codes 95972 and 95973 describe intraoperative (at initial insertion/ revision) or subsequent electronic analysis of an implanted complex spinal cord or peripheral (except cranial nerve) neurostimulator pulse generator system, with programming. Codes 95974 and 95975 describe intraoperative (at initial insertion/revision) or subsequent electronic analysis of an implanted complex cranial nerve neurostimulator pulse generator system, with programming. Codes 95978 and 95979 describe initial or subsequent electronic analysis of an implanted brain neurostimulator pulse generator system, with programming.

(For insertion of neurostimulator pulse generator, see 61885, 63685, 63688, 64590)

(For revision or removal of neurostimulator pulse generator or receiver, see 61888, 63688, 64595)

(For implantation of neurostimulator electrodes, see 61850-61875, 63650-63655, 64553-64580. For revision or removal of neurostimulator electrodes, see 61880, 63660, 64585)

95970   Electronic analysis of implanted neurostimulator pulse generator system (eg, rate, pulse amplitude and duration, configuration of wave form, battery status, electrode selectability, output modulation, cycling, impedance and patient compliance measurements); simple or complex brain, spinal cord, or peripheral (ie, cranial nerve, peripheral nerve, autonomic nerve, neuromuscular) neurostimulator pulse generator/transmitter, without reprogramming

95971   simple spinal cord, or peripheral (ie, peripheral nerve, autonomic nerve, neuromuscular) neurostimulator pulse generator/transmitter, with intraoperative or subsequent programming

95972   complex spinal cord, or peripheral (except cranial nerve) neurostimulator pulse generator/transmitter, with intraoperative or subsequent programming, first hour

+ 95973   complex spinal cord, or peripheral (except cranial nerve) neurostimulator pulse generator/transmitter, with intraoperative or subsequent programming, each additional 30 minutes after first hour (List separately in addition to code for primary procedure)

(Use 95973 in conjunction with 95972)

95974   complex cranial nerve neurostimulator pulse generator/transmitter, with intraoperative or subsequent programming, with or without nerve interface testing, first hour

+ 95975   complex cranial nerve neurostimulator pulse generator/transmitter, with intraoperative or subsequent programming, each additional 30 minutes after first hour (List separately in addition to code for primary procedure)

(Use 95975 in conjunction with 95974)

95978 Electronic analysis of implanted neurostimulator pulse generator system (eg, rate, pulse amplitude and duration, battery status, electrode selectability and polarity, impedance and patient compliance measurements), complex deep brain neurostimulator pulse generator/transmitter, with initial or subsequent programming; first hour

+ 95979 each additional 30 minutes after first hour (List separately in addition to code for primary procedure)

(Use 95979 in conjunction with 95978)

Other Procedures

95990 Refilling and maintenance of implantable pump or reservoir for drug delivery, spinal (intrathecal, epidural) or brain (intraventricular);

(For analysis and/or reprogramming of implantable infusion pump, see 62367-62368)

(For refill and maintenance of implanted infusion pump or reservoir for systemic drug therapy (eg, chemotherapy or insulin, use 96530)

95991 administered by physician

95999 Unlisted neurological or neuromuscular diagnostic procedure

Motion Analysis

Codes 96000-96004 describe services performed as part of a major therapeutic or diagnostic decision making process. Motion analysis is performed in a dedicated motion analysis laboratory (ie, a facility capable of performing videotaping from the front, back and both sides, computerized 3-D kinematics, 3-D kinetics, and dynamic electromyography). Code 96000 may include 3-D kinetics and stride characteristics. Codes 96002-96003 describe dynamic electromyography.

Code 96004 should only be reported once regardless of the number of study(ies) reviewed/interpreted.

(For performance of needle electromyography procedures, see 95860-95875)

(For gait training, use 97116)

96000 Comprehensive computer-based motion analysis by video-taping and 3-D kinematics;

96001 with dynamic plantar pressure measurements during walking

96002 Dynamic surface electromyography, during walking or other functional activities, 1-12 muscles

96003 Dynamic fine wire electromyography, during walking or other functional activities, 1 muscle

(Do not report 96002, 96003 in conjunction with 95860-95864, 95869-95872)

96004 Physician review and interpretation of comprehensive computer based motion analysis, dynamic plantar pressure measurements, dynamic surface electromyography during walking or other functional activities, and dynamic fine wire electromyography, with written report

Central Nervous System Assessments/Tests (eg, Neuro-Cognitive, Mental Status, Speech Testing)

The following codes are used to report the services provided during testing of the cognitive function of the central nervous system. The testing of cognitive processes, visual motor responses, and abstractive abilities is accomplished by the combination of several types of testing procedures. It is expected that the administration of these tests will generate material that will be formulated into a report.

(For development of cognitive skills, see 97532, 97533)

(For mini-mental status examination performed by a physician, see **Evaluation and Management** services codes)

▶(96100 has been deleted. To report, see 96101, 96102, 96103)◀

● **96101** Psychological testing (includes psychodiagnostic assessment of emotionality, intellectual abilities, personality and psychopathology, eg, MMPI, Rorshach, WAIS), per hour of the psychologist's or physician's time, both face-to-face time with the patient and time interpreting test results and preparing the report

● **96102** Psychological testing (includes psychodiagnostic assessment of emotionality, intellectual abilities, personality and psychopathology, eg, MMPI and WAIS), with qualified health care professional interpretation and report, administered by technician, per hour of technician time, face-to-face

● **96103** Psychological testing (includes psychodiagnostic assessment of emotionality, intellectual abilities, personality and psychopathology, eg, MMPI), administered by a computer, with qualified health care professional interpretation and report

96105 Assessment of aphasia (includes assessment of expressive and receptive speech and language function, language comprehension, speech production ability, reading, spelling, writing, eg, by Boston Diagnostic Aphasia Examination) with interpretation and report, per hour

96110   Developmental testing; limited (eg, Developmental Screening Test II, Early Language Milestone Screen), with interpretation and report

96111   extended (includes assessment of motor, language, social, adaptive and/or cognitive functioning by standardized developmental instruments) with interpretation and report

▶(96115 has been deleted. To report, use 96116)◀

● **96116**   Neurobehavioral status exam (clinical assessment of thinking, reasoning and judgment, eg, acquired knowledge, attention, language, memory, planning and problem solving, and visual spatial abilities), per hour of the psychologist's or physician's time, both face-to-face time with the patient and time interpreting test results and preparing the report

▶(96117 has been deleted. To report, see 96118, 96119, 96120)◀

● **96118**   Neuropsychological testing (eg, Halstead-Reitan Neuropsychological Battery, Wechsler Memory Scales and Wisconsin Card Sorting Test), per hour of the psychologist's or physician's time, both face-to-face time with the patient and time interpreting test results and preparing the report

● **96119**   Neuropsychological testing (eg, Halstead-Reitan Neuropsychological Battery, Wechsler Memory Scales and Wisconsin Card Sorting Test), with qualified health care professional interpretation and report, administered by technician, per hour of technician time, face-to-face

● **96120**   Neuropsychological testing (eg, Wisconsin Card Sorting Test), administered by a computer, with qualified health care professional interpretation and report

Health and Behavior Assessment/Intervention

Health and behavior assessment procedures are used to identify the psychological, behavioral, emotional, cognitive, and social factors important to the prevention, treatment, or management of physical health problems.

The focus of the assessment is not on mental health but on the biopsychosocial factors important to physical health problems and treatments. The focus of the intervention is to improve the patient's health and well-being utilizing cognitive, behavioral, social, and/or psychophysiological procedures designed to ameliorate specific disease-related problems.

▶Codes 96150-96155 describe services offered to patients who present with primary physical illnesses, diagnoses, or symptoms and may benefit from assessments and interventions that focus on the biopsychosocial factors related to the patient's health status. These services do not represent preventive medicine counseling and risk factor reduction interventions.◀

For patients that require psychiatric services (90801-90899) as well as health and behavior assessment/intervention (96150-96155), report the predominant service performed. Do not report 96150-96155 in conjunction with 90801-90899 on the same date.

Evaluation and Management services codes (including **Preventive Medicine, Individual Counseling** codes 99401-99404, and **Preventive Medicine, Group Counseling** codes 99411-99412), should not be reported on the same day.

(For health and behavior assessment and/or intervention performed by a physician, see **Evaluation and Management** or **Preventive Medicine** services codes)

96150   Health and behavior assessment (eg, health-focused clinical interview, behavioral observations, psychophysiological monitoring, health-oriented questionnaires), each 15 minutes face-to-face with the patient; initial assessment

96151   re-assessment

96152   Health and behavior intervention, each 15 minutes, face-to-face; individual

96153   group (2 or more patients)

96154   family (with the patient present)

96155   family (without the patient present)

Chemotherapy Administration

▶Chemotherapy administration codes 96401-96549 apply to parenteral administration of non-radionuclide anti-neoplastic drugs; and also to anti-neoplastic agents provided for treatment of noncancer diagnoses (eg, cyclophosphamide for auto-immune conditions) or to substances such as monoclonal antibody agents, and other biologic response modifiers. These services can be provided by any physician. Chemotherapy services are typically highly complex and require direct physician supervision for any or all purposes of patient assessment, provision of consent, safety oversight and intra-service supervision of staff. Typically, such chemotherapy services require advanced practice training and competency for staff who provide these services; special considerations for preparation, dosage or disposal; and commonly, these services entail significant patient risk and frequent monitoring. Examples are frequent changes in the infusion rate, prolonged presence of nurse administering the solution for patient monitoring and infusion adjustments, and frequent conferring with the physician about these issues.◀

▶If performed to facilitate the infusion or injection, the following services are included and are not reported separately:

▲=Revised code   ●=New code   ▶◀=Contains new or revised text

a. Use of local anesthesia

b. IV start

c. Access to indwelling IV, subcutaneous catheter or port

d. Flush at conclusion of infusion

e. Standard tubing, syringes and supplies

f. Preparation of chemotherapy agent(s)◄

►(For declotting a catheter or port, use 36550)◄

►Report separate codes for each parenteral method of administration employed when chemotherapy is administered by different techniques. The administration of medications (eg, antibiotics, steroidal agents, antiemetics, narcotics, analgesics) administered independently or sequentially as supportive management of chemotherapy administration, should be separately reported using 90760, 90761, 90765, 90779 as appropriate.◄

►Report both the specific service as well as code(s) for the specific substance(s) or drug(s) provided. The fluid used to administer the drug(s) is considered incidental hydration and is not separately reportable.◄

►When administering multiple infusions, injections or combinations, only one "initial" service code should be reported, unless protocol requires that two separate IV sites must be used. The "initial" code that best describes the key or primary reason for the encounter should always be reported irrespective of the order in which the infusions or injections occur. If an injection or infusion is of a subsequent or concurrent nature, even if it is the first such service within that group of services, then a subsequent or concurrent code from the appropriate section should be reported (eg, the first IV push given subsequent to an initial one-hour infusion is reported using a subsequent IV push code).◄

►When reporting codes for which infusion time is a factor, use the actual time over which the infusion is administered.◄

►If a significant separately identifiable Evaluation and Management service is performed, the appropriate E/M service code should be reported using modifier 25 in addition to 96401-96549. For same day E/M service, a different diagnosis is not required.◄

►Regional (isolation) chemotherapy perfusion should be reported using the codes for arterial infusion (96420-96425). Placement of the intra-arterial catheter should be reported using the appropriate code from the **Cardiovascular Surgery** section. Placement of arterial and venous cannula(s) for extracorporeal circulation via a membrane oxygenator perfusion pump should be reported using 36823. Code 36823 includes dose calculation and administration of the chemotherapy agent by injection into the perfusate. Do not report 96409-96425 in conjunction with 36823.◄

►(For home infusion services, see 99601-99602)◄

►Injection and Intravenous Infusion Chemotherapy◄

►Intravenous or intra-arterial push is defined as: a) an injection in which the healthcare professional who administers the substance/drug is continuously present to administer the injection and observe the patient, or b) an infusion of 15 minutes or less.◄

►(96400 has been deleted. To report, see 96401, 96402)◄

● 96401   Chemotherapy administration, subcutaneous or intramuscular; non-hormonal anti-neoplastic

● 96402   hormonal anti-neoplastic

▲ 96405   Chemotherapy administration; intralesional, up to and including 7 lesions

▲ 96406   intralesional, more than 7 lesions

►(96408 has been deleted. To report, use 96409)◄

● 96409   intravenous, push technique, single or initial substance/drug

►(96410 has been deleted. To report, use 96413)◄

+● 96411   intravenous, push technique, each additional substance/drug (List separately in addition to code for primary procedure)

►(Use 96411 in conjunction with 96409, 96413)◄

►(96412 has been deleted. To report, use 96415)◄

● 96413   Chemotherapy administration, intravenous infusion technique; up to 1 hour, single or initial substance/drug

►(96414 has been deleted. To report, use 96416)◄

+● 96415   each additional hour, 1 to 8 hours (List separately in addition to code for primary procedure)

►(Use 96415 in conjunction with 96413)◄

►(Report 96415 for infusion intervals of greater than 30 minutes beyond 1-hour increments)◄

►(Report 90761 to identify hydration, or 90766, 90767, 90775 to identify therapeutic, prophylactic, or diagnostic drug infusion or injection, if provided as a secondary or subsequent service in association with 96413)◄

● 96416   initiation of prolonged chemotherapy infusion (more than 8 hours), requiring use of a portable or implantable pump

►(For refilling and maintenance of a portable pump or an implantable infusion pump or reservoir for drug delivery, see 96521-96523)◄

+● 96417   each additional sequential infusion (different substance/drug), up to 1 hour (List separately in addition to code for primary procedure)

►(Use 96417 in conjunction with 96413)◄

►(Report only once per sequential infusion. Report 96415 for additional hour(s) of sequential infusion)◄

►Intra-Arterial Chemotherapy◄

96420   Chemotherapy administration, intra-arterial; push technique

96422   infusion technique, up to one hour

+▲ 96423   infusion technique, each additional hour up to 8 hours (List separately in addition to code for primary procedure)

(Use 96423 in conjunction with 96422)

►(Report 96423 for infusion intervals of greater than 30 minutes beyond 1-hour increments)◄

(For regional chemotherapy perfusion via membrane oxygenator perfusion pump to an extremity, use 36823)

96425   infusion technique, initiation of prolonged infusion (more than 8 hours), requiring the use of a portable or implantable pump

►(For refilling and maintenance of a portable pump or an implantable infusion pump or reservoir for drug delivery, see 96521-96523)◄

►Other Chemotherapy◄

►Code 96523 does not require direct physician supervision. Codes 96521-96523 may be reported when these devices are used for therapeutic drugs other than chemotherapy.◄

►(For collection of blood specimen from a completely implantable venous access device, use 36540)◄

96440   Chemotherapy administration into pleural cavity, requiring and including thoracentesis

96445   Chemotherapy administration into peritoneal cavity, requiring and including peritoneocentesis

96450   Chemotherapy administration, into CNS (eg, intrathecal), requiring and including spinal puncture

(For intravesical (bladder) chemotherapy administration, use 51720)

(For insertion of subarachnoid catheter and reservoir for infusion of drug, see 62350, 62351, 62360-62362; for insertion of intraventricular catheter and reservoir, see 61210, 61215)

►(96520 has been deleted. To report, use 96521)◄

● **96521**   Refilling and maintenance of portable pump

● **96522**   Refilling and maintenance of implantable pump or reservoir for drug delivery, systemic (eg, intravenous, intra-arterial)

►(For refilling and maintenance of an implantable infusion pump for spinal or brain drug infusion, use 95990-95991)◄

● **96523**   Irrigation of implanted venous access device for drug delivery systems

►(Do not report 96523 if an injection or infusion is provided on the same day)◄

►(96530 has been deleted. To report, use 96522)◄

96542   Chemotherapy injection, subarachnoid or intraventricular via subcutaneous reservoir, single or multiple agents

►(96545 has been deleted)◄

(For radioactive isotope therapy, use 79005)

96549   Unlisted chemotherapy procedure

Photodynamic Therapy

(To report ocular photodynamic therapy, use 67221)

96567   Photodynamic therapy by external application of light to destroy premalignant and/or malignant lesions of the skin and adjacent mucosa (eg, lip) by activation of photosensitive drug(s), each phototherapy exposure session

+ 96570   Photodynamic therapy by endoscopic application of light to ablate abnormal tissue via activation of photosensitive drug(s); first 30 minutes (List separately in addition to code for endoscopy or bronchoscopy procedures of lung and esophagus)

+ 96571   each additional 15 minutes (List separately in addition to code for endoscopy or bronchoscopy procedures of lung and esophagus)

(96570, 96571 are to be used in addition to bronchoscopy, endoscopy codes)

(Use 96570, 96571 in conjunction with 31641, 43228 as appropriate)

Special Dermatological Procedures

Dermatologic services are typically consultative, and any of the five levels of consultation (99241-99255) may be appropriate.

In addition, services and skills outlined under **Evaluation and Management** levels of service appropriate to dermatologic illnesses should be coded similarly.

(For whole body photography, see Category III code 0044T, 0045T)

(For intralesional injections, see 11900, 11901)

(For Tzanck smear, use 87207)

96900   Actinotherapy (ultraviolet light)

Medicine

96902 Microscopic examination of hairs plucked or clipped by the examiner (excluding hair collected by the patient) to determine telogen and anagen counts, or structural hair shaft abnormality

96910 Photochemotherapy; tar and ultraviolet B (Goeckerman treatment) or petrolatum and ultraviolet B

96912 psoralens and ultraviolet A (PUVA)

96913 Photochemotherapy (Goeckerman and/or PUVA) for severe photoresponsive dermatoses requiring at least four to eight hours of care under direct supervision of the physician (includes application of medication and dressings)

96920 Laser treatment for inflammatory skin disease (psoriasis); total area less than 250 sq cm

96921 250 sq cm to 500 sq cm

96922 over 500 sq cm

96999 Unlisted special dermatological service or procedure

Physical Medicine and Rehabilitation

Codes 97001-97755 should be used to report each distinct procedure performed. Do not append modifier 51 to 97001-97755.

(For muscle testing, range of joint motion, electromyography, see 95831 et seq)

(For biofeedback training by EMG, use 90901)

(For transcutaneous nerve stimulation (TNS), use 64550)

97001 Physical therapy evaluation

97002 Physical therapy re-evaluation

97003 Occupational therapy evaluation

97004 Occupational therapy re-evaluation

97005 Athletic training evaluation

97006 Athletic training re-evaluation

Modalities

Any physical agent applied to produce therapeutic changes to biologic tissue; includes but not limited to thermal, acoustic, light, mechanical, or electric energy.

Supervised

The application of a modality that does not require direct (one-on-one) patient contact by the provider.

97010 Application of a modality to one or more areas; hot or cold packs

97012 traction, mechanical

97014 electrical stimulation (unattended)

(For acupuncture with electrical stimulation, see 97813, 97814)

97016 vasopneumatic devices

97018 paraffin bath

▶(97020 has been deleted. To report, use 97024)◀

97022 whirlpool

▲ **97024** diathermy (eg, microwave)

97026 infrared

97028 ultraviolet

Constant Attendance

The application of a modality that requires direct (one-on-one) patient contact by the provider.

97032 Application of a modality to one or more areas; electrical stimulation (manual), each 15 minutes

97033 iontophoresis, each 15 minutes

97034 contrast baths, each 15 minutes

97035 ultrasound, each 15 minutes

97036 Hubbard tank, each 15 minutes

97039 Unlisted modality (specify type and time if constant attendance)

Therapeutic Procedures

A manner of effecting change through the application of clinical skills and/or services that attempt to improve function.

Physician or therapist required to have direct (one-on-one) patient contact.

97110 Therapeutic procedure, one or more areas, each 15 minutes; therapeutic exercises to develop strength and endurance, range of motion and flexibility

97112 neuromuscular reeducation of movement, balance, coordination, kinesthetic sense, posture, and/or proprioception for sitting and/or standing activities

97113 aquatic therapy with therapeutic exercises

97116 gait training (includes stair climbing)

(Use 96000-96003 to report comprehensive gait and motion analysis procedures)

97124 massage, including effleurage, petrissage and/or tapotement (stroking, compression, percussion)

(For myofascial release, use 97140)

97139 Unlisted therapeutic procedure (specify)

97140 Manual therapy techniques (eg, mobilization/manipulation, manual lymphatic drainage, manual traction), one or more regions, each 15 minutes

97150   Therapeutic procedure(s), group (2 or more individuals)

(Report 97150 for each member of group)

(Group therapy procedures involve constant attendance of the physician or therapist, but by definition do not require one-on-one patient contact by the physician or therapist)

(For manipulation under general anesthesia, see appropriate anatomic section in **Musculoskeletal System**)

(For osteopathic manipulative treatment (OMT), see 98925-98929)

▶(97504 has been deleted. To report, use 97760)◀

▶(97520 has been deleted. To report, use 97761)◀

97530   Therapeutic activities, direct (one-on-one) patient contact by the provider (use of dynamic activities to improve functional performance), each 15 minutes

97532   Development of cognitive skills to improve attention, memory, problem solving, (includes compensatory training), direct (one-on-one) patient contact by the provider, each 15 minutes

97533   Sensory integrative techniques to enhance sensory processing and promote adaptive responses to environmental demands, direct (one-on-one) patient contact by the provider, each 15 minutes

97535   Self-care/home management training (eg, activities of daily living (ADL) and compensatory training, meal preparation, safety procedures, and instructions in use of assistive technology devices/adaptive equipment) direct one-on-one contact by provider, each 15 minutes

97537   Community/work reintegration training (eg, shopping, transportation, money management, avocational activities and/or work environment/modification analysis, work task analysis, use of assistive technology device/adaptive equipment), direct one-on-one contact by provider, each 15 minutes

(For wheelchair management/propulsion training, use 97542)

▲ 97542   Wheelchair management (eg, assessment, fitting, training), each 15 minutes

97545   Work hardening/conditioning; initial 2 hours

+ 97546   each additional hour (List separately in addition to code for primary procedure)

(Use 97546 in conjunction with 97545)

Active Wound Care Management

Active wound care procedures are performed to remove devitalized and/or necrotic tissue and promote healing. Provider is required to have direct (one-on-one) patient contact.

(Do not report 97597-97602 in conjunction with 11040-11044)

97597   Removal of devitalized tissue from wound(s), selective debridement, without anesthesia (eg, high pressure waterjet with/without suction, sharp selective debridement with scissors, scalpel and forceps), with or without topical application(s), wound assessment, and instruction(s) for ongoing care, may include use of a whirlpool, per session; total wound(s) surface area less than or equal to 20 square centimeters

97598   total wound(s) surface area greater than 20 square centimeters

(97601 has been deleted. To report, use 97597, 97598)

97602   Removal of devitalized tissue from wound(s), non-selective debridement, without anesthesia (eg, wet-to-moist dressings, enzymatic, abrasion), including topical application(s), wound assessment, and instruction(s) for ongoing care, per session

97605   Negative pressure wound therapy (eg, vacuum assisted drainage collection), including topical application(s), wound assessment, and instruction(s) for ongoing care, per session; total wound(s) surface area less than or equal to 50 square centimeters

97606   total wound(s) surface area greater than 50 square centimeters

Tests and Measurements

Requires direct one-on-one patient contact.

(For muscle testing, manual or electrical, joint range of motion, electromyography or nerve velocity determination, see 95831-95904)

▶(97703 has been deleted. To report, use 97762)◀

97750   Physical performance test or measurement (eg, musculoskeletal, functional capacity), with written report, each 15 minutes

97755   Assistive technology assessment (eg, to restore, augment or compensate for existing function, optimize functional tasks and/or maximize environmental accessibility), direct one-on-one contact by provider, with written report, each 15 minutes

(To report augmentative and alternative communication devices, see 92605, 92607)

▶Orthotic Management and Prosthetic Management◀

● 97760   Orthotic(s) management and training (including assessment and fitting when not otherwise reported), upper extremity(s), lower extremity(s) and/or trunk, each 15 minutes

▶(Code 97760 should not be reported with 97116 for the same extremity)◀

● 97761   Prosthetic training, upper and/or lower extremity(s), each 15 minutes

● 97762   Checkout for orthotic/prosthetic use, established patient, each 15 minutes

Medicine

Other Procedures

▶(For extracorporeal shock wave musculoskeletal therapy, see Category III codes 0019T, 0101T, 0102T)◀

(97780 has been deleted. To report, see 97810, 97811)

(97781 has been deleted. To report, see 97813, 97814)

97799   Unlisted physical medicine/rehabilitation service or procedure

Medical Nutrition Therapy

97802   Medical nutrition therapy; initial assessment and intervention, individual, face-to-face with the patient, each 15 minutes

97803   re-assessment and intervention, individual, face-to-face with the patient, each 15 minutes

97804   group (2 or more individual(s)), each 30 minutes

(For medical nutrition therapy assessment and/or intervention performed by a physician, see **Evaluation and Management** or **Preventive Medicine** service codes)

Acupuncture

Acupuncture is reported based on 15-minute increments of personal (face-to-face) contact with the patient, not the duration of acupuncture needle(s) placement.

If no electrical stimulation is used during a 15-minute increment, use 97810, 97811. If electrical stimulation of any needle is used during a 15-minute increment, use 97813, 97814.

▶Only one code may be reported for each 15-minute increment. Use either 97810 or 97813 for the initial 15-minute increment. Only one initial code is reported per day.◀

▶Evaluation and Management services may be reported separately, using modifier 25, if the patient's condition requires a significant separately identifiable E/M service, above and beyond the usual preservice and postservice work associated with the acupuncture services. The time of the E/M service is not included in the time of the acupuncture service.◀

97810   Acupuncture, 1 or more needles; without electrical stimulation, initial 15 minutes of personal one-on-one contact with the patient

▶(Do not report 97810 in conjunction with 97813)◀

+▲ 97811   without electrical stimulation, each additional 15 minutes of personal one-on-one contact with the patient, with re-insertion of needle(s) (List separately in addition to code for primary procedure)

▶(Use 97811 in conjunction with 97810, 97813)◀

▲ 97813   with electrical stimulation, initial 15 minutes of personal one-on-one contact with the patient

▶(Do not report 97813 in conjunction with 97810)◀

+▲ 97814   with electrical stimulation, each additional 15 minutes of personal one-on-one contact with the patient, with re-insertion of needle(s) (List separately in addition to code for primary procedure)

▶(Use 97814 in conjunction with 97810, 97813)◀

Osteopathic Manipulative Treatment

Osteopathic manipulative treatment (OMT) is a form of manual treatment applied by a physician to eliminate or alleviate somatic dysfunction and related disorders. This treatment may be accomplished by a variety of techniques.

Evaluation and Management services may be reported separately if, using modifier 25, the patient's condition requires a significant separately identifiable E/M service, above and beyond the usual preservice and postservice work associated with the procedure. The E/M service may be caused or prompted by the same symptoms or condition for which the OMT service was provided. As such, different diagnoses are not required for the reporting of the OMT and E/M service on the same date.

Body regions referred to are: head region; cervical region; thoracic region; lumbar region; sacral region; pelvic region; lower extremities; upper extremities; rib cage region; abdomen and viscera region.

98925   Osteopathic manipulative treatment (OMT); one to two body regions involved

98926   three to four body regions involved

98927   five to six body regions involved

98928   seven to eight body regions involved

98929   nine to ten body regions involved

Chiropractic Manipulative Treatment

Chiropractic manipulative treatment (CMT) is a form of manual treatment to influence joint and neurophysiological function. This treatment may be accomplished using a variety of techniques.

The chiropractic manipulative treatment codes include a pre-manipulation patient assessment. Additional Evaluation and Management services may be reported separately using modifier 25, if the patient's condition requires a significant separately identifiable E/M service, above and beyond the usual preservice and postservice work associated with the procedure. The E/M service

Medicine

may be caused or prompted by the same symptoms or condition for which the CMT service was provided. As such, different diagnoses are not required for the reporting of the CMT and E/M service on the same date.

For purposes of CMT, the five spinal regions referred to are: cervical region (includes atlanto-occipital joint); thoracic region (includes costovertebral and costotransverse joints); lumbar region; sacral region; and pelvic (sacro-iliac joint) region. The five extraspinal regions referred to are: head (including temporoman- dibular joint, excluding atlanto-occipital) region; lower extremities; upper extremities; rib cage (excluding costotransverse and costovertebral joints) and abdomen.

98940 Chiropractic manipulative treatment (CMT); spinal, one to two regions

98941   spinal, three to four regions

98942   spinal, five regions

98943   extraspinal, one or more regions

▶Education and Training for Patient Self-Management◀

▶The following codes are used to report educational and training services prescribed by a physician and provided by a qualified, nonphysician healthcare professional using a standardized curriculum to an individual or a group of patients for the treatment of established illness(s)/disease(s) or to delay comorbidity(s). Education and training for patient self-management may be reported with these codes only when using a standardized curriculum as described below. This curriculum may be modified as necessary for the clinical needs, cultural norms and health literacy of the individual patient(s).◀

▶The purpose of the educational and training services is to teach the patient (may include caregiver(s)) how to effectively self-manage the patient's illness(s)/disease(s) or delay disease comorbidity(s) in conjunction with the patient's professional healthcare team. Education and training related to subsequent reinforcement or due to changes in the patient's condition or treatment plan are reported in the same manner as the original education and training. The type of education and training provided for the patient's clinical condition will be identified by the appropriate diagnosis code(s) reported.◀

▶The qualifications of the nonphysician healthcare professionals and the content of the educational and training program must be consistent with guidelines or standards established or recognized by a physician society, nonphysician healthcare professional society/association, or other appropriate source.◀

▶(For counseling and education provided by a physician to an individual, see the appropriate Evaluation and Management codes)◀

▶(For counseling and education provided by a physician to a group, use 99078)◀

▶(For counseling and/or risk factor reduction intervention provided by a physician to patient(s) without symptoms or established disease, see 99401-99412)◀

▶(For medical nutrition therapy, see 97802-97804)◀

▶(For health and behavior assessment/intervention that is not part of a standardized curriculum, see 96150-96155)◀

● **98960** Education and training for patient self-management by a qualified, nonphysician health care professional using a standardized curriculum, face-to-face with the patient (could include caregiver/family) each 30 minutes; individual patient

● **98961**   2-4 patients

● **98962**   5-8 patients

Special Services, Procedures and Reports

The procedures with code numbers 99000 through 99091 provide the reporting physician or other qualified healthcare professional with the means of identifying the completion of special reports and services that are an adjunct to the basic services rendered. The specific number assigned indicates the special circumstances under which a basic procedure is performed.

Code 99091 should be reported no more than once in a 30-day period to include the physician or health care provider time involved with data accession, review and interpretation, modification of care plan as necessary (including communication to patient and/or caregiver), and associated documentation.

If the services described by 99091 are provided on the same day the patient presents for an E/M service, these services should be considered part of the E/M service and not separately reported.

Do not report 99091 if it occurs within 30 days of care plan oversight services 99374-99380. Do not report 99091 if other more specific CPT codes exist (eg, 93014, 93227, 93233, 93272 for cardiographic services; 95250 for continuous glucose monitoring). Do not report 99091 for transfer and interpretation of data from hospital or clinical laboratory computers.

▶Codes 99050-99060 are reported in addition to an associated basic service. Typically only a single adjunct code from among 99050-99060 would be reported per patient encounter. However, there may be circumstances in which reporting multiple adjunct codes per patient encounter may be appropriate.◀

Medicine

Miscellaneous Services

99000 Handling and/or conveyance of specimen for transfer from the physician's office to a laboratory

99001 Handling and/or conveyance of specimen for transfer from the patient in other than a physician's office to a laboratory (distance may be indicated)

99002 Handling, conveyance, and/or any other service in connection with the implementation of an order involving devices (eg, designing, fitting, packaging, handling, delivery or mailing) when devices such as orthotics, protectives, prosthetics are fabricated by an outside laboratory or shop but which items have been designed, and are to be fitted and adjusted by the attending physician

(For routine collection of venous blood, use 36415)

99024 Postoperative follow-up visit, normally included in the surgical package, to indicate that an evaluation and management service was performed during a postoperative period for a reason(s) related to the original procedure

(As a component of a surgical "package," see **Surgery Guidelines**)

(99025 has been deleted)

99026 Hospital mandated on call service; in-hospital, each hour

99027 out-of-hospital, each hour

(For physician standby services requiring prolonged physician attendance, use 99360, as appropriate. Time spent performing separately reportable procedure(s) or service(s) should not be included in the time reported as mandated on call service)

▲ **99050** Services provided in the office at times other than regularly scheduled office hours, or days when the office is normally closed (eg, holidays, Saturday or Sunday), in addition to basic service

● **99051** Service(s) provided in the office during regularly scheduled evening, weekend, or holiday office hours, in addition to basic service

▶(99052 has been deleted)◀

● **99053** Service(s) provided between 10:00 PM and 8:00 AM at 24-hour facility, in addition to basic service

▶(99054 has been deleted)◀

▲ **99056** Service(s) typically provided in the office, provided out of the office at request of patient, in addition to basic service

▲ **99058** Service(s) provided on an emergency basis in the office, which disrupts other scheduled office services, in addition to basic service

● **99060** Service(s) provided on an emergency basis, out of the office, which disrupts other scheduled office services, in addition to basic service

99070 Supplies and materials (except spectacles), provided by the physician over and above those usually included with the office visit or other services rendered (list drugs, trays, supplies, or materials provided)

▶(For supply of spectacles, use the appropriate supply codes)◀

99071 Educational supplies, such as books, tapes, and pamphlets, provided by the physician for the patient's education at cost to physician

99075 Medical testimony

99078 Physician educational services rendered to patients in a group setting (eg, prenatal, obesity, or diabetic instructions)

99080 Special reports such as insurance forms, more than the information conveyed in the usual medical communications or standard reporting form

(Do not report 99080 in conjunction with 99455, 99456 for the completion of Workmen's Compensation forms)

99082 Unusual travel (eg, transportation and escort of patient)

99090 Analysis of clinical data stored in computers (eg, ECGs, blood pressures, hematologic data)

(For physician/health care professional collection and interpretation of physiologic data stored/transmitted by patient/caregiver, see 99091)

(Do not report 99090 if other more specific CPT codes exist, eg, 93014, 93227, 93233, 93272 for cardiographic services; 95250 for continuous glucose monitoring, 97750 for musculoskeletal function testing)

99091 Collection and interpretation of physiologic data (eg, ECG, blood pressure, glucose monitoring) digitally stored and/or transmitted by the patient and/or caregiver to the physician or other qualified health care professional, requiring a minimum of 30 minutes of time

Qualifying Circumstances for Anesthesia

(For explanation of these services, see **Anesthesia Guidelines**)

✛ **99100** Anesthesia for patient of extreme age, under 1 year and over 70 (List separately in addition to code for primary anesthesia procedure)

(For procedure performed on infants less than 1 year of age at time of surgery, see 00326, 00561, 00834, 00836)

✛ **99116** Anesthesia complicated by utilization of total body hypothermia (List separately in addition to code for primary anesthesia procedure)

+ 99135   Anesthesia complicated by utilization of controlled hypotension (List separately in addition to code for primary anesthesia procedure)

+ 99140   Anesthesia complicated by emergency conditions (specify) (List separately in addition to code for primary anesthesia procedure)

        (An emergency is defined as existing when delay in treatment of the patient would lead to a significant increase in the threat to life or body part.)

▶Moderate (Conscious) Sedation◀

▶Moderate (conscious) sedation is a drug induced depression of consciousness during which patients respond purposefully to verbal commands, either alone or accompanied by light tactile stimulation. No interventions are required to maintain a patent airway, and spontaneous ventilation is adequate. Cardiovascular function is usually maintained.◀

▶Moderate sedation does not include minimal sedation (anxiolysis), deep sedation or monitored anesthesia care (00100-01999).◀

▶When providing moderate sedation, the following services are included and NOT reported separately:

■ Assessment of the patient (not included in intraservice time);

■ Establishment of IV access and fluids to maintain patency, when performed;

■ Administration of agent(s);

■ Maintenance of sedation;

■ Monitoring of oxygen saturation, heart rate and blood pressure; and

■ Recovery (not included in intraservice time).◀

▶Intraservice time starts with the administration of the sedation agent(s), requires continuous face-to-face attendance, and ends at the conclusion of personal contact by the physician providing the sedation.◀

▶Do not report 99143-99150 in conjunction with 94760-94762.◀

▶Do not report 99143-99145 in conjunction with codes listed in Appendix G. Do not report 99148-99150 in conjunction with codes listed in Appendix G when performed in the nonfacility setting.◀

▶When a second physician other than the healthcare professional performing the diagnostic or therapeutic services provides moderate sedation in the facility setting (eg, hospital, outpatient hospital/ambulatory surgery center, skilled nursing facility) for the procedures listed in Appendix G, the second physician reports 99148-99150. However, for the circumstance in which these services are performed by the second physician in the nonfacility setting (eg, physician office, freestanding imaging center), codes 99148-99150 are not reported.◀

        ▶(99141, 99142 have been deleted. To report, see 99143-99145)◀

⊘● **99143**   Moderate sedation services (other than those services described by codes 00100-01999) provided by the same physician performing the diagnostic or therapeutic service that the sedation supports, requiring the presence of an independent trained observer to assist in the monitoring of the patient's level of consciousness and physiological status; under 5 years of age, first 30 minutes intra-service time

⊘● **99144**   age 5 years or older, first 30 minutes intra-service time

+● **99145**   each additional 15 minutes intra-service time (List separately in addition to code for primary service)

        ▶(Use 99145 in conjunction with 99143, 99144)◀

⊘● **99148**   Moderate sedation services (other than those services described by codes 00100-01999), provided by a physician other than the health care professional performing the diagnostic or therapeutic service that the sedation supports; under 5 years of age, first 30 minutes intra-service time

⊘● **99149**   age 5 years or older, first 30 minutes intra-service time

+● **99150**   each additional 15 minutes intra-service time (List separately in addition to code for primary service)

        ▶(Use 99150 in conjunction with 99148, 99149)◀

Other Services and Procedures

99170   Anogenital examination with colposcopic magnification in childhood for suspected trauma

        ▶(For conscious sedation, use 99143-99150)◀

99172   Visual function screening, automated or semi-automated bilateral quantitative determination of visual acuity, ocular alignment, color vision by pseudoisochromatic plates, and field of vision (may include all or some screening of the determination(s) for contrast sensitivity, vision under glare)

        (This service must employ graduated visual acuity stimuli that allow a quantitative determination of visual acuity (eg, Snellen chart). This service may not be used in addition to a general ophthalmological service or an E/M service)

        (Do not report 99172 in conjunction with 99173)

Medicine

99173   Screening test of visual acuity, quantitative, bilateral

(The screening test used must employ graduated visual acuity stimuli that allow a quantitative estimate of visual acuity (eg, Snellen chart). Other identifiable services unrelated to this screening test provided at the same time may be reported separately (eg, preventive medicine services). When acuity is measured as part of a general ophthalmological service or of an E/M service of the eye, it is a diagnostic examination and not a screening test.)

(Do not report 99173 in conjunction with 99172)

99175   Ipecac or similar administration for individual emesis and continued observation until stomach adequately emptied of poison

(For diagnostic intubation, see 82926-82928, 89130-89141)

(For gastric lavage for diagnostic purposes, see 91055)

99183   Physician attendance and supervision of hyperbaric oxygen therapy, per session

(Evaluation and Management services and/or procedures (eg, wound debridement) provided in a hyperbaric oxygen treatment facility in conjunction with a hyperbaric oxygen therapy session should be reported separately)

99185   Hypothermia; regional

99186   total body

99190   Assembly and operation of pump with oxygenator or heat exchanger (with or without ECG and/or pressure monitoring); each hour

99191   3/4 hour

99192   1/2 hour

99195   Phlebotomy, therapeutic (separate procedure)

99199   Unlisted special service, procedure or report

Home Health Procedures/Services

These codes are used by non-physician health care professionals. Physicians should utilize the home visit codes 99341-99350, and utilize CPT codes other than 99500-99600 for any additional procedure/service provided to a patient living in a residence.

The following codes are used to report services provided in a patient's residence (including assisted living apartments, group homes, non-traditional private homes, custodial care facilities, or schools).

Health care professionals who are authorized to use Evaluation and Management Home Visit codes (99341-99350) may report 99500-99600 in addition to 99341-99350 if both services are performed. Evaluation and Management services may be reported separately, using modifier 25, if the patient's condition requires a

significant separately identifiable E/M service, above and beyond the home health service(s)/procedure(s) codes 99500-99600.

99500   Home visit for prenatal monitoring and assessment to include fetal heart rate, non-stress test, uterine monitoring, and gestational diabetes monitoring

99501   Home visit for postnatal assessment and follow-up care

99502   Home visit for newborn care and assessment

99503   Home visit for respiratory therapy care (eg, bronchodilator, oxygen therapy, respiratory assessment, apnea evaluation)

99504   Home visit for mechanical ventilation care

99505   Home visit for stoma care and maintenance including colostomy and cystostomy

99506   Home visit for intramuscular injections

99507   Home visit for care and maintenance of catheter(s) (eg, urinary, drainage, and enteral)

99509   Home visit for assistance with activities of daily living and personal care

(To report self-care/home management training, see 97535)

(To report home medical nutrition assessment and intervention services, see 97802-97804)

(To report home speech therapy services, see 92507-92508)

99510   Home visit for individual, family, or marriage counseling

99511   Home visit for fecal impaction management and enema administration

99512   Home visit for hemodialysis

(For home infusion of peritoneal dialysis, use 99601, 99602)

(99551-99569 have been deleted. To report, see 99601-99602)

99600   Unlisted home visit service or procedure

Home Infusion Procedures/Services

99601   Home infusion/specialty drug administration, per visit (up to 2 hours);

+ 99602   each additional hour (List separately in addition to code for primary procedure)

(Use 99602 in conjunction with 99601)

Category II Codes

The following section of *Current Procedural Terminology (CPT)* contains a set of supplemental tracking codes that can be used for performance measurement. It is anticipated that the use of Category II codes for performance measurement will decrease the need for record abstraction and chart review, and thereby minimize administrative burden on physicians, other health care professionals, hospitals, and entities seeking to measure the quality of patient care. These codes are intended to facilitate data collection about the quality of care rendered by coding certain services and test results that support nationally established performance measures and that have an evidence base as contributing to quality patient care.

The use of these codes is optional. The codes are not required for correct coding and may not be used as a substitute for Category I codes.

►These codes describe clinical components that may be typically included in evaluation and management services or clinical services and, therefore, do not have a relative value associated with them. Category II codes may also describe results from clinical laboratory or radiology tests and other procedures, identified processes intended to address patient safety practices, or services reflecting compliance with state or federal law.◄

►Category II codes described in this section make use of alphabetical characters as the 5th character in the string (ie, 4 digits followed by the letter **F**). These digits are not intended to reflect the placement of the code in the regular (Category I) part of the CPT codebook. To promote understanding of these codes and their associated measures, users are referred to Appendix H, which contains information about performance measurement exclusion modifiers, measures, and their source.◄

CPT Category II codes are arranged according to the following categories derived from standard clinical documentation format:

Composite Measures 0001F

Patient Management 0500F

Patient History 1000F

Physical Examination. 2000F

Diagnostic/Screening Processes
or Results. 3000F

Therapeutic, Preventive or Other
Interventions 4000F

Follow-up or Other
Outcomes . . . . 5000F (no codes at this time)

Patient Safety . . . . 6000F (no codes at this time)

►Cross-references to the measures associated with each Category II code and its source are included for reference in Appendix H. Users should review the complete measure(s) associated with each code prior to implementation.◄

►Category II codes are reviewed by the Performance Measures Advisory Group (PMAG), an advisory body to the CPT Editorial Panel and the CPT/HCPAC Advisory Committee. The PMAG is comprised of performance measurement experts representing the Agency for Healthcare Research and Quality (AHRQ), the American Medical Association (AMA), the Centers for Medicare and Medicaid Services (CMS), the Joint Commission on Accreditation of Healthcare Organizations (JCAHO), the National Committee for Quality Assurance (NCQA), and the Physician Consortium for Performance Improvement. The PMAG may seek additional expertise and/or input from other national health care organizations, as necessary, for the development of tracking codes. These may include national medical specialty societies, other national health care professional associations, accrediting bodies, and federal regulatory agencies.◄

Category II codes are published biannually: January 1 and July 1. The most current listing, along with guidelines and forms for submitting code change proposals for Category II codes, may be accessed on the Internet at http://www.ama-assn.org/go/cpt.

> ►(For blood pressure measured, use 2000F)◄
>
> (0002F has been deleted. To report, use 1000F)
>
> (0003F has been deleted. To report, use 1001F)
>
> (0004F has been deleted. To report, use 4000F)
>
> ►(For tobacco use cessation intervention, pharmacologic therapy, use 4001F)◄
>
> (0006F has been deleted. To report, use 4002F)
>
> (0007F has been deleted. To report, use 4006F)
>
> (0008F has been deleted. To report, use 4009F)
>
> (0009F has been deleted. To report, use 1002F)
>
> (0010F has been deleted)
>
> (0011F has been deleted. To report, use 4011F)

►Modifiers◄

►The following performance measurement modifiers may be used for Category II codes to indicate that a service specified in the associate measure(s) was considered but, due to either medical or patient circumstance(s) documented in the medical record, the service was not provided. These modifiers serve as denominator exclusions from the performance measure.◄

►Category II modifiers should only be reported with Category II codes—they should not be reported with Category I or Category III codes. In addition, unless otherwise noted in special guidelines, parenthetic notes, or code descriptor language, the modifiers included in the Category II section may be used with any code listed in the Category II section.◄

►**1P** Performance Measure Exclusion Modifier due to Medical Reasons:

Includes, for example:

- Patient allergic history,

- Potential adverse drug interaction,

- Acquired or congenital absence of organ/limb,

- Other documented clinical contraindication.

2P Performance Measure Exclusion Modifier due to Patient Choice:

Includes, for example:

- Patient refusal,

- Economic,

- Social,

- Religious.◄

Composite Measures

Composite measures codes combine several measures grouped within a single code descriptor to facilitate reporting for a clinical condition when all components are met. If only some of the components are met, or if services are provided in addition to those included in the composite code, they may be reported individually using the corresponding CPT Category II codes for those services.

● **0001F** Heart failure assessed (includes assessment of all the following components):

Blood pressure measured (2000F)[1]

Level of activity assessed (1003F)[1]

Clinical symptoms of volume overload (excess) assessed (1004F)[1]

Weight, recorded (2001F)[1]

Auscultation of the heart performed (2003F)[1]

Clinical signs of volume overload (excess) assessed (2002F)[1]

►(To report blood pressure measured, use 2000F)◄

● **0005F** Osteoarthritis assessed

Includes assessment of all the following components:

Osteoarthritis symptoms and functional status assessed (1006F)[1]

Use of anti-inflammatory or over-the-counter (OTC) analgesic medications assessed (1007F)[1]

Initial examination of the involved joint(s) (includes visual inspection, palpation, range of motion) (2004F)[1]

►(To report tobacco use cessation intervention, use 4001F)◄

Patient Management

Patient management codes describe utilization measures or measures of patient care provided for specific clinical purposes (eg, prenatal care, pre- and post-surgical care).

0500F Initial prenatal care visit (report at first prenatal encounter with health care professional providing obstetrical care. Report also date of visit and, in a separate field, the date of the last menstrual period - LMP)[2]

0501F Prenatal flow sheet documented in medical record by first prenatal visit (documentation includes at minimum blood pressure, weight, urine protein, uterine size, fetal heart tones, and estimated date of delivery). Report also: date of visit and, in a separate field, the date of the last menstrual period - LMP (Note: If reporting 0501F Prenatal flow sheet, it is not necessary to report 0500F Initial prenatal care visit)[1]

0502F Subsequent prenatal care visit

[Excludes: patients who are seen for a condition unrelated to pregnancy or prenatal care (eg, an upper respiratory infection; patients seen for consultation only, not for continuing care)]

0503F Postpartum care visit[2]

Patient History

Patient history codes describe measures for select aspects of patient history or review of systems.

1000F Tobacco use, smoking, assessed[1]

1001F Tobacco use, non-smoking, assessed[1]

Footnotes

[1] Physician Consortium for Performance Improvement, www.ama-assn.org/go/quality

[2] National Committee on Quality Assurance (NCQA), Health Employer Data Information Set (HEDIS®), www.ncqa.org

1002F Anginal symptoms and level of activity, assessed[1]

● **1003F** Level of activity assessed[1]

● **1004F** Clinical symptoms of volume overload (excess) assessed[1]

● **1005F** Asthma symptoms evaluated (includes physician documentation of numeric frequency of symptoms or patient completion of an asthma assessment tool/survey/questionnaire)[1]

● **1006F** Osteoarthritis symptoms and functional status assessed (may include the use of a standardized scale or the completion of an assessment questionnaire, such as the SF-36, AAOS Hip & Knee Questionnaire)[1]

[Instructions: Report when osteoarthritis is addressed during the patient encounter]

● **1007F** Use of anti-inflammatory or analgesic over-the-counter (OTC) medications for symptom relief assessed[1]

● **1008F** Gastrointestinal and renal risk factors assessed for patients on prescribed or OTC non-steroidal anti-inflammatory drug (NSAID)[1]

Physical Examination

Physical examination codes describe aspects of physical examination or clinical assessment.

2000F Blood pressure, measured[1]

● **2001F** Weight recorded[1]

● **2002F** Clinical signs of volume overload (excess) assessed[1]

● **2003F** Auscultation of the heart performed[1]

● **2004F** Initial examination of the involved joint(s) (includes visual inspection, palpation, range of motion)[1]

[Instructions: Report only for initial osteoarthritis visit or for visits for new joint involvement]

Diagnostic/Screening Processes or Results

Diagnostic/screening processes or results codes describe results of tests ordered (clinical laboratory tests, radiological or other procedural examinations).

● **3000F** Blood pressure ≤ 140/90 mm Hg[2]

● **3002F** Blood pressure > 140/90 mm Hg[2]

Therapeutic, Preventive or Other Interventions

Therapeutic, preventive or other interventions codes describe pharmacologic, procedural, or behavioral therapies, including preventive services such as patient education and counseling.

4000F Tobacco use cessation intervention, counseling[1]

4001F Tobacco use cessation intervention, pharmacologic therapy[1]

4002F Statin therapy, prescribed[1]

● **4003F** Patient education, written/oral, appropriate for patients with heart failure performed[1]

4006F Beta-blocker therapy, prescribed[1]

4009F Angiotensin converting enzyme (ACE) inhibitor therapy, prescribed[1]

4011F Oral antiplatelet therapy prescribed (eg, aspirin, clopidogrel/Plavix, or combination of aspirin and dipyridamole/Aggrenox)[1]

● **4012F** Warfarin therapy prescribed[1]

● **4014F** Written discharge instructions provided to heart failure patients discharged home. (Instructions include all of the following components: activity level, diet, discharge medications, follow-up appointment, weight monitoring, what to do if symptoms worsen)[3]

[Excludes patients < 18 years of age]

● **4015F** Persistent asthma, long term control medication [inhaled corticosteroids or an acceptable alternative treatment, (cromolyn sodium, leukotriene modifier, nedocromil, OR sustained release theophylline)], prescribed[1]

[Note: There are no medical exclusion criteria]

►(Do not report modifier 1P with 4015F)◄

►(To report patient reasons for not prescribing, use modifier 2P)◄

● **4016F** Anti-inflammatory/analgesic agent prescribed[1]

[Use for prescribed or continued medication(s), including over-the-counter medication(s)]

● **4017F** Gastrointestinal prophylaxis for NSAID use prescribed[1]

● **4018F** Therapeutic exercise for the involved joint(s) instructed or physical or occupational therapy prescribed[1]

Category II Codes

Footnotes

[1] Physician Consortium for Performance Improvement, www.ama-assn.org/go/quality

[2] National Committee on Quality Assurance (NCQA), Health Employer Data Information Set (HEDIS®), www.ncqa.org

[3] Joint Commission on Accreditation of Healthcare Organizations (JCAHO), ORYX Initiative Performance Measures, www.jcaho.org/pms

Follow-up or Other Outcomes

Follow-up or other outcomes codes describe review and
communication of test results to patients, patient
satisfaction or experience with care, patient functional
status, and patient morbidity and mortality.

No codes exist at this time.

Patient Safety

Patient safety codes that describe patient safety practices.

No codes exist at this time.

Category III Codes

The following section contains a set of temporary codes for emerging technology, services, and procedures. Category III codes will allow data collection for these services/procedures. Use of unlisted codes does not offer the opportunity for the collection of specific data. If a Category III code is available, this code must be reported instead of a Category I unlisted code. This is an activity that is critically important in the evaluation of health care delivery and the formation of public and private policy. The use of the codes in this section will allow physicians and other qualified health care professionals, insurers, health services researchers, and health policy experts to identify emerging technology, services, and procedures for clinical efficacy, utilization and outcomes.

The inclusion of a service or procedure in this section neither implies nor endorses clinical efficacy, safety or the applicability to clinical practice. The codes in this section do not conform to the usual requirements for CPT Category I codes established by the Editorial Panel. For Category I codes, the Panel requires that the service/procedure be performed by many health care professionals in clinical practice in multiple locations and that FDA approval, as appropriate, has already been received. The nature of emerging technology, services, and procedures is such that these requirements may not be met. For these reasons, temporary codes for emerging technology, services, and procedures have been placed in a separate section of the CPT codebook and the codes are differentiated from Category I CPT codes by the use of alphanumeric characters.

Services/procedures described in this section make use of alphanumeric characters. These codes have an alpha character as the 5th character in the string, preceded by four digits. The digits are not intended to reflect the placement of the code in the Category I section of CPT nomenclature. Codes in this section may or may not eventually receive a Category I CPT code. In either case, a given Category III code will be archived after five years of its inception unless it is demonstrated that a temporary code is still needed. New codes in this section are released semi-annually via the AMA/CPT internet site, to expedite dissemination for reporting. The full set of temporary codes for emerging technology, services, and procedures are published annually in the CPT codebook. Go to www.ama-assn.org/go/cpt for the most current listing.

(0001T has been deleted. To report, use 34803)

(0002T has been deleted. To report, use 34805)

0003T Cervicography

(0005T-0007T have been deleted. To report, see 0075T, 0076T)

⊙ **0008T** Upper gastrointestinal endoscopy including esophagus, stomach, and either the duodenum and/or jejunum as appropriate, with suturing of the esophagogastric junction

(0009T has been deleted. To report, use 58356)

►(0010T has been deleted. To report, use 86480)◄

(0012T has been deleted. To report, use 29866)

(0013T has been deleted. To report, see 29867, 27415)

(0014T has been deleted. To report, use 29868)

0016T Destruction of localized lesion of choroid (eg, choroidal neovascularization), transpupillary thermotherapy

0017T Destruction of macular drusen, photocoagulation

0018T Delivery of high power, focal magnetic pulses for direct stimulation to cortical neurons

▲ **0019T** Extracorporeal shock wave involving musculoskeletal system, not otherwise specified, low energy

►(For application of high energy extracorporeal shock wave involving musculoskeletal system not otherwise specified, use 0101T)◄

►(For application of high energy extracorporeal shock wave involving lateral humeral epicondyle, use 0102T)◄

►(0020T has been deleted. To report, use 28890)◄

0021T Insertion of transcervical or transvaginal fetal oximetry sensor

►(0023T has been deleted. To report, use 87900)◄

0024T Non-surgical septal reduction therapy (eg, alcohol ablation), for hypertrophic obstructive cardiomyopathy, with coronary arteriograms, with or without temporary pacemaker

(0025T has been deleted. To report, use 76514)

0026T Lipoprotein, direct measurement, intermediate density lipoproteins (IDL) (remnant lipoproteins)

0027T Endoscopic lysis of epidural adhesions with direct visualization using mechanical means (eg, spinal endoscopic catheter system) or solution injection (eg, normal saline) including radiologic localization and epidurography

(For diagnostic epidurography, use 64999)

0028T Dual energy x-ray absorptiometry (DEXA) body composition study, one or more sites

0029T Treatment(s) for incontinence, pulsed magnetic neuromodulation, per day

0030T Antiprothrombin (phospholipid cofactor) antibody, each Ig class

0031T   Speculoscopy;

0032T   with directed sampling

▶(0033T has been deleted. For endovascular repair of descending thoracic aorta, involving coverage of left subclavian artery origin, use 33880)◀

▶(0034T has been deleted. For endovascular repair of descending thoracic aorta, not involving coverage of left subclavian artery origin, use 33881)◀

▶(0035T has been deleted. For proximal extension during endovascular repair of descending thoracic aorta, use 33883. Distal extensions are included in 33880, 33881. Distal extensions performed after endovascular repair of descending thoracic aorta are reported with 33886)◀

▶(0036T has been deleted. For additional proximal extensions use 33884. Additional distal extensions during endovascular repair of descending thoracic aorta are included in 33880, 33881. Additional distal extensions placed after endovascular repair of thoracic aorta are included in 33886)◀

▶(0037T has been deleted. For open subclavian to carotid artery transposition performed in conjunction with endovascular thoracic aortic repair by neck incision, use 33889)◀

▶(0038T has been deleted. For endovascular repair of descending thoracic aorta, involving coverage of left subclavian artery origin, radiological supervision and interpretation, use 75956)◀

▶(0039T has been deleted. For endovascular repair of descending thoracic aorta, not involving coverage of left subclavian artery origin, radiological supervision and interpretation, use 75957)◀

▶(0040T has been deleted. For placement of proximal extension prosthesis for endovascular repair of descending thoracic aorta, radiological supervision and interpretation, use 75958. For placement of distal extension prosthesis after thoracic endovascular repair of descending thoracic aorta, radiological supervision and interpretation, use 75959)◀

0041T   Urinalysis infectious agent detection, semi-quantitative analysis of volatile compounds

0042T   Cerebral perfusion analysis using computed tomography with contrast administration, including post-processing of parametric maps with determination of cerebral blood flow, cerebral blood volume, and mean transit time

0043T   Carbon monoxide, expired gas analysis (eg, $ETCO_c$/hemolysis breath test)

0044T   Whole body integumentary photography, at request of a physician, for monitoring of high-risk patients; with dysplastic nevus syndrome or familial melanoma

0045T   with history of dysplastic nevi or personal history of melanoma

0046T   Catheter lavage of a mammary duct(s) for collection of cytology specimen(s), in high risk individuals (GAIL risk scoring or prior personal history of breast cancer), each breast; single duct

0047T   each additional duct

0048T   Implantation of a ventricular assist device, extracorporeal, percutaneous transseptal access, single or dual cannulation

+ 0049T   Prolonged extracorporeal percutaneous transseptal ventricular assist device, greater than 24 hours, each subsequent 24 hour period (List separately in addition to code for primary procedure)

(Use 0049T in conjunction with 0048T)

0050T   Removal of a ventricular assist device, extracorporeal, percutaneous transseptal access, single or dual cannulation

0051T   Implantation of a total replacement heart system (artificial heart) with recipient cardiectomy

(For implantation of heart assist or ventricular assist device, see 33975, 33976)

0052T   Replacement or repair of thoracic unit of a total replacement heart system (artificial heart)

(For replacement or repair of other implantable components in a total replacement heart system (artificial heart), use 0053T)

0053T   Replacement or repair of implantable component or components of total replacement heart system (artificial heart), excluding thoracic unit

(For replacement or repair of a thoracic unit of a total replacement heart system (artificial heart), use 0052T)

+ 0054T   Computer-assisted musculoskeletal surgical navigational orthopedic procedure, with image-guidance based on fluoroscopic images (List separately in addition to code for primary procedure)

+ 0055T   Computer-assisted musculoskeletal surgical navigational orthopedic procedure, with image-guidance based on CT/MRI images (List separately in addition to code for primary procedure)

(When CT and MRI are both performed, report 0055T only once)

+ 0056T   Computer assisted musculoskeletal surgical navigational orthopedic procedure, image-less (List separately in addition to code for primary procedure)

(0057T has been deleted. To report, use 43257)

0058T   Cryopreservation; reproductive tissue, ovarian

0059T   oocyte(s)

(For cryopreservation of embryo(s), sperm and testicular reproductive tissue, see 89258, 89259, 89335)

0060T   Electrical impedance scan of the breast, bilateral (risk assessment device for breast cancer)

Category III Codes

0061T   Destruction/reduction of malignant breast tumor including breast carcinoma cells in the margins, microwave phased array thermotherapy, disposable catheter with combined temperature monitoring probe and microwave sensor, externally applied microwave energy, including interstitial placement of sensor

(For imaging guidance performed in conjunction with 0061T, see 76942, 76986)

0062T   Percutaneous intradiscal annuloplasty, any method, unilateral or bilateral including fluoroscopic guidance; single level

+ 0063T   one or more additional levels (List separately in addition to 0062T for primary procedure)

(For CT or MRI guidance and localization for needle placement and annuloplasty in conjunction with 0062T, 0063T, see 76360, 76393)

0064T   Spectroscopy, expired gas analysis (eg, nitric oxide/carbon dioxide test)

0065T   Ocular photoscreening, with interpretation and report, bilateral

(Do not report 0065T in conjunction with 99172 or 99173)

0066T   Computed tomographic (CT) colonography (ie, virtual colonoscopy); screening

0067T   diagnostic

(Do not report 0066T or 0067T in conjunction with 72192-72194, 74150-74170)

+ 0068T   Acoustic heart sound recording and computer analysis; with interpretation and report (List separately in addition to codes for electrocardiography)

(Use 0068T in conjunction with 93000)

+ 0069T   acoustic heart sound recording and computer analysis only (List separately in addition to codes for electrocardiography)

(Use 0069T in conjunction with 93005)

+ 0070T   interpretation and report only (List separately in addition to codes for electrocardiography)

(Use 0070T in conjunction with 93010)

0071T   Focused ultrasound ablation of uterine leiomyomata, including MR guidance; total leiomyomata volume less than 200 cc of tissue

0072T   total leiomyomata volume greater or equal to 200 cc of tissue

(Do not report 0071T, 0072T in conjunction with 51702 or 76394)

0073T   Compensator-based beam modulation treatment delivery of inverse planned treatment using three or more high resolution (milled or cast) compensator convergent beam modulated fields, per treatment session

(For treatment planning, use 77301)

(Do not report 0073T in conjunction with 77401-77416, 77418)

Online Medical Evaluation

An online medical evaluation is a type of Evaluation and Management (E/M) service provided by a physician or qualified health care professional to a patient using internet resources in response to the patient's online inquiry. Reportable services involve the physician's personal timely response to the patient's inquiry and must involve permanent storage (electronic or hard copy) of the encounter. This service should not be reported for patient contacts (eg, telephone calls) considered to be pre-service or post-service work for other E/M or non E/M services. A reportable service would encompass the sum of communication (eg, related telephone calls, prescription provision, laboratory orders) pertaining to the online patient encounter or problem(s).

0074T   Online evaluation and management service, per encounter, provided by a physician, using the Internet or similar electronic communications network, in response to a patient's request, established patient

0075T   Transcatheter placement of extracranial vertebral or intrathoracic carotid artery stent(s), including radiologic supervision and interpretation, percutaneous; initial vessel

+ 0076T   each additional vessel (List separately in addition to code for primary procedure)

(Use 0076T in conjunction with 0075T)

(When the ipsilateral extracranial vertebral or intrathoracic carotid arteriogram (including imaging and selective catheterization) confirms the need for stenting, then 0075T and 0076T include all ipsilateral extracranial vertebral or intrathoracic selective carotid catheterization, all diagnostic imaging for ipsilateral extracranial vertebral or intrathoracic carotid artery stenting, and all related radiologic supervision and interpretation. If stenting is not indicated, then the appropriate codes for selective catheterization and imaging should be reported in lieu of code 0075T or 0076T.)

0077T   Implanting and securing cerebral thermal perfusion probe, including twist drill or burr hole, to measure absolute cerebral tissue perfusion

(0078T-0081T should be reported in accordance with the Endovascular Abdominal Aneurysm Repair guidelines established for 34800-34826)

▲ 0078T   Endovascular repair using prosthesis of abdominal aortic aneurysm, pseudoaneurysm or dissection, abdominal aorta involving visceral branches (superior mesenteric, celiac and/or renal artery(s))

(Do not report 0078T in conjunction with 34800-34805, 35081, 35102, 35452, 35454, 35472, 37205-37208)

(Report 0078T in conjunction with 35454, 37205-37208 when these procedures are performed outside the target zone of the endoprosthesis)

Category III Codes

+ 0079T   Placement of visceral extension prosthesis for endovascular repair of abdominal aortic aneurysm involving visceral vessels, each visceral branch (List separately in addition to code for primary procedure)

(Use 0079T in conjunction with 0078T)

(Do not report 0079T in conjunction with 34800-34805, 35081, 35102, 35452, 35454, 35472, 37205-37208)

(Report 0079T in conjunction with 35454, 37205-37208 when these procedures are performed outside the target zone of the endoprosthesis)

0080T   Endovascular repair of abdominal aortic aneurysm, pseudoaneurysm or dissection, abdominal aorta involving visceral vessels (superior mesenteric, celiac or renal), using fenestrated modular bifurcated prosthesis (two docking limbs), radiological supervision and interpretation

(Do not report 0080T in conjunction with 34800-34805, 35081, 35102, 35452, 35454, 35472, 37205-37208)

(Report 0080T in conjunction with 35454, 37205-37208 when these procedures are performed outside the target zone of the endoprosthesis)

+ 0081T   Placement of visceral extension prosthesis for endovascular repair of abdominal aortic aneurysm involving visceral vessels, each visceral branch, radiological supervision and interpretation (List separately in addition to code for primary procedure)

(Use 0081T in conjunction with 0080T)

(Do not report 0081T in conjunction with 34800-34805, 35081, 35102, 35452, 35454, 35472, 37205-37208)

(Report 0081T in conjunction with 35454, 37205-37208 when these procedures are performed outside the target zone of the endoprosthesis)

0082T   Stereotactic body radiation therapy, treatment delivery, one or more treatment areas, per day

(Do not report 0082T in conjunction with 77401-77416, 77418)

0083T   Stereotactic body radiation therapy, treatment management, per day

(Do not report 0083T in conjunction with 77427-77432)

0084T   Insertion of a temporary prostatic urethral stent

0085T   Breath test for heart transplant rejection

0086T   Left ventricular filling pressure indirect measurement by computerized calibration of the arterial waveform response to Valsalva maneuver

0087T   Sperm evaluation, Hyaluronan binding assay

0088T   Submucosal radiofrequency tissue volume reduction of tongue base, one or more sites, per session (ie, for treatment of obstructive sleep apnea syndrome)

● **0089T**   Actigraphy testing, recording, analysis and interpretation (minimum of three-day recording)

● **0090T**   Total disc arthroplasty (artificial disc), anterior approach, including diskectomy to prepare interspace (other than for decompression); single interspace, cervical

● **0091T**   single interspace, lumbar

+● **0092T**   each additional interspace (List separately in addition to code for primary procedure)

►(Use 0092T in conjunction with 0090T, 0091T)◄

● **0093T**   Removal of total disc arthroplasty, anterior approach; single interspace, cervical

● **0094T**   single interspace, lumbar

+● **0095T**   each additional interspace (List separately in addition to code for primary procedure)

►(Use 0095T in conjunction with 0093T, 0094T)◄

● **0096T**   Revision of total disc arthroplasty, anterior approach; single interspace, cervical

►(Do not report 0096T in conjunction with 0093T)◄

● **0097T**   single interspace, lumbar

►(Do not report 0097T in conjunction with 0094T)◄

+● **0098T**   each additional interspace (List separately in addition to code for primary procedure)

►(Use 0098T in conjunction with 0096T, 0097T)◄

►(Do not report 0098T in conjunction with 0095T)◄

►(Do not report 0090T-0097T in conjunction with 22851, 49010, when performed at the same level)◄

►(0090T-0097T include fluoroscopy when performed)◄

►(For decompression, see 63001-63048)◄

● **0099T**   Implantation of intrastromal corneal ring segments

● **0100T**   Placement of a subconjunctival retinal prosthesis receiver and pulse generator, and implantation of intra-ocular retinal electrode array, with vitrectomy

● **0101T**   Extracorporeal shock wave involving musculoskeletal system, not otherwise specified, high energy

►(For application of low energy musculoskeletal system extracorporeal shock wave, use 0019T)◄

● **0102T**   Extracorporeal shock wave, high energy, performed by a physician, requiring anesthesia other than local, involving lateral humeral epicondyle

►(For application of low energy musculoskeletal system extracorporeal shock wave, use 0019T)◄

● **0103T**   Holotranscobalamin, quantitative

● **0104T**   Inert gas rebreathing for cardiac output measurement; during rest

● **0105T**   during exercise

● **0106T**   Quantitative sensory testing (QST), testing and interpretation per extremity; using touch pressure stimuli to assess large diameter sensation

● **0107T**   using vibration stimuli to assess large diameter fiber sensation

● **0108T**   using cooling stimuli to assess small nerve fiber sensation and hyperalgesia

● **0109T**   using heat-pain stimuli to assess small nerve fiber sensation and hyperalgesia

● **0110T**   using other stimuli to assess sensation

● **0111T**   Long-chain (C20-22) omega-3 fatty acids in red blood cell (RBC) membranes

▶(For very long chain fatty acids, use 82726)◀

▶Medication Therapy Management◀

▶Medication Therapy Management Service(s) (MTMS) describe face-to-face patient assessment and intervention as appropriate, by a pharmacist. MTMS is provided to optimize the response to medications or to manage treatment-related medication interactions or complications.◀

▶MTMS includes the following documented elements: review of the pertinent patient history, medication profile (prescription and non-prescription), and recommendations for improving health outcomes and treatment compliance. These codes are not to be used to describe the provision of product-specific information at the point of dispensing or any other routine dispensing-related activities.◀

● **0115T**   Medication therapy management service(s) provided by a pharmacist, individual, face-to-face with patient, initial 15 minutes, with assessment, and intervention if provided; initial encounter

● **0116T**   subsequent encounter

+● **0117T**   each additional 15 minutes (List separately in addition to code for primary service)

▶(Use 0117T in conjunction with 0115T, 0116T)◀

● **0120T**   Ablation, cryosurgical, of fibroadenoma, including ultrasound guidance, each fibroadenoma

▶(Do not report 0120T in conjunction with 90772)◀

● **0123T**   Fistulization of sclera for glaucoma, through ciliary body

● **0124T**   Conjunctival incision with posterior juxtascleral placement of pharmacological agent (does not include supply of medication)

● **0126T**   Common carotid intima-media thickness (IMT) study for evaluation of atherosclerotic burden or coronary heart disease risk factor assessment

● **0130T**   Validated, statistically reliable, randomized, controlled, single-patient clinical investigation of FDA approved chronic care drugs, provided by a pharmacist, interpretation and report to the prescribing health care professional

● **0133T**   Upper gastrointestinal endoscopy, including esophagus, stomach, and either the duodenum and/or jejunum as appropriate, with injection of implant material into and along the muscle of the lower esophageal sphincter (eg, for treatment of gastroesophageal reflux disease)

● **0135T**   Ablation, renal tumor(s), unilateral, percutaneous, cryotherapy

● **0137T**   Biopsy, prostate, needle, saturation sampling for prostate mapping

▶(Do not report 0137T in conjunction with 76942)◀

● **0140T**   Exhaled breath condensate pH

Category III Codes

Notes

⊘=Modifier 51 exempt ⊙=Conscious sedation ✚=Add-on code ✗=FDA approval pending

Appendix A

Modifiers

This list includes all of the modifiers applicable to *CPT 2006* codes.

21   **Prolonged Evaluation and Management Services:** When the face-to-face or floor/unit service(s) provided is prolonged or otherwise greater than that usually required for the highest level of evaluation and management service within a given category, it may be identified by adding modifier 21 to the evaluation and management code number. A report may also be appropriate.

22   **Unusual Procedural Services:** When the service(s) provided is greater than that usually required for the listed procedure, it may be identified by adding modifier 22 to the usual procedure number. A report may also be appropriate.

23   **Unusual Anesthesia:** Occasionally, a procedure, which usually requires either no anesthesia or local anesthesia, because of unusual circumstances must be done under general anesthesia. This circumstance may be reported by adding modifier 23 to the procedure code of the basic service.

24   **Unrelated Evaluation and Management Service by the Same Physician During a Postoperative Period:** The physician may need to indicate that an evaluation and management service was performed during a postoperative period for a reason(s) unrelated to the original procedure. This circumstance may be reported by adding modifier 24 to the appropriate level of E/M service.

25   **Significant, Separately Identifiable Evaluation and Management Service by the Same Physician on the Same Day of the Procedure or Other Service:** The physician may need to indicate that on the day a procedure or service identified by a CPT code was performed, the patient's condition required a significant, separately identifiable E/M service above and beyond the other service provided or beyond the usual preoperative and postoperative care associated with the procedure that was performed. ▶A significant, separately identifiable E/M service is defined or substantiated by documentation that satisfies the relevant criteria for the respective E/M service to be reported (see **Evaluation and Management Services Guidelines** for instructions on determining level of E/M service).◀ The E/M service may be prompted by the symptom or condition for which the procedure and/or service was provided. As such, different diagnoses are not required for reporting of the E/M service. **Note:** This modifier is not used to report an E/M service that resulted in a decision to perform surgery (see modifier 57).

26   **Professional Component:** Certain procedures are a combination of a physician component and a technical component. When the physician component is reported separately, the service may be identified by adding modifier 26 to the usual procedure number.

32   **Mandated Services:** Services related to *mandated* consultation and/or related services (eg, PRO, third party payer, governmental, legislative or regulatory requirement) may be identified by adding modifier 32 to the basic procedure.

47   **Anesthesia by Surgeon:** Regional or general anesthesia provided by the surgeon may be reported by adding modifier 47 to the basic service. (This does not include local anesthesia.) **Note:** Modifier 47 would not be used as a modifier for the anesthesia procedures.

50   **Bilateral Procedure:** Unless otherwise identified in the listings, bilateral procedures that are performed at the same operative session, should be identified by adding modifier 50 to the appropriate five digit code.

51   **Multiple Procedures:** When multiple procedures, other than E/M services, are performed at the same session by the same provider, the primary procedure or service may be reported as listed. The additional procedure(s) or service(s) may be identified by appending modifier 51 to the additional procedure or service code(s). **Note:** This modifier should not be appended to designated "add-on" codes (see Appendix D).

52   **Reduced Services:** Under certain circumstances a service or procedure is partially reduced or eliminated at the physician's discretion. Under these circumstances the service provided can be identified by its usual procedure number and the addition of modifier 52, signifying that the service is reduced. This provides a means of reporting reduced services without disturbing the identification of the basic service. **Note:** For hospital outpatient reporting of a previously scheduled procedure/service that is partially reduced or cancelled as a result of extenuating circumstances or those that threaten the well-being of the patient prior to or after administration of anesthesia, see modifiers 73 and 74 (see modifiers approved for ASC hospital outpatient use).

53   **Discontinued Procedure:** Under certain circumstances, the physician may elect to terminate a surgical or diagnostic procedure. Due to extenuating circumstances or those that threaten the well being of the patient, it may be necessary to indicate that a surgical or diagnostic procedure was started but discontinued. This circumstance may be reported by adding modifier 53 to the code reported by the physician for the discontinued procedure. **Note:** This modifier is not used to report the elective cancellation of a procedure prior to the patient's anesthesia induction and/or surgical preparation in the operating suite. For outpatient hospital/ambulatory surgery center (ASC) reporting of a previously scheduled procedure/service that is partially reduced or cancelled as a result of extenuating circumstances or those that threaten the well being of the patient prior to or after administration of anesthesia, see modifiers 73 and 74 (see modifiers approved for ASC hospital outpatient use).

54 Surgical Care Only: When one physician performs a surgical procedure and another provides preoperative and/or postoperative management, surgical services may be identified by adding modifier 54 to the usual procedure number.

55 Postoperative Management Only: When one physician performed the postoperative management and another physician performed the surgical procedure, the postoperative component may be identified by adding modifier 55 to the usual procedure number.

56 Preoperative Management Only: When one physician performed the preoperative care and evaluation and another physician performed the surgical procedure, the preoperative component may be identified by adding modifier 56 to the usual procedure number.

57 Decision for Surgery: An evaluation and management service that resulted in the initial decision to perform the surgery may be identified by adding modifier 57 to the appropriate level of E/M service.

58 Staged or Related Procedure or Service by the Same Physician During the Postoperative Period: The physician may need to indicate that the performance of a procedure or service during the postoperative period was: a) planned prospectively at the time of the original procedure (staged); b) more extensive than the original procedure; or c) for therapy following a diagnostic surgical procedure. This circumstance may be reported by adding modifier 58 to the staged or related procedure. **Note:** This modifier is not used to report the treatment of a problem that requires a return to the operating room (see modifier 78).

59 Distinct Procedural Service: Under certain circumstances, the physician may need to indicate that a procedure or service was distinct or independent from other services performed on the same day. Modifier 59 is used to identify procedures/services that are not normally reported together, but are appropriate under the circumstances. This may represent a different session or patient encounter, different procedure or surgery, different site or organ system, separate incision/excision, separate lesion, or separate injury (or area of injury in extensive injuries) not ordinarily encountered or performed on the same day by the same physician. However, when another already established modifier is appropriate it should be used rather than modifier 59. Only if no more descriptive modifier is available, and the use of modifier 59 best explains the circumstances, should modifier 59 be used.

62 Two Surgeons: When two surgeons work together as primary surgeons performing distinct part(s) of a procedure, each surgeon should report his/her distinct operative work by adding modifier 62 to the procedure code and any associated add-on code(s) for that procedure as long as both surgeons continue to work together as primary surgeons. Each surgeon should report the co-surgery once using the same procedure code. If additional procedure(s) (including add-on procedure(s)) are performed during the same surgical session, separate code(s) may also be reported with modifier 62 added. **Note:** If a co-surgeon acts as an assistant in the performance of additional procedure(s) during the same surgical session, those services may be reported using separate procedure code(s) with the modifier 80 or modifier 82 added, as appropriate.

63 Procedure Performed on Infants less than 4 kg: Procedures performed on neonates and infants up to a present body weight of 4 kg may involve significantly increased complexity and physician work commonly associated with these patients. This circumstance may be reported by adding modifier 63 to the procedure number. **Note:** Unless otherwise designated, this modifier may only be appended to procedures/services listed in the 20000-69999 code series. Modifier 63 should not be appended to any CPT codes listed in the **Evaluation and Management Services, Anesthesia, Radiology, Pathology/Laboratory, or Medicine** sections.

66 Surgical Team: Under some circumstances, highly complex procedures (requiring the concomitant services of several physicians, often of different specialties, plus other highly skilled, specially trained personnel, various types of complex equipment) are carried out under the "surgical team" concept. Such circumstances may be identified by each participating physician with the addition of modifier 66 to the basic procedure number used for reporting services.

76 Repeat Procedure by Same Physician: The physician may need to indicate that a procedure or service was repeated subsequent to the original procedure or service. This circumstance may be reported by adding modifier 76 to the repeated procedure/service.

77 Repeat Procedure by Another Physician: The physician may need to indicate that a basic procedure or service performed by another physician had to be repeated. This situation may be reported by adding modifier 77 to the repeated procedure/service.

78 Return to the Operating Room for a Related Procedure During the Postoperative Period: The physician may need to indicate that another procedure was performed during the postoperative period of the initial procedure. When this subsequent procedure is related to the first, and requires the use of the operating room, it may be reported by adding modifier 78 to the related procedure. (For repeat procedures on the same day, see modifier 76.)

79 Unrelated Procedure or Service by the Same Physician During the Postoperative Period: The physician may need to indicate that the performance of a procedure or service during the postoperative period was unrelated to the original procedure. This circumstance may be reported by using modifier 79. (For repeat procedures on the same day, see modifier 76.)

80 **Assistant Surgeon:** Surgical assistant services may be identified by adding modifier 80 to the usual procedure number(s).

81 **Minimum Assistant Surgeon:** Minimum surgical assistant services are identified by adding modifier 81 to the usual procedure number.

82 **Assistant Surgeon (when qualified resident surgeon not available):** The unavailability of a qualified resident surgeon is a prerequisite for use of modifier 82 appended to the usual procedure code number(s).

90 **Reference (Outside) Laboratory:** When laboratory procedures are performed by a party other than the treating or reporting physician, the procedure may be identified by adding modifier 90 to the usual procedure number.

91 **Repeat Clinical Diagnostic Laboratory Test:** In the course of treatment of the patient, it may be necessary to repeat the same laboratory test on the same day to obtain subsequent (multiple) test results. Under these circumstances, the laboratory test performed can be identified by its usual procedure number and the addition of modifier 91. **Note:** This modifier may not be used when tests are rerun to confirm initial results; due to testing problems with specimens or equipment; or for any other reason when a normal, one-time, reportable result is all that is required. This modifier may not be used when other code(s) describe a series of test results (eg, glucose tolerance tests, evocative/suppression testing). This modifier may only be used for laboratory test(s) performed more than once on the same day on the same patient.

99 **Multiple Modifiers:** Under certain circumstances two or more modifiers may be necessary to completely delineate a service. In such situations modifier 99 should be added to the basic procedure, and other applicable modifiers may be listed as part of the description of the service.

Anesthesia Physical Status Modifiers

The Physical Status modifiers are consistent with the American Society of Anesthesiologists ranking of patient physical status, and distinguishing various levels of complexity of the anesthesia service provided. All anesthesia services are reported by use of the anesthesia five-digit procedure code (00100-01999) with the appropriate physical status modifier appended.

Example: 00100-P1

Under certain circumstances, when another established modifier(s) is appropriate, it should be used in addition to the physical status modifier.

Example: 00100-P4-53

Physical Status Modifier P1: A normal healthy patient

Physical Status Modifier P2: A patient with mild systemic disease

Physical Status Modifier P3: A patient with severe systemic disease

Physical Status Modifier P4: A patient with severe systemic disease that is a constant threat to life

Physical Status Modifier P5: A moribund patient who is not expected to survive without the operation

Physical Status Modifier P6: A declared brain-dead patient whose organs are being removed for donor purposes

Modifiers Approved for Ambulatory Surgery Center (ASC) Hospital Outpatient Use

CPT Level I Modifiers

25 **Significant, Separately Identifiable Evaluation and Management Service by the Same Physician on the Same Day of the Procedure or Other Service:** The physician may need to indicate that on the day a procedure or service identified by a CPT code was performed, the patient's condition required a significant, separately identifiable E/M service above and beyond the other service provided or beyond the usual preoperative and postoperative care associated with the procedure that was performed. ▶A significant, separately identifiable E/M service is defined or substantiated by documentation that satisfies the relevant criteria for the respective E/M service to be reported (see **Evaluation and Management Services Guidelines** for instructions on determining level of E/M service).◀ The E/M service may be prompted by the symptom or condition for which the procedure and/or service was provided. As such, different diagnoses are not required for reporting of the E/M service. **Note:** This modifier is not used to report an E/M service that resulted in a decision to perform surgery. (see modifier 57).

27 **Multiple Outpatient Hospital E/M Encounters on the Same Date:** For hospital outpatient reporting purposes, utilization of hospital resources related to separate and distinct E/M encounters performed in multiple outpatient hospital settings on the same date may be reported by adding modifier 27 to each appropriate level outpatient and/or emergency department E/M code(s). This modifier provides a means of reporting circumstances involving evaluation and management services provided by physician(s) in more than one (multiple) outpatient hospital setting(s) (eg, hospital emergency department, clinic). **Note:** This modifier is not to be used for physician reporting of multiple E/M services performed by the same physician on the same date. For physician reporting of all outpatient evaluation and management services provided by the same physician on the same date and performed in multiple outpatient setting(s) (eg, hospital emergency department, clinic), see **Evaluation and Management, Emergency Department, or Preventive Medicine Services** codes.

50 **Bilateral Procedure:** Unless otherwise identified in the listings, bilateral procedures that are performed at the same operative session should be identified by adding modifier 50 to the appropriate five digit code.

52 Reduced Services: Under certain circumstances a service or procedure is partially reduced or eliminated at the physician's discretion. Under these circumstances the service provided can be identified by its usual procedure number and the addition of modifier 52, signifying that the service is reduced. This provides a means of reporting reduced services without disturbing the identification of the basic service. **Note:** For hospital outpatient reporting of a previously scheduled procedure/service that is partially reduced or cancelled as a result of extenuating circumstances or those that threaten the well-being of the patient prior to or after administration of anesthesia, see modifiers 73 and 74.

58 Staged or Related Procedure or Service by the Same Physician During the Postoperative Period: The physician may need to indicate that the performance of a procedure or service during the postoperative period was: a) planned prospectively at the time of the original procedure (staged); b) more extensive than the original procedure; or c) for therapy following a diagnostic surgical procedure. This circumstance may be reported by adding modifier 58 to the staged or related procedure. **Note:** This modifier is not used to report the treatment of a problem that requires a return to the operating room (see modifier 78).

59 Distinct Procedural Service: Under certain circumstances, the physician may need to indicate that a procedure or service was distinct or independent from other services performed on the same day. Modifier 59 is used to identify procedures/services that are not normally reported together, but are appropriate under the circumstances. This may represent a different session or patient encounter, different procedure or surgery, different site or organ system, separate incision/excision, separate lesion, or separate injury (or area of injury in extensive injuries) not ordinarily encountered or performed on the same day by the same physician. However, when another already established modifier is appropriate it should be used rather than modifier 59. Only if no more descriptive modifier is available, and the use of modifier 59 best explains the circumstances, should modifier 59 be used.

73 Discontinued Out-Patient Hospital/Ambulatory Surgery Center (ASC) Procedure Prior to the Administration of Anesthesia: Due to extenuating circumstances or those that threaten the well being of the patient, the physician may cancel a surgical or diagnostic procedure subsequent to the patient's surgical preparation (including sedation when provided, and being taken to the room where the procedure is to be performed), but prior to the administration of anesthesia (local, regional block(s) or general). Under these circumstances, the intended service that is prepared for but cancelled can be reported by its usual procedure number and the addition of modifier 73. **Note:** The elective cancellation of a service prior to the administration of anesthesia and/or surgical preparation of the patient should not be reported. For physician reporting of a discontinued procedure, see modifier 53.

74 Discontinued Out-Patient Hospital/Ambulatory Surgery Center (ASC) Procedure After Administration of Anesthesia: Due to extenuating circumstances or those that threaten the well being of the patient, the physician may terminate a surgical or diagnostic procedure after the administration of anesthesia (local, regional block(s), general) or after the procedure was started (incision made, intubation started, scope inserted, etc). Under these circumstances, the procedure started but terminated can be reported by its usual procedure number and the addition of modifier 74. **Note:** The elective cancellation of a service prior to the administration of anesthesia and/or surgical preparation of the patient should not be reported. For physician reporting of a discontinued procedure, see modifier 53.

76 Repeat Procedure by Same Physician: The physician may need to indicate that a procedure or service was repeated subsequent to the original procedure or service. This circumstance may be reported by adding modifier 76 to the repeated procedure/service.

77 Repeat Procedure by Another Physician: The physician may need to indicate that a basic procedure or service performed by another physician had to be repeated. This situation may be reported by adding modifier 77 to the repeated procedure/service.

78 Return to the Operating Room for a Related Procedure During the Postoperative Period: The physician may need to indicate that another procedure was performed during the postoperative period of the initial procedure. When this subsequent procedure is related to the first, and requires the use of the operating room, it may be reported by adding modifier 78 to the related procedure. (For repeat procedures on the same day, see 76.)

79 Unrelated Procedure or Service by the Same Physician During the Postoperative Period: The physician may need to indicate that the performance of a procedure or service during the postoperative period was unrelated to the original procedure. This circumstance may be reported by using modifier 79. (For repeat procedures on the same day, see 76.)

91 Repeat Clinical Diagnostic Laboratory Test: In the course of treatment of the patient, it may be necessary to repeat the same laboratory test on the same day to obtain subsequent (multiple) test results. Under these circumstances, the laboratory test performed can be identified by its usual procedure number and the addition of modifier 91. **Note:** This modifier may not be used when tests are rerun to confirm initial results; due to testing problems with specimens or equipment; or for any other reason when a normal, one-time, reportable result is all that is required. This modifier may not be used when other code(s) describe a series of test results (eg, glucose tolerance tests, evocative/suppression testing). This modifier may only be used for laboratory test(s) performed more than once on the same day on the same patient.

Level II (HCPCS/National) Modifiers

E1 Upper left, eyelid

E2 Lower left, eyelid

E3 Upper right, eyelid

E4 Lower right, eyelid

F1 Left hand, second digit

F2 Left hand, third digit

F3 Left hand, fourth digit

F4 Left hand, fifth digit

F5 Right hand, thumb

F6 Right hand, second digit

F7 Right hand, third digit

F8 Right hand, fourth digit

F9 Right hand, fifth digit

FA Left hand, thumb

GG Performance and payment of a screening mammogram and diagnostic mammogram on the same patient, same day

GH Diagnostic mammogram converted from screening mammogram on same day

LC Left circumflex coronary artery (Hospitals use with codes 92980-92984, 92995, 92996)

LD Left anterior descending coronary artery (Hospitals use with codes 92980-92984, 92995, 92996)

LT Left side (used to identify procedures performed on the left side of the body)

QM Ambulance service provided under arrangement by a provider of services

QN Ambulance service furnished directly by a provider of services

RC Right coronary artery (Hospitals use with codes 92980-92984, 92995, 92996)

RT Right side (used to identify procedures performed on the right side of the body)

T1 Left foot, second digit

T2 Left foot, third digit

T3 Left foot, fourth digit

T4 Left foot, fifth digit

T5 Right foot, great toe

T6 Right foot, second digit

T7 Right foot, third digit

T8 Right foot, fourth digit

T9 Right foot, fifth digit

TA Left foot, great toe

Appendix B

Summary of Additions, Deletions, and Revisions

Appendix B shows the actual changes that were made to the code descriptors. New codes appear with a bullet (●) and are indicated as "Code added." Revised codes are preceded with a triangle (▲). Within revised codes, the deleted language appears with a ~~strikethrough~~, while new text appears underlined. Codes with which conscious sedation would not be separately reported when performed at the same session by the same provider are denoted with the bullseye (◉).

Revisions to the headings, notes, introductory paragraphs, and cross-references are not included in this Appendix, but are identified in the main text of the book with the "► ◄" symbols and presented in green. Codes listed as "Grammatical change" contain minor revisions that do not alter the original intent of the codes, and therefore are not preceded with a triangle (▲).

Evaluation and Management

~~99261~~ **~~Follow-up inpatient consultation~~** ~~for an established patient, which requires at least two of these three key components:~~

- ~~■ a problem focused interval history;~~
- ~~■ a problem focused examination;~~
- ~~■ medical decision making that is straightforward or of low complexity.~~

~~Counseling and/or coordination of care with other providers or agencies are provided consistent with nature of the problem(s) and the patient's and/or family's needs.~~

~~Usually, the patient is stable, recovering or improving. Physicians typically spend 10 minutes at the bedside and on the patient's hospital floor or unit.~~

~~99262~~ **~~Follow-up inpatient consultation~~** ~~for an established patient which requires at least two of these three key components:~~

- ~~■ an expanded problem focused interval history;~~
- ~~■ an expanded problem focused examination;~~
- ~~■ medical decision making of moderate complexity.~~

~~Counseling and/or coordination of care with other providers or agencies are provided consistent with the nature of the problem(s) and the patient's and/or family's needs.~~

~~Usually, the patient is responding inadequately to therapy or has developed a minor complication. Physicians typically spend 20 minutes at the bedside and on the patient's hospital floor or unit.~~

~~99263~~ **~~Follow-up inpatient consultation~~** ~~for an established patient which requires at least two of these three key components:~~

- ~~■ a detailed interval history;~~
- ~~■ a detailed examination;~~
- ~~■ medical decision making of high complexity.~~

~~Counseling and/or coordination of care with other providers or agencies are provided consistent with the nature of the problem(s) and the patient's and/or family's needs.~~

~~Usually, the patient is unstable or has developed a significant complication or a significant new problem. Physicians typically spend 30 minutes at the bedside and on the patient's hospital floor or unit.~~

~~99271~~ **~~Confirmatory consultation~~** ~~for a new or established patient, which requires these three key components:~~

- ~~■ a problem focused history;~~
- ~~■ a problem focused examination; and~~
- ~~■ straightforward medical decision making.~~

~~Counseling and/or coordination of care with other providers or agencies are provided consistent with the nature of the problem(s) and the patient's and/or family's needs.~~

~~Usually, the presenting problem(s) are self limited or minor.~~

~~99272~~ **~~Confirmatory consultation~~** ~~for a new or established patient, which requires these three key components:~~

- ~~■ an expanded problem focused history;~~
- ~~■ an expanded problem focused examination; and~~
- ~~■ straightforward medical decision making.~~

~~Counseling and/or coordination of care with other providers or agencies are provided consistent with the nature of the problem(s) and the patient's and/or family's needs.~~

~~Usually, the presenting problem(s) are of low severity.~~

~~99273~~ **~~Confirmatory consultation~~** ~~for a new or established patient, which requires these three key components:~~

- ~~■ a detailed history;~~
- ~~■ a detailed examination; and~~
- ~~■ medical decision making of low complexity.~~

~~Counseling and/or coordination of care with other providers or agencies are provided consistent with the nature of the problem(s) and the patient's and/or family's needs.~~

~~Usually, the presenting problem(s) are of moderate severity.~~

~~99274~~ **~~Confirmatory consultation~~** ~~for a new or established patient, which requires these three key components:~~

- ~~■ a comprehensive history;~~
- ~~■ a comprehensive examination; and~~
- ~~■ medical decision making of moderate complexity.~~

~~Counseling and/or coordination of care with other providers or agencies are provided consistent with the nature of the problem(s) and the patient's and/or family's needs.~~

~~Usually, the presenting problem(s) are of moderate to high severity.~~

99275 ~~Confirmatory consultation for a new or established patient, which requires these three key components:~~

■ ~~a comprehensive history;~~

■ ~~a comprehensive examination; and~~

■ ~~medical decision making of high complexity.~~

~~Counseling and/or coordination of care with other providers or agencies are provided consistent with the nature of the problem(s) and the patient's and/or family's needs.~~

~~Usually, the presenting problem(s) are of moderate to high severity.~~

● 99300 Code added

99301 ~~Evaluation and management of a new or established patient involving an annual nursing facility assessment which requires these three key components:~~

■ ~~a detailed interval history;~~

■ ~~a comprehensive examination; and~~

■ ~~medical decision making that is straightforward or of low complexity.~~

~~Counseling and/or coordination of care with other providers or agencies are provided consistent with the nature of the problem(s) and the patient's and/or family's needs.~~

~~Usually, the patient is stable, recovering or improving. The review and affirmation of the medical plan of care is required. Physicians typically spend 30 minutes at the bedside and on the patient's facility floor or unit.~~

99302 ~~Evaluation and management of a new or established patient involving a nursing facility assessment which requires these three key components:~~

■ ~~a detailed interval history;~~

■ ~~a comprehensive examination; and~~

■ ~~medical decision making of moderate to high complexity.~~

~~Counseling and/or coordination of care with other providers or agencies are provided consistent with the nature of the problem(s) and the patient's and/or family's needs.~~

~~Usually, the patient has developed a significant complication or a significant new problem and has had a major permanent change in status.~~

~~The creation of a new medical plan of care is required. Physicians typically spend 40 minutes at the bedside and on the patient's facility floor or unit.~~

99303 ~~Evaluation and management of a new or established patient involving a nursing facility assessment at the time of initial admission or readmission to the facility, which requires these three key components:~~

■ ~~a comprehensive history;~~

■ ~~a comprehensive examination; and~~

■ ~~medical decision making of moderate to high complexity.~~

~~Counseling and/or coordination of care with other providers or agencies are provided consistent with the nature of the problem(s) and the patient's and/or family's needs.~~

~~The creation of a medical plan of care is required. Physicians typically spend 50 minutes at the bedside and on the patient's facility floor or unit.~~

● 99304 Code added

● 99305 Code added

● 99306 Code added

● 99307 Code added

● 99308 Code added

● 99309 Code added

● 99310 Code added

99311 ~~Subsequent nursing facility care, per day, for the evaluation and management of a new or established patient, which requires at least two of these three key components:~~

■ ~~a problem focused interval history;~~

■ ~~a problem focused examination;~~

■ ~~medical decision making that is straightforward or of low complexity.~~

~~Counseling and/or coordination of care with other providers or agencies are provided consistent with the nature of the problem(s) and the patient's and/or family's needs.~~

~~Usually, the patient is stable, recovering or improving. Physicians typically spend 15 minutes at the bedside and on the patient's facility floor or unit.~~

99312 ~~Subsequent nursing facility care, per day, for the evaluation and management of a new or established patient, which requires at least two of these three key components:~~

■ ~~an expanded problem focused interval history;~~

■ ~~an expanded problem focused examination;~~

■ ~~medical decision making of moderate complexity.~~

~~Counseling and/or coordination of care with other providers or agencies are provided consistent with the nature of the problem(s) and the patient's and/or family's needs.~~

~~Usually, the patient is responding inadequately to therapy or has developed a minor complication. Physicians typically spend 25 minutes at the bedside and on the patient's facility floor or unit.~~

99313 ~~Subsequent nursing facility care, per day, for the evaluation and management of a new or established patient, which requires at least two of these three key components:~~

■ ~~a detailed interval history;~~

■ ~~a detailed examination;~~

■ ~~medical decision making of moderate to high complexity.~~

~~Counseling and/or coordination of care with other providers or agencies are provided consistent with the nature of the problem(s) and the patient's and/or family's needs.~~

~~Usually, the patient has developed a significant complication or a significant new problem. Physicians typically spend 35 minutes at the bedside and on the patient's facility floor or unit.~~

● 99318 Code added

99321 ~~Domiciliary or rest home visit~~ ~~for the evaluation and management of a new patient which requires these three key components:~~

■ ~~a problem focused history;~~

■ ~~a problem focused examination; and~~

■ ~~medical decision making that is straightforward or of low complexity.~~

~~Counseling and/or coordination of care with other providers or agencies are provided consistent with the nature of the problem(s) and the patient's and/or family's needs.~~

~~Usually, the presenting problem(s) are of low severity.~~

99322 ~~Domiciliary or rest home visit~~ ~~for the evaluation and management of a new patient, which requires these three key components:~~

■ ~~an expanded problem focused history;~~

■ ~~an expanded problem focused examination; and~~

■ ~~medical decision making of moderate complexity.~~

~~Counseling and/or coordination of care with other providers or agencies are provided consistent with the nature of the problem(s) and the patient's and/or family's needs.~~

~~Usually, the presenting problem(s) are of moderate severity.~~

99323 ~~Domiciliary or rest home visit~~ ~~for the evaluation and management of a new patient, which requires these three key components:~~

■ ~~a detailed history;~~

■ ~~a detailed examination; and~~

■ ~~medical decision making of high complexity.~~

~~Counseling and/or coordination of care with other providers or agencies are provided consistent with the nature of the problem(s) and the patient's and/or family's needs.~~

~~Usually, the presenting problem(s) are of high complexity.~~

● 99324   Code added

● 99325   Code added

● 99326   Code added

● 99327   Code added

● 99328   Code added

99331 ~~Domiciliary or rest home visit~~ ~~for the evaluation and management of an established patient, which requires at least two of these three key components:~~

■ ~~a problem focused interval history;~~

■ ~~a problem focused examination;~~

■ ~~medical decision making that is straightforward or of low complexity.~~

~~Counseling and/or coordination of care with other providers or agencies are provided consistent with the nature of the problem(s) and the patient's and/or family's needs.~~

~~Usually, the patient is stable, recovering or improving.~~

99332 ~~Domiciliary or rest home visit~~ ~~for the evaluation and management of an established patient, which requires at least two of these three key components:~~

■ ~~an expanded problem focused interval history;~~

■ ~~an expanded problem focused examination;~~

■ ~~medical decision making of moderate complexity.~~

~~Counseling and/or coordination of care with other providers or agencies are provided consistent with the nature of the problem(s) and the patient's and/or family's needs.~~

~~Usually, the patient is responding inadequately to therapy or has developed a minor complication.~~

99333 ~~Domiciliary or rest home visit~~ ~~for the evaluation and management of an established patient, which requires at least two of these three key components:~~

■ ~~a detailed interval history;~~

■ ~~a detailed examination;~~

■ ~~medical decision making of high complexity.~~

~~Counseling and/or coordination of care with other providers or agencies are provided consistent with the nature of the problem(s) and the patient's and/or family's needs.~~

~~Usually, the patient is unstable or has developed a significant complication or a significant new problem.~~

● 99334   Code added

● 99335   Code added

● 99336   Code added

● 99337   Code added

● 99339   Code added

● 99340   Code added

Anesthesia

01964   ~~Anesthesia for abortion procedures~~

● 01965   Code added

● 01966   Code added

Surgery

▲ 15000   Surgical preparation or creation of recipient site by excision of open wounds, burn eschar, or scar (including subcutaneous tissues), or incisional release of scar contracture; first 100 sq cm or one percent of body area of infants and children

● 15040   Code added

▲ 15100   Split-thickness autograft ~~graft~~, trunk, arms, legs; first 100 sq cm or less, or one percent of body area of infants and children (except 15050)

● 15110   Code added

+● 15111   Code added

● 15115   Code added

+● 15116   Code added

▲ 15120   Split-thickness autograft ~~graft~~, face, scalp, eyelids, mouth, neck, ears, orbits, genitalia, hands, feet, and/or multiple digits; first 100 sq cm or less, or one percent of body area of infants and children (except 15050)

● 15130	Code added	
+● 15131	Code added	
● 15135	Code added	
+● 15136	Code added	
● 15150	Code added	
+● 15151	Code added	
+● 15152	Code added	
● 15155	Code added	
+● 15156	Code added	
+● 15157	Code added	
● 15170	Code added	
+● 15171	Code added	
● 15175	Code added	
+● 15176	Code added	
● 15300	Code added	
+● 15301	Code added	
● 15320	Code added	
+● 15321	Code added	
● 15330	Code added	
+● 15331	Code added	
● 15335	Code added	
+● 15336	Code added	
● 15340	Code added	
+● 15341	Code added	

15342 ~~Application of bilaminate skin substitute/neodermis; 25 sq cm~~

+ 15343 ~~each additional 25 sq cm (List separately in addition to code for primary procedure)~~

15350 ~~Application of allograft, skin; 100 sq cm or less~~

+ 15351 ~~each additional 100 sq cm (List separately in addition to code for primary procedure)~~

● 15360	Code added	
+● 15361	Code added	
● 15365	Code added	
+● 15366	Code added	

▲ 15400 Application of ~~x~~Xenograft, skin (dermal), for temporary wound closure; trunk, arms, legs; first ~~;~~ 100 sq cm or less, or one percent of body area of infants and children

+▲ 15401 each additional 100 sq cm, or each additional one percent of body area of infants and children, or part thereof (List separately in addition to code for primary procedure)

● 15420	Code added	
+● 15421	Code added	
● 15430	Code added	
+● 15431	Code added	

15810 ~~Salabrasion; 20 sq cm or less~~

15811 ~~over 20 sq cm~~

16010 ~~Dressings and/or debridement, initial or subsequent; under anesthesia, small~~

16015 ~~under anesthesia, medium or large, or with major debridement~~

▲ 16020 Dressings and/or debridement of partial-thickness burns, initial or subsequent; ~~without anesthesia, office or hospital,~~ small (less than 5% total body surface area)

▲ 16025 ~~without anesthesia,~~ medium (eg, whole face or whole extremity, or 5% to 10% total body surface area)

▲ 16030 ~~without anesthesia,~~ large (eg, more than one extremity, or greater than 10% total body surface area)

21493 ~~Closed treatment of hyoid fracture; without manipulation~~

21494 ~~with manipulation~~

● 22010	Code added	
● 22015	Code added	
● 22523	Code added	
● 22524	Code added	
+● 22525	Code added	
● 28890	Code added	

▲ 30130 Excision inferior turbinate, partial or complete, any method

▲ 30140 Submucous resection inferior turbinate, partial or complete, any method

▲ 30801 Cautery and/or ablation, mucosa of inferior turbinates, unilateral or bilateral, any method~~, (separate procedure)~~; superficial

▲ 30930 Fracture nasal inferior turbinate(s), therapeutic

▲ 31526 diagnostic, with operating microscope or telescope

▲ 31531 with operating microscope or telescope

▲ 31536 with operating microscope or telescope

▲ 31541 with operating microscope or telescope

▲ 31561 with operating microscope or telescope

▲ 31571 with operating microscope or telescope

31585 ~~Treatment of closed laryngeal fracture; without manipulation~~

31586 ~~with closed manipulative reduction~~

● 32503	Code added	
● 32504	Code added	

32520 ~~Resection of lung; with resection of chest wall~~

32522 ~~with reconstruction of chest wall, without prosthesis~~

32525 ~~with major reconstruction of chest wall, with prosthesis~~

▲ 33502 Repair of anomalous coronary artery from pulmonary artery origin; by ligation

● 33507	Code added	
● 33548	Code added	
+● 33768	Code added	
● 33880	Code added	
● 33881	Code added	
● 33883	Code added	
+● 33884	Code added	
● 33886	Code added	

● 33889   Code added

● 33891   Code added

~~33918~~   ~~Repair of pulmonary atresia with ventricular septal defect, by unifocalization of pulmonary arteries; without cardiopulmonary bypass~~

~~33919~~   ~~with cardiopulmonary bypass~~

● 33925   Code added

● 33926   Code added

▲ 34833   Open iliac artery exposure with creation of conduit for delivery of ~~infrarenal~~ aortic or iliac endovascular prosthesis, by abdominal or retroperitoneal incision, unilateral

▲ 34834   Open brachial artery exposure to assist in the deployment of ~~infrarenal~~ aortic or iliac endovascular prosthesis by arm incision, unilateral

● 36598   Code added

⊙● 37184   Code added

+⊙● 37185   Code added

+⊙● 37186   Code added

⊙● 37187   Code added

⊙● 37188   Code added

▲ 37209   Exchange of a previously placed ~~arterial~~ intravascular catheter during thrombolytic therapy

● 37718   Code added

~~37720~~   ~~Ligation and division and complete stripping of long or short saphenous veins~~

● 37722   Code added

~~37730~~   ~~Ligation and division and complete stripping of long and short saphenous veins~~

~~42325~~   ~~Fistulization of sublingual salivary cyst (ranula);~~

~~42326~~   ~~with prosthesis~~

~~43638~~   ~~Gastrectomy, partial, proximal, thoracic or abdominal approach including esophagogastrostomy, with vagotomy;~~

~~43639~~   ~~with pyloroplasty or pyloromyotomy~~

● 43770   Code added

● 43771   Code added

● 43772   Code added

● 43773   Code added

● 43774   Code added

▲ 43848   Revision, open, of gastric restrictive procedure for morbid obesity, other than adjustable gastric band (separate procedure)

● 43886   Code added

● 43887   Code added

● 43888   Code added

● 44180   Code added

● 44186   Code added

● 44187   Code added

● 44188   Code added

~~44200~~   ~~Laparoscopy, surgical; enterolysis (freeing of intestinal adhesion) (separate procedure)~~

~~44201~~   ~~jejunostomy (eg, for decompression or feeding)~~

▲ 44202   Laparoscopy, surgical; enterectomy, resection of small intestine, single resection and anastomosis

+● 44213   Code added

● 44227   Code added

~~44239~~   ~~Unlisted laparoscopy procedure, rectum~~

▲ 44310   Ileostomy or jejunostomy, non-tube ~~(separate procedure)~~

▲ 44320   Colostomy or skin level cecostomy; ~~(separate procedure)~~

▲ 45119   Proctectomy, combined abdominoperineal pull-through procedure (eg, colo-anal anastomosis), with creation of colonic reservoir (eg, J-pouch), with ~~or without proximal~~ diverting ~~ostomy~~ enterostomy when performed

● 45395   Code added

● 45397   Code added

● 45400   Code added

● 45402   Code added

● 45499   Code added

▲ 45540   Proctopexy (eg, for prolapse); abdominal approach

▲ 45550   ~~Proctopexy combined~~ with sigmoid resection, abdominal approach

● 45990   Code added

● 46505   Code added

● 46710   Code added

● 46712   Code added

● 50250   Code added

⊙● 50382   Code added

⊙● 50384   Code added

⊙● 50387   Code added

● 50389   Code added

⊙● 50592   Code added

▲ 50688   Change of ureterostomy tube or externally accessible ureteral stent via ileal conduit

● 51999   Code added

▲ 52647   ~~Non-contact l~~Laser coagulation of prostate, including control of postoperative bleeding, complete (vasectomy, meatotomy, cystourethroscopy, urethral calibration and/or dilation, and internal urethrotomy are included if performed)

▲ 52648   ~~Contact l~~Laser vaporization ~~with or without transurethral resection~~ of prostate, including control of postoperative bleeding, complete (vasectomy, meatotomy, cystourethroscopy, urethral calibration and/or dilation, ~~and~~ internal urethrotomy and transurethral resection of prostate are included if performed)

● 57295   Code added

▲ 57421   with biopsy(s) of vagina/cervix

+● 58110   Code added

● 61630   Code added

● 61635   Code added

● 61640   Code added

+● 61641   Code added

+● 61642   Code added

▲ 64613 ~~cervical spinal~~ neck muscle(s) (eg, for spasmodic torticollis, spasmodic dysphonia)

● 64650 Code added

● 64653 Code added

▲ 67901 Repair of blepharoptosis; frontalis muscle technique with suture or other material (eg, banked fascia)

▲ 67902 frontalis muscle technique with autologous fascial sling (includes obtaining fascia)

~~69410 Focal application of phase control substance, middle ear (baffle technique)~~

Radiology

▲ 75900 Exchange of a previously placed ~~arterial~~ intravascular catheter during thrombolytic therapy with contrast monitoring, radiological supervision and interpretation

● 75956 Code added

● 75957 Code added

● 75958 Code added

● 75959 Code added

▲ 76012 Radiological supervision and interpretation, percutaneous vertebroplasty or vertebral augmentation including cavity creation, per vertebral body; under fluoroscopic guidance

~~76375 Coronal, sagittal, multiplanar, oblique, 3-dimensional and/or holographic reconstruction of computed tomography, magnetic resonance imaging, or other tomographic modality~~

● 76376 Code added

● 76377 Code added

▲ 77412 Radiation treatment delivery, three or more separate treatment areas, custom blocking, tangential ports, wedges, rotational beam, compensators, ~~special particle~~ electron beam ~~(eg, electron or neutrons)~~; up to 5 MeV

● 77421 Code added

● 77422 Code added

● 77423 Code added

~~78160 Plasma radioiron disappearance (turnover) rate~~

~~78162 Radioiron oral absorption~~

~~78170 Radioiron red cell utilization~~

~~78172 Chelatable iron for estimation of total body iron~~

~~78455 Venous thrombosis study (eg, radioactive fibrinogen)~~

Pathology and Laboratory

● 80195 Code added

▲ 82270 Blood, occult, by peroxidase activity (eg, guaiac), qualitative; feces, ~~1-3~~ consecutive collected specimens with single determination, for colorectal neoplasm screening (ie, patient was provided three cards or single triple card for consecutive collection) ~~simultaneous determinations~~

● 82271 Code added

● 82272 Code added

~~82273 other sources~~

▲ 83036 ~~glycated~~ glycosylated (A1C)

● 83037 Code added

▲ 83630 Lactoferrin, fecal~~;~~; qualitative

● 83631 Code added

● 83695 Code added

● 83700 Code added

● 83701 Code added

● 83704 Code added

~~83715 Lipoprotein, blood; electrophoretic separation and quantitation~~

~~83716 high resolution fractionation and quantitation of lipoproteins including lipoprotein subclasses when performed (eg, electrophoresis, nuclear magnetic resonance, ultracentrifugation)~~

▲ 83898 amplification of patient nucleic acid, each nucleic acid sequence ~~(eg, PCR, LCR), single primer pair, each primer pair~~

● 83900 Code added

+▲ 83901 amplification of patient nucleic acid, multiplex, each additional nucleic acid sequence ~~each multiplex reaction~~ (List separately in addition to code for primary procedure)

● 83907 Code added

● 83908 Code added

● 83909 Code added

● 83914 Code added

▲ 84238 non-endocrine ~~(eg, acetylcholine)~~ (specify receptor)

~~86064 B cells, total count~~

● 86200 Code added

● 86355 Code added

● 86357 Code added

● 86367 Code added

~~86379 Natural killer (NK) cells, total count~~

● 86480 Code added

~~86585 tuberculosis, tine test~~

~~86587 Stem cells (ie, CD34), total count~~

● 86923 Code added

● 86960 Code added

● 87209 Code added

● 87900 Code added

+▲ 87904 each additional ~~1 through 5~~ drug~~s~~ tested (List separately in addition to code for primary procedure)

▲ 88175 with screening by automated system and manual rescreening or review, under physician supervision

● 88333 Code added

● 88334 Code added

● 88384 Code added

● 88385 Code added

● 88386 Code added

● 89049 Code added

Medicine

⊘ ✐ ● 90649   Code added

⊘ ✐ ▲ 90680   Rotavirus vaccine, ~~tetravalent,~~pentavalent, 3 dose schedule, live, for oral use

⊘ ▲ 90713   Poliovirus vaccine, inactivated, (IPV), for subcutaneous or intramuscular use

⊘ ● 90714   Code added

⊘ ✐ ▲ 90715   Tetanus, diphtheria toxoids and acellular pertussis vaccine (TdaPp), for use in individuals 7 years or older, for intramuscular use

⊘ ✐ ● 90736   Code added

● 90760   Code added

+● 90761   Code added

● 90765   Code added

+● 90766   Code added

+● 90767   Code added

+● 90768   Code added

● 90772   Code added

● 90773   Code added

● 90774   Code added

+● 90775   Code added

● 90779   Code added

~~90780   Intravenous infusion for therapy/diagnosis, administered by physician or under direct supervision of physician; up to one hour~~

+ ~~90781   each additional hour, up to eight (8) hours (List separately in addition to code for primary procedure)~~

~~90782   Therapeutic, prophylactic or diagnostic injection (specify material injected); subcutaneous or intramuscular~~

~~90783   intra-arterial~~

~~90784   intravenous~~

~~90788   Intramuscular injection of antibiotic (specify)~~

~~90799   Unlisted therapeutic, prophylactic or diagnostic injection~~

▲ 90870   Electroconvulsive therapy (includes necessary monitoring)~~; single seizure~~

~~90871   multiple seizures, per day~~

~~90939   Hemodialysis access flow study to determine blood flow in grafts and arteriovenous fistulae by an indicator dilution method, hook-up; transcutaneous measurement and disconnection~~

▲ 90940   Hemodialysis access flow study to determine blood flow in grafts and arteriovenous fistulae by an indicator method~~measurement and disconnection~~

● 91022   Code added

~~92330   Prescription, fitting, and supply of ocular prosthesis (artificial eye), with medical supervision of adaptation~~

~~92335   Prescription of ocular prosthesis (artificial eye) and direction of fitting and supply by independent technician, with medical supervision of adaptation~~

~~92390   Supply of spectacles, except prosthesis for aphakia and low vision aids~~

~~92391   Supply of contact lenses, except prosthesis for aphakia~~

~~92392   Supply of low vision aids (A low vision aid is any lens or device used to aid or improve visual function in a person whose vision cannot be normalized by conventional spectacle correction. Includes reading additions up to 4D.)~~

~~92393   Supply of ocular prosthesis (artificial eye)~~

~~92395   Supply of permanent prosthesis for aphakia; spectacles~~

~~92396   contact lenses~~

▲ 92506   Evaluation of speech, language, voice, communication, and/or auditory processing~~, and/or aural rehabilitation status~~

▲ 92507   Treatment of speech, language, voice, communication, and/or auditory processing disorder~~(includes aural rehabilitation)~~; individual

~~92510   Aural rehabilitation following cochlear implant (includes evaluation of aural rehabilitation status and hearing, therapeutic services) with or without speech processor programming~~

▲ 92520   Laryngeal function studies (ie, aerodynamic testing and acoustic testing)

▲ 92568   Acoustic reflex testing; threshold

▲ 92569   Acoustic reflex ~~decay~~ ~~test~~

● 92626   Code added

+● 92627   Code added

● 92630   Code added

● 92633   Code added

▲ 95250   Ambulatory continuous glucose monitoring of ~~for up to 72 hours by continuous recording and storage of glucose values from~~ interstitial tissue fluid via a subcutaneous sensor for up to 72 hours; ~~(includes~~sensor placement, hook-up, calibration of monitor, patient ~~initiation and~~training, removal of sensor, and printout of recording~~, disconnection, downloading with printout of data)~~

● 95251   Code added

~~95858   with electromyographic recording~~

● 95865   Code added

● 95866   Code added

+● 95873   Code added

+● 95874   Code added

~~96100   Psychological testing (includes psychodiagnostic assessment of personality, psychopathology, emotionality, intellectual abilities, eg, WAIS-R, Rorschach, MMPI) with interpretation and report, per hour~~

● 96101   Code added

● 96102   Code added

● 96103   Code added

~~96115   Neurobehavioral status exam (clinical assessment of thinking, reasoning and judgment, eg, acquired knowledge, attention, memory, visual spatial abilities, language functions, planning) with interpretation and report, per hour~~

● 96116   Code added

~~96117   Neuropsychological testing battery (eg, Halstead-Reitan, Luria, WAIS-R) with interpretation and report, per hour~~

● 96118   Code added

● 96119   Code added

● 96120   Code added

~~96400~~   ~~Chemotherapy administration, subcutaneous or intramuscular, with or without local anesthesia~~

● 96401   Code added

● 96402   Code added

▲ 96405   Chemotherapy administration, ~~intralesional~~; intralesional, up to and including 7 lesions

▲ 96406   intralesional, more than 7 lesions

~~96408~~   ~~Chemotherapy administration, intravenous; push technique~~

● 96409   Code added

~~96410~~   ~~infusion technique, up to one hour~~

+● 96411   Code added

+ ~~96412~~   ~~infusion technique, one to 8 hours, each additional hour (List separately in addition to code for primary procedure)~~

● 96413   Code added

~~96414~~   ~~infusion technique, initiation of prolonged infusion (more than 8 hours), requiring the use of a portable or implantable pump~~

+● 96415   Code added

● 96416   Code added

+● 96417   Code added

+▲ 96423   infusion technique, ~~one to 8 hours,~~ each additional hour up to 8 hours (List separately in addition to code for primary procedure)

~~96520~~   ~~Refilling and maintenance of portable pump~~

● 96521   Code added

● 96522   Code added

● 96523   Code added

~~96530~~   ~~Refilling and maintenance of implantable pump or reservoir for drug delivery, systemic (eg, intravenous, intra-arterial)~~

~~96545~~   ~~Provision of chemotherapy agent~~

~~97020~~   ~~microwave~~

▲ 97024   diathermy (eg, microwave)

~~97504~~   ~~Orthotic(s) fitting and training, upper extremity(ies), lower extremity(ies), and/or trunk, each 15 minutes~~

~~97520~~   ~~Prosthetic training, upper and/or lower extremities, each 15 minutes~~

▲ 97542   Wheelchair management~~, propulsion training~~ (eg, assessment, fitting, training), each 15 minutes

~~97703~~   ~~Checkout for orthotic/prosthetic use, established patient, each 15 minutes~~

● 97760   Code added

● 97761   Code added

● 97762   Code added

+▲ 97811   without electrical stimulation, each additional 15 minutes of personal one-on-one contact with the patient, with re-insertion of needle(s) (List separately in addition to code for primary procedure)

▲ 97813   ~~Acupuncture, one or more needles,~~ with electrical stimulation~~;~~, initial 15 minutes of personal one-on-one contact with the patient

+▲ 97814   with electrical stimulation, each additional 15 minutes of personal one-on-one contact with the patient, with re-insertion of needle(s) (List separately in addition to code for primary procedure)

● 98960   Code added

● 98961   Code added

● 98962   Code added

▲ 99050   Services ~~requested after posted~~ provided in the office ~~hours~~ at times other than regularly scheduled office hours, or days when the office is normally closed (eg, holidays, Saturday or Sunday), in addition to basic service

● 99051   Code added

~~99052~~   ~~Services requested between 10:00 PM and 8:00 AM in addition to basic service~~

● 99053   Code added

~~99054~~   ~~Services requested on Sundays and holidays in addition to basic service~~

▲ 99056   Service(s) typically provided ~~at request of patient in a location other than physician's office which are normally provided in the~~ in the office, provided out of the office at request of patient, in addition to basic service

▲ 99058   ~~Office s~~Service(s) provided on an emergency basis in the office, which disrupts other scheduled office services, in addition to basic service

● 99060   Code added

⊘ ~~99141~~   ~~Sedation with or without analgesia (conscious sedation); intravenous, intramuscular or inhalation~~

⊘ ~~99142~~   ~~oral, rectal and/or intranasal~~

⊘● 99143   Code added

⊘● 99144   Code added

+● 99145   Code added

⊘● 99148   Code added

⊘● 99149   Code added

+● 99150   Code added

Category II Codes

● 0001F   Code added

● 0005F   Code added

● 1003F   Code added

● 1004F   Code added

● 1005F   Code added

● 1006F   Code added

● 1007F   Code added

● 1008F   Code added

● 2001F   Code added

● 2002F   Code added

● 2003F   Code added

● 2004F   Code added

● 3000F   Code added

● 3002F   Code added

● **4003F**   Code added

● **4012F**   Code added

● **4014F**   Code added

● **4015F**   Code added

● **4016F**   Code added

● **4017F**   Code added

● **4018F**   Code added

Category III Codes

~~**0010T**~~   ~~Tuberculosis test, cell-mediated immunity measurement of gamma-interferon antigen response~~

▲ **0019T**   Extracorporeal shock wave ~~therapy,~~ involving musculoskeletal system, not otherwise specified, low energy

~~**0020T**~~   ~~involving plantar fascia~~

~~**0023T**~~   ~~Infectious agent drug susceptibility phenotype prediction using genotypic comparison to known genotypic/phenotypic database, HIV-1~~

~~**0033T**~~   ~~Endovascular repair of descending thoracic aortic aneurysm, pseudoaneurysm or dissection; involving coverage of left subclavian artery origin, initial endoprosthesis~~

~~**0034T**~~   ~~not involving coverage of left subclavian artery origin, initial endoprosthesis~~

~~**0035T**~~   ~~Placement of proximal or distal extension prosthesis for endovascular repair of descending thoracic aortic aneurysm, pseudoaneurysm or dissection; initial extension~~

+ ~~**0036T**~~   ~~each additional extension (List separately in addition to code for primary procedure)~~

~~**0037T**~~   ~~Open subclavian to carotid artery transposition performed in conjunction with endovascular thoracic aneurysm repair, by neck incision, unilateral~~

~~**0038T**~~   ~~Endovascular repair of descending thoracic aortic aneurysm, pseudoaneurysm or dissection involving coverage of left subclavian artery origin, initial endoprosthesis, radiological supervision and interpretation~~

~~**0039T**~~   ~~Endovascular repair of descending thoracic aortic aneurysm, pseudoaneurysm or dissection not involving coverage of left subclavian artery origin, initial endoprosthesis, radiological supervision and interpretation~~

~~**0040T**~~   ~~Placement of proximal or distal extension prosthesis for endovascular repair of descending thoracic aortic aneurysm, pseudoaneurysm or dissection, each extension, radiological supervision and interpretation~~

▲ **0078T**   Endovascular repair using prosthesis of abdominal aortic aneurysm, pseudoaneurysm or dissection, abdominal aorta involving visceral branches~~vessels~~ (superior mesenteric, celiac and/or renal artery(s)), ~~using fenestrated modular bifurcated prosthesis (two docking limbs)~~

● **0089T**   Code added

● **0090T**   Code added

● **0091T**   Code added

+● **0092T**   Code added

● **0093T**   Code added

● **0094T**   Code added

+● **0095T**   Code added

● **0096T**   Code added

● **0097T**   Code added

+● **0098T**   Code added

● **0099T**   Code added

● **0100T**   Code added

● **0101T**   Code added

● **0102T**   Code added

● **0103T**   Code added

● **0104T**   Code added

● **0105T**   Code added

● **0106T**   Code added

● **0107T**   Code added

● **0108T**   Code added

● **0109T**   Code added

● **0110T**   Code added

● **0111T**   Code added

● **0115T**   Code added

● **0116T**   Code added

+● **0117T**   Code added

● **0120T**   Code added

● **0123T**   Code added

● **0124T**   Code added

● **0126T**   Code added

● **0130T**   Code added

● **0133T**   Code added

● **0135T**   Code added

● **0137T**   Code added

● **0140T**   Code added

Appendix C

Clinical Examples

As described in *CPT 2006*, clinical examples of the CPT codes for Evaluation and Management (E/M) services are intended to be an important element of the coding system. The clinical examples, when used with the E/M descriptors contained in the full text of *CPT*, provide a comprehensive and powerful tool for physicians to report the services provided to their patients.

The American Medical Association is pleased to provide you with these clinical examples for *CPT 2006*. The clinical examples that are provided in this supplement are limited to Office or Other Outpatient Services, Hospital Inpatient Services, Consultations, Critical Care, Prolonged Services and Care Plan Oversight.

These clinical examples do not encompass the entire scope of medical practice. Inclusion or exclusion of any particular specialty group does not infer any judgment of importance or lack thereof; nor does it limit the applicability of the example to any particular specialty.

Of utmost importance is that these clinical examples are just that: examples. A particular patient encounter, depending on the specific circumstances, must be judged by the services provided by the physician for that particular patient. Simply because the patient's complaints, symptoms, or diagnoses match those of a particular clinical example, does not automatically assign that patient encounter to that particular level of service. The three key components (history, examination, and medical decision making) must be met and documented in the medical record to report a particular level of service.

Office or Other Outpatient Services

New Patient

99201 Initial office visit for a 50-year-old male from out-of-town who needs a prescription refill for a nonsteroidal anti-inflammatory drug. (Anesthesiology)

Initial office visit for a 40-year-old female, new patient, requesting information about local pain clinics. (Anesthesiology/Pain Medicine)

Initial office visit for a 10-year-old girl for determination of visual acuity as part of a summer camp physical (does not include determination of refractive error). (Ophthalmology)

Initial office visit for an out-of-town patient requiring topical refill. (Dermatology)

Initial office visit for a 65-year-old male for reassurance about an isolated seborrheic keratosis on upper back. (Plastic Surgery)

Initial office visit for an out-of-state visitor who needs refill of topical steroid to treat lichen planus. (Dermatology)

Initial office visit for an 86-year-old male, out-of-town visitor, who needs prescription refilled for an anal skin preparation that he forgot. (General Surgery/Colon & Rectal Surgery)

Initial office visit for a transient patient with alveolar osteitis for repacking. (Oral & Maxillofacial Surgery)

Initial office visit for a patient with a pedunculated lesion of the neck which is unsightly. (Dermatology)

Initial office visit for a 10-year-old male, for limited subungual hematoma not requiring drainage. (Internal Medicine)

Initial office visit with an out-of-town visitor who needs a prescription refilled because she forgot her hay fever medication. (Allergy & Immunology/Internal Medicine)

Initial office visit with a 9-month-old female with diaper rash. (Pediatrics)

Initial office visit with a 10-year-old male with severe rash and itching for the past 24 hours, positive history for contact with poison oak 48 hours prior to the visit. (Family Medicine)

Initial office visit with a 5-year-old female to remove sutures from simple wound placed by another physician. (Plastic Surgery)

Initial office visit for a 22-year-old male with a small area of sunburn requiring first aid. (Dermatology/Family Medicine/Internal Medicine)

Initial office visit for the evaluation and management of a contusion of a finger. (Orthopaedic Surgery)

99202 Initial office visit for a 13-year-old patient with comedopapular acne of the face unresponsive to over-the-counter medications. (Family Medicine)

Initial office visit for a patient with a clinically benign lesion or nodule of the lower leg which has been present for many years. (Dermatology)

Initial office visit for a patient with a circumscribed patch of dermatitis of the leg. (Dermatology)

Initial office visit for a patient with papulosquamous eruption of elbows. (Dermatology)

Initial office visit for a 9-year-old patient with erythematous, grouped, vesicular eruption of the lip of three days' duration. (Pediatrics)

Initial office visit for an 18-year-old male referred by an orthodontist for advice regarding removal of four wisdom teeth. (Oral & Maxillofacial Surgery)

Initial office visit for a 14-year-old male, who was referred by his orthodontist, for advice on the exposure of impacted maxillary cuspids. (Oral & Maxillofacial Surgery)

Initial office visit for a patient presenting with itching patches on the wrists and ankles. (Dermatology)

Initial office visit for a 30-year-old male for evaluation and discussion of treatment of rhinophyma. (Plastic Surgery)

Initial office visit for a 16-year-old male with severe cystic acne, new patient. (Dermatology)

Initial office evaluation for gradual hearing loss, 58-year-old male, history and physical examination, with interpretation of complete audiogram, air bone, etc. (Otolaryngology)

Initial evaluation and management of recurrent urinary infection in female. (Internal Medicine)

Initial office visit with a 10-year-old girl with history of chronic otitis media and a draining ear. (Pediatrics)

Initial office visit for a 10-year-old female with acute maxillary sinusitis. (Family Medicine)

Initial office visit for a patient with recurring episodes of herpes simplex who has developed a clustering of vesicles on the upper lip. (Internal Medicine)

Initial office visit for a 25-year-old patient with single season allergic rhinitis. (Allergy & Immunology)

Initial office visit to plan transient dialysis for a 56-year-old stable dialysis patient who has accompanying records. (Nephrology)

99203 Initial office visit for a 76-year-old male with a stasis ulcer of three months' duration. (Dermatology)

Initial office visit for a 30-year-old female with pain in the lateral aspect of the forearm. (Physical Medicine & Rehabilitation)

Initial office visit for a 15-year-old patient with a four-year history of moderate comedopapular acne of the face, chest, and back with early scarring. Discussion of use of systemic medication. (Dermatology)

Initial office visit for a patient with papulosquamous eruption of the elbow with pitting of nails and itchy scalp. (Dermatology)

Initial office visit for a 57-year-old female who complains of painful parotid swelling for one week's duration. (Oral & Maxillofacial Surgery)

Initial office visit for a patient with an ulcerated non-healing lesion or nodule on the tip of the nose. (Dermatology)

Initial office visit for a patient with dermatitis of the antecubital and popliteal fossae. (Dermatology)

Initial office visit for a 22-year-old female with irregular menses. (Family Medicine)

Initial office visit for a 50-year-old female with dyspepsia and nausea. (Family Medicine)

Initial office visit for a 53-year-old laborer with degenerative joint disease of the knee with no prior treatment. (Orthopaedic Surgery)

Initial office visit for a 60-year-old male with Dupuytren's contracture of one hand with multiple digit involvement. (Orthopaedic Surgery)

Initial office visit for a 33-year-old male with painless gross hematuria without cystoscopy. (Internal Medicine)

Initial office visit for a 55-year-old female with chronic blepharitis. There is a history of use of many medications. (Ophthalmology)

Initial office visit for an 18-year-old female with a two-day history of acute conjunctivitis. Extensive history of possible exposures, prior normal ocular history, and medication use is obtained. (Ophthalmology)

Initial office visit for a 14-year-old male with unilateral anterior knee pain. (Physical Medicine & Rehabilitation)

Initial office visit of an adult who presents with symptoms of an upper-respiratory infection that has progressed to unilateral purulent nasal discharge and discomfort in the right maxillary teeth. (Otolaryngology, Head & Neck Surgery)

Initial office visit of a 40-year-old female with symptoms of atopic allergies including eye and sinus congestion, often associated with infections. She would like to be tested for allergies. (Otolaryngology, Head & Neck Surgery)

Initial office visit of a 65-year-old with nasal stuffiness. (Otolaryngology, Head & Neck Surgery)

Initial office visit for initial evaluation of a 48-year-old man with recurrent low back pain radiating to the leg. (General Surgery)

Initial office visit for evaluation, diagnosis and management of painless gross hematuria in a new patient, without cystoscopy. (Internal Medicine)

Initial office visit with couple for counseling concerning voluntary vasectomy for sterility. Spent 30 minutes discussing procedure, risks and benefits, and answering questions. (Urology)

Initial office visit of a 49-year-old male with nasal obstruction. Detailed exam with topical anesthesia. (Plastic Surgery)

Initial office visit for evaluation of a 13-year-old female with progressive scoliosis. (Physical Medicine & Rehabilitation)

Initial office visit for a 21-year-old female desiring counseling and evaluation of initiation of contraception. (Family Practice/Internal Medicine/Obstetrics & Gynecology)

Initial office visit for a 49-year-old male presenting with painless blood per rectum associated with bowel movement. (Colon & Rectal Surgery)

Initial office visit for a 19-year-old football player with three-day-old acute knee injury; now with swelling and pain. (Orthopaedic Surgery)

99204 Initial office visit for a 13-year-old female with progressive scoliosis. (Orthopaedic Surgery)

Initial office visit for a 34-year-old female with primary infertility for evaluation and counseling. (Obstetrics & Gynecology)

Initial office visit for a 6-year-old male with multiple upper respiratory infections. (Allergy & Immunology)

Initial office visit for a patient with generalized dermatitis of 80 percent of the body surface area. (Dermatology)

Initial office visit for an adolescent who was referred by school counselor because of repeated skipping school. (Psychiatry)

Initial office visit for a 50-year-old machinist with a generalized eruption. (Dermatology)

Initial office visit for a 45-year-old female who has been abstinent from alcohol and benzodiazepines for three months but complains of headaches, insomnia, and anxiety. (Psychiatry)

Initial office visit for a 60-year-old male with recent change in bowel habits, weight loss, and abdominal pain. (Abdominal Surgery/General Surgery)

Initial office visit for a 50-year-old male with an aortic aneurysm who is considering surgery. (General Surgery)

Initial office visit for a 17-year-old female with depression. (Internal Medicine)

Initial office visit of a 40-year-old with chronic draining ear, imbalance, and probable cholesteatoma. (Otolaryngology, Head & Neck Surgery)

Initial office visit for initial evaluation of a 63-year-old male with chest pain on exertion. (Cardiology/Internal Medicine)

Initial office visit for evaluation of a 70-year-old patient with recent onset of episodic confusion. (Internal Medicine)

Initial office visit for a 7-year-old female with juvenile diabetes mellitus, new to area, past history of hospitalization times three. (Pediatrics)

Initial office visit of a 50-year-old female with progressive solid food dysphagia. (Gastroenterology)

Initial office visit for a 34-year-old patient with primary infertility, including counseling. (Obstetrics & Gynecology)

Initial office visit for evaluation of a 70-year-old female with polyarthralgia. (Rheumatology)

Initial office visit for a patient with papulosquamous eruption involving 60 percent of the cutaneous surface with joint pain. Combinations of topical and systemic treatments discussed. (Dermatology)

99205 Initial office visit for a patient with disseminated lupus erythematosus with kidney disease, edema, purpura, and scarring lesions on the extremities plus cardiac symptoms. (Dermatology/General Surgery/Internal Medicine)

Initial office visit for a 25-year-old female with systemic lupus erythematosus, fever, seizures, and profound thrombocytopenia. (Rheumatology/Allergy & Immunology)

Initial office visit for an adult with multiple cutaneous blisters, denuded secondarily infected ulcerations, oral lesions, weight loss, and increasing weakness refractory to high dose corticosteroid. Initiation of new immunosuppressive therapy. (Dermatology)

Initial office visit for a 28-year-old male with systemic vasculitis and compromised circulation to the limbs. (Rheumatology)

Initial office visit for a 41-year-old female new to the area requesting rheumatologic care, on disability due to scleroderma and recent hospitalization for malignant hypertension. (Rheumatology)

Initial office visit for a 52-year-old female with acute four extremity weakness and shortness of breath one week post-flu vaccination. (Physical Medicine & Rehabilitation)

Initial office visit for a 60-year-old male with previous back surgery; now presents with back and pelvic pain, two-month history of bilateral progressive calf and thigh tightness and weakness when walking, causing several falls. (Orthopaedic Surgery)

Initial office visit for an adolescent referred from ER after making suicide gesture. (Psychiatry)

Initial office visit for a 49-year-old female with a history of headaches and dependence on opioids. She reports weight loss, progressive headache, and depression. (Psychiatry)

Initial office visit for a 50-year-old female with symptoms of rash, swellings, recurrent arthritic complaints, and diarrhea and lymphadenopathy. Patient has had a 25 lb. weight loss and was recently camping in the Amazon. (Allergy & Immunology)

Initial office visit for a 34-year-old uremic Type I diabetic patient referred for ESRD modality assessment and planning. (Nephrology)

Initial office visit for a 75-year-old female with neck and bilateral shoulder pain, brisk deep tendon reflexes, and stress incontinence. (Physical Medicine & Rehabilitation)

Initial office visit for an 8-year-old male with cerebral palsy and spastic quadriparesis. (Physical Medicine & Rehabilitation)

Initial office visit for a 73-year-old male with known prostate malignancy, who presents with severe back pain and a recent onset of lower extremity weakness. (Physical Medicine & Rehabilitation)

Initial office visit for a 38-year-old male with paranoid delusions and a history of alcohol abuse. (Psychiatry)

Initial office visit for a 12-week-old with bilateral hip dislocations and bilateral club feet. (Orthopaedic Surgery)

Initial office visit for a 29-year-old female with acute orbital congestion, eyelid retraction, and bilateral visual loss from optic neuropathy. (Ophthalmology)

Initial office visit for a 70-year-old diabetic patient with progressive visual field loss, advanced optic disc cupping and neovascularization of retina. (Ophthalmology)

Initial office visit for a newly diagnosed Type I diabetic patient. (Endocrinology)

Initial office evaluation of a 65-year-old female with exertional chest pain, intermittent claudication, syncope and a murmur of aortic stenosis. (Cardiology)

Initial office visit for a 73-year-old male with an unexplained 20 lb. weight loss. (Hematology/Oncology)

Initial office evaluation, patient with systemic lupus erythematosus, fever, seizures and profound thrombocytopenia. (Allergy & Immunology/Internal Medicine/Rheumatology)

Initial office evaluation and management of patient with systemic vasculitis and compromised circulation to the limbs. (Rheumatology)

Initial office visit for a 24-year-old homosexual male who has a fever, a cough, and shortness of breath. (Infectious Disease)

Initial outpatient evaluation of a 69-year-old male with severe chronic obstructive pulmonary disease, congestive heart failure, and hypertension. (Family Medicine)

Initial office visit for a 17-year-old female, who is having school problems and has told a friend she is considering suicide. The patient and her family are consulted in regard to treatment options. (Psychiatry)

Initial office visit for a female with severe hirsutism, amenorrhea, weight loss and a desire to have children. (Endocrinology/Obstetrics & Gynecology)

Initial office visit for a 42-year-old male on hypertensive medication, newly arrived to the area, with diastolic blood pressure of 110, history of recurrent calculi, episodic headaches, intermittent chest pain and orthopnea. (Internal Medicine)

Established Patient

99211 Office visit for an 82-year-old female, established patient, for a monthly B12 injection with documented Vitamin B12 deficiency. (Geriatrics/Internal Medicine/Family Medicine)

Office visit for a 50-year-old male, established patient, for removal of uncomplicated facial sutures. (Plastic Surgery)

Office visit for an established patient who lost prescription for lichen planus. Returned for new copy. (Dermatology)

Office visit for an established patient undergoing orthodontics who complains of a wire which is irritating his/her cheek and asks you to check it. (Oral & Maxillofacial Surgery)

Office visit for a 50-year-old female, established patient, seen for her gold injection by the nurse. (Rheumatology)

Office visit for a 73-year-old female, established patient, with pernicious anemia for weekly B12 injection. (Gastroenterology)

Office visit for an established patient for dressing change on a skin biopsy. (Dermatology)

Office visit for a 19-year-old, established patient, for removal of sutures from a two cm. laceration of forehead, which you placed four days ago in ER. (Plastic Surgery)

Office visit of a 20-year-old female, established patient, who receives an allergy vaccine injection and is observed for a reaction by the nurse. (Otolaryngology, Head & Neck Surgery)

Office visit for a 45-year-old male, established patient, with chronic renal failure for the administration of erythropoietin. (Nephrology)

Office visit for an established patient, a Peace Corps enlistee, who requests documentation that third molars have been removed. (Oral & Maxillofacial Surgery)

Office visit for a 69-year-old female, established patient, for partial removal of antibiotic gauze from an infected wound site. (Plastic Surgery)

Office visit for a 9-year-old, established patient, successfully treated for impetigo, requiring release to return to school. (Dermatology/Pediatrics)

Office visit for an established patient requesting a return-to-work certificate for resolving contact dermatitis. (Dermatology)

Office visit for an established patient who is performing glucose monitoring and wants to check accuracy of machine with lab blood glucose by technician who checks accuracy and function of patient machine. (Endocrinology)

Follow-up office visit for a 65-year-old female with a chronic indwelling percutaneous nephrostomy catheter seen for routine pericatheter skin care and dressing change. (Interventional Radiology)

Outpatient visit with 19-year-old male, established patient, for supervised drug screen. (Addiction Medicine)

Office visit with 12-year-old male, established patient, for cursory check of hematoma one day after venipuncture. (Internal Medicine)

Office visit with 31-year-old female, established patient, for return to work certificate. (Anesthesiology)

Office visit for a 42-year-old, established patient, to read tuberculin test results. (Allergy & Immunology)

Office visit for 14-year-old, established patient, to re-dress an abrasion. (Orthopaedic Surgery)

Office visit for a 45-year-old female, established patient, for a blood pressure check. (Obstetrics & Gynecology)

Office visit for a 23-year-old, established patient, for instruction in use of peak flow meter. (Allergy & Immunology)

Office visit for prescription refill for a 35-year-old female, established patient, with schizophrenia who is stable but has run out of neuroleptic and is scheduled to be seen in a week. (Psychiatry)

99212 Office visit for an 11-year-old, established patient, seen in follow-up for mild comedonal acne of the cheeks on topical desquamating agents. (Dermatology/Family Medicine/Pediatrics)

Office visit for a 10-year-old female, established patient, who has been swimming in a lake, now presents with a one-day history of left ear pain with purulent drainage. (Family Medicine)

Office visit of a child, established patient, with chronic secretory otitis media. (Otolaryngology, Head & Neck Surgery)

Office visit for an established patient seen in follow-up of clearing patch of localized contact dermatitis. (Family Medicine/Dermatology)

Office visit for an established patient returning for evaluation of response to treatment of lichen planus on wrists and ankles. (Dermatology)

Office visit for an established patient with tinea pedis being treated with topical therapy. (Dermatology)

Office visit for an established patient with localized erythematous plaque of psoriasis with topical hydration. (Dermatology)

Office visit for a 50-year-old male, established patient, recently seen for acute neck pain, diagnosis of spondylosis, responding to physical therapy and intermittent cervical traction. Returns for evaluation for return to work. (Neurology)

Office visit for an established patient with recurring episodes of herpes simplex who has developed a clustering of vesicles on the upper lip. (Oral & Maxillofacial Surgery)

Evaluation for a 50-year-old male, established patient, who has experienced a recurrence of knee pain after he discontinued NSAID. (Anesthesiology/Pain Medicine)

Office visit for an established patient with an irritated skin tag for reassurance. (Dermatology)

Office visit for a 40-year-old, established patient, who has experienced a systemic allergic reaction following administration of immunotherapy. The dose must be readjusted. (Allergy & Immunology)

Office visit for a 33-year-old, established patient, for contusion and abrasion of lower extremity. (Orthopaedic Surgery)

Office visit for a 22-year-old male, established patient, one month after I & D of "wrestler's ear." (Plastic Surgery)

Office visit for a 21-year-old, established patient, who is seen in follow-up after antibiotic therapy for acute bacterial tonsillitis. (Otolaryngology, Head & Neck Surgery)

Office visit for a 4-year-old, established patient, with tympanostomy tubes, check-up. (Otolaryngology, Head & Neck Surgery)

Office visit for an established patient who has had needle aspiration of a peritonsillar abscess. (Otolaryngology, Head & Neck Surgery)

Follow-up office examination for evaluation and treatment of acute draining ear in a 5-year-old with tympanotomy tubes. (Otolaryngology, Head & Neck Surgery)

Office visit, established patient, 6-year-old with sore throat and headache. (Family Medicine/Pediatrics)

Office evaluation for possible purulent bacterial conjunctivitis with one- to two-day history of redness and discharge, 16-year-old female, established patient. (Pediatrics/Internal Medicine/Family Medicine)

Office visit with a 65-year-old female, established patient, returns for three-week follow-up for resolving severe ankle sprain. (Orthopaedic Surgery)

Office visit, sore throat, fever and fatigue in a 19-year-old college student, established patient. (Internal Medicine)

Office visit with a 33-year-old female, established patient, recently started on treatment for hemorrhoidal complaints, for re-evaluation. (Colon & Rectal Surgery)

Office visit with a 36-year-old male, established patient, for follow-up on effectiveness of medicine management of oral candidiasis. (Oral & Maxillofacial Surgery)

Office visit for a 27-year-old female, established patient, with complaints of vaginal itching. (Obstetrics & Gynecology)

Office visit for a 65-year-old male, established patient, with eruptions on both arms from poison oak exposure. (Allergy & Immunology/Internal Medicine)

99213 Office visit for an established patient with new lesions of lichen planus in spite of topical therapies. (Dermatology)

Office visit for the quarterly follow-up of a 45-year-old male with stable chronic asthma requiring regular drug therapy. (Allergy & Immunology)

Office visit for a 13-year-old, established patient, with comedopapular acne of the face which has shown poor response to topical medication. Discussion of use of systemic medication. (Dermatology)

Office visit for a 62-year-old female, established patient, for follow-up for stable cirrhosis of the liver. (Internal Medicine/Family Medicine)

Office visit for a 3-year-old, established patient, with atopic dermatitis and food hypersensitivity for quarterly follow-up evaluation. The patient is on topical lotions and steroid creams as well as oral antihistamines. (Allergy & Immunology)

Office visit for an 80-year-old female, established patient, to evaluate medical management of osteoarthritis of the temporomandibular joint. (Rheumatology)

Office visit for a 70-year-old female, established patient, one year post excision of basal cell carcinoma of nose with nasolabial flap. Now presents with new suspicious recurrent lesion and suspicious lesion of the back. (Plastic Surgery)

Office visit for a 68-year-old female, established patient, with polymyalgia rheumatic, maintained on chronic low-dose corticosteroid, with no new complaints. (Rheumatology)

Office visit for a 3-year-old female, established patient, for earache and dyshidrosis of feet. (Pediatrics/Family Medicine)

Office visit for an established patient for 18 months post-operative follow-up of TMJ repair. (Oral & Maxillofacial Surgery)

Office visit for a 45-year-old male, established patient, being re-evaluated for recurrent acute prostatitis. (Urology)

Office visit for a 43-year-old male, established patient, with known reflex sympathetic dystrophy. (Anesthesiology)

Office visit for an established patient with an evenly pigmented superficial nodule of leg which is symptomatic. (Dermatology)

Office visit for an established patient with psoriasis involvement of the elbows, pitting of the nails, and itchy scalp. (Dermatology)

Office visit for a 27-year-old male, established patient, with deep follicular and perifollicular inflammation unable to tolerate systemic antibiotics due to GI upset, requires change of systemic medication. (Dermatology)

Office visit for a 16-year-old male, established patient, who is on medication for exercise-induced bronchospasm. (Allergy & Immunology)

Office visit for a 60-year-old, established patient, with chronic essential hypertension on multiple drug regimen, for blood pressure check. (Family Medicine)

Office visit for a 20-year-old male, established patient, for removal of sutures in hand. (Family Medicine)

Office visit for a 58-year-old female, established patient, with unilateral painful bunion. (Orthopaedic Surgery)

Office visit for a 45-year-old female, established patient, with known osteoarthritis and painful swollen knees. (Rheumatology)

Office visit for a 25-year-old female, established patient, complaining of bleeding and heavy menses. (Obstetrics & Gynecology)

Office visit for a 55-year-old male, established patient, with hypertension managed by a beta blocker/thiazide regime; now experiencing mild fatigue. (Nephrology)

Office visit for a 65-year-old female, established patient, with primary glaucoma for interval determination of intraocular pressure and possible adjustment of medication. (Ophthalmology)

Office visit for a 56-year-old man, established patient, with stable exertional angina who complains of new onset of calf pain while walking. (Cardiology)

Office visit for a 63-year-old female, established patient, with rheumatoid arthritis on auranofin and ibuprofen, seen for routine follow-up visit. (Rheumatology)

Office visit for an established patient with Graves' disease, three months post I-131 therapy, who presents with lassitude and malaise. (Endocrinology)

Office visit for the quarterly follow-up of a 63-year-old male, established patient, with chronic myofascial pain syndrome, effectively managed by doxepin, who presents with new onset urinary hesitancy. (Pain Medicine)

Office visit for the biannual follow-up of an established patient with migraine variant having infrequent, intermittent, moderate to severe headaches with nausea and vomiting, which are sometimes effectively managed by ergotamine tartrate and an antiemetic, but occasionally requiring visits to an emergency department. (Pain Medicine)

Office visit for an established patient after discharge from a pain rehabilitation program to review and adjust medication dosage. (Pain Medicine)

Office visit with 55-year-old male, established patient, for management of hypertension, mild fatigue, on beta blocker/thiazide regimen. (Family Medicine/Internal Medicine)

Outpatient visit with 37-year-old male, established patient, who is three years post total colectomy for chronic ulcerative colitis, presents for increased irritation at his stoma. (General Surgery)

Office visit for a 70-year-old diabetic hypertensive established patient with recent change in insulin requirement. (Internal Medicine/Nephrology)

Office visit with 80-year-old female, established patient, for follow-up osteoporosis, status-post compression fractures. (Rheumatology)

Office visit for an established patient with stable cirrhosis of the liver. (Gastroenterology)

Routine, follow-up office evaluation at a three-month interval for a 77-year-old female, established patient, with nodular small cleaved-cell lymphoma. (Hematology/Oncology)

Quarterly follow-up office visit for a 45-year-old male, established patient, with stable chronic asthma, on steroid and bronchodilator therapy. (Pulmonary Medicine)

Office visit for a 50-year-old female, established patient, with insulin-dependent diabetes mellitus and stable coronary artery disease, for monitoring. (Family Medicine/Internal Medicine)

99214 Office visit for an established patient now presenting with generalized dermatitis of 80 percent of the body surface area. (Dermatology)

Office visit for a 32-year-old female, established patient, with new onset right lower quadrant pain. (Family Medicine)

Office visit for reassessment and reassurance/counseling of a 40-year-old female, established patient, who is experiencing increased symptoms while on a pain management treatment program. (Pain Medicine)

Office visit for a 30-year-old, established patient, under management for intractable low back pain, who now presents with new onset right posterior thigh pain. (Pain Medicine)

Office visit for an established patient with frequent intermittent, moderate to severe headaches requiring beta blocker or tricyclic antidepressant prophylaxis, as well as four symptomatic treatments, but who is still experiencing headaches at a frequency of several times a month that are unresponsive to treatment. (Pain Medicine)

Office visit for an established patient with psoriasis with extensive involvement of scalp, trunk, palms, and soles with joint pain. Combinations of topical and systemic treatments discussed and instituted. (Dermatology)

Office visit for a 55-year-old male, established patient, with increasing night pain, limp, and progressive varus of both knees. (Orthopaedic Surgery)

Follow-up visit for a 15-year-old withdrawn patient with four-year history of papulocystic acne of the face, chest, and back with early scarring and poor response to past treatment. Discussion of use of systemic medication. (Dermatology)

Office visit for a 28-year-old male, established patient, with regional enteritis, diarrhea, and low-grade fever. (Internal Medicine)

Office visit for a 25-year-old female, established patient, following recent arthrogram and MR imaging for TMJ pain. (Oral & Maxillofacial Surgery)

Office visit for a 32-year-old female, established patient, with large obstructing stone in left mid-ureter, to discuss management options including urethroscopy with extraction or ESWL. (Urology)

Evaluation for a 28-year-old male, established patient, with new onset of low back pain. (Anesthesiology/Pain Medicine)

Office visit for a 28-year-old female, established patient, with right lower quadrant abdominal pain, fever, and anorexia. (Internal Medicine/Family Medicine)

Office visit for a 45-year-old male, established patient, four months follow-up of L4-5 diskectomy, with persistent incapacitating low back and leg pain. (Orthopaedic Surgery)

Outpatient visit for a 77-year-old male, established patient, with hypertension, presenting with a three-month history of episodic substernal chest pain on exertion. (Cardiology)

Office visit for a 25-year-old female, established patient, for evaluation of progressive saddle nose deformity of unknown etiology. (Plastic Surgery)

Office visit for a 65-year-old male, established patient, with BPH and severe bladder outlet obstruction, to discuss management options such as TURP. (Urology)

Office visit for an adult diabetic established patient with a past history of recurrent sinusitis who presents with a one-week history of double vision. (Otolaryngology, Head & Neck Surgery)

Office visit for an established patient with lichen planus and 60 percent of the cutaneous surface involved, not responsive to systemic steroids, as well as developing symptoms of progressive heartburn and paranoid ideation. (Dermatology)

Office visit for a 52-year-old male, established patient, with a 12-year history of bipolar disorder responding to lithium carbonate and brief psychotherapy. Psychotherapy and prescription provided. (Psychiatry)

Office visit for a 63-year-old female, established patient, with a history of familial polyposis, status post-colectomy with sphincter sparing procedure, who now presents with rectal bleeding and increase in stooling frequency. (General Surgery)

Office visit for a 68-year-old male, established patient, with the sudden onset of multiple flashes and floaters in the right eye due to a posterior vitreous detachment. (Ophthalmology)

Office visit for a 55-year-old female, established patient, on cyclosporin for treatment of resistant, small vessel vasculitis. (Rheumatology)

Follow-up office visit for a 55-year-old male, two months after iliac angioplasty with new onset of contralateral extremity claudication. (Interventional Radiology)

Office visit for a 68-year-old male, established patient, with stable angina, two months post myocardial infarction, who is not tolerating one of his medications. (Cardiology)

Weekly office visit for 5FU therapy for an ambulatory established patient with metastatic colon cancer and increasing shortness of breath. (Hematology/Oncology)

Follow-up office visit for a 60-year-old male, established patient, whose post-traumatic seizures have disappeared on medication and who now raises the question of stopping the medication (Neurology)

Office evaluation on new onset RLQ pain in a 32-year-old woman, established patient. (Urology/General Surgery/Internal Medicine/Family Medicine)

Office evaluation of 28-year-old, established patient, with regional enteritis, diarrhea and low-grade fever. (Family Medicine/Internal Medicine)

Office visit with 50-year-old female, established patient, diabetic, blood sugar controlled by diet. She now complains of frequency of urination and weight loss, blood sugar of 320 and negative ketones on dipstick. (Internal Medicine)

Follow-up office visit for a 45-year-old, established patient, with rheumatoid arthritis on gold, methotrexate, or immunosuppressive therapy. (Rheumatology)

Office visit for a 60-year-old male, established patient, two years post-removal of intracranial meningioma, now with new headaches and visual disturbance. (Neurosurgery)

Office visit for a 68-year-old female, established patient, for routine review and follow-up of non-insulin dependent diabetes, obesity, hypertension and congestive heart failure. Complains of vision difficulties and admits dietary noncompliance. Patient is counseled concerning diet and current medications adjusted. (Family Medicine)

99215 Office visit for an established patient who developed persistent cough, rectal bleeding, weakness, and diarrhea plus pustular infection on skin. Patient on immunosuppressive therapy. (Dermatology)

Office visit for an established patient with disseminated lupus erythematosus, extensive edema of extremities kidney disease, and weakness requiring monitored course on azathioprene, corticosteroid and complicated by acute depression. (Dermatology/Internal Medicine/Rheumatology)

Office visit for an established patient with progressive dermatomyositis and recent onset of fever, nasal speech, and regurgitation of fluids through the nose. (Dermatology)

Office visit for a 28-year-old female, established patient, who is abstinent from previous cocaine dependence, but reports progressive panic attacks and chest pains. (Psychiatry)

Office visit for an established adolescent patient with history of bipolar disorder treated with lithium; seen on urgent basis at family's request because of severe depressive symptoms. (Psychiatry)

Office visit for an established patient having acute migraine with new onset neurological symptoms and whose headaches are unresponsive to previous attempts at management with a combination of preventive and abortive medication. (Pain Medicine)

Office visit for an established patient with exfoliative lichen planus with daily fever spikes, disorientation, and shortness of breath. (Dermatology)

Office visit for a 25-year-old, established patient, two years post-burn with bilateral ectropion, hypertrophic facial burn scars, near absence of left breast, and burn syndactyly of both hands. Discussion of treatment options following examination. (Plastic Surgery)

Office visit for a 6-year-old, established patient, to review newly diagnosed immune deficiency with recommendations for therapy including IV immunoglobulin and chronic antibiotics. (Allergy & Immunology)

Office visit for a 36-year-old, established patient, three months status post-transplant, with new onset of peripheral edema, increased blood pressure, and progressive fatigue. (Nephrology)

Office visit for an established patient with Kaposi's sarcoma who presents with fever and widespread vesicles. (Dermatology)

Office visit for a 27-year-old female, established patient, with bipolar disorder who was stable on lithium carbonate and monthly supportive psychotherapy but now has developed symptoms of hypomania. (Psychiatry)

Office visit for a 25-year-old male, established patient with a history of schizophrenia who has been seen bi-monthly but is complaining of auditory hallucinations. (Psychiatry)

Office visit for a 62-year-old male, established patient, three years post-op abdominal perineal resection, now with a rising carcinoembryonic antigen, weight loss, and pelvic pain. (Abdominal Surgery)

Office visit for a 42-year-old male, established patient, nine months post-op emergency vena cava shunt for variceal bleeding, now presents with complaints of one episode of "dark" bowel movement, weight gain, tightness in abdomen, whites of eyes seem "yellow" and occasional drowsiness after eating hamburgers. (Abdominal Surgery)

Office visit for a 68-year-old male, established patient, with biopsy-proven rectal carcinoma, for evaluation and discussion of treatment options. (General Surgery)

Office visit for a 60-year-old, established patient, with diabetic nephropathy with increasing edema and dyspnea. (Endocrinology)

Office visit with 30-year-old male, established patient for three-month history of fatigue, weight loss, intermittent fever, and presenting with diffuse adenopathy and splenomegaly. (Family Medicine)

Office visit for restaging of an established patient with new lymphadenopathy one year post-therapy for lymphoma. (Hematology/Oncology)

Office visit for evaluation of recent onset syncopal attacks in a 70-year-old woman, established patient. (Internal Medicine)

Follow-up visit, 40-year-old mother of three, established patient, with acute rheumatoid arthritis, anatomical Stage 3, ARA function Class 3 rheumatoid arthritis, and deteriorating function. (Rheumatology)

Follow-up office visit for a 65-year-old male, established patient, with a fever of recent onset while on outpatient antibiotic therapy for endocarditis. (Infectious Disease)

Office visit for a 75-year-old, established patient, with ALS (amyotrophic lateral sclerosis), who is no longer able to swallow. (Neurology)

Office visit for a 70-year-old female, established patient, with diabetes mellitus and hypertension, presenting with a two-month history of increasing confusion, agitation and short-term memory loss. (Family Medicine/Internal Medicine)

Hospital Inpatient Services

Initial Hospital Care

New or Established Patient

99221 Initial hospital visit following admission for a 42-year-old male for observation following an uncomplicated mandible fracture. (Plastic Surgery/Oral & Maxillofacial Surgery)

Initial hospital visit for a 40-year-old patient with a thrombosed synthetic arteriovenous conduit. (Nephrology)

Initial hospital visit for a healthy 24-year-old male with an acute onset of low back pain following a lifting injury. (Internal Medicine/Anesthesiology/Pain Medicine)

Initial hospital visit for a 69-year-old female with controlled hypertension, scheduled for surgery. (Internal Medicine/Cardiology)

Initial hospital visit for a 24-year-old healthy female with benign tumor of palate. (Oral & Maxillofacial Surgery)

Initial hospital visit for a 14-year-old female with infectious mononucleosis and dehydration. (Internal Medicine)

Initial hospital visit for a 62-year-old female with stable rheumatoid arthritis, admitted for total joint replacement. (Rheumatology)

Initial hospital visit for a 12-year-old patient with a laceration of the upper eyelid, involving the lid margin and superior canaliculus, admitted prior to surgery for IV antibiotic therapy. (Plastic Surgery)

Initial hospital visit for a 69-year-old female with controlled hypertension, scheduled for surgery. (Cardiology)

Hospital admission, examination, and initiation of treatment program for a 67-year-old male with uncomplicated pneumonia who requires IV antibiotic therapy. (Internal Medicine)

Hospital admission for an 18-month-old with 10 percent dehydration. (Pediatrics)

Hospital admission for a 12-year-old with a laceration of the upper eyelid involving the lid margin and superior canaliculus, admitted prior to surgery for IV antibiotic therapy. (Ophthalmology)

Hospital admission for a 32-year-old female with severe flank pain, hematuria and presumed diagnosis of ureteral calculus as determined by Emergency Department physician. (Urology)

Initial hospital visit for a patient with several large venous stasis ulcers not responding to outpatient therapy. (Dermatology)

Initial hospital visit for 21-year-old pregnant patient (nine weeks gestation) with hyperemesis gravidarum. (Obstetrics & Gynecology)

Initial hospital visit for a 73-year-old female with acute pyelonephritis who is otherwise generally healthy. (Geriatrics)

Initial hospital visit for 62-year-old patient with cellulitis of the foot requiring bedrest and intravenous antibiotics. (Orthopaedic Surgery)

99222   Initial hospital visit for a 50-year-old patient with lower quadrant abdominal pain and increased temperature, but without septic picture. (General Surgery/Abdominal Surgery/Colon & Rectal Surgery)

Initial hospital visit for airway management, due to a benign laryngeal mass. (Otolaryngology, Head & Neck Surgery)

Initial hospital visit for a 66-year-old female with an L-2 vertebral compression fracture with acute onset of paralytic ileus; seen in the office two days previously. (Orthopaedic Surgery)

Initial hospital visit and evaluation of a 15-year-old male admitted with peritonsillar abscess or cellulitis requiring intravenous antibiotic therapy. (Otolaryngology, Head & Neck Surgery)

Initial hospital visit for a 42-year-old male with vertebral compression fracture following a motor vehicle accident. (Orthopaedic Surgery)

Initial hospital visit for a patient with generalized atopic dermatitis and secondary infection. (Dermatology)

Initial hospital visit for a 3-year-old patient with high temperature, limp, and painful hip motion of 18 hours' duration. (Pediatrics/Orthopaedic Surgery)

Initial hospital visit for a young adult, presenting with an acute asthma attack unresponsive to outpatient therapy. (Allergy & Immunology)

Initial hospital visit for an 18-year-old male who has suppurative sialoadenitis and dehydration. (Oral & Maxillofacial Surgery)

Initial hospital visit for a 65-year-old female for acute onset of thrombotic cerebrovascular accident with contralateral paralysis and aphasia. (Neurology)

Initial hospital visit for a 50-year-old male chronic paraplegic patient with pain and spasm below the lesion. (Anesthesiology)

Partial hospital admission for an adolescent patient from chaotic blended family, transferred from inpatient setting, for continued treatment to control symptomatic expressions of hostility and depression. (Psychiatry)

Initial hospital visit for a 15-year-old male with acute status asthmaticus, unresponsive to outpatient therapy. (Internal Medicine)

Initial hospital visit for a 61-year-old male with history of previous myocardial infarction, who now complains of chest pain. (Internal Medicine)

Initial hospital visit of a 15-year-old on medications for a sore throat over the last two weeks. The sore throat has worsened and patient now has dysphagia. The exam shows large necrotic tonsils with an adequate airway and small palpable nodes. The initial mono test was negative. (Otolaryngology, Head & Neck Surgery)

Initial hospital evaluation of a 23-year-old allergy patient admitted with eyelid edema and pain on fifth day of oral antibiotic therapy. (Otolaryngology, Head & Neck Surgery)

Hospital admission, young adult patient, failed previous therapy and now presents in acute asthmatic attack. (Family Medicine/Allergy & Immunology)

Hospital admission of a 62-year-old smoker, established patient, with bronchitis in acute respiratory distress. (Internal Medicine/Pulmonary Medicine)

Hospital admission, examination, and initiation of a treatment program for a 65-year-old female with new onset of right-sided paralysis and aphasia. (Neurology)

Hospital admission, examination, and initiation of treatment program for a 66-year-old chronic hemodialysis patient with fever and a new pulmonary infiltrate. (Nephrology)

Hospital admission for an 8-year-old febrile patient with chronic sinusitis and severe headache, unresponsive to oral antibiotics. (Allergy & Immunology)

Hospital admission for a 40-year-old male with submaxillary cellulitis and trismus from infected lower molar. (Oral & Maxillofacial Surgery)

99223   Initial hospital visit for a 45-year-old female, who has a history of rheumatic fever as a child and now has anemia, fever, and congestive heart failure. (Cardiology)

Initial hospital visit for a 50-year-old male with acute chest pain and diagnostic electrocardiographic changes of an acute anterior myocardial infarction. (Cardiology/Family Medicine/Internal Medicine)

Initial hospital visit of a 75-year-old with progressive stridor and dysphagia with history of cancer of the larynx treated by radiation therapy in the past. Exam shows a large recurrent tumor of the glottis with a mass in the neck. (Otolaryngology, Head & Neck Surgery)

Initial hospital visit for a 70-year-old male admitted with chest pain, complete heart block, and congestive heart failure. (Cardiology)

Initial hospital visit for an 82-year-old male who presents with syncope, chest pain, and ventricular arrhythmias. (Cardiology)

Initial hospital visit for a 75-year-old male with history of arteriosclerotic coronary vascular disease, who is severely dehydrated, disoriented, and experiencing auditory hallucinations. (Psychiatry)

Initial hospital visit for a 70-year-old male with alcohol and sedative-hypnotic dependence, admitted by family for severe withdrawal, hypertension, and diabetes mellitus. (Psychiatry)

Initial hospital visit for a persistently suicidal latency-aged child whose parents have requested admission to provide safety during evaluation, but are anxious about separation from her. (Psychiatry)

Initial psychiatric visit for an adolescent patient without previous psychiatric history, who was transferred from the medical ICU after a significant overdose. (Psychiatry)

Initial hospital visit for a 35-year-old female with severe systemic lupus erythematosus on corticosteroid and cyclophosphamide, with new onset of fever, chills, rash, and chest pain. (Rheumatology)

Initial hospital visit for a 52-year-old male with known rheumatic heart disease who presents with anasarca, hypertension, and history of alcohol abuse. (Cardiology)

Initial hospital visit for a 55-year-old female with a history of congenital heart disease; now presents with cyanosis. (Cardiology)

Initial hospital visit for a psychotic, hostile, violently combative adolescent, involuntarily committed, for seclusion and restraint in order to provide for safety on unit. (Psychiatry)

Initial hospital visit for a now subdued and sullen teenage male with six-month history of declining school performance, increasing self-endangerment, and resistance of parental expectations, including running away past weekend after physical fight with father. (Psychiatry)

Initial partial hospital admission for a 17-year-old female with history of borderline mental retardation who has developed auditory hallucinations. Parents are known to abuse alcohol, and Child Protective Services is investigating allegations of sexual abuse of a younger sibling. (Psychiatry)

Initial hospital visit of a 67-year old male admitted with a large neck mass, dysphagia, and history of myocardial infarction three months before. (Otolaryngology, Head & Neck Surgery)

Initial hospital visit for a patient with suspected cerebrospinal fluid rhinorrhea which developed two weeks after head injury. (Otolaryngology, Head & Neck Surgery)

Initial hospital visit for a 25-year-old female with history of poly-substance abuse and psychiatric disorder. The patient appears to be psychotic with markedly elevated vital signs. (Psychiatry)

Initial hospital visit for a 70-year-old male with cutaneous T-cell lymphoma who has developed fever and lymphadenopathy. (Internal Medicine)

Initial hospital visit for a 62-year-old female with known coronary artery disease, for evaluation of increasing edema, dyspnea on exertion, confusion, and sudden onset of fever with productive cough. (Internal Medicine)

Initial hospital visit for a 3-year-old female with 36-hour history of sore throat and high fever; now with sudden onset of lethargy, irritability, photophobia, and nuchal rigidity. (Pediatrics)

Initial hospital visit for a 26-year-old female for evaluation of severe facial fractures (LeFort's II/III). (Plastic Surgery)

Initial hospital visit for a 55-year-old female for bilateral mandibular fractures resulting in flail mandible and airway obstruction. (Plastic Surgery)

Initial hospital visit for a 71-year-old patient with a red painful eye four days following uncomplicated cataract surgery due to endophthalmitis. (Ophthalmology)

Initial hospital visit for a 45-year-old patient involved in a motor vehicle accident who suffered a perforating corneoscleral laceration with loss of vision. (Ophthalmology)

Initial hospital visit for a 58-year-old male who has Ludwig's angina and progressive airway compromise. (Oral & Maxillofacial Surgery)

Initial hospital visit for a patient with generalized systemic sclerosis, receiving immunosuppressive therapy because of recent onset of cough, fever, and inability to swallow. (Dermatology)

Initial hospital visit for an 82-year-old male who presents with syncope, chest pain, and ventricular arrhythmias. (Cardiology)

Initial hospital visit for a 62-year-old male with history of previous myocardial infarction, comes in with recurrent, sustained ventricular tachycardia. (Cardiology)

Initial hospital visit for a chronic dialysis patient with infected PTFE fistula, septicemia, and shock. (Nephrology)

Initial hospital visit for a 1-year-old male, victim of child abuse, with central nervous system depression, skull fracture, and retinal hemorrhage. (Family Medicine/Neurology)

Initial hospital visit for a 25-year-old female with recent C4-5 quadriplegia, admitted for rehabilitation. (Physical Medicine & Rehabilitation)

Initial hospital visit for an 18-year-old male, post-traumatic brain injury with multiple impairment. (Physical Medicine & Rehabilitation)

Initial partial hospital admission for 16-year-old male, sullen and subdued, with six-month history of declining school performance, increasing self-endangerment, and resistance to parental expectations. (Psychiatry)

Initial hospital visit for a 16-year-old primigravida at 32 weeks gestation with severe hypertension (200/110), thrombocytopenia, and headache. (Obstetrics & Gynecology)

Initial hospital visit for a 49-year-old male with cirrhosis of liver with hematemesis, hepatic encephalopathy, and fever. (Gastroenterology)

Initial hospital visit for a 55-year-old female in chronic pain who has attempted suicide. (Psychiatry)

Initial hospital visit for a 70-year-old male, with multiple organ system disease, admitted with history of being aneuric and septic for 24 hours prior to admission. (Urology)

Initial hospital visit for a 3-year-old female with 36-hour history of sore throat and high fever, now with sudden onset of lethargy, irritability, photophobia, and nuchal rigidity. (Internal Medicine)

Initial hospital visit for a 78-year-old male, transfers from nursing home with dysuria and pyuria, increasing confusion, and high fever. (Internal Medicine)

Initial hospital visit for a 1-day-old male with cyanosis, respiratory distress, and tachypnea. (Cardiology)

Initial hospital visit for a 3-year-old female with recurrent tachycardia and syncope. (Cardiology)

Initial hospital visit for a thyrotoxic patient who presents with fever, atrial fibrillation, and delirium. (Endocrinology)

Initial hospital visit for a 50-year-old Type I diabetic who presents with diabetic ketoacidosis with fever and obtundation. (Endocrinology)

Initial hospital visit for a 40-year-old female with anatomical stage 3, ARA functional class 3 rheumatoid arthritis on methotrexate, corticosteroid, and nonsteroidal anti-inflammatory drugs. Patient presents with severe arthritis flare, new oral ulcers, abdominal pain, and leukopenia. (Rheumatology)

Initial hospital exam of a pediatric patient with high fever and proptosis. (Otolaryngology, Head & Neck Surgery)

Initial hospital visit for a 25-year-old patient admitted for the first time to the rehab unit, with recent C-4-5 quadriplegia. (Physical Medicine & Rehabilitation)

Hospital admission, examination, and initiation of treatment program for a previously unknown 58-year-old male who presents with acute chest pain (Cardiology)

Hospital admission, examination, and initiation of induction chemotherapy for a 42-year-old patient with newly diagnosed acute myelogenous leukemia. (Hematology/Oncology)

Hospital admission following a motor vehicle accident of a 24-year-old male with fracture dislocation of C5-6; neurologically intact. (Neurosurgery)

Hospital admission for a 78-year-old female with left lower lobe pneumonia and a history of coronary artery disease, congestive heart failure, osteoarthritis and gout. (Family Medicine)

Hospital admission, examination, and initiation of treatment program for a 65-year-old immunosuppressed male with confusion, fever, and a headache. (Infectious Disease)

Hospital admission for a 9-year-old with vomiting, dehydration, fever, tachypnea and an admitting diagnosis of diabetic ketoacidosis. (Pediatrics)

Initial hospital visit for a 65-year-old male who presents with acute myocardial infarction, oliguria, hypotension, and altered state of consciousness. (Cardiology)

Initial hospital visit for a hostile/resistant adolescent patient who is severely depressed and involved in poly-substance abuse. Patient is experiencing significant conflict in his chaotic family situation and was suspended from school following an attack on a teacher with a baseball bat. (Psychiatry)

Initial hospital visit for 89-year-old female with fulminant hepatic failure and encephalopathy. (Gastroenterology)

Initial hospital visit for a 42-year-old female with rapidly progressing scleroderma, malignant hypertension, digital infarcts, and oligurea. (Rheumatology)

Subsequent Hospital Care

99231 Subsequent hospital visit for a 65-year-old female, post-open reduction and internal fixation of a fracture. (Physical Medicine & Rehabilitation)

Subsequent hospital visit for a 33-year-old patient with pelvic pain who is responding to pain medication and observation. (Obstetrics & Gynecology)

Subsequent hospital visit for a 21-year-old female with hyperemesis who has responded well to intravenous fluids. (Obstetrics & Gynecology)

Subsequent hospital visit to re-evaluate post-op pain and titrate patient-controlled analgesia for a 27-year-old female. (Anesthesiology)

Follow-up hospital visit for a 35-year-old female, status post-epidural analgesia. (Anesthesiology/Pain Medicine)

Subsequent hospital visit for a 56-year-old male, post-gastrectomy, for maintenance of analgesia using an intravenous dilaudid infusion. (Anesthesiology)

Subsequent hospital visit for a 4-year-old on day three receiving medication for uncomplicated pneumonia. (Allergy & Immunology)

Subsequent hospital visit for a 30-year-old female with urticaria which has stabilized with medication. (Allergy & Immunology)

Subsequent hospital visit for a 76-year-old male with venous stasis ulcers. (Dermatology)

Subsequent hospital visit for a 24-year-old female with otitis externa, seen two days before in consultation, now to have otic wick removal. (Otolaryngology, Head & Neck Surgery)

Subsequent hospital visit for a 27-year-old with acute labyrinthitis. (Otolaryngology, Head & Neck Surgery)

Subsequent hospital visit for a 10-year-old male admitted for lobar pneumonia with vomiting and dehydration; is becoming afebrile and tolerating oral fluids. (Family Medicine/Pediatrics)

Subsequent hospital visit for a 62-year-old patient with resolving cellulitis of the foot. (Orthopaedic Surgery)

Subsequent hospital visit for a 25-year-old male admitted for supra-ventricular tachycardia and converted on medical therapy. (Cardiology)

Subsequent hospital visit for a 27-year-old male two days after open reduction and internal fixation for malar complex fracture. (Plastic Surgery)

Subsequent hospital visit for a 76-year-old male with venous stasis ulcers. (Geriatrics)

Subsequent hospital visit for a 67-year-old female admitted three days ago with bleeding gastric ulcer; now stable. (Gastroenterology)

Subsequent hospital visit for stable 33-year-old male, status post-lower gastrointestinal bleeding. (General Surgery/Gastroenterology)

Subsequent hospital visit for a 29-year-old auto mechanic with effort thrombosis of left upper extremity. (General Surgery)

Subsequent hospital visit for a 14-year-old female in middle phase of inpatient treatment, who is now behaviorally stable and making satisfactory progress in treatment. (Psychiatry)

Subsequent hospital visit for an 18-year-old male with uncomplicated asthma who is clinically stable. (Allergy & Immunology)

Subsequent hospital visit for a 55-year-old male with rheumatoid arthritis, two days following an uncomplicated total joint replacement. (Rheumatology)

Subsequent hospital visit for a 60-year-old dialysis patient with an access infection, now afebrile on antibiotic. (Nephrology)

Subsequent hospital visit for a 36-year-old female with stable post-rhinoplasty epistaxis. (Plastic Surgery)

Subsequent hospital visit for a 66-year-old female with L-2 vertebral compression fracture with resolving ileus. (Orthopaedic Surgery)

Subsequent hospital visit for a patient with peritonsillar abscess. (Otolaryngology, Head & Neck Surgery)

Subsequent hospital visit for an 18-year-old female responding to intravenous antibiotic therapy for ear or sinus infection. (Otolaryngology, Head & Neck Surgery)

Subsequent hospital visit for a 70-year-old male admitted with congestive heart failure who has responded to therapy. (Cardiology)

Follow-up hospital visit for a 32-year-old female with left ureteral calculus; being followed in anticipation of spontaneous passage. (Urology)

Subsequent hospital visit for a 4-year-old female, admitted for acute gastroenteritis and dehydration, requiring IV hydration; now stable. (Family Medicine)

Subsequent hospital visit for a 50-year-old Type II diabetic who is clinically stable and without complications requiring regulation of a single dose of insulin daily. (Endocrinology)

Subsequent hospital visit to reassesses the status of a 65-year-old patient post-open reduction and internal fixation of hip fracture, on the rehab unit. (Physical Medicine & Rehabilitation)

Subsequent hospital visit for a 78-year-old male with cholangiocarcinoma managed by biliary drainage. (Interventional Radiology)

Subsequent hospital visit for a 50-year-old male with uncomplicated myocardial infarction who is clinically stable and without chest pain. (Family Medicine/Cardiology/Internal Medicine)

Subsequent hospital visit for a stable 72-year-old lung cancer patient undergoing a five-day course of infusion chemotherapy. (Hematology/Oncology)

Subsequent hospital visit, two days post admission for a 65-year-old male with a CVA (cerebral vascular accident) and left hemiparesis, who is clinically stable. (Neurology/Physical Medicine and Rehabilitation)

Subsequent hospital visit for now stable, 33-year-old male, status post lower gastrointestinal bleeding. (General Surgery)

Subsequent visit on third day of hospitalization for a 60-year-old female recovering from an uncomplicated pneumonia. (Infectious Disease/Internal Medicine/Pulmonary Medicine)

Subsequent hospital visit for a 3-year-old patient in traction for a congenital dislocation of the hip. (Orthopaedic Surgery)

Subsequent hospital visit for a 4-year-old female, admitted for acute gastroenteritis and dehydration, requiring IV hydration; now stable. (Family Medicine/Internal Medicine)

Subsequent hospital visit for 50-year-old female with resolving uncomplicated acute pancreatitis. (Gastroenterology)

99232 Subsequent hospital visit for a patient with venous stasis ulcers who developed fever and red streaks adjacent to the ulcer. (Dermatology/Internal Medicine/Family Medicine)

Subsequent hospital visit for a 66-year-old male for dressing changes and observation. Patient has had a myocutaneous flap to close a pharyngeal fistula and now has a low-grade fever. (Plastic Surgery)

Subsequent hospital visit for a 54-year-old female admitted for myocardial infarction, but who is now having frequent premature ventricular contractions. (Internal Medicine)

Subsequent hospital visit for an 80-year-old patient with a pelvic rim fracture, inability to walk, and severe pain; now 36 hours post-injury, experiencing urinary retention. (Orthopaedic Surgery)

Subsequent hospital visit for a 17-year-old female with fever, pharyngitis, and airway obstruction, who after 48 hours develops a maculopapular rash. (Pediatrics/Family Medicine)

Follow-up hospital visit for a 32-year-old patient admitted the previous day for corneal ulcer. (Dermatology)

Follow-up visit for a 67-year-old male with congestive heart failure who has responded to antibiotics and diuretics, and has now developed a monoarthropathy. (Internal Medicine)

Follow-up hospital visit for a 58-year-old male receiving continuous opioids who is experiencing severe nausea and vomiting. (Pain Medicine)

Subsequent hospital visit for a patient after an auto accident who is slow to respond to ambulation training. (Physical Medicine & Rehabilitation)

Subsequent hospital visit for a 14-year-old with unstable bronchial asthma complicated by pneumonia. (Allergy & Immunology)

Subsequent hospital visit for a 50-year-old diabetic, hypertensive male with back pain not responding to conservative inpatient management with continued radiation of pain to the lower left extremity. (Orthopaedic Surgery)

Subsequent hospital visit for a 37-year-old female on day five of antibiotics for bacterial endocarditis, who still has low-grade fever. (Cardiology)

Subsequent hospital visit for a 54-year-old patient, post MI (myocardial infarction), who is out of the CCU (coronary care unit) but is now having frequent premature ventricular contractions on telemetry. (Cardiology/Internal Medicine)

Subsequent hospital visit for a patient with neutropenia, a fever responding to antibiotics, and continued slow gastrointestinal bleeding on platelet support. (Hematology/Oncology)

Subsequent hospital visit for a 50-year-old male admitted two days ago for sub-acute renal allograft rejection. (Nephrology)

Subsequent hospital visit for a 35-year-old drug addict, not responding to initial antibiotic therapy for pyelonephritis. (Urology)

Subsequent hospital visit of an 81-year-old male with abdominal distention, nausea, and vomiting. (General Surgery)

Subsequent hospital care for a 62-year-old female with congestive heart failure, who remains dyspneic and febrile. (Internal Medicine)

Subsequent hospital visit for a 73-year-old female with recently diagnosed lung cancer, who complains of unsteady gait. (Pulmonary Medicine)

Subsequent hospital visit for a 20-month-old male with bacterial meningitis treated one week with antibiotic therapy; has now developed a temperature of 101.0. (Pediatrics)

Subsequent hospital visit for 13-year-old male admitted with left lower quadrant abdominal pain and fever, not responding to therapy. (General Surgery)

Subsequent hospital visit for a 65-year-old male with hemiplegia and painful paretic shoulder. (Physical Medicine & Rehabilitation)

99233   Subsequent hospital visit for a 38-year-old male, quadriplegic with acute autonomic hyperreflexia, who is not responsive to initial care. (Physical Medicine & Rehabilitation)

Follow-up hospital visit for a teenage female who continues to experience severely disruptive, violent and life-threatening symptoms in a complicated multi-system illness. Family/social circumstances also a contributing factor. (Psychiatry)

Subsequent hospital visit for a 42-year-old female with progressive systemic sclerosis (scleroderma), renal failure on dialysis, congestive heart failure, cardiac arrhythmias, and digital ulcers. (Allergy & Immunology)

Subsequent hospital visit for a 50-year-old diabetic, hypertensive male with nonresponding back pain and radiating pain to the lower left extremity, who develops chest pain, cough, and bloody sputum. (Orthopaedic Surgery)

Subsequent hospital visit for a 64-year-old female, status post-abdominal aortic aneurysm resection, with non-responsive coagulopathy, who has now developed lower GI bleeding. (Abdominal Surgery/Colon & Rectal Surgery/General Surgery)

Follow-up hospital care of a patient with pansinusitis infection complicated by a brain abscess and asthma; no response to current treatment. (Otolaryngology, Head & Neck Surgery)

Subsequent hospital visit for a patient with a laryngeal neoplasm who develops airway compromise, suspected metastasis. (Otolaryngology, Head & Neck Surgery)

Subsequent hospital visit for a 49-year-old male with significant rectal bleeding, etiology undetermined, not responding to treatment. (Abdominal Surgery/General Surgery/Colon & Rectal Surgery)

Subsequent hospital visit for a 50-year-old male, post-aortocoronary bypass surgery; now develops hypotension and oliguria. (Cardiology)

Subsequent hospital visit for an adolescent patient who is violent, unsafe, and noncompliant, with multiple expectations for participation in treatment plan and behavior on the treatment unit. (Psychiatry)

Subsequent hospital visit for an 18-year-old male being treated for presumed PCP psychosis. Patient is still moderately symptomatic with auditory hallucinations and is insisting on signing out against medical advice. (Psychiatry)

Subsequent hospital visit for an 8-year-old female with caustic ingestion, who now has fever, dyspnea, and dropping hemoglobin. (Gastroenterology)

Follow-up hospital visit for a chronic renal failure patient on dialysis who develops chest pain and shortness of breath and a new onset pericardial friction rub. (Nephrology)

Subsequent hospital visit for a 44-year-old patient with electrical burns to the left arm with ascending infection. (Orthopaedic Surgery)

Subsequent hospital visit for a patient with systemic sclerosis who has aspirated and is short of breath. (Dermatology)

Subsequent hospital visit for a 65-year-old female, status post-op resection of abdominal aortic aneurysm, with suspected ischemic bowel. (General Surgery)

Subsequent hospital visit for a 50-year-old male, post-aortocoronary bypass surgery, now develops hypotension and oliguria. (Cardiology)

Subsequent hospital visit for a 65-year-old male, following an acute myocardial infarction, who complains of shortness of breath and new chest pain. (Cardiology)

Subsequent hospital visit for a 65-year-old female with rheumatoid arthritis (stage 3, class 3) admitted for urosepsis. On the third hospital day, chest pain, dyspnea and fever develop. (Rheumatology)

Follow-up hospital care of a pediatric case with stridor, laryngomalacia, established tracheostomy, complicated by multiple medical problems in PICU. (Otolaryngology, Head & Neck Surgery)

Subsequent hospital visit for a 60-year-old female, four days post uncomplicated inferior myocardial infarction who has developed severe chest pain, dyspnea, diaphoresis and nausea. (Family Medicine)

Subsequent hospital visit for a patient with AML (acute myelogenous leukemia), fever, elevated white count and uric acid undergoing induction chemotherapy. (Hematology/Oncology)

Subsequent hospital visit for a 38-year-old quadriplegic male with acute autonomic hyperreflexia, who is not responsive to initial care. (Physical Medicine & Rehabilitation)

Subsequent hospital visit for a 65-year-old female post-op resection of abdominal aortic aneurysm, with suspected ischemic bowel. (General Surgery)

Subsequent hospital visit for a 60-year-old female with persistent leukocytosis and a fever seven days after a sigmoid colon resection for carcinoma. (Infectious Disease)

Subsequent hospital visit for a chronic renal failure patient on dialysis, who develops chest pain, shortness of breath and new onset of pericardial friction rub. (Nephrology)

Subsequent hospital visit for a 65-year-old male with acute myocardial infarction who now demonstrates complete heart block and congestive heart failure. (Cardiology)

Subsequent hospital visit for a 25-year-old female with hypertension and systemic lupus erythematosus, admitted for fever and respiratory distress. On the third hospital day, the patient presented with purpuric skin lesions and acute renal failure. (Allergy & Immunology)

Subsequent hospital visit for a 55-year-old male with severe chronic obstructive pulmonary disease and bronchospasm; initially admitted for acute respiratory distress requiring ventilatory support in the ICU. The patient was stabilized, extubated and transferred to the floor, but has now developed acute fever, dyspnea, left lower lobe rhonchi and laboratory evidence of carbon dioxide retention and hypoxemia. (Family Medicine/Internal Medicine)

Subsequent hospital visit for 46-year-old female, known liver cirrhosis patient, with recent upper gastrointestinal hemorrhage from varices; now with worsening ascites and encephalopathy. (Gastroenterology)

Subsequent hospital visit for 62-year-old female admitted with acute subarachnoid hemorrhage, negative cerebral arteriogram, increased lethargy and hemiparesis with fever. (Neurosurgery)

Consultations

Office or Other Outpatient Consultations

New or Established Patient

99241   Initial office consultation for a 40-year-old female in pain from blister on lip following a cold. (Oral & Maxillofacial Surgery)

Initial office consultation for a 62-year-old construction worker with olecranon bursitis. (Orthopaedic Surgery)

Office consultation with 25-year-old postpartum female with severe symptomatic hemorrhoids. (Colon & Rectal Surgery)

Office consultation with 58-year-old male, referred for follow-up of creatinine level and evaluation of obstructive uropathy, relieved two months ago. (Nephrology)

Office consultation for 30-year-old female tennis player with sprain or contusion of the forearm. (Orthopaedic Surgery)

Office consultation for a 45-year-old male, requested by his internist, with asymptomatic torus palatinus requiring no further treatment. (Oral & Maxillofacial Surgery)

99242   Initial office consultation for a 20-year-old male with acute upper respiratory tract symptoms. (Allergy & Immunology)

Initial office consultation for a 29-year-old soccer player with painful proximal thigh/groin injury. (Orthopaedic Surgery)

Initial office consultation for a 66-year-old female with wrist and hand pain, numbness of finger tips, suspected median nerve compression by carpal tunnel syndrome. (Plastic Surgery)

Initial office consultation for a patient with a solitary lesion of discoid lupus erythematosus on left cheek to rule out malignancy or self-induced lesion. (Dermatology)

Office consultation for management of systolic hypertension in a 70-year-old male scheduled for elective prostate resection. (Geriatrics)

Office consultation with 27-year-old female, with old amputation, for evaluation of existing above-knee prosthesis. (Physical Medicine & Rehabilitation)

Office consultation with 66-year-old female with wrist and hand pain, and finger numbness, secondary to suspected carpal tunnel syndrome. (Orthopaedic Surgery)

Office consultation for 61-year-old female, recently on antibiotic therapy, now with diarrhea and leukocytosis. (Abdominal Surgery)

Office consultation for a patient with papulosquamous eruption of elbow with pitting of nails and itchy scalp. (Dermatology)

Office consultation for a 30-year-old female with single season allergic rhinitis. (Allergy & Immunology)

99243   Initial office consultation for a 60-year-old male with avascular necrosis of the left femoral head with increasing pain. (Orthopaedic Surgery)

Office consultation for a 31-year-old woman complaining of palpitations and chest pains. Her internist had described a mild systolic click. (Cardiology)

Office consultation for a 65-year-old female with persistent bronchitis. (Infectious Disease)

Office consultation for a 65-year-old man with chronic low-back pain radiating to the leg. (Neurosurgery)

Office consultation for 23-year-old female with Crohn's disease not responding to therapy. (Abdominal Surgery/Colon & Rectal Surgery)

Office consultation for 25-year-old patient with symptomatic knee pain and swelling, with torn anterior cruciate ligament and/or torn meniscus. (Orthopaedic Surgery)

Office consultation for a 67-year-old patient with osteoporosis and mandibular atrophy with regard to reconstructive alternatives. (Oral & Maxillofacial Surgery)

Office consultation for 39-year-old patient referred at a perimenopausal age for irregular menses and menopausal symptoms. (Obstetrics & Gynecology)

99244   Initial office consultation for a 28-year-old male, HIV+, with a recent change in visual acuity. (Ophthalmology)

Initial office consultation for a 15-year-old male with failing grades, suspected drug abuse. (Pediatrics)

Initial office consultation for a 36-year-old factory worker, status four months post-occupational low back injury and requires management of intractable low back pain. (Pain Medicine)

Initial office consultation for a 45-year-old female with a history of chronic arthralgia of TMJ and associated myalgia and sudden progressive symptomatology over last two to three months. (Oral & Maxillofacial Surgery)

Initial office consultation for evaluation of a 70-year-old male with appetite loss and diminished energy. (Psychiatry)

Initial office consultation for an elementary school-aged patient, referred by pediatrician, with multiple systematic complaints and recent onset of behavioral discontrol. (Psychiatry)

Initial office consultation for a 23-year-old female with developmental facial skeletal anomaly and subsequent abnormal relationship of jaw(s) to cranial base. (Oral & Maxillofacial Surgery)

Initial office consultation for a 45-year-old myopic patient with a one-week history of floaters and a partial retinal detachment. (Ophthalmology)

Initial office consultation for a 65-year-old female with moderate dementia, mild unsteadiness, back pain fatigue on ambulation, intermittent urinary incontinence. (Neurosurgery)

Initial office consultation for a 33-year-old female referred by endocrinologist with amenorrhea and galactorrhea, for evaluation of pituitary tumor. (Neurosurgery)

Initial office consultation for a 34-year-old male with new onset nephrotic syndrome. (Nephrology)

Initial office consultation for a 39-year-old female with intractable chest wall pain secondary to metastatic breast cancer. (Anesthesiology/Pain Medicine)

Initial office consultation for a patient with multiple giant tumors of jaws. (Oral & Maxillofacial Surgery)

Initial office consultation for a patient with a failed total hip replacement with loosening and pain upon walking. (Orthopaedic Surgery)

Initial office consultation for a 60-year-old female with three-year history of intermittent tic-like unilateral facial pain; now constant pain for six weeks without relief by adequate carbamazepine dosage. (Neurosurgery)

Initial office consultation for a 45-year-old male heavy construction worker with prior lumbar disk surgery two years earlier; now gradually recurring low back and unilateral leg pain for three months, unable to work for two weeks. (Neurosurgery)

Initial office consultation of a patient who presents with a 30-year history of smoking and right neck mass. (Otolaryngology, Head & Neck Surgery)

Office consultation with 38-year-old female, with inflammatory bowel disease, who now presents with right lower quadrant pain and suspected intra-abdominal abscess. (General Surgery/Colon & Rectal Surgery)

Office consultation with 72-year-old male with esophageal carcinoma, symptoms of dysphagia and reflux. (Thoracic Surgery)

Office consultation for discussion of treatment options for a 40-year-old female with a two-centimeter adenocarcinoma of the breast. (Radiation Oncology)

Office consultation for young patient referred by pediatrician because of patient's short attention span, easy distractibility and hyperactivity. (Psychiatry)

Office consultation for 66-year-old female, history of colon resection for adenocarcinoma six years earlier, now with severe mid-back pain; x-rays showing osteoporosis and multiple vertebral compression fractures. (Neurosurgery)

Office consultation for a patient with chronic pelvic inflammatory disease who now has left lower quadrant pain with a palpable pelvic mass. (Obstetrics & Gynecology)

Office consultation for a patient with long-standing psoriasis with acute onset of erythroderma, pustular lesions, chills and fever. Combinations of topical and systemic treatments discussed and instituted. (Dermatology)

99245 Initial office consultation for a 35-year-old multiple-trauma male patient with complex pelvic fractures, for evaluation and formulation of management plan. (Orthopaedic Surgery)

Initial emergency room consultation for 10-year-old male in status epilepticus, recent closed head injury, information about medication not available. (Neurosurgery)

Initial emergency room consultation for a 23-year-old patient with severe abdominal pain, guarding, febrile, and unstable vital signs. (Obstetrics & Gynecology)

Office consultation for a 67-year-old female longstanding uncontrolled diabetic who presents with retinopathy, nephropathy, and a foot ulcer. (Endocrinology)

Office consultation for a 37-year-old male for initial evaluation and management of Cushing's disease. (Endocrinology)

Office consultation for a 60-year-old male who presents with thyrotoxicosis, exophthalmos, frequent premature ventricular contractions and congestive heart failure. (Endocrinology)

Initial office consultation for a 36-year-old patient, one year status post occupational herniated cervical disk treated by laminectomy, requiring management of multiple sites of intractable pain, depression, and narcotic dependence. (Pain Medicine)

Office consultation for a 58-year-old man with a history of MI and CHF who complains of the recent onset of rest angina and shortness of breath. The patient has a systolic blood pressure of 90mmHG and is in Class IV heart failure. (Cardiology)

Emergency room consultation for a 1-year-old with a three-day history of fever with increasing respiratory distress who is thought to have cardiac tamponade by the ER physician. (Cardiology)

Office consultation in the emergency room for a 25-year-old male with severe, acute, closed head injury. (Neurosurgery)

Office consultation for a 23-year-old female with Stage II A Hodgkins disease with positive supraclavicular and mediastinal nodes. (Radiation Oncology)

Office consultation for a 27-year-old juvenile diabetic patient with severe diabetic retinopathy, gastric atony, nephrotic syndrome and progressive renal failure, now with a serum creatinine of 2.7, and a blood pressure of 170/114. (Nephrology)

Office consultation for independent medical evaluation of a patient with a history of complicated low back and neck problems with previous multiple failed back surgeries. (Orthopaedic Surgery)

Office consultation for an adolescent referred by pediatrician for recent onset of violent and self-injurious behavior. (Psychiatry)

Office consultation for a 6-year-old male for evaluation of severe muscle and joint pain and a diffuse rash. Patient well until 4-6 weeks earlier, when he developed arthralgia, myalgias, and a fever of 102 for one week. (Rheumatology)

Initial Inpatient Consultations

New or Established Patient

99251 Initial hospital consultation for a 27-year-old female with fractured incisor post-intubation. (Oral & Maxillofacial Surgery)

Initial hospital consultation for an orthopaedic patient on IV antibiotics who has developed an apparent candida infection of the oral cavity. (Oral & Maxillofacial Surgery)

Initial inpatient consultation for a 30-year-old female complaining of vaginal itching, post orthopaedic surgery. (Obstetrics & Gynecology)

Initial inpatient consultation for a 36-year-old male on orthopaedic service with complaint of localized dental pain. (Oral & Maxillofacial Surgery)

99252 Initial hospital consultation for a 45-year-old male, previously abstinent alcoholic, who relapsed and was admitted for management of gastritis. The patient readily accepts the need for further treatment. (Addiction Medicine)

Initial hospital consultation for a 35-year-old dialysis patient with episodic oral ulcerations. (Oral & Maxillofacial Surgery)

Initial inpatient preoperative consultation for a 43-year-old woman with cholecystitis and well-controlled hypertension. (Cardiology)

Initial inpatient consultation for recommendation of antibiotic prophylaxis for a patient with a synthetic heart valve who will undergo urologic surgery. (Internal Medicine)

Initial inpatient consultation for possible drug induced skin eruption in 50-year-old male. (Dermatology)

Preoperative inpatient consultation for evaluation of hypertension in a 60-year-old male who will undergo a cholecystectomy. Patient had a normal annual check-up in your office four months ago. (Internal Medicine)

Initial inpatient consultation for 66-year-old patient with wrist and hand pain and finger numbness, secondary to carpal tunnel syndrome. (Orthopaedic Surgery/Plastic Surgery)

Initial inpatient consultation for a 66-year-old male smoker referred for pain management immediately status post-biliary tract surgery done via sub-costal incision. (Anesthesiology/Pain Medicine)

99253 Initial hospital consultation for a 50-year-old female with incapacitating knee pain due to generalized rheumatoid arthritis. (Orthopaedic Surgery)

Initial hospital consultation for a 60-year-old male with avascular necrosis of the left femoral heel with increasing pain. (Orthopaedic Surgery)

Initial hospital consultation for a 45-year-old female with compound mandibular fracture and concurrent head, abdominal and/or orthopaedic injuries. (Oral & Maxillofacial Surgery)

Initial hospital consultation for a 22-year-old female, paraplegic, to evaluate wrist and hand pain. (Orthopaedic Surgery)

Initial hospital consultation for a 40-year-old male with 10-day history of incapacitating unilateral sciatica, unable to walk now, not improved by bed rest. (Neurosurgery)

Initial hospital consultation, requested by pediatrician, for treatment recommendations for a patient admitted with persistent inability to walk following soft tissue injury to ankle. (Physiatry)

Initial hospital consultation for a 27-year-old previously healthy male who vomited during IV sedation and may have aspirated gastric contents. (Anesthesiology)

Initial hospital consultation for a 33-year-old female, post-abdominal surgery, who now has a fever. (Internal Medicine)

Initial inpatient consultation for a 57-year-old male, post lower endoscopy, for evaluation of abdominal pain and fever. (General Surgery)

Initial inpatient consultation for rehabilitation of a 73-year-old female one week after surgical management of a hip fracture. (Physical Medicine & Rehabilitation)

Initial inpatient consultation for diagnosis/management of fever following abdominal surgery. (Internal Medicine)

Initial inpatient consultation for a 35-year-old female with a fever and pulmonary infiltrate following cesarean section. (Pulmonary Medicine)

Initial inpatient consultation for a 42-year-old non-diabetic patient, post-op cholecystectomy, now with an acute urinary tract infection. (Nephrology)

Initial inpatient consultation for 53-year-old female with moderate uncomplicated pancreatitis. (Gastroenterology)

Initial inpatient consultation for 45-year-old patient with chronic neck pain with radicular pain of the left arm. (Orthopaedic Surgery)

Initial inpatient consultation for 8-year-old patient with new onset of seizures who has a normal examination and previous history. (Neurology)

99254 Initial hospital consultation for a 15-year-old patient with painless swelling of proximal humerus with lytic lesion by x-ray. (Orthopaedic Surgery)

Initial hospital consultation for evaluation of a 29-year-old female with a diffusely positive medical review of systems and history of multiple surgeries. (Psychiatry)

Initial hospital consultation for a 70-year-old diabetic female with gangrene of the foot. (Orthopaedic Surgery)

Initial inpatient consultation for a 47-year-old female with progressive pulmonary infiltrate, hypoxemia, and diminished urine output. (Anesthesiology)

Initial hospital consultation for a 13-month-old with spasmodic cough, respiratory distress, and fever. (Allergy & Immunology)

Initial hospital consultation for a patient with failed total hip replacement with loosening and pain upon walking. (Orthopaedic Surgery)

Initial hospital consultation for a 62-year-old female with metastatic breast cancer to the femoral neck and thoracic vertebra. (Orthopaedic Surgery)

Initial hospital consultation for a 39-year-old female with nephrolithiasis requiring extensive opioid analgesics, whose vital signs are now elevated. She initially denied any drug use, but today gives history of multiple substance abuse, including opioids and prior treatment for a personality disorder. (Psychiatry)

Initial hospital consultation for a 70-year-old female without previous psychiatric history, who is now experiencing nocturnal confusion and visual hallucinations following hip replacement surgery. (Psychiatry)

Initial inpatient consultation for evaluation of a 63-year-old in the ICU with diabetes and chronic renal failure who develops acute respiratory distress syndrome 36 hours after a mitral valve replacement. (Anesthesiology)

Initial inpatient consultation for a 66-year-old female with enlarged supraclavicular lymph nodes, found on biopsy to be malignant. (Hematology/Oncology)

Initial inpatient consultation for a 43-year-old female for evaluation of sudden painful visual loss, optic neuritis and episodic paresthesia. (Ophthalmology)

Initial inpatient consultation for evaluation of a 71-year-old male with hyponatremia (serum sodium 114) who was admitted to the hospital with pneumonia. (Nephrology)

Initial inpatient consultation for a 72-year-old male with emergency admission for possible bowel obstruction. (Internal Medicine/General Surgery)

Initial inpatient consultation for a 35-year-old female with fever, swollen joints, and rash of one-week duration. (Rheumatology)

99255 Initial inpatient consultation for a 76-year-old female with massive, life-threatening gastrointestinal hemorrhage and chest pain. (Gastroenterology)

Initial inpatient consultation for a 75-year-old female, admitted to intensive care with acute respiratory distress syndrome, who is hypersensitive, has a moderate metabolic acidosis, and a rising serum creatinine. (Nephrology)

Initial hospital consultation for patient with a history of complicated low back pain and neck problems with previous multiple failed back surgeries. (Orthopaedic Surgery/Neurosurgery)

Initial hospital consultation for a 66-year-old female, two days post-abdominal aneurysm repair, with oliguria and hypertension of one-day duration. (Nephrology/Internal Medicine)

Initial hospital consultation for a patient with shotgun wound to face with massive facial trauma and airway obstruction. (Oral & Maxillofacial Surgery)

Initial hospital consultation for patient with severe pancreatitis complicated by respiratory insufficiency, acute renal failure, and abscess formation. (General Surgery/Colon & Rectal Surgery)

Initial hospital consultation for a 35-year-old multiple-trauma male patient with complex pelvic fractures to evaluate and formulate management plan. (Orthopaedic Surgery)

Initial inpatient consultation for adolescent patient with fractured femur and pelvis who pulled out IVs and disconnected traction in attempt to elope from hospital. (Psychiatry)

Initial hospital consultation for a 16-year-old primigravida at 32 weeks gestation requested by a family practitioner for evaluation of severe hypertension, thrombocytopenia, and headache. (Obstetrics & Gynecology)

Initial hospital consultation for a 58-year-old insulin-dependent diabetic with multiple antibiotic allergies, now with multiple fascial plane abscesses and airway obstruction. (Oral & Maxillofacial Surgery)

Initial inpatient consultation for a 55-year-old male with known cirrhosis and ascites, now with jaundice, encephalopathy, and massive hematemesis. (Gastroenterology)

Initial hospital consultation for a 25-year-old male, seen in emergency room with severe, closed head injury. (Neurosurgery)

Initial hospital consultation for a 2-day-old male with single ventricle physiology and subaortic obstruction. Family counseling following evaluation for multiple, staged surgical procedures. (Thoracic Surgery)

Initial hospital consultation for a 45-year-old male admitted with subarachnoid hemorrhage and intracranial aneurysm on angiogram. (Neurosurgery)

Initial inpatient consultation for myxedematous patient who is hypoventilating and obtunded. (Endocrinology)

Initial hospital consultation for a 45-year-old patient with widely metastatic lung carcinoma, intractable back pain, and a history that includes substance dependence, NSAID allergy, and two prior laminectomies with fusion for low back pain. (Pain Medicine)

Initial hospital consultation for evaluation of treatment options in a 50-year-old patient with cirrhosis, known peptic ulcer disease, hypotension, encephalopathy, and massive acute upper gastrointestinal bleeding which cannot be localized by endoscopy. (Interventional Radiology)

Initial inpatient consultation in the ICU for a 70-year-old male who experienced a cardiac arrest during surgery and was resuscitated. (Cardiology)

Initial inpatient consultation for a patient with severe pancreatitis complicated by respiratory insufficiency, acute renal failure and abscess formation. (Gastroenterology)

Initial inpatient consultation for a 70-year-old cirrhotic male admitted with ascites, jaundice, encephalopathy, and massive hematemesis. (Gastroenterology)

Initial inpatient consultation in the ICU for a 51-year-old patient who is on a ventilator and has a fever two weeks after a renal transplantation. (Infectious Disease)

Initial inpatient consultation for evaluation and formulation of plan for management of multiple trauma patient with complex pelvic fracture, 35-year-old male. (General Surgery/Orthopaedic Surgery)

Initial inpatient consultation for a 50-year-old male with a history of previous myocardial infarction, now with acute pulmonary edema and hypotension. (Cardiology)

Initial inpatient consultation for 45-year-old male with recent, acute subarachnoid hemorrhage, hesitant speech, mildly confused, drowsy. High risk group for HIV+ status. (Neurosurgery)

Initial inpatient consultation for 36-year-old female referred by her internist to evaluate a patient being followed for abdominal pain and fever. The patient has developed diffuse abdominal pain, guarding, rigidity and increased fever. (Obstetrics & Gynecology)

Emergency Department Services

New or Established Patient

99281   Emergency department visit for a patient for removal of sutures from a well-healed, uncomplicated laceration. (Emergency Medicine)

Emergency department visit for a patient for tetanus toxoid immunization. (Emergency Medicine)

Emergency department visit for a patient with several uncomplicated insect bites. (Emergency Medicine)

99282   Emergency department visit for a 20-year-old student who presents with a painful sunburn with blister formation on the back. (Emergency Medicine)

Emergency department visit for a child presenting with impetigo localized to the face. (Emergency Medicine)

Emergency department visit for a patient with a minor traumatic injury of an extremity with localized pain, swelling, and bruising. (Emergency Medicine)

Emergency department visit for an otherwise healthy patient whose chief complaint is a red, swollen cystic lesion on his/her back. (Emergency Medicine)

Emergency department visit for a patient presenting with a rash on both legs after exposure to poison ivy. (Emergency Medicine)

Emergency department visit for a young adult patient with infected sclera and purulent discharge from both eyes without pain, visual disturbance or history of foreign body in either eye. (Emergency Medicine)

99283   Emergency department visit for a sexually active female complaining of vaginal discharge who is afebrile and denies experiencing abdominal or back pain. (Emergency Medicine)

Emergency department visit for a well-appearing 8-year-old who has a fever, diarrhea and abdominal cramps, is tolerating oral fluids and is not vomiting. (Emergency Medicine)

Emergency department visit for a patient with an inversion ankle injury, who is unable to bear weight on the injured foot and ankle. (Emergency Medicine)

Emergency department visit for a patient who has a complaint of acute pain associated with a suspected foreign body in the painful eye. (Emergency Medicine)

Emergency department visit for a healthy, young adult patient who sustained a blunt head injury with local swelling and bruising without subsequent confusion, loss of consciousness or memory deficit. (Emergency Medicine)

99284 Emergency department visit for a 4-year-old who fell off a bike sustaining a head injury with brief loss of consciousness. (Emergency Medicine)

Emergency department visit for an elderly female who has fallen and is now complaining of pain in her right hip and is unable to walk. (Emergency Medicine)

Emergency department visit for a patient with flank pain and hematuria. (Emergency Medicine)

Emergency department visit for a female presenting with lower abdominal pain and a vaginal discharge. (Emergency Medicine)

99285 Emergency department visit for a patient with a complicated overdose requiring aggressive management to prevent side effects from the ingested materials. (Emergency Medicine)

Emergency department visit for a patient with a new onset of rapid heart rate requiring IV drugs. (Emergency Medicine)

Emergency department visit for a patient exhibiting active, upper gastrointestinal bleeding. (Emergency Medicine)

Emergency department visit for a previously healthy young adult patient who is injured in an automobile accident and is brought to the emergency department immobilized and has symptoms compatible with intra-abdominal injuries or multiple extremity injuries. (Emergency Medicine)

Emergency department visit for a patient with an acute onset of chest pain compatible with symptoms of cardiac ischemia and/or pulmonary embolus. (Emergency Medicine)

Emergency department visit for a patient who presents with a sudden onset of "the worst headache of her life," and complains of a stiff neck, nausea, and inability to concentrate. (Emergency Medicine)

Emergency department visit for a patient with a new onset of a cerebral vascular accident. (Emergency Medicine)

Emergency department visit for acute febrile illness in an adult, associated with shortness of breath and an altered level of alertness. (Emergency Medicine)

Critical Care Services

99291 First hour of critical care of a 65-year-old man with septic shock following relief of ureteral obstruction caused by a stone.

First hour of critical care of a 15-year-old with acute respiratory failure from asthma.

First hour of critical care of a 45-year-old who sustained a liver laceration, cerebral hematoma, flailed chest, and pulmonary contusion after being struck by an automobile.

First hour of critical care of a 65-year-old woman who, following a hysterectomy, suffered a cardiac arrest associated with a pulmonary embolus.

First hour of critical care of a 6-month-old with hypovolemic shock secondary to diarrhea and dehydration.

First hour of critical care of a 3-year-old with respiratory failure secondary to pneumocystis carinii pneumonia.

Prolonged Services

Prolonged Physician Service With Direct (Face-to-Face) Patient Contact

Office or Other Outpatient

99354/ 99355 A 20-year-old female with history of asthma presents with acute bronchospasm and moderate respiratory distress. Initial evaluation shows respiratory rate 30, labored breathing and wheezing heard in all lung fields. Office treatment is initiated which includes intermittent bronchial dilation and subcutaneous epinephrine. Requires intermittent physician face-to-face time with patient over a period of 2-3 hours. (Family Medicine/Internal Medicine)

Inpatient

99356 A 34-year-old primigravida presents to hospital in early labor. Admission history and physical reveals severe preeclampsia. Physician supervises management of preeclampsia, IV magnesium initiation and maintenance, labor augmentation with pitocin, and close maternal-fetal monitoring. Physician face-to-face involvement includes 40 minutes of continuous bedside care until the patient is stable, then is intermittent over several hours until the delivery. (Family Medicine/Internal Medicine/Obstetrics & Gynecology)

Prolonged Physician Service Without Direct Patient (Face-to-Face) Contact

99358/ 99359 A 65-year-old new patient with multiple problems is seen and evaluated. After the visit, the physician requires extensive time to talk with the patient's daughter, to review complex, detailed medical records transferred from previous physicians and to complete a comprehensive treatment plan. This plan also requires the physician to personally initiate and coordinate the care plan with a local home health agency and a dietician. (Family Medicine/Internal Medicine)

Physician Standby Services

99360   A 24-year-old patient is admitted to OB unit attempting VBAC. Fetal monitoring shows increasing fetal distress. Patient's blood pressure is rising and labor progressing slowly. A primary care physician is requested by the OB/GYN to standby in the unit for possible cesarean delivery and neonatal resuscitation. (Family Medicine/Internal Medicine)

Care Plan Oversight Services

99375   First month of care plan oversight for terminal care of a 58-year-old woman with advanced intraabdominal ovarian cancer. Care plan includes home oxygen, diuretics IV for edema and ascites control and pain control management involving IV morphine infusion when progressive ileus occurred. Physician phone contacts with nurse, family, and MSW. Discussion with MSW concerning plans to withdraw supportive measures per patient wishes. Documentation includes review and modification of care plan and certifications from nursing, MSW, pharmacy, and DME. (Family Medicine/Internal Medicine)

Appendix D

Summary of CPT Add-on Codes

This listing is a summary of CPT add-on codes for *CPT 2006*. The codes listed below are identified in *CPT 2006* with a ✚ symbol.

01953	15421	33884	44955	63295	83901	96411
01968	15431	33924	47001	63308	87187	96415
01969	15787	33961	47550	64472	87904	96417
11001	16036	34808	48400	64476	88155	96423
11008	17003	34813	49568	64480	88185	96570
11101	17310	34826	49905	64484	88311	96571
11201	19001	35390	56606	64623	88312	97546
11732	19126	35400	57267	64627	88313	97811
11922	19291	35500	58110	64727	88314	97814
13102	19295	35572	58611	64778	90466	99100
13122	19297	35681	59525	64783	90468	99116
13133	22103	35682	60512	64787	90472	99135
13153	22116	35683	61316	64832	90474	99140
15001	22216	35685	61517	64837	90761	99145
15101	22226	35686	61609	64859	90766	99150
15111	22328	35697	61610	64872	90767	99290
15116	22522	35700	61611	64874	90768	99292
15121	22525	36218	61612	64876	90775	99354
15131	22534	36248	61641	64901	92547	99355
15136	22585	36476	61642	64902	92608	99356
15151	22614	36479	61795	66990	92627	99357
15152	22632	37185	61864	67225	92973	99358
15156	26125	37186	61868	67320	92974	99359
15157	26861	37206	62148	67331	92978	99602
15171	26863	37208	62160	67332	92979	0049T
15176	27358	37250	63035	67334	92981	0054T
15201	27692	37251	63043	67335	92984	0055T
15221	31620	38102	63044	67340	92996	0056T
15241	31632	38746	63048	69990	92998	0063T
15261	31633	38747	63057	74301	93320	0068T
15301	31637	43635	63066	75774	93321	0069T
15321	32501	44015	63076	75946	93325	0070T
15331	33141	44121	63078	75964	93571	0076T
15336	33225	44128	63082	75968	93572	0079T
15341	33508	44139	63086	75993	93609	0081T
15361	33530	44203	63088	75996	93613	0092T
15366	33572	44213	63091	75998	93621	0095T
15401	33768	44701	63103	76082	93622	0098T
				76083	93623	0117T
				76125	93662	
				76802	95873	
				76810	95874	
				76812	95920	
				76937	95962	
				78020	95967	
				78478	95973	
				78480	95975	
				78496	95979	

Appendix E

Summary of CPT Codes Exempt from Modifier 51

This listing is a summary of CPT codes that are exempt from the use of modifier 51 but have NOT been designated as CPT add-on procedures/services. The codes listed below are identified in *CPT 2006* with a ⊘ symbol.

17004	32020	90585	90712	93555
17304	33517	90586	90713	93556
17305	33518	90632	90714	93600
17306	33519	90633	90715	93602
17307	33521	90634	90716	93603
20660	33522	90636	90717	93610
20690	33523	90645	90718	93612
20692	35600	90646	90719	93615
20900	36620	90647	90720	93616
20902	36660	90648	90721	93618
20910	38792	90649	90723	93619
20912	44500	90655	90725	93620
20920	61107	90656	90727	93624
20922	61210	90657	90732	93631
20924	62284	90658	90733	93640
20926	90281	90660	90734	93641
20930	90283	90665	90735	93642
20931	90287	90669	90736	93650
20936	90288	90675	90740	93651
20937	90291	90676	90743	93652
20938	90296	90680	90744	93660
20974	90371	90690	90746	95900
20975	90375	90691	90747	95903
22840	90376	90692	90748	95904
22841	90378	90693	90749	99143
22842	90379	90698	93501	99144
22843	90384	90700	93503	99148
22844	90385	90701	93505	99149
22845	90386	90702	93508	
22846	90389	90703	93510	
22847	90393	90704	93511	
22848	90396	90705	93514	
22851	90399	90706	93524	
31500	90476	90707	93526	
32000	90477	90708	93527	
32002	90581	90710	93528	
			93529	
			93530	
			93531	
			93532	
			93533	
			93539	
			93540	
			93541	
			93542	
			93543	
			93544	
			93545	

Appendix F

Summary of CPT Codes Exempt from Modifier 63

The listing is a summary of CPT codes that are exempt from the use of modifier 63. The codes listed below are additionally identified in *CPT 2006* with the parenthetical instruction "(Do not report modifier 63 in conjunction with …)"

30540	39503	63704
30545	43313	63706
31520	43314	65820
33401	43520	
33403	43831	
33470	44055	
33472	44126	
33502	44127	
33503	44128	
33505	46070	
33506	46705	
33610	46715	
33611	46716	
33619	46730	
33647	46735	
33670	46740	
33690	46742	
33694	46744	
33730	47700	
33732	47701	
33735	49215	
33736	49491	
33750	49492	
33755	49495	
33762	49496	
33778	49600	
33786	49605	
33922	49606	
33960	49610	
33961	49611	
36415	53025	
36420	54000	
36450	54150	
36460	54160	
36510	63700	
36660	63702	

Appendix G

Summary of CPT Codes That Include Moderate (Conscious) Sedation

▶The following list of procedures includes conscious sedation as an inherent part of providing the procedure. These codes are identified in the CPT codebook with a ⊙ symbol.◀

▶Since these services include moderate sedation, it is not appropriate for the same physician to report both the service and the sedation codes 99143-99145. It is expected that if conscious sedation is provided to the patient as part of one of these services, it is provided by the same physician who is providing the service.◀

▶In the unusual event when a second physician other than the health care professional performing the diagnostic or therapeutic services provides moderate sedation in the facility setting (eg, hospital, outpatient hospital/ambulatory surgery center, skilled nursing facility) for the procedures listed in Appendix G, the second physician can report 99148–99150. However, for the circumstance in which these services are performed by the second physician in the nonfacility setting (eg, physician office, freestanding imaging center), codes 99148-99150 would not be reported. Moderate sedation does not include minimal sedation (anxiolysis), deep sedation, or monitored anesthesia care (00100-01999).◀

▶The inclusion of a procedure on this list does not prevent separate reporting of an associated anesthesia procedure/service (CPT codes 00100-01999) when performed by a physician other than the health care professional performing the diagnostic or therapeutic procedure. In such cases the person providing anesthesia services shall be present for the purpose of continuously monitoring the patient and shall not act as a surgical assistant. When clinical conditions of the patient require such anesthesia services, or in the circumstances when the patient does not require sedation, the operating physician is not required to report the procedure as a reduced service using modifier 52.◀

19298	32019	33218	35474	43234	44372
20982	32020	33220	35475	43235	44373
31615	32201	33222	35476	43236	44376
31620	33010	33223	36555	43237	44377
31622	33011	33233	36557	43238	44378
31623	33206	33234	36558	43239	44379
31624	33207	33235	36560	43240	44380
31625	33208	33240	36561	43241	44382
31628	33210	33241	36563	43242	44383
31629	33211	33244	36565	43243	44385
31635	33212	33249	36566	43244	44386
31645	33213	35470	36568	43245	44388
31646	33214	35471	36570	43246	44389
31656	33216	35472	36571	43247	44390
31725	33217	35473	36576	43248	44391
			36578	43249	44392
			36581	43250	44393
			36582	43251	44394
			36583	43255	44397
			36585	43256	44500
			36590	43257	44901
			36870	43258	45303
			37184	43259	45305
			37185	43260	45307
			37186	43261	45308
			37187	43262	45309
			37188	43263	45315
			37203	43264	45317
			37215	43265	45320
			37216	43267	45321
			43200	43268	45327
			43201	43269	45332
			43202	43271	45333
			43204	43272	45334
			43205	43453	45335
			43215	43456	45337
			43216	43458	45338
			43217	44360	45339
			43219	44361	45340
			43220	44363	45341
			43226	44364	45342
			43227	44365	45345
			43228	44366	45355
			43231	44369	45378
			43232	44370	45379

45380	93314	93652
45381	93315	0008T
45382	93316	
45383	93317	
45384	93318	
45385	93501	
45386	93505	
45387	93508	
45391	93510	
45392	93511	
47011	93514	
48511	93524	
49021	93526	
49041	93527	
49061	93528	
50021	93529	
50382	93530	
50384	93539	
50387	93540	
50592	93541	
58823	93542	
66720	93543	
69300	93544	
77600	93545	
77605	93555	
77610	93556	
77615	93561	
92953	93562	
92960	93571	
92961	93572	
92973	93609	
92974	93613	
92975	93615	
92978	93616	
92979	93618	
92980	93619	
92981	93620	
92982	93621	
92984	93622	
92986	93624	
92987	93640	
92995	93641	
92996	93642	
93312	93650	
93313	93651	

Appendix H

Alphabetic Index of Performance Measures by Clinical Condition or Topic

Note: Prior to coding, the user must review the complete description of the code in the Category II section of the CPT codebook and the complete description of its associated measure by accessing the measure developer's Web site provided in the footnoted reference.

Performance Measure Exclusion Modifiers	**-1P Performance Measure Exclusion Modifier due to Medical Reasons** Includes, for example: - patient allergic history, - potential adverse drug interaction, - acquired or congenital absence of organ/limb, - other documented clinical contraindication **-2P Performance Measure Exclusion Modifier due to Patient Choice** Includes, for example: - patient refusal, - economic, - social, - religious	Performance measurement exclusion modifiers may be used to indicate that a service specified by a performance measure was considered but, due to either medical or patient circumstance(s) documented in the medical record, the service was not provided. These modifiers serve as denominator exclusions from the performance measure.

Brief Description of Performance Measure & Source	CPT Code(s)	Brief Code Descriptor
Asthma		
Asthma Assessment[1]—Percentage of patients aged 5-40 years with asthma who were evaluated during at least one office visit during the reporting year for the frequency (numeric) of daytime and nocturnal asthma symptoms (To be counted in calculations of this measure, symptom frequency must be numerically quantified. Measure may also be met by physician documentation or patient completion of an asthma assessment tool/survey/questionnaire. Assessment tool may include the QualityMetric Asthma Control Test™, National Asthma Education & Prevention Program (NAEPP) Asthma Symptoms and Peak Flow Diary). **Numerator:** Patients in the denominator who were evaluated during at least one office visit during the reporting year for the frequency (numeric) of daytime and nocturnal asthma symptoms **Denominator:** All patients aged 5-40 years with asthma **Inclusion(s):** None **Exclusion(s):** None	1005F	Asthma symptoms evaluated
Asthma Pharmacologic Therapy[1]—Percentage of patients aged 5-40 years with mild, moderate, or severe *persistent* asthma who were prescribed either the preferred long-term control medication (inhaled corticosteroids)* or an acceptable alternative treatment **Numerator:** Patients in the denominator who were prescribed either the preferred[a] long-term control medication (inhaled corticosteroids)* or an acceptable alternative treatment[b] (cromolyn sodium, leukotriene modifier, nedocromil, OR sustained release theophylline) **Denominator:** All patients aged 5-40 years with mild, moderate, or severe persistent asthma	4015F	Persistent asthma, long-term control medication prescribed

(continued)

[1]Physician Consortium for Performance Improvement, www.ama-assn.org/go/quality
[2]National Committee on Quality Assurance (NCQA), Health Employer Data Information Set (HEDIS®), www.ncqa.org
[3]Joint Commission on Accreditation of Healthcare Organizations (JCAHO), ORYX Initiative Performance Measures, www.jcaho.org/pms

Brief Description of Performance Measure & Source	CPT Code(s)	Brief Code Descriptor
Asthma, cont'd		
Inclusion(s): None **Exclusion(s):** Documentation of patient reasons (eg, economic, social, religious) for not prescribing either the preferred long-term control medication or an acceptable alternative treatment (There are no medical exclusion criteria) [a, b]Refer to complete description of measure on the Consortium's Internet site for list of medications, treatment recommendations, dosages *In patients with moderate or severe persistent asthma, strong evidence indicates that use of inhaled long-term acting beta$_2$-agonists (LABA) in combination with ICS leads to improvements in lung function and symptoms and reduced supplemental bronchodilator use. LABA is not recommended for use as monotherapy		
Congestive Heart Failure (CHF)		
Composite Measure: Heart Failure Assessment[1]—See individual measures listed below for: level of activity assessed (1003F), clinical symptoms of volume overload (excess) assessed (1004F), blood pressure measured (2000F), weight recorded (2001F), clinical signs of volume overload (excess) assessed (2002F), and auscultation of the heart performed (2003F)	**0001F**	Heart failure assessed (includes assessments 1003F, 1004F, 2000F, 2001F, 2002F, and 2003F)
Assessment of Activity Level[1]—Percentage of heart failure patient visits with assessment of activity level **Numerator:** Patient visits in the denominator with assessment of current level of activity OR documentation of standardized scale or completion of assessment tool (includes use of New York Heart Association Functional Classification of Congestive Heart Failure; Kansas City Cardiomyopathy Questionnaire; Minnesota™ Living with Heart Failure Questionnaire; or Guyatt's Chronic Heart Failure Questionnaire) **Denominator:** All patient visits for patients aged ≥18 years with heart failure **Inclusion(s):** None **Exclusion(s):** None	**1003F**	Level of activity assessed
Assessment of Clinical Symptoms of Volume Overload (Excess)[1]—Percentage of heart failure patient visits with assessment of clinical symptoms of volume overload (excess) **Numerator:** Patient visits in the denominator with assessment of clinical symptoms of volume overload (excess) OR documentation of standardized scale or completion of assessment tool (includes New York Heart Association Functional Classification of Congestive Heart Failure; Kansas City Cardiomyopathy Questionnaire; Minnesota™ Living with Heart Failure Questionnaire; or Guyatt's Chronic Heart Failure Questionnaire) **Denominator:** All patient visits for patients aged ≥ 18 years with heart failure **Inclusion(s):** None **Exclusion(s):** None	**1004F**	Clinical symptoms of volume overload (excess) assessed
Blood Pressure Measurement[1]—Percentage of patients in the denominator who had a blood pressure measurement during the last office visit **Numerator:** Patients who had a blood pressure measurement during the last office visit **Denominator:** All patients with CHF **Inclusion(s):** None **Exclusion(s):** None	**2000F**	Blood pressure measured
Weight Measurement[1]—Percentage of heart failure patient visits with weight measurement **Numerator:** Patient visits in the denominator with weight measurement recorded **Denominator:** All patient visits for patients aged ≥ 18 years with heart failure **Inclusion(s):** None **Exclusion(s):** None	**2001F**	Weight recorded

[1]Physician Consortium for Performance Improvement, www.ama-assn.org/go/quality
[2]National Committee on Quality Assurance (NCQA), Health Employer Data Information Set (HEDIS®), www.ncqa.org
[3]Joint Commission on Accreditation of Healthcare Organizations (JCAHO), ORYX Initiative Performance Measures, www.jcaho.org/pms

Brief Description of Performance Measure & Source	CPT Code(s)	Brief Code Descriptor
Congestive Heart Failure (CHF), cont'd		
Assessment of Clinical Signs of Volume Overload (Excess)[1]—Percentage of patient visits with assessment of clinical signs of volume overload (excess) **Numerator:** Patient visits in the denominator with assessment of clinical signs of volume overload (excess) **Denominator:** All patient visits for patients aged ≥ 18 years with heart failure **Inclusions(s):** None **Exclusion(s):** None	2002F	Clinical signs of volume overload (excess) assessed
Examination of the Heart[1]—Percentage of patient visits with examination of the heart **Numerator:** Patient visits in the denominator with examination of the heart **Denominator:** All patient visits for patients aged ≥ 18 years with heart failure **Inclusion(s):** None **Exclusion(s):** None	2003F	Auscultation of the heart performed
Patient Education[1]—Percentage of heart failure patients who were provided with patient education on disease management and health behavior changes during one or more visit(s) within a six-month period **Numerator:** Patients in the denominator who were provided with written and/or verbal education at one or more visit(s) during a six-month care period under evaluation Patient education (includes one or more of the following: weight monitoring; diet (sodium restriction); symptom management; physical activity; smoking cessation; medication instruction; minimizing or avoiding use of NSAIDs; follow-up plans for next appointment or visiting nurse; referral for specific educational or management programs; or prognosis/end-of-life issues) **Denominator:** All patients aged ≥ 18 years with heart failure and with one or more visit(s) during a six-month period **Inclusion(s)(Denominator):** Patients with one or more visit(s) during a six-month period **Exclusion(s):** None	4003F	Patient education, written/oral, appropriate for patients with heart failure performed
Beta-Blocker Therapy[1]—Percentage of heart failure patients who also have LVSD who were prescribed beta-blocker therapy **Numerator:** Patients in the denominator who were prescribed beta-blocker therapy **Denominator:** All heart failure patients aged ≥ 18 years with left ventricular ejection fraction (LVEF) ≤ 40% or with moderately or severely depressed left ventricular systolic function **Inclusion(s):** None **Exclusion(s):** Documentation that a beta-blocker was not indicated; documentation of medical or patient reason(s) for not prescribing beta-blocker (eg, bradycardia < 50 bpm without beta-blocker therapy, history of Class IV heart failure, history of second- or third-degree AV block without permanent pacemaker)	4006F	Beta-blocker therapy prescribed
Heart Failure Angiotensin Converting Enzyme (ACE) Inhibitor for left ventricular systolic dysfunction (LVSD)[1]—Percentage of heart failure patients who also have LVSD and who were prescribed ACE inhibitor therapy **Numerator:** Heart failure patients in the denominator aged ≥ 18 years who are prescribed an ACE inhibitor at hospital discharge **Denominator:** All heart failure patients with aged ≥ 18 years with left ventricular ejection fraction (LVEF) < 40% or with moderately or severely depressed left ventricular systolic function **Inclusion(s):** None **Exclusion(s) (Denominator):** Documentation that ACE inhibitor was not indicated (eg, patients on angiotensin receptor blockers (ARB)); documentation of medical reason(s) for not prescribing ACE inhibitor therapy (eg, allergy, angioedema due to ACE inhibitor, anuric renal failure due to ACE inhibitor, pregnancy, moderate or severe aortic stenosis); documentation of patient reasons for not prescribing ACE inhibitor therapy (economic, social, or religious)	4009F	Angiotensin Converting Enzyme (ACE) inhibitor therapy prescribed

[1]Physician Consortium for Performance Improvement, www.ama-assn.org/go/quality
[2]National Committee on Quality Assurance (NCQA), Health Employer Data Information Set (HEDIS®), www.ncqa.org
[3]Joint Commission on Accreditation of Healthcare Organizations (JCAHO), ORYX Initiative Performance Measures, www.jcaho.org/pms

Brief Description of Performance Measure & Source	CPT Code(s)	Brief Code Descriptor
Congestive Heart Failure (CHF), cont'd		
Warfarin Therapy for Patients with Atrial Fibrillation[1]—Percentage of heart failure patients who also have paroxysmal or chronic atrial fibrillation who were prescribed warfarin therapy **Numerator:** Patients in the denominator who were prescribed warfarin therapy **Denominator:** All heart failure patients aged ≥ 18 years with paroxysmal or chronic atrial fibrillation **Inclusion(s):** None **Exclusion(s):** Documentation that warfarin was not indicated; documentation of medical reasons(s) for not prescribing warfarin (eg, allergy to warfarin, risk of bleeding or bleeding disorder, compliance, etc); documentation of patient reason(s) (eg, economic, social, and/or religious) for not prescribing warfarin	4012F	Warfarin therapy prescribed
Heart Failure Discharge Instructions[3]—Percentage of hospitalized heart failure patients in the denominator who received written discharge instructions **Numerator:** Heart failure patients in the denominator with documentation that they or their caregivers were given written discharge instructions or other educational material addressing all of the following: activity level, diet, discharge medications, follow-up appointment, weight monitoring, what to do if symptoms worsen **Denominator:** Heart failure patients discharged home **Inclusion(s):** none **Exclusion(s):** Patients aged < 18 years	4014F	Written discharge instructions provided to heart failure patients discharged home
Coronary Artery Disease (CAD)		
Smoking Cessation Evaluation[1]—Percentage of patients evaluated for smoking or other tobacco use **Numerator:** Patients evaluated for smoking or other tobacco use **Denominator:** All patients **Inclusion(s):** None **Exclusion(s):** None	1000F 1001F	Tobacco use, smoking, assessed Tobacco use, non-smoking, assessed
Symptom & Activity Assessment[1]—Percentage of CAD patients who were evaluated for both level of activity and anginal symptoms during one or more office visits **Numerator:** Patients who were evaluated for both level of activity and anginal symptoms during one or more office visits **Denominator:** All patients with CAD **Inclusion(s):** None **Exclusion(s):** None	1002F	Anginal symptoms and level of activity assessed
Blood Pressure Measurement[1]—Percentage of patients who had a blood pressure measurement during the last office visit **Numerator:** Patients who had a blood pressure measurement during the last office visit **Denominator:** All patients with CAD **Inclusion(s):** None **Exclusion(s):** None	2000F	Blood pressure measured
Smoking Cessation Intervention[1]—Percentage of patients identified as cigarette smokers who received smoking cessation intervention **Numerator:** Patients identified as smokers or other tobacco users who were offered an intervention for tobacco use cessation, either counseling or pharmacologic therapy during one or more office visits. **Denominator:** All patients identified as smokers or other tobacco users **Inclusion(s):** None **Exclusion(s):** None	4000F 4001F	Tobacco use cessation counseling Tobacco use cessation intervention, pharmacologic therapy

[1]Physician Consortium for Performance Improvement, www.ama-assn.org/go/quality
[2]National Committee on Quality Assurance (NCQA), Health Employer Data Information Set (HEDIS®), www.ncqa.org
[3]Joint Commission on Accreditation of Healthcare Organizations (JCAHO), ORYX Initiative Performance Measures, www.jcaho.org/pms

Brief Description of Performance Measure & Source	CPT Code(s)	Brief Code Descriptor
Coronary Artery Disease (CAD), cont'd		
Drug Therapy for Lowering Cholesterol[1]—Percentage of patients who were prescribed a statin (based on current ACC/AHA guidelines) **Numerator:** Patients who were prescribed a statin **Denominator:** All patients with CAD **Inclusion(s):** None **Exclusion(s):** Documentation that a statin was not indicated; documentation of medical or patient reason(s) for not prescribing a statin	4002F	Statin therapy prescribed
Beta-Blocker Therapy- Prior Myocardial Infarction (MI)[1]—Percentage of CAD patients who also have prior MI who were prescribed beta-blocker therapy **Numerator:** Patients who were prescribed beta-blocker therapy **Denominator:** All patients with CAD **Inclusion(s):** Patients with prior MI **Exclusion(s):** Documentation that a beta-blocker was not indicated; documentation of medical or patient reason(s) for not prescribing a beta-blocker	4003F	Beta-blocker therapy prescribed
Angiotensin Converting Enzyme (ACE) Inhibitor Therapy[1]—Percentage of CAD patients who also have diabetes and/or left ventricular systolic dysfunction (LVSD) who were prescribed ACE inhibitor therapy **Numerator:** Patients who were prescribed ACE inhibitor therapy **Denominator:** All patients with CAD who also have diabetes and/or LVSD **Inclusion(s):** Patients with CAD who also have diabetes and/or LVSD, left ventricular ejection fraction (LVEF) < 40% or moderately or severely depressed left ventricular systolic function) **Exclusion(s):** Documentation that ACE inhibitor was not indicated (eg, patients on angiotensin receptor blockers; documentation of medical or patient reason(s) for not prescribing ACE inhibitor	4004F	Angiotensin Converting Enzyme (ACE) inhibitor prescribed
Antiplatelet Therapy[1]—Percentage of patients who were prescribed antiplatelet therapy **Numerator:** Patients who were prescribed antiplatelet therapy **Denominator:** All patients with CAD **Inclusion(s):** None **Exclusion(s):** Documentation that antiplatelet therapy was not indicated; documentation of medical or patient reason(s) for not prescribing a beta-blocker	5005F	Oral antiplatelet therapy prescribed
Hypertension (HTN)		
Blood Pressure Measurement[1]—Percentage of patient visits with blood pressure recorded for patients aged ≥ 18 years **Numerator:** Patient visits in the denominator with blood pressure measurement recorded **Denominator:** All patient visits for patients aged ≥ 18 years with hypertension **Inclusion(s):** None **Exclusion(s):** None	2000F	Blood pressure measured
Controlling High Blood Pressure[2]—Percentage of patients whose blood pressure is adequately controlled (BP ≤ 140/90) during the measurement year **Numerator:** Patients in the denominator whose blood pressure is adequately controlled (BP ≤ 140/90) during the measurement year **Denominator:** Patients aged 46 to 85 years with a diagnosis of hypertension and medical record review to confirm diagnosis and continuously enrolled for the measurement year **Inclusion(s):** None **Exclusion(s):** Exclude from eligible population all members diagnosed with end-stage renal disease anytime on or prior to December 31 of the measurement year	3000F 3002F	Blood pressure ≤ 140/90 mm Hg Blood pressure > 140/90 mm Hg

[1]Physician Consortium for Performance Improvement, www.ama-assn.org/go/quality
[2]National Committee on Quality Assurance (NCQA), Health Employer Data Information Set (HEDIS®), www.ncqa.org
[3]Joint Commission on Accreditation of Healthcare Organizations (JCAHO), ORYX Initiative Performance Measures, www.jcaho.org/pms

Brief Description of Performance Measure & Source	CPT Code(s)	Brief Code Descriptor
Osteoarthritis (Adult)		
Composite Measure: Osteoarthritis Assessment—See individual measures listed below for: Osteoarthritis symptoms and functional status assessed (1006F), use of anti-inflammatory or over-the-counter (OTC) analgesic medications assessed (1007F), initial examination of the involved joint(s) (includes visual inspection, palpation, range of motion) (2004F)	0005F	Osteoarthritis assessed includes assessments 1006F, 1007F, 2004F
Symptom and Functional Assessment[1]—Percentage of osteoarthritis patient visits with assessment for current level of satisfaction with symptoms and functional status **Numerator:** Patient visits in the denominator with assessment for current level of satisfaction with symptoms and functional status **Denominator:** All patient visits for patients aged ≥ 21 years with osteoarthritis of the knee **Inclusion(s):** None **Exclusion(s):** None **Note:** Use when osteoarthritis is addressed during the patient encounter	1006F	Osteoarthritis symptoms and functional status assessed
Assessment for Use of Anti-inflammatory or Analgesic OTC medications[1] Percentage of osteoarthritis patient visits with assessment for use of anti-inflammatory or analgesic over-the-counter (OTC) medications **Numerator:** Patient visits in the denominator with assessment for use of anti-inflammatory or analgesic OTC medications **Denominator:** All patient visits for patients aged ≥ 21 years with osteoarthritis of the knee **Inclusion(s):** None **Exclusion(s):** None **Note:** Use when osteoarthritis is addressed during the patient encounter	1007F	Use of anti-inflammatory or analgesic over-the-counter (OTC) medications assessed
Non-steroidal Anti-inflammatory Drug (NSAID) Risk Assessment[1] Percentage of patients on prescribed or OTC NSAIDs who were assessed for gastrointestinal and renal risk factors **Numerator:** Patients who were assessed for all of the following risk factors: • GI bleed • History of peptic ulcer disease • Concomitant use of glucocorticoids or anticoagulants • Smoking • Significant alcohol use • Age > 65 years • Renal disease (Creatinine (Cr) > 2.0 mg/dl) • Hypertension • Heart failure • Concomitant use of diuretic or angiotensin converting enzyme (ACE) inhibitor **Denominator:** All patients aged ≥ 21 years with osteoarthritis **Inclusion(s):** None **Exclusion(s):** None	1008F	Gastrointestinal and renal risk factors assessed
Physical Examination of the Knee[1] Percentage of osteoarthritis patients for whom a physical examination of the knee was performed during the initial visit **Numerator:** Patients in the denominator for whom a physical examination of the knee was performed during the initial visit <div align="right">(continued)</div>	2004F	Initial examination of the involved joint(s)

[1]Physician Consortium for Performance Improvement, www.ama-assn.org/go/quality
[2]National Committee on Quality Assurance (NCQA), Health Employer Data Information Set (HEDIS®), www.ncqa.org
[3]Joint Commission on Accreditation of Healthcare Organizations (JCAHO), ORYX Initiative Performance Measures, www.jcaho.org/pms

Brief Description of Performance Measure & Source	CPT Code(s)	Brief Code Descriptor
Osteoarthritis (Adult), cont'd		
Denominator: All patients aged ≥ 21 years with osteoarthritis of the knee **Inclusion(s):** None **Exclusion(s):** None **Note:** Use only for initial osteoarthritis visit or for visits for new joint involvement		
Anti-inflammatory/Analgesic Therapy[1] Percentage of patient visits during which an anti-inflammatory agent or analgesic was considered **Numerator:** Patient visits in the denominator during which an anti-inflammatory agent or analgesic was considered **Denominator:** All patient visits for patients aged ≥ 21 years with osteoarthritis of the knee **Inclusion(s) (Numerator):** Documentation that an anti-inflammatory agent or analgesic was not indicated; documentation of medical reason(s) for not prescribing an anti-inflammatory agent or analgesic (eg, allergy, drug interaction, contraindication); documentation of patient reasons(s) for not prescribing an anti-inflammatory agent or analgesic (eg, economic, social, religious); documentation that an anti-inflammatory agent or analgesic was prescribed **Exclusion(s):** None	4016F	Anti-inflammatory/analgesic agent prescribed
Gastrointestinal Prophylaxis[1] Percentage of patients visits during which GI prophylaxis was considered **Numerator:** Patient visits in the denominator during which GI prophylaxis was considered **Denominator:** All patient visits for patients aged ≥ 21 years with osteoarthritis on prescribed or OTC NSAIDs **Inclusion(s) (Numerator):** Documentation that GI prophylaxis was not indicated (eg, patients on COX-2 inhibitors); documentation of medical reason(s) for not prescribing GI prophylaxis (eg, allergy, drug interaction, contraindication); documentation of patient reason(s) for not prescribing GI prophylaxis (eg, economic, social, or religious); documentation that GI prophylaxis was prescribed **Exclusion(s):** None	4017F	Gastrointestinal prophylaxis for NSAID use prescribed
Therapeutic Exercise for the Knee[1] Percentage of patient visits during which therapeutic exercise for the involved joint(s) (therapeutic exercised instructed or physical therapy prescribed) was considered **Numerator:** Patient visits during which therapeutic exercise for the knee was considered **Denominator:** All patient visits for patients aged ≥ 21 years with OA of the knee **Inclusion(s) (Numerator):** Documentation that therapeutic exercise was not indicated; documentation of medical reason(s) for not instructing therapeutic exercise for the knee or prescribing physical therapy for the knee; documentation of patient reason(s) for not instructing therapeutic exercise for the knee or prescribing physical therapy for the knee (eg, economic, social, religious); documentation that therapeutic exercise for the knee was instructed; documentation that physical therapy for the knee was prescribed **Exclusion(s):** None	4018F	Therapeutic exercise for the involved joint(s) instructed or physical therapy prescribed

[1]Physician Consortium for Performance Improvement, www.ama-assn.org/go/quality
[2]National Committee on Quality Assurance (NCQA), Health Employer Data Information Set (HEDIS®), www.ncqa.org
[3]Joint Commission on Accreditation of Healthcare Organizations (JCAHO), ORYX Initiative Performance Measures, www.jcaho.org/pms

Brief Description of Performance Measure & Source	CPT Code(s)	Brief Code Descriptor
Prenatal-Postpartum Care		
Timeliness of Prenatal Care[2]—Percentage of patients in the denominator who received prenatal care **Numerator:** Number of women in the denominator who received a prenatal care visit as a member of the managed care organization (MCO) in the first trimester or within 42 days of enrollment in the MCO **Denominator:** Women who had live births between November 6th of the year prior to the measurement year and November 5th of the measurement year, who were continuously enrolled at least 43 days prior to delivery through 56 days after delivery **Inclusion(s):** None **Exclusion(s):** None	0500F	Initial prenatal care visit
Prenatal Flow Sheet[1]—Percentage of patients in the denominator with a prenatal flow sheet in use by the first physician visit **Numerator:** Percentage of patients in the denominator with a flow sheet in use by the date of the first physician visit, which contains at a minimum: blood pressure, weight, urine protein, uterine size, fetal heart tones, and estimated date of delivery **Denominator:** Pregnant women seen for prenatal care **Inclusion(s):** None **Exclusion(s):** Patients seen for consultation only, not for continuing care	0501F	Prenatal flow sheet documented
Frequency of Ongoing Prenatal Care[2]—Percentage of patients in the denominator with expected number of prenatal visits **Numerator:** Number of women in the denominator who had an unduplicated count of < 21%, 21%-40%, 41%-60%, 61%-80%, or ≥ 81% of the expected number of prenatal care visits, adjusted for the month of pregnancy at time of enrollment and gestational age **Denominator:** Women who had live births during the measurement year **Inclusion(s):** None **Exclusion(s):** MCOs must exclude members for whom a prenatal visit is not indicated	0502F	Subsequent prenatal care visit
Postpartum Care[2]—Percentage of patients in the denominator who had a postpartum visit between 21 and 56 days after delivery **Numerator:** Number of women in the denominator who had a postpartum visit on or between 21 days and 56 days after delivery **Denominator:** Women who had live births between November 6th of the year prior to the measurement year and November 5th of the measurement year, who were continuously enrolled at least 43 days prior to delivery through 56 days after delivery **Inclusion(s):** None **Exclusion(s):** None	0503F	Postpartum care visit

[1]Physician Consortium for Performance Improvement, www.ama-assn.org/go/quality
[2]National Committee on Quality Assurance (NCQA), Health Employer Data Information Set (HEDIS®), www.ncqa.org
[3]Joint Commission on Accreditation of Healthcare Organizations (JCAHO), ORYX Initiative Performance Measures, www.jcaho.org/pms

Appendix I

Genetic Testing Code Modifiers

This listing of modifiers is intended for reporting with molecular laboratory procedures related to genetic testing. Genetic testing modifiers should be used in conjunction with CPT and HCPCS codes to provide diagnostic granularity of service to enable providers to submit complete and precise genetic testing information without altering test descriptors. These modifiers are categorized by mutation. The first (numeric) digit indicates the disease category and the second (alpha) digit denotes gene type. Introductory guidelines in the molecular diagnostic and molecular cytogenetic code sections of CPT provide further guidance in interpretation and application of genetic testing modifiers.

Neoplasia (solid tumor, excluding sarcoma and lymphoma)

0A	BRCA1 (Hereditary breast/Ovarian cancer)
0B	BRCA2 (Hereditary breast cancer)
0C	Neurofibromin (Neurofibromatosis, type 1)
0D	Merlin (Neurofibromatosis, type 2)
0E	c-RET (Multiple endocrine neoplasia, types 2A/B, familial medullary thyroid carcinoma)
0F	VHL (Von Hippel Lindau disease, renal carcinoma)
0G	SDHD (Hereditary paraganglioma)
0H	SDHB (Hereditary paraganglioma)
0I	ERRB2, commonly called Her-2/neu
0J	MLH1 (HNPCC, mismatch repair genes)
0K	MSH2, MSH6, or PMS2 (HNPCC, mismatch repair genes)
0L	APC (Hereditary polyposis coli)
0M	Rb (Retinoblastoma)
0N	TP53, commonly called p53
0O	PTEN (Cowden's syndrome)
0P	KIT, also called CD117 (gastrointestinal stromal tumor)
0Z	Solid tumor gene, not otherwise specified

Neoplasia (sarcoma)

1A	WT1 or WT2 (Wilm's tumor)
1B	PAX3, PAX7, or FOXO1A (Alveolar rhabdomyosarcoma)
1C	FLI1, ERG, ETV1, or EWSR1 (Ewing's sarcoma, desmoplastic round cell)
1D	DDIT3 or FUS (Myxoid liposarcoma)
1E	NR4A3, RBF56, or TCF12 (Myxoid chondrosarcoma)
1F	SSX1, SSX2, or SYT (Synovial sarcoma)
1G	MYCN (Neuroblastoma)
1H	COL1A1 or PDGFB (Dermatofibrosarcoma protuberans)
1I	TFE3 or ASPSCR1 (Alveolar soft parts sarcoma)
1J	JAZF1 or JJAZ1 (Endometrial stromal sarcoma)
1Z	Sarcoma gene, not otherwise specified

Neoplasia (lymphoid/hematopoietic)

2A	RUNX1 or CBFA2T1, commonly called AML1 or ETO, genes associated with t(8;21) AML1—also ETO (Acute myelogenous leukemia)
2B	BCR or ABL1, genes associated with t(9;22) (Chronic myelogenous or acute leukemia) BCR—also ABL (Chronic myeloid, acute lymphoid leukemia)
2C	PBX1 or TCF3, genes associated with t(1;19) (Acute lymphoblastic leukemia) CGF1
2D	CBFB or MYH11, genes associated with inv 16 (Acute myelogenous leukemia) CBF beta (leukemia)
2E	MLL (acute leukemia)
2F	PML or RARA, genes associated with t(15;17) (Acute promyelocytic leukemia) PML/RAR alpha (Promyelocytic leukemia)
2G	ETV6, commonly called TEL, gene associated with t(12;21) (acute leukemia) TEL (Leukemia)
2H	BCL2 (B cell lymphoma, follicle center cell origin) bcl-2 (Lymphoma)
2I	CCND1, commonly called BCL1, cyclin D1 (Mantle cell lymphoma, myeloma) bcl-1 (Lymphoma)
2J	MYC (Burkitt lymphoma) c-myc (Lymphoma)
2K	IgH (Lymphoma/leukemia)
2L	IGK (Lymphoma/leukemia)
2M	TRB, T cell receptor beta (Lymphoma/leukemia)
2N	TRG, T cell receptor gamma (Lymphoma/leukemia)

2O   SIL or TAL1 (T cell leukemia)

2T   BCL6 (B cell lymphoma)

2Q   API1 or MALT1 (MALT lymphoma)

2R   NPM or ALK, genes associated with t(2;5) (Anaplastic large cell lymphoma)

2S   FLT3 (Acute myelogenous leukemia)

2Z   Lymphoid/hematopoietic neoplasia, not otherwise specified

Non-neoplastic hematology/coagulation

3A   F5, commonly called Factor V (Leiden, others) (Hypercoagulable state)

3B   FACC (Fanconi anemia)

3C   FACD (Fanconi anemia)

3D   HBB, beta globin (Thalassemia, Sickle cell anemia, other hemoglobinopathies)

3E   HBA, commonly called alpha globin (Thalassemia)

3F   MTHFR (Elevated homocystinemia)

3G   F2, commonly called prothrombin (20210, others) (Hypercoagulable state) Prothrombin (Factor II, 20210A) (Hypercoagulable state)

3H   F8, commonly called Factor VIII (Hemophilia A/VWF)

3I   F9, commonly called Factor IX (Hemophilia B)

3K   F13, commonly called Factor XIII (bleeding or hypercoagulable state) Beta globin

3Z   Non-neoplastic hematology/coagulation, not otherwise specified

Histocompatibility/blood typing/ identity/microsatellite

4A   HLA-A

4B   HLA-B

4C   HLA-C

4D   HLA-D

4E   HLA-DR

4F   HLA-DQ

4G   HLA-DP

4H   Kell

4I   Fingerprint for engraftment (post-allogeneic progenitor cell transplant)

4J   Fingerprint for donor allelotype (allogeneic transplant)

4K   Fingerprint for recipient allelotype (allogeneic transplant)

4L   Fingerprint for leukocyte chimerism (allogeneic solid organ transplant)

4M   Fingerprint for maternal versus fetal origin

4N   Microsatellite instability

4O   Microsatellite loss (loss of heterozygosity)

4Z   Histocompatiblity/blood typing, not otherwise specified

Neurologic, non-neoplastic

5A   ASPA, commonly called Aspartoacylase A (Canavan disease)

5B   FMR-1 (Fragile X, FRAXA, syndrome)

5C   FRDA, commonly called Frataxin (Freidreich ataxia)

5D   HD, commonly called Huntington (Huntington's disease)

5E   GABRA5, NIPA1, UBE3A, or ANCR GABRA (Prader Willi-Angelman syndrome)

5F   GJB2, commonly called Connexin-26 (Hereditary hearing loss) Connexin-32 (GJB2) (Hereditary deafness)

5G   GJB1, commonly called Connexin-32 (X-linked Charcot-Marie-Tooth disease)

5H   SNRPN (Prader Willi-Angelman syndrome)

5I   SCA1, commonly called Ataxin-1 (Spinocerebellar ataxia, type 1)

5J   SCA2, commonly called Ataxin-2 (Spinocerebellar ataxia, type 2)

5K   MJD, commonly called Ataxin-3 (Spinocerebellar ataxia, type 3, Machado-Joseph disease)

5L   CACNA1A (Spinocerebellar ataxia, type 6)

5M   ATXN7 Ataxin-7 (Spinocerebellar ataxia, type 7)

5N   PMP-22 (Charcot-Marie-Tooth disease, type 1A)

5O   MECP2 (Rett syndrome)

5Z   Neurologic, non-neoplastic, not otherwise specified

Muscular, non-neoplastic

6A DMD, commonly called dystrophin (Duchenne/Becker muscular dystrophy)

6B DMPK (Myotonic dystrophy, type 1)

6C ZNF-9 (Myotonic dystrophy, type 2)

6D SMN1/SMN2 (Autosomal recessive spinal muscular atrophy)

6E MTTK, commonly called tRNAlys (myotonic epilepsy, MERRF)

6F MTTL1, commonly called tRNAleu (mitochondrial encephalomyopathy, MELAS)

6Z Muscular, not otherwise specified

Metabolic, other

7A APOE, commonly called apolipoprotein E (Cardiovascular disease or Alzheimer's disease)

7B NPC1 or NPC2, commonly called sphingomyelin phosphodiesterase (Nieman-Pick disease)

7C GBA, commonly called acid beta glucosidase (Gaucher disease)

7D HFE (Hemochromatosis)

7E HEXA, commonly called hexosaminidase A (Tay-Sachs disease)

7F ACADM (medium chain acyl CoA dehydrogenase deficiency)

7Z Metabolic, other, not otherwise specified

Metabolic, transport

8A CFTR (Cystic fibrosis)

8B PRSS1 (Hereditary pancreatitis)

8Z Metabolic, transport, not otherwise specified

Metabolic-pharmacogenetics

9A TPMT, commonly called (thiopurine methyltransferase) (patients on antimetabolite therapy)

9B CYP2 genes, commonly called cytochrome p450 (drug metabolism)

9C ABCB1, commonly called MDR1 or p-glycoprotein (drug transport)

9D NAT2 (drug metabolism)

9L Metabolic-pharmacogenetics, not otherwise specified

Dysmorphology

9M FGFR1 (Pfeiffer and Kallman syndromes)

9N FGFR2 (Crouzon, Jackson-Weiss, Apert, Saethre-Chotzen syndromes)

9O FGFR3 (Achondroplasia, Hypochondroplasia, Thanatophoric dysplasia, types I and II, Crouzon syndrome with acanthosis nigricans, Muencke syndromes)

9P TWIST (Saethre-Chotzen syndrome)

9Q DGCR, commonly called CATCH-22 (DiGeorge and 22q11 deletion syndromes)

9Z Dysmorphology, not otherwise specified

Appendix J

Electrodiagnostic Medicine Listing of Sensory, Motor, and Mixed Nerves

This summary assigns each sensory, motor, and mixed nerve with its appropriate nerve conduction study code in order to enhance accurate reporting of 95900, 95903, and 95904. Each nerve constitutes one unit of service.

Codes 95900 and 95903 involve the following motor nerves:

I. Upper extremity/cervical plexus/brachial plexus motor nerves
   A. Axillary motor nerve to the deltoid
   B. Long thoracic motor nerve to the serratus anterior
   C. Median nerve
      1. Median motor nerve to the abductor pollicis brevis
      2. Median motor nerve, anterior interosseous branch, to the flexor pollicis longus
      3. Median motor nerve, anterior interosseous branch, to the pronator quadratus
      4. Median motor nerve to the first lumbrical
      5. Median motor nerve to the second lumbrical
   D. Musculocutaneous motor nerve to the biceps brachii
   E. Radial nerve
      1. Radial motor nerve to the extensor carpi ulnaris
      2. Radial motor nerve to the extensor digitorum communis
      3. Radial motor nerve to the extensor indicis proprius
      4. Radial motor nerve to the brachioradialis
   F. Suprascapular nerve
      1. Suprascapular motor nerve to the supraspinatus
      2. Suprascapular motor nerve to the infraspinatus
   G. Thoracodorsal motor nerve to the latissimus dorsi
   H. Ulnar nerve
      1. Ulnar motor nerve to the abductor digiti minimi
      2. Ulnar motor nerve to the palmar interosseous
      3. Ulnar motor nerve to the first dorsal interosseous
      4. Ulnar motor nerve to the flexor carpi ulnaris
   I. Other
II. Lower extremity motor nerves
   A. Femoral motor nerve to the quadriceps
      1. Femoral motor nerve to vastus medialis
      2. Femoral motor nerve to vastus lateralis
      3. Femoral motor nerve to vastus intermedialis
      4. Femoral motor nerve to rectus femoris
   B. Ilioinguinal motor nerve
   C. Peroneal (fibular) nerve
      1. Peroneal motor nerve to the extensor digitorum brevis
      2. Peroneal motor nerve to the peroneus brevis
      3. Peroneal motor nerve to the peroneus longus
      4. Peroneal motor nerve to the tibialis anterior
   D. Plantar motor nerve
   E. Sciatic nerve
   F. Tibial nerve
      1. Tibial motor nerve, inferior calcaneal branch, to the abductor digiti minimi
      2. Tibial motor nerve, medial plantar branch, to the abductor hallucis
      3. Tibial motor nerve, lateral plantar branch, to the flexor digiti minimi brevis
   G. Other

III. Cranial nerves and trunk
   A. Cranial nerve VII (facial motor nerve)
      1. Facial nerve to the frontalis
      2. Facial nerve to the nasalis
      3. Facial nerve to the orbicularis oculi
      4. Facial nerve to the orbicularis oris
   B. Cranial nerve XI (spinal accessory motor nerve)
   C. Cranial nerve XII (hypoglossal motor nerve)
   D. Intercostal motor nerve
   E. Phrenic motor nerve to the diaphragm
   F. Recurrent laryngeal nerve
   G. Other
IV. Nerve roots
   A. Cervical nerve root stimulation
      1. Cervical level 5 (CT)
      2. Cervical level 6 (C6)
      3. Cervical level 7 (C7)
      4. Cervical level 8 (C8)
   B. Thoracic nerve root stimulation
      1. Thoracic level 1 (T1)
      2. Thoracic level 2 (T2)
      3. Thoracic level 3 (T3)
      4. Thoracic level 4 (T4)
      5. Thoracic level 5 (T5)
      6. Thoracic level 6 (T6)
      7. Thoracic level 7 (T7)
      8. Thoracic level 8 (T8)
      9. Thoracic level 9 (T9)
      10. Thoracic level 10 (T10)
      11. Thoracic level 11 (T11)
      12. Thoracic level 12 (T12)
   C. Lumbar nerve root stimulation
      1. Lumbar level 1 (L1)
      2. Lumbar level 2 (L2)
      3. Lumbar level 3 (L3)
      4. Lumbar level 4 (L4)
      5. Lumbar level 5 (L5)
   D. Sacral nerve root stimulation
      1. Sacral level 1 (S1)
      2. Sacral level 2 (S2)
      3. Sacral level 3 (S3)
      4. Sacral level 4 (S4)

Code 95904 involves the following sensory and mixed nerves:

I. Upper extremity sensory and mixed nerves
   A. Lateral antebrachial cutaneous sensory nerve
   B. Medial antebrachial cutaneous sensory nerve
   C. Medial brachial cutaneous sensory nerve
   D. Median nerve
      1. Median sensory nerve to the first digit
      2. Median sensory nerve to the second digit
      3. Median sensory nerve to the third digit
      4. Median sensory nerve to the fourth digit
      5. Median palmar cutaneous sensory nerve
      6. Median palmar mixed nerve
   E. Posterior antebrachial cutaneous sensory nerve

    F. Radial sensory nerve
        1. Radial sensory nerve to the base of the thumb
        2. Radial sensory nerve to digit 1
    G. Ulnar nerve
        1. Ulnar dorsal cutaneous sensory nerve
        2. Ulnar sensory nerve to the fourth digit
        3. Ulnar sensory nerve to the fifth digit
        4. Ulnar palmar mixed nerve
    H. Intercostal sensory nerve
    I. Other

II. Lower extremity sensory and mixed nerves
    A. Lateral femoral cutaneous sensory nerve
    B. Medial calcaneal sensory nerve
    C. Medial femoral cutaneous sensory nerve
    D. Peroneal nerve
        1. Deep peroneal sensory nerve
        2. Superficial peroneal sensory nerve, medial dorsal cutaneous branch
        3. Superficial peroneal sensory nerve, intermediate dorsal cutaneous branch
    E. Posterior femoral cutaneous sensory nerve
    F. Saphenous nerve
        1. Saphenous sensory nerve (distal technique)
        2. Saphenous sensory nerve (proximal technique)
    G. Sural nerve
        1. Sural sensory nerve, lateral dorsal cutaneous branch
        2. Sural sensory nerve
    H. Tibial sensory nerve (digital nerve to toe 1)
    I. Tibial sensory nerve (medial plantar nerve)
    J. Tibial sensory nerve (lateral plantar nerve)
    K. Other

III. Head and trunk sensory nerves
    A. Dorsal nerve of the penis
    B. Greater auricular nerve
    C. Ophthalmic branch of the trigeminal nerve
    D. Pudendal sensory nerve
    E. Suprascapular sensory nerves
    F. Other

The following table provides a reasonable maximum number of studies performed per diagnostic category necessary for a physician to arrive at a diagnosis in 90% of patients with that final diagnosis. The numbers in each column represent the number of studies recommended. The appropriate number of studies to be performed is based upon the physician's discretion.

Indication	Needle EMG (95860-95864 95867-95870)	Nerve Conduction Studies (95900, 95903, 95904)		Other EMG Studies (95934, 95936, 95937)	
		Motor NCS With and/or Without F Wave	Sensory NCS	H-Reflex	Neuromuscular Junction Testing (Repetitive Stimulation)
Carpal tunnel (unilateral)	1	3	4		
Carpal tunnel (bilateral)	2	4	6		
Radiculopathy	2	3	2	2	
Mononeuropathy	1	3	3	2	
Polyneuropathy/mononeuropathy multiplex	3	4	4	2	
Myopathy	2	2	2		2
Motor neuronopathy (eg, ALS)	4	4	2		2
Plexopathy	2	4	6	2	
Neuromuscular junction	2	2	2		3
Tarsal tunnel syndrome (unilateral)	1	4	4		
Tarsal tunnel syndrome (bilateral)	2	5	6		
Weakness, fatigue, cramps, or twitching (focal)	2	3	4		2
Weakness, fatigue, cramps, or twitching (general)	4	4	4		2
Pain, numbness, or tingling (unilateral)	1	3	4	2	
Pain, numbness, or tingling (bilateral)	2	4	6	2	

Appendix K

Product Pending FDA Approval

Some vaccine products have been assigned a CPT Category I code in anticipation of future approval from the Food and Drug Administration (FDA). Following is a list of the vaccine product codes pending FDA approval status that are identified in the CPT codebook with the ∕ symbol. Upon revision of the approval status by the FDA, notation of this revision will be provided via the AMA CPT "Category I Vaccine Codes" Internet listings (www.ama-assn.org/ama/pub/category/10902.html) and in subsequent publications of the CPT codebook.

90649

90680

90698

90710

90715

90736

Appendix L

Vascular Families

Note: Assignment of branches to first, second, and third order in this table makes the assumption that the starting point is catheterization of the aorta. This categorization would not be accurate, for instance, if a femoral or carotid artery were catheterized directly in an antegrade direction. Arteries highlighted in bold are those more commonly reported during arteriographic procedures.

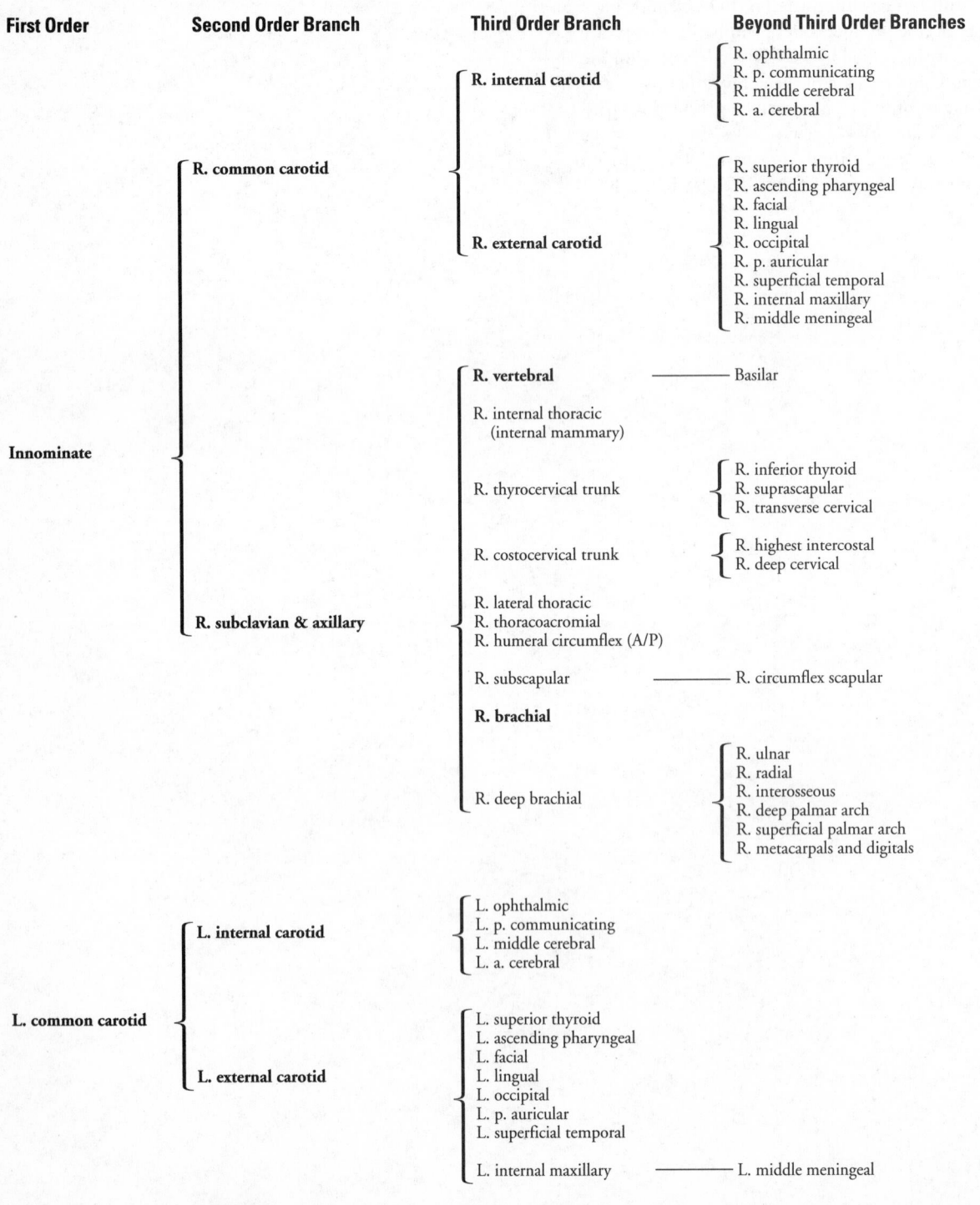

First Order	Second Order Branch	Third Order Branch	Beyond Third Order Branches
		R. internal carotid	R. ophthalmic R. p. communicating R. middle cerebral R. a. cerebral
	R. common carotid	**R. external carotid**	R. superior thyroid R. ascending pharyngeal R. facial R. lingual R. occipital R. p. auricular R. superficial temporal R. internal maxillary R. middle meningeal
Innominate		**R. vertebral**	Basilar
		R. internal thoracic (internal mammary)	
		R. thyrocervical trunk	R. inferior thyroid R. suprascapular R. transverse cervical
		R. costocervical trunk	R. highest intercostal R. deep cervical
	R. subclavian & axillary	R. lateral thoracic R. thoracoacromial R. humeral circumflex (A/P)	
		R. subscapular	R. circumflex scapular
		R. brachial	
		R. deep brachial	R. ulnar R. radial R. interosseous R. deep palmar arch R. superficial palmar arch R. metacarpals and digitals
	L. internal carotid	L. ophthalmic L. p. communicating L. middle cerebral L. a. cerebral	
L. common carotid	**L. external carotid**	L. superior thyroid L. ascending pharyngeal L. facial L. lingual L. occipital L. p. auricular L. superficial temporal	
		L. internal maxillary	L. middle meningeal

R = right, L = left, A = anterior, P = posterior

First Order	Second Order Branch	Third Order Branch	Beyond Third Order Branches

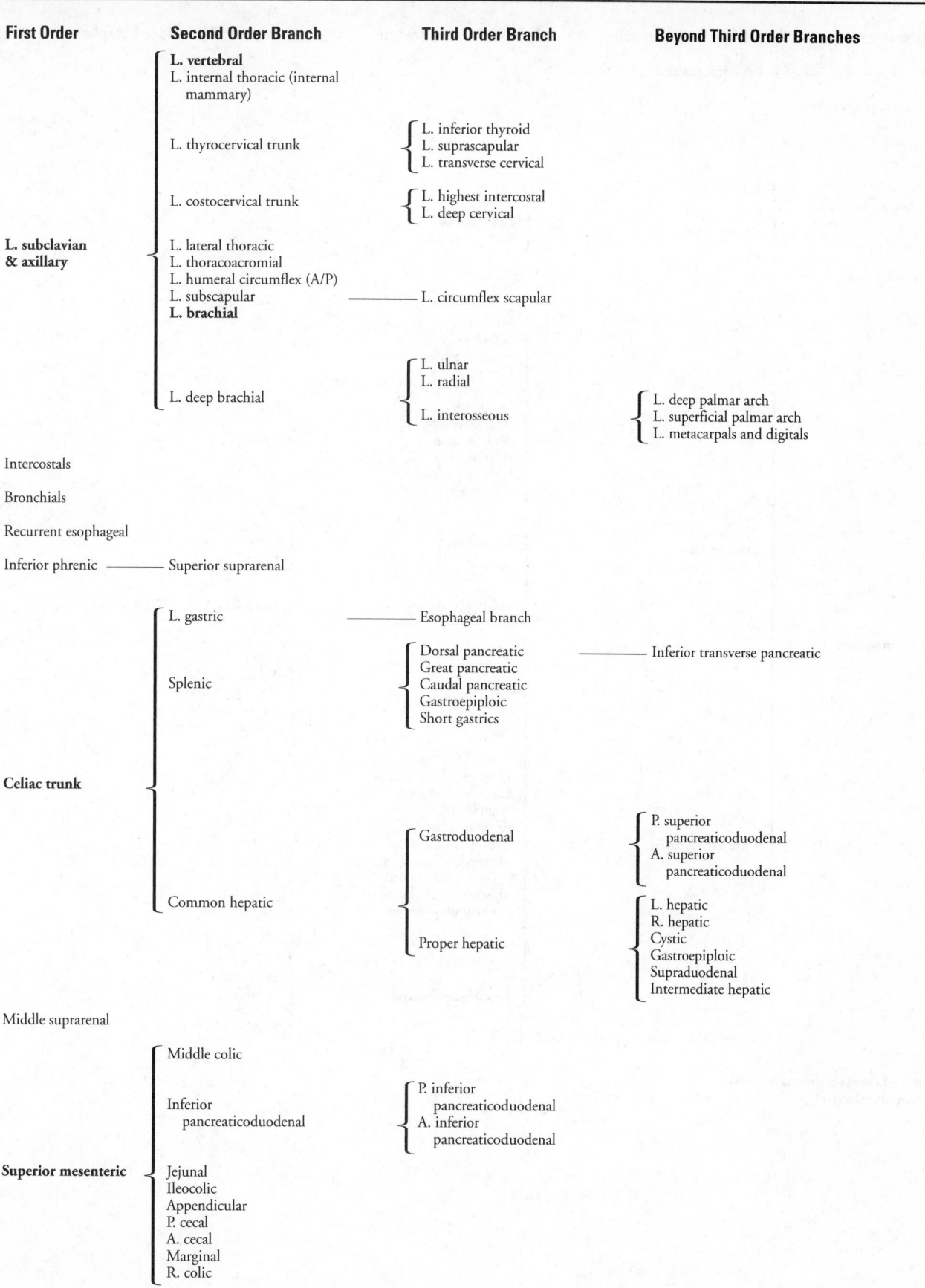

L. subclavian & axillary

- **L. vertebral**
- L. internal thoracic (internal mammary)
- L. thyrocervical trunk
  - L. inferior thyroid
  - L. suprascapular
  - L. transverse cervical
- L. costocervical trunk
  - L. highest intercostal
  - L. deep cervical
- L. lateral thoracic
- L. thoracoacromial
- L. humeral circumflex (A/P)
- L. subscapular —— L. circumflex scapular
- **L. brachial**
- L. deep brachial
  - L. ulnar
  - L. radial
  - L. interosseous
    - L. deep palmar arch
    - L. superficial palmar arch
    - L. metacarpals and digitals

Intercostals

Bronchials

Recurrent esophageal

Inferior phrenic —— Superior suprarenal

Celiac trunk

- L. gastric —— Esophageal branch
- Splenic
  - Dorsal pancreatic —— Inferior transverse pancreatic
  - Great pancreatic
  - Caudal pancreatic
  - Gastroepiploic
  - Short gastrics
- Common hepatic
  - Gastroduodenal
    - P. superior pancreaticoduodenal
    - A. superior pancreaticoduodenal
  - Proper hepatic
    - L. hepatic
    - R. hepatic
    - Cystic
    - Gastroepiploic
    - Supraduodenal
    - Intermediate hepatic

Middle suprarenal

Superior mesenteric

- Middle colic
- Inferior pancreaticoduodenal
  - P. inferior pancreaticoduodenal
  - A. inferior pancreaticoduodenal
- Jejunal
- Ileocolic
- Appendicular
- P. cecal
- A. cecal
- Marginal
- R. colic

R = right, L = left, A = anterior, P = posterior

First Order	Second Order Branch	Third Order Branch	Beyond Third Order Branches

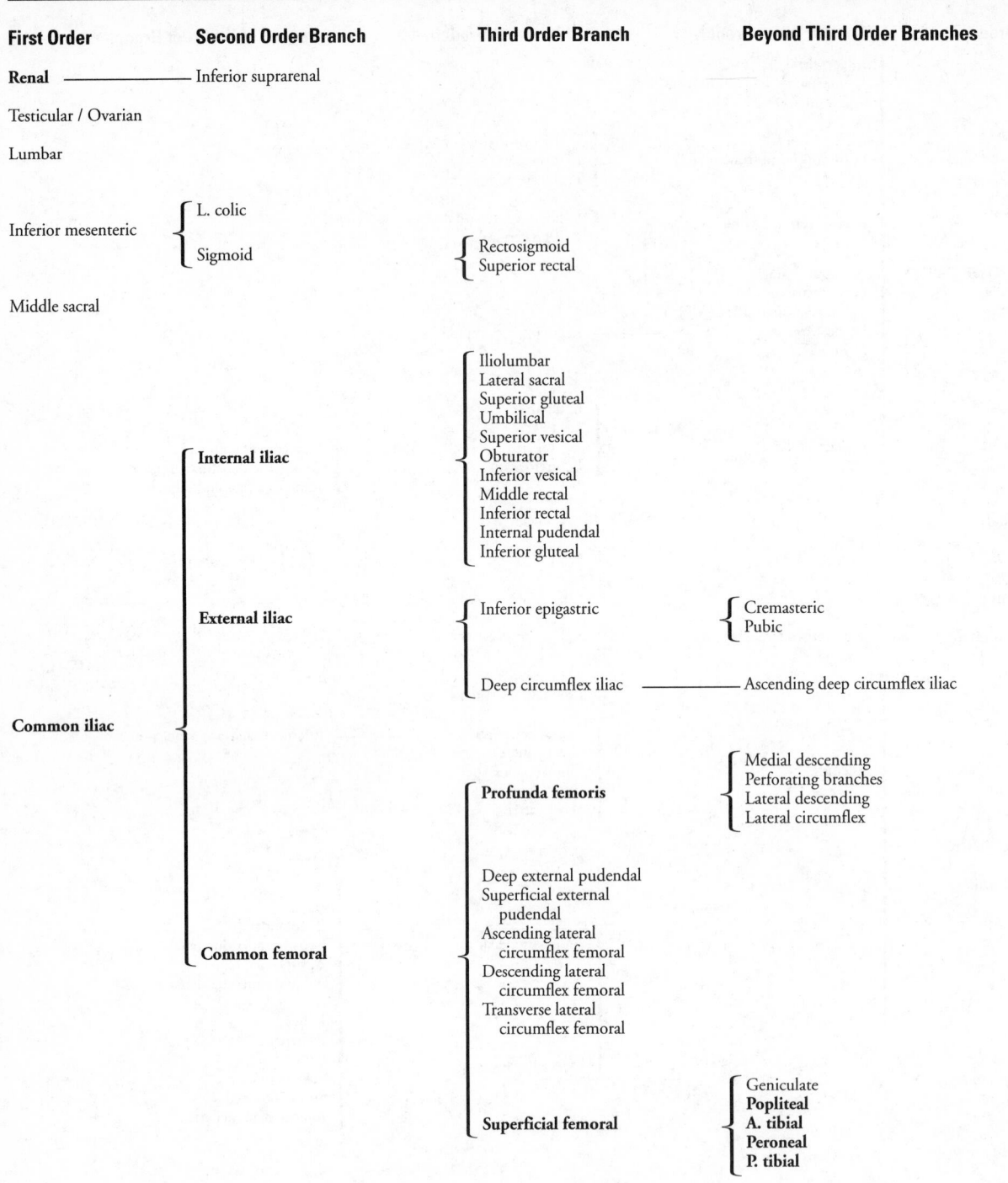

Renal ————— Inferior suprarenal

Testicular / Ovarian

Lumbar

Inferior mesenteric
- L. colic
- Sigmoid → Rectosigmoid / Superior rectal

Middle sacral

Common iliac

Internal iliac →
- Iliolumbar
- Lateral sacral
- Superior gluteal
- Umbilical
- Superior vesical
- Obturator
- Inferior vesical
- Middle rectal
- Inferior rectal
- Internal pudendal
- Inferior gluteal

External iliac →
- Inferior epigastric → Cremasteric / Pubic
- Deep circumflex iliac ————— Ascending deep circumflex iliac

Common femoral →
- **Profunda femoris** → Medial descending / Perforating branches / Lateral descending / Lateral circumflex
- Deep external pudendal
- Superficial external pudendal
- Ascending lateral circumflex femoral
- Descending lateral circumflex femoral
- Transverse lateral circumflex femoral
- **Superficial femoral** → Geniculate / **Popliteal** / **A. tibial** / **Peroneal** / **P. tibial**

R. & L. main pulmonary arteries (venous selective)

Reference: Kadir S. *Atlas of Normal and Variant Angiographic Anatomy.* Philadephia, Pa: WB Saunders Co; 1991.
R = right, L = left, A = anterior, P = posterior

Index

Instructions for the Use of the CPT Index

Main Terms

The index is organized by main terms. Each main term can stand alone, or be followed by up to three modifying terms. There are four primary classes of main entries:

1. Procedure or service.
   For example: Endoscopy; Anastomosis; Splint

2. Organ or other anatomic site.
   For example: Tibia; Colon; Salivary Gland

3. Condition.
   For example: Abscess; Entropion; Tetralogy of Fallot

4. Synonyms, Eponyms and Abbreviations.
   For example: EEG; Bricker Operation; Clagett Procedure

Modifying Terms

A main term may be followed by a series of up to three indented terms that modify the main term. When modifying terms appear, one should review the list, as these subterms do have an effect on the selection of the appropriate code for the procedure.

Code Ranges

Whenever more than one code applies to a given index entry, a code range is listed. If several non-sequential codes apply, they will be separated by a comma. For example:

Esophagus
    Reconstruction 43300, 43310, 43313

If two or more sequential codes apply, they will be separated by a hyphen. For example:

Debridement
    Burns 01951-01953, 16010-16030

Conventions

As a space saving convention, certain words infer some meaning. This convention is primarily used when a procedure or service is listed as a subterm. For example:

Knee
    Incision (of)

In this example, the word in parentheses (of) does not appear in the index, but it is inferred. As another example:

Pancreas
    Anesthesia (for procedures on)

In this example, as there is no such entity as pancreas anesthesia, the words in parentheses are inferred. That is, anesthesia for procedures on the pancreas.

The alphabetic index is NOT a substitute for the main text of *CPT*. Even if only one code appears, the user must refer to the main text to ensure that the code selection is accurate.

A

A Vitamin
See Vitamin, A

A-II
See Angiotensin II

Abbe-Estlander Procedure
See Reconstruction; Repair, Cleft Lip

Abdomen
Abdominal Wall
  Removal
    Mesh 11008
    Prosthesis 11008
  Repair
    Hernia 49491-49496, 49501, 49507,
                   49521, 49590
  Tumor
    Excision 22900
    Unlisted Services and Procedures 22999
Abscess
  Incision and Drainage 49020, 49040
    Open 49040
    Percutaneous 49021
Angiography 74175, 75635
Artery
  Ligation 37617
Biopsy 49000
Bypass Graft 35907
Cannula/Catheter
  Removal 49422
Celiotomy
  for Staging 49220
CT Scan 74150-74175, 75635
Cyst
  Destruction/Excision 49200-49201
Drainage
  Fluid 49080-49081
Ectopic Pregnancy 59130
Endometrioma
  Destruction/Excision 49200-49201
Exploration 49000-49002
  Blood Vessel 35840
  Staging 58960
Incision 49000
  Staging 58960
Incision and Drainage
  Pancreatitis 48000
Injection
  Air 49400
  Contrast Material 49400
Insertion
  Catheter 49419-49421
  Venous Shunt 49425
Intraperitoneal
  Catheter Removal 49422
  Shunt
    Ligation 49428
    Removal 49429
Laparotomy
  Staging 49220
Magnetic Resonance Imaging
(MRI) 74181-74183

Needle Biopsy
  Mass 49180
Peritoneocentesis 49080-49081
Radical Resection 51597
Repair
  Blood Vessel 35221
    with Other Graft 35281
    with Vein Graft 35251
  Hernia 49491-49525, 49560-49587
  Suture 49900
Revision
  Venous Shunt 49426
Suture 49900
Tumor
  Destruction/Excision 49200-49201
Ultrasound 76700-76705
Unlisted Services and Procedures 49999
Wound Exploration
  Penetrating 20102
X-Ray 74000-74022

Abdominal Aorta
See Aorta, Abdominal

Abdominal Aortic Aneurysm
See Aorta, Abdominal, Aneurysm

Abdominal Deliveries
See Cesarean Delivery

Abdominal Hysterectomy
See Hysterectomy, Abdominal

Abdominal Lymphangiogram
See Lymphangiography, Abdomen

Abdominal Paracentesis
See Abdomen, Drainage

Abdominal Radiographies
See Abdomen, X-Ray

Abdominal Wall
Debridement
  Infected 11005-11006
Reconstruction 49905
Removal
  Mesh 11008
  Prosthesis 11008
Surgery 22999
Tumor
  Excision 22900

Abdominohysterectomy
See Hysterectomy, Abdominal

Abdominopelvic Amputation
See Amputation, Interpelviabdominal

Abdominoplasty 15831

Ablation
Anal
  Polyp 46615
  Tumor 46615
Bone
  Tumor 20982
Colon
  Tumor 45339
Cryosurgical
  Fibroadenoma 0120T
  Renal Mass 50250

Renal Tumor
  Percutaneous 0135T
CT Scan Guidance 76362
Endometrial 58353-58356, 58563
Endometrium
  Ultrasound Guidance 58356
Heart
  Arrhythmogenic Focus 93650-93652
    See Cardiology; Diagnostic, Intracardiac
    Pacing and Mapping
Liver
  Tumor
    Laparoscopic 47370-47371
    Open 47380-47382
Magnetic Resonance Guidance 76394
Prostate 55873
Renal Cyst 50541
Renal Mass 50542
  Radiofrequency 50592
Renal Tumor
  Cryotherapy
    Percutaneous 0135T
Turbinate Mucosa 30801-30802
Ultrasound
  Guidance 76940
  Uterine Tumor 0071T-0072T
Uterine Tumor
  Ultrasound, Focused 0071T-0072T
Vein
  Endovenous 36475-36479

Abortion
See Obstetrical Care
Incomplete 59812
Induced
  by Dilation and Curettage 59840
  by Dilation and Evacuation 59841
  by Saline 59850-59851
  by Vaginal Suppositories 59855-59856
  with Hysterectomy 59100, 59852, 59857
Missed
  First Trimester 59820
  Second Trimester 59821
Septic 59830
Spontaneous 59812
Therapeutic
  by Saline 59850
    with Dilation and Curettage 59851
    with Hysterectomy 59852

Abrasion
Skin
  Chemical Peel 15788-15793
  Dermabrasion 15780-15783
  Lesion 15786-15787

Abscess
Abdomen 49040-49041
  Incision and Drainage
    Open 49040
    Percutaneous 49021
Anal
  Incision and Drainage 46045-46050
Ankle 27603
Appendix
  Incision and Drainage 44900
    Open 44900
    Percutaneous 44901

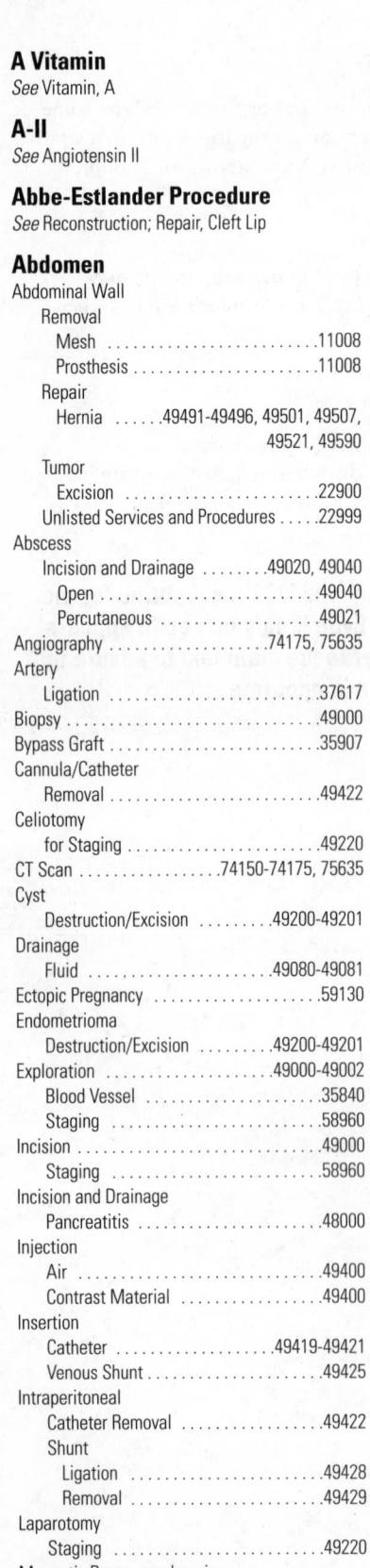

Arm, Lower 25028
　Excision 25145
　Incision and Drainage 25035
Arm, Upper
　Incision and Drainage 23930-23935
Auditory Canal, External 69020
Bartholin's Gland
　Incision and Drainage 56420
Bladder
　Incision and Drainage 51080
Brain
　Drainage 61150-61151
　Excision 61514, 61522
　Incision and Drainage 61320-61321
Breast
　Incision and Drainage 19020
Carpals
　Incision, Deep 25035
Clavicle
　Sequestrectomy 23170
Drainage
　with X-Ray 75989
Ear, External
　Complicated 69005
　Simple 69000
Elbow
　Incision and Drainage 23930-23935
Epididymis
　Incision and Drainage 54700
Excision
　Olecranon Process 24138
　Radius 24136
　Ulna 24138
Eyelid
　Incision and Drainage 67700
Facial Bones
　Excision 21026
Finger 26010-26011
　Incision and Drainage 26034
Foot
　Incision 28005
Gums
　Incision and Drainage 41800
Hand
　Incision and Drainage 26034
Hematoma
　Incision and Drainage 27603
Hip
　Incision and Drainage 26990-26992
Humeral Head 23174
Humerus
　Excision 24134
　Incision and Drainage 23935
Kidney
　Incision and Drainage 50020
　　Open 50020
　　Percutaneous 50021
Leg, Lower
　Incision and Drainage 27603
Liver 47010
　Drainage
　　Open 47010
　Injection 47015
　Repair 47300
Localization
　Nuclear Medicine 78806-78807
Lung
　Percutaneous Drainage 32200-32201

Lymph Node
　Incision and Drainage 38300-38305
Lymphocele Drainage 49062
Mandible
　Excision 21025
Mouth
　Incision and Drainage 40800-40801,
　　　　　　　　41005-41009, 41015-41018
Nasal Septum
　Incision and Drainage 30020
Neck
　Incision and Drainage 21501-21502
Ovarian
　Incision and Drainage 58820-58822
　　Abdominal Approach 58822
　　Vaginal Approach 58820
Ovary
　Drainage
　　Percutaneous 58823
Palate
　Incision and Drainage 42000
Paraurethral Gland
　Incision and Drainage 53060
Parotid Gland Drainage 42300-42305
Pelvic
　Drainage
　　Percutaneous 58823
Pelvis
　Incision and Drainage ..26990-26992, 45000
Pericolic
　Drainage
　　Percutaneous 58823
Perineum
　Incision and Drainage 56405
Perirenal or Renal
　Drainage 50020-50021
　　Percutaneous 50021
Peritoneum
　Incision and Drainage
　　Open 49020
　　Percutaneous 49021
Prostate
　Incision and Drainage 55720-55725
　Transurethral Drainage 52700
Radius
　Incision, Deep 25035
Rectum
　Incision and Drainage 45005-45020,
　　　　　　　　　　46040, 46060
Retroperitoneal 49060-49061
　Drainage
　　Open 49060
　　Percutaneous 49061
Salivary Gland
　Drainage 42300-42320
Scapula
　Sequestrectomy 23172
Scrotum
　Incision and Drainage 54700, 55100
Shoulder
　Drainage 23030
Skene's Gland
　Incision and Drainage 53060
Skin
　Incision and Drainage 10060-10061
　Puncture Aspiration 10160
Soft Tissue
　Incision 20000-20005

Spine
　Incision and Drainage 22010-22015
Subdiaphragmatic 49040-49041
Sublingual Gland
　Drainage 42310-42320
Submaxillary Gland
　Drainage 42310-42320
Subphrenic 49040-49041
Testis
　Incision and Drainage 54700
Thoracostomy 32020
Thorax
　Incision and Drainage 21501-21502
Throat
　Incision and Drainage 42700-42725
Tongue
　Incision and Drainage 41000-41006
Tonsil
　Incision and Drainage 42700
Ulna
　Incision, Deep 25035
Urethra
　Incision and Drainage 53040
Uvula
　Incision and Drainage 42000
Vagina
　Incision and Drainage 57010
Vulva
　Incision and Drainage 56405
Wrist
　Excision 25145
　Incision and Drainage 25028, 25035
X-Ray 76080

Abscess, Nasal
See Nose, Abscess

Abscess, Parotid Gland
See Parotid Gland, Abscess

Absorptiometry
Dual Energy
　Body Composition 0028T
　Bone 76075
　　Appendicular 76076
　　Axial Skeleton 76075
　　Vertebral 76077
Dual Photon
　Bone 78351
Radiographic
　Photodensity 76078
Single Photon
　Bone 78350

Absorption Spectrophotometry, Atomic
See Atomic Absorption Spectroscopy

Accessory Nerve, Spinal
See Nerves, Spinal Accessory

Accessory, Toes
See Polydactyly, Toes

ACE
See Angiotensin Converting Enzyme (ACE), Performance Measures

Acetabuloplasty 27120-27122

Acetabulum
Fracture
   Closed Treatment 27220-27222
   Open Treatment 27226-27228
   with Manipulation 27222
   without Manipulation 27220
Reconstruction 27120
   with Resection, Femoral Head 27122
Tumor
   Excision 27076

Acetaldehyde
Blood 82000

Acetaminophen
Urine 82003

Acetic Anhydrides 84600

Acetone
Blood or Urine 82009-82010

Acetone Body 82009-82010

Acetylcholinesterase
Blood or Urine 82013

AcG
See Clotting Factor

Achilles Tendon
Incision 27605-27606
Lengthening 27612
Repair 27650-27654

Achillotomy
See Tenotomy, Achilles Tendon

Acid
Gastric 82926-82928

Acid Diethylamide, Lysergic
See Lysergic Acid Diethylamide

Acid Fast Bacilli (AFB)
Culture 87116

Acid Fast Bacillus Culture
See Culture, Acid Fast Bacilli

Acid Fast Stain 88312

Acid Perfusion Test
Esophagus 91012, 91030

Acid Phosphatase 84060-84066

Acid Probes, Nucleic
See Nucleic Acid Probe

Acid Reflux Test
Esophagus 91034-91038

Acid, Adenylic
See Adenosine Monophosphate (AMP)

Acid, Aminolevulinic
See Aminolevulinic Acid (ALA)

Acid, Ascorbic
See Ascorbic Acid

Acid, Deoxyribonucleic
See Deoxyribonucleic Acid

Acid, Folic
See Folic Acid

Acid, Glycocholic
See Cholylglycine

Acid, Lactic
See Lactic Acid

Acid, N-Acetylneuraminic
See Sialic Acid

Acid, Phenylethylbarbituric
See Phenobarbital

Acid, Uric
See Uric Acid

Acidity /Alkalinity
See pH

Acids, Amino
See Amino Acids

Acids, Bile
See Bile Acids

Acids, Fatty
See Fatty Acid

Acids, Guanylic
See Guanosine Monophosphate

Acids, N-Acetylneuraminic
See Sialic Acid

Acne Surgery
Incision and Drainage
   Abscess 10060-10061
   Comedones 10040
   Cyst 10040
   Milia, Multiple 10040
   Pustules 10040

Acne Treatment
Abrasion 15786-15787
Chemical Peel 15788-15793
Cryotherapy 17340
Dermabrasion 15780-15783
Exfoliation
   Chemical 17360

Acoustic Evoked Brain Stem Potential
See Evoked Potential, Auditory Brainstem

Acoustic Neuroma
See Brain, Tumor, Excision; Brainstem; Mesencephalon; Skull Base Surgery

Acoustic Recording
Heart Sounds
   with Computer Analysis 0068T-0070T

Acromioclavicular Joint
Arthrocentesis 20605
Arthrotomy 23044
   with Biopsy 23101
Dislocation 23540-23552
   Open Treatment 23550-23552
X-Ray 73050

Acromion
Excision
   Shoulder 23130

Acromionectomy
Partial 23130

Acromioplasty 23415-23420
Partial 23130

ACTH
See Adrenocorticotropic Hormone (ACTH)

ACTH Releasing Factor
See Corticotropic Releasing Hormone (CRH)

Actigraphy
Sleep Study 0089T

Actinomyces
Antibody 86602

Actinomycosis 86000

Actinomycotic Infection
See Actinomycosis

Actinotherapy 96900
See Dermatology

Activated Factor X
See Thrombokinase

Activated Partial Thromboplastin Time
See Thromboplastin, Partial, Time

Activation, Lymphocyte
See Blastogenesis

Activities of Daily Living
See Physical Medicine/Therapy/Occupational Therapy

Activity, Glomerular Procoagulant
See Thromboplastin

Acupuncture
with Electrical Stimulation 97813-97814
without Electrical Stimulation 97810-97811

Acute Poliomyelitis
See Polio

Acylcarnitines 82016-82017

Adamantinoma, Pituitary
See Craniopharyngioma

Addam Operation
See Dupuytren's Contracture

Adductor Tenotomy of Hip
See Tenotomy, Hip, Adductor

Adenoidectomy 42820-42821,
                            42830-42836

Adenoids
Excision 42830-42836
   with Tonsils 42820-42821
Unlisted Services and Procedures 42999

Adenoma
Pancreas
    Excision 48120
Thyroid Gland Excision 60200

Adenosine 3'5' Monophosphate
See Cyclic AMP

Adenosine Diphosphate
Blood 82030

Adenosine Monophosphate (AMP)
Blood 82030

Adenovirus
Antibody 86603
Antigen Detection
    Enzyme Immunoassay 87301
    Immunofluorescense 87260

Adenovirus Vaccine
See Vaccines

Adenylic Acid
See Adenosine Monophosphate (AMP)

ADH
See Antidiuretic Hormone

Adhesions
Epidural 0027T, 62263-62264
Eye
    Corneovitreal 65880
    Incision
        Anterior Segment 65860-65870
        Posterior Segment 65875
Intermarginal
    Construction 67880
    Transposition of Tarsal Plate 67882
Intestinal
    Enterolysis 44005
    Laparoscopic 44180
Intracranial
    Lysis 62161
Intrauterine
    Lysis 58559
Labial
    Lysis 56441
Lungs
    Lysis 32124
Pelvic
    Lysis 58660, 58662, 58740
Penile
    Lysis
        Post-circumcision 54162
Preputial
    Lysis 54450
Urethral
    Lysis 53500

Adipectomy
See Lipectomy

ADL
See Activities of Daily Living

Administration
Immunization
    Each Additional Vaccine/Toxoid 90472,
                                        90474
        with Counseling 90466, 90468

One Vaccine/Toxoid 90471, 90473
    with Counseling 90465, 90467

ADP
See Adenosine Diphosphate

ADP Phosphocreatine Phosphotransferase
See CPK

Adrenal Cortex Hormone
See Corticosteroids

Adrenal Gland
Biopsy 60540-60545
Excision
    Laparoscopy 60650
    Retroperitoneal Tumor 60545
Exploration 60540-60545
Nuclear Medicine
    Imaging 78075

Adrenal Medulla
See Medulla

Adrenalectomy 60540
Anesthesia 00866
Laparoscopic 50545

Adrenalin
See Catecholamines
Blood 82383
Urine 82384

Adrenaline-Noradrenaline
Testing 82382-82384

Adrenocorticotropic Hormone (ACTH) ...80400-80406, 80412, 80418, 82024
Blood or Urine 82024
Stimulation Panel 80400-80406

Adrenogenital Syndrome .56805, 57335

Adult T Cell Leukemia Lymphoma Virus I
See HTLV I

Advanced Life Support
See Emergency Department Services
Physician Direction 99288

Advancement
Genioglossus 21199
Tendon
    Foot 28238

Advancement Flap
See Skin, Adjacent Tissue Transfer

Aerosol Inhalation
See Pulmonology, Therapeutic
Pentamidine 94642

AFB
See Acid Fast Bacilli (AFB)

Afferent Nerve
See Sensory Nerve

AFP
See Alpha-Fetoprotein

After Hours Medical Services 99050

Agents, Anticoagulant
See Clotting Inhibitors

Agglutinin
Cold 86156-86157
Febrile 86000

Aggregation
Platelet 85576

AHG
See Clotting Factor

AICD (Pacing Cardioverter-Defibrillator)
See Defibrillator, Heart; Pacemaker, Heart

Aid, Hearing
See Hearing Aid

AIDS Antibodies
See Antibody, HIV

AIDS Virus
See HIV-1

Akin Operation
See Bunion Repair

ALA
See Aminolevulinic Acid (ALA)

Alanine 2 Oxoglutarate Aminotransferase
See Transaminase, Glutamic Pyruvic

Alanine Amino (ALT) 84460

Alanine Transaminase
See Transaminase, Glutamic Pyruvic

Albarran Test
See Water Load Test

Albumin
Ischemia modified 82045
Serum 82040
Urine 82042-82044

Alcohol
Breath 82075
Ethyl
    Blood 82055
    Urine 82055
Ethylene Glycol 82693

Alcohol Dehydrogenase
See Antidiuretic Hormone

Alcohol, Isopropyl
See Isopropyl Alcohol

Alcohol, Methyl
See Methanol

Aldolase
Blood 82085

Aldosterone
Blood 82088
Suppression Evaluation 80408
Urine 82088

Alimentary Canal
See Gastrointestinal Tract

Alkaline Phosphatase 84075-84080
Leukocyte 85540
WBC 85540

Alkaloids
See Specific Drug
Urine 82101

Allergen Bronchial Provocation Tests
See Allergy Tests; Bronchial Challenge Test

Allergen Challenge, Endobronchial
See Bronchial Challenge Test

Allergen Immunotherapy
Allergen
   Prescription/Supply/Injection ..95120-95125
     with Extract Supply 95144
      Injection 95115-95117
Antigens 95144
IgE 86003-86005
IgG 86001
Insect Venom
   Prescription/Supply 95145-95149
   Prescription/Supply/Injection ..95130-95134
Prescription/Supply 95165
   Insect, Whole Body 95170
Rapid Desensitization 95180

Allergy Services/Procedures
See Office and/or Other Outpatient Services;
Allergen and Immunotherapy
Education and Counseling 99201-99215
Unlisted Services and Procedures 95199

Allergy Tests
Challenge Test
   Bronchial 95070-95071
   Ingestion 95075
Eye Allergy 95060
Food Allergy 95075
Intradermal
   Allergen Extract 95024-95028
   Biologicals 95015
   Drugs 95015
   Incremental 95027
   Venoms 95015
Nasal Mucous Membrane Test 95065
Nose Allergy 95065
Patch
   Application Tests 95044
   Photo Patch 95052
Photosensitivity 95056
Provocative Testing 95078
Skin Tests
   Allergen Extract 95004
   Biologicals 95010
   Drugs 95010
   Venoms 95010

Allogeneic Donor
Lymphocyte Infusion 38242

Allogeneic Transplantation
See Homograft

Allograft
Aortic Valve 33406, 33413
Bone
   Structural 20931
Cartilage
   Knee 27415
Lung Transplant 32850
Skin 15300-15336
Spine Surgery
   Morselized 20930
   Structural 20931

Allograft Preparation
Heart 33933, 33944
Intestines 44715-44721
Kidney 50323-50329
Liver 47143-47147
Lung 32855-32856, 33933
Pancreas 48551-48552
Renal 50323-50329

Alloplastic Dressing
Burns 15000-15001

Allotransplantation
Intestines 44135-44136
Renal 50360-50365
   Removal 50370

Almen Test
See Blood, Feces

Alpha-1 Antitrypsin 82103-82104

Alpha-2 Antiplasmin 85410

Alpha-Fetoprotein
Amniotic Fluid 82106
Serum 82105

Alphatocopherol 84446

ALT
See Transaminase, Glutamic Pyruvic

Altemeier Procedure
See Anus; Rectum, Prolapse, Excision

Aluminum
Blood 82108

Alveola
Fracture
   Closed Treatment 21421
   Open Treatment 21422-21423

Alveolar Cleft
Ungrafted Bilateral 21147
Ungrafted Unilateral 21146

Alveolar Nerve
Avulsion 64738
Incision 64738
Transection 64738

Alveolar Ridge
Fracture
   Closed Treatment 21440
   Open Treatment 21445

Alveolectomy 41830

Alveoloplasty 41874

Alveolus
Excision 41830

Amide, Procaine
See Procainamide

Amikacin
Assay 80150

Amine
Vaginal Fluid 82120

Amino Acids 82127-82139

Aminolevulinic Acid (ALA)
Blood or Urine 82135

Aminotransferase
See Transaminase

Aminotransferase, Alanine
See Transaminase, Glutamic Pyruvic

Aminotransferase, Aspartate
See Transaminase, Glutamic Oxaloacetic

Amitriptyline
Assay 80152

Ammonia
Blood 82140
Urine 82140

Amniocenteses
See Amniocentesis

Amniocentesis 59000
See Chromosome Analysis
Induced Abortion 59850
   with Dilation and Curettage 59851
   with Dilation and Evacuation 59851
   with Hysterectomy 59852
Urine
   with Amniotic Fluid Reduction 59001

Amnioinfusion
Transabdominal 59070

Amnion
Amniocentesis 59000
   with Amniotic Fluid Reduction 59001
Amnioinfusion
   Transabdominal 59070

Amniotic Fluid
Alpha-Fetoprotein 82106
Scan 82143
Testing 83661, 83663-83664

Amniotic Membrane
See Amnion

Amobarbital 82205

AMP
See Adenosine Monophosphate (AMP)

AMP, Cyclic
See Cyclic AMP

Amphetamine
Blood or Urine 82145

Amputation
See Radical Resection; Replantation
Ankle 27888
Arm, Lower 25900-25905, 25915
   Revision 25907-25909
Arm, Upper 24900-24920
   and Shoulder 23900-23921
   Revision 24925-24930
   with Implant 24931-24935
Cervix
   Total 57530
Ear
   Partial 69110
   Total 69120
Finger .26910-26952
Foot 28800-28805
Hand at Metacarpal 25927
   at Wrist 25920
     Revision .25922
   Revision 25924, 25929-25931
Interpelviabdominal 27290
Interthoracoscapular 23900
Leg, Lower 27598, 27880-27882
   Revision 27884-27886
Leg, Upper 27590-27592
   at Hip 27290-27295
   Revision 27594-27596
Metacarpal 26910
Metatarsal 28810
Penis
   Partial 54120
   Radical 54130-54135
   Total 54125
Thumb .26910-26952
Toe 28810-28825
Tuft of Distal Phalanx 11752
Upper Extremity 24940
   Cineplasty 24940

Amputation through Hand
See Hand, Amputation

Amputation, Nose
See Resection, Nose

Amylase
Blood 82150
Urine 82150

ANA
See Antinuclear Antibodies (ANA)

Anabolic Steroid
See Androstenedione

Anal Abscess
See Abscess, Anal

Anal Bleeding
See Anus, Hemorrhage

Anal Fistula
See Fistula, Anal

Anal Fistulectomy
See Excision, Fistula, Anal

Anal Fistulotomy
See Fistulotomy, Anal

Anal Sphincter
Dilation 45905
Incision 46080

Anal Ulceration
See Anus, Fissure

Analgesia
See Anesthesia; Sedation

Analgesic Cutaneous Electrostimulation
See Application, Neurostimulation

Analysis
Computer Data .99090
Electroencephalogram
   Digital 95957
Electronic
   Drug Infusion Pump 62367-62368
   Pacing Cardioverter-
   Defibrillator 93741-93744
     See Pacemaker, Heart
   Pulse Generator 95970-95971
Physiologic Data, Remote 99091
Protein
   Tissue
     Western Blot 88372
Semen
   Sperm Isolation 89260-89261

Analysis, Spectrum
See Spectrophotometry

Anaspadias
See Epispadias

Anastomosis
Arteriovenous Fistula
   Direct 36821
   with Bypass Graft 35686
   with Graft 36825-36830, 36832
Artery
   to Aorta 33606
   to Artery
     Cranial .61711
Bile Duct
   to Bile Duct 47800
   to Intestines 47760, 47780
Bile Duct to Gastrointestinal 47785
Broncho-Bronchial 32486
Caval to Mesenteric 37160
Cavopulmonary 33768
Colorectal 44620
Epididymis
   to Vas Deferens
     Bilateral 54901
     Unilateral 54900
Excision
   Trachea 31780-31781
Fallopian Tube 58750
Gallbladder to Intestines 47720-47740
Hepatic Duct to Intestines 47765, 47802
Ileo-Anal 45113
Intestine to Intestine 44130

Intestines
   Colo-anal 45119
   Cystectomy 51590
   Enterocystoplasty 51960
   Resection
     Laparoscopic 44202-44205
Intrahepatic Portosystemic . . .37182-37183
Jejunum 43825
Microvascular
   Free Transfer
     Jejunum 43496
Nerve
   Facial to Hypoglossal 64868
   Facial to Phrenic 64870
Oviduct 58750
Pancreas to Intestines 48180, 48520-48540
Portocaval 37140
Pulmonary 33606
Renoportal 37145
Splenorenal 37180-37181
Stomach 43825
   to Duodenum 43810, 43855
     Revision 43850
   to Jejunum 43820, 43860-43865
Tubotubal 58750
Ureter
   to Bladder 50780-50785
   to Colon 50810-50815
     Removal 50830
   to Intestine 50800, 50820-50825
     Removal 50830
   to Kidney 50727-50750
   to Ureter 50727, 50760-50770
Vein
   Saphenopopliteal 34530
Vein to Vein 37140-37160, 37182-37183

Anastomosis of Lacrimal Sac to Conjunctival Sac
See Conjunctivorhinostomy

Anastomosis of Pancreas
See Pancreas, Anastomosis

Anastomosis, Aorta-Pulmonary Artery
See Aorta, Anastomosis, to Pulmonary Artery

Anastomosis, Bladder, to Intestine
See Enterocystoplasty

Anastomosis, Hepatic Duct
See Hepatic Duct, Anastomosis

Anderson Tibial Lengthening .27715
See Ankle; Tibia, Osteoplasty, Lengthening

Androstanediol Glucuronide . . .82154

Androstanolone
See Dihydrotestosterone

Androstenedione
Blood or Urine .82157

Androstenolone
See Dehydroepiandrosterone

Androsterone
Blood or Urine .82160

Anesthesia

See Analgesia
Abbe-Estlander Procedure 00102
Abdomen
   Abdominal Wall 00700, 00730,
           00800-00802, 00820, 00836
    Halsted Repair 00750-00756
    Blood Vessels 00770, 00880-00882
    Endoscopy 00740, 00810
    Extraperitoneal 00860-00862,
           00866-00868, 00870
    Hernia Repair 00830-00836
    Halsted Repair 00750-00756
    Intraperitoneal ..00790-00797, 00840-00842
Abdominoperineal Resection 00844
Abortion
   Incomplete 01965
   Induced 01966
Achilles Tendon Repair 01472
Acromioclavicular Joint 01620
Adrenalectomy 00866
Amniocentesis 00842
Aneurysm
   Axillary-Brachial 01652
   Knee 01444
   Popliteal Artery 01444
Angiography 01920
Ankle 00400, 01462-01522
Anorectal Procedure 00902
Anus 00902
Arm
   Lower ...00400, 01810-01820, 01830-01860
   Upper 00400, 01710-01782
Arrhythmias 00410
Arteriography 01916
Arteriovenous Fistula 01432
Arthroplasty
   Hip 01214-01215
   Knee 01402
Arthroscopic Procedures
   Ankle 01464
   Elbow 01732-01740
   Foot 01464
   Hip 01202
   Knee 01382, 01400
   Shoulder 01622-01630
   Wrist 01829-01830
Auditory Canal, External
   Removal Foreign Body 69205
Axilla 00400, 01610-01682
Back Skin 00300
Batch-Spittler-McFaddin Operation 01404
Biopsy 00100
   Liver 00702
Bladder 00870, 00912
Brain 00210-00218, 00220-00222
Breast 00402-00406
Bronchi 00542
   Intrathoracic Repair of Trauma 00548
   Reconstruction 00539
Bronchoscopy 00520
Burns
   Debridement and/or
   Excision 01951-01953
   Dressings and/or
   Debridement 16020, 16025, 16030
Burr Hole 00214

Bypass Graft
   Leg, Lower 01500
   Leg, Upper 01270
   Shoulder, Axillary 01654-01656
Cardiac Catheterization 01920
Cast
   Knee 01420
Cast Application
   Forearm, Wrist and Hand 01860
   Leg 01490
   Pelvis 01130
   Shoulder 01680-01682
Central Venous Circulation 00532
Cervical Cerclage 00948
Cervix 00948
Cesarean Delivery 01961, 01963
Chemonucleolysis 00634
Chest 00400-00410, 00470-00474,
   00522, 00530-00539, 00542-00548, 00550
Chest Skin 00400
Childbirth
   Cesarean Delivery 01961, 01963,
          01968-01969
   External Cephalic Version 01958
   Vaginal Delivery 01960, 01967
Clavicle 00450-00454
Cleft Lip Repair 00102
Cleft Palate Repair 00172
Colpectomy 00942
Colporrhaphy 00942
Colpotomy 00942
Corneal Transplant 00144
Cranioplasty 00215
Culdoscopy 00950
Cystectomy 00864
Cystolithotomy 00870
Cystourethroscopy
   Local 52265
   Spinal 52260
Decortication 00542
Defibrillator 00534, 00560
Diaphragm 00540-00541
Disarticulation
   Hip 01212
   Knee 01404
   Shoulder 01634
Diskography 01905
Dressing Change 15852
Drug Administration
   Epidural or Subarachnoid 01996
Ear 00120-00126
Elbow 00400, 01710-01782
Electrocoagulation
   Intracranial Nerve 00222
Electroconvulsive Therapy 00104
Embolectomy
   Arm, Upper 01772
   Femoral 01274
   Femoral Artery 01274
   Forearm, Wrist and Hand 01842
   Leg, Lower 01502
Endoscopy
   Arm, Lower 01830
   Gastrointestinal 00740
   Intestines 00810
   Uterus 00952
   Vagina 00950
Esophagus 00320, 00500

External Cephalic Version 01958
External Fixation System
   Adjustment/Revision 20693
   Removal 20694
Eye 00140-00148
   Cornea 00144
   Iridectomy 00147
   Iris 00147
Eyelid 00103
Facial Bones 00190-00192
Fallopian Tube
   Ligation 00851
Femoral Artery
   Ligation 01272
Femur 01220-01234, 01340, 01360
Fibula 01390-01392
Foot 00400, 01462-01522
Forearm 00400, 01810-01820, 01830-01860
Fowler-Stephens Orchiopexy 00930
Gastrocnemius Recession 01474
Gastrointestinal Endoscopy 00740
Genitalia
   Female 00940-00948, 00950-00952,
          01958-01969
   Male 00920-00928, 00930-00938
Great Vessels of Chest 00560-00563
Hand 00400, 01810-01820, 01830-01860
Harrington Rod Technique 00670
Head 00222, 00300
   Muscles 00300
   Nerves 00300
Heart 00560-00566, 00580
   Coronary Artery Bypass Grafting 00566
   Electrophysiology/Ablation 00537
   Transplant 00580
Hepatectomy
   Partial 00792
Hernia Repair
   Abdomen
     Lower 00830-00836
     Upper 00750-00752, 00756
Hip 01200-01202, 01210-01215
Humerus 01620, 01730, 01742-01744, 01758
Hysterectomy 01962
   Cesarean 01963, 01969
   Radical 00846
   Vaginal 00944
Hysterosalpingography 00952
Hysteroscopy 00952
Induced Abortion 01966
Inferior Vena Cava Ligation 00882
Injections
   Nerve 01991-01992
Integumentary System
   Anterior Trunk 00400
   Arm, Upper 00400
   Axilla 00400
   Elbow 00400
   Extremity 00400
   Forearm 00400
   Hand 00400
   Head 00300
   Knee 00400
   Leg, Lower 00400
   Leg, Upper 00400
   Neck 00300
   Perineum 00400
   Popliteal Area 00400

Posterior Pelvis 00300
Posterior Trunk 00300
Shoulder 00400
Wrist 00400
Intestines
Endoscopy 00810
Intracranial Procedures 00210-00218,
00220-00222
Intraoral Procedures 00170-00176
Intrathoracic Procedures
Bronchi 00539, 00548
Trachea 00539, 00548
Intrathoracic System 00500, 00520-00529,
00530-00539, 00540-00548,
00550, 00560-00566, 00580
Iridectomy 00147
Keen Operation 00604
Kidney 00862, 00868, 00872-00873
Knee 00400, 01320, 01340, 01360,
01380-01404, 01420-01444
Knee Skin 00400
Laminectomy 00604
Laparoscopy 00790-00792, 00840
Larynx 00320, 00326
Leg
Lower 00400, 01462-01522
Upper 01200-01202, 01210-01234,
01250-01260, 01270-01274
Lens 00142
Leriche Operation 00622
Life Support for Organ Donor 01990
Ligation
Fallopian Tube 00851
Lithotripsy 00872-00873
Liver 00702, 00796
Transplant 00796
Liver Hemorrhage 00792
Local
Intravenous 01995
Lumbar Puncture 00635
Lungs 00522, 00539, 00540-00548
Transplant 00580
Lymphadenectomy 00934-00936
Lymphatic System 00320
Mammoplasty 00402
Marcellation Operation 00944
Mediastinoscopy 00528-00529
Mediastinum 00528-00529, 00540-00541
Mouth 00170-00172
Myelography 01905
Myringotomy 69421
Neck 00300, 00320-00322, 00350-00352
Nephrectomy 00862
Neuraxial
Cesarean Delivery 01968-01969
Labor 01967-01969
Vaginal Delivery 01967
Neurectomy 01180-01190
Nose 00160-00164
Removal
Foreign Body 30310
Omphalocele 00754
Ophthalmoscopy 00148
Orchiectomy 00926-00928
Orchiopexy .00930
Torek Procedure 00930
Organ Harvesting
Brain-Dead Patient 01990

Osteoplasty
Tibia/Fibula 01484
Osteotomy
Humerus 01742
Tibia/Fibula 01484
Other Procedures 01990, 01995-01999
Otoscopy 00124
Pacemaker Insertion 00530
Pacing Cardioverter/Defibrillator 00534
Pancreas 00794
Pancreatectomy 00794
Panniculectomy 00802
Patella 01390-01392
Pectus Excavatum 00474
Pelvic Exenteration 00848
Pelvis 00400, 00865, 01112, 01120-01150,
01160, 01170-01173, 01180-01190
Amputation 01140
Bone 01120
Bone Marrow 01112
Examination 57400
Extraperitoneal 00864
Intraperitoneal 00844-00848
Repair 01173
Skin 00300, 00400
Penis 00932-00938
Pericardial Sac 00560-00563
Perineum 00904-00908
Pharynx 00174-00176
Phleborrhaphy
Arm, Upper 01782
Forearm, Wrist and Hand 01852
Pleura 00540-00541
Needle Biopsy 00522
Pneumocentesis 00524
Popliteal Area 00400, 01320, 01430-01444
Prognathism 00192
Prostate 00865, 00908, 00914
Prostatectomy
Perineal .00908
Radical 00865
Walsh Modified Radical 00865
Radiological Procedures 01905-01922
Arterial
Therapeutic 01924-01926
Venous/Lymphatic
Therapeutic 01930-01933
Renal Procedures 00862
Repair of Skull 00215
Replacement
Ankle 01486
Elbow 01760
Hip 01212-01215
Knee 01402
Shoulder .01638
Wrist 01832
Restriction
Gastric
for Obesity 00797
Retropharyngeal Tumor Excision 00174
Rib Resection 00470-00474
Sacroiliac Joint 01160, 01170, 27096
Salivary Glands 00100
Scheie Procedure 00147
Sedation
Moderate 99148-99150
with Independent
Observation 99143-99145

Seminal Vesicles 00922
Shoulder 00400, 00450-00454, 01610-01682
Dislocation
Closed Treatment 23655
Shunt
Spinal Fluid 00220
Sinuses
Accessory 00160-00164
Skull 00190
Skull Fracture
Elevation .00215
Special Circumstances
Emergency 99140
Extreme Age 99100
Hypotension 99135
Hypothermia 99116
Spinal Instrumentation 00670
Spinal Manipulation 00640
Spine and Spinal Cord 00600-00604,
00620, 00670
Cervical 00600-00604, 00640, 00670
Injection 62310-62319
Lumbar 00630-00635, 00640, 00670
Thoracic 00620-00622, 00640, 00670
Vascular .00670
Sternoclavicular Joint 01620
Sternum 00550
Stomach
Restriction
for Obesity 00797
Strayer Procedure 01474
Subdural Taps 00212
Suture Removal 15850-15851
Sympathectomy
Lumbar 00632
Thoracolumbar 00622
Symphysis Pubis 01160, 01170
Tenodesis 01716
Tenoplasty .01714
Tenotomy 01712
Testis 00924-00928, 00930
Thoracoplasty 00472
Thoracoscopy 00528-00529, 00540-00541
Thoracotomy 00540-00541
Thorax 00400-00410,
00450-00454, 00470-00474
Thromboendarterectomy 01442
Thyroid 00320-00322
Tibia 01390-01392, 01484
Trachea 00320, 00326, 00542
Reconstruction 00539
Transplantation
Cornea 00144
Heart 00580
Kidney 00868
Liver 00796, 01990
Lungs 00580
Organ Harvesting 01990
Transurethral Procedures 00910-00918
Tubal Ligation 00851
Tuffier Vaginal Hysterectomy 00944
TURP 00914
Tympanostomy 00120
Tympanotomy 00126
Unlisted Services and Procedures 01999
Urethra 00910, 00918, 00920, 00942
Urethrocystoscopy 00910
Urinary Bladder 00864, 00870, 00912

Urinary Tract 00860
Uterus 00952
Vagina 00940-00942, 00950
   Dilation 57400
   Removal
      Foreign Body 57415
Vaginal Delivery 01960
Vas Deferens
   Excision 00921
Vascular Access 00532
Vascular Shunt 01844
Vascular Surgery
   Abdomen, Lower 00880-00882
   Abdomen, Upper 00770
   Arm, Lower 01840-01852
   Arm, Upper 01770-01782
   Brain 00216
   Elbow 01770-01782
   Hand .01840-01852
   Knee .01430-01444
   Leg, Lower 01500-01522
   Leg, Upper 01260, 01270-01274
   Neck .00350-00352
   Shoulder 01650-01670
   Wrist .01840-01852
Vasectomy 00921
Venography 01916
Ventriculography 00214, 01920
Vertebral Process
   Fracture/Dislocation
      Closed Treatment 22315
Vertebroplasty 01905
Vitrectomy 00145
Vitreoretinal Surgery 00145
Vitreous Body 00145
Vulva 00906
Vulvectomy 00906
Wertheim Operation 00846
Wrist 00400, 01810-01860

Anesthesia Local

See Anesthesia, Local

Aneurysm Repair

See Aorta; Artery
Abdominal Aorta 0078T, 0079T, 0080T, 0081T,
                34800-34805, 34825-34832,
                35081-35103, 75952-75953
Axillary Artery 35011-35013
Basilar Artery 61698, 61702
Brachial Artery 35011-35013
Carotid Artery 35001-35002,
            61613, 61697, 61700, 61703
Celiac Artery 35121-35122
Femoral Artery 35141-35142
Hepatic Artery 35121-35122
Iliac Artery . . .34900, 35131-35132, 75953-75954
Innominate Artery 35021-35022
Intracranial Artery 61705-61708
Mesenteric Artery 35121-35122
Popliteal Artery 35151-35152

Radial Artery 35045
Renal Artery 35121-35122
Splenic Artery 35111-35112
Subclavian Artery . . .35001-35002, 35021-35022
Thoracoabdominal Aorta 33877
Ulnar Artery 35045
Vascular Malformation or Carotid-Cavernous
Fistula 61710
Vertebral Artery 61698, 61702

Angel Dust

See Phencyclidine

Angina Assessment

See Performance Measure

Angiocardiographies

See Heart, Angiography

Angiography

See Aortography
Abdomen 74175, 74185, 75635, 75726
Abdominal Aorta 0080T, 0081T, 75635,
                      75952-75953
Adrenal 75731-75733
Aorta
   Injection 93544
Arm Artery 73206, 75710-75716
Arteriovenous Shunt 75790
Brachial Artery .75658
Brain 70496
Carotid Artery 75660-75671
   Cervical
      Bilateral 75680
      Unilateral 75676
Chest .71275, 71555
Coronary Artery 93556
   Flow Velocity Measurement During
   Angiography 93571-93572
Coronary Bypass 93556
Endovascular Repair . .0080T, 0081T, 75952-75953
Extremity, Lower 73725
Extremity, Upper 73225
Fluorescein 92235
Head 70496, 70544-70546
   Artery 75650
Heart Vessels
   Injection 93545
Indocyanine-green 92240
Left Heart
   Injection 93543
Leg Artery 73706, 75635, 75710-75716
Lung
   Injection 93541
      See Cardiac Catheterization, Injection
Mammary Artery 75756
   See Aortography
Neck 70498, 70547-70549
   Artery 75650
Nuclear Medicine 78445
Other Artery 75774
Pelvic Artery 72198, 75736
Pelvis 72191
Pulmonary 75741-75746

Renal Artery 75722-75724
Right Heart
   Injection 93542
Spinal Artery 75705
Spinal Canal 72159
Thorax 71275
Transcatheter Therapy
   Embolization 75894, 75898
   Infusion 75894, 75898
Vertebral 75685

Angioma

See Lesion, Skin

Angioplasties, Coronary Balloon

See Percutaneous Transluminal Angioplasty

Angioplasty

Aorta
   Intraoperative 35452
   Percutaneous 35472
Axillary Artery
   Intraoperative 35458
Brachiocephalic Artery
   Intraoperative 35458
   Percutaneous 35475
Coronary Artery
   Percutaneous Transluminal 92982-92984
Femoral Artery
   Intraoperative 35456
   Percutaneous 35474
Iliac Artery
   Intraoperative 35454
   Percutaneous 35473
Intracranial
   Percutaneous 61630
Percutaneous Transluminal
Angioplasty 92982-92984
   See Angioplasty; Percutaneous, Transluminal
Popliteal Artery
   Intraoperative 35456
   Percutaneous 35474
Pulmonary Artery
   Percutaneous Transluminal 92997-92998
Renal Artery
   Intraoperative 35450
   Percutaneous 35471
Subclavian Artery
   Intraoperative 35458
Tibioperoneal Artery
   Intraoperative 35459
   Percutaneous 35470
Transluminal
   Arterial 75962-75968
   Venous 75978
Venous
   Intraoperative 35460
   Percutaneous 35476
Visceral Artery
   Intraoperative 35450
   Percutaneous 35471

Angioscopy

Non-Coronary Vessels 35400

Angiotensin Converting Enzyme (ACE)

(ACE) 82164
See Performance Measures

Angiotensin Forming Enzyme
See Renin

Angiotensin I 84244
Riboflavin 84252

Angiotensin II
Blood or Urine 82163

Angle Deformity
Reconstruction
    Toe 28313

Anhydride, Carbonic
See Carbon Dioxide

Anhydrides, Acetic
See Acetic Anhydrides

Animal Inoculation 87001-87003,
87250

Ankle
See Fibula; Leg, Lower; Tibia; Tibiofibular Joint
Abscess
    Incision and Drainage 27603
Amputation 27888
Arthrocentesis 20605
Arthrodesis 27870
Arthrography 73615
Arthroplasty 27700-27703
Arthroscopy
    Surgical 29891-29899
Arthrotomy 27610-27612, 27620-27626
Biopsy 27613-27614, 27620
Bursa
    Incision and Drainage 27604
Disarticulation 27889
Dislocation
    Closed Treatment 27840-27842
    Open Treatment 27846-27848
Exploration 27610, 27620
Fracture
    Lateral 27786-27814
    Medial 27760-27766, 27808-27814
    Trimalleolar 27816-27823
Fusion 27870
Hematoma
    Incision and Drainage 27603
Incision 27607
Injection
    Radiologic 27648
Lesion
    Excision 27630
Magnetic Resonance Imaging
(MRI) 73721-73723
Manipulation 27860
Removal
    Foreign Body 27610, 27620
    Implant 27704
    Loose Body 27620
Repair
    Achilles Tendon 27650-27654
    Ligament 27695-27698
    Tendon 27612, 27680-27687
Strapping 29540
Synovium
    Excision 27625-27626
Tenotomy 27605-27606

Tumor
    Excision 27615-27619
Unlisted Services and Procedures 27899
X-Ray 73600-73610
    with Contrast 73615

Ankylosis (Surgical)
See Arthrodesis

Annuloplasty
Percutaneous, Intradiscal 0062T, 0063T

Anogenital Region
See Perineum

Anoplasty
Stricture 46700-46705

Anorectal Exam (Surgical) 45990

Anorectal Myectomy
See Myomectomy, Anorectal

Anorectal Procedure
Biofeedback 90911

Anorectovaginoplasty 46744-46746

Anoscopy
Ablation
    Polyp 46615
    Tumor 46615
Biopsy 46606
Dilation 46604
Exploration 46600
Hemorrhage 46614
Removal
    Foreign Body 46608
    Polyp 46610-46612
    Tumor 46610-46612

Antebrachium
See Forearm

Antecedent, Plasma Thromboplastin
See Plasma Thromboplastin, Antecedent

Antepartum Care
Cesarean Delivery 59510
    Previous 59610, 59618
Vaginal Delivery 59425-59426

Anterior Ramus of Thoracic Nerve
See Intercostal Nerve

Anthrax Vaccine
See Vaccines

Anthrogon
See Follicle Stimulating Hormone (FSH)

Anti Australia Antigens
See Antibody, Hepatitis B

Anti D Immunoglobulin
See Immune Globulins, Rho (D)

Anti-Human Globulin Consumption Test
See Coombs Test

Anti-Phospholipid Antibody
See Antibody, Phospholipid

Antiactivator, Plasmin
See Alpha-2 Antiplasmin

Antibiotic Administration
Injection 90788

Antibiotic Sensitivity 87181-87184,
87188
Enzyme Detection 87185
Minimum Bactericidal Concentration 87187
Minimum Inhibitory Concentration 87186

Antibodies, Thyroid-Stimulating
See Immunoglobulin, Thyroid Stimulating

Antibodies, Viral
See Viral Antibodies

Antibody
See Antibody Identification; Microsomal Antibody
Actinomyces 86602
Adenovirus 86603
Antinuclear 86038-86039
Antiphosphatidylserine (Phospholipid) ...86148
Antiprothrombin 0030T
Antistreptolysin O 86060-86063
Aspergillus 86606
Bacterium 86609
Bartonella 86611
Beta 2 Glycoprotein I 86146
Blastomyces 86612
Blood Crossmatch 86920-86923
Bordetella 86615
Borrelia 86618-86619
Brucella 86622
Campylobacter 86625
Candida 86628
Cardiolipin 86147
Chlamydia 86631-86632
Coccidioides 86635
Coxiella Burnetii 86638
Cryptococcus 86641
Cyclic Citrullinated Peptide (CCP) 86200
Cytomegalovirus 86644-86645
Cytotoxic Screen 86807-86808
Deoxyribonuclease 86215
Deoxyribonucleic Acid (DNA) 86225-86226
Diphtheria 86648
Ehrlichia 86666
Encephalitis 86651-86654
Enterovirus 86658
Epstein-Barr Virus 86663-86665
Fluorescent 86255-86256
Francisella Tularensis 86668
Fungus 86671
Giardia Lamblia 86674
Growth Hormone 86277
Helicobacter Pylori 86677
Helminth 86682
Hemophilus Influenza 86684
Hepatitis
    Delta Agent 86692
Hepatitis A 86708-86709
Hepatitis B
    Core 86704
    IgM 86705
    Surface 86706
Hepatitis Be 86707
Hepatitis C 86803-86804

Herpes Simplex 86694-86696
Heterophile 86308-86310
Histoplasma 86698
HIV 86689, 86701-86703
HIV-1 . . . . .86701, 86703
HIV-2 86702-86703
HTLV-I 86687, 86689
HTLV-II 86688
Influenza Virus 86710
Insulin 86337
Intrinsic Factor 86340
Islet Cell 86341
Legionella 86713
Leishmania .86717
Leptospira 86720
Listeria Monocytogenes 86723
Lyme Disease 86617
Lymphocytic Choriomeningitis 86727
Lymphogranuloma Venereum 86729
Microsomal .86376
Mucormycosis 86732
Mumps 86735
Mycoplasma 86738
Neisseria Meningitidis 86741
Nocardia 86744
Nuclear Antigen 86235
Other Virus .86790
Parvovirus 86747
Phospholipid 86147
Phospholipid Cofactor 0030T
Plasmodium .86750
Platelet 86022-86023
Protozoa 86753
Red Blood Cell 86850-86870
Respiratory Syncytial Virus 86756
Rickettsia 86757
Rotavirus 86759
Rubella 86762
Rubeola 86765
Salmonella .86768
Shigella 86771
Sperm 89325
Streptokinase 86590
Tetanus 86774
Thyroglobulin 86800
Toxoplasma 86777-86778
Treponema Pallidum 86781
Trichinella 86784
Varicella-Zoster 86787
White Blood Cell 86021
Yersinia 86793

Antibody Identification

Leukocyte Antibodies 86021
Platelet 86022-86023
Red Blood Cell
   Pretreatment 86970-86972
Serum
   Pretreatment 86975-86978

Antibody Neutralization Test
See Neutralization Test

Antibody Receptor
See FC Receptor

Anticoagulant
See Clotting Inhibitors

Antidiabetic Hormone
See Glucagon

Antidiuretic Hormone 84588

Antidiuretic Hormone Measurement
See Vasopressin

AntiDNA Autoantibody
See Antinuclear Antibodies (ANA)

Antigen
Allergen Immunotherapy 95144
Carcinoembryonic 82378
Prostate Specific 84152-84153

Antigen Bronchial Provocation Tests
See Bronchial Challenge Test

Antigen Detection
Direct Fluorescence 87265-87272, 87276,
           87278, 87280, 87285-87290
   Bordetella 87265
   Chlamydia Trachomatis 87270
   Cryptosporidium 87272
   Cytomegalovirus 87271
   Enterovirus 87267
   Giardia .87269
   Influenza A 87276
   Legionella Pneumophila 87278
   Not Otherwise Specified 87299
   Respiratory Syncytial Virus 87280
   Treponema Pallidum 87285
   Varicella-Zoster 87290
Enzyme Immunoassay 87301-87451
   Adenovirus 87301
   Chlamydia Trachomatis 87320
   Clostridium Difficile 87324
   Cryptococcus Neoformans 87327
   Cryptosporidium 87328
   Cytomegalovirus 87332
   Entamoeba Histolytica Dispar Group . .87336
   Entamoeba Histolytica Group 87337
   Escherichia coli O157 87335
   Giardia .87329
   Helicobacter Pylori 87338-87339
   Hepatitis B Surface Antigen (HBsAg) . .87340
   Hepatitis B Surface Antigen (HBsAg)
   Neutralization 87341
   Hepatitis Be Antigen (HBeAg) 87350
   Hepatitis Delta Agent 87380
   Histoplasma capsulatum 87385
   HIV-1 87390
   HIV-2 87391
   Influenza A 87400
   Influenza B 87400
   Multiple Step Method 87301-87449
     Polyvalent 87451
   Not Otherwise Specified 87449, 87451
   Respiratory Syncytial Virus 87420
   Rotavirus 87425
   Shigella-like Toxin 87427
   Single Step Method 87450
   Streptococcus, Group A 87430
Immunofluorescence 87260-87300
   Adenovirus 87260
   Herpes Simplex 87273-87274
   Influenza B 87275
   Legionella Micdadei 87277
   Not Otherwise Specified 87299
   Parainfluenza Virus 87279
   Pneumocystis Carinii 87281
   Polyvalent 87300
   Rubeola .87283

Antigen, Australia
See Hepatitis Antigen, B Surface

Antigen, CD4
See CD4

Antigen, CD8
See CD8

Antigens, CD142
See Thromboplastin

Antigens, CD143
See Angiotensin Converting Enzyme (ACE)

Antigens, E
See Hepatitis Antigen, Be

Antigens, Hepatitis
See Hepatitis Antigen

Antigens, Hepatitis B
See Hepatitis Antigen, B

Antihemophilic Factor B
See Christmas Factor

Antihemophilic Factor C
See Plasma Thromboplastin, Antecedent

Antihemophilic Globulin (AHG) 85240

Antihuman Globulin 86880-86886

Antimony 83015

Antinuclear Antibodies (ANA) .86038-86039

Antiplasmin, Alpha-2 85410

Antiplatelet Therapy
See Performance Measures

Antiprotease, Alpha 1
See Alpha-1 Antitrypsin

Antiprothrombin Antibody 0030T

Antistreptococcal Antibody 86215

Antistreptokinase Titer 86590

Antistreptolysin O 86060-86063

Antithrombin III 85300-85301

Antithrombin VI
See Fibrin Degradation Products

Antitoxin Assay 87230

Antiviral Antibody
See Viral Antibodies

Antrostomy
Sinus
　　Maxillary 31256-31267

Antrotomy
Sinus
　　Maxillary 31020-31032
Transmastoid 69501

Antrum of Highmore
See Sinus, Maxillary

Antrum Puncture
Sinus
　　Maxillary 31000
　　Sphenoid 31002

Anus
See Hemorrhoids; Rectum
Ablation 46615
Abscess
　　Incision and Drainage 46045-46050
Biofeedback 90911
Biopsy
　　Endoscopy 46606
Crypt
　　Excision 46210-46211
Dilation
　　Endoscopy 46604
Endoscopy
　　Biopsy 46606
　　Dilation 46604
　　Exploration 46600
　　Hemorrhage 46614
　　Removal
　　　　Foreign Body 46608
　　　　Polyp 46610, 46612
　　　　Tumor 46610, 46612
Excision
　　Tag 46220, 46230
Exploration
　　Endoscopy 46600
　　Surgical 45990
Fissure
　　Destruction 46940-46942
　　Excision 46200
Fistula
　　Excision 46270-46285
　　Repair 46706
Hemorrhage
　　Endoscopic Control 46614
Hemorrhoids
　　Clot Excision 46320
　　Destruction 46934-46936
　　Excision 46250-46262
　　Injection 46500
　　Ligation 46221, 46945-46946
　　Stapling 46947
　　Suture 46945-46946
Imperforated
　　Repair 46715-46742
Incision
　　Septum 46070
Lesion
　　Destruction 46900-46917, 46924
　　Excision 45108, 46922
Manometry 91122
Placement
　　Seton 46020

Reconstruction 46742
　　Congenital Absence 46730-46740
　　Sphincter 46750-46751, 46760-46762
　　with Graft 46753
　　with Implant 46762
Removal
　　Foreign Body 46608
　　Seton 46030
　　Suture 46754
　　Wire 46754
Repair
　　Anovaginal Fistula 46715-46716
　　Cloacal Anomaly 46748
　　Fistula 46706
　　Stricture 46700-46705
Sphincter
　　Chemodenervation 46505
　　Electromyography 51784-51785
　　Needle 51785
Unlisted Services and Procedures 46999

Aorta
Abdominal
　　Aneurysm 0078T, 0079T, 0080T, 0081T,
　　　　34800-34805, 34825-34832,
　　　　35081-35103, 75952-75953
　　Thromboendarterectomy 35331
Anastomosis
　　to Pulmonary Artery 33606
Angiogram
　　Radiologic Injection 93544
　　　　See Cardiac Catheterization, Injection
Angioplasty 35452
Aortography 75600-75630
Balloon 33967, 33970
Catheterization
　　Catheter 36200
　　Intracatheter/Needle 36160
Circulation Assist 33967, 33970
Conduit to Heart 33404
Excision
　　Coarctation 33840-33851
Insertion
　　Balloon Device 33967
　　Graft 33330-33335
　　Intracatheter/Needle 36160
Removal
　　Balloon Assist Device 33968, 33971
Repair 33320-33322, 33802-33803
　　Coarctation 33840-33851
　　Graft 33860-33877
　　Hypoplastic or Interrupted Aortic Arch
　　　　with Cardiopulmonary Bypass 33853
　　　　without Cardiopulmonary Bypass ...33852
　　Sinus of Valsalva 33702-33720
Suspension 33800
Suture 33320-33322
Thoracic
　　Repair 75956-75959
　　　　Endovascular 33880-33891
Valve
　　Incision 33415
　　Repair 33400-33403
　　　　Left Ventricle 33414
　　　　Supravalvular Stenosis 33417
　　Replacement 33405-33413
X-Ray with Contrast 75600-75630

Aorta-Pulmonary ART Transposition
See Transposition, Great Arteries

Aortic Sinus
See Sinus of Valsalva

Aortic Stenosis
Repair 33415
　　Supravalvular 33417

Aortic Valve
See Heart, Aortic Valve

Aortic Valve Replacement
See Replacement, Aortic Valve

Aortocoronary Bypass
See Coronary Artery Bypass Graft (CABG)

Aortocoronary Bypass for Heart Revascularization
See Artery, Coronary, Bypass

Aortography 75600-75605,
　　　　　　　　　　　　　　75630, 93544
See Angiography
Serial 75625
with Iliofemoral Artery 75630

Aortoiliac
Embolectomy 34151-34201
Thrombectomy 34151-34201

Aortopexy 33800

Aortoplasty
Supravalvular Stenosis 33417

AP
See Voiding Pressure Studies

Apert-Gallais Syndrome
See Adrenogenital Syndrome

Aphasia Testing 96105
See Neurology, Diagnostic

Apheresis
Therapeutic 36511-36516

Apical-Aortic Conduit 33404

Apicectomy
with Mastoidectomy 69605
　　Petrous 69530

Apoaminotransferase, Aspartate
See Transaminase, Glutamic Oxaloacetic

Apolipoprotein
Blood or Urine 82172

Appendectomy 44950-44960
Laparoscopic 44970

Appendiceal Abscess
See Abscess, Appendix

Appendico-Vesicostomy
Cutaneous 50845

Appendix
Abscess
  Incision and Drainage
    Open 44900
    Percutaneous 44901
Excision 44950-44960

Application
Allergy Tests 95044
Bone Fixation Device
  Multiplane 20692
  Uniplane 20690
Caliper 20660
Cranial Tongs 20660
Fixation Device
  Shoulder 23700
Halo
  Cranial 20661
    Thin Skull Osteology 20664
  Femoral 20663
  Maxillofacial Fixation 21100
  Pelvic 20662
Interdental Fixation Device 21110
Neurostimulation 64550
Radioelement 77761-77778
  Surface 77789
  with Ultrasound 76965
Stereotactic Frame 20660

Application of External Fixation Device
See Fixation Device, Application, External

APPT
See Thromboplastin, Partial, Time

Aquatic Therapy
See Physical Medicine/Therapy/Occupational Therapy

Aqueous Shunt
to Extraocular Reservoir 66180
  Revision 66185

Arch, Zygomatic
See Zygomatic Arch

Arm
See Radius; Ulna; Wrist
Lower
  Abscess 25028
  Amputation 24900-24920, 25900-25905,
                    25915
    Cineplasty 24940
    Revision 25907-25909
  Angiography 73206
  Artery
    Ligation 37618
  Biopsy 25065-25066
  Bursa
    Incision and Drainage 25031
  Bypass Graft 35903
  Cast 29075
  CT Scan 73200-73206
  Decompression 25020-25025
  Exploration
    Blood Vessel 35860
  Fasciotomy 24495, 25020-25025
  Hematoma 25028

Lesion, Tendon Sheath
  Excision 25110
Magnetic Resonance Imaging
(MRI) 73218-73220, 73223
Reconstruction
  Ulna 25337
Removal
  Foreign Body 25248
Repair
  Blood Vessel with Other Graft 35266
  Blood Vessel with Vein Graft 35236
  Decompression 24495
  Muscle 25260-25263, 25270
    Secondary 25265
  Secondary
    Muscle 25272-25274
    Tendon 25272-25274
  Tendon 25260-25263, 25270,
         25280-25295, 25310-25316
    Secondary 25265
  Tendon Sheath 25275
Replantation 20805
Splint 29125-29126
Tenotomy 25290
Tumor
  Excision 25075-25077
Ultrasound 76880
Unlisted Services and Procedures 25999
X-Ray 73090
  with Upper Arm 73092
Removal
  Foreign Body
    Forearm or Wrist 25248
Repair
  Muscle 24341
  Tendon 24341
Upper
  Abscess
    Incision and Drainage 23930
      See Elbow; Humerus
  Amputation 23900-23921, 24900-24920
    Cineplasty 24940
    Revision 24925-24930
    with Implant 24931-24935
  Anesthesia 00400, 01710-01782
  Angiography 73206
  Artery
    Ligation 37618
  Biopsy 24065-24066
  Bypass Graft 35903
  Cast 29065
  CT Scan 73200-73206
  Exploration
    Blood Vessel 35860
  Hematoma
    Incision and Drainage 23930
  Magnetic Resonance Imaging
  (MRI) 73218-73220, 73223
  Muscle Revision 24330-24331
  Removal
    Cast 29705
    Foreign Body 24200-24201
  Repair
    Blood Vessel with Other Graft 35266
    Blood Vessel with Vein Graft 35236
    Muscle Transfer 24301, 24320
    Tendon 24332
    Tendon Lengthening 24305

    Tendon Revision 24320
    Tendon Transfer 24301
    Tenotomy 24310
  Replantation 20802
  Splint 29105
  Tumor
    Excision 24075-24077
  Ultrasound 76880
  Unlisted Services and Procedures 24999
  Wound Exploration
    Penetrating 20103
X-Ray
  with Lower Arm
    Infant 73092

Arnold-Chiari Malformation Repair
See Decompression, Skull

Arrest, Epiphyseal
See Epiphyseal Arrest

Arrhythmogenic Focus
Heart
  Catheter Ablation 93650-93652
  Destruction 33250-33251, 33261

Arsenic 83015
Blood or Urine 82175

ART
See Syphilis Test

Arterial Catheterization
See Cannulation, Arterial

Arterial Dilatation, Transluminal
See Angioplasty, Transluminal

Arterial Grafting for Coronary Artery Bypass
See Bypass Graft, Coronary Artery, Arterial

Arterial Pressure
See Blood Pressure

Arterial Puncture 36600

Arteriography, Aorta
See Aortography

Arteriosus, Ductus
See Ductus Arteriosus

Arteriosus, Truncus
See Truncus Arteriosus

Arteriotomy
See Incision, Artery; Transection, Artery

Arteriovenous Anastomosis 36818-36820

Arteriovenous Fistula
Cannulization
  Vein 36815
Repair
  Abdomen 35182
    Acquired or Traumatic 35189
  Head 35180
    Acquired or Traumatic 35188
  Lower Extremity 35184
    Acquired or Traumatic 35190

Neck 35180
　Acquired or Traumatic 35188
Thorax 35182
　Acquired or Traumatic 35189
Upper Extremity 35184
　Acquired or Traumatic 35190
Revision
　Hemodialysis Graft or Fistula
　　with Thrombectomy 36833
　　without Thrombectomy 36832
Thrombectomy
　Dialysis Graft
　　without Revision 36831
　Graft 36870

Arteriovenous Malformation
Cranial
　Repair 61680-61692, 61705-61708
Spinal
　Excision 63250-63252
　Injection 62294
　Repair 63250-63252

Arteriovenous Shunt
Angiography 75790
Catheterization 36145

Artery
Abdomen
　Angiography 75726
　Catheterization 36245-36248
　Ligation 37617
Adrenal
　Angiography 75731-75733
Anastomosis
　Cranial 61711
Angioplasty 75962-75968
Aorta
　Angioplasty 35452
　Atherectomy 35481, 35491
Aortoiliac
　Embolectomy 34151-34201
　Thrombectomy 34151-34201
Aortoiliofemoral 35363
Arm
　Angiography 75710-75716
　Harvest of Artery for Coronary Artery
　　Bypass Graft 35600
Atherectomy
　Open 35480-35485
　Percutaneous 35490-35495
Axillary
　Aneurysm 35011-35013
　Angioplasty 35458
　Bypass Graft 35516-35522, 35533,
　　　　　　35616-35623, 35650, 35654
　Embolectomy 34101
　Thrombectomy 34101
　Thromboendarterectomy 35321
Basilar
　Aneurysm 61698, 61702
Biopsy
　Transcatheter 75970
Brachial
　Aneurysm 35011-35013
　Angiography 75658
　Bypass Graft ...35510, 35512, 35522-35525
　Catheterization 36120

Embolectomy 34101
Exploration 24495
Exposure 34834
Thrombectomy 34101
Thromboendarterectomy 35321
Brachiocephalic
　Angioplasty 35458
　Atherectomy 35484, 35494
　Catheterization 36215-36218
Bypass Graft
　with Composite Graft 35681-35683
Cannulization
　for Extra Corporeal Circulation 36823
　to Vein 36810-36815
Carotid
　Aneurysm 35001-35002, 61697-61705
　　Vascular Malformation or Carotid
　　Cavernous Fistula 61710
　Angiography 75660-75680
　Bypass Graft ...33891, 35501-35510, 35526,
　　　　　　35601-35606, 35626, 35642
　Catheterization 36100
　Decompression ..61590-61591, 61595-61596
　Embolectomy 34001
　Exploration 35701
　Ligation 37600-37606, 61611-61612
　Thrombectomy 34001
　Thromboendarterectomy 35301, 35390
　Transection 61611-61612
　Transposition 33889
Carotid, Common
　Intima-Media Thickness (IMT) Study ..0126T
Celiac
　Aneurysm 35121-35122
　Bypass Graft 35531, 35631
　Embolectomy 34151
　Thrombectomy 34151
　Thromboendarterectomy 35341
Chest
　Ligation 37616
Coronary
　Angiography 93556
　Atherectomy 92995-92996
　Bypass 33517-33519
　　Arterial 33533-33536
　Bypass Venous Graft 33510-33516
　Graft 33503-33505
　Ligation 33502
　Repair 33500-33507
　Thrombectomy
　　Percutaneous 92973
Digital
　Sympathectomy 64820
Ethmoidal
　Ligation 30915
Extra Corporeal Circulation
　for Regional Chemotherapy
　of Extremity 36823
Extracranial
　Vascular Studies
　　Non-Invasive, Physiologic 93875
Extremities
　Vascular Studies 93922-93923
Extremity
　Bypass Graft Revision 35879-35881
　Catheterization 36140
　Ligation 37618

Femoral
　Aneurysm 35141-35142
　Angioplasty 35456
　Atherectomy 35483, 35493
　Bypass Graft 35521, 35533, 35546,
　　35551-35558, 35566, 35621, 35646-35647,
　　　　　　35651-35661, 35666, 35700
　Bypass In-Situ 35583-35585
　Embolectomy 34201
　Exploration 35721
　Exposure 34812-34813
　Thrombectomy 34201
　Thromboendarterectomy 35371-35381
Great Vessel
　Repair 33770-33781
Head
　Angiography 75650
Hepatic
　Aneurysm 35121-35122
Iliac
　Aneurysm 35131-35132, 75954
　Angioplasty 35454
　Atherectomy 35482, 35492
　Bypass Graft ...35541, 35563, 35641, 35663
　Embolectomy 34151-34201
　Exposure 34820, 34833
　Graft 34900
　Occulsion Device 34808
　Thrombectomy 34151-34201
　Thromboendarterectomy 35351,
　　　　　　　　　　35361-35363
Iliofemoral
　Bypass Graft ...35548-35549, 35565, 35665
　Thromboendarterectomy 35355, 35363
　X-Ray with Contrast 75630
Innominate
　Aneurysm 35021-35022
　Embolectomy 34001-34101
　Thrombectomy 34001-34101
　Thromboendarterectomy 35311
Leg
　Angiography 75710-75716
　Catheterization 36245-36248
Mammary
　Angiography 75756
Maxillary
　Ligation 30920
Mesenteric
　Aneurysm 35121-35122
　Bypass Graft 35531, 35631
　Embolectomy 34151
　Thrombectomy 34151
　Thromboendarterectomy 35341
Middle Cerebral Artery, Fetal
　Vascular Studies 76821
Neck
　Angiography 75650
　Ligation 37615
Nose
　Incision 30915-30920
Other Angiography 75774
Other Artery
　Exploration 35761
Pelvic
　Angiography 75736
　Catheterization 36245-36248
Peripheral Arterial Rehabilitation 93668

Peroneal
  Bypass Graft 35566-35571, 35666-35671
  Bypass In-Situ 35585-35587
  Embolectomy 34203
  Thrombectomy 34203
  Thromboendarterectomy 35381
Popliteal
  Aneurysm 35151-35152
  Angioplasty 35456
  Atherectomy 35483, 35493
  Bypass Graft ..35551-35556, 35571, 35623,
              35651, 35656, 35671, 35700
  Bypass In-Situ 35583, 35587
  Embolectomy 34203
  Exploration 35741
  Thrombectomy 34203
  Thromboendarterectomy 35381
Pulmonary
  Anastomosis 33606
  Angiography 75741-75746
  Repair 33690, 33925-33926
Radial
  Aneurysm 35045
  Embolectomy 34111
  Sympathectomy 64821
  Thrombectomy 34111
Rehabilitation 93668
Reimplantation
  Carotid 35691, 35694-35695
  Subclavian 35693-35695
  Vertebral 35691-35693
  Visceral 35697
Renal
  Aneurysm 35121-35122
  Angiography 75722-75724
  Angioplasty 35450
  Atherectomy 35480, 35490
  Bypass Graft 35536, 35560, 35631-35636
  Embolectomy 34151
  Thrombectomy 34151
  Thromboendarterectomy 35341
Repair
  Aneurysm 36834, 61697-61708
  Angioplasty 75962-75968
Revision
  Hemodialysis Graft or Fistula
    with Thrombectomy 36833
    without Thrombectomy 36832
Spine
  Angiography 75705
Splenic
  Aneurysm 35111-35112
  Bypass Graft 35536, 35636
Subclavian
  Aneurysm 35001-35002, 35021-35022
  Angioplasty 35458
  Bypass Graft 35506-35507, 35511-35516,
              35526, 35606-35616, 35626, 35645
  Embolectomy 34001-34101
  Thrombectomy 34001-34101
  Thromboendarterectomy 35301-35311
  Transposition 33889
  Unlisted Services and Procedures 37799
Superficial Palmar Arch
  Sympathectomy 64823
Temporal
  Biopsy 37609
  Ligation 37609

Thoracic
  Catheterization 36215-36218
Thrombectomy 37184-37186
  Hemodialysis Graft or Fistula 36831
  Other than Hemodialysis Graft
  or Fistula 35875, 36870
Tibial
  Bypass Graft 35566-35571,
              35623, 35666-35671
  Bypass In-Situ 35585-35587
  Embolectomy 34203
  Thrombectomy 34203
  Thromboendarterectomy 35381
Tibioperoneal
  Angioplasty 35459, 35470
  Atherectomy 35485, 35495
Transcatheter Therapy
  with Angiography 75894-75898
Transposition
  Carotid 35691, 35694-35695
  Subclavian 35693-35695
  Vertebral 35691-35693
Ulnar
  Aneurysm 35045
  Embolectomy 34111
  Sympathectomy 64822
  Thrombectomy 34111
Unlisted Services and Procedures 37799
Vertebral
  Aneurysm 35005, 61698, 61702
  Angiography 75685
  Bypass Graft 35508, 35515, 35642-35645
  Catheterization 36100
  Decompression 61597
  Thromboendarterectomy 35301
Visceral
  Angioplasty 35450
  Atherectomy 35480, 35490
  Reimplantation 35697

Artery Catheterization, Pulmonary
See Catheterization, Pulmonary Artery

Arthrectomy
Elbow 24155

Arthrocentesis
Intermediate Joint 20605
Large Joint 20610
Small Joint 20600

Arthrodeses
See Arthrodesis

Arthrodesis
Ankle 27870
  Tibiotalar and Fibulotalar Joints 29899
Carpometacarpal Joint
  Hand 26843-26844
  Thumb.....................26841-26842
Cervical Anterior
  with Discectomy 22554
Elbow 24800-24802
Finger Joint 26852
  Interphalangeal 26860-26863
  Metacarpophalangeal 26850
Foot Joint 28730-28735, 28740
  Pantalar 28705
  Subtalar 28725

Triple 28715
  with Advancement 28737
  with Lengthening 28737
Hand Joint 26843-26844
Hip Joint 27284-27286
Intercarpal Joint 25820
  with Autograft 25825
Interphalangeal Joint 26860-26863
  Great Toe 28755
    with Tendon Transfer 28760
Knee 27580
Metacarpophalangeal Joint 26850-26852
Metatarsophalangeal Joint
  Great Toe 28750
Pubic Symphysis 27282
Radioulnar Joint
  with Resection of Ulna 25830
Sacroiliac Joint 27280
Shoulder
  See Shoulder, Arthrodesis
Shoulder Joint 23800
  with Autogenous Graft 23802
Talus
  Pantalar 28705
  Subtalar 28725
  Triple 28715
Tarsal Joint 28730-28735, 28740
  with Advancement 28737
  with Lengthening 28737
Tarsometatarsal Joint 28730-28735, 28740
Thumb Joint 26841-26842
Tibiofibular Joint 27871
Vertebra
  Additional Interspace
    Anterior/Anterolateral Approach 22585
    Lateral Extracavitary 22534
    Posterior 22632
  Cervical
    Anterior/Anterolateral Approach 22548
    Posterior/Posterolateral and/or Lateral
    Transverse Process 22590-22600
  Lumbar
    Anterior/Anterolateral Approach 22558
    Lateral Extracavitary 22533
    Posterior/Interbody 22630
    Posterior/Posterolateral and/or Lateral
    Transverse Process 22612
  Spinal Deformity
    Anterior Approach 22808-22812
    Posterior Approach 22800-22804
  Spinal Fusion
    Exploration 22830
  Thoracic
    Anterior/Anterolateral Approach 22556
    Lateral Extracavitary 22532
    Posterior/Posterolateral and/or Lateral
    Transverse Process 22610
Vertebrae
  Posterior 22614
Wrist............................25800
  with Graft 25810
  with Sliding Graft 25805

Arthrography
Ankle 73615
  Injection 27648
Elbow 73085
  Injection 24220

Hip 73525
    Injection 27093-27095
Knee 73580
    Injection 27370
Sacroiliac Joint 73542
    Injection 27096
Shoulder 73040
    Injection 23350
Temporomandibular Joint (TMJ) . . .70328-70332
    Injection 21116
Wrist 73115
    Injection 25246

Arthroplasties, Knee Replacement
See Prosthesis, Knee

Arthroplasty
Ankle 27700-27703
Elbow 24360
    Total Replacement 24363
    with Implant 24361-24362
Hip 27132
    Partial Replacement 27125
    Revision 27134-27138
    Total Replacement 27130
Interphalangeal Joint 26535-26536
Intervertebral Disc
    Removal 0093T-0095T
    Revision 0096T-0098T
    Total Replacement 0090T-0092T
Knee 27437-27443, 27446-27447
    Revision 27486-27487
    with Prosthesis 27438, 27445
Metacarpophalangeal Joint 26530-26531
Radius 24365
    with Implant 24366
Reconstruction
    Prosthesis
        Hip 27125
Shoulder Joint
    with Implant 23470-23472
Temporomandibular Joint 21240-21243
Wrist 25447
    Carpal 25443
    Lunate 25444
    Navicular .25443
    Radius 25441
    Revision .25449
    Total Replacement 25446
    Trapezium .25445
    Ulna 25442
    with Implant 25441-25445
Wrist (Pseudarthrosis Type) 25332

Arthroplasty, Hip, Total
See Hip, Total Replacement

Arthroplasty, Shoulder
See Repair, Shoulder

Arthropods
Examination 87168

Arthroscopy
Diagnostic
    Elbow 29830
    Hip 29860
    Knee 29870
    Metacarpophalangeal Joint 29900

Shoulder 29805
Temporomandibular Joint 29800
Wrist 29840
Surgical
    Ankle 29891-29899
    Elbow 29834-29838
    Hip 29861-29863
    Knee 29871-29889
        Cartilage Allograft 29867
        Cartilage Autograft 29866
        Meniscal Transplantation 29868
    Metacarpophalangeal Joint 29901-29902
    Shoulder 29806-29827
    Temporomandibular Joint 29804
    Wrist 29843-29848
Unlisted Services and Procedures 29999

Arthroscopy of Ankle
See Ankle, Arthroscopy

Arthrotomy
Acromioclavicular Joint 23044
Ankle 27610-27612, 27620
Ankle Joint 27625-27626
Carpometacarpal Joint 26070
    with Biopsy, Synovium
        with Synovial Biopsy 26100
Elbow 24000
    Capsular Release 24006
    with Joint Exploration 24101
    with Synovectomy 24102
    with Synovial Biopsy 24100
Finger Joint .26075
    Interphalangeal
        with Synovial Biopsy 26110
    Metacarpophalangeal
        with Biopsy, Synovium 26105
Glenohumeral Joint 23040
Hip 27033
    for Infection
        with Drainage 27030
        with Synovectomy 27054
Interphalangeal Joint 26080, 26110
    Toe 28024, 28054
Intertarsal Joint 28020, 28050
Knee 27310, 27330-27335, 27403, 29868
Metacarpophalangeal Joint 26075, 26105
Metatarsophalangeal Joint 28022, 28052
Shoulder 23044, 23105-23107
Shoulder Joint 23100-23101
    Exploration and/or Removal of Loose or
    Foreign Body 23107
Sternoclavicular Joint 23044
Tarsometatarsal Joint 28020, 28050
Temporomandibular Joint 21010
with Biopsy
    Acromioclavicular Joint 23101
    Glenohumeral Joint 23100
    Hip Joint 27052
    Knee Joint 27330
    Sacroiliac Joint
        Hip Joint 27050
    Sternoclavicular Joint 23101
with Synovectomy
    Glenohumeral Joint 23105
    Sternoclavicular Joint 23106
Wrist 25040, 25100-25107

Arthrotomy for Removal of Prosthesis of Ankle
See Ankle, Removal, Implant

Arthrotomy for Removal of Prosthesis of Hip
See Hip, Removal, Prosthesis

Arthrotomy for Removal of Prosthesis of Wrist
See Prosthesis, Wrist, Removal

Articular Ligament
See Ligament

Artificial Abortion
See Abortion

Artificial Cardiac Pacemaker
See Heart, Pacemaker

Artificial Eye
See Prosthesis

Artificial Genitourinary Sphincter
See Prosthesis, Urethral Sphincter

Artificial Insemination 58976
See In Vitro Fertilization
Intra-Cervical 58321
Intra-Uterine 58322
Sperm Washing 58323

Artificial Knee Joints
See Prosthesis, Knee

Artificial Penis
See Penile Prosthesis

Artificial Pneumothorax
See Pneumothorax, Therapeutic

Arytenoid
Excision
    Endoscopic 31560-31561

Arytenoid Cartilage
Excision 31400
Repair 31400

Arytenoidectomy 31400
Endoscopic .31560

Arytenoidopexy 31400

Ascorbic Acid
Blood 82180

Aspartate Aminotransferase
See Transaminase, Glutamic Oxaloacetic

Aspergillus
Antibody 86606

Aspiration
See Puncture Aspiration
Amniotic Fluid
    Diagnostic 59000
    Therapeutic 59001
Bladder 51000-51010
Bone Marrow 38220

Brain Lesion
Stereotactic 61750-61751
Bronchi
Endoscopy 31645-31646
Bursa 20600-20610
Catheter
Nasotracheal 31720
Tracheobronchial 31725
Cyst
Bone 20615
Kidney 50390
Pelvis 50390
Spinal Cord .62268
Thyroid 60001
Duodenal 89100-89105
Fetal Fluid 59074
Ganglion Cyst 20612
Hydrocele
Tunica Vaginalis 55000
Joint 20600-20610
Laryngoscopy
Direct 31515
Lens Material 66840
Liver 47015
Lung 32420
Nucleus of Disk
Lumbar 62287
Orbital Contents 67415
Pelvis
Endoscopy .49322
Pericardium 33010-33011
Pleural Cavity 32000-32002
Puncture
Cyst
Breast 19000-19001
Spinal Cord
Stereotaxis 63615
Syrinx
Spinal Cord 62268
Thyroid 60001
Trachea
Nasotracheal 31720
Puncture 31612
Tunica Vaginalis
Hydrocele 55000
Vitreous 67015

Aspiration Lipectomies
See Liposuction

Aspiration of Bone Marrow from Donor for Transplant
See Bone Marrow, Harvesting

Aspiration, Chest
See Thoracentesis

Aspiration, Lung Puncture
See Pneumocentesis

Aspiration, Nail
See Evacuation, Hematoma, Subungual

Aspiration, Spinal Puncture
See Spinal Tap

Assay Tobramycin
See Tobramycin

Assay, Very Long Chain Fatty Acids
See Fatty Acid, Very Long Chain

Assisted Circulation
See Circulation Assist

AST
See Transaminase, Glutamic Oxaloacetic

Astragalectomy 28130

Astragalus
See Talus

Asymmetry, Face
See Hemifacial Microsomia

Ataxia Telangiectasia
Chromosome Analysis 88248

Ataxy, Telangiectasia
See Ataxia Telangiectasia

Atherectomies, Coronary
See Artery, Coronary, Atherectomy

Atherectomy
See X-Ray, Artery
Open
Aorta 35481
Brachiocephalic 35484
Femoral 35483
Iliac 35482
Popliteal 35483
Renal 35480
Tibioperoneal 35485
Visceral 35480
Percutaneous
Aorta 35491
Brachiocephalic 35494
Coronary 92995-92996
See Artery, Coronary
Femoral 35493
Iliac 35492
Popliteal 35493
Renal 35490
Tibioperoneal 35495
Visceral 35490
X-Ray
Peripheral Artery 75992-75993
Renal Artery 75994
Visceral Artery 75995-75996

ATLV
See HTLV I

ATLV Antibodies
See Antibody, HTLV-I

Atomic Absorption Spectroscopy 0064T, 82190

ATP Creatine Phosphotransferase
See CPK

Atresia, Choanal
See Choanal Atresia

Atresia, Congenital
Auditory Canal, External
Reconstruction 69320

Atria
Reconstruction 33253

Atrial Electrogram
See Cardiology, Diagnostic
Esophageal Recording 93615-93616

Atrial Fibrillation
See Fibrillation, Atrial

Atrioseptopexy
See Heart, Repair, Atrial Septum

Atrioseptoplasty
See Heart, Repair, Atrial Septum

Attachment
See Fixation

Atticotomy 69631, 69635

Audiologic Function Tests
See Ear, Nose and Throat; Hearing Evaluation
Acoustic Reflex .92568
Acoustic Reflex Decay 92569
Audiometry
Bekesy 92560-92561
Comprehensive 92557
Conditioning Play 92582
Groups 92559
Pure Tone 92552-92553
Select Picture 92583
Speech 92555-92556
Visual Reinforcement 92579
Central Auditory Function 92620-92621
Electrocochleography 92584
Evoked Otoacoustic Emission 92587-92588
Filtered Speech .92571
Lombard Test 92573
Loudness Balance 92562
Screening 92551
Sensorineural Acuity 92575
Short Increment Sensitivity Index 92564
Staggered Spondaic Word Test 92572
Stenger Test 92565, 92577
Synthetic Sentence Test 92576
Tinnitus Assessment 92625
Tone Decay 92563

Audiometry
Bekesy 92560-92561
Brainstem Evoked Response 92585-92586
Comprehensive .92557
Conditioning Play 92582
Groups 92559
See Ear, Nose and Throat
Pure Tone 92552-92553
Select Picture .92583
Speech 92555-92556
Tympanometry .92567

Auditory Brain Stem Evoked Response
See Evoked Potential, Auditory Brainstem

Auditory Canal
Decompression .61591
External
Abscess
Incision and Drainage 69020

Biopsy 69105
Lesion
  Excision 69140-69155
Reconstruction
  for Congenital Atresia 69320
  for Stenosis 69310
Removal
  Cerumen 69210
  Ear Wax 69210
  Foreign Body 69200-69205
Internal
Decompression 69960

Auditory Canal Atresia, External
See Atresia, Congenital, Auditory Canal, External

**Auditory Evoked Otoacoustic
Emission** 92587-92588

**Auditory Evoked
Potentials** 92585-92586
See Audiologic Function Tests

Auditory Labyrinth
See Ear, Inner

Auditory Meatus
X-Ray 70134

Auditory Tube
See Eustachian Tube

Augmentation
Chin 21120, 21123
Malar 21270
Mandibular Body
  with Bone Graft 21127
  with Prosthesis 21125
Osteoplasty
  Facial Bones 21208
Percutaneous
  Spine 22523-22535

Augmentation Mammoplasty
See Breast, Augmentation

Augmented Histamine Test 91052
See Gastric Analysis Test

Aural Rehabilitation 92626-92633

Auricle (Heart)
See Atria

Auricular Fibrillation
See Fibrillation, Atrial

Auricular Prosthesis 21086

Australia Antigen
See Hepatitis Antigen, B Surface

Autograft
Bone
  Local 20936
  Morselized 20937
  Structural 20938
Chondrocytes
  Knee 27412

for Spine Surgery
  Local 20936
  Morselized 20937
  Structural 20938
Skin
  Dermal 15130-15136
  Epidermal 15110-15116, 15150-15157
  Harvesting
    for Tissue Culture 15040

Autologous Blood Transfusion
See Autotransfusion

Autologous Transplantation
See Autograft

Automated Data
Nuclear Medicine 78890-78891

**Autonomic Nervous System
Function**
See Neurology, Diagnostic; Neurophysiologic
Testing

Autoprothrombin C
See Thrombokinase

Autoprothrombin I
See Proconvertin

Autoprothrombin II
See Christmas Factor

Autoprothrombin III
See Stuart-Prower Factor

Autopsy
Coroner's Exam 88045
Forensic Exam 88040
Gross and Micro Exam 88020-88029
Gross Exam 88000-88016
Organ 88037
Regional 88036
Unlisted Services and Procedures 88099

Autotransfusion
Blood 86890-86891

Autotransplant
See Autograft

Autotransplantation
Renal 50380

AV Fistula
See Arteriovenous Fistula

AV Shunt
See Arteriovenous Shunt

Avulsion
Nails 11730-11732
Nerve 64732-64772

Axillary Arteries
See Artery, Axillary

Axillary Nerve
Injection
  Anesthetic 64417

Axis, Dens
See Odontoid Process

B

B Antibodies, Hepatitis
See Antibody, Hepatitis B

B Antigens, Hepatitis
See Hepatitis Antigen, B

B Complex Vitamins
B-12 Absorption 78270-78272

B-Cells
Count 86355

B-DNA
See Deoxyribonucleic Acid

b-Hexosaminidase 83080

B1 Vitamin
See Thiamine

B6 Vitamin
See Vitamin, B-6

B12 Vitamin
See Cyanocobalamin

Babcock Operation
See Ligation, Vein, Saphenous

Bacillus Calmette Guerin Vaccine
See BCG Vaccine

Back/Flank
Biopsy 21920-21925
Repair
  Hernia 49540
Strapping 29220
Tumor
  Excision 21930
  Radical Resection 21935
Wound Exploration
  Penetrating 20102

Backbone
See Spine

Bacteria Culture
Additional Methods 87077
Aerobic 87040-87071
Anaerobic 87073-87076
Blood 87040
Other Source 87070-87075
Screening 87081
Stool 87045-87046
Urine 87086-87088

Bacterial Endotoxins 87176

**Bacterial Overgrowth
Breath Test** 91065

Bactericidal Titer, Serum 87197

Bacterium
Antibody 86609

BAER
See Evoked Potential, Auditory Brainstem

Baker Tube
Intestine Decompression 44021

Baker's Cyst .27345

Balanoplasty
See Penis, Repair

Baldy-Webster Operation
See Uterus, Repair, Suspension

Balkan Grippe
See Q Fever

Balloon Angioplasties, Coronary
See Percutaneous Transluminal Angioplasty

Balloon Angioplasty
See Angioplasty

Balloon Assisted Device
Aorta 33967-33974, 93727

Band, Pulmonary Artery
See Banding, Artery, Pulmonary

Banding
Artery
   Fistula 37607
   Pulmonary 33690

Bank, Blood
See Blood Banking

Bankart Procedure
See Capsulorrhaphy, Anterior

Barany Caloric Test
See Caloric Vestibular Test

Barbiturates
Blood or Urine .82205

Bardenheuer Operation
See Ligation, Artery, Chest

Bariatric Surgery 43644-43645,
   43770-43774, 43842-43848, 43886-43888

Barium 83015

Barium Enema 74270-74280

Barker Operation
See Talus, Excision

Barr Bodies .88130

Barr Procedure
See Tendon, Transfer, Leg, Lower

Bartholin's Gland
Abscess
   Incision and Drainage 56420
Cyst
   Repair 56440
Excision 56740
Marsupialization 56440

Bartonella
Antibody 86611

Bartonella Detection 87470-87472

Basic Life Services 99450

Basic Proteins, Myelin
See Myelin Basic Protein

Basilar Arteries
See Artery, Basilar

Batch-Spittler-McFaddin Operation
See Disarticulation, Knee

BCG Vaccine
See Vaccines

Be Antigens, Hepatitis
See Hepatitis Antigen, Be

Bed Sores
See Debridement; Pressure Ulcer (Decubitus);
Skin Graft and Flap

Bekesy Audiometry
See Audiometry, Bekesy

Belsey IV Procedure
See Fundoplasty

Bender-Gestalt Test 96101-96103

Benedict Test for Urea
See Urinalysis, Qualitative

Benign Cystic Mucinous Tumor
See Ganglion

**Benign Neoplasm of Cranial
Nerves**
See Cranial Nerve

Bennett Fracture
See Phalanx; Thumb, Fracture

Bennett Procedure
See Repair, Leg, Upper, Muscle; Revision

Benzidine Test
See Blood, Feces

Benzodiazepine
Assay 80154

Benzoyl Cholinesterase
See Cholinesterase

Bernstein Test
See Acid Perfusion Test, Esophagus

Beryllium 83015

**Beta 2 Glycoprotein I
Antibody** 86146

Beta Blocker Therapy
See Performance Measures

Beta Glucosidase 82963

Beta Hypophamine
See Antidiuretic Hormone

Beta Lipoproteins
See Lipoprotein, LDL

Beta Test
See Psychiatric Diagnosis

Beta-2-Microglobulin
Blood 82232
Urine 82232

Beta-hydroxydehydrogenase . .80406

Bethesda System 88164-88167

Bicarbonate 82374

Biceps Tendon
Insertion 24342

Bichloride, Methylene
See Dichloromethane

Bicuspid Valve
See Mitral Valve

Bifrontal Craniotomy 61557

**Bilaminate Skin
Substitute/Neodermis**
See Tissue
Repair
   See Tissue, Culture
     Repair; Tissue, Culture, Skin Grafts

Bile Acids 82239
Blood 82240

Bile Duct
See Gallbladder
Anastomosis
   Cyst 47716
   with Intestines 47760, 47780-47785
Biopsy
   Endoscopy .47553
Catheterization 75982
Change Catheter Tube 75984
Cyst
   Excision 47715
   Repair 47716
Destruction
   Calculi (Stone) 43265
Dilation
   Endoscopy 43271, 47555-47556
Drainage
   Transhepatic 75980
Endoscopy
   Biopsy 47553
   Destruction
     Calculi (Stone) 43265
     Tumor 43272
   Dilation 43271, 47555-47556
   Exploration .47552
   Intraoperative 47550
   Removal
     Calculi (Stone) 43264, 47554
     Foreign Body 43269
     Stent 43269
   Specimen Collection 43260
   Sphincter Pressure 43263
   Sphincterotomy 43262
   Tube Placement 43267-43268
Exploration
   Atresia 47700
   Endoscopy .47552
Incision
   Sphincter 43262, 47460
Incision and Drainage 47420-47425

Insertion

Catheter 47510, 47525, 75982
   Revision 47530
Stent 47511, 47801
Nuclear Medicine
   Imaging 78223
Reconstruction
   Anastomosis 47800
Removal
   Calculi (Stone) 43264, 47420-47425
      Percutaneous 47630
   Foreign Body 43269
   Stent 43269
Repair 47701
   Cyst 47716
   Gastrointestinal Tract 47785
   with Intestines 47760, 47780
Tube Placement
   Nasobiliary .43267
   Stent 43268
Tumor
   Destruction .43271
   Excision 47711-47712
Unlisted Services and Procedures 47999
X-Ray
   Guide Dilation 74360
   with Contrast 74300-74320
      Calculus Removal 74327
      Guide Catheter 74328, 74330

Bile Duct, Common, Cystic Dilatation

See Cyst, Choledochal

Bilirubin

Blood 82247-82248
Feces 82252
Total
   Direct 82247-82248
   Transcutaneous 88400

Billroth I or II

See Gastrectomy, Partial

Bilobectomy .32482

Bimone

See Testosterone

Binding Globulin, Testosterone-Estradiol

See Globulin, Sex Hormone Binding

Binet Test 96101-96103

Binet-Simon Test 96101-96103

Binocular Microscopy 92504

Biofeedback

See Training, Biofeedback
Anorectal 90911
Psychiatric Treatment 90875-90876

Biofeedback Training

See Training, Biofeedback

Bioimpedance

Breast 0060T
Thorax 93701

Biological Skin Grafts

See Allograft, Skin

Biometry

Eye 76516-76519, 92136

Biopsies, Needle

See Needle Biopsy

Biopsy

See Brush Biopsy; Needle Biopsy
Abdomen 49000
Adrenal Gland 60540-60545
Anal
   Endoscopy .46606
Ankle 27613-27614, 27620
Arm, Lower 25065-25066
Arm, Upper 24065-24066
Artery
   Temporal 37609
Auditory Canal, External 69105
Back/Flank 21920-21925
Bile Duct
   Endoscopy .47553
Bladder 52354
   Cystourethroscope 52204
   Cystourethroscopy 52224, 52250
Blood Vessel
   Transcatheter 75970
Bone 20220-20245
Bone Marrow .38221
Brain 61140
   Stereotactic 61750-61751
Brainstem 61575-61576
Breast 19100-19103
   Stereotactic Localization 76095
Bronchi
   Catheterization 31717
   Endoscopic 31625-31629, 31632-31633
Brush
   Bronchi 31717
   Renal Pelvis 52007
   Ureter 52007
   with Cystourethroscopy 52204
Carpometacarpal Joint
   Synovium 26100
Cervix 57454-57455, 57460,
             57500, 57520
Chorionic Villus 59015
Colon 44025, 44100
   Endoscopy 44389, 45380, 45391-45392
   Multiple
      with Colostomy, Cecostomy 44322
Colon-Sigmoid
   Endoscopy 45305, 45331
Conjunctiva 68100
Cornea 65410
Duodenum 44010
Ear
   External 69100
Elbow 24065-24066, 24101
   Synovium 24100
Embryo Blastomere 89290-89291
Endometrium 58100-58110, 58558
Epididymis 54800-54820
Esophagus
   Endoscopy .43202
Eye Muscle 67350
Eyelid 67810

Forearm
   Soft Tissue 25065-25066
Gallbladder
   Endoscopy .43261
Gastrointestinal, Upper
   Endoscopy .43239
Hand Joint
   Synovium 26100
Heart 93505
Hip 27040-27041
   Joint 27052
Hypopharynx .42802
Ileum
   Endoscopy .44382
Interphalangeal Joint
   Finger 26110
   Toe 28054
Intertarsal Joint
   Toe 28050
Intestines, Small 44020, 44100
   Endoscopy 44361, 44377
Kidney 50200-50205
   Endoscopic 50555-50557,
           50574-50576, 52354
Knee .27323-27324
   Synovium 27330
Knee Joint
   Synovium 27330
Lacrimal Gland 68510
Lacrimal Sac .68525
Larynx
   Endoscopy 31510, 31576
Leg
   Lower 27613-27614
   Upper 27323-27324
Lip 40490
Liver 47000-47001, 47100
Lung
   Needle 32405
   Thoracotomy 32095-32100
Lymph Nodes 38500-38530
   Injection Procedure
     for Identification of Sentinel Node . .38792
   Laparoscopic 38570-38572
   Needle 38505
   Open 38500, 38510-38530
      Superficial 38500
Mediastinum .39400
   Needle 32405
Metacarpophalangeal Joint 26105
Metatarsophalangeal Joint 28052
Mouth 40808, 41108
Muscle 20200-20206
Nail 11755
Nasopharynx 42804-42806
Neck 21550
Nerve 64795
Nose
   Endoscopic .31237
   Intranasal 30100
Oocyte Polar Body 89290-89291
Orbit 61332
   Exploration 67400, 67450
   Fine Needle Aspiration 67415
Oropharynx 42800
Ovary 58900
Palate 42100
Pancreas 48100

Pelvis 27040-27041
Penis 54100
   Deep Structures 54105
Percutaneous Needle
   Spinal Cord 62269
Perineum 56605-56606
Peritoneum
   Endoscopic 47561
Pharynx 42800-42806
Pleura
   Needle 32400-32402
   Thoracotomy 32095-32100
Pleural
   Open 32402
Prostate 0137T, 55700-55705
Rectum 45100
Retroperitoneal Area 49010
Sacroiliac Joint 27050
Salivary Gland 42405
Shoulder
   Deep 23066
   Soft Tissue 23065
Shoulder Joint 23100-23101
Sinus
   Sphenoid 31050-31051
Skin Lesion 11100-11101
Spinal Cord 63275-63290
   Percutaneous 62269
   Stereotaxis 63615
Stomach 43600-43605
Tarsometatarsal Joint
   Synovial 28050
Testis .54500-54505
Thorax 21550
Throat .42800-42806
Tongue 41100-41105
Transcatheter .37200
Ureter 52354
   Endoscopic 50955-50957, 50974-50976
Urethra 52204, 52354, 53200
Uterus
   Endometrial 58100-58110
   Endoscopic 58558
Uvula 42100
Vagina 57100-57105, 57421
Vertebral Body 20250-20251
Vulva 56605-56606, 56821
with Arthrotomy
   Acromioclavicular Joint 23101
   Glenohumeral Joint 23100
   Sternoclavicular Joint 23101
with Cystourethroscopy 52354
Wrist 25065-25066, 25100-25101

Biopsy, Skin
See Skin, Biopsy

Biopsy, Vein
See Vein, Biopsy

Biostatistics
See Biometry

Biosterol
See Vitamin, A

Biotinidase 82261

Birthing Room
Newborn Care 99431

Bischof Procedure
See Laminectomy, Surgical

Bismuth 83015

Bizzozero's Corpuscle/Cell
See Blood, Platelet

Bladder
Abscess
   Incision and Drainage 51080
Anastomosis .51960
Aspiration 51000-51010
Biopsy 52204
Catheterization 51045, 51701-51703
Change Tube 51705-51710
Creation
   Stoma 51980
Cyst
   Urachal
      Excision 51500
Destruction
   Endoscopic 52214-52224, 52354
Dilation
   Ureter 52260-52265, 52341-52342,
                        52344-52345
Diverticulum
   Excision 51525
   Incision 52305
   Resection 52305
Endoscopy 52000
   Biopsy 52204, 52354
   Catheterization 52005, 52010
   Destruction 52214-52224, 52400
   Dilation 52260-52265
   Diverticulum 52305
   Evacuation
      Clot 52001
   Excision
      Tumor 52234-52240, 52355
   Exploration .52351
   Injection 52283
   Lithotripsy .52353
   Radiotracer .52250
   Removal
      Calculus 52310-52315, 52352
      Foreign Body 52310-52315
   Sphincter Surgery 52277
   Tumor
      Excision 52355
   Ureter Surgery 52290-52300
   Urethral Syndrome 52285
   with Urethrotomy 52270-52276
Excision
   Partial 51550-51565
   Total 51570, 51580, 51590-51597
      with Nodes 51575, 51585, 51595
   Transurethral 52640
   Tumor 52234-52240
Incision
   Catheter 51045
   with Destruction 51020-51030
   with Radiotracer 51020
Incision and Drainage 51040
Injection
   Radiologic 51600-51610
Insertion
   Stent 51045, 52334

Instillation
   Drugs 51720
Irrigation 51700
Laparoscopy .51999
Lesion
   Destruction 51030
Neck
   Endoscopy
      Injection of Implant Material 51715
   Excision 51520
Nuclear Medicine
   Residual Study 78730
Radiotracer 52250
Reconstruction
   and Urethra 51800-51820
   with Intestines 51960
Removal
   Calculus 51050, 52310-52315
   Foreign Body 52310-52315
   Urethral Stent 52310-52315
Repair
   Diverticulum 52305
   Exstrophy .51940
   Fistula 44660-44661,
             45800-45805, 51880-51925
   Neck 51845
   Wound 51860-51865
Resection 52500
Sphincter Surgery 52277
Suspension 51990
Suture
   Fistula 44660-44661,
             45800-45805, 51880-51925
   Wound 51860-51865
Tumor
   Excision 51530
Unlisted Services and Procedures 53899
Urethrocystography 74450-74455
Urethrotomy 52270-52276
Urinary Incontinence Procedures
   Laparoscopy 51990-51992
   Pulsed Magnetic Neuromodulation . . .0029T
X-Ray 74430
   with Contrast 74450-74455

**Bladder Voiding Pressure
Studies** 51795

**Blalock-Hanlon
Procedure** 33735-33737
See Septostomy, Atrial

Blalock-Taussig Procedure
See Shunt, Great Vessel

Blast Cells
See Stem Cell

Blast Transformation
See Blastogenesis

Blastocyst Implantation
See Implantation

Blastocyst Transfer
See Embryo Transfer

Blastogenesis 86353

Blastomyces
Antibody 86612

Blastomycosis, European
See Cryptococcus

Bleeding
See Hemorrhage

Bleeding Disorder
See Coagulopathy

Bleeding Time 85002

Bleeding Tube
Passage and Placement 91100

Bleeding, Anal
See Anus, Hemorrhage

Bleeding, Uterine
See Hemorrhage, Uterus

Bleeding, Vaginal
See Hemorrhage, Vagina

Blepharoplasty 15820-15823
See Canthoplasty
Anesthesia 00103

Blepharoptosis
Repair 67901-67909
   Frontalis Muscle Technique 67901
      with Fascial Sling 67902
   Superior Rectus Technique with
   Fascial Sling .67906
   Tarso Levator Resection/Advancement
      External Approach 67904
      Internal Approach 67903

Blepharorrhaphy
See Tarsorrhaphy

Blepharospasm
Chemodenervation 64612

Blepharotomy 67700

Blister
See Bulla

Blom-Singer Prosthesis 31611

Blood
See Blood Cell Count, Complete Blood Count
Bleeding Time .85002
Collection, for Autotransfusion
   Intraoperative 86891
   Preoperative 86890
Feces .82270, 82272
   by Hemoglobin Immunoassay 82274
Gastric Contents 82273
Hemoglobin Concentration 85046
Nuclear Medicine
   Flow Imaging 78445
   Red Cell 78140
   Red Cell Survival 78130-78135
Osmolality 83930
Other Source 82273
Plasma
   Exchange 36514-36516
Platelet
   Aggregation 85576
   Automated Count 85049
   Count 85008
   Manual Count 85032

Stem Cell
   Count 86367
   Donor Search 38204
   Harvesting 38205-38206
   Transplantation 38240-38242
      Cell Concentration 38215
      Cryopreservation 38207, 88240
      Plasma Depletion 38214
      Platelet Depletion 38213
      Red Blood Cell Depletion 38212
      T-cell Depletion 38210
      Thawing 38208-38209, 88241
      Tumor Cell Depletion 38211
      Washing .38209
Transfusion 36430
   Exchange .36455
      Newborn 36450
   Fetal 36460
   Push
      Infant 36440
Unlisted Services and Procedures 85999
Urine 83491
Viscosity 85810

Blood Banking
Frozen Blood Preparation 86930-86932
Frozen Plasma Preparation 86927
Physician Services 86077-86079

Blood Cell
CD4 and CD8
   Including Ratio 86360
Enzyme Activity 82657
Exchange 36511-36513
Sedimentation Rate
   Automated 85652
   Manual 85651

Blood Cell Count
Automated 85049
B-Cells 86355
Blood Smear 85007-85008
Differential WBC Count 85004-85007, 85009
Hematocrit 85014
Hemoglobin 85018
Hemogram
   Added Indices 85025-85027
   Automated 85025-85027
   Manual 85032
Microhematocrit 85013
Natural Killer (NK) Cells 86357
Red Blood Cells 85032-85041
Reticulocyte 85044-85046
Stem Cells 86367
T-Cells 86359-86361
White Blood Cells 85032, 85048, 89055

Blood Cell Count, Red
See Red Blood Cell (RBC), Count

Blood Cell Count, White
See White Blood Cell, Count

Blood Cell, Red
See Red Blood Cell (RBC)

Blood Cell, White
See Leukocyte

Blood Clot
Assay 85396
Clot Lysis Time 85175
Clot Retraction 85170
Clotting Factor 85250-85293
Clotting Factor Test 85210-85244
Clotting Inhibitors . . .85300-85302, 85305, 85307
Coagulation Time 85345-85348

Blood Coagulation Defect
See Coagulopathy

Blood Coagulation Disorders
See Clot

Blood Coagulation Factor
See Clotting Factor

Blood Coagulation Factor I
See Fibrinogen

Blood Coagulation Factor II
See Prothrombin

Blood Coagulation Factor III
See Thromboplastin

Blood Coagulation Factor IV
See Calcium

Blood Coagulation Factor VII
See Proconvertin

Blood Coagulation Factor VIII
See Clotting Factor

Blood Coagulation Factor IX
See Christmas Factor

Blood Coagulation Factor X
See Stuart-Prower Factor

Blood Coagulation Factor X, Activated
See Thrombokinase

Blood Coagulation Factor XI
See Plasma Thromboplastin, Antecedent

Blood Coagulation Factor XIII
See Fibrin Stabilizing Factor

Blood Coagulation Test
See Coagulation

Blood Component Removal
See Apheresis

Blood Count, Complete
See Complete Blood Count (CBC)

Blood Flow Check, Graft 15860, 90940

Blood Gases
CO_2 82803
HCO_3 82803
O_2 Saturation 82805-82810
pCO_2 82803
pH 82800-82803
pO_2 82803

Blood Letting
See Phlebotomy

Blood Lipoprotein
See Lipoprotein

Blood Occult
See Occult, Blood

Blood Pool Imaging 78472-78473,
78481-78483, 78494-78496

Blood Pressure
See Performance Measures
Left Ventricular Filling 0086T
Monitoring, 24 Hour 93784-93790
Venous 93770

Blood Products
Irradiation 86945
Pooling 86965
Splitting 86985
Volume Reduction 86960

Blood Sample
Fetal 59030

Blood Serum
See Serum

Blood Smear 85060

Blood Syndrome
Chromosome Analysis 88245-88248

Blood Tests
Nuclear Medicine
   Plasma Volume 78110-78111
   Platelet Survival 78190-78191
   Red Cell Volume 78120-78121
   Whole Blood Volume 78122
Panels
   Electrolyte 80051
   General Health Panel 80050
   Hepatic Function 80076
   Hepatitis, Acute 80074
   Lipid Panel 80061
   Metabolic
      Basic 80048
      Comprehensive 80053
   Obstetric Panel 80055
   Renal Function 80069
Volume Determination 78122

Blood Transfusion, Autologous
See Autotransfusion

Blood Typing
ABO Only 86900
Antigen Screen 86903-86904
Crossmatch 86920-86923
Other RBC Antigens 86905
Paternity Testing 86910-86911
Rh (D) 86901
Rh Phenotype 86906

Blood Urea Nitrogen 84520-84525

Blood Vessels
See Artery; Vein
Angioscopy
   Non-Coronary 35400
Endoscopy
   Surgical 37500

Excision
   Arteriovenous Malformation . . .63250-63252
Exploration
   Abdomen 35840
   Chest 35820
   Extremity 35860
   Neck 35800
Great
   Suture 33320-33322
Harvest
   Endoscopic 33508
   Lower Extremity Vein 35572
   Upper Extremity Artery 35600
   Upper Extremity Vein 35500
Kidney
   Repair 50100
Repair
   Abdomen
     See Aneurysm Repair; Fistula, Repair
     with Composite Graft 35681-35683
     with Other Graft 35281
     with Vein Graft 35251
   Aneurysm 61705-61708
   Arteriovenous Malformation . . .61680-61692,
      61705-61710, 63250-63252
   Chest
     with Composite Graft 35681-35683
     with Other Graft 35271-35276
     with Vein Graft 35241-35246
   Direct 35201-35226
   Finger 35207
   Graft Defect 35870
   Hand 35207
   Lower Extremity 35226
     with Composite Graft 35681-35683
     with Other Graft 35281
     with Vein Graft 35251
   Neck
     with Composite Graft 35681-35683
     with Other Graft 35261
     with Vein Graft 35231
   Upper Extremity 35206
     with Composite Graft 35681-35683
     with Other Graft 35266
     with Vein Graft 35236
   Shunt Creation
     Direct 36818, 36821
     Thomas Shunt 36835
     with Bypass Graft 35686
     with Graft 36825-36830
   Shunt Revision
     with Graft 36832

Blood, Occult
See Occult Blood

Bloom Syndrome
Chromosome Analysis 88245

Blot Test, Ink
See Inkblot Test

Blotting, Western
See Western Blot

Blow-Out Fracture
Orbital Floor 21385-21395

Blue, Dome Cyst
See Breast, Cyst

BMT
See Bone Marrow, Transplantation

Boarding Home Care 99324-99337

Bodies, Acetone
See Acetone Body

Bodies, Barr
See Barr Bodies

Bodies, Carotid
See Carotid Body

Bodies, Ciliary
See Ciliary Body

Bodies, Heinz
See Heinz Bodies

Bodies, Inclusion
See Inclusion Bodies

Bodies, Ketone
See Ketone Body

Body Cast
Halo 29000
Removal 29700, 29710-29715
Repair 29720
Risser Jacket 29010-29015
Turnbuckle Jacket 29020-29025
Upper Body and Head 29040
Upper Body and Legs 29046
Upper Body and One Leg 29044
Upper Body Only 29035

Body Composition
Dual Energy X-Ray Absorptiometry 0028T

Body Fluid
Crystal Identification 89060

Body of Vertebra
See Vertebral Body

Body Section
X-Ray 76100
   Motion 76101-76102

Body System, Neurologic
See Nervous System

Boil
See Furuncle

Boil, Vulva
See Abscess, Vulva

Bone
See Specific Bone
Ablation
   Tumor 20982
Biopsy 20220-20245
CT Scan
   Density Study 76070-76071
Cyst
   Drainage 20615
   Injection 20615
Dual Energy X-Ray
Absorptiometry 76075-76077

Excision
　Epyphyseal Bar 20150
　Facial Bones 21026
　Mandible 21025
Fixation
　Caliper 20660
　Cranial Tong 20660
　Halo 20661-20663, 21100
　Interdental 21110
　Multiplane 20692
　Pin/Wire 20650
　Skeletal
　　Humeral Epicondyle
　　　Percutaneous 24566
　Stereotactic Frame 20660
　Uniplane 20690
Insertion
　Needle 36680
　Osseointegrated Implant
　　for External Speech Processor/Cochlear
　　Stimulator 69714-69718
Nuclear Medicine
　Density Study 78350-78351
　Imaging 78300-78320
　SPECT 78320
　Unlisted Services and Procedures 78399
Protein .83937
Removal
　Fixation Device 20670-20680
Replacement
　Osseointegrated Implant
　　for External Speech Processor/Cochlear
　　Stimulator 69717-69718
X-Ray
　Age Study 76020
　Dual Energy Absorptiometry . . .76075-76077
　Length Study 76040
　Osseous Survey 76061-76065

Bone 4-Carboxyglutamic Protein
See Osteocalcin

Bone Conduction Hearing Device, Electromagnetic
Implantation/Replacement 69710
Removal/Repair 69711

Bone Density Study
Appendicular Skeleton 76071, 76076
Axial Skeleton 76070, 76075
Ultrasound 76977
Vertebral Fracture Assessment 76077

Bone Graft
Augmentation
　Mandibular Body 21127
Femur 27170
Fracture
　Orbit .21408
Harvesting 20900-20902
Malar Area 21210
Mandible 21215
Mandibular Ramus 21194
Maxilla .21210
Microvascular Anastomosis
　Fibula 20955
　Other 20962
Nasal Area 21210
Nasomaxillary Complex Fracture 21348

Open Treatment
　Craniofacial Separation 21436
Osteocutaneous Flap 20969-20973
Reconstruction
　Mandibular Rami 21194
　Midface 21145-21160
Skull 61316
　Excision 62148
Spine Surgery
　Allograft
　　Morselized 20930
　　Structural 20931
　Autograft
　　Local 20936
　　Morselized 20937
　　Structural 20938
Vascular Pedicle 25430

Bone Healing
Electrical Stimulation
　Invasive 20975
　Noninvasive 20974
Ultrasound Stimulation 20979

Bone Infection
See Osteomyelitis

Bone Marrow
Aspiration 38220
Harvesting 38230
Magnetic Resonance Imaging (MRI) 76400
Needle Biopsy 38221
Nuclear Medicine
　Imaging 78102-78104
Smear .85097
T-Cell Transplantation 38240-38242
Trocar Biopsy 38221

Bone Plate
Mandible 21244

Bone Scan
See Bone, Nuclear Medicine; Nuclear Medicine

Bone Spur
See Exostosis

Bone Wedge Reversal
Osteotomy 21122

Bone, Carpal
See Carpal Bone

Bone, Cheek
See Cheekbone

Bone, Facial
See Facial Bone

Bone, Hyoid
See Hyoid Bone

Bone, Metatarsal
See Metatarsal

Bone, Nasal
See Nasal Bone

Bone, Navicular
See Navicular

Bone, Scan
See Bone, Nuclear Medicine; Nuclear Medicine Imaging

Bone, Semilunar
See Lunate

Bone, Sesamoid
See Sesamoid Bone

Bone, Tarsal
See Ankle Bone

Bone, Temporal
See Temporal Bone

Bordetella
Antibody 86615
Antigen Detection
　Direct Fluorescence 87265

Borrelia
Antibody 86618-86619

Borrelia burgdorferi ab
See Antibody, Lyme Disease

Borreliosis, Lyme
See Lyme Disease

Borthen Operation
See Iridotasis

Bost Fusion
See Arthrodesis, Wrist

Bosworth Operation
See Acromioclavicular Joint, Dislocation; Arthrodesis, Vertebrae; Fasciotomy,

Bottle Type Procedure 55060

Botulinum Toxin
See Chemodenervation

Boutonniere Deformity 26426-26428

Bowel
See Intestine

Bowleg Repair 27455-27457

Boyce Operation
See Nephrotomy

Boyd Hip Disarticulation
See Amputation, Leg, Upper; Radical Resection; Replantation

Brace
See Cast
for Leg Cast 29358

Brachial Arteries
See Artery, Brachial

Brachial Plexus
Decompression 64713
Injection
　Anesthetic 64415-64416
Neuroplasty 64713
Release 64713
Repair/Suture 64861

Brachiocephalic Artery
See Artery, Brachiocephalic

Brachycephaly 21175

Brachytherapy 77761-77778, 77789
Dose Plan 77326-77328
Remote Afterloading
   1-4 Positions 77781
   5-8 Positions 77782
   9-12 Positions 77783
   Over 12 Positions 77784
   Over 4 Positions 77781-77784
Unlisted Services and Procedures 77799

Bradykinin
Blood or Urine 82286

Brain
See Brainstem; Mesencephalon; Skull Base
Surgery
Abscess
   Drainage 61150-61151
   Excision 61514, 61522
   Incision and Drainage 61320-61321
Adhesions
   Lysis 62161
Anesthesia 00210-00218, 00220-00222
Angiography 70496
Biopsy 61140
   Stereotactic 61750-61751
Catheter
   Irrigation 62194, 62225
   Replacement 62160, 62194, 62225
Cisternography 70015
Computer Assisted
   Surgery 61795
Cortex
   Magnetic Stimulation 0018T
Craniopharyngioma
   Excision 61545
CT Scan 0042T, 70450-70470, 70496
Cyst
   Drainage 61150-61151, 62161-62162
   Excision 61516, 61524, 62162
Doppler, Transcranial 93886-93893
Epileptogenic Focus
   Excision 61534, 61536
Excision
   Amygdala 61566
   Choroid Plexus 61544
   Hemisphere 61542-61543
   Hippocampus 61566
   Other Lobe 61323, 61539-61540
   Temporal Lobe 61537-61538
Exploration
   Infratentorial 61305
   Supratentorial 61304
Hematoma
   Drainage 61154
   Incision and Drainage 61312-61315
Implantation
   Chemotherapy Agent 61517
   Electrode 61850-61875
   Pulse Generator 61885-61886
   Receiver 61885-61886
   Thermal Perfusion Probe 0077T

Incision
   Corpus Callosum 61541
   Frontal Lobe 61490
   Mesencephalic Tract 61480
   Subpial 61567
Insertion
   Catheter 61210
   Electrode 61531-61533, 61850-61875
   Pulse Generator 61885-61886
   Receiver 61885-61886
   Reservoir 61210-61215
Lesion
   Aspiration Stereotactic 61750-61751
   Excision 61534, 61536,
      61600-61608, 61615-61616
Magnetic Resonance Imaging
(MRI) 70551-70553
   Intraoperative 70557-70559
Meningioma
   Excision 61512, 61519
Myelography 70010
Nuclear Medicine
   Blood Flow 78610-78615
   Cerebrospinal Fluid 78630-78650
   Imaging 78600-78607
     Vascular Flow 78610
Positron Emission Tomography 78608-78609
Removal
   Electrode 61535, 61880
   Foreign Body 61570, 62163
   Pulse Generator 61888
   Receiver 61888
   Shunt 62256-62258
Repair
   Dura 61618
   Wound 61571
Shunt
   Creation 62180-62192, 62200-62223
   Removal 62256-62258
   Replacement ...62160, 62194, 62225-62230,
      62256-62258
   Reprogramming 62252
Skull
   Transcochlear Approach 61596
   Transcondylar Approach 61597
   Transpetrosal Approach 61598
   Transtemporal Approach 61595
Skull Base
   Craniofacial Approach 61580-61585
   Infratemporal Approach 61590-61591
   Orbitocranial Zygomatic Approach 61592
Stereotactic
   Aspiration 61750-61751
   Biopsy 61750-61751
   Create Lesion ...61720-61735, 61790-61791
   Localization for Placement
   Therapy Fields 61770
   Radiation Treatment 77432
   Radiosurgery 61793
   Surgery 61795
   Trigeminal Tract 61791
Transection
   Subpial 61567
Tumor
   Excision 61510, 61518, 61520-61521,
      61526-61530, 61545, 62164
X-Ray
   with Contrast 70010-70015

Brain Coverings
See Meninges

Brain Death
Determination 95824

Brain Stem
See Brainstem

Brain Stem Auditory Evoked Potential
See Evoked Potential, Auditory Brainstem

Brain Surface Electrode
Stimulation 95961-95962

Brain Tumor, Acoustic Neuroma
See Brain, Tumor, Excision

Brain Tumor, Craniopharyngioma
See Craniopharyngioma

Brain Tumor, Meningioma
See Meningioma

Brain Ventriculography
See Ventriculography

Brainstem
See Brain
Biopsy 61575-61576
Decompression 61575-61576
Evoked Potentials 92585-92586
Lesion
   Excision 61575-61576

Branchial Cleft
Cyst
   Excision 42810-42815

Branchioma
See Branchial Cleft, Cyst

Breast
Abscess
   Incision and Drainage 19020
Augmentation 19324-19325
Bioimpedance 0060T
Biopsy 19100-19103
Catheter Placement
   for Interstitial Radioelement
   Application 19296-19298
Cyst
   Puncture Aspiration 19000-19001
Excision
   Biopsy 19100-19103
   Capsules 19371
   Chest Wall Tumor 19260-19272
   Cyst 19120
   Lactiferous Duct Fistula 19112
   Lesion 19120-19126, 19160
     by Needle Localization 19125-19126
   Mastectomy 19140-19240
   Nipple Exploration 19110
Exploration 19020
Implants
   Insertion 19340-19342
   Preparation of Moulage 19396
   Removal 19328-19330
   Supply 19396

Incision
　　Capsules 19370
Injection
　　Radiologic 19030
Magnetic Resonance Imaging
(MRI) 76093-76094
Mammoplasty
　　Augmentation 19324-19325
　　Reduction 19318
Mastopexy 19316
Metallic Localization Clip Placement 19295
Needle Biopsy 19100
Needle Wire Placement 19290-19291
Periprosthetic Capsulectomy 19371
Periprosthetic Capsulotomy 19370
Reconstruction 19357-19369
　　Augmentation 19324-19325
　　Mammoplasty 19318-19325
　　Nipple 19350-19355
　　　　Areola 19350
　　Revision 19380
　　with Free Flap 19364
　　with Latissimus Dorsi Flap 19361
　　with Other Techniques 19366
　　with Tissue Expander 19357
　　with Transverse Rectus Abdominis
　　　　Myocutaneous Flap 19367-19369
Reduction 19318
Removal
　　Capsules 19371
　　Modified Radical 19240
　　Partial 19140-19162
　　Radical 19200-19220
　　Simple, Complete 19180
　　Subcutaneous 19182
Repair
　　Suspension 19316
Stereotactic Localization 76095
Ultrasound 76645
Unlisted Services and Procedures 19499
X-Ray 76090-76092
　　Localization Nodule 76096
　　with Computer-aided Detection .76082-76083

Breath Odor Alcohol
See Alcohol, Breath

Breath Test
Alcohol, Ethyl 82075
Heart Transplant Rejection Detection 0085T
Helicobacter Pylori ...78267-78268, 83013-83014
Hydrogen 91065

Breathing, Inspiratory Positive-Pressure
See Intermittent Positive Pressure Breathing (IPPB)

Bricker Procedure
Intestines Anastomosis 50820

Bristow Procedure
See Capsulorrhaphy, Anterior

Brock Operation
See Valvotomy, Pulmonary Valve

Broken, Nose
See Fracture, Nasal Bone

Bronchi
Aspiration
　　Endoscopic 31645-31646
Biopsy
　　Endoscopic 31625-31629, 31632-31633
Catheterization
　　Insertion 31710
　　with Bronchial Brush Biopsy 31717
Endoscopy
　　Aspiration 31645-31646
　　Biopsy 31625-31629, 31632-31633
　　Destruction
　　　　Tumor 31641
　　Dilation 31630-31631, 31636-31638
　　Excision
　　　　Lesion 31640
　　Exploration 31622
　　Foreign Body Removal 31635
　　Fracture 31630
　　Injection 31656
　　Lesion 31640-31641
　　Stenosis 31641
　　Tumor 31640-31641
　　Ultrasound 31620
Exploration
　　Endoscopic 31622
Fracture
　　Endoscopy 31630
Injection
　　X-Ray 31656, 31715
Instillation
　　Contrast Material 31708
Needle Biopsy 31629, 31633
Reconstruction 31770
　　Graft Repair 31770
　　Stenosis 31775
Removal
　　Foreign Body 31635
Repair
　　Fistula 32815
Stenosis
　　Endoscopic Treatment 31641
Stent
　　Placement 31636-31637
　　Revision 31638
Tumor
　　Excision 31640
Ultrasound 31620
Unlisted Services and Procedures 31899
X-Ray
　　with Contrast 71040-71060

Bronchial Allergen Challenge
See Bronchial Challenge Test

Bronchial Alveolar Lavage 31624

Bronchial Brush Biopsy
with Catheterization 31717

Bronchial Brushings/Protected Brushing 31623

Bronchial Challenge Test
See Allergy Tests
with Antigens, Gases 95070
with Chemicals 95071

Bronchial Provocation Tests
See Bronchial Challenge Test

Bronchioalveolar Lavage
See Lung, Lavage

Broncho-Bronchial Anastomosis 32486

Bronchoalveolar Lavage
See Lung, Lavage

Bronchography 71040-71060
Catheterization 31710
Injection
　　Transtracheal 31715
Instillation
　　Contrast Material 31708
Segmental
　　Injection 31656

Bronchoplasty 32501
See Reconstruction, Bronchi
Excision Stenosis and Anastomosis 31775
Graft Repair 31770

Bronchopneumonia, Hiberno-Vernal
See Q Fever

Bronchopulmonary Lavage
See Lung, Lavage

Bronchoscopy
Alveolar Lavage 31624
Aspiration 31645-31646
Biopsy 31625-31629, 31632-31633
Brushing/Protected Brushing 31623
Catheter Placement
　　Intracavitary Radioelement 31643
Dilation 31630-31631, 31636-31638
Exploration 31622
Fracture 31630
Injection 31656
Needle Biopsy 31629, 31633
Removal
　　Foreign Body 31635
　　Tumor 31640-31641
Stenosis 31641
Stent Placement 31631, 31636-31637
Stent Revision 31638
Ultrasound 31620
X-Ray Contrast 31656

Bronchospasm Evaluation
See Pulmonology, Diagnostic, Spirometry

Bronkodyl
See Theophylline

Brow Ptosis
Repair 67900

Brucella 86000
Antibody 86622

Bruise
See Hematoma

Brunschwig Operation 58240
See Hip; Pelvis, Exenteration

Brush Biopsy
See Biopsy; Needle Biopsy
Bronchi 31717

Brush Border ab
See Antibody, Heterophile

Bucca
See Cheek

Buccal Mucosa
See Mouth, Mucosa

Bulbourethral Gland
Excision .... .53250

Bulla
Incision and Drainage
    Puncture Aspiration .... .10160
Lung
    Excision-Plication .... .32141
        Endoscopic .... .32655

BUN
See Blood Urea Nitrogen; Urea Nitrogen

Bunion Repair 28296-28299
Chevron Procedure .... .28296
Concentric Procedure .... .28296
Joplin Procedure .... .28294
Keller Procedure .... .28292
Lapidus Procedure .... .28297
Mayo Procedure .... .28292
McBride Procedure .... .28292
Mitchell Procedure .... .28296
Silver Procedure .... .28290
with Implant .... .28293

Burgess Amputation
See Disarticulation, Ankle

Burhenne Procedure
See Bile Duct, Removal, Calculi (Stone);
Gallbladder

Burkitt Herpesvirus
See Epstein-Barr Virus

Burns
Allograft 15300-15321, 15330-15336
Debridement 01951-01953,
                    15000-15001, 16020-16030
Dressings 16020-16030
Escharotomy 16035-16036
Excision 01951-01953, 15000-15001
Initial Treatment .... .16000
Tissue Culture Skin Grafts 15100-15157
Xenograft 15400-15431

Burr Hole
Anesthesia .... .00214
Skull
    Biopsy Brain .... .61140
    Catheterization .... .61210
    Drainage
        Abscess 61150-61151
        Cyst 61150-61151
        Hematoma 61154-61156
    Exploration
        Infratentorial .... .61253
        Supratentorial .... .61250
    for Implant of Neurostimulator
    Array 61863-61868
    Injection, Contrast Media .... .61120

Insertion
    Catheter .... .61210
    Reservoir .... .61210

Burrow's Operation
See Skin, Adjacent Tissue Transfer

Bursa
Ankle .... .27604
Arm, Lower .... .25031
Elbow
    Excision .... .24105
    Incision and Drainage .... .23931
Femur
    Excision .... .27062
Foot
    Incision and Drainage .... .28001
Hip
    Incision and Drainage .... .26991
Injection 20600-20610
Ischial
    Excision .... .27060
Joint
    Aspiration 20600-20610
    Drainage 20600-20610
    Injection 20600-20610
Knee
    Excision .... .27340
Leg, Lower .... .27604
Palm
    Incision and Drainage 26025-26030
Pelvis
    Incision and Drainage .... .26991
Shoulder
    Drainage .... .23031
Wrist .... .25031
    Excision 25115-25116

Bursectomy
See Excision, Bursa

Bursitis, Radiohumeral
See Tennis Elbow

Bursocentesis
See Aspiration, Bursa

Button
Nasal Septal Prosthesis
    Insertion .... .30220

Butyrylcholine Esterase
See Cholinesterase

Bypass Graft
Axillary Artery 35516-35522, 35533,
                    35616-35623, 35650, 35654
Brachial Artery .... .35510, 35512, 35522-35525
Carotid Artery ..... .33891, 35501-35510, 35526,
                    35601-35606, 35626, 35642
Celiac Artery .... .35531, 35631
Coronary Artery
    Angiography .... .93556
    Arterial 33533-33536
    Venous Graft 33510-33516
Excision
    Abdomen .... .35907
    Extremity .... .35903
    Neck .... .35901
    Thorax .... .35905

Femoral Artery .... .35521, 35533, 35546,
            35551-35558, 35566, 35621, 35646-35647,
                    35651-35661, 35666, 35700
Harvest
    Endoscopic .... .33508
    Upper Extremity Vein .... .35500
Iliac Artery .... .35541, 35563, 35641, 35663
Iliofemoral Artery 35548-35549, 35565, 35665
Mesenteric Artery .... .35531, 35631
Peroneal Artery 35566-35571, 35666-35671
Placement
    Vein Patch .... .35685
Popliteal Artery 35551-35558, 35571, 35623,
                    35651, 35656, 35671, 35700
Renal Artery ...... .35536, 35560, 35631-35636
Reoperation .... .35700
Repair
    Abdomen .... .35907
    Extremity .... .35903
    Lower Extremity
        with Composite Graft 35681-35683
    Neck .... .35901
    Thorax .... .35905
Revascularization
    Extremity .... .35903
    Neck .... .35901
    Thorax .... .35905
Revision
    Lower Extremity
        with Angioplasty .... .35879
        with Vein Interposition .... .35881
    Secondary Repair .... .35870
Splenic Artery .... .35536, 35636
Subclavian Artery .. .35506-35507, 35511-35516,
            35526, 35606-35616, 35626, 35645
Thrombectomy 37184-37186
    Other than Hemodialysis Graft
    or Fistula 35875-35876
Tibial Artery .. .35566-35571, 35623, 35666-35671
Vertebral Artery ..... .35508, 35515, 35642-35645
with Composite Graft .... .35681

Bypass In-Situ
Femoral Artery 35583-35585
Peroneal Artery 35585-35587
Popliteal Artery .... .35583, 35587
Tibial Artery 35585-35587
Ventricular Restoration .... .33548

Bypass, Cardiopulmonary
See Cardiopulmonary Bypass

C

C Vitamin
See Ascorbic Acid

C-13
Urea Breath Test 83013-83014
Urease Activity 83013-83014

C-14
Urea Breath Test 78267-78268
Urease Activity 83013-83014

C-Peptide 80432, 84681

C-Reactive Protein 86140-86141

C-Section
See Cesarean Delivery

CABG
See Coronary Artery Bypass Graft (CABG)

Cadmium
Urine 82300

Caffeine Halothane Contracture Test (CHCT) 89049

Calcaneal Spur
See Heel Spur

Calcaneus
Craterization 28120
Cyst
    Excision 28100-28103
Diaphysectomy 28120
Excision 28118-28120
Fracture
    Open Treatment 28415-28420
    Percutaneous Fixation 28406
    with Manipulation 28405-28406
    without Manipulation 28400
Repair
    Osteotomy 28300
Saucerization 28120
Tumor
    Excision 27647, 28100-28103
X-Ray 73650

Calcareous Deposits
Subdeltoid
    Removal 23000

Calcifediol
Blood or Urine 82306

Calcifediol Assay
See Calciferol

Calciferol
Blood or Urine 82307

Calcification
See Calcium, Deposits

Calciol
See Vitamin, D-3

Calcitonin
Blood or Urine 82308
Stimulation Panel 80410

Calcium
Blood
    Infusion Test 82331
Deposits
    See Removal, Calculi (Stone); Removal,
    Foreign Bodies
Ionized 82330
Total 82310
Urine 82340

Calcium-Binding Protein, Vitamin K-Dependent
See Osteocalcin

Calcium-Pentagastrin Stimulation 80410

Calculus
Analysis 82355-82370
Destruction
    Bile Duct 43265
    Pancreatic Duct 43265
Removal
    Bile Duct 43264, 47554, 74327
    Bladder 51050, 52310-52318, 52352
    Kidney 50060-50081, 50130, 50561,
                     50580, 52352
    Pancreatic Duct 43264
    Ureter 50610-50630, 50961, 50980,
        51060-51065, 52320-52325, 52352
    Urethra 52310-52315, 52352

Calculus of Kidney
See Calculus, Removal, Kidney

Caldwell-Luc Procedure
See Sinus, Maxillary; Sinusotomy; Sternum, Fracture
Orbital Floor Blowout Fracture 21385
Sinusotomy 31030-31032

Caliper
Application/Removal 20660

Callander Knee Disarticulation
See Disarticulation, Knee

Callosum, Corpus
See Corpus Callosum

Calmette Guerin Bacillus Vaccine
See BCG Vaccine

Caloric Vestibular Test 92533

Calycoplasty 50405

Camey Enterocystoplasty 50825

CAMP
See Cyclic AMP

Campbell Procedure 27422

Campylobacter
Antibody 86625

Campylobacter Pylori
See Helicobacter Pylori

Canal, Ear
See Auditory Canal

Canal, Semicircular
See Semicircular Canal

Canaloplasty 69631, 69635

Candida
Antibody 86628
Skin Test 86485

Cannulation 36821
Arterial 36620-36625
Sinus
    Maxillary 31000
    Sphenoid 31002
Thoracic Duct 38794

Cannulation, Renoportal
See Anastomosis, Renoportal

Cannulization
See Catheterization
Arteriovenous 36145, 36810-36815
Declotting 36550, 36860-36861
ECMO 36822
External
    Declotting 36860-36861
Vas Deferens 55200
Vein to Vein 36800

Canthocystostomy
See Conjunctivorhinostomy

Canthopexy
Lateral 21282
Medial 21280

Canthoplasty 67950

Canthorrhaphy 67880-67882

Canthotomy 67715

Canthus
Reconstruction 67950

Cap, Cervical
See Cervical Cap

Capsule
See Capsulodesis
Elbow
    Arthrotomy 24006
    Excision 24006
Foot 28264
Interphalangeal Joint
    Excision 26525
    Incision 26525
Knee 27435
Metacarpophalangeal Joint
    Excision 26520
    Incision 26520
Metatarsophalangeal Joint
    Release 28289
Shoulder
    Incision 23020
Wrist
    Excision 25320

Capsulectomy
Breast
    Periprosthetic 19371

Capsulodesis
Metacarpophalangeal Joint 26516-26518

Capsulorrhaphy
Anterior 23450-23462
Multi-Directional Instability 23466
Posterior 23465
Wrist 25320

Capsulotomy
Breast
    Periprosthetic 19370
Foot 28260-28262
Hip
    with Release, Flexor Muscles 27036
Interphalangeal Joint 28272

Knee 27435
Metacarpophalangeal Joint 26520
Metatarsophalangeal Joint 28270
Toe 28270-28272
Wrist 25085

Captopril 80416-80417

Carbamazepine
Assay 80156-80157

Carbazepin
See Carbamazepine

Carbinol
See Methanol

**Carbohydrate Deficient
Transferrin** 82373

Carbon Dioxide
Blood or Urine .82374

Carbon Monoxide
Blood 82375-82376

Carbon Tetrachloride 84600

Carboxycathepsin
See Angiotensin Converting Enzyme (ACE)

Carboxyhemoglobin 82375-82376

Carbuncle
Incision and Drainage 10060-10061

Carcinoembryonal Antigen
See Antigen, Carcinoembryonic

Carcinoembryonic Antigen 82378

Cardiac
See Coronary

Cardiac Arrhythmia, Tachycardia
See Tachycardia

Cardiac Atria
See Atria

Cardiac Catheterization
Combined Left and Right Heart 93526-93529
Combined Right and Retrograde Left
    Congenital Cardiac Anomalies 93531
Combined Right and Transseptal Left
    Congenital Cardiac Anomalies . .93532-93533
for Biopsy 93505
for Dilution Studies 93561-93562
Imaging .93555-93556
Injection .93539-93545
    See Catheterization, Cardiac
Left Heart 93510-93524
Pacemaker 33210
Right
    Congenital Cardiac Anomalies 93530
Right Heart 93501-93503

Cardiac Electroversion
See Cardioversion

Cardiac Event Recorder
Implantation 33282
Removal 33284

**Cardiac Magnetic Resonance
Imaging (CMRI)**
Complete Study 75554
Limited Study .75555
Morphology 75553
Velocity Flow Mapping 75556

Cardiac Massage
Thoracotomy 32160

Cardiac Muscle
See Myocardium

Cardiac Neoplasm
See Heart, Tumor

Cardiac Output
Indicator Dilution 93561-93562
Inert Gas Rebreathing 0104T-0105T

Cardiac Pacemaker
See Heart, Pacemaker

Cardiac Rehabilitation 93797-93798

Cardiac Septal Defect
See Septal Defect

Cardiac Transplantation
See Heart, Transplantation

Cardiectomy
Donor 33930, 33940

Cardioassist 0049T, 92970-92971

Cardiolipin Antibody 86147

Cardiology
See Electrocardiography
Diagnostic
    Acoustic Recording with Computer Analysis
        Heart Sounds 0068T-0069T, 0070T
    Atrial Electrogram
        Esophageal Recording 93615-93616
    Cardio-Defibrillator
        Evaluation and Testing 93640-93642,
                                                      93741-93744
    Echocardiography
        Doppler 93303-93321, 93662
        Intracardiac 93662
        Transesophageal 93318
        Transthoracic 93303-93317, 93350
    Electrocardiogram
        Evaluation 93000, 93010, 93014
        Microvolt T-wave Alternans 93025
        Monitoring 93224-93237
        Patient-Demand 93268-93272
        Rhythm 93040-93042
        Tracing .93005
        Transmission 93012
    Ergonovine Provocation Test 93024
    Hemodynamic Monitoring
    Non-invasive 0086T
    Implantable Loop Recorder System . . .93727
    Intracardiac Pacing and Mapping 93631
        3-D Mapping 93613
        Follow-up Study 93624
        Stimulation and Pacing 93623

Intracardiac Pacing and Recording
    Arrhythmia Induction 93618-93620
    Bundle of His 93600
    Comprehensive 93619-93622
    Intra-Atrial 93602, 93610
    Right Ventricle 93603
    Tachycardia Sites 93609
    Ventricular 93612
Intravascular Ultrasound 92978-92979
Left Ventricular Pressure
Measurement 0086T
Pacemaker Testing 93642
    Antitachycardia System 93724
    Dual Chamber 93731-93733
    Leads .93641
    Single Chamber 93734-93736
Perfusion Imaging 78460-78461
    See Nuclear Medicine
Stress Tests
    Cardiovascular 93015-93018
    Drug Induced 93024
    Multiple Gated Acquisition (MUGA) .78473
Tilt Table Evaluation 93660
Therapeutic
Cardio-Defibrillator
    Initial Set-up and Programming 93745
Cardioassist 92970-92971
Cardioversion 92960-92961
Intravascular Ultrasound 92978-92979
Pacing
    Transcutaneous, Temporary 92953
Thrombolysis 92975-92977
Thrombolysis, Coronary 92977
Valvuloplasty
    Percutaneous 92986-92990

Cardiomyotomy
See Esophagomyotomy

Cardioplasty 43320

Cardiopulmonary Bypass 33926
See Heart; Lung, Transplantation

**Cardiopulmonary
Resuscitation** 92950

Cardiotomy 33310-33315

Cardiovascular Stress Test
See Exercise Stress Tests

Cardioversion 92960-92961

Care Plan Oversight Services
See Physician Services

Care, Custodial
See Nursing Facility Services

Care, Intensive
See Intensive Care

Care, Neonatal Intensive
See Intensive Care, Neonatal

Care, Self
See Self Care

Carneous Mole
See Abortion

Carnitine 82379

Carotene 82380

Caroticum, Glomus
See Carotid Body

Carotid Artery
Aneurysm Repair
    Vascular Malformation or Carotid-Cavernous
    Fistula 61710
Excision 60605
Ligation 37600-37606
Stent, Transcatheter Placement 0075T-0076T
Transection
    with Skull Base Surgery 61609

Carotid Body
Lesion
    Carotid Artery 60605
    Excision 60600

Carpal Bone
See Wrist
Arthroplasty
    with Implant 25443
Cyst
    Excision 25130-25136
Dislocation
    Closed Treatment 25690
    Open Treatment 25695
Excision 25210-25215
    Partial 25145
Fracture
    Closed Treatment 25622, 25630
    Open Treatment 25628, 25645
    with Manipulation 25624, 25635
    without Manipulation 25630
Incision and Drainage 26034
Insertion
    Vascular Pedicle 25430
Osteoplasty 25394
Repair 25431-25440
Sequestrectomy 25145
Tumor
    Excision 25130-25136

Carpal Tunnel
Injection
    Therapeutic 20526

Carpal Tunnel Syndrome
Decompression 64721

Carpals
Incision and Drainage 25035

Carpectomy 25210-25215

Carpometacarpal Joint
Arthrodesis
    Hand 26843-26844
    Thumb 26841-26842
Arthrotomy 26070
Biopsy
    Synovium 26100
Dislocation
    Closed Treatment 26670
        with Manipulation 26675-26676
    Open Treatment 26685-26686

Exploration 26070
Fusion
    Hand 26843-26844
    Thumb 26841-26842
Removal
    Foreign Body 26070
Repair 25447
Synovectomy 26130

Cartilage Graft
Ear to Face 21235
Harvesting 20910-20912
Rib to Face 21230

Cartilage, Arytenoid
See Arytenoid

Cartilage, Ear
See Ear Cartilage

Cartilaginous Exostoses
See Exostosis

Case Management Services
Team Conferences 99361-99373
Telephone Calls 99361-99373

Cast
See Brace; Splint
Body
    Risser Jacket 29010-29015
Body Cast
    Halo 29000
    Turnbuckle Jacket 29020-29025
    Upper Body and Head 29040
    Upper Body and Legs 29046
    Upper Body and One Leg 29044
    Upper Body Only 29035
Clubfoot 29450
Cylinder 29365
Finger 29086
Hand 29085
Hip 29305-29325
Leg
    Rigid Total Contact 29445
Long Arm 29065
Long Leg 29345-29355, 29365, 29450
Long Leg Brace 29358
Patellar Tendon Bearing (PTB) 29435
Removal 29700-29715
Repair 29720
Short Arm 29075
Short Leg 29405-29435, 29450
Shoulder 29049-29058
Walking 29355, 29425
    Revision 29440
Wedging 29740-29750
Windowing 29730
Wrist 29085

Casting
Unlisted Services and Procedures 29799

Castration
See Orchiectomy

Castration, Female
See Oophorectomy

CAT Scan
See CT Scan

Cataract
Excision 66830
Incision 66820-66821
    Laser 66821
    Stab Incision 66820
Removal/Extraction
    Extracapsular 66982, 66984
    Intracapsular 66983

Catecholamines 80424, 82382-82384
Blood 82383
Urine 82382

Cathepsin-D 82387

Catheter
See Cannulization; Venipuncture
Aspiration
    Nasotracheal 31720
    Tracheobronchial 31725
Bladder 51701-51703
    Irrigation 51700
Breast Cytology 0046T, 0047T
Declotting 36550
Exchange
    Intravascular 37209, 75900
    Peritoneal 49423
Intracatheter
    Irrigation 99507
    Obstruction Clearance 36596
Pericatheter
    Obstruction
        Clearance 36595
Placement
    Breast
        for Interstitial Radioelement
        Application 19296-19298
    Bronchus
        for Intracavitary Radioelement
        Application 31643
Removal
    Central Venous 36589
    Peritoneum 49422
    Spinal Cord 62355
Repair
    Central Venous 36575
Replacement
    Central Venous 36580-36581, 36584
Repositioning 36597

Catheterization
See Catheter
Abdomen 49420-49421
Abdominal Artery 36245-36248
Aorta 36160-36215
Arterial
    Cutdown 36625
    Intracatheter/Needle 36100-36140
    Percutaneous 36620
Arteriovenous Shunt 36145
Bile Duct 47530
    Change 47525
    Percutaneous 47510
Bladder 51010, 51045

Brachiocephalic Artery 36215-36218
Brain 61210
    Replacement 62160, 62194, 62225
Bronchography 31710
Cardiac
    Combined Left and Right
        Heart 93526-93529
    Combined Right and Retrograde Left
        for Congenital Cardiac
        Anomalies .93531
    Combined Right and Transseptal Left
        for Congenital Cardiac
        Anomalies 93532-93533
    Flow Directed 93503
    for Biopsy 93505
    for Dilution Studies 93561-93562
    Imaging 93555-93556
    Injection 93539-93545
    Left Heart 93510-93524
    Pacemaker 33210
    Right Heart 36013, 93501
        for Congenital Cardiac Anomalies . . .93530
Central 36555-36566
Cerebral Artery 36215
Cystourethroscopy
    Ejaculatory Duct 52010
    Ureteral 52005
Ear, Middle 69405
Eustachian Tube 69405
Fallopian Tube 58345, 74742
Intracardiac
    Ablation 93650-93652
Jejunum
    for Enteral 44015
Kidney
    Drainage 50392
    with Ureter 50393
Legs 36245-36248
Nasotracheal 31720
Newborn
    Umbilical Vein 36510
Pelvic Artery 36245-36248
Peripheral 36568-36571
Placement
    Arterial Coronary Conduit
        without Concomitant Left Heart
            Catheterization 93508
    Coronary Artery
        without Concomitant Left Heart
            Catheterization 93508
    Venous Coronary Bypass Graft
        without Concomitant Left Heart
            Catheterization 93508
Pleural Cavity 32019
Portal Vein 36481
Pulmonary Artery 36013-36015
Radioelement Application 55859
Removal
    Fractured Catheter 75961
    Obstructive Material
        Intracatheter 36596
        Pericatheter 36595
Salivary Duct 42660
Skull 61107
Spinal Cord 62350-62351
Thoracic Artery 36215-36218

Tracheobronchi 31725
Transglottic 31700
Umbilical Artery 36660
Umbilical Vein 36510
Ureter
    Endoscopic 50553, 50572, 50953,
                    50972, 52005
    Injection 50394, 50684
    Manometric Studies 50396, 50686
Uterus
    Radiology 58340
Vena Cava 36010
Venous
    Central Line 36555-36556, 36568-36569,
                      36580, 36584
    First Order 36011
    Intracatheter/Needle 36000
    Organ Blood .36500
    Second Order 36012
    Umbilical Vein 36510
Ventricular 61020-61026, 61210-61215

Cauda Equina
See Spinal Cord
Decompression 63005-63011, 63017, 63047-
            63048, 63055-63057, 63087-63091
Exploration 63005-63011, 63017

Cauterization
Anal Fissure 46940-46942
Cervix 57522
    Cryocautery .57511
    Electro or Thermal 57510
    Laser Ablation 57513
Chemical
    Granulation Tissue 17250
Everted Punctum 68705
Nasopharyngeal Hemorrhage 42970
Nose
    Hemorrhage 30901-30906
Skin Lesion 11055-11057, 17000-17004
Skin Tags .11200-11201
Turbinate Mucosa 30801-30802

Cavernitides, Fibrous
See Peyronie Disease

Cavernosography
Corpora 54230

Cavernosometry 54231

Cavities, Pleural
See Pleural Cavity

Cavus Foot Correction 28309

CBC
See Blood Cell Count; Complete Blood Count
(CBC)

CCL4
See Carbon Tetrachloride

CCU Visit
See Critical Care Services

CD142 Antigens
See Thromboplastin

CD143 Antigens
See Angiotensin Converting Enzyme (ACE)

CD4 86360

CD8 86360

CEA
See Carcinoembryonic Antigen

Cecil Repair
See Urethroplasty

Cecostomy 44300
Laparoscopic 44188

Celiac Plexus
Destruction 64680
Injection
    Anesthetic 64530
    Neurolytic 64680

Celiac Trunk Artery
See Artery, Celiac

Celioscopy
See Endoscopy, Peritoneum

Celiotomy 49000
Abdomen
    for Staging 49220

Cell Count
Body Fluid 89050-89051

Cell, Blood
See Blood Cell

Cell, Islet
See Islet Cell

Cell, Mother
See Stem Cell

Cell-Stimulating Hormone, Interstitial
See Luteinizing Hormone (LH)

Cellobiase
See Beta Glucosidase

Cellular Inclusion
See Inclusion Bodies

Central Shunt 33764

Central Venous Catheter Placement
Insertion
    Central 36555-36558
    Peripheral 36568-36569
Repair 36575
Replacement 36580-36585
Repositioning 36597

Central Venous Catheter Removal 36589

Cephalic Version
of Fetus
    External 59412

Cephalocele
See Encephalocele

Cephalogram, Orthodontic
See Orthodontic Cephalogram

Cerclage
Cervix 57700
   Abdominal 59325
   Removal Under Anesthesia 59871
   Vaginal 59320

Cerebellopontine Angle Tumor
See Brain, Tumor, Excision; Brainstem;
Mesencephalon; Skull Base Surgery

Cerebral Cortex Decortication
See Decortication

Cerebral Death
See Brain Death

Cerebral Hernia
See Encephalocele

Cerebral Perfusion Analysis ...0042T

Cerebral Thermography
See Thermogram, Cephalic

Cerebral Ventriculographies
See Ventriculography

Cerebral Vessels
Angioplasty 61630
Dilation
   Intracranial Vasospasm 61640-61642
Occlusion 61623
Placement
   Stent 61635

Cerebrose
See Galactose

Cerebrospinal Fluid 86325
Nuclear Imaging 78630-78650

Cerebrospinal Fluid Leak 63744
Brain
   Repair 61618-61619, 62100
Nasal/Sinus Endoscopy
   Repair 31290-31291
Spinal Cord
   Repair 63707-63709

Cerebrospinal Fluid
Shunt 63740, 63746
Creation 62180-62192, 62200-62223
Irrigation 62194
Removal 62256-62258
Replacement 62160, 62194, 62225-62230
Reprogramming 62252

Ceruloplasmin 82390

Cerumen
Removal 69210

Cervical Cap 57170

Cervical
Lymphadenectomy 38720-38724

Cervical Mucus
Penetration Test 89330

Cervical Plexus
Injection
   Anesthetic 64413

Cervical Pregnancy 59140

Cervical Puncture 61050-61055

Cervical Smears 88141, 88155,
             88164-88167, 88174-88175
See Cytopathology

Cervical Spine
See Vertebra, Cervical

Cervical Sympathectomy
See Sympathectomy, Cervical

Cervicectomy 57530

Cervicography 0003T

Cervicoplasty 15819

Cervicothoracic Ganglia
See Stellate Ganglion

Cervix
See Cytopathology
Amputation
   Total 57530
Biopsy 57500, 57520
   Colposcopy 57454-57455, 57460
Cauterization 57522
   Cryocautery 57511
   Electro or Thermal 57510
   Laser Ablation 57513
Cerclage 57700
   Abdominal 59325
   Removal Under Anesthesia 59871
   Vaginal 59320
Cervicography 0003T
Colposcopy 57452-57461
Conization 57461, 57520-57522
Curettage
   Endocervical 57454, 57456, 57505
Dilation
   Canal 57800
   Stump 57820
Dilation and Curettage 57820
Ectopic Pregnancy 59140
Excision
   Radical 57531
   Stump
     Abdominal Approach 57540-57545
     Vaginal Approach 57550-57556
   Total 57530
Exploration
   Endoscopy 57452
Insertion
   Dilation 59200
   Laminaria 59200
   Prostaglandin 59200
   Sensor, Fetal Oximetry 0021T
Repair
   Cerclage 57700
   Abdominal 59325
   Suture 57720
   Vaginal 59320
Unlisted Services and Procedures 58999

Cesarean Delivery
Antepartum Care 59610, 59618
Delivery
   after Attempted Vaginal Delivery 59618
     Delivery Only 59620
     Postpartum Care 59622
     Routine Care 59610, 59618
Delivery Only 59514
Postpartum Care 59515
Routine Care 59510
Tubal Ligation at Time of 58611
with Hysterectomy 59525

CGMP
See Cyclic GMP

Chalazion
Excision 67805
   Multiple
     Different Lids 67805
     Same Lid 67801
   Single 67800
   Under Anesthesia 67808

Challenge Tests
Bronchial Ingestion 95070-95075

Chambers Procedure 28300

Change
Catheter
   Bile Duct 75984
Fetal Position
   by Manipulation 59412
Tube or Stent
   Endoscopic
     Bile or Pancreatic Duct 43269

Change of, Dressing
See Dressings, Change

Change, Gastrostomy Tube
See Gastrostomy Tube, Change of

CHCT
See Caffeine Halothane Contracture Test

Cheek
Bone
   Excision 21030, 21034
   Fracture
     Closed Treatment with
      Manipulation 21355
     Open Treatment 21360-21366
     Reconstruction 21270
Fascia Graft 15840
Muscle Graft 15841-15845
Muscle Transfer 15845

Cheilectomy
Metatarsophalangeal Joint Release 28289

Cheiloplasty
See Lip, Repair

Cheiloschisis
See Cleft Lip

Cheilotomy
See Incision, Lip

Chemical Cauterization
Granulation Tissue 17250

Chemical Exfoliation 17360

Chemical Peel 15788-15793

Chemiluminescent Assay 82397

Chemistry Tests
Clinical
    Unlisted Services and Procedures 84999

Chemocauterization
Corneal Epithelium 65435
    with Chelating Agent 65436

Chemodenervation
Anal Sphincter 46505
Eccrine Glands
    Axillae 64650
    Feet 64652
    Hands 64651
    Other Area 64653
Electrical Stimulation for Guidance 95873
Extraocular Muscle 67345
Extremity Muscle 64614
Facial Muscle 64612
Neck Muscle 64613
Needle Electromyography for Guidance ...95874
Trunk Muscle 64614

Chemonucleolysis 62292

Chemosurgery
Mohs Technique 17304-17310
Skin Lesion 17004, 17110, 17270, 17280

Chemotaxis Assay 86155

Chemotherapy
Arterial Catheterization 36640
Bladder Instillation 51720
CNS 61517, 96450
Extracorporeal Circulation
    Extremity 36823
Home Infusion Procedures 99601-99602
Intra-Arterial 96420-96425
Intralesional 96405-96406
Intramuscular 96400-96402
Intravenous 96408-96415, 96417
    Infusion Pump 96416
Kidney Instillation 50391
Peritoneal Cavity 96445
Pleural Cavity 96440
Pump Services
    Implantable 96522
    Maintenance 95990-95991
    Portable 96521
Reservoir Filling 96542
Subcutaneous 96400-96402
Supply of Agent 96545
Unlisted Services and Procedures 96549
Ureteral Instillation 50391

Chest
See Mediastinum; Thorax
Angiography 71275
Artery
    Ligation 37616

CT Scan 71250-71275
Exploration
    Blood Vessel 35820
Magnetic Resonance Imaging
(MRI) 71550-71552
Repair
    Blood Vessel 35211-35216
        with Other Graft 35271-35276
        with Vein Graft 35241-35246
Ultrasound 76604
Wound Exploration
    Penetrating 20101
X-Ray 71010-71035
    Complete (Four Views)
        with Fluoroscopy 71034
    Insertion Pacemaker 71090
    Partial (Two Views)
        with Fluoroscopy 71023
    Stereo 71015
    with Fluoroscopy 71090

Chest Cavity
Bypass Graft 35905
Endoscopy
    Exploration 32601-32606
    Surgical 32650-32665

Chest Wall
See Pulmonology, Therapeutic
Manipulation 94667-94668
Reconstruction 49904
    Trauma 32820
Repair 32905
    Closure 32810
    Fistula 32906
Tumor
    Excision 19260-19272
Unlisted Services and Procedures 32999

Chest Wall Fistula
See Fistula, Chest Wall

Chest, Funnel
See Pectus Excavatum

Chevron Procedure 28296

Chiari Osteotomy of the Pelvis
See Osteotomy, Pelvis

Chicken Pox Vaccine 90716

Child Procedure
See Excision, Pancreas, Partial

Chin
Repair
    Augmentation 21120
    Osteotomy 21121-21123

Chinidin
See Quinidine

Chiropractic Manipulation
See Manipulation, Chiropractic

Chiropractic Treatment
Spinal
    Extraspinal 98940-98943

Chlamydia
Antibody 86631-86632
Antigen Detection
    Direct Fluorescence 87270
    Enzyme Immunoassay 87320
Culture 87110

Chloramphenicol 82415

Chloride
Blood 82435
Other Source 82438
Spinal Fluid 82438
Urine 82436

Chloride, Methylene
See Dichloromethane

Chlorinated Hydrocarbons 82441

Chlorohydrocarbon
See Chlorinated Hydrocarbons

Chlorpromazine 84022

Choanal Atresia
Repair 30540-30545

Cholangiography
Injection 47500-47505
Intraoperative 74300-74301
Percutaneous 74320
    with Laparoscopy 47560-47561
Postoperative 74305
Repair
    with Bile Duct Exploration 47700
    with Cholecystectomy ..47563, 47605, 47620

Cholangiopancreatography 43260
See Bile Duct; Pancreatic Duct
Repair
    See Bile Duct; Pancreatic Duct
        with Biopsy 43261
        with Surgery 43262-43267, 43269

Cholangiostomy
See Hepaticostomy

Cholangiotomy
See Hepaticostomy

Cholecalciferol
See Vitamin, D-3

Cholecystectomy 47562-47564,
                                        47600-47620
Any Method 47562-47564
    with Cholangiography ..47563, 47605, 47620
    with Exploration Common
    Duct 47564, 47610

Cholecystenterostomy 47570,
                                         47720-47741

Cholecystography 74290-74291

Cholecystotomy 47480, 48001
Percutaneous 47490

Choledochoplasty
See Bile Duct, Repair

Choledochoscopy 47550

Choledochostomy 47420-47425

Choledochotomy 47420-47425

Choledochus, Cyst
See Cyst, Choledochal

Cholera Vaccine
Injectable 90725

Cholesterol
Measurement 83721
Serum 82465
Testing 83718-83719

Choline Esterase I
See Acetylcholinesterase

Choline Esterase II
See Cholinesterase

Cholinesterase
Blood 82480-82482

Cholylglycine
Blood 82240

Chondroitin Sulfate 82485

Chondromalacia Patella
Repair 27418

Chondropathia Patellae
See Chondromalacia Patella

Chondrosteoma
See Exostosis

Chopart Procedure 28800-28805
See Amputation, Foot; Radical Resection;
Replantation

Chordotomies
See Cordotomy

Chorioangioma
See Lesion, Skin

Choriogonadotropin
See Chorionic Gonadotropin

Choriomeningitides, Lymphocytic
See Lymphocytic Choriomeningitis

Chorionic Gonadotropin 80414,
84702-84703
Stimulation 80414-80415

Chorionic Growth Hormone
See Lactogen, Human Placental

Chorionic Tumor
See Hydatidiform Mole

Chorionic Villi
See Biopsy, Chorionic Villus

Chorionic Villus
Biopsy 59015

Choroid
Destruction
　Lesion 0016T, 67220-67225

Choroid Plexus
Excision 61544

Christmas Factor 85250

Chromaffinoma, Medullary
See Pheochromocytoma

Chromatin, Sex
See Barr Bodies

Chromatography
Column/Mass Spectrometry 82541-82544
Gas Liquid or HPLC 82486, 82491-82492
Paper 82487-82488
Thin-Layer 82489

Chromium 82495

Chromogenic Substrate Assay .85130

Chromosome Analysis
See Amniocentesis
Added Study 88280-88289
Amniotic Fluid 88267-88269
　Culture 88235
Biopsy Culture
　Tissue 88233
Bone Marrow Culture 88237
Chorionic Villus 88267
　5 Cells 88261
　15-20 Cells 88262
　20-25 Cells 88264
　45 Cells 88263
　Culture 88235
for Breakage Syndromes 88245-88249
Fragile-X 88248
Lymphocyte Culture 88230
Pregnancy Associated Plasma Protein-A ...84163
Skin Culture
　Tissue 88233
Tissue Culture 88239
Unlisted Services and Procedures 88299

Chromotubation 58350
Oviduct 58350

Chronic Erection
See Priapism

Chronic Interstitial Cystitides
See Cystitis, Interstitial

Ciliary Body
Cyst
　Destruction
　　Cryotherapy 66720
　　Cyclodialysis 66740
　　Cyclophotocoagulation 66710-66711
　　Diathermy 66700
　　Nonexcisional 66770
Destruction
　Cyclophotocoagulation 66710-66711
　Endoscopic 66711
Lesion
　Destruction 66770
Repair 66680

Cimino Type Procedure 36821

Cinefluorographies
See Cineradiography

Cineplasty
Arm, Lower or Upper 24940

Cineradiography
Esophagus 74230
Pharynx 70371, 74230
Speech Evaluation 70371
Swallowing Evaluation 74230
Unlisted Services and Procedures ..76120-76125

Circulation Assist
Aortic 33967, 33970
Balloon 33967, 33970
External 33960-33961

Circulation, Extracorporeal
See Extracorporeal Circulation

Circulatory Assist
See Circulation Assist

Circumcision
Repair 54163
Surgical Excision 54161
　Newborn 54160
with Clamp or Other Device 54152
　Newborn 54150

Cisternal Puncture 61050-61055

Cisternography 70015
Nuclear 78630

Citrate
Blood or Urine 82507

Clagett Procedure
See Chest Wall, Repair, Closure

Clavicle
Craterization 23180
Cyst
　Excision 23140
　　with Allograft 23146
　　with Autograft 23145
Diaphysectomy 23180
Dislocation
　Acromioclavicular Joint
　　Closed Treatment 23540-23545
　　Open Treatment 23550-23552
　Sternoclavicular Joint
　　Closed Treatment 23520-23525
　　Open Treatment 23530-23532
　　without Manipulation 23540
Excision 23170
　Partial 23120, 23180
　Total 23125
Fracture
　Closed Treatment
　　with Manipulation 23505
　　without Manipulation 23500
　Open Treatment 23515
Pinning, Wiring 23490
Prophylactic Treatment 23490
Repair Osteotomy 23480-23485
Saucerization 23180

Sequestrectomy 23170
Tumor
   Excision 23140, 23146, 23200
      with Autograft 23145
      Radical Resection 23200
X-Ray 73000

Clavicula
See Clavicle

Claviculectomy
Partial 23120
Total 23125

Claw Finger Repair 26499

Cleft Cyst, Branchial
See Branchial Cleft, Cyst

Cleft Foot
Reconstruction .28360

Cleft Hand
Repair 26580

Cleft Lip
Repair 40700-40761
Rhinoplasty 30460-30462

Cleft Palate
Repair 42200-42225
Rhinoplasty 30460-30462

Cleft, Branchial
See Branchial Cleft

Clinical Act of Insertion
See Insertion

Clinical Chemistry Test
See Chemistry Tests, Clinical

Clinical Investigation
FDA-approved Drugs
  Single Patient
    by Pharmacist 0130T

Clinical Pathology
See Pathology, Clinical

Clitoroplasty
Intersex State 56805

**Closed [Transurethral] Biopsy of
Bladder**
See Biopsy, Bladder, Cystourethroscopy

Clostridial Tetanus
See Tetanus

Clostridium Botulinum Toxin
See Chemodenervation

Clostridium Difficile
Antigen Detection
  Enzyme Immunoassay 87324
by Immunoassay
  with Direct Optical Observation 87803

Clostridium Tetani ab
See Antibody, Tetanus

Closure 12001-13160
Anal Fistula 46288
Atrioventricular Valve 33600
Cystostomy 51880
Enterostomy 44625-44626
  Laparoscopic 44227
Lacrimal Fistula 68770
Lacrimal Punctum
  Plug 68761
  Thermocauterization, Ligation or Laser
  Surgery 68760
Rectovaginal Fistula 57300-57308
Semilunar Valve 33602
Septal Defect .33615
Sternotomy 21750
Ventricular Tunnel 33722

Closure of Esophagostomy
See Esophagostomy, Closure

Closure of Gastrostomy
See Gastrostomy, Closure

Closure, Atrial Septal Defect
See Heart, Repair, Atrial Septum

**Closure, Cranial Sutures,
Premature**
See Craniosynostosis

Closure, Fistula, Vesicouterine
See Fistula, Vesicouterine, Closure

Closure, Meningocele Spinal
See Meningocele Repair

Closure, Vagina
See Vagina, Closure

Clot 34401-34490, 35875-35876, 50230
See Thrombectomy; Thromboendarterectomy

Clot Lysis Time 85175

Clot Retraction 85170

Clotting Disorder
See Coagulopathy

Clotting Factor 85210-85293

Clotting Inhibitors . . .85300-85305, 85307

Clotting Operation
See Excision, Nail Fold

Clotting Test
Protein C 85303, 85307
Protein S 85306

Clotting Time
See Coagulation Time

Clubfoot Cast 29450
Wedging 29750

CMG
See Cystometrogram

CMRI
See Cardiac Magnetic Resonance Imaging

CMV
See Cytomegalovirus

CNPB
See Continuous Negative Pressure Breathing
(CNPB); Pulmonology, Therapeutic

Co-Factor I, Heparin
See Antithrombin III

CO2
See Carbon Dioxide

Coagulation
Unlisted Services and Procedures 85999

Coagulation Defect
See Coagulopathy

Coagulation Factor
See Clotting Factor

Coagulation Factor I
See Fibrinogen

Coagulation Factor II
See Prothrombin

Coagulation Factor III
See Thromboplastin

Coagulation Factor IV
See Calcium

Coagulation Factor VII
See Proconvertin

Coagulation Factor VIII
See Clotting Factor

Coagulation Factor IX
See Christmas Factor

Coagulation Factor X
See Stuart-Prower Factor

Coagulation Factor Xa
See Thrombokinase

Coagulation Factor XI
See Plasma Thromboplastin, Antecedent

Coagulation Factor XII
See Hageman Factor

Coagulation Factor XIII
See Fibrin Stabilizing Factor

Coagulation Time 85345-85348

Coagulation, Blood
See Blood Clot

Coagulation, Light
See Photocoagulation

Coagulin
See Thromboplastin

Coagulopathy 85390
Assay 85130

Cocaine
Blood or Urine 82520
Screen 82486

Coccidioides
Antibody 86635

Coccidioidin Test
See Streptokinase, Antibody

Coccidioidomycosis
Skin Test 86490

Coccygeal Spine Fracture
See Coccyx, Fracture

Coccygectomy 15920-15922, 27080

Coccyx
Excision 27080
Fracture
    Closed Treatment 27200
    Open Treatment 27202
Tumor
    Excision 49215
X-Ray 72220

Cochlear Device
Insertion 69930
Programming 92601-92604

Codeine
Alkaloid Screening 82101

Codeine Screen 82486

Cofactor Protein S
See Protein S

Coffey Operation
See Uterus, Repair, Suspension

Cognitive Function Tests 96116
See Neurology, Diagnostic

Cognitive Skills Development 97532
See Physical Medicine/Therapy/Occupational Therapy

Cold Agglutinin 86156-86157

Cold Pack Treatment 97010

Cold Preservation
See Cryopreservation

Cold Therapies
See Cryotherapy

Colectomy
Partial 44140
    Laparoscopic 44213
    with Anastomosis 44140
        Laparoscopic 44204, 44207-44208
    with Coloproctostomy 44145-44146
    with Colostomy 44141-44144
        Laparoscopic 44206, 44208
    with Ileocolostomy
        Laparoscopic 44205
    with Ileostomy 44144
    with Ileum Removal 44160
    with Transcanal Approach 44147
Total
    Laparoscopic 44210-44212
      with Proctectomy and
      Ileostomy 44210-44212
      without Proctectomy 44210

Open
    with Anastomosis 44152
    with Complete Proctectomy 45121
    with Ileal Reservoir 44153
    with Ileostomy 44150-44151
    with Proctectomy 44155-44156

Collagen Cross Links 82523

Collagen Injection 11950-11954

Collar Bone
See Clavicle

Collateral Ligament
Ankle
    Repair 27695-27698
Interphalangeal Joint 26545
Knee Joint
    Repair 27409
Knee Repair 27405
Metacarpophalangeal Joint 26540-26542
Repair
    Ankle 27695-27698

Collection and Processing
Allogenic Blood
    Harvesting of Stem Cells 38205
Autologous Blood
    Harvesting of Stem Cells 38206
    Intraoperative 86891
    Preoperative 86890
Specimen
    Capillary Blood 36416
    Venous Blood 36415, 36540
Washings
    Esophagus 91000
    Stomach .91055

Colles Fracture 25600-25620

Colles Fracture Reversed
See Smith Fracture

Collins Syndrome, Treacher
See Treacher-Collins Syndrome

Collis Procedure
See Gastroplasty with Esophagogastric Fundoplasty

Colon
See Colon-Sigmoid
Biopsy 44025, 44100, 44322
    Endoscopic 44389, 45380, 45391-45392
Colostomy
    Revision 44340-44346
Colotomy 44322
    Colostomy 44320
CT Scan
    Colonography 0066T, 0067T
    Virtual Colonoscopy 0066T, 0067T
Destruction
    Lesion 44393, 45383
    Tumor 44393, 45383
Endoscopy
    Biopsy 44389, 45380, 45391-45392
    Destruction
        Lesion 44393
        Tumor 44393, 45383

    Dilation 45386
Exploration 44388, 45378, 45381, 45386
Hemorrhage 44391, 45382
Injection, Submucosal 45381
Placement
    Stent 45387
Removal
    Foreign Body 44390, 45379
    Polyp 44392, 45384-45385
    Tumor 45384-45385
Specimen Collection 45380
Ultrasound 45391-45392
via Colotomy 45355
via Stoma 44388-44397
Virtual 0066T, 0067T
Excision
    Partial 44140-44147, 44160
      Laparoscopic 44204-44208
    Total 44150-44156
      Laparoscopic 44210-44212
Exploration .44025
    Endoscopy 44388, 45378, 45381, 45386
Hemorrhage
    Endoscopic Control 44391, 45382
Hernia 44050
Incision
    Creation
        Stoma 44320-44322
    Exploration 44025
    Revision
        Stoma 44340-44346
Lavage
    Intraoperative 44701
Lesion
    Destruction 45383
    Excision 44110-44111
Lysis
    Adhesions 44005
Obstruction 44025-44050
Reconstruction
    Bladder from 50810
Removal
    Foreign Body 44025, 44390, 45379
    Polyp 44392
Repair
    Diverticula 44605
    Fistula 44650-44661
    Hernia 44050
    Malrotation 44055
    Obstruction 44050
    Ulcer 44605
    Volvulus .44050
    Wound 44605
Splenic Flexure
    Mobilization
        Laparoscopic 44213
Stoma Closure 44620-44625
Suture
    Diverticula 44605
    Fistula 44650-44661
    Plication .44680
    Stoma 44620-44625
    Ulcer 44605
    Wound 44605
Tumor
    Destruction 45383

Ultrasound
  Endoscopic 45391-45392
X-Ray with Contrast
  Barium Enema 74270-74280

Colon-Sigmoid
See Colon
Biopsy
  Endoscopy 45331
Dilation
  Endoscopy 45340
Endoscopy
  Ablation
    Polyp 45339
    Tumor 45339
  Biopsy 45331
  Dilation 45340
  Exploration 45330, 45335
  Hemorrhage 45334
  Needle Biopsy 45342
  Placement
    Stent 45327, 45345
  Removal
    Foreign Body 45332
    Polyp 45333, 45338
    Tumor 45333, 45338
  Ultrasound 45341-45342
  Volvulus 45337
Exploration
  Endoscopy 45330, 45335
Hemorrhage
  Endoscopy .45334
Needle Biopsy
  Endoscopy .45342
Removal
  Foreign Body 45332
Repair
  Volvulus
    Endoscopy 45337
Ultrasound
  Endoscopy 45341-45342

Colonna Procedure
See Acetabulum, Reconstruction

Colonography
CT Scan .0066T, 0067T

Colonoscopy
Biopsy 45380, 45392
Collection Specimen 45380
  via Colotomy 45355
Destruction
  Lesion 45383
  Tumor 45383
Dilation 45386
Hemorrhage Control 45382
Injection
  Submucosal 45381
Placement
  Stent 45387
Removal
  Foreign Body 45379
  Polyp 45384-45385
  Tumor 45384-45385
Ultrasound 45391-45392
via Stoma 44388-44390
  Biopsy 44389

Destruction
  of Lesion 44393
  of Tumor 44393
Exploration 44388
Hemorrhage .44391
Placement
  Stent 44397
Removal
  Foreign Body 44390
  Polyp 44392, 44394
  Tumor 44392, 44394
Virtual 0066T, 0067T

Color Vision Examination 92283

Colorrhaphy 44604

Colostomy 44320, 45563
Abdominal
  Establishment 50810
Home Visit 99505
Intestine, Large
  with Suture 44605
Laparoscopic 44188
Colostomy 44188
Perineal
  Establishment 50810
Revision 44340
  Paracolostomy Hernia 44345-44346

Colotomy .44025

Colpectomy
Partial 57106
Total 57110
with Hysterectomy 58275-58280
  with Repair of Enterocele 58280

Colpo-Urethrocystopexy 58152,
                                    58267, 58293
Marshall-Marchetti-Krantz Procedure . . .58152,
                                    58267, 58293
Pereyra Procedure 58267, 58293

Colpoceliocentesis
See Colpocentesis

Colpocentesis 57020

Colpocleisis 57120

Colpocleisis Complete
See Vagina, Closure

Colpohysterectomies
See Excision, Uterus, Vaginal

Colpoperineorrhaphy 57210

Colpopexy
Extra-Peritoneal 57282
Intra-Peritoneal 57283
Laparoscopic 57425
Open 57280

Colpoplasty
See Repair, Vagina

Colporrhaphy
Anterior 57240, 57289
  with Insertion of Mesh 57267
  with Insertion of Prosthesis 57267

Anteroposterior 57260-57265
  with Enterocele Repair 57265
  with Insertion of Mesh 57267
  with Insertion of Prosthesis 57267
Nonobstetrical 57200
Posterior 57250
  with Insertion of Mesh 57267
  with Insertion of Prosthesis 57267

Colposcopy
Biopsy 56821, 57421, 57454-57455, 57460
  Endometrium 58110
Cervix 57421, 57452-57461
Exploration .57452
Loop Electrode Biopsy 57460
Loop Electrode Conization 57461
Perineum 99170
Vagina 57420-57421
Vulva 56820
  Biopsy 56821

Colpotomy
Drainage
  Abscess 57010
Exploration .57000

Colprosterone
See Progesterone

Column Chromatography/Mass
Spectrometry 82541-82544

Columna Vertebralis
See Spine

Combined Heart-Lung
Transplantation
See Transplantation, Heart-Lung

Combined Right and Left Heart
Cardiac Catheterization
See Cardiac Catheterization, Combined Left and
Right Heart

Comedones
Removal 10040

Commissurotomy
Right Ventricle 33476-33478

Common Sensory Nerve
Repair/Suture 64834

Common Truncus
See Truncus Arteriosus

Communication Device
Non-Speech-Generating . . .92605-92606
Speech-Generating 92606-92609

Community/Work Reintegration
Training 97537
  See Physical Medicine/Therapy/Occupational
  Therapy

Compatibility Test
Blood .86920, 86923

Complement
Antigen 86160
Fixation Test 86171

Functional Activity .... .86161
Hemolytic
    Total .... .86162
Total .... .86162

**Complete Blood Count
(CBC)** 85025-85027
See Blood Cell Count

Complete Colectomy
See Colectomy, Total

Complete Pneumonectomy
See Pneumonectomy, Completion

**Complete Transposition of Great
Vessels**
See Transposition, Great Arteries

Complex, Factor IX
See Christmas Factor

Complex, Vitamin B
See B Complex Vitamins

Component Removal, Blood
See Apheresis

Composite Graft 15760-15770,
                           35681-35683

Compound B
See Corticosterone

Compound F
See Cortisol

Compression, Nerve, Median
See Carpal Tunnel Syndrome

**Computed Tomographic
Scintigraphy**
See Emission Computerized Tomography

Computed Tomography (CT)
See CT Scan; Specific Anatomic Site

Computer Analysis
Acoustic Recording
    Heart Sounds
        with Computer Analysis ..... .0068T-0069T,
                             0070T

Computer Assisted Navigation
Orthopedic Surgery .... .0054T, 0055T, 0056T

Computer Data Analysis .... .99090

Computer-aided Detection
Mammography 76082-76083

**Computer-Assisted Psychological
Testing** .... .96103

**Computerized Emission
Tomography**
See Emission Computerized Tomography

Concentration of Specimen .... .87015

Concentration, Hydrogen-Ion
See pH

Concentration, Minimum Inhibitory
See Minimum Inhibitory Concentration

Concentric Procedure .... .28296

Concha Bullosa Resection
with Nasal/Sinus Endoscopy .... .31240

Conchae Nasale
See Nasal Turbinate

Conduction, Nerve
See Nerve Conduction

Conduit, Ileal
See Ileal Conduit

Condyle
Humerus
    Fracture
        Closed Treatment 24576-24577
        Open Treatment .... .24579
        Percutaneous .... .24582
Metatarsal
    Excision .... .28288
Phalanges
    Toe
        Excision .... .28126

Condyle, Mandibular
See Mandibular Condyle

Condylectomy
Temporomandibular Joint .... .21050
with Skull Base Surgery 61596-61597

Condyloma
Destruction 54050-54065

Conference
Medical
    with Interdisciplinary Team 99361-99373

Confirmation
Drug .... .80102

Confirmatory Consultations
See Consultations

**Congenital Arteriovenous
Malformation**
See Arteriovenous Malformation

Congenital Elevation of Scapula
See Sprengel's Deformity

Congenital Heart Septum Defect
See Septal Defect

Congenital Kidney Abnormality
Nephrolithotomy .... .50070
Pyeloplasty .... .50405
Pyelotomy .... .50135

Congenital Laryngocele
See Laryngocele

Congenital Vascular Anomaly
See Vascular Malformation

Conisation
See Cervix, Conization

Conization
Cervix .... .57461, 57520-57522

Conjoint Psychotherapy .... .90847
See Psychiatric Treatment, Family

Conjunctiva
Biopsy .... .68100
Cyst
    Incision and Drainage .... .68020
Fistulize for Drainage
    with Tube .... .68750
    without Tube .... .68745
Graft .... .65782
    Harvesting .... .68371
Harvesting .... .68371
Incision .... .0124T
Insertion Stent .... .68750
Lesion
    Destruction .... .68135
    Excision 68110-68130
        Over 1 cm .... .68115
        with Adjacent Sclera .... .68130
Reconstruction 68320-68335
    Symblepharon
        with Graft .... .68335
    with Flap
        Bridge or Partial .... .68360
        Total .... .68362
Repair
    Symblepharon
        Division .... .68340
        with Graft .... .68335
        without Graft .... .68330
    Wound
        Direct Closure .... .65270
        Mobilization and Rearrangement .. .65272-
                                 65273
Unlisted Services and Procedures ...... .68399

**Conjunctivo-Tarso-Muller
Resection** .... .67908

Conjunctivocystorhinostomy
See Conjunctivorhinostomy

Conjunctivodacryocystostomy
See Conjunctivorhinostomy

Conjunctivoplasty 68320-68330
Reconstruction Cul de Sac
    with Extensive Rearrangement .... .68326
    with Graft .... .68326
        Buccal Mucous Membrane .... .68328
with Extensive Rearrangement .... .68320
with Graft .... .68320
    Buccal Mucous Membrane .... .68325

Conjunctivorhinostomy
with Tube .... .68750
without Tube .... .68745

Conscious Sedation
See Sedation

Construction
Finger
    Toe to Hand Transfer 26551-26556

Neobladder 51596
Vagina
    with Graft 57292
    without Graft 57291

Consultation
See Second Opinion; Third Opinion
Clinical Pathology 80500-80502
Follow-up Inpatient
Initial Inpatient 99251-99255
    New or Established Patient . . .99251-99255
Office and/or Other Outpatient 99241-99245
    New or Established Patient . . .99241-99245
Psychiatric, with Family 90887
Radiation Therapy
    Radiation Physics 77336-77370
Surgical Pathology 88321-88325
    Intraoperation 88329-88334
X-Ray 76140

Consumption Test, Antiglobulin
See Coombs Test

Contact Lens Services
Fittings and Prescription 92070, 92310-92313
Modification 92325
Prescription 92314-92317
Replacement 92326

Continuous Negative Pressure Breathing (CNPB) 94662

Continuous Positive Airway Pressure (CPAP) 94660
See Pulmonology, Therapeutic

Contouring
Silicone Injections 11950-11954
Tumor
    Facial Bone .21029

Contraception
Cervical Cap
    Fitting 57170
Diaphragm
    Fitting 57170
Intrauterine Device (IUD)
    See Insertion, Intrauterine Device (IUD);
    Intrauterine Device (IUD); Removal,
    Intrauterine Device (IUD)
    Insertion 58300
    Removal 58301

Contraceptive Capsules, Implantable
Insertion 11975
Removal 11976
    with Reinsertion 11977

Contraceptive Device, Intrauterine
See Intrauterine Device (IUD)

Contracture
Elbow
    Release
      with Radical Resection of Capsule . .24149
Palm
    Release 26121-26125
Thumb
    Release 26508

Contracture of Palmar Fascia
See Dupuytren's Contracture

Contralateral Ligament
Repair
    Knee 27405

Contrast Aortogram
See Aortography

Contrast Bath Therapy 97034
See Physical Medicine/Therapy/Occupational
Therapy

Contrast Material
Injection
    via Peritoneal Catheter 49424
Instillation
    Bronchography 31708
    Laryngography 31708

Contrast Phlebogram
See Venography

Contusion
See Hematoma

Converting Enzyme, Angiotensin
See Angiotensin Converting Enzyme (ACE)

Coombs Test 86880

Copper .82525

Coprobilinogen
Feces 84577

Coproporphyrin 84120

Coracoacromial Ligament Release .23415

Coracoid Process Transfer 23462

Cord, Spermatic
See Spermatic Cord

Cord, Spinal
See Spinal Cord

Cord, Vocal
See Vocal Cords

Cordectomy 31300

Cordocenteses
See Cordocentesis

Cordocentesis 59012

Cordotomy 63194-63199

Corectomy
See Excision, Iris

Coreoplasty 66762

Cornea
Biopsy 65410
Curettage 65435-65436
    with Chelating Agent 65436
Epithelium
    Excision 65435-65436
      with Chelating Agent 65436

Lesion
    Destruction .65450
    Excision 65400
      with Graft 65426
      without Graft 65420
Pachymetry 76514
Prosthesis 65770
Pterygium
    Excision 65420
Puncture 65600
Relaxing Incisions 65772-65775
Repair
    Astigmatism 65772-65775
    Wedge Resection 65775
    with Glue 65286
    Wound
      Nonperforating 65275
      Perforating 65280-65285
      Tissue Glue 65286
Reshape
    Epikeratoplasty 65765
    Keratomileusis 65760
    Keratoprosthesis 65767
Scraping
    Smear 65430
Tattoo 65600
Thickness Measurement 76514
Transplantation
    Autograft or Homograft
      Lamellar 65710
      Penetrating 65730-65755
      for Aphakia 65750

Coronary
Atherectomy
    Percutaneous 92995-92996
Thrombectomy
    Percutaneous 92973

Coronary Angioplasty, Transluminal Balloon
See Percutaneous Transluminal Angioplasty

Coronary Artery
Insertion
    Stent 92980-92981
Ligation 33502
Placement
    Radiation Delivery Device 92974
Repair .33500-33507

Coronary Artery Bypass Graft (CABG) 33503-33505, 33510-33516
Arterial .33533-33536
Arterial Graft 33548
Arterial-Venous 33517-33523
Harvest
    Upper Extremity Artery 35600
Reoperation 33530
Venous .33510-33516

Coronary Endarterectomy 33572

Coroner's Exam 88045

Coronoidectomy
Temporomandibular Joint 21070

Corpectomy 63101-63103

Corpora Cavernosa
Corpus Spongiosum Shunt 54430
Glans Penis Fistulization 54435
Injection 54235
Irrigation
    Priapism 54220
Saphenous Vein Shunt 54420
X-Ray with Contrast 74445

Corpora Cavernosa, Plastic Induration
See Peyronie Disease

Corpora Cavernosography 74445

Corpus Callosum
Transection 61541

Corpus Vertebrae (Vertebrale)
See Vertebral Body

Correction of Cleft Palate
See Cleft Palate, Repair

Correction of Lid Retraction
See Repair, Eyelid, Retraction

Correction of Malrotation of Duodenum
See Ladd Procedure

Correction of Syndactyly
See Syndactyly, Repair

Correction of Ureteropelvic Junction
See Pyeloplasty

Cortex Decortication, Cerebral
See Decortication

Cortical Mapping
Transection
    by Electric Stimulation 95961-95962

Corticoids
See Corticosteroids

Corticoliberin
See Corticotropic Releasing Hormone (CRH)

Corticosteroid Binding Globulin
See Transcortin

Corticosteroid Binding Protein
See Transcortin

Corticosteroids
Blood 83491
Urine 83491

Corticosterone
Blood or Urine 82528

Corticotropic Releasing Hormone (CRH) 80412

Cortisol 80400-80406, 80418-80420,
                 80436, 82530
Stimulation 80412
Total 82533

Cortisol Binding Globulin 84449

Costectomy
See Resection, Ribs

Costen Syndrome
See Temporomandibular Joint (TMJ)

Costotransversectomy 21610

Cothromboplastin
See Proconvertin

Cotte Operation 58400-58410
See Repair, Uterus, Suspension; Revision

Cotton Procedure
Bohler Procedure 28405

Counseling
See Preventive Medicine

Counseling and/or Risk Factor Reduction Intervention— Preventive Medicine, Individual Counseling
See Preventive Medicine, Counseling and/or Risk Factor Reduction Intervention, Individual Counseling

Count, Blood Cell
See Blood Cell Count

Count, Blood Platelet
See Blood, Platelet, Count

Count, Cell
See Cell Count

Count, Complete Blood
See Complete Blood Count (CBC)

Count, Erythrocyte
See Red Blood Cell (RBC), Count

Count, Leukocyte
See White Blood Cell, Count

Count, Reticulocyte
See Reticulocyte, Count

Counterimmuno-electrophoresis 86185

Counters, Cell
See Cell Count

Countershock, Electric
See Cardioversion

Coventry Tibial Wedge Osteotomy
See Osteotomy, Tibia

Cowper's Gland
Excision 53250

Coxa
See Hip

Coxiella Burnetii
Antibody 86638

Coxsackie
Antibody 86658

CPAP
See Continuous Positive Airway Pressure

CPK
Blood 82550-82552

CPR (Cardiopulmonary Resuscitation) 92950

Cranial Bone
Halo
    Thin Skull Osteology 20664
Reconstruction
    Extracranial 21181-21184
Tumor
    Excision 61563-61564

Cranial Halo 20661

Cranial Nerve
See Specific Nerve
Avulsion 64732-64760, 64771
Decompression 61458, 64716
Implantation
    Electrode 64553, 64573
Incision 64732-64752, 64760, 65771
Injection
    Anesthetic 64400-64408, 64412
    Neurolytic 64600-64610
Insertion
    Electrode 64553, 64573
Neuroplasty 64716
Release 64716
Repair
    Suture, with or without Graft . . .64864-64865
Section 61460
Transection 64732-64760, 64771
Transposition 64716

Cranial Nerve II
See Optic Nerve

Cranial Nerve V
See Trigeminal Nerve

Cranial Nerve VII
See Facial Nerve

Cranial Nerve X
See Vagus Nerve

Cranial Nerve XI
See Accessory Nerve

Cranial Nerve XII
See Hypoglossal Nerve

Cranial Tongs
Application/Removal 20660
Removal 20665

Craniectomy 61501
See Craniotomy
Decompression 61322-61323, 61340-61343
Exploratory 61304-61305
Extensive, for Multiple Suture Craniosynostosis . .
                 61558-61559
for Electrode 61860-61875
Release Stenosis 61550-61552
Surgical 61312-61315, 61320-61323,
        61440-61480, 61500-61516, 61518-61522

Craniofacial Procedures
Unlisted Services and Procedures 21299

Craniofacial Separation
Closed Treatment .21431
Open Treatment 21432-21436
Wire Fixation 21431

Craniomegalic Skull
Reduction 62115-62117

Craniopharyngioma
Excision 61545

Cranioplasty 62120
Encephalocele Repair 62120
for Defect 62140-62141, 62145
with Autograft 62146-62147
with Bone Graft 61316, 62146-62147

Craniostenosis
See Craniosynostosis

Craniosynostosis
Bifrontal Craniotomy 61557
Extensive Craniectomy 61558-61559

Craniotomy
See Burr Hole; Craniectomy; Drill Hole; Puncture
Bifrontal 61557
Decompression 61322-61323
Exploratory 61304-61305
for Craniosynostosis 61556-61557
for Encephalocele 62121
for Implant of Neurostimulators 61850-61875
Frontal 61556
Parietal 61556
Surgery 61312-61315, 61320-61323, 61440,
　　　　61490, 61546, 61570-61571, 61582-61583,
　　　　　　　61590, 61592, 61760, 62120
with Bone Flap 61510-61516, 61526-61530,
　　　　　　　61533-61545, 61566-61567

Cranium
See Skull

Craterization
Calcaneus 28120
Clavicle 23180
Femur 27070-27071, 27360
Fibula .27360, 27641
Hip 27070
Humerus 23184, 24140
Ileum 27070
Metacarpal 26230
Metatarsal 28122
Olecranon Process 24147
Phalanges
　　Finger 26235-26236
　　Toe 28124
Pubis 27070
Radius .24145, 25151
Scapula 23182
Talus 28120
Tarsal 28122
Tibia 27360, 27640
Ulna 24147, 25150

Creatine 82553-82554
Blood or Urine 82540

Creatine Kinase
Total 82550

Creatine Phosphokinase
Blood 82552
Total 82550

Creatinine
Blood 82565
Clearance 82575
Other Source 82570
Urine 82570-82575

Creation
Arteriovenous
　　Fistula/Autogenous Graft 36825
Colonic Reservoir 45119
Complete Heart Block 93650
Defect 40720
Ileal Reservoir 44153, 45113
Lesion .61790, 63600
Mucofistula 44144
Pericardial Window 32659
Recipient Site 15000
Shunt
　　Cerebrospinal Fluid 62200
　　Subarachnoid
　　　Lumbar-Peritoneal 63740
　　Subarachnoid-Subdural 62190
　　Ventriculo 62220
Sigmoid Bladder .50810
Speech Prosthesis 31611
Stoma
　　Bladder 51980
　　Kidney 50395
　　Renal Pelvis .50395
　　Tympanic Membrane 69433-69436
　　Ureter 50860
Ventral Hernia 39503

CRF
See Corticotropic Releasing Hormone (CRH)

CRH
See Corticotropic Releasing Hormone (CRH)

Cricoid Cartilage Split
Larynx 31587

Cricothyroid Membrane
Incision 31605

Cristobalite
See Silica

Critical Care Services 99289-99292
See Emergency Department Services; Prolonged
Attendance
Evaluation and Management 99291-99292
Gastric Intubation 91105
Interfacility Transport 99289-99290
Ipecac Administration for Poison 99175
Neonatal
　　Initial 99295
　　Low Birth Weight Infant 99298-99300
　　Subsequent .99296
Pediatric
　　Initial 99293
　　Interfacility Transport 99289-99290
　　Subsequent 99294, 99299-99300

Cross Finger Flap 15574

Crossmatch 86920-86923

Crossmatching, Tissue
See Tissue Typing

Cruciate Ligament
Arthroscopic Repair 29888-29889
Repair 27407-27409
　　Knee
　　　with Collateral Ligament 27409

Cryoablation
See Cryosurgery

Cryofibrinogen 82585

Cryofixation
See Cryopreservation

Cryoglobulin 82595

Cryopreservation
Cells 38207-38209, 88240-88241
Embryo 89258
for Transplantation . .32850, 33930, 33940, 44132,
　　　47133, 47140, 48550, 50300-50320, 50547
Freezing and Storage 38207, 88240
Oocyte 0059T
Ovarian Tissue 0058T
Sperm 89259
Testes 89335
Thawing
　　Embryo 89352
　　Oocytes 89353
　　Reproductive Tissue 89354
　　Sperm 89356

Cryosurgery 17000-17286, 47371, 47381
See Destruction
Fibroadenoma 0120T
Labyrinthotomy 69801
Lesion
　　Kidney 50250
　　Mouth 40820
　　Penis 54056, 54065
　　Vagina 57061-57065
　　Vulva 56501-56515

Cryotherapy
Acne 17340
Destruction
　　Ciliary Body .66720
Lesion
　　Cornea 65450
　　Retina 67208, 67227
Retinal Detachment
　　Prophylaxis .67141
　　Repair 67101
Trichiasis
　　Correction 67825

Cryptectomy 46210-46211

Cryptococcus
Antibody 86641
Antigen Detection
　　Enzyme Immunoassay 87327

Cryptococcus Neoformans
Antigen Detection
    Enzyme Immunoassay 87327

Cryptorchism
See Testis, Undescended

Cryptosporidium
Antigen Detection
    Direct Fluorescence 87272
    Enzyme Immunoassay 87328

Crystal Identification
Any Body Fluid 89060

CSF
See Cerebrospinal Fluid Leak

CT Scan
3D Rendering 76376-76377
Bone
    Density Study 76070-76071
Drainage 75989
Follow-up Study .76380
Guidance
    Localization 76355
    Needle Placement 76360
    Radiation Therapy 76370
    Vertebroplasty 76013
    Visceral Tissue Ablation 76362
Unlisted Services and Procedures 76497
with Contrast 70460
    Abdomen .74160
    Arm 73201
    Brain 0042T, 70460
    Cerebral Blood Flow/Volume 0042T
    Ear 70481
    Face 70487
    Head 70460
    Leg 73701
    Maxilla 70487
    Neck 70491
    Orbit 70481
    Pelvis 72193
    Sella Turcica 70481
    Spine
        Cervical 72126
        Lumbar 72132
        Thoracic 72129
    Thorax 71260
without and with Contrast
    Abdomen 74170-74175, 75635
    Arm 73202-73206
    Brain 70470, 70496
    Chest 71275
    Ear 70482
    Face 70488
    Head 70470, 70496
    Leg 73702-73706, 75635
    Maxilla 70488
    Neck 70492, 70498
    Orbit 70482
    Pelvis 72191, 72194
    Sella Turcica 70482
    Spine
        Cervical 72127
        Lumbar 72133
        Thoracic 72130
    Thorax 71270-71275

without Contrast 70450
    Abdomen .74150
    Arm 73200
    Brain 70450
    Colon
        Colonography 0066T, 0067T
        Virtual Colonoscopy 0066T, 0067T
    Ear 70480
    Face 70486
    Head 70450
    Leg 73700
    Maxilla 70486
    Neck 70490
    Orbit 70480
    Pelvis 72192
    Sella Turcica 70480
    Spine
        Cervical 72125
        Lumbar 72131
        Thoracic 72128
    Thorax 71250

CT Scan, Radionuclide
See Emission Computerized Tomography

Cuff, Rotator
See Rotator Cuff

Culdocentesis
See Colpocentesis

Culture
Acid Fast Bacilli 87116
Amniotic Fluid
    Chromosome Analysis 88235
Bacteria
    Additional Methods 87077
    Aerobic 87040-87070
    Anaerobic 87073-87076
    Blood 87040
    Other 87070-87073
    Screening 87081
    Stool 87045-87046
    Urine 87086-87088
Bone Marrow
    Chromosome Analysis 88237
Chlamydia 87110
Chorionic Villus
    Chromosome Analysis 88235
Fertilized Oocytes
    for In Vitro Fertilization 89250
        Co-Culture of Embryo 89251
Fungus
    Blood 87103
    Hair 87101
    Identification 87106
    Nail 87101
    Other 87102
    Skin 87101
Lymphocyte
    Chromosome Analysis 88230
Mold 87107
Mycobacteria 87116-87118
Mycoplasma 87109
Oocyte/Embryo 89250
    Co-Culture of Oocyte/Embryo 89251
    Extended Culture 89272
Pathogen
    by Kit 87084

Skin
    Chromosome Analysis 88233
Tissue
    Toxin/Antitoxin 87230
    Virus 87252-87253
Tubercle Bacilli 87116
Typing 87140-87158
Unlisted Services and Procedures 87999
Yeast 87106

Curettage
See Dilation and Curettage
Cervix
    Endocervical 57454, 57456, 57505
Cornea 65435-65436
    Chelating Agent 65436
Hydatidiform Mole 59870
Postpartum 59160

Curettage and Dilatation
See Dilation and Curettage

Curettage, Uterus
See Uterus, Curettage

Curettement
Skin Lesion 11055-11057, 17004, 17110,
                     17270, 17280

Curietherapy
See Brachytherapy

Custodial Care
See Domiciliary Services; Nursing Facility
Services

Cutaneolipectomy
See Lipectomy

Cutaneous Electrostimulation, Analgesic
See Application, Neurostimulation

Cutaneous Tag
See Skin, Tags

Cutaneous Tissue
See Integumentary System

Cutaneous-Vesicostomy
See Vesicostomy, Cutaneous

CVS
See Biopsy, Chorionic Villus

Cyanacobalamin
See Cyanocobalamin

Cyanide
Blood 82600
Tissue 82600

Cyanocobalamin 82607-82608

Cyclic AMP 82030

Cyclic GMP 83008

Cyclic Somatostatin
See Somatostatin

Cyclocryotherapy
See Cryotherapy, Destruction, Ciliary Body

Cyclodialysis
Destruction
   Ciliary Body 66740

Cyclophotocoagulation
Destruction
   Ciliary Body 66710-66711

Cyclosporine
Assay 80158

Cyst
Abdomen
   Destruction/Excision 49200-49201
Ankle
   Capsule 27630
   Tendon Sheath 27630
Bartholin's Gland Excision 56740
   See Bartholin's Gland, Cyst
   Repair 56440
Bile Duct 47715-47716
Bladder
   Excision 51500
Bone
   Drainage 20615
   Injection 20615
Brain
   Drainage .61150-61151, 61156, 62161-62162
   Excision 61516, 61524, 62162
Branchial Cleft
   Excision 42810-42815
Breast
   Incision and Drainage 19020
   Puncture Aspiration 19000-19001
Calcaneus 28100-28103
Carpal 25130-25136
Choledochal 47715-47716
Ciliary Body
   Destruction 66770
Clavicle
   Excision 23140-23146
Conjunctiva 68020
Dermoid
   Nose
     Excision 30124-30125
Drainage
   Contrast Injection 49424
   with X-Ray 76080
Excision
   Cheekbone 21030
   Clavicle 23140
     with Allograft 23146
     with Autograft 23145
   Femur 27355-27358
   Ganglion
     See Ganglion
   Humerus
     with Allograft 23156
     with Autograft 23155
   Hydatid
     See Echinococcosis
   Lymphatic
     See Lymphocele
   Maxilla 21030
   Mediastinum 32662
   Olecranon Process
     with Allograft 24126
     with Autograft 24125
   Pericardial 32661

Pilonidal 11770-11772
Radius
   with Allograft 24126
   with Autograft 24125
Scapula 23140
   with Allograft 23146
   with Autograft 23145
Ulna
   with Allograft 24126
   with Autograft 24125
Zygoma 21030
Facial Bones
   Excision 21030
Femur 27065-27067
Fibula 27635-27638
Ganglion
   Aspiration/Injection 20612
Gums
   Incision and Drainage 41800
Hip 27065-27067
Humerus
   Excision 23150-23156, 24110
   with Allograft 24116
   with Autograft 24115
Ileum 27065-27067
Incision and Drainage 10060-10061
   Pilonidal 10080-10081
Iris
   Destruction 66770
Kidney
   Ablation 50541
   Aspiration 50390
   Excision 50280-50290
   Injection 50390
   X-Ray 74470
Knee
   Baker's 27345
   Excision 27347
Leg, Lower
   Capsule 27630
   Tendon Sheath 27630
Liver 47010
   Drainage 47010
   Open 47010
   Repair 47300
Lung
   Incision and Drainage 32200
   Removal 32140
Lymph Node
   Axillary/Cervical
     Excision 38550-38555
Mandible
   Excision 21040, 21046-21047
Maxilla
   Excision 21030, 21048-21049
Mediastinal
   Excision 39200
Metacarpal 26200-26205
Metatarsal 28104-28107
Mouth 41005-41009, 41015-41018
   Incision and Drainage 40800-40801
Mullerian Duct
   Excision 55680
Nose
   Excision 30124-30125
Olecranon 24120

Ovarian
   Excision 58925
   Incision and Drainage 58800-58805
Pancreas 48500
   Anastomosis 48520-48540
   Excision 48120
Pelvis
   Aspiration 50390
   Injection 50390
Pericardial
   Excision 33050
Phalanges
   Finger 26210-26215
   Toe 28108
Pilonidal
   Excision 11770-11772
   Incision and Drainage 10080-10081
Pubis 27065-27067
Radius 24120, 25120-25126
Rathke's Pouch
   See Craniopharyngioma
Removal
   Skin 10040
Retroperitoneal
   Destruction/Excision 49200-49201
Salivary Gland Creation
   Destruction/Excision
     Drainage 42409
     Excision 42408
Scapula
   Excision 23140-23146
Seminal Vesicle
   Excision 55680
Skin
   Puncture Aspiration 10160
Spinal Cord
   Aspiration 62268
   Incision and Drainage 63172-63173
Sublingual Gland Drainage 42409
   Excision 42408
Talus 28100-28103
Tarsal 28104-28107
Thyroglossal Duct
   Excision 60280-60281
   Incision and Drainage 60000
Thyroid Gland Aspiration 60001
   Excision 60200
   Injection 60001
Tibia 27635-27638
Tongue 41000-41006, 41015
Ulna 24120, 25120-25126
Urachal
   Bladder
     Excision 51500
Vaginal
   Excision 57135
Wrist 25130-25136
   Excision 25111-25112
Zygoma
   Excision 21030

Cyst Ovary
See Ovary, Cyst

Cystatins, Kininogen
See Kininogen

Cystectomy
Complete 51570
 with Bilateral Pelvic
 Lymphadenectomy 51575, 51585, 51595
 with Continent Diversion 51596
 with Ureteroileal Conduit 51590
 with Ureterosigmoidostomy 51580
Ovarian 58925
 Laparoscopic 58661
Partial
 Complicated 51555
 Reimplantation of Ureters 51565
 Simple 51550

Cystic Hygroma
See Hygroma

Cystine
Urine 82615

Cystitis
Interstitial 52260-52265

Cystography 74430
Injection 52281
 Radiologic 51600

Cystolithotomy 51050

Cystometrogram 51725-51726

Cystoplasty 51800

Cystorrhaphy 51860-51865

Cystoscopy 52000

Cystoscopy, with Biopsy
See Biopsy, Bladder, Cystourethroscopy

Cystostomy
Change Tube 51705-51710
Closure 51880
Home Visit 99505
with Fulguration 51020
with Insertion Radioactive Material 51020
with Urethrectomy
 Female 53210
 Male 53215

Cystotomy
Excision
 Bladder Diverticulum 51525
 Bladder Tumor 51530
 Repair of Ureterocele 51535
 Vesical Neck 51520
Repair Ureterocele 51535
with Calculus Basket Extraction 51065
with Destruction Intravesical Lesion 51030
with Drainage 51040
with Fulguration 51020
with Insertion
 Radioactive Material 51020
 Ureteral Catheter 51045
with Removal Calculus 51050, 51065

Cystourethrogram, Retrograde
See Urethrocystography, Retrograde

Cystourethropexy
See Vesicourethropexy

Cystourethroplasty 51800-51820

Cystourethroscopy 52000, 52351,
 52601, 52647-52648, 53500
Biopsy 52204, 52354
 Brush 52007
Calibration and/or Dilation Urethral Stricture or
Stenosis 52281
Catheterization
 Ejaculatory Duct 52010
 Ureteral 52005
Destruction
 Lesion 52400
Dilation
 Bladder 52260-52265
 Intra-Renal Stricture 52343, 52346
 Ureter 52341-52342, 52344-52345
 Urethra 52281
Evacuation
 Clot 52001
Female Urethral Syndrome 52285
Incision
 Ejaculatory Duct 52402
Injection of Implant Material 52327
Insertion
 Indwelling Ureteral Stent 50947, 52332
 Radioactive Substance 52250
 Ureteral Guide Wire 52334
 Urethral Stent 52282
Lithotripsy 52353
Manipulation of Ureteral Calculus 52330
Meatotomy
 Ureteral 52290-52305
Removal
 Calculus ..52310-52315, 52320-52325, 52352
 Foreign Body 52310-52315
 Urethral Stent 52310-52315
Resection
 Ejaculatory Duct 52402
 External Sphincter 52277
 Tumor 52355
Urethral Syndrome 52285
Vasectomy
 Transurethral 52402
Vasotomy
 Transurethral 52402
with Direct Vision Internal Urethrotomy ...52276
with Ejaculatory Duct Catheterization 52010
with Fulguration 52214, 52354
 Lesion 52224
 Tumor 52234-52240
with Internal Urethrotomy
 Female 52270
 Male 52275
with Steroid Injection 52283
with Ureteral Catheterization 52005
with Ureteral Meatotomy 52290-52305

Cytochrome Reductase, Lactic
See Lactic Dehydrogenase

Cytogenetic Study
Molecular
 DNA Probe 88271-88275, 88291, 88365
Unlisted Services and Procedures 88299

Cytomegalovirus
Antibody 86644-86645
Antigen Detection
 Direct Fluorescence 87271
 Enzyme Immunoassay 87332
 Nucleic Acid 87495-87497

Cytometries, Flow
See Flow Cytometry

Cytopathology
Cervical or Vaginal
 Requiring Interpretation by Physician ..88141
 Thin Layer Prep 88142-88143,
 88174-88175
Concentration Technique 88108
 See Saccomonno Technique
Evaluation 88172
Fluids, Washings, Brushings 88104-88108
Forensic 88125
Other Source 88160-88162
Selective Cellular Enhancement Technique .88112
Smears
 Cervical or Vaginal 88141-88167,
 88174-88175
Unlisted Services and Procedures 88199

Cytoscopy
See Bladder, Endoscopy

Cytosol Aminopeptidase
See Leucine Aminopeptidase

Cytotoxic Screen
Lymphocyte 86805-86806
Percent Reactive Antibody (PRA) ...86807-86808
Serum Antibodies 86807-86808

D

D & C Yellow No. 7
See Fluorescein

D 2, Vitamin
See Calciferol

D and C
See Dilation and Curettage

D and E
See Dilation and Evacuation

D Galactose
See Galactose

D Glucose
See Glucose

D Vitamin
See Vitamin, D

D-Xylose Absorption Test 84620

Dacryoadenectomy
Partial 68505
Total 68500

Dacryocystectomy 68520

Dacryocystogram
See Dacryocystography

Dacryocystography 68850, 70170
Nuclear Imaging 78660

Dacryocystorhinostomy 68720
Total
        with Nasal/Sinus Endoscopy 31239

Dacryocystostomies
See Dacryocystotomy

Dacryocystotomy 68420

Daily Living Activities
See Activities of Daily Living

Damus-Kaye-Stansel Procedure
See Anastomosis, Pulmonary

Dana Operation
See Rhizotomy

Dandy Operation
See Ventriculocisternostomy

Dark Adaptation Examination ..92284

Dark Field Examination ...87164-87166

Darkroom Test
See Glaucoma, Provocative Test

Darrach Procedure
See Excision, Ulna, Partial

Day Test
See Blood, Feces

**de Quervain's Disease
Treatment** 25000

Death, Brain
See Brain Death

Debridement
Brain 62010
Burns 01951-01953, 16020-16030
Mastoid Cavity
        Complex 69222
        Simple 69220
Metatarsophalangeal Joint 28289
Muscle
        Infected 11004-11006
Nails 11720-11721
Nose
        Endoscopic 31237
Pancreatic Tissue 48005
Skin
        Eczematous 11000-11001
        Full Thickness 11041
        Infected 11000-11006
        Partial Thickness 11040
        Subcutaneous Tissue 11042-11044
            Infected 11004-11006
        with Open Fracture and/or
        Dislocation 11010-11012
Sternum 21627

Wound
        Non-Selective 97602
        Selective 97597-97598

Debulking Procedure
Ovary/Pelvis 58952-58954

Decompression
See Section
Arm, Lower 24495, 25020-25025
Auditory Canal, Internal 69960
Brainstem 61575-61576
Cauda Equina 63011, 63017, 63047-63048,
                        63056-63057, 63087-63091
Cranial Nerve 61458
Esophagogastric Varices 37181
Facial Nerve 61590
        Intratemporal
            Lateral to Geniculate Ganglion 69720,
                                        69740
            Medial to Geniculate Ganglion 69725,
                                        69745
        Total 69955
Finger 26035
Gasserian Ganglion
        Sensory Root 61450
Hand 26035-26037
Intestines
        Small 44021
Jejunostomy
Laparoscopic 44186
Leg
        Fasciotomy 27600-27602
Nerve 64702-64727
        Root 63020-63048, 63055-63103
Nucleus of Disk
        Lumbar 62287
Optic Nerve 67570
Orbit 61330
        Removal of Bone 67414, 67445
Skull 61322-61323, 61340-61345
Spinal Cord 63001-63017, 63045-63103
        Cauda Equina 63005
Tarsal Tunnel Release 28035
Volvulus 45321, 45337
with Nasal/Sinus Endoscopy
        Optic Nerve 31294
        Orbit Wall 31292-31293
Wrist 25020-25025

Decortication
Lung
        Endoscopic 32651-32652
        Partial 32225
        Total 32220
        with Parietal Pleurectomy 32320

Decubiti
See Pressure Ulcer (Decubitus)

Decubitus Ulcers
See Debridement; Pressure Ulcer (Decubitus);
Skin Graft and Flap

Deetjeen's Body
See Blood, Platelet

Defect, Coagulation
See Coagulopathy

Defect, Heart Septal
See Septal Defect

Defect, Septal Closure, Atrial
See Heart, Repair, Atrial Septum

Deferens, Ductus
See Vas Deferens

Defibrillation
See Cardioversion

Defibrillator, Heart
See Pacemaker, Heart
Evaluation and Testing 93640-93642,
                                    93741-93744
Insertion Single/Dual Chamber
        Electrodes 33216-33217,
                        33224-33225, 33245-33249
        Pulse Generator 33240, 33246
Removal Single/Dual Chamber
        Electrodes 33243-33244
        Pulse Generator 33241
Repair 33218-33220
Repositioning Single/Dual Chamber
        Electrodes 33215, 33226
Revise Pocket Chest 33223
Wearable Device 93741-93742, 93745

Deformity, Boutonniere
See Boutonniere Deformity

Deformity, Sprengel's
See Sprengel's Deformity

**Degenerative, Articular Cartilage,
Patella**
See Chondromalacia Patella

Degradation Products, Fibrin
See Fibrin Degradation Products

Dehydroepiandrosterone 82626

**Dehydroepiandrosterone
Sulfate** 82627

**Dehydrogenase,
6-Phosphogluconate**
See Phosphogluconate-6, Dehydrogenase

Dehydrogenase, Alcohol
See Antidiuretic Hormone

**Dehydrogenase,
Glucose-6-Phosphate**
See Glucose-6-Phosphate, Dehydrogenase

Dehydrogenase, Glutamate
See Glutamate Dehydrogenase

Dehydrogenase, Isocitrate
See Isocitric Dehydrogenase

Dehydrogenase, Lactate
See Lactic Dehydrogenase

Dehydrogenase, Malate
See Malate Dehydrogenase

Dehydroisoandrosterone Sulfate
See Dehydroepiandrosterone Sulfate

Delay of Flap
Skin Graft 15600-15630

Deligation
Ureter 50940

Deliveries, Abdominal
See Cesarean Delivery

Delivery
See Cesarean Delivery; Vaginal Delivery

Delorme Operation
See Pericardiectomy

Denervation
Hip
　Femoral 27035
　Obturator 27035
　Sciatic 27035

Denervation, Sympathetic
See Excision, Nerve, Sympathetic

Denis-Browne Splint 29590

Dens Axis
See Odontoid Process

**Denver Developmental
Screening Test** 96101-96103

Denver Krupic Procedure
See Aqueous Shunt, to Extraocular Reservoir

Denver Shunt
Patency Test 78291

Denver-Krupin Procedure 66180

Deoxycorticosterone
See Desoxycorticosterone

Deoxycortisol 80436, 82634

Deoxyephedrine
See Methamphetamine

Deoxyribonuclease
Antibody 86215

Deoxyribonuclease I
See DNAse

Deoxyribonucleic Acid
Antibody 86225-86226

Depilation
See Removal, Hair

Depletion
Plasma 38214
Platelet 38213
T-Cell 38210
Tumor Cell 38211

Deposit Calcium
See Calcium, Deposits

Depth Electrode
Insertion 61760

Derma-Fat-Fascia Graft 15770

Dermabrasion 15780-15783

Dermatology
Actinotherapy 96900
Examination of Hair
　Microscopic 96902
Ultraviolet A Treatment 96912
Ultraviolet B Treatment 96910-96913
Ultraviolet Light Treatment 96900-96913
Unlisted Services and Procedures 96999

Dermatoplasty
Septal 30620

Dermoid
See Cyst, Dermoid

Derrick-Burnet Disease
See Q Fever

Descending Abdominal Aorta
See Aorta, Abdominal

Desipramine
Assay 80160

Desmotomy
See Ligament, Release

Desoxycorticosterone 82633

Desoxycortone
See Desoxycorticosterone

Desoxyephedrine
See Methamphetamine

Desoxynorephedrin
See Amphetamine

Desoxyphenobarbital
See Primidone

Desquamation
See Exfoliation

Destruction
Acne 17340-17360
　Cryotherapy .17340
Arrhythmogenic Focus
　Heart 33250-33251, 33261
Bladder 51020, 52214-52224, 52354
Calculus
　Bile Duct 43265
　Kidney 50590
　Pancreatic Duct 43265
Chemical Cauterization
　Granulation Tissue 17250
Ciliary Body
　Cryotherapy .66720
　Cyclodialysis 66740
　Cyclophotocoagulation 66710-66711
　Diathermy 66700
　Endoscopic .66711
Cyst
　Abdomen 49200-49201
　Ciliary Body .66770
　Iris 66770
　Retroperitoneal 49200-49201
Endometrial ablation 58356
Endometriomas
　Abdomen 49200-49201
　Retroperitoneal 49200-49201

Fissure
　Anal 46940-46942
Hemorrhoids 46934-46936
Kidney 52354
　Endoscopic 50557, 50576
Lesion
　Anal 46900-46917, 46924
　Bladder 51030
　Breast 0061T
　Choroid 0016T, 67220-67225
　Ciliary Body .66770
　Colon 45383
　Conjunctiva .68135
　Cornea 65450
　Eyelid 67850
　Facial 17000-17004, 17280-17286
　Gastrointestinal, Upper 43258
　Gums 41850
　Intestines
　　Large 44393
　　Small 44369
　Iris 66770
　Mouth 40820
　Nose
　　Intranasal 30117-30118
　Palate 42160
　Penis
　　Cryosurgery 54056
　　Electrodesiccation 54055
　　Extensive .54065
　　Laser Surgery 54057
　　Simple 54050-54060
　　Surgical Excision 54060
　Pharynx 42808
　Prostate 45320
　　Thermotherapy 53850-53853
　　　Microwave 53850
　　　Radio Frequency 53852
　Rectum 45320
　Retina
　　Cryotherapy, Diathermy 67208, 67227
　　Photocoagulation 0017T, 67210, 67228
　　Radiation by Implantation
　　of Source .67218
　Skin
　　Benign 17000-17250
　　Malignant 17260-17286, 96567
　　Premalignant 96567
　Spinal Cord 62280-62282
　Ureter 52341-52342, 52344-52345
　Urethra 52400, 53265
　Uvula 42160
　Vagina
　　Extensive .57065
　　Simple 57061
　Vascular, Cutaneous 17106-17108
　Vulva
　　Extensive .56515
　　Simple 56501
Molluscum Contagiosum 17110
Muscle Endplate
　Extraocular 67345
　Extremity 64614
　Facial 64612
　Neck 64613
　Trunk 64614

Nerve 64600-64640, 64680-64681
   Laryngeal, Recurrent 31595
Polyp
   Aural 69540
   Nose 30110-30115
   Urethra 53260
Prostate 55873
Prostate Tissue
   Transurethral
      Thermotherapy 53850-53853
Sinus
   Frontal 31080-31085
Skene's Gland 53270
Skin Lesion
   Benign 17000-17004
      15 or More Lesions 17004
      2-14 Lesions 17003
   Malignant 17260-17286
      by Photodynamic Therapy 96567
   Premalignant 17000-17004
      by Photodynamic Therapy 96567
      15 or More Lesions 17004
      2-14 Lesions 17003
Tonsil
   Lingual 42870
Tumor
   Abdomen 49200-49201
   Bile Duct 43272
   Breast 0061T
   Chemosurgery 17304-17310
   Colon 45383
   Intestines
      Large 44393
      Small 44369
   Pancreatic Duct 43272
   Rectum 45190, 46937-46938
   Retroperitoneal 49200-49201
   Urethra 53220
Tumor or Polyp
   Rectum 45320
Turbinate Mucosa 30801-30802
Ureter 52354
   Endoscopic 50957, 50976
Urethra 52214-52224, 52354
   Prolapse 53275
Warts
   Flat 17110-17111
   with Cystourethroscopy 52354

Determination, Blood Pressure
See Blood Pressure

Developmental Testing . . .96110-96111

Device
Adjustable Gastric Band 43770-43774
Iliac Artery Occlusion Device
   Insertion 34808
Subcutaneous Port
   for Gastric Restrictive
      Procedure 43770, 43774, 43886-43888
Venous Access
   Collection of Blood Specimen 36540
   Fluoroscopic Guidance 36598, 75998
   Insertion
      Central 36560-36566
      Peripheral 36570-36571
      Irrigation .96523

Obstruction Clearance 36595-36596
   Imaging 75901-75902
   Removal 36590
   Repair 36576
   Replacement 36582-36583, 36585
      Catheter .36578
Ventricular Assist
   Extracorporeal Removal 0050T

Device Handling 99002

Device, Intrauterine
See Intrauterine Device (IUD)

Device, Orthotic
See Orthotics

Dexamethasone
Suppression Test 80420

DHA Sulfate
See Dehydroepiandrosterone Sulfate

DHEA
See Dehydroepiandrosterone

DHEA Sulfate
See Dehydroepiandrosterone Sulfate

DHT
See Dihydrotestosterone

Diagnosis, Psychiatric
See Psychiatric Diagnosis

Diagnostic Amniocentesis
See Amniocentesis

Diagnostic Aspiration of Anterior Chamber of Eye
See Eye, Paracentesis, Anterior Chamber, with Diagnostic Aspiration of Aqueous

Diagnostic Radiologic Examination
See Radiology, Diagnostic

Diagnostic Skin and Sensitization Tests
See Allergy Tests

Diagnostic Ultrasound
See Echography

Diagnostic Ultrasound of Heart
See Echocardiography

Dialyses, Peritoneal
See Dialysis, Peritoneal

Dialysis
Arteriovenous Fistula
   Revision
      without Thrombectomy 36832
Arteriovenous Shunt 36145
   Revision
      with Thrombectomy 36833
   Thrombectomy 36831
End Stage Renal Disease 90918-90925
Hemodialysis 90935-90937
   Blood Flow Study 90940
Hemoperfusion .90997

Patient Training
   Completed Course 90989
   Per Session 90993
Peritoneal 90945-90947
Unlisted Services and Procedures 90999

Dialysis, Extracorporeal
See Hemodialysis

Diaphragm
Repair
   for Eventration 39545
   Hernia 39502-39541
   Laceration .39501
Resection 39560-39561
Unlisted Procedures 39599
Vagina
   Fitting 57170

Diaphragm Contraception
See Contraception, Diaphragm

Diaphysectomy
Calcaneus 28120
Clavicle 23180
Femur 27360
Fibula .27360, 27641
Humerus 23184, 24140
Metacarpal 26230
Metatarsal 28122
Olecranon Process 24147
Phalanges
   Finger 26235-26236
   Toe 28124
Radius 24145, 25151
Scapula 23182
Talus 28120
Tarsal 28122
Tibia .27360, 27640
Ulna .24147, 25150

Diastase
See Amylase

Diastasis
See Separation

Diathermy 97024
See Physical Medicine/Therapy/Occupational Therapy
Destruction
   Ciliary Body .66700
Lesion
   Retina 67208, 67227
Retinal Detachment
   Prophylaxis 67141
   Repair 67101

Diathermy, Surgical
See Electrocautery

Dibucaine Number 82638

Dichloride, Methylene
See Dichloromethane

Dichlorides, Ethylene
See Dichloroethane

Dichloroethane 84600

Dichloromethane 84600

Diethylamide, Lysergic Acid
See Lysergic Acid Diethylamide

Diethylether 84600

Differential Count
See White Blood Cell Count

Differentiation Reversal Factor
See Prothrombin

Diffusion Test, Gel
See Immunodiffusion

Digestive Tract
See Gastrointestinal Tract

Digit
See Finger; Toe
Replantation 20816-20822

Digital Artery
Sympathectomy 64820

Digital Slit-Beam Radiograph
See Scanogram

Digits
Pinch Graft 15050

Digoxin
Assay 80162

Dihydrocodeinone 82646

Dihydrocodeinone Screen 82486

Dihydroepitestosterone
See Dihydrotestosterone

Dihydrohydroxycodeinone
See Oxycodinone

Dihydromorphinone 82486, 82649

Dihydrotestosterone 82651

Dihydroxyethanes
See Ethylene Glycol

Dihydroxyvitamin D 82652

Dilatation, Transluminal Arterial
See Angioplasty, Transluminal

Dilation
See Dilation and Curettage
Anal
  Endoscopy 46604
  Sphincter 45905
Bile Duct
  Endoscopy 43271, 47555-47556
  Stricture 74363
Bladder
  Cystourethroscopy 52260-52265
Bronchi
  Endoscopy 31630, 31636-31638
Cerebral Vessels
  Intracranial Vasospasm 61640-61642
Cervix
  Canal 57800
  Stump 57820

Colon
  Endoscopy 45386
Colon-Sigmoid
  Endoscopy 45340
Esophagus 43450-43458
  Balloon 43220, 43249
  Endoscopy 43220-43226, 43249
  Surgical 43510
Intestines, Small
  Endoscopy 44370
Kidney 50395
  Intra-Renal Stricture 52343, 52346
Lacrimal Punctum 68801
Larynx
  Endoscopy 31528-31529
Pancreatic Duct
  Endoscopy 43271
Rectum
  Endoscopy 45303
  Sphincter 45910
Salivary Duct 42650-42660
Trachea
  Endoscopy 31630-31631, 31636-31638
Ureter 50395, 52341-52342, 52344-52345
  Endoscopy ...50553, 50572, 50953, 50972
Urethra 52260-52265
  General 53665
  Suppository and/or Instillation .53660-53661
Urethral
  Stenosis 52281
  Stricture 52281, 53600-53621
Vagina 57400

Dilation and Curettage 59840
See Curettage; Dilation
Cervix 57800-57820
Corpus Uteri 58120
Hysteroscopy 58558
Postpartum 59160
with Amniotic Injections 59851
with Vaginal Suppositories 59856

Dilation and Evacuation 59841
with Amniotic Injections 59851

Dimethadione 82654

Dioxide, Carbon
See Carbon Dioxide

Dioxide, Silicon
See Silica

Dipeptidyl Peptidase A
See Angiotensin Converting Enzyme (ACE)

Diphenylhydantoin
See Phenytoin

Diphosphate, Adenosine
See Adenosine Diphosphate

Diphtheria
See Vaccines
Antibody 86648

Dipropylacetic Acid
Assay 80164

Direct Pedicle Flap
Formation 15570-15576

Disability Evaluation Services
Basic Life and/or Disability Evaluation 99450
Work-Related or Medical
Disability Evaluation 99455-99456

Disarticulation
Ankle 27889
Hip 27295
Knee 27598
Wrist 25920, 25924
  Revision 25922

Disarticulation of Shoulder
See Shoulder, Disarticulation

Disc, Intervertebral
See Intervertebral Disk

Discectomies
See Diskectomy

Discectomies, Percutaneous
See Diskectomy, Percutaneous

Discharge Services
See Hospital Services
Hospital 99238-99239
Nursing Facility 99315-99316
Observation Care 99234-99236

Discharge, Body Substance
See Drainage

Discission
Cataract
  Laser Surgery 66821
  Stab Incision 66820
Vitreous Strands 67030

Discography
See Diskography

Discolysis
See Chemonucleolysis

Disease
Durand-Nicolas-Favre
  See Lymphogranuloma Venereum
Erb-Goldflam
  See Myasthenia Gravis
Heine-Medin
  See Polio
Hydatid
  See Echinococcosis
Lyme
  See Lyme Disease
Ormond
  See Retroperitoneal Fibrosis
Peyronie
  See Peyronie Disease
Posada-Wernicke
  See Coccidioidomycosis

Disease/Organ Panel
See Organ/Disease Panel

Disk Chemolyses, Intervertebral
See Chemonucleolysis

Diskectomy 63075-63078
Additional Segment 22226
Arthrodesis
    Additional Interspace 22534, 22585
    Cervical 22554
    Lumbar 22533, 22558, 22630
    Thoracic 22532, 22556
Cervical 22220
Lumbar 22224, 22630
Percutaneous 62287
Thoracic 22222

Diskography
Cervical Disk 72285
Injection 62290-62291
Lumbar Disk 72295
Thoracic 72285

Dislocated Elbow
See Dislocation, Elbow

Dislocated Hip
See Dislocation, Hip Joint

Dislocated Jaw
See Dislocation, Temporomandibular Joint

Dislocated Joint
See Dislocation

Dislocated Shoulder
See Dislocation, Shoulder

Dislocation
Acromioclavicular Joint
    Open Treatment 23550-23552
Ankle
    Closed Treatment 27840-27842
    Open Treatment 27846-27848
Carpal
    Closed Treatment 25690
    Open Treatment 25695
Carpometacarpal Joint 26670
    Closed Treatment
      with Manipulation 26675-26676
    Open Treatment 26685-26686
    Percutaneous Fixation 26676
Clavicle
    Closed Treatment 23540-23545
    Open Treatment 23550-23552
    with Manipulation 23545
    without Manipulation 23540
Closed Treatment
    Carpometacarpal Joint 26670-26675
    Metacarpophalangeal 26700-26706
    Thumb 26641
Elbow
    Closed Treatment 24600-24605, 24640
    Open Treatment 24615
Hip Joint
    Closed Treatment 27250-27252, 27265-27266
    Congenital 27256-27259
    Open Treatment .27253-27254, 27258-27259
    without Trauma 27265-27266
Interphalangeal Joint
    Closed Treatment 26770-26775
    Open Treatment 26785
    Percutaneous Fixation 26776

Toe
    Closed Treatment 28660-28665
    Open Treatment 28675
    Percutaneous Fixation 26770-26776, 28666
    with Manipulation 26770
Knee 27560-27562
    Closed Treatment 27550-27552,
                 27560-27562
    Open Treatment 27556-27558,
                 27566, 27730
    Recurrent 27420-27424
Lunate
    Closed Treatment 25690
    Open Treatment 25695
    with Manipulation 25690, 26670-26676,
                 26700-26706
Metacarpophalangeal Joint
    Closed Treatment 26700-26706
    Open Treatment 26715
Metatarsophalangeal Joint
    Closed Treatment 28630-28635
    Open Treatment 28645
    Percutaneous Fixation 28636
Open Treatment 26685-26686
Patella
    Closed Treatment 27560-27562
    Open Treatment 27566
    Recurrent 27420-27424
Pelvic Ring
    Closed Treatment 27193-27194
    Open Treatment 27217-27218
    Percutaneous Fixation 27216
    without Manipulation 27193-27194
Percutaneous Fixation
    Metacarpophalangeal 26705
Peroneal Tendons 27675-27676
Radio-Ulnar Joint 25520-25526
Radius
    Closed Treatment 24640
    with Fracture
      Closed Treatment 24620
      Open Treatment 24635
Shoulder
    Closed Treatment with
    Manipulation 23650-23655
    Open Treatment 23660
    with Greater Tuberosity Fracture
      Closed Treatment 23665
      Open Treatment 23670
    with Surgical or Anatomical Neck
    Fracture
      Closed Treatment 23675
      Open Treatment 23680
Skin
    Debridement 11010-11012
Sternoclavicular Joint
    Closed Treatment
      with Manipulation 23525
      without Manipulation 23520
    Open Treatment 23530-23532
Talotarsal Joint
    Closed Treatment 28570-28575
    Open Treatment 28546
    Percutaneous Fixation 28576
Tarsal
    Closed Treatment 28540-28545
    Open Treatment 28555
    Percutaneous Fixation 28546

Tarsometatarsal Joint
    Closed Treatment 28600-28605
    Open Treatment 28615
    Percutaneous Fixation 28606
Temporomandibular Joint
    Closed Treatment 21480-21485
    Open Treatment 21490
Thumb
    Closed Treatment 26641-26645
    Open Treatment 26665
    Percutaneous Fixation 26650
    with Fracture 26645
      Open Treatment 26665
      Percutaneous Fixation 26650-26665
    with Manipulation 26641-26650
Tibiofibular Joint
    Closed Treatment 27830-27831
    Open Treatment 27832
Vertebra
    Additional Segment
      Open Treatment 22328
    Cervical
      Open Treatment 22326
      Closed Treatment 22305
      with Manipulation, Casting
      and/or Bracing 22315
      without Manipulation 22310
    Lumbar
      Open Treatment 22325
    Thoracic
      Open Treatment 22327
Wrist
    Closed Treatment 25660, 25675, 25680
    Intercarpal 25660
      Open Treatment 25670
    Open Treatment 25670, 25685
    Percutaneous Fixation 25671
    Radiocarpal 25660
      Open Treatment 25670
    Radioulnar
      Closed Treatment 25675
      Open Treatment 25676
      Percutaneous Fixation 25671
    with Fracture
      Closed Treatment 25680
      Open Treatment 25685
    with Manipulation 25660, 25675, 25680

Dislocation, Radiocarpal Joint
See Radiocarpal Joint, Dislocation

Disorder
Blood Coagulation
    See Coagulopathy
Penis
    See Penis
Retinal
    See Retina

Displacement Therapy
Nose 30210

Dissection
Hygroma, Cystic
    Axillary/Cervical 38550-38555
Lymph Nodes 38542

Dissection, Neck, Radical
See Radical Neck Dissection

Distention
See Dilation

Diverticula, Meckel's
See Diverticulum, Meckel's

Diverticulectomy .... .44800
Esophagus 43130-43135

Diverticulectomy, Meckel's
See Meckel's Diverticulum, Excision

Diverticulum
Bladder
    See Bladder, Diverticulum
Meckel's
    Excision .... .44800
Repair
    Urethra 53400-53405

Division
Muscle
    Foot .... .28250
Plantar Fascia
    Foot .... .28250

Division, Isthmus, Horseshoe Kidney
See Symphysiotomy, Horseshoe Kidney

Division, Scalenus Anticus Muscle
See Muscle Division, Scalenus Anticus

Dl-Amphetamine
See Amphetamine

DMO
See Dimethadione

DNA
Antibody 86225-86226

DNA Endonuclease
See DNAse

DNA Probe
See Cytogenetics Studies; Nucleic Acid Probe

DNAse
Antibody .... .86215

Domiciliary Services
See Nursing Facility Services
Assisted Living 99339-99340
Discharge Services 99315-99316
Established Patient 99334-99337
New Patient 99324-99328

Donor Procedures
Conjunctival Graft .... .68371
Heart Excision .... .33940
Heart/Lung Excision .... .33930
Liver Segment 47140-47142
Stem Cells
    Donor Search .... .38204

Dopamine
See Catecholamines
Blood 82383-82384
Urine .... .82382, 82384

Doppler Echocardiography 76827-
         76828, 93307-93308, 93320-93350
Extracranial .... .93875
Intracardiac .... .93662
Transesophageal .... .93318
Transthoracic 93303-93317

Doppler Scan
Arterial Studies
    Extremities 93922-93924
    Fetal
        Middle Cerebral Artery .... .76821
        Umbilical Artery .... .76820
Extremities .... .93965
Intracranial Arteries 93886-93893

Dorsal Vertebra
See Vertebra, Thoracic

Dose Plan
See Dosimetry

Dosimetry
Radiation Therapy .... .77300, 77331
    Brachytherapy 77326-77328
    Intensity Modulation .... .77301
    Teletherapy 77305-77321

Double-Stranded DNA
See Deoxyribonucleic Acid

Doxepin
Assay .... .80166

DPH
See Phenytoin

Drainage
See Excision; Incision; Incision and Drainage
Abdomen
    Abdomen Fluid 49080-49081
Abscess
    Appendix 44900-44901
        Percutaneous .... .44901
    Brain 61150-61151
    Eyelid .... .67700
    Liver 47010-47011
    Ovary
        Percutaneous .... .58823
    Pelvic
        Percutaneous .... .58823
    Pericolic
        Percutaneous .... .58823
    Perirenal or Renal 50020-50021
        Percutaneous .... .50021
    Prostate .... .52700
    Retroperitoneal 49060-49061
        Percutaneous .... .49061
    Subdiaphragmatic or
    Subphrenic 49040-49041
        Percutaneous 49040-49041
    with X-Ray .... .75989
Amniotic Fluid
    Diagnostic Aspiration .... .59000
    Therapeutic Aspiration .... .59001
Bile Duct
    Transhepatic .... .75980
Brain Fluid .... .61070
Bursa 20600-20610

Cerebrospinal Fluid 61000-61020, 61050,
                61070, 62272
Cervical Fluid .... .61050
Cisternal Fluid .... .61050
Cyst
    Bone .... .20615
    Brain 61150-61151, 62161-62162
    Breast 19000-19001
    Ganglion .... .20612
    Liver 47010-47011
        Percutaneous .... .47011
    Salivary Gland .... .42409
    Sublingual Gland .... .42409
Extraperitoneal Lymphocele
    Laparoscopic .... .49323
    Open .... .49062
Eye
    Anterior Chamber Paracentesis
      with Diagnostic Aspiration of
      Aqueous .... .65800
      with Therapeutic Release of
      Aqueous .... .65805
    Removal Blood .... .65815
    Removal of Vitreous and/or Discission
      Anterior Hyaloid Membrane .... .65810
Fetal Fluid .... .59074
Ganglion Cyst .... .20612
Hematoma
    Brain 61154-61156
    Vagina 57022-57023
Hematoma, Subungual .... .11740
Joint 20600-20610
Liver
    Abscess or Cyst 47010-47011
        Percutaneous .... .47011
Lymphocele
    Endoscopic .... .49323
Onychia 10060-10061
Orbit .... .67405, 67440
Pancreas
    See Anastomosis, Pancreas to Intestines
    Pseudocyst 48510-48511
        Percutaneous .... .48511
Paronychia 10060-10061
Pericardial Sac .... .32659
Pericardium
    See Aspiration, Pericardium
Pseudocyst
    Gastrointestinal, Upper
      Transmural Endoscopic .... .43240
    Pancreas .... .48510
      Open .... .48510
      Percutaneous .... .48511
Puncture
    Chest 32000-32002
Skin .... .10040, 10060-10061, 10080-10081,
                10120-10180
Spinal Cord
    Cerebrospinal Fluid .... .62272
Subdural Fluid 61000-61001
Urethra
    Extravasation 53080-53085
Ventricular Fluid .... .61020

Drainage Implant, Glaucoma
See Aqueous Shunt

Dressings
Burns 16020-16030
Change
   Anesthesia 15852

DREZ Procedure
See Incision, Spinal Cord; Incision and Drainage

DRIL
See Revascularization, Distal

Drill Hole
Skull
   Catheter 61107
   Drain Hematoma 61108
   Exploration 61105
   Implant Electrode 61850, 61863-61868

Drinking Test for Glaucoma
See Glaucoma, Provocative Test

Drug
See Drug Assay; Specific Drug
Analysis
   Tissue Preparation 80103
Confirmation 80102
Infusion 62360-62362

Drug Assay
Amikacin 80150
Amitriptyline 80152
Benzodiazepine 80154
Carbamazepine 80156-80157
Cyclosporine 80158
Desipramine 80160
Digoxin 80162
Dipropylacetic Acid 80164
Doxepin 80166
Ethosuximide 80168
Gentamicin 80170
Gold 80172
Haloperidol 80173
Imipramine 80174
Lidocaine 80176
Lithium 80178
Nortriptyline 80182
Phenobarbital 80184
Phenytoin 80185-80186
Primidone 80188
Procainamide 80190-80192
Quantitative
   Other 80299
Quinidine 80194
Salicylate 80196
Sirolimus 80195
Tacrolimus 80197
Theophylline 80198
Tobramycin 80200
Topiramate 80201
Vancomycin 80202

Drug Delivery Implant
Insertion 11981
Irrigation 96523
Maintenance and Refill
   Brain 95990
   Epidural 95990-95991
   Intra-arterial 96522

Intrathecal 95990-95991
Intravenous 96522
Intraventricular 95990-95991
Removal 11982-11983
   with Reinsertion 11983

Drug Instillation
See Instillation, Drugs

Drug Management
by Pharmacist 0115T, 0116T, 0117T
Psychiatric 90862
Validation 0130T

Drug Screen 80100-80101, 82486

Drugs, Anticoagulant
See Clotting Inhibitors

DST
See Dexamethasone, Suppression Test

DT Shots 90702

DTaP Immunization 90721

DTaP-HepB-IPV Immunization
........................90723

DTP Immunization 90701, 90720

Dual Photon Absorptiometry
See Absorptiometry, Dual Photon

Dual X-Ray Absorptiometry (DXA)
Appendicular 76076
Axial Skeleton 76075
Body Composition 0028T
Vertebral Fracture 76077

Duct, Bile
See Bile Duct

Duct, Hepatic
See Hepatic Duct

Duct, Mammary
Lavage 0046T, 0047T

Duct, Nasolacrimal
See Nasolacrimal Duct

Duct, Omphalomesenteric
See Omphalomesenteric Duct

Duct, Pancreatic
See Pancreatic Duct

Duct, Salivary
See Salivary Duct

Duct, Stensen's
See Parotid Duct

Duct, Thoracic
See Thoracic Duct

Ductogram, Mammary
See Galactogram

Ductus Arteriosus
Repair 33820-33824

Ductus Deferens
See Vas Deferens

Duhamel Procedure
See Proctectomy, Total

Dunn Operation
See Arthrodesis, Foot Joint

Duodenotomy 44010

Duodenum
Biopsy 44010
Exclusion 48547
Exploration 44010
Incision 44010
Motility Study 91022
Removal
   Foreign Body 44010
X-Ray 74260

Duplex Scan
See Vascular Studies
Arterial Studies
   Aorta 93978-93979
   Extracranial 93880-93882
   Lower Extremity 93925-93926
   Penile 93980-93981
   Upper Extremity 93930-93931
   Visceral 93975-93979
Hemodialysis Access 93990
Venous Studies
   Extremity 93970-93971
   Penile 93980-93981

Dupuy-Dutemp Operation
See Reconstruction, Eyelid; Revision

**Dupuytren's
Contracture** 26040-26045

Durand-Nicolas-Favre Disease
See Lymphogranuloma Venereum

Dust, Angel
See Phencyclidine

Duvries Operation
See Tenoplasty

Dwyer Procedure
See Osteotomy, Calcaneus

DXA
See Dual X-Ray Absorptiometry (DXA)

Dynamometry
See Osteotomy, Calcaneus
Venous Studies
   See Osteotomy, Calcaneus
   with Ophthalmoscopy 92260

E

E Antigens
See Hepatitis Antigen, Be

E B Virus
See Epstein-Barr Virus

E Vitamin
See Tocopherol

E1
See Estrone

E2
See Estradiol

E3
See Estriol

Ear
Collection of Blood 36415-36416
Drum 69420-69421, 69433-69436,
69450, 69610-69620

   See Tympanic Membrane
External
   Abscess Incision and Drainage
      Complicated 69005
      Simple 69000
   Biopsy 69100
   Excision
      Partial 69110
      Total 69120
   Hematoma
      Incision and Drainage 69000-69005
   Reconstruction 69300
   Unlisted Services and Procedures 69399
Inner
   CT Scan 70480-70482
   Excision
      Labyrinth 69905-69910
   Exploration
      Endolymphatic Sac 69805-69806
   Incision 69820
      Labyrinth 69801-69802
      Semicircular Canal 69840
   Insertion
      Cochlear Device 69930
   Semicircular Canal 69820
   Unlisted Services and Procedures 69949
Middle
   Catheterization 69405
   CT Scan 70480-70482
   Exploration 69440
   Inflation
      with Catheterization 69400
      without Catheterization 69401
   Insertion
      Catheter 69405
   Lesion
      Excision 69540
   Reconstruction
      Tympanoplasty with Antrotomy
      or Mastoidotomy 69635-69637
      Tympanoplasty with
      Mastoidectomy 69641-69646
      Tympanoplasty without
      Mastoidectomy 69631-69633
   Removal
      Ventilating Tube 69424
   Repair
      Oval Window 69666
      Round Window 69667
   Revision
      Stapes 69662

Tumor
   Excision 69550-69554
   Unlisted Services and Procedures 69799
Outer
   CT Scan 70480-70482

Ear Canal
See Auditory Canal

Ear Cartilage
Graft
   to Face 21235

Ear Lobes
Pierce 69090

Ear Protector Attenuation 92596
See Hearing Aid Services

Ear Wax
See Cerumen

Ear, Nose, and Throat
See Hearing Aid Services; Otorhinolaryngology,
Diagnostic
Audiologic Function Tests
   Acoustic Reflex 92568
   Acoustic Reflex Decay 92569
   Audiometry
      Bekesy 92560-92561
      Comprehensive 92557
      Conditioning Play 92582
      Evoked Response 92585-92586
      Groups 92559
      Pure Tone 92552-92553
      Select Picture 92583
      Speech 92555-92556
   Brainstem Evoked Response . . .92585-92586
   Central Auditory Function 92620-92621
   Ear Protector Evaluation 92596
   Electrocochleography 92584
   Filtered Speech 92571
   Hearing Aid Evaluation 92590-92595
   Lombard Test 92573
   Loudness Balance 92562
   Screening Test 92551
   Sensorineural Acuity 92575
   Short Increment Sensitivity
   Index (SISI) 92564
   Staggered Spondaic Word Test 92572
   Stenger Test 92565, 92577
   Synthetic Sentence Test 92576
   Tone Decay 92563
   Tympanometry 92567
Audiometry
   Evoked Otoacoustic Emissions . .92587-92588
   Visual Reinforcement 92579
Binocular Microscopy 92504
Facial Nerve Function Study 92516
Hearing, Language and Speech Evaluation .92506
Laryngeal Function Study 92520
Nasal Function Study 92512
Nasopharyngoscopy 92511
Vestibular Function Tests
   Additional Electrodes 92547
   Caloric Tests 92533, 92543
   Nystagmus
      Optokinetic 92534, 92544
      Positional 92532, 92542
      Spontaneous 92531, 92541

Posturography .92548
Torsion Swing Test 92546
Tracking Tests .92545

Ebstein Anomaly Repair 33468

Eccrine Glands
Chemodenervation
   Axillae 64650
   Feet 64999
   Hands 64999
   Other Area .64653

ECG
See Electrocardiography

Echinococcosis 86171, 86280

Echocardiography
Cardiac 93320-93350
   Intracardiac 93662
   Transesophageal 93318
   Transthoracic 93303-93317
Doppler 93303-93317, 93320-93321, 93662
Fetal Heart 76825-76826
   Doppler
      Complete .76827
      Follow-up or Repeat Study 76828
   for Congenital Anomalies
      Transesophageal 93315-93317
      Transthoracic 93303-93304
Intracardiac 93662
Transesophageal 93318
   for Congenital Anomalies 93315-93317
Transthoracic 93303-93318, 93350
   for Congenital Anomalies 93303-93304

Echoencephalography 76506

Echography
Abdomen 76700-76705
Arm 76880
Breast 76645
Cardiac 93303-93317, 93320-93321,
93350, 93662
   Guidance 76932
Chest 76604
Extracranial Arteries 93880-93882
Eyes .76510-76529
Follow-up 76970
Head 76536
Heart
   Imaging Guidance 76932
Hip
   Infant 76885-76886
Intracranial Arteries 93886-93893
Intraoperative 76986
Kidney
   Transplant .76778
Leg 76880
Neck 76536
Pelvis 76856-76857
Placement Therapy Fields 76950
Pregnant Uterus 76801-76828
Prostate 76872-76873
Retroperitoneal 76770-76775
Scrotum 76870
Spine 76800
Transvaginal 76817, 76830

Unlisted Ultrasound Procedures 76999
Vagina 76817, 76830

Echotomography
See Echography

ECMO
See Extracorporeal Membrane Oxygenation

ECS
See Emission Computerized Tomography

ECSF (Erythrocyte Colony Stimulating Factor)
See Erythropoietin

ECT
See Emission Computerized Tomography

Ectasia
See Dilation

Ectopic Pregnancy
See Obstetrical Care
Abdominal 59130
Cervix 59140
Interstitial
    Partial Resection Uterus 59136
    Total Hysterectomy 59135
Laparoscopy 59150
    with Salpingectomy and/or
    Oophorectomy 59151
Tubal 59121
    with Salpingectomy and/or
    Oophorectomy 59120

Ectropion
Repair
    Excision Tarsal Wedge 67916
    Extensive 67917
    Suture 67914
    Thermocauterization 67915

Education Services
Group 98961-98962, 99078
Individual

Education Supplies 99071

EEG
See Electroencephalography (EEG)

Egg
See Ova

Ehrlichia
Antibody 86666

EKG
See Electrocardiography

Elastase .82656

Elbow
See Humerus; Radius; Ulna
Abscess
    Incision and Drainage 23930, 23935
Anesthesia 00400, 01710-01782
Arthrectomy 24155
Arthrocentesis 20605
Arthrodesis 24800-24802

Arthroplasty 24360
    Total Replacement 24363
    with Implant 24361-24362
Arthroscopy
    Diagnostic .29830
    Surgical 29834-29838
Arthrotomy 24000
    Capsular Release 24006
    with Joint Exploration 24101
    with Synovectomy 24102
    with Synovial Biopsy 24101
Biopsy 24065-24066, 24101
Bursa
    Incision and Drainage 23931
Dislocation
    Closed Treatment 24600-24605, 24640
    Open Treatment 24615
    Subluxate .24640
Excision 24155
    Bursa 24105
    Synovium .24102
Exploration 24000, 24101
Fracture
    Monteggia 24620-24635
    Open Treatment 24586-24587
Hematoma
    Incision and Drainage 23930
Implant
    Removal 24164
Incision and Drainage 24000
Injection
    Arthrography
        Radiologic 24220
Magnetic Resonance Imaging (MRI) 73221
Manipulation .24300
Radical Resection
    Capsule, Soft Tissue and Bone
        with Contracture Release 24149
Removal
    Foreign Body 24000, 24101, 24200-24201
    Implant 24160
    Loose Body 24101
Repair
    Epicondylitis 24350
    Fasciotomy 24350-24356
    Flexorplasty 24330
    Hemiepiphyseal Arrest 24470
    Ligament 24343-24346
    Muscle 24341
    Muscle Transfer 24301
    Tendon 24340-24342
        Lengthening 24305
        Transfer 24301
    Tennis Elbow 24350-24356
Steindler Advancement 24330
Strapping 29260
Tumor
    Excision 24075-24077
Unlisted Procedures, Humerus and Elbow . .24999
X-Ray .73070-73080
    with Contrast 73085

Elbow, Golfer
See Tennis Elbow

Elbows, Tennis
See Tennis Elbow

Electric Countershock
See Cardioversion

Electric Stimulation
See Electrical Stimulation

Electric Stimulation, Transcutaneous
See Application, Neurostimulation

Electrical Stimulation
Bone Healing
    Invasive 20975
    Noninvasive 20974
Brain Surface 95961-95962
Guidance
    for Chemodenervation 95873
Physical Therapy
    Attended, Manual 97032
    Unattended 97014

Electro-Hydraulic Procedure 52325

Electro-Oculography 92270

Electroanalgesia
See Application, Neurostimulation

Electrocardiography
24 Hour Monitoring 93224-93237
Evaluation 93000, 93010, 93014
Patient-Demand Recording
    Transmission and Evaluation 93270
Patient-Demand Transmission and Evaluation
    Transmission and Evaluation
        Interpretation 93272
        Monitoring 93271
Rhythm
    Evaluation .93042
    Microvolt T-wave Alternans 93025
    Tracing 93041
    Tracing and Evaluation 93040
Signal Averaged 93278
Transmission .93012

Electrocautery 17000-17286
See Destruction

Electrochemistry
See Electrolysis

Electroconvulsive Therapy 90870

Electrocorticogram
Intraoperative .95829

Electrode, Depth
See Depth Electrode
Electrode Array Intracranial 61850-61868,
                                        61885, 61886
Peripheral Nerve 64553-64565, 64573-64581
Retinal 0100T
Spinal .63650-63655

Electrodesiccation 17000-17286
Lesion
    Penis 54055

Electroejaculation 55870

Electroencephalography (EEG) 95816
Brain Death 95824
Coma 95822
Digital Analysis 95957
Electrode Placement 95830
Intraoperative 95955
Monitoring ...95812-95813, 95950-95953, 95956
   with Drug Activation 95954
   with Physical Activation 95954
   with WADA Activation 95958
Sleep 95822, 95827
Standard 95819

Electrogastrography 91132-91133

Electrogram, Atrial
Esophageal Recording 93615-93616

Electrolysis 17380

Electromyographs
See Electromyography, Needle

Electromyography
Anorectal with Biofeedback 90911
Fine Wire
   Dynamic 96004
Needle
   Extremities 95861-95864
   Extremity 95860
   Face and Neck Muscles ...95867-95868
   Guidance
     for Chemodenervation 95874
   Hemidiaphragm 95866
   Larynx 95865
   Ocular 92265
   Other than Thoracic Paraspinal 95870
   Single Fiber Electrode 95872
   Thoracic Paraspinal Muscles 95869
Sphincter Muscles
   Anus 51784-51785
     Needle 51785
   Urethra 51784-51785
     Needle 51785
Surface
   Dynamic 96002-96004

Electron Microscopy 88348-88349

Electronic Analysis
Drug Infusion Pump 62367-62368
Implantable Loop Recorder System 93727
Neurostimulator Pulse Generator ...95970-95979
Pacing Cardioverter-Defibrillator ...93741-93744

Electrophoresis
Counterimmuno- 86185
Immuno- 86320-86327
Immunofixation 86334-86335
Protein 84165-84166
Unlisted Services and Procedures 82664

Electrophysiology Procedure 93600-93660

Electroretinogram
See Electroretinography

Electroretinography 92275

Electrostimulation, Analgesic Cutaneous
See Application, Neurostimulation

Electrosurgery
Trichiasis
   Correction 67825

Electroversion, Cardiac
See Cardioversion

Elevation, Scapula, Congenital
See Sprengel's Deformity

Elliot Operation
See Excision, Lesion, Sclera

Eloesser Procedure
See Thoracostomy, Empyema

Eloesser Thoracoplasty
See Thoracoplasty

Embolectomy
Aortoiliac Artery 34151-34201
Axillary Artery 34101
Brachial Artery 34101
Carotid Artery 34001
Celiac Artery 34151
Femoral 34201
Iliac 34151-34201
Innominate Artery 34001-34101
Mesentery Artery 34151
Peroneal Artery 34203
Popliteal Artery 34203
Pulmonary Artery 33910-33916
Radial Artery 34111
Renal Artery 34151
Subclavian Artery 34001-34101
Tibial Artery 34203
Ulnar Artery 34111

Embryo
Biopsy 89290-89291
Cryopreservation 89258
Cryopreserved
   Preparation
     Thawing 89352
Culture 89250
   with Co-Culture Oocyte 89251
Hatching
   Assisted
     Microtechnique 89253
Preparation
   for Transfer 89255
Storage 89342

Embryo Implantation
See Implantation

Embryo Transfer
In Vitro Fertilization 58974-58976
   Intrafallopian Transfer 58976
   Intrauterine Transfer 58974

Embryo/Fetus Monitoring
See Monitoring, Fetal

Embryonated Eggs
Inoculation 87250

Emergency Department Services 99281-99288
See Critical Care; Emergency Department Services
Anesthesia 99140
Physician Direction of Advanced Life Support 99288

Emesis Induction 99175

EMG
See Electromyography, Needle

EMI Scan
See CT Scan

Emission Computerized Tomography 78607

Emission-Computed Tomography, Single-Photon
See SPECT

Emmet Operation
See Vagina, Repair, Obstetric

Empyema
Closure
   Chest Wall 32810
Thoracostomy 32020-32036

Empyema, Lung
See Abscess, Thorax

Empyemectomy 32540

Encephalitis
Antibody 86651-86654

Encephalitis Virus Vaccine 90735

Encephalocele
Repair 62120
   Craniotomy 62121

Encephalon
See Brain

End-Stage Renal Disease Services 90918-90925

End-Expiratory Pressure, Positive
See Pressure Breathing, Positive

Endarterectomy
Coronary Artery 33572
Pulmonary 33916

Endemic Flea-Borne Typhus
See Murine Typhus

Endobronchial Challenge Tests
See Bronchial Challenge Test

Endocavitary Fulguration
See Electrocautery

Endocrine System
Unlisted Services and Procedures ..60699, 78099

Endocrine, Pancreas
See Islet Cell

Endolymphatic Sac
Exploration
    with Shunt 69806
    without Shunt 69805

Endometrial Ablation 58353
Curettage 58356
Exploration
    via Hysteroscopy 58563

Endometrioma
Abdomen
    Destruction/Excision 49200-49201
Retroperitoneal
    Destruction/Excision 49200-49201

Endometriosis, Adhesive
See Adhesions, Intrauterine

Endometrium
Ablation 58356
Biopsy 58100-58110, 58558

Endonuclease, DNA
See DNAse

Endoscopic Retrograde Cannulation of Pancreatic Duct (ERCP)
See Cholangiopancreatography

Endoscopies, Pleural
See Thoracoscopy

Endoscopy
See Arthroscopy; Thoracoscopy
Adrenal Gland
    Biopsy 60650
    Excision 60650
Anus
    Biopsy 46606
    Dilation 46604
    Exploration 46600
    Hemorrhage 46614
    Removal
      Foreign Body 46608
      Polyp 46610, 46612
      Tumor 46610, 46612
Bile Duct
    Biopsy 47553
    Destruction
      Calculi (Stone) 43265
      Tumor 43272
    Dilation 43271, 47555-47556
    Exploration 47552
    Intraoperative 47550
    Percutaneous 47552-47555
    Removal
      Calculi (Stone) 43264, 47554
      Foreign Body 43269
      Stent 43269
    Specimen Collection 43260
    Sphincter Pressure 43263
    Sphincterotomy 43262
    Tube Placement 43267-43268
Bladder 52000
    Biopsy 52204, 52354
    Catheterization 52005, 52010
    Destruction 52354
      Lesion 52400

Evacuation
    Clot 52001
Excision
    Tumor 52355
    Exploration 52351
    Lithotripsy 52353
Removal
    Calculus 52352
    Urethral Stent 52282
Bladder Neck
    Injection of Implant Material 51715
Brain
    Shunt
      Creation 62201
Bronchi
    Aspiration 31645-31646
    Biopsy 31625-31629, 31632-31633
    Destruction
      Lesion 31641
      Tumor 31641
    Dilation 31630-31631, 31636-31638
    Exploration 31622
    Injection 31656
    Lesion
      Destruction 31641
    Needle Biopsy 31629, 31633
    Placement
      Stent 31631, 31636-31637
    Revision
      Stent 31638
    Specimen Collection 31623-31624
    Stenosis 31641
    Tumor
      Destruction 31641
    Ultrasound 31620
Cervix
    Biopsy 57454-57455, 57460
    Curettage 57454, 57456
    Exploration 57452
    Loop Electrode Biopsy 57460
    Loop Electrode Conization 57461
Chest Cavity
    Exploration 32601-32606
    Surgical 32650-32665
Colon
    Biopsy 44389, 45380, 45392
    Destruction
      Lesion 44393, 45383
      Tumor 44393, 45383
    Exploration 45378
    Hemorrhage 44391, 45382
    Injection 45381
    Placement
      Stent 45387
    Removal
      Foreign Body 44390, 45379
      Polyp 44392, 45384-45385
      Tumor 44392, 45384-45385
    Specimen Collection 45380
    Ultrasound 45391-45392
    via Colotomy 45355
    via Stoma 44388-44393, 44397
    Virtual 0066T, 0067T
Colon-Sigmoid
    Ablation
      Polyp 45339
      Tumor 45339
    Biopsy 45331

Dilation 45340
Exploration 45330, 45335
Hemorrhage 45334
Needle Biopsy 45342
Placement
    Stent 45327, 45345
Removal
    Foreign Body 45332
    Polyp 45333, 45338
    Tumor 45333, 45338
    Specimen Collection 45331
    Ultrasound 45341-45342
    Volvulus 45337
Esophagus
    Biopsy 43202
    Dilation 43220-43226
    Exploration 43200
    Hemorrhage 43227
    Injection 43201, 43204
    Insertion Stent 43219
    Needle Biopsy 43232
    Removal
      Foreign Body 43215
      Polyp 43216-43217, 43228
      Tumor 43216, 43228
    Ultrasound 43231-43232
    Vein Ligation 43205
Eye 66990
Foot
    Plantar Fasciotomy 29893
Gastrointestinal
    Upper
      Biopsy 43239
      Catheterization 43241
      Destruction of Lesion 43258
      Dilation 43245, 43248-43249
      Drainage of Pseudocyst 43240
      Exploration 43234-43235
      Foreign Body 43247
      Gastric Bypass 43644-43645
      Gastroenterostomy 43644-43645
      Hemorrhage 43255
      Inject Varices 43243
      Injection 0133T, 43236
      Needle Biopsy 43238, 43242
      Removal 43247, 43250-43251
      Roux-En-Y 43644
      Stent Placement 43256
      Suturing 0008T
      Thermal Radiation 43257
      Tube Placement 43246
      Ultrasound ...43237-43242, 43259, 76975
      Vein Ligation 43244
    Ileum
      via Stoma 44383
    Intestines, Small
      Biopsy 44361, 44377
      Destruction
        Lesion 44369
        Tumor 44369
      Diagnostic 44376
      Exploration 44360
      Hemorrhage 44366, 44378
      Insertion
        Stent 44370, 44379
        Tube 44379
      Pelvic Pouch 44385-44386

Removal
    Foreign Body 44363
    Lesion 44365
    Polyp 44364-44365
Tube Placement 44372
Tube Revision 44373
via Stoma 44380-44383
Tumor 44364-44365
Intracranial 62160-62165
Kidney
    Biopsy 50555, 50574-50576, 52354
    Catheterization 50553, 50572
    Destruction 50557, 50576, 52354
    Dilation of Ureter 50553
    Excision
        Tumor 52355
    Exploration .52351
    Lithotripsy .52353
    Removal
        Calculus 50561, 50580, 52352
        Foreign Body 50561, 50580
    via Incision 50562-50580
    via Stoma 50551-50561
Larynx
    Biopsy 31510, 31535-31536
    Direct 31515-31571
    Exploration 31505, 31520-31526, 31575
    Fiberoptic 31575-31579
    Indirect 31505-31513
    Operative 31530-31561
    Removal
        Foreign Body 31530-31531
        Lesion 31511, 31545-31546
            See Endoscopic
Lysis
    Device 0027T
Mediastinoscopy
    Biopsy 39400
    Exploration .39400
Nose
    Diagnostic 31231-31235
    Surgical 31237-31294
    Unlisted Services and Procedures 31299
Pancreatic Duct
    Destruction
        Calculi (Stone) 43265
        Tumor 43272
    Dilation 43271
    Removal
        Calculi (Stone) 43264
        Foreign Body 43269
        Stent 43269
    Specimen Collection 43260
    Sphincter Pressure 43263
    Sphincterotomy 43262
    Tube Placement 43267-43268
Pelvis
    Aspiration 49322
    Destruction of Lesion 58662
    Lysis of Adhesions 58660
    Oviduct Surgery 58670-58671
    Removal of Adnexal Structures 58661
Peritoneum
    Biopsy 47561
    Drainage
        Lymphocele 49323, 54690
        Radiologic 47560

Rectum
    Biopsy 45305
    Destruction
        Tumor 45320
    Dilation 45303
    Exploration .45300
    Hemorrhage 45317
    Removal
        Foreign Body 45307
        Polyp 45308-45315
        Tumor 45308-45315
    Volvulus 45321
Spleen
    Removal 38120
Testis
    Removal 54690
Trachea
    Dilation 31630-31631, 31636-31638
    via Tracheostomy 31615
Ureter
    Biopsy . . .50955-50957, 50974-50976, 52354
    Catheterize 50953, 50972
    Destruction 50957, 50976, 52354
    Excision
        Tumor 52355
    Exploration .52351
    Injection of Implant Material 52327
    Lithotripsy .52353
    Manipulation of Ureteral Calculus . . .52330
    Placement
        Stent 50947
    Removal
        Calculus 50961, 50980, 52352
        Foreign Body 50961, 50980
    Resection 52355
    via Incision 50970-50980
    via Stoma 50951-50961
Ureteral
    Biopsy 52007
    Catheterization 52005
Urethra 52000
    Biopsy 52204, 52354
    Catheterization 52010
    Destruction 52354
        Lesion 52400
    Evacuation
        Clot 52001
    Excision
        Tumor 52355
    Exploration .52351
    Incision
        Ejaculatory Duct 52402
    Injection of Implant Material 51715
    Lithotripsy .52353
    Removal
        Calculus .52352
    Resection
        Ejaculatory Duct 52402
        Vasectomy 52402
        Vasotomy 52402
Uterus
    Anesthesia .00952
    Hysteroscopy
        Diagnostic 58555
        with Division/Resection Intrauterine
        Septum .58560
        with Lysis of Intrauterine
        Adhesions 58559

Placement
    Fallopian Tube 58565
Removal
    Endometrial 58563
    Impacted Foreign Body 58562
    Leiomyomata 58561
    Surgical with Biopsy 58558
Vagina
    Anesthesia .00950
    Biopsy 57454
    Exploration .57452
Vascular
    Surgical 33508, 37500-37501
Virtual
    Colon 0066T, 0067T

Endosteal Implant
Reconstruction
    Mandible 21248-21249
    Maxilla 21248-21249

Endothelioma, Dural
See Meningioma

Endotracheal Intubation
See Insertion, Endotracheal Tube

Endotracheal Tube
Intubation 31500

Endovascular Repair 0078T, 0079T,
                    0080T, 0081T, 33880-33891,
          34800-34805, 34812-34826, 34833-34900
Angiography 75952-75959

Endovascular Therapy
Ablation
    Vein 36475-36479
Occlusion 61623

Enema
Home Visit for Fecal Impaction 99511
Intussusception 74283
Therapeutic
    for Intussusception 74283

Energies, Electromagnetic
See Irradiation

ENT
See Ear, Nose, and Throat; Otorhinolaryngology,
Diagnostic
Therapeutic
    See Otorhinolaryngology

Entamoeba Histolytica
Antigen Detection
    Enzyme Immunoassay 87336-87337

Enterectomy 44120-44121,
                    44126-44128, 44137, 44202
Donor 44132-44133
with Enterostomy 44125

Enterocele
Repair 57556
    Hysterectomy
        with Colpectomy 58280

Enterocystoplasty 51960
Camey 50825

Enteroenterostomy
See Anastomosis, Intestines

Enterolysis 44005
Laparoscopic 44180

Enteropancreatostomy
See Anastomosis, Pancreas to Intestines

Enterorrhaphy 44602-44603, 44615

Enterostomy 44300
Closure 44625-44626
with Enterectomy
    Intestine, Small 44125

Enterotomy 44615

Enterovirus
Antibody 86658

Entropion
Repair 67921-67924
    Excision Tarsal Wedge 67923
    Suture 67921
    Thermocauterization 67922

Enucleation
Eye
    with Implant 65103
        Muscles Attached 65105
    without Implant 65101
Pleural 32540

Enucleation, Cyst, Ovarian
See Cystectomy, Ovarian

Environmental Intervention
for Psychiatric Patients 90882

Enzyme Activity 82657
Radioactive Substrate 82658

Enzyme, Angiotensin Converting
See Angiotensin Converting Enzyme (ACE)

Enzyme, Angiotensin-Forming
See Renin

EOG
See Electro-oculography

Eosinocyte
See Eosinophils

Eosinophils
Nasal Smear 89190

Epiandrosterone 82666

Epicondylitides, Lateral Humeral
See Tennis Elbow

Epicondylitis, Radiohumeral
See Tennis Elbow

Epidemic Parotitis
See Mumps

Epididymectomy
Bilateral 54861
Unilateral 54860

Epididymis
Abscess
    Incision and Drainage 54700
Anastomosis
    to Vas Deferens
        Bilateral 54901
        Unilateral 54900
Biopsy 54800-54820
Epididymography 74440
Excision
    Bilateral 54861
    Unilateral 54860
Exploration
    Biopsy 54820
Hematoma
    Incision and Drainage 54700
Lesion
    Excision
        Local 54830
        Spermatocele 54840
Needle Biopsy 54800
Spermatocele
    Excision 54840
Unlisted Services and Procedures 55899
X-Ray with Contrast 74440

Epididymograms 55300

Epididymography 74440

Epididymoplasty
See Repair, Epididymis

Epididymovasostomy
Bilateral 54901
Unilateral 54900

Epidural
Electrode
    Insertion 61531
    Removal 61535
Injection 62281-62282, 62310-62319,
                                  64479-64484
Lysis 0027T, 62263-62264

Epidural Anesthesia
See Anesthesia, Epidural

Epidurography 72275

Epigastric
Hernia Repair 49572

Epiglottidectomy 31420

Epiglottis
Excision 31420

Epikeratoplasty 65767

Epilation
See Removal, Hair

Epinephrine
See Catecholamines
Blood 82383-82384
Urine 82384

Epiphyseal Arrest
Femur 20150, 27185, 27475, 27479-27485, 27742
Fibula 20150, 27477-27485, 27730-27742

Radius 20150, 25450-25455
Tibia ..20150, 27477-27485, 27730, 27734-27742
Ulna 20150, 25450-25455

Epiphyseal Separation
Radius
    Closed Treatment 25600
    Open Treatment 25620

Epiphysiodesis
See Epiphyseal Arrest

Epiphysis
See Bone; Specific Bone

Epiploectomy 49255

Episiotomy 59300

Epispadias
Penis
    Reconstruction 54385
Repair 54380-54390
    with Exstrophy of Bladder 54390
    with Incontinence 54380-54390

Epistaxis 30901-30906
with Nasal/Sinus Endoscopy 31238

EPO
See Erythropoietin

Epstein-Barr Virus
Antibody 86663-86665

Equina, Cauda
See Cauda Equina

ERCP
See Bile Duct; Cholangiopancreatography;
Pancreatic Duct

ERG
See Electroretinography

Ergocalciferol
See Calciferol

Ergocalciferols
See Calciferol

Ergonovine Provocation Test ...93024

Erythrocyte
See Red Blood Cell (RBC)

Erythrocyte ab
See Antibody, Red Blood Cell

Erythrocyte Count
See Red Blood Cell (RBC), Count

Erythropoietin 82668

Escharotomy
Burns 16035-16036

Escherichia coli 0157
Antigen Detection
    Enzyme Immunoassay 87335

ESD
See Endoscopy, Gastrointestinal, Upper

Esophageal Acid Infusion Test
See Acid Perfusion Test

Esophageal Polyp
See Polyp, Esophagus

Esophageal Tumor
See Tumor, Esophagus

Esophageal Varices
Ligation 43205, 43400
Transection/Repair 43401

Esophagectomy
Partial 43116-43124
Total 43107-43113, 43124

Esophagoenterostomy
with Total Gastrectomy 43620

Esophagogastroduodenoscopies
See Endoscopy, Gastrointestinal, Upper

Esophagogastromyotomy
See Esophagomyotomy

Esophagogastrostomy 43320

Esophagojejunostomy 43340-43341

Esophagomyotomy .32665, 43330-43331

Esophagorrhaphy
See Esophagus, Suture

Esophagoscopies
See Endoscopy, Esophagus

Esophagostomy 43350-43352
Closure 43420-43425

Esophagotomy 43020, 43045

Esophagotracheal Fistula
See Fistula, Tracheoesophageal

Esophagus
Acid Perfusion Test 91030
Acid Reflux Tests 91034-91038
Balloon Distension
　Provocation Study 91040
Biopsy
　Endoscopy 43202
Cineradiography 74230
Dilation 43450-43458
　Endoscopic ...43220-43226, 43248-43249
　Surgical 43510
Endoscopy
　Biopsy 43202
　Dilation 43220-43226
　Exploration 43200
　Hemorrhage 43227
　Injection 43201, 43204
　　Sphincter 0133T
　Insertion Stent 43219
　Needle Biopsy 43232
　Removal
　　Foreign Body 43215
　　Polyp 43216-43217, 43228
　　Tumor 43216, 43228
　Ultrasound 43231-43232
　Vein Ligation 43205

Excision
　Diverticula 43130-43135
　Partial 43116-43124
　Total 43107-43113, 43124
Exploration
　Endoscopy 43200
Hemorrhage 43227
Incision 43020, 43045
　Muscle 43030
Injection
　Sclerosing Agent 43204
　Submucosal 43201
Insertion
　Stent 43219
　Tamponade 43460
　Tube 43510
Intubation with Specimen Collection 91000
Lesion
　Excision 43100-43101
Ligation 43405
Motility Study 78258, 91010-91012
Needle Biopsy
　Endoscopy 43232
Nuclear Medicine
　Imaging (Motility) 78258
　Reflux Study 78262
Reconstruction 43300, 43310, 43313
　Creation
　　Stoma 43350-43352
　Esophagostomy 43350
　Fistula 43305, 43312, 43314
　Gastrointestinal 43360-43361
Removal
　Foreign Bodies ..43020, 43045, 43215, 74235
　Lesion 43216
　Polyp 43216-43217, 43228
Repair 43300, 43310, 43313
　Esophagogastric Fundoplasty ..43324-43325
　　Laparoscopic 43280
　Esophagogastrostomy 43320
　Esophagojejunostomy 43340-43341
　Fistula ..43305, 43312, 43314, 43420-43425
　Muscle 43330-43331
　Pre-existing Perforation 43405
　Varices 43401
　Wound 43410-43415
Suture 43405
　Wound 43410-43415
Ultrasound
　Endoscopy 43231-43232
Unlisted Services and Procedures ..43289, 43499
Vein
　Ligation 43205, 43400
Video 74230
X-Ray 74220

Esophagus Neoplasm
See Tumor, Esophagus

Esophagus, Varix
See Esophageal Varices

Established Patient
Domiciliary or Rest Home Visit 99334-99337
Emergency Department Services ..99281-99285
Home Services 99347-99350
Hospital Inpatient Services 99221-99239
Hospital Observation Services 99217-99220

Initial Inpatient Consultations 99251-99255
Office and/or Other Outpatient
Consultations 99241-99245
Office Visit 99211-99215
Online Evaluation and Management
Services 0074T
Outpatient Visit 99211-99215

Establishment
Colostomy
　Abdominal 50810
　Perineal 50810

Estes Operation
See Ovary, Transposition

Estlander Procedure 40525

Estradiol 82670
Response 80414

Estriol
Blood or Urine 82677

Estrogen
Blood or Urine 82671-82672
Receptor 84233

Estrone
Blood or Urine 82679

Ethanediols
See Ethylene Glycol

Ethanol
Blood 82055
Breath 82075
Urine 82055

Ethchlorovynol
See Ethchlorvynol

Ethchlorvinol
See Ethchlorvynol

Ethchlorvynol
Blood 82690
Urine 82690

Ethmoid
Fracture
　with Fixation 21340

Ethmoid, Sinus
See Sinus, Ethmoid

Ethmoidectomy 31200-31205
Endoscopic 31254-31255
Skull Base Surgery 61580-61581
with Nasal/Sinus Endoscopy 31254-31255

Ethosuccimid
See Ethosuximide

Ethosuximide 80168
Assay 80168

Ethyl Alcohol
See Ethanol

Ethylene Dichlorides
See Dichloroethane

Ethylene Glycol 82693

Ethylmethylsuccimide
See Ethosuximide

Etiocholanalone Measurement
See Etiocholanolone

Etiocholanolone 82696

ETOH
See Alcohol, Ethyl

Euglobulin Lysis 85360

European Blastomycosis
See Cryptococcus

Eustachian Tube
Catheterization 69405
Inflation
    Myringotomy 69420
        Anesthesia 69421
    with Catheterization 69400
    without Catheterization 69401
Insertion
    Catheter 69405

Eutelegenesis
See Artificial Insemination

Evacuation
Cervical Pregnancy 59140
Hematoma
    Brain 61312-61315
    Subungual 11740
Hydatidiform Mole 59870

Evaluation and Management
Assistive Technology
    Assessment 97755
Athletic Training
    Evaluation 97005
    Re-evaluation 97006
Basic Life and/or Disability
Evaluation Services 99450
Care Plan Oversight Services 99339-99340,
                                  99374-99380
    Home Health Agency Care 99374
    Home or Rest Home Care 99339-99340
    Hospice 99377-99378
    Nursing Facility 99379-99380
Case Management Services 99361-99373
Consultation 99241-99255
Critical Care 99291-99292
    Interfacility Pediatric Transport .99289-99290
Domiciliary or Rest Home
    Established Patient 99334-99337
    New Patient 99324-99328
Emergency Department 99281-99288
Health Behavior
    Assessment 96150
    Family Intervention 96154-96155
    Group Intervention 96153
    Individual Intervention 96152
    Re-assessment 96151
Home Services 99341-99350
Hospital 99221-99233
    Discharge 99238-99239

Hospital Services
    Observation Care 99217-99220
Insurance Exam 99455-99456
Internet Communication 0074T
Low Birthweight Infant 99298-99300
Medical
    with Individual Psychotherapy
        Hospital or Residential Care 90817,
                90819, 90822, 90824, 90827, 90829
        Office or Outpatient ..90805, 90807, 90809
    with Individual Psychotherapy, Interactive
        Office or Outpatient ..90811, 90813, 90815
Neonatal Critical Care 99295-99296
Newborn Care 99431-99440
Nursing Facility
    See Nursing Facility Services
    Annual Assessment 99318
    Discharge 99315-99316
    Initial Care 99304-99306
    Other 99318
    Subsequent Care 99307-99310
Occupation Therapy Evaluation 97003
    Re-evaluation 97004
Office and Other Outpatient 99201-99215
Online 0074T
Pediatric Critical Care 99293-99294
Pediatric Interfacility Transport ...99289-99290
Physical Therapy Evaluation 97001
    Re-evaluation 97002
Physician Standby Services 99360
Preventive Services 99381-99429
Prolonged Services 99356-99357
Psychiatric
    Records or Reports 90885
Unlisted Services and Procedures 99499
Work-Related and/or Medical Disability
Evaluation 99450

Evaluation Studies, Drug, Pre-Clinical
See Drug Screen

Evisceration
Ocular Contents
    with Implant 65093
    without Implant 65091

Evisceration, Pelvic
See Exenteration, Pelvis

Evocative/Suppression Test 80400-80440
Stimulation Panel 80410

Evoked Potential
See Audiologic Function Tests
Auditory Brainstem 92585-92586
Central Motor
    Transcranial Motor Stimulation .95928-95929
Somatosensory Testing 95925-95927
Visual, CNS 95930

Evoked Potential, Auditory
See Auditory Evoked Potentials

Ewart Procedure
See Palate, Reconstruction, Lengthening

Excavatum, Pectus
See Pectus Excavatum

Exchange
Drainage Catheter
    Under Radiologic Guidance 49423
Intraocular Lens 66986
Intravascular Catheter 37209, 75900

Exchange Transfusion
See Blood, Transfusion, Exchange

Excision
See Debridement; Destruction
Abscess
    Brain 61514, 61522
    Olecranon Process 24138
    Radius 24136
    Ulna 24138
Acromion
    Shoulder 23130
Adenoids 42830-42836
Adenoma
    Thyroid Gland 60200
Adrenal Gland 60540
    Laparoscopic 60650
    with Excision Retroperitoneal Tumor ..60545
Alveolus 41830
Anal Crypt 46210-46211
Anal Fissure 46200
Anal Tag 46220, 46230
Aorta
    Coarctation 33840-33851
Appendix 44950-44960
Arteriovenous Malformation
    Spinal 63250-63252
Arytenoid Cartilage 31400
    Endoscopic 31560-31561
Atrial Septum 33735-33737
Bartholin's Gland 56740
Bladder
    Diverticulum 51525
    Neck 51520
    Partial 51550-51565
    Total 51570, 51580, 51590-51597
        with Nodes 51575, 51585, 51595
    Transurethral 52640
    Tumor 51530
Bladder Neck Contracture
    Postoperative 52640
Bone
    Facial 21026
    Mandible 21025
    Postoperative
        Femur 20150
        Fibula 20150
        Radius 20150
        Tibia 20150
        Ulna 20150
Bone Abscess
    Facial 21026
    Mandible 21025
Brain
    Amygdala 61566
    Epileptogenic Focus 61536
    Hemisphere 61542-61543
    Hippocampus 61566
    Other Lobe 61323, 61539-61540
    Temporal Lobe 61537-61538
Brain Lobe
    See Lobectomy, Brain

Breast
- Biopsy .19100-19103
- Chest Wall Tumor 19260-19272
- Cyst 19120-19126
- Lactiferous Duct Fistula 19112
- Lesion .19120-19126
  - by Needle Localization 19125-19126
- Mastectomy 19140-19240
- Nipple Exploration 19110

Bulbourethral Gland 53250

Bullae
- Lung 32141
  - Endoscopic 32655

Burns 01951-01953, 15000-15001

Bursa
- Elbow 24105
- Femur 27062
- Ischial 27060
- Knee 27340
- Wrist 25115-25116

Bypass Graft 35901-35907

Calcaneus 28118-28120

Calculi (Stone)
- Parotid Gland 42330, 42340
- Salivary Gland 42330-42340
- Sublingual Gland 42330
- Submandibular Gland 42330-42335

Carotid Artery 60605

Carpal 25145, 25210-25215

Cartilage
- Knee Joint 27332-27333
- Shoulder Joint 23101
- Temporomandibular Joint 21060
- Wrist 25107

Caruncle
- Urethra 53265

Cataract
- Secondary .66830

Cervix
- Radical 57531
- Stump
  - Abdominal Approach 57540-57545
  - Vaginal Approach 57550-57556
- Total 57530

Chalazion
- Multiple
  - Different Lids 67805
  - Same Lid 67801
- Single 67800
- with Anesthesia 67808

Chest Wall
- Tumor 19260-19272

Choroid Plexus .61544

Clavicle
- Partial 23120, 23180
- Sequestrectomy 23170
- Total 23125
- Tumor
  - Radical Resection 23200

Coccyx 27080

Colon
- Excision
  - Partial 44140-44147, 44160
    - with Anastomosis 44140
  - Total 44150-44156

Laparoscopic
- with Anastomosis 44204, 44207-44208
- with Colostomy 44206, 44208
- with Ileocolostomy 44205

Condyle
- Temporomandibular Joint 21050

Constricting Ring
- Finger 26596

Cornea
- Epithelium .65435
  - with Chelating Agent 65436
- Scraping 65430

Coronoidectomy 21070

Cowper's Gland .53250

Cranial Bone
- Tumor 61563-61564

Cyst
- *See* Ganglion Cyst
- Bile Duct 47715
- Bladder 51500
- Brain 61516, 61524, 62162
- Branchial 42810-42815
- Calcaneus 28100-28103
- Carpal 25130-25136
- Cheekbone .21030
- Clavicle 23140
  - with Allograft 23146
  - with Autograft 23145
- Facial Bones 21030
- Femur 27065-27067, 27355-27358
- Fibula 27635-27638
- Finger 26160
- Foot 28090
- Hand 26160
- Hip .27065-27067
- Humerus 23150, 24110
  - with Allograft 23156, 24116
  - with Autograft 23155, 24115
- Ileum 27065-27067
- Kidney 50280-50290
- Knee 27345-27347
- Lung 32140
- Mandible 21040, 21046-21047
- Maxilla 21030, 21048-21049
- Mediastinal 39200
- Mediastinum 32662
- Metacarpal 26200-26205
- Metatarsal 28104-28107
- Mullerian Duct 55680
- Nose 30124-30125
- Olecranon .24120
- Olecranon Process
  - with Allograft 24126
  - with Autograft 24125
- Ovarian 58925
  - *See* Cystectomy, Ovarian
- Pericardial .33050
  - Endoscopic 32661
- Phalanges 26210-26215
- Toe 28108
- Pilonidal 11770-11772
- Pubis 27066-27067
- Radius 24120, 25120-25126
  - with Allograft 24126
  - with Autograft 24125
- Salivary Gland 42408

Scapula 23140
- with Allograft 23146
- with Autograft 23145

Seminal Vesicle .55680

Sublingual Gland 42408

Talus 28100-28103

Tarsal 28104-28107

Thyroglossal Duct 60280-60281

Thyroid Gland 60200

Tibia 27635-27638

Toe 28092

Ulna 24120, 25120-25126
- with Allograft 24126
- with Autograft 24125

Urachal
- Bladder 51500
- Vaginal 57135

Destruction of the Vestibule of the Mouth
- *See* Mouth, Vestibule of, Excision, Destruction

Diverticulum, Meckel's
- *See* Meckel's Diverticulum, Excision

Ear, External
- Partial 69110
- Total 69120

Elbow Joint 24155

Electrode 57522

Embolectomy/Thrombectomy
- Aortoiliac Artery 34151-34201
- Axillary Artery 34101
- Brachial Artery 34101
- Carotid Artery 34001
- Celiac Artery 34151
- Femoral Artery 34201
- Heart 33310-33315
- Iliac Artery 34151-34201
- Innominate Artery 34001-34101
- Mesentery Artery 34151
- Peroneal Artery 34203
- Popliteal Artery 34203
- Radial Artery 34111
- Renal Artery 34151
- Subclavian Artery 34001-34101
- Tibial Artery 34203
- Ulnar Artery 34111

Embolism
- Pulmonary Artery 33910-33916

Empyema
- Lung 32540
- Pleural 32540

Epididymis
- Bilateral 54861
- Unilateral 54860

Epiglottis 31420

Esophagus
- Diverticula 43130-43135
- Partial 43116-43124
- Total 43107-43113, 43124

Eye
- *See* Enucleation, Eye

Fallopian Tube
- Salpingectomy 58700
- Salpingo-Oophorectomy 58720

Fascia
- *See* Fasciectomy

Femur 27360
- Partial 27070-27071

Fibula 27360, 27455-27457, 27641

Fistula
  Anal 46270-46285
Foot
  Fasciectomy 28060
  Radical 28060-28062
Gallbladder 47600-47620
  Cholecystectomy 47562-47564
    with Cholangiography 47563
    with Exploration Common Duct 47564
Ganglion Cyst
  Knee 27347
  Wrist 25111-25112
Gingiva 41820
Gums 41820
  Alveolus 41830
  Operculum .41821
Heart
  Donor 33940
Heart/Lung
  Donor 33930
Hemangioma 11400-11446
Hemorrhoids 46221, 46250
  Clot 46320
  Complex 46260-46262
  Simple 46255
  with Fissurectomy 46257-46258
Hip
  Partial 27070-27071
Hippocampus 61566
Humeral Head
  Resection 23195
  Sequestrectomy 23174
Humerus 23184, 23220-23222, 24134, 24140,
                                24150-24151
Hydrocele
  Spermatic Cord 55500
  Tunica Vaginalis 55040-55041
    Bilateral .55041
    Unilateral 55040
Hygroma, Cystic
  Axillary/Cervical 38550-38555
Hymenotomy 56700
  See Hymen, Excision
Ileum
  Ileoanal Reservoir 45136
  Partial 27070-27071
Inner Ear
  See Ear, Inner, Excision
Interphalangeal Joint
  Toe 28160
Intervertebral Disk
  Decompression 63075-63078
  Hemilaminectomy 63040, 63043-63044
  Herniated 63020-63044, 63055-63066
Intestine
  Laparoscopic
    with Anastomosis 44202-44203
Intestines
  Donor 44132-44133
Intestines, Small 44120-44128
  Transplantation 44137
Iris
  Iridectomy
    Optical .66635
    Peripheral 66625
    Sector 66630

  with Corneoscleral or
    Corneal Section 66600
  with Cyclectomy 66605
Kidney
  Donor 50300-50320, 50547
  Partial 50240
  Recipient 50340
  Transplantation 50370
  with Ureters 50220-50236
Kneecap 27350
Labyrinth
  Transcanal .69905
  with Mastoidectomy 69910
Lacrimal Gland
  Partial 68505
  Total 68500
Lacrimal Sac .68520
Larynx
  Partial 31367-31382
  Total 31360-31365
  with Pharynx 31390-31395
Lesion
  Anal 45108, 46922
  Ankle 27630
    Arthroscopic 29891
  Auditory Canal, External
    Exostosis 69140
    Radical with Neck Dissection 69155
    Radical without Neck Dissection . . .69150
    Soft Tissue 69145
  Bladder 52224
  Brain 61534, 61536-61540
  Brainstem 61575-61576
  Carotid Body 60600-60605
  Colon 44110-44111
  Conjunctiva 68110-68130
    over 1 cm 68115
    with Adjacent Sclera 68130
  Cornea 65400
    without Graft 65420
  Ear, Middle 69540
  Epididymis
    Local 54830
    Spermatocele 54840
  Esophagus 43100-43101
  Eye 65900
  Eyelid
    Multiple, Different Lids 67805
    Multiple, Same Lid 67801
    Single 67800
    Under Anesthesia 67808
    without Closure 67840
  Femur 27062
  Finger 26160
  Foot 28080, 28090
  Gums 41822-41828
  Hand 26160
  Intestines .44110
    Small 43250, 44111
  Intraspinal 63265-63273
  Knee 27347
  Larynx
    Endoscopic 31545-31546
  Leg, Lower 27630
  Meniscus .27347
  Mesentery .44820
  Mouth 40810-40816, 41116

Nerve 64774-64792
Neuroma 64778
Nose
  Intranasal 30117-30118
Orbit 61333
  Lateral Approach 67420
  Removal 67412
Palate 42104-42120
Pancreas 48120
Penis 54060
  Surgical Excision Penile
  Plaque 54110-54112
Pharynx 42808
Rectum 45108
Sclera 66130
Skin
  Benign 11400-11471
  Malignant 11600-11646
Skull 61500, 61615-61616
Spermatic Cord 55520
Spinal Cord 63300-63308
Stomach 43611
Talus
  Arthroscopic 29891
Testis 54512
Tibia
  Arthroscopic 29891
Toe 28092
Tongue 41110-41114
Urethra 52224, 53265
Uterus 59100
  Leiomyomata . .58140, 58545-58546, 58561
Uvula 42104-42107
Wrist Tendon 25110
Lesion, Arthroscopic
  Ankle 29891
  Talus 29891
  Tibia 29891
Lesion, Tendon Sheath
  Arm, Lower 25110
Lip 40500-40530
  Frenum 40819
Liver
  Extensive .47122
  Lobectomy 47125-47130
  Partial . . .47120, 47125-47130, 47140-47142
  Total 47133
Lung
  Bronchus Resection 32486
  Bullae
    Endoscopic 32655
  Completion 32488
  Emphysematous 32491
  Lobe 32480-32482
  Segment .32484
  Total 32440-32445
  Tumor, Apical Tumor
    with Resection 32503
    with Reconstruction 32504
  Wedge Resection 32500
    Endoscopic 32657
Lung/Heart
  Donor 33930
Lymph Nodes 38500, 38510-38530
  Abdominal 38747
  Inguinofemoral 38760-38765

Limited, for Staging
　Para-Aortic 38562
　Pelvic 38562
　Retroperitoneal 38564
Pelvic 38770
Radical
　Axillary 38740-38745
　Cervical 38720-38724
　Suprahyoid 38700
Retroperitoneal Transabdominal 38780
Thoracic 38746
Mandibular
　Exostosis 21031
Mastoid
　Complete 69502
　Radical 69511
　　Modified 69505
　　Petrous Apicectomy 69530
　Simple 69501
Maxilla
　Exostosis 21032
Maxillary Torus Palatinus 21032
Meningioma
　Brain 61512, 61519
Meniscectomy
　Temporomandibular Joint 21060
Metacarpal 26230
Metatarsal 28110-28114, 28122, 28140
　Condyle 28288
Mouth
　Frenum 40819
Mucosa
　Gums 41828
　Mouth 40818
Nail Fold 11765
Nails 11750-11752
Nerve
　Foot 28030
　Leg, Upper 27315-27320
　Sympathetic 64802-64818
Neurofibroma 64788-64790
Neurolemmoma 64788-64792
Neuroma 64774-64786
Nose
　Dermoid Cyst
　　Complex 30125
　　Simple 30124
　Polyp 30110-30115
　Rhinectomy 30150-30160
　Skin 30120
　Submucous Resection
　　Nasal Septum 30520
　　Turbinate 30140
　Turbinate 30130-30140
Odontoid Process 22548
Olecranon Process 24147
Omentum 49255
Ovary 58720
　Partial
　　Oophorectomy 58940
　　Ovarian Malignancy 58943
　　Peritoneal Malignancy 58943
　　Tubal Malignancy 58943
　　Wedge Resection 58920
　Total 58940-58943
Oviduct 58720
Palate 42120, 42145

Pancreas
　Ampulla of Vater 48148
　Duct 48148
　Partial 48140-48146, 48150,
　　　　　　　　48153-48154, 48160
　Peripancreatic Tissue 48005
　Total 48155-48160
Parathyroid Gland 60500-60502
Parotid Gland 42340
　Partial 42410-42415
　Total 42420-42426
Patella 27350
　See Patellectomy
Penile Adhesions
　Post-circumcision 54162
Penis
　Frenulum 54164
　Partial 54120
　Prepuce 54150-54161, 54163
　Radical 54130-54135
　Total 54125
Pericardium 33030-33031
　Endoscopic 32659
Petrous Temporal
　Apex 69530
Phalanges
　Finger 26235-26236
　Toe 28124-28126, 28150-28160
Pharynx 42145
　Partial 42890
　Resection 42892-42894
　with Larynx 31390-31395
Pituitary Gland 61546-61548
Pleura 32310-32320
　Endoscopic 32656
Polyp
　Intestines 43250
　Nose
　　Extensive 30115
　　Simple 30110
　Sinus 31032
　Urethra 53260
Pressure Ulcers 15920-15999
　See Skin Graft and Flap
Prostate
　Abdominoperineal 45119
　Partial 55801, 55821-55831
　Perineal 55801-55815
　Radical 55810-55815, 55840-55845
　Regrowth 52630
　Residual Obstructive Tissue 52620
　Retropubic 55831-55845
　Suprapubic 55821
　Transurethral 52601, 52612-52614
Pterygium
　with Graft 65426
Pubis
　Partial 27070-27071
Radical Synovium Wrist 25115-25116
Radius 24130, 24136, 24145,
　　　　　　　24152-24153, 25145
　Styloid Process 25230
Rectum
　Partial 45111, 45113-45116, 45123
　Prolapse 45130-45135
　Stricture 45150
　Total 45119-45120
　with Colon 45121

Redundant Skin of Eyelid
　See Blepharoplasty
Ribs 21600-21616, 32900
Scapula
　Ostectomy 23190
　Partial 23182
　Sequestrectomy 23172
　Tumor
　　Radical Resection 23210
Sclera 66160
Scrotum 55150
Semilunar Cartilage of Knee
　See Knee, Meniscectomy
Seminal Vesicle 55650
Sesamoid Bone
　Foot 28315
Sinus
　Ethmoid 31200-31205
　Maxillary 31225-31230
Skene's Gland 53270
Skin
　Excess 15831-15839
　Lesion
　　Benign 11400-11471
　　Malignant 11600-11646
　Nose 30120
Skin Graft
　Preparation of Site 15000
Skull 61501
Spermatic Veins 55530-55540
　Abdominal Approach 55535
　Hernia Repair 55540
Spleen 38100-38102
　Laparoscopic 38120
Stapes
　with Footplate Drill Out 69661
　without Foreign Material 69660
Sternum 21620, 21630-21632
Stomach
　Partial 43631-43635, 43845
　Total 43620-43622
Sublingual Gland 42450
Submandibular Gland 42440, 42508
Sweat Glands
　Axillary 11450-11451
　Inguinal 11462-11463
　Perianal 11470-11471
　Perineal 11470-11471
　Umbilical 11470-11471
Synovium
　Ankle 27625-27626
　Carpometacarpal Joint 26130
　Elbow 24102
　Hip Joint 27054
　Interphalangeal Joint 26140
　Intertarsal Joint 28070
　Knee Joint 27334-27335
　Metacarpophalangeal Joint 26135
　Metatarsophalangeal Joint 28072
　Shoulder 23105-23106
　Tarsometatarsal Joint 28070
　Wrist 25105, 25118-25119
Talus 28120, 28130
Tarsal 28116, 28122
Temporal Bone 69535
Temporal, Petrous
　Apex 69530

Tendon
    Finger 26180, 26390, 26415
    Hand 26390, 26415
    Palm 26170
Tendon Sheath
    Finger 26145
    Foot 28086-28088
    Palm 26145
    Wrist 25115-25116
Testis
    Laparoscopic 54690
    Partial 54522
    Radical 54530-54535
    Simple 54520
    Tumor 54530-54535
Thrombectomy
    Axillary Vein 34490
    Bypass Graft 35875-35876
    Femoropopliteal Vein 34401-34451
    Iliac Vein 34401-34451
    Subclavian Vein 34471-34490
    Vena Cava 34401-34451
Thromboendarterectomy
    Aorta, Abdominal 35331
    Aortoiliofemoral 35363
    Axillary Artery 35321
    Brachial Artery 35321
    Carotid Artery 35301, 35390
    Celiac Artery 35341
    Femoral Artery 35371-35381
    Iliac 35361-35363
    Iliac Artery 35351
    Iliofemoral Artery 35355, 35363
    Innominate Artery 35311
    Mesenteric Artery 35341
    Peroneal Artery 35381
    Popliteal Artery 35381
    Renal Artery 35341
    Subclavian Artery 35301-35311
    Tibial Artery 35381
    Vertebral Artery 35301
Thymus Gland 60521
Thyroid Gland for Malignancy
    Partial 60210-60225
    Removal All Thyroid Tissue 60260
    Secondary 60260
    Total 60240
        Cervical Approach 60271
        Limited Neck Dissection 60252
        Radical Neck Dissection 60254
        Sternal Split/Transthoracic
        Approach 60270
Tibia 27360, 27640
Tongue
    Complete 41140-41155
    Frenum 41115
    Partial 41120-41135
    with Mouth Resection 41150-41153
    with Radical Neck 41135, 41145-41155
Tonsils 42825-42826
    Lingual 42870
    Radical 42842-42845
    Tag 42860
    with Adenoids 42820-42821
Torus Mandibularis 21031
Trachea
    Stenosis 31780-31781
Transcervical Approach 60520

Tricuspid Valve 33460
Tumor
    Abdominal Wall 22900
    Acetabulum 27076
    Ankle 27615-27619
    Arm, Lower 25075-25077
    Arm, Upper 24075-24077
    Back/Flank 21930
    Bile Duct 47711-47712
    Bladder 51530, 52234-52240, 52355
    Brain 61510, 61518, 61520-61521,
              61526-61530, 61545, 62164
    Bronchi 31640
    Calcaneus 27647, 28100-28103
    Carpal 25130-25136
    Cheekbone 21030, 21034, 21048-21049
    Clavicle 23140
    with Allograft 23146
    with Autograft 23145
    Ear, Middle
        Extended 69554
        Transcanal 69550
        Transmastoid 69552
    Elbow 24075-24077
    Esophagus
        Endoscopic Ablation 43228
    Facial Bones 21029-21030,
          21034-21040, 21046-21049
    Facial Tissue 21015
    Femur . . .27065-27067, 27355-27358, 27365
    Fibula 27635-27638, 27646
    Finger 26115-26117
    Foot 28043-28046
    Gums 41825-41827
    Hand 26115-26117
    Heart 33120-33130
    Hip 27047-27049, 27065-27067
        Radical 27075-27076
    Humerus 23150, 23220-23222,
              24110-24115
        with Allograft 23156, 24116
        with Autograft 23155, 24116
    Ileum 27065-27067
    Innominate 27077
    Intestines
        Small .43250
    Ischial 27078-27079
    Kidney 52355
    Knee 27327-27329, 27365
    Lacrimal Gland
        Frontal Approach 68540
        Involving Osteotomy 68550
    Larynx 31300
        Endoscopic 31540-31541, 31578
    Leg, Lower 27615-27619
    Leg, Upper 27327-27329
    Mandible 21040-21047
    Maxilla 21030, 21034, 21048-21049
    Mediastinal 39220
    Mediastinum 32662
    Metacarpal 26200-26205
        Radical 26250-26255
    Metatarsal . . .28104-28107, 28173
    Neck 21555-21557
    Olecranon Process 24120
        with Allograft 24126
        with Autograft 24125
    Parotid Gland 42410-42426

Pelvis 27047-27049
Pericardial 33050
Pericardium 32661
Phalanges 26210-26215, 26260-26262
    Toe 26215, 28108, 28175
Pituitary Gland 61546-61548, 62165
Presacral 49215
Pubis 27065-27067
Radius . . .24120-24125, 25120-25126, 25170
Rectum 45160-45170
Sacrococcygeal 49215
Scapula .23140
    with Allograft 23146
    with Autograft 23145
Shoulder 23075-23077
Skull 61500
Spermatocele
    See Spermatocele, Excision
Spinal Cord 63275-63290
Spleen, Total
    See Splenectomy, Total
Sternum 21630
Stomach 43610
Talus 27647, 28100-28103
Tarsal 28104-28107, 28171
Thorax 21555-21557
Thyroid .60200
Tibia 27635-27638, 27645-27646
Trachea
    Cervical 31785
    Thoracic 31786
Ulna 24120-24125, 25120-25126, 25170
Ureter 52355
Urethra 52234-52240, 52355, 53220
Uterus
    Abdominal Approach 58140, 58146
    Vaginal Approach 58145
Vagina .57135
Vertebra, Lumbar 22102
Vertebra, Thoracic 22101
Wrist 25075-25077
Zygoma 21030, 21034
Turbinate 30130-30140
Tympanic Nerve 69676
Ulcer
    Stomach 43610
Ulna 24147, 25145
    Complete 25240
    Partial 25150-25151, 25240
Umbilicus 49250
Ureter
    See Ureterectomy
Ureterocele 51535
Urethra
    Diverticulum 53230-53235
    Prolapse 53275
    Total
        Female 53210
        Male 53215
Uterus
    Laparoscopic 58550
    Leiomyomata 58546
    Partial 58180
    Radical 58210, 58285
    Removal Tubes and/or
    Ovaries 58262-58263, 58291,
              58552, 58554
    with Colpectomy 58275-58280

with Colpo-Urethrocystopexy 58267, 58293
with Repair of Enterocele . . .58270, 58292, 58294
Total 58150-58152, 58200
Vaginal . .58260, 58290-58294, 58550, 58553
Uvula 42140-42145
Vagina
　Closure 57120
　Complete
　　with Removal of Paravaginal Tissue .57111
　　with Removal of Paravaginal Tissue
　　with Lymphadenectomy 57112
　　with Removal of Vaginal Wall 57110
　Partial
　　with Removal of Paravaginal Tissue .57107
　　with Removal of Paravaginal Tissue
　　with Lymphadenectomy 57109
　　with Removal of Vaginal Wall 57106
　Septum 57130
　Total 57110
　with Hysterectomy 58275-58280
　Repair of Enterocele 58280
Varicocele
　Spermatic Cord 55530-55540
　　Abdominal Approach 55535
　　Hernia Repair 55540
Vas Deferens 55250
Vascular Malformation
　Finger 26115
　Hand 26115
Vein
　Varicose 37765-37766
Vertebra
　Additional Segment 22103, 22116
　Cervical 22110
　　for Tumor 22100, 22110
　Lumbar 22102
　　for Tumor .22114
　Thoracic 22112
　　for Tumor .22101
Vertebral Body
　Decompression 63081-63103
　Lesion 63300-63308
Vitreous 67039
　Total
　　Pars Plana Approach 67036
　　with Epiretinal Membrane
　　Stripping 67038
　　with Retinal Surgery 67038
Vulva
　Radical
　　Complete 56633-56640
　　Partial 56630-56632
　Simple
　　Complete 56625
　　Partial 56620

Exclusion
Duodenum 48547
Small Intestine 44700

Exenteration
Eye
　Removal Orbital Contents 65110
　Therapeutic Removal of Bone 65112
　with Muscle or Myocutaneous Flap . .65114
Pelvis 45126, 58240

Exercise Stress Tests 93015-93018
Exercise Test
See Electromyography, Needle
Ischemic Limb .95875

Exercise Therapy 97110-97113
See Physical Medicine/Therapy/Occupational Therapy

Exfoliation
Chemical 17360

Exocrine, Pancreas
See Pancreas

Exomphalos
See Omphalocele

Exostectomy 28288, 28290

Exostoses
See Exostosis

Exostoses, Cartilaginous
See Exostosis

Exostosis
Excision 69140

Expander, Skin, Inflatable
See Tissue, Expander

Expired Gas Analysis 94680-94690, 94770
See Pulmonology, Diagnostic
Carbon Monoxide
　Breath Test .0043T
Spectroscopic .0064T

Exploration
Abdomen 49000-49002
　Penetrating Wound 20102
　Staging 58960
Adrenal Gland 60540-60545
Anal
　Endoscopy 46600
Ankle 27610, 27620
Anus
　Surgical 45990
Arm, Lower 25248
Artery
　Brachial 24495
　Carotid 35701
　Femoral 35721
　Other 35761
　Popliteal 35741
Back
　Penetrating Wound 20102
Bile Duct
　Atresia 47700
　Endoscopy 47552-47553
Blood Vessel
　Abdomen 35840
　Chest 35820
　Extremity 35860
　Neck 35800
Brain
　Infratentorial 61305
　Supratentorial 61304

via Burr Hole
　Infratentorial 61253
　Supratentorial 61250
Breast 19020
Bronchi
　Endoscopy 31622
Bronchoscopy .31622
Cauda Equina 63005-63011, 63017
Chest
　Penetrating Wound 20101
Colon
　Endoscopic 44388, 45378
Colon-Sigmoid
　Endoscopic 45330, 45335
Common Bile Duct
　with Cholecystectomy 47610
Duodenum 44010
Ear, Inner
　Endolymphatic Sac
　　with Shunt .69806
　　without Shunt 69805
Ear, Middle 69440
Elbow 24000, 24101
Epididymis 54820
Esophagus
　Endoscopy 43200
Extremity
　Penetrating Wound 20103
Finger Joint 26075-26080
Flank
　Penetrating Wound 20102
Gallbladder 47480
Gastrointestinal Tract, Upper
　Endoscopy 43234-43236
Hand Joint 26070
Heart .33310-33315
Hepatic Duct .47400
Hip 27033
Interphalangeal Joint
　Toe 28024
Intertarsal Joint 28020
Intestines, Small
　Endoscopy 44360
　Enterotomy .44020
Kidney 50010, 50045, 50120
Knee 27310, 27331
Lacrimal Duct .68810
　Canaliculi 68840
　with Anesthesia 68811
　with Insertion Tube or Stent 68815
Larynx 31320
　Endoscopy 31505, 31520-31526, 31575
Liver
　Wound 47361-47362
Mediastinum 39000-39010
Metatarsophalangeal Joint 28022
Nasolacrimal Duct 68810
　with Anesthesia 68811
　with Insertion Tube or Stent 68815
Neck
　Lymph Nodes 38542
　Penetrating Wound 20100
Nipple 19110
Nose
　Endoscopy 31231-31235
Orbit .61332-61334
　with/without Biopsy 67450
　without Bone Flap 67400

Parathyroid Gland 60500-60505
Pelvis 49320
Prostate 55860
    with Nodes 55862-55865
Rectum
    Endoscopic 45300
    Injury 45562-45563
    Surgical 45990
Retroperitoneal Area 49010
Scrotum 55110
Shoulder Joint 23040-23044, 23107
Sinus
    Frontal 31070-31075
    Maxillary 31020-31030
Skull 61105
Spinal Cord 63001-63011,
                    63015-63017, 63040-63044
Spine Fusion 22830
Stomach 43500
Tarsometatarsal Joint 28020
Testis
    Undescended 54550-54560
Toe Joint 28024
Ureter 50600
Vagina 57000
    Endocervical 57452
Wrist 25101, 25248
    Joint 25040

Exploration, Larynx by Incision
See Laryngotomy, Diagnostic

Exploratory Laparotomy
See Abdomen, Exploration

Expression
Lesion
    Conjunctiva 68040

Exteriorization, Small Intestine
See Enterostomy

External Auditory Canal
See Auditory Canal

External Cephalic Version 59412

External Ear
See Ear, External

External Extoses
See Exostosis

External Fixation
Adjustment/Revision 20693
Application 20690-20692
Mandibular Fracture
    Open Treatment 21454
    Percutaneous Treatment 21452
Removal 20694

Extirpation, Lacrimal Sac
See Dacryocystectomy

Extracorporeal Circulation 33960-33961
for Regional Chemotherapy
    Extremity 36823

Extracorporeal Dialyses
See Hemodialysis

Extracorporeal Membrane Oxygenation
Cannulization 36822

Extracorporeal Photochemotherapies
See Photopheresis

Extracorporeal Shock Wave Therapy
See Lithotripsy
Musculoskeletal 0019T
Plantar Fascia 28890

Extracranial
Intracranial 61623

Extraction
Lens
    Extracapsular 66940
    Intracapsular 66920
        for Dislocated Lens 66930

Extraction, Cataract
See Cataract, Excision

Extradural Anesthesia
See Anesthesia, Epidural

Extradural Injection
See Epidural, Injection

Extraocular Muscle
See Eye Muscles

Extrauterine Pregnancy
See Ectopic Pregnancy

Extravasation Blood
See Hemorrhage

Extremity
Lower
    Harvest of Vein for Bypass Graft 35500
    Harvest of Vein for Vascular
    Reconstruction 35572
    Revision 35879-35881
Upper
    Harvest of Artery for Coronary Artery
    Bypass Graft 35600
    Harvest of Vein for Bypass Graft 35500
    Repair
        Blood Vessel 35206
Wound Exploration
    Penetrating Wound 20103

Eye
See Ciliary Body; Cornea; Iris; Lens; Retina;
Sclera; Vitreous
Biometry 76516-76519, 92136
Drainage
    Anterior Chamber
        Discission of Anterior Hyaloid
        Membrane 65810
        with Diagnostic Aspiration of
        Aqueous 65800
        with Removal of Blood 65815
        with Removal of Vitreous and/or with
        Therapeutic Release of Aqueous 65805
Endoscopy 66990
Goniotomy 65820

Incision
    Adhesions
        Anterior Synechiae 65860, 65870
        Corneovitreal Adhesions 65880
        Goniosynechiae 65865
        Posterior Synechiae 65875
    Anterior Chamber 65820
    Conjunctiva 0124T
    Trabeculae 65850
Injection
    Air 66020
    Medication 66030
Insertion
    Implantation
        Corneal Ring Segments 0099T
        Drug Delivery System 67027
        Electrode Array 0100T
        Foreign Material for
        Reinforcement 65155
        Muscles Attached 65140
        Muscles, Not Attached 65135
        Reinsertion 65150
        Scleral Shell 65130
Interferometry
    Biometry 92136
Lesion
    Excision 65900
Nerve
    Destruction 67345
Paracentesis
    Anterior Chamber
        Removal of Blood 65815
        Removal or Vitreous and/or Discission
        Anterior Hyaloid Membrane 65810
        with Diagnostic Aspiration of
        Aqueous 65800
        with Therapeutic Release of
        Aqueous 65805
Radial Keratotomy 65771
Reconstruction
    Graft
        Conjunctiva 65782
        Stem Cell 65781
    Transplantation
        Amniotic Membrane 65780
Removal
    Blood Clot 65930
    Bone 65112
    Foreign Body
        Conjunctival Embedded 65210
        Conjunctival Superficial 65205
        Corneal with Slit Lamp 65222
        Corneal without Slit Lamp 65220
        Intraocular 65235-65265
    Implant 65175
        Anterior Segment 65920
        Muscles, Not Attached 65103
        Posterior Segment 67120-67121
Repair
    Conjunctiva
        by Mobilization and Rearrangement with
        Hospitalization 65273
        by Mobilization and Rearrangement
        without Hospitalization 65272
        Direct Closure 65270
    Cornea
        Nonperforating 65275
        Perforating 65280-65285

Muscles 65290
Sclera
  Anterior Segment 66250
  with Graft 66225
  with Tissue Glue 65286
  without Graft 66220
  Trabeculae 65855
  Wound
    by Mobilization and
    Rearrangement 65272-65273
    Direct Closure 65270
Shunt, Aqueous
  to Extraocular Reservoir 66180
Ultrasound 76510-76514
  Biometry 76516-76519
  Foreign Body 76529
Unlisted Services and Procedures
  Anterior Segment 66999
  Posterior Segment 67299
with Muscle or Myocutaneous Flap 65114
  Muscles Attached 65105
  Ocular Contents
    with Implant 65093
    without Implant 65091
  Orbital Contents 65110
    without Implant 65101
X-Ray 70030

Eye Allergy Test 95060
See Allergy Tests

Eye Evisceration
See Evisceration, Ocular Contents

Eye Exam
Established Patient 92012-92014
New Patient 92002-92004
Radiologic 70030
with Anesthesia 92018-92019

Eye Exercises
Training 92065

Eye Muscles
Biopsy 67350
Repair
  Strabismus
    Adjustable Sutures 67335
    Exploration and/or Repair Detached
    Extraocular Muscle 67340
    on Patient with Previous Surgery . . .67331
    One Vertical Muscle 67314
    Posterior Fixation Suture 67334
    Recession or Resection 67311-67312
    Release of Scar Tissue without Detaching
    Extraocular Muscle 67343
    Two or More Vertical Muscles 67316
    with Scarring Extraocular Muscles . .67332
    with Superior Oblique Muscle 67318
Transposition 67320
Unlisted Services and Procedures 67399

Eye Prosthesis
See Prosthesis

Eye Socket
See Orbit; Orbital Contents; Orbital Floor;
Periorbital Region

Eyebrow
Repair
  Ptosis 67900

Eyeglasses
See Spectacle Services

Eyelashes
Repair Trichiasis
  Epilation
    by Forceps Only 67820
    by Other than Forceps 67825
  Incision of Lid Margin 67830
    with Free Mucous Membrane Graft . .67835

Eyelid
Abscess
  Incision and Drainage 67700
Biopsy 67810
Blepharoplasty 15820-15823
Chalazion
  Excision .67805
    Multiple 67801-67805
    Single .67800
    with Anesthesia 67808
Closure by Suture 67875
Incision
  Canthus .67715
  Sutures 67710
Injection
  Subconjunctival 68200
Lesion
  Destruction 67850
  Excision
    Multiple 67801-67805
    Single .67800
    with Anesthesia 67808
    without Closure 67840
Reconstruction
  Canthus .67950
  Total 67973-67975
  Total Eyelid
    Lower 67973-67975
    Second Stage 67975
    Upper .67974
  Transfer of Tarsoconjunctival Flap from
  Opposing Eyelid 67971
Removal
  Foreign Body 67938
Repair 21280-21282
  Blepharoptosis
    Conjunctivo-Tarso-Muller's
    Muscle-Levator Resection 67908
    Frontalis Muscle Technique . .67901-67904
    Reduction Overcorrection of Ptosis . .67909
    Superior Rectus Technique with Fascial
    Sling 67906
  Ectropion
    Blepharoplasty 67914
    Suture .67914
  Entropion
    Excision Tarsal Wedge 67923
    Extensive 67924
    Suture .67921
    Thermocauterization 67922

Excisional 67961
  over One-Fourth of Lid Margin 67966
Lagophthalmos 67912
Lashes
  Epilation, by Forceps Only 67820
  Epilation, by Other than Forceps 67825
  Lid Margin 67830-67835
Wound
  Full Thickness 67935
  Partial Thickness 67930
Repair with Graft
  Retraction 67911
Skin Graft
  Full Thickness 67961
  Split 67961
Suture 67880
  with Transposition of Tarsal Plate 67882
Tissue Transfer, Adjacent 67961
Unlisted Services and Procedures 67999

Eyelid Ptoses
See Blepharoptosis

F

Face
CT Scan 70486-70488
Lesion
  Destruction 17000-17004, 17280-17286
Magnetic Resonance Imaging
(MRI) 70540-70543
Tumor Resection 21015

Face Lift 15824-15828

Facial Asymmetries
See Hemifacial Microsomia

Facial Bone
See Mandible; Maxilla
Tumor
  Excision .21034

Facial Bones
Abscess
  Excision .21026
Reconstruction
  Secondary 21275
Repair 21208-21209
Tumor
  Excision 21029-21030
  Resection
    Radical 21015
X-Ray .70140-70150

Facial Nerve
Anastomosis
  to Hypoglossal 64868
  to Phrenic Nerve 64870
  to Spinal Accessory 64866
Avulsion 64742

Decompression 61590, 61596
  Intratemporal
    Lateral to Geniculate
      Ganglion 69720, 69740
    Medial to Geniculate
      Ganglion 69725, 69745
    Total 69955
Function Study .92516
Incision 64742
Injection
  Anesthetic .64402
Mobilization 61590
Repair
  Lateral to Geniculate Ganglion 69740
  Medial to Geniculate Ganglion 69745
Repair/Suture
  with or without Graft 64864-64865
Suture
  Lateral to Geniculate Ganglion 69740
  Medial to Geniculate Ganglion 69745
Transection 64742

Facial Nerve Paralysis
Graft .15840-15845
Repair 15840-15845

Facial Prosthesis
Impression 21088

Facial Rhytidectomy
See Face Lift

Factor I
See Fibrinogen

Factor II
See Prothrombin

Factor III
See Thromboplastin

Factor IV
See Calcium

Factor VII
See Proconvertin

Factor VIII
See Clotting Factor

Factor IX
See Christmas Factor

Factor X
See Stuart-Prower Factor

Factor X, Activated
See Thrombokinase

Factor Xa Inhibitor
See Antithrombin III

Factor XI
See Plasma Thromboplastin, Antecedent

Factor XII
See Hageman Factor

Factor XIII
See Fibrin Stabilizing Factor

Factor, ACTH-Releasing
See Corticotropic Releasing Hormone (CRH)

Factor, Antinuclear
See Antinuclear Antibodies (ANA)

Factor, Blood Coagulation
See Clotting Factor

Factor, Fitzgerald
See Fitzgerald Factor

Factor, Fletcher
See Fletcher Factor

Factor, Hyperglycemic-Glycogenolytic
See Glucagon

Factor Inhibitor Test 85335

Factor, Intrinsic
See Intrinsic Factor

Factor, Rheumatoid
See Rheumatoid Factor

Factor, Sulfation
See Somatomedin

Fallopian Tube
Anastomosis .58750
Catheterization 58345, 74742
Destruction
  Endoscopy 58670
Ectopic Pregnancy 59121
  with Salpingectomy and/or
  Oophorectomy 59120
Excision 58700-58720
Ligation 58600-58611
Lysis
  Adhesions .58740
Occlusion 58615
  Endoscopy 58671
Placement
  Implant for Occlusion 58565
Repair 58752
  Anastomosis 58750
  Create Stoma 58770
Tumor
  Resection 58950, 58952-58956
Unlisted Services and Procedures 58999
X-Ray 74742

Fallopian Tube Pregnancy
See Ectopic Pregnancy, Tubal

Fallot, Tetralogy of
See Tetralogy of Fallot

Family Psychotherapy
See Psychotherapy, Family

Fanconi Anemia
Chromosome Analysis 88248

Farnsworth-Munsell Color Test
See Color Vision Examination

Farr Test
See Gammaglobulin, Blood

Fasanella-Servat Procedure . . .67908

Fascia Graft 15840

Fascia Lata Graft
Harvesting 20920-20922

Fascial Defect
Repair 50728

Fascial Graft
Free
  Microvascular Anastomosis 15758
Open Treatment
  Sternoclavicular Dislocation 23532

Fasciectomy
Foot 28060
  Radical 28060-28062
Palm .26121-26125

Fasciocutaneous Flaps . . .15732-15738

Fasciotomy
Arm, Lower 24495, 25020-25025
Elbow 24350-24356
Foot 28008
Hand Decompression 26037
Hip 27025
Knee 27305, 27496-27499
Leg, Lower 27600-27602, 27892-27894
Leg, Upper . . .27305, 27496-27499, 27892-27894
Palm .26040-26045
Plantar
  Endoscopic 29893
Thigh 27025
Toe 28008
Wrist .25020-25025

FAST
See Allergen Immunotherapy

Fat
Feces .82705-82715
Removal
  Lipectomy 15876-15879

Fat Stain
Feces 89125
Respiratory Secretions 89125
Sputum 89125
Urine 89125

Fatty Acid
Blood 82725
Long-Chain Omega-3
  Red blood cell (RBC) membranes 0111T
Very Long Chain 82726

Favre-Durand Disease
See Lymphogranuloma Venereum

FC Receptor 86243

FDP
See Fibrin Degradation Products

Feedback, Psychophysiologic
See Biofeedback; Training, Biofeedback

Female Castration
See Oophorectomy

Female Gonad
See Ovary

Femoral Arteries
See Artery, Femoral

Femoral Nerve
Injection
    Anesthetic 64447-64448

Femoral Stem Prosthesis
See Arthroplasty, Hip

Femoral Vein
See Vein, Femoral

Femur
See Hip; Knee; Leg, Upper
Abscess
    Incision 27303
Bursa
    Excision 27062
Craterization 27070, 27360
Cyst
    Excision 27065-27067, 27355-27358
Diaphysectomy 27360
Drainage 27303
Excision 27070, 27360
    Epiphyseal Bar 20150
Fracture 27244
Fracture
    Closed Treatment 27501-27503
    Distal 27508, 27510, 27514
    Distal, Medial or Lateral Condyle 27509
    Epiphysis 27516-27519
    Intertrochanteric 27244
    Intertrochanteric
        Closed Treatment 27238
        Treatment with Implant 27244
        with Implant 27245
        with Manipulation 27240
    Neck
        Closed Treatment 27230-27232
        Open Treatment 27236
        Percutaneous Fixation 27235
    Open Treatment 27245, 27506-27507,
                27511-27513
    Percutaneous Fixation 27509
    Pertrochanteric 27244
    Pertrochanteric
        Closed Treatment 27238
        Treatment with Implant 27244
        with Implant 27245
        with Manipulation 27240
    Shaft 27500, 27502, 27506-27507
    Subtrochanteric 27244
    Subtrochanteric
        Closed Treatment 27238
        Treatment with Implant 27244
        with Implant 27245
        with Manipulation 27240
    Supracondylar 27501-27503, 27509,
                27511-27513
    Transcondylar 27501-27503, 27509,
                27511-27513

Trochanteric
    Closed Treatment 27246
    Open Treatment 27248
    with Manipulation 27503
    without Manipulation 27501
Halo 20663
Lesion
    Excision 27062
Osteoplasty
    Lengthening 27466-27468
    Shortening 27465, 27468
Osteotomy
    without Fixation 27448
Prophylactic Treatment 27187, 27495
Realignment 27454
Reconstruction 27468
    at Knee 27442-27443, 27446
    Lengthening 27466-27468
    Shortening 27465, 27468
Repair 27470-27472
    Epiphysis 27181, 27475, 27742
        Arrest 27185
    Muscle Transfer 27110
    Osteotomy 27140, 27151-27156,
             27161-27165, 27450-27454
    with Graft 27170
Saucerization 27070, 27360
Tumor
    Excision ..27065-27067, 27355-27358, 27365
X-Ray 73550

Fenestration Procedure
Semicircular Canal 69820
    Revision 69840
Tracheostomy 31610

Fenestration, Pericardium
See Pericardiostomy

Fern Test 87210
See Smear and Stain, Wet Mount

Ferric Chloride
Urine 81005

Ferrihemoglobin
See Methemoglobin

Ferritin
Blood or Urine 82728

Ferroxidase
See Ceruloplasmin

Fertility Control
See Contraception

Fertility Test
Semen Analysis 89300-89321
Sperm Analysis
    Cervical Mucus Penetration Test 89330
    Hamster Penetration 89329

Fertilization
Assisted
    Oocyte
        Microtechnique 89280-89281
Oocyte
    with Co-Culture 89251

Fertilization in Vitro
See In Vitro Fertilization

Fetal Biophysical Profile .76818-76819

Fetal Contraction Stress Test .59020

Fetal Hemoglobin 85461

Fetal Lung Maturity Assessment;
Lecithin Sphingomyelin Ratio .83661

Fetal Monitoring
See Monitoring, Fetal

Fetal Non-Stress Test 59025
Ultrasound 76818

Fetal Procedure
Amnioinfusion 59070
Cord Occlusion 59072
Fluid Drainage 59074
Shunt Placement 59076
Unlisted Fetal Invasive Procedure 59897
Unlisted Laparoscopy Procedure 59898
Unlisted Procedure, Maternity Care
and Delivery 59899

Fetal Testing
Amniotic Fluid
    Lung Maturity 83661, 83663-83664
Heart 76825-76826
    Doppler
        Complete 76827
        Follow-up or Repeat Study 76828
Hemoglobin 83030-83033, 85460
Ultrasound 76801-76828
    Heart 76825
    Middle Cerebral Artery 76821
    Umbilical Artery 76820

Fetuin
See Alpha-Fetoprotein

Fever, Australian Q
See Q Fever

Fever, Japanese River
See Scrub Typhus

Fibrillation
Atrial 33253

Fibrillation, Heart
See Heart, Fibrillation

Fibrin Degradation
Products 85362-85380

Fibrin Deposit
Removal 32150

Fibrin Stabilizing
Factor 85290-85291

Fibrinase
See Plasmin

Fibrinogen 85384-85385

Fibrinolysin
See Plasmin

Fibrinolysins 85390

Fibrinolysis
Alpha-2 Antiplasmin .... .85410
Assay .... .85396
Plasmin .... .85400
Plasminogen 85420-85421
Plasminogen Activator .... .85415

Fibroadenoma
Ablation
   Cryosurgical .... .0120T
Excision 19120-19126

Fibroblastoma, Arachnoidal
See Meningioma

Fibrocutaneous Tags 11200-11201

Fibromatosis, Dupuytren's
See Dupuytren's Contracture

Fibromatosis, Penile
See Peyronie Disease

Fibromyoma
See Leiomyomata

Fibronectin, Fetal .... .82731

Fibrosis, Penile
See Peyronie Disease

Fibrosis, Retroperitoneal
See Retroperitoneal Fibrosis

Fibrous Cavernitides
See Peyronie Disease

Fibrous Dysplasia ... .21029, 21181-21184

Fibula
See Ankle; Knee; Tibia
Bone Graft with Microvascular
Anastomosis .... .20955
Craterization .... .27360, 27641
Cyst
   Excision 27635-27638
Diaphysectomy .... .27360, 27641
Excision .... .27360, 27641
   Epiphyseal Bar .... .20150
Fracture
   Malleolus 27786-27814
   Shaft 27780-27784
Incision .... .27607
Osteoplasty
   Lengthening .... .27715
Repair
   Epiphysis 27477-27485, 27730-27742
   Osteotomy 27707-27712
Saucerization .... .27360, 27641
Tumor
   Excision 27635-27638, 27646
X-Ray .... .73590

Figure of Eight Cast .... .29049

Filariasis .... .86280

Filtering Operation
See Incision, Sclera, Fistulization; Incision and Drainage

Filtration Implant, Glaucoma
See Aqueous Shunt

Fimbrioplasty .... .58760
Laparoscopic .... .58672

Fine Needle Aspiration 10021-10022
Evaluation 88172-88173

Finger
See Phalanx, Finger
Abscess
   Bone
      Incision and Drainage .... .26034
   Incision and Drainage 26010-26011
Amputation 26951-26952
   with Exploration or Removal .... .26910
Arthrocentesis .... .20600
Arthrodesis
   Interphalangeal Joint 26860-26863
   Metacarpophalangeal Joint 26850-26852
Bone
   Incision and Drainage .... .26034
Cast .... .29086
Collection of Blood 36415-36416
Decompression .... .26035
Excision
   Constricting Ring .... .26596
   Tendon .... .26180, 26390, 26415
Insertion
   Tendon Graft .... .26392
Magnetic Resonance Imaging (MRI) ...... .73221
Reconstruction
   Extra Digit .... .26587
   Toe to Hand Transfer 26551-26556
Removal
   Implantation .... .26320
   Tube .... .26392, 26416
Repair
   Blood Vessel .... .35207
   Claw Finger .... .26499
   Extra Digit .... .26587
   Macrodactylia .... .26590
   Tendon
      Extensor 26415-26434,
             26445-26449, 26460
      Flexor 26356-26358,
             26440-26442, 26455
   Volar Plate .... .26548
   Web Finger 26560-26562
Replantation 20816-20822
Reposition .... .26555
Sesamoidectomy .... .26185
Splint 29130-29131
Strapping .... .29280
Tendon Sheath
   Excision .... .26145
   Incision .... .26055
   Incision and Drainage .... .26020
Tenotomy .... .26060, 26460
   Flexor .... .26455
Tumor
   Excision 26115-26117
Unlisted Services and Procedures .... .26989
X-Ray .... .73140

Finger Flap
Tissue Transfer .... .14350

Finger Joint
See Intercarpal Joint

Finney Operation
See Gastroduodenostomy

FISH
See Fluorescent In Situ Hybridization

Fishberg Concentration Test
See Water Load Test

Fissure in Ano
See Anus, Fissure

Fissurectomy .... .46200

Fissurectomy, Anal
See Anus, Fissure, Excision

Fistula
Anal
   Repair .... .46288, 46706
Autogenous Graft .... .36825
Bronchi
   Repair .... .32815
Carotid-Cavernous
   Repair .... .61710
Chest Wall
   Repair .... .32906
Conjunctiva
   with Tube or Stent .... .68750
   without Tube .... .68745
Enterovesical
   Closure 44660-44661
Ileoanal Pouch
   Repair 46710-46712
Kidney 50520-50526
Lacrimal Gland Closure .... .68770
   Dacryocystorhinostomy .... .68720
Nose
   Repair 30580-30600
Oval Window .... .69666
Postauricular .... .69700
Rectovaginal
   Abdominal Approach .... .57305
   Transperineal Approach .... .57308
   with Concomitant Colostomy .... .57307
Round Window .... .69667
Sclera
   Iridencleisis or Iridotasis .... .66165
   Sclerectomy with Punch or Scissors
   with Iridectomy .... .66160
   Thermocauterization with Iridectomy .. .66155
   Trabeculectomy ab Externo in
   Absence Previous Surgery .... .66170
   Trabeculectomy ab Externo with
   Scarring .... .66172
   Trephination with Iridectomy .... .66150
Suture
   Kidney 50520-50526
   Ureter 50920-50930
Trachea .... .31755
Tracheoesophageal
   Repair .... .43305, 43312, 43314
   Speech Prosthesis .... .31611
Ureter 50920-50930
Urethra 53400-53405
Urethrovaginal .... .57310
   with Bulbocavernosus Transplant ..... .57311
Vesicouterine
   Closure 51920-51925

Vesicovaginal
   Closure .... .51900
   Transvesical and Vaginal Approach ...57330
   Vaginal Approach .... .57320
X-Ray .... .76080

Fistula Arteriovenous
See Arteriovenous Fistula

Fistulectomy
Anal .... .46060, 46270-46285
   See Hemorrhoids

Fistulization
Conjunction
   to Nasal Cavity .... .68745
Esophagus 43350-43352
Intestines 44300-44346
Lacrimal Sac
   to Nasal Cavity .... .68720
Penis .... .54435
Pharynx .... .42955
Repair Salivary Cyst
Sclera
   for Glaucoma .... .0123T
Tracheopharyngeal .... .31755

Fistulization, Interatrial
See Septostomy, Atrial

Fistulotomy
Anal .... .46270, 46280

Fitting
Cervical Cap .... .57170
Contact Lens .... .92070, 92310-92313
   See Contact Lens Services
Diaphragm .... .57170
Low Vision Aid 92354-92355
   See Spectacle Services
Spectacle Prosthesis 92352-92353
Spectacles 92340-92342

Fitzgerald Factor .... .85293

Fixation
Interdental
   without Fracture .... .21497

Fixation (Device)
See Application; Bone, Fixation; Spinal
Instrumentation
Application
   External 20690-20692
Pelvic
   Insertion .... .22848
Removal
   External .... .20694
   Internal 20670-20680
Sacrospinous Ligament
   Vaginal Prolapse .... .57282
Shoulder .... .23700
Skeletal
   Humeral Epycondyle
     Percutaneous .... .24566
Spinal
   Insertion 22841-22847
   Prosthetic .... .22851
   Reinsertion .... .22849

Fixation Test, Complement
See Complement, Fixation Test

Fixation, External
See External Fixation

Fixation, Kidney
See Nephropexy

Fixation, Rectum
See Proctopexy

Fixation, Tongue
See Tongue, Fixation

Flank
See Back/Flank

Flap
See Skin Graft and Flap
Free
   Breast Reconstruction .... .19364
Grafts 15574-15650, 15842
Latissimus Dorsi
   Breast Reconstruction .... .19361
Omentum .... .49905
Omentum
   Free
     with Microvascular Anastomosis ...49906
Transverse Rectus Abdominis Myocutaneous
   Breast Reconstruction 19367-19369

Flatfoot Correction .... .28735

Flea Typhus
See Murine Typhus

Fletcher Factor .... .85292

Flow Cytometry 88184-88189

Flow-Volume Loop
See Pulmonology, Diagnostic
Pulmonary .... .94375

Flu Vaccines ...90645-90648, 90655-90660

Fluid Collection
Incision and Drainage
   Skin .... .10140

Fluid, Amniotic
See Amniotic Fluid

Fluid, Body
See Body Fluid

Fluid, Cerebrospinal
See Cerebrospinal Fluid

Fluorescein
Angiography, Ocular .... .92287
Intravenous Injection
   Vascular Flow Check, Graft .... .15860

Fluorescein Angiography
See Angiography, Fluorescein

Fluorescent In Situ
Hybridization .... .88365

Fluoride
Blood .... .82735
Urine .... .82735

Fluoroscopy
Bile Duct
   Calculus Removal .... .74327
   Guide Catheter .... .74328, 74330
Chest
   Bronchoscopy 31622-31640
   Complete (Four Views) .... .71034
   Partial (Two Views) .... .71023
Drain Abscess .... .75989
GI Tract
   Guide Intubation .... .74340
Hourly 76000-76001
Introduction
   GI Tube .... .74340
Larynx .... .70370
Nasogastric .... .43752
Needle Biopsy .... .76003
Orogastric .... .43752
Pancreatic Duct
   Guide Catheter 74329-74330
Pharynx .... .70370
Renal
   Guide Catheter .... .74475
Spine/Paraspinous
   Guide Catheter/Needle .... .76005
Unlisted Services and Procedures .... .76496
Ureter
   Guide Catheter .... .74480
Venous Access Device .... .36598, 75998
Vertebra
   Osteoplasty .... .76012

Flurazepam
Blood or Urine .... .82742

Flush Aortogram 75722-75724

FNA
See Fine Needle Aspiration

Foam Stability Test .... .83662

Fold, Vocal
See Vocal Cords

Foley Operation Pyeloplasty
See Pyeloplasty

Foley Y-Pyeloplasty 50400-50405

Folic Acid .... .82747
Blood .... .82746

Follicle Stimulating Hormone
(FSH) .... .80418, 80426, 83001

Folliculin
See Estrone

Follitropin
See Follicle Stimulating Hormone (FSH)

Follow-up Inpatient Consultations
See Consultation, Follow-up Inpatient

Follow-up Services
See Hospital Services; Office and/or Other
Outpatient Services
Post-Op .... .99024

Fontan Procedure
See Repair, Heart, Anomaly; Revision

Food Allergy Test 95075
See Allergy Tests

Foot
See Metatarsal; Tarsal
Amputation 28800-28805
Bursa
   Incision and Drainage 28001
Capsulotomy 28260-28264
Cast 29450
Fasciectomy 28060
   Radical 28060-28062
Fasciotomy 28008
   Endoscopic 29893
Incision 28002-28005
Joint
   See Talotarsal Joint; Tarsometatarsal Joint
   Magnetic Resonance Imaging
   (MRI) 73721-73723
Lesion
   Excision 28080, 28090
Magnetic Resonance Imaging
(MRI) 73718-73720
Nerve
   Excision 28030
   Incision 28035
Neuroma
   Excision 28080
Reconstruction
   Cleft Foot 28360
Removal
   Foreign Body 28190-28193
Repair
   Muscle 28250
   Tendon 28200-28230, 28234-28238
Replantation 20838
Sesamoid
   Excision 28315
Splint 29590
Strapping 29540, 29590
Suture
   Tendon 28200-28210
Tendon Sheath
   Excision 28086-28088
Tenotomy 28230, 28234
Tumor
   Excision 28043-28046
Unlisted Services and Procedures 28899
X-Ray 73620-73630

Foot Abscess
See Abscess, Foot

Foot Navicular Bone
See Navicular

Forearm 20805
See Arm, Lower

Forehead
Reconstruction 21179-21180, 21182-21184
   Midface 21159-21160
Reduction 21137-21139

Forehead and Orbital Rim
Reconstruction 21172-21180

Foreign Body Removal
Pharynx 42809
Shoulder 23331

Forensic Exam 88040
Cytopathology 88125
Phosphatase, Acid 84061

Foreskin of Penis
See Penis, Prepuce

Formycin Diphosphate
See Fibrin Degradation Products

Fournier's Gangrene
See Debridement, Skin, Subcutaneous Tissue,
Infected

Fowler-Stephens Orchiopexy
See Orchiopexy

Fowler-Stephens Procedure ...54650

Fox Operation
See Entropion, Repair

Fraction, Factor IX
See Christmas Factor

Fracture
Acetabulum
   Closed Treatment 27220-27222
   Open Treatment 27226-27228
   with Manipulation 27222
   without Manipulation 27220
Alveola
   Closed Treatment 21421
   Open Treatment 21422-21423
Alveolar Ridge
   Closed Treatment 21440
   Open Treatment 21445
Ankle
   Closed Treatment 27816-27818
   Lateral 27786-27814
   Medial 27760-27766, 27808-27814
   Open Treatment 27822-27823
   Trimalleolar 27816-27823
   with Manipulation 27818
   without Manipulation 27816
Ankle Bone
   Medial 27760-27762
Bennett's
   See Thumb, Fracture
Bronchi
   Endoscopy 31630
Calcaneus
   Closed Treatment 28400-28405
   Open Treatment 28415-28420
   Percutaneous Fixation 28436
   with Manipulation 28405-28406
   without Manipulation 28400
Carpal
   Closed Treatment
     with Manipulation 25624, 25635
     without Manipulation 25622, 25630
   Open Treatment 25628, 25645
Carpal Scaphoid
   Closed Treatment 25622
Cheekbone
   Open Treatment 21360-21366
   with Manipulation 21355

Clavicle
   Closed Treatment
     with Manipulation 23505
     without Manipulation 23500
   Open Treatment 23515
Closed Treatment 27520
Coccyx
   Closed Treatment 27200
   Open Treatment 27202
Colles
   See Colles Fracture
Colles-Reversed
   See Smith Fracture
Elbow
   Monteggia
     Closed Treatment 24620
     Open Treatment 24635
   Open Treatment 24586-24587
Femur 27244
Femur
   Closed Treatment 27230, 27238-27240,
      27246, 27500-27503, 27508,
      27510, 27516-27517
   with Manipulation 27232
   Distal 27508, 27510, 27514
   Epiphysis 27516-27519
   Intertrochanteric
     Closed Treatment 27238
     Intramedullary Implant 27245
     Treatment with Implant 27244-27245
     with Manipulation 27240
   Neck
     Closed Treatment 27230
     Open Treatment 27236
     Percutaneous Fixation 27235
     with Manipulation 27232
   Open Treatment 27245, 27248,
      27506-27507, 27511-27514, 27519
   Percutaneous Fixation 27235, 27509
   Pertrochanteric
     Closed Treatment 27238
     Intramedullary Implant Shaft 27245,
      27500, 27502, 27506-27507
     Open Treatment 27244-27245
     with Manipulation 27240
   Subtrochanteric
     Closed Treatment 27238
     Intramedullary Implant 27245
     Open Treatment 27244-27245
     with Manipulation 27240
   Supracondylar 27501-27503, 27509,
      27511-27513
   Transcondylar 27501-27503, 27509,
      27511-27513
   Trochanteric
     Closed Treatment 27246
     Open Treatment 27248
   with Manipulation 27232, 27502-27503,
      27510
   without Manipulation 27230, 27238,
      27246, 27500-27501, 27508,
      27516-27517, 27520
Fibula
   Closed Treatment 27780-27781,
      27786-27788, 27808-27810
   Malleolus 27786-27814
   Open Treatment 27784, 27792, 27814

Shaft 27780-27786, 27808
  with Manipulation 27788, 27810
  without Manipulation 27780-27781
Frontal Sinus
  Open Treatment 21343-21344
Great Toe
  Closed Treatment 28490
  without Manipulation 28490
Heel
  Open Treatment 28415-28420
  with Manipulation 28405-28406
  without Manipulation 28400
Humerus
  Closed Treatment 24500-24505
    with Manipulation 23605
    without Manipulation 23600
  Condyle
    Closed Treatment 24576-24577
    Open Treatment 24579
    Percutaneous 24582
  Epicondyle
    Closed Treatment 24560-24565
    Open Treatment 24575
    Skeletal Fixation
      Percutaneous 24566
  Greater Tuberosity Fracture
    Closed Treatment with
    Manipulation 23625
    Closed Treatment without
    Manipulation 23620
    Open Treatment 23630
  Open Treatment 23615-23616
  Shaft 24500-24505, 24516
    Open Treatment 24515
  Supracondylar
    Closed Treatment 24530-24535
    Open Treatment 24545-24546
    Percutaneous Fixation 24538
  Transcondylar
    Closed Treatment 24530-24535
    Open Treatment 24545-24546
    Percutaneous Fixation 24538
  with Dislocation
    Closed Treatment 23665
    Open Treatment 23670
  with Shoulder Dislocation
    Closed Treatment 23675
    Open Treatment 23680
Hyoid Bone
  Open Treatment 21495
Ilium
  Open Treatment 27215, 27218
  Percutaneous Fixation 27216
Knee 27520
  Arthroscopic Treatment 29850-29851
  Open Treatment 27524
Larynx
  Open Treatment 31584
Malar Area
  Open Treatment 21360-21366
  with Bone Graft 21366
  with Manipulation 21355

Mandible
  Closed Treatment
    Interdental Fixation 21453
    with Manipulation 21451
    without Manipulation 21450
  Open Treatment 21454-21470
    External Fixation 21454
    with Interdental Fixation 21462
    without Interdental Fixation 21461
  Percutaneous Treatment 21452
Maxilla
  Closed Treatment 21421
  Open Treatment 21422-21423
Metacarpal
  Closed Treatment 26600-26605
    with Fixation 26607
  Open Treatment 26615
  Percutaneous Fixation 26608
  with Manipulation 26605-26607
  without Manipulation 26600
Metatarsal
  Closed Treatment 28470-28475
  Open Treatment 28485
  Percutaneous Fixation 28476
  with Manipulation 28475-28476
  without Manipulation 28450, 28470
Monteggia
  See Fracture, Ulna; Monteggia Fracture
Nasal Bone
  Closed Treatment 21310-21320
  Open Treatment 21325-21335
  with Manipulation 21315-21320
  without Manipulation 21310
Nasal Septum
  Closed Treatment 21337
  Open Treatment 21336
Nasal Turbinate
  Therapeutic 30930
Nasoethmoid
  Open Treatment 21338-21339
  Percutaneous Treatment 21340
  with Fixation 21340
Nasomaxillary
  Closed Treatment 21345
  Open Treatment 21346-21348
  with Bone Grafting 21348
  with Fixation 21345-21347
Navicular
  Closed Treatment 25622
  Open Treatment 25628
  with Manipulation 25624
Odontoid
  Open Treatment
    with Graft 22319
    without Graft 22318
Orbit
  Closed Treatment
    with Manipulation 21401
    without Manipulation 21400
  Open Treatment 21406-21408
    Blowout Fracture 21385-21395
Orbital Floor
  Blow Out 21385-21395
Palate
  Closed Treatment 21421
  Open Treatment 21422-21423

Patella
  Closed Treatment
    without Manipulation 27520
  Open Treatment 27524
Pelvic Ring
  Closed Treatment 27193-27194
  Open Treatment
    Anterior 27217
    Posterior 27218
  Percutaneous Fixation 27216
  without Manipulation 27193-27194
Phalanges
  Articular
    Closed Treatment 26740
    Open Treatment 26746
    with Manipulation 26742
  Closed Treatment 26742, 28510
    Articular 26740
    Distal 26750
    with Manipulation 26755
  Distal 26755-26756
    Closed Treatment 26750
    Open Treatment 26765
    Percutaneous Fixation 26756
  Finger/Thumb
    Closed Treatment 26720-26725
    Shaft 26720, 26727
    with Manipulation 26725-26727
  Great Toe 28490
    Closed Treatment 28495
    Open Treatment 28505
    Percutaneous Fixation 28496
    with Manipulation 28495-28496
  Open Treatment 26735, 26746
    Distal 26765
  Shaft
    Closed Treatment 26725
    Open Treatment 26735
    Percutaneous Fixation 26727
  Toe
    Closed Treatment 28515
    Open Treatment 28525
    with Manipulation 28515
    without Manipulation 28510
  with Manipulation 26742, 26755
  without Manipulation 26740, 26750
Radius
  Closed Treatment 25560-25565
  Colles 25600-25605
  Distal 25600-25611
    Open Treatment 25620
    Smith 25600-25620
  Head/Neck
    Closed Treatment 24650-24655
    Open Treatment 24665-24666
  Open Treatment 25515, 25620
  Percutaneous Fixation 25611
  Shaft 25500, 25525-25526
    Closed Treatment . . .25500-25505, 25520
    Open Treatment 25515, 25525-25526,
                        25574
  with Manipulation 25565, 25605
  with Ulna 25560-25565
    Open Treatment 25575
  without Manipulation 25560, 25600

Rib
   Closed Treatment 21800
   External Fixation 21810
   Open Treatment 21805
Scaphoid
   Closed Treatment 25622
   Open Treatment 25628
   with Dislocation
      Closed Treatment 25680
      Open Treatment 25685
   with Manipulation 25624
Scapula
   Closed Treatment
      with Manipulation 23575
      without Manipulation 23570
   Open Treatment 23585
Sesamoid
   Closed Treatment 28530
   Foot 28530-28531
   Open Treatment 28531
Skin
   Debridement 11010-11012
Skull 62000-62010
   Closed Treatment 21300
Sternum
   Closed Treatment 21820
   Open Treatment 21825
Talus
   Closed Treatment 28430-28435
   Open Treatment 28445
   with Manipulation 28435-28436
   without Manipulation 28430
Tarsal
   Open Treatment 28465
   Percutaneous Fixation 28456
   with Manipulation 28455-28456
Thumb
   with Dislocation 26645-26650
   Open Treatment 26665
Tibia 27759
Tibia
   Arthroscopic Treatment 29855-29856
   Closed Treatment 27530-27532, 27538,
            27750-27752, 27760-27762,
            27808-27810, 27824-27825
   Distal 27824-27828
   Intercondylar 27538-27540
   Malleolus 27760-27766, 27808-27814
   Open Treatment 27535-27536, 27540,
          27758, 27766, 27814, 27826-27828
   Percutaneous Fixation 27756
   Plateau 27530-27536, 29855-29856
   Shaft 27750-27759
   with Manipulation 27752, 27760-27762,
                         27810
   without Manipulation 27530, 27750,
           27760-27762, 27808, 27825
Trachea
   Endoscopy .31630
Ulna
   See Elbow; Humerus; Radius
   Closed Treatment 25560-25565
   Olecranon
      Closed Treatment 24670-24675
      Open Treatment 24685
   Open Treatment 25574-25575

Shaft
   Closed Treatment 25530-25535
   Open Treatment 25545, 25574
Styloid Process
   Closed Cell 25650
   Open Treatment 25652
   Percutaneous Fixation 25651
   with Dislocation
      Closed Treatment 24620
      Monteggia 24620-24635
      Open Treatment 24635
   with Manipulation 25535, 25565
   with Radius 25560-25565
   Open Treatment 25575
   without Manipulation 25530, 25560
Vertebra
   Additional Segment
      Open Treatment 22328
   Cervical
      Open Treatment 22326
   Closed Treatment
      with Manipulation, Casting and/or
      Bracing 22315
      without Manipulation 22310
   Lumbar
      Open Treatment 22325
   Posterior
      Open Treatment 22325-22327
   Thoracic
      Open Treatment 22327
   with Shoulder Dislocation
      Closed Treatment 23675
      Open Treatment 23680
Vertebral Process
   Closed Treatment 22305
Wrist
   with Dislocation
      Closed Treatment 25680
      Open Treatment 25685
Zygomatic Arch
   Open Treatment 21356-21366
   with Manipulation 21355

Fragile-X
Chromosome Analysis 88248

Fragility
Red Blood Cell
   Mechanical 85547
   Osmotic 85555-85557

Frames, Stereotactic
See Stereotactic Frame

Francisella 86000
Antibody 86668

Fredet-Ramstedt Procedure 43520

Free E3
See Estriol

Free Skin Graft
See Skin, Grafts, Free

Free T4
See Thyroxine, Free

Frei Disease
See Lymphogranuloma Venereum

Frenectomy 40819, 41115

Frenectomy, Lingual
See Excision, Tongue, Frenum

Frenotomy 40806, 41010

Frenulectomy 40819

Frenuloplasty 41520

Frenum
Lip
   Incision 40806
      See Lip

Frenumectomy 40819

Frickman Operation
See Proctopexy

Frontal Craniotomy 61556

Frontal Sinus
See Sinus, Frontal

Frontal Sinusotomy
See Exploration, Sinus, Frontal

Frost Suture 67875

**Frozen Blood
Preparation** 86930-86932

Fructose .84375
Semen 82757

**Fructose Intolerance
Breath Test** 91065

Fruit Sugar
See Fructose

FSF 85290-85291

FSH
See Follicle Stimulating Hormone (FSH)

FSP
See Fibrin Degradation Products

FT-4 84439

Fulguration
See Destruction
Bladder 51020
Cystourethroscopy with 52214
   Lesion .52224
   Tumor 52234-52240
Ureter 50957, 50976
Ureterocele
   Ectopic 52301
   Orthotopic 52300

Fulguration, Endocavitary
See Electrocautery

Full Thickness Graft 15200-15261

Function Test, Lung
See Pulmonology, Diagnostic

Function Test, Vestibular
See Vestibular Function Tests

Function, Study, Nasal
See Nasal Function Study

Functional Ability
See Activities of Daily Living

Fundoplasty
Esophagogastric 43324-43325
   Laparoscopic 43280
   with Gastroplasty 43326

Fundoplication
See Fundoplasty, Esophagogastric

Fungus
Antibody 86671
Culture
   Blood 87103
   Hair 87101
   Identification 87106
   Nail 87101
   Other 87102
   Skin 87101
Tissue Exam 87220

Funnel Chest
See Pectus Excavatum

Furuncle
Incision and Drainage 10060-10061

Furuncle, Vulva
See Abscess, Vulva

Fusion
See Arthrodesis
Pleural Cavity 32005
Thumb
   in Opposition 26820

Fusion, Epiphyseal-Diaphyseal
See Epiphyseal Arrest

Fusion, Joint
See Arthrodesis

Fusion, Joint, Ankle
See Ankle, Arthrodesis

Fusion, Joint, Interphalangeal, Finger
See Arthrodesis, Finger Joint, Interphalangeal

G

Gago Procedure
See Repair, Tricuspid Valve; Revision

Gait Training 97116
See Physical Medicine/Therapy/Occupational Therapy

Galactogram 76086-76088
Injection 19030

Galactokinase
Blood 82759

Galactose
Blood 82760
Urine 82760

Galactose-1-Phosphate
Uridyl Transferase 82775-82776

Gall Bladder
See Gallbladder

Gallbladder
See Bile Duct
Anastomosis
   with Intestines 47720-47741
Excision 47562-47564, 47600-47620
Exploration 47480
Incision 47490
Incision and Drainage 47480
Nuclear Medicine
   Imaging 78223
Removal
   Calculi (Stone) 47480
Repair
   with Gastroenterostomy 47741
   with Intestines 47720-47740
Unlisted Services and Procedures 47999
X-Ray with Contrast 74290-74291

Galvanocautery
See Electrocautery

Galvanoionization
See Iontophoresis

Gamete Intrafallopian Transfer (GIFT) 58976

Gamete Transfer
In Vitro Fertilization 58976

Gamma Camera Imaging
See Nuclear Medicine

Gamma Glutamyl Transferase 82977

Gamma Seminoprotein
See Antigen, Prostate Specific

Gammacorten
See Dexamethasone

Gammaglobulin
Blood 82784-82787

Gamulin Rh
See Immune Globulins, Rho (D)

Ganglia, Trigeminal
See Gasserian Ganglion

Ganglion
See Gasserian Ganglion
Cyst
   Aspiration/Injection 20612
   Drainage 20612
   Wrist
      Excision 25111-25112
Injection
   Anesthetic 64505, 64510

Ganglion Cervicothoracicum
See Stellate Ganglion

Ganglion Pterygopalatinum
See Sphenopalatine Ganglion

Ganglion, Gasser's
See Gasserian Ganglion

Gardner Operation
See Meningocele Repair

Gardnerella Vaginalis Detection 87510-87512

Gasser Ganglion
See Gasserian Ganglion

Gasserian Ganglion
Sensory Root
   Decompression 61450
   Section 61450
Stereotactic 61790

Gastrectomy
Partial 43631-43635, 43845
   with Gastrojejunostomy 43632
Total 43621-43622
   with Esophagoenterostomy 43620
with Gastroduodenostomy 43631

Gastric Acid 82926-82928

Gastric Analysis Test 91052

Gastric Intubation ...89130-89141, 91105

Gastric Lavage, Therapeutic ...91105

Gastric Tests
Manometry 91020

Gastric Ulcer Disease
See Stomach, Ulcer

Gastrin 82938-82941

Gastrocnemius Recession
Leg, Lower 27687

Gastroduodenostomy 43810, 43850-43855

Gastroenterology, Diagnostic
Breath Hydrogen Test 91065
Esophagus Tests
   Acid Perfusion 91030
   Acid Reflux 91034-91038
   Balloon Distension Provocation Study .91040
   Intubation with Specimen Collection ..91000
   Motility Study 91010-91012
Gastric Tests
   Manometry 91020
Gastroesophageal Reflux Test
   See Acid Reflux
Intestine
   Bleeding Tube 91100
Manometry 91020
Rectum
   Sensation, Tone, and Compliance Test .91120
Rectum/Anus
   Manometry 91122

Stomach
  Intubation with Specimen Prep 91055
  Saline Load Test 91060
  Stimulation of Secretion 91052
Unlisted Services and Procedures 91299

Gastroenterostomy
for Obesity 43644-43645, 43842-43848

Gastroesophageal Reflux Test .91034-91038

Gastrointestinal Endoscopies
See Endoscopy, Gastrointestinal

Gastrointestinal Exam
Nuclear Medicine
  Blood Loss Study 78278
  Protein Loss Study 78282
  Shunt Testing 78291
  Unlisted Services and Procedures 78299

Gastrointestinal Tract
Imaging
  Intraluminal 91110
Reconstruction 43360-43361
Upper
  Dilation 43249
X-Ray 74240-74245
  Guide Dilator 74360
  Guide Intubation 74340-74350
  with Contrast 74246-74249

Gastrointestinal, Upper
Biopsy
  Endoscopy 43239
Dilation
  Endoscopy 43245
  Esophagus 43248
Endoscopy
  Catheterization 43241
  Destruction
    Lesion 43258
  Dilation 43245
  Drainage
    Pseudocyst 43240
  Exploration 43234-43235
  Hemorrhage 43255
  Inject Varices 43243
  Injection 0133T, 43236
  Needle Biopsy 43238, 43242
  Removal
    Foreign Body 43247
    Lesion 43251
    Polyp 43251
    Tumor 43251
  Stent Placement 43256
  Suturing
    Esophagogastric junction 0008T
  Thermal Radiation 43257
  Tube Placement 43246
  Ultrasound 43237-43238,
                              43242, 43259, 76975
Exploration
  Endoscopy 43234-43235
Hemorrhage
  Endoscopic Control 43255
Injection
  Submucosal 43236
  Varices 43243

Lesion
  Destruction 43258
Ligation of Vein 43244
Needle Biopsy
  Endoscopy 43238, 43242
Removal
  Foreign Body 43247
  Lesion 43250
  Polyp 43250-43251
  Tumor 43250
Tube Placement
  Endoscopy 43246
Ultrasound
  Endoscopy 43237-43238,
                              43242, 43259, 76975

Gastrojejunostomy 43860-43865
with Duodenal Exclusion 48547
with Partial Gastrectomy 43632
with Vagotomy 43825
without Vagotomy 43820

Gastroplasty
Revision
  for Obesity 43644-43645, 43842-43848

Gastroplasty with Esophagogastric Fundoplasty 43326, 43842-43843

Gastrorrhaphy 43840

Gastroschises
See Gastroschisis

Gastroschisis 49605

Gastrostomy
Closure 43870
Laparoscopic
  Temporary 43653
Temporary .43830
  Laparoscopic 43653
  Neonatal 43831
with Pancreatic Drain 48001
with Pyloroplasty 43640
with Vagotomy 43640

Gastrostomy Tube
Change of .43760
Directed Placement
  Endoscopic 43246
Insertion
  Percutaneous 43750
Percutaneous 43750
Repositioning 43761

Gastrotomy 43500-43501, 43510

GDH
See Glutamate Dehydrogenase

Gel Diffusion 86331

Gel Diffusion Test
See Immunodiffusion

Gene Product
See Protein

Genioplasty 21120-21123
Augmentation 21120, 21123
Osteotomy 21121-21123

Genitourinary Sphincter, Artificial
See Prosthesis, Urethral Sphincter

Genotype Analysis
by Nucleic Acid
  Infectious Agent
    Hepatitis C Virus 87902
    HIV-1 Protease/Reverse
    Transcriptase 87901

Gentamicin 80170
Assay 80170

Gentamycin Level
See Gentamicin

Gentiobiase
See Beta Glucosidase

Genus: Human Cytomegalovirus Group
See Cytomegalovirus

GERD
See Gastroesophageal Reflux Test

German Measles
See Rubella

Gestational Trophoblastic Tumor
See Hydatidiform Mole

GGT
See Gamma Glutamyl Transferase

GI Tract
See Gastrointestinal Tract

Giardia
Antigen Detection
  Enzyme Immunoassay 87329
  Immunofluorescence 87269

Giardia Lamblia
Antibody 86674

Gibbons Stent 52332

GIF
See Somatostatin

GIFT
See Gamete Intrafallopian Transfer

Gill Operation 63012

Gillies Approach
Fracture
  Zygomatic Arch 21356

Gingiva
See Gums

Gingiva, Abcess
See Abscess
Fracture
  See Abscess, Gums; Gums
  Zygomatic Arch
    See Abscess, Gums; Gums, Abscess

Gingivectomy 41820

Gingivoplasty 41872

Girdlestone Laminectomy
See Laminectomy

Girdlestone Procedure
See Acetabulum, Reconstruction

Gla Protein (Bone)
See Osteocalcin

Gland
See Specific Gland

Gland, Adrenal
See Adrenal Gland

Gland, Bartholin's
See Bartholin's Gland

Gland, Bulbourethral
See Bulbourethral Gland

Gland, Lacrimal
See Lacrimal Gland

Gland, Mammary
See Breast

Gland, Parathyroid
See Parathyroid Gland

Gland, Parotid
See Parotid Gland

Gland, Pituitary
See Pituitary Gland

Gland, Salivary
See Salivary Glands

Gland, Sublingual
See Sublingual Gland

Gland, Sweat
See Sweat Glands

Gland, Thymus
See Thymus Gland

Gland, Thyroid
See Thyroid Gland

Glasses
See Spectacle Services

Glaucoma
Cryotherapy 66720
Cyclophotocoagulation 66710-66711
Diathermy 66700
Fistulization of Sclera 66150
Provocative Test .92140

Glaucoma Drainage Implant
See Aqueous Shunt

Glenn Procedure 33766-33767

Glenohumeral Joint
Arthrotomy 23040
    with Biopsy .23100
    with Synovectomy 23105
Exploration 23107
Removal
    Foreign or Loose Body 23107

Glenoid Fossa
Reconstruction .21255

GLN
See Glutamine

Globulin
Antihuman 86880-86886
Immune .90281-90399
Sex Hormone Binding 84270

Globulin, Corticosteroid-Binding
See Transcortin

Globulin, Rh Immune
See Immune Globulins, Rho (D)

Globulin, Thyroxine-Binding
See Thyroxine Binding Globulin

Glomerular Procoagulant Activity
See Thromboplastin

Glomus Caroticum
See Carotid Body

Glossectomies
See Excision, Tongue

Glossopexy
See Tongue, Fixation

Glossorrhaphy
See Suture, Tongue

Glucagon 82943
Tolerance Panel 80422-80424
Tolerance Test .82946

Glucose 80422-80424, 80430-80435,
                                            95250-95251
Blood Test 82947-82950, 82962
Body Fluid 82945
Interstitial Fluid
    Continuous Monitoring 95250-95251
Tolerance Test 82951-82952
    with Tolbutamide 82953

Glucose Phosphate Isomerase
See Phosphohexose Isomerase

Glucose Phosphate Isomerase Measurement
See Phosphohexose Isomerase

Glucose-6-Phosphate
Dehydrogenase 82955-82960

Glucosidase 82963

Glucuronide Androstanediol . . .82154

Glue
Cornea Wound .65286
Sclera Wound 65286

Glukagon
See Glucagon

Glutamate Dehydrogenase
Blood 82965

Glutamate Pyruvate Transaminase
See Transaminase, Glutamic Pyruvic

Glutamic Alanine Transaminase
See Transaminase, Glutamic Pyruvic

Glutamic Aspartic Transaminase
See Transaminase, Glutamic Oxaloacetic

Glutamic Dehydrogenase
See Glutamate Dehydrogenase

Glutamine .82975

Glutamyltransferase, Gamma . .82977

Glutathione 82978

Glutathione Reductase 82979

Glutethimide 82980

Glycanhydrolase, N-Acetylmuramide
See Lysozyme

Glycated Hemoglobins
See Glycohemoglobin

Glycated Protein 82985

Glycerol Phosphoglycerides
See Phosphatidylglycerol

Glycerol, Phosphatidyl
See Phosphatidylglycerol

Glycerophosphatase
See Alkaline Phosphatase

Glycinate, Theophylline Sodium
See Theophylline

Glycocholic Acid
See Cholylglycine

Glycohemoglobin 83036

Glycol, Ethylene
See Ethylene Glycol

Glycols, Ethylene
See Ethylene Glycol

Glycosaminoglycan
See Mucopolysaccharides

GMP
See Guanosine Monophosphate

GMP, Cyclic
See Cyclic GMP

Goeckerman Treatment . .96910-96913

Gol-Vernet Operation
See Pyelotomy, Exploration

Gold
Assay 80172

Goldwaite Procedure 27422

Golfer's Elbow
See Tennis Elbow

Gonadectomy, Female
See Oophorectomy

Gonadectomy, Male
See Excision, Testis

Gonadotropin
Chorionic 84702-84703
FSH 83001
ICSH 83002
LH 83002

Gonadotropin Panel 80426

Gonioscopy 92020

Goniotomy 65820

Gonococcus
See Neisseria Gonorrhoeae

Goodenough Harris Drawing Test 96101-96103

GOTT
See Transaminase, Glutamic Oxaloacetic

GPUT
See Galactose-1-Phosphate, Uridyl Transferase

Graft
See Bone Graft; Bypass Graft
Anal 46753
Aorta 33840-33851, 33860-33877
Artery
   Coronary 33503-33505
Bone
   See Bone Marrow, Transplantation
   Harvesting 20900-20902
   Microvascular Anastomosis 20955-20962
   Osteocutaneous Flap with Microvascular
   Anastomosis 20969-20973
   Vascular Pedicle 25430
Bone and Skin 20969-20973
Cartilage
   Ear to Face 21235
   Harvesting 20910-20912
      See Cartilage Graft
   Rib to Face 21230
Conjunctiva 65782
   Harvesting 68371
Cornea
   with Lesion Excision 65426
Cornea Transplant
   in Aphakia 65750
   in Pseudophakia 65755
   Lamellar 65710
   Penetrating 65730
Dura
   Spinal Cord 63710
Endovascular 34900
Eye
   Amniotic Membrane 65780
   Conjunctiva 65782
   Stem Cell 65781
Facial Nerve Paralysis 15840-15845
Fascia
   Cheek 15840
Fascia Lata
   Harvesting 20920-20922
Gum Mucosa 41870
Heart
   See Heart, Transplantation

Heart Lung
   See Transplantation, Heart-Lung
Kidney
   See Kidney, Transplantation
Liver
   See Liver, Transplantation
Lung
   See Lung, Transplantation
Muscle
   Cheek 15841-15845
Nail Bed
   Reconstruction 11762
Nerve 64885-64907
Oral Mucosa 40818
Organ
   See Transplantation
Pancreas
   See Pancreas, Transplantation
Skin
   Biological
      See Allograft, Skin
   Blood Flow Check, Graft 15860
      See Skin Graft and Flap
   Harvesting
      for Tissue Culture 15040
   Vascular Flow Check, Graft 15860
Tendon
   Finger 26392
   Hand 26392
   Harvesting 20924
Tissue
   Harvesting 20926
Vein
   Cross-Over 34520

Grain Alcohol
See Alcohol, Ethyl

Granulation Tissue
Cauterization, Chemical 17250

Gravi, Myasthenia
See Myasthenia Gravis

Gravities, Specific
See Specific Gravity

Great Toe
Free Osteocutaneous Flap with
Microvascular Anastomosis 20973

Great Vessels
Shunt
   Aorta to Pulmonary Artery
      Ascending 33755
      Descending 33762
   Central 33764
   Subclavian to Pulmonary Artery 33750
   Vena Cava to Pulmonary Artery . 33766-33767
Unlisted Services and Procedures 33999

Great Vessels Transposition
See Transposition, Great Arteries

Greater Tuberosity Fracture
with Shoulder Dislocation
   Closed Treatment 23665
   Open Treatment 23670

Greater Vestibular Gland
See Bartholin's Gland

Green Operation
See Scapulopexy

Gridley Stain 88312

Grippe, Balkan
See Q Fever

Gritti Operation
See Amputation, Leg, Upper; Radical Resection;
Replantation

Groin Area
Repair
   Hernia 49550-49557

Group Health Education . 98961-98962,
                                 99078

Grouping, Blood
See Blood Typing

Growth Factors, Insulin-Like
See Somatomedin

Growth Hormone 83003
Human 80418, 80428-80430, 86277

Growth Hormone Release Inhibiting Factor
See Somatostatin

GTT
See Hydatidiform Mole

Guaiac Test
See Blood, Feces

Guanosine Monophosphate 83008

Guanosine Monophosphate, Cyclic
See Cyclic GMP

Guanylic Acids
See Guanosine Monophosphate

Guard Stain 88313

Gullet
See Esophagus

Gums
Abscess
   Incision and Drainage 41800
Alveolus
   Excision 41830
Cyst
   Incision and Drainage 41800
Excision
   Gingiva 41820
   Operculum 41821
Graft
   Mucosa 41870
Hematoma
   Incision and Drainage 41800
Lesion
   Destruction 41850
   Excision 41822-41828
Mucosa
   Excision 41828
Reconstruction
   Alveolus 41874
   Gingiva 41872

Removal
      Foreign Body 41805
Tumor
      Excision 41825-41827
Unlisted Services and Procedures 41899

Gunning-Lieben Test
See Acetone, Blood or Urine

Guthrie Test 84030

H

H Flu
See Hemophilus Influenza

H-Reflex Study 95934-95936

HAA (Hepatitis Associated Antigen)
See Hepatitis Antigen, B Surface

HAAb
See Antibody, Hepatitis

Haemoglobin F
See Fetal Hemoglobin

Haemorrhage
See Hemorrhage

Haemorrhage Rectum
See Hemorrhage, Rectum

Hageman Factor 85280

HAI Test
See Hemagglutination Inhibition Test

Hair
Electrolysis 17380
KOH Examination 87220
Microscopic Evaluation 96902
Transplant
      Punch Graft 15775-15776
      Strip Graft 15220-15221

Hair Removal
See Removal, Hair

Hallux
See Great Toe

Halo
Body Cast 29000
Cranial 20661
      for Thin Skull Osteology 20664
Femur 20663
Maxillofacial 21100
Pelvic 20662
Removal 20665

Haloperidol
Assay 80173

Halsted Mastectomy
See Mastectomy, Radical

Halsted Repair
See Hernia, Repair, Inguinal

Ham Test
See Hemolysins

Hammertoe Repair 28285-28286

Hamster Penetration Test 89329

Hand
See Carpometacarpal Joint; Intercarpal Joint
Amputation
      at Metacarpal 25927
      at Wrist 25920
         Revision 25922
      Revision 25924, 25929-25931
Arthrodesis
      Carpometacarpal Joint 26843-26844
      Intercarpal Joint 25820-25825
Bone
      Incision and Drainage 26034
Cast 29085
Decompression 26035-26037
Fracture
      Metacarpal 26600
Insertion
      Tendon Graft 26392
Magnetic Resonance Imaging
(MRI) 73218-73223
Reconstruction
      Tendon Pulley 26500-26504
Removal
      Implantation 26320
      Tube/Rod 26390-26392, 26416
Repair
      Blood Vessel 35207
      Cleft Hand 26580
      Muscle 26591-26593
Tendon
      Extensor 26410-26416, 26426-26428,
                                26433-26437
      Flexor 26350-26358, 26440
      Profundus 26370-26373
Replantation 20808
Strapping 29280
Tendon
      Excision 26390
      Extensor 26415
Tenotomy 26450, 26460
Tumor
      Excision 26115-26117
Unlisted Services and Procedures 26989
X-Ray 73120-73130

Hand Abscess
See Abscess, Hand

Hand Phalange
See Finger, Bone

Hand(s) Dupuytrens Contracture(s)
See Dupuytren's Contracture

Handling
Device 99002
Radioelement 77790
Specimen 99000-99001

Hanganutziu Deicher Antibodies
See Antibody, Heterophile

Haptoglobin 83010-83012

Hard Palate
See Palate

Harelip Operation
See Cleft Lip, Repair

Harii Procedure 25430

Harrington Rod
Insertion 22840
Removal 22850

Hartmann Procedure
Laparoscopic 44206
Open 44143

Harvesting
Bone Graft 20900-20902
Bone Marrow 38230
Cartilage Graft 20910-20912
Conjunctival Graft 68371
Eggs
      In Vitro Fertilization 58970
Endoscopic
      Vein for Bypass Graft 33508
Fascia Lata Graft 20920-20922
Intestines 44132-44133
Kidney 50300-50320, 50547
Liver 47133, 47140-47142
Lower Extremity Vein
      for Vascular Reconstruction 35572
Skin
      for Tissue Culture 15040
Stem Cell 38205-38206
Tendon Graft 20924
Tissue Grafts 20926
Upper Extremity Artery
      for Coronary Artery Bypass Graft 35600
Upper Extremity Vein
      for Bypass Graft 35500

Hauser Procedure 27420

Hayem's Elementary Corpuscle
See Blood, Platelet

Haygroves Procedure
See Reconstruction, Acetabulum; Revision

HBcAb
See Antibody, Hepatitis

HBeAb
See Antibody, Hepatitis

HBeAg
See Hepatitis Antigen, Be

HBsAb
See Antibody, Hepatitis

HBsAg (Hepatitis B Surface Antigen)
See Hepatitis Antigen, B Surface

HCG
See Chorionic Gonadotropin

HCO3
See Bicarbonate

HCV Antibodies
See Antibody, Hepatitis C

HDL
See Lipoprotein

Head
Angiography 70496, 70544-70546
CT Scan 70450-70470, 70496
Excision 21015-21070
Fracture and/or Dislocation 21300-21497
Incision 21010, 61316, 62148
Introduction or Removal 21076-21116
Lipectomy, Suction Assisted 15876
Magnetic Resonance Angiography
(MRA) 70544-70546
Nerve
    Graft 64885-64886
Other Procedures 21299, 21499
Repair/Revision and/or
Reconstruction 21120-21296
Ultrasound Exam 76506, 76536
Unlisted Services and Procedures 21499
X-Ray 70350

Head Rings, Stereotactic
See Stereotactic Frame

Headbrace
Application 21100
Application/Removal 20661

Heaf Test
See TB Test

Health Behavior
See Evaluation and Management, Health
Behavior

Health Risk Assessment Instrument
See Preventive Medicine

Hearing Aid
Bone Conduction
    Implantation 69710
    Removal 69711
    Repair 69711
    Replacement 69710

Hearing Aid Check 92592-92593

Hearing Aid Services
Electroacoustic Test 92594-92595
Examination 92590-92591

Hearing Tests
See Audiologic Function Tests; Hearing
Evaluation

Hearing Therapy 92507-92508,
                                92601-92604

Heart
Ablation
    Ventricular Septum
        Non-surgical 0024T
Allograft Preparation 33933
Angiography
    Injection 93542-93543
        See Cardiac Catheterization; Injection

Aortic Arch
    with Cardiopulmonary Bypass 33853
    without Cardiopulmonary Bypass 33852
Aortic Valve
    Repair
        Left Ventricle 33414
        Replacement 33405-33413
Arrhythmogenic Focus
    Catheter Ablation 93650-93652
    Destruction 33250-33251, 33261
Atria
    See Atria
Biopsy 93505
    Imaging Guidance 76932
    Ultrasound
        Imaging Guidance 76932
Blood Vessel
    Repair 33320-33322
Cardiac Output Measurements 0104T-0105T,
                                93561-93562
Cardiac Rehabilitation 93797-93798
Cardioassist 92970-92971
    Ventricular Assist Device
        Extracorporeal 0049T
Cardiopulmonary Bypass
    with Lung Transplant 32852, 32854
Catheterization 93501, 93510-93533
    Combined Right and Retrograde Left
        for Congenital Cardiac Anomalies ...93531
    Combined Right and Transseptal Left for
        Congenital Cardiac
        Anomalies 93532-93533
    Flow Directed 93503
    Right
        for Congenital Cardiac Anomalies ...93530
            See Catheterization, Cardiac
Closure
    Septal Defect 33615
    Valve
        Atrioventricular 33600
        Semilunar 33602
Commissurotomy
    Right Ventricle 33476-33478
Destruction
    Arrhythmogenic Focus 33250, 33261
Electrical Recording
    3-D Mapping 93613
    Acoustic Heart Sound ...0068T-0069T, 0070T
    Atria 93602
    Atrial Electrogram, Esophageal
    (or Trans-esophageal) 93615-93616
    Bundle of His 93600
    Comprehensive 93619-93622
    Right Ventricle 93603
    Tachycardia Sites 93609
Electroconversion 92960-92961
Electrophysiologic Follow-up Study 93624
Excision
    Donor 33930, 33940
    Tricuspid Valve 33460
Exploration 33310-33315
Fibrillation
    Atrial 33253
Great Vessels
    See Great Vessels
Heart-Lung Bypass
    See Cardiopulmonary Bypass

Heart-Lung Transplantation
    See Transplantation, Heart-Lung
Hemodynamic Monitoring
    Non-invasive 0086T
Implantation
    Artificial Heart
        Intracorporeal 0051T
    Total Replacement Heart System
        Intracorporeal 0051T
    Ventricular Assist Device 33976
        Extracorporeal 0048T
        Intracorporeal 33979
Incision
    Atrial 33253
    Exploration 33310-33315
Injection
    Radiologic 93542-93543
        See Cardiac Catheterization, Injection
Insertion
    Balloon Device 33973
    Defibrillator 33246
    Electrode 33210-33211, 33216-33217,
                                33224-33225
    Pacemaker 33200-33208
    Catheter 33210
    Pulse Generator 33212-33213
    Ventricular Assist Device 33975
Intraoperative Pacing and Mapping 93631
Ligation
    Fistula 37607
Magnetic Resonance Imaging
(MRI) 75552-75553
Mitral Valve
    See Mitral Valve
Muscle
    See Myocardium
Myocardium
    Imaging 78466-78469
    Perfusion Study 78460-78465
Nuclear Medicine
    Blood Flow Study 78414
    Blood Pool Imaging 78472-78473,
                        78481-78483, 78494-78496
    Myocardial Imaging 78466-78469
    Myocardial Perfusion 78460-78465
    Shunt Detection 78428
    Unlisted Services and Procedures 78499
Open Chest Massage 32160
Output
    See Cardiac Output
Pacemaker
    Conversion 33214
    Insertion 33200-33208
        Pulse Generator 33212-33213
    Removal 33233-33237
    Replacement 33206-33208
    Catheter 33210
    Upgrade 33214
Pacing
    Arrhythmia Induction 93618
    Atria 93610
    Transcutaneous
        Temporary 92953
        Ventricular 93612
Pacing Cardioverter-Defibrillator
    Evaluation and Testing 93640-93642,
                                93740-93745

Insertion Single/Dual Chamber
Electrodes 33216-33217,
33224-33225, 33245-33249
Pulse Generator 33240, 33246
Repositioning Single/Dual Chamber
Electrodes 33215, 33226
Wearable Device 93741-93742, 93745
Positron Emission Tomography (PET) 78459
Perfusion Study 78491-78492
Pulmonary Valve
See Pulmonary Valve
Rate Increase
See Tachycardia
Reconstruction
Atrial Septum 33735-33737
Vena Cava 34502
Recording, Acoustic 0068T
Reduction
Ventricular Septum
Non-surgical 0024T
Removal
Balloon Device 33974
Electrode 33238
Ventricular Assist Device 33977-33978
Extracorporeal 0050T
Intracorporeal 33980
Removal Single/Dual Chamber
Electrodes 33243-33244
Pulse Generator 33241
Repair .33218-33220
Repair
Anomaly 33615-33617
Aortic Sinus 33702-33722
Artificial Heart
Intracorporeal 0052T, 0053T
Atrial Septum 33253, 33641, 33647
Atrioventricular Canal 33660-33665
Complete 33670
Prosthetic Valve 33670
Atrioventricular Valve 33660-33665
Cor Triatriatum 33732
Electrode 33218
Fenestration .93580
Infundibular 33476-33478
Mitral Valve 33420-33430
Myocardium .33542
Outflow Tract 33476-33478
Postinfarction 33542-33545
Prosthetic Valve Dysfunction 33496
Septal Defect 33608-33610, 33660,
33813-33814, 93581
Sinus of Valsalva 33702-33722
Sinus Venosus 33645
Tetralogy of Fallot 33692-33697, 33924
Total Replacement Heart System
Intracorporeal 0052T, 0053T
Tricuspid Valve 33463-33468
Ventricle 33548, 33611-33612
Obstruction 33619
Ventricular Septum 33545, 33647,
33681-33688, 33692-33697, 93581
Ventricular Tunnel 33722
Wound 33300-33305
Replacement
Artificial Heart
Intracorporeal 0052T, 0053T
Electrode 33210-33211, 33217
Mitral Valve 33430

Total Replacement Heart System
Intracorporeal 0052T, 0053T
Tricuspid Valve 33465
Repositioning
Electrode 33215, 33217, 33226
Tricuspid Valve 33468
Resuscitation .92950
Septal Defect
See Septal Defect
Stimulation and Pacing 93623
Thrombectomy 33310-33315
Transplantation 33935, 33945
Allograft Preparation 33933, 33944
Tricuspid Valve
See Tricuspid Valve
Tumor
Excision 33120-33130
Unlisted Services and Procedures 33999
Ventriculography
See Ventriculography
Ventriculomyectomy 33416
Wound
Repair 33300-33305

Heart Sounds

Acoustic Recording
with Computer Analysis . .0068T-0069T, 0070T

Heart Vessels

Angioplasty
Percutaneous 92982-92984
See Angioplasty; Percutaneous
Transluminal Angioplasty
Insertion
Graft 33330-33335
Thrombolysis 92975-92977
Valvuloplasty
See Valvuloplasty
Percutaneous 92986-92990

Heat Unstable Haemoglobin

See Hemoglobin, Thermolabile

Heavy Lipoproteins

See Lipoprotein

Heavy Metal 83015-83018

Heel

See Calcaneus
Collection of Blood 36415-36416
X-Ray 73650

Heel Bone

See Calcaneus

Heel Fracture

See Calcaneus, Fracture

Heel Spur

Excision 28119

Heine Operation

See Cyclodialysis

Heine-Medin Disease

See Polio

Heinz Bodies 85441-85445

Helicobacter Pylori

Antibody 86677
Antigen Detection
Enzyme Immunoassay 87338-87339
Blood Test 83009
Breath Test 78267-78268, 83013-83014
Stool 87338
Urease Activity 83009, 83013-83014

Heller Operation

See Esophagomyotomy

Heller Procedure 32665, 43330-43331

Helminth

Antibody 86682

Hemagglutination Inhibition Test 86280

Hemangioma

See Lesion, Skin; Tumor

Hemapheresis

See Apheresis

Hematochezia

See Blood, Feces

Hematologic Test

See Blood Tests

Hematology

Unlisted Services and Procedures 85999

Hematoma

Ankle 27603
Arm, Lower 25028
Arm, Upper
Incision and Drainage 23930
Brain
Drainage 61154-61156
Evacuation 61312-61315
Incision and Drainage 61312-61315
Drain 61108
Ear, External
Complicated 69005
Simple 69000
Elbow
Incision and Drainage 23930
Epididymis
Incision and Drainage 54700
Gums
Incision and Drainage 41800
Hip 26990
Incision and Drainage
Neck 21501-21502
Skin 10140
Thorax 21501-21502
Knee 27301
Leg, Lower 27603
Leg, Upper 27301
Mouth 41005-41009, 41015-41018
Incision and Drainage 40800-40801
Nasal Septum
Incision and Drainage 30020
Nose
Incision and Drainage 30000, 30020
Pelvis 26990

Scrotum
  Incision and Drainage 54700
Shoulder
  Drainage 23030
Skin
  Incision and Drainage 10140
  Puncture Aspiration 10160
Subdural 61108
Subungual
  Evacuation 11740
Testis
  Incision and Drainage 54700
Tongue 41000-41006, 41015
Vagina
  Incision and Drainage 57022-57023
Wrist 25028

Hematopoietic Stem Cell Transplantation
See Stem Cell, Transplantation

Hematopoietin
See Erythropoietin

Hematuria
See Blood, Urine

Hemic System
Unlisted Procedure 38999

Hemiepiphyseal Arrest
Elbow 24470

Hemifacial Microsomia
Reconstruction
  Mandibular Condyle 21247

Hemilaminectomy 63020-63044

Hemilaryngectomy 31370-31382

Hemipelvectomies
See Amputation, Interpelviabdominal

Hemiphalangectomy
Toe 28160

Hemispherectomy
Partial 61543
Total 61542

Hemocytoblast
See Stem Cell

Hemodialyses
See Hemodialysis

Hemodialysis 90935-90937
Blood Flow Study 90940
Duplex Scan of Access 93990

Hemodynamic Monitoring
Non-invasive Left Ventricular 0086T

Hemofiltration 90945-90947

Hemoglobin
Analysis
  O_2 Affinity 82820
Carboxyhemoglobin 82375-82376
Chromatography 83021
Concentration .85046
Electrophoresis 83020

Fetal 83030-83033, 85460-85461
Fractionation and Quantitation 83020
Glycosylated (A1C) 83036-83037
Methemoglobin 83045-83050
Non-Automated 83026
Plasma 83051
Sulfhemoglobin 83055-83060
Thermolabile 83065-83068
Urine 83069

Hemoglobin F
Fetal
  Chemical 83030
  Qualitative 83033

Hemoglobin, Glycosylated
See Glycohemoglobin

Hemogram
Added Indices 85025-85027
Automated 85025-85027
Manual 85014-85018, 85032

Hemolysins 85475
with Agglutinins 86940-86941

Hemolytic Complement
See Complement, Hemolytic

Hemolytic Complement, Total
See Complement, Hemolytic, Total

Hemoperfusion 90997

Hemophil
See Clotting Factor

Hemophilus Influenza
Antibody 86684

Hemorrhage
Abdomen 49002
Anal
  Endoscopic Control 46614
Bladder
  Postoperative 52606
Chest Cavity
  Endoscopic Control 32654
Colon
  Endoscopic Control 44391, 45382
Colon-Sigmoid
  Endoscopic Control 45334
Esophagus
  Endoscopic Control 43227
Gastrointestinal, Upper
  Endoscopic Control 43255
Intestines, Small
  Endoscopic Control 44366, 44378
Liver
  Control 47350
Lung 32110
Nasal
  Cauterization 30901-30906
  Endoscopic Control 31238
Nasopharynx 42970-42972
Oropharynx 42960-42962
Rectum
  Endoscopic Control 45317
Throat .42960-42962

Uterus
  Postpartum .59160
Vagina 57180

Hemorrhoidectomy
Complex 46260
  with Fissurectomy 46261-46262
External Complete 46250
Ligature 46221
Simple 46255
  with Fissurectomy 46257-46258

Hemorrhoidopexy 46947

Hemorrhoids
Destruction 46934-46936
Incision
  External 46083
Injection
  Sclerosing Solution 46500
Ligation 46945-46946
Stapling 46947
Suture .46945-46946

Hemosiderin 83070-83071

Hemothorax
Thoracostomy 32020

Heparin 85520
See Clotting Inhibitors
Neutralization 85525
Protamine Tolerance Test 85530

Heparin Cofactor I
See Antithrombin III

Hepatectomy
Extensive 47122
Left Lobe 47125
Partial
  Donor 47140-47142
  Lobe 47120
Right Lobe 47130
Total
  Donor 47133

Hepatic Abscess
See Abscess, Liver

Hepatic Arteries
See Artery, Hepatic

Hepatic Artery Aneurysm
See Artery, Hepatic, Aneurysm

Hepatic Duct
Anastomosis
  with Intestines 47765, 47802
Exploration 47400
Incision and Drainage 47400
Nuclear Medicine
  Imaging 78223
Removal
  Calculi (Stone) 47400
Repair
  with Intestines 47765, 47802
Unlisted Services and Procedures 47999

Hepatic Haemorrhage
See Hemorrhage, Liver

Hepatic Portal Vein
See Vein, Hepatic Portal

Hepatic Portoenterostomies
See Hepaticoenterostomy

Hepatic Transplantation
See Liver, Transplantation

Hepaticodochotomy
See Hepaticostomy

Hepaticoenterostomy 47802

Hepaticostomy 47400

Hepaticotomy 47400

Hepatitis A and Hepatitis B 90636

Hepatitis A Vaccine
Adolescent/Pediatric
   2 Dose Schedule 90633
   3 Dose Schedule 90634
Adult Dosage 90632

Hepatitis Antibody
A 86708-86709
B
   B Core 86704-86705
   B Surface 86706
   Be 86707
C 86803-86804
Delta Agent 86692
IgG 86704, 86708
IgM 86704-86705, 86708-86709

Hepatitis Antigen
B 87515-87517
B Surface 87340-87341
Be 87350
C 87520-87522
Delta Agent 87380
G 87525-87527

Hepatitis B and Hib 90748

Hepatitis B Vaccine
Dosage
   Adolescent 90743
   Adult 90746
   Immunosuppressed 90740, 90747
   Pediatric/Adolescent 90744

Hepatitis B Virus E Antibody
See Antibody, Hepatitis

Hepatitis B Virus Surface ab
See Antibody, Hepatitis B, Surface

Hepatorrhaphy
See Liver, Repair

Hepatotomy
Abscess 47010-47011
   Percutaneous 47011
Cyst 47010-47011
   Percutaneous 47011

Hernia Repair
Abdominal 49590
   Incisional 49560
   Recurrent 49565
Diaphragmatic 39502-39541
Epigastric 49570
   Incarcerated 49572
Femoral 49550
   Incarcerated 49553
   Recurrent 49555
   Recurrent Incarcerated 49557
Incisional
   Incarcerated 49561
Inguinal 49491, 49495-49500, 49505
   Incarcerated 49492, 49496, 49501,
               49507, 49521
   Laparoscopic 49650-49651
   Recurrent 49520
   Sliding 49525
   Strangulated 49492
Lumbar 49540
Lung 32800
Orchiopexy 54640
Recurrent Incisional
   Incarcerated 49566
   Reducible 49565
Umbilicus
   Incarcerated 49582, 49587
   Reducible 49580, 49585
with Spermatic Cord 55540
   Spigelian 49590

Hernia, Cerebral
See Encephalocele

Hernia, Rectovaginal
See Rectocele

Hernia, Umbilical
See Omphalocele

Heroin Screen 82486

Heroin, Alkaloid Screening 82101

Herpes Simplex
Antibody 86696
Antigen Detection
   Immunofluorescence 87273-87274
   Nucleic Acid 87528-87530
Identification
   Smear and Stain 87207

Herpes Smear and Stain 87207

Herpes Virus-4 (Gamma), Human
See Epstein-Barr Virus

Herpes Virus-6
Detection 87531-87533

Herpetic Vesicle
Destruction 54050-54065

Heteroantibodies
See Antibody, Heterophile

Heterograft
Skin 15400-15401, 15420-15421

Heterologous Transplant
See Xenograft

Heterologous Transplantation
See Heterograft

Heterophile Antibody 86308-86310

Heterotropia
See Strabismus

Hex B
See b-Hexosaminidase

Hexadecadrol
See Dexamethasone

Hexosephosphate Isomerase
See Phosphohexose Isomerase

Heyman Procedure 27179, 28264

Hg Factor
See Glucagon

HGB
See Hemoglobin, Concentration

HGH
See Growth Hormone, Human

HHV-4
See Epstein-Barr Virus

HIAA
See Hydroxyindolacetic Acid, Urine

Hib Vaccine
4 Dose Schedule
   HbOC 90645
   PRP-T 90648
PRP-D
   Booster 90646
PRP-OMP
   3 Dose Schedule 90647

Hibb Operation
See Spinal Cord; Spine, Fusion; Vertebra;
Vertebral Body; Vertebral Process

Hickmann Catheterization
See Cannulization; Catheterization, Venous,
Central Line; Venipuncture

Hidradenitis
See Sweat Gland
Excision 11450-11471
Suppurative
   Incision and Drainage 10060-10061

High Altitude
Simulation Test 94452-94453

High Density Lipoprotein
See Lipoprotein

High Molecular Weight Kininogen
See Fitzgerald Factor

Highly Selective Vagotomy
See Vagotomy, Highly Selective

Highmore Antrum
See Sinus, Maxillary

Hill Procedure 43324
Laparoscopic 43280

Hinton Positive
See RPR

Hip

See Femur; Pelvis
Abscess
   Incision and Drainage 26990
Arthrocentesis 20610
Arthrodesis 27284-27286
Arthrography 73525
Arthroplasty 27130-27132
Arthroscopy 29860-29863
Arthrotomy 27030-27033
Biopsy 27040-27041
Bone
   Drainage 26992
Bursa
   Incision and Drainage 26991
Capsulectomy
   with Release, Flexor Muscles 27036
Cast 29305-29325
Craterization 27070
Cyst
   Excision 27065-27067
Denervation 27035
Echography
   Infant 76885-76886
Endoprosthesis
   See Prosthesis, Hip
Excision 27070
Exploration 27033
Fasciotomy 27025
Fusion 27284-27286
Hematoma
   Incision and Drainage 26990
Injection
   Radiologic 27093-27096
Reconstruction
   Total Replacement 27130
Removal
   Cast 29710
   Foreign Body 27033, 27086-27087
    Arthroscopic 29861
   Loose Body
    Arthroscopic 29861
   Prosthesis 27090-27091
Repair
   Muscle Transfer 27100-27105, 27111
   Osteotomy 27146-27156
   Tendon 27097
Saucerization 27070
Stem Prostheses
   See Arthroplasty, Hip
Strapping 29520
Tenotomy
   Abductor Tendon 27006
   Adductor Tendon 27000-27003
   Iliopsoas 27005
Total Replacement 27130-27132
Tumor
   Excision 27047-27049, 27065-27067
   Radical 27075-27076
Ultrasound
   Infant 76885-76886
X-Ray 73500-73520, 73540
   Intraoperative 73530
   with Contrast 73525

Hip Joint

Arthroplasty 27132
   Revision 27134-27138

Arthrotomy 27052
Biopsy 27052
Capsulotomy
   with Release, Flexor Muscles 27036
Dislocation 27250-27252
   Congenital 27256-27259
   Open Treatment 27253-27254
   without Trauma 27265-27266
Manipulation 27275
Reconstruction
   Revision 27134-27138
Synovium
   Excision 27054
    Arthroscopic 29863
Total Replacement 27132

Hip Stem Prostheses

See Arthroplasty, Hip

Hippocampus

Excision 61566

Histamine 83088

Histamine Release Test 86343

Histochemistry 88318-88319

Histocompatibility Testing

See Tissue Typing

Histoplasma

Antibody 86698
Antigen 87385

Histoplasma capsulatum

Antigen Detection
   Enzyme Immunoassay 87385

Histoplasmin Test

See Histoplasmosis, Skin Test

Histoplasmoses

See Histoplasmosis

Histoplasmosis

Skin Test 86510

History and Physical

See Evaluation and Management, Office and/or
Other Outpatient Services
Pelvic Exam 57410

HIV

Antibody 86701-86703
   Confirmation Test 86689

HIV-1

Antigen Detection
   Enzyme Immunoassay 87390

HIV-2

Antigen Detection
   Enzyme Immunoassay 87391

HK3 Kallikrein

See Antigen, Prostate Specific

HLA Typing 86812-86817

HMRK

See Fitzgerald Factor

HMW Kininogen

See Fitzgerald Factor

Hoffman Apparatus 20690

Hofmeister Operation

See Gastrectomy, Total

Holotranscobalamin 0103T

Holten Test

See Creatinine, Urine, Clearance

Home Services

Activities of Daily Living 99509
Catheter Care 99507
Enema Administration 99511
Established Patient 99347-99350
Hemodialysis 99512
Home Infusion Procedures 99601-99602
Individual or Family Counseling 99510
Intramuscular Injections 99506
Mechanical Ventilation 99504
New Patient 99341-99345
Newborn Care 99502
Postnatal Assessment 99501
Prenatal Monitoring 99500
Respiratory Therapy 99503
Sleep Studies 95805-95811
Stoma Care 99505
Unlisted Services and Procedures 99600

Home Visit

See House Calls

Homocyst(e)ine 83090

Urine 82615

Homogenization, Tissue 87176

Homograft

Skin 15300-15336

Homologous Grafts

See Graft

Homologous Transplantation

See Homograft

Homovanillic Acid

Urine 83150

Hormone Assay

ACTH 82024
Aldosterone
   Blood or Urine 82088
Androstenedione
   Blood or Urine 82157
Androsterone
   Blood or Urine 82160
Angiotensin II 82163
Corticosterone 82528
Cortisol
   Total 82533
Dehydroepiandrosterone 82626
Dihydroelestosterone 82651
Dihydrotestosterone 82651
Epiandrosterone 82666
Estradiol 82670
Estriol 82677
Estrogen 82671-82672

Hormone Assay, Estrone (continued)

Estrone .... .82679
Follicle Stimulating Hormone .... .83001
Growth Hormone .... .83003
Hydroxyprogesterone 83498-83499
Luteinizing Hormone .... .83002
Somatotropin .... .83003
Testosterone .... .84403
Vasopressin .... .84588

Hormone Pellet Implantation .... .11980

Hormone, Adrenocorticotrophic
See Adrenocorticotropic Hormone (ACTH)

Hormone, Corticotropin-Releasing
See Corticotropic Releasing Hormone (CRH)

Hormone, Growth
See Growth Hormone

Hormone, Human Growth
See Growth Hormone, Human

Hormone, Interstitial Cell-Stimulating
See Luteinizing Hormone (LH)

Hormone, Parathyroid
See Parathormone

Hormone, Pituitary Lactogenic
See Prolactin

Hormone, Placental Lactogen
See Lactogen, Human Placental

Hormone, Somatotropin Release-Inhibiting
See Somatostatin

Hormone, Thyroid-Stimulating
See Thyroid Stimulating Hormone (TSH)

Hormone-Binding Globulin, Sex
See Globulin, Sex Hormone Binding

Hormones, Adrenal Cortex
See Corticosteroids

Hormones, Antidiuretic
See Antidiuretic Hormone

Hospital Discharge Services
See Discharge Services, Hospital

Hospital Services
Inpatient Services 99238-99239
  Discharge Services 99238-99239
  Initial Care
    New or Established Patient . .99221-99233
  Initial Hospital Care 99221-99223
  Newborn 99431-99433
  Prolonged Services 99356-99357
  Subsequent Hospital Care 99231-99233
Observation
  Discharge Services 99234-99236
  Initial Care 99218-99220
    New or Established Patient . .99218-99220
Same Day Admission
  Discharge Services 99234-99236
Subsequent Newborn Care .... .99433

Hot Pack Treatment .... .97010
See Physical Medicine and Rehabilitation

House Calls 99341-99350

Howard Test
See Cystourethroscopy, Catheterization, Ureter

HPL
See Lactogen, Human Placental

HTLV I
Antibody
  Confirmatory Test .... .86689
  Detection .... .86687

HTLV II
Antibody .... .86688

HTLV III
See HIV

HTLV III Antibodies
See Antibody, HIV

HTLV IV
See HIV-2

Hubbard Tank Therapy .... .97036
See Physical Medicine/Therapy/Occupational Therapy

Hue Test .... .92283

Huggin Operation
See Orchiectomy, Simple

Huhner Test .... .89300, 89320

Human Chorionic Gonadotropin
See Chorionic Gonadotropin

Human Chorionic Somatomammotropin
See Lactogen, Human Placental

Human Cytomegalovirus Group
See Cytomegalovirus

Human Growth Hormone (HGH) ..... .80418, 80428-80430

Human Herpes Virus 4
See Epstein-Barr Virus

Human Immunodeficiency Virus
See HIV

Human Immunodeficiency Virus 1
See HIV-1

Human Immunodeficiency Virus 2
See HIV-2

Human Papillomavirus Detection 87620-87622

Human Placental Lactogen
See Lactogen, Human Placental

Human T Cell Leukemia Virus I
See HTLV I

Human T Cell Leukemia Virus I Antibodies
See Antibody, HTLV I

Human T Cell Leukemia Virus II
See HTLV II

Human T Cell Leukemia Virus II Antibodies
See Antibody, HTLV II

Humeral Epicondylitides, Lateral
See Tennis Elbow

Humeral Fracture
See Fracture, Humerus

Humerus
See Arm, Upper; Shoulder
Abscess
  Incision and Drainage .... .23935
Craterization .... .23184, 24140
Cyst
  Excision .... .23150, 24110
    with Allograft .... .23156, 24116
    with Autograft .... .23155, 24115
Diaphysectomy .... .23184, 24140
Excision .... .23174, 23184, 23195, 24134, 24140,
    24150-24151
Fracture
  Closed Treatment 24500-24505
    with Manipulation .... .23605
    without Manipulation .... .23600
  Condyle
    Closed Treatment 24576-24577
    Open Treatment .... .24579
    Percutaneous Fixation .... .24582
  Epicondyle
    Closed Treatment 24560-24565
    Open Treatment .... .24575
    Skeletal Fixation
      Percutaneous .... .24566
  Greater Tuberosity Fracture
    Closed Treatment with
    Manipulation .... .23625
    Closed Treatment without
    Manipulation .... .23620
    Open Treatment .... .23630
  Open Treatment 23615-23616
  Shaft 24500-24505, 24516
    Open Treatment .... .24515
  Supracondylar
    Closed Treatment 24530-24535
    Open Treatment 24545-24546
    Percutaneous Fixation .... .24538
  Transcondylar
    Closed Treatment 24530-24535
    Open Treatment 24545-24546
    Percutaneous Fixation .... .24538
  with Dislocation 23665-23670
Osteomyelitis .... .24134
Pinning, Wiring .... .23491, 24498
Prophylactic Treatment .... .23491, 24498
Radical Resection 23220-23222
Repair .... .24430
  Nonunion, Malunion 24430-24435
  Osteoplasty .... .24420
  Osteotomy 24400-24410
  with Graft .... .24435

Resection Head 23195
Saucerization 23184, 24140
Sequestrectomy 23174, 24134
Tumor
    Excision 23150, 23220-23222, 24110
      with Allograft 23156, 24116
      with Autograft 23155, 24115
X-Ray 73060

Hummelshein Operation
See Strabismus, Repair

Humor Shunt, Aqueous
See Aqueous Shunt

HVA
See Homovanillic Acid

Hyaluron Binding Assay 0087T

Hybridization Probes, DNA
See Nucleic Acid Probe

Hydatid Disease
See Echinococcosis

Hydatid Mole
See Hydatidiform Mole

Hydatidiform Mole
Evacuation and Curettage 59870
Excision 59100

Hydration 90760-90761

Hydrocarbons, Chlorinated
See Chlorinated Hydrocarbons

Hydrocele
Aspiration 55000
Excision
  Bilateral
    Tunica Vaginalis 55041
  Unilateral
    Spermatic Cord 55500
    Tunica Vaginalis 55040
Repair 55060

Hydrochloric Acid, Gastric
See Acid, Gastric

Hydrochloride, Vancomycin
See Vancomycin

Hydrocodon
See Dihydrocodeinone

Hydrogen Ion Concentration
See pH

Hydrolase, Acetylcholine
See Acetylcholinesterase

Hydrolase, Triacylglycerol
See Lipase

Hydrolases, Phosphoric Monoester
See Phosphatase

Hydrotherapy (Hubbard Tank) 97036
See Physical Medicine/Therapy/Occupational Therapy

Hydrotubation 58350

Hydroxyacetanilide
See Acetaminophen

Hydroxycorticosteroid 83491

Hydroxyindolacetic Acid ...83497
Urine 83497

Hydroxypregnenolone 80406, 84143

Hydroxyprogesterone 80402-80406, 83498-83499

Hydroxyproline 83500-83505

Hydroxytyramine
See Dopamine

Hygroma
Cystic
  Axillary/Cervical
    Excision 38550-38555

Hymen
Excision 56700
Incision 56720

Hymenal Ring
Revision 56700

Hymenectomy 56700

Hymenotomy 56720

Hyoid
Bone
  Fracture
    Open Treatment 21495
Muscle
  Incision and Suspension 21685

Hyperbaric Oxygen Pressurization 99183

Hypercycloidal X-Ray 76101-76102

Hyperdactylies
See Supernumerary Digit

Hyperglycemic Glycogenolytic Factor
See Glucagon

Hyperhidrosis 64650, 64653

Hypertelorism of Orbit
See Orbital Hypertelorism

Hyperthermia Therapy
See Thermotherapy

Hyperthermia Treatment ..77600-77620

Hypnotherapy 90880

Hypodermis
See Subcutaneous Tissue

Hypogastric Plexus
Destruction 64681
Injection
  Anesthetic 64517
  Neurolytic 64681

Hypoglossal Nerve
Anastomosis
  to Facial Nerve 64868

Hypoglossal-Facial Anastomosis
See Anastomosis, Nerve, Facial to Hypoglossal

Hypopharynges
See Hypopharynx

Hypopharynx
Biopsy 42802

Hypophysectomy 61546-61548, 62165

Hypophysis
See Pituitary Gland

Hypopyrexia
See Hypothermia

Hypospadias
Repair 54300, 54352
  Complications 54340-54348
  First Stage 54304
    Proximal Penile or Penoscrotal 54332
  One Stage
    Meatal Advancement 54322
    Perineal 54336
  Urethroplasty
    Local Skin Flaps 54324
    Local Skin Flaps and Mobilization of Urethra 54326
    Local Skin Flaps, Skin Graft Patch and/or Island Flap 54328
  Urethroplasty for Second Stage .54308-54316
    Free Skin Graft 54316
  Urethroplasty for Third Stage 54318

Hypothermia 99185-99186

Hypoxia
Breathing Response 94450
High Altitude Simulation Test 94452-94453

Hysterectomy
Abdominal
  Radical 58210
  Resection of Ovarian Malignancy 58951, 58953-58956
  Supracervical 58180
  Total 58150, 58200, 58956
    with Colpo-Urethrocystopexy 58152
    with Omentectomy 58956
    with Partial Vaginectomy 58200
Cesarean
  after Cesarean Delivery 59525
  with Closure of Vesicouterine Fistula ..51925
Removal
  Lesion 59100
Vaginal 58260-58270, 58290-58294, 58550-58554
  Laparoscopic 58550
  Radical 58285

Removal Tubes/Ovaries 58262-58263,
58291-58292, 58552, 58554
Repair of Enterocele .58263, 58292, 58294
with Colpectomy 58275-58280
with Colpo-Urethrocystopexy .58267, 58293

Hysterolysis
See Lysis, Adhesions, Uterus

Hysteroplasty 58540

Hysterorrhaphy 58520, 59350

Hysterosalpingography 74740
Catheterization 58345
Injection Procedure 58340

Hysterosalpingostomy
See Implantation, Tubouterine

Hysteroscopy
Ablation
Endometrial 58563
Diagnostic 58555
Lysis
Adhesions 58559
Placement
Fallopian Tube Implants 58565
Removal
Impacted Foreign Body 58562
Leiomyomata 58561
Resection
of Intrauterine Septum 58560
Surgical with Biopsy 58558
Unlisted Services and Procedures ..58578, 58579

Hysterosonography
See Ultrasound; Sonohysterography

Hysterotomy 59100
See Ligation, Uterus
Induced Abortion
with Amniotic Injections 59852
with Vaginal Suppositories 59857

Hysterotrachelectomy
See Amputation, Cervix

I

I, Angiotensin
See Angiotensin I

I Antibodies, HTLV
See Antibody, HTLV-I

I, Coagulation Factor
See Fibrinogen

I, Heparin Co-Factor
See Antithrombin III

ICCE
See Extraction, Lens, Intracapsular

Ichthyosis, Sex Linked
See Syphilis Test

ICSH
See Luteinizing Hormone (LH)

Identification
Oocyte
from Follicular Fluid 89254
Sperm
from Aspiration 89257
from Tissue 89264

IDH
See Isocitric Dehydrogenase, Blood

IG
See Immune Globulins

IgE 86003-86005

IgG 86001

II, Coagulation Factor
See Prothrombin

II, Cranial Nerve
See Optic Nerve

Ileal Conduit
Visualization 50690

Ileoscopy
via Stoma 44383

Ileostomy 44310, 45136
Continent (Kock Procedure) 44316
Laparoscopic 44186, 44187
Non-Tube 44187
Revision 44312-44314

Iliac Arteries
See Artery, Iliac

Iliac Crest
Free Osteocutaneous Flap with Microvascular
Anastomosis 20970

Iliohypogastric Nerve
Injection
Anesthetic 64425

Ilioinguinal Nerve
Injection
Anesthetic 64425

Ilium
Craterization 27070
Cyst
Excision 27065-27067
Excision 27070
Fracture
Open Treatment 27215, 27218
Saucerization 27070
Tumor
Excision 27065-27067

Ilizarov Procedure
Monticelli Type 20692
See Application, Bone Fixation Device

IM Injection
See Injection, Intramuscular

Imaging
See Vascular Studies

Imaging, Gamma Camera
See Nuclear Medicine

Imaging, Magnetic Resonance
See Magnetic Resonance Imaging (MRI)

Imaging, Ultrasonic
See Echography

Imbrication
Diaphragm 39545

Imidobenzyle
See Imipramine

Imipramine
Assay 80174

Immune Complex Assay 86332

Immune Globulin
Administration 90780-90784

Immune Globulin E
See IgE

Immune Globulins
Antitoxin
Botulinum 90287
Diphtheria 90296
Botulism 90288
Cytomegalovirus 90291
Hepatitis B 90371
Human 90281-90283
Rabies 90375-90376
Respiratory Syncytial Virus 90378-90379
Rho (D) 90384-90386
Tetanus 90389
Unlisted Immune Globulin 90399
Vaccinia 90393
Varicella-Zoster 90396

Immunization Administration
Each Additional Vaccine/Toxoid ...90472, 90474
with Counseling 90466, 90468
One Vaccine/Toxoid 90471, 90473
with Counseling 90465, 90467

Immunization, Mumps
See Mumps, Immunization

Immunoassay
Analyte 83519-83520
Infectious Agent ...86317-86318, 87449-87451
Nonantibody 83516-83519
Tumor Antigen 86294, 86316
CA 125 86304
CA 15-3 86300
CA 19-9 86301

Immunoblotting, Western
See Western Blot

Immunochemical, Lysozyme
(Muramidase)
See Lysozyme

Immunocytochemistry 88342

Immunodeficiency Virus Type 1, Human
See HIV 1

Immunodeficiency Virus Type 2, Human
See HIV 2

Immunodeficiency Virus, Human
See HIV

Immunodiffusion 86329-86331

Immunoelectrophoresis .86320-86327, 86334-86335

Immunofixation Electrophoresis 86334-86335

Immunofluorescent Study 88346-88347

Immunogen
See Antigen

Immunoglobulin 82787
Platelet Associated 86023
Thyroid Stimulating 84445

Immunoglobulin E
See IgE

Immunoglobulin Receptor Assay 86243

Immunologic Skin Test
See Skin, Tests

Immunology
Unlisted Services and Procedures 86849

Immunotherapies, Allergen
See Allergen Immunotherapy

Impedance Testing 92567
See Audiologic Function Tests

Imperfectly Descended Testis
See Testis, Undescended

Implant Removal
See Specific Anatomical Site

Implant, Breast
See Breast, Implants

Implant, Glaucoma Drainage
See Aqueous Shunt

Implant, Orbital
See Orbital Implant

Implant, Penile
See Penile Prosthesis

Implant, Penile Prosthesis, Inflatable
See Penile Prosthesis, Insertion, Inflatable

Implant, Subperiosteal
See Subperiosteal Implant

Implant, Ureters into, Bladder
See Anastomosis, Ureter, to Bladder

Implantation
Artificial Heart
   Intracorporeal 0051T
Bone
   for External Speech Processor/Cochlear
   Stimulator 69714-69718
Brain
   Chemotherapy 61517
   Thermal Perfusion Probe 0077T
Cardiac Event Recorder 33282
Contraceptive Capsules 11975, 11977
Drug Delivery Device 11981, 11983, 61517
Electrode
   Brain 61850-61875
   Nerve 64553-64581
   Spinal Cord 63650-63655
Eye
   Anterior Segment 65920
   Aqueous Shunt to Extraocular Placement or
   Replacement of Pegs 65125
   Corneal Ring Segments 0099T
   Posterior Segment
      Extraocular 67120
      Intraocular 67121
   Reservoir 66180
   Vitreous
      Drug Delivery System 67027
Fallopian Tube 58565
Hearing Aid Hormone Pellet(s)
   Bone Conduction 69710
Hip Prosthesis
   See Arthroplasty, Hip
Hormone Pellet 11980
Intraocular Lens
   See Insertion, Intraocular Lens
Joint
   See Arthroplasty
Mesh
   Hernia Repair 49568
   Vaginal Repair 57267
Nerve
   into Bone 64787
   into Muscle 64787
Neurostimulators
   Pulse Generator 61885
   Receiver 61886
Ovum 58976
Pulse Generator
   Brain 61885-61886
   Spinal Cord Electrode Array 63685
Receiver
   Brain 61885-61886
   Spinal Cord 63685
Removal 20670-20680
   Elbow 24164
   Radius 24164
Reservoir Vascular Access Device
   Declotting 36550
Retinal Electrode Array 0100T
Total Replacement Heart System
   Intracorporeal 0051T
Tubouterine 58752
Ventricular Assist Device 33976
   Extracorporeal 0048T
   Intracorporeal 33979

Impression, Maxillofacial
Auricular Prosthesis 21086
Definitive Obturator Prosthesis 21080
Facial Prosthesis 21088
Interim Obturator 21079
Mandibular Resection Prosthesis 21081
Nasal Prosthesis 21087
Oral Surgical Splint 21085
Orbital Prosthesis 21077
Palatal Augmentation Prosthesis 21082
Palatal Lift Prosthesis 21083
Speech Aid Prosthesis 21084
Surgical Obturator 21076

IMT
See Intima-Media Thickness Study

In Situ Hybridization
See Nucleic Acid Probe, Cytogenetic Studies, Morphometric Analysis

In Vitro Fertilization 58321-58322

In Vivo NMR Spectroscopy
See Magnetic Resonance Spectroscopy

Incision
See Incision and Drainage
Abdomen 49000
   Exploration 58960
Abscess
   Soft Tissue 20000-20005
Accessory Nerve 63191
Anal
   Fistula 46270, 46280
   Septum 46070
   Sphincter 46080
Ankle 27607
   Tendon 27605-27606
Anus
   See Anus, Incision
Aortic Valve
   for Stenosis 33415
Artery
   Nose 30915-30920
Atrial Septum 33735-33737
Bile Duct
   Sphincter 43262, 47460
Bladder
   Catheterization 51045
   with Destruction 51020-51030
   with Radiotracer 51020
Bladder Diverticulum 52305
Brachial Artery
   Exposure 34834
Brain
   Amygdalohippocampectomy 61566
   Subpial 61567
Breast
   Capsules 19370
Burn Scab 16035-16036
Cataract
   Secondary
      Laser Surgery 66821
      Stab Incision Technique 66820
Chest
   Biopsy 32095-32100

Colon
  Exploration 44025
  Stoma
    Creation 44320-44322
    Revision 44340-44346
Cornea
  for Astigmatism 65772
Corpus Callosum 61541
Cricothyroid Membrane 31605
Dentate Ligament 63180-63182
Duodenum 44010
Ear, Inner
  Labyrinth
    with Mastoidectomy 69802
    with or without Cryosurgery 69801
  Elbow 24000
Esophagus 43020, 43045
  Muscle 43030
Exploration
  Heart 33310-33315
  Kidney 50010
Eye
  Adhesions .65880
    Anterior Segment 65860-65865
    Anterior Synechiae 65870
    Corneovitreal 65880
    Posterior 65875
  Anterior Chamber 65820
  Conjunctiva 0124T
  Trabeculae 65850
Eyelid
  Canthus 67715
  Sutures 67710
Femoral Artery
  Exposure 34812-34813
Fibula 27607
Finger
  Decompression 26035
  Tendon 26060, 26455-26460
  Tendon Sheath 26055
Foot 28005
  Capsule 28260-28264
  Fasciotomy 28008
  for Infection 28002-28003
  Tendon 28230, 28234
Frontal Lobe .61490
Gallbladder 47490
Hand Decompression 26035-26037
  Tendon 26450, 26460
Heart
  Exploration 33310-33315
Hemorrhoids
  External 46083
Hepatic Ducts
  See Hepaticostomy
Hip
  Denervation 27035
  Exploration 27033
  Fasciotomy 27025
  Joint Capsule
    for Flexor Release 27036
  Tendon
    Abductor 27006
    Adductor 27000-27003
    Iliopsoas 27005
Hymen
  See Hymen, Incision
Hymenotomy 56720

Hyoid
  Muscle 21685
Iliac Artery
  Exposure 34820, 34833
Intercarpal Joint
  Dislocation 25670
Interphalangeal Joint
  Capsule 26525
Intestines (Except Rectum)
  See Enterotomy
Intestines, Small 44010
  Biopsy 44020
  Creation
    Pouch 44316
    Stoma 44300-44310, 44314
  Decompression 44021
  Exploration 44020
  Incision 44020
  Removal
    Foreign Body 44020
  Revision
    Stoma 44312
Iris 66500-66505
Kidney 50010, 50045
Knee
  Capsule 27435
  Exploration 27310
  Fasciotomy 27305
  Removal of Foreign Body 27310
Lacrimal Punctum 68440
Lacrimal Sac
  See Dacryocystotomy
Larynx 31300-31320
Leg, Lower
  Fasciotomy 27600-27602
Leg, Upper
  Fasciotomy 27305
  Tenotomy 27306-27307, 27390-27392
Lip
  Frenum 40806
Liver
  See Hepatotomy
Lung
  Biopsy 32095-32100
  Decortication
    Partial 32225
    Total 32220
Lymphatic Channels 38308
Mastoid
  See Mastoidotomy
Medullary Tract 61470
Mesencephalic Tract 61480
Metacarpophalangeal Joint
  Capsule 26520
Mitral Valve 33420-33422
Muscle
  See Myotomy
Nerve 64573-64580,
                    64585, 64595, 64702-64772
  Foot 28035
  Root 63185-63190
  Sacral 64581
  Vagus 43640-43641
Nose
  See Rhinotomy
Orbit
  See Orbitotomy

Palm
  Fasciotomy 26040-26045
Pancreas
  Sphincter .43262
Penis
  Prepuce 54000-54001
  Newborn .54000
Pericardium
  with Clot Removal 33020
  with Foreign Body Removal 33020
  with Tube .33015
Pharynx
  Stoma 42955
Pleura
  Biopsy 32095-32100
Pleural Cavity
  Empyema 32035-32036
  Pneumothorax 32020
Prostate
  Exposure
    Bilateral Pelvic Lymphadenectomy . .55865
    Insertion Radioactive Substance 55860
    Lymph Node Biopsy 55862
    Transurethral 52450
Pterygomaxillary Fossa 31040
Pulmonary Valve 33470-33474
Pyloric Sphincter 43520
Retina
  Encircling Material 67115
Sclera
  Fistulization
    Iridencleisis or Iridotasis 66165
    Sclerectomy with Punch or Scissors
      with Iridectomy 66160
    Thermocauterization with
      Iridectomy 66155
    Trabeculectomy ab Externo in Absence
      Previous Surgery 66170
    Trephination with Iridectomy 66150
Semicircular Canal
  Fenestration 69820
  Revision 69840
Seminal Vesicle 55600-55605
  Complicated 55605
Shoulder
  Bone 23035
  Capsular Contracture Release 23020
  Removal
    Calcareous Deposits 23000
    Tenomyotomy 23405-23406
Shoulder Joint 23040-23044
Sinus
  Frontal 31070-31087
  Maxillary 31020-31032
    Endoscopic 31256-31267
  Multiple 31090
  Sphenoid
    Sinusotomy 31050-31051
Skin 10040, 10060-10061,
                    10080-10081, 10120-10180
Skull 61316, 62148
  Suture 61550-61552
Spinal Cord 63200
  Tract 63170, 63194-63199
Stomach
  Creation
    Stoma 43830-43832

Exploration 43500
Pyloric Sphincter 43520
Synovectomy 26140
Temporomandibular Joint 21010
Tendon
Arm, Upper 24310
Thigh
Fasciotomy .27025
Thorax
Empyema 32035-32036
Pneumothorax 32020
Thyroid Gland
See Thyrotomy
Tibia 27607
Toe
Capsule 28270-28272
Fasciotomy .28008
Tendon 28232-28234
Tenotomy 28010-28011
Tongue
Frenum 41010
Trachea
Emergency 31603-31605
Planned 31600-31601
with Flaps .31610
Tympanic Membrane 69420
with Anesthesia 69421
Ureter 50600
Ureterocele 51535
Urethra 53000-53010
Meatus 53020-53025
Uterus
Remove Lesion 59100
Vagina
Exploration .57000
Vas Deferens .55200
for X-Ray 55300
Vestibule of the Mouth
See Mouth, Vestibule of, Incision
Vitreous Strands
Laser Surgery 67031
Pars Plana Approach 67030
Wrist .25100-25105
Capsule 25085
Decompression 25020-25025
Tendon Sheath 25000-25001

Incision and Drainage

See Drainage; Incision
Abdomen
Fluid 49080-49081
Pancreatitis .48000
Abscess
Abdomen 49020, 49040
Open 49040
Percutaneous 49021
Anal 46045-46050
Ankle 27603
Appendix 44900
Open 44900
Percutaneous 44901
Arm, Lower 25028
Arm, Upper 23930-23931
Auditory Canal, External 69020
Bartholin's Gland 56420
Bladder 51080
Brain 61320-61321
Breast 19020

Ear, External
Complicated 69005
Simple 69000
Elbow 23930
Epididymis .54700
Eyelid 67700
Finger 26010-26011
Gums 41800
Hip 26990
Kidney 50020
Open 50020
Percutaneous 50021
Knee 27301
Leg, Lower 27603
Leg, Upper 27301
Liver 47010
Open 47010
Percutaneous 47011
Lung 32200
Percutaneous 32201
Lymph Node 38300-38305
Mouth 40800-40801, 41005-41009,
41015-41018
Nasal Septum 30020
Neck 21501-21502
Nose 30000, 30020
Ovary 58820-58822
Abdominal Approach 58822
Palate 42000
Paraurethral Gland 53060
Parotid Gland 42300-42305
Pelvis 26990, 45000
Perineum 56405
Peritoneum 49020
Percutaneous 49021
Prostate 55720-55725
Rectum . .45005-45020, 46040, 46050-46060
Retroperitoneal 49060
Open 49060
Salivary Gland 42300-42320
Scrotum 54700, 55100
Skene's Gland 53060
Skin 10060-10061
Subdiaphragmatic
Percutaneous 49040-49041
Sublingual Gland 42310-42320
Submaxillary Gland 42310-42320
Subphrenic
Percutaneous 49040-49041
Testis 54700
Thorax 21501-21502
Throat 42700-42725
Tongue 41000-41006, 41015
Tonsil 42700
Urethra 53040
Uvula 42000
Vagina 57010
Vulva 56405
Wrist 25028
Ankle 27610
Bile Duct 47420-47425
Bladder 51040
Bulla
Skin
Puncture Aspiration 10160
Bursa
Ankle 27604
Arm, Lower 25031

Elbow 23931
Foot 28001
Hip 26991
Knee 27301
Leg, Lower 27604
Leg, Upper 27301
Palm 26025-26030
Pelvis 26991
Wrist 25031
Carbuncle
Skin 10060-10061
Carpals 25035, 26034
Comedones
Skin 10040
Cyst
Conjunctiva 68020
Gums 41800
Liver
Open 47010
Percutaneous 47011
Lung 32200
Percutaneous 32201
Mouth 40800-40801, 41005-41009,
41015-41018
Ovarian 58800-58805
Skin 10040, 10060-10061
Pilonidal 10080-10081
Puncture Aspiration 10160
Spinal Cord 63172-63173
Thyroid Gland 60000
Tongue 41000-41006, 41015, 60000
Elbow
Abscess 23935
Arthrotomy 24000
Femur 27303
Fluid Collection
Skin 10140
Foreign Body
Skin 10120-10121
Furuncle 10060-10061
Gallbladder .47480
Hematoma
Ankle 27603
Arm, Lower 25028
Arm, Upper 23930
Brain 61312-61315
Ear, External
Complicated 69005
Simple 69000
Elbow 23930
Epididymis .54700
Gums 41800
Hip 26990
Knee 27301
Leg, Lower 27603
Leg, Upper 27301
Mouth 40800-40801, 41005-41009,
41015-41018
Nasal Septum 30020
Neck 21501-21502
Nose 30000, 30020
Pelvis 26990
Scrotum 54700
Skin 10140
Puncture Aspiration 10160
Skull 61312-61315
Testis 54700
Thorax 21501-21502

Tongue 41000-41006, 41015
Vagina .57022-57023
Wrist 25028
Hepatic Duct 47400
Hip
   Bone 26992, 27030
Humerus
   Abscess 23935
Interphalangeal Joint
   Toe 28024
Intertarsal Joint .28020
Kidney 50040, 50125
Knee .27303, 27310
Lacrimal Gland .68400
Lacrimal Sac 68420
Liver
   Abscess or Cyst 47010-47011
      Percutaneous 47011
Mediastinum 39000-39010
Metatarsophalangeal Joint 28022
Milia, Multiple .10040
Onychia 10060-10061
Orbit .67405, 67440
Paronychia 10060-10061
Pelvic
   Bone 26992
Penis 54015
Pericardium 33025
Phalanges
   Finger 26034
Pilonidal Cyst 10080-10081
Pustules
   Skin 10040
Radius 25035
Seroma
   Skin 10140
Shoulder
   Abscess 23030
   Arthrotomy
      Acromioclavicular Joint 23044
      Sternoclavicular Joint 23044
   Bursa 23031
   Hematoma 23030
Shoulder Joint
   Arthrotomy
      Glenohumeral Joint 23040
Spine
   Abscess 22010-22015
Tarsometatarsal Joint 28020
Tendon Sheath
   Finger 26020
   Palm 26020
Thorax
   Deep 21510
Toe 28024
Ulna 25035
Ureter 50600
Vagina 57020
Wound Infection
   Skin 10180
Wrist .25028, 25040

Incisional Hernia Repair
See Hernia, Repair, Incisional

Inclusion Bodies
Fluid 88106
Smear .87207, 87210

Incomplete Abortion
See Abortion, Incomplete

Indicator Dilution Studies
. 93561-93562

Induced Abortion
See Abortion

Induced Hyperthermia
See Thermotherapy

Induced Hypothermia
See Hypothermia

Induratio Penis Plastica
See Peyronie Disease

Infant, Newborn, Intensive Care
See Intensive Care, Neonatal

Infantile Paralysis
See Polio

Infection
Immunoassay 86317-86318
Rapid Test 86403-86406

Infection, Actinomyces
See Actinomycosis

Infection, Bone
See Osteomyelitis

Infection, Filarioidea
See Filariasis

Infection, Postoperative Wound
See Postoperative Wound Infection

Infection, Wound
See Wound, Infection

Infectious Agent
Antigen Detection
   Direct Fluorescence 87265-87272, 87276,
               87278, 87280, 87285-87290
     Bordetella .87265
     Chlamydia Trachomatis 87270
     Cryptosporidium 87272
     Cytomegalovirus 87271
     Enterovirus 87267
     Giardia 87269
     Influenza A 87276
     Legionella Pneumophila 87278
     Respiratory Syncytial Virus 87280
     Treponema Pallidum 87285
     Varicella-Zoster 87290
   Enzyme Immunoassay
     Adenovirus 87301
     Chlamydia Trachomatis 87320
     Clostridium Difficile 87324
     Cryptococcus Neoformans 87327
     Cryptosporidium 87328
     Cytomegalovirus 87332
     Entamoeba Histolytica Dispar Group .87336
     Entamoeba Histolytica Group 87337
     Escherichia Coli 0157 87335
     Giardia 87329
     Helicobacter Pylori 87338-87339
     Hepatitis B Surface Antigen
     (HBsAg) .87340

     Hepatitis B Surface Antigen (HBsAg)
     Neutralization 87341
     Hepatitis Be Antigen (HBeAg) 87350
     Hepatitis, Delta Agent 87380
     Histoplasma capsulatum 87385
     HIV-1 87390
     HIV-2 87391
     Influenza A 87400
     Influenza B 87400
     Multiple Step Method 87301-87449,
                       87451
      See specific agent
     Not Otherwise Specified 87449, 87451
     Respiratory Syncytial Virus 87420
     Rotavirus .87425
     Shiga-like Toxin 87427
     Single Step Method 87450
     Streptococcus, Group A 87430
   Immunofluorescence . . .87260, 87273-87275,
      87277, 87279, 87281-87283, 87299-87300
     Adenovirus 87260
     Herpes Simplex 87273-87274
     Influenza B 87275
     Legionella Micdadei 87277
     Not Otherwise Specified 87299
     Parainfluenza Virus 87279
     Pneumocystis Carinii 87281
     Polyvalent 87300
     Rubeola 87283
  Concentration .87015
  Detection
   by Immunoassay
     Chlamydia Trachomatis 87810
     Clostridium Difficile 87803
     Influenza .87804
     Neisseria Gonorrheae 87850
     Not Otherwise Specified 87899
     Respiratory Syncytial Virus 87807
     Streptococcus, Group A 87880
     Streptococcus, Group B 87802
     with Direct Optical
      Observation 87802-87899
   by Nucleic Acid
     Bartonella Henselae 87470-87472
     Bartonella Quintana 87470-87472
     Borrelia Burgdorferi 87475-87477
     Candida Species 87480-87482
     Chlamydia Pneumoniae 87485-87487
     Chlamydia Trachomatis 87490-87492
     Cytomegalovirus 87495-87497
     Gardnerella Vaginalis 87510-87512
     Hepatitis B Virus 87515-87517
     Hepatitis C 87520-87522
     Hepatitis G 87525-87527
     Herpes Simplex Virus 87528-87530
     Herpes Virus-6 87531-87533
     HIV-1 87534-87536
     HIV-2 87537-87539
     Legionella Pneumophila 87540-87542
     Multiple Organisms 87800-87801
     Mycobacteria
      Avium-Intracellulare 87560-87562
      Mycobacteria Species 87550-87552
      Mycobacteria Tuberculosis . . .87555-87557
      Mycoplasma Pneumoniae 87580-87582
      Neisseria Gonorrheae 87590-87592
      Not Otherwise Specified 87797-87799
      Papillomavirus, Human 87620-87622

Streptococcus, Group A 87650-87652
Trichomonas Vaginalis 87660
Urinalysis 0041T
Genotype Analysis
by Nucleic Acid
Hepatitis C Virus 87902
HIV-1 Protease/Reverse
Transcriptase 87901
Phenotype Analysis
by Nucleic Acid
HIV-1 Drug Resistance 87903-87904
Phenotype Prediction
by Genetic Database 87900

Infectious Mononucleosis Virus
See Epstein-Barr Virus

Inflammatory Process
Localization
Nuclear Medicine 78805-78807

Inflation
Ear, Middle
Eustachian Tube
with Catheterization 69400
without Catheterization 69401
Eustachian Tube
Myringotomy 69420
Anesthesia 69424

Influenza A
Antigen Detection
Direct Fluorescence 87276
Enzyme Immunoassay 87400

Influenza B
Antigen Detection
Enzyme Immunoassay 87400
Immunofluorescence 87275

Influenza Vaccine
See Vaccines

Influenza Virus
Antibody 86710
by Immunoassay
with Direct Optical Observation 87804

Infraorbital Nerve
Avulsion 64734
Incision 64734
Transection 64734

Infrared Light Treatment 97026
See Physical Medicine/Therapy/Occupational
Therapy

**Infratentorial
Craniectomy** 61520-61521

Infusion
Amnion
Transabdominal 59072
Cerebral
Intravenous
for Thrombolysis 37195
Intra-Arterial 90773
Unlisted 90779
Intraosseous 36680

Intravenous 90779
Diagnostic/Prophylactic/
Therapeutic 90760-90761, 90765-90768
Radioelement 77750
Transcatheter Therapy 37201-37202

Infusion Pump
Electronic Analysis
Spinal Cord 62367-62368
Insertion
Intra-Arterial 36260
Intraarterial
Removal 36262
Revision 36261
Intravenous
Insertion 36563
Repair 36576
Replacement 36583
Maintenance 95990-95991, 96521-96522
See Chemotherapy, Pump Services
Spinal Cord 62361-62362
Ventricular Catheter 61215

Infusion Therapy 62350-62351,
62360-62362
See Injection, Chemotherapy
Arterial Catheterization 36640
Chemotherapy 96401-96549
Home Infusion Procedures 99601-99602
Intravenous 90760-90768
Pain 62360-62362, 62367-62368
Transcatheter Therapy 75896

Ingestion Challenge Test 95075
See Allergy Tests

Inguinal Hernia Repair
See Hernia, Repair, Inguinal

INH
See Drug Assay

Inhalation
Pentamidine 94642

Inhalation Provocation Tests
See Bronchial Challenge Test

Inhalation Treatment 94640,
94664, 99503
See Pulmonology, Therapeutic

Inhibin A 86336

Inhibition Test, Hemagglutination
See Hemagglutination Inhibition Test

Inhibition, Fertilization
See Contraception

Inhibitor, Alpha 1-Protease
See Alpha-1 Antitrypsin

Inhibitor, Alpha 2-Plasmin
See Alpha-2 Antiplasmin

Inhibitory Concentration, Minimum
See Minimum Inhibitory Concentration

Initial Inpatient Consultations
See Consultation, Initial Inpatient

Injection
See Allergen Immunotherapy; Infusion
Abdomen
Air 49400
Contrast Material 49400
Angiography
Pulmonary 75746
Ankle
Radial 27648
Antibiotic
See Antibiotic Administration
Antigen (Allergen) 95115-95125
Aorta (Aortography)
Radiologic 93544
Aponeurosis 20550
Bladder
Radiologic 51600-51610
Brain Canal 61070
Bronchography
Segmental 31656
Bursa 20600-20610
Cardiac Catheterization 93539-93545
Carpal Tunnel
Therapeutic 20526
Chemotherapy 96401-96549
Cistern
Medication or Other 61055
Contrast
via Catheter 36598, 49424
Corpora Cavernosa 54235
Cyst
Bone 20615
Kidney 50390
Pelvis 50390
Thyroid 60001
Elbow
Arthrography
Radiologic 24220
Epidural
See Epidural, Injection
Esophageal Sphincter
Endoscopy 0133T
Esophageal Varices
Endoscopy 43243
Esophagus
Sclerosing Agent 43204
Submucosal 43201
Extremity
Pseudoaneurysm 36002
Eye
Air 66020
Medication 66030
Eyelid
Subconjunctival 68200
Ganglion
Anesthetic 64505, 64510
Ganglion Cyst 20612
Gastric Secretion Stimulant 91052
Gastric Varices
Endoscopy 43243
Heart Vessels
Cardiac Catheterization 93539-93545
See Catheterization, Cardiac
Radiologic 93545
Hemorrhoids
Sclerosing Solution 46500

Hip
    Radiologic 27093-27095
Insect Venom 95130-95134
Intervertebral Disk
    Chemonucleolysis Agent 62292
    Radiological 62290-62291
Intra-Arterial 90773, 90779
    Thrombolytic 37184-37186
Intra-Amniotic 59852
Intradermal
    for Tattooing 11920-11922
Intralesional
    Skin 11900-11901
Intramuscular 90772
    Therapeutic 90772, 99506
Intravenous 90779
    Diagnostic 90779
        Thrombolytic 37187-37188
    Unlisted 90779
    Vascular Flow Check, Graft 15860
Intravenous Push 90774-90775
Joint 20600-20610
Kidney
    Drugs 50391
    Radiologic 50394
Knee
    Radiologic 27370
Lacrimal Gland
    Radiologic 68850
Left Heart
    Radiologic 93543
Lesion
    Skin 11900-11901
Ligament 20550
Liver 47015
    Radiologic 47500-47505
Mammary Ductogram/Galactogram 19030
Muscle Endplate
    Extremity 64614
    Facial 64612
    Neck 64613
    Trunk 64614
Nerve
    Anesthetic 01991-01992, 64400-64530
    Neurolytic Agent .64600-64640, 64680-64681
Orbit
    Retrobulbar
        Alcohol 67505
        Medication 67500
    Tenon's Capsule 67515
Pancreatography 48400
Paraveretebral Facet Joint/Nerve . .64470-64476
Penis
    for Erection 54235
    Peyronie Disease 54200
      with Surgical Exposure of Plague . . .54205
    Radiology 54230
    Vasoactive Drugs 54231
Peritoneal Cavity Air
    See Pneumoperitoneum
Radiologic
    Breast 19030

Rectum
    Sclerosing Solution 45520
Right Heart
    See Cardiac Catheterization, Injection
    Radiologic 93542
Sacroiliac Joint
    for Arthrography 27096
Salivary Duct 42660
Salivary Gland
    Radiologic 42550
Sclerosing Agent
    Esophagus 43204
    Intravenous 36470-36471
Sentinel Node Identification 38792
Shoulder
    Arthrography
        Radiologic 23350
Shunt
    Peritoneal
        Venous 49427
Sinus Tract 20500
    Diagnostic 20501
Spider Veins
    Telangiectasia 36468-36469
Spinal Artery 62294
Spinal Cord
    Anesthetic 62310-62319
    Blood 62273
    Neurolytic Agent 62280-62282
    Other 62310-62311
    Radiological 62284
Steroids
    Urethral Stricture 52283
Subcutaneous 90772
    Silicone 11950-11954
    Therapeutic 90772, 90782
Temporomandibular Joint
    Arthrography 21116
Tendon Origin, Insertion 20551
Tendon Sheath 20550
Therapeutic
    Extremity Pseudoaneurysm 36002
    Lung 32960
    Thyroid .60001
    Turbinate 30200
Thoracic Cavity
    See Pleurodesis, Chemical
Trachea 31612
    Puncture 31612
Transtracheal
    Bronchography 31715
Trigger Point(s)
    One or Two Muscles 20552
    Three or More Muscles 20553
Turbinate 30200
Ureter
    Drugs 50391
    Radiologic 50684

Venography 36005
Ventricle
    Dye 61120
    Medication or Other 61026
Vitreous 67028
    Fluid Substitute 67025
Vocal Cords
    Therapeutic 31513, 31570-31571
Wrist
    Carpal Tunnel
        Therapeutic 20526
    Radiologic 25246

Inner Ear
See Ear, Inner

Innominate
Tumor
    Excision .27077

Innominate Arteries
See Artery, Brachiocephalic

Inorganic Sulfates
See Sulfate

Insemination
Artificial 58321-58322, 89268

Insertion
See Implantation; Intubation; Transplantation
Baffle
Balloon
    Intra-Aortic 33967, 33973
Breast
    Implants 19340-19342
Cannula
    Arteriovenous 36810-36815
    ECMO 36822
    Extra Corporeal Circulation
        for Regional Chemotherapy
        of Extremity 36823
    Thoracic Duct 38794
    Vein to Vein 36800
Catheter
    Abdomen 49419-49421
    Abdominal Artery 36245-36248
    Aorta 36200
    Bile Duct 47525-47530, 75982
        Percutaneous 47510
    Bladder 51045, 51701-51703
    Brachiocephalic Artery 36215-36218
    Brain 61210, 61770
    Breast
        for Interstitial Radioelement
        Application 19296-19298
    Bronchi 31710, 31717
    Bronchus
        for Intracavitary Radioelement
        Application 31643
    Cardiac
        See Catheterization, Cardiac
        Flow Directed 93503
    Ear, Middle 69405
    Eustachian Tube 69405
    Gastrointestinal, Upper 43241

Jejunum 44015
Kidney 50392
Lower Extremity Artery 36245-36248
Nasotracheal 31720
Pelvic Artery 36245-36248
Pleural Cavity 32019
Portal Vein .36481
Prostate 55859
Pulmonary Artery 36013-36015
Right Heart .36013
Skull 61107
Spinal Cord 62350-62351
Suprapubic .51010
Thoracic Artery 36215-36218
Trachea 31700
Tracheobronchial 31725
Ureter via Kidney 50393
Urethra 51701-51703
Vena Cava .36010
Venous 36011-36012, 36400-36410,
                   36420-36425, 36500-36510,
                   36555-36558, 36568-36569
Cervical Dilation 59200
Cochlear Device 69930
Contraceptive Capsules 11975, 11977
Drug Delivery Implant 11981, 11983
Electrode
    Brain 61531-61533, 61760,
                                 61850-61875
    Heart 33210-33211, 33216-33217,
                         33224-33225, 93620-93622
    Nerve 64553-64581
    Retina 0100T
    Sphenoidal .95830
    Spinal Cord 63650-63655
Endotracheal Tube 31500
Gastrostomy Tube
    Laparoscopic 43653
    Percutaneous 43750
Graft
    Aorta 33330-33335
    Heart Vessel 33330-33335
Guide
    Kidney Pelvis 50395
Guide Wire
    Endoscopy 43248
    Esophagoscopy 43248
        with Dilation 43226
Heyman Capsule
    Uterus
        for Brachytherapy 58346
Iliac Artery
    Occlusion Device 34808
Implant
    Bone
        for External Speech Processor/Cochlear
        Stimulator 69714-69718
Infusion Pump
    Intra-Arterial 36260
    Intravenous 36563
    Spinal Cord 62361-62362
Intracatheter/Needle
    Aorta 36160
    Arteriovenous Shunt 36145
    Intra-Arterial 36100-36140
    Intravenous 36000
    Kidney 50392

Intraocular Lens 66983
    Manual or Mechanical
    Technique 66982, 66984
    Not Associated with Concurrent Cataract
    Removal 66985
Intrauterine Device (IUD) 58300
IVC Filter 75940
Jejunostomy Tube
    Endoscopy 44372
Keel
    Laryngoplasty 31580
Laminaria 59200
Mesh
    Pelvic Floor 57267
Nasobiliary Tube
    Endoscopy 43267
Nasopancreatic Tube
    Endoscopy 43267
Needle
    Bone 36680
    Intraosseous 36680
    Prostate 55859
Needle Wire
    Trachea 31730
Neurostimulator
    Pulse Generator 64590
    Receiver 64590
Nose
    Septal Prosthesis 30220
Obturator
    Larynx 31527
Ocular Implant
    in Scleral Shell 65130
    Muscles Attached 65140
    Muscles, Not Attached 65135
    with Foreign Material 65155
    with/without Conjunctival Graft 65150
Orbital Transplant 67550
Oviduct
    Chromotubation 58350
    Hydrotubation 58350
Ovoid
    Vagina
        for Brachytherapy 57155
Pacemaker
    Fluoroscopy/Radiography 71090
    Heart 33200-33208, 33212-33213
Pacing Cardio-Defibrillator
    Electrodes 33245-33246
    Leads 33216-33220, 33224-33225,
                         33243-33245
    Pulse Generator only 33240-33241
Packing
    Vagina 57180
Penile Prosthesis, Inflatable
    See Penile Prosthesis, Insertion, Inflatable
Pessary
    Vagina 57160
Pin
    Skeletal Traction 20650
Probe
    Brain 61770
Prostaglandin 59200
Prostate
    Radioactive Substance 55860
Prosthesis
    Knee 27438, 27445
    Nasal Septal 30220

Palate 42281
Pelvic Floor 57267
Penis
    Inflatable 54401-54405
    Noninflatable 54400
    Speech 31611
    Testis 54660
    Urethral Sphincter 53444-53445
Pulse Generator
    Brain 61885-61886
    Heart 33212-33213
    Spinal Cord 63685
Radioactive Material
    Bladder 51020
    Cystourethroscopy 52250
Receiver
    Brain 61885-61886
    Spinal Cord 63685
Reservoir
    Brain 61210-61215
    Spinal Cord 62360
    Subcutaneous 49419
Sensor, Fetal Oximetry
    Cervix 0021T
    Vagina 0021T
Shunt 36835
    Abdomen
        Vein 49425
        Venous .49426
    Intrahepatic Portosystemic 37182
Spinal Instrument 22849
    Spinous Process 22841
Spinal Instrumentation
    Anterior 22845-22847
    Internal Spinal Fixation 22841
    Pelvic Fixation 22848
    Posterior Nonsegmental
        Harrington Rod Technique 22840
    Posterior Segmental 22842-22844
    Prosthetic Device 22851
Stent
    Bile Duct 43268, 47801
        Percutaneous 47511
    Bladder 51045
    Conjunctiva 68750
    Coronary 92980-92981
    Esophagus 43219
    Gastrointestinal, Upper 43256
    Ileum 44383
    Indwelling .50605
    Lacrimal Duct 68815
    Pancreatic Duct 43268
    Small Intestines 44370, 44379
    Ureter 50688
    Ureter via Kidney 50393
    Ureteral 50947, 52332
    Urethral 0084T, 52282
Tamponade
    Esophagus 43460
Tandem
    Uterus
        for Brachytherapy 57155
Tendon Graft
    Finger 26392
    Hand 26392
Testicular Prosthesis
    See Prosthesis, Testicular, Insertion

Tissue Expanders
    Skin 11960-11971
Tube
    Bile Duct 43268
    Esophagus 43510
    Gastrointestinal, Upper 43241
    Ileum .44383
    Kidney 50398
    Pancreatic Duct 43268
    Small Intestines 44379
    Trachea 31730
    Ureter 50688
Ureteral Guide Wire 52334
Vascular Pedicle
    Carpal Bone 25430
Venous Access Device
    Central 36560-36566
    Peripheral 36570-36571
Ventilating Tube 69433
Ventricular Assist Device 33975
Wire
    Skeletal Traction 20650

Inspiratory Positive Pressure Breathing

See Intermittent Positive Pressure Breathing (IPPB)

Instillation

Contrast Material
    Bronchography 31708
    Laryngography 31708
Drugs
    Bladder 51720
    Kidney 50391
    Ureter 50391

Instillation, Bladder

See Bladder, Instillation

Instrumentation

See Application; Bone, Fixation; Spinal Instrumentation
Spinal
    Insertion 22840-22848, 22851
    Reinsertion 22849
    Removal 22850, 22852-22855

Insufflation, Eustachian Tube

See Eustachian Tube, Inflation

Insulin

Insulin 80422, 80432-80435
Antibody 86337
Blood 83525
Free 83527

Insulin C-Peptide Measurement

See C-Peptide

Insulin Like Growth Factors

See Somatomedin

Insurance

Basic Life and/or Disability
Evaluation Services 99450
Examination 99450-99456

Integumentary System

Biopsy .11100-11101
Breast
    Excision 19100-19272
    Incision 19000-19030
    Metallic Localization Clip Placement . .19295
    Preoperative Placement of Needle
    Localization 19290-19291
    Reconstruction 19316-19396
    Repair 19316-19396
    Unlisted Services and Procedures 19499
Burns 15000-15001, 15100-15101,
    15120-15121, 15400-15401, 16000-16036
Debridement 11000-11006, 11010-11044
Destruction
    See Dermatology
    Actinotherapy 96900
    Benign or Premalignant Lesion .17000-17250
    Chemical Exfoliation 17360
    Cryotherapy 17340
    Electrolysis Epilation 17380
    Malignant Lesion 17260-17286
    by Photodynamic Therapy 96567
    Mohs Micrographic Surgery . .17304-17310
    Photodynamic Therapy 96567-96571
    Unlisted Services and Procedures 17999
Drainage 10040, 10060-10061,
    10080-10081, 10120-10180
Excision
    Benign Lesion 11400-11471
    Debridement 11000-11006, 11010-11044
    Malignant Lesion 11600-11646
Incision 10040, 10060-10061,
    10080-10081, 10120-10180
Introduction 11900-11977
    Drug Delivery Implant 11981, 11983
Nails 11720-11765
Paring .11055-11057
Pressure Ulcers 15920-15999
Removal
    Drug Delivery Implant 11982-11983
Repair
    Adjacent Tissue
    Transfer/Rearrangement 14000-14350
    Complex 13100-13160
    Flaps
    Other 15740-15776
    Free Skin Grafts .15000-15001, 15050-15136,
    15200-15321, 15420-15431
    Intermediate 12031-12057
    Other Procedures 15780-15879
    Simple 12001-12021
    Skin and/or Deep Tissue 15570-15738
Shaving of Epidermal or
Dermal Lesion 11300-11313
Skin Replacement Surgery and Skin Substitutes
    Grafts
    Acellular Dermal
    Replacement 15170-15176
    Allograft and Tissue Cultured
    Allogenic Skin Substitute 15300-15366
    Autograft/Tissue Cultured
    Autograft 15040-15157
    Xenograft 15400-15431
Skin Tags
    Removal 11200-11201

Integumentum Commune

See Integumentary System

Intelligence Test 96101-96102

Computer-Assisted 96103

Intensive Care

Low Birthweight Infant
    Subsequent Care 99298-99300

Intercarpal Joint

Arthrodesis 25820-25825
Dislocation
    Closed Treatment 25660
Repair 25447

Intercostal Nerve

Destruction 64620
Injection
    Anesthetic 64420-64421
    Neurolytic 64620

Interdental Fixation

Device
    Application 21110
Mandibular Fracture
    Closed Treatment 21453
    Open Treatment 21462
without Fracture 21497

Interdental Papilla

See Gums

Interdental Wire Fixation

Closed Treatment
    Craniofacial Separation 21431

Interferometry

Eye
    Biometry 92136

Intermediate Care Facilities (ICFs)

See Nursing Facility Services

Intermittent Positive Pressure Breathing (IPPB)

See Continuous Negative Pressure Breathing (CNPB); Continuous Positive Airway Pressure (CPAP)

Internal Breast Prostheses

See Breast, Implants

Internal Ear

See Ear, Inner

Internal Rigid Fixation

Reconstruction
    Mandibular Rami 21196

Internet E/M Service 0074T

Interphalangeal Joint

Arthrodesis 26860-26863
Arthroplasty 26535-26536
Arthrotomy 26080, 28054
Biopsy
    Synovium 26110
Capsule
    Excision 26525
    Incision 26525

Dislocation
    Closed Treatment 26770
    Open Treatment 26785
    Percutaneous Fixation 26776
    with Manipulation 26340
Exploration 26080
Fracture
    Closed Treatment 26740
    Open Treatment 26746
    with Manipulation 26742
Fusion 26860-26863
Great Toe
    Arthrodesis .28755
      with Tendon Transfer 28760
    Fusion 28755
      with Tendon Transfer 28760
Removal of Foreign Body 26080
Repair
    Collateral Ligament 26545
    Volar Plate .26548
Synovectomy .26140
Toe 28272
    Arthrotomy .28024
    Dislocation 28660-28665, 28675
      Percutaneous Fixation 28666
    Excision 28160
    Exploration .28024
    Removal
      Foreign Body 28024
      Loose Body 28024
    Synovial
      Biopsy 28054

Interruption
Vein
    Femoral 37650
    Iliac 37660
    Vena Cava .37620

Intersex State
Clitoroplasty 56805
Vaginoplasty 57335

Intersex Surgery
Female to Male 55980
Male to Female 55970

Interstitial Cell Stimulating Hormone
See Luteinizing Hormone (LH)

Interstitial Cystitides, Chronic
See Cystitis, Interstitial

Interstitial Cystitis
See Cystitis, Interstitial

Interstitial Fluid Pressure
Monitoring 20950

Interstitual Cell Stimulating Hormone
See Luteinizing Hormone (LH)

Intertarsal Joint
Arthrotomy 28020, 28050
Exploration 28020
Removal
    Foreign Body 28020
    Loose Body 28020

Synovial
    Biopsy 28050
    Excision 28070

Interthoracoscapular Amputation
See Amputation, Interthoracoscapular

Intertrochanteric Femur Fracture
See Femur, Fracture, Intertrochanteric

Intervertebral Chemonucleolysis
See Chemonucleolysis

Intervertebral Disk
Arthroplasty
    Cervical Interspace 0090T
    Each Additional Interspace 0092T
    Lumbar Interspace 0091T
    Removal 0093T, 0094T, 0095T
    Revision 0096T-0098T

Intervertebral Disk
Diskography
    Cervical 72285
    Lumbar 72295
    Thoracic 72285
Excision
    Decompression 63075-63078
    Herniated 63020-63044, 63055-63066
Injection
    Chemonucleolysis Agent 62292
    X-Ray 62290-62291

Intestinal Anastomosis
See Anastomosis, Intestines

Intestinal Invagination
See Intussusception

Intestinal Peptide, Vasoactive
See Vasoactive Intestinal Peptide

Intestine
Biopsy 44100
Lesion
    Excision 44110-44111
Unlisted Services and Procedures . .44238-44239,
                            44799

Intestines
Allotransplantation 44135-44136
    Removal 44137
Anastomosis 44625-44626
    Laparoscopic 44227
Bleeding Tube 91100
Closure
    Enterostomy
      Large or Small 44625-44626
      Stoma 44620-44625
Excision
    Donor 44132-44133
Exclusion 44700
Laparoscopic Resection
    with Anastomosis 44202-44208
Lysis of Adhesions
    Laparoscopic 44180
Nuclear Medicine
    Imaging 78290
Reconstruction
    Bladder 50820
    Colonic Reservoir 45119

Repair
Diverticula 44605
Obstruction 44615
Ulcer 44605
Wound 44605
Resection
    Laparoscopic 44227
Suture
    Diverticula .44605
    Stoma 44620-44625
    Ulcer 44605
    Wound 44605
Transplantation
    Allograft Preparation 44715-44721
    Donor Enterectomy 44132-44133
    Removal of Allograft 44137

Intestines, Large
See Anus; Cecum; Colon; Rectum

Intestines, Small
Anastomosis 43845, 44130
Biopsy 44020
    Endoscopy .44361
Catheterization
    Jejunum 44015
Decompression 44021
Destruction
    Lesion 44369
    Tumor 44369
Endoscopy 44364
    Biopsy 44361, 44377
    Control of Bleeding 44366, 44378
      via Stoma 44382
    Destruction
      Lesion 44369
      Tumor 44369
    Diagnostic .44376
    Exploration .44360
    Hemorrhage 44366
    Insertion
      Stent 44370, 44379
      Tube 44379
    Pelvic Pouch 44385-44386
    Removal
      Foreign Body 44363
      Lesion 44365
      Polyp 44364-44365
      Tumor 44364-44365
    Tube Placement 44372
    Tube Revision 44373
    via Stoma .44380
Enterostomy .44300
Excision 44120-44128
    Partial with Anastomosis 44140
Exclusion 44700
Exploration 44020
Gastrostomy Tube 44373
Hemorrhage .44378
Hemorrhage Control 44366
Ileostomy 44310-44314, 45136
    Continent 44316
Incision 44020
    Creation
      Pouch 44316
      Stoma 44300-44310, 44314
    Decompression 44021
    Exploration .44020

Revision
    Stoma 44312
    Stoma Closure 44620-44626
Insertion
    Catheter 44015
    Jejunostomy Tube 44372
Jejunostomy 44310
Lysis
    Adhesions .44005
Removal
    Foreign Body 44020, 44363
Repair
    Diverticula 44602-44603
    Enterocele
        Abdominal Approach 57270
        Vaginal Approach 57268
    Fistula 44640-44661
    Hernia 44050
    Malrotation 44055
    Obstruction 44050
    Ulcer 44602-44603
    Volvulus 44050
    Wound 44602-44603
Revision
    Jejunostomy Tube 44373
Specimen Collection 89100-89105
Suture
    Diverticula 44602-44603
    Fistula 44640-44661
    Plication 44680
    Ulcer 44602-44603
    Wound 44602-44603
X-Ray 74245, 74249-74251
    Guide Intubation 74355

Intestinovesical Fistula
See Fistula, Enterovesical

Intima-Media Thickness (IMT) Study
Artery
    Carotid, Common 0126T

Intimectomy
See Endarterectomy

Intra Arterial Injections
See Injection, Intraarterial

Intra-Abdominal Voiding Pressure Studies 51797

Intra-Osseous Infusion
See Infusion, Intraosseous

Intracapsular Extraction of Lens
See Extraction, Lens, Intracapsular

Intracardiac Echocardiography 93662

Intracranial
Biopsy 61140
Extracranial 61623
Microdissection 69990

Intracranial Arterial Perfusion
Thrombolysis 61624

Intracranial Neoplasm, Acoustic Neuroma
See Brain, Tumor, Excision

Intracranial Neoplasm, Craniopharyngioma
See Craniopharyngioma

Intracranial Neoplasm, Meningioma
See Meningioma

Intrafallopian Transfer, Gamete
See GIFT

Intraluminal Angioplasty
See Angioplasty

Intramuscular Injection
See Injection, Intramuscular

Intraocular Lens
Exchange 66986
Insertion 66983
    Manual or Mechanical
    Technique 66982, 66984
    Not Associated with Concurrent Cataract
    Removal 66985

Intratracheal Intubation
See Insertion, Endotracheal Tube

Intrauterine Contraceptive Device
See Intrauterine Device (IUD)

Intrauterine Device (IUD)
Insertion 58300
Removal 58301

Intrauterine Synechiae
See Adhesions, Intrauterine

Intravascular Stent
See Transcatheter, Placement, Intravascular Stents
X-Ray 75960

Intravascular Ultrasound
Intraoperative 37250-37251

Intravenous Infusion
Diagnosis 90765-90768
Hydration 90760-90761

Intravenous Injection
See Injection, Intravenous

Intravenous Pyelogram
See Urography, Intravenous

Intravenous Therapy
See Injection, Chemotherapy
Pain Management 90773-90775

Intravesical Instillation
See Bladder, Instillation

Intravitreal Injection
Pharmacologic Agent 67028

Intrinsic Factor 83528
Antibody 86340

Introduction
Breast
    Metallic Localization Clip Placement . .19295
    Preoperative Placement, Needle 19290-19291
Contraceptive Capsules
    Implantable 11975-11977
Drug Delivery Implant 11981, 11983
Gastrointestinal Tube 44500
    with Fluoroscopic Guidance 74340
Tissue Expanders
    Skin 11960-11971

Intubation
See Insertion
Endotracheal Tube 31500
Eustachian Tube
    See Catheterization, Eustachian Tube
Gastric 89130-89141, 91105
Specimen Collection
    Esophagus 91000
    Stomach 91055

Intubation Tube
See Endotracheal Tube

Intussusception
Barium Enema .74283
Reduction
    Laparotomy 44050

Invagination, Intestinal
See Intussusception

Inversion, Nipple
See Nipples, Inverted

Iodide Test
See Nuclear Medicine, Thyroid, Uptake

Iodine Test
See Starch Granules, Feces

Ionization, Medical
See Iontophoresis

Iontophoreses
See Iontophoresis

Iontophoresis 97033
Sweat Collection 89230

IP
See Allergen Immunotherapy

Ipecac Administration 99175

IPPB
See Intermittent Positive Pressure Breathing; Pulmonology, Therapeutic

Iridectomy
by Laser Surgery 66761
Peripheral for Glaucoma 66625
with Corneoscleral or Corneal Section 66600
with Sclerectomy with Punch or Scissors . .66160
with Thermocauterization 66155
with Transfixion as for Iris Bombe 66605
with Trephination 66150

Iridencleisis 66165

Iridodialysis 66680

Iridoplasty 66762

Iridotasis 66165

Iridotomy
by Laser Surgery 66761
by Stab Incision 66500
Excision
   Optical 66635
   Peripheral 66625
   with Corneoscleral or Corneal
   Section 66600
   with Cyclectomy 66605
Incision
   Stab 66500
   with Transfixion as for Iris Bombe 66505
Optical 66635
Peripheral 66625
Sector 66630

Iris
Cyst
   Destruction 66770
Excision
   Iridectomy
     Optical 66635
     Peripheral 66625
     Sector 66630
     with Corneoscleral or
     Corneal Section 66600
     with Cyclectomy 66605
Incision
   Iridotomy
     Stab 66500
     with Transfixion as for Iris Bombe ...66505
Lesion
   Destruction 66770
Repair
   with Ciliary Body 66680
     Suture 66682
Revision
   Laser Surgery 66761
   Photocoagulation 66762
Suture
   with Ciliary Body 66682

Iron 83540

Iron Binding Capacity 83550

Iron Hematoxylin Stain 88312

Iron Stain 85536, 88313

Irradiation
Blood Products 86945

Irrigation
Bladder 51700
Catheter
   Brain 62194, 62225
Corpora Cavernosa
   Priapism 54220
Penis
   Priapism 54220
Peritoneal
   See Peritoneal Lavage
Rectum
   for Fecal Impaction 91123

Shunt
   Spinal Cord 63744
Sinus
   Maxillary 31000
   Sphenoid 31002
Vagina 57150
Venous Access Device 96523

Irving Sterilization
See Ligation, Fallopian Tube, Oviduct

Ischial
Bursa
   Excision 27060
Tumor
   Excision 27078-27079

Ischiectomy 15941

Island Pedicle Flaps 15740

Islands of Langerhans
See Islet Cell

Islet Cell
Antibody 86341

Isocitrate Dehydrogenase
See Isocitric Dehydrogenase

Isocitric Dehydrogenase
Blood 83570

Isolation
Sperm 89260-89261

Isomerase, Glucose 6 Phosphate
See Phosphohexose Isomerase

Isopropanol
See Isopropyl Alcohol

Isopropyl Alcohol 84600

Isthmusectomy
Thyroid Gland 60210-60225

IUD
See Intrauterine Device (IUD)

IV
See Injection, Chemotherapy; Intravenous
Therapy

IV Infusion Therapy
See Allergen Immunotherapy; Chemotherapy;
Infusion; Injection, Chemotherapy

IV Injection
See Injection, Intravenous

IV, Coagulation Factor
See Calcium

IVC Filter
Placement 75940

IVF
See Artificial Insemination; In Vitro Fertilization

Ivy Bleeding Time 85002

IX Complex, Factor
See Christmas Factor

J

Jaboulay Operation
See Gastroduodenostomy

Jaboulay Operation Gastroduodenostomy
See Gastroduodenostomy

Jannetta Procedure
See Decompression, Cranial Nerve; Section

Japanese, River Fever
See Scrub Typhus

Jatene Type 33770-33781

Jaw Joint
See Facial Bones; Mandible; Maxilla

Jaws
Muscle Reduction 21295-21296
X-Ray
   for Orthodontics 70355

Jejunostomy
Catheterization 44015
Insertion
   Catheter 44015
Laparoscopic 44186-44187
Non-Tube 44187, 44310
with Pancreatic Drain 48001

Jejunum
Creation
   Stoma
     Laparoscopic 44186
Transfer
   with Microvascular Anastomosis
     Free 43496

Johannsen Procedure 53400

Johanson Operation
See Reconstruction, Urethra

Joint
See Specific Joint
Acromioclavicular
   See Acromioclavicular Joint
Arthrocentesis 20600-20610
Aspiration 20600-20610
Dislocation
   See Dislocation
Drainage 20600-20610
Finger
   See Intercarpal Joint
Fixation (Surgical)
   See Arthrodesis
Foot
   See Foot, Joint
Hip
   See Hip Joint
Injection 20600-20610
Intertarsal
   See Intertarsal Joint
Knee
   See Knee Joint

Ligament
   See Ligament
Metacarpophalangeal
   See Metacarpophalangeal Joint
Metatarsophalangeal
   See Metatarsophalangeal Joint
Nuclear Medicine
   Imaging 78300, 78315
Radiology
   Stress Views .76006
Sacroiliac
   See Sacroiliac Joint
Shoulder
   See Glenohumeral Joint
Sternoclavicular
   See Sternoclavicular Joint
Survey 76066
Temporomandibular
   See Temporomandibular Joint (TMJ)
   Dislocation Temporomandibular
      See Dislocation, Temporomandibular Joint
   Implant
      See Prosthesis, Temporomandibular Joint
Wrist
   See Radiocarpal Joint

Joint Syndrome, Temporomandibular
See Temporomandibular Joint (TMJ)

Jones and Cantarow Test
See Blood Urea Nitrogen; Urea Nitrogen, Clearance

Jones Procedure 28760

Joplin Procedure 28294

Jugal Bone
See Cheekbone

Jugular Vein
See Vein, Jugular

K

K-Wire Fixation
Tongue 41500

Kader Operation
See Incision, Stomach, Creation, Stoma; Incision and Drainage

Kala Azar Smear 87207

Kallidin I /Kallidin 9
See Bradykinin

Kallikrein HK3
See Antigen, Prostate Specific

Kallikreinogen
See Fletcher Factor

Kasai Procedure 47701

Kedani Fever
See Scrub Typhus

Keel
Insertion/Removal
   Laryngoplasty 31580

Keen Operation
See Laminectomy

Kelikian Procedure 28280

Keller Procedure 28292

Kelly Urethral Plication 57220

Keratectomy
Partial
   for Lesion 65400

Keratomileusis 65760

Keratophakia 65765

Keratoplasty
Lamellar 65710
Penetrating 65730
   in Aphakia .65750
   in Pseudophakia 65755

Keratoprosthesis 65770

Keratotomy
Radial 65771

Ketogenic Steroids 83582

Ketone Body
Acetone 82009-82010

Ketosteroids 83586-83593

Kidner Procedure 28238

Kidney
Abscess
   Incision and Drainage 50020
      Open 50020
      Percutaneous 50021
Anesthesia 00862
Biopsy 50200-50205
   Endoscopic 50555-50557, 52354
Catheterization
   Endoscopic .50572
Cyst
   Ablation 50541
   Aspiration 50390
   Excision 50280-50290
   Injection 50390
   X-Ray 74470
Destruction
   Calculus 50590
   Endoscopic 50557, 50576, 52354
Dilation 50395
Endoscopy
   Biopsy 50555, 50574-50576, 52354
   Catheterization 50553, 50572
   Destruction 50557, 50576, 52354
   Dilation
      Intra-Renal Stricture 52343, 52346
      Ureter 50553

Excision
   Tumor 52355
   Exploration .52351
   Lithotripsy 52353
   Removal
      Calculus 50561, 50580, 52352
      Foreign Body 50561, 50580
   via Incision 50562-50580
   via Stoma 50551-50561
Excision
   Donor 50300-50320, 50547
   Partial 50240
   Recipient 50340
   Transplantation 50370
   with Ureters 50220-50236
Exploration 50010, 50045, 50120
Incision 50010, 50045
Incision and Drainage 50040, 50125
Injection
   Drugs 50391
   Radiologic 50394
Insertion
   Catheter 50392-50393
   Guide 50395
   Intracatheter 50392
   Stent 50393
   Tube 50398
Instillation
   Drugs 50391
Lithotripsy 50590
Manometry
   Pressure 50396
Mass
   Ablation 50542
      Cryosurgical 50250
      Radiofrequency 50592
Needle Biopsy .50200
Nuclear Medicine
   Blood Flow .78715
   Function Study 78725
   Imaging 78700-78710
   Unlisted Services and Procedures 78799
Removal
   Calculus 50060-50081, 50130, 50561
   Foreign Body 50561, 50580
   Tube
      Nephrostomy 50389
Repair
   Blood Vessels 50100
   Fistula 50520-50526
   Horseshoe Kidney 50540
   Renal Pelvis 50400-50405
   Wound 50500
Solitary 50405
Suture
   Fistula 50520-50526
   Horseshoe Kidney 50540
Transplantation
   Allograft Preparation 50323-50329
   Anesthesia
      Donor 00862
      Recipient .00868
   Donor 00862
   Donor Nephrectomy 50300-50320, 50547
   Implantation of Graft 50360
   Recipient Nephrectomy 50340, 50365
   Reimplantation Kidney 50380
   Removal Transplant Renal Autograft . .50370

Tumor
  Ablation
    Cryotherapy .... .0135T
Ultrasound 76770-76778
X-Ray with Contrast
  Guide Catheter .... .74475

Kidney Stone
See Calculus, Removal, Kidney

Killian Operation
See Sinusotomy, Frontal

Kinase, Creatine
See CPK

Kineplasty
See Cineplasty

Kinetic Therapy .... .97530
See Physical Medicine/Therapy/Occupational Therapy

Kininase A
See Angiotensin Converting Enzyme (ACE)

Kininogen .... .85293

Kininogen, High Molecular Weight
See Fitzgerald Factor

Kleihauer-Betke Test .... .85460

Kloramfenikol
See Chloramphenicol

Knee
See Femur; Fibula; Patella; Tibia
Abscess .... .27301
Arthrocentesis .... .20610
Arthrodesis .... .27580
Arthroplasty 27440-27445, 27447
  Revision 27486-27487
Arthroscopy
  Diagnostic .... .29870
  Surgical 29866-29868, 29871-29889
Arthrotomy ...... .27310, 27330-27335, 27403
Biopsy 27323-27324, 27330-27331
  Synovium .... .27330
Bone
  Drainage .... .27303
Bursa .... .27301
  Excision .... .27340
Cyst
  Excision 27345-27347
Disarticulation .... .27598
Dislocation 27550-27552, 27560-27562
  Open Treatment 27556-27558, 27566
Drainage .... .27310
Excision
  Cartilage 27332-27333
  Ganglion .... .27347
  Lesion .... .27347
  Synovium 27334-27335
Exploration .... .27310, 27331
Fasciotomy .... .27305, 27496-27499
Fracture 27520-27524
  Arthroscopic Treatment 29850-29851
Fusion .... .27580
Hematoma .... .27301
Incision
  Capsule .... .27435

Injection
  X-Ray .... .27370
Magnetic Resonance Imaging
(MRI) 73721-73723
Manipulation .... .27570
Meniscectomy 27332-27333
Reconstruction 27437-27438
  Ligament 27427-27429
  with Prosthesis .... .27445
Removal
  Foreign Body .... .27310, 27331, 27372
  Loose Body .... .27331
  Prosthesis .... .27488
Repair
  Ligament 27405-27409
    Collateral .... .27405
    Collateral and Cruciate .... .27409
    Cruciate 27407-27409
  Meniscus .... .27403
  Tendon 27380-27381
Replacement .... .27447
Retinacular
  Release .... .27425
Strapping .... .29530
Suture
  Tendon 27380-27381
Transplantation
  Chondrocytes .... .27412
  Meniscus .... .29868
  Osteochondral
    Allograft .... .27415, 29867
    Autograft .... .27412, 29866
Tumor
  Excision 27327-27329, 27365
Unlisted Services and Procedures .... .27599
X-Ray 73560-73564
  Arthrography .... .73580
  Bilateral .... .73565
X-Ray with Contrast
  Arthrography .... .73580

Knee Joint
Arthroplasty .... .27446

Knee Prosthesis
See Prosthesis, Knee

Kneecap
Excision .... .27350
Repair
  Instability 27420-27424

Knock-Knee Repair 27455-27457

Kocher Operation 23650-23680
See Clavicle; Scapula; Shoulder, Dislocation, Closed Treatment

Kocher Pylorectomy
See Gastrectomy, Partial

Kock Pouch .... .44316
Formation .... .50825

Kock Procedure .... .44316

KOH
See Hair, Nails, Tissue, Examination for Fungi

Kraske Procedure .... .45116

Krause Operation
See Gasserian Ganglion, Sensory Root, Decompression

Kroenlein Procedure .... .67420

Krukenberg Procedure .... .25915

Kuhlmann Test 96101-96103

Kyphectomy
More than Two Segments .... .22819
Up to Two Segments .... .22818

Kyphoplasty 22523-22525

L

L Ascorbic Acid
See Ascorbic Acid

L Aspartate 2 Oxoglutarate Aminotransferase
See Transaminase, Glutamic Oxaloacetic

L Glutamine
See Glutamine

L-Alanine
See Aminolevulinic Acid (ALA)

L-Leucylnaphthylamidase
See Leucine Aminopeptidase

L/S Ratio
Amniotic Fluid .... .83661

Labial Adhesions
Lysis .... .56441

Labyrinth
See Ear, Inner

Labyrinthectomy .... .69905
with Mastoidectomy .... .69910
with Skull Base Surgery .... .61596

Labyrinthotomy
with Mastoidectomy .... .69802
with/without Cryosurgery .... .69801

Laceration Repair
See Specific Site

Lacrimal Duct
Canaliculi
  Repair .... .68700
Exploration .... .68810
  Canaliculi .... .68840
  Stent .... .68815
  with Anesthesia .... .68811
Insertion
  Stent .... .68815
Removal
  Dacryolith .... .68530
  Foreign Body .... .68530
X-Ray with Contrast .... .70170

Lacrimal Gland

Biopsy 68510
Close Fistula .68770
Excision
　　Partial 68505
　　Total 68500
Fistulization .68720
Incision and Drainage 68400
Injection
　　X-Ray .68850
Nuclear Medicine
　　Tear Flow 78660
Removal
　　Dacryolith 68530
　　Foreign Body 68530
Repair
　　Fistula .68770
Tumor
　　Excision
　　　　Frontal Approach 68540
　　　　with Osteotomy 68550
X-Ray 70170

Lacrimal Punctum

Closure
　　by Plug 68761
　　by Thermocauterization, Ligation or Laser
　　Surgery 68760
Dilation 68801
Incision 68440
Repair 68705

Lacrimal Sac

Biopsy 68525
Excision 68520
Incision and Drainage 68420

Lacrimal System

Unlisted Services and Procedures 68899

**Lactase Deficiency Breath
Test** 91065

Lactate 83605

Lactate Dehydrogenase . . .83615-83625

Lactic Acid 83605

Lactic Cytochrome Reductase
See Lactate Dehydrogenase

Lactic Dehydrogenase
See Lactate Dehydrogenase

Lactiferous Duct
See Mammary Duct; Mammary Ductogram
Excision 19112
Exploration 19110

Lactoferrin
Fecal .83630-83631

Lactogen, Human Placental 83632

Lactogenic Hormone
See Prolactin

Lactose
Urine .83633-83634

Ladd Procedure 44055

Lagophthalmos
Repair 67912

Laki Lorand Factor
See Fibrin Stabilizing Factor

Lamblia Intestinalis
See Giardia Lamblia

Lambrinudi Operation
See Arthrodesis, Foot Joint

Lamellar Keratoplasties
See Keratoplasty, Lamellar

Laminaria
Insertion 59200

Laminectomy . .62351, 63001, 63005-63011,
　　　　　　　　　63015-63044, 63180-63200,
　　　　　　　　　63265-63290, 63300-63655
Lumbar 22630, 63012
Surgical 63170-63172
with Facetectomy 63045-63048

Laminoplasty
Cervical 63050-63051

Langerhans Islands
See Islet Cell

Language Evaluation 92506

Language Therapy 92507-92508

LAP
See Leucine Aminopeptidase

Laparoscopic Appendectomy
See Appendectomy, Laparoscopic

Laparoscopic Biopsy of Ovary
See Biopsy, Ovary, Laparoscopic

Laparoscopy
Abdominal 49320-49329
Adrenal Gland
　　Biopsy 60650
　　Excision 60650
Adrenalectomy 50545
Appendectomy 44970
Aspiration 49322
Biopsy 47561, 49321
　　Lymph Nodes 38570
Bladder
　　Repair
　　　　Sling Operation 51992
　　　　Urethral Suspension 51990
　　　　Unlisted 51999
Cecostomy .44188
　　Laparoscopic 44188
Cholangiography 47560-47561
Cholecystectomy 47562-47564
Cholecystenterostomy 47570
Colectomy
　　Laparoscopic 44213
　　Partial 44204-44208, 44213
　　Total 44210-44212
Colostomy .44188
Destruction
　　Lesion 58662
Diagnostic .49320

Drainage
　　Extraperitoneal Lymphocele 49323
Ectopic Pregnancy 59150
　　with Salpingectomy and/or
　　Oophorectomy 59151
Enterectomy 44202
Enterolysis .44180
Enterostomy
　　Closure 44227
Esophagogastric Fundoplasty 43280
Fimbrioplasty 58672
Gastric Restrictive Procedures 43644-43645,
　　　　　　　　　　　　　　　43770-43774
Gastrostomy
　　Temporary 43653
Hernia Repair
　　Initial .49650
　　Recurrent 49651
Ileostomy 44187
In Vitro Fertilization 58976
　　Retrieve Oocyte 58970
　　Transfer Embryo 58974
　　Transfer Gamete 58976
Incontinence Repair 51990-51992
Jejunostomy 44186-44187
Kidney
　　Ablation 50541-50542
Ligation
　　Veins, Spermatic 55550
Liver
　　Ablation
　　　　Tumor 47370-47371
Lymphadenectomy 38571-38572
Lymphatic 38570-38589
Lysis of Adhesions 58660
Lysis of Intestinal Adhesions 44180
Nephrectomy 50545-50548
　　Partial 50543
Orchiectomy 54690
Orchiopexy .54692
Oviduct Surgery 58670-58671, 58679
Pelvis 49320
Proctectomy
　　Complete 45395
　　with Creation of Colonic Reservoir 45397
Proctopexy
　　for Prolapse 45400-45402
Prostatectomy 55866
Pyeloplasty .50544
Rectum
　　Resection 45395, 45397
　　Unlisted 45499
Removal
　　Fallopian Tube 58661
　　Leiomyomata 58545-58546
　　Ovaries 58661
　　Spleen 38120
　　Testis .54690
Resection
　　Intestines
　　　　with Anastomosis 44202-44203
　　Rectum 45395, 45397
Salpingostomy 58673
Splenectomy 38120-38129
Splenic Flexure
　　Mobilization 44213
Stomach 43651-43659
　　Gastric Bypass 43644-43645

Gastroenterostomy 43644-43645
   Roux-En-Y 43644
Unlisted Services and Procedures 38129,
      38589, 43289, 43659, 44238, 44979,
      45499, 47379, 47579, 49329, 49659,
      50549, 50949, 51999, 54699, 55559,
      58578-58579, 58679, 59898
Ureterolithotomy 50945
Ureteroneocystostomy 50947-50948
Urethral Suspension 51990
Vaginal Hysterectomy 58550-58554
Vaginal Suspension 57425
Vagus Nerves
   Transection 43651-43652
with X-Ray 47560

Laparotomy
Exploration 47015, 49000-49002
Hemorrhage Control 49002
Second Look 58960
Staging 49220, 58960
with Biopsy 49000

Laparotomy, Exploratory
See Abdomen, Exploration

Lapidus Procedure 28297

Large Bowel
See Anus; Cecum; Rectum

Laroyenne Operation
See Vagina, Abscess, Incision and Drainage

Laryngeal Function Study 92520

Laryngeal Sensory Testing 92614-92617

Laryngectomy 31360-31382
Partial 31367-31382
Subtotal .31367-31368

Laryngocele
Removal 31300

Laryngofissure 31300

Laryngography 70373
Instillation
   Contrast Material 31708

Laryngopharyngectomy
See Excision, Larynx, with Pharynx

Laryngopharynx
See Hypopharynx

Laryngoplasty
Burns 31588
Cricoid Split 31587
Laryngeal Stenosis 31582
Laryngeal Web 31580
Open Reduction of Fracture 31584

Laryngoscopy
Diagnostic 31505
Direct 31515-31571
Exploration 31505, 31520-31526, 31575
Fiberoptic 31575-31579
   with Stroboscopy 31579
Indirect .31505-31513

Newborn 31520
Operative 31530-31561

Laryngotomy 31300
Diagnostic 31320

Larynx
Aspiration
   Endoscopy .31515
Biopsy
   Endoscopy 31510, 31535-31536, 31576
Dilation
   Endoscopic 31528-31529
Electromyography
   Needle 95865
Endoscopy
   Direct .31515-31571
   Excision 31545-31546
   Exploration 31505, 31520-31526, 31575
   Fiberoptic 31575-31579
      with Stroboscopy 31579
   Indirect 31505-31513
   Operative 31530-31561
Excision
   Lesion .31512, 31578
      Endoscopic 31545-31546
   Partial .31367-31382
   Total 31360-31365
   with Pharynx 31390-31395
Exploration
   Endoscopic 31505, 31520-31526, 31575
Fracture 31584
Insertion
   Obturator 31527
Nerve
   Destruction .31595
Reconstruction
   Burns 31588
   Cricoid Split 31587
   Other 31588
   Stenosis 31582
   Web 31580
Removal
   Foreign Body
      Endoscopic . . .31511, 31530-31531, 31577
   Lesion
      Endoscopic . . .31512, 31545-31546, 31578
Repair
   Reinnervation Neuromuscular
      Pedicle .31590
Stroboscopy 31579
Tumor
   Excision 31300
      Endoscopic 31540-31541
Unlisted Services and Procedures 31599
Vocal Cord(s)
   Injection 31513, 31570-31571
X-Ray 70370
   with Contrast 70373

Laser Surgery
Anus 46614, 46917
Cautery
   Esophagus 43227
Lens, Posterior 66821
Lacrimal Punctum 68760
Lesion
   Mouth 40820
   Nose .30117-30118

Penis 54057
Skin 17000-17004, 17106-17111,
             17260-17286
Myocardium 33140-33141
Prostate .52647-52648
Spine
   Diskectomy .62287
Tumors
   Urethra and Bladder 52234
Urethra and Bladder 52214

Laser
Treatment 17000-17286, 96920-96922
See Destruction

Lateral Epicondylitis
See Tennis Elbow

Latex Fixation 86403-86406

LATS
See Thyrotropin Releasing Hormone (TRH)

Latzko Operation
See Repair, Vagina, Fistula; Revision

LAV
See HIV

LAV Antibodies
See Antibody, HIV

LAV-2
See HIV-2

Lavage
Colon 44701
Lung
   Bronchial 31624
   Total 32997
Mammary Duct 0046T, 0047T
Peritoneal 49080

LCM
See Lymphocytic Choriomeningitis

LD
See Lactate Dehydrogenase

LDH 83615-83625

LDL
See Lipoprotein, LDL

Lead 83655

Leadbetter Procedure 53431

Lecithin-Sphingomyelin Ratio .83661

Lecithinase C
See Tissue Typing

Lee and White Test 85345

LEEP Procedure 57460

LeFort I Procedure
Midface Reconstruction 21141-21147, 21155,
             21160
Palatal or Maxillary Fracture 21421-21423

LeFort II Procedure
Midface Reconstruction 21150-21151
Nasomaxillary Complex Fracture . . .21345-21348

LeFort III Procedure
Craniofacial Separation 21431-21436
Midface Reconstruction 21154-21159

LeFort Procedure
Vagina 57120

Left Atrioventricular Valve
See Mitral Valve

Left Heart Cardiac Catheterization
See Cardiac Catheterization, Left Heart

Leg
Cast
   Rigid Total Contact 29445
Lower
   See Ankle; Fibula; Knee; Tibia
   Abscess
     Incision and Drainage 27603
   Amputation 27598, 27880-27882
     Revision 27884-27886
   Angiography .73706
   Artery
     Ligation 37618
   Biopsy 27613-27614
   Bursa
     Incision and Drainage 27604
   Bypass Graft 35903
   Cast 29405-29435, 29450
   CT Scan 73700-73706
   Decompression 27600-27602
   Exploration
     Blood Vessel 35860
   Fasciotomy 27600-27602, 27892-27894
   Hematoma
     Incision and Drainage 27603
   Lesion
     Excision 27630
   Magnetic Resonance Imaging
   (MRI) .73718-73720
   Repair
     Blood Vessel 35226
     Blood Vessel with Other Graft 35286
     Blood Vessel with Vein Graft 35256
     Fascia 27656
     Tendon 27658-27692
     Splint 29515
     Strapping .29580
   Suture
     Tendon 27658-27665
   Tumor
     Excision 27615-27619
   Ultrasound .76880
   Unlisted Services and Procedures 27899
   Unna Boot .29580
   X-Ray 73592
Upper
   See Femur
   Abscess 27301
   Amputation 27590-27592
     at Hip 27290-27295
     Revision 27594-27596
   Angiography 73706, 75635
   Artery
     Ligation 37618
   Biopsy 27323-27324
   Bursa 27301
   Bypass Graft 35903

Cast 29345-29355, 29365, 29450
Cast Brace 29358
CT Scan 73700-73706, 75635
Exploration
   Blood Vessel 35860
Fasciotomy 27305, 27496-27499,
                   27892-27894
Halo Application 20663
Hematoma 27301
Magnetic Resonance Imaging
(MRI) .73718-73720
Neurectomy 27315-27320
Removal
   Cast 29705
   Foreign Body 27372
Repair
   Blood Vessel with Other Graft 35286
   Blood Vessel with Vein Graft 35256
   Muscle 27385-27386, 27400, 27430
   Tendon 27393-27400
   Splint 29505
   Strapping .29580
   Suture
     Muscle 27385-27386
   Tenotomy 27306-27307, 27390-27392
Tumor
   Excision 27327-27329
Ultrasound 76880
Unlisted Services and Procedures 27599
Unna Boot 29580
X-Ray 73592
Wound Exploration
   Penetrating 20103

Leg Length Measurement X-Ray
See Scanogram

Legionella
Antibody 86713
Antigen 87277-87278, 87540-87542

Legionella Micdadei
Antigen Detection
   Immunofluorescence 87277

Legionella Pneumophila
Antigen Detection
   Direct Fluorescence 87278

Leiomyomata
Removal 58140, 58545-58546, 58561

Leishmania
Antibody 86717

Lengthening, Tendon
See Tendon, Lengthening

Lens
Extracapsular .66940
Intracapsular .66920
   Dislocated .66930
Intraocular
   Exchange 66986
   Reposition .66825
Prosthesis
   Insertion 66983
     Manual or Mechanical
     Technique 66982, 66984
     Not Associated with Concurrent Cataract
     Removal .66985

Removal
   Lens Material
     Aspiration Technique 66840
     Extracapsular 66940
     Intracapsular 66920-66930
     Pars Plana Approach 66852
     Phacofragmentation Technique 66850

Lens Material
Aspiration Technique 66840
Pars Plana Approach 66852
Phacofragmentation Technique 66850

Leptomeningioma
See Meningioma

Leptospira
Antibody 86720

Leriche Operation 64809
See Sympathectomy, Thoracolumbar

Lesion
See Tumor
Anal
   Destruction 46900-46917, 46924
   Excision 45108, 46922
Ankle
   Tendon Sheath 27630
Arm, Lower
   Tendon Sheath
     Excision 25110
Auditory Canal, External
   Excision
     Exostosis .69140
     Radical with Neck Dissection 69155
     Radical without Neck Dissection 69150
     Soft Tissue 69145
Bladder
   Destruction 51030
Brain
   Excision 61534, 61536,
          61600-61608, 61615-61616
   Radiation Treatment 77432
Brainstem
   Excision 61575-61576
Breast
   Excision 19120-19126
Carotid Body
   Excision 60600-60605
Chemotherapy 96405-96406
   Destruction 67220-67225
Choroid
   Destruction 0016T
Ciliary Body
   Destruction 66770
Colon
   Destruction 44393, 45383
   Excision 44110-44111
Conjunctiva
   Destruction 68135
   Excision 68110-68130
     Over 1 cm 68115
     with Adjacent Sclera 68130
   Expression .68040
Cornea
   Destruction 65450
   Excision 65400
     of Pterygium 65420-65426

Destruction
    Ureter . . .52341-52342, 52344-52345, 52354
Ear, Middle
    Excision 69540
Epididymis
    Excision 54830
Esophagus
    Ablation 43228
    Excision 43100-43101
    Removal 43216
Excision 59100
    Bladder 52224
    Urethra 52224, 53265
Eye
    Excision 65900
Eyelid
    Destruction 67850
    Excision
        Multiple, Different Lids 67805
        Multiple, Same Lid 67801
        Single 67800
        Under Anesthesia 67808
        without Closure 67840
Facial
    Destruction 17000-17004, 17280-17286
Femur
    Excision 27062
Finger
    Tendon Sheath 26160
Foot
    Excision 28080, 28090
Gums
    Destruction 41850
    Excision 41822-41828
Hand Tendon Sheath 26160
Intestines
    Excision 44110
Intestines, Small
    Destruction 44369
    Excision 44111
Iris
    Destruction 66770
Larynx
    Excision 31545-31546
Leg, Lower
    Tendon Sheath 27630
Lymph Node
    Incision and Drainage 38300-38305
Mesentery
    Excision 44820
Mouth
    Destruction 40820
    Excision 40810-40816, 41116
    Vestibule
        Destruction 40820
        Repair 40830
Nerve
    Excision 64774-64792
Nose
    Intranasal
        External Approach 30118
        Internal Approach 30117
Orbit
    Excision 61333, 67412
Palate
    Destruction 42160
    Excision 42104-42120

Pancreas
    Excision 48120
Pelvis
    Destruction 58662
Penis
    Destruction
        Cryosurgery 54056
        Electrodesiccation 54055
        Extensive .54065
        Laser Surgery 54057
        Simple 54050-54060
        Surgical Excision 54060
    Excision 54060
        Penile Plaque 54110-54112
Pharynx
    Destruction 42808
    Excision 42808
Rectum
    Excision 45108
Removal
    Larynx 31512, 31578
Resection 52354
Retina
    Destruction
        Extensive 67227-67228
        Localized 0017T, 67208-67210
        Radiation by Implantation of Source . . .67218
Sciatic Nerve
    Excision 64786
Sclera
    Excision 66130
Skin
    Abrasion 15786-15787
    Biopsy 11100-11101
    Destruction
        Benign 17000-17250
        Malignant 17260-17286
        by Photodynamic Therapy 96567
    Excision
        Benign 11400-11471
        Malignant 11600-11646
        Injection 11900-11901
        Paring or Curettement 11055-11057
        Shaving 11300-11313
Skin Tags
    Removal 11200-11201
Skull
    Excision . .61500, 61600-61608, 61615-61616
Spermatic Cord
    Excision 55520
Spinal Cord
    Destruction 62280-62282
    Excision 63265-63273
Stomach
    Excision 43611
Testis
    Excision 54512
Toe
    Excision 28092
Tongue
    Excision 41110-41114
Uvula
    Destruction 42145
    Excision 42104-42107
Vagina
    Destruction 57061-57065

Vulva
    Destruction
        Extensive .56515
        Simple 56501
Wrist Tendon
    Excision 25110

Leu 2 Antigens
See CD8

Leucine Aminopeptidase 83670

Leukemia Lymphoma Virus I, Adult T Cell
See HTLV I

Leukemia Lymphoma Virus I Antibodies, Human T Cell
See Antibody, HTLV-I

Leukemia Lymphoma Virus II Antibodies, Human T Cell
See Antibody, HTLV-II

Leukemia Virus II, Hairy Cell Associated, Human T Cell
See HTLV II

Leukoagglutinins 86021

Leukocyte
See White Blood Cell
Alkaline Phosphatase 85540
Antibody 86021
Count 85032, 85048, 89055
Histamine Release Test 86343
Phagocytosis 86344
Transfusion 86950

Levarterenol
See Noradrenalin

Levator Muscle Repair
See Blepharoptosis, Repair

LeVeen Shunt
Insertion 49425
Patency Test 78291
Revision 49426

Levulose
See Fructose

LGV
See Lymphogranuloma Venereum

LH
See Luteinizing Hormone (LH)

LHR
See Leukocyte Histamine Release Test

Lid Suture
See Blepharoptosis, Repair

Lidocaine
Assay 80176

Lift, Face
See Face Lift

Ligament

See Specific Site
Collateral
Repair
Knee
with Cruciate Ligament 27409
Dentate
Section 63180-63182
Injection 20550
Release
Coracoacromial 23415
Transverse Carpal 29848
Repair
Elbow 24343-24346
Knee Joint 27405-27409

Ligation

Artery
Abdomen 37617
Carotid 37600-37606
Chest 37616
Coronary 33502
Ethmoidal 30915
Extremity 37618
Fistula 37607
Maxillary 30920
Neck 37615
Temporal 37609
Esophageal Varices 43204, 43400
Fallopian Tube
Oviduct 58600-58611, 58670
Gastroesophageal 43405
Hemorrhoids 46945-46946
Oviducts 59100
Salivary Duct 42665
Shunt
Aorta
Pulmonary 33924
Peritoneal
Venous 49428
Thoracic Duct 38380
Abdominal Approach 38382
Thoracic Approach 38381
Vas Deferens 55450
Vein
Clusters 37785
Esophagus 43205, 43244, 43400
Femoral 37650
Gastric 43244
Iliac 37660
Jugular, Internal 37565
Perforate 37760
Saphenous 37700-37735, 37780
Vena Cava 37620

Ligature Strangulation

Skin Tags 11200-11201

Light Coagulation

See Photocoagulation

Light Scattering Measurement

See Nephelometry

Light Therapy, UV

See Actinotherapy

Limb

See Extremity

Limited Lymphadenectomy for Staging

See Lymphadenectomy, Limited, for Staging

Limited Neck Dissection

with Thyroidectomy 60252

Limited Resection Mastectomies

See Breast, Excision, Lesion

Lindholm Operation

See Tenoplasty

Lingual Bone

See Hyoid Bone

Lingual Frenectomy

See Excision, Tongue, Frenum

Lingual Nerve

Avulsion 64740
Incision 64740
Transection 64740

Lingual Tonsil

See Tonsils, Lingual

Linton Procedure 37760

Lip

Biopsy 40490
Excision 40500-40530
Frenum 40819
Incision
Frenum 40806
Reconstruction 40525-40527
Repair 40650-40654
Cleft Lip 40700-40761
Fistula 42260
Unlisted Services and Procedures 40799

Lip, Cleft

See Cleft Lip

Lipase 83690

Lipectomy

Excision 15831-15839
Suction Assisted 15876-15879

Lipectomy, Aspiration

See Liposuction

Lipids

Feces 82705-82710

Lipo-Lutin

See Progesterone

Lipolysis, Aspiration

See Liposuction

Lipophosphodiesterase I

See Tissue Typing

Lipoprotein

(a) 83695
Blood 0026T, 83695-83721
LDL 83700-83704, 83721

Lipoprotein, Alpha

See Lipoprotein

Lipoprotein, Pre-Beta

See Lipoprotein, Blood

Liposuction 15876-15879

Lisfranc Operation

See Amputation, Foot; Radical Resection; Replantation

Listeria Monocytogenes

Antibody 86723

Lithium

Assay 80178

Litholapaxy 52317-52318

Lithotripsy

See Extracorporeal Shock Wave Therapy
Bile Duct Calculi (Stone)
Endoscopy 43265
Bladder 52353
Kidney 50590, 52353
Pancreatic Duct Calculi (Stone)
Endoscopy 43265
Ureter 52353
Urethra 52353
with Cystourethroscopy 52353

Lithotrity

See Litholapaxy

Liver

See Hepatic Duct
Ablation
Tumor 47380-47382
Laparoscopic 47370-47371
Abscess
Aspiration 47015
Incision and Drainage
Open 47010
Percutaneous 47011
Injection 47015
Aspiration 47015
Biopsy 47100
Cyst
Aspiration 47015
Incision and Drainage
Open 47010
Percutaneous 47011
Excision
Extensive 47122
Partial ...47120, 47125-47130, 47140-47142
Total 47133
Injection 47015
Radiologic 47505
X-Ray 47500
Lobectomy 47125-47130
Partial 47120
Needle Biopsy 47000-47001
Nuclear Medicine
Function Study 78220
Imaging 78201-78216
Vascular Flow 78206
Repair
Abscess 47300
Cyst 47300
Wound 47350-47362
Suture
Wound 47350-47362

Transplantation 47135-47136
    Allograft Preparation 47143-47147
Trisegmentectomy 47122
Unlisted Services and Procedures . .47379, 47399

Living Activities, Daily
See Activities of Daily Living

Lobectomy
Brain 61323, 61537-61540
Contralateral Subtotal
    Thyroid Gland 60212, 60225
Liver 47120-47130
Lung 32480-32482
    Sleeve 32486
Parotid Gland 42410-42415
Segmental 32663
Sleeve 32486
Temporal Lobe 61537-61538
Thyroid Gland Partial 60210-60212
    Total 60220-60225
Total 32663

Lobotomy
Frontal 61490

Local Excision Mastectomies
See Breast, Excision, Lesion

Local Excision of Lesion or Tissue of Femur
See Excision, Lesion, Femur

Localization of Nodule
Radiographic
    Breast 76096

Log Hydrogen Ion Concentration
See pH

Lombard Test
See Audiologic Function Test

Long Acting Thyroid Stimulator
See Thyrotropin Releasing Hormone (TRH)

Long-Term Care Facility Visits
See Nursing Facility Services

Longmire Operation
See Anastomosis, Hepatic Duct to Intestines

Loopogram
See Urography, Antegrade

Loose Body
Removal
    Ankle 27620
    Carpometacarpal Joint 26070
    Elbow 24101
    Interphalangeal Joint 28020
      Toe 28024
    Knee Joint 27331
    Metatarsophalangeal Joint 28022
    Tarsometatarsal Joint 28020
    Toe 28022
    Wrist 25101

Lord Procedure
See Anal Sphincter, Dilation

Louis Bar Syndrome
See Ataxia Telangiectasia

Low Birth Weight Intensive Care Services 99298-99300

Low Density Lipoprotein
See Lipoprotein, LDL

Low Vision Aids
See Spectacle Services
Fitting 92354-92355

Lower Extremities
See Extremity, Lower

Lower GI Series
See Barium Enema

LRH
See Luteinizing Releasing Factor

LSD
See Lysergic Acid Diethylamide

LTH
See Prolactin

Lumbar
See Spine
Aspiration, Disk
    Percutaneous 62287

Lumbar Plexus
Decompression 64714
Injection
    Anesthetic .64449
Neuroplasty 64714
Release 64714
Repair/Suture .64862

Lumbar Puncture
See Spinal Tap

Lumbar Spine Fracture
See Fracture, Vertebra, Lumbar

Lumbar Sympathectomy
See Sympathectomy, Lumbar

Lumbar Vertebra
See Vertebra, Lumbar

Lumen Dilation 74360

Lumpectomy 19160-19162

Lunate
Arthroplasty
    with Implant 25444
Dislocation
    Closed Treatment 25690
    Open Treatment 25695

Lung
Abscess
    Incision and Drainage
      Open 32200
      Percutaneous 32200-32201
Aspiration 32420
Biopsy 32095-32100

Bullae
    Excision 32141
      Endoscopic 32655
Cyst
    Incision and Drainage
      Open 32200
    Removal 32140
Decortication
    Endoscopic 32651-32652
    Partial 32225
    Total 32220
    with Parietal Pleurectomy 32320
Empyema
    Excision 32540
Excision
    Bronchus Resection 32486
    Completion 32488
    Donor
      Heart-Lung 33930
      Lung 32850
    Emphysematous 32491
    Empyema 32540
    Lobe 32480-32482
    Segment 32484
    Total 32440-32445
    Tumor 32503-32504
    Wedge Resection 32500
      Endoscopic 32657
Foreign Body
    Removal 32151
Hemorrhage .32110
Lavage
    Bronchial 31624
    Total 32997
Lysis
    Adhesions .32124
Needle Biopsy 32405
Nuclear Medicine
    Imaging, Perfusion 78580-78585
    Imaging, Ventilation 78586-78594
    Unlisted Services and Procedures 78599
Pneumocentesis 32420
Pneumolysis .32940
Pneumothorax 32960
Puncture 32420
Removal
    Bronchoplasty 32501
    Completion Pneumonectomy 32488
    Extrapleural 32445
    Single Lobe 32480
    Single Segment 32484
    Sleeve Lobectomy 32486
    Sleeve Pneumonectomy 32442
    Total Pneumonectomy 32440-32445
    Two Lobes .32482
    Volume Reduction 32491
    Wedge Resection 32500
Repair
    Hernia 32800
Segmentectomy 32484
Tear
    Repair 32110
Thoracotomy
    Biopsy 32095-32100
    Cardiac Massage 32160
    for Post-Op Complications 32120

Removal
   Bullae 32141
   Cyst 32140
   Intrapleural Foreign Body 32150
   Intrapulmonary Foreign Body 32151
  Repair 32110
  with Excision-Plication of Bullae 32141
  with Open Intrapleural
   Pneumonolysis 32124
Transplantation 32851-32854, 33935
  Allograft Preparation ..32855-32856, 33933
  Donor Pneumonectomy
   Heart-Lung 33930
   Lung 32850
Tumor
  Removal 32503-32504
Unlisted Services and Procedures 32999

Lung Function Tests
See Pulmonology, Diagnostic

Lung Volume Reduction
Emphysematous 32491

Lupus Anticoagulant Assay 85705

Lupus Band Test
See Immunofluorescent Study

Luteinizing Hormone (LH) 80418, 80426, 83002

Luteinizing Releasing Factor ...83727

Luteotropic Hormone
See Prolactin

Luteotropin
See Prolactin

Luteotropin, Placental
See Lactogen, Human Placental

Lyme Disease 86617-86618

Lyme Disease ab
See Antibody, Lyme Disease

Lyme Disease Vaccine
See Vaccination

Lymph Duct
Injection 38790

Lymph Nodes
Abscess
  Incision and Drainage 38300-38305
Biopsy 38500, 38510-38530, 38570
  Needle 38505
Dissection 38542
Excision 38500, 38510-38530
  Abdominal 38747
  Inguinofemoral 38760-38765
  Laparoscopic 38571-38572
  Limited, for Staging
   Para-Aortic 38562
   Pelvic 38562
   Retroperitoneal 38564
  Pelvic 38770

Radical
  Axillary 38740-38745
  Cervical 38720-38724
  Suprahyoid 38720-38724
  Retroperitoneal Transabdominal 38780
  Thoracic 38746
Exploration 38542
Hygroma, Cystic
  Axillary/Cervical
   Excision 38550-38555
Nuclear Medicine
  Imaging 78195
Removal
  Abdominal 38747
  Inguinofemoral 38760-38765
  Pelvic 38770
  Retroperitoneal Transabdominal 38780
  Thoracic 38746

Lymph Vessels
Imaging
  Lymphangiography
   Abdomen 75805-75807
   Arm 75801-75803
   Leg 75801-75803
   Pelvis 75805-75807
  Nuclear Medicine 78195
Incision 38308

Lymphadenectomy
Abdominal 38747
Bilateral Inguinofemoral ..54130, 56632, 56637
Bilateral Pelvic 51575, 51585, 51595, 54135, 55845, 55865
  Total 38571-38572, 57531, 58210
Diaphragmatic Assessment 58960
Gastric 38747
Inguinofemoral 38760-38765
Inguinofemoral, Iliac and Pelvic 56640
Injection
  Sentinel Node 38792
Limited Para-Aortic, Resection of Ovarian
Malignancy 58951, 58954
Limited Pelvic 55842, 55862, 58954
Limited, for Staging
  Para-Aortic 38562
  Pelvic 38562
  Retroperitoneal 38564
Mediastinal 21632
Peripancreatic 38747
Portal 38747
Radical
  Axillary 38740-38745
  Cervical 38720-38724
  Pelvic 54135, 55845
  Suprahyoid 38700
Regional 50230
Retroperitoneal Transabdominal 38780
Thoracic 38746
Unilateral Inguinofemoral 56631, 56634

Lymphadenitis
Incision and Drainage 38300-38305

Lymphadenopathy Associated Antibodies/Virus
See Antibody, HIV

Lymphangiogram
See Lymphangiography

Lymphangiography
Abdomen 75805-75807
Arm 75801-75803
Injection 38790
Leg 75801-75803
Pelvis 75805-75807

Lymphangioma, Cystic
See Hygroma; Lymph Nodes, Hygroma

Lymphangiotomy 38308

Lymphatic Channels
Incision 38308

Lymphatic Cyst
See Lymphocele

Lymphatic System
Unlisted Procedure 38999

Lymphatics
See Specific Procedure

Lymphoblast Transformation
See Blastogenesis

Lymphocele
Drainage
  Laparoscopic 49323
  Open 49062

Lymphocoele
See Lymphocele

Lymphocyte
Culture 86821-86822
Toxicity Assay 86805-86806
Transformation 86353

Lymphocyte, Thymus-Dependent
See T-Cells

Lymphocytes, CD4
See CD4

Lymphocytes, CD8
See CD8

Lymphocytic Choriomeningitis
Antibody 86727

Lymphocytotoxicity 86805-86806

Lymphogranuloma Venereum
Antibody 86729

Lymphoma Virus, Burkitt
See Epstein-Barr Virus

Lynch Procedure 31075

Lysergic Acid Diethylamide ...80102-80103, 80299

Lysergide
See Lysergic Acid Diethylamide

Lysis
Adhesions
    Epidural 0027T, 62263-62264
    Fallopian Tube 58740
    Foreskin 54450
    Intestinal 44005
    Labial 56441
    Lung 32124
    Nose 30560
    Ovary 58740
    Oviduct .58740
    Penile
       Post-Circumcision 54162
    Ureter 50715-50725
    Urethra .53500
    Uterus .58559
Euglobulin .85360
Labial
    Adhesions 56441
Nose
    Intranasal Synechia 30560

Lysozyme 85549

M

MacEwen Operation
See Hernia, Repair, Inguinal

Machado Test
See Complement, Fixation Test

MacLean-De Wesselow Test
See Blood Urea Nitrogen; Urea Nitrogen, Clearance

Macrodactylia
Repair 26590

Madlener Operation
See Tubal Ligation

Magnesium 83735

Magnet Operation
See Ciliary Body; Cornea; Eye, Removal, Foreign Body; Iris; Lens; Retina; Sclera; Vitreous

Magnetic Resonance
Unlisted Services and Procedures 76498

Magnetic Resonance Angiography (MRA)
Abdomen .74185
Arm 73225
Chest 71555
Head 70544-70546
Leg 73725
Neck 70547-70549
Pelvis 72198
Spine 72159

Magnetic Resonance Imaging (MRI)
3D Rendering 76376-76377
Abdomen 74181-74183

Ankle 73721-73723
Arm 73218-73220, 73223
Bone Marrow Study 76400
Brain 70551-70553
    Intraoperative 70557-70559
Breast 76093-76094
Chest 71550-71552
Elbow 73221
Face 70540-70543
Finger Joint 73221
Foot 73718-73719
Foot Joints 73721-73723
Guidance
    Needle Placement 76393
    Visceral Tissue Ablation 76394
Hand 73218-73220, 73223
Heart 75552
    Complete Study 75554
    Flow Mapping 75556
    Limited Study 75555
    Morphology 75553
Joint
    Lower Extremity 73721-73723
    Upper Extremity 73221-73223
Knee 73721-73723
Leg 73718-73720
Neck 70540-70543
Orbit 70540-70543
Pelvis 72195-72197
Spectroscopy 76390
Spine
    Cervical 72141-72142, 72156-72158
    Lumbar 72148-72158
    Thoracic 72146-72147, 72156-72158
Temporomandibular Joint (TMJ) 70336
Toe 73721-73723
Unlisted .76498
Wrist 73221

Magnetic Resonance Spectroscopy 76390

Magnetic Stimulation
Brain Cortex 0018T

Magnetoencephalography (MEG) 95965-95967

Magnuson Procedure 23450

MAGPI Operation 54322

MAGPI Procedure
See Hypospadias, Repair

Major Vestibular Gland
See Bartholin's Gland

Malar Area
Augmentation 21270
Bone Graft 21210
Fracture
    Open Treatment 21360-21366
    with Bone Graft 21366
    with Manipulation 21355
Reconstruction 21270

Malar Bone
See Cheekbone

Malaria Antibody 86750

Malaria Smear 87207

Malate Dehydrogenase 83775

Maldescent, Testis
See Testis, Undescended

Male Circumcision
See Circumcision

Malformation, Arteriovenous
See Arteriovenous Malformation

Malic Dehydrogenase
See Malate Dehydrogenase

Malignant Hyperthermia Susceptibility
Caffeine Halothane Contracture
Test (CHCT) 89049

Malleolus
See Ankle; Fibula; Leg, Lower; Tibia; Tibiofibular Joint

Mallet Finger Repair 26432

Maltose
Tolerance Test 82951-82952

Malunion Repair
Femur
    with Graft 27472
    without Graft 27470
Metatarsal 28322
Tarsal Joint 28320

Mammalian Oviduct
See Fallopian Tube

Mammaplasty
See Breast, Reconstruction; Mammoplasty

Mammary Abscess
See Abscess, Breast

Mammary Arteries
See Artery, Mammary

Mammary Duct
Catheter Lavage for Cytology 0046T, 0047T
X-Ray with Contrast 76086-76088

Mammary Ductogram
Injection .19030

Mammary Stimulating Hormone
See Prolactin

Mammillaplasty
See Nipples, Reconstruction

Mammogram
Breast
    Localization Nodule 76096

Mammography 76090-76092
Screening 76092
with Computer-Aided Detection 76082-76083

Mammoplasty
Augmentation 19324-19325
Reduction 19318

Mammotomy
See Incision, Breast; Incision and Drainage, Breast; Mastotomy

Mammotropic Hormone, Pituitary
See Prolactin

Mammotropic Hormone, Placental
See Lactogen, Human Placental

Mammotropin
See Prolactin

Mandated Services
On Call Services 99027

Mandible
See Facial Bones; Maxilla; Temporomandibular Joint (TMJ)
Abscess
    Excision 21025
Bone Graft 21215
Cyst
    Excision 21040, 21046-21047
Fracture
    Closed Treatment
      with Interdental Fixation 21453
      with Manipulation 21451
      without Manipulation 21450
    Open Treatment 21454-21470
      External Fixation 21454
      with Interdental Fixation 21462
      without Interdental Fixation 21461
    Percutaneous Treatment 21452
Osteotomy 21198-21199
Reconstruction
    with Implant 21244-21246, 21248-21249
Removal
    Foreign Body 41806
Torus Mandibularis
    Excision 21031
Tumor
    Excision 21040-21047
X-Ray 70100-70110

Mandibular Body
Augmentation
    with Bone Graft 21127
    with Prosthesis 21125

Mandibular Condyle
Fracture
    Open Treatment 21465
Reconstruction .21247

Mandibular Condylectomy
See Condylectomy

Mandibular Fracture
See Fracture, Mandible

Mandibular Rami
Reconstruction
    with Bone Graft 21194
    with Internal Rigid Fixation 21196
    without Bone Graft 21193
    without Internal Rigid Fixation 21195

Mandibular Resection Prosthesis .21081

Mandibular Staple Bone Plate
Reconstruction
    Mandible 21244

Manganese .83785

Manipulation
Chest Wall 94667-94668
Chiropractic 98940-98943
Dislocation and/or Fracture 25535
    Acetabulum 27222
    Acromioclavicular 23545
    Ankle 27810, 27818, 27860
    Carpometacarpal 26670-26676
    Clavicular .23505
    Elbow 24300, 24640
    Femoral 27232, 27502, 27510, 27517
      Pertrochanteric 27240
    Fibula 27781, 27788
    Finger 26725-26727, 26742, 26755
    Greater Tuberosity
      Humeral 23625
    Hand 26670-26676
    Heel 28405-28406
    Hip 27257
    Hip Socket .27222
    Humeral 23605, 24505, 24535, 24577
      Epicondyle 24565
    Intercarpal .25660
    Interphalangeal Joint . . .26340, 26770-26776
    Lunate 25690
    Malar Area .21355
    Mandibular 21451
    Metacarpal 26605-26607
    Metacarpophalangeal . .26700-26706, 26742
    Metacarpophalangeal Joint 26340
    Metatarsal 28475-28476
    Nasal Bone 21315-21320
    Orbit 21401
    Phalangeal Shaft 26727
      Distal, Finger or Thumb 26755
      Phalanges, Finger/Thumb 26725
    Phalanges
      Finger 26742, 26755, 26770-26776
      Finger/Thumb 26727
      Great Toe 28495-28496
      Toes 28515
    Radial 24655, 25565
    Radial Shaft 25505
    Radiocarpal 25660
    Radioulnar .25675
    Scapular 23575
    Shoulder 23650-23655
      with Greater Tuberosity 23665
    Shoulder Dislocation
    Sternoclavicular 23525
      with Neck Fracture 23675
    Talus 28435-28436
    Tarsal 28455-28456
    Thumb 26641-26650
    Tibial 27532, 27752
    Trans-Scaphoperilunar 25680
    Ulnar 24675, 25535, 25565
    Vertebral 22315
    Wrist . . .25259, 25624, 25635, 25660, 25675,
                 25680, 25690
Foreskin 54450
Globe .92018-92019

Hip 27275
Interphalangeal Joint, Proximal 26742
Knee 27570
Osteopathic 98925-98929
Shoulder
    Application of Fixation Apparatus 23700
Spine
    with Anesthesia 22505
Tibial, Distal 27762

Manometric Studies
Kidney
    Pressure 50396
Rectum/Anus .91122
Ureter
    Pressure 50686
Ureterostomy .50686

Manometry
Rectum 90911

Mantoux Test
See TB Test, Skin Test

Manual Therapy 97140

Maquet Procedure 27418

Marcellation Operation
See Hysterectomy, Vaginal

Marrow, Bone
See Bone Marrow

**Marshall-Marchetti-Krantz
Procedure** 51840-51841, 58152,
                     58267, 58293

Marsupialization
Bartholin's Gland Cyst 56440
Cyst
    Sublingual Salivary 42409
Liver
    Cyst or Abscess 47300
Pancreatic Cyst 48500
Skin 10040
Urethral Diverticulum 53240

Mass
Kidney
    Ablation 50542
      Cryosurgical 50250

**Mass Spectrometry and Tandem
Mass Spectrometry**
Analyte
    Qualitative .83788
    Quantitative 83789

Massage
Cardiac 32160
Therapy 97124
    See Physical Medicine/Therapy/Occupational Therapy

Masseter Muscle/Bone
Reduction 21295-21296

Mastectomy
Gynecomastia .19140
Modified Radical 19240
Partial .19160-19162

Radical 19200-19220
Simple, Complete 19180
Subcutaneous 19182

Mastectomy, Halsted
See Mastectomy, Radical

Mastoid
Excision
   Complete 69502
   Radical 69511
     Modified 69505
     Petrous Apicectomy 69530
   Simple .69501
Obliteration 69670
Repair
   by Excision 69601-69603
   Fistula .69700
   with Apicectomy 69605
   with Tympanoplasty 69604

Mastoid Cavity
Debridement 69220-69222

Mastoidectomy
Osseointegrated Implant
   for External Speech Processor/Cochlear
   Stimulator 69715, 69718
with Apicectomy 69605
with Skull Base Surgery 61590, 61597
   Decompression 61595
   Facial Nerve 61595
with Tympanoplasty 69604, 69641-69646
   Cochlear Device Implantation 69930
   Complete 69502
     Revision 69601
   Ossicular Chain Reconstruction 69605
   Radical 69511
     Modified 69505
     Revision 69602-69603
   Simple .69501
   with Labyrinthectomy 69910
   with Labyrinthotomy 69802
   with Petrous Apicectomy 69530

Mastoidotomy 69635-69637
with Tympanoplasty 69635
   Ossicular Chain Reconstruction 69636
   and Synthetic Prosthesis 69636

Mastoids
Polytomography 76101-76102
X-Ray 70120-70130

Mastopexy 19316

Mastotomy 19020

Maternity Care
See Abortion; Cesarean Delivery; Ectopic
Pregnancy; Obstetrical Care

**Maternity Care and
Delivery** 59612-59622, 59898

Maxilla
See Facial Bones; Mandible
Bone Graft 21210
CT Scan 70486-70488
Cyst
   Excision 21048-21049

Excision 21030, 21032-21034
Fracture
     Closed Treatment 21345, 21421
     Open Treatment .21346-21348, 21422-21423
     with Fixation 21345-21347
Osteotomy 21206
Reconstruction
   with Implant 21245-21246, 21248-21249
Tumor
   Excision 21048-21049

Maxillary Arteries
See Artery, Maxillary

Maxillary Sinus
See Sinus, Maxillary

Maxillary Torus Palatinus
Tumor Excision 21032

Maxillectomy 31225-31230

Maxillofacial Fixation
Application
   Halo Type Appliance 21100

Maxillofacial Impressions
Auricular Prosthesis 21086
Definitive Obturator Prosthesis 21080
Facial Prosthesis 21088
Interim Obturator Prosthesis 21079
Mandibular Resection Prosthesis 21081
Nasal Prosthesis 21087
Oral Surgical Splint 21085
Orbital Prosthesis 21077
Palatal Augmentation Prosthesis 21082
Palatal Lift Prosthesis 21083
Speech Aid Prosthesis 21084
Surgical Obturator Prosthesis 21076

Maxillofacial Procedures
Unlisted Services and Procedures 21299

**Maxillofacial
Prosthetics** 21076-21089
Unlisted Services and Procedures 21089

Maydl Operation 45563, 50810
See Colostomy

Mayo Hernia Repair
See Hernia, Repair, Umbilicus

Mayo Operation
See Varicose Vein, Removal

Mayo Procedure 28292

McBride Procedure 28292

McBurney Operation
See Hernia, Repair, Inguinal

McCannel Procedure 66682

McDonald Operation
See Repair, Cervix, Cerclage, Abdominal; Revision

McIndoe Procedure
See Vagina, Construction

McKissock Surgery
See Breast, Reduction

McVay Operation
See Hernia, Repair, Inguinal

Measles Uncomplicated
See Rubeola

Measles Vaccine
See Vaccines

Measles, German
See Rubella

Meat Fibers
Feces 89160

Meatoplasty 69310

Meatotomy 53020-53025
Cystourethroscopy 52281
Infant 53025
Prostate
   Laser Coagulation 52647
   Laser Vaporization 52648
Transurethral Electrosurgical Resection
   Prostate .52601
Ureter 52290
Ureteral
   Cystourethroscopy 52290-52305

Meckel's Diverticulum
Excision 44800
Unlisted Services and Procedures 44899

Median Nerve
Decompression 64721
Neuroplasty .64721
Release 64721
Repair/Suture
   Motor 64835
Transposition 64721

Median Nerve Compression
See Carpal Tunnel Syndrome

Mediastinal Cyst
See Cyst, Mediastinal; Mediastinum, Cyst

Mediastinoscopy 39400

Mediastinotomy
Cervical Approach 39000
Transthoracic Approach 39010

Mediastinum
See Chest; Thorax
Cyst
   Excision 32662, 39200
Endoscopy
   Biopsy 39400
   Exploration 39400
Exploration 39000-39010
Incision and Drainage 39000-39010
Needle Biopsy 32405
Removal
   Foreign Body 39000-39010
Tumor
   Excision 32662, 39220
Unlisted Procedures 39499

**Medical Disability Evaluation
Services** 99455-99456

Medical Testimony 99075

Medicine, Preventive
See Preventive Medicine

Medicine, Pulmonary
See Pulmonology

Medulla
Tractotomy 61470

Medullary Tract
Incision 61470
Section 61470

Meibomian Cyst
See Chalazion

Membrane Oxygenation, Extracorporeal
See Extracorporeal Membrane Oxygenation

Membrane, Mucous
See Mucosa

Membrane, Tympanic
See Ear, Drum

Meninges
Tumor
    Excision 61512, 61519

Meningioma
Excision 61512, 61519
Tumor
    Excision 61512, 61519

Meningitis, Lymphocytic Benign
See Lymphocytic Choriomeningitis

Meningocele Repair 63700-63702

Meningococcal
See Vaccines

Meningococcal Vaccine
See Vaccines

Meningococcus
See Neisseria Meningitidis

Meningomyelocele
See Myelomeningocele

Meniscectomy
Knee Joint 27332-27333
Temporomandibular Joint 21060

Meniscus
Knee
    Excision 27332-27333
    Repair 27403
    Transplantation 29868

Mental Nerve
Avulsion 64736
Incision 64736
Transection 64736

Meprobamate 83805

Mercury 83015, 83825

Merskey Test
See Fibrin Degradation Products

Mesencephalic Tract
Incision 61480
Section 61480

Mesencephalon
Tractotomy 61480

Mesenteric Arteries
See Artery, Mesenteric

Mesentery
Lesion
    Excision 44820
Repair 44850
Suture 44850
Unlisted Services and Procedures 44899

Mesh
Implantation
    Hernia 49568
Insertion
    Pelvic Floor 57267
Removal
    Abdominal Infected 11008

Metabisulfite Test
See Red Blood Cell (RBC), Sickling

Metabolite 82520

Metacarpal
Amputation 26910
Craterization 26230
Cyst
    Excision 26200-26205
Diaphysectomy 26230
Excision 26230
    Radical
      for Tumor 26250-26255
Fracture
    Closed Treatment 26605
      with Fixation 26607
    Open Treatment 26615
    Percutaneous Fixation 26608
    with Manipulation 26605-26607
    without Manipulation 26600
Ostectomy
    Radical
      for Tumor 26250-26255
Repair
    Lengthening 26568
    Nonunion 26546
    Osteotomy 26565
Saucerization 26230
Tumor
    Excision 26200-26205

Metacarpophalangeal Joint
Arthrodesis 26850-26852
Arthroplasty 26530-26531
Arthroscopy
    Diagnostic 29900
    Surgical 29901-29902
Arthrotomy 26075
Biopsy
    Synovium 26105

Capsule
    Excision 26520
    Incision 26520
Capsulodesis 26516-26518
Dislocation
    Closed Treatment 26700
    Open Treatment 26715
    Percutaneous Fixation 26705-26706
    with Manipulation 26340
Exploration 26075
Fracture
    Closed Treatment 26740
    Open Treatment 26746
    with Manipulation 26742
Fusion 26516-26518, 26850-26852
Removal of Foreign Body 26075
Repair
    Collateral Ligament 26540-26542
Synovectomy 26135

Metadrenaline
See Metanephrines

Metals, Heavy
See Heavy Metal

Metamfetamine
See Methamphetamine

Metanephrines 83835

Metatarsal
See Foot
Amputation 28810
Condyle
    Excision 28288
Craterization 28122
Cyst
    Excision 28104-28107
Diaphysectomy 28122
Excision 28110-28114, 28122, 28140
Fracture
    Closed Treatment
      with Manipulation 28475-28476
      without Manipulation 28470
    Open Treatment 28485
    Percutaneous Fixation 28476
Free Osteocutaneous Flap with Microvascular
Anastomosis 20972
Repair 28322
    Lengthening 28306-28307
    Osteotomy 28306-28309
Saucerization 28122
Tumor
    Excision 28104-28107, 28173

Metatarsectomy 28140

Metatarsophalangeal Joint
Arthrotomy 28022, 28052
Cheilectomy 28289
Dislocation 28630-28635, 28645
    Percutaneous Fixation 28636
Exploration 28022
Great Toe
    Arthrodesis 28750
    Fusion 28750
Removal
    of Foreign Body 28022
    of Loose Body 28022

Repair
   Hallux Rigidus 28289
Synovial
   Biopsy 28052
   Excision 28072
Toe 28270

Methadone 83840

Methaemoglobin
See Methemoglobin

Methamphetamine
Blood or Urine .82145

Methanol 84600

Methbipyranone
See Metyrapone

Methemalbumin 83857

Methemoglobin 83045-83050

Methenamine Silver Stain 88312

Methopyrapone
See Metyrapone

Methoxyhydroxymandelic Acid
See Vanillylmandelic Acid

Methsuximide 83858

Methyl Alcohol
See Methanol

Methylamphetamine
See Methamphetamine

Methylene Bichloride
See Dichloromethane

Methylfluorprednisolone
See Dexamethasone

Methylmorphine
See Codeine

Metroplasty
See Hysteroplasty

Metyrapone .80436

MIC
See Minimum Inhibitory Concentration

Micro-Ophthalmia
Orbit Reconstruction 21256

Microalbumin
Urine 82043-82044

Microbiology 87001-87999

Microdissection 88380

Microfluorometries, Flow
See Flow Cytometry

Microglobulin, Beta 2
Blood 82232
Urine 82232

Micrographic Surgery
Mohs Technique 17304-17310

Micrographic Surgery, Mohs
See Mohs Micrographic Surgery

Micropigmentation
Correction 11920-11922

Microscope, Surgical
See Operating Microscope

Microscopic Evaluation
Hair 96902

Microscopies, Electron
See Electron Microscopy

Microscopy
Ear Exam 92504

Microsomal Antibody 86376

Microsomia, Hemifacial
See Hemifacial Microsomia

Microsurgery
Operating Microscope 69990

Microvascular Anastomosis
Bone Graft
   Fibula 20955
   Other 20962
Fascial Flap, Free 15758
Muscle Flap, Free 15756
Osteocutaneous Flap with 20969-20973
Skin Flap, Free 15757

Microvite A
See Vitamin, A

Microwave Therapy 97024
See Physical Medicine/Therapy/Occupational
Therapy

Midbrain
See Brain; Brainstem; Mesencephalon; Skull
Base Surgery

Midcarpal Medioccipital Joint
Arthrotomy 25040

**Middle Cerebral Artery
Velocimetry** 76821

Middle Ear
See Ear, Middle

Midface
Reconstruction
   Forehead Advancement 21159-21160
   with Bone Graft 21145-21160, 21188
   without Bone Graft 21141-21143

**Migration Inhibitory Factor
(MIF)** 86378

Mile Operation
See Colectomy, Total, with Proctectomy

Milia, Multiple
Removal 10040

Miller Procedure 28737

**Miller-Abbott
Intubation** 44500, 74340

Minerva Cast 29035
Removal 29710

**Minimum Inhibitory
Concentration** 87186

**Minimum Lethal
Concentration** 87187

**Minnesota Multiphasic Personality
Inventory**
See MMPI

Miscarriage
Incomplete Abortion 59812
Missed Abortion
   First Trimester 59820
   Second Trimester 59821
Septic Abortion 59830

Missed Abortion
See Abortion

Mitchell Procedure 28296

Mitogen Blastogenesis 86353

Mitral Valve
Incision 33420-33422
Repair .33420-33427
   Incision 33420-33422
Replacement .33430

Mitrofanoff Operation 50845
See Appendico-Vesicostomy

Miyagawanella
See Chlamydia

MLC
See Lymphocyte, Culture

MMPI 96101-96103
Computer-Assisted 96103

MMR Shots 90707
See Vaccines

Mobilization
Splenic Flexure 44139
   Laparoscopic 44213
Stapes 69650

Modified Radical Mastectomy
See Mastectomy, Modified Radical

**Mohs Micrographic
Surgery** 17304-17310

Molar Pregnancy
See Hydatidiform Mole

Mold
Culture 87107

Mole, Carneous
See Abortion

Mole, Hydatid
See Hydatidiform Mole

Molecular Cytogenetics 88271-88275
Interpretation and Report 88291

Molecular Diagnostics . . .83890-83914
Amplification 83898-83901
Cell Lysis 83907
Dot/Slot Production 83893
Enzymatic Digestion 83892
Extraction 83890-83891
Interpretation .83912
Molecular Isolation (Extraction) 83890
Mutation Identification 83904-83906
    Enzymatic Ligation 83914
Mutation Scanning 83903
Nucleic Acid Amplification 83900, 83901,
                                        83908
Nucleic Acid Extraction 83907
Nucleic Acid Probe 83896
Nucleic Acid Transfer 83897
Polymerase Reaction Chain 83898
Reverse Transcription 83902
Separation 83894
Separation and Identification
    High Resolution Technique 83909

Molecular Oxygen Saturation
See Oxygen Saturation

Molecular Probes 88384-88386
Multiple
    Array-Based Evaluation 88384-88386

Molluscum Contagiosum
Destruction 17110-17111, 54050-54065

Molteno Procedure 66180

Monilia
See Candida

Monitoring
Blood Pressure, 24 Hour 93784-93790
Electrocardiogram 93224-93237
    See Electrocardiography
Electroencephalogram 95812-95813,
                                        95950-95953, 95956
    with Drug Activation 95954
    with Physical Activation 95954
    with WADA Activation 95958
Fetal
    During Labor 59050-59051, 99500
        Interpretation Only 59051
Glucose
    Interstitial Fluid 95250-95251
Interstitial Fluid Pressure 20950
Seizure .61531, 61760

Monitoring, Sleep
See Polysomnography

Monoethylene Glycol
See Ethylene Glycol

Mononucleosis Virus, Infectious
See Epstein-Barr Virus

Monophosphate, Adenosine
See Adenosine Monophosphate (AMP)

Monophosphate, Adenosine Cyclic
See Cyclic AMP

Monophosphate, Guanosine
See Guanosine Monophosphate

Monophosphate, Guanosine Cyclic
See Cyclic GMP

Monospot Test
See Rapid Test for Infection

Monoxide, Carbon
See Carbon Monoxide

Monteggia Fracture 24620-24635

Monticelli Procedure
See Application, Bone Fixation Device

Morbilli
See Rubeola

Morphine Methyl Ether
See Codeine

Morphometric Analysis
Nerve 88356
Skeletal Muscle 88355
Tumor 88358-88361, 88367-88368

Morton's Neuroma
See Neuroma, Foot, Excision
Excision 28080

Moschcowitz Operation
See Repair, Hernia, Femoral; Revision

Mosenthal Test
See Urinalysis, Routine

Mother Cell
See Stem Cell

Motility Study
Duodenal 91022
Esophagus 91010-91012
    Imaging 78258
Sperm 89300

Motion Analysis
by Video and 3D Kinematics 96000, 96004
Computer-based 96000, 96004

Mouth
Abscess
    Incision and Drainage 40800-40801,
                                        41005-41009, 41015-41018
Biopsy .40808, 41108
Cyst
    Incision and Drainage 40800-40801,
                                        41005-41009, 41015-41018
Excision
    Frenum 40819
Hematoma
    Incision and Drainage 40800-40801,
                                        41005-41009, 41015-41018
Lesion
    Destruction .40820
    Excision 40810-40816, 41116
Vestibule
    Destruction .40820
    Repair 40830

Mucosa
Excision 40818
Reconstruction 40840-40845
Removal
    Foreign Body 40804-40805
Repair
    Laceration 40830-40831
Unlisted Services and Procedures . .40899, 41599
Vestibule
    Excision
        Destruction 40808-40820
    Incision 40800-40806
    Other Procedures 40899
    Removal
        Foreign Body 40804
    Repair 40830-40845

Move
See Transfer
Finger 26555
Toe Joint 26556
Toe to Hand 26551-26554

Moynihan Test
See Gastrointestinal Tract, X-Ray, with Contrast

MPD Syndrome
See Temporomandibular Joint (TMJ)

MPR
See Multifetal Pregnancy Reduction

MR Spectroscopy
See Magnetic Resonance Spectroscopy

MRA
See Magnetic Resonance Angiography

MRI
See Magnetic Resonance Imaging (MRI)

MSLT
See Multiple Sleep Latency Testing (MSLT)

Mucin
Synovial Fluid .83872

Mucocele
Sinusotomy
    Frontal 31075

Mucopolysaccharides 83864-83866

Mucormycoses
See Mucormycosis

Mucormycosis
Antibody 86732

Mucosa
Cautery .30801-30802
Destruction
    Cautery 30801-30802
    Photodynamic Therapy 96567
Ectopic Gastric Imaging 78290
Excision of Lesion
    Alveolar, Hyperplastic 41828
    Vestibule of Mouth 40810-40818
    via Esophagoscopy 43228
    via Small Intestinal Endoscopy 44369
    via Upper GI Endoscopy 43258
Periodontal Grafting 41870

Turbinates .30801-30802
Urethra, Mucosal Advancement 53450
Vaginal Biopsy 57100-57105

Mucosa, Buccal
See Mouth, Mucosa

Mucous Cyst
Antibody
　　Hand or Finger 26160

Mucous Membrane
See Mouth, Mucosa
Cutaneous
　　Biopsy .11100-11101
　　Excision
　　　　Benign Lesion 11440-11446
　　　　Malignant Lesion 11640-11646
　　Layer Closure, Wounds 12051-12057
　　Simple Repair, Wounds 12011-12018
Excision
　　Sphenoid Sinus 31288
Lid Margin
　　Correction of Trichiasis 67835
　　Nasal Test 95065
　　Ophthalmic Test 95060
Rectum
　　Proctoplasty for Prolapse 45505

Mucus Cyst
See Mucous Cyst

MUGA (Multiple Gated Acquisition) 78472-78478, 78483

Muller Procedure
See Sleep Study

Multifetal Pregnancy Reduction 59866

Multiple Sleep Latency Testing (MSLT) 95805

Multiple Valve Procedures
See Valvuloplasty

Mumford Operation
See Claviculectomy, Partial

Mumford Procedure 29824

Mumps
Antibody 86735
Immunization 90704, 90707, 90710
Vaccine 90704
　　MMR 90707
　　MMRV 90710

Muramidase 85549

Murine Typhus 86000

Muscle
See Specific Muscle
Abdomen
　　See Abdominal Wall
Biopsy 20200-20206
Debridement
　　Infected 11004-11006
Heart
　　See Myocardium

Neck
　　See Neck Muscle
Removal
　　Foreign Body 20520-20525
Repair
　　Forearm 25260-25274
　　Wrist 25260-25274
Revision
　　Arm, Upper 24330-24331
Transfer
　　Arm, Upper 24301, 24320
　　Elbow 24301
　　Femur 27110
　　Hip 27100-27105, 27111
　　Shoulder 23395-23397, 24301, 24320

Muscle Compartment Syndrome
Detection 20950

Muscle Denervation
See Denervation

Muscle Division
Scalenus Anticus 21700-21705
Sternocleidomastoid 21720-21725

Muscle Flaps 15732-15738
Free 15756

Muscle Grafts 15841-15845

Muscle Testing
Dynamometry, Eye 92260
Extraocular Multiple Muscles 92265
Manual 95831-95834

Muscle, Oculomotor
See Eye Muscles

Muscles
Repair
　　Extraocular .65290

Musculo-Skeletal System
See Musculoskeletal System

Musculoplasty
See Muscle, Repair

Musculoskeletal System
Unlisted Services and Procedures 20999,
　　24999, 25999, 26989, 27299, 27599, 27899
Unlisted Services and Procedures, Head . . .21499

Musculotendinous (Rotator) Cuff
Repair 23410-23412

Mustard Procedure
See Repair, Great Arteries; Revision

Myasthenia Gravis
Tensilon Test 95857

Myasthenic, Gravis
See Myasthenia Gravis

Mycobacteria
Culture 87116
　　Identification 87118
Detection 87550-87562
Sensitivity Studies 87190

Mycoplasma
Antibody 86738
Culture 87109
Detection 87580-87582

Mycota
See Fungus

Myectomy, Anorectal
See Myomectomy, Anorectal

Myelencephalon
See Medulla

Myelin Basic Protein
Cerebrospinal Fluid 83873

Myelography
Brain 70010
Spine
　　Cervical 72240
　　Lumbosacral 72265
　　Thoracic 72255
　　Total 72270

Myelomeningocele
Repair .63704-63706

Myelotomy 63170

Myocardial
Perfusion Imaging . . .78460-78465, 78478-78480
　　See Nuclear Medicine
Positron Emission Tomography (PET) 78459

Myocardial Imaging 78466-78469
Positron Emission Tomography
　　Perfusion Study 78491-78492
Repair
　　Postinfarction 33542

Myocutaneous Flaps 15732-15738, 15756

Myofascial Pain Dysfunction Syndrome
See Temporomandibular Joint (TMJ)

Myofibroma
See Leiomyomata

Myoglobin .83874

Myomectomy
Anorectal 45108
Uterus 58140-58146, 58545-58546

Myoplasty
See Muscle, Repair

Myotomy
Esophagus 43030
Hyoid 21685

Myringoplasty 69620

Myringostomy
See Myringotomy

Myringotomy 69420-69421

Myxoid Cyst
See Ganglion

N

N. Meningitidis
See Neisseria Meningitidis

Naffziger Operation
See Decompression, Orbit; Section

Nagel Test
See Color Vision Examination

Nail Bed
Reconstruction 11762
Repair 11760

Nail Fold
Excision
    Wedge 11765

Nail Plate Separation
See Nails, Avulsion

Nails
Avulsion 11730-11732
Biopsy 11755
Debridement 11720-11721
Drainage 10060-10061
Evacuation
    Hematoma, Subungual 11740
Excision 11750-11752
KOH Examination 87220
Removal 11730-11732, 11750-11752
Trimming 11719

Narcosynthesis
Diagnostic and Therapeutic 90865

Nasal Abscess
See Nose, Abscess

Nasal Area
Bone Graft 21210

Nasal Bleeding
See Epistaxis

Nasal Bone
Fracture
    Closed Treatment 21310-21320
    Open Treatment 21325-21335
    with Manipulation 21315-21320
    without Manipulation 21310
X-Ray 70160

Nasal Deformity
Repair 40700-40761

Nasal Function Study 92512

Nasal Polyp
See Nose, Polyp

Nasal Prosthesis
Impression 21087

Nasal Septum
Abscess
    Incision and Drainage 30020

Fracture
    Closed Treatment 21337
    Open Treatment 21336
Hematoma
    Incision and Drainage 30020
Repair 30630
Submucous Resection 30520

Nasal Sinuses
See Sinus; Sinuses

Nasal Smear
Eosinophils 89190

Nasal Turbinate
Fracture
    Therapeutic 30930

Nasoethmoid Complex
Fracture
    Open Treatment 21338-21339
    Percutaneous Treatment 21340
Reconstruction 21182-21184

Nasogastric Tube
Placement 43752

Nasolacrimal Duct
Exploration 68810
    with Anesthesia 68811
Insertion
    Stent 68815
X-Ray
    with Contrast 70170

Nasomaxillary
Fracture
    Closed Treatment 21345
    Open Treatment 21346-21348
    with Bone Grafting 21348

Nasopharynges
See Nasopharynx

Nasopharyngoscopy 92511

Nasopharynx
See Pharynx
Biopsy 42804-42806
Hemorrhage 42970-42972
Unlisted Services and Procedures 42999

Natriuretic Peptide 83880

Natural Killer (NK) Cells
Count 86357

Natural Ostium
Sinus
    Maxillary 31000
    Sphenoid 31002

Navicular
Arthroplasty
    with Implant 25443
Fracture
    Closed Treatment 25622
    Open Treatment 25628
    with Manipulation 25624
Navigation
    Computer Assisted 0054T-0056T
Repair 25440

Neck
Angiography 70498, 70547-70549
Artery
    Ligation 37615
Biopsy 21550
Bypass Graft 35901
CT Scan 70490-70492, 70498
Dissection, Radical
    See Radical Neck Dissection
Exploration
    Blood Vessel 35800
    Lymph Nodes 38542
Incision and Drainage
    Abscess 21501-21502
    Hematoma 21501-21502
Lipectomy, Suction Assisted 15876
Magnetic Resonance Angiography
(MRA) 70547-70549
Magnetic Resonance Imaging
(MRI) 70540-70543
Nerve
    Graft 64885-64886
Repair
    Blood Vessel 35201
    with Other Graft 35261
    with Vein Graft 35231
Skin
    Revision 15819
Tumor
    Excision 21555-21556
    Excision/Resection 21557
Ultrasound Exam 76536
Unlisted Services and Procedures,
Surgery 21899
Urinary Bladder
    See Bladder, Neck
Wound Exploration
    Penetrating 20100
X-Ray 70360

Neck Muscle
Division
    Scalenus Anticus 21700-21705
    Sternocleidomastoid 21720-21725

Necropsy
Coroner's Exam 88045
Forensic Exam 88040
Gross and Micro Exam 88020-88029
Gross Exam 88000-88016
Organ 88037
Regional 88036
Unlisted Services and Procedures 88099

Needle Biopsy
See Biopsy
Abdomen Mass 49180
Bone 20220-20225
Bone Marrow 38221
Breast 19100
Colon
    Endoscopy 45392
Colon-Sigmoid
    Endoscopy 45342
CT Scan Guidance 76360
Epididymis 54800
Esophagus
    Endoscopy 43232

Fluoroscopic Guidance 76003
Gastrointestinal, Upper
    Endoscopy 43238, 43242
Kidney 50200
Liver 47000-47001
Lung 32405
Lymph Nodes 38505
Mediastinum 32405
Muscle 20206
Pancreas 48102
Pleura 32400
Prostate 0137T, 55700
Retroperitoneal Mass 49180
Salivary Gland .42400
Spinal Cord 62269
Testis 54500
Thyroid Gland .60100
Transbronchial 31629, 31633

Needle Localization
Breast
    Placement 19290-19291
    with Lesion Excision 19125-19126
Magnetic Resonance Guidance 76393

Needle Manometer Technique .20950

Needle Wire
Introduction
    Trachea 31730
Placement
    Breast 19290-19291

Neer Procedure 23470

Neisseria Gonorrheae 87590-87592, 87850

Neisseria Meningitidis
Antibody 86741

Neobladder
Construction 51596

Neonatal Critical Care
See Newborn Care
Initial 99295
Subsequent 99296

Neoplasm
Cancer Photoradiation Therapy
    See Photochemotherapy
Cardiac
    See Heart, Tumor
Colon
    See Colon, Tumor
Esophageal
    See Tumor, Esophagus
Spinal Cord
    See Spinal Cord, Neoplasm
Unspecified Nature of Brain
    See Brain, Tumor

Neoplastic Growth
See Tumor

Nephelometry 83883

Nephrectomy
Donor 50300-50320, 50547
Laparoscopic 50545-50548
Partial 50240
    Laparoscopic 50543
Recipient 50340
with Ureters 50220-50236, 50546, 50548

Nephrolith
See Calculus, Removal, Kidney

Nephrolithotomy 50060-50075

Nephropexy 50400-50405

Nephroplasty
See Kidney, Repair

Nephropyeloplasty
See Pyeloplasty

Nephrorrhaphy 50500

Nephroscopy
See Endoscopy, Kidney

Nephrostogram 50394

Nephrostolithotomy
Percutaneous 50080-50081

Nephrostomy 50040
Change Tube .50398
Endoscopic 50562-50570
Percutaneous .52334
with Drainage .50040
X-Ray with Contrast
    Guide Dilation 74485

Nephrostomy Tract
Establishment .50395

Nephrotomogram
See Nephrotomography

Nephrotomography 74415

Nephrotomy 50040-50045
with Exploration 50045

Nerve
Cranial
    See Cranial Nerve
Facial
    See Facial Nerve
Intercostal
    See Intercostal Nerve
Lingual
    See Lingual Nerve
Median
    See Median Nerve
Obturator
    See Obturator Nerve
Peripheral
    See Peripheral Nerve
Phrenic
    See Phrenic Nerve
Sciatic
    See Sciatic Nerve
Spinal
    See Spinal Nerve

Tibial
    See Tibial Nerve
Ulnar
    See Ulnar Nerve
Vestibular
    See Vestibular Nerve

Nerve Conduction
Motor Nerve 95900-95903
Sensory Nerve or Mixed 95904

Nerve II, Cranial
See Optic Nerve

Nerve Root
See Cauda Equina; Spinal Cord
Decompression 63020-63048, 63055-63103
Incision 63185-63190
Section 63185-63190

Nerve Stimulation, Transcutaneous
See Application, Neurostimulation

Nerve Teasing 88362

Nerve V, Cranial
See Trigeminal Nerve

Nerve VII, Cranial
See Facial Nerve

Nerve X, Cranial
See Vagus Nerve

Nerve XI, Cranial
See Accessory Nerve

Nerve XII, Cranial
See Hypoglossal Nerve

Nerves
Anastomosis
    Facial to Hypoglossal 64868
    Facial to Phrenic 64870
    Facial to Spinal Accessory 64866
Avulsion 64732-64772
Biopsy 64795
Decompression 64702-64727
Destruction 64600-64681
    Laryngeal, Recurrent 31595
Foot
    Excision 28030
    Incision 28035
Graft 64885-64907
Implantation
    Electrode 64553-64581
    to Bone 64787
    to Muscle .64787
Incision 43640-43641, 64732-64772
Injection
    Anesthetic 01991-01992, 64400-64530
    Neurolytic Agent 64600-64681
Insertion
    Electrode 64553-64581
Lesion
    Excision 64774-64792
Neurofibroma
    Excision 64788-64792
Neurolemmoma
    Excision 64788-64792

Neurolytic
  Internal 64727
Neuroma
  Excision 64774-64786
Neuroplasty .64702-64721
Removal
  Electrode 64585
Repair
  Graft 64885-64907
  Microdissection 69990
  Suture 64831-64876
Spinal Accessory
  Incision 63191
  Section 63191
Suture .64831-64876
Sympathectomy
  Excision 64802-64818
Transection 43640-43641, 64732-64772
Transposition 64718-64721
Unlisted Services and Procedures 64999

Nervous System
Nuclear Medicine
  Unlisted Services and Procedures 78699

Nesidioblast
See Islet Cell

Neural Conduction
See Nerve Conduction

Neural Ganglion
See Ganglion

Neurectomy
Foot 28030
Gastrocnemius 27320
Hamstring Muscle 27315
Leg, Upper 27315-27320
Popliteal 27320
Tympanic 69676

Neuroendoscopy
Intracranial 62160-62165

Neurofibroma
Cutaneous Nerve
  Excision 64788
Extensive
  Excision 64792
Peripheral Nerve
  Excision 64790

Neurolemmoma
Cutaneous Nerve
  Excision 64788
Extensive
  Excision 64792
Peripheral Nerve
  Excision 64790

Neurologic System
See Nervous System

Neurology
Diagnostic
  Anal Sphincter 51785
  Autonomic Nervous Function
    Heart Rate Response 95921-95923
    Pseudomotor Response 95921-95923
    Sympathetic Function 95921-95923

Brain Cortex Magnetic Stimulation 0018T
Brain Surface Electrode
  Stimulation 95961-95962
Central Motor
  Transcranial Motor
    Stimulation 95928-95929
Electrocorticogram
  Intraoperative 95829
Electroencephalogram (EEG) . . .95812-95827,
                                      95955
  Brain Death 95824
  Electrode Placement 95830
  Intraoperative 95955
  Monitoring . . .95812-95813, 95950-95953,
                                    95956
  Physical or Drug Activation 95954
  Sleep 95822, 95827
  Standard 95819
  WADA Activation 95958
Electroencephalography (EEG)
  Digital Analysis 95957
Electromyography
  See Electromyography
  Fine Wire
    Dynamic 96004
  Ischemic Limb Exercise Test 95875
  Needle 51785, 95860-95872
  Surface
    Dynamic 96002-96004
Higher Cerebral Function
  Aphasia Test 96105
  Cognitive Function Tests 96116
  Developmental Tests 96110-96111
  Neurobehavioral Status 96116
  Neuropsychological Testing . .96118-96120
  Neuropsychological Testing, Computer-
  Assisted 96120
Magnetoencephalography
(MEG) 95965-95967
Motion Analysis
  by Video and 3D Kinematics .96000, 96004
  Computer-based 96000, 96004
Muscle Testing
  Manual 95831-95834
Nerve Conduction
  Motor Nerve 95900-95903
  Sensory Nerve or Mixed 95904
Neuromuscular Junction Tests 95937
Neurophysiological Testing
  Intraoperative 95920
Neuropsychological Testing 96118-96120
  Computer-Assisted 96120
Plantar Pressure Measurements
  Dynamic 96001, 96004
Polysomnography 95808-95811
Range of Motion 95851-95852
Reflex
  H-Reflex 95933-95934
  Blink Reflex 95933
Sleep Study 95807-95810
Somatosensory Testing 95925-95927
Tensilon Test 95857
Unlisted Services and Procedures 95999
Urethral Sphincter 51785
Visual Evoked Potential, CNS 95930

Neurolysis
Nerve 64704-64708
  Internal 64727

Neuroma
Acoustic
  See Brain, Tumor, Excision
Excision
  Cutaneous Nerve 64774
  Digital Nerve 64776-64778
  Foot 28080
  Foot Nerve 64782-64783
  Hand Nerve 64782-64783
  Peripheral Nerve 64784
  Sciatic Nerve 64786
Interdigital
  See Mortons Neuroma; Neuroma, Foot,
  Excision

Neuromuscular Junction
Tests 95937

Neuromuscular Pedicle
Reinnervation
  Larynx 31590

Neuromuscular
Reeducation 97112
See Physical Medicine/Therapy/Occupational
Therapy

Neurophysiologic Testing
Autonomic Nervous Function
  Heart Rate Response 95921-95923
  Pseudomotor Response 95921-95923
  Sympathetic Function 95921-95923
Intraoperative, Per Hour 95920

Neuroplasty 64712
Cranial Nerve 64716
Digital Nerve 64702-64704
Peripheral Nerve 64708-64714, 64718-64721

Neuropsychological
Testing 96118-96120
Computer-Assisted 96120

Neurorrhaphy 64831-64876
Peripheral Nerve
  with Graft 64885-64907

Neurostimulators
Analysis .95970-95979
Application 64550
Implantation 64553-64565
Insertion
  Pulse Generator 61885-61886, 64590
  Receiver 61885-61886, 64590
Removal
  Electrodes 61880
  Pulse Generator 61888, 64595
  Receiver 61888, 64595
Replacement 61885

Neurotomy, Sympathetic
See Gasserian Ganglion, Sensory Root,
Decompression

Neurovascular Pedicle
Flaps 15750

Neutralization Test
Virus 86382

New Patient
Domiciliary or Rest Home Visit 99324-99328
Emergency Department Services . . .99281-99288
Home Services 99341-99345
Hospital Inpatient Services 99221-99239
Hospital Observation Services 99217-99220
Initial Inpatient Consultations 99251-99255
Initial Office Visit 99201-99205
    See Evaluation and Management; Office and
    Other Outpatient
Office and/or Other Outpatient
Consultations 99241-99245

Newborn Care 99431-99440, 99502
Attendance at Delivery 99436
Birthing Room 99431
Blood Transfusion 36450
    See Neonatal Intensive Care
Circumcision
    Clamp or Other Device 54150
    Surgical Excision 54160
History and Examination 99431, 99435
Laryngoscopy 31520
Normal .99431-99433
Prepuce Slitting .54000
Preventive
    Office 99432
Resuscitation 99440
Standby for Cesarean Delivery 99360
Subsequent Hospital Care 99433
Umbilical Artery Catheterization 36660

Nickel 83885

Nicolas-Durand-Favre Disease
See Lymphogranuloma Venereum

Nicotine 83887

Nidation
See Implantation

Nipples
See Breast
Inverted 19355
Reconstruction 19350

Nissen Operation
See Fundoplasty, Esophagogastric

Nissen Procedure 43324
Laparoscopic 43280

Nitrate Reduction Test
See Urinalysis

**Nitroblue Tetrazolium Dye
Test** 86384

Nitrogen, Blood Urea
See Blood Urea Nitrogen

NMR Imaging
See Magnetic Resonance Imaging (MRI)

NMR Spectroscopies
See Magnetic Resonance Spectroscopy

No Man's Land
Tendon Repair 26356-26358

Noble Procedure
See Repair; Suture

Nocardia
Antibody 86744

**Nocturnal Penile Rigidity
Test** 54250

**Nocturnal Penile Tumescence
Test** 54250

Node Dissection, Lymph
See Dissection, Lymph Nodes

Node, Lymph
See Lymph Nodes

Nodes
See Lymph Nodes

Non-Invasive Vascular Imaging
See Vascular Studies

Non-Office Medical Services . .99056
Emergency Care .99060

Non-Stress Test, Fetal 59025

Nonunion Repair
Femur
    with Graft .27472
    without Graft 27470
Metatarsal 28322
Tarsal Joint 28320

Noradrenalin
Blood .82383-82384
Urine 82384

Norchlorimipramine
See Imipramine

Norepinephrine
See Catecholamines
Blood .82383-82384
Urine 82384

Nortriptyline
Assay 80182

Norwood Procedure 33611-33612,
33619
See Repair, Heart, Ventricle; Revision

Nose
Abscess
    Incision and Drainage 30000, 30020
Artery
    Incision 30915-30920
Biopsy
    Intranasal 30100
Dermoid Cyst
    Excision
        Complex 30125
        Simple 30124
Displacement Therapy 30210

Endoscopy
    Diagnostic 31231-31235
    Surgical 31237-31294
Excision
    Rhinectomy 30150-30160
Fracture
    Closed Treatment 21345
    Open Treatment 21325-21336,
        21338-21339, 21346-21347
    Percutaneous Treatment 21340
    with Fixation 21330, 21340, 21345-21347
Hematoma
    Incision and Drainage 30000, 30020
Hemorrhage
    Cauterization 30901-30906
Insertion
    Septal Prosthesis 30220
Intranasal
    Lesion
        External Approach 30118
        Internal Approach 30117
Lysis of Adhesions 30560
Polyp
    Excision
        Extensive 30115
        Simple 30110
Reconstruction
    Cleft Lip/Cleft Palate 30460-30462
    Dermatoplasty 30620
    Primary 30400-30420
    Secondary 30430-30450
    Septum 30520
Removal
    Foreign Body 30300
        Anesthesia 30310
        Lateral Rhinotomy 30320
Repair
    Adhesions .30560
    Cleft Lip 40700-40761
    Fistula 30580-30600, 42260
    Rhinophyma 30120
    Septum 30540-30545, 30630
    Synechia 30560
    Vestibular Stenosis 30465
Skin
    Excision 30120
    Surgical Planing 30120
Submucous Resection Turbinate
    Excision 30140
Turbinate
    Excision 30130-30140
    Fracture 30930
    Injection 30200
Turbinate Mucosa
    Cauterization 30801-30802
Unlisted Services and Procedures 30999

Nose Bleed 30901-30906
See Hemorrhage, Nasal

NTD 86384
See Nitroblue Tetrazolium Dye Test

Nuclear Antigen
Antibody 86235

Nuclear Imaging
See Nuclear Medicine

Nuclear Magnetic Resonance Imaging
See Magnetic Resonance Imaging (MRI)

Nuclear Magnetic Resonance Spectroscopy
See Magnetic Resonance Spectroscopy

Nuclear Medicine
Adrenal Gland Imaging 78075
Automated Data 78890-78891
Bile Duct
   Imaging 78223
Bladder
   Residual Study 78730
Blood
   Bone
      Density Study 78350-78351
      Imaging 78300-78320
      SPECT 78320
      Ultrasound 76977
      Unlisted Services and Procedures ...78399
   Flow Imaging 78445
   Iron
      Red Cells 78140
   Platelet Survival 78190-78191
   Red Cell Survival 78130-78135
   Red Cells 78120-78121
   Unlisted Services and Procedures 78199
   Whole Blood Volume 78122
Bone Marrow
   Imaging 78102-78104
Brain
   Blood Flow 78610-78615
   Cerebrospinal Fluid 78630-78650
   Imaging 78600-78609
      Vascular Flow 78610
Endocrine System
   Unlisted Services and Procedures 78099
Esophagus
   Imaging (Motility) 78258
   Reflux Study 78262
Gallbladder
   Imaging 78223
Gastric Mucosa
   Imaging 78261
Gastrointestinal
   Blood Loss Study 78278
   Protein Loss Study 78282
   Shunt Testing 78291
   Unlisted Services and Procedures 78299
Genitourinary System
   Unlisted Services and Procedures 78799
Heart
   Blood Flow 78414
   Blood Pool Imaging 78472-78473,
         78481-78483, 78494-78496
   Myocardial Imaging 78459, 78466-78469
   Myocardial Perfusion 78460-78465,
         78478-78480
   Shunt Detection 78428
   Unlisted Services and Procedures 78499
Hepatic Duct
   Imaging 78223
Inflammatory Process 78805-78807

Intestines
   Imaging 78290
Kidney
   Blood Flow 78715
   Function Study 78725
   Imaging 78700-78707, 78710
Lacrimal Gland Tear Flow 78660
Liver
   Function Study 78220
   Imaging 78201-78216
   Vascular Flow 78206
Lung
   Imaging Perfusion 78580-78585
   Imaging Ventilation 78586-78594
   Unlisted Services and Procedures 78599
Lymph Nodes 78195
Lymphatics 78195
   Unlisted Services and Procedures 78199
Musculoskeletal System
   Unlisted Services and Procedures 78399
Nervous System
   Unlisted Services and Procedures 78699
Parathyroid Gland Imaging 78070
Pulmonary Perfusion Imaging 78588
Salivary Gland Function Study 78232
   Imaging 78230-78231
Spleen
   Imaging 78185, 78215-78216
   Unlisted Services and Procedures 78199
Stomach
   Blood Loss Study 78278
   Emptying Study 78264
   Protein Loss Study 78282
   Reflux Study 78262
   Vitamin B-12 Absorption 78270-78272
Testes
   Imaging 78760-78761
Therapeutic
   Interstitial 79300
   Intra-Arterial 79445
   Intra-Articular 79440
   Intracavitary 79200
   Intravenous 79101
   Intravenous Infusion 79403
   Oral 79005
   Thyroid 79200-79300
   Unlisted Services and Procedures 79999
Thyroid
   Imaging 78010
   Imaging for Metastases 78015-78018
   Imaging with Flow 78011
   Imaging with Uptake 78006
   Metastases Uptake 78020
   Uptake 78000-78003
Tumor Imaging
   Positron Emission Tomography .78811-78816
     with Computed Tomography ..78814-78816
Tumor Localization 78800-78804
Unlisted Services and Procedures 78999
Urea Breath Test 78267-78268
Ureter
   Reflux Study 78740
Vein
   Thrombosis Imaging 78456-78458

Nucleases, DNA
See DNAse

Nucleic Acid Probe 83896
Amplified Probe Detection
   Infectious Agent
      Bartonella Henselae 87471
      Bartonella Quintana 87471
      Borrelia Burgdorferi 87476
      Candida Species 87481
      Chlamydia Pneumoniae 87486
      Chlamydia Trachomatis 87491
      Cytomegalovirus 87496
      Gardnerella Vaginalis 87511
      Hepatitis B Virus 87516
      Hepatitis C 87521
      Hepatitis G 87526
      Herpes Simplex Virus 87529
      Herpes Virus-6 87532
      HIV-1 87535
      HIV-2 87538
      Legionella Pneumophila 87541
      Multiple Organisms 87801
      Mycobacteria Avium-Intracellulare ..87561
      Mycobacteria Species 87551
      Mycobacteria Tuberculosis 87556
      Mycoplasma Pneumoniae 87581
      Neisseria Gonorrheae 87591
      Not Otherwise Specified 87798, 87801
      Papillomavirus, Human 87621
      Streptococcus, Group A 87651
Direct Probe Detection
   Infectious Agent
      Bartonella Henselae 87470
      Bartonella Quintana 87470
      Borrelia Burgdorferi 87475
      Candida Species 87480
      Chlamydia Pneumoniae 87485
      Chlamydia Trachomatis 87490
      Cytomegalovirus 87495
      Gardnerella Vaginalis 87510
      Hepatitis B Virus 87515
      Hepatitis C 87520
      Hepatitis G 87525
      Herpes Simplex Virus 87528
      Herpes Virus-6 87531
      HIV-1 87534
      HIV-2 87537
      Legionella Pneumophila 87540
      Multiple Organisms 87800
      Mycobacteria Avium-Intracellulare ..87560
      Mycobacteria Species 87550
      Mycobacteria Tuberculosis 87555
      Mycoplasma Pneumoniae 87580
      Neisseria Gonorrheae 87590
      Not Otherwise Specified 87797
      Papillomavirus, Human 87620
      Streptococcus, Group A 87650
      Trichomonas Vaginalis 87660
Genotype Analysis
   Infectious Agent
      Hepatitis C Virus 87902
      HIV-1 87901

In Situ Hybridization 88365-88368
Phenotype Analysis
　Infectious Agent
　　HIV-1 Drug Resistance 87903-87904
Quantification
　Infectious Agent
　　Bartonella Henselae 87472
　　Bartonella Quintana 87472
　　Borrelia Burgdorferi 87477
　　Candida Species 87482
　　Chlamydia Pneumoniae 87487
　　Chlamydia Trachomatis 87492
　　Cytomegalovirus 87497
　　Gardnerella Vaginalis 87512
　　Hepatitis B Virus 87517
　　Hepatitis C 87522
　　Hepatitis G 87527
　　Herpes Simplex Virus 87530
　　Herpes Virus-6 87533
　　HIV-1 87536
　　HIV-2 87539
　　Legionella Pneumophila 87542
　　Mycobacteria Avium-Intracellulare ..87562
　　Mycobacteria Species 87552
　　Mycobacteria Tuberculosis 87557
　　Mycoplasma Pneumoniae 87582
　　Neisseria Gonorrheae 87592
　　Not Otherwise Specified 87799
　　Papillomavirus, Human 87622
　　Streptococcus, Group A 87652

Nucleolysis, Intervertebral Disk
See Chemonucleolysis

Nucleotidase 83915

Nursemaid Elbow 24640

**Nursing Facility Discharge
Services**
See Discharge Services, Nursing Facility

Nursing Facility Services
Annual Assessment 99318
Care Plan Oversight Services 99379-99380
Comprehensive Assessments
Discharge Services 99315-99316
Initial Care 99304-99306
Subsequent Care 99307-99310

Nuss Procedure
with Thoracoscopy 21743
without Thoracoscopy 21742

Nutrition Therapy
Group 97804
Home Infusion 99601-99602
Initial Assessment 97802
Reassessment 97803

Nystagmus Tests
See Vestibular Function Tests
Optokinetic 92534, 92544
Positional 92532, 92542
Spontaneous 92531, 92541

O

O₂ Saturation
See Oxygen Saturation

Ober-Yount Procedure 27025
See Fasciotomy, Hip

Obliteration
Mastoid 69670
Vagina
　Total 57110-57112
　Vault......................57120

Oblongata, Medulla
See Medulla

Observation 99234-99236
See Evaluation and Management; Hospital
Services

Obstetrical Care
Abortion
　Induced
　　by Amniocentesis Injection ..59850-59852
　　　See Abortion; Cesarean Delivery;
　　　Ectopic Pregnancy
　　by Dilation and Curettage 59840
　　by Dilation and Evaluation 59841
　Missed
　　First Trimester 59820
　　Second Trimester 59821
　Spontaneous 59812
　Therapeutic 59840-59852
Antepartum Care 59425-59426
Cesarean Delivery 59618-59622
　Only 59514
　Postpartum Care 59515
　Routine 59510
　with Hysterectomy 59525
Curettage
　Hydatidiform Mole 59870
Evacuation
　Hydatidiform Mole 59870
External Cephalic Version 59412
Miscarriage
　Surgical Completion 59812-59821
Placenta Delivery 59414
Postpartum Care 59430, 59514
Septic Abortion 59830
Total (Global) 59400, 59610, 59618
Unlisted Services and Procedures ..59898-59899
Vaginal
　after Cesarean 59610-59614
Vaginal Delivery 59409-59410
　Delivery after Cesarean 59610-59614

Obstruction
See Occlusion

Obstruction Clearance
Venous Access Device 36595-36596

Obstruction Colon
See Colon, Obstruction

Obturator Nerve
Avulsion 64763-64766
Incision 64763-64766
Transection 64763-64766

Obturator Prosthesis 21076
Definitive 21080
Insertion
　Larynx 31527
Interim 21079

Occipital Nerve, Greater
Avulsion 64744
Incision 64744
Injection
　Anesthetic 64405
Transection 64744

Occlusion
Extracranial
　Intracranial 61623
Fallopian Tube
　Oviduct...............58565, 58615
Penis
　Vein 37790
Umbilical Cord 59072

Occlusive Disease of Artery
See Repair, Artery; Revision

Occult Blood 82270-82272
by Hemoglobin Immunoassay 82274

Occupational Therapy
Evaluation 97003-97004

Ocular Implant
See Orbital Implant
Insertion
　in Scleral Shell 65130
　Muscles Attached 65140
　Muscles, Not Attached 65135
Modification 65125
Reinsertion 65150
　with Foreign Material 65155
Removal 65175

Ocular Muscle
See Eye Muscles

Ocular Orbit
See Orbit

Ocular Photoscreening 0065T

Ocular Prostheses
See Prosthesis, Ocular

Oculomotor Muscle
See Eye Muscles

Oddi Sphincter
See Sphincter of Oddi

Odontoid Dislocation
Open Treatment/Reduction 22318
　with Grafting 22319

Odontoid Fracture
Open Treatment/Reduction 22318
　with Grafting 22319

Odontoid Process
Excision 22548

Oesophageal Neoplasm
See Tumor, Esophagus

Oesophageal Varices
See Esophageal Varices

Oesophagus
See Esophagus

Oestradiol
See Estradiol

Office and/or Other Outpatient Services
See History and Physical
Consultation
Established Patient 99211-99215
New Patient 99201-99205
Normal Newborn 99432
Office Visit
    Established Patient 99211-99215
    New Patient 99201-99205
Outpatient Visit
    Established Patient 99211-99215
    New Patient 99201-99205
    Prolonged Services 99354-99355

Office Medical Services
After Hours 99050
Emergency Care 99058
Extended Hours 99051

Office or Other Outpatient Consultations
See Consultation, Office and/or Other Outpatient

Olecranon
See Elbow; Humerus; Radius; Ulna
Bursa
    Arthrocentesis 20605
Cyst
    Excision 24125-24126
Tumor
    Cyst 24120
    Excision 24125-24126

Olecranon Process
Craterization 24147
Diaphysectomy 24147
Excision 24147
    Abscess 24138
Fracture
    See Elbow; Humerus; Radius
    Closed Treatment 24670-24675
    Open Treatment 24685
Osteomyelitis 24138, 24147
Saucerization 24147
Sequestrectomy 24138

Oligoclonal Immunoglobulins .83916

Omentectomy 49255, 58950-58956
Laparotomy 58960
Oophorectomy 58943
Resection Ovarian Malignancy 58950-58952
Resection Peritoneal Malignancy ..58950-58956
Resection Tubal Malignancy 58950-58956

Omentum
Excision 49255, 58950-58956
Flap 49904-49905
    Free
      with Microvascular Anastomosis ...49906
Unlisted Services and Procedures 49999

Omphalectomy 49250

Omphalocele
Repair 49600-49611

Omphalomesenteric Duct
Excision 44800

Omphalomesenteric Duct, Persistent
See Diverticulum, Meckel's

Oncoprotein
HER-2/neu 83950

One Stage Prothrombin Time 85610-85611
See Prothrombin Time

Onychectomy
See Excision, Nails

Onychia
Drainage 10060-10061

Oocyte
Assisted Fertilization
    Microtechnique 89280-89281
Biopsy 89290-89291
Cryopreservation 0059T
Culture
    Extended 89272
    Less than 4 Days 89250
    with Co-Culture 89251
Identification
    Follicular Fluid 89254
Insemination 89268
Retrieval
    for In Vitro Fertilization 58970
Storage 89346
Thawing 89356

Oophorectomy .58262-58263, 58291-58292,
    58552, 58554, 58661, 58940-58943
Ectopic Pregnancy
    Laparoscopic Treatment 59120
    Surgical Treatment 59120

Oophorectomy, Partial
See Excision, Ovary, Partial

Oophorocystectomy
See Cystectomy, Ovarian

Open Biopsy, Adrenal Gland
See Adrenal Gland, Biopsy

Operating Microscope 69990

Operation
Blalock-Hanlon
    See Septostomy, Atrial
Blalock-Taussig Subclavian-Pulmonary
Anastomosis
    See Pulmonary Artery, Shunt, Subclavian

Borthen
    See Iridotasis
Dana
    See Rhizotomy
Dunn
    See Arthrodesis, Foot Joint
Duvries
    See Tenoplasty
Estes
    See Ovary, Transposition
Foley Pyeloplasty
    See Pyeloplasty
Fontan
    See Repair, Heart, Anomaly
Fox
    See Fox Operation
Gardner
    See Meningocele Repair
Green
    See Scapulopexy
Harelip
    See Cleft Lip, Repair
Heine
    See Cyclodialysis
Heller
    See Esophagomyotomy
Iris, Inclusion
    See Iridencleisis
Jaboulay Gastroduodenostomy
    See Gastroduodenostomy
Johanson
    See Reconstruction, Urethra
Keller
    See Keller Procedure
Krause
    See Gasserian Ganglion, Sensory Root,
    Decompression
Mumford
    See Claviculectomy, Partial
Nissen
    See Fundoplasty, Esophagogastric
Peet
    See Nerves, Sympathectomy, Excision
Ramstedt
    See Pyloromyotomy
Richardson Hysterectomy
    See Hysterectomy, Abdominal, Total
Schanz
    See Femur, Osteotomy
Schlatter Total Gastrectomy
    See Excision, Stomach, Total
Smithwick
    See Excision, Nerve, Sympathetic
Winiwarter Cholecystoenterostomy
    See Anastomosis, Gallbladder to Intestines

Operation Microscopes
See Operating Microscope

Operculectomy 41821

Operculum
See Gums

Ophthalmic Mucous Membrane Test 95060
See Allergy Tests

Ophthalmology

Unlisted Services and Procedures 92499
   See Ophthalmology, Diagnostic

Ophthalmology, Diagnostic

Color Vision Exam .92283
Computerized Scanning 92135
Computerized Screening 0065T, 99172
Dark Adaptation 92284
Electro-oculography 92270
Electromyography, Needle 92265
Electroretinography 92275
Endoscopy 66990
Eye Exam
   Established Patient 92012-92014
   New Patient 92002-92004
   with Anesthesia 92018-92019
Glaucoma Provocative Test 92140
Gonioscopy 92020
Ocular Photography
   External 92285
   Internal 92286-92287
Ophthalmoscopy 92225-92226
   with Dynamometry 92260
   with Fluorescein Angiography 92235
   with Fluorescein Angioscopy 92230
   with Fundus Photography 92250
   with Indocyanine-Green Angiography . .92240
Photoscreening 0065T
Refractive Determination 92015
Sensorimotor Exam 92060
Tonography 92120
   with Provocation 92130
Tonometry
   Serial 92100
Ultrasound 76511-76529
Visual Acuity Screen 99172-99173
Visual Field Exam 92081-92083
Visual Function Screen 0065T, 99172

Ophthalmoscopy 92225-92226

See Ophthalmology, Diagnostic

Opiates 83925

Opinion, Second

See Confirmatory Consultations

Optic Nerve

Decompression 67570
   with Nasal/Sinus Endoscopy 31294

Optokinetic Nystagmus Test

See Nystagmus Tests, Optokinetic

Oral Lactose Tolerance
Test 82951-82953

See Glucose, Tolerance Test

Oral Mucosa

See Mouth, Mucosa

Oral Surgical Splint 21085

Orbit

See Orbital Contents; Orbital Floor; Periorbital
Region
Biopsy 61332
   Exploration 67450
   Fine Needle Aspiration or Orbital
   Contents 67415
   Orbitotomy without Bone Flap 67400
CT Scan 70480-70482
Decompression 61330
   Bone Removal 67414, 67445
Exploration 61332, 67400, 67450
   Lesion
      Excision .61333
Fracture
   Closed Treatment
      with Manipulation 21401
      without Manipulation 21400
   Open Treatment 21406-21408
      Blowout Fracture 21385-21395
Incision and Drainage 67405, 67440
Injection
   Retrobulbar 67500-67505
   Tenon's Capsule 67515
Insertion
   Implant 67550
Lesion
   Excision 67412, 67420
Magnetic Resonance Imaging
(MRI) 70540-70543
Removal
   Decompression 67445
   Exploration 61334
   Foreign Body 61334, 67413, 67430
   Implant 67560
Sella Turcica 70482
Unlisted Services and Procedures 67599
X-Ray 70190-70200

Orbit Area

Reconstruction
   Secondary 21275

Orbit Wall

Decompression
   with Nasal/Sinus Endoscopy . . .31292-31293

Orbital Contents

Aspiration 67415

Orbital Floor

See Orbit; Periorbital Region
Fracture
   Blow Out 21385-21395

Orbital Hypertelorism

Osteotomy
   Periorbital 21260-21263

Orbital Implant

See Ocular Implant
Insertion 67550
Removal 67560

Orbital Prosthesis 21077

Orbital Rim and Forehead

Reconstruction 21172-21180

Orbital Rims

Reconstruction 21182-21184

Orbital Transplant 67560

Orbital Walls

Reconstruction 21182-21184

Orbitocraniofacial Reconstruction

Secondary 21275

Orbitotomy

with Bone Flap
   for Exploration 67450
   Lateral Approach 67420
   with Drainage 67440
   with Removal Foreign Body 67430
   with Removal of Bone for
   Decompression 67445
with Removal Foreign Body 67413
with Removal of Bone for Decompression .67414
without Bone Flap
   for Exploration 67400
   with Drainage Only 67405
   with Removal Lesion 67412

Orchidectomies

See Excision, Testis

Orchidopexy

See Orchiopexy

Orchidoplasty

See Repair, Testis

Orchiectomy

Laparoscopic 54690
Partial 54522
Radical
   Abdominal Exploration 54535
   Inguinal Approach 54530
Simple 54520

Orchiopexy

Abdominal Approach 54650
Inguinal Approach 54640
Intra-Abdominal Testis 54692

Orchioplasty

See Repair, Testis

Organ Grafting

See Transplantation

Organ or Disease-Oriented Panel

Electrolyte 80051
General Health Panel 80050
Hepatic Function Panel 80076
Hepatitis Panel .80074
Lipid Panel 80061
Metabolic
   Basic 80048
   Comprehensive 80053
Obstetric Panel .80055
Renal Function .80069

Organ System, Neurologic

See Nervous System

Organic Acids 83918-83921

Ormond Disease
See Retroperitoneal Fibrosis

Orogastric Tube
Placement 43752

Oropharynx
Biopsy 42800

Orthodontic Cephalogram 70350

Orthomyxoviridae
See Influenza Virus

Orthomyxovirus
See Influenza Virus

Orthopantogram 70355

Orthopedic Cast
See Cast

Orthopedic Surgery
Computer Assisted Navigation 0054T-0056T
Stereotaxis
    Computer Assisted 0054T-0056T

Orthoptic Training 92065

Orthoroentgenogram 76040

Orthosis
See Orthotics

Orthotics
Check-Out 97762
Management and Training 97760

Os Calcis Fracture
See Calcaneus, Fracture

Osmolality
Blood 83930
Urine 83935

Osseous Survey 76061-76065

Osseous Tissue
See Bone

Ossicles
Excision
    Stapes
        with Footplate Drill Out 69661
        without Foreign Material 69660-69661
Reconstruction
    Ossicular Chain
        Tympanoplasty with
        Antrotomy or Mastoidotomy . .69636-69637
        Tympanoplasty with
        Mastoidectomy 69642, 69644, 69646
        Tympanoplasty without
        Mastoidectomy 69632-69633
Release
    Stapes 69650
Replacement
    with Prosthesis 69633, 69637

Ostectomy
Metacarpal 26250-26255
Metatarsal 28288
Phalanges
    Finger 26260-26262
Pressure Ulcer
    Ischial 15941, 15945
    Sacral 15933, 15935, 15937
    Trochanteric 15951, 15953, 15958
Scapula 23190
Sternum 21620

Osteocalcin 83937

Osteocartilaginous Exostoses
See Exostosis

Osteochondroma
See Exostosis

Osteocutaneous Flap
with Microvascular Anastomosis . . .20969-20973

Osteoma
Sinusotomy
    Frontal 31075

Osteomyelitis 20000-20005
Elbow
    Incision and Drainage 23935
Excision
    Clavicle 23180
    Facial 21026
    Humerus, Proximal 23184
    Mandible 21025
    Scapula 23182
Femur/Knee
    Incision and Drainage 27303
Finger
    Incision 26034
Hand Incision .26034
Hip
    Incision, Deep 26992
Humerus 24134
    Incision and Drainage 23935
Incision
    Foot 28005
    Shoulder 23035
    Thorax 21510
Olecranon Process 24138, 24147
Pelvis
    Incision, Deep 26992
Radius .24136, 24145
Sequestrectomy
    Clavicle 23170
    Humeral Head 23174
    Scapula 23172
    Skull 61501

Osteopathic Manipulation 98925-98929

Osteoplasty
Carpal Bone 25394
Facial Bones
    Augmentation 21208
    Reduction .21209
Femoral Neck .27179

Femur 27179
    Lengthening 27466-27468
    Shortening 27465, 27468
Fibula
    Lengthening 27715
Humerus 24420
Metacarpal 26568
Phalanges, Finger 26568
Radius .25390-25393
Tibia
    Lengthening 27715
Ulna 25390-25393
Vertebra 76012-76013
    Lumbar 22521-22522
    Thoracic 22520, 22522

Osteotomy
Calcaneus 28300
Chin 21121-21123
Clavicle 23480-23485
Femur .27140, 27151
    Femoral Neck 27161
    for Slipped Epiphysis 27181
    with Fixation 27165
    with Open Reduction of Hip 27156
    with Realignment 27454
    without Fixation 27448-27450
Fibula 27707-27712
Hip 27146-27151
    Femoral
        with Open Reduction 27156
    Femur 27151
Humerus 24400-24410
Mandible 21198-21199
    Extra-Oral 21047
    Intra-Oral .21046
Maxilla 21206
    Extra-Oral 21049
    Intra-Oral .21048
Metacarpal 26565
Metatarsal 28306-28309
Orbit Reconstruction 21256
Pelvis 27158
Periorbital
    Orbital Hypertelorism 21260-21263
    Osteotomy with Graft 21267-21268
Phalanges
    Finger 26567
    Toe 28299, 28310-28312
Radius
    and Ulna 25365, 25375
    Distal Third 25350
    Middle or Proximal Third 25355
    Multiple 25370
Skull Base 61582-61585, 61592
Spine
    Anterior 22220-22226
    Posterior
        Posterolateral 22210-22214
Talus 28302
Tarsal .28304-28305
Tibia 27455-27457, 27705, 27709-27712
Ulna 25360
    and Radius 25365, 25375
    Multiple 25370

Vertebra
   Additional Segment
     Anterior Approach 22226
     Posterior/Posterolateral Approach . .22216
   Cervical
     Anterior Approach 22220
     Posterior/Posterolateral Approach . .22210
   Lumbar
     Anterior Approach 22224
     Posterior/Posterolateral Approach . .22214
   Thoracic
     Anterior Approach 22222
     Posterior/Posterolateral Approach . .22212
with Graft
   Reconstruction
     Periorbital Region 21267-21268

Otolaryngology
Diagnostic
   Exam Under Anesthesia 92502

Otomy
See Incision

Otoplasty 69300

Otorhinolaryngology
Unlisted Services and Procedures 92700

**Ouchterlony
Immunodiffusion** 86331

Outer Ear
See Ear, Outer

Outpatient Visit
See History and Physical; Office and/or Other
Outpatient Services

Output, Cardiac
See Cardiac Output

Ova
Smear 87177

Oval Window
Repair Fistula 69666

Oval Window Fistula
See Fistula, Oval Window

Ovarian Cyst
See Cyst, Ovarian; Ovary, Cyst

Ovarian Vein Syndrome
Ureterolysis 50722

Ovariectomies
See Oophorectomy

Ovariolysis .58740

Ovary
Abscess
   Incision and Drainage 58820-58822
     Abdominal Approach 58822
Biopsy 58900
Cryopreservation 0058T
Cyst
   Incision and Drainage 58800-58805

Excision 58662, 58720
   Cyst 58925
   Partial
     Oophorectomy 58661, 58940
     Ovarian Malignancy 58943
     Peritoneal Malignancy 58943
     Tubal Malignancy 58943
     Wedge Resection 58920
   Total 58940-58943
Laparoscopy 58660-58662, 58679
Lysis
   Adhesions 58660, 58740
Radical Resection 58950-58952
Transposition 58825
Tumor
   Resection 58950-58956
Unlisted Services and Procedures . .58679, 58999
Wedge Resection 58920

Oviduct
Anastomosis 58750
Chromotubation 58350
Ectopic Pregnancy 59120-59121
Excision 58700-58720
Fulguration
   Laparoscopic 58670
Hysterosalpingography 74740
Laparoscopy 58679
Ligation 58600-58611
Lysis
   Adhesions 58740
Occlusion 58615
   Laparoscopic 58671
Repair 58752
   Anastomosis 58750
   Create Stoma 58770
Unlisted Services and Procedures . .58679, 58999
X-Ray with Contrast 74740

Ovocyte
See Oocyte

Ovulation Tests 84830

Ovum Implantation
See Implantation

Ovum Transfer Surgery
See Gamete Intrafallopian Transfer

Oxalate 83945

Oxidase, Ceruloplasmin
See Ceruloplasmin

Oxidoreductase, Alcohol-Nad+
See Antidiuretic Hormone

Oximetry (Noninvasive)
See Pulmonology, Diagnostic
Blood O_2 Saturation
   Ear or Pulse 94760-94762

Oxoisomerase
See Phosphohexose Isomerase

Oxosteroids
See Ketosteroids

Oxycodinone 80102-80103, 83925

Oxygen Saturation 82805-82810

**Oxygenation, Extracorporeal
Membrane**
See Extracorporeal Membrane Oxygenation

Oxyproline
See Hydroxyproline

Oxytocin Stress Test, Fetal 59020

P

P & P
See Proconvertin

P B Antibodies
See Antibody, Heterophile

P-Acetamidophenol
See Acetaminophen

Pacemaker, Heart
See Defibrillator, Heart
Conversion 33214
Electronic Analysis 93641-93642
   Antitachycardia System 93724
   Dual Chamber . .93731-93732, 93743-93744
   Single Chamber . .93734-93735, 93741-93742
   Wearable Device 93741-93742, 93745
Insertion .33200-33208
   Electrode 33210-33211, 33216-33217,
                          33224-33225
   Pulse Generator Only 33212-33213
Removal .33233-33237
   via Thoracotomy 33236-33237
Repair
   Electrode 33218-33220
Replacement
   Catheter 33210
   Electrode 33210-33211
   Insertion 33206-33208
   Pulse Generator 33212-33213
Repositioning
   Electrode 33215, 33226
Revise Pocket
   Chest 33222
Telephonic Analysis 93733, 93736
Upgrade 33214

Pachymetry
Eye 76514

Packing
Nasal Hemorrhage 30901-30906

Pain Management
Epidural/Intrathecal 62350-62351,
                  62360-62362, 99601-99602
Intravenous Therapy 90783-90784

**Palatal Augmentation
Prosthesis** .21082

Palatal Lift Prosthesis 21083

Palate
Abscess
    Incision and Drainage 42000
Biopsy 42100
Excision 42120, 42145
Fracture
    Closed Treatment 21421
    Open Treatment 21422-21423
Lesion
    Destruction 42160
    Excision 42104-42120
Prosthesis 42280-42281
Reconstruction
    Lengthening 42226-42227
Repair
    Cleft Palate 42200-42225
    Laceration 42180-42182
    Vomer Flap 42235
Unlisted Services and Procedures 42299

Palate, Cleft
See Cleft Palate

Palatoplasty 42200-42225

Palatoschisis
See Cleft Palate

Palm
Bursa
    Incision and Drainage 26025-26030
Fasciectomy 26121-26125
Fasciotomy 26040-26045
Tendon
    Excision 26170
Tendon Sheath
    Excision 26145
    Incision and Drainage 26020

Palsy, Seventh Nerve
See Facial Nerve Paralysis

Pancreas
Anastomosis
    to Intestines 48180
    with Intestines 48520-48540
Anesthesia 00794
Biopsy 48100
    Needle Biopsy 48102
Cyst
    Anastomosis 48520-48540
    Repair 48500
Debridement
    Peripancreatic Tissue 48005
Excision
    Ampulla of Vater 48148
    Duct 48148
    Partial ...48140-48146, 48150, 48154, 48160
    Peripancreatic Tissue 48005
    Total 48155-48160
Lesion
    Excision 48120
Needle Biopsy 48102
Placement
    Drainage 48000-48001

Pseudocyst
    Drainage
        Open 48510
        Percutaneous 48511
Removal
    Calculi (Stone) 48020
Removal Transplanted Allograft 48556
Repair
    Cyst 48500
Suture 48545
Transplantation 48160, 48550, 48554-48556
    Allograft Preparation 48550-48552
Unlisted Services and Procedures 48999
X-Ray with Contrast 74300-74305
    Injection Procedure 48400

Pancreas, Endocrine Only
See Islet Cell

Pancreatectomy
Donor 48550
Partial 48140-48146, 48150-48154, 48160
Total 48155-48160
with Transplantation 48160

Pancreatic DNAse
See DNAse

Pancreatic Duct
Destruction
    Calculi (Stone) 43265
Dilation
    Endoscopy 43271
Endoscopy
    Collection
        Specimen 43260
    Destruction
        Calculi (Stone) 43265
        Tumor 43272
    Dilation 43271
    Removal (Endoscopic)
        Calculi (Stone) 43264
        Foreign Body 43269
        Stent 43269
    Sphincter Pressure 43263
    Sphincterotomy 43262
    Tube Placement 43267-43268
Incision
    Sphincter 43262
Removal
    Calculi (Stone) 43264
    Foreign Body 43269
    Stent 43269
Tube Placement
    Nasopancreatic 43267
    Stent 43268
Tumor
    Destruction 43272
X-Ray with Contrast
    Guide Catheter 74329-74330

Pancreatic Elastase 1 (PE1) 82656

Pancreatic Islet Cell AB
See Antibody, Islet Cell

Pancreaticojejunostomy 48180

Pancreatography
Injection Procedure 48400
Intraoperative 74300-74301
Postoperative 74305

Pancreatojejunostomies
See Pancreaticojejunostomy

Pancreatorrhaphy 48545

Pancreatotomy
See Incision, Pancreas

Pancreozymin-Secretin Test ...82938

Panel
See Organ or Disease Oriented Panel

Panniculectomy
See Lipectomy

Pap Smears 88141-88155,
           88164-88167, 88174-88175

Paper Chromatographies
See Chromatography, Paper

Paper, Chromatography
See Chromatography, Paper

Papilla, Interdental
See Gums

Papillectomy 46220

Papilloma
Destruction
    Anus 46900-46924
    Penis 54050-54065

PAPP D
See Lactogen, Human Placental

Para-Tyrosine
See Tyrosine

Paracentesis
Abdomen 49080-49081
Eye
    Anterior Chamber
        with Diagnostic Aspiration of
        Aqueous 65800
        with Removal of Blood 65815
        with Removal Vitreous and/or Discission
        of Anterior Hyaloid Membrane 65810
        with Therapeutic Release of
        Aqueous 65805
Thorax 32000-32002

Paracervical Nerve
Injection
    Anesthetic 64435

Paraffin Bath Therapy 97018
See Physical Medicine/Therapy/Occupational
Therapy

Paraganglioma, Medullary
See Pheochromocytoma

Parainfluenza Virus
Antigen Detection
    Immunofluorescence 87279

Paralysis, Facial Nerve
See Facial Nerve Paralysis

Paralysis, Infantile
See Polio

Paranasal Sinuses
See Sinus; Sinuses

Parasites
Blood 87207-87209
Examination 87169
Smear 87177

Parasitic Worms
See Helminth

Parathormone 83970

Parathyrin
See Parathormone

**Parathyroid
Autotransplantation** 60512

Parathyroid Gland
Autotransplant 60512
Excision 60500-60502
Exploration 60500-60505
Nuclear Medicine
   Imaging 78070

Parathyroid Hormone 83970

**Parathyroid Hormone
Measurement**
See Parathormone

Parathyroid Transplantation
See Transplantation, Parathyroid

Parathyroidectomy 60500-60505

Paraurethral Gland
Abscess
   Incision and Drainage 53060

Paravertebral Nerve
Destruction 64622-64627
Injection
   Anesthetic 64470-64484
   Neurolytic 64622-64627

Parietal Cell Vagotomies
See Vagotomy, Highly Selective

Parietal Craniotomy 61556

Paring
Skin Lesion
   Benign Hyperkeratotic 11055-11057
      More than 4 Lesions 11057
      Single Lesion 11055
      2 to 4 Lesions 11056

Paronychia
Incision and Drainage 10060-10061

Parotid Duct
Diversion 42507-42510
Reconstruction 42507-42510

Parotid Gland
Abscess
   Incision and Drainage 42300-42305
Calculi (Stone)
   Excision 42330, 42340
Excision
   Partial 42410-42415
   Total 42420-42426
Tumor
   Excision 42410-42426

Parotitides, Epidemic
See Mumps

Pars Abdominalis Aortae
See Aorta, Abdominal

Partial Colectomy
See Colectomy, Partial

Partial Cystectomy
See Cystectomy, Partial

Partial Esophagectomy
See Esophagectomy, Partial

Partial Gastrectomy
See Excision, Stomach, Partial

Partial Glossectomy
See Excision, Tongue, Partial

Partial Hepatectomy
See Excision, Liver, Partial

Partial Mastectomies
See Breast, Excision, Lesion

Partial Nephrectomy
See Excision, Kidney, Partial

Partial Pancreatectomy
See Pancreatectomy, Partial

Partial Splenectomy
See Splenectomy, Partial

Partial Thromboplastin Time
See Thromboplastin, Partial, Time

Partial Ureterectomy
See Ureterectomy, Partial

Particle Agglutination 86403-86406

Parvovirus
Antibody 86747

Patch
Allergy Tests 95044
   See Allergy Tests

Patella
See Knee
Dislocation 27560-27566
Excision 27350
   with Reconstruction 27424
Fracture 27520-27524
Reconstruction 27437-27438
Repair
   Chondromalacia 27418
   Instability 27420-27424

Patella, Chondromalacia
See Chondromalacia Patella

**Patellar Tendon Bearing
(PTB) Cast** 29435

Patellectomy
with Reconstruction 27424

Paternity Testing 86910-86911

Patey's Operation
See Mastectomy, Radical

Pathologic Dilatation
See Dilation

Pathology
Clinical
   Consultation 80500-80502
Surgical 88355
   Consultation 88321-88325
      Intraoperative 88329-88334
   Decalcification Procedure 88311
   Electron Microscopy 88348-88349
   Gross and Micro Exam
      Level II 88302
      Level III 88304
      Level IV 88305
      Level V 88307
      Level VI 88309
   Gross Exam
      Level I 88300
   Histochemistry 88318-88319
   Immunocytochemistry 88342
   Immunofluorescent Study 88346-88347
   Morphometry
      Nerve 88356
      Skeletal Muscle 88355
      Tumor 88358-88361
   Nerve Teasing 88362
   Special Stain 88312-88314
   Staining 88312-88314
   Tissue Hybridization 88365
   Unlisted Services and Procedures 88399,
                                        89240

Patterson's Test
See Blood Urea Nitrogen

Paul-Bunnell Test
See Antibody; Antibody Identification;
Microsomal Antibody

PBG
See Porphobilinogen

PCP
See Phencyclidine

PCR
See Polymerase Chain Reaction

Peans' Operation
See Amputation, Leg, Upper, at Hip; Radical
Resection; Replantation

Pectoral Cavity
See Chest Cavity

Pectus Carinatum
Reconstructive Repair 21740-21742
　　with Thoracoscopy 21743

Pectus Excavatum
Reconstructive Repair 21740-21742
　　with Thoracoscopy 21743

Pediatric Critical Care 99293-99294

Pediatric Intensive Care 99293

Pedicle Fixation
Insertion 22842-22844

Pedicle Flap
Formation 15570-15576
Island 15740
Neurovascular 15750
Transfer 15650

PEEP
See Pressure Breathing, Positive

Peet Operation
See Nerves, Sympathectomy, Excision

Pelvi-Ureteroplasty
See Pyeloplasty

Pelvic Adhesions
See Adhesions, Pelvic

Pelvic Exam 57410

Pelvic Exenteration 51597

Pelvic Fixation
Insertion 22848

Pelvic Lymphadenectomy 58240

Pelvimetry 74710

Pelviolithotomy 50130

Pelvis
See Hip
Abscess
　　Incision and Drainage 26990, 45000
Angiography 72191
Biopsy 27040-27041
Bone
　　Drainage 26992
Brace Application 20662
Bursa
　　Incision and Drainage 26991
CT Scan 72191-72194
Cyst
　　Aspiration 50390
　　Injection 50390
Destruction
　　Lesion 58662
Endoscopy
　　Destruction of Lesion 58662
　　Lysis of Adhesions 58660
　　Oviduct Surgery 58670-58671
Exclusion
　　Small Intestine 44700
Exenteration 45126, 58240
Halo 20662

Hematoma
　　Incision and Drainage 26990
Lysis
　　Adhesions 58660
Magnetic Resonance Angiography 72198
Magnetic Resonance Imaging
(MRI) 72195-72197
Removal
　　Foreign Body 27086-27087
Repair
　　Osteotomy 27158
　　Tendon 27098
Ring
　　Dislocation 27193-27194, 27216-27218
　　Fracture 27216-27218
　　　Closed Treatment 27193-27194
Tumor
　　Excision 27047-27049
Ultrasound 76856-76857
Unlisted Services and Procedures for Hips and
Hip Joint 27299
X-Ray 72170-72190, 73540
　　Manometry 74710

Pemberton Osteotomy of Pelvis
See Osteotomy, Pelvis

Penectomy
See Amputation, Penis

Penetrating Keratoplasties
See Keratoplasty, Penetrating

Penile Induration
See Peyronie Disease

Penile Prosthesis
Insertion
　　Inflatable 54401-54405
　　Noninflatable 54400
Removal
　　Inflatable 54406, 54410-54417
　　Semi-Rigid 54415-54417
Repair
　　Inflatable 54408
Replacement
　　Inflatable 54410-54411, 54416-54417
　　Semi-Rigid 54416-54417

Penile Rigidity Test 54250

Penile Tumescence Test 54250

Penis
Amputation
　　Partial 54120
　　Radical 54130-54135
　　Total 54125
Biopsy 54100-54105
Circumcision
　　Repair 54163
　　Surgical Excision
　　　Newborn 54160
　　with Clamp or Other Device 54152
　　　Newborn 54150
Excision
　　Partial 54120
　　Prepuce 54150-54161, 54163
　　Total 54125-54135

Frenulum
　　Excision 54164
Incision
　　Prepuce 54000-54001
Incision and Drainage 54015
Injection
　　for Erection 54235
　　Peyronie Disease 54200
　　　Surgical Exposure Plague 54205
　　Vasoactive Drugs 54231
　　X-Ray 54230
Insertion
　　Prosthesis
　　　Inflatable 54401-54405
　　　Noninflatable 54400
Irrigation
　　Priapism 54220
Lesion
　　Destruction
　　　Cryosurgery 54056
　　　Electrodesiccation 54055
　　　Extensive 54065
　　　Laser Surgery 54057
　　　Simple 54050-54060
　　　Surgical Excision 54060
　　Excision 54060
　　　Penile Plaque 54110-54112
Nocturnal Penile Tumescence Test 54250
Occlusion
　　Vein 37790
Plaque
　　Excision 54110-54112
Plethysmography 54240
Prepuce
　　Stretch 54450
Reconstruction
　　Angulation 54360
　　Chordee 54300-54304, 54328
　　Complications 54340-54348
　　Epispadias 54380-54390
　　Hypospadias 54328-54352
　　Injury 54440
Removal
　　Foreign Body 54115
　　Prosthesis
　　　Inflatable 54406, 54410-54417
　　　Semi-Rigid 54415-54417
Repair
　　Fistulization 54435
　　Priapism with Shunt 54420-54430
　　Prosthesis
　　　Inflatable 54408
Replacement
　　Prosthesis
　　　Inflatable 54410-54411, 54416-54417
　　　Semi-Rigid 54416-54417
Revascularization 37788
Rigidity Test 54250
Test Erection 54250
Unlisted Services and Procedures 55899
Venous Studies 93980-93981

Penis Adhesions
Lysis
　　Post-circumcision 54162

Penis Prostheses
See Penile Prosthesis

Pentagastrin Test
See Gastric Analysis Test

Pentamidine
See Inhalation Treatment

Peptidase P
See Angiotensin Converting Enzyme (ACE)

Peptidase S
See Leucine Aminopeptidase

Peptide, Connecting
See C-Peptide

Peptide, Vasoactive Intestinal
See Vasoactive Intestinal Peptide

Peptidyl Dipeptidase A
See Angiotensin Converting Enzyme (ACE)

Percutaneous Abdominal Paracentesis
See Abdomen, Drainage

Percutaneous Atherectomies
See Artery, Atherectomy

Percutaneous Biopsy, Gallbladder/Bile Ducts
See Bile Duct, Biopsy

Percutaneous Discectomies
See Diskectomy, Percutaneous

Percutaneous Electric Nerve Stimulation
See Application, Neurostimulation

Percutaneous Lumbar Diskectomy 62287
See Aspiration, Nucleus of Disk, Lumbar; Puncture Aspiration

Percutaneous Lysis 62263-62264

Percutaneous Nephrostomies
See Nephrostomy, Percutaneous

Percutaneous Transluminal Angioplasty
Artery
　　Aortic 35472
　　Brachiocephalic 35475
　　Coronary 92982-92984
　　Femoral-Popliteal 35474
　　Iliac 35473
　　Pulmonary 92997-92998
　　Renal 35471
　　Tibioperoneal 35470
　　Visceral 35471
Venous 35476

Percutaneous Transluminal Coronary Angioplasty
See Percutaneous Transluminal Angioplasty

Pereyra Procedure . .51845, 57289, 58267

Performance Measures
ACE Inhibitor Therapy 4009F
Anginal Symptom Assessment 1002F
Antiplatelet Therapy 4011F

Beta-Blocker Therapy 4006F
Blood Pressure .2000F
Composite Measures
　　Heart Failure Assessment 0001F
　　Osteoarthritis Assessment 0005F
Diagnostic/Screening Processes or Results
　　Blood Pressure 3000F, 3002F
Patient History
　　Activity Level Assessment 1003F
　　Anti-Inflammatory or Analgesic
　　Medications Assessment 1007F
　　Asthma Assessment 1005F
　　Non-Steroidal Anti-Inflammatory
　　Drug (NSAID) 1008F
　　Osteoarthritis Assessment 1006F
　　Tobacco Use 1000F-0501F
　　Volume Overload Assessment 1004F
Patient Management
　　Postpartum Care Visit 0503F
　　Prenatal Care Visit, Initial 0500F
　　Prenatal Care Visit, Subsequent 0502F
　　Prenatal Flow Sheet 0501F
Physical Examination
　　Heart Auscultation 2003F
　　Osteoarthritis Assessment 2004F
　　Volume Overload Assessment 2002F
　　Weight 2001F
Therapeutic, Preventive or Other Interventions
　　Anti-Inflammatory/Analgesic
　　Agent 4016F
　　Asthma Medication 4015F
　　Gastrointestinal Prophylaxis for NSAID
　　Use 4017F
　　Heart Failure Education 4003F
　　　Written Discharge Instructions 4014F
　　Statin Therapy 4002F
　　Therapeutic Exercise 4018F
　　Warfarin Therapy 4012F
Tobacco Use
　　Assessment 1000F-1001F
　　Counseling 4000F
　　Pharmacologic Therapy 4001F

Performance Test
See Physical Medicine/Therapy/Occupational Therapy
Performance Test, Physical Therapy 97750
Psychological Test 96101-96103
　　Computer-Assisted 96103

Perfusion
Brain
　　Imaging 0042T
Myocardial 78460-78465, 78478-78480
　　Imaging 78466-78469
Positron Emission Tomography (PET)
　　Myocardial Imaging 78491-78492

Perfusion Pump
See Infusion Pump

Perfusion, Intracranial Arterial
Thrombolysis 61624

Pericardectomies
See Excision, Pericardium

Pericardial Cyst
See Cyst, Pericardial

Pericardial Sac
Drainage 32659

Pericardial Window
for Drainage 33025

Pericardial Window Technic
See Pericardiostomy

Pericardiectomy
Complete .33030-33031
Subtotal .33030-33031
Total
　　Endoscopic 32660

Pericardiocentesis 33010-33011
Ultrasound Guidance 76930

Pericardiostomy
Tube 33015

Pericardiotomy
Removal
　　Clot 33020
　　Foreign Body 33020

Pericardium
Cyst
　　Excision 32661, 33050
Excision 32659, 33030-33031
Incision
　　Removal
　　　Clot 33020
　　　Foreign Body 33020
　　with Tube .33015
Incision and Drainage 33025
Puncture Aspiration 33010-33011
Removal
　　Clot
　　　Endoscopic 32658
　　Foreign Body
　　　Endoscopic 32658
Tumor
　　Excision 32661, 33050

Peridural Anesthesia
See Anesthesia, Epidural

Peridural Injection
See Epidural, Injection

Perineal Prostatectomy
See Prostatectomy, Perineal

Perineoplasty 56810

Perineorrhaphy
Repair
　　Rectocele .57250

Perineum
Abscess
　　Incision and Drainage 56405
Colposcopy 99170
Debridement
　　Infected 11004, 11006
Removal
　　Prosthesis .53442
Repair 56810
X-Ray with Contrast 74775

Perionychia
See Paronychia

Periorbital Region
Reconstruction
    Osteotomy with Graft 21267-21268
Repair-Osteotomy 21260-21263

Peripheral Artery Disease (PAD)
Rehabilitation 93668

Peripheral Nerve
Repair/Suture
    Major .64856, 64859

Periprosthetic Capsulectomy
Breast 19371

Peristaltic Pumps
See Infusion Pump

Peritoneal Dialysis 90945-90947

Peritoneal Free Air
See Pneumoperitoneum

Peritoneal Lavage 49080

Peritoneocentesis 49080-49081

Peritoneoscopy
See Endoscopy, Peritoneum

Peritoneum
Abscess
    Incision and Drainage 49020
        Percutaneous 49021
Chemotherapy Administration 96445
    See Chemotherapy
Endoscopy
    Biopsy 47561
    Drainage
        Lymphocele 49323
    X-Ray 47560
Exchange
    Drainage Catheter 49423
Injection
    Contrast
        via Catheter 49424
Ligation
    Shunt 49428
Removal
    Cannula/Catheter 49422
    Foreign Body 49085
    Shunt 49429
Tumor
    Resection 58950-58956
Unlisted Services and Procedures 49999
Venous Shunt
    Injection 49427
X-Ray 74190

Persistent Truncus Arteriosus
See Truncus Arteriosus

Persistent, Omphalomesenteric Duct
See Diverticulum, Meckel's

Personal Care
See Self Care

Personality Test 96101-96103
Computer-Assisted 96103

Pessary
Insertion 57160

Pesticides
Chlorinated Hydrocarbons 82441

PET
See Positron Emission Tomography

Petrous Temporal
Excision
    Apex 69530

Peyronie Disease
Injection 54200
Surgical Exposure 54205
with Graft 54110-54112

pH
See Blood
Exhaled Breath Condensate 0140T
Other Fluid 83986
Urine 83986

Phacoemulsification
Removal
    Extracapsular Cataract 66982, 66984
    Secondary Membranous Cataract 66850

Phagocytosis
White Blood Cells 86344

Phalangectomy
Toe 28150
    Partial 28160

Phalanges (Hand)
See Finger, Bone

Phalanx, Finger
Craterization 26235-26236
Cyst
    Excision 26210-26215
Diaphysectomy 26235-26236
Excision 26235-26236
    Radical
        for Tumor 26260-26262
Fracture
    Articular
        Closed Treatment 26740
        Open Treatment 26746
        with Manipulation 26742
    Distal 26755-26756
        Closed Treatment 26750
        Open Treatment 26765
        Percutaneous Fixation 26756
    Open Treatment 26735
        Distal 26765
    Shaft 26720-26727
        Open Treatment 26735
Incision and Drainage 26034
Ostectomy
    Radical
        for Tumor 26260-26262
Repair
    Lengthening 26568
    Nonunion .26546
    Osteotomy 26567

Saucerization 26235-26236
Thumb
    Fracture
        Shaft 26720-26727
Tumor
    Excision 26210-26215

Phalanx, Great Toe
See Phalanx, Toe
Fracture 28490
    Open Treatment 28505
    with Manipulation 28495-28496
Percutaneous Fixation 28496
without Manipulation 28490

Phalanx, Toe
Condyle
    Excision 28126
Craterization 28124
Cyst
    Excision 28108
Diaphysectomy 28124
Excision 28124, 28150-28160
Fracture
    Open Treatment 28525
    with Manipulation 28515
    without Manipulation 28510
Repair
    Osteotomy 28310-28312
Saucerization .28124
Tumor
    Excision 28108, 28175

Pharmaceutic Preparations
See Drug

Pharmacotherapies
See Chemotherapy

Pharyngeal Tonsil
See Adenoids

Pharyngectomy
Partial 42890

Pharyngolaryngectomy . . .31390-31395

Pharyngoplasty 42950

Pharyngorrhaphy
See Suture, Pharynx

Pharyngostomy 42955

Pharyngotomy
See Incision, Pharynx

Pharyngotympanic Tube
See Eustachian Tube

Pharynx
See Nasopharynx; Throat
Biopsy 42800-42806
Cineradiography 70371, 74230
Creation
    Stoma 42955
Excision 42145
    Partial 42890
    Resection 42892-42894
    with Larynx 31390-31395
Hemorrhage 42960-42962

Lesion
  Destruction 42808
  Excision 42808
Reconstruction 42950
Removal
  Foreign Body 42809
Repair
  with Esophagus 42953
Unlisted Services and Procedures 42999
Video Study 70371, 74230
X-Ray 70370, 74210

Phencyclidine 83992

Phenobarbital 82205
Assay 80184

Phenothiazine 84022

Phenotype Analysis
by Nucleic Acid
  Infectious Agent
    HIV-1 Drug Resistance 87903-87904

Phenotype Prediction
by Genetic Database
  HIV-1 Drug Susceptibility 87900

Phenylalanine 84030

Phenylalanine-Tyrosine Ratio 84030

Phenylketones 84035

Phenylketonuria
See Phenylalanine

Phenytoin
Assay 80185-80186

Pheochromocytoma 80424

Pheresis
See Apheresis

Phlebectasia
See Varicose Vein

Phlebectomy
Varicose Veins 37765-37766

Phlebographies
See Venography

Phleborrhaphy
See Suture, Vein

Phlebotomy
Therapeutic 99195

Phoria
See Strabismus

Phosphatase
Alkaline 84075, 84080
  Blood 84078
Forensic Examination 84061

Phosphatase Acid 84060
Blood 84066

Phosphate, Pyridoxal
See Pyridoxal Phosphate

Phosphatidyl Glycerol
See Phosphatidylglycerol

Phosphatidylcholine Cholinephosphohydrolase
See Tissue Typing

Phosphatidylglycerol 84081

Phosphocreatine Phosphotransferase, ADP
See CPK

Phosphogluconate-6
Dehydrogenase 84085

Phosphoglycerides, Glycerol
See Phosphatidylglycerol

Phosphohexose Isomerase 84087

Phosphohydrolases
See Phosphatase

Phosphokinase, Creatine
See CPK

Phospholipase C
See Tissue Typing

Phospholipid Antibody 86147

Phospholipid Cofactor Antibody 0030T

Phosphomonoesterase
See Phosphatase

Phosphoric Monoester Hydrolases
See Phosphatase

Phosphorus 84100
Urine 84105

Phosphotransferase, ADP Phosphocreatine
See CPK

Photo Patch
Allergy Test 95052
  See Allergy Tests

Photochemotherapies, Extracorporeal
See Photopheresis

Photochemotherapy 96910-96913
See Dermatology
Endoscopic Light 96570-96571

Photocoagulation
Endolaser Panretinal
  Vitrectomy 67040
Focal Endolaser
  Vitrectomy 67040
Iridoplasty 66762

Lesion
  Cornea 65450
  Retina 0017T, 67210, 67227-67228
Retinal Detachment
  Prophylaxis 67145
  Repair 67105

Photodensity
Radiographic
  Absorptiometry 76078

Photodynamic Therapy
External 96567

Photography
Skin
  Diagnostic 0044T, 0045T

Photography, Ocular
See Ophthalmosocpy, Diagnostic

Photopheresis
Extracorporeal 36522

Photophoresis
See Actinotherapy; Photochemotherapy

Photoradiation Therapies
See Actinotherapy

Photoscreen
Ocular 0065T

Photosensitivity Testing 95056
See Allergy Tests

Phototherapies
See Actinotherapy

Phototherapy, Ultraviolet
See Actinotherapy

Phrenic Nerve
Anastomosis
  to Facial Nerve 64870
Avulsion 64746
Incision 64746
Injection
  Anesthetic 64410
Transection 64746

Physical Medicine/Therapy/ Occupational Therapy
See Neurology, Diagnostic
Activities of Daily Living 97535, 99509
Aquatic Therapy
  with Exercises 97113
Athletic Training
  Evaluation 97005
  Re-Evaluation 97006
Check-Out
  Orthotic/Prosthetic 97762
Cognitive Skills Development 97532
Community/Work Reintegration 97537
Evaluation 97001-97002
Kinetic Therapy 97530
Manual Therapy 97140

Modalities
  Contrast Baths 97034
  Diathermy Treatment 97024
  Electric Simulation
    Unattended 97014
  Electric Stimulation
    Attended, Manual 97032
  Hot or Cold Pack 97010
  Hydrotherapy (Hubbard Tank) 97036
  Infrared Light Treatment 97026
  Iontophoresis 97033
  Microwave Therapy 97024
  Paraffin Bath 97018
  Traction 97012
  Ultrasound 97035
  Ultraviolet Light 97028
  Unlisted Services and Procedures 97039
  Vasopneumatic Device 97016
  Whirlpool Therapy 97022
Orthotics Training 97760
Osteopathic Manipulation 98925-98929
Procedures
  Aquatic Therapy 97113
  Gait Training 97116
  Group Therapeutic 97150
  Massage Therapy 97124
  Neuromuscular Reeducation 97112
  Physical Performance Test 97750
  Therapeutic Exercises 97110
  Traction Therapy 97140
  Work Hardening 97545-97546
Prosthetic Training 97761
Sensory Integration 97533
Therapeutic Activities 97530
Unlisted Services and Procedures ..97139, 97799
Wheelchair Management 97542
Work Reintegration 97537

Physical Therapy
See Physical Medicine/Therapy/Occupational Therapy

Physician Services
Care Plan Oversight Services 99339-99340,
                              99374-99380
  Domiciliary Facility 99339-99340
  Home Health Agency Care 99374
  Home or Rest Home Care 99339-99340
  Hospice 99377-99378
  Nursing Facility 99379-99380
Direction, Advanced Life Support 99288
Prolonged
  with Direct Patient Contact 99354-99357
    Outpatient/Office 99354-99355
  with Direct Patient Services
    Inpatient 99356-99357
  without Direct Patient Contact .99358-99359
Standby 99360
Supervision, Care Plan Oversight
Services 99339-99340, 99374-99380

Piercing of Ear Lobe 69090

Piles
See Hemorrhoids

Pilonidal Cyst
Excision 11770-11772
Incision and Drainage 10080-10081

Pin
See Wire
Insertion/Removal
  Skeletal Traction 20650
Prophylactic Treatment
  Femur 27187
  Humerus 24498
  Shoulder 23490-23491

Pinch Graft 15050

Pinna
See Ear, External

Pinworms
Examination 87172

Pirogoff Procedure 27888

Pituitary Epidermoid Tumor
See Craniopharyngioma

Pituitary Gland
Excision 61546-61548
Tumor
  Excision 61546-61548, 62165

Pituitary Growth Hormone
See Growth Hormone

Pituitary Lactogenic Hormone
See Prolactin

Pituitectomy
See Excision, Pituitary Gland

PKU
See Phenylalanine

Placement
Adjustable Gastric Band 43770
Broncheal Stent 31636-31637
Catheter
  Breast
    for Interstitial Radioelement
    Application 19296-19298
  Bronchus
    for Intracavitary Radioelement
    Application 31643
    See Catheterization
Catheter, Cardiac 93503
  See Catheterization, Cardiac
Colonic Stent 44397, 45327, 45345, 45387
Drainage
  Pancreas 48001
Endovascular Prosthesis
  Aorta 33883-33886
Guidance
  Catheter
    Abscess 75989
    Bile 75982
    Specimen 75989
  Prosthesis
    Thoracic Aorta 75958-75959
Intravascular Stent
  Coronary 92980-92981
  Intracranial 61635
IVC Filter 75940
Jejunostomy Tube
  Endoscopic 44372

Metallic Localization Clip
  Breast 19295
Nasogastric Tube 43752
Needle
  Bone 36680
Needle Wire
  Breast 19290-19291
Orogastric Tube 43752
Radiation Delivery Device
  Intracoronary Artery 92974
Seton
  Anal 46020
Subconjuntival Retinal Prosthesis 0100T
Tracheal Stent 31631
Ureteral Stent 50947

Placenta
Delivery 59414

Placental Lactogen
See Lactogen, Human Placental

Placental Villi
See Chorionic Villus

Plagiocephaly 21175

Plague Vaccine 90727

Planing
Nose
  Skin 30120

Plantar Digital Nerve
Decompression 64726

Plantar Pressure Measurements
Dynamic 96001, 96004

Plasma
Frozen Preparation 86927

Plasma Prokallikrein
See Fletcher Factor

Plasma Protein-A, Pregnancy-Associated (PAPP-A) 84163

Plasma Test
Volume Determination 78110-78111

Plasma Thromboplastin
Antecedent 85270
Component 85250

Plasmin 85400

Plasmin Antiactivator
See Alpha-2 Antiplasmin

Plasminogen 85420-85421

Plasmodium
Antibody 86750

Plastic Repair of Mouth
See Mouth, Repair

Plate, Bone
See Bone Plate

Platelet
See Blood Cell Count, Complete Blood Count
Aggregation 85576
Antibody 86022-86023
Assay 85055
Blood 85025
Count 85032, 85049
Neutralization 85597

Platelet Cofactor I
See Clotting Factor

Platelet Test
Survival Test 78190-78191

Platysmal Flap 15825

PLC
See Lymphocyte, Culture; Tissue Typing

Pleoptic Training 92065

Plethysmography
See Vascular Studies
Extremities 93922-93923
　　Veins 93965
Penis 54240
Total Body 93720-93722

Pleura
Biopsy 32095-32100, 32400-32402
Decortication 32320
Empyema
　　Excision 32540
Excision 32310-32320
　　Endoscopic 32656
Foreign Body
　　Removal 32150-32151
Needle Biopsy 32400
Removal
　　Foreign Body 32653
Repair 32215
Thoracotomy 32095-32100
Unlisted Services and Procedures 32999

Pleural Cavity
Aspiration 32000-32002
Catheterization 32019
Chemotherapy Administration 96440
　　See Chemotherapy
Fusion 32005
Incision
　　Empyema 32035-32036
　　Pneumothorax 32020
Puncture and Drainage 32000-32002
Thoracostomy 32035-32036

Pleural Endoscopies
See Thoracoscopy

Pleural Scarification
for Repeat Pneumothorax 32215

Pleural Tap
See Thoracentesis

Pleurectomy
Anesthesia 00542
Parietal 32310-32320
　　Endoscopic 32656

Pleuritis, Purulent
See Abscess, Thorax

Pleurocentesis
See Thoracentesis

Pleurodesis
Chemical 32005
Endoscopic 32650

Pleurosclerosis
See Pleurodesis

Pleurosclerosis, Chemical
See Pleurodesis, Chemical

Plexectomy, Choroid
See Choroid Plexus, Excision

Plexus Brachialis
See Brachial Plexus

Plexus Cervicalis
See Cervical Plexus

Plexus Coeliacus
See Celiac Plexus

Plexus Lumbalis
See Lumbar Plexus

Plexus, Choroid
See Choroid Plexus

PLGN
See Plasminogen

Plication, Sphincter, Urinary Bladder
See Bladder, Repair, Neck

Pneumocentesis
Lung 32420

Pneumocisternogram
See Cisternography

Pneumococcal Vaccine
See Vaccines

Pneumocystis Carinii
Antigen Detection
　　Immunofluorescence 87281

Pneumogastric Nerve
See Vagus Nerve

Pneumogram
Pediatric 94772

Pneumolysis 32940

Pneumonectomy 32440-32500
Completion 32488
Donor 32850, 33930
Sleeve 32442
Total 32440-32445

Pneumonology
See Pulmonology

Pneumonolysis 32940
Intrapleural 32652
Open Intrapleural 32124

Pneumonostomy 32200-32201

Pneumonotomy
See Incision, Lung

Pneumoperitoneum 49400

Pneumoplethysmography
Ocular 93875

Pneumothorax
Chemical Pleurodesis 32005
Pleural Scarification for Repeat 32215
Therapeutic
　　Injection Intrapleural Air 32960
Thoracentesis with Tube Insertion 32002

Polio
Antibody 86658
Vaccine 90712-90713

Poliovirus Vaccine, Inactivated
See Vaccines

Pollicization
Digit 26550

Polya Gastrectomy
See Gastrectomy, Partial

Polydactylism
See Supernumerary Digit

Polydactylous Digit
Reconstruction 26587
Repair 26587

Polydactyly, Toes 28344

Polymerase Chain Reaction 83898

Polyp
Antrochoanal
　　Removal 31032
Esophagus
　　Ablation 43228
Nose
　　Excision
　　　Endoscopic 31237-31240
　　　Extensive 30115
　　　Simple 30110
Sphenoid Sinus
　　Removal 31051
Urethra
　　Excision 53260

Polypectomy
Nose
　　Endoscopic 31237
Uterus 58558

Polypeptide, Vasoactive Intestinal
See Vasoactive Intestinal Peptide

Polysomnography 95808-95811

Polyuria Test
See Water Load Test

Pomeroy's Operation
See Tubal Ligation

Pooling
Blood Products 86965

Popliteal Arteries
See Artery, Popliteal

Popliteal Synovial Cyst
See Baker's Cyst

Poradenitistras
See Lymphogranuloma Venereum

PORP (Partial Ossicular Replacement Prosthesis) 69633, 69637

Porphobilinogen
Urine 84106-84110

Porphyrin Precursors 82135

Porphyrins
Feces .84126-84127
Urine .84119-84120

Port Film 77417

Portal Vein
See Vein, Hepatic Portal

Porter-Silber Test
See Corticosteroid, Blood

Portoenterostomies, Hepatic
See Hepaticoenterostomy

Portoenterostomy 47701

Posadas-Wernicke Disease
See Coccidioidomycosis

Positional Nystagmus Test
See Nystagmus Tests, Positional

Positive End Expiratory Pressure
See Pressure Breathing, Positive

Positive-Pressure Breathing, Inspiratory
See Intermittent Positive Pressure Breathing (IPPB)

Positron Emission Tomography (PET)
Brain .78608-78609
Heart 78459
Myocardial Imaging
  Perfusion Study 78491-78492
Tumor .78811-78813
  with Computed Tomography . .78814-78816

Post-Op Visit 99024

Postauricular Fistula
See Fistula, Postauricular

Postcaval Ureter
See Retrocaval Ureter

Postmortem
See Autopsy

Postop Vas Reconstruction
See Vasovasorrhaphy

Postoperative Wound Infection
Incision and Drainage 10180

Postpartum Care
Cesarean Delivery 59515
  after Attempted Vaginal Delivery 59622
  Previous 59610, 59614-59618, 59622
Vaginal Delivery 59430
  after Previous Cesarean Delivery 59614

Potassium .84132
Urine 84133

Potential, Auditory Evoked
See Auditory Evoked Potentials

Potential, Evoked
See Evoked Potential

Potts-Smith Procedure 33762

Pouch, Kock
See Kock Pouch

PPP
See Fibrin Degradation Products

PRA
See Cytotoxic Screen

Prealbumin 84134

Prebeta Lipoproteins
See Lipoprotein, Blood

Pregl's Test
See Cystourethroscopy, Catheterization, Urethral

Pregnancy
Abortion
  Induced 59855-59857
    by Amniocentesis Injection . .59850-59852
    by Dilation and Curettage 59840
    by Dilation and Evaluation 59841
  Septic 59830
  Therapeutic
    by Dilation and Curettage 59851
    by Hysterectomy 59852
    by Saline 59850
Cesarean Delivery 59618-59622
  Only 59514
  Postpartum Care 59514-59515
  Routine Care 59510
  Vaginal Birth After 59610-59614
  with Hysterectomy 59525
Ectopic
  Abdominal 59130
  Cervix 59140
  Interstitial
    Partial Resection Uterus 59136
    Total Hysterectomy 59135
  Laparoscopy
    with Salpingectomy and/or
    Oophorectomy 59151
    without Salpingectomy and/or
    Oophorectomy 59150
  Tubal 59121
    with Salpingectomy and/or
    Oophorectomy 59120

Miscarriage
Surgical Completion
  Any Trimester 59812
  First Trimester 59820
  Second Trimester 59821
Molar
  See Hydatidiform Mole
Multifetal Reduction 59866
Placenta Delivery 59414
Vaginal Delivery 59409-59410
  after Cesarean Delivery 59610-59614
  Antepartum Care 59425-59426
  Postpartum Care 59430
  Total Obstetrical Care . .59400, 59610, 59618

Pregnancy Test 84702-84703
Urinalysis 81025

Pregnanediol 84135

Pregnanetriol 84138

Pregnenolone 84140

Prekallikrein
See Fletcher Factor

Prekallikrein Factor 85292

Premature, Closure, Cranial Suture
See Craniosynostosis

Prenatal Procedure 59897
Amnioinfusion
  Transabdominal 59070
Drainage
  Fluid 59074
Occlusion
  Umbilical Cord 59072
Shunt 59076

Prenatal Testing
Amniocentesis 59000
  with Amniotic Fluid Reduction 59001
Chorionic Villus Sampling 59015
Cordocentesis 59012
Fetal Blood Sample 59030
Fetal Monitoring 59050
  Interpretation Only 59051
Non-Stress Test, Fetal 59025, 99500
Oxytocin Stress Test 59020
Stress Test
  Oxytocin 59020
Ultrasound 76801-76817
  Fetal Biophysical Profile 76818-76819
  Fetal Heart 76825

Prentiss Operation
See Orchiopexy, Inguinal Approach

Preparation
for Transfer
  Embryo .89255
for Transplantation
  Heart 33933, 33944
  Heart/Lung 33933
  Intestines 44715-44721
  Kidney 50323-50329
  Liver 47143-47147

Lung 32855-32856, 33933
Pancreas 48551-48552
Renal 50323-50329
Thawing
  Embryo
   Cryopreserved 89352
  Oocytes
   Cryopreserved 89356
  Reproductive Tissue
   Cryopreserved 89354
  Sperm
   Cryopreserved 89353

Presacral Sympathectomy
See Sympathectomy, Presacral

Prescription
Contact Lens 92310-92317
  See Contact Lens Services

Pressure Breathing
See Pulmonology, Therapeutic
Negative
  Continuous (CNP) 94662
Positive
  Continuous (CPAP) 94660

Pressure Measurement of Sphincter of Oddi
See Sphincter of Oddi, Pressure Measurement

Pressure Ulcer (Decubitus)
See Debridement; Skin Graft and Flap

Pressure Ulcers
Excision 15920-15999

Pressure, Blood
See Blood Pressure

Pressure, Venous
See Blood Pressure, Venous

Pretreatment
Red Blood Cell
  Antibody Identification 86970-86972
Serum
  Antibody Identification 86975-86978

Prevention & Control
See Prophylaxis

Preventive Medicine 99381-99397
See Immunization; Newborn Care, Normal; Office and/or Other Outpatient Services; Performance Measures, Prophylatic Treatment
Administration/Interpretation of Health Risk Assessment 99420
Counseling and/or Risk Factor Reduction Intervention 99401-99429
  Group Counseling 99411-99412
  Individual Counseling 99401-99404
Established Patient 99382-99397
New Patient 99381-99387
Newborn Care 99432
Respiratory Pattern Recording 94772
Unlisted Services and Procedures 99429

Priapism
Repair
  Fistulization 54435
  with Shunt 54420-54430

Primidone
Assay 80188

PRL
See Prolactin

Pro-Insulin C Peptide
See C-Peptide

Proalbumin
See Prealbumin

Probes, DNA
See Nucleic Acid Probe

Probes, Nucleic Acid
See Nucleic Acid Probe

Procainamide
Assay 80190-80192

Process
See Anatomic term (eg coracoid, odontoid)

Procidentia
Rectum
  Excision 45130-45135
  Repair 45900

Procoagulant Activity, Glomerular
See Thromboplastin

Proconvertin 85230

Proctectasis
See Dilation, Rectum

Proctectomy
Partial
  Open 45111, 45113-45116, 45123
Total 45110, 45112, 45119-45120
  Laparoscopic 45395-45397
  Open 45111,45113-45116,45123
  with Colon 45121
with Colectomy/Ileostomy
  Laparoscopic 44212
  Open 44155

Proctocele
See Rectocele

Proctopexy
Laparoscopic 45400-45402
  with Sigmoid Resection 45402
Open 45540-45541
  with Sigmoid Excision 45550

Proctoplasty 45500-45505

Proctorrhaphy
See Rectum, Suture

Proctoscopies
See Anoscopy

Proctosigmoidoscopy
Ablation
  Polyp or Lesion 45320
Biopsy 45305

Destruction
  Tumor 45320
Dilation 45303
Exploration 45300
Hemorrhage Control 45317
Placement
  Stent 45327
Removal
  Foreign Body 45307
  Polyp 45308-45315
  Tumor 45315
Volvulus Repair 45321

Products, Gene
See Protein

Proetz Therapy
Nose 30210

Profibrinolysin
See Plasminogen

Progenitor Cell
See Stem Cell

Progesterone 84144

Progesterone Receptors 84234

Progestin Receptors
See Progesterone Receptors

Proinsulin 84206

Projective Test 96101-96103

Prokallikrein
See Fletcher Factor

Prokallikrein, Plasma
See Fletcher Factor

Prokinogenase
See Fletcher Factor

Prolactin 80418, 80440, 84146

Prolapse
See Procidentia

Prolapse, Rectal
See Procidentia, Rectum

Prolastin
See Alpha-1 Antitrypsin

Prolonged Services 99354-99357, 99360
without Direct Patient Contact 99358-99359

Prophylactic Treatment
See Preventive Medicine
Femoral Neck and Proximal Femur
  Nailing 27187
  Pinning 27187
  Wiring 27187
Femur 27495
  Nailing 27495
  Pinning 27495
  Wiring 27495
Humerus
  Pinning, Wiring 24498

Radius 25490, 25492
   Nailing 25490, 25492
   Pinning 25490, 25492
   Plating 25490, 25492
   Wiring 25490, 25492
Shoulder
   Clavicle 23490
   Humerus 23491
Tibia 27745
Ulna 25491-25492
   Nailing 25491-25492
   Pinning 25491-25492
   Plating 25491-25492
   Wiring 25491-25492

Prophylaxis
Retina
   Detachment
      Cryotherapy, Diathermy 67141
      Photocoagulation 67145

Prostaglandin 84150
Insertion 59200

Prostanoids
See Prostaglandin

Prostate
Ablation
   Cryosurgery 55873
Abscess
   Drainage 52700
   Incision and Drainage 55720-55725
Biopsy 0137T, 55700-55705
Brachytherapy
   Needle Insertion 55859
Coagulation
   Laser 52647
Destruction
   Cryosurgery 55873
   Thermotherapy 53850-53853
      Microwave 53850
      Radio Frequency 53852
Excision
   Partial 55801, 55821-55831
   Perineal 55801-55815
   Radical 55810-55815, 55840-55845
   Retropubic 55831-55845
   Suprapubic 55821
   Transurethral . . .52402, 52601, 52612-52614
Exploration
   Exposure 55860
   with Nodes 55862-55865
Incision
   Exposure 55860-55865
   Transurethral 52450
Insertion
   Radioactive Substance 55860
Needle Biopsy 0137T, 55700
Thermotherapy
   Transurethral 53850-53853
Ultrasound 76872-76873
Unlisted Services and Procedures 55899
   Urinary System 53899
Urethra
   Stent Insertion 0084T
   Transurethral Balloon Dilation 52510
Vaporization
   Laser 52648

Prostate Specific
Antigen 84152-84154

Prostatectomy 52601
Laparascopic 55866
Perineal
   Partial 55801
   Radical 55810-55815
Retropubic
   Partial 55831
   Radical 55840-55845, 55866
Suprapubic
   Partial 55821
Transurethral 52612-52614

Prostatic Abscess
See Abscess, Prostate

Prostatotomy 55720-55725

Prosthesis
Augmentation
   Mandibular Body 21125
Auricular 21086
Breast
   Insertion 19340-19342
   Removal 19328-19330
   Supply 19396
Check-Out 97762
   See Physical Medicine/Therapy/Occupational
   Therapy
Cornea 65770
Endovascular
   Thoracic Aorta 33883-33886
Facial 21088
Hernia
   Mesh 49568
Hip
   Removal 27090-27091
Intestines 44700
Knee
   Insertion 27438, 27445
Lens
   Insertion 66982-66985
   Manual or Mechanical
   Technique 66982-66984
   Not Associated with Concurrent Cataract
   Removal .66985
Mandibular Resection 21081
Nasal 21087
Nasal Septum
   Insertion .30220
Obturator 21076
   Definitive 21080
   Interim 21079
Ocular 21077, 65770, 66982-66985, 92358
   Loan 92358
Orbital 21077
   Partial or Total 69633, 69637
Orthotic
   Check-Out 97762
   Training .97761
Ossicle Reconstruction
   Chain 69633
Palatal Augmentation 21082
Palatal Lift 21083
Palate 42280-42281

Penile
   Insertion 54400-54405
   Removal 54406, 54410-54417
   Repair 54408
   Replacement 54410-54411, 54416-54417
Perineum
   Removal .53442
Skull Plate
   Removal .62142
   Replacement 62143
Spectacle
   Fitting 92352-92353
   Repair 92371
Speech Aid 21084
Spinal
   Insertion .22851
Synthetic 69633, 69637
Temporomandibular Joint
   Arthroplasty 21243
Testicular
   Insertion .54660
Training 97761
Urethral Sphincter
   Insertion 53444-53445
   Removal 53446-53447
   Repair 53449
   Replacement 53448
Vagina
   Insertion .57267
Wrist
   Removal 25250-25251

Protease F
See Plasmin

Protein
A, Plasma (PAPP-A) 84163
C-Reactive 86140-86141
Electropheresis 84165-84166
Glycated 82985
Myelin Basic .83873
Osteocalcin 83937
Other Fluids .84166
Prealbumin 84134
Serum 84155, 84165
Total 84155-84160
Urine 84156
Western Blot 84181-84182, 88372

Protein Analysis, Tissue
Western Blot .88371

Protein Blotting
See Western Blot

Protein C Activator 85337

Protein C Antigen 85302

Protein C Assay 85303

Protein C Resistance Assay 85307

Protein S
Assay 85306
Total 85305

Prothrombase
See Thrombokinase

Prothrombin .85210

Prothrombin Time 85610-85611

Prothrombinase
See Thromboplastin

Prothrombokinase 85230

Protime
See Prothrombin Time

Proton Treatment Delivery
Complex 77525
Intermediate 77523
Simple 77520-77522

Protoporphyrin 84202-84203

Protozoa
Antibody 86753

Provitamin A
See Vitamin, A

Provocation Test
for Allergies 95078
   See Allergy Tests
for Glaucoma 92140

Provocation Tonography 92130

Prower Factor
See Stuart-Prower Factor

PSA
See Prostate Specific Antigen

Pseudocyst, Pancreas
See Pancreas, Pseudocyst

PSG
See Polysomnography

Psoriasis Treatment 96910-96922
See Dermatology; Photochemotherapy

Psychiatric Diagnosis
Evaluation of Records or Reports 90885
Interventional Evaluation
   Interactive 90802
Interview and Evaluation 90801-90802
Psychological Testing 96101-96103
   Computer-Assisted 96103
Unlisted Services and Procedures 90899

Psychiatric Treatment
See Psychotherapy
Biofeedback Training 90875-90876
Consultation with Family 90887
Drug Management 90862
Electroconvulsive Therapy 90870
Environmental Intervention 90882
Family 90846-90849, 99510
Group 90853-90857
Hypnotherapy 90880
Individual
   Insight-Oriented
      Home Visit .99510
      Hospital or Residential Care . .90816-90822
      Office or Outpatient 90804-90809

Interactive
   Home Visit .99510
   Hospital or Residential Care . .90823-90829
   Office or Outpatient 90810-90815
Narcosynthesis Analysis 90865
Psychoanalysis .90845
Report Preparation 90889
Residential
   Facility Care 90816-90829
Unlisted Services and Procedures 90899

Psychoanalysis 90845

Psychophysiologic Feedback
See Biofeedback

Psychotherapy
Family 90846-90849, 99510
Group 90853-90857
   Insight-Oriented
      Hospital or Residential Care . .90816-90822
      Office or Outpatient 90804-90809
   Interactive
      Hospital or Residential Care . .90823-90829
      Office or Outpatient 90810-90815

PTA 85270

PTA (Factor XI)
See Clotting Factor

PTC Factor .85250

PTCA
See Percutaneous Transluminal Angioplasty

Pteroylglutamic Acid
See Folic Acid

Pterygium
Excision 65420
   with Graft 65426

Pterygomaxillary Fossa
Incision 31040

Pterygopalatine Ganglion
See Sphenopalatine Ganglion

PTH
See Parathormone

Ptosis
See Blepharoptosis; Procidentia

PTT
See Thromboplastin, Partial, Time

Ptyalectasis
See Dilation, Salivary Duct

Pubic Symphysis 27282

Pubis
Craterization 27070
Cyst
   Excision 27065-27067
Excision 27070
Saucerization .27070
Tumor
   Excision 27065-27067

Pudendal Nerve
Avulsion 64761
Destruction 64630
Incision 64761
Injection
   Anesthetic 64430
   Neurolytic 64630
Transection 64761

Puestow Procedure 48180

Pulled Elbow
See Nursemaid Elbow

Pulmonary Artery
Banding 33690
Catheterization 36013-36015
Embolism 33910-33916
   Excision 33910-33916
Percutaneous Transluminal
Angioplasty 92997-92998
Reimplantation .33788
Repair 33690, 33917-33920
   Reimplantation 33788
Shunt
   from Aorta 33755-33762, 33924
   from Vena Cava 33766-33767
   Subclavian 33750
Transection 33922

Pulmonary Function Test
See Pulmonology, Diagnostic

Pulmonary Haemorrhage
See Hemorrhage, Lung

Pulmonary Perfusion Imaging
Nuclear Medicine 78588

Pulmonary Valve
Incision .33470-33474
Repair .33470-33474
Replacement 33475

Pulmonary Vein
Repair 33730

Pulmonology
Diagnostic
   Airway Closing Volume 94370
   Bronchodilation 94664
   Carbon Dioxide Response Curve 94400
   Carbon Monoxide Diffusion Capacity . .94720
   Expired Gas Analysis . . .0043T, 0064T, 94250
      CO_2 94770
      O_2 and CO_2 94681
      O_2 Update, Direct 94680
      O_2 Uptake, Indirect 94690
   Flow-Volume Loop 94375
   Function Study 78596
   Functional Residual Capacity 94240
   Hemoglobin O_2 Affinity 82820
   High Altitude Simulation
   Test (HAST) 94452-94453
   Hypoxia Response Curve 94450
   Inhalation Treatment 94640
   Maldistribution of Inspired Air 94350
   Maximum Breathing Capacity 94200
   Maximum Voluntary Ventilation 94200
   Membrane Compliance 94750
   Membrane Diffusion Capacity 94725

Nitrogen Washout Curve 94350
Oximetry
    Ear or Pulse 94760-94762
Resistance to Airflow 94360
Spirometry 94010-94070
    Evaluation 94010-94070
    Patient Initiated with
    Bronchospasm 94014-94016
Sputum Mobilization with
    Inhalants 94664
Stress Test 94621
Stress Test, Pulmonary 94620
Thoracic Gas Volume 94260
Therapeutic
    Expired Gas Analysis 94250
    Inhalation
        Pentamidine 94642
    Inhalation Treatment . . .94640, 94664, 99503
    Manipulation of Chest Wall 94667-94668
    Pressure Ventilation
        Negative CNPB 94662
        Positive CPAP 94660
    Unlisted Services and Procedures 94799
    Ventilation Assist 94656-94657, 99504
Unlisted Services and Procedures 94799

Pulse Generator
Electronic Analysis 95970-95971
Heart
    Insertion/Replacement 33212-33213

Pulse Rate Increased
See Tachycardia

Pulsed Magnetic Neuromodulation
Urinary Incontinence 0029T

Pump
See Chemotherapy, Pump Services; Infusion Pump

Pump Services
Oxygenator/Heat Exchanger 99190-99192

Pump Stomach for Poison 91105

Pump, Infusion
See Infusion Pump

Punch Graft 15775-15776

Puncture
Artery 36600
Chest
    Drainage 32000-32002
Cisternal
    See Cisternal Puncture
Lumbar
    See Spinal Tap
Lung 32420
Pericardium 33010-33011
Pleural Cavity
    Drainage 32000-32002
Skull
    Drain Fluid 61000-61020
        Cistern .61050
        Inject Cistern 61055
        Inject Ventricle 61026
    Shunt
        Drain Fluid 61070
        Injection 61070

Spinal Cord
    Diagnostic .62270
    Drain Fluid .62272
    Lumbar 62270
Tracheal
    Aspiration and/or Injection 31612

Puncture Aspiration
Abscess
    Skin 10160
Bulla 10160
Cyst
    Breast 19000-19001
    Skin 10160
Hematoma 10160

Puncturing
See Puncture

Pure-Tone Audiometry
See Audiometry, Pure Tone

Pustules
Removal 10040

Putti-Platt Procedure 23450

PUVA
See Dermatology; Photochemotherapy; Ultraviolet Light Therapy

Pyelogram
See Urography, Intravenous; Urography, Retrograde

Pyelography 74400, 74425
Injection 50394

Pyelolithotomy 50130
Anatrophic 50075
Coagulum 50130

Pyeloplasty 50400-50405, 50544
Repair
    Horseshoe Kidney 50540
Secondary 50405

Pyeloscopy
with Cystourethroscopy 52351
    Biopsy 52354
    Destruction 52354
    Lithotripsy 52353
    Removal
        Calculus 52352
    Tumor Excision 52355

Pyelostogram 50394

Pyelostolithotomy
Percutaneous 50080-50081

Pyelostomy 50125, 50400-50405
Change Tube .50398

Pyelotomy
Complicated .50135
Endoscopic 50570
Exploration 50120
with Drainage 50125
with Removal Calculus 50130

Pyeloureterogram
Antegrade 50394

Pyeloureteroplasty
See Pyeloplasty

Pyloric Sphincter
Incision 43520
Reconstruction 43800

Pyloromyotomy 43520

Pyloroplasty 43800
with Vagotomy 43640

Pyothorax
See Abscess, Thorax

Pyridoxal Phosphate 84207

Pyrophosphate, Adenosine
See Adenosine Diphosphate

Pyrophosphorylase, Udp Galactose
See Galactose-1-Phosphate, Uridyl Transferase

Pyruvate 84210-84220

Q

Q Fever 86000, 86638

Q Fever ab
See Antibody, Coxiella Burnetii

QST
See Quantitative Sensory Testing

Quadrantectomy 19160-19162

Quadriceps Repair 27430

Quantitative Sensory Testing (QST)
Cooling Stimuli 0108T
Heat-Pain Stimuli 0109T
Other Stimuli 0110T
Touch Pressure Stimuli 0106T
Vibration Stimuli 0107T

Quick Test
See Prothrombin Time

Quinidine
Assay 80194

Quinine 84228

R

Rabies Vaccine
See Vaccines

Rachicentesis
See Spinal Tap

Radial Arteries
See Artery, Radial

Radial Head, Subluxation
See Nursemaid Elbow

Radial Keratotomy 65771

Radiation
See Irradiation

Radiation Physics
Consultation 77336-77370
Unlisted Services and Procedures 77399

Radiation Therapy 77280-77295
Consultation
    Radiation Physics 77336-77370
CT Scan Guidance 76370
Dose Plan 77300, 77305-77331
    Brachytherapy 77326-77328
    Intensity Modulation 77301
    Teletherapy 77305-77321
Field Set-up 77280-77295
Planning 77261-77263, 77299
Special 77470
Stereotactic
    Body 0082T, 0083T
    Cerebral Lesions 77432
    Guidance 77421
Treatment Delivery
    Beam Modulation 0073T
    High Energy Neutron Radiation .77422-77423
    Intensity Modulation 77418
    Proton Beam 77520-77525
    Single Area 77402-77406, 77422
    Stereotactic
        Body 0082T
    Superficial 77401
    3 or More Areas 77412-77416
    2 Areas 77407-77411
    Weekly 77427
Treatment Device 77332-77334
Treatment Management
    1 or 2 Fractions Only 77431
    Stereotactic
        Body 0083T
        Cerebral 77432
    Unlisted Services and Procedures 77499
    Weekly 77427

Radiation, X
See X-Ray

Radical Excision of Lymph Nodes
See Excision, Lymph Nodes, Radical

Radical Mastectomies, Modified
See Mastectomy, Modified Radical

Radical Neck Dissection
Laryngectomy 31365-31368
Pharyngolaryngectomy 31390-31395
with Auditory Canal Surgery 69155
with Thyroidectomy 60254
with Tongue Excision 41135, 41145, 41153-41155

Radical Resection
See Resection, Radical
Abdomen 51597
Acetabulum 27076
Ankle 27615
Arm, Lower 25077
Calcaneus 27647
Elbow
    Capsule, Soft Tissue, Bone
        with Contracture Release 24149
Face 21015
Fibula 27646
Finger 26117
Foot 28046
Forearm 25077
Hand 26115
Hip
    Soft Tissue 27049
    Tumor or Infection 27075-27076
Humerus 23220-23222
Innominate 27077
Ischial 27078-27079
Knee 27329
Leg
    Lower 27615
    Upper 27329
Metacarpal 26250-26255
Metatarsal 28173
Mouth
    with Tongue Excision 41150, 41155
Ovarian Tumor
    Bilateral Salpingo-Oophorectomy-
    Omentectomy 58950-58956
    with Radical Dissection for
    Debulking 58952-58954
    with Total Abdominal
    Hysterectomy 58951, 58953-58956
Pelvis
    Soft Tissue 27049
Peritoneal Tumor
    Bilateral Salpingo-Oophorectomy-
    Omentectomy 58952-58956
    with Radical Dissection for
    Debulking 58952-58954
Phalanges
    Finger 26260-26262
    Toe 28175
Radius 25170
Scalp 21015
Scapula 23210
Shoulder 23077
Sternum 21630-21632
Talus
    Tumor 27647
Tarsal 28171
Tibia 27645
Tonsil 42842-42845
Tumor
    Back/Flank 21935
    Femur 27365
    Knee 27329, 27365
    Leg, Upper 27329
    Neck 21557
    Thorax 21557
Ulna 25170
Wrist 25077

Radical Vaginal Hysterectomy
See Hysterectomy, Vaginal, Radical

Radical Vulvectomy
See Vulvectomy, Radical

Radio-Cobalt B12 Schilling Test
See Vitamin, B12, Absorption Study

Radioactive Colloid Therapy ...79300

Radioactive Substance
Insertion
    Prostate 55860

Radiocarpal Joint
Arthrotomy 25040
Dislocation
    Closed Treatment 25660

Radiocinematographies
See Cineradiography

Radioelement
Application 77761-77778
    Surface 77789
    with Ultrasound 76965
Handling 77790
Infusion 77750

Radioelement Substance
Catheter Placement
    Breast 19296-19298
    Bronchus 31643
    Prostate 55859
Needle Placement
    Prostate 55859

Radiography
See Radiology, Diagnostic; X-Ray

Radioimmunosorbent Test
See Gammaglobulin, Blood

Radioisotope Brachytherapy
See Brachytherapy

Radioisotope Scan
See Nuclear Medicine

Radiological Marker
Preoperative Placement
    Excision of Breast Lesion 19125-19126

Radiology
See Nuclear Medicine, Radiation Therapy, X-Ray, Ultrasound
Diagnostic
    Unlisted Services and Procedures 76499
Stress Views 76006

Radionuclide CT Scan
See Emission Computerized Tomography

Radionuclide Imaging
See Nuclear Medicine

Radionuclide Therapy
See Radiopharmaceutical Therapy

Radionuclide Tomography, Single-Photon Emission-Computed
See SPECT

Radiopharmaceutical Therapy
Interstitial 79300
Intra-Arterial 79445
Intra-Articular 79440
Intracavitary 79200
Intravenous 79101, 79403
Oral 79005
Unlisted Services and Procedures 79999

Radiotherapeutic
See Radiation Therapy

Radiotherapies
See Irradiation

Radiotherapy, Surface
See Application, Radioelement, Surface

Radioulnar Joint
Arthrodesis
　　with Resection of Ulna 25830
Dislocation
　　Closed Treatment 25675
　　Open Treatment 25676
　　Percutaneous Fixation 25671

Radius
See Arm, Lower; Elbow; Ulna
Arthroplasty 24365
　　with Implant 24366, 25441
Craterization 24145, 25151
Cyst
　　Excision 24125-24126, 25120-25126
Diaphysectomy 24145, 25151
Dislocation
　　Partial 24640
　　Subluxate 24640
　　with Fracture
　　　　Closed Treatment 24620
　　　　Open Treatment 24635
Excision 24130, 24136, 24145, 24152-24153
　　Epiphyseal Bar 20150
　　Partial 25145
　　Styloid Process 25230
Fracture 25605
　　Closed Treatment 25500-25505, 25520,
　　　　　　　　　　　　　　　　　　25600-25605
　　　　with Manipulation 25605
　　　　without Manipulation 25600
　　Distal 25600-25611
　　　　Open Treatment 25620
　　Head/Neck
　　　　Closed Treatment 24650-24655
　　　　Open Treatment 24665-24666
　　Open Treatment 25515, 25525-25526,
　　　　　　　　　　　　　　　　　　　　　25574
　　Percutaneous Fixation 25611
　　Shaft 25500-25526
　　　　Open Treatment 25574
　　with Ulna 25560-25565
　　　　Open Treatment 25575
Implant
　　Removal 24164
Incision and Drainage 25035
Osteomyelitis 24136, 24145
Osteoplasty 25390-25393
Prophylactic Treatment 25490, 25492

Repair
　　Epiphyseal Arrest 25450-25455
　　Epiphyseal Separation
　　　　Closed .25600
　　　　Closed with Manipulation 25605
　　　　Open Treatment 25620
　　　　Percutaneous Fixation 25611
　　Malunion or Nonunion 25400, 25415
　　Osteotomy 25350-25355, 25370-25375
　　　　and Ulna 25365
　　　　with Graft 25405, 25420-25426
Saucerization 24145, 25151
Sequestrectomy 24136, 25145
Tumor
　　Cyst 24120
　　Excision . .24125-24126, 25120-25126, 25170

Ramstedt Operation
See Pyloromyotomy

Ramus Anterior, Nervus Thoracicus
See Intercostal Nerve

Range of Motion Test
Extremities or Trunk 95851
Eye 92018-92019
Hand 95852

Rapid Heart Rate
See Tachycardia

Rapid Plasma Reagin
Test 86592-86593

Rapid Test for
Infection 86308, 86403-86406
Monospot Test 86308

Rapoport Test 52005

Raskind Procedure 33735-33737

Rat Typhus
See Murine Typhus

Rathke Pouch Tumor
See Craniopharyngioma

Rays, Roentgen
See X-Ray

Raz Procedure 51845
See Repair, Bladder, Neck

RBC
See Red Blood Cell (RBC)

RBC ab
See Antibody, Red Blood Cell

Reaction
Lip
　　without Reconstruction 40530

Reaction, Polymerase Chain
See Polymerase Chain Reaction

Realignment
Femur
　　with Osteotomy 27454
Knee
　　Extensor 27422

Receptor
See CD4; Estrogen, Receptor; FC Receptor;
Progesterone Receptors

Receptor Assay
Hormone 84233-84235
Non Hormone .84238

Recession
Gastrocnemius
　　Leg, Lower .27687

Reconstruction
See Revision
Abdominal Wall
　　Omental Flap 49905
Acetabulum 27120-27122
Anal
　　Congenital Absence 46730-46740
　　Fistula 46742
　　Graft 46753
　　Sphincter 46750-46751, 46760-46762
　　with Implant 46762
Ankle .27700-27703
Apical-Aortic Conduit 33404
Atrial 33253
Auditory Canal, External 69310-69320
Bile Duct
　　Anastomosis 47800
Bladder
　　and Urethra 51800-51820
　　from Colon .50810
　　from Intestines 50820, 51960
Breast .19357-19369
　　Augmentation 19324-19325
　　Mammoplasty 19318-19325
　　Nipple 19350-19355
　　Revision 19380
　　Transverse Rectus Abdominis Myocutaneous
　　　　Flap 19367-19369
　　with Free Flap 19364
　　with Latissimus Dorsi Flap 19361
　　with Other Techniques 19366
　　with Tissue Expander 19357
Bronchi 32501
　　Graft Repair 31770
　　Stenosis 31775
Canthus 67950
Carpal 25443
Carpal Bone 25394, 25430
Cheekbone 21270
Chest Wall 32504
　　Omental Flap 49904
　　Trauma 32820
Cleft Palate 42200-42225
Conduit
　　Apical-Aortic 33404
Conjunctiva 68320-68335
　　with Flap
　　　　Bridge or Partial 68360
　　　　Total 68362
Cranial Bone
　　Extracranial 21181-21184
Ear, Middle
　　Tympanoplasty with Antrotomy or
　　Mastoidotomy
　　　　with Ossicular Chain
　　　　Reconstruction 69636-69637

Tympanoplasty with Mastoidectomy . .69641
   Radical or Complete 69644-69645
   with Intact or Reconstructed
     Wall 69643-69644
   with Ossicular Chain
     Reconstruction 69642
Tympanoplasty without
  Mastoidectomy 69631
   with Ossicular Chain
     Reconstruction 69632-69633
Elbow 24360
  Total Replacement 24363
  with Implant 24361-24362
Esophagus 43300, 43310, 43313
  Creation
    Stoma 43350-43352
  Esophagostomy 43350
  Fistula 43305, 43312, 43314
  Gastrointestinal 43360-43361
Eye
  Graft
    Conjunctiva 65782
    Stem Cell 65781
  Transplantation
    Amniotic Membrane 65780
Eyelid
  Canthus 67950
  Second Stage 67975
  Total 67973-67975
  Total Eyelid
    Lower, One Stage 67973
    Upper, One Stage 67974
  Transfer Tarsoconjunctival Flap from
    Opposing Eyelid 67971
Facial Bones
  Secondary .21275
Fallopian Tube
  See Repair
Femur
  Lengthening 27466-27468
  Shortening 27465, 27468
Fibula
  Lengthening 27715
Finger
  Polydactylous 26587
Foot
  Cleft 28360
Forehead 21172-21180, 21182-21184
Glenoid Fossa .21255
Gums
  Alveolus 41874
  Gingiva 41872
Hand
  Tendon Pulley 26500-26504
  Toe to Finger Transfer 26551-26556
Heart
  Atrial 33253
  Atrial Septum 33735-33737
  Pulmonary Artery Shunt 33924
  Vena Cava .34502
Hip
  Replacement 27130-27132
  Secondary 27134-27138
Hip Joint
  with Prosthesis 27125
Interphalangeal Joint 26535-26536
  Collateral Ligament 26545

Intestines, Small
  Anastomosis 43845, 44130
Knee 27437-27438
  Femur 27442-27443, 27446
  Ligament 27427-27429
  Replacement 27447
  Revision 27486-27487
  Tibia 27440-27443, 27446
  with Prosthesis 27438, 27445
Kneecap
  Instability 27420-27424
Larynx
  Burns 31588
  Cricoid Split 31587
  Other 31545-31546, 31588
  Stenosis 31582
  Web 31580
Lip 40525-40527, 40761
Lunate 25444
Malar Augmentation
  Prosthetic Material 21270
  with Bone Graft 21210
Mandible
  with Implant 21244-21246, 21248-21249
Mandibular Condyle 21247
Mandibular Rami
  with Bone Graft 21194
  with Internal Rigid Fixation 21196
  without Bone Graft 21193
  without Internal Rigid Fixation 21195
Maxilla
  with Implant 21245-21246, 21248-21249
Metacarpophalangeal Joint 26530-26531
Midface
  Forehead Advancement 21159-21160
  with Bone Graft 21145-21160, 21188
  without Bone Graft 21141-21143
Mouth 40840-40845
Nail Bed 11762
Nasoethmoid Complex 21182-21184
Navicular 25443
Nose
  Cleft Lip/Cleft Palate 30460-30462
  Dermatoplasty 30620
  Primary 30400-30420
  Secondary 30430-30450
  Septum 30520
Orbit 21256
Orbit Area
  Secondary .21275
Orbit with Bone Grafting 21182-21184
Orbital Rim 21172-21180
Orbital Rims 21182-21184
Orbital Walls 21182-21184
Orbitocraniofacial
  Secondary Revision 21275
Oviduct
  Fimbrioplasty 58760
Palate
  Cleft Palate 42200-42225
  Lengthening 42226-42227
Parotid Duct
  Diversion 42507-42510
Patella 27437-27438
  Instability 27420-27424

Penis
  Angulation .54360
  Chordee 54300-54304
  Complications 54340-54348
  Epispadias 54380-54390
  Hypospadias 54332, 54352
    One Stage Distal with
     Urethroplasty 54324-54328
    One Stage Perineal 54336
Periorbital Region
  Osteotomy with Graft 21267-21268
Pharynx 42950
Pyloric Sphincter 43800
Radius 24365, 25390-25393, 25441
  Arthroplasty
    with Implant 24366
Shoulder Joint
  with Implant 23470-23472
Skull 21172-21180
  Defect 62140-62141, 62145
Spinal Elements 63051, 63295
Sternum 21740-21742
  with Thoracoscopy 21743
Stomach
  for Obesity 43644-43645, 43845-43848
  Gastric Bypass 43644-43645, 43846
  Roux-En-Y 43644, 43846
  with Duodenum .43810, 43850-43855, 43865
  with Jejunum 43820-43825, 43860
Superior-Lateral Orbital Rim
and Forehead 21172-21175
Supraorbital Rim and Forehead 21179-21180
Symblepharon 68335
Temporomandibular Joint
  Arthroplasty 21240-21243
Throat 42950
Thumb
  from Finger 26550
  Opponensplasty 26490-26496
Tibia
  Lengthening 27715
  Tubercle 27418
Toe
  Angle Deformity 28313
  Extra Toes .28344
  Hammertoe 28285-28286
  Macrodactyly 28340-28341
  Polydactylous 26587
  Syndactyly .28345
  Webbed Toe 28345
Tongue
  Frenum 41520
Trachea
  Carina 31766
  Cervical 31750
  Fistula 31755
  Intrathoracic 31760
Trapezium 25445
Tympanic Membrane 69620
Ulna 25390-25393, 25442
  Radioulnar .25337
Ureter 50700
  with Intestines 50840

Urethra 53410-53440, 53445
   Complications 54340-54348
   Hypospadias
      One Stage Distal with Meatal
      Advancement 54322
      One Stage Distal with
      Urethroplasty 54324-54328
      Suture to Bladder 51840-51841
      Urethroplasty for Second
      Stage 54308-54316
      Urethroplasty for Third Stage 54318
Uterus 58540
Vas Deferens
   See Vasovasorrhaphy
Vena Cava 34502
   with Resection 37799
Wound Repair 13100-13160
Wrist 25332
   Capsulectomy 25320
   Capsulorrhaphy 25320
   Realign 25335
Zygomatic Arch 21255

Rectal Bleeding
See Hemorrhage, Rectum

Rectal Prolapse
See Procidentia, Rectum

Rectal Sphincter
Dilation 45910

Rectocele
Repair 45560

Rectopexy
See Proctopexy

Rectoplasty
See Proctoplasty

Rectorrhaphy
See Rectum, Suture

Rectovaginal Fistula
See Fistula, Rectovaginal

Rectovaginal Hernia
See Rectocele

Rectum
See Anus
Abscess
   Incision and Drainage 45005-45020,
                    46040, 46060
Biopsy 45100
Dilation
   Endoscopy 45303
Endoscopy
   Destruction
      Tumor 45320
   Dilation 45303
   Exploration 45300
   Hemorrhage 45317
   Removal
      Foreign Body 45307
      Polyp 45308-45315
      Tumor 45308-45315
   Volvulus 45321

Excision
   Partial 45111, 45113-45116, 45123
   Total 45110, 45112, 45119-45120
   with Colon 45121
Exploration
   Endoscopic 45300
   Surgical 45990
Hemorrhage
   Endoscopic 45317
Injection
   Sclerosing Solution 45520
Laparoscopy 45499
Lesion
   Excision 45108
Manometry 91122
Prolapse
   Excision 45130-45135
Pulsed Irrigation
   Fecal Impaction 91123
Removal
   Fecal Impaction 45915
      by Pulsed Irrigation 91123
   Foreign Body 45307, 45915
Repair
   Fistula 45800-45825
   Injury 45562-45563
   Prolapse 45505-45541, 45900
   Rectocele 45560
   Stenosis 45500
   with Sigmoid Excision 45550
Sensation, Tone, and Compliance Test 91120
Stricture
   Excision 45150
Suture
   Fistula 45800-45825
   Prolapse 45540-45541
Tumor
   Destruction 45190, 45320, 46937-46938
   Excision 45160-45170
Unlisted Services and Procedures 45999

Red Blood Cell (RBC)
Antibody 86850-86870
   Pretreatment 86970-86972
Count 85032-85041
Fragility
   Mechanical 85547
   Osmotic 85555-85557
Hematocrit 85014
Morphology 85007
Platelet Estimation 85007
Sedimentation Rate
   Automated 85652
   Manual 85651
Sequestration 78140
Sickling 85660
Survival Test 78130-78135
Volume Determination 78120-78121

Red Blood Cell ab
See Antibody, Red Blood Cell

Reductase, Glutathione
See Glutathione Reductase

Reductase, Lactic Cytochrome
See Lactic Dehydrogenase

Reduction
Forehead 21137-21139
Lung Volume 32491
Mammoplasty 19318
Masseter Muscle/Bone 21295-21296
Osteoplasty
   Facial Bones 21209
Pregnancy
   Multifetal 59866
Skull
   Craniomegalic 62115-62117
Ventricular Septum
   Non-Surgical 0024T

Reflex Test
Blink Reflex 95933
H-Reflex 95934-95936

Reflux Study 78262
Gastroesophageal 91034-91038

Refraction 92015

Rehabilitation
Artery
   Occlusive Disease 93668
Auditory
   Post-Lingual Hearing Loss 92633
   Pre-Lingual Hearing Loss 92630
   Status Evaluation 92626-92627
Cardiac 93797-93798

Rehabilitative
See Rehabilitation

Rehfuss Test
See Gastroenterology, Diagnostic, Stomach

Reichstein's Substance S
See Deoxycortisol

Reimplantation
Arteries
   Aorta
      Prosthesis 35697
   Carotid 35691, 35694-35695
   Subclavian 35693-35695
   Vertebral 35691-35693
   Visceral 35697
Kidney 50380
Ovary 58825
Pulmonary Artery 33788
Ureter, to Bladder 50780-50785
Ureters 51565

Reinnervation
Larynx
   Neuromuscular Pedicle 31590

Reinsch Test 83015

Reinsertion
Drug Delivery Implant 11983
Implantable Contraceptive Capsules 11977
Spinal Fixation Device 22849

Relative Density
See Specific Gravity

Release

Carpal Tunnel 64721
Elbow Contracture
    with Radical Release of Capsule 24149
Flexor Muscles
    Hip 27036
Muscle
    Knee 27422
Nerve 64702-64726
    Neurolytic 64727
Retina
    Encircling Material 67115
Spinal Cord 63200
Stapes 69650
Tarsal Tunnel 28035
Tendon 24332, 25295

Release-Inhibiting Hormone, Somatotropin

See Somatostatin

Removal

Adjustable Gastric Band 43772-43774
Allograft
    Intestinal 44137
Artificial Intervertebral Disc
    Cervical Interspace 0093T, 0095T
    Lumbar Interspace 0094T, 0095T
Balloon
    Intra-Aortic 33974
Balloon Assist Device
    Intra-Aortic 33968, 33971
Blood Clot
    Eye 65930
Blood Component
    Apheresis 36511-36516
Breast
    Capsules 19371
    Implants 19328-19330
    Modified Radical 19240
    Partial 19140-19162
    Radical 19200-19220
    Simple, Complete 19180
    Subcutaneous 19182
Calcareous Deposits
    Subdeltoid 23000
Calculi (Stone)
    Bile Duct 43264, 47420-47425
        Percutaneous 47554, 47630
    Bladder 51050, 52310-52318, 52352
    Gallbladder 47480
    Hepatic Duct 47400
    Kidney 50060-50081, 50130, 50561,
                    50580, 52352
    Pancreas 48020
    Pancreatic Duct 43264
    Salivary Gland 42330-42340
    Ureter 50610-50630, 50961, 50980,
         51060-51065, 52320-52330, 52352
    Urethra 52310-52315, 52352
Cardiac Event Recorder 33284
Cast 29700-29715
Cataract
    with Replacement
        Extracapsular 66982, 66984
        Intracapsular 66983
        Not Associated with Concurrent 66983

Catheter
    Central Venous 36589
    Fractured 75961
    Peritoneum 49422
    Spinal Cord 62355
Cerclage
    Cervix 59871
Cerumen
    Auditory Canal, External 69210
Clot
    Pericardium 33020
        Endoscopic 32658
Comedones 10040
Contraceptive Capsules 11976-11977
Cranial Tongs 20665
Cyst 10040
Dacryolith
    Lacrimal Duct 68530
    Lacrimal Gland 68530
Defibrillator
    Heart 33244
        Pulse Generator Only 33241
        via Thoracotomy 33243
Drug Delivery Implant 11982-11983
Ear Wax
    Auditory Canal, External 69210
Electrode
    Brain 61535, 61880
    Heart 33238
    Nerve 64585
    Spinal Cord 63660
Embolus
    See Embolectomy
External Fixation System 20694
Eye
    Bone 67414, 67445
    Ocular Contents
        with Implant 65093
        without Implant 65091
    Orbital Contents Only 65110
    with Bone 65112
    with Implant
        Muscles Attached 65105
        Muscles, Not Attached 65103
    with Muscle or Myocutaneous Flap ...65114
    without Implant 65101
Fallopian Tube
    Laparoscopy 58661
Fat
    Lipectomy 15876-15879
Fecal Impaction
    Rectum 45915
Fibrin Deposit 32150
Fixation Device 20670-20680
Foreign Bodies 65205-65265
    Anal 46608
    Ankle Joint 27610, 27620
    Arm
        Lower 25248
        Upper 24200-24201
    Auditory Canal, External 69200
        with Anesthesia 69205
    Bile Duct 43269
    Bladder 52310-52315
    Brain 61570, 62163
    Bronchi 31635
    Colon 44025, 44390, 45379
    Colon-Sigmoid 45332

Conjunctival Embedded 65210
Cornea
    with Slit Lamp 65222
    without Slit Lamp 65220
Duodenum 44010
Elbow 24000, 24101, 24200-24201
Esophagus 43020, 43045, 43215, 74235
External Eye 65205
Eyelid 67938
Finger 26075-26080
Foot 28190-28193
Gastrointestinal, Upper 43247
Gum 41805
Hand 26070
Hip 27033, 27086-27087
Hysteroscopy 58562
Interphalangeal Joint
    Toe 28024
Intertarsal Joint 28020
Intestines, Small 44020, 44363
Intraocular 65235
Kidney 50561, 50580
Knee Joint 27310, 27331, 27372
Lacrimal Duct 68530
Lacrimal Gland 68530
Larynx 31511, 31530-31531, 31577
Leg, Upper 27372
Lung 32151
Mandible 41806
Mediastinum 39000-39010
Metatarsophalangeal Joint 28022
Mouth 40804-40805
Muscle 20520-20525
Nose 30300
    Anesthesia 30310
    Lateral Rhinotomy 30320
Orbit 61334, 67413, 67430
    with Bone Flap 67430
    without Bone Flap 67413
Pancreatic Duct 43269
Patella
    See Patellectomy
Pelvis 27086-27087
Penile Tissue 54115
Penis 54115
Pericardium 33020
    Endoscopic 32658
Peritoneum 49085
Pharynx 42809
Pleura 32150-32151
    Endoscopic 32653
Posterior Segment
    Magnetic Extraction 65260
    Nonmagnetic Extraction 65265
Rectum 45307, 45915
Scrotum 55120
Shoulder 23040-23044
    Complicated 23332
    Deep 23331
    Subcutaneous 23330
Skin
    with Debridement 11010-11012
Stomach 43500
Subcutaneous Tissue 10120-10121
    with Debridement 11010-11012
Tarsometatarsal Joint 28020
Tendon Sheath 20520-20525
Toe 28022

Ureter .50961, 50980
Urethra .52310-52315
Uterus 58562
Vagina 57415
Wrist 25040, 25101, 25248
Foreign Body
 Elbow 24101
Hair
 Electrolysis 17380
Halo 20665
Hearing Aid
 Bone Conduction 69711
Hematoma
 Brain 61312-61315
Implantation 20670-20680
 Ankle 27704
 Contraceptive Capsules 11976-11977
 Elbow 24160
 Eye 67120-67121
 Finger 26320
 Hand 26320
 Radius 24164
 Wrist 25449
Infusion Pump
 Intra-Arterial 36262
 Intravenous 36590
 Spinal Cord 62365
Intra-Aortic Balloon 33974
 Assist Device 33968, 33971
Intrauterine Device (IUD) 58301
Keel
 Laryngoplasty 31580
Lacrimal Gland
 Partial 68505
 Total 68500
Lacrimal Sac
 Excision 68520
Laryngocele 31300
Leiomyomata 58545-58546, 58561
Lens .66920-66940
Lens Material 66840-66852
Lesion
 Conjunctiva 68040
 Larynx 31512, 31578
  Endoscopic 31545-31546
Loose Body
 Ankle 27620
 Carpometacarpal Joint 26070
 Elbow 24101
 Interphalangeal Joint
  Toe 28024
 Intertarsal Joint 28020
 Knee Joint 27331
 Metatarsophalangeal Joint 28022
 Tarsometatarsal Joint 28020
 Toe 28022
 Wrist 25101
Lung
 Apical Tumor 32503-32504
 Bronchoplasty 32501
 Completion Pneumonectomy 32488
 Cyst 32140
 Extrapleural 32445
 Single Lobe 32480
 Single Segment 32484
 Sleeve Lobectomy 32486
 Sleeve Pneumonectomy 32442

Total Pneumonectomy 32440-32445
Two Lobes 32482
Volume Reduction 32491
Wedge Resection 32500
Lymph Nodes
 Abdominal .38747
 Inguinofemoral 38760-38765
 Pelvic 38770
 Retroperitoneal
  Transabdominal 38780
 Thoracic 38746
Mammary Implant 19328-19330
Mastoid
 Air Cells 69670
Mesh
 Abdominal Wall 11008
Milia, Multiple 10040
Nails 11730-11732, 11750-11752
Neurostimulators
 Pulse Generator 64595
 Receiver 64595
Ocular Implant 65175, 65920
Orbital Implant 67560
Ovaries
 Laparoscopy 58661
Pacemaker
 Heart 33233-33237
Patella, Complete 27424
Plate
 Skull 62142
Polyp
 Anal 46610, 46612
 Antrochoanal 31032
 Colon 44392, 45385
 Colon-Sigmoid 45333
 Endoscopy 44364-44365, 44394
 Esophagus 43217, 43250
 Gastrointestinal, Upper 43250-43251
 Rectum 45315
 Sphenoid Sinus 31051
Prosthesis
 Abdomen 49606
 Abdominal Wall 11008
 Hip 27090-27091
 Knee 27488
 Penis 54406, 54410-54417
 Perineum 53442
 Skull 62142
 Urethral Sphincter 53446-53447
 Wrist 25250-25251
Pulse Generator
 Brain 61888
 Spinal Cord 63688
Pustules 10040
Receiver
 Brain 61888
 Spinal Cord 63688
Reservoir
 Spinal Cord 62365
Seton
 Anal 46030
Shoulder Joint
 Foreign or Loose Body 23107
Shunt
 Brain 62256-62258
 Heart 33924
 Peritoneum 49429
 Spinal Cord 63746

Skin Tags 11200-11201
Sling
 Urethra 53442
 Vagina 57287
Spinal Instrumentation
 Anterior 22855
 Posterior Nonsegmental
  Harrington Rod 22850
 Posterior Segmental 22852
Stent
 Bile Duct 43269
 Pancreatic Duct 43269
 Ureteral 50382-50387
Subcutaneous Port
 for Gastric Restrictive
 Procedure 43887-43888
Suture
 Anal 46754
 Anesthesia 15850-15851
Thrombus
 See Thrombectomy
Tissue Expanders
 Skin 11971
Transplant Intestines 44137
Transplant Kidney 50370
Tube
 Ear, Middle 69424
 Finger 26392, 26416
 Hand 26392, 26416
 Nephrostomy 50389
Tumor
 Temporal Bone 69970
Ureter
 Ligature 50940
Urethral Stent
 Bladder 52310-52315
 Urethra 52310-52315
Vein
 Clusters 37785
 Perforation .37760
 Saphenous 37718, 37722, 37735, 37780
 Varicose 37765-37766
Venous Access Device 36590
 Obstruction 75901-75902
Ventilating Tube
 Ear, Middle 69424
Ventricular Assist Device 33977-33978
 Extracorporeal 0050T
 Intracorporeal 33980
Vitreous
 Anterior Approach 67005-67010
Wire
 Anal 46754

Renal Abscess
See Abscess, Kidney

Renal Arteries
See Artery, Renal

Renal Autotransplantation
See Autotransplantation, Renal

Renal Calculus
See Calculus, Removal, Kidney

Renal Cyst
See Cyst, Kidney

Renal Dialyses
See Hemodialysis

Renal Disease Services
See Dialysis

Renal Transplantation
See Kidney, Transplantation

Renin 80408, 80416, 84244
Peripheral Vein 80417

Renin-Converting Enzyme 82164

Reoperation
Carotid
   Thromboendarterectomy 35390
Coronary Artery Bypass
   Valve Procedure 33530
Distal Vessel Bypass 35700

Repair
See Revision
Abdomen 49900
   Hernia 49491-49525, 49565, 49570,
              49582-49590
   Omphalocele 49600-49611
   Suture 49900
Abdominal Wall .15831
Anal
   Anomaly 46744-46748
   Fistula 46288, 46706, 46715-46716
   Stricture 46700-46705
Anastomosis
   Cyst 47716
Aneurysm
   Aorta 33877, 33880-33886, 34800-34805,
     34825-34832, 75952-75953, 0078T, 0079T,
                     0080T, 0081T
   Arteriovenous 36834
   Iliac Artery .75954
   Intracranial Artery 61697-61708
Ankle
   Ligament 27695-27698
   Tendon . . .27612, 27650-27654, 27680-27687
Aorta 33320-33322, 33802-33803
   Coarctation 33840-33851
   Graft 33860-33877
   Sinus of Valsalva 33702-33720
   Thoracic 75956-75959
     Endovascular 33880-33891
Aortic Arch
   with Cardiopulmonary Bypass 33853
   without Cardiopulmonary Bypass 33852
Aortic Valve 33400-33403
   Obstruction
     Outflow Tract 33414
     Septic Hypertrophy 33416
     Stenosis .33415
Arm
   Lower 25260-25263, 25270
     Fasciotomy 24495
     Secondary 25265, 25272-25274
     Tendon 25290
     Tendon Sheath 25275
     Muscle 24341
     Tendon 24332, 24341, 25280, 25295,
                  25310-25316

Upper
   Muscle Revision 24330-24331
   Muscle Transfer 24301, 24320
   Tendon Lengthening 24305
   Tendon Revision 24320
   Tendon Transfer 24301
   Tenotomy .24310
Arteriovenous Aneurysm 36834
Arteriovenous Fistula
   Abdomen .35182
     Acquired or Traumatic 35189
   Head 35180
     Acquired or Traumatic 35188
   Lower Extremity 35184
     Acquired or Traumatic 35190
   Neck 35180
     Acquired or Traumatic 35188
   Thorax 35182
     Acquired or Traumatic 35189
   Upper Extremity 35184
     Acquired or Traumatic 35190
Arteriovenous Malformation
   Intracranial 61680-61692
   Intracranial Artery 61705-61708
   Spinal Artery 62294
   Spinal Cord 63250-63252
Artery
   Angioplasty 75962-75968
   Aorta 35452, 35472
   Axillary 35458
   Brachiocephalic 35458, 35475
   Bypass Graft 35501-35571, 35601-35683,
              35691-35695, 35700
   Bypass In-Situ 35583-35587
   Bypass Venous Graft 33510-33516,
              35510-35525
   Coronary .33507
   Femoral 35456, 35474
   Iliac 34900, 35454, 35473
   Occlusive Disease 35001, 35005-35021,
     35045-35081, 35091, 35102, 35111, 35121,
             35131, 35141, 35151
   Popliteal 35456, 35474
   Pulmonary 33690
   Renal 35450
   Renal or Visceral 35471
   Subclavian 35458
   Thromboendarterectomy 35301-35321,
              35341-35390
   Tibioperoneal 35459, 35470
   Viscera 35450, 35471
Arytenoid Cartilage 31400
Atrial Fibrillation 33253
Bile Duct 47701
   Cyst 47716
   with Intestines 47760, 47780-47785
   Wound 47900
Bladder
   Exstrophy .51940
   Fistula 44660-44661, 45800-45805,
              51880-51925
   Neck 51845
   Resection .52500
   Wound 51860-51865
Blepharoptosis
   Frontalis Muscle Technique
     with Fascial Sling 67902

Blood Vessel
   Abdomen .35221
     with Other Graft 35281
     with Vein Graft 35251
   Chest 35211-35216
     with Other Graft 35271-35276
     with Vein Graft 35241-35246
   Finger 35207
   Graft Defect 35870
   Hand 35207
   Kidney 50100
   Lower Extremity 35226
     with Other Graft 35286
     with Vein Graft 35256
   Neck 35201
     with Other Graft 35261
     with Vein Graft 35231
   Upper Extremity 35206
     with Other Graft 35266
     with Vein Graft 35236
Body Cast 29720
Brain
   Wound 61571
Breast
   Suspension 19316
Bronchi
   Fistula 32815
Brow Pyrosis .67900
Bunion 28290-28299
Bypass Graft 35901-35907
   Fistula 35870
Calcaneus
   Osteotomy 28300
Cannula 36860-36861
Carpal 25440
Carpal Bone .25431
Cervix
   Cerclage .57700
     Abdominal 59320-59325
   Suture 57720
Chest Wall 32905
   Closure 32810
   Fistula 32906
Chin
   Augmentation 21120, 21123
   Osteotomy 21121-21123
Clavicle
   Osteotomy 23480-23485
Cleft Hand 26580
Cleft Lip 40525-40527, 40700-40761
   Nasal Deformity 40700-40701,
              40720-40761
Cleft Palate
   See Cleft Palate Repair
Colon
   Fistula 44650-44661
   Hernia 44050
   Malrotation 44055
   Obstruction 44050
Cornea
   See Cornea, Repair
Coronary Chamber Fistula 33500-33501
Cyst
   Bartholin's Gland 56440
   Liver 47300
   Repair 47716

Diaphragm
    for Eventration 39545
    Hernia 39502-39541
    Laceration 39501
Ductus Arteriosus 33820-33824
Ear, Middle
    Oval Window Fistula 69666
    Round Window Fistula 69667
Elbow
    Fasciotomy 24350-24356
    Hemiepiphyseal Arrest 24470
    Ligament 24343-24346
    Muscle 24341
    Muscle Transfer 24301
    Tendon 24340-24342
        Each .24341
    Tendon Lengthening 24305
    Tendon Transfer 24301
    Tennis Elbow 24350-24356
Encephalocele 62121
Enterocele
    Hysterectomy 58270, 58294
Epididymis 54900-54901
Epispadias 54380-54390
Esophagus 43300, 43310, 43313
    Esophagogastrostomy 43320
    Esophagojejunostomy 43340-43341
    Fistula . . .43305, 43312, 43314, 43420-43425
    Fundoplasty 43324-43325
    Muscle 43330-43331
    Pre-Existing Perforation 43405
    Varices .43401
    Wound 43410-43415
Eye
    Ciliary Body 66680
        Suture .66682
    Conjunctiva 65270-65273
        Wound 65270-65273
    Cornea .65275
        Astigmatism 65772-65775
        with Glue 65286
        Wound 65275-65285
    Fistula
        Lacrimal Gland 68770
    Iris
        Suture .66682
        with Ciliary Body 66680
    Lacrimal Duct
        Canaliculi 68700
    Lacrimal Punctum 68705
    Retina
        Detachment 67101-67112
    Sclera
        Reinforcement 67250-67255
        Staphyloma 66220-66225
        with Glue 65286
        with Graft 66225
        Wound 65286, 66250
    Strabismus
        Chemodenervation 67345
    Symblepharon
        Division 68340
        with Graft 68335
        without Graft 68330
    Trabeculae 65855

Eye Muscles
    Strabismus
        Adjustable Sutures 67335
        One Horizontal Muscle 67311
        One Vertical Muscle 67314
        Posterior Fixation Suture
        Technique 67334-67335
        Previous Surgery, Not Involving
        Extraocular Muscles 67331
        Release Extensive Scar Tissue 67343
        Superior Oblique Muscle 67318
        Two Horizontal Muscles 67312
        Two or More Vertical Muscles 67316
    Wound
        Extraocular Muscle 65290
Eyebrow
    Ptosis 67900
Eyelashes
    Epilation
        by Forceps 67820
        by Other than Forceps 67825
    Incision of Lid Margin 67830
        with Free Mucous Membrane
        Graft .67835
Eyelid 21280-21282
    Ectropion 67916-67917
        Suture .67914
        Thermocauterization 67915
    Entropion 67924
        Excision Tarsal Wedge 67923
        Suture 67921-67924
        Thermocauterization 67922
    Excisional 67961-67966
    Lagophthalmos 67912
    Ptosis
        Conjunctivo-Tarso-Muller's
        Muscle-Levator Resection 67908
        Frontalis Muscle Technique . .67901-67902
        Levator Resection 67903-67904
        Reduction of Overcorrection 67909
        Superior Rectus Technique 67906
        Retraction 67911
    Wound
        Suture 67930-67935
Facial Bones 21208-21209
Facial Nerve
    Paralysis 15840-15845
    Suture
        Intratemporal, Lateral to Geniculate
        Ganglion 69740
        Intratemporal, Medial to Geniculate
        Ganglion 69745
Fallopian Tube 58752
    Anastomosis 58750
    Create Stoma 58770
Fascial Defect 50728
Femur 27470-27472
    Epiphysis 27475-27485, 27742
        Arrest .27185
        by Pinning 27176
        by Traction 27175
        Open Treatment 27177-27178
        Osteoplasty 27179
        Osteotomy 27181
    Muscle Transfer 27110

Osteotomy 27140, 27151, 27450-27454
    Femoral Neck 27161
    with Fixation 27165
    with Open Reduction 27156
    with Graft 27170
Fibula
    Epiphysis 27477-27485, 27730-27742
    Osteotomy 27707-27712
Finger
    Claw Finger 26499
    Macrodactylia 26590
    Polydactylous 26587
    Syndactyly 26560-26562
    Tendon
        Extensor 26415-26434, 26445-26449
        Flexor 26356-26358, 26440-26442
        Joint Stabilization 26474
        PIP Joint 26471
        Toe Transfer 26551-26556
        Trigger 26055
        Volar Plate 26548
        Web Finger 26560-26562
Fistula
    Carotid-Cavernous 61710
    Ileoanal Pouch 46710-46712
    Mastoid 69700
    Rectovaginal 57308
Foot
    Fascia .28250
    Muscle .28250
    Tendon 28200-28226, 28238
Gallbladder
    with Gastroenterostomy 47741
    with Intestines 47720-47740
Great Arteries 33770-33781
Great Vessel 33320-33322
Hallux Valgus 28290-28299
Hamstring .27097
Hand
    Cleft Hand 26580
    Muscle 26591-26593
    Tendon
        Extensor 26410-26416, 26426-26428,
                           26433-26437
        Flexor 26350-26358, 26440
        Profundus 26370-26373
Hearing Aid
    Bone Conduction 69711
Heart
    Anomaly 33600-33617
    Aortic Sinus 33702-33722
    Artificial Heart
        Intracorporeal 0052T, 0053T
    Atrial 33253
    Atrioventricular Canal 33660-33665
        Complete 33670
    Atrioventricular Valve 33660-33665
    Blood Vessel 33320-33322
    Cor Triatriatum 33732
    Fibrillation 33253
    Infundibular 33476-33478
    Mitral Valve 33420-33427
    Myocardium 33542
    Outflow Tract 33476-33478
    Postinfarction 33542-33545
    Prosthetic Valve 33670, 33852-33853
    Prosthetic Valve Dysfunction 33496
    Pulmonary Artery Shunt 33924

Pulmonary Valve 33470-33474
Septal Defect 33545, 33608-33610,
             33681-33688, 33692-33697
  Atrial and Ventricular 33647
  Atrium .33641
Sinus of Valsalva 33702-33722
Sinus Venosus 33645
Tetralogy of Fallot 33692-33697
Total Replacement Heart System
  Intracorporeal 0052T, 0053T
Tricuspid Valve 33465
Ventricle 33548, 33611-33612
  Obstruction 33619
Ventricular Tunnel 33722
Wound 33300-33305
Hepatic Duct
with Intestines 47765, 47802
Hernia 50728
Abdomen 49565, 49590
  Incisional 49560
Epigastric 49570
  Incarcerated 49572
Femoral .49550
  Incarcerated 49553
  Recurrent 49555
  Recurrent Incarcerated 49557
  Reducible Recurrent 49555
Incisional
  Incarcerated 49561
  Recurrent Incarcerated 49566
Inguinal 49491-49521
  Initial .49650
  Recurrent 49651
  Sliding .49525
Intestinal 44025-44050
Lumbar .49540
Lung 32800
Orchiopexy 54640
Reducible 49565, 49570
  Femoral 49550
  Incisional 49560
  Inguinal 49500, 49505
  Recurrent 49520
Sliding .49525
Spigelian 49590
Umbilical 49580, 49585
  Incarcerated 49582, 49587
  Reducible 49580
with Spermatic Cord 54640
Hip
Muscle Transfer 27100-27105, 27111
Osteotomy 27146-27156
Tendon .27097
Humerus 24420-24430
Osteotomy 24400-24410
with Graft 24435
Ileostomy
See Ileostomy, Repair
Interphalangeal Joint
Volar Plate 26548
Intestine
Large
  Ulcer 44605
  Wound .44605
Intestines
Enterocele
  Abdominal Approach 57270
  Vaginal Approach 57268

Large
  Closure Enterostomy 44620-44626
  Diverticula 44605
  Obstruction 44615
Intestines, Small
  Closure Enterostomy 44620-44626
  Diverticula 44602-44603
  Fistula 44640-44661
  Hernia .44050
  Malrotation 44055
  Obstruction 44025-44050
  Ulcer 44602-44603
  Wound 44602-44603
Introitus
Vagina .56800
Iris, Ciliary Body 66680
Jejunum
Free Transfer
  with Microvascular Anastomosis . . .43496
Kidney
Fistula 50520-50526
Horseshoe 50540
Renal Pelvis 50400-50405
Wound .50500
Knee
Cartilage 27403
Instability 27420
Ligament 27405-27409
  Collateral 27405
  Collateral and Cruciate 27409
  Cruciate 27407-27409
Meniscus 27403
Tendon 27380-27381
Larynx
Fracture 31584
Reinnervation
  Neuromuscular Pedicle 31590
Leg
Lower
  Fascia .27656
  Tendon 27658-27692
Upper
  Muscle 27385-27386, 27400, 27430
  Tendon 27393-27400
Ligament
See Ligament, Repair
Lip 40650-40654
Cleft Lip 40700-40761
Fistula .42260
Liver
Abscess 47300
Cyst 47300
Wound 47350-47361
Lung
Hernia .32800
Pneumolysis 32940
Tear 32110
Mastoidectomy
Complete 69601
Modified Radical 69602
Radical .69603
with Apicectomy 69605
with Tympanoplasty 69604
Maxilla
Osteotomy 21206
Mesentery 44850

Metacarpal
  Lengthening 26568
  Nonunion 26546
  Osteotomy 26565
Metacarpophalangeal Joint
  Capsulodesis 26516-26518
  Collateral Ligament 26540-26542
  Fusion 26516-26518
Metatarsal 28322
Osteotomy 28306-28309
Microsurgery 69990
Mitral Valve 33420-33427
Mouth
Laceration 40830-40831
Vestibule of 40830-40845
Musculotendinous Cuff 23410-23412
Nail Bed 11760
Nasal Deformity
Cleft Lip 40700-40761
Nasal Septum 30630
Navicular 25440
Neck Muscles
Scalenus Anticus 21700-21705
Sternocleidomastoid 21720-21725
Nerve 64876
Graft 64885-64907
Microrepair 69990
Suture 64831-64876
Nose
Adhesions 30560
Fistula 30580-30600, 42260
Rhinophyma 30120
Septum 30540-30545, 30630
Synechia 30560
Vestibular Stenosis 30465
Omphalocele 49600-49611
Osteotomy
Femoral Neck 27161
Radius
  and Ulna 25365
Ulna
  and Radius 25365
Vertebra
  Additional Segment 22216, 22226
  Cervical 22210, 22220
  Lumbar 22214, 22224
  Thoracic 22212, 22222
Oviduct .58752
Create Stoma 58770
Pacemaker
Heart
  Electrode 33218-33220
Palate
Laceration 42180-42182
Vomer Flap 42235
Pancreas
Cyst 48500
Pseudocyst 48510-48511
  Percutaneous 48511
Paravaginal Defect 57284
Pectus Carinatum 21740-21742
with Thoracoscopy 21743
Pectus Excavatum 21740-21742
with Thoracoscopy 21743
Pelvic Floor
Prosthetic Insertion 57267

Pelvis
   Osteotomy 27158
   Tendon 27098
Penis
   Fistulization 54435
   Injury 54440
   Priapism 54420-54435
   Shunt 54420-54430
Perineum 56810
Periorbital Region
   Osteotomy 21260-21263
Phalanx
   Finger
      Lengthening 26568
      Osteotomy 26567
      Nonunion 26546
   Toe
      Osteotomy 28310-28312
Pharynx
   with Esophagus 42953
Pleura 32215
Prosthesis
   Penis 54408
Pulmonary Artery 33917-33920, 33925-33926
   Reimplantation 33788
Pulmonary Valve 33470-33474
Quadriceps
   See Quadriceps, Repair
Radius
   Epiphyseal 25450-25455
   Malunion or Nonunion 25400, 25415
   Osteotomy 25350-25355, 25370-25375
   with Graft 25405, 25420-25426
Rectocele
   See Rectocele, Repair
Rectovaginal Fistula 57308
Rectum
   Fistula 45800-45825
   Injury 45562-45563
   Prolapse 45505-45541, 45900
   Rectocele 45560
   Stenosis 45500
   with Sigmoid Excision 45550
Retinal Detachment with Diathermy
   See Diathermy, Retinal Detachment, Repair
Rotator Cuff
   See Rotator Cuff, Repair
Salivary Duct 42500-42505
   Fistula .42600
Scapula
   Fixation 23400
   Scapulopexy 23400
Sclera
   See Sclera, Repair
Scrotum 55175-55180
Septal Defect 33813-33814
Shoulder
   Capsule 23450-23466
   Cuff 23410-23412
   Ligament Release 23415
   Muscle Transfer 23395-23397
   Musculotendinous Rotator
      Cuff 23415-23420
   Tendon 23410-23412, 23430-23440
   Tenomyotomy 23405-23406
Simple, Integumentary System
   See Integumentary System, Repair, Simple

Sinus
   Ethmoid
      Cerebrospinal Fluid Leak 31290
   Sphenoid
      Cerebrospinal Fluid Leak 31291
Sinus of Valsalva 33702-33722
Skin
   Wound
      Complex 13100-13160
      Intermediate 12031-12057
      Simple 12020-12021
Skull
   Cerebrospinal Fluid Leak 62100
   Encephalocele 62120
Spica Cast .29720
Spinal Cord .63700
   Cerebrospinal Fluid Leak 63707-63709
   Meningocele 63700-63702
   Myelomeningocele 63704-63706
Spinal Meningocele
   See Meningocele, Repair
Spine
   Lumbar Vertebra 22524, 22525
   Osteotomy 22210-22226
   Thoracic Vertebra 22523, 22525
Spleen 38115
Stomach
   Esophagogastrostomy 43320
   Fistula .43880
   Fundoplasty 43324-43325
   Laceration 43501-43502
   Stoma .43870
   Ulcer 43501
Talus
   Osteotomy 28302
Tarsal 28320
   Osteotomy 28304-28305
Testis
   Injury 54670
   Suspension 54620-54640
   Torsion .54600
Throat
   Pharyngoesophageal 42953
   Wound .42900
Thumb
   Muscle .26508
   Tendon .26510
Tibia 27720-27725
   Epiphysis 27477-27485, 27730-27742
   Osteotomy 27455-27457, 27705,
                  27709-27712
   Pseudoarthrosis 27727
Toe
   Bunion 28290-28299
   Muscle .28240
   Tendon .28240
   Webbing 28280, 28345
Toes
   Macrodactylia 26590
   Polydactylous 26587
Tongue 41250-41252
   Fixation 41500
   Laceration 41250-41252
   Mechanical 41500
   Suture .41510

Trachea
   Fistula .31755
      with Plastic Repair 31825
      without Plastic Repair 31820
   Stenosis 31780-31781
   Stoma 31613-31614
   Scar 31830
      with Plastic Repair 31825
      without Plastic Repair 31820
   Wound
      Cervical 31800
      Intrathoracic 31805
Tricuspid Valve 33463-33465
Truncus Arteriosus
   Rastelli Type 33786
Tunica Vaginalis
   Hydrocele 55060
Tympanic Membrane 69450, 69610
Ulna
   Epiphyseal 25450-25455
   Malunion or Nonunion 25400, 25415
   Osteotomy 25360, 25370-25375,
                 25425-25426
   with Graft 25405, 25420
Umbilicus
   Omphalocele 49600-49611
Ureter
   Anastomosis 50740-50825
   Continent Diversion 50825
   Deligation 50940
   Fistula 50920-50930
   Lysis Adhesions 50715-50725
   Suture .50900
   Urinary Undiversion 50830
Ureterocele 51535
Urethra
   Artificial Sphincter 53449
   Diverticulum 53240, 53400-53405
   Fistula . . .45820-45825, 53400-53405, 53520
   Stoma .53520
   Stricture 53400-53405
   Urethrocele 57230
   Wound 53502-53515
Urethral Sphincter 57220
Urinary Incontinence 53431-53440, 57284
Uterus
   Fistula 51920-51925
   Rupture 58520, 59350
   Suspension 58400-58410
Vagina
   Anterior
      See Colporrhaphy, Anterior
   Cystocele 57240, 57260
   Enterocele 57265
   Fistula 46715-46716, 51900
      Rectovaginal 57300-57307
      Transvesical and Vaginal Approach . .57330
      Urethrovaginal 57310-57311
      Vesicovaginal 57320-57330
   Hysterectomy 58267, 58293
   Incontinence 57284, 57288
   Pereyra Procedure 57289
   Postpartum 59300
   Prolapse 57282, 57284
   Rectocele 57250-57260
   Suspension 57280-57284
      Laparoscopic 57425
   Wound 57200-57210

Vaginal Wall Prolapse
  See Colporrhaphy
Vas Deferens
  Suture .... .55400
Vein
  Angioplasty 35460, 35476, 75978
  Femoral 34501
  Graft 34520
  Pulmonary 33730
  Transposition 34510
Vulva
  Postpartum 59300
Wound
  Complex 13100-13160
  Intermediate 12031-12057
  Simple 12001-12021
Wound Dehiscence
  Complex 13160
  Simple 12020-12021
Wrist 25260-25263, 25270, 25447
  Bone 25440
  Carpal Bone 25431
  Cartilage 25107
  Removal
    Implant 25449
  Secondary 25265, 25272-25274
  Tendon 25280-25316
  Tendon Sheath 25275
  Total Replacement 25446

Repeat Surgeries
See Reoperation

Replacement
Adjustable Gastric Band 43773
Aortic Valve 33405-33413
Arthroplasties, Hip
  See Arthroplasty, Hip
Artificial Heart
  Intracorporeal 0052T, 0053T
Cerebrospinal Fluid Shunt 62160, 62194,
                                62225-62230
Contact Lens
  See Contact Lens Services
Elbow
  Total 24363
Electrode
  Heart 33210-33211, 33216-33217
Eye
  Drug Delivery System 67121
Gastrostomy Tube 43760
Hearing Aid
  Bone Conduction 69710
Hip 27130-27132
  Revision 27134-27138
Implant
  Bone
    for External Speech Processor/Cochlear
      Stimulator 69717-69718
Intervertebral Disc
  Cervical Interspace 0090T
  Each Additional Interspace 0092T
  Lumbar Interspace 0091T
Knee
  Total 27447
Mitral Valve 33430
Nephrostomy Tube
  See Nephrostomy, Change Tube

Nerve 64726
Neurostimulator
  Pulse Generator/Receiver
    Intracranial 61885
    Peripheral Nerve 64590
    Spinal 63685
Ossicles
  with Prosthesis 69633, 69637
Ossicular Replacement
  See TORP (Total Ossicular Replacement
  Prosthesis)
Pacemaker 33206-33208
  Catheter 33210
  Electrode 33210-33211, 33216-33217
Pacing Cardioverter-Defibrillator
  Leads 33243-33244
  Pulse Generator Only 33241
Penile
  Prosthesis 54410-54411, 54416-54417
Prosthesis
  Skull 62143
  Urethral Sphincter 53448
Pulmonary Valve 33475
Pulse Generator
  Brain 61885
  Peripheral Nerve 64590
  Spinal Cord 63685
Receiver
  Brain 61885
  Peripheral Nerve 64590
  Spinal Cord 63685
Skin
  Acellular Dermal Matrix 15170-15176
Skull Plate 62143
Spinal Cord
  Reservoir 62360
Stent
  Ureteral 50382, 50387
Subcutaneous Port
  for Gastric Restrictive Procedure 43888
Tissue Expanders
  Skin 11970
Total Replacement
  See Hip, Total Replacement
Total Replacement Heart System
  Intracorporeal 0052T, 0053T
Tricuspid Valve 33465
Ureter
  with Intestines 50840
Venous Access Device 36582-36583, 36585
  Catheter 36578
Venous Catheter
  Central 36580-36581, 36584

Replantation
Arm, Upper 20802
Digit 20816-20822
Foot 20838
Forearm 20805
Hand 20808
Thumb 20824-20827

Report Preparation
Extended, Medical 99080
Psychiatric 90889

Reposition
Toe to Hand 26551-26556

Repositioning
Central Venous Catheter 36597
Electrode
  Heart 33215-33217, 33226
Gastrostomy Tube 43761
Heart
  Defibrillator
    Leads 33215-33216, 33226, 33249
Intraocular Lens 66825
Tricuspid Valve 33468

Reproductive Tissue
Cryopreserved
  Preparation
    Thawing 89354
Storage 89344

Reprogramming
Shunt
  Brain 62252

Reptilase Test 85635

Reptilase Time
See Thrombin Time

Resection
Aortic Valve
  Stenosis 33415
Bladder Diverticulum 52305
Bladder Neck
  Transurethral 52500
Brain Lobe
  See Lobectomy, Brain
Chest Wall 19260-19272
Diaphragm 39560-39561
Endaural
  See Ear, Inner, Excision
Humeral Head 23195
Intestines, Small
  Laparoscopic 44202-44203
Lung 32503-32504
Mouth
  with Tongue Excision 41153
Myocardium
  Aneurysm 33542
  Septal Defect 33545
Nasal Septum Submucous
  See Nasal Septum, Submucous Resection
Nose
  Septum 30520
Ovary, Wedge
  See Overy, Wedge Resection
Palate 42120
Phalangeal Head
  Toe 28153
Prostate Transurethral
  See Prostatectomy, Transurethral
Radical
  Arm, Upper 24077
  Elbow 24077
    with Contracture Release 24149
  Foot 28046
  Humerus 24150-24151
  Radius 24152-24153
  Tumor
    Ankle 27615
    Calcaneus or Talus 27647
    Clavicle 23200

Femur 27365
Fibula 27646
Humerus 23220
Humerus with Autograft 23221
Humerus with Prosthetic
   Replacement 23222
Knee 27329, 27365
Leg, Lower 27615
Leg, Upper 27329
Metatarsal 28173
Phalanx, Toe 28175
Scapula 23210
Tarsal 28171
Tibia 27645
Ribs 19260-19272, 32900
Synovial Membrane
  See Synovectomy
Temporal Bone 69535
Ulna
  Arthrosedis
    Radioulnar Joint 25830
Ureterocele
  Ectopic 52301
  Orthotopic 52300
Vena Cava
  with Reconstruction 37799

Resonance Spectroscopy, Magnetic
See Magnetic Resonance Spectroscopy

Respiration, Positive-Pressure
See Pressure Breathing, Positive

Respiratory Pattern Recording
Preventive
  Infant 94772

Respiratory Syncytial Virus
Antibody 86756
Antigen Detection
  Direct Fluorescence 87280
  Direct Optical Observation 87807
  Enzyme Immunoassay 87420

Respiratory Syncytial Virus Immune Globulin
See Immune Globulins
Antigen Detection
  See Immune Globulins, Respiratory Syncytial Virus

Response, Auditory Evoked
See Auditory Evoked Potentials

Rest Home Visit
See Domiciliary Services

Resuscitation
Cardiac
  See Cardiac Massage
Cardio-Pulmonary
  See Cardio-Pulmonary Resuscitation
Newborn 99440

Reticulocyte
Count 85044-85045

Retina
Incision
  Encircling Material 67115

Lesion
  Extensive
    Destruction 67227-67228
  Localized
    Destruction 0017T, 67208-67218
Repair
  Detachment
    by Scleral Buckling 67112
    Cryotherapy or Diathermy 67101
    Injection of Air 67110
    Photocoagulation 67105
    Scleral Dissection 67107
    with Vitrectomy 67108, 67112
  Prophylaxis
    Detachment 67141-67145
Retinopathy
  Destruction
    Cryotherapy, Diathermy 67227
    Photocoagulation 67228

Retinacular
Knee
  Release 27425

Retinopathy
Destruction
  Cryotherapy, Diathermy 67227
  Photocoagulation 67228

Retraction, Clot
See Clot Retraction

Retrieval
Transcatheter Foreign Body 37203

Retrocaval Ureter
Ureterolysis 50725

Retrograde Cholangiopancreatographies, Endoscopic
See Cholangiopancreatography

Retrograde Cystourethrogram
See Urethrocystography, Retrograde

Retrograde Pyelogram
See Urography, Retrograde

Retroperitoneal Area
Abscess
  Incision and Drainage
    Open 49060
    Percutaneous 49061
Biopsy 49010
Cyst
  Destruction/Excision 49200-49201
Endometriomas
  Destruction/Excision 49200-49201
Exploration 49010
Needle Biopsy
  Mass 49180
Tumor
  Destruction/Excision 49200-49201

Retroperitoneal Fibrosis
Ureterolysis 50715

Retropubic Prostatectomies
See Prostatectomy, Retropubic

Revascularization
Distal Upper Extremity
  with Interval Ligation 36838
Interval Ligation
  Distal Upper Extremity 36838
Penis 37788
Transmyocardial 33140-33141

Reversal, Vasectomy
See Vasovasorrhaphy

Reverse T3
See Triiodothyronine, Reverse

Reverse Triiodothyronine
See Triiodothyronine, Reverse

Revision
See Reconstruction
Adjustable Gastric Band 43771
Aorta 33404
Atrial 33253
Blepharoplasty 15820-15823
Broncheal Stent 31638
Bronchus 32501
Bypass Graft
  Vein Patch 35685
Cervicoplasty 15819
Colostomy
  See Colostomy, Revision
Cornea
  Prosthesis 65770
  Reshaping
    Epikeratoplasty 65767
    Keratomileusis 65760
    Keratophakia 65765
Defibrillator Site
  Chest 33223
Ear, Middle 69662
External Fixation System 20693
Eye
  Aqueous Shunt 66185
Gastric Restrictive Procedure 43848
Gastrostomy Tube 44373
Hip Replacement
  See Replacement, Hip, Revision
Hymenal Ring 56700
Ileostomy
  See Ileostomy, Revision
Infusion Pump
  Intraarterial 36261
  Intravenous 36576-36578, 36582-36583
Iris
  Iridoplasty 66762
  Iridotomy 66761
Jejunostomy Tube 44373
Lower Extremity Arterial Bypass ...35879-35881
Pacemaker Site
  Chest 33222
Rhytidectomy 15824-15829
Semicircular Canal
  Fenestration 69840
Shunt
  Intrahepatic Portosystemic 37183
Sling 53442
Stapedectomy
  See Stapedectomy, Revsion
Stomach
  for Obesity 43848

Subcutaneous Port
    for Gastric Restrictive Procedure 43886
Tracheostomy
    Scar 31830
Urinary-Cutaneous Anastomosis ...50727-50728
Vagina
    Prosthetic Graft 57295
    Sling
      Stress Incontinence 57287
Venous Access Device 36576-36578,
           36582-36583, 36585
Ventricle
    Ventriculomyectomy 33416
    Ventriculomyotomy 33416

Rh (D)
See Blood Typing

Rh Immune Globulin
See Immune Globulins, Rho (D)

Rheumatoid Factor 86430-86431

Rhinectomy
Partial 30150
Total 30160

Rhinomanometry 92512

Rhinopharynx
See Nasopharynx

Rhinophyma
Repair 30120

Rhinoplasty
Cleft Lip/Cleft Palate 30460-30462
Primary 30400-30420
Secondary 30430-30450

Rhinoscopy
See Endoscopy, Nose

Rhinotomy
Lateral 30118, 30320

Rhizotomy 63185-63190

Rho Variant Du 86905

Rhytidectomy 15824-15829

Rhytidoplasties
See Face Lift

Rib
Antibody 86756
Antigen Detection
    by Immunoassay
      with Direct Optical Observation
      Direct Fluorescense 87280
      Enzyme Immunoassay 87420
Excision 21600-21616, 32900
Fracture
    Closed Treatment 21800
    External Fixation 21810
    Open Treatment 21805
Graft
    to Face 21230
Resection 19260-19272, 32900
X-Ray 71100-71111

Riboflavin 84252

Richardson Operation Hysterectomy
See Hysterectomy, Abdominal, Total

Richardson Procedure 53460

Rickettsia
Antibody 86757

Ridell Operation
See Sinusotomy, Frontal

Ridge, Alveolar
See Alveolar Ridge

Right Atrioventricular Valve
See Tricuspid Valve

Right Heart Cardiac Catheterization
See Cardiac Catheterization, Right Heart

Ripstein Operation
See Proctopexy

Risk Factor Reduction Intervention
See Performance Measures, Preventive Medicine

Risser Jacket 29010-29015
Removal 29710

Rocky Mountain Spotted Fever 86000

Roentgen Rays
See X-Ray

Roentgenographic
See X-Ray

Roentgenography
See Radiology, Diagnostic

Ropes Test 83872

Rorschach Test 96101

Ross Procedure 33413

Rotation Flap
See Skin, Adjacent Tissue Transfer

Rotator Cuff
Repair 23410-23420

Rotavirus
Antibody 86759
Antigen Detection
    Enzyme Immunoassay 87425

Rotavirus Vaccine 90680

Round Window
Repair Fistula 69667

Round Window Fistula
See Fistula, Round Window

Roux-En-Y Procedure 43621,
    43633-43634, 43644, 43846, 47740-47741,
         47780-47785, 48540

RPR 86592-86593

RSV
See Immune Globulins; Respiratory Syncytial Virus

RT3
See Triiodothyronine, Reverse

Rubbing Alcohol
See Isopropyl Alcohol

Rubella
Antibody 86762
Vaccine 90706

Rubella HI Test
See Hemagglutination Inhibition Test

Rubella/Mumps
See Vaccines

Rubeola
Antibody 86765
Antigen Detection
    Immunofluorescence 87283

Rubeolla
See Rubeola

Russell Viper Venom Time 85612-85613

S

Sac, Endolymphatic
See Endolymphatic Sac

Saccomanno Technique 88108

Sacral Nerve
Implantation
    Electrode 64561, 64581
Insertion
    Electrode 64561, 64581

Sacroiliac Joint
Arthrodesis 27280
Arthrotomy 27050
Biopsy 27050
Dislocation
    Open Treatment 27218
Fusion 27280
Injection for Arthrography 27096
X-Ray 72200-72202, 73542

Sacrum
Tumor
    Excision 49215
X-Ray 72220

Sahli Test
See Gastroenterology, Diagnostic, Stomach

Salicylate
Assay 80196

Saline Load Test 91060

Saline-Solution Abortion
See Abortion, Induced, by Saline

Salivary Duct
Catheterization 42660
Dilation 42650-42660
Ligation 42665
Repair 42500-42505
    Fistula 42600

Salivary Gland Virus
See Cytomegalovirus

Salivary Glands
Abscess
    Incision and Drainage 42310-42320
Biopsy 42405
Calculi (Stone)
    Excision 42330-42340
Cyst
    Drainage 42409
    Excision 42408
Injection
    X-Ray 42550
Needle Biopsy 42400
Nuclear Medicine
    Function Study 78232
    Imaging 78230-78231
Parotid
    Abscess 42300-42305
Unlisted Services and Procedures 42699
X-Ray 70380-70390
    with Contrast 70390

Salmonella
Antibody 86768

Salpingectomy 58262-58263,
    58291-58292, 58552, 58554, 58661, 58700
Ectopic Pregnancy
    Laparoscopic Treatment 59151
    Surgical Treatment 59120
Oophorectomy 58943

Salpingo-Oophorectomy 58720
Resection Ovarian Malignancy 58950-58956
Resection Peritoneal Malignancy ...58950-58956
Resection Tubal Malignancy 58950-58956

Salpingohysterostomy
See Implantation, Tubouterine

Salpingolysis 58740

Salpingoneostomy 58673, 58770

Salpingoplasty
See Fallopian Tube, Repair

Salpingostomy 58673, 58770
Laparoscopic 58673

Salter Osteotomy of the Pelvis
See Osteotomy, Pelvis

Sampling
See Biopsy; Brush Biopsy; Needle Biopsy

Sang-Park Procedure 33735-33737

Sao Paulo Typhus
See Rocky Mountain Spotted Fever

Saucerization
Calcaneus 28120
Clavicle 23180
Femur 27070, 27360
Fibula 27360, 27641
Hip 27070
Humerus 23184, 24140
Ileum 27070
Metacarpal 26230
Metatarsal 28122
Olecranon Process 24147
Phalanges
    Finger 26235-26236
    Toe 28124
Pubis 27070
Radius 24145, 25151
Scapula 23182
Talus 28120
Tarsal 28122
Tibia 27360, 27640
Ulna 24147, 25150

Saundby Test
See Blood, Feces

Scabies
See Tissue, Examination for Ectoparasites

Scalenotomy
See Muscle Division, Scalenus Anticus

Scalenus Anticus
Division 21700-21705

Scaling
See Exfoliation

Scalp
Tumor Resection
    Radical 21015

Scalp Blood Sampling 59030

Scan
See Specific Site, Nuclear Medicine
Abdomen
    See Abdomen, CT Scan
CT
    See CT Scan
MRI
    See Magnetic Resonance Imaging
PET
    See Positron Emission Tomography
Radionuclide
    See Emission Computerized Tomography

Scanning, Radioisotope
See Nuclear Medicine

Scanogram 76040

Scaphoid
Fracture
    Closed Treatment 25622
    Open Treatment 25628
    with Manipulation 25624

Scapula
Craterization 23182
Cyst
    Excision 23140
        with Allograft 23146
        with Autograft 23145
Diaphysectomy 23182
Excision 23172, 23190
    Partial 23182
Fracture
    Closed Treatment
        with Manipulation 23575
        without Manipulation 23570
    Open Treatment 23585
Ostectomy 23190
Repair
    Fixation 23400
    Scapulopexy 23400
Saucerization 23182
Sequestrectomy 23172
Tumor
    Excision 23140, 23210
        with Allograft 23146
        with Autograft 23145
        Radical Resection 23210
X-Ray 73010

Scapulopexy 23400

Scarification
Pleural 32215

Scarification of Pleura
See Pleurodesis

Schanz Operation
See Femur, Osteotomy

Schauta Operation
See Hysterectomy, Vaginal, Radical

Schede Procedure 32905-32906

Scheie Procedure
See Iridectomy

Schilling Test 78270
See Vitamin B-12 Absorption Study

Schlatter Operation Total Gastrectomy
See Excision, Stomach, Total

Schlicter Test 87197
See Bactericidal Titer, Serum

Schocket Procedure 66180
See Aqueous Shunt

Schonbein Test
See Blood, Feces

Schuchard Procedure
Osteotomy
    Maxilla 21206

Schwannoma, Acoustic
See Brain, Tumor, Excision

Sciatic Nerve
Decompression 64712
Injection
    Anesthetic 64445-64446
Lesion
    Excision 64786
Neuroma
    Excision 64786
Neuroplasty 64712
Release 64712
Repair/Suture 64858

Scintigraphy
See Nuclear Medicine
Computed Tomographic
    See Emission Computerized Tomography

Scissoring
Skin Tags .11200-11201

Sclera
Excision
    Sclerectomy with Punch or Scissors . . .66160
Fistulization
    for Glaucoma 0123T
    Iridencleisis or Iridotasis 66165
    Sclerectomy with Punch or Scissors with
    Iridectomy .66160
    Thermocauterization with Iridectomy . .66155
    Trabeculectomy ab Externo in Absence of
    Previous Surgery 66170
    Trephination with Iridectomy 66150
Incision
    Fistulization
        Iridencleisis or Iridotasis 66165
        Sclerectomy with Punch or Scissors with
        Iridectomy 66160
        Thermocauterization with Iridectomy 66155
        Trabeculectomy ab Externo in Absence of
        Previous Surgery 66170
        Trephination with Iridectomy 66150
Lesion
    Excision 66130
Repair
    Reinforcement
        with Graft 67255
        without Graft 67250
    Staphyloma
        with Graft 66225
        without Graft 66220
    with Glue 65286
    Wound
        Operative .66250
        Tissue Glue 65286

Scleral Buckling Operation
See Retina, Repair, Detachment

Scleral Ectasia
See Staphyloma, Sclera

Sclerectomy .66160

Sclerotherapy
Venous .36468-36471

Sclerotomy
See Incision, Sclera

Screening, Drug
See Drug Screen

Scribner Cannulization 36810

Scrotal Varices
See Varicocele

Scrotoplasty 55175-55180

Scrotum
Abscess
    Incision and Drainage 54700, 55100
Excision 55150
Exploration 55110
Hematoma
    Incision and Drainage 54700
Removal
    Foreign Body 55120
Repair .55175-55180
Ultrasound 76870
Unlisted Services and Procedures 55899

Scrub Typhus 86000

Second Look Surgery
See Reoperation

Second Opinion
See Confirmatory Consultations

Section
See Decompression
Cesarean
    See Cesarean Delivery
Cranial Nerve .61460
    Spinal Access 63191
Dentate Ligament 63180-63182
Gasserian Ganglion
    Sensory Root 61450
Medullary Tract 61470
Mesencephalic Tract 61480
Nerve Root 63185-63190
Spinal Accessory Nerve 63191
Spinal Cord Tract 63194-63199
Tentorium Cerebelli 61440
Vestibular Nerve
    Transcranial Approach 69950
    Translabyrinthine Approach 69915

Sedation
Moderate 99143-99150
    with Independent Observation . .99143-99145

Seddon-Brookes Procedure . . .24320

Sedimentation Rate
Blood Cell
    Automated 85652
    Manual 85651

Segmentectomy
Breast .19160-19162
Lung 32484

Seidlitz Powder Test
See X-Ray, with Contrast

Selective Cellular Enhancement
Technique 88112

Selenium 84255

Self Care
See Physical Medicine/Therapy/Occupational
Therapy
Training 97535, 98960-98962, 99509

Sella Turcica
CT Scan 70480-70482
X-Ray 70240

Semen
See Sperm

Semen Analysis 89300-89321
Sperm Analysis
    Antibodies 89325
with Sperm Isolation 89260-89261

Semenogelase
See Antigen, Prostate Specific

Semicircular Canal
Incision
    Fenestration 69820
    Revised 69840

Semilunar
Bone
    See Lunate
Ganglion
    See Gasserian Ganglion

Seminal Vesicle
Cyst
    Excision 55680
Excision 55650
Incision 55600-55605
Mullerian Duct
    Excision 55680
Unlisted Services and Procedures 55899

Seminal Vesicles
Vesiculography 74440
X-Ray with Contrast 74440

Seminin
See Antigen, Prostate Specific

Semiquantitative 81005

Sengstaaken Tamponade
Esophagus 43460

Senning Procedure 33774-33777
See Repair, Great Arteries; Revision

Senning Type 33774-33777

Sensitivity Study
Antibiotic
    Agar 87181
    Disc 87184
    Enzyme Detection 87185
    Macrobroth 87188
    MIC 87186
    Microtiter 87186
    MLC 87187
    Mycobacteria 87190
Antiviral Drugs
    HIV-1
        Tissue Culture 87904

Sensor, Fetal Oximetry
Insertion
    Cervix 0021T
    Vagina 0021T

Sensorimotor Exam 92060

Sensory Nerve
Common
    Repair/Suture 64834

Sentinel Node
Injection Procedure 38792

Separation
Craniofacial
    Closed Treatment 21431
    Open Treatment 21432-21436

Septal Defect
Repair 33813-33814

Septectomy
Atrial 33735-33737
    Balloon (Rashkind Type) 92992
    Blade Method (Park) 92993
Closed
    See Septostomy, Atrial
Submucous Nasal
    See Nasal Septum, Submucous Resection

Septic Abortion
See Abortion, Septic

Septoplasty 30520

Septostomy
Atrial 33735-33737
    Balloon (Rashkind Type) 92992
    Blade Method (Park) 92993

Septum, Nasal
See Nasal Septum

Sequestrectomy
Carpal 25145
Clavicle 23170
Humeral Head 23174
Humerus 24134
Olecranon Process 24138
Radius 24136, 25145
Scapula 23172
Skull 61501
Ulna .24138, 25145

Serialography
Aorta 75625

Serodiagnosis, Syphilis
See Serologic Test for Syphilis

Serologic Test for
Syphilis 86592-86593

Seroma
Incision and Drainage
    Skin 10140

Serotonin .84260

Serum
Albumin
    See Albumin, Serum
Antibody Identification
    Pretreatment 86975-86978
CPK
    See Creatine Kinase, Total
Serum Immune Globulin 90281-90283

Sesamoid Bone
Excision 28315
Finger
    Excision 26185
Foot
    Fracture 28530-28531
Thumb
    Excision 26185

Sesamoidectomy
Toe 28315

Sever Procedure
See Contracture, Palm, Release

Severing of Blepharorrhaphy
See Tarsorrhaphy, Severing

Sex Change Operation
Female to Male 55980
Male to Female 55970

Sex Chromatin
See Barr Bodies

Sex Chromatin
Identification 88130-88140

Sex Hormone Binding
Globulin .84270

Sex-Linked Ichthyoses
See Syphilis Test

SGOT 84450

SGPT 84460

Shaving
Skin Lesion 11300-11313

SHBG
See Sex Hormone Binding Globulin

Shelf Procedure
See Osteotomy, Hip

Shiga-Like Toxin
Antigen Detection
    Enzyme Immunoassay 87427

Shigella
Antibody 86771

Shirodkar Operation
See Repair, Cervix, Cerclage, Abdominal

Shock Wave (Extracorporeal)
Therapy 0019T, 0101T-0102T, 28890

Shock Wave Lithotripsy 50590

Shock Wave, Ultrasonic
See Ultrasound

Shop Typhus of Malaya
See Murine Typhus

Shoulder
See Clavicle; Scapula
Abscess
    Drainage .23030
Amputation 23900-23921
Arthrocentesis 20610
Arthrodesis .23800
    with Autogenous Graft 23802
Arthrography
    Injection
        Radiologic 23350
Arthroscopy
    Diagnostic 29805
    Surgical 29806-29827
Arthrotomy
    with Removal Loose or Foreign Body . .23107
Biopsy
    Deep 23066
    Soft Tissue 23065
Blade
    See Scapula
Bone
    Excision
        Acromion 23130
        Clavicle 23120-23125
        Incision 23035
    Tumor
        Excision 23140-23146
Bursa
    Drainage .23031
Capsular Contracture Release 23020
Cast
    Figure Eight 29049
    Removal .29710
    Spica 29055
    Velpeau .29058
Disarticulation 23920-23921
Dislocation
    Closed Treatment
        with Manipulation 23650-23655
Exploration .23107
Hematoma
    Drainage .23030
Manipulation
    Application of Fixation Apparatus 23700
Prophylactic Treatment 23490-23491
Radical Resection 23077
Removal
    Calcareous Deposits 23000
    Cast 29710
    Foreign Body
        Complicated 23332
        Deep 23331
        Subcutaneous 23330
    Foreign or Loose Body 23107
Repair
    Capsule 23450-23466
    Ligament Release 23415
    Muscle Transfer 23395-23397
    Rotator Cuff 23410-23420
    Tendon 23410-23412, 23430-23440
    Tenomyotomy 23405-23406
Strapping 29240
Surgery
    Unlisted Services and Procedures 23929

Tumor
Excision 23075-23077
Unlisted Services and Procedures 23929
X-Ray 73020-73030
X-Ray with Contrast 73040

Shoulder Joint
See Clavicle; Scapula
Arthroplasty
with Implant 23470-23472
Arthrotomy
with Biopsy 23100-23101
with Synovectomy 23105-23106
Dislocation
Open Treatment 23660
with Greater Tuberosity Fracture
Closed Treatment 23665
Open Treatment 23670
with Surgical or Anatomical Neck Fracture
Closed Treatment with Manipulation 23675
Open Treatment 23680
Excision
Torn Cartilage 23101
Exploration 23040-23044
Incision and Drainage 23040-23044
Removal
Foreign Body 23040-23044
X-Ray 73050

Shunt(s)
Aqueous
to Extraocular Reservoir 66180
Revision 66185
Arteriovenous
See Arteriovenous Shunt
Brain
Creation 62180-62223
Removal 62256-62258
Replacement 62160, 62194,
62225-62230, 62258
Reprogramming 62252
Cerebrospinal Fluid
See Cerebrospinal Fluid Shunt
Creation
Arteriovenous
Direct 36821
ECMO 36822
Thomas Shunt 36835
Transposition 36818-36820
with Bypass Graft 35686
with Graft 36825-36830
Cerebrospinal Fluid 62200
Thomas Shunt 36835
Fetal 59076
Great Vessel
Aorta
Pulmonary 33924
Aorta to Pulmonary Artery
Ascending 33755
Descending 33762
Central 33764
Subclavian Pulmonary Artery 33750
Vena Cava to Pulmonary Artery .33766-33768
Intra-Atrial 33735-33737
LeVeen
See LeVeen Shunt
Nonvascular
X-Ray 75809

Peritoneal
Venous
Injection 49427
Ligation 49428
Removal 49429
X-Ray 75809
Pulmonary Artery
See Pulmonary Artery, Shunt
Revision
Arteriovenous 36832
Spinal Cord
Creation 63740-63741
Irrigation 63744
Removal 63746
Replacement 63744
Superior Mesenteric-Caval
See Anastomosis, Caval to Mesenteric
Ureter to Colon 50815
Ventriculocisternal with Valve
See Ventriculocisternostomy

Shuntogram 75809

Sialic Acid 84275

Sialodochoplasty 42500-42505

Sialogram
See Sialography

Sialography 70390

Sickling
Electrophoresis 83020

Siderocytes 85536

Siderophilin
See Transferrin

Sigmoid
See Colon-Sigmoid

Sigmoid Bladder
Cystectomy 51590

Sigmoidoscopy
Ablation
Polyp 45339
Tumor 45339
Biopsy 45331
Collection
Specimen 45331
Exploration 45330, 45335
Hemorrhage Control 45334
Injection
Submucosal 45335
Needle Biopsy 45342
Placement
Stent 45345
Removal
Foreign Body 45332
Polyp 45333, 45338
Tumor 45333, 45338
Repair
Volvulus 45337
Ultrasound 45341-45342

Signal-Averaged Electrocardiography
See Electrocardiogram

Silica 84285

Silicon Dioxide
See Silica

Silicone
Contouring Injections 11950-11954

Silver Operation
See Keller Procedure

Silver Procedure 28290

Simple Mastectomies
See Mastectomy

Single Photon Absorptiometry
See Absorptiometry, Single Photon

Single Photon Emission Computed Tomography
See SPECT

Sinu, Sphenoid
See Sinuses, Sphenoid

Sinus
Ethmoidectomy
Excision 31254
Pilonidal
See Cyst, Pilonidal

Sinus of Valsalva
Repair 33702-33722

Sinus Venosus
Repair 33645

Sinusectomy, Ethmoid
See Ethmoidectomy

Sinuses
Ethmoid
Excision 31200-31205
with Nasal/Sinus Endoscopy .31254-31255
Repair of Cerebrospinal Leak 31290
Frontal
Destruction 31080-31085
Exploration 31070-31075
with Nasal/Sinus Endoscopy 31276
Fracture
Open Treatment 21343-21344
Incision 31070-31087
Injection 20500
Diagnostic 20501
Maxillary
Antrostomy 31256-31267
Excision 31225-31230
Exploration 31020-31032
with Nasal/Sinus Endoscopy 31233
Incision 31020-31032, 31256-31267
Irrigation 31000
Skull Base 61581
Surgery 61581
Multiple
Incision 31090
Paranasal
Incision 31090
Sphenoid
Biopsy 31050-31051
Exploration 31050-31051
with Nasal/Sinus Endoscopy 31235

Incision .31050-31051
    with Nasal/Sinus Endoscopy .31287-31288
Irrigation 31002
Repair of Cerebrospinal Leak 31291
Sinusotomy 31050-31051
Skull Base Surgery 61580-61581
Unlisted Services and Procedures 31299
X-Ray 70210-70220

Sinusoidal Rotational Testing
See Ear, Nose and Throat

Sinusoscopy
Sinus
    Maxillary 31233
    Sphenoid 31235

Sinusotomy
See Sinus, Multiple
Combined 31090
Frontal Sinus
    Exploratory 31070-31075
    Nonobliterative 31086-31087
    Obliterative 31080-31085
Maxillary 31020-31032
Multiple
    Paranasal 31090
Sphenoid Sinus 31050-31051

Sirolimus
Drug Assay 80195

SISI Test 92564

Sistrunk Operation
See Cyst, Thyroid Gland, Excision

Size Reduction, Breast
See Breast, Reduction

Skeletal Fixation
Humeral Epicondyle
    Percutaneous 24566

Skeletal Traction
Insertion/Removal
    Pin/Wire 20650

Skene's Gland
Abscess
    Incision and Drainage 53060
Destruction 53270
Excision 53270

Skilled Nursing Facilities (SNFs)
See Nursing Facility Services

Skin
Abrasion .15786-15787
    Chemical Peel 15788-15793
    Dermabrasion 15780-15783
Abscess
    See Abscess, Skin
Adjacent Tissue Transfer 14000-14350
Allogenic Substitute 15340-15341
    Dermal 15360-15366
Allografts
    See Allograft, Skin
Biopsy .11100-11101
Chemical Exfoliation 17360
Cyst
    See Cyst, Skin

Debridement 11000-11006, 11010-11044
    Eczematous 11000-11001
    Full Thickness 11041
    Infected 11000-11006
    Partial Thickness 11040
    Subcutaneous Tissue 11042-11044
        Infected 11004-11006
    with Open Fracture and/or
    Dislocation 11010-11012
Decubitus Ulcer(s)
    See Pressure Ulcer (Decubitus)
Desquamation
    See Exfoliation
Destruction
    Benign Lesions
        Fifteen or More Lesions 17004
        First Lesion 17000
        Two - Fourteen Lesions 17003
    Flat Warts 17110-17111
    Lesions 17106-17108
    Malignant Lesions 17260-17286
        by Photodynamic Therapy 96567
    Premalignant Lesions
        by Photodynamic Therapy 96567
        Fifteen or More Lesions 17004
        First Lesion 17000
        Two - Fourteen Lesions 17003
Excision
    Debridement 11000-11006, 11010-11044
    Excess Skin 15831-15839
    Hemangioma 11400-11446
    Lesion
        Benign 11400-11446
        Malignant 11600-11646
Expanders
    See Tissue, Expander
Fasciocutaneous Flaps 15732-15738
Grafts
    Free 15050-15321, 15340-15366,
                         15420-15431, 15757
    Harvesting
        for Tissue Culture 15040
Homografts
    See Homograft, Skin
Incision and Drainage 10040, 10060-10061,
               10080-10081, 10120-10180
    See Incision, Skin
Lesion
    See Lesion; Tumor
    Verrucous
        See Warts
Muscle Flaps 15732-15738
Myocutaneous Flaps 15732-15738
Nose
    Surgical Planing 30120
Paring .11055-11057
Photography
    Diagnostic 0044T, 0045T
Removal
    Skin Tags 11200-11201
Revision
    Blepharoplasty 15820-15823
    Cervicoplasty 15819
    Rhytidectomy 15824-15829
Shaving 11300-11313
Tags
    Removal 11200-11201

Tests
    See Allergy Tests
    Candida .86485
    Coccidioidomycosis 86490
    Histoplasmosis 86510
    Other Antigen 86586
    Tuberculosis 86580
Unlisted Services and Procedures 17999
Wound Repair
    Complex 13100-13160
    Intermediate 12031-12057
    Simple 12001-12021

Skin Graft and Flap
Acellular Dermal Replacement 15170-15176
Allogenic Skin Substitute 15340-15341
    Dermal Skin Substitute 15360-15366
Allograft 15300-15321
    Acellular Dermal 15330-15336
Composite Graft 15760-15770
Cross Finger Flap 15574
Delay .15600-15630
Delay of Flap 15600-15630
Derma-Fat-Fascia 15770
Dermal Autograft 15130-15136
Epidermal Autograft .15110-15116, 15150-15157
Fascial
    Free 15758
Fasciocutaneous 15732-15738
Formation 15570-15576
Free
    Microvascular Anastomosis 15756-15758
Free Skin Graft
    Full Thickness 15200-15261
Island Pedicle Flap 15740
Muscle 15732-15738, 15842
    Free 15756
Myocutaneous 15732-15738, 15756
Pedicle Flap
    Formation 15570-15576
    Island .15740
    Neurovascular 15750
    Transfer 15650
Pinch Graft 15050
Platysmal .15825
Punch Graft 15775-15776
Punch Graft for Hair Transplant 15775-15776
Recipient Site Preparation 15000-15001
Skin
    Free 15757
Split Graft 15100-15101, 15120-15121
Superficial Musculoaponeurotic System . . .15829
Tissue Transfer 14000-14350
Tissue-Cultured 15100-15101, 15120-15121
Transfer .15650
Vascular Flow Check 15860
Xenograft Skin 15400-15421
    Acellular Implant 15430-15431

Skull
Burr Hole
    Biopsy Brain 61140
    Drainage
        Abscess 61150-61151
        Cyst 61150-61151
        Hematoma 61154-61156
    Exploration
        Infratentorial 61253
        Supratentorial 61250

Insertion
Catheter 61210
EEG Electrode 61210
Reservoir 61210
Intracranial
Biopsy 61140
with Injection 61120
Decompression 61322-61323, 61340-61345
Orbit 61330
Drill Hole
Catheter 61107
Drainage Hematoma 61108
Exploration 61105
Excision 61501
Exploration
Drill Hole 61105
Fracture 62000-62010
Closed Treatment 21300
Hematoma
Drainage 61108
Incision
Suture 61550-61552
Insertion
Catheter 61107
Lesion
Excision ..61500, 61600-61608, 61615-61616
Orbit
Biopsy 61332
Excision
Lesion 61333
Exploration 61332-61334
Removal Foreign Body 61334
Puncture
Cervical 61050
Cisternal 61050
Drain Fluid 61070
Injection 61070
Subdural 61000-61001
Ventricular Fluid 61020
Reconstruction 21172-21180
Defect 62140-62141, 62145
Reduction
Craniomegalic 62115-62117
Removal
Plate 62142
Prosthesis 62142
Repair
Cerebrospinal Fluid Leak 62100
Encephalocele 62120
Replacement
Plate 62143
Prosthesis 62143
Tumor
Excision 61500
X-Ray 70250-70260

Skull Base Surgery
Anterior Cranial Fossa
Bicoronal Approach 61586
Craniofacial Approach 61580-61583
Extradural 61600-61601
LeFort I Osteotomy Approach 61586
Orbitocranial Approach 61584-61585
Transzygomatic Approach 61586
Carotid Aneurysm 61613
Carotid Artery 61610
Transection/Ligation 61609-61612

Craniotomy 62121
Dura
Repair of Cerebrospinal Fluid
Leak 61618-61619
Middle Cranial Fossa
Extradural 61605, 61607
Infratemporal Approach 61590-61591
Intradural 61606, 61608
Orbitocranial Zygomatic Approach 61592
Posterior Cranial Fossa
Extradural 61615
Intradural 61616
Transcondylar Approach 61596-61597
Transpetrosal Approach 61598
Transtemporal Approach 61595

Sleep Study 95806-95807
Actigraphy 0089T

Sliding Inlay Graft, Tibia
See Ankle; Tibia, Repair

Sling Operation
Incontinence 53440
Removal 53442
Stress Incontinence 51992, 57287
Vagina 57287-57288

Small Bowel
See Intestines, Small
Neoplasm
See Tumor, Intestines, Small

SMAS Flap 15829

Smear
Cervical
See Cervical Smears
Papanicolaou
See Pap Smears

Smear and Stain
See Cytopathology, Smears
Cornea 65430
Fluorescent 87206
Gram or Giesma 87205
Ova/Parasites 87177, 87209
Parasites 87207-87209
Wet Mount 87210

Smith Fracture 25600-25620

Smith-Robinson Operation
See Arthrodesis, Vertebra

Smithwick Operation
See Excision, Nerve, Sympathetic

SO₄
See Sulfate

Soave Procedure 45120

Sodium 84295, 84302
Urine 84300

Sodium Glycinate, Theophylline
See Theophylline

Sofield Procedure 24410

Soft Tissue
See Tissue, Soft

Solar Plexus
See Celiac Plexus

Solitary Cyst
See Bone, Cyst

**Somatomammotropin,
Chorionic** 83632

Somatomedin 84305

Somatosensory Testing
Lower Limbs 95926
Trunk or Head 95927
Upper Limbs 95925

Somatostatin 84307

Somatotropin 83003

**Somatotropin Release Inhibiting
Hormone**
See Somatostatin

Somatropin
See Growth Hormone, Human

Somnographies
See Polysomnography

Somophyllin T
See Theophylline

Sonography
See Echography

Sonohysterography 76831
Saline Infusion
Injection Procedure 58340

Sore, Bed
See Pressure Ulcer (Decubitus)

Spasm Eyelid
See Blepharospasm

Special Services
After Hours Medical Services 99050
Analysis
Remote Physiologic Data 99091
Computer Data Analysis 99090
Device Handling 99002
Emergency Care In Office 99058
Emergency Care Out of Office 99060
Extended Hours Medical Services ..99051-99053
Group Education 99078
Self-Management 98961-98962
Hyperbaric Oxygen 99183
Hypothermia 99185-99186
Individual Education
Self-management 98960
Medical Testimony 99075
Non-Office Medical Services 99056
On Call Services 99026-99027
Phlebotomy 99199
Post-Op Visit 99024
Pump Services 99190-99192

Reports and Forms
   Medical, Extended 99080
   Psychiatric 90889
Specimen Handling 99000-99001
Supply of Materials 99070
   Educational 99071
Unlisted Services and Procedures 99199
Unusual Travel 99082

Specific Gravity
Body Fluid 84315

Specimen Collection
Intestines 89100-89105
Stomach 89130-89141

Specimen Concentration 87015

Specimen Handling 99000-99001

SPECT 78607
See Emission Computerized Tomography
Abscess Localization 78807
Bone 78320
Cerebrospinal Fluid 78647
Heart
   Multiple 78465
   Single 78464
Kidney 78710
Liver 78205
Tumor Localization 78803

Spectacle Services
Fitting
   Low Vision Aid 92354-92355
   Spectacle Prosthesis 92352-92353
   Spectacles 92340-92342
Repair 92370-92371

Spectrometry
Mass
   Analyte
      Qualitative 83788
      Quantitative 83789

Spectrophotometry 84311
Atomic Absorption
   See Atomic Absorption Spectroscopy

Spectroscopy
Atomic Absorption 82190
Expired Breath Analysis 0064T
Magnetic Resonance 76390

Spectrum Analyses
See Spectrophotometry

Speculoscopy 0031T
with Direct Sampling 0032T

Speech Evaluation 92506
Cine 70371
for Prosthesis 92597, 92607-92608
Video 70371

Speech Prosthesis 21084, 92609
Creation 31611
Evaluation for Speech 92597, 92607-92608
Insertion 31611

Speech Therapy 92507-92508

Sperm
Cryopreserved
   Preparation
      Thawing 89353
Storage 89343

Sperm Analysis
Antibodies 89325
Cervical Mucus Penetration Test 89330
Cryopreservation 89259
Hamster Penetration Test 89329
Hyaluron Binding Assay 0087T
Identification
   Aspiration 89257
   from Testis Tissue 89264
Isolation 89260-89261

Sperm Evaluation, Cervical Mucus Penetration Test
See Huhner Test

Sperm Washing 58323

Spermatic Cord
Hydrocele
   Excision .55500
Laparoscopy 55559
Lesion
   Excision .55520
Repair
   Veins 55530-55540
      Abdominal Approach 55535
      with Hernia Repair 55540
Varicocele
   Excision 55530-55540

Spermatic Veins
Excision 55530-55540
Ligation 55550

Spermatocele
Excision 54840

Spermatocystectomy
See Spermatocele, Excision

Sphenoid Sinus
See Sinuses, Sphenoid

Sphenoidotomy
Excision
   with Nasal/Sinus Endoscopy . . .31287-31288

Sphenopalatine Ganglion
Injection
   Anesthetic 64505

Sphincter
See Specific Sphincter
Anal
   See Anal Sphincter
Artificial Genitourinary
   See Prosthesis, Urethral Sphincter
Pyloric
   See Pyloric Sphincter

Sphincter of Oddi
Pressure Measurement
   Endoscopy 43263

Sphincteroplasty
Anal 46750-46751, 46760-46761
   with Implant 46762
Bile Duct 47460
Bladder Neck
   See Bladder, Repair, Neck

Sphincterotomy 52277
Anal 46080
Bile Duct 47460

Spica Cast
Hip 29305-29325
Repair 29720
Shoulder 29055

Spinal Accessory Nerve
Anastomosis
   to Facial Nerve 64866
Incision 63191
Injection
   Anesthetic 64412
Section 63191

Spinal Column
See Spine

Spinal Cord
See Cauda Equina; Nerve Root
Biopsy 63275-63290
Cyst
   Aspiration 62268
   Incision and Drainage 63172-63173
Decompression 63001-63003
   with Cervical Laminoplasty 63050-63051
Drain Fluid 62272
Exploration 63001-63044
Graft
   Dura 63710
Implantation
   Electrode 63650-63655
   Pulse Generator 63685
   Receiver .63685
Incision 63200
   Dentate Ligament 63180-63182
   Tract 63170, 63194-63199
Injection
   Anesthetic 62310-62319
   Blood 62273
   CT Scan .62284
   Neurolytic Agent 62280-62282
   Other 62310-62311
   X-Ray 62284
Insertion
   Electrode 63650-63655
   Pulse Generator 63685
   Receiver .63685
Lesion
   Destruction 62280-62282
   Excision 63265-63273, 63300-63308
Needle Biopsy .62269
Neoplasm
   Excision 63275-63290
Puncture (Tap)
   Diagnostic 62270
   Drain Fluid 62272
   Lumbar 62270
Reconstruction
   Dorsal Spine Elements 63295

Release 63200
Removal
　　Catheter 62355
　　Electrode 63660
　　Pulse Generator 63688
　　Pump 62365
　　Receiver 63688
　　Reservoir 62365
Repair
　　Cerebrospinal Fluid Leak 63707-63709
　　Meningocele 63700-63702
　　Myelomeningocele 63704-63706
Section
　　Dentate Ligament 63180-63182
　　Tract 63194-63199
Shunt
　　Create 63740-63741
　　Irrigation 63744
　　Removal 63746
　　Replacement 63744
Stereotaxis
　　Aspiration 63615
　　Biopsy 63615
　　Creation Lesion 63600
　　Excision Lesion 63615
　　Stimulation .63610
Syrinx
　　Aspiration 62268
Tumor
　　Excision 63275-63290

Spinal Cord Neoplasms
See Spinal Cord
Tumor
　　See Spinal Cord, Tumor; Tumor
　　Excision
　　　　See Spinal Cord, Tumor; Tumor, Spinal
　　　　Cord

Spinal Fluid
See Cerebrospinal Fluid

Spinal Fracture
See Fracture, Vertebra

Spinal Instrumentation
Anterior 22845-22847
　　Removal 22855
Internal Fixation 22841
Pelvic Fixation .22848
Posterior Nonsegmental
　　Harrington Rod Technique 22840
　　Removal 22850
Posterior Segmental 22842-22844
　　Removal 22852
Prosthetic Device 22851
Reinsertion of Spinal Fixation Device 22849

Spinal Manipulation
See Manipulation, Chiropractic

Spinal Nerve
Avulsion 64772
Transection 64772

Spinal Tap
See Cervical Puncture; Cisternal Puncture;
Subdural Tap; Ventricular Puncture
Drainage Fluid .62272
Lumbar 62270

Spine
See Spinal Cord; Vertebra; Vertebral Body;
Vertebral Process
Allograft
　　Morselized .20930
　　Structural 20931
Augmentation
　　Lumbar Vertebra 22524, 22525
　　Thoracic Vertebra 22523, 22525
Autograft
　　Local 20936
　　Morselized .20937
　　Structural 20938
Biopsy .20250-20251
CT Scan
　　Cervical 72125-72127
　　Lumbar 72131-72133
　　Thoracic 72128-72130
Fixation 22842
Fusion
　　Anterior 22808-22812
　　Anterior Approach 22548-22585, 22812
　　Exploration .22830
　　Lateral Extracavitary 22532-22534
　　Posterior Approach 22590-22802
Incision and Drainage
　　Abscess 22010-22015
Insertion
　　Instrumentation 22840-22848, 22851
Kyphectomy 22818-22819
Magnetic Resonance Angiography 72159
Magnetic Resonance Imaging
　　Cervical 72141-72142, 72156-72158
　　Lumbar 72148-72158
　　Thoracic 72146-72147, 72156-72158
Manipulation
　　with Anesthesia 22505
Myelography
　　Cervical 72240
　　Lumbosacral 72265
　　Thoracic 72255
　　Total 72270
Reconstruction
　　Dorsal Spine Elements 63295
Reinsertion
　　Instrumentation 22849
Removal
　　Instrumentation 22850, 22852-22855
Repair, Osteotomy
　　Anterior 22220-22226
　　Posterior 22210-22214
　　　　Cervical Laminoplasty 63050-63051
　　Posterolateral 22216
Ultrasound 76800
Unlisted Services and Procedures,
Surgery 22899
X-Ray .72020, 72090
　　Absorptiometry 76075, 76077
　　Cervical 72040-72052
　　Lumbosacral 72100-72120
　　Standing 72069
　　Thoracic 72070-72074
　　Thoracolumbar 72080
　　Total 72010

with Contrast
　　Cervical 72240
　　Lumbosacral 72265
　　Thoracic 72255
　　Total 72270

Spine Chemotherapy
Administration .96450
　　See Chemotherapy

Spirometry 94010-94070
See Pulmonology, Diagnostic
Patient Initiated 94014-94016

Splanchnicectomy
See Nerves, Sympathectomy, Excision

Spleen
Excision 38100-38102
　　Laparoscopic 38120
Injection
　　Radiologic 38200
Nuclear Medicine
　　Imaging 78185, 78215-78216
Repair 38115

Splenectomy
Laparoscopic .38120
Partial 38101
Partial with Repair, Ruptured Spleen 38115
Total 38100
　　En bloc 38102

Splenoplasty
See Repair, Spleen

Splenoportography 75810
Injection Procedures 38200

Splenorrhaphy 38115

Splint
See Casting; Strapping
Arm
　　Long 29105
　　Short 29125-29126
Finger .29130-29131
Foot 29590
Leg
　　Long 29505
　　Short 29515
Oral Surgical 21085
Ureteral
　　See Ureteral Splinting

Split Grafts 15100-15101, 15120-15121

Split Renal Function Test
See Cystourethroscopy, Catheterization, Ureteral

Splitting
Blood Products 86985

Spontaneous Abortion
See Abortion

Sprengel's Deformity 23400

Spring Water Cyst
See Cyst, Pericardial

Spur, Bone
See Exostosis
Calcaneal
  See Heel Spur

Sputum Analysis .... .89220

SRIH
See Somatostatin

Ssabanejew-Frank Operation
See Incision, Stomach, Creation, Stoma; Incision and Drainage

Stabilizing Factor, Fibrin
See Fibrin Stabilizing Factor

Stable Factor .... .85230

Stallard Procedure
See Conjunctivorhinostomy

Stamey Procedure .... .51845
See Repair, Bladder, Neck

Standby Services
Physician .... .99360

Stanford-Binet Test
See Psychiatric Diagnosis

Stanftan
See Binet Test

Stapedectomy
Revision .... .69662
with Footplate Drill Out .... .69661
without Foreign Material .... .69660

Stapedotomy
Revision .... .69662
with Footplate Drill Out .... .69661
without Foreign Material .... .69660

Stapes
Excision
  with Footplate Drill Out .... .69661
  without Foreign Material .... .69660
Mobilization
  See Mobilization, Stapes
Release .... .69650
Revision .... .69662

Staphyloma
Sclera
  Repair
    with Graft .... .66225
    without Graft .... .66220

Starch Granules
Feces .... .89225

State Operation
See Proctectomy

Statin Therapy
See Performance Measures

Statistics/Biometry
See Biometry

Steindler Stripping .... .28250

Stellate Ganglion
Injection
  Anesthetic .... .64510

Stem Cell
Cell Concentration .... .38215
Count .... .86367
Cryopreservation .... .38207, 88240
Donor Search .... .38204
Harvesting 38205-38206
Limbal
  Allograft .... .65781
Plasma Depletion .... .38214
Platelet Depletion .... .38213
Red Blood Cell Depletion .... .38212
T-Cell Depletion .... .38210
Thawing 38208-38209, 88241
Transplantation 38240-38242
Tumor Cell Depletion .... .38211
Washing .... .38209

Stem, Brain
See Brainstem

Stenger Test .... .92565, 92577
See Audiologic Function Test; Ear, Nose and Throat

Stenosis
Aortic
  See Aortic Stenosis
Bronchi .... .31641
  Reconstruction .... .31775
Excision
  Trachea 31780-31781
Laryngoplasty .... .31582
Reconstruction
  Auditory Canal, External .... .69310
Repair
  Trachea 31780-31781
Tracheal
  See Trachea Stenosis
Urethral
  See Urethral Stenosis

Stensen Duct
See Parotid Duct

Stent
Indwelling
  Insertion
    Ureter .... .50605
Placement
  Bronchoscopy .... .31631, 31636-31637
  Colonoscopy .... .45387
    via Stoma .... .44397
  Endoscopy
    Gastrointestinal, Upper .... .43256
  Enteroscopy .... .44370
  Proctosigmoidoscopy .... .45327
  Sigmoidoscopy .... .45345
  Transcatheter
    Intravascular ..37205-37208, 37215-37216
    Extracranial .... .0075T-0076T
  Ureteroneocystomy 50947-50948
Removal
  Ureteral 50382-50387
Replacement
  Ureteral .... .50382, 50387

Revision
  Bronchoscopy .... .31638
Transcatheter
  Intravascular
    Intracranial .... .61635
Urethra .... .52282
  Prostatic .... .0084T

Stent, Intravascular
See Transcatheter, Placement, Intravascular Stents

Stents, Tracheal
See Tracheal Stent

Stereotactic Frame
Application/Removal .... .20660

Stereotaxis
Aspiration
  Brain Lesion .... .61750
    with CT Scan and/or MRI .... .61751
  Spinal Cord .... .63615
Biopsy
  Aspiration
    Brain Lesion .... .61750
  Brain .... .61750
    with CT Scan and/or MRI .... .61751
  Breast .... .76095
  Spinal Cord .... .63615
Computer Assisted
  Brain Surgery .... .61795
  Orthopedic Surgery .... .0054T-0056T
Creation Lesion
  Brain
    Deep 61720-61735
    Percutaneous .... .61790
  Gasserian Ganglion .... .61790
  Spinal Cord .... .63600
  Trigeminal Tract .... .61791
CT Scan
  Aspiration .... .61751
  Biopsy .... .61751
Excision Lesion
  Brain .... .61750
  Spinal Cord .... .63615
Focus Beam
  Radiosurgery .... .61793
Localization
  Brain .... .61770
Radiation Therapy ...0082T, 0083T, 77421, 77432
Stimulation
  Spinal Cord .... .63610

Sterile Coverings
See Dressings

Sternal Fracture
See Fracture, Sternum

Sternoclavicular Joint
Arthrotomy .... .23044
  with Biopsy .... .23101
  with Synovectomy .... .23106
Dislocation
  Closed Treatment
    with Manipulation .... .23525
    without Manipulation .... .23520
  Open Treatment 23530-23532
    with Fascial Graft .... .23532

Sternocleidomastoid
Division 21720-21725

Sternotomy
Closure 21750

Sternum
Debridement 21627
Excision 21620, 21630-21632
Fracture
    Closed Treatment 21820
    Open Treatment 21825
Ostectomy 21620
Radical Resection 21630-21632
Reconstruction 21740-21742, 21750
    with Thoracoscopy 21743
X-Ray 71120-71130

Steroid-Binding Protein, Sex
See Globulin, Sex Hormone Binding

Steroids
Anabolic
    See Androstenedione
Injection
    Urethral Stricture 52283
Ketogenic
    Urine 83582

STH (Somatotropic Hormone)
See Growth Hormone

Stimulating Antibody, Thyroid
See Immunoglobulin, Thyroid Stimulating

Stimulation
Electric
    See Electrical Stimulation
Lymphocyte
    See Blastogenesis
Spinal Cord
    Stereotaxis 63610
Transcutaneous Electric
    See Application, Neurostimulation

Stimulator, Long-Acting Thyroid
See Thyrotropin Releasing Hormone (TRH)

Stimulators, Cardiac
See Heart, Pacemaker

Stimulus Evoked Response 51792

Stoffel Operation
See Rhizotomy

Stoma
Creation
    Bladder 51980
    Kidney 50551-50561
    Stomach
        Neonatal 43831
        Temporary 43830-43831
    Ureter 50860
Ureter
    Endoscopy via 50951-50961

Stomach
Anastomosis
    with Duodenum 43810, 43850-43855
    with Jejunum . . .43820-43825, 43860-43865
Biopsy 43600-43605

Creation
  Stoma
    Temporary 43830-43831
  Temporary Stoma
    Laparoscopic 43653
Electrogastrography 91132-91133
Excision
    Partial 43631-43635, 43845
    Total 43620-43622
Exploration .43500
Gastric Bypass 43644-43645, 43846
    Revision 43848
Gastric Restrictive Procedures 43770-43774,
                 43848, 43886-43888
Incision 43830-43832
    Exploration 43500
    Pyloric Sphincter 43520
    Removal
        Foreign Body 43500
Intubation with Specimen Prep 91055
Nuclear Medicine
    Blood Loss Study 78278
    Emptying Study 78264
    Imaging .78261
    Protein Loss Study 78282
    Reflux Study 78262
    Vitamin B-12 Absorption 78270-78272
Reconstruction
    for Obesity 43644-43645, 43842-43847
    Roux-En-Y 43644, 43846
Removal
    Foreign Body 43500
Repair 48547
    Fistula .43880
    Fundoplasty 43324-43325
        Laparoscopic 43280
    Laceration 43501-43502
    Stoma .43870
    Ulcer 43501
Saline Load Test 91060
Specimen Collection 89130-89141
Stimulation of Secretion 91052
Suture
    Fistula .43880
    for Obesity 43842-43843
    Stoma .43870
    Ulcer 43840
    Wound .43840
Tumor
    Excision 43610-43611
Ulcer
    Excision 43610
Unlisted Services and Procedures . .43659, 43999

Stomatoplasty
See Mouth, Repair

Stone, Kidney
See Calculus, Removal, Kidney

Stookey-Scarff Procedure
See Ventriculocisternostomy

Stool Blood
See Blood, Feces

Storage
Embryo 89342
Oocyte 89346
Reproductive Tissue 89344
Sperm 89343

Strabismus
Chemodenervation 67345
Repair
    Adjustable Sutures 67335
    Extraocular Muscles 67340
    One Horizontal Muscle 67311
    One Vertical Muscle 67314
    Posterior Fixation Suture
    Technique 67334-67335
    Previous Surgery, Not Involving Extraocular
    Muscles 67331
    Release Extensive Scar Tissue 67343
    Superior Oblique Muscle 67318
    Transposition 67320
    Two Horizontal Muscles 67312
    Two or More Vertical Muscles 67316

Strapping
See Cast; Splint
Ankle 29540
Back 29220
Chest 29200
Elbow 29260
Finger 29280
Foot 29540, 29590
Hand 29280
Hip 29520
Knee 29530
Shoulder 29240
Thorax 29200
Toes 29550
Unlisted Services and Procedures 29799
Unna Boot .29580
Wrist 29260

Strassman Procedure 58540

Strayer Procedure
Leg, Lower .27687

Streptococcus pneumoniae Vaccine
See Vaccines

Streptococcus, Group A
Antigen Detection
    Enzyme Immunoassay 87430
    Nucleic Acid 87650-87652
Direct Optical Observation 87880

Streptococcus, Group B
by Immunoassay
    with Direct Optical Observation 87802

Streptokinase, Antibody 86590

Stress Tests
Cardiovascular 93015-93024
Multiple Gated Acquisition (MUGA) .78472-78473
Myocardial Perfusion Imaging 78460-78465
Pulmonary 94620-94621
    See Pulmonology, Diagnostic

Stricture
Repair
    Urethra 53400-53405
Urethra
   See Urethral Stenosis

Stricturoplasty
Intestines 44615

Stroboscopy
Larynx 31579

STS 86592-86593
See Syphilis Test

Stuart-Prower Factor 85260

Study, Color Vision
See Color Vision Examination

Sturmdorf Procedure 57520

Styloid Process
Radial
    Excision 25230

Styloidectomy
Radial 25230

Stypven Time
See Russell Viper Venom Time

Subacromial Bursa
Arthrocentesis .20610

Subclavian Arteries
See Artery, Subclavian

Subcutaneous Injection
See Injection, Subcutaneous

Subcutaneous Mastectomies
See Mastectomy, Subcutaneous

Subcutaneous Tissue
Excision .15831-15839

Subdiaphragmatic Abscess
See Abscess, Subdiaphragmatic

Subdural Electrode
Insertion 61531-61533
Removal 61535

Subdural Hematonia
See Hematoma, Subdural

Subdural Puncture 61105-61108

Subdural Tap 61000-61001

Sublingual Gland
Abscess
    Incision and Drainage 42310-42320
Calculi (Stone)
    Excision 42330
Cyst
    Drainage 42409
    Excision 42408
Excision 42450

Subluxation
Elbow 24640

Submandibular Gland
Calculi (Stone)
    Excision 42330-42335
Excision 42440

Submaxillary Gland
Abscess
    Incision and Drainage 42310-42320

Submucous Resection of Nasal Septum
See Nasal Septum, Submucous Resection

Subperiosteal Implant
Reconstruction
    Mandible 21245-21246
    Maxilla 21245-21246

Subphrenic Abscess
See Abscess, Subdiaphragmatic

Substance S, Reichstein's
See Deoxycortisol

Subtrochanteric Fracture
See Femur, Fracture, Subtrochanteric

Sucrose Hemolysis Test
See Red Blood Cell (RBC), Fragility, Osmotic

Suction Lipectomies
See Liposuction

Sudiferous Gland
See Sweat Glands

Sugar Water Test
See Red Blood Cell (RBC), Fragility, Osmotic

Sugars 84375-84379

Sugiura Procedure
See Esophagus, Repair, Varices

Sulfate
Chondroitin
   See Chondroitin Sulfate
DHA
   See Dehydroepiandrosterone Sulfate
Urine 84392

Sulfation Factor
See Somatomedin

Sulphates
See Sulfate

Sumatran Mite Fever
See Scrub Typhus

Superficial Musculoaponeurotic System (SMAS) Flap
Rhytidectomy .15829

Supernumerary Digit
Reconstruction 26587
Repair 26587

Supply
Chemotherapeutic Agent 96545
   See Chemotherapy
Educational Materials 99071

Low Vision Aids
   See Spectacle Services
Materials 99070
Prosthesis
    Breast 19396

Suppositories, Vaginal
See Pessary

Suppression 80400-80408

Suppression/Testing
See Evocative/Suppression Test

Suppressor T Lymphocyte Marker
See CD8

Suppurative Hidradenitides
See Hidradenitis, Suppurative

Suprahyoid
Lymphadenectomy 38700

Supraorbital Nerve
Avulsion 64732
Incision 64732
Transection 64732

Supraorbital Rim and Forehead
Reconstruction 21179-21180

Suprapubic Prostatectomies
See Prostatectomy, Suprapubic

Suprarenal
Gland
   See Adrenal Gland
Vein
   See Vein, Adrenal

Suprascapular Nerve
Injection
    Anesthetic .64418

Suprasellar Cyst
See Craniopharyngioma

Surface CD4 Receptor
See CD4

Surface Radiotherapy
See Application, Radioelement, Surface

Surgeries
Breast-Conserving
   See Breast, Excision, Lesion
Conventional
   See Celiotomy
Laser
   See Laser Surgery
Mohs
   See Mohs Micrographic Surgery
Repeat
   See Reoperation

Surgical
Avulsion
   See Avulsion
Cataract Removal
   See Cataract, Excision
Collapse Therapy; Thoracoplasty
   See Thoracoplasty

Diathermy
   See Electrocautery
Galvanism
   See Electrolysis
Incision
   See Incision
Microscopes
   See Operating Microscope
Pathology
   See Pathology, Surgical
Planing
   Nose
      Skin 30120
Pneumoperitoneum
   See Pneumoperitoneum
Removal, Eye
   See Enucleation, Eye
Revision
   See Reoperation
Services
   Post-Op Visit 99024

Surveillance
See Monitoring

Suspension
Aorta 33800
Kidney
   See Nephropexy
Muscle
   Hyoid 21685
Vagina
   See Colpopexy

Suture
See Repair
Abdomen 49900
Aorta 33320-33322
Bile Duct
   Wound 47900
Bladder
   Fistulization 44660-44661,
         45800-45805, 51880-51925
     Vesicouterine 51920-51925
     Vesicovaginal 51900
   Wound 51860-51865
Cervix 57720
Colon
   Diverticula 44604-44605
   Fistula 44650-44661
   Plication 44680
   Stoma 44620-44625
   Ulcer 44604-44605
   Wound 44604-44605
Esophagus
   Wound 43410-43415
Eyelid 67880
   Closure of 67875
   with Transposition of Tarsal Plate 67882
   Wound
     Full Thickness 67935
     Partial Thickness 67930
Facial Nerve
   Intratemporal
     Lateral to Geniculate Ganglion 69740
     Medial to Geniculate Ganglion 69745
Foot
   Tendon 28200-28210

Gastroesophageal 0008T, 43405
Great Vessel 33320-33322
Hemorrhoids 46945-46946
Hepatic Duct
   See Hepatic Duct, Repair
Intestine
   Large
     Diverticula 44605
     Ulcer 44605
     Wound 44605
Intestines
   Large
     Diverticula 44604
     Ulcer 44604
     Wound 44604
   Small
     Diverticula 44602-44603
     Fistula 44640-44661
     Plication 44680
     Ulcer 44602-44603
     Wound 44602-44603
     Stoma 44620-44625
Iris
   with Ciliary Body 66682
Kidney
   Fistula 50520-50526
   Horseshoe 50540
   Wound 50500
Leg, Lower
   Tendon 27658-27665
Leg, Upper
   Muscle 27385-27386
Liver
   Wound 47350-47361
Mesentery 44850
Nerve 64831-64876
Pancreas 48545
Pharynx
   Wound 42900
Rectum
   Fistula 45800-45825
   Prolapse 45540-45541
Removal
   Anesthesia 15850-15851
Spleen
   See Splenorrhapy
Stomach
   Fistula 43880
   Laceration 43501-43502
   Stoma 43870
   Ulcer 43501, 43840
   Wound 43840
Tendon
   Foot 28200-28210
   Knee 27380-27381
Testis
   Injury 54670
   Suspension 54620-54640
Thoracic Duct
   Abdominal Approach 38382
   Cervical Approach 38380
   Thoracic Approach 38381
Throat
   Wound 42900
Tongue
   to Lip 41510

Trachea
   Fistula
     with Plastic Repair 31825
     without Plastic Repair 31820
   Stoma
     with Plastic Repair 31825
     without Plastic Repair 31820
   Wound
     Cervical 31800
     Intrathoracic 31805
Ulcer 44604-44605
Ureter 50900
   Deligation 50940
   Fistula 50920-50930
Urethra
   Fistula 45820-45825, 53520
   Stoma 53520
   to Bladder 51840-51841
   Wound 53502-53515
Uterus
   Fistula 51920-51925
   Rupture 58520, 59350
   Suspension 58400-58410
Vagina
   Cystocele 57240, 57260
   Enterocele 57265
   Fistula
     Rectovaginal 57300-57307
     Transvesical and Vaginal Approach ..57330
     Urethrovaginal 57310-57311
     Vesicovaginal 51900, 57320-57330
   Rectocele 57250-57260
   Suspension 57280, 57283
   Wound 57200-57210
Vas Deferens 55400
Vein
   Femoral 37650
   Iliac 37660
   Vena Cava 37620
Wound 44604-44605

**Swallowing
Evaluation** 92526, 92610-92613,
              92616-92617
Cine 74230
Treatment 92526
Video 74230

Swanson Procedure 28309

Sweat Collection
Iontophoresis 89230

Sweat Glands
Excision
   Axillary 11450-11451
   Inguinal 11462-11463
   Perianal 11470-11471
   Perineal 11470-11471
   Umbilical 11470-11471

Sweat Test 82435
See Chloride, Blood

Swenson Procedure 45120

Syme Procedure 27888

Sympathectomy
Artery
    Digital 64820
    Radial 64821
    Superficial Palmar Arch 64823
    Ulnar 64822
Cervical 64802
Cervicothoracic 64804
Digital Artery
    with Magnification 64818
Lumbar 64820
Presacral 58410
Thoracic 32664
Thoracolumbar 64809
with Rib Excision 21616

Sympathetic Nerve
Excision 64802-64818
Injection
    Anesthetic 64508, 64520-64530

Sympathins
See Catecholamines

Symphysiotomy
Horseshoe Kidney 50540

Symphysis, Pubic
See Pubic Symphysis

Syncytial Virus, Respiratory
See Respiratory Syncytial Virus

Syndactylism, Toes
See Webbed, Toe

Syndactyly
Repair 26560-26562

Syndesmotomy
See Ligament, Release

Syndrome
Adrenogenital
    See Adrenogenital Syndrome
Ataxia-Telangiectasia
    See Ataxia Telangiectasia
Bloom
    See Bloom Syndrome
Carpal Tunnel
    See Carpal Tunnel Syndrome
Costen's
    See Temporomandibular Joint (TMJ)
Erb -Goldflam
    See Myasthenia Gravis
Ovarian Vein
    See Ovarian Vein Syndrome
Synechiae, Intrauterine
    See Adhesions, Intrauterine
Treacher Collins
    See Treacher-Collins Syndrome
Urethral
    See Urethral Syndrome

Syngesterone
See Progesterone

Synostosis (Cranial)
See Craniosynostosis

Synovectomy
Arthrotomy with
    Glenohumeral Joint 23105
    Sternoclavicular Joint 23106
Elbow 24102
Excision
    Carpometacarpal Joint 26130
    Finger Joint 26135-26140
    Hip Joint 27054
    Interphalangeal Joint 26140
    Knee Joint 27334-27335
    Metacarpophalangeal Joint 26135
    Palm 26145
Wrist 25105, 25118-25119
    Radical 25115-25116

Synovial
Bursa
    See Bursa
Cyst
    See Ganglion
Membrane
    See Synovium
Popliteal Space
    See Baker's Cyst

Synovium
Biopsy
    Carpometacarpal Joint 26100
    Interphalangeal Joint 26110
    Knee Joint 27330
    Metacarpophalangeal Joint
        with Synovial Biopsy 26105
Excision
    Carpometacarpal Joint 26130
    Finger Joint 26135-26140
    Hip Joint 27054
    Interphalangeal Joint 26140
    Knee Joint 27334-27335

Syphilis ab
See Antibody, Treponema Pallidum

Syphilis Test 86592-86593

Syrinx
Spinal Cord
    Aspiration 62268

System
Endocrine
    See Endocrine System
Hemic
    See Hemic System
Lymphatic
    See Lymphatic System
Musculoskeletal
    See Musculoskeletal System
Nervous
    See Nervous System

T

T Cell Leukemia Virus I Antibodies, Adult
See Antibody, HTLV-I

T Cell Leukemia Virus I, Human
See HTLV I

T Cell Leukemia Virus II Antibodies, Human
See Antibody, HTLV-II

T Cell Leukemia Virus II, Human
See HTLV II

T Lymphotropic Virus Type III Antibodies, Human
See Antibody, HIV

T-3
See Triiodothyronine

T-4 ....84436-84439, 86360

T-7 Index
See Thyroxine, Total

T-8
See CD8; T-Cells, Ratio

T-Cell T8 Antigens
See CD8

T-Cells
CD4
    Absolute 86361
Count 86359
Ratio 86360

T-Phyl
See Theophylline

T3 Free
See Triiodothyronine, Free

T4 Molecule
See CD4

T4 Total
See Thyroxine, Total

Taarnhoj Procedure
See Decompression, Gasserian Ganglion, Sensory Root; Section

Tachycardia
Heart
    Recording 93609

Tacrolimus
Drug Assay 80197

Tag, Skin
See Skin, Tags

Tail Bone
Excision 27080
Fracture 27200-27202

Takeuchi Procedure .... .33505

Talectomy
See Astragalectomy

Talotarsal Joint
Dislocation 28570-28575, 28585
   Percutaneous Fixation 28576

Talus
Arthrodesis
   Pantalar .... .28705
   Subtalar .... .28725
   Triple .... .28715
Arthroscopy
   Surgical 29891-29892
Craterization .... .28120
Cyst
   Excision 28100-28103
Diaphysectomy 28120
Excision 28120, 28130
Fracture
   Open Treatment 28445
   Percutaneous Fixation 28436
   with Manipulation 28435-28436
   without Manipulation 28430
Repair
   Osteochondritis Dissecans 29892
   Osteotomy .... .28302
Saucerization .... .28120
Tumor
   Excision 27647, 28100-28103

Tap
Cisternal
   See Cisternal Puncture
Lumbar Diagnostic
   See Spinal Tap

Tarsal
Fracture
   Percutaneous Fixation 28456

Tarsal Bone
See Ankle Bone

Tarsal Joint
See Foot
Arthrodesis 28730-28735, 28740
   with Advancement 28737
   with Lengthening 28737
Craterization .... .28122
Cyst
   Excision 28104-28107
Diaphysectomy 28122
Dislocation 28540-28545, 28555
   Percutaneous Fixation 28545-28546
Excision 28116, 28122
Fracture
   Open Treatment 28465
   with Manipulation 28455-28456
   without Manipulation 28450
Fusion 28730-28735, 28740
   with Advancement 28737
   with Lengthening 28737
Repair .... .28320
   Osteotomy 28304-28305
Saucerization .... .28122
Tumor
   Excision 28104-28107, 28171

Tarsal Strip Procedure 67917-67924

Tarsal Tunnel Release .... .28035

Tarsal Wedge Procedure .67916, 67923

Tarsometatarsal Joint
Arthrodesis 28730-28735, 28740
Arthrotomy 28020, 28050
Dislocation 28600-28605, 28615
   Percutaneous Fixation 28606
Exploration .... .28020
Fusion 28730-28735, 28740
Removal
   Foreign Body 28020
   Loose Body .... .28020
Synovial
   Biopsy 28050
   Excision .... .28070

Tarsorrhaphy .... .67875
Median .... .67880
Severing .... .67710
   with Transposition of Tarsal Plate ..... .67882

Tattoo
Cornea .... .65600
Skin 11920-11922

TB Test
Antigen Response 86480
Skin Test 86580

TBG
See Thyroxine Binding Globulin

TBS
See Bethesda System

TCT
See Thrombin Time

Td Shots
See Tetanus Immunization; Vaccines

Team Conference
Case Management Services 99361-99373

Tear Duct
See Lacrimal Duct

Tear Gland
See Lacrimal Gland

Technique
Pericardial Window
   See Pericardiostomy
Projective
   See Projective Test

Teeth
X-Ray 70300-70320

Telangiectasia
Chromosome Analysis 88248
Injection .... .36468

Telangiectasia, Cerebello-Oculocutaneous
See Ataxia Telangiectasia

Telephone
Case Management Services 99361-99373
Pacemaker Analysis 93733, 93736
Transmission of ECG 93012

Teletherapy
Dose Plan 77305-77321

Temperature Gradient Studies .... .93740

Temporal Arteries
See Artery, Temporal

Temporal Bone
Electromagnetic Bone Conduction Hearing Device
   Implantation/Replacement 69710
   Removal/Repair 69711
Excision .... .69535
Resection .... .69535
Tumor
   Removal .... .69970
Unlisted Services and Procedures 69979

Temporal, Petrous
Excision
   Apex 69530

Temporomandibular Joint (TMJ)
Arthrocentesis .... .20605
Arthrography 70328-70332
   Injection .... .21116
Arthroplasty 21240-21243
Arthroscopy
   Diagnostic .... .29800
   Surgical .... .29804
Arthrotomy .... .21010
Cartilage
   Excision .... .21060
Condylectomy .... .21050
Coronoidectomy .... .21070
Dislocation
   Closed Treatment 21480-21485
   Open Treatment .... .21490
Injection
   Radiologic .... .21116
Magnetic Resonance Imaging (MRI) ..... .70336
Meniscectomy .... .21060
Prostheses
   See Prosthesis, Temporomandibular Joint
Reconstruction
   See Reconstruction, Temporomandibular Joint
X-Ray with Contrast 70328-70332

Tenago Procedure .... .53431

Tendinosuture
See Suture, Tendon

Tendon
Achilles
   See Achilles Tendon
Arm, Upper
   Revision .... .24320
Finger
   Excision .... .26180
Forearm
   Repair 25260-25274
Graft
   Harvesting .... .20924

Insertion
  Biceps Tendon .24342
Lengthening
  Ankle 27685-27686
  Arm, Upper .24305
  Elbow 24305
  Finger 26476, 26478
  Forearm 25280
  Hand .26476, 26478
  Leg, Lower 27685-27686
  Leg, Upper 27393-27395
  Toe 28240
  Wrist 25280
Palm
  Excision 26170
Release
  Arm, Lower 25295
  Arm, Upper 24332
  Wrist 25295
Shortening
  Ankle 27685-27686
  Finger 26477, 26479
  Hand .26477, 26479
  Leg, Lower 27685-27686
Transfer
  Arm, Lower 25310-25312, 25316
  Arm, Upper 24301
  Elbow 24301
  Finger 26497-26498
  Hand .26480-26489
  Leg, Lower 27690-27692
  Leg, Upper 27400
  Pelvis 27098
  Thumb 26490-26492, 26510
  Wrist 25310-25312, 25316
Transplant
  Leg, Upper 27396-27397
Wrist
  Repair 25260-25274

Tendon Origin

Insertion
  Injection 20551

Tendon Pulley Reconstruction of Hand

See Hand, Reconstruction, Tendon Pulley

Tendon Sheath

Arm
  Lower
    Repair 25275
Finger
  Incision 26055
  Incision and Drainage 26020
  Lesion 26160
Foot
  Excision 28086-28088
Hand Lesion 26160
Injection 20550
Palm
  Incision and Drainage 26020
Removal
  Foreign Body 20520-20525
Wrist
  Excision, Radical 25115-25116
  Incision 25000-25001
  Repair 25275

Tenectomy, Tendon Sheath

See Excision, Lesion, Tendon Sheath

Tennis Elbow

Repair 24350-24356

Tenodesis

Biceps Tendon
  at Elbow .24340
  Shoulder .23430
Finger .26471-26474
Wrist 25300-25301

Tenolysis

Ankle 27680-27681
Arm, Lower 25295
Arm, Upper 24332
Finger
  Extensor 26445-26449
  Flexor 26440-26442
Foot 28220-28226
Hand Extensor 26445-26449
  Flexor 26440-26442
Leg, Lower 27680-27681
Wrist 25295

Tenomyotomy

Shoulder 23405-23406

Tenon's Capsule

Injection 67515

Tenoplasty

Anesthesia 01714

Tenorrhaphy

See Suture, Tendon

Tenosuspension

See Tenodesis

Tenosuture

See Suture, Tendon

Tenotomy

Achilles Tendon 27605-27606
Ankle 27605-27606
Arm, Lower 25290
Arm, Upper 24310
Finger 26060, 26455-26460
Foot .28230, 28234
Hand 26450, 26460
Hip
  Iliopsoas Tendon 27005
Hip, Abductor 27006
Hip, Adductor 27000-27003
Leg, Upper 27306-27307, 27390-27392
Toe 28010-28011, 28232-28234, 28240
Wrist 25290

TENS

See Application, Neurostimulation; Physical Medicine/Therapy/Occupational Therapy

Tensilon Test 95857

Tension, Ocular

See Glaucoma

Tentorium Cerebelli

Section 61440

Terman-Merrill Test 96101-96103

Termination, Pregnancy

See Abortion

Test

Antiglobulin
  See Coombs Test
Aphasia
  See Aphasia Testing
Bender Visual-Motor Gestalt
  See Bender-Gestalt Test
Binet
  See Binet Test
Blood
  See Blood Tests
Blood Coagulation
  See Coagulation
Breath
  See Breath Test
Cervical Mucus Penetration
  See Cervical Mucus Penetration Test
Clinical Chemistry
  See Chemistry Tests, Clinical
Complement Fixation
  See Complement, Fixation Test
Exercise
  See Exercise Stress Tests
Fern
  See Smear and Stain, Wet Mount
Fetal, Nonstress
  See Fetal Non-Stress Test
Function, Vestibular
  See Vestibular Function Tests
Gel Diffusion
  See Immunodiffusion
Glucose Tolerance
  See Glucose, Tolerance Test
Hearing
  See Audiologic Function Tests
Hemagglutination Inhibition
  See Hemagglutination Inhibition Test
Ink Blot
  See Inkblot Test
Intelligence
  See Intelligence Test
Lung Function
  See Pulmonology, Diagnostic
Neutralization
  See Neutralization Test
Papanicolaou
  See Pap Smears
Pregnancy
  See Pregnancy Test
Quick
  See Prothrombin Time
Radioimmunosorbent
  See Gammaglobulin, Blood
Rorschach
  See Rorschach Test
Schilling
  See Schilling Test
Skin
  See Skin, Tests
Stanford-Binet
  See Psychiatric Diagnosis
Tuberculin
  See Skin, Tests, Tuberculosis

Test Tube Fertilization
See In Vitro Fertilization

Tester, Color Vision
See Color Vision Examination

Testes
Cryopreservation 89335
Nuclear Medicine
    Imaging 78760-78761
Undescended
    See Testis, Undescended

Testicular Vein
See Spermatic Veins

Testimony, Medical 99075

Testing, Histocompatibility
See Tissue Typing

Testing, Neurophysiologic
Intraoperative 95920

Testing, Neuropsychological 96118-96120
Computer-Assisted 96120

Testing, Range of Motion
See Range of Motion Test

Testis
Abscess
    Incision and Drainage 54700
Biopsy 54500-54505
Excision
    Laparoscopic 54690
    Partial 54522
    Radical 54530-54535
    Simple 54520
Hematoma
    Incision and Drainage 54700
Insertion
    Prosthesis 54660
Lesion
    Excision 54512
Needle Biopsy 54500
Repair
    Injury 54670
    Suspension 54620-54640
    Torsion 54600
Suture
    Injury 54670
    Suspension 54620-54640
Transplantation
    to Thigh 54680
Tumor
    Excision 54530-54535
Undescended
    Exploration 54550-54560
Unlisted Services and Procedures . 54699, 55899

Testosterone 84402
Response 80414
    Stimulation 80414-80415
Total 84403

Testosterone Estradiol Binding Globulin
See Globulin, Sex Hormone Binding

Tetanus 86280
Antibody 86774
Immunoglobulin 90389
Vaccine 90703

Tetrachloride, Carbon
See Carbon Tetrachloride

Tetralogy of Fallot ... 33692-33697, 33924

Thal-Nissen Procedure 43325

Thawing
See Frozen Blood Preparation
Cryopreserved
    Embryo 89352
    Oocytes 89356
    Reproductive Tissue 89354
    Sperm 89353
Previously Frozen Cells 38208-38209

Thawing and Expansion
of Frozen Cell 88241

THBR
See Thyroid Hormone Binding Ratio

Theleplasty
See Nipples, Reconstruction

Theophylline
Assay 80198

Therapeutic
Abortion
    See Abortion, Therapeutic
Apheresis
    See Apheresis, Therapeutic
Drug Assay
    See Drug Assay
Mobilization
    See Mobilization
Photopheresis
    See Photopheresis
Radiology
    See Radiology, Therapeutic

Therapies
Cold
    See Cryotherapy
Exercise
    See Exercise Therapy
Family
    See Psychotherapy, Family
Language
    See Language Therapy
Milieu
    See Environmental Intervention
Occupational
    See Occupational Therapy
Photodynamic
    See Photochemotherapy
Photoradiation
    See Actinotherapy
Physical
    See Physical Medicine/Therapy/Occupational
    Therapy
Speech
    See Speech Therapy

Tocolytic
    See Tocolysis
Ultraviolet
    See Actinotherapy

Therapy
ACE Inhibitor Therapy
    See Performance Measures
Beta Blocker Therapy
    See Performance Measures
Desensitization
    See Allergen Immunotherapy
Hemodialysis
    See Hemodialysis
Hot Pack
    See Hot Pack Treatment
Pharmacologic; for Cessation of Tobacco Use
    See Performance Measures
Radiation
    See Irradiation
Speech
    See Speech Therapy
Statin Therapy, Prescribed
    See Performance Measures

Thermocauterization
Ectropion
    Repair 67922
Lesion
    Cornea 65450

Thermocoagulation
See Electrocautery

Thermogram
Cephalic 93760
Peripheral 93762

Thermographies
See Thermogram

Thermography, Cerebral
See Thermogram, Cephalic

Thermotherapy
Prostate 53850-53853
    Microwave 53850
    Radiofrequency 53852

Thiamine 84425

Thiersch Operation 15050
See Pinch Graft

Thiersch Procedure 46753

Thigh
Fasciotomy 27025
    See Femur; Leg, Upper

Thin Layer Chromatographies
See Chromatography, Thin-Layer

Thiocyanate 84430

Third Disease
See Rubella

Third Opinion
See Confirmatory Consultations

Thompson Procedure .... .27430

Thompson Test
See Smear and Stain, Routine

Thoracectomy
See Thoracoplasty

Thoracentesis 32000-32002

Thoracic
Anterior Ramus
    See Intercostal Nerve
Arteries
    See Artery, Thoracic
Cavity
    See Chest Cavity
Duct
    See Lymphatics
    Cannulation .... .38794
    Ligation .... .38380
        Abdominal Approach .... .38382
        Thoracic Approach .... .38381
    Suture
        Abdominal Approach .... .38382
        Cervical Approach .... .38380
        Thoracic Approach .... .38381
Empyema
    See Abscess, Thorax
Surgery
    Video-Assisted
        See Thoracoscopy
Vertebra
    See Vertebra, Thoracic
Wall
    See Chest Wall

Thoracocentesis
See Thoracentesis

Thoracoplasty .... .32905
with Closure Bronchopleural Fistula ..... .32906

Thoracoscopy
Diagnostic 32601-32606
    with Biopsy .... .32602, 32604, 32606
    without Biopsy .... .32601, 32603, 32605
Surgical 32650-32665
    with Control Traumatic Hemorrhage .. .32654
    with Creation Pericardial Window .... .32659
    with Esophagomyotomy .... .32665
    with Excision Mediastinal Cyst, Tumor
        and/or Mass .... .32662
    with Excision Pericardial Cyst, Tumor
        and/or Mass .... .32661
    with Excision-Plication of Bullae ...... .32655
    with Lobectomy .... .32663
    with Parietal Pleurectomy .... .32656
    with Partial Pulmonary Decortication . .32651
    with Pleurodesis .... .32650
    with Removal Intrapleural Foreign
        Body .... .32653
    with Removal of Clot/Foreign Body .. .32658
    with Sternum Reconstruction ...... .21743
    with Thoracic Sympathectomy ...... .32664
    with Total Pericardiectomy .... .32660
    with Total Pulmonary Decortication . .32652
    with Wedge Resection of Lung ...... .32657

Thoracostomy
Empyema 32035-32036
Tube, with/without Water Seal .... .32020

Thoracotomy
Cardiac Massage .... .32160
for Pacing Cardioverter-Defibrillator
Pads 33245-33246
for Post-Op Complications .... .32120
Hemorrhage .... .32110
Removal
    Bullae .... .32141
    Cyst .... .32140
    Defibrillator .... .33243
    Electrodes .... .33238
    Foreign Body
        Intrapleural .... .32150
        Intrapulmonary .... .32151
    Pacemaker 33236-33237
    with Biopsy 32095-32100
    with Excision-Plication of Bullae .... .32141
    with Lung Repair .... .32110
    with Open Intrapleural Pneumolysis .32124
Transmyocardial Laser Revascularization ..33140-
                                                    33141

Thorax
See Chest; Chest Cavity; Mediastinum
Angiography .... .71275
Bioimpedance .... .93701
Biopsy .... .21550
CT Scan 71250-71275
Incision
    Empyema 32035-32036
    Pneumothorax .... .32020
Incision and Drainage
    Abscess 21501-21502
    Deep .... .21510
    Hematoma 21501-21502
Strapping .... .29200
Tumor
    Excision 21555-21556
    Excision/Resection .... .21557
Unlisted Services and Procedures, Surgery .21899

Three Glass Test
See Urinalysis, Glass Test

Three-Day Measles
See Rubella

Throat
See Pharynx
Abscess
    Incision and Drainage 42700-42725
Biopsy 42800-42806
Hemorrhage 42960-42962
Reconstruction .... .42950
Removal
    Foreign Body .... .42809
Repair
    Pharyngoesophageal .... .42953
    Wound .... .42900
Suture
    Wound .... .42900
Unlisted Services and Procedures .... .42999

Thrombectomy
See Thromboendarterectomy
Aortoiliac Artery 34151-34201
Arteriovenous Fistula
    Graft .... .36870
Axillary Artery .... .34101
Axillary Vein .... .34490
Brachial Artery .... .34101
Bypass Graft
    Other than Hemodialysis Graft or
    Fistula 35875-35876
Carotid Artery .... .34001
Celiac Artery .... .34151
Dialysis Graft
    without Revision .... .36831
Femoral .... .34201
Femoropopliteal Vein 34421-34451
Iliac 34151-34201
Iliac Vein 34401-34451
Innominate Artery 34001-34101
Mesentery Artery .... .34151
Percutaneous
    Coronary Artery .... .92973
    Fluoroscopic Guidance 37184-37188
    Mechanical Arterial 37184-37186
    Mechanical Venous 37187-37188
Peroneal Artery .... .34203
Popliteal Artery .... .34203
Radial Artery .... .34111
Renal Artery .... .34151
Subclavian Artery 34001-34101
Subclavian Vein 34471-34490
Tibial Artery .... .34203
Ulnar Artery .... .34111
Vena Cava 34401-34451
Vena Caval .... .50230

Thrombin Inhibitor I
See Antithrombin III

Thrombin Time 85670-85675

Thrombocyte (Platelet)
See Blood, Platelet

Thrombocyte ab
See Antibody, Platelet

Thromboendarterectomy
See Thrombectomy
Aorta, Abdominal .... .35331
Aortoiliofemoral Artery .... .35363
Axillary Artery .... .35321
Brachial Artery .... .35321
Carotid Artery .... .35301, 35390
Celiac Artery .... .35341
Femoral Artery 35371-35381
Iliac Artery .... .35351, 35361-35363
Iliofemoral Artery .... .35355, 35363
Innominate Artery .... .35311
Mesenteric Artery .... .35341
Peroneal Artery .... .35381
Popliteal Artery .... .35381
Renal Artery .... .35341
Subclavian Artery 35301-35311
Tibial Artery .... .35381
Vertebral Artery .... .35301

Thrombokinase 85260

Thrombolysin
See Plasmin

Thrombolysis
Catheter Exchange
  Intravascular 37209, 75900
Cerebral
  Intravenous Infusion 37195
Coronary Vessels 92975-92977
Cranial Vessels 37195

Thrombolysis Biopsy Intracranial
Arterial Perfusion 61624

Thrombolysis Intracranial 65205
See Ciliary Body; Cornea; Eye, Removal, Foreign
Body; Iris; Lens; Retina; Sclera; Vitreous

Thrombomodulin 85337

Thromboplastin
Inhibition 85705
Inhibition Test 85347
Partial Time 85730-85732

**Thromboplastin Antecedent,
Plasma**
See Plasma Thromboplastin, Antecedent

Thromboplastinogen
See Clotting Factor

Thromboplastinogen B
See Christmas Factor

Thumb
See Phalanx
Amputation 26910-26952
Arthrodesis
  Carpometacarpal Joint 26841-26842
Dislocation
  with Fracture 26645-26650
    Open Treatment 26665
    with Manipulation 26641
Fracture
  with Dislocation 26645-26650
    Open Treatment 26665
Fusion
  in Opposition 26820
Reconstruction
  from Finger 26550
  Opponensplasty 26490-26496
Repair
  Muscle 26508
  Muscle Transfer 26494
  Tendon Transfer 26510
Replantation 20824-20827
Sesamoidectomy 26185
Unlisted Services and Procedures 26989

Thymectomy 60520-60521
Sternal Split/Transthoracic
Approach 60521-60522
Transcervical Approach 60520

Thymotaxin
See Beta-2-Microglobulin

Thymus Gland 60520
Excision 60520-60521

Thyramine
See Amphetamine

Thyrocalcitonin
See Calcitonin

Thyroglobulin 84432
Antibody 86800

Thyroglossal Duct
Cyst
  Excision 60280-60281

Thyroid Gland
Cyst
  Aspiration 60001
  Excision .60200
  Incision and Drainage 60000
  Injection .60001
Excision
  for Malignancy
    Limited Neck Dissection 60252
    Radical Neck Dissection 60254
  Partial 60210-60225
  Secondary 60260
  Total 60240, 60271
    Cervical Approach 60271
    Removal All Thyroid Tissue 60260
    Sternal Split/Transthoracic
    Approach 60270
    Transcervical Approach 60520
Metastatic Cancer
  Nuclear Imaging 78015-78018
Needle Biopsy 60100
Nuclear Medicine
  Imaging .78010
  Imaging for Metastases 78015-78018
  Imaging with Flow 78011
  Imaging with Uptake 78006-78007
  Metastases Uptake 78020
  Uptake 78000-78003
Tumor
  Excision .60200

**Thyroid Hormone Binding
Ratio** 84479

Thyroid Hormone Uptake 84479

**Thyroid Stimulating Hormone
(TSH)** 80418, 80438-80440, 84443

**Thyroid Stimulating Hormone
Receptor ab**
See Thyrotropin Releasing Hormone (TRH)

**Thyroid Stimulating Immune
Globulins** 84445

Thyroid Stimulator, Long Acting
See Thyrotropin Releasing Hormone (TRH)

Thyroid Suppression Test
See Nuclear Medicine, Thyroid, Uptake

Thyroidectomy
Partial 60210-60225
Secondary 60260

Total 60240, 60271
  Cervical Approach 60271
  for Malignancy
    Limited Neck Dissection 60252
    Radical Neck Dissection 60254
  Removal All Thyroid Tissue 60260
  Sternal Split/Transthoracic Approach . .60270

Thyrolingual Cyst
See Cyst, Thyroglossal Duct

Thyrotomy 31300

Thyrotropin Receptor Ab
See Thyrotropin Releasing Hormone (TRH)

**Thyrotropin Releasing Hormone
(TRH)** 80438-80439

Thyroxine
Free 84439
Neonatal .84437
Total 84436
True 84436

Thyroxine Binding Globulin 84442

Tibia
See Ankle
Arthroscopy Surgical 29891-29892
Craterization 27360, 27640
Cyst
  Excision 27635-27638
Diaphysectomy 27360, 27640
Excision 27360, 27640
  Epiphyseal Bar 20150
Fracture
  Arthroscopic Treatment 29855-29856
    Plafond 29892
  Closed Treatment 27824-27825
  Distal 27824-27828
  Intercondylar 27538-27540
  Malleolus 27760-27766, 27808-27814
  Open Treatment 27535-27536,
                          27758-27759, 27826-27828
  Plateau 29855-29856
    Closed Treatment 27530-27536
  Shaft 27752-27759
  with Manipulation 27825
  without Manipulation 27824
Incision 27607
Osteoplasty
  Lengthening 27715
Prophylactic Treatment 27745
Reconstruction 27418
  at Knee 27440-27443, 27446
Repair 27720-27725
  Epiphysis 27477-27485, 27730-27742
  Osteochondritis Dissecans
    Arthroscopy 29892
    Osteotomy 27455-27457, 27705,
                                  27709-27712
  Pseudoarthrosis 27727
Saucerization 27360, 27640
Tumor
  Excision 27635-27638, 27645
X-Ray 73590

Tibial
Arteries
   See Artery, Tibial
Nerve
   Repair/Suture
      Posterior 64840

Tibiofibular Joint
Arthrodesis 27871
Dislocation 27830-27832
Disruption
   Open Treatment 27829
Fusion 27871

TIG
See Immune Globulins, Tetanus

Time
Bleeding
   See Bleeding Time
Prothrombin
   See Prothrombin Time
Reptilase
   See Thrombin Time

Tinnitus
Assessment 92625

Tissue
Culture
   Chromosome Analysis 88230-88239
   Homogenization 87176
   Non-neoplastic Disorder 88230, 88237
   Skin Grafts 15100-15101, 15120-15121
      Harvesting 15040
   Solid Tumor 88239
   Toxin/Antitoxin 87230
   Virus 87252-87253
Enzyme Activity 82657
Examination for Ectoparasites 87220
Examination for Fungi 87220
Expander
   Breast Reconstruction with 19357
   Insertion
      Skin 11960
   Removal
      Skin 11971
   Replacement
      Skin 11970
Grafts
   Harvesting .20926
Granulation
   See Granulation Tissue
Homogenization 87176
Hybridization In Situ 88365-88368
Mucosal
   See Mucosa
Preparation
   Drug Analysis 80103
Skin Harvest for Culture 15040
Soft
   Abscess 20000-20005
Transfer
   Adjacent
      Eyelids .67961
      Skin 14000-14350
   Facial Muscles 15845
   Finger Flap 14350
   Toe Flap 14350

Typing
   HLA Antibodies 86812-86817
   Lymphocyte Culture 86821-86822

Tissue Culture
from Skin Harvest 15040
Skin Grafts 15150-15157, 15340-15366

Tissue Factor
See Thromboplastin

TLC
See Chromatography, Thin-Layer
Screen 84375

TMJ
See Temporomandibular Joint (TMJ)
Prostheses
   See Prosthesis, Temporomandibular Joint

Tobacco
See Performance Measures

Tobramycin
Assay 80200

Tocolysis 59412

Tocopherol 84446

Toe
See Interphalangeal Joint, Toe;
Metatarsophalangeal Joint; Phalanx
Amputation 28810-28825
Capsulotomy 28270-28272
Fasciotomy 28008
Fracture
   See Fracture, Phalanges, Toe
Lesion
   Excision 28092
Reconstruction
   Angle Deformity 28313
   Extra Toes 28344
   Hammertoe 28285-28286
   Macrodactyly 28340-28341
   Syndactyly 28345
   Webbed Toe 28345
Repair
   Bunion 28290-28299
   Muscle 28240
   Tendon 28232-28234, 28240
   Webbed .28280
   Webbed Toe 28345
Tenotomy 28010-28011, 28232-28234
Unlisted Services and Procedures 28899

Toe Flap
Tissue Transfer 14350

Toes
Arthrocentesis 20600
Dislocation
   See Specific Joint
Magnetic Resonance Imaging
(MRI) .73721-73723
Reconstruction
   Extra Digit 26587
Repair
   Extra Digit 26587
   Macrodactylia 26590
Reposition to Hand 26551-26556

Strapping 29550
X-Ray 73660

Tolbutamide Tolerance Test 82953

Tolerance Test
Glucagon 82946
Glucose 82951-82952
   with Tolbutamide 82953
Heparin-Protamine 85530
Insulin 80434-80435
Maltose 82951-82952
Tolbutamide 82953

Tomodensitometries
See CT Scan

Tomographic Scintigraphy, Computed
See Emission Computerized Tomography

Tomographic SPECT
Myocardial Imaging 78469

Tomographies, Computed X-Ray
See CT Scan

Tomography, Computerized Axial
Abdomen
   See Abdomen, CT Scan
Head
   See Head, CT Scan

Tomography, Emission Computed
See Positron Emission Tomography
Single Photon
   See SPECT

Tompkins Metroplasty 58540
See Uterus, Reconstruction

Tongue
Abscess
   Incision and Drainage . .41000-41006, 41015
Biopsy .41100-41105
Cyst
   Incision and Drainage 41000-41006,
                       41015, 60000
Excision
   Complete 41140-41155
   Frenum 41115
   Partial 41120-41135
   with Mouth Resection 41150-41153
   with Radical Neck 41135, 41145,
                      41153-41155
Fixation 41500
Hematoma
   Incision and Drainage . .41000-41006, 41015
Incision
   Frenum 41010
Lesion
   Excision 41110-41114
Reconstruction
   Frenum 41520
Reduction for Sleep Apnea 0088T
Repair
   See Repair, Tongue
   Laceration 41250-41252
   Suture 41510
Suture 41510
Unlisted Services and Procedures 41599

Tonography 92120
with Provocation 92130

Tonometry, Serial 92100

Tonsil, Pharyngeal
See Adenoids

Tonsillectomy 42820-42826

Tonsils
Abscess
    Incision and Drainage 42700
Excision 42825-42826
    Lingual 42870
    Radical 42842-42845
    Tag 42860
    with Adenoids 42820-42821
Lingual
    Destruction 42870
Unlisted Services and Procedures 42999

Topiramate
Assay 80201

Torek Procedure
See Orchiopexy

Torkildsen Procedure 62180

**TORP (Total Ossicular Replacement
Prosthesis)** 69633, 69637

Torsion Swing Test 92546

Torula
See Cryptococcus

Torus Mandibularis
Tumor Excision 21031

Total
Abdominal Hysterectomy
    See Hysterectomy, Abdominal, Total
Bilirubin Level
    See Bilirubin, Total
Catecholamines
    See Catecholamines, Urine
Cystectomy
    See Bladder, Excision, Total
Dacryoadenectomy
    See Dacryoadenectomy, Total
Elbow Replacement
    See Replacement, Elbow, Total
Esophagectomy
    See Esophagectomy, Total
Gastrectomy
    See Excision, Stomach, Total
Hemolytic Complement
    See Complement, Hemolytic, Total
Hip Arthroplasty
    See Hip, Total Replacement
Knee Arthroplasty
    See Prosthesis, Knee
Mastectomies
    See Mastectomy
Ostectomy of Patella
    See Patellectomy
Splenectomy
    See Splenectomy, Total

Touroff Operation 37615
See Ligation, Artery, Neck

Toxicology Screen 80100-80103

Toxin Assay 87230

Toxin, Botulinum
See Chemodenervation

Toxoplasma
Antibody 86777-86778

Trabeculectomies
See Trabeculoplasty

Trabeculectomy ab Externo
in Absence of Previous Surgery 66170
with Scarring Previous Surgery 66172

Trabeculoplasty
by Laser Surgery 65855

Trabeculotomy ab Externo
Eye 65850

Trachea
Aspiration 31720
    Catheter 31720-31725
Catheterization 31700
Dilation 31630-31631, 31636-31638
Endoscopy
    via Tracheostomy 31615
Excision
    Stenosis 31780-31781
Fistula
    with Plastic Repair 31825
    without Plastic Repair 31820
Fracture
    Endoscopy 31630
Incision
    Emergency 31603-31605
    Planned 31600-31601
    with Flaps 31610
Instillation
    Contrast Material 31708
Introduction
    Needle Wire 31730
Puncture
    Aspiration and/or Injection 31612
Reconstruction
    Carina 31766
    Cervical 31750
    Fistula 31755
    Intrathoracic 31760
Repair
    Cervical 31750
    Fistula 31755
    Intrathoracic 31760
    Stoma 31613-31614
Revision
    Stoma
        Scars 31830
Scar
    Revision 31830
Stenosis
    Excision 31780-31781
    Repair 31780-31781

Stoma
    Repair
        with Plastic Repair 31825
        without Plastic Repair 31820
    Revision
        Scars 31830
Tumor
    Excision
        Cervical 31785
        Thoracic 31786
Unlisted Services and Procedures
    Bronchi 31899
Wound
    Suture
        Cervical 31800
        Intrathoracic 31805

Tracheal
Stent
    Placement 31631
Tubes
    See Endotracheal Tube

Trachelectomy 57530
Radical 57531

Tracheloplasty
See Cervicoplasty

Trachelorrhaphy 57720

Tracheo-Esophageal Fistula
See Fistula, Tracheoesophageal

Tracheobronchoscopy
through Tracheostomy 31615

Tracheoplasty
Cervical 31750
Intrathoracic 31760
Tracheopharyngeal Fistulization 31755

Tracheostoma
Revision 31613-31614

Tracheostomy
Emergency 31603-31605
Planned 31600-31601
Revision
    Scar 31830
Surgical Closure
    with Plastic Repair 31825
    without Plastic Repair 31820
Tracheobronchoscopy through 31615
with Flaps 31610

Tracheotomy
Tube Change 31502

Tracking Tests (Ocular) 92545
See Ear, Nose and Throat

Tract, Urinary
See Urinary Tract

Traction Therapy
See Physical Medicine/Therapy/Occupational
Therapy
Manual 97140
Mechanical 97012

Tractotomy
Medulla 61470
Mesencephalon 61480

Training
Activities of Daily Living 97535, 99509
Biofeedback 90901-90911
Cognitive Skills 97532
Community/Work Reintegration 97537
Home Management 97535, 99509
Orthoptic/Pleoptic 92065
Orthotics 97760
Prosthetics 97761
Self Care 97535, 98960-98962, 99509
Sensory Integration 97533
Walking (Physical Therapy) 97116
Wheelchair Management 97542

TRAM Flap
Breast Reconstruction 19367-19369

Trans-Scaphoperilunar
Fracture/Dislocation
   Closed Treatment 25680
   Open Treatment 25685

Transaminase
Glutamic Oxaloacetic 84450
Glutamic Pyruvic 84460

Transcatheter
Biopsy 37200
Closure
  Percutaneous
    Heart 93580-93581
Embolization
  Percutaneous 37204
    Cranial 61624-61626
Occlusion
  Percutaneous 37204
    Cranial 61624-61626
Placement
  Intravascular Stents 0075T-0076T,
           37205-37208, 37215-37216
Therapy
  Embolization 75894
  Infusion 37201-37202, 75896-75898
  Perfusion
    Cranial 61624-61626
  Retrieval 75961

Transcatheter Foreign Body
Retrieval 37203

Transcortin 84449

Transcranial
Doppler Study (TCP) 93886-93893
Stimulation, Motor 95928-95929

Transcutaneous Electric Nerve Stimulation
See Application, Neurostimulation

Transdermal Electrostimulation
See Application, Neurostimulation

Transection
Artery
  Carotid 61610, 61612

Blood Vessel
  Kidney 50100
Brain
  Subpial 61567
Carotid
  with Skull Base Surgery 61609
Nerve 64732-64772
  Vagus 43640-43641
Pulmonary Artery 33922

Transesophageal
Doppler Echocardiography 93312-93318

Transfer
Blastocyst
  See Embryo Transfer
Gamete Intrafallopian
  See GIFT
Jejunum
  with Microvascular Anastomosis
    Free 43496
Preparation
  Embryo 89255
    Cryopreserved 89352
Surgical
  See Transposition
Tendon
  See Tendon, Transfer
Toe to Hand 26551-26556

Transferase
Aspartate Amino 84450
Glutamic Oxaloacetic 84450

Transferrin 84466

Transformation
Lymphocyte 86353

Transfusion
Blood 36430
  Exchange 36450-36455
  Fetal 36460
  Push
    Infant 36440
Blood Parts
  Exchange 36511-36516
Unlisted Services and Procedures 86999
White Blood Cells 86950

Transfusion of, Blood, Autologous
See Autotransfusion

Transluminal
Angioplasty
  Arterial 75962-75968
Atherectomies
  See Artery, Atherectomy
Coronary Balloon Dilatation
  See Percutaneous Transluminal Angioplasty

Transmyocardial Laser Revascularization 33140-33141

Transosteal Bone Plate
Reconstruction
  Mandible 21244

Transpeptidase, Gamma-Glutamyl
See Gamma Glutamyl Transferase

Transplant
See Graft
Bone
  See Bone Graft
Hair
  See Hair, Transplant

Transplantation
See Graft
Allogenic
  See Homograft
Autologous
  See Autograft
Bone Marrow 38240-38242
Cartilage
  Knee
    Allograft 27415, 29867
    Autograft 27412, 29866
Chondrocytes
  Knee 27412
Conjunctiva 65782
Cornea
  Autograft/Homograft
    Lamellar 65710
    Penetrating 65730-65755
    for Aphakia 65750
Eye
  Amniotic Membrane 65780
  Conjunctiva 65782
  Stem Cell 65781
Hair
  Punch Graft 15775-15776
  Strip 15220-15221
Heart 33945
  Allograft Preparation 33933, 33944
Heart-Lung 33935
Heterologous
  See Heterograft
Intestines
  Allograft Preparation 44715-44721
  Allotransplantation 44135-44136
  Donor Enterectomy 44132-44133
  Removal of Allograft 44137
Liver 47135
  Allograft Preparation 47143-47147
  Heterotopic 47136
Lung
  Allograft Preparation ...32855-32856, 33933
  Anesthesia 00580
  Donor Pneumonectomy 32850
  Double, with Cardiopulmonary
    Bypass 32854
  Double, without Cardiopulmonary
    Bypass 32853
  Single, with Cardiopulmonary
    Bypass 32852
  Single, without Cardiopulmonary
    Bypass 32851
Meniscus
  Knee 29868
Muscle
  See Muscle Flaps
Pancreas 48160, 48550, 48554-48556
  Allograft Preparation 48551-48552
Parathyroid 60512

Renal
    Allograft Preparation 50323-50329
    Allotransplantation .... .50360
      with Recipient Nephrectomy .... .50365
    Autotransplantation .... .50380
    Donor Nephrectomy 50300-50320, 50547
    Recipient Nephrectomy .... .50340
    Removal Transplanted Renal Allograft .50370
Skin
    See Dermatology
Stem Cells 38240-38242
    Cell Concentration .... .38215
    Cryopreservation .... .38207
    Harvesting 38205-38206
    Plasma Depletion .... .38214
    Platelet Depletion .... .38213
    Red Blood Cell Depletion .... .38212
    T-Cell Depletion .... .38210
    Thawing .... .38208
    Tumor Cell Depletion .... .38211
    Washing .... .38209
Testis
    to Thigh .... .54680
Tissue, Harvesting
    See Graft, Tissue, Harvesting

Transpleural Thoracoscopy
See Thoracoscopy

Transposition
Arteries
    Carotid .... .33889, 35691, 35694-35695
    Subclavian .... .33889, 35693-35695
    Vertebral 35691-35693
Cranial Nerve .... .64716
Eye Muscles .... .67320
Great Arteries
    Repair 33770-33781
Nerve 64718-64721
Ovary .... .58825
Peripheral Nerve
    Major .... .64856
Vein Valve .... .34510

Transthoracic Echocardiography
See Echocardiography

Transthyretin
See Prealbumin

Transureteroureterostomy ..... .50770

Transurethral Balloon Dilation
Prostatic Urethra .... .52510

Transurethral Fulguration
Postoperative Bleeding .... .52606

Transurethral Procedure
See Specific Procedure
Prostate
    Incision .... .52450
    Resection 52612-52614
    Thermotherapy 53850-53853
      Microwave .... .53850
      Radiofrequency .... .53852

Trapezium
Arthroplasty
    with Implant .... .25445

Travel, Unusual .... .99082

Treacher-Collins Syndrome
Midface Reconstruction 21150-21151

Treatment, Tocolytic
See Tocolysis

Trendelenburg Operation
See Varicose Vein, Removal, Secondary Varicosity

Trephine Procedure
Sinusotomy
    Frontal .... .31070

Treponema Pallidum
Antibody
    Confirmation Test .... .86781
Antigen Detection
    Direct Fluorescence .... .87285

TRH
See Thyrotropin Releasing Hormone (TRH)

Triacylglycerol
See Triglycerides

Triacylglycerol Hydrolase
See Lipase

Tributyrinase
See Lipase

Trichiasis
Repair .... .67825
    Epilation, by Forceps .... .67820
    Epilation, by Other than Forceps ..... .67825
    Incision of Lid Margin .... .67830
      with Free Mucous Membrane Graft .67835

Trichina
See Trichinella

Trichinella
Antibody .... .86784
Trichogram .... .96902

Trichomonas vaginalis
Antigen Detection
    Nucleic Acid .... .87660

Trichrome Stain .... .88313

Tricuspid Valve
Excision .... .33460
Repair 33463-33465
Replacement .... .33465
Repositioning .... .33468

Tridymite
See Silica

Trigeminal Ganglia
See Gasserian Ganglion

Trigeminal Nerve
Destruction 64600-64610
Injection
    Anesthetic .... .64400
    Neurolytic 64600-64610

Trigeminal Tract
Stereotactic
    Create Lesion .... .61791

Trigger Finger Repair .... .26055

Trigger Point
Injection
    One or Two Muscles .... .20552
    Two or More Muscles .... .20553

Triglyceridase
See Lipase

Triglyceride Lipase
See Lipase

Triglycerides .... .84478

Trigonocephaly .... .21175

Triiodothyronine
Free .... .84481
Reverse .... .84482
Total .... .84480
True .... .84480

Triolean Hydrolase
See Lipase

Trioxopurine
See Uric Acid

Tripcellim
See Trypsin

Trisegmentectomy .... .47122

Trocar Biopsy
Bone Marrow .... .38221

Trochanteric Femur Fracture
See Femur, Fracture, Trochanteric

Trophoblastic Tumor GTT
See Hydatidiform Mole

Troponin .... .84484
Qualitative .... .84512
Quantitative .... .84484

Truncal Vagotomies
See Vagotomy, Truncal

Truncus Arteriosus
Repair .... .33786

Truncus Brachiocephalicus
See Artery, Brachiocephalic

Trunk, Brachiocephalic
See Artery, Brachiocephalic

Trypanosomiases
See Trypanosomiasis

Trypanosomiasis .... .86171, 86280

Trypsin
Duodenum .... .84485
Feces 84488-84490

**Trypsin Inhibitor, Alpha
1-Antitrypsin**
See Alpha-1 Antitrypsin

Trypure
See Trypsin

Tsalicylate Intoxication
See Salicylate

TSH
See Thyroid Stimulating Hormone

TSI
See Thyroid Stimulating Immunoglobulin

Tsutsugamushi Disease
See Scrub Typhus

TT
See Thrombin Time

TT-3
See Triiodothyronine, True

TT-4
See Thyroxine, True

Tuba Auditoria (Auditiva)
See Eustachian Tube

Tubal Embryo Stage Transfer
See Embryo Transfer

Tubal Ligation 58600
Laparoscopic 58670
with Cesarean Delivery 58611

Tubal Occlusion
See Fallopian Tube
with Cesarean Delivery
   See Fallopian Tube, Occlusion; Occlusion
   Create Lesion
      See Fallopian Tube, Occlusion; Occlusion,
      Fallopian Tube

Tubal Pregnancy 59121
with Salpingectomy and/or
Oophorectomy 59120

Tube Change
Tracheotomy 31502

Tube Placement
Endoscopic
   Bile Duct, Pancreatic Duct 43268
   Nasobiliary, Nasopancreatic
     for Drainage 43267
Gastrostomy Tube 43750
Nasogastric Tube 43752
Orogastric Tube 43752

Tube, Fallopian
See Fallopian Tube

Tubectomy
See Excision, Fallopian Tube

Tubed Pedicle Flap
Formation 15570-15576

Tubercle Bacilli
Culture 87116

Tubercleplasty
Tibia
   Anterior 27418

Tuberculin Test
See Skin, Tests, Tuberculosis

Tuberculosis
Antigen Response Test 86480
Culture 87116
Skin Test 86580

Tuberculosis Vaccine
(BCG) 90585-90586

Tubes
Endotracheal
   See Endotracheal Tube
Gastrostomy
   See Gastrostomy Tube

Tudor 'Rabbit Ear'
See Urethra, Repair

Tuffier Vaginal Hysterectomy
See Hysterectomy, Vaginal

Tumor
See Craniopharyngioma
Abdomen
   Destruction/Excision 49200-49201
Abdominal Wall
   Excision 22900
Acetabulum
   Excision 27076
Ankle 27615-27619
Arm, Lower 25075-25077
Arm, Upper
   Excision 24075-24077
Back/Flank
   Excision 21930
   Radical Resection 21935
Bile Duct
   Destruction 43272
   Extrahepatic 47711
   Intrahepatic 47712
Bladder 52234-52240
   Excision 51530, 52355
Bone
   Ablation 20982
Brain 61510
   Excision 61518, 61520-61521,
          61526-61530, 61545, 62164
Breast
   Excision 19120-19126
Bronchi
   Excision 31640
Calcaneus 28100-28103
   Excision 27647
Carpal 25130-25136
Cheekbone 21030, 21034
Chest Wall
   Excision 19260-19272
Clavicle
   Excision 23140, 23200
   with Allograft 23146
   with Autograft 23145
Coccyx 49215
Colon
   Destruction 44393, 45383
Cranial Bone
   Reconstruction 21181-21184
Destruction
   Chemosurgery 17304-17310
   Urethra 53220

Ear, Middle
   Extended 69554
   Transcanal 69550
   Transmastoid 69552
Elbow
   Excision 24075-24077
Esophagus
   Ablation 43228
Excision
   Femur 27355-27358
Facial Bone 21029-21030, 21034
Fallopian Tube
   Resection 58950, 58952-58956
Femoral 27355-27358
Femur 27065-27067
   Excision 27365
Fibroid
   See Leiomyomata
Fibula 27635-27638
   Excision 27646
Finger
   Excision 26115-26117
Foot 28043-28046
Forearm
   Radical Resection 25077
Gastrostomy
   See Lesion
Gums
   Excision 41825-41827
Hand
   Excision 26115-26117
Heart
   Excision 33120-33130
Hip 27047-27049, 27065-27067
   Excision 27075-27076
Humerus
   Excision 23150, 23220-23222, 24110
   with Allograft 23156, 24116
   with Autograft 23155, 24115
Ileum 27065-27067
Immunoassay for Antigen 86294, 86316
   CA 125 86304
   CA 15-3 86300
   CA 19-9 86301
Innominate
   Excision 27077
Intestines, Small
   Destruction 44369
Ischial
   Excision 27078-27079
Kidney
   Ablation
     Cryotherapy 0135T
     Radiofrequency 50592
   Excision 50562, 52355
Knee
   Excision 27327-27329, 27365
Lacrimal Gland
   Excision
     Frontal Approach 68540
     with Osteotomy 68550
Larynx
   Excision 31300
   Endoscopic 31540-31541, 31578
   Incision 31300
Leg, Lower 27615-27619

Leg, Upper
  Excision 27327-27329
Localization
  Nuclear Medicine 78800-78804
Mandible 21044-21047
Maxilla 21030, 21034, 21048-21049
Maxillary Torus Palatinus 21032
Mediastinal
  Excision .39220
Mediastinum 32662
Meningioma 61512
  Excision .61519
Metacarpal 26200-26205, 26250-26255
Metatarsal 28104-28107
  Excision .28173
Neck
  Excision 21555-21556
  Radical Resection 21557
Olecranon
  Excision .24120
Olecranon Process
  with Allograft
    Excision 24126
  with Autograft
    Excision 24125
Ovary
  Resection 58950-58956
Pancreatic Duct
  Destruction 43272
Parotid Gland
  Excision 42410-42426
Pelvis .27047-27049
Pericardial
  Endoscopic 32661
  Excision .33050
Peritoneum
  Resection 58950-58956
Phalanges
  Finger 26210-26215, 26260-26262
  Toe 28108
    Excision 28175
Pituitary Gland
  Excision 61546-61548, 62165
Positron Emission Tomography
(PET) 78811-78816
Pubis .27065-27067
Radiation Therapy 77295
Radius 25120-25126, 25170
  Excision .24120
  with Allograft
    Excision 24126
  with Autograft
    Excision 24125
Rectum
  Destruction 45190, 45320, 46937-46938
  Excision 45160-45170
Resection
  Face 21015
  Scalp 21015
  with Cystourethroscopy 52355
Retroperitoneal
  Destruction/Excision 49200-49201
Sacrum 49215
Scapula
  Excision 23140, 23210
    with Allograft 23146
    with Autograft 23145

Shoulder
  Excision 23075-23077
Skull
  Excision .61500
Soft Tissue
  Elbow
    Excision 24075
  Finger
    Excision 26115
  Forearm
    Radical Resection 25077
  Hand
    Excision 26115
  Wrist
    Excision 25075
    Radical Resection 25077
Spinal Cord
  Excision 63275-63290
Stomach
  Excision 43610-43611
Talus 28100-28103
  Excision .27647
Tarsal 28104-28107
  Excision .28171
Temporal Bone
  Removal .69970
Testis
  Excision 54530-54535
Thorax
  Excision 21555-21556
  Radical Resection 21557
Thyroid
  Excision .60200
Tibia 27365, 27635-27638
  Excision .27645
Torus Mandibularis 21031
Trachea
  Excision
    Cervical 31785
    Thoracic 31786
Ulna 25120-25126, 25170
  Excision .24120
  with Allograft
    Excision 24126
  with Autograft
    Excision 24125
Ureter
  Excision .52355
Urethra 52234-52240, 53220
  Excision .52355
Uterus
  Excision 58140-58146
Vagina
  Excision .57135
Vertebra
  Additional Segment
    Excision 22116
  Cervical
    Excision 22100
  Lumbar 22102
  Thoracic
    Excision 22101
Wrist 25075-25077, 25135-25136
  Radical Resection 25077

Tunica Vaginalis
Hydrocele
  Aspiration 55000
  Excision 55040-55041
  Repair 55060

Turbinate
Excision 30130-30140
Fracture
  Therapeutic 30930
Injection 30200
Submucous Resection
  Nose Excision 30140

Turbinate Mucosa
Cauterization 30801-30802

Turcica, Sella
See Sella Turcica

Turnbuckle Jacket 29020-29025
Removal 29715

TURP
See Prostatectomy, Transurethral

Tylectomy
See Breast, Excision, Lesion

Tylenol
Urine 82003

Tympanic Membrane
Create Stoma 69433-69436
Incision 69420-69421
Reconstruction 69620
Repair 69450, 69610

Tympanic Nerve
Excision 69676

Tympanolysis 69450

Tympanomastoidectomy
See Tympanoplasty

Tympanometry 92567
See Audiologic Function Tests

Tympanoplasty
See Myringoplasty
Radical or Complete 69645
  with Ossicular Chain Reconstruction . .69646
with Antrotomy or Mastoidotomy 69635
  with Ossicular Chain Reconstruction . .69636
    and Synthetic Prosthesis 69637
with Mastoidectomy 69641
  with Intact or Reconstructed Wall 69643
    and Ossicular Chain Reconstruction .69644
  with Ossicular Chain Reconstruction . .69642
without Mastoidectomy 69631
  with Ossicular Chain Reconstruction . .69632
    and Synthetic Prosthesis 69633

Tympanostomy 69433-69436

Tympanotomy
See Myringotomy

Typhoid Vaccine 90690-90693
AKD 90693
Oral 90690
Polysaccharide 90691

Typhus
Endemic
    See Murine Typhus
Mite-Borne
    See Scrub Typhus
Sao Paulo
    See Rocky Mountain Spotted Fever
Tropical
    See Scrub Typhus

Typing, Blood
See Blood Typing

Typing, HLA
See HLA Typing

Typing, Tissue
See Tissue Typing

Tyrosine 84510

Tzank Smear 87207

U

Uchida Procedure
See Tubal Ligation

UDP Galactose Pyrophosphorylase
See Galactose-1-Phosphate, Uridyl Transferase

UFR
See Uroflowmetry

Ulcer
Anal
    See Anus, Fissure
Decubitus
    See Debridement; Pressure Ulcer (Decubitus);
    Skin Graft and Flap
Pinch Graft 15050
Pressure 15920-15999
Stomach
    Excision 43610

Ulcerative, Cystitis
See Cystitis, Interstitial

Ulna
See Arm, Lower; Elbow; Humerus; Radius
Arthrodesis
    Radioulnar Joint
        with Resection 25830
Arthroplasty
    with Implant 25442
Centralization or Wrist 25335
Craterization 24147, 25150-25151
Cyst
    Excision 24125-24126, 25120-25126
Diaphysectomy 24147, 25150-25151
Excision 24147
    Abscess 24138
    Complete 25240
    Epiphyseal Bar 20150
    Partial 25145-25151, 25240

Fracture
    Closed Treatment 25530-25535
    Olecranon 24670-24675
        Open Treatment 24685
    Open Treatment 25545
    Shaft 25530-25545
        Open Treatment 25574
    Styloid
        Closed Treatment 25650
        Open Treatment 25652
        Percutaneous Fixation 25651
    with Dislocation
        Closed Treatment 24620
        Open Treatment 24635
    with Manipulation 25535
    with Radius 25560-25565
        Open Treatment 25575
    without Manipulation 25530
Incision and Drainage 25035
Osteoplasty 25390-25393
Prophylactic Treatment 25491-25492
Reconstruction
    Radioulnar 25337
Repair
    Epiphyseal Arrest 25450-25455
    Malunion or Nonunion 25400, 25415
    Osteotomy 25360, 25370-25375
        and Radius 25365
    with Graft 25405, 25420-25426
Saucerization 24147, 25150-25151
Sequestrectomy 24138, 25145
Tumor
    Cyst 24120
    Excision ..24125-24126, 25120-25126, 25170

Ulnar Arteries
See Artery, Ulnar

Ulnar Nerve
Decompression 64718
Neuroplasty 64718-64719
Reconstruction 64718-64719
Release 64718-64719
Repair/Suture
    Motor 64836
Transposition 64718-64719

Ultrasonic
See Ultrasound

Ultrasonic Cardiography
See Echocardiography

Ultrasonic Procedure 52325

Ultrasonography
See Echography

Ultrasound
See Echocardiography; Echography
3D Rendering 76376-76377
Abdomen 76700-76705
Arm 76880
Artery
    Intracranial 93886-93893
    Middle Cerebral 76821
    Umbilical 76820
Bladder 51798
Bone Density Study 76977
Breast 76645

Bronchi
    Endoscopy 31620
Chest 76604
Colon
    Endoscopic 45391-45392
Colon-Sigmoid
    Endoscopic 45341-45342
Drainage
    Abscess 75989
Echoencephalography
    See Echoencephalography
Esophagus
    Endoscopy 43231-43232
Eye 76510-76513
    Arteries 93875
    Biometry 76516-76519
    Foreign Body 76529
    Pachymetry 76514
Fetus 76818-76828
Follow-Up 76970
for Physical Therapy 97035
Gastrointestinal 76975
Gastrointestinal, Upper
    Endoscopic 43237-43238, 43242, 43259
Guidance
    Amniocentesis 59001, 76946
    Amnioinfusion 59070
    Arteriovenous Fistulae 76936
    Chorionic Villus Sampling 76945
    Cryosurgery 55873
    Drainage
        Fetal Fluid 59074
    Endometrial Ablation 58356
    Fetal Cordocentesis 76941
    Fetal Transfusion 76941
    Heart Biopsy 76932
    Needle Biopsy 43232, 43238, 43242,
                         45342, 45392, 76942
    Occlusion
        Umbilical Cord 59072
    Ova Retrieval 76948
    Pericardiocentesis 76930
    Pseudoaneurysm 76936
    Radiation Therapy 76950
    Radioelement 76965
    Shunt Placement
        Fetal 59076
    Thoracentesis 76942
    Tissue Ablation 76940
    Vascular Access 76937
Head 76506, 76536
Heart
    Fetal 76825
Hips
    Infant 76885-76886
Hysteronsonography 76831
Intraoperative 76986
Intravascular
    Intraoperative 37250-37251
Kidney 76770, 76778
Leg 76880
Neck 76536
Non-Coronary
    Intravascular 75945-75946
Pelvis 76856-76857
Pregnant Uterus 76801-76817
Prostate 76873

Rectal 76872-76873
Retroperitoneal 76770-76775
Scrotum 76870
Sonohysterography 76831
Spine 76800
Stimulation to Aid Bone Healing 20979
Umbilical Artery 76820
Unlisted Services and Procedures 76999
Uterus
    Tumor Ablation 0071T-0072T
Vagina 76830

Ultraviolet Light Therapy
Dermatology
    Ultraviolet A 96912
    Ultraviolet B 96910
for Dermatology 96900
for Physical Medicine 97028

Umbilectomy 49250

Umbilical
Artery Ultrasound 76820
Hernia
    See Omphalocele
Vein Catheterization
    See Catheterization, Umbilical Vein

Umbilical Cord
Occlusion 59072

Umbilicus
Excision 49250
Repair
    Hernia 49580-49587
    Omphalocele 49600-49611

Undescended Testicle
See Testis, Undescended

Unfertilized Egg
See Ova

Unguis
See Nails

Unilateral Simple Mastectomy
See Mastectomy

Unlisted Services and Procedures 99499, 99600
Abdomen 22999, 49329, 49999
Allergy/Immunology 95199
Anal 46999
Anesthesia 01999
Arm 25999
Arthroscopy 29999
Autopsy 88099
Bile Duct 47999
Bladder 51999
Brachytherapy 77799
Breast 19499
Bronchi 31899
Cardiac 33999
Cardiovascular Studies 93799
Casting 29799
Cervix 58999
Chemistry Procedure 84999
Chemotherapy 96549
Chest 32999
Coagulation 85999

Colon 44799
Conjunctiva Surgery 68399
Craniofacial 21299
CT Scan 76497
Cytogenetic Study 88299
Cytopathology 88199
Dermatology 96999
Dialysis 90999
Diaphragm 39599
Ear
    External 69399
    Inner 69949
    Middle 69799
Endocrine System 60699
Epididymis 55899
Esophagus 43289, 43499
Evaluation and Management Services 99499
Eye Muscle 67399
Eye Surgery
    Anterior Segment 66999
    Posterior Segment 67299
Eyelid 67999
Fluoroscopy 76496
Forearm 25999
Gallbladder 47999
Gastroenterology Test 91299
Gum 41899
Hand 26989
Hemic System 38999
Hepatic Duct 47999
Hip Joint 27299
Home Services 99600
Hysteroscopy 58579
Immunization 90749
Immunology 86849
Infusion 90779
Injection 90779
Injection of Medication 90779
Intestine 44238, 44799
Kidney 49659
Lacrimal System 68899
Laparoscopy 38129, 38589, 43289, 43659,
            44238, 44979, 47379, 47579, 49329,
            49659, 50549, 50949, 54699, 55559,
            58578, 58679, 59898, 60659
Larynx 31599
Lip 40799
Liver 47379, 47399
Lungs 32999
Lymphatic System 38999
Magnetic Resonance 76498
Maxillofacial 21299
Maxillofacial Prosthetics 21089
Meckel's Diverticulum 44899
Mediastinum 39499
Mesentery Surgery 44899
Microbiology 87999
Mouth 40899, 41599
Musculoskeletal 25999, 26989
Musculoskeletal Surgery
    Abdominal Wall 22999
    Neck 21899
    Spine 22899
    Thorax 21899
Musculoskeletal System 20999
    Ankle 27899
    Arm, Upper 24999
    Elbow 24999

Head 21499
Knee 27599
Leg, Lower 27899
Leg, Upper 27599
Necropsy 88099
Nervous System Surgery 64999
Neurology/Neuromuscular Testing 95999
Nose 30999
Nuclear Medicine 78999
    Blood 78199
    Bone 78399
    Endocrine System 78099
    Genitourinary System 78799
    Heart 78499
    Hematopoietic System 78199
    Lymphatic System 78199
    Musculoskeletal System 78399
    Nervous System 78699
    Therapeutic 79999
Obstetrical Care 59898-59899
Omentum 49329, 49999
Ophthalmology 92499
Orbit 67599
Otorhinolaryngology 92700
Ovary 58679, 58999
Oviduct 58679, 58999
Palate 42299
Pancreas Surgery 48999
Pathology 89240
Pelvis 27299
Penis 55899
Peritoneum 49329, 49999
Pharynx 42999
Physical Therapy 97039, 97139, 97799
Pleura 32999
Pressure Ulcer 15999
Preventive Medicine 99429
Prostate 55899
Psychiatric 90899
Pulmonology 94799
Radiation Physics 77399
Radiation Therapy 77499
    Planning 77299
Radiology, Diagnostic 76499
Radionuclide Therapy 79999
Radiopharmaceutical Therapy 79999
Rectum 45499, 45999
Salivary Gland 42699
Scrotum 55899
Seminal Vesicle 55899
Shoulder Surgery 23929
Sinuses 31299
Skin 17999
Special Services and Reports 99199
Spine 22899
Stomach 43659, 43999
Strapping 29799
Surgical Pathology 88399
Temporal Bone 69979
Testis 54699, 55899
Throat 42999
Tongue 41599
Tonsil/Adenoid 42999
Toxoid 90749
Trachea 31899
Transfusion 86999
Ultrasound 76999
Ureter 50949

Urinary System 53899
Uterus 58578-58579, 58999
Uvula 42299
Vaccine 90749
Vagina 58999
Vas Deferens 55899
Vascular 37799
Vascular Endoscopy 37501
Vascular Injection 36299
Vascular Studies 93799
Wrist 25999

Unna Paste Boot 29580
Removal 29700

UPP
See Urethra Pressure Profile

Upper
Digestive System Endoscopy
   See Endoscopy, Gastrointestinal, Upper
Extremity
   See Arm, Upper; Elbow; Humerus
Gastrointestinal Bleeding
   See Gastrointestinal, Upper, Hemorrhage
Gastrointestinal Endoscopy, Biopsy
   See Biopsy
   Planning
      See Biopsy, Gastrointestinal, Upper
      Endoscopy; Endoscopy, Gastrointestinal
GI Tract
   See Gastrointestinal Tract, Upper

Urachal Cyst
See Cyst, Urachal

Urea Breath Test 78267-78268, 83014

Urea Nitrogen
See Blood Urea Nitrogen
Clearance 84545
Quantitative 84520
Semiquantitative 84525
Urine 84540

Urea Nitrogen, Blood
See Blood Urea Nitrogen

Urecholine Supersensitivity Test
See Cystometrogram

Ureter
Anastomosis
   to Bladder 50780-50785
   to Colon 50810-50815
   to Intestine 50800, 50820-50825
   to Kidney 50740-50750
   to Ureter 50760-50770
Biopsy 50955-50957, 50974-50976, 52007
Catheterization 52005
Continent Diversion 50825
Creation
   Stoma 50860
Destruction
   Endoscopic 50957, 50976
Dilation 52341-52342, 52344-52345
   Endoscopic 50553, 50572, 50953, 50972
Endoscopy
   Biopsy 50955-50957, 50974-50976,
                 52007, 52354
   Catheterization 50953, 50972, 52005

Destruction 50957, 50976, 52354
Dilation 52341-52342, 52344-52345
Excision
   Tumor 52355
Exploration 52351
Injection of Implant Material 52327
Insertion
   Stent 50947, 52332-52334
Lithotripsy 52353
Manipulation of Ureteral Calculus 52330
Removal
   Calculus 50961, 50980, 52320-52325,
                     52352
   Foreign Body 50961, 50980
Resection 52355
via Incision 50970-50980
via Stoma 50951-50961
Exploration 50600
Incision and Drainage 50600
Injection
   Drugs 50391
   Radiologic 50684, 50690
Insertion
   Catheter 50393
   Stent 50393, 50688, 50947, 52332-52334
   Tube 50688
Instillation
   Drugs 50391
Lesion
   Destruction 52354
Lithotripsy 52353
Lysis
   Adhesions 50715-50725
Manometric Studies
   Pressure 50686
Meatotomy 52290
Nuclear Medicine
   Reflux Study 78740
Postcaval
   See Retrocaval Ureter
Reconstruction 50700
   with Intestines 50840
Reflux Study 78740
Reimplantation 51565
Removal
   Anastomosis 50830
   Calculus 50610-50630, 50961,
           51060-51065, 52320-52325
   Foreign Body 50961
   Stent 50382-50387
Repair 50900
   Anastomosis 50740-50825
   Continent Diversion 50825
   Deligation 50940
   Fistula 50920-50930
   Lysis Adhesions 50715-50725
   Ureterocele 51535
   Ectopic 52301
   Orthotopic 52300
   Urinary Undiversion 50830
Replacement
   Stent 50382, 50387
   with Intestines 50840
Resection 52355
Revision
   Anastomosis 50727-50728

Stent
   Change 50688
   Insertion 50688
Suture 50900
   Deligation 50940
   Fistula 50920-50930
Tube
   Change 50688
   Insertion 50688
Tumor Resection 52355
Unlisted Services and Procedures 50949,
                     53899
X-Ray with Contrast
   Guide Catheter 74480
   Guide Dilation 74485

Ureteral
Catheterization
   See Catheterization, Ureter
Guide Wire Insertion 52334
Meatotomy
   See Meatotomy, Ureteral
Splinting 50400-50405
Stent Insertion 52332

Ureterectomy 50650-50660
Partial 50220, 50546
Total 50548

Ureterocalycostomy 50750

Ureterocele
Excision 51535
Fulguration
   Ectopic 52301
   Orthotopic 52300
Incision 51535
Repair 51535
Resection
   Ectopic 52301
   Orthotopic 52300

Ureterocolon Conduit 50815

Ureteroenterostomy 50800
Revision 50830

Ureterography
Injection Procedure 50684

Ureteroileal Conduit 50820
Cystectomy 51590
Removal 50830

Ureterolithotomy 50610-50630
Laparoscopy 50945
Transvesical 51060

Ureterolysis
for Ovarian Vein Syndrome 50722
for Retrocaval Ureter 50725
for Retroperitoneal Fibrosis 50715

Ureteroneocystostomy ...50780-50785,
              50830, 51565
Laparoscopic 50947-50948

Ureteroplasty 50700

Ureteropyelography 50951, 52005
Injection Procedure 50684, 50690

Ureteropyelostomy 50740

Ureteroscopy
Dilation
   Intra-Renal Stricture 52346
   Ureter 52344-52345
Third Stage with Cystourethroscopy 52351
   Biopsy 52354
   Destruction 52354
   Lithotripsy 52353
   Removal
      Calculus 52352
   Tumor Excision 52355

Ureterosigmoidostomy 50810
Revision 50830

Ureterostomy 50860, 50951
Injection Procedure 50684
Manometric Studies 50686

Ureterostomy Stent
Change 50688

Ureterostomy Tube
Change 50688

Ureterotomy 50600
Insertion Indwelling Stent 50605

Ureteroureterostomy 50760-50770,
                              50830

Urethra
Abscess
   Incision and Drainage 53040
Adhesions
   Lysis 53500
Artificial Sphincter
   Repair 53449
Biopsy 52204, 53200
Destruction 52214-52224
Dilation 52260-52265, 53600-53621
   General 53665
   Suppository and/or Instillation ...53660-53661
Diverticulum
   See Urethral Diverticulum
Drainage
   Extravasation 53080-53085
Endoscopy 52000
   Biopsy 52204, 52354
   Catheterization 52010
   Destruction 52354, 52400
   Evacuation
      Clot 52001
   Excision
      Tumor 52355
   Exploration 52351
   Incision
      Ejaculatory Duct 52402
   Injection of Implant Material 51715
   Lithotripsy 52353
   Removal
      Calculus 52352
   Resection
      Ejaculatory Duct 52402
   Vasectomy 52402
   Vasotomy 52402

Excision
   Diverticulum 53230-53235
   Total
      Female 53210
      Male 53215
Incision 53000-53010
   Meatus 53020-53025
Incision and Drainage 53060
Insertion
   Stent 0084T, 52282
Lesion
   Destruction 53265
   Excision 53260
Paraurethral Gland
   Incision and Drainage 53060
Polyp
   Destruction 53260
   Excision 53260
Pressure Profile 51772
Prolapse
   Destruction 53275
   Excision 53275
   Repair 53275
Prostate
   Transurethral Balloon Dilation 52510
Radiotracer 52250
Reconstruction 53410-53440, 53445
   and Bladder 51800-51820
   Complications 54340-54348
   Hypospadias
      One Stage 54322-54328
      Second Stage 54308-54316
      Third Stage 54318
   Meatus 53450-53460
Removal
   Calculus 52310-52315
   Foreign Body 52310-52315
   Sling 53442
   Urethral Stent 52310-52315
Repair
   Diverticulum 53240, 53400-53405
   Fistula ...45820-45825, 53400-53405, 53520
   Sphincter 57220
   Stricture 53400-53405
   Urethrocele 57230
   Wound 53502-53515
Skene's Gland
   Incision and Drainage 53060
Sphincter 52277
   Electromyography 51784-51785
      Needle 51785
   Insertion
      Prosthesis 53444
   Reconstruction 53445
   Removal
      Prosthesis 53446-53447
   Repair
      Prosthesis 53449
   Replacement
      Prosthesis 53448
Suture
   Fistula 45820-45825, 53520
   to Bladder 51840-51841
   Wound 53502-53515
Tumor
   Destruction 53220
   Excision 53220
Unlisted Services and Procedures 53899

Urethrocystography 74450-74455
Urethrotomy 52270-52276
X-Ray with Contrast 74450-74455

Urethral
Diverticulum
   Marsupialization 53240
Meatus, Dorsal
   See Epispadias
Sphincter
   Biofeedback Training 90911
   Insertion
      Prosthesis 53444
   Removal
      Prosthesis 53446-53447
   Replacement
      Prosthesis 53448
Stenosis
   Dilation 52281
Stent
   Insertion 0084T, 52282
   Removal
      Bladder 52310-52315
      Urethra 52310-52315
Stricture
   Dilation 52281, 53600-53621
   Injection
      Steroids 52283
Syndrome
   Cystourethroscopy 52285

Urethrectomy
Total
   Female 53210
   Male 53215

Urethrocele
See Urethra, Prolapse

Urethrocystography 74450-74455
Contrast and/or Chain 51605
Retrograde 51610
Voiding 51600

Urethrocystopexy
See Vesicourethropexy

Urethromeatoplasty 53450-53460

Urethropexy 51840-51841

Urethroplasty 46744-46746
First Stage 53400
One Stage
   Hypospadias 54322-54328
Reconstruction
   Female Urethra 53430
   Male Anterior Urethra 53410
   Prostatic/Membranous Urethra
      First Stage 53420
      One Stage 53415
      Second Stage 53425
Second Stage 53405
   Hypospadias 54308-54316
Third Stage
   Hypospadias 54318

Urethrorrhaphy 53502-53515

Urethroscopy
See Endoscopy, Urethra

Urethrostomy 53000-53010

Urethrotomy 53000-53010
Direct Vision
 with Cystourethroscopy 52276
Internal 52601, 52647-52648
with Cystourethroscopy
 Female 52270
 Male 52275

Uric Acid
Blood 84550
Other Source 84560
Urine 84560

Uridyltransferase, Galactose-1-Phosphate
See Galactose-1-Phosphate, Uridyl Transferase

Uridylyltransferase, Galactosephosphate
See Galactose-1-Phosphate, Uridyl Transferase

Urinalysis 0041T, 81000-81099
Automated 81001, 81003
Glass Test 81020
Microalbumin 82043-82044
Microscopic 81015
Pregnancy Test 81025
Qualitative 81005
Routine 81002
Screen 81007
Semiquantitative 0041T, 81005
Unlisted Services and Procedures 81099
Volume Measurement 81050
without Microscopy 81002

Urinary Bladder
See Bladder

Urinary Catheter Irrigation
See Irrigation, Catheter

Urinary Concentration Test
See Water Load Test

Urinary Sphincter, Artificial
See Prosthesis, Urethral Sphincter

Urinary Tract
X-Ray with Contrast 74400-74425

Urine
Albumin
 See Albumin, Urine
Blood
 See Blood, Urine
Colony Count 87086
Pregnancy Test 81025
Tests 81001

Urobilinogen
Feces 84577
Urine 84578-84583

Urodynamic Tests
Bladder Capacity
 Ultrasound 51798
Cystometrogram 51725-51726
Electromyography Studies
 Needle 51785

Residual Urine
 Ultrasound 51798
Stimulus Evoked Response 51792
Urethra Pressure Profile 51772
Uroflowmetry 51736-51741
Voiding Pressure Studies
 Bladder 51795
 Intra-Abdominal 51797

Uroflowmetry 51736-51741

Urography
Antegrade 74425
Infusion 74410-74415
Intravenous 74400-74415
Retrograde 74420

Uroporphyrin 84120

Urothromboplastin
See Thromboplastin

Uterine
Adhesion
 See Adhesions, Intrauterine
Cervix
 See Cervix
Endoscopies
 See Endoscopy, Uterus
Haemorrhage
 See Hemorrhage, Uterus

Uterus
Ablation
 Endometrium 58353-58356
 Tumor
  Ultrasound, Focused 0071T-0072T
Biopsy
 Endometrium 58100-58110
 Endoscopic 58558
Catheterization
 X-Ray 58340
Chromotubation 58350
Curettage 58356
 Postpartum 59160
Dilation and Curettage 58120
 Postpartum 59160
Ectopic Pregnancy
 Interstitial
  Partial Resection Uterus 59136
  Total Hysterectomy 59135
Endoscopy
 Endometrial Ablation 58563
 Exploration 58555
 Surgery 58558-58565
 Treatment 58558-58565
Excision
 Laparoscopic 58550
 Partial 58180
 Radical 58210, 58285
 Removal of Tubes and/or
 Ovaries 58262-58263, 58291-58293, 58552, 58554
 Total 58150-58152, 58200, 58953-58956
 Vaginal 58260-58270, 58290-58294, 58550-58554
  with Colpectomy 58275-58280
  with Colpo-Urethrocystopexy 58267
  with Repair of Enterocele 58270, 58294

Hemorrhage
 Postpartum 59160
Hydatidiform Mole
 Excision 59100
Hydrotubation 58350
Hysterosalpingography 74740
Incision
 Remove Lesion 59100
Insertion
 Heyman Capsule
  for Brachytherapy 58346
 Intrauterine Device (IUD) 58300
 Tandem
  for Brachytherapy 57155
Laparoscopy 58578
Lesion
 Excision 58545-58546, 59100
Reconstruction 58540
Removal
 Intrauterine Device (IUD) 58301
Repair
 Fistula 51920-51925
 Rupture 58520, 59350
 Suspension 58400
  with Presacral Sympathectomy 58410
Sonohysterography 76831
Suture
 Rupture 59350
Tumor
 Ablation
  Ultrasound, Focused 0071T-0072T
 Excision
  Abdominal Approach 58140, 58146
  Vaginal Approach 58145
Unlisted Services and Procedures 58578, 58999
X-Ray with Contrast 74740

UTP Hexose 1 Phosphate Uridylyltransferase
See Galactose-1-Phosphate, Uridyl Transferase

UV Light Therapy
See Actinotherapy

Uvula
Abscess
 Incision and Drainage 42000
Biopsy 42100
Excision 42140-42145
Lesion
 Destruction 42145
 Excision 42104-42107
Unlisted Services and Procedures 42299

Uvulectomy 42140

V

V Flap Procedure
One Stage Distal Hypospadias Repair 54322

V, Cranial Nerve
See Trigeminal Nerve

V-Y Operation, Bladder, Neck
See Bladder, Repair, Neck

V-Y Plasty
See Skin, Adjacent Tissue Transfer

Vaccination
See Allergen Immunotherapy; Immunization;
Vaccines

Vaccines
Adenovirus .90476-90477
Anthrax 90581
Chicken Pox 90716
Cholera
   Injectable 90725
Diphtheria and Tetanus (Td) 90714
Diphtheria Toxoid 90719
Diphtheria, Tetanus (DT) 90702
Diphtheria, Tetanus, Acellular
Pertussis (DTaP) .90700
Diphtheria, Tetanus, Acellular Pertussis and
Hemophilus Influenza B (Hib) (DTaP-Hib) . . .90721
Diphtheria, Tetanus, Acellular Pertussis,
Haemophilus Influenza Type B, and
Inactivated Poliovirus (DTaP-Hib-IPV) 90698
Diphtheria, Tetanus, Acellular Pertussis,
Hepatitis B, and Inactivated Poliovirus
(DTaP-HepB-IPV) .90723
Diphtheria, Tetanus, and Acellular Pertussis
(TdaP) 90715
Diphtheria, Tetanus, Whole Cell
Pertussis (DTP) 90701
Diphtheria, Tetanus, Whole Cell Pertussis and
Hemophilus Influenza B (Hib) (DTP-Hib) 90720
Encephalitis, Japanese 90735
Hemophilus Influenza B 90645-90648
Hepatitis A 90632-90634
Hepatitis A and Hepatitis B 90636
Hepatitis B 90740-90747
Hepatitis B and Hemophilus Influenza B
(HepB-Hib) 90748
Human Papilloma Virus (HPV) 90649
Influenza 90655-90660
Lyme Disease 90665
Measles 90705
Measles and Rubella 90708
Measles, Mumps and Rubella (MMR) 90707
Measles, Mumps, Rubella and Varicella
(MMRV) 90710
Meningococcal 90733-90734
Mumps 90704
Plague 90727
Pneumococcal 90669, 90732
Poliovirus, Inactivated
   Intramuscular .90713
   Subcutaneous 90713
Poliovirus, Live
   Oral 90712
Rabies 90675-90676
Rotavirus 90680
Rubella 90706
Tetanus and Diphtheria 90718
Tetanus and Diphtheria (Td) 90714
Tetanus Toxoid 90703
Tetanus, Diphtheria, and Acellular
Pertussis (TdaP) .90715
Tuberculosis (BCG) 90585-90586

Typhoid 90690-90693
Unlisted Vaccine/Toxoid 90749
Varicella (Chicken Pox) 90716
Yellow Fever 90717
Zoster (Shingles) 90736

Vagina
Abscess
   Incision and Drainage 57010
Amines Test 82120
Biopsy
   Colposcopy 57421
   Endocervical .57454
   Extensive 57105
   Simple 57100
Closure 57120
Colposcopy . . .57420-57421, 57455-57456, 57461
Construction
   with Graft 57292
   without Graft .57291
Cyst
   Excision 57135
Dilation 57400
Endocervical
   Biopsy 57454
   Exploration 57452
Excision
   Closure 57120
   Complete
      with Removal of Paravaginal Tissue .57111
      with Removal of Paravaginal Tissue with
      Lymphadenectomy 57112
      with Removal of Vaginal Wall 57110
   Partial
      with Removal of Paravaginal Tissue .57107
      with Removal of Paravaginal Tissue with
      Lymphadenectomy 57109
      with Removal of Vaginal Wall 57106
   Total 57110
   with Hysterectomy 58275-58280
      with Repair of Enterocele 58280
Exploration
   Endocervical .57452
   Incision 57000
Hematoma
   Incision and Drainage 57022-57023
Hemorrhage 57180
Hysterectomy 58290, 58550-58554
Incision and Drainage 57020
Insertion
   Ovoid
      for Brachytherapy 57155
   Packing for Bleeding 57180
   Pessary 57160
   Sensor, Fetal Oximetry 0021T
Irrigation 57150
Lesion
   Destruction 57061-57065
      Extensive 57065
      Simple 57061
Prolapse
   Sacrospinous Ligament Fixation 57282
Removal
   Foreign Body .57415
   Prosthetic Graft 57295
   Sling
      Stress Incontinence 57287

Repair 56800
   Cystocele 57240, 57260
      Combined Anteroposterior . . .57260-57265
      Posterior .57240
   Enterocele 57265
   Fistula 51900
      Rectovaginal 57300-57308
      Transvesical and Vaginal Approach . .57330
      Urethrovaginal 57310-57311
      Vesicovaginal 51900, 57320-57330
   Hysterectomy 58267, 58293
   Incontinence 57284, 57288
   Obstetric 59300
   Paravaginal Defect 57284
   Pereyra Procedure 57289
   Prolapse 57282-57284
   Prosthesis Insertion 57267
   Rectocele
      Combined Anteroposterior . . .57260-57265
      Posterior .57250
   Suspension 57280-57283
      Laparoscopic 57425
   Urethral Sphincter 57220
   Wound 57200-57210
      Colpoperineorrhaphy 57210
      Colporrhaphy 57200
Revision
   Prosthetic Graft 57295
   Sling
      Stress Incontinence 57287
Septum
   Excision 57130
Suspension 57280-57283
   Laparoscopic 57425
Suture
   Cystocele 57240, 57260
   Enterocele 57265
   Fistula 51900, 57300-57330
   Rectocele 57250-57260
   Wound 57200-57210
Tumor
   Excision 57135
Ultrasound 76830
Unlisted Services and Procedures 58999
X-Ray with Contrast 74775

Vaginal Delivery 59400, 59610-59614
after Previous Cesarean Delivery . . .59610-59612
   Attempted 59618-59622
Antepartum Care 59400
Cesarean Delivery after Attempted 59618
   Delivery Only .59620
   Postpartum Care 59622
Delivery after Previous
   Vaginal Delivery Only
      Postpartum Care 59614
Delivery Only 59409
External Cephalic Version 59412
Placenta 59414
Postpartum Care 59410
Routine Care 59400

Vaginal Hysterectomy 58552-58554

Vaginal Smear
See Pap Smears

Vaginal Suppositories
Induced Abortion .59855
    with Dilation and Curettage 59856
    with Hysterectomy 59857

Vaginectomy
See Colpectomy

Vaginoplasty
Intersex State 57335

Vaginorrhaphy
See Colporrhaphy

Vaginoscopy
Biopsy 57454
Exploration 57452

Vaginotomy
See Colpotomy

Vagotomy
Abdominal 64760
Highly Selective 43641
Parietal Cell 43641, 64755
Selective 43640
Transthoracic 64752
Truncal 43640
with Gastroduodenostomy Revision,
Reconstruction .43855
with Gastrojejunostomy Revision,
Reconstruction .43865
with Partial Distal Gastrectomy 43635

Vagus Nerve
Avulsion
    Abdominal 64760
    Selective 64755
    Thoracic 64752
Incision 43640-43641
    Abdominal 64760
    Selective 64755
    Thoracic 64752
Injection
    Anesthetic 64408
Transection 43640-43641
    Abdominal 64760
    Selective 43652, 64755
    Thoracic 64752
    Truncal 43651

Valentine's Test
See Urinalysis, Glass Test

Valproic Acid
See Dipropylacetic Acid

Valproic Acid Measurement
See Dipropylacetic Acid

Valsalva Sinus
See Sinus of Valsalva

Valva Atrioventricularis Sinistra (Valva Mitralis)
See Mitral Valve

Valve
Aortic
    See Heart, Aortic Valve
Bicuspid
    See Mitral Valve

Mitral
    See Mitral Valve
Pulmonary
    See Pulmonary Valve
Tricuspid
    See Tricuspid Valve

Valve Stenoses, Aortic
See Aortic Stenosis

Valvectomy
Tricuspid Valve 33460

Valvotomy
Mitral Valve 33420-33422
Pulmonary Valve 33470-33474
Reoperation 33530

Valvuloplasty
Aortic Valve 33400-33403
Femoral Vein 34501
Mitral Valve 33425-33427
Percutaneous Balloon
    Aortic Valve .92986
    Mitral Valve .92987
    Pulmonary Valve 92990
Prosthetic Valve 33496
Reoperation 33530
Tricuspid Valve 33463-33465

Van Deen Test
See Blood, Feces

Van Den Bergh Test
See Bilirubin, Blood

Vancomycin
Assay 80202

Vanillylmandelic Acid
Urine 84585

Vanilmandelic Acid
See Vanillylmandelic Acid

Varicella (Chicken Pox)
See Vaccines

Varicella-Zoster
Antibody 86787
Antigen Detection
    Direct Fluorescence 87290

Varices Esophageal
See Esophageal Varices

Varicocele
Spermatic Cord
    Excision 55530-55540

Varicose Vein
Ablation 36475-36479
Removal 37720, 37730, 37765-37785
Secondary Varicosity 37785
with Tissue Excision 37735-37760

Vas Deferens
Anastomosis
    to Epididymis 54900-54901
Excision 55250
Incision 55200
    for X-Ray 55300

Ligation 55450
Repair
    Suture 55400
Unlisted Services and Procedures 55899
Vasography 74440
X-Ray with Contrast 74440

Vascular Flow Check, Graft 15860

Vascular Injection
Unlisted Services and Procedures 36299

Vascular Lesion
Cranial
    Excision 61600-61608, 61615-61616
Cutaneous
    Destruction 17106-17108

Vascular Malformation
Cerebral
    Repair 61710
Finger
    Excision 26115
Hand
    Excision 26115

Vascular Procedure
Brachytherapy
    Intracoronary Artery 92974
Intravascular Ultrasound
    Coronary Vessels 92978-92979
Stent
    Intracoronary 92980-92981

Vascular Procedures
Angioscopy
    Non-Coronary Vessels 35400
Endoscopy
    Surgical 37500
Harvest
    Lower Extremity Vein 35572
Intravascular Ultrasound
    Non-Coronary Vessels 75945-75946
Thrombolysis
    Coronary Vessels 92975-92977
    Cranial Vessels 37195

Vascular Rehabilitation
See Peripheral Artery Disease Rehabilitation (PAD)

Vascular Studies
See Doppler Scan, Duplex, Plethysmography
Angioscopy
    Non-Coronary Vessels 35400
Aorta 93978-93979
Arterial Studies (Non-Invasive)
    Extracranial 93875-93882
    Extremities 93922-93924
    Intracranial 93886-93890
    Lower Extremity 93925-93926
    Middle Cerebral Artery, Fetal 76821
    Umbilical Artery, Fetal 76820
Artery Studies
    Upper Extremity 93930-93931
Blood Pressure Monitoring,
24 Hour 93784-93790
Cardiac Catheterization
    Imaging 93555-93556
Hemodialysis Access 93990

Kidney
  Multiple Study
    with Pharmacological Intervention ..78709
  Single Study
    with Pharmacological Intervention ..78708
Penile Vessels 93980-93981
Plethysmography
  Total Body 93720-93722
Temperature Gradient 93740
Thermogram
  Cephalic 93760
  Peripheral 93762
Unlisted Services and Procedures 93799
Venous Studies
  Extremity 93965-93971
  Venous Pressure 93770
Visceral Studies 93975-93979

Vascular Surgery
Arm, Upper
  Anesthesia 01770-01782
Elbow
  Anesthesia 01770-01782
Endoscopy 37500
Unlisted Services and Procedures 37799

Vasectomy 55250
Laser Coagulation of Prostate 52647
Laser Vaporization 52648
Reversal
  See Vasovasorrhaphy
Transurethral
  Cystourethroscopic 52402
Transurethral Electrosurgical Resection of
Prostate 52601
Transurethral Resection of Prostate 52648

Vasoactive Drugs
Injection
  Penis 54231

Vasoactive Intestinal
Peptide 84586

Vasogram
See Vasography

Vasography 74440

Vasointestinal Peptide
See Vasoactive Intestinal Peptide

Vasopneumatic Device
Therapy 97016
See Physical Medicine/Therapy/Occupational
Therapy

Vasopressin 84588

Vasotomy 55200, 55300
Transurethral
  Cystourethroscopic 52402

Vasovasorrhaphy 55400

Vasovasostomy 55400

VATS
See Thoracoscopy

VDRL 86592-86593

Vein
Ablation
  Endovenous 36475-36479
Adrenal
  Venography 75840-75842
Anastomosis
  Caval to Mesenteric 37160
  Intrahepatic Portosystemic 37182-37183
  Portocaval 37140
  Reniportal 37145
  Saphenopopliteal 34530
  Splenorenal 37180-37181
  to Vein 37140-37160, 37182-37183
Angioplasty 75978
  Transluminal 35460
Arm
  Harvest of Vein for Bypass Graft 35500
  Venography 75820-75822
Axillary
  Thrombectomy 34490
Biopsy
  Transcatheter 75970
Cannulization
  to Artery 36810-36815
  to Vein 36800
Catheterization
  Central Insertion 36555-36558
  Organ Blood 36500
  Peripheral Insertion 36568-36569
  Removal 36589
  Repair 36575
  Replacement 36578-36581, 36584
  Umbilical 36510
Division
  Saphenous 37718, 37722
Endoscopic Harvest
  for Bypass Graft 33508
External Cannula
  Declotting 36860-36861
Extremity
  Non-Invasive Studies 93965-93971
Femoral
  Repair 34501
Femoropopliteal
  Thrombectomy 34421-34451
Guidance
  Fluoroscopic 75998
  Ultrasound 76937
Hepatic Portal
  Splenoportography 75810
  Venography 75885-75887
Iliac
  Thrombectomy 34401-34451
Injection
  Sclerosing Agent 36468-36471
Insertion
  IVC Filter 75940
Interrupt
  Femoral 37650
  Iliac 37660
  Vena Cava 37620
Jugular
  Venography 75860
Leg
  Harvest for Vascular Reconstruction ...35572
  Venography 75820-75822

Ligation
  Clusters 37785
  Esophagus 43205
  Jugular 37565
  Perforation 37760
  Saphenous 37700-37735, 37780
  Secondary 37785
Liver
  Venography 75889-75891
Neck
  Venography 75860
Nuclear Medicine
  Thrombosis Imaging 78456-78458
Orbit
  Venography 75880
Placement
  IVC Filter 75940
Portal
  Catheterization 36481
Pulmonary
  Repair 33730
Removal
  Clusters 37785
  Saphenous 37720, 37730-37735, 37780
  Varicose 37765-37766
Renal
  Venography 75831-75833
Repair
  Aneurysm 36834
  Angioplasty 75978
  Graft 34520
Sampling
  Venography 75893
Sinus
  Venography 75870
Skull
  Venography 75870-75872
Spermatic
  Excision 55530-55540
  Ligation 55550
Splenic
  Splenoportography 75810
Stripping
  Saphenous 37718-37735
Subclavian
  Thrombectomy 34471-34490
Thrombectomy 37187-37188
  Other than Hemodialysis Graft or
  Fistula 35875-35876
Unlisted Services and Procedures 37799
Valve Transposition 34510
Varicose
  See Varicose Vein
Vena Cava
  Thrombectomy 34401-34451
  Venography 75825-75827

Velpeau Cast 29058

Vena Cava
Catheterization 36010
Reconstruction 34502
Resection with Reconstruction 37799

Vena Caval
Thrombectomy 50230

Venereal Disease Research Laboratory
See VDRL

Venesection
See Phlebotomy

Venipuncture
See Cannulation; Catheterization
Breast
    Cytology 0045T
Child/Adult
    Cutdown 36425
    Percutaneous 36410
Infant
    Cutdown 36420
    Percutaneous 36400-36406
Routine 36415

Venography
Adrenal 75840-75842
Arm 75820-75822
Epidural 75872
Hepatic Portal 75885-75887
Injection 36005
Jugular 75860
Leg 75820-75822
Liver 75889-75891
Neck 75860
Nuclear Medicine 78445, 78457-78458
Orbit 75880
Renal 75831-75833
Sagittal Sinus 75870
Vena Cava 75825-75827
Venous Sampling 75893

Venorrhaphy
See Suture, Vein

Venotomy
See Phlebotomy

Venous Access Device
Fluoroscopic Guidance 75998
Insertion
    Central 36560-36566
    Peripheral 36570-36571
Irrigation 96523
Obstruction Clearance 36595-36596
    Guidance 75901-75902
Removal 36590
Repair 36576
Replacement 36582-36583, 36585
    Catheter Only 36578

Venous Blood Pressure
See Blood Pressure, Venous

Venovenostomy
See Anastomosis, Vein

Ventilating Tube
Insertion 69433
Removal 69424

Ventilation Assist ...94656-94657, 99504
See Pulmonology, Therapeutic

Ventricular Puncture 61020-61026,
61105-61120

Ventriculocisternostomy 62180,
62200-62201

Ventriculography
Anesthesia
    Brain 00214
    Cardiac 01920
Nuclear Imaging 78635

Ventriculomyectomy 33416

Ventriculomyotomy 33416

Vermiform Appendix
See Appendix

Vermilionectomy 40500

Verruca Plana
See Warts, Flat

Verruca(e)
See Warts

Version, Cephalic
See Cephalic Version

Vertebra
See Spinal Cord; Spine; Vertebral Body; Vertebral Process
Additional Segment
    Excision 22103, 22116
Arthrodesis
    Anterior 22548-22585
    Exploration 22830
    Lateral Extracavitary 22532-22534
    Posterior 22590-22802
    Spinal Deformity
        Anterior Approach 22808-22812
        Posterior Approach 22800-22804
Cervical
    Excision
        for Tumor 22100, 22110
    Fracture 23675-23680
Fracture/Dislocation
    Additional Segment
        Open Treatment 22328
    Cervical
        Open Treatment 22326
    Lumbar
        Open Treatment 22325
    Thoracic
        Open Treatment 22327
Kyphectomy 22818-22819
Lumbar
    Excision
        for Tumor 22102, 22114
Osteoplasty
    CT Scan 76013
    Fluoroscopy 76012
    Lumbar 22521-22522
    Thoracic 22520-22522
Osteotomy
    Additional Segment
        Anterior Approach 22226
        Posterior/Posterolateral Approach ..22216
    Cervical
        Anterior Approach 22220
        Posterior/Posterolateral Approach ..22210

Lumbar
    Anterior Approach 22224
    Posterior/Posterolateral Approach ..22214
Thoracic
    Anterior Approach 22222
    Posterior/Posterolateral Approach ..22212
Thoracic
    Excision
        for Tumor 22101, 22112

Vertebrae
See Vertebra
Arthrodesis
    Anterior 22548-22585
    Lateral Extracavitary 22532-22534
    Spinal Deformity 22818-22819

Vertebral
Arteries
    See Artery, Vertebral
Body
    Biopsy 20250-20251
    Excision
        Decompression 63081-63103
        Lesion 63300-63308
        with Skull Base Surgery 61597
    Fracture/Dislocation
        Closed Treatment 22305
        without Manipulation 22310
    Kyphectomy 22818-22819
Column
    See Spine
Corpectomy 63081-63103, 63300-63308
Fracture
    See Fracture, Vertebra
Process
    Fracture/Dislocation
        Closed Treatment
        with Manipulation, Casting and/or
        Bracing 22315

Very Low Density Lipoprotein
See Lipoprotein, Blood

Vesication
See Bulla

Vesicle, Seminal
See Seminal Vesicle

Vesico-Psoas Hitch 50785

Vesicostomy
Cutaneous 51980

Vesicourethropexy 51840-51841

Vesicovaginal Fistula
See Fistula, Vesicovaginal

Vesiculectomy 55650

Vesiculogram, Seminal
See Vesiculography

Vesiculography 55300, 74440

Vesiculotomy 55600-55605
Complicated 55605

Vessel, Blood
See Blood Vessels

Vessels Transposition, Great
See Transposition, Great Arteries

Vestibular Function Tests
See Ear, Nose and Throat
Additional Electrodes 92547
Caloric Test 92533
Caloric Vestibular Tests 92543
Nystagmus
　Optokinetic 92534, 92544
　Positional 92532, 92542
　Spontaneous 92531, 92541
Posturography 92548
Sinusoidal Rotational Testing 92546
Torsion Swing Test 92546
Tracking Test 92545

Vestibular Nerve
Section
　Transcranial Approach 69950
　Translabyrinthine Approach 69915

Vestibule of Mouth
See Mouth, Vestibule of

Vestibuloplasty 40840-40845

Vidal Procedure
See Varicocele, Spermatic Cord, Excision

Video
Esophagus 74230
Pharynx .70371, 74230
Speech Evaluation 70371
Swallowing Evaluation 74230

Video-Assisted Thoracoscopic Surgery
See Thoracoscopy

Videoradiography
Unlisted Services and Procedures . .76120-76125

VII, Coagulation Factor
See Proconvertin

VII, Cranial Nerve
See Facial Nerve

VIII, Coagulation Factor
See Clotting Factor

Villus, Chorionic
See Chorionic Villus

Villusectomy
See Synovectomy

VIP
See Vasoactive Intestinal Peptide

Viral Antibodies 86280

Viral Warts
See Warts

Virtual Colonoscopy
Diagnostic 0067T
Screening 0066T

Virus
AIDS
　See HIV-1
Burkitt Lymphoma
　See Epstein-Barr Virus
Human Immunodeficiency
　See HIV
Influenza
　See Influenza Virus
Respiratory Syncytial
　See Respiratory Syncytial Virus
Salivary Gland
　See Cytomegalovirus

Virus Identification
Immunofluorescence 87254

Virus Isolation 87250-87255

Visceral Larval Migrans 86280

Viscosities, Blood
See Blood, Viscosity

Visit, Home
See House Calls

Visual Acuity Screen 99172-99173

Visual Field Exam 92081-92083

Visual Function Screen . . .0065T, 99172

Visual Reinforcement Audiometry 92579
See Audiologic Function Tests

Visualization
Ileal Conduit 50690

Vital Capacity Measurement . . .94150

Vitamin 84591
A 84590
B Complex
　See B Complex Vitamins
B-1 84425
B-12 82607-82608
　Absorption Study 78270-78272
　Holotranscobalamin 0103T
B-2 84252
B-6 84207
B-6 Measurement
　See Pyridoxal Phosphate
BC
　See Folic Acid
C 82180
D 82307, 82652
D, 25-Hydroxy Measurement
　See Calcifediol
D-2
　See Calciferol
D-3 82306
E 84446
K 84597
K Dependent Bone Protein
　See Osteocalcin
K-Dependent Protein S
　See Protein S

Vitelline Duct
See Omphalomesenteric Duct

Vitrectomy
Anterior Approach
　Partial 67005
Pars Plana Approach 67036
Subtotal 67010
with Endolaser Panretinal
Photocoagulation 67040
with Epiretinal Membrane Stripping 67038
with Focal Endolaser Photocoagulation 67039
with Implantation or Replacement
　Drug Delivery System 67027

Vitreous
Aspiration 67015
Excision
　Pars Planta Approach 67036
　with Epiretinal Membrane Stripping . . .67038
　with Focal Endolaser
　Photocoagulation 67039
Implantation
　Drug Delivery System 67027
Incision
　Strands 67030-67031
Injection
　Fluid Substitute 67025
　Pharmacologic Agent 67028
Removal
　Anterior Approach 67005
　Subtotal 67010
Replacement
　Drug Delivery System 67027
Strands
　Discission 67030
　Severing 67031
Subtotal 67010

VLDL
See Lipoprotein, Blood

VMA
See Vanillylmandelic Acid

Vocal Cords
Injection
　Endoscopy 31513
　Therapeutic 31570-31571

Voice Box
See Larynx

Voice Button 31611

Voiding Pressure Studies
Abdominal 51797
Bladder 51795

Volatiles 84600

Volhard's Test
See Water Load Test

Volkman Contracture 25315-25316

Volume Reduction
Blood Products .86960

Volume Reduction, Lung
See Lung Volume Reduction

Von Kraske Proctectomy
See Proctectomy, Partial

VP
See Voiding Pressure Studies

Vulva
Abscess
   Incision and Drainage 56405
Colposcopy 56820
   Biopsy 56821
Excision
   Complete 56625, 56633-56640
   Partial 56620, 56630-56632
   Radial 56630-56631, 56633-56640
     Complete 56633-56640
     Partial 56630-56632
   Simple
     Complete 56625
     Partial 56620
Lesion
   Destruction 56501-56515
Perineum
   Biopsy 56605-56606
   Incision and Drainage 56405
Repair
   Obstetric 59300

Vulvectomy
Complete 56625, 56633-56640
Partial 56620, 56630-56632
Radical 56630-56631, 56633-56640
   Complete
     with Bilateral Inguinofemoral
     Lymphadenectomy 56637
     with Inguinofemoral, Iliac, and Pelvic
     Lymphadenectomy 56640
     with Unilateral Inguinofemoral
     Lymphadenectomy 56634
   Partial
     with Bilateral Inguinofemoral
     Lymphadenectomy 56632
     with Unilateral Inguinofemoral
     Lymphadenectomy 56631
   Simple
     Complete 56625
     Partial 56620

VZIG
See Immune Globulins, Varicella-Zoster

W

W-Plasty
See Skin, Adjacent Tissue Transfer

WADA Activation Test 95958
See Electroencephalography

WAIS 96101-96102

Waldius Procedure 27445

Wall, Abdominal
See Abdominal Wall

Walsh Modified Radical Prostatectomy
See Prostatectomy

Warts
Flat
   Destruction 17110-17111

Washing
Sperm 58323

Wasserman Test
See Syphilis Test

Wassmund Procedure
Osteotomy
   Maxilla 21206

Water Load Test 89235

Water Wart
See Molluscum Contagiosum

Waterston Procedure 33755

Watson-Jones Procedure 27695-27698

Wave, Ultrasonic Shock
See Ultrasound

WBC
See White Blood Cell

Webbed
Toe
   Repair 28280

Wedge Excision
Osteotomy 21122

Wedge Resection
Ovary 58920

Well-Baby Care 99381, 99391, 99432

Wellness Behavior
See Evaluation and Management, Health Behavior

Wernicke-Posadas Disease
See Coccidioidomycosis

Westergren Test
See Sedimentation Rate, Blood Cell

Western Blot
HIV 86689
Protein 84181-84182
Tissue Analysis 88371-88372

Wheelchair Management
Training 97542

Wheelchair Management/Propulsion
See Physical Medicine/Therapy/Occupational Therapy

Wheeler Knife Procedure
See Discission, Cataract

Wheeler Procedure
See Blepharoplasty, Entropion
Discission Secondary Membranous
Cataract 66820

Whipple Procedure 48150

Whirlpool Therapy 97022
See Physical Medicine/Therapy/Occupational Therapy

White Blood Cell
Alkaline Phosphatase 85540
Antibody 86021
Count 85032, 85048, 89055
Differential 85004-85007, 85009
Histamine Release Test 86343
Phagocytosis 86344
Transfusion
   See Leukocyte, Transfusion

Whitemead Operation
See Hemorrhoidectomy, Complex

Whitman Astragalectomy
See Talus, Excision

Whitman Procedure 27120

Wick Catheter Technique 20950

Widal Serum Test
See Agglutinin, Febrile

Window
Oval
   See Oval Window
Round
   See Round Window

Window Technic, Pericardial
See Pericardiostomy

Windpipe
See Trachea

Winiwarter Operation
See Anastomosis, Gallbladder to Intestines

Winter Procedure 54435

Wintrobe Test
See Sedimentation Rate, Blood Cell

Wire
See Pin
Insertion/Removal
   Skeletal Traction 20650
Interdental
   without Fracture 21497

Wiring
Prophylactic Treatment
   Humerus 24498

Wirsung Duct
See Pancreatic Duct

Witzel Operation 43500, 43520, 43830-43832
See Incision, Stomach, Creation, Stoma; Incision and Drainage

Womb
See Uterus

Wood Alcohol
See Methanol

Work Hardening 97545-97546
See Physical Medicine/Therapy/Occupational
Therapy

**Work Related Evaluation
Services** 99455-99456

Worm
See Helminth

Wound
Closure
　Temporary
　　Skin Allograft 15300-15321
　　Skin Xenograft 15420-15421
Debridement
　Non-Selective 97602
　Selective 97597-97598
Dehiscence
　Repair 12020-12021, 13160
Exploration
　Penetrating
　　Abdomen/Flank/Back 20102
　　Chest 20101
　　Extremity 20103
　　Neck 20100
　　Penetrating Trauma 20100-20103
Infection
　Incision and Drainage
　　Postoperative 10180
Negative Pressure Therapy 97605-97606
Repair
　Complex 13100-13160
　Intermediate 12031-12057
　Simple 12001-12021
　Urethra 53502-53515
Suture
　Bladder 51860-51865
　Kidney 50500
　Trachea
　　Cervical 31800
　　Intrathoracic 31805
　Urethra 53502-53515
Vagina
　Repair 57200-57210

Wrist
See Arm, Lower; Carpal Bone
Abscess 25028
Arthrocentesis 20605
Arthrodesis 25800
　with Graft 25810
　with Sliding Graft 25805
Arthrography 73115
Arthroplasty 25332, 25443, 25447
　Revision 25449
　Total Replacement 25446
　with Implant 25441-25442, 25444-25445
Arthroscopy
　Diagnostic 29840
　Surgical 29843-29848
Arthrotomy 25040, 25100-25105
　for Repair 25107

Biopsy 25065-25066, 25100-25101
Bursa
　Excision 25115-25116
　Incision and Drainage 25031
Capsule
　Incision 25085
Cast 29085
Cyst 25130-25136
Decompression 25020-25025
Disarticulation 25920
　Reamputation 25924
　Revision 25922
Dislocation
　Closed Treatment 25660
　Intercarpal 25660
　　Open Treatment 25670
　Open Treatment 25670, 25676
　Percutaneous Fixation 25671
　Radiocarpal 25660
　　Open Treatment 25670
　Radioulnar
　　Closed Treatment 25675
　　Percutaneous Fixation 25671
　with Fracture
　　Closed Treatment 25680
　　Open Treatment 25685
　with Manipulation 25259, 25660, 25675
Excision
　Carpal 25210-25215
　Cartilage 25107
Exploration 25040, 25101
Fasciotomy 25020-25025
Fracture 25645
　Closed Treatment 25622, 25630
　Open Treatment 25628
　with Dislocation 25680-25685
　with Manipulation 25259, 25624, 25635
Ganglion Cyst
　Excision 25111-25112
Hematoma 25028
Incision 25040, 25100-25105
　Tendon Sheath 25000-25001
Injection
　Carpal Tunnel
　　Therapeutic 20526
　X-Ray 25246
Joint
　See Radiocarpal Joint
Lesion, Tendon Sheath
　Excision 25110
Magnetic Resonance Imaging (MRI) 73221
Reconstruction
　Capsulectomy 25320
　Capsulorrhaphy 25320
　Carpal Bone 25394, 25430
　Realign 25335
Removal
　Foreign Body 25040, 25101, 25248
　Implant 25449
　Loose Body 25101
　Prosthesis 25250-25251
Repair 25447
　Bone 25440
　Carpal Bone 25431
　Muscle 25260, 25270
　　Secondary ... 25263-25265, 25272-25274
　Tendon 25260, 25270, 25280-25316
　　Secondary ... 25263-25265, 25272-25274

Tendon Sheath 25275
Strapping 29260
Synovium
　Excision 25105, 25115-25119
Tendon Sheath
　Excision 25115-25116
Tenodesis 25300-25301
Tenotomy 25290
Tumor 25130-25136
　Excision 25075-25077
Unlisted Services and Procedures 25999
X-Ray 73100-73110
　with Contrast 73115

X

X, Coagulation Factor
See Stuart-Prower Factor

X, Cranial Nerve
See Vagus Nerve

X-Linked Ichthyoses
See Syphilis Test

X-Ray
Abdomen 74000-74022
Abscess 76080
Acromioclavicular Joint 73050
Ankle 73600-73610
Arm, Lower 73090
Arm, Upper 73092
Artery
　Atherectomy 75992-75996
Auditory Meatus 70134
Bile Duct
　Guide Dilation 74360
Body Composition
　Dual Energy Absorptiometry 0028T
Body Section 76100
　Motion 76101-76102
Bone
　Age Study 76020
　Dual Energy Absorptiometry ... 76075-76077
　Length Study 76040
　Osseous Survey 76061-76065
　Ultrasound 76977
Breast 76090-76092
　Localization Nodule 76096
　with Computer-aided Detection . 76082-76083
Calcaneus 73650
Chest 71010-71035
　Complete (Four Views)
　　with Fluoroscopy 71034
　　Insert Pacemaker 71090
　Partial (Two Views)
　　with Fluoroscopy 71023
　　Stereo 71015
　　with Fluoroscopy 71090
Clavicle 73000
Coccyx 72220
Consultation 76140
Duodenum 74260
Elbow 73070-73080

Esophagus 74220
Eye 70030
Facial Bones 70140-70150
Fallopian Tube 74742
Femur 73550
Fibula 73590
Finger 73140
Fistula 76080
Foot .73620-73630
Gastrointestinal Tract 74240-74245
　　Guide Dilation 74360
　　Guide Intubation 74340-74350
Hand .73120-73130
Head 70350
Heel 73650
Hip 73500-73520, 73540
　　Intraoperative 73530
Humerus 73060
Intestines, Small 74245, 74249-74251
　　Guide Intubation 74355
Intravascular Stent 75960
Jaws 70355
Joint
　　Stress Views 76006
Knee 73560-73564, 73580
　　Bilateral 73565
Larynx 70370
Leg 73592
Lumen Dilator 74360
Mandible 70100-70110
Mastoids 70120-70130
Nasal Bone 70160
Neck 70360
Nose to Rectum
　　Foreign Body 76010
Orbit .70190-70200
Pelvis 72170-72190, 73540
　　Manometry 74710
Peritoneum 74190
Pharynx 70370, 74210
Ribs .71100-71111
Sacroiliac Joint 72200-72202, 73542
Sacrum 72220
Salivary Gland 70380
Scapula 73010
Sella Turcica .70240
Shoulder 73020-73030, 73050
Sinus Tract 76080
Sinuses 70210-70220
Skull .70250-70260
Specimen/Surgical 76098
Spine 72020, 72090
　　Cervical 72040-72052
　　Lumbosacral 72100-72120
　　Thoracic 72070-72074
　　Thoracolumbar 72080
　　Total 72010
Standing
　　Spine 72069
Sternum 71120-71130
Teeth 70300-70320
Tibia 73590
Toe 73660
Total Body
　　Foreign Body 76010
Unlisted Services and Procedures . .76120-76125

with Contrast
　　Ankle 73615
　　Aorta 0080T, 0081T, 75600-75630,
　　　　　　　　　　　　　　　　　　75952-75953
　　Artery
　　　　Abdominal 75726
　　　　Additional Vessels 75774
　　　　Adrenal 75731-75733
　　　　Arm 75710-75716
　　　　Arteriovenous Shunt 75790
　　　　Brachial 75658
　　　　Carotid 75660-75680
　　　　Coronary 93556
　　　　Coronary Bypass 93556
　　　　Head and Neck 75650
　　　　Iliac 75953
　　　　Leg 75710-75716
　　　　Mammary 75756
　　　　Pelvic .75736
　　　　Pulmonary 75741-75746
　　　　Renal 75722-75724
　　　　Spine .75705
　　　　Transcatheter Therapy 75894-75898
　　　　Vertebral 75685
　　Bile Duct 74300-74320
　　　　Calculus Removal 74327
　　　　Catheterization 75982-75984
　　　　Drainage 75980-75982
　　　　Guide Catheter 74328, 74330
　　Bladder 74430, 74450-74455
　　Brain 70010-70015
　　Bronchi 71040-71060
　　Central Venous Access Device 36598
　　Colon
　　　　Barium Enema 74270-74280
　　Corpora Cavernosa 74445
　　Elbow 73085
　　Epididymis 74440
　　Gallbladder 74290-74291
　　Gastrointestinal Tract 74246-74249
　　Hip 73525
　　Iliofemoral Artery 75630
　　Intervertebral Disk
　　　　Cervical 72285
　　　　Lumbar 72295
　　　　Thoracic 72285
　　Joint
　　　　Stress Views 76006
　　Kidney
　　　　Cyst 74470
　　　　Guide Catheter 74475
　　Knee 73560-73564, 73580
　　Lacrimal Duct 70170
　　Larynx 70373
　　Lymph Vessel
　　　　Abdomen 75805-75807
　　　　Arm 75801-75803
　　　　Leg 75801-75803
　　Mammary Duct 76086-76088
　　Nasolacrimal Duct 70170
　　　　Guide Dilation 74485
　　Oviduct 74740
　　Pancreas 74300-74305
　　Pancreatic Duct
　　　　Guide Catheter 74329-74330
　　Perineum .74775
　　Peritoneum 74190
　　Salivary Gland 70390

Seminal Vesicles 74440
Shoulder 73040
Spine
　　Cervical 72240
　　Lumbosacral 72265
　　Thoracic 72255
　　Total 72270
Subtraction Method 76350
Temporomandibular Joint
(TMJ) 70328-70332
Ureter
　　Guide Catheter 74480
　　Guide Dilation 74485
Urethra 74450-74455
Urinary Tract 74400-74425
Uterus 74740
Vas Deferens .74440
Vein
　　Adrenal 75840-75842
　　Arm 75820-75822
　　Hepatic Portal 75810, 75885-75887
　　Jugular 75860
　　Leg 75820-75822
　　Liver 75889-75891
　　Neck 75860
　　Orbit 75880
　　Renal 75831-75833
　　Sampling 75893
　　Sinus 75870
　　Skull 75870-75872
　　Splenic 75810
　　Vena Cava 75825-75827
Wrist 73115
Wrist 73100-73110

X-Ray Tomography, Computed
See CT Scan

Xa, Coagulation Factor
See Thrombokinase

Xenoantibodies
See Antibody, Heterophile

Xenograft 15400-15401
Skin
　　Acellular Implant 15430-15431
　　Dermal 15420-15421

Xenografts, Skin
See Heterograft, Skin

Xenotransplantation
See Heterograft

Xerography
See Xeroradiography

Xeroradiography 76150

XI, Coagulation Factor
See Plasma Thromboplastin, Antecedent

XI, Cranial Nerve
See Accessory Nerve

XII, Coagulation Factor
See Hageman Factor

XII, Cranial Nerve
See Hypoglossal Nerve

XIII, Coagulation Factor
See Fibrin Stabilizing Factor

Xylose Absorption Test
Blood 84620
Urine 84620

Y

Yeast
Culture 87106

Yellow Fever Vaccine 90717

Yersinia
Antibody 86793

Z

Ziegler Procedure
Discission Secondary Membranous Cataract ....
                       66820

Zinc 84630

Zinc Manganese Leucine Aminopeptidase
See Leucine Aminopeptidase

Zygoma
See Cheekbone

Zygomatic Arch
Fracture
    Open Treatment 21356-21366
    with Manipulation 21355

Clinical Examples in Radiology

A guide to understanding the practical application of radiology CPT® codes.

The American Medical Association (AMA) and American College of Radiology (ACR) partnered on this new publication *Clinical Examples in Radiology, a practical guide to coding*. The goal of this quarterly newsletter is to provide authoritative advice and guidance that is concise, practical, and of value in the day-to-day practice of coding professionals, physician practices, and billing services. Inside each issue you'll receive:

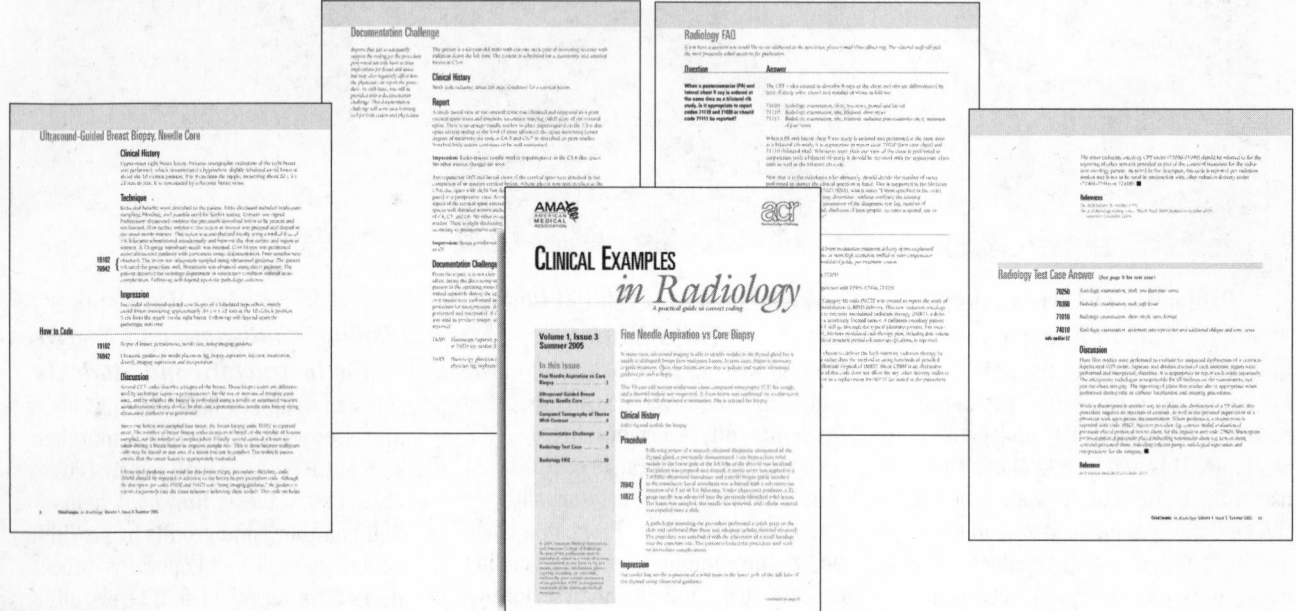

Clinical Examples.
Several, carefully selected procedure reports, covering all areas of radiology, dissected and annotated by nationally recognized experts in radiology coding.

Documentation Challenge.
A real-life radiology operative report—and the ensuing insightful and detailed commentary—will help you approach difficult cases and provide concrete suggestions to follow to improve your procedure reporting and coding.

Radiology Coding Q&A.
Highlights several coding questions. Subscribers can e-mail questions directly to the newsletter staff. Selected questions will be answered in future issues.

Self Quiz.
Test your knowledge with each issue's radiology test case and compare your answer to the correct answer and explanation provided.

In addition to four quarterly, 12-page newsletter issues, you will receive two special report bulletins per year.
Each bulletin covers on-going code changes, brief clarifications of existing CPT codes, "hot" coding topics in radiology, and more.

Earn CEU credits toward AAPC, AHIMA, and RCC certifications with on-line, interactive tests.

Download the Inaugural issue for FREE at www.ama-assn.org/go/cpt, and click on CPT Products and Services.

Subscribe Now! Call **800-621-8335** *or visit* ***www.amabookstore.com***.

CLINICAL EXAMPLES IN RADIOLOGY, A Practical Guide to Correct Coding Order #: CE151505CGW	**Two Year Subscription Price** (8 quarterly issues plus 4 special report bulletins) Price: $360.00 AMA/ACR Member Price: $285.00	**One Year Subscription Price** (4 quarterly issues plus 2 special report bulletins) Price: $225.00 AMA/ACR Member Price: $179.00

American College of Radiology

AMERICAN MEDICAL ASSOCIATION